POSTCARDS FROM ABSURDISTAN

FRONTISPIECE. Jan Reegen, *Rita*, 1950, tempera, on a protectorate newspaper and a Union of Czech Youth poster, 62.5 by 43.5 cm, Galerie Ztichlá klika v Praze. From Marie Klimešová, *Roky ve dnech: české umění 1945–1957*, Prague, 2010.

Postcards from Absurdistan

PRAGUE AT THE END OF HISTORY

DEREK SAYER

PRINCETON UNIVERSITY PRESS

PRINCETON & OXFORD

Published by Princeton University Press
41 William Street, Princeton, New Jersey 08540
99 Banbury Road, Oxford OX2 6JX

press.princeton.edu

All Rights Reserved
Library of Congress Cataloging-in-Publication Data

Names: Sayer, Derek, author.
Title: Postcards from Absurdistan : Prague at the end of history / Derek Sayer.
Other titles: Prague at the end of history
Description: Princeton : Princeton University Press, 2022. | Includes bibliographical references and index.
Identifiers: LCCN 2022006939 (print) | LCCN 2022006940 (ebook) | ISBN 9780691185453 (hardback) | ISBN 9780691239514 (ebook)
Subjects: LCSH: Prague (Czech Republic)—Civilization—20th century.
Classification: LCC DB2622 .S29 2022 (print) | LCC DB2622 (ebook) | DDC 943.712—dc23/eng/20220215
LC record available at https://lccn.loc.gov/2022006939
LC ebook record available at https://lccn.loc.gov/2022006940

British Library Cataloging-in-Publication Data is available

Editorial: Priya Nelson, Barbara Shi
Jacket Design: Chris Ferrante
Production: Danielle Amatucci
Publicity: Alyssa Sanford, Kate Farquhar-Thomson

Jacket Credit: bpk Bildagentur / Land Niedersachsen / Stefan Behrens / Art Resource, NY

This book has been composed in Arno Pro

Printed on acid-free paper. ∞

Printed in the United States of America

10 9 8 7 6 5 4 3 2 1

In memory of my mother Kathy, my sister Alison, and my dog Luci

I prefer, once again, walking by night to believing myself a man who walks by daylight.

—ANDRÉ BRETON, *NADJA*

CONTENTS

ILLUSTRATIONS

SPEAKING AT THE FOURTH CONGRESS of the Czechoslovak Writers' Union in Prague on 27 June 1967, Milan Kundera told his audience: "The entire story of this nation between democracy, fascist subjugation, Stalinism and socialism . . . contains within it everything essential that has made the twentieth century the twentieth century. This perhaps makes it possible for us to pose more substantial questions, to create perhaps more meaningful myths than those who have not undergone this anabasis. In this century this nation lived through perhaps more than many other nations, and if its mind was alert, perhaps it knows more too."[1] As if to underline his point, just over a year later the troops of five Warsaw Pact nations crossed the Czechoslovak border to crush the most ambitious attempt to reconcile communism and democracy seen anywhere in the world. In the spirit of Kundera's observation, *Postcards from Absurdistan: Prague at the End of History* is the final volume in a loose trilogy of cultural histories that take Prague, rather than Paris, London, or New York, as a vantage point from which to reexamine different facets of modernity and modernism—both terms I would prefer to write in the plural. While the books complement one another, each is intended to stand alone. *The Coasts of Bohemia: A Czech History* (1998)[2] charted the shifting sands of national identity and historical memory in relation to changing configurations of political power in Bohemia—the land currently known as Czechia or the Czech Republic[3]—from the 1780s to the 1950s. *Prague, Capital of the Twentieth Century: A Surrealist History* (2013) zoomed in on the Bohemian capital during the earlier decades of the twentieth century, focusing on the fraught relations between avant-garde art and revolutionary politics.[4] Between the world wars Prague became the world's second center of surrealism after Paris, and the interwoven stories of the Paris and Prague surrealist groups and their attempts to reconcile Marx's "*transformer le monde*" (transform the world) with Rimbaud's "*changer la vie*" (change life) formed the backbone of my narrative.[5] Offering more twisted tales of politics and the arts, *Postcards from Absurdistan* is a companion and sequel to *Prague, Capital of the Twentieth Century*. It could be seen as an elegy for that century—its hopes, its dreams, its delusions.

I begin in 1920, in the aftermath of World War I, with the love affair between Franz Kafka and Milena Jesenská as a window into the complexities of language, ethnicity, and class that would soon disappear from Prague's landscape under the combined onslaught of fascism and communism. But most of my story is set in the eventful half century between 1938 and 1989, a period I cover in far more detail here than in either of the previous two books. During these decades the city saw the end of Tomáš Masaryk's democratic first Czechoslovak Republic following the Munich Agreement of September 1938, the German invasion of 15 March 1939, six years of Nazi occupation, and the murder of more than a quarter of a million Czechoslovak Jews in the Holocaust; liberation by the Soviet Red Army in May 1945, the ethnic cleansing of three million Bohemian Germans by their forcible expulsion from the country in 1945–1946, Klement Gottwald's communist coup of Victorious February 1948, and the Stalinist terror of the 1950s; the creative explosion of the 1960s cultural thaw, the reform communism of Alexander Dubček's Prague Spring, the Soviet invasion of 21 August 1968, and twenty years of so-called normalization under Gustáv Husák. The period—and an era—ends with the Velvet Revolution of November 1989, which catapulted the dissident playwright Václav Havel into Prague Castle and precipitated the breakup of Czechoslovakia in 1992. I argued in *Prague, Capital of the Twentieth Century* that "this is a place in which modernist dreams have time and again unraveled; a location in which the masks have sooner or later always come off to reveal the grand narratives of progress for the childish fairy tales they are."[6] These were the years of peak unraveling.

I do not attempt to impose an artificial coherence on a history that conspicuously lacks it. In the words of Walter Benjamin (whose study of nineteenth-century Paris in *The Arcades Project* has been a continual inspiration for my work on Prague), I want to allow "the rags, the refuse" that gets lost in the grander narratives of modernity, to "come into their own." As I explained in the introduction to *Prague, Capital of the Twentieth Century*, I am interested in "the details that derail"; my method is that of Benjamin's "literary montage," whose intent is "to discover in the analysis of the small individual moment the crystal of the total event."[7] I weave a tapestry out of such moments, letting the people who populate my pages speak in their own voices as much as possible. The result is a cornucopia of what Jean-François Lyotard has called *petits récits*.[8] The fragments out of which *Postcards from Absurdistan* is woven are intended to function as *images*, as Humphrey Jennings defines that term in *Pandaemonium*, the "imaginative history of the Industrial Revolution" that inspired Danny Boyle's acclaimed opening ceremony at the 2012 London Olympic Games. "What I call *Images*," Jennings writes, "are quotations from writings of the period in question . . . which either in the writing or in the nature of the matter itself or both have revolutionary and symbolic and illuminatory quality. I mean that *they contain in little a whole world*—they are the knots in a great net of tangled time and space—the moments at which the situation of humanity is clear—even if only for the flash time of the photographer or the lighting."[9] Benjamin speaks similarly of "dialectical images" in which "it's not that what is past casts its light on what is present, or what is present its light on what is past; rather, image is that wherein what has been comes together in a flash with the now to form a constellation." This "moment of awakening," he goes on, "is identical with the 'now of recognizability' in which things put on their true—surrealist—face."[10]

The images through which I try to bring Prague's twentieth-century past into dialogue with our twenty-first-century present include not only quotations from written sources—poems, novels, short stories, plays, letters, diaries, memoirs, interviews, newspapers, transcripts of radio broadcasts, minutes of meetings, government reports, laws, proclamations, political tracts—but also buildings, paintings, sculptures, photographs, book covers, exhibitions, stage sets, films, TV programs, cartoons, operas, songs, postage stamps, banknotes, funeral ceremonies, and jokes. In this regard—and irrespective of any contribution this book might make to the sociology of modernity—I hope *Postcards from Absurdistan* helps extend knowledge of modern Czech cultural history among English-speaking readers, even though it does not pretend to provide a comprehensive survey. For this period in particular, that history includes several waves of the diaspora that novelist Josef Škvorecký has called the "Bohemia of the soul."[11] Whether they were Czechs, Germans, or Jews, many Praguers did not have to wait for sociologists to breathlessly proclaim a "new mobilities paradigm" to know the limitations the "*sedentarist* bias," which "treats as normal stability, meaning, and place, and treats as abnormal distance, change, and placelessness," imposes on the writing of history.[12] I offer no apology for following my protagonists through Paris and Tokyo, Moscow and New York, Pondicherry and Casablanca, Terezín and Auschwitz, Mexico City and the deserts of Utah, even if it sometimes disrupts the tidy flow of the narrative just as it disrupted the flow of their lives. Mobility—voluntary and otherwise—is but one of many features of the modern world that Western scholarship has marginalized and that the vantage point of Prague brings into sharp relief. I hope this is not the only way this book challenges cartographies and chronologies of modernity inherited from the twentieth century that continue to haunt us today. At a time when democracy is once more under global assault, this is not just another story of quarrels in a faraway country, between peoples of whom we know nothing.[13] The dark half century of Prague's modernity considered here holds up an unsettling mirror to our own historical crossroads.

As ever, Princeton University Press has been a pleasure to work with. I owe particular thanks to my editors Eric Crahan and (from July 2020) Priya Nelson, who were unfailingly supportive of this project even though both inherited it, and to editorial assistant Barbara Shi, who worked closely and efficiently with me to see the manuscript through the editorial process and into production. Art director Dimitri Karetnikov and permissions manager Lisa Black provided invaluable advice regarding the illustrations. Larisa Martin did a scrupulous job of copy editing. In choosing images, I avoided overlap with *Coasts of Bohemia and Prague, Capital of the Twentieth Century* (hence there are no reproductions of Karel Teige or Toyen, whose work was plentifully represented in the earlier volumes), and although the abstract Czech *informel* art of the midcentury plays an important part in my narrative, it gains little from being reproduced in black and white. I am indebted to Jessika Hoffmeister, Pavel Hrnčíř, Viktor Stoilov, and Veronika Tuckerová for putting me in touch with rights holders for images and to Jan Placák for allowing us to freely reproduce works owned by his Galerie Ztichlá klika. Helena Lukas and Jindřich Toman were generous in providing permissions to reproduce works for which they held copyright as heirs, as well as supplying copies from their respective archives.

Petr Zídek and Lucie Zídková kindly sent me scans of printed materials I was unable to access because of the COVID-19 pandemic. It was Lucie who introduced me to the Holocaust memorial at Bubny Station during what she described as our "Kamil Lhoták walk" through Holešovice on my last pre-COVID visit to the city in September 2018, where I presented an early version of the Prelude to this book as "The Prague Address" at the European International Studies Association (EISA) 12th Pan-European Conference on International Relations. I owe thanks to Benjamin Tallis for inviting me to give the Address and to the City of Prague for providing EISA with funds that defrayed the costs of my travel and accommodations. Michael Beckerman, Helena Čapková, Andrea Orzoff, David Vichnar, Yoke-Sum Wong, and Kimberly Elman Zarecor all made the time to read sections of the manuscript during what has been an exceptionally demanding period for everyone teaching in universities, and the book has greatly benefited from their comments and corrections, as it has from those of two anonymous readers for PUP. To Ivan Margolius, Zeese Papanikolas, and Jindřich Toman, who read through the entire manuscript (in Zeese's case several times over) as it was taking shape, I owe more than I can say. I hope they will take some pleasure in seeing their criticisms and suggestions reflected in the final product, and not just in correction of missing or misplaced diacritics. Yoke-Sum would have read all of it too, she says, like she did its predecessor, but thanks to COVID we never did get to Paris.

Calgary, Alberta
February 2022

Prelude

17 NOVEMBER

An era can be said to end when its basic illusions are exhausted. . . . A retreat
began from the old confidence in reason itself; nothing any longer could be
what it seemed. . . . A sort of political surrealism came dancing through the
ruins of what had nearly been a beautifully moral and rational world.

—ARTHUR MILLER[1]

IN THE CZECH REPUBLIC 17 November is a national holiday, officially known
as the Day of Struggle for Freedom and Democracy. It used to be called the
International Day of the Students, and in some quarters the name change remains controversial.[2] The holiday commemorates two events that occurred on
the same day, fifty years apart. The first, which I discuss in more detail later,
took place in 1939. Following Slovakia's secession from Czechoslovakia under
Nazi tutelage, Adolf Hitler's Wehrmacht occupied the Czech Lands on
15 March 1939 and incorporated them into the Third Reich as the Protectorate
of Bohemia and Moravia. Demonstrations broke out in Prague on 28 October,
the day Czechoslovakia had declared its independence from Austria-Hungary
in 1918. Police fired on the protesters, wounding medical student Jan Opletal,
who later died of his injuries. There was further trouble after Opletal's funeral
on 15 November, when groups of students roamed through the city center
vandalizing bilingual signs, chanting anti-German slogans, and singing patriotic
songs. In the early hours of 17 November security forces stormed student dormitories, deported more than twelve hundred students to concentration camps,
and shot nine alleged ringleaders. All Czech universities and other institutions

1

of postsecondary education were declared closed for three years, and they remained shut for the rest of the war. The next year the International Students' Council, a London-based refugee body, proclaimed 17 November International Students' Day. It has been celebrated around the world ever since.

During the Cold War the Communist Party of Czechoslovakia (Komunistická strana Československa, hereafter KSČ) commandeered 17 November for its own agenda. An important part of communist legitimacy stemmed from the party's resistance credentials during World War II, and the regime assiduously cultivated the memory of the German occupation. Over time, and especially after the Soviet invasion of 21 August 1968, the 17 November commemorations became largely formulaic. But at the fiftieth anniversary of the Nazis' closure of Czech universities, unusual circumstances prevailed. For weeks, East German refugees had been pouring through Prague on their way to West Germany. Even as the KSČ was still resisting the tide of reform sweeping the Soviet bloc, the East German government opened the Berlin Wall on 9 November 1989. On 17 November a crowd of fifteen thousand assembled at the Albertov campus of Charles University to listen to pro-democracy speakers. Josef Šárka, a participant in Jan Opletal's funeral fifty years earlier, told them, "I am glad you are fighting for the same thing as we fought for back then."[3] After the rally the students marched to Vyšehrad Cemetery, where prominent Czech writers, artists, and musicians have been buried since the nineteenth century. They lit candles, sang the national anthem, and laid flowers on the grave of nineteenth-century romantic poet Karel Hynek Mácha. From Vyšehrad they set out for Wenceslas Square, marching along the Vltava riverbank toward the National Theater. On Národní Avenue, just down the road from the theater, they were beaten up by riot police. The police action triggered ten days of nightly demonstrations that forced the Communist Party to relinquish its monopoly on power.

Thereafter 17 November became a day not only for remembering the victims of 1939 but also for affirming the democratic values of what soon became known as the Velvet Revolution. Students marked both by laying flowers at Albertov every year. But in 2015 the celebrations took a strange turn. That year more than a million refugees crossed Europe's borders. Notwithstanding vehement opposition from university authorities, the far-right Anti-Islamic Bloc organized a rally "in support of the views of the president on immigration and Islam" at the time and place the 17 November commemoration normally took place. A month earlier Czech Republic president Miloš Zeman had warned that "Islamic refugees will not respect Czech laws and habits, they will apply sharia law, so unfaithful women will be stoned to death and thieves will have their hands cut off."[4] When the students arrived at Albertov to lay their flowers as usual, police barred their entry. Only people with preprinted cards reading "Long Live Zeman!" were allowed past the barriers.

Zeman himself spoke at the rally, where he told the crowd that people opposed to Islam and refugees should not be "branded" as Islamophobes, fascists, or racists. "What joins these two anniversaries over the abyss of time of fifty years?" he asked:

> I think there are two things. First, the disagreement of our nation with occupation, be it open as in the case of the German occupation, or poorly hidden but real as in the case of the Soviet occupation. This nation deserves to rule itself and no one, repeat no one, from outside can dictate what it should and shouldn't do. But the second reminder from both 17 Novembers is possibly just as serious. Then people went out into the streets to protest against manipulation, to protest against the fact that they were pressured to believe a single correct opinion . . . that they were not allowed to think differently than those who manipulated them.[5]

Afterward Zeman stood side by side with Anti-Islamic Bloc founder Martin Konvička to sing the Czech national anthem. Konvička had previously gained notoriety for publicly advocating concentration camps for Muslims. Foreign guests on the platform included English Defence League founder "Tommy Robinson" (Stephen Yaxley-Lennon) and leader of the far-right German anti-Islamic movement Pegida. Banners carried by the crowd read "Fuck Islam!" and "Ban Islam!" (in English).

Zeman went further in his 2015 Christmas and New Year message to the nation, telling his compatriots, "I am profoundly convinced that we are facing an organized invasion and not a spontaneous movement of refugees."[6] Zeman was narrowly (51.4 to 48.6 percent) reelected Czech president in 2018, winning majorities in every region of the country except Prague, where he was trounced by his liberal opponent Jiří Drahoš. Drahoš also bettered Zeman in the cities of Brno and Plzeň, though not in the onetime coal and steel metropolis (and working-class KSČ stronghold) of Ostrava, where Zeman took 62 percent of the vote. Though there are always national specificities to be taken into account, these demographic divides are remarkably similar to those underlying other contemporary populist revolts against "globalizing urban elites" across much of Europe and North America. Those unexpected triumphs included the victory of the Brexit campaign in the United Kingdom's referendum on leaving the European Union in June 2016 and Donald Trump's election as US president in November of the same year.

FIGURE 0.1. Otakar Příhoda and Miroslav Krátký's 17 November memorial, Národní Avenue, Prague, 1990. Photograph by author, 2021.

For more than eighty years the date 17 November has been a resonant signifier in the Czech imagination, not unlike the Fourth of July—or September 11—for Americans. It is a day set apart from others. But there is no simple continuity in its signification. Something more complicated, contradictory, and fluid has been happening—what we might call the eternal return of the never-quite-the-same. The only constant is the recurrence of the signifier itself: the day in the calendar, 17 November. What is signified by that date repeatedly changes according to the shifting needs of successive presents. With an absurdity that is thoroughly typical of Prague, by 2015 the memory of Jan Opletal, killed protesting the fascist occupation, had been hijacked by neofascists protesting a nonexistent "invasion" of Muslim refugees. Roman Tyč drew attention to this mutability of the signified in his artistic protest of 17 November 2009. Otakar Příhoda and Miroslav Krátký's memorial to the events of 1989, which had been installed in 1990 at the place where the police attacked the students on Národní Avenue, consists of a bronze sculpture of several upraised hands above the inscription "17.11.1989." Some of the hands are making the peace sign. On the Day of Struggle for Freedom and Democracy in 2009 Tyč added two matching bronze side panels to the memorial, challenging the kitsch of its symbolism. He titled his work *Není co slavit* (There is nothing to celebrate). On the left panel, where the inscription read "17.11.1939," the hands were raised in the Nazi salute. On the right panel, where the inscription read "17.11.2009," the hands were making the middle finger "Fuck you!" gesture. Tyč's panels were removed by police the following day. The artist later explained:

> The plaque itself was simply crying out for the completing information. All these hands are Czech, unlike the gestures they display. It is not beside the point to put what has happened here and what is happening here into context. The Czechs *Heil*-ed back then, and when all is said and done, they do the same today, after the years the victorious victory maybe isn't so victorious after all.[7]

———

I subtitled this book *Prague at the End of History* with deliberate irony, because history was declared *at an end* no fewer than three times during Bohemia's turbulent twentieth century: by the Nazis, when they incorporated Prague into their "thousand-year Reich"; by the communists, who proclaimed socialism "achieved" in 1960 and saw the future as an inexorable march forward to communism; and by many Western commentators, who were no less confident that the 1989 revolutions in Europe heralded (in Francis Fukuyama's words) "the universalization of Western liberal democracy as the final form of human government."[8] Each was the illusion of its epoch. Each was spectacularly wrong. In Prague the dreamworlds of modernity have repeatedly disintegrated to return us to a no-man's-land of recurring nightmares to which Czech dissidents gave the name Absurdistan. This is the territory explored in this book. Its features have been unsparingly exposed in Prague's twentieth-century literature and arts as well as in Czech popular culture, often by way of a rich vein of frequently vulgar and sometimes obscene black comedy that stretches from Franz Kafka's *The Castle* and *The Trial* and Jaroslav Hašek's *Good Soldier Švejk* to Miloš Forman's *The Firemen's Ball*, Bohumil Hrabal's *Closely Watched Trains* and *I Served the King of England*, and the satirical public art of David Černý, who first shot to fame when he painted pink the Soviet tank commemorating the city's liberation by the Red Army in May 1945.[9]

Absurdistan is what modernity looks like once we take our modernist blinkers off. It is a land where, as surrealist poet Petr Král observed while exiled in Paris in the 1980s, you can turn a corner and stumble across "the Russian steppes between two baroque domes, like an antechamber of the Gulag comfortably situated in the suburbs of Paris or Munich."[10] The *domeček* (little house)—as the communist secret police torture chamber at 214 Kapucínská Street, just behind the lovely Italianate Loreta Church in Hradčany, was popularly known—comes into view.[11] Across the square from the Loreta Church is the Černín Palace, where Czechoslovakia's foreign minister Jan Masaryk either jumped or was thrown to his death from his apartment window three weeks after the 1948 KSČ coup. In Absurdistan the future is certain, but the past is always unpredictable. In Absurdistan it's the shop next door that doesn't have any bananas; *this* is the shop where we don't have any meat. In Absurdistan Soviet jazz will not be played. Ivan Ivanovich has fucked his balalaika. These are all communist-era jokes, but Absurdistan was here long before communism and is still here after it. Back in the days when Bohemia was still part of Austria-Hungary, Karel Sabina, the librettist for Bedřich Smetana's *The Bartered Bride*, the Czech "national opera," turned out to be an Austrian police informer. And where else but in postcommunist Absurdistan would a prime minister have to resign because his chief of staff and lover used the secret police to spy on his estranged wife, as Czech Republic premier Petr Nečas did in 2013? Josef K. and the Good Soldier Švejk may be long gone, but Jára Cimrman, the fictional genius born in 1966 on the radio program *Nealkoholická vinárna U Pavouka* (The nonalcoholic wine bar at the spider), was voted "The Greatest Czech" in a 2005 television survey ahead of Jan Hus, Comenius, Tomáš Masaryk, and Václav Havel. From the Jára Cimrman Theater in the working-class (but nowadays rapidly gentrifying) Prague quarter of Žižkov, the beloved Czech polymath presides over "not only parodies of pseudoscience and enlightenment but of any kind of noetic optimism and positivism."[12]

Absurdistan is where Bob Dylan was looking out from when he wrote "Desolation Row." It is no place for kitsch. I use the word here as Milan Kundera defined it: "the need to gaze into the mirror of the beautifying lie and to be moved to tears of gratification at one's own reflection."[13] Absurdistan is ground zero for the surrealists' *humor noir*, that "SENSE . . . of the theatrical (and joyless) pointlessness of everything" that André Breton called "the mortal enemy of sentimentality."[14] "Humor," Kundera writes, is "the divine flash that reveals the world in its moral ambiguity and man in his profound incompetence to judge others . . . the intoxicating relativity of human things; the strange pleasure that comes of the certainty that there is no certainty."[15] Aficionados of gallows humor will find plenty to divert them in twentieth-century Prague—not least, the publication of documents in 2008 outing Kundera as an alleged police informer in his youth.[16]

The sociologist Anthony Giddens characterizes modernity as "a shorthand term for modern society, or industrial civilization," that is "associated with (1) a certain set of attitudes towards the world, the idea of the world as open to transformation, by human intervention; (2) a complex of economic institutions, especially industrial production and a market economy; (3) a certain range of political institutions, including the nation-state and mass democracy. Largely as a result of these characteristics," Giddens maintains, "modernity is vastly more dynamic than any previous type of social order. It is a society . . . which, unlike any preceding culture, lives in the future, rather than the past."[17] Viewed from Absurdistan, this is the kitsch version of the modern condition. While all of Giddens's features are visible in Prague, so are other, less salubrious facets of the modern world. There are economic institutions that are indisputably modern and heavily industrial but not linked to a market economy: Five-Year Plans and the rest of the apparatus of a command economy, which was simultaneously an extraordinarily powerful instrument of social control. There are political institutions that play a key part in the organization of social life, but they are mass-democratic only in name. Alongside the flags, anthems, parades, and other rituals of the modern state, both fascism and communism politicized the minutiae of the everyday and policed it through a vast machinery of surveillance while refining the spectacle of terror as an instrument of power. These, too, are quintessentially modern phenomena: nothing says twentieth century quite like the concentration camp, the gulag, the street committee, and the show trial. We cannot begin to conceptualize *this* modernity without recognizing genocide, ethnic cleansing, racism, and xenophobia as constitutive elements of modern national states—and, since we are all subjects of national states whether we like it or not, of our modern subjectivities. If we were to develop a gallery of Absurdistani social types in the manner of German sociologist Georg Simmel, it would have to include the revolutionary, the apparatchik, the interrogator, the collaborator, the refugee, the dissident, the outsider, and the survivor, not to mention the innocent bystander who is always looking the other way and Václav Havel's greengrocer, whose knowing complicity allows the whole show to go on.[18] But often, it is by no means certain who is who. In Absurdistan yesterday's revolutionary is today's apparatchik and today's apparatchik is tomorrow's entrepreneur. Historical periodization loses its purchase as the boundaries between political regimes and social systems blur. The distinctions between collaboration and resistance, acquiescence and dissent get lost in a perpetually shifting landscape of endless shades of gray.

The optimism of 1989 didn't last long. History didn't end. But in the wake of 9/11, the 2008 financial crisis, the worldwide resurgence of populist nationalism, the COVID-19 pandemic, and runaway global warming, it might be easier to get a hearing now for a more skeptical view of modernity than it was back then. I see no good reason to regard democratic modernity as the norm and authoritarian or totalitarian modernity as a deviation. Indeed, the Nazi and communist versions of the end of history might be seen as the very epitome of Giddens's "society . . . which . . . lives in the future, rather than the past." After all, what better exemplifies the supremely modernist "idea of the world as open to transformation, by human intervention," than the Nazis' "triumph of the will" and the communists' "scientific socialism"? At the very least, Prague's variety of modern experiences ought to induce us to expand our understanding of what is and is not part of the modern condition—or whether there is such a singular thing at all. Better yet, we might venture further down the path opened up by Max Weber, Hannah Arendt, and Zygmunt Bauman, among others,[19] and ask whether it isn't the everyday practices of "modern society, or industrial civilization" that nourish these *fleurs du mal* in the first place. This book does not answer these questions. But it should provide plentiful food for thought for anyone who wishes to ponder them further. Twentieth-century Prague offers a more unsettling looking glass than Kundera's mirror of kitsch. My hope is that it is one in which we can see aspects of ourselves in the other and vice versa—and shudder as well as laugh, caught short by the sudden recognition of Rimbaud's truth: "*Je est un autre.*"[20]

ACT 1

Recto 1918–1945

Years ago we saw no-man's-land, in a film, and because the film was set in 1918 we thought, naïvely, that it was the past. Then we went home with a feeling of pride in the free and radiant future toward which the people of today are walking hand in hand. Back then we had not yet experienced what strange twists and detours, switches and blind alleys history creates.

—MILENA JESENSKÁ, "V ZEMI NIKOHO,"
PŘÍTOMNOST, 29 DECEMBER 1938

1

Kafkárna

But as long as we are not quite so perfect, as long as the statement alone does not suffice for faith and understanding, as long as we must place our fingers in the wounds, like Thomas, we have the right to convince ourselves the wounds exist, and that they are deep.

—MILENA JESENSKÁ[1]

Love Letters

"She is a living fire, of a kind I have never seen before," Franz Kafka wrote to his friend Max Brod early in May 1920, "yet at the same time she is extremely tender, courageous, bright."[2] Milena Jesenská is best known to English-language readers—if she is known at all—as the recipient of Kafka's *Briefe an Milena* (*Letters to Milena*), first published in German by Willi Haas in 1952 and translated into English the next year. Milena gave Willi the letters for safekeeping after Hitler's Wehrmacht occupied Prague in March 1939. Haas had neither Jesenská's nor Kafka's permission to publish them, and Milena's daughter Jana Černá insists that both would have wanted the correspondence to be kept private.[3] But it wasn't, so we can place our fingers in the wounds like Doubting Thomas and convince ourselves that they are deep. Milena's letters to Franz have not survived, so we see her here entirely through Kafka's eyes. Franz's lanky shadow continues to loom over most of the secondary literature on Jesenská available in English, too. Margarete Buber-Neumann's memoir-cum-biography *Milena, Kafkas Freundin* (Milena, Kafka's lover) was first translated as *Mistress to Kafka: The Life and Death of Milena*, a title that was a titillating travesty of both Jesenská's relationship to Kafka and Buber-Neumann's book.

It was later republished as *Milena: The Tragic Story of Kafka's Great Love*. Jana Černá's reminiscences of her mother, titled in Czech *Adresát Milena Jesenská* (The addressee Milena Jesenská), became *Kafka's Milena*. Mary Hockaday promises to flesh out "Kafka's muse"—a description Milena scarcely merits, given the brevity of their affair—as "a radical-thinking, thoroughly independent woman and journalist in her own right," but her biography is titled *Kafka, Love and Courage*.[4] Somehow the subject of the book gets relegated to the subtitle: *The Life of Milena Jesenská*.

Despite her clickbait title, Hockaday devotes just two and a half chapters out of twelve to Jesenská's involvement with Kafka. This is probably about right, considering that, for all its intensity, Franz and Milena's "dream-like amorous association," as Jana Černá describes it, was short-lived, mostly epistolary, and likely not consummated.[5] When the correspondence began, Franz was engaged to his second fiancée Julie Wohryzek in Prague, and Milena was unhappily married to her first husband Ernst Pollak in Vienna. Franz would soon dump Julie (in the late afternoon of 5 July 1920 on Charles Square), but Milena proved incapable of leaving Ernst. "In spite of everything," Kafka lamented, her "fire . . . burns only for him."[6] The Pollaks had a fashionably modern open marriage, an arrangement that Milena accepted with reluctance. Ernst at one point installed his supposedly beautiful but brainless lover Mizzi Beer in their apartment in a ménage à trois,[7] while Milena had liaisons of her own with the writer Hermann Broch and the aristocratic Austrian communist Franz Xaver Schaffgotsch. It was Schaffgotsch who introduced her to the writings of Rosa Luxemburg, the communist leader murdered in Berlin by Freikorps thugs during the Spartacist Uprising of January 1919. Milena would later translate Luxemburg's *Letters from Prison* into Czech.[8] Kafka wrote the bulk of his letters to Milena over an eight-month period between April and November 1920. During this time they met just twice, for four days in Vienna at the end of June (according to Franz, "the first was unsure, the second was oversure, the third day was full of regret, and the fourth was the good one")[9] and for a mutually unsatisfying one-day tryst in the little Czechoslovak-Austrian border town of Gmünd in late August. Franz tried to break off the correspondence in November, telling her, "What you are for me, Milena, beyond the whole world we inhabit, cannot be found in all the daily scraps of paper which I have sent you . . . these letters are pure anguish, *they are caused by incurable anguish and they cause incurable anguish*."[10] Milena continued her lovelorn visits to the post office until January 1921,[11] when she received a letter from the High Tatra mountains where Franz was being treated for tuberculosis. "Make it impossible for us to meet, and do not write," he implored; "please fulfill my request in silence, it is the only thing that can enable me to go on living, everything else causes further destruction."[12] They did meet a few times after that in Prague, but no longer as lovers. Kafka described Milena's visits as "kind and noble" but "somewhat forced, too, like the visits one pays an invalid."[13] Franz entrusted Milena with his diaries, dating back to 1910, in October 1921. When he next wrote, at the end of March 1922, he addressed her as Frau Milena, using the formal *Sie*.[14] They saw each other for the last time in June 1923.

Milena Jesenská was more than just *Kafkas Freundin*, and their affair was but one episode, albeit a significant one, in her eventful life. That said, these letters provide as good a way as any into the convolutions of Prague at the beginning of the end of history. Whether in the intimacy of love letters or in the cockpit of the public sphere, it was a time and place where the implications of language for identity could not be avoided. Early in the correspondence, when their connection was still that of author to translator (Milena's Czech translation of Kafka's story "The Stoker" appeared in the communist poet S. K. Neumann's magazine *Kmen* [Stem] in April 1920), Franz asked Milena if she could write to him in Czech rather than German. "Of course I understand Czech," he explained. "I've meant to ask you several times already why you never write in Czech. Not to imply that your command of German leaves anything to be desired . . . I wanted to read you in Czech because, after all, you do belong to that language, because only there can Milena be found in her entirety."[15] By her own account, Milena "did not know a word of German" when she arrived in Vienna in March 1918 as a "young girl" (*malá holka*). This may have been an exaggeration, but Franz Schaffgotsch recalled that she still spoke German badly two years later.[16] Max Brod, too, described Milena's German at the time as "imperfect."[17] But it is not linguistic competence that is at issue here. "If I write in German," Milena told her friend Willi Schlamm in 1938, "I only say half of what I have to say . . . I am controlled, caustic, good-humored. In Czech I am sentimental and 'abominably fond of truth.' What do you prefer?"[18] By that date there can be no doubt of Milena's capabilities in German, but she is speaking of the ineffable connections between language and being. So was Kafka. "*The limits of my language mean the limits of my world*," wrote their Viennese contemporary Ludwig Wittgenstein in his *Tractatus Logico-Philosophicus*, a work he completed during a leave from the Austrian army in the summer of 1918.[19] In Prague, Wittgenstein's celebrated dictum was no more than a simple description of everyday realities. Franz and Milena were both dyed-in-the-wool Praguers, but even as they walked the same streets they inhabited different worlds.

Besides, Kafka was Jewish. He was sharply reminded of that fact at dinner one evening in the Pension Ottoburg in Merano, where he was convalescing (and "making plans day and night—against my own clear will—about how I could seduce the chambermaid") when he began his correspondence with Milena.[20] "The company in my present pension," he wrote to Max Brod, "are all German and Christian." Usually Franz ate at a small table by himself:

> But today when I went into the dining room the colonel (the general was not there yet) invited me so cordially to the common table that I had to give in. So now the thing took its course. After the first few words it came out that I was from Prague. Both of them—the general, who sat opposite me, and the colonel—were acquainted with Prague. Was I Czech? No. So now explain to those true German military eyes what you really are. Someone else suggested "German-Bohemian," someone else "Little Quarter" [*Kleinseite*, in Czech *Malá Strana*, the Lesser Town]. Then the subject was dropped and people went on eating, but the general, with his sharp ears linguistically schooled in the Austrian army, was not satisfied. After we had eaten, he once more began to wonder about the sound of my German, perhaps more bothered by what he saw than what he heard. At that point I tried to explain that by my being Jewish. At this his scientific curiosity, to be sure, was satisfied, but not his human feelings. At the same moment, probably by sheer chance, for all the others could not have heard our conversation, but perhaps there was some connection after all, the whole company rose to leave (though yesterday they lingered on together for a long while; I heard that, since my door is adjacent to the dining room).[21]

Explain what you really are. For Prague Jews of Kafka's generation, that was a tall order.

Ratcatcher's Beauties

Franz Kafka was born on 3 July 1883 in a baroque house on the corner of Maiselova and Kaprova Streets, just off the Old Town Square (Staroměstské náměstí). Only the portal survives today. The rest of the building was demolished during the slum clearance initiated by the Prague City Council in 1894, which razed the centuries-old Jewish ghetto and replaced it with upscale apartment houses in a hodgepodge of historicist and art nouveau styles, leaving only a scattering of synagogues, the Old Jewish Cemetery, and the Jewish Town Hall with its backward-turning clock as mementos. In Czech the clearance was known as the *asanace*, from the Latin *sanitas*, the root of the terms *sanity*, *sanitation*, and *cordon sanitaire*. The little plaza where the house stood is now called Franz Kafka Square (náměstí Franze Kafky). It acquired the name only in 2000; for much of the latter half of the twentieth century Prague's most famous writer was officially forgotten in his homeland, having been doubly othered as "a Prague-Jewish author writing in German."[22] The Kafka family lived for years on Pařížská (then called Mikulášská) Street, the main thoroughfare of the new quarter, in an apartment house on the corner of the embankment opposite the newly built Svatopluk Čech Bridge (Čechův most) from 1907 and in the Oppelt House on the corner of the Old Town Square from 1913. If the "shy young poet Gustav Janouch, who worshipped Kafka, brought him his first poems, [and] engaged him in discussions," is to be believed, the ghetto remained a constant presence in Kafka's world long after it had gone.[23] "I came when it had already disappeared," Franz supposedly told the boy, who was the son of one of his colleagues at the Workers' Accident Insurance Institute of the Kingdom of Bohemia:

> But . . . In us all it still lives—the dark corners, the secret alleys, shuttered windows, squalid courtyards, rowdy pubs, and sinister inns. We walk through the broad streets of the newly built town. But our steps and our glances are uncertain. Inside we tremble just as before in the ancient streets of our misery. Our heart knows nothing of the slum clearance which has been achieved. The unhealthy old Jewish town within us is far more real than the new hygienic town around us. With our eyes open we walk through a dream: ourselves only a ghost of a vanished age.[24]

Janouch is too delicate to mention the Fifth Quarter's numerous brothels, which made the district as notorious as its appalling mortality statistics.[25] U Denice, which the journalist and playwright Karel Ladislav Kukla described as "the eldorado of . . . Prague street girls,"[26] stood a couple doors down from the Jewish Town Hall and the Old-New Synagogue on Rabínská (today Maiselova) Street. Kukla's two-volume *Konec bahna Prahy* (The end of the Prague cesspit, 1927), "an illustrated review of real stories, dramas, and humorous sketches from the darkest as well as the most wonderful havens of moral squalor, despair, darkness, gallows humor, prostitution, and crime in the saloons, bars, alleyways, pubs, hospitals, lunatic asylums, dives, and gutters of Greater Prague"—which seems to cover all the bases—affectionately gathered the city's *fleurs du mal*.[27] With *Ze všech koutů Prahy* (From all corners of Prague, 1894), *Noční Prahou* (Prague by night, 1905), and *Podzemní Praha* (Underground Prague, 1920), *Konec bahna Prahy* completed what Kukla proudly called his "Unknown Prague" tetralogy. One of his sources was Paul Leppin, a literary connoisseur of the "ratcatcher's beauty" of the city's underworld whom Max Brod dubbed the "chosen bard of the painfully disappearing old Prague."[28] At the Salon Aaron on Cikánská (Gypsy, today Eliška Krásnohorská) Street, wrote Leppin, "satisfied, voluptuous prostitutes flaunted themselves in flowing silk gowns . . . [and] the laughter fluttered within like a captive bird in a cage." The pride of the house was the strawberry-blonde Jana, who was more desired than her companions because she "gave to each man from the tensile, agonizing, restless sweetness that imbued her."[29] Leppin tells her story—or, rather, a heavily mythologized version of it—in his tale "The Ghost of the Jewish Ghetto," published in *Das Paradies der Andern* (*Others' Paradise*, 1920). The action climaxes with Jana (Johanna in Leppin's German) escaping the public hospital where she had been taken during an epidemic and making her way back to the Salon Aaron, only to find that it had been torn down. "A troop of drunken soldiers was passing by. . . . Amid the debris of the gutted bordellos, Johanna gave herself to the men whom chance had placed in her path." The sex trade survived the *asanace*, as it would everything else modernity threw at it, and the whores moved on. "Clacking in high-heeled shoes, depravity fled to the outer edge of the suburbs. A city for the rich and fashionable rose up in the old squares."[30]

Kafka was not unmarked by this environment. "I passed by the brothel as by the house of a beloved," he recorded in his diary in the spring of 1910. Is it beside the point to note that the Czech word *nevěstka* (prostitute) is a diminutive of *nevěsta* (bride)? The female sex was clearly on Franz's mind, as it often was; a couple lines later he floats an image of "the seamstresses in the downpour of rain" apropos nothing at all.[31] When not sampling the bordellos of Paris and Milan (as they did while on vacation in 1911),[32] Franz and Max patronized the whorehouses at home. Brod, Leppin, and their fellow writers Egon Erwin Kisch and Franz Werfel were regulars at the Salon Gogo in the House of the Red Peacock on Kamzíková Street, where the young Werfel charmed the ladies by impersonating Caruso with his beautiful tenor renditions of operatic arias. Opened by Abraham Goldschmidt around 1865, the Gogo was the most luxurious of Prague's houses of pleasure. Gustav Mahler was a frequent customer during his tenure as resident conductor a few steps away at the Estates Theater in 1885–1886, though he reputedly didn't like being

FIGURE 1.1. Hansi Szokoll and Franz Kafka, c. 1907. Photographer unknown.
Photograph © Archiv Klaus Wagenbach.

disturbed by the girls when composing at the piano in the yellow Japanese room on the second floor. Visits from Otto von Bismarck and the future (and last) Habsburg emperor Karl I lent further distinction to the establishment.[33] In 1908 Kafka fell in love with a twenty-one-year-old wine bar waitress named Hansi Szokoll, with whom he was photographed wearing a bowler hat like Sabina in Milan Kundera's *Nesnesitelná lehkost bytí* (*The Unbearable Lightness of Being*, 1984), accompanied by a dog. The photo is famous. Hansi is not. Sometimes she is cropped out of the picture; she seldom merits more than a paragraph or two in Kafka biographies. But Franz spent a very satisfying Sunday evening in June "in the dusk on the sofa beside dear H.'s bed while she pummeled [*schlug*] her boyish body under the red blanket." What Hansi was up to is anyone's guess, but this was the selfsame body that Kafka told Brod "entire cavalry regiments had ridden across."[34] The next month Franz took an aging streetwalker to a hotel. She complained that "people aren't as sweet to whores as they are to lovers. I didn't comfort her," he wrote Max, "because she didn't comfort me either."[35] This wasn't just a passing youthful phase. "I intentionally walk through the streets where there are whores," reads an entry in Kafka's diary five years later. "Walking past them excites me, the remote but nevertheless existent possibility of going with one. Is that grossness? But I know no better, and doing this seems basically innocent to me and causes me almost no regret."[36]

If Franz lived in truth, it was a down-and-dirty, pornographic, unvarnished truth. But this was not, or at least not until recent scholarship began to unpick the Kafka myth,[37] the authorized version. Max Brod began Kafka's unlikely transubstantiation into a latter-day prophet of all modern ills when he fictionalized his friend as the saintly Richard Garta in his roman à clef *Zauberreich der Liebe* (The enchanted kingdom of love, 1926), which appeared just two years after Franz's death. "Kafka is more than any other modern writer," Brod claimed later, "he is the 20th-century Job."[38] When Max published Kafka's diaries in 1948 he laundered the sacred text, omitting "things that were too intimate."[39] Take, for example, this passage from October 1911, in which Brod excised all the words in angle brackets:[40]

<In Suha [*sic*] b[rothel]> the day before the day before yesterday. The one, a Jewish girl with a narrow face, or rather, a face that tapers down to a narrow chin, but is widened out by an expansive, wavy hairdo. The three small doors that lead from the inside of the building into the salon. The guests as though in a guardroom on the stage, drinks on the table are barely touched. <The flat-faced girl in an angular dress that does not begin to move until way down at the hemline.> Several girls here dressed like the marionettes for children's theatres that are sold in the Christmas market, that is, with ruching and gold stuck on and loosely sewn so that one can rip them with one pull and they then fall apart in one's fingers.[41]

The precision of Kafka's prose is unnerving—especially if you happen to know the Christmas market that still takes place every year in the Old Town Square. So is the precision of Brod's scalpel. His suppression of the fact that this entire scene is set in a brothel—Šuha on the corner of Benediktská and Dlouhá Streets, a more down-home Prague cathouse than the Gogo—takes the sting out of the marionette analogy and obscures its point, while lending the passage an air of inexplicable "Kafkaesque" mystery. In sanitizing Kafka's life, argues Milan Kundera, Brod censored the essence of Kafka's art. For "at the root of Kafka's novels . . . [lies] a profound antiromanticism; it shows up everywhere: in the way Kafka sees society as well as in the way he constructs a sentence; but its origin may lie in Kafka's vision of sex." Kundera instances K's ecstatic coitus with Frieda "among the beer puddles and the other filth covering the floor" in *The Castle*, a congress that is made all the more grotesque because, unknown to the lovers, "above them, on the bar counter, sit the two assistants: they were watching the couple the whole time."[42] Ratcatcher's beauty is right. Not for nothing did André Breton include an excerpt from Kafka's novella "The Metamorphosis" in his *Anthology of Black Humor*.[43]

Kafka likely would have agreed—a little ruefully, perhaps—with the young Czech psychoanalytic theorist Bohuslav Brouk, who wrote in his afterword to Jindřich Štyrský's *Emilie přichází ke mně ve snu* (*Emily Comes to Me in a Dream*, 1933) that "there is nothing as intensely dispiriting for those who have sublimated the substance of the body than their animality spontaneously making its presence felt. Just consider how the signs of uncontrollable shits deject the hero during a triumphal campaign, or how painfully the nabobs bear their sexual appetites towards their despised inferiors."[44] Comprising a dream narrative and ten pornographic photomontages, *Emily* was first produced in a private limited edition of sixty-nine copies to avoid the censor. It was the last of six volumes in Štyrský's *Edice 69* (Edition 69, 1931–1933), a series of "works of outstanding literary merit and . . . graphic art that will have long-lasting artistic value" but whose "print-runs [were] kept to a minimum by the exclusively erotic nature of the work."[45] Earlier publications in the series included the Marquis de Sade's *Justine* (illustrated by Toyen, née Marie Čermínová) and Vítězslav Nezval's autobiographical coming-of-age novella *Sexuální nocturno* (*Sexual Nocturne*, illustrated by Štyrský). Nezval, Štyrský, Toyen, and Brouk were founding members of the Czechoslovak Surrealist Group in March 1934. The Czech art historian Karel Srp finds it "almost unbelievable that one of the most important books in twentieth-century Czech art reaches the hands of a broader public" for the first time only in 2001, when *Emily* was reprinted in facsimile, but it rather proves Brouk's point.[46]

Pornography is a mirror in which decent folks don't like to see themselves reflected. For the surrealists, the erotic was a methodology for unveiling discomforting truths. Franz Kafka is not the first or the last man or woman to be possessed by undignified desires that cannot be sanitized or romanticized away, and Prague is not the first or the last modern city to clean up the ancient dens of iniquity blighting its center only to have the whores and their johns resurface elsewhere. "The body will continue to demonstrate mortality as the fate of all humans," Brouk continues. "It is for this reason that any reference to human animality so gravely affects those who dream of its antithesis. They take offense not only at any mention of animality in life, but in science, literature, and the arts as well, as this would disturb their reveries by undermining their rationalist airs and social pretensions. By imposing acts both sexual and excremental on their perception, their superhuman fantasies are destroyed, laying bare the vanity of their efforts to free themselves from the power of nature, which has, in assuming mortality, equipped them with a sex and an irrepressible need to satisfy its hunger."[47] *Inter faeces et urinam nascimur.*

Language Games

Kafka's biographer Reiner Stach suggests that while Franz's sisters Valli (Valerie), Elli (Gabriele), and Ottla (Ottilie) might have been shocked by their big brother's visits to prostitutes, his parents were more likely reassured of his masculine normality.[48] His father Hermann, after all, once offered to accompany Franz to a brothel where he could ease his bodily urges rather than see him marry Julie Wohryzek, a mere cobbler's daughter ("If you're scared of that sort of place, I'll come with you").[49] The Kafkas were respectable people with solid bourgeois values. Franz's mother Julie, née Löwy, came from a merchant and brewing family in Poděbrady in eastern Bohemia. The Löwys moved to Prague when Julie was twenty and lived on the Old Town Square in a house where Bedřich Smetana once ran a music school. Like most upper-middle-class Bohemian Jews, they spoke German. Hermann Kafka came from humbler stock. He was raised in the village of Osek near Strakonice in southern Bohemia, where his father Jakob was a kosher butcher. The 1890 census recorded 381 inhabitants in Osek, all of whom declared Czech to be their "language of everyday use."[50] An 1852 census listed twenty Jewish families living in the village, enough to sustain a synagogue.[51] The language of instruction during Hermann's scant few years at the Jewish elementary school in Osek was German, though postcards written in his hand suggest that his grasp of formal German was poor. But he possessed "the Kafka will to life, business, and conquest" in abundance and was amply blessed with "strength, health, appetite, loudness of voice, eloquence, self-satisfaction, worldly dominance, endurance, presence of mind, knowledge of human nature, [and] a certain way of doing things on a grand scale" (I quote Franz).[52] Like hundreds of thousands of other immigrants from the Czech-speaking countryside, Hermann found his way to Prague, where he arranged his marriage through a Jewish matchmaker. With the aid of Julie's dowry he opened a shop on Celetná Street in 1882, selling "linen, fashionable knitted ware, sunshades and umbrellas, walking sticks and cotton goods."[53] On his letterhead Hermann styled himself Heřman Kafka, using the Czech rather than the German spelling of his name.[54] This may have saved the store from damage during the language riots of November 1897, sparked by the fall of Count Kazimir Badeni's government in Vienna following Bohemian-German protests against his decree that all civil servants in Bohemia be bilingual by 1901. Hermann's business prospered, and in 1912 he moved his shop to the corner of the Kinský Palace in the Old Town Square.

During Franz's childhood the family moved several times before settling into the House at the Minute (Dům U Minuty) beside the Old Town Hall in June 1889. The renaissance sgraffiti that are such a striking feature of the façade today were only uncovered in 1919. The Kafkas lived there for seven years before relocating in September 1896 to a larger apartment across the square at 3 Celetná Street, in the same building as Hermann's shop. By that time Franz had acquired his three sisters and lost two brothers. Busy with the business, where they both worked six and a half days a week, Hermann and Julie left Franz's care largely to the domestic staff, including the cook Františka Nedvědová, the maid Marie Zemanová, and the nurse Anna Čukalová, all of whom were Czech Catholics.[55] Franz told his first fiancée Felice Bauer that in his early years he "lived alone for a very long time, battling with nurses, old nannies, spiteful cooks, unhappy governesses, since my parents were always at the shop."[56] Nedvědová, he later wrote to Milena, was "a small dry thin person with a pointed nose, hollow cheeks, somewhat jaundiced but firm, energetic, and superior," who tormented him as she walked him to school with threats that she would tell the teacher how naughty he had been at home.[57] Housekeeper Marie Wernerová, who initially arrived as a governess for Kafka's sisters around 1910 and eventually moved in for good, was a Czech Jewish country girl who spoke little or no German.[58] Franz was still exchanging Christmas presents and corresponding with Slečna (Miss),[59] as Wernerová was known in the family, at the end of his life.[60] Kafka was proud of his proficiency in Czech, but in a characteristically self-mocking way ("I apologize for my mistakes with particular elegance").[61] He appreciated the "linguistic music" of Božena Němcová's beloved novel *Babička* (*The Grandmother*, 1855),[62] a foundation of modern Czech literature, and admired "the vitality of spoken Czech."[63] But it was in German that Franz learned his lessons at the German Boys Elementary School on the Meat Market (Masná ulice), the Old Town Gymnasium (located on the second floor of the Kinský Palace), and the Karl-Ferdinand German University of Prague, where he received his doctorate in law in 1906.[64] Prague University, founded by Charles IV in 1349 and the oldest in Central Europe, had fractured into separate Czech and German institutions in 1882.

"I have never lived among Germans," Franz told Milena after she complied with his request to write to him in Czech. "German is my mother tongue and as such more natural to me," he explained, "but I consider Czech much more affectionate, which is why your letter removes several uncertainties; I see you more clearly, the movements of your body, your hands, so quick, so resolute, it's almost like a meeting."[65] But when Milena asked him a few days later, "Are you a Jew?" (*Jste žid?*), he responds with a harsher corporeal metaphor: "Don't you see how the fist is pulled back in the word '*jste*' so as to gain muscle power? And then in the word '*žid*' the happy blow, flying unerringly forward. The Czech language often produces such strange effects on the German ear." The word *nechápu* (I don't comprehend), he continues, is "a strange word in Czech and even in your mouth it is so severe, so callous, cold-eyed, stingy . . . [that it] prohibits the other person from expressing anything to the contrary."[66] Remarking on some "perfectly good German" phrases in his sister Ottla's letters that "did not express what they were intended to say," he observes that "these are, of course, translations from the Czech . . . which German refuses to assimilate, at least as far as I, a half-German, can judge."[67] A year later Ottla would marry a Czech Catholic, Josef David, against her parents' will but with Franz's strong support. The linguistic estrangement was still worse with Franz's mother. "Yesterday it occurred to me that I did not always love my mother as she deserved and as I could," he noted in his diary in October 1911, "only because the German language prevented it. . . . 'Mutter' is peculiarly German for the Jew, it unconsciously contains, together with the Christian splendor, Christian coldness also, the Jewish woman who is called 'Mutter' therefore becomes not only comic but strange."[68] A month earlier, following his visit to a Milanese brothel, Kafka recorded in his diary, "At home it was with the German bordello girls that one lost a sense of one's nationality for a moment, here it was with the French girls."[69] A decade later Franz told Max Brod that, in the Yiddish-German of central European Jews, the verb *mauscheln* "consists of a bumptious, tacit, or self-pitying appropriation of someone else's property, something not earned, but stolen by means of a relatively casual gesture. Yet it remains someone else's property, even though there is no evidence of a single solecism."[70] The root of the word *mauscheln* is the name Moshe (Moses); the Langenscheidt German dictionary lists among its meanings "to talk Yiddish," "to mumble," "to mutter," and "to cheat," and it gives *tricksen, mogeln, täuschen, schummeln,* and *schwindeln* as synonyms. Franz's world was *unheimlich* (uncanny) to its core.[71]

"The people who understand Czech best (apart from Czech Jews, of course), are the gentlemen from *Naše řeč* [Our language], second best are the readers of that journal, third best the subscribers—of which I am one," he joked with Milena.[72] *Naše řeč* still exists and is nowadays published under the auspices of the Czech Academy of Sciences Institute for the Czech Language. It celebrated its hundredth birthday in 2017. Franz might have been amused by an article on a common but untranslatable Czech word that appeared in 2009:

> There is also a special expression associated with the Prague socio-cultural context—*kafkárna*. This word that remains difficult to interpret, let alone translate, denotes an absurd feeling of hopelessness, disarray, and dislocation that is typical of Franz Kafka's work. . . . Most commonly, the word *kafkárna* is used to describe a nonsensical, logically inexplicable, chaotic, ridiculous, or hopeless **situation**, **state** and **feeling** to which one gradually resigns oneself, although one does not identify with it and it escapes one's conscious understanding. . . . The word may also describe a place that is peculiar, strange, out of the ordinary in a negative sense, a place governed by absurd laws.[73]

And what of those languages with which Kafka might have identified as a Jew? When Emperor Joseph II "emancipated" Jews in the 1780s, his aim was to make them "more useful and serviceable to the State."[74] It was a Faustian bargain. Joseph's reforms gave Jews substantial civil rights (though not full civic equality) while curtailing their communal autonomy and banning the continued use of Yiddish or Hebrew in community record keeping. German became the language of instruction in all Jewish elementary schools. By the time Kafka introduced a recital of Yiddish poetry by the Warsaw-born actor Isaac Meir Levi (alias Yitzhak Löwy/Jacques Levi/Jack Lewi) at the Jewish Town Hall on 11 February 1912, Prague Jews had long since lost any language of their own. Franz began his talk with the observation that "many of you are so frightened of Yiddish that one can almost see it in your faces." It frightened them because, like the demolished ghetto, it represented a past they thought they had left behind. Franz assured his audience that "once Yiddish has taken hold of you and moved you—and Yiddish is everything, the words, the Chasidic melody, and the essential character of this Eastern European Jewish actor himself . . . you will come to feel the true unity of Yiddish, and so strongly that it will frighten you, yet it will no longer be fear of Yiddish but of yourselves."[75] Fascinated by the Yiddish theater of eastern Europe, Kafka attended performances at the Café Savoy by Löwy's players from Lviv at least twenty times in 1911.[76] But deep down he knew there was no place in that true unity for him. "Both the intention and the implementation of everything

Löwy does is childlike and absurd," he wrote a year or so later, disillusioned.[77] Neither Prague nor Kafka belonged to eastern Europe.

Franz was not convinced by Zionist promises of a New Jerusalem either. He made some serious attempts to learn Hebrew, most desperately during the last year of his life when he was living in Berlin with his last lover, Dora Diamant, a runaway seamstress from a Hassidic family in Poland. But unlike Max Brod, whose Zionist ardor dated from Martin Buber's 1909 lectures to Bar Kochba (the Association of Jewish University Students of Prague), Kafka remained skeptical about a Jewish national renaissance—or at least his place in it. He found Buber "dreary. No matter what he says," he confessed to Felice Bauer in January 1913, "there is always something missing."[78] Later that year, since he happened to be in town for a conference in connection with his job at the Workers' Accident Insurance Institute for the Kingdom of Bohemia, he dropped in on the eleventh Zionist World Congress in Vienna. "I sat in . . . as if it were an event totally alien to me," he reported to Brod, "and if I didn't quite throw spitballs at the delegates, as did a girl in the opposite gallery, I was bored enough to."[79] "What have I in common with Jews?" Kafka asked in his diary in January 1914, famously responding: "I have hardly anything in common with myself."[80] "We both know numerous typical examples of the Western Jew," he wrote to Milena in a fit of lacerating clarity in November 1920. "As far as I am concerned I'm the most Western-Jewish of them all . . . nothing has been granted me, everything must be earned, not only the present and future, but the past as well":

> It's a little as if instead of just having to wash up, comb one's hair, etc., before every walk—which is difficult enough—a person is constantly missing everything he needs to take with him, and so each time he has to sew his clothes, make his boots, manufacture his hat, cut his walking stick, etc. Of course it's impossible to do all of that well; it may hold up for a few blocks, but then suddenly, at the Graben [Na Příkopě], for example, everything falls apart and he's left standing there naked with rags and pieces. And now the torture of running back to the Altstädter Ring [Old Town Square]! And in the end he runs into an angry mob on the Eisengasse [Železná Street], hot in pursuit of Jews.
>
> Don't misunderstand me, Milena. I'm not saying such a man is lost, not at all, but he is lost the minute he goes to the Graben where he is a disgrace to himself and the world.[81]

A few days previously Czech mobs had occupied the offices of the Bohemian-German newspaper the *Prager Tagblatt* (Prague daily) and trashed the archives in the Jewish Town Hall. The rioters on Železná Street may have been on their way to the Estates Theater, Prague's oldest, which is best remembered today for staging the world première of Mozart's *Don Giovanni* in 1787. To the chagrin of Czech nationalists, the Estates had stopped offering Czech plays and had become an exclusively German-language venue nearly sixty years earlier, after the Provisional Theater, predecessor of the volubly Czech National Theater, opened in 1862.[82] Yelling "The Estates to the Nation!" the Czechs forcibly expelled the German players. The National Theater took over the premises and performed Bedřich Smetana's *Prodaná nevěsta* (*The Bartered Bride*, 1866) that same night. Czechoslovakia's first president, Tomáš Garrigue Masaryk, supposedly refused to set foot in the building ever again. By then, *The Bartered Bride*—a jolly rural romp wherein the comely Mařenka and her resourceful suitor Jeník outwit her scheming parents and the buffo marriage broker Kecal to the accompaniment of Czech peasant dances and lusty male choruses serenading good Czech beer—had become *the* Czech national opera, a status it retains to the present day. "I've been spending every afternoon outside on the streets, bathing in anti-Semitic hate," Franz wrote to Milena. "Isn't it natural to leave a place where one is so hated? (Zionism or national feeling isn't needed for this at all.) The heroism of staying on," he added, "is nonetheless merely the heroism of cockroaches which cannot be exterminated, even from the bathroom."[83] Coming from the author of "The Metamorphosis," the cockroach image is devastating. That story begins: "As Gregor Samsa awoke one morning from uneasy dreams he found himself transformed in his bed into a gigantic insect [the word Kafka uses is *Ungeziefer*, or vermin]."[84] Franz ended his correspondence with Milena a couple weeks later. The timing may have been sheer chance, but perhaps there was some connection after all.

Kafka was neither saint nor prophet. But he *was* blessed—or cursed—with what Milena, writing to Max Brod a few months later, described as "terrible clairvoyance." By this she meant exceptional insight, rather than the faculty of perceiving future events. Franz did not "foresee the Holocaust" (or the gulag or the Moscow trials),[85] but this is not to say that his writings do not illuminate the roots of such obscenities in the everyday life of the modern world. "At one time or another we have all taken refuge in a lie, in blindness, enthusiasm, optimism, a conviction, pessimism, or something else," Milena continued. "But [Kafka] has never fled to any refuge, not one. He is absolutely incapable of lying, just as he is incapable of getting drunk." That is why "Frank [as she always called him] is unable to live. Frank is incapable of living. Frank will never recover. Frank will soon die."[86] Kafka died of tuberculosis in an Austrian sanitarium in the summer of 1924. He was forty years old. Given what happened subsequently, he was perhaps better off being out of it. In her obituary for the *Národní listy* (National paper), Milena quoted one of his letters from memory: "When heart and soul can't bear it any longer, the lung takes on half the burden."[87] But she found universal significance in Kafka's "moving, pure naïveté"—or at least in the body of work to which it gave rise:

> He has written the most significant books of modern German literature, books that embody the struggle of today's generation throughout the world—while refraining from all tendentiousness. They are true, stark, and painful, to the point of being naturalistic even where they are symbolic. They are full of dry scorn and the sensitive perspective of a man who saw the world so clearly that he couldn't bear it, a man who was bound to die since he refused to make concessions or take refuge, as others do, in various fallacies of reason, or the unconscious. . . . All of his books paint the horror of secret misunderstandings, of innocent guilt between people. He was an artist and a man of such anxious conscience he could hear even where others, deaf, felt themselves secure.[88]

German Prague!

When Max Brod described "old Austrian Prague" as a "city of three nationalities,"[89] it seemed a self-evidently accurate portrayal of the city in which he was raised. But a century earlier that would not have been true. Nations are not timeless. Czech and German speakers and Jewish believers had lived side by side in the Bohemian lands for more than a millennium, sometimes harmoniously, sometimes not. The social significance of language shifted back and forth over the course of time. A case can be made for the existence of a strong sense of language-based Czech identity during the Middle Ages, which manifested itself most forcefully during the fifteenth-century Hussite Wars.[90] But with the absorption of the Kingdom of Bohemia into the Austrian Empire after the crown passed to the Habsburgs in 1526, and especially after the Rising of the Bohemian Estates was defeated at the Battle of the White Mountain on the western outskirts of Prague in 1620, language came to divide social strata rather than ethnic groups. German became the language of state, literature, and learning, the lingua franca of the upper classes, while Czech was reduced to the vulgar tongue of the common folk. As a written language, Czech went into seemingly terminal decline. The transformation of linguistic differences into bases for *national* communities was a more recent development, bound up with other social changes associated with the onset of modernity. Czech speakers were welded into a coherent nation only in the nineteenth century, during what the Czechs call their national revival (*národní obrození*). This Slavic "insurgency" left non-Czech speakers with little choice but to redefine themselves in ethnic terms too.[91] In fact, the term *revival* (*obrození*) is a misnomer. The process is better understood as a new imagining of community and inventing of tradition, even if some of the raw materials out of which they were fabricated were of undeniably ancient provenance.

The revival began in the 1780s with a small coterie of scholarly awakeners (*buditele*) who occupied themselves with Czech language, literature, legend, history, and folklore under the patronage of German-speaking aristocrats whose loyalties were to the land of Bohemia rather than to the Czech (or German) nation. The awakeners' labors had little popular impact until after 1850, when the growth of modern industry brought a flood of Czech-speaking country folk to the cities. Which language was used in state and municipal offices, courts, schools, colleges and universities, and other arenas of everyday life suddenly became a fraught political issue. I have told this story at length in *The Coasts of Bohemia*.[92] Suffice it to say here that after Czechs gained a majority on the Prague City Council and elected the first modern Czech mayor in 1861, they never looked back. By the end of the century Prague was demographically and otherwise "a Czech city, so Czech, that it was perhaps more Czech only during the Hussite times and the times that immediately followed," when "Prague Germans . . . were violently expelled from the city."[93] Here I quote from *Ottův slovník naučný* (*Otto's Encyclopedia*, 1888–1909), a magnificent twenty-eight-volume work produced with the participation of much of the faculty at the Czech University and rivaled in size and scholarship only by the *Encyclopedia Britannica*. By this time the Hussite Wars loomed large in the Czech imagination as an era of past glory when, in the words of historian and "father of the nation" (*Otec národa*) František Palacký, "a nation not great in numbers . . . stood up in arms against all the immense forces and powers through which the temporal and spiritual authorities of the age governed throughout the whole of Christendom."[94] The image of Czechs standing up "against all" (*proti všem*) had an obvious contemporary resonance.

It is impossible to give precise figures for this "second Czechicization of Prague."[95] The boundaries within which censuses were undertaken and the criteria they employed to establish (or obfuscate) nationality changed over the period. Further complicating matters, once national affiliation became a political hot potato, many people responded to census questions strategically. Jews shifted their declared "language of everyday use," which was taken as a proxy for nationality, with the prevailing political wind. *Otto's Encyclopedia* demanded in 1903 that "Prague Jewry, who were mostly born in Czech regions, would at long last stop seeing material advantage in declaring their language of everyday use to be German upon moving to Prague."[96] In fact, the proportion of Prague Jews declaring their language to be German fell from 74 percent in the 1890 census to 45 percent in 1900. This change is only partially explained by fresh Jewish immigration from Czech-speaking rural areas. The *Svůj k svému!* (Each to his own!) business boycott of 1892, the anti-Semitism in Czech newspaper coverage of the conflict over the replacement of bilingual street signs by Czech-only signs in 1893, and the 1897 language riots (during which Czech mobs smashed synagogue windows in Smíchov and Žižkov) were persuasive reasons for Jews to think twice about identifying as German. Hermann Kafka declared Czech to be the everyday language of his household in the 1890, 1900, and 1910 censuses, as did all other members of the family—except for Franz, who in 1910 recorded his language of everyday use as German.[97]

Whatever the difficulties in interpreting the statistics, the overall pattern is clear. A less than accurate census of 1851 broke down Prague's population as 53 percent Czech, 33 percent German, and 11 percent Jewish (of which 8 percent spoke German and 3 percent Czech). A city census of 1869 divided the population into 80.5 percent Czech and 17.9 percent German, which was probably closer to the mark. Jews were included in these numbers; when residents were identified by religion, Jews accounted for 8.28 percent of Prague's inhabitants.[98] These figures relate to the four historical towns of the city center and the former Jewish ghetto, known since 1850 as Josefov (after Joseph II). In 1890 German speakers made up 18.7 percent of the inhabitants in the Old Town (Staré Město), 16.2 percent in the New Town (Nové Město), 17.4 percent in the Lesser Town (Malá Strana), 8.2 percent in Hradčany, and 23.5 percent in Josefov.[99] Vyšehrad, Holešovice-Bubny, and Libeň, which were incorporated into the city between 1883 and 1901, were overwhelmingly Czech speaking. So were the contiguous towns of Karlín, Smíchov, Vinohrady, and Žižkov, which remained legally independent until they were annexed to Greater Prague (Hlavní město Praha) in 1922. The suburban population surpassed that of the historical center by 1890. In 1900 the Prague conurbation was 93.1 percent Czech speaking and 6.7 percent German speaking. In the 1921 census, when the new Czechoslovak state allowed people to define their own nationality for the first time, self-declared Germans constituted just 4.6 percent of the city's inhabitants.[100] During the seventy years in which Prague grew from a provincial town of 150,000 people to a 625,000-strong national capital, the proportion of the population self-identifying as German (speaking) had fallen to barely a tenth of what it had been.

Prague Germans did not just disappear into a sea of Czechs, as these raw numbers might lead us to expect. "The twenty-five thousand Germans, who constituted only 5 percent of the population of Prague at the time," recalled Egon Erwin Kisch in his memoir *Marktplatz der Sensationen* (*Sensation Fair*, 1942), "possessed two magnificent theaters [the Estates Theater, built in 1783, and the New German Theater, opened in 1888], a huge concert hall [the Rudolfinum, built in 1876–1884], two colleges [German University and German Polytechnic], five high schools, and four advanced vocational institutes, two newspapers with a morning and an evening edition each [*Bohemia* and *Prager Tagblatt*], large meeting halls, and a lively social life."[101] Albert Einstein, who took up what turned out to be a short-lived position as a professor at the German University of Prague in April 1911, had mixed first impressions of the city. "It is different here than in Zurich," he wrote. "The air is full of soot, the water is life-threatening, the people are superficial, shallow, and uncouth, if also, as it seems, in general good-hearted." But, as he happily noted, "I have a spacious institute with a magnificent library and I don't have to struggle with the difficulties of the language, which with my awful ponderousness in learning languages comes heavily into consideration for me!" He could live, and live well, entirely in German, including playing his violin and debating Kant's *Critique of Pure Reason* at Berta Fanta's renowned salon held at the Unicorn Apothecary House on the Old Town Square.[102]

"If you didn't have a title or weren't rich," Kisch observed, "you just didn't belong." Even if, he might have added, German *was* your language of everyday use. German Prague was an "almost exclusively ... upper middle class" enclave of mine owners, industrial magnates, wealthy merchants, and bank directors who rubbed shoulders with high-ranking military officers, state officials, and university professors. Kisch bluntly asserts that "There was no German proletariat."[103] This was only half true. Although language had long divided social classes, by the end of the century the commanding heights of the economy were no longer exclusively in German hands. Osvald Polívka's Land Bank building, replete with patriotic frescoes by Mikoláš Aleš, opened its doors in 1895 on Na Příkopě—the Graben where Franz Kafka disgraced himself and the world—next door to the German Casino, which had been the center of

Prague-German social life since 1862. Working-class Germans didn't hang out at the casino.[104] They lived in the cheaper, mostly Czech areas of the city and were more likely to intermarry with Czechs. In this way, Prague Germans' self-perception as elites may have inadvertently hastened their demographic decline.

The greater irony, in retrospect, is that a large number of Prague's Germans—almost half in 1900—were Jews. Anti-Semitism was on the rise across the empire as pan-Austrian liberalism, with which Prague's Jews had strongly identified since 1848, gave way to rival ethnic nationalisms. Karl Lueger, the rabidly anti-Semitic mayor of Vienna from 1897 to 1910, had his Czech counterpart in Karel Baxa, who served as mayor of Prague from 1919 to 1937. Baxa had first made his name in 1899 during the Hilsner trial, which split opinion in Austria-Hungary much as the Dreyfus case had in France. A Jewish vagrant, Leopold Hilsner, was convicted on the flimsiest of evidence of the alleged "ritual murder" of a nineteen-year-old Czech girl, Anežka Hrůzová, in Polná in southeastern Bohemia. Tomáš Masaryk intervened on behalf of the defendant, penning the Czech equivalent of Émile Zola's *J'accuse!* It did not make him popular among many of his compatriots. Baxa acted pro bono for the victim's family and had no qualms about playing the blood libel card. "'You Hilsner!' was the cry that greeted Jewish children on their way to school," according to Kisch, "accompanied by the significant gesture of a finger being drawn across the bare neck. This was supposed to depict the characteristic cut that played a role in the trial."[105]

Twenty years later Kafka angrily alluded to the case in one of his letters to Milena: "I don't understand how whole nations of people could ever have thought of ritual murder before these recent events (at most they may have felt general fear and jealousy, but here there is no question, we see 'Hilsner' committing the crime step by step . . .)." The context for his outburst was Czech reaction to the suicide of Josef Reiner, the Christian editor of the liberal Prague newspaper *Tribuna*, following the discovery of his wife's affair with Willi Haas, a Jew. This is the same *Tribuna* that had recently begun to carry Milena's writings and the same Willi Haas who later published *Letters to Milena*. As it happens, the woman in question, who subsequently married Haas, was Milena's close friend Jarmila Ambrožová. "First of all what most terrifies me about the story is the conviction that the Jews are necessarily bound to fall upon you Christians," Franz explained to Milena, "just as predatory animals are bound to murder. . . . It is impossible for you to imagine this in all its fullness and power, even if you understand everything else in the story better than I do."[106] He could have cited a long history of Czech anti-Semitism to underline his point. Jan Neruda, author of the Czech classic *Malostranské povídky* (Tales from the Lesser Town, 1878, published in English as *Prague Tales*), called for "emancipation from the Jews" in his pamphlet *Pro strach židovský* (The Jewish fear, 1869), while the liberal Czech journalist and "martyr" of the 1848 revolution Karel Havlíček Borovský characterized the Jewish population as "a separate, Semitic nation that lives only incidentally in our midst and sometimes understands or knows our language." Havlíček (as he is generally known) had no doubt that "he who wants to be a Czech must cease to be a Jew."[107]

Less than a fifth of Prague Jews identified themselves as Jewish by nationality when given the opportunity to do so for the first time in the 1921 census. More than half gave their nationality as Czechoslovak—prudently, perhaps, given the atmosphere of the times. But nearly a quarter of the city's self-declared *German* minority still identified their religion as Judaism.[108] That identity was no doubt as conflicted as Kafka's, but there is no reason to question that they *felt* more German than Czech—even if only "half German"—and, like the majority of Prague Jews at the time, did not experience Jewishness as a *nationality* at all. Hugo Bergmann, Kafka's classmate through elementary and high school and a mainstay at Berta Fanta's salon, was a deeply committed Zionist. He nevertheless wrote: "My mother tongue is German, I attended only German schools, speak and think in German. These are in general the signposts by which in this country one judges membership to the German people or the Czech people. By these criteria I am thus German as much as anybody else."[109] Max Brod—who was instrumental in persuading Tomáš Masaryk to recognize Jews as a national minority in the new state—was more nuanced, describing himself as "a Jewish writer of the German tongue." He claimed a "distant love" (*Distanzliebe*) for the German culture that was and wasn't his:

> I do not feel myself to be a member of the German people, but am a friend of Germanness and also, by language and education . . . culturally related to Germanness. I am a friend of Czechness, yet am in essential ways . . . detached from Czechness. I cannot find a simpler formulation for an existence in the Jewish diaspora of a nationally divided city.[110]

But Brod was adamant that "for me Prague is home. And I do not have another real home. My family has lived in Prague as far back as I can trace it on my father's side. And Prague is the main setting not just in some but in *all* of my novels. In the 46 years of my life I have never been away from Prague for more than a few weeks."[111] Max championed the composer Leoš Janáček, the expressionist artists of Osma (The Eight),[112] and Jaroslav Hašek's *Osudy do-brého vojáka Švejka za světové války* (The fortunes of the good soldier Švejk in the world war, to give *The Good Soldier Švejk* its full title), when none of them found much support in Czech cultural circles. The critic F. X. Šalda captured something important when he wrote that Brod's *Tycho Brahes Weg zu Gott* (Tycho Brahe's path to God)—an "old-Prague" historical novel set "in a time when the old is not true any more and the new is not true yet"—was "not a *German* novel, it is a *Jewish* novel. . . . And this most characteristic Jewishness is so beautiful in Brod's book, and when all is said and done it is very close and comprehensible to genuine Czech national feeling [*češství*]."[113]

Two years younger than Kafka, Egon Erwin Kisch was another bright Jewish boy with literary ambitions. The raging reporter, as he called himself,[114] started his career in 1906 writing about Prague's underworld of crime and prostitution for the German-language daily *Bohemia*. Kisch fought in the Austrian army in World War I, was radicalized by the Russian Revolution, took part in the Vienna Uprising of November 1918, and joined the newly founded Austrian Communist Party in June 1919. Back in Prague after the war he collaborated with Jaroslav Hašek and others at the Revoluční scéna (Revolutionary stage) cabaret theater, which staged its anarchic sketches in the basement of the Hotel Adria on Wenceslas Square. He reportedly danced the first tango in Prague with Emča Revoluce (Ema of the Revolution, née Ema Czadská) at one of Hašek's favorite watering holes, the Montmartre Café on Řetězová Street in the Old Town. The bohemian haunt, which opened its doors nightly when everywhere else was closing, had recently been remodeled in Czech cubist style by the young architect and set designer Jiří Kroha, who covered the walls with murals "manifesting the opposition of youth against every sort of official line."[115] Egon moved on to Berlin in 1921 and made that city his base until Adolf Hitler seized power in 1933. Kisch has a legitimate claim to be the inventor of modern reportage. A counterpart of the photomontages of John Heartfield or the paintings of George Grosz and Otto Dix, his articles reflected the Weimar Republic's *neue Sachlichkeit* (new objectivity) aesthetic, eschewing expressionist soul-searching for hard-edged engagement with contemporary life. In the late 1920s Kisch became a publicist for the Comintern, publishing collections based on his travels through Soviet Russia (*Zaren, Popen, Bolschewiken* [Tsars, priests, and Bolsheviks], 1927), North Africa (*Wagnisse in aller Welt* [Worldwide exploits], 1927), the United States (*Paradies Amerika* [Paradise America], 1930), Soviet Central Asia (*Asien gründlich verändert* [*Changing Asia*], 1932), and China (*China geheim* [*Secret China*], 1933). He was arrested the day after the Reichstag fire in 1933 and was briefly imprisoned before being escorted over the Czechoslovak border. More foreign adventures followed, including a trip to Australia during which he jumped ship (literally) in Melbourne, breaking his leg when he landed hard on the dock. He successfully fought the Australian government's attempt to deport him as an undesirable agitator. Like André Malraux, Arthur Koestler, Ilya Ehrenburg, Ernest Hemingway, George Orwell, and photojournalists Robert Capa, Gerda Taro, and David Seymour, Egon made his way to Spain in 1937–1938. He spent World War II in Mexico City, where he wrote *Sensation Fair*.

No doubt by then Kisch's portrayal of the fin de siècle Prague of his youth was colored by geographic and temporal distance, but the absurdities ring true. He recalled the city's "national ghettoes" with retrospective incredulity. "What was obvious to any Czech," he wrote, "must have seemed unbelievable to anyone not from Prague." The segregated worlds of his hometown were every bit as surreal as any other place his travels had taken him:

> The Prague German had nothing to do with the city's half million Czechs except what related to business. He never lit his cigar with a match from the Czech School Fund, any more than a Czech would light his with a match from the little box of the German School Association. No German ever set foot in the Czech Citizens' Club [Měšťanská beseda], and no Czech ever deigned to visit the German Casino. Even the instrumental concerts were monolingual, and the same for the swimming pools, the parks, the playgrounds, most restaurants, coffee-houses, and stores. The promenade of the Czechs was Ferdinandstrasse [today's Národní Avenue], whereas the Germans preferred the Graben. . . . The Germans had their own churches, and the Czechs theirs. The German and Czech universities, and the Czech and German technical institutes, were as remote from one another as if one were located on the North Pole and the other on the South Pole. . . . For the botanical garden of one university a plant was ordered from the South Seas that could be seen blossoming in the garden of the other university had a wall not stood in the way.[116]

A Little Bit of Sulfur, a Little Bit of Hell

Kisch fails to mention one exception to this linguistic apartheid—though it is the exception that proves the rule. Prague-German bachelors of Kisch's and Kafka's generation were happy to amuse themselves in the arms of Czech

FIGURE 1.2. Milena Jesenská, c. 1920. Photographer
unknown. From Jaroslava Vondráčková,
Kolem Mileny Jesenské, Prague, 1991.

servants, shop assistants, factory girls, and barmaids, who gained the reputation for uninhibited hotness that is common to young women in such situations the world over. James Hawes points out that "Kafka's powerful sexual
imagination seems to have been forever haunted by poor young servant-girl
figures"—the housemaid whose seduction of sixteen-year-old Karl Rossmann
triggers the action in *Amerika*; Josef K's typist, washerwoman, and lawyer's
maid in *The Trial*; the barmaid Frieda in *The Castle*—while George Gibian
argues that Milena Jesenská "stood for the very essence of what [Kafka] romanticized and thirsted for, such as closeness to the earth, directness—Czech
attitudes, Czech health."[117] This erotic mobilization of the nature-culture opposition is familiar from other colonial contexts. Max Brod sentimentalized

this "theater of Germanic sexual imperialism," where (as Hawes puts it) "the sweet girls and their well-off beaux, when not speaking the international language of sex and money, quite literally *spoke different languages*,"[118] in his novel *Das Tschechische Dienstmädchen* (The Czech maidservant, 1909). "The young author appears to believe that national issues can be resolved in bed," snorted Leo Herrmann in the Zionist weekly *Selbstwehr* (Self-defense).[119] Quite how is unclear, since the heroine Pepí Vlková ends up like Anna Karenina and Emma Bovary and drowns herself in the Vltava. The book was generally well received in the Czech press. Jiří Karásek ze Lvovic, a leading light of the "decadent" group that formed around the journal *Moderní revue* (Modern review) in the 1890s, was "surprised by the author's lack of prejudice—no diatribes against Czechs."[120]

Kafka told Milena about one such amorous encounter that took place when he was twenty, still living with his parents above the shop in Celetná Street, and studying for the state law exams. One summer night he was distracted from the rigors of Roman law by a shopgirl standing in the doorway of the clothing store below, directly opposite his bedroom window. They soon "came to an understanding using sign language," and he followed her home. The girl (Franz never names her) got rid of another admirer, and they ended up in a hotel in the Lesser Town. "It was all enticing, exciting, and disgusting," Franz wrote, "and as we walked home over the Karlsbrücke [Charles Bridge] toward morning—it was still hot and beautiful—I was actually happy." Franz met the girl again for an encore before going to the country for his summer holiday, where he "played around a bit with another girl, and could no longer bear the sight of the shopgirl from Prague." It was one of those moments of terrible clairvoyance when the little obscenities of sex turned into metaphors for the larger *kafkárna* of the world:

> She kept on following me with her uncomprehending eyes. And although the girl had done something slightly disgusting in the hotel (not worth mentioning), had said something slightly obscene (not worth mentioning), I don't mean to say this was the sole reason for my animosity (in fact, I'm sure it wasn't); nonetheless the memory remained. I knew then and there that I would never forget it and at the same time I knew—or thought I knew—that deep down, this disgust and filth were a necessary part of the whole, and it was precisely this (which she had indicated to me by one slight action, one small word), which had drawn me with such amazing force into this hotel, which otherwise I would have avoided with all my remaining strength.

And it's stayed that way ever since. My body, often quiet for years, would then again be shaken by this longing for some very particular, trivial, disgusting thing, something slightly repulsive, embarrassing, obscene, which I always found even in the best cases—some insignificant odor, a little bit of sulfur, a little bit of hell. This urge had something of the eternal Jew—senselessly being drawn along, senselessly wandering through a senselessly obscene world.[121]

In November 1911, as part of the arrangements surrounding his sister Elli's marriage to the young businessman Karl Herrmann, Kafka became an unlikely partner in Prague's first asbestos factory, which was located in the proletarian suburb of Žižkov. Hermann Kafka was still trying to make a practical man out of his only surviving son and heir. Contrary to popular belief, Franz's day job as a senior civil servant writing legal briefs at the Workers' Accident Insurance Institute of the Kingdom of Bohemia was a cushy position that paid him well, secured him a pension, and got him exempted from military service during World War I. It required his presence in the office only six hours a day. Nevertheless, finding that the combination of his job and his afternoon visits to the factory left him with little time to pursue what he saw as his true vocation, writing,[122] Franz bailed and the asbestos company eventually went bust. This did nothing to improve his relationship with his father, who had sunk considerable capital into the enterprise. The impressions Franz jotted down in his diary of a Prague with which he had hitherto had little contact were probably the only positive things that came from this venture. As usual, they were remarkably sharp, though what they mostly showed was the cavernous gulf between the old, painfully disappearing Prague, whose underbelly Paul Leppin and other fin de siècle writers so lovingly caressed in both Czech and German, and the prosaic modern surroundings in which most Praguers lived and worked.

"Yesterday in the factory," Franz writes: "The girls, in their unbearably dirty and untidy clothes, their hair disheveled as though they had just got up, the expressions on their faces fixed by the incessant noise of the transmission belts and by the individual machines . . . they aren't people, you don't greet them, you don't apologize when you bump into them . . . they stand there in petticoats, they are at the mercy of the pettiest power." But after six o'clock, when the machines stopped and the workers had cleaned themselves up as best they could, "then at last they are women again, despite pallor and bad teeth they can smile . . . and you do not know how to behave when one of them holds your winter coat for you to put on."[123] Nothing in this passage lets on that Franz is describing *his* factory, *his* employees, and *his* power; the metamorphosis of helpless hands in petticoats into women becomes just another metaphor for the impersonal, dehumanizing machinery of modernity. Perhaps because the only Czech winner of the Nobel Prize in literature to date also hailed from Žižkov, Kafka's ruminations remind me of the alternating currents in one of Jaroslav Seifert's best-loved poems, the sweetly vicious "Píseň o dívkách" (Song about girls, 1923). The poem has two stanzas: the first ends, "and every one is different"; the second ends, "and all of them are the same."[124] Seifert too sought his sentimental education in Prague's brothels, even if his first sight of "a girl's naked breasts" led him to "beat a fearful retreat" from Břetislavova Street in the Lesser Town back to Žižkov.[125] That encounter, which the poet described tenderly and hilariously sixty years later in his memoir *Všecky krásy světa* (All the beauties of the world, 1981), took place during the last month of World War I. K. L. Kukla tells us that Břetislavova Street had by then displaced the alleys of the Fifth Quarter as "the most shameful street in Prague."[126]

The journey home provided Kafka with ample food for thought on the psychogeography of his native city. The tram passed "people outside, lights in stores, walls of viaducts ... backs and faces over and over again, a highway leading from the business street of the suburb with nothing human on it save people going home, the glaring electric lights of the railway station burned into the darkness, the low, tapering chimneys of a gasworks." A poster advertising an upcoming performance by a singer "gropes its way along the walls as far as an alley near the cemeteries"—presumably the Christian cemeteries at Olšany, which border the New Jewish Cemetery where Franz would eventually be buried—"from where it then returned to me out of the cold of the fields into the livable warmth of the city." Though we accept foreign cities as a fact, he muses, "the suburbs of our native city ... are also foreign to us." There, people live "partly within our city, partly on the miserable, dark edge of the city that is furrowed like a great ditch, although they all have an area of interest in common with us that is greater than any other group of people outside the city." Franz enters and leaves Prague's suburbs, he says, "with a weak mixed feeling of anxiety, of abandonment, of sympathy, of curiosity, of conceit, of joy in traveling, of fortitude, and return with pleasure, seriousness, and calm, especially from Žižkov."[127]

We could be reading the testimony of a brave white New Yorker venturing into Harlem before it got gentrified or a Parisian flâneur who strays beyond the Boulevard Périphérique into the dark continent of the *banlieues*. Otto's

Encyclopedia paints a rather different picture of life on the other side of the tracks—as it literally was: Žižkov is separated from the Old Town and the New Town by the railroad tracks leading to what are today the Masaryk and Main Stations. With more than seventy-two thousand people living there at the time Kafka was writing, "almost all Czech and of the Catholic religion," Žižkov was Prague's most populous suburb and the third largest city in Bohemia. Most of its inhabitants were manual workers employed in the large Prague and Karlín factories or in the many smaller workshops in Žižkov itself, like Herrmann & Co.'s asbestos factory. The area's streets, which "bear the names of leading men of the Czech nation as well as memorable places in Czech history, mainly from the Hussite times," were "very lively and busy, especially during mornings, afternoons, and evening." Recognized as a municipality in 1881, Žižkov takes its name from the Hussite commander Jan Žižka of Trocnov, whose peasant army defeated the crusading forces of Emperor Sigismund at the Battle of Vítkov Hill on 14 July 1420. As for Kafka's "miserable, dark edge of the city," Žižkov prided itself on being "lit by electric light." It was "among the first Czech towns to install such lighting (in 1889)," *Otto's Encyclopedia* boasted, "much earlier than Prague."[128]

2

A Modern Woman

The age has divided in two. Behind us remains the old time, which is condemned to molder in libraries, and in front of us sparkles a new day.

—"US DEVĚTSIL," 1920[1]

Am I, above All, a Czech?

Milena Jesenská was born in Žižkov on 10 August 1896 in an apartment house at 4 Prokopovo Square, overlooking what was then the district's main fruit and vegetable market. In contrast to the "museumlike zones" in which "nothing was moved, nothing thrown away" of Prague's Old and New Towns, writes Reiner Stach, Žižkov was "dominated by a present devoid of history, and sparked by a recurring sense that a new era was about to dawn, with steadily intensifying visions for the future." I get the contrast Stach is trying to draw between a decrepit German Prague with a "crippling fixation on the past" and a lusty, youthful Czech Prague—the same kind of imagery Kafka sometimes used when comparing himself to Milena.[2] But this is an oversimplification. Writing in *Česká otázka* (The Czech question) in 1894, Tomáš Masaryk, who was then a professor of sociology at the Czech University, warned *Czechs* that "thus far we have been far more diverted from the present toward the past than is good for us, and this one-sidedness hides a serious danger for the national cause."[3] Built in 1875, Prokopovo Square was named after Prokop Holý (Prokop the Bald), the radical Hussite leader who was killed at the fratricidal Battle of Lipany that ended the Hussite Wars in 1434. Since 2005 the space has been graced by Karel Nepraš's tongue-in-cheek equestrian statue of Jaroslav Hašek, who, after returning in 1920 from five years in revolutionary Russia, moved in with his friend Franta Sauer on neighboring Jeronýmova Street and began writing *The Good Soldier Švejk*. Jeronýmova Street took its name from Jeroným Pražský (Jerome of Prague), who was burned at the stake by the Council of Constance in 1416, a year after Jan Hus. Sauer led the mob that destroyed the Marian Column in the Old Town Square on 3 November 1918, a week after Czechoslovakia declared independence from Austria-Hungary, in the mistaken belief that the pillar commemorated the Catholic victory at the Battle of the White Mountain in 1620. Modernity does not exclude history—or should I say histories? It cultivates them.

Milena's father Jan Jesenský was an up-and-coming young dentist who went on to become a professor of stomatology at the Czech University in 1911. Her mother, Milena Hejzlarová, was the daughter of an inspector of schools in Náchod in northeastern Bohemia, and her dowry helped Jan set up in private practice. The family moved into the city center when Milena was five. In 1902 they settled into a palatial top-floor apartment in a Secession building on the corner of Ovocná (Fruit) Street and Wenceslas Square (Václavské náměstí), which still stands. Dr. Jesenský had his dental surgery on the second floor. Milena spent her formative years living at the heart of the Golden Cross, the commercial core of downtown Prague, which, far from resembling a museum, was embarking on a giddy modernization that continued through the interwar years. The *asanace* was not the only force reshaping the city. Commerce was just as rapacious. One alarmed response was the founding in 1900 of the Klub za starou Prahu (Club for Old Prague), which was dedicated to "monitoring changes in the city, expressing views on renovations and new buildings in Prague, and wherever there are threats to monuments or the historic face of the city doing everything it can to defend them."[4] Wenceslas Square acquired electric lighting in 1889. The trams were electrified and extended to the suburbs in 1896–1902. The *Bestia Triumphans* of modernity trampled gothic, renaissance, and baroque houses to make way for offices, banks, shops, hotels, cinemas, cafés, and arcades.[5] By the late 1920s only one building on Wenceslas Square predated the nineteenth century, and most had gone up in the previous fifty years. The area throbbed with neon signs. Across the street from the Jesenskýs' apartment, Efraim Löbl's silk and textiles store on the corner of Můstek and Na Příkopě boasted kinetic illuminations by the sculptor Zdeněk Pešánek that coordinated with the city's first traffic lights, which were installed in 1930.

Ovocná Street was renamed 28 October (28. října) Street in February 1919 to mark the date of Czechoslovakia's declaration of independence the year before. Part of the semicircle of avenues that follow the walls and moat that

FIGURE 2.1. Jaroslav Hašek memorial, Prokopovo Square, 2005. The sculpture was designed by Karel Nepraš and finished by his daughter, Karolína Neprašová, after his death. Photograph by author, 2016.

once separated the Old and New Towns, it linked Na Příkopě with Ferdinandova Avenue, which was concurrently renamed Národní třída (National Avenue). At the other end of Na Příkopě, Francis Joseph Square became Republic Square (Náměstí Republiky), and Eliščina Avenue, named after Emperor Francis Joseph's wife Elisabeth, became Revolutionary Avenue (Revoluční třída).[6] These changes were part of a comprehensive purge of reminders of Habsburg rule. Emperor Francis I was hauled down from his monument on the Masaryk Embankment (today's Smetana Embankment; Masaryk has moved upriver), and the statue of Jan Josef Václav Radecký, the Czech field marshal who masterminded Austria's victories during the First War of Italian Independence in 1848–1849, was removed from the Lesser Town Square (Malostranské náměstí). The Francis Bridge became the Bridge of the Legions (Most Legií), in honor of the Czechoslovak legions formed from exiles, deserters, and prisoners of war who fought with the Allies on both the eastern and western fronts against Germany and Austria-Hungary during World War I. After being rechristened the First of May Bridge in 1960, its name reverted to Bridge of the Legions in 1990. The communists were not enamored of the legions, whose sixty-thousand-strong army got caught up in the Russian Civil War and ended up fighting the Bolsheviks across Siberia to Vladivostok, whence the legionnaires were finally evacuated by ship to Europe in September 1920. The legions' proximity may have been a factor in triggering the execution of Tsar Nicholas II and his family in Yekaterinburg on 16–17 July 1918. Radecký still languishes in the lapidarium of the National Museum at the Výstaviště exhibition grounds in Holešovice, along with shards of the Marian Column from the Old Town Square, but Francis made it back to his pedestal in 2003. Perhaps enough time had passed by then to forget old wrongs. Or maybe not. A proposal to erect a replica of the Marian Column in its original site was rejected by the Prague City Council after a three-hour debate in 2017.[7] The writer Lenka Procházková, who organized the petition opposing the restoration, protested that "the Marian column was a symbol of the humiliation of the Czech people. Replacing it would be similar to, for example, re-building the statue of Stalin at Letná."[8] The city council's 2017 decision was reversed in January 2020.[9] Taking advantage of the lack of tourists thronging the square during the Czech Republic's COVID-19 lockdown, Petr Váňa's replica of the Marian Column was installed on 4 July 2020.[10]

The Stalin statue, which once gazed over the city from Letná Plain, is a powerful metaphor. Work began in February 1952. The colossus took fourteen thousand tons of granite, six hundred workers, and 495 days to complete.

Three weeks before it was unveiled in 1955 its sculptor Otakar Švec committed suicide. Obligated to enter the competition, he had submitted a design so over the top that he thought it had no chance of winning. The monument was thirty meters high, twelve meters across, and twenty-two meters deep; the block from which Stalin's head was carved weighed fifty-two metric tons. Intended to convey "the unity of Stalin's person with the people and the eternal brother-hood of the Czechoslovak people with the Soviet people in the struggle for the realization of the great ideas of peace and socialism," Švec's sculpture de-picted four "representatives of the Soviet people" and "four representatives of the Czechoslovak people," in the best socialist realist style, marching behind Stalin into the Promised Land.[11] Whatever the intended symbolism, the en-semble rapidly became known as the "lineup for meat" (fronta na maso). Czechs made fun of the female partisan on the Soviet side of the procession, whose eyes were firmly fixed on the future but whose hand appeared to be reaching back into the fly of the soldier behind her. By the time the monstros-ity was completed, Stalin was dead. A year after its unveiling Nikita Khrush-chev made his "secret speech" to the Twentieth Congress of the Communist Party of the Soviet Union (CPSU) denouncing Stalin's crimes. The Czechs were slow to de-Stalinize, but the memorial was blown up in 1962. Rumor has it that Stalin's ear was recycled as a swimming pool in a Prague backyard, but that may be an urban legend.[12]

Jan Jesenský would not have approved of restoring the Marian Column. A supporter of the virulently nationalist Young Czech party that dominated Bohemia politics in the 1890s, Milena's father was (in his granddaughter Jana Černá's words) a "chauvinist and anti-Semite, for whom Germans were The Enemy, Jews a dirty word and Ernst Pollak's relationship with his daughter a disaster."[13] Jan's sister Růžena was cut from the same cloth. A significant per-sonality in her time, Milena's aunt was a novelist, poet, playwright, and regular contributor to the Young Czechs' newspaper Národní listy. She also published in the first Czech women's magazine Ženské listy (The women's paper), the popular cultural weekly Zlatá Praha (Golden Prague), and Moderní revue, which was founded in 1894 by Arnošt Procházka and Jiří Karásek ze Lvovic as the organ of "the young movement in Czech literature," with the aim of being "open to everything modern."[14] Kafka may have swooned on seeing a fellow traveler reading one of Růžena Jesenská's feuilletons on the train home after his four days with Milena in Vienna ("I borrow it, begin reading aimlessly, put it down and then sit there with your face, looking just the way it did when we parted at the station"),[15] but Max Brod delivered a harsher judgment. "Because of her chauvinistic Czech attitudes and philistine outlook," he sniffed, "she was held in distaste in our circles."[16] Jan Jesenský buttressed his nationalist credentials by claiming descent from Johannes Jessenius, an anatomist and rector of the University of Prague who was one of twenty-seven leaders of the Rising of the Bohemian Estates executed in the Old Town Square on 21 June 1621. Twenty-seven crosses embedded in the cobblestones mark where the scaffold stood. That claim was spurious, as Jesenius left only daughters. So did Jan Jesenský. Milena's only sibling, a boy named Jan after his father, died in infancy.

In an article published in *Přítomnost* (The present) shortly after the Germans' 15 March 1939 invasion, Milena related a childhood memory in which, as in one of Walter Benjamin's dialectical images, past and present momentarily came together to form a constellation in which things put on their true—surrealist—face. "Back then," she writes, "it was a suffocating era of Austrian and Czech friction and great mutual dislike, an era that carried within it the roots of many later ugly events." The Jesenskýs' apartment was at the meeting point of the streets where, on Sunday mornings, Czechs and Germans ritually acted out their ethnic solitudes. Na Příkopě (or, as it was and is colloquially known, Příkopy) was the German concourse, while the Czechs paraded along Ferdinandova Avenue. Milena recalled:

> Then came one Sunday I will likely never forget as long as I live. . . . The Austrian students in their colored caps were marching [along Na Příkopě] from the Powder Tower, not along the sidewalk, but down the center of the street. They were singing, they walked in unison, with a resounding, disciplined step. All of a sudden a crowd of Czechs approached from Wenceslas Square—and they too were not walking on the sidewalk but down the middle of the street. They walked in silence. Mom held my hand by the window, a little more tightly than was necessary. And in the front row of the Czechs walked my Dad. I recognized him from the window and was very pleased, but Mom went white as a sheet.

The police intervened, shots were fired, and a man lay "like a discarded rag" on the cobblestones. "Příkopy was somehow suddenly empty, but one person remained standing in front of the guns—my Dad. I remember quite clearly, absolutely clearly, how he stood. Quietly, with his hands at his sides." The date was likely 3 November 1905, and Milena was nine years old.[17]

Looking back on the confrontation three decades later, Milena had little time for nineteenth-century bombast of the "against all" variety. She states clearly, "We are not, and we never were in a position to take a stand against someone." But she insists that "it is necessary to know how to remain standing. With head bared and sincere love in our heart, with profound dignity, sincerity, and honesty, to remain standing beside everything that is Czech."[18] Such sentiments came as a surprise to many of her readers, for Milena had spent her life rebelling against the nationalism of her father's and aunt's generation. But if they thought the prodigal daughter had returned to the national ghetto, they were mistaken. When "an admirable man of action and a great patriot" with whom "just a year ago I would certainly have differed greatly in worldview" read her recent articles and complimented her with the words, "Let your opinions be what they may, I see that above all, you are a Czech," Milena tartly responded, "I am *self-evidently* [*samozřejmě*] a Czech, but *above all* [*především*] I try to be a decent human being." There was steel inside that sentiment. She pointedly titled the article "Am I above All a Czech?"[19]

In 1907, when she was eleven, Milena started at the Minerva girls' gymnasium (academic high school) in Vojtěšská Street near the National Theater. Eliška Krásnohorská had established the school in 1890 with the aim of preparing Czech girls for university. It was the first girls' gymnasium not just in Bohemia but throughout the entire Austrian Empire. Minerva girls were the crème de la Czech crème, and they knew it. "*Dívko z Minervy, nervi mi mý nervy*" (Minerva girl, don't rattle my nerves) was a popular rhyme of the time. Jana Černá writes that "Milena's relationship with her father was one of the strangest of its kind I ever encountered . . . its blend of terror, love, revulsion, hatred and respect so greatly resembled Kafka's relationship with *his* father, that that alone must have been a link between them."[20] Father and daughter had their moments, like their long weekend walks together in the countryside. Jan enrolled Milena in the muscularly patriotic Sokol gymnastic society and encouraged her to swim, play tennis, and ski.[21] But things went downhill after Milena's mother, who had never been healthy, died in January 1913. Sixteen-year-old Milena was left alone with an irascible father who would rather be at work, out playing cards at his club, or in the arms of one or another mistress.

After Milena graduated from Minerva in 1915 Jesenský enrolled her in medical school, but she dropped out after just four semesters. She couldn't stand the smell of blood, and she recoiled at what she saw when assisting her father in his dental surgery—Jan's skills were in high demand during World War I for reconstructing soldiers' shattered faces. A spell at Prague Musical Conservatory was even shorter lived. Milena enlivened her late teens by modeling nude for painters, experimenting with morphine and cocaine filched from Dad's medicine cabinet, and running up unpaid bills. She stole not only from her father but also from shops and friends' apartments. Her friend Jaroslava (Slávka) Vondráčková describes one argument she witnessed when Milena showed up asking her father for money at the Tůmovka café, where Dr. Jesenský was meeting with Slávka's brother-in-law. "Always the same debts you have to pay for this girl," Jan fumed. "And she's still running around with that Jew, she won't see reason. And at home I have to hide ducats, gold for teeth, drugs and even my newest socks from her." But "finally Jesenský gave her the money and the men went off to the club to play cards. And drink beer, maybe wine. Lots of it."[22] Therein, perhaps, lay the problem.

Not the least of Milena's affronts was her flouting of the invisible barriers between Czech and German Prague. Speaking on Radio Free Europe in 1953, the dramatist and critic Josef Kodíček recalled another Sunday morning on Na Příkopě. It was 1915, ten years after Jan Jesenský's standoff with the Austrian police. The war that had broken out the previous fall, marooning Czechs from their Serbian and Russian Slavic brothers, did nothing to ease ethnic tensions. The Germans were promenading as usual along their Graben under the watchful eye of Prince Franz Anton von Thun und Hohenstein, governor of Bohemia. "Just then two young girls stroll by, arm in arm," Kodíček reminisced. "They are both something to look at. The first Prague girls to give themselves a deliberately boyish look. . . . They are probably the first Czech girls of the pre-war generation to extend their world from the Czech promenade on Ferdinand Avenue to Na Příkopě . . . Milena and Miss Staša. Clearly it's Milena who sets the tone."[23] Unfettered by corsets, hosiery, or convention,[24] Milena and her schoolmates Staša Procházková (later Jílovská) and Jarmila Ambrožová (later Haasová) extended their forays to the Café Arco on the corner of Hybernská and Dlážděná Streets, close to what is now Masaryk Station. Bohumil Kubišta, Emil Filla, and other painters of the Eight had frequented the café when it opened in the fall of 1907, the same year Max Brod hailed the group's first exhibition as a "springtime in Prague."[25] The Arco had one of the best collections of domestic and foreign art magazines in the city. It remained a place in which Czech and German writers and artists mingled, but it is better remembered today as the venue where the young German Jewish literati of what Brod baptized the Prague Circle *brodelt und kafkat, werfelt und kischt*. The play on the names of Max Brod, Franz Kafka, Franz Werfel, and Egon Erwin Kisch is usually attributed to the Viennese critic Karl Kraus, although his authorship is apocryphal. Other "Arconauts" included Willi Haas, Oskar Baum, Otto Pick, Paul Kornfeld, František Langer, and Johannes Urzidil. The café's interior was designed by Jan Kotěra, a pupil of Otto Wagner, who is often described as the father of modern Czech architecture.

Milena probably first met Kafka in the Arco, though Stach believes these "stylish groupies" made little impression on Franz other than as "a welcome erotic element; no one pictured them as future journalists and translators, despite their solid literary education."[26] *Her* eyes were firmly fixed on "that Jew"—Ernst Pollak, a translator at the Austrian National Bank whose critical acumen was prized among the Arconauts. A friend of Franz Werfel and Willi Haas, Pollak was urbane, cultivated, and ten years older than Milena. He "holds me and many other women under a type of spell," she later confessed to Max Brod.[27] To Jan Jesenský's dismay, Ernst and Milena became lovers. In 1916 Milena got pregnant and her father nursed her through an abortion, but still she would not drop her Jew. The following June, in a last throw of the dice, Jan used his medical contacts—one of whom was the father of Milena's friend Staša—to have Milena committed to an asylum in Veleslavín in the western suburbs of Prague, where she was diagnosed as suffering from "a pathological deficiency of moral concepts and inhibitions."[28] At twenty, she was still under Jan's paternal authority. Slávka Vondráčková suggests that Milena's kleptomania was an equally important reason for her confinement as her relationship with Pollak.[29] The experience left Milena with a lifelong antipathy toward psychiatry, where "everything can be abnormal, and every word is a new weapon for the torturer."[30] "You see what a sanatorium means," the distraught Pollak wrote to Willi Haas, "what used to be called a convent or a prison." He begged for Milena's hand in marriage, but Jesenský refused his consent.[31] Milena spent nine months imprisoned in Veleslavín before her father finally gave in. One of his conditions was that the lovers leave town. Milena was released on 7 March 1918, married Ernst on 16 March, and left for Vienna a few days later.

Enriching the Old, Domestic Repertoire

It was in Vienna, under the most inauspicious of circumstances both political (within months the Austrian Empire would collapse and the Austrian economy with it) and personal ("my husband . . . is unfaithful to me one hundred times a year"),[32] that Milena Jesenská—or, as she had become, Milena Pollak—began her career as a journalist. Ernst's salary at the bank could not support their lifestyle. Milena tried teaching Czech and working as a porter at railway stations, but neither paid the bills. In the fall of 1919 Staša Jílovská put her in touch with Arne Laurin (né Arnošt Lustig),[33] an editor at *Tribuna* who later became chief editor of the *Prager Presse*, a state-funded left-wing daily set up under Tomáš Masaryk's patronage to help integrate the German minority into the new Czechoslovak state. Laurin was one of the "Friday Men" (*Pátečníci*)—and they were all men—who met on Friday afternoons in the 1920s at Josef and Karel Čapek's Vinohrady villa to discuss this and that, along with Masaryk, Edvard Beneš, *Tribuna*'s chief editor Ferdinand Peroutka, Josef Kodíček, economist Josef Macek, writers František Langer, Karel Poláček, and Eduard Bass, and other eminent intellectuals. Milena's first translation appeared in *Tribuna* on 9 November 1919. Her first article, titled simply "Vienna," came out on 30 December. She focused on the surrealities of postwar life in the old imperial metropolis—what Milan Kundera calls the "density of unexpected encounters."[34] "There is no heating, no coal, no wood, no coke," she writes. "Trains are not running throughout the country, the factories stop at every minute, shops close at five o'clock, in the restaurants and cafés carbide lamps flicker from eight o'clock on. . . . It's the same with food. If you are extremely frugal—in both quantity and quality—your weekly paycheck will just cover a single, wretched dinner." Yet "fifteen theaters are sold out daily in Vienna despite the enormous price of tickets. . . . Twenty cabarets, twenty bars, masses of restaurants where it is impossible to eat for under 200K [crowns], all full. . . . Cinemas—in almost every street, cafés—in almost every street—are overflowing. The fashion boutiques on Kärtnerstrasse are full of people. Furs, dresses, material, hats, shoes . . . Vienna eats with its mouth full, Vienna dances, Vienna enjoys itself, sings and plays waltzes and operettas more nonsensically than ever . . . Vienna is mad—or is the world mad?"[35]

"The Coffee-House," published in *Tribuna* a few months later, paints a jaundiced picture of "those expressly 'literary' cafés, known from afar, cafés known to the whole city, meeting places of the intellectual and bohemian world like the Prague Union, the Vienna Central, the Berlin des Westens, the Paris Montmartre"—and, Milena might have added, Prague's Café Arco. She ticks off the clientele on her fingers: "the celebrities . . . who already have a name in the official world," those "capitalists of the spirit" who "are rare guests"; "the journalists from every sort of newspaper, the famous, the less famous, and those who are not famous at all"; aspiring writers "who carry their first poems in their breast pockets and read them aloud . . . whenever the chance arises"; "but mostly, mostly: the horde of human flotsam, the horde of most astonishing characters from the most mysterious backgrounds, the horde of people who will never get anywhere and will never do anything, the heroically resigned and quiet melancholics whom the world does not know about and never will know about." Where Ernst Pollak, who held court for hours in the Central and Herrenhof Cafés, fit into this classification Milena does not say. As she told Kafka, she was not yet ready to leave her husband, despite her loneliness. But clearly she did not relish the prospect of becoming just another of "the women who are brought along [who] slowly move from table to table, whether because 'that's the way it goes' or because of marriage, infidelity, divorce. In the end they belong to the café, they lose their surnames and are called by their nicknames alone, they become friends, with the growing count of cigarettes smoked and the growing count of lovers they lose their true femininity, they grow stale, they grow boring, they grow ugly."[36]

The hallmarks of Jesenská's writing are already apparent in these pieces: a conversational style, an eye for detail, a nose for paradox and irony, an ability to make metaphors out of the everyday. She is passionate and compassionate, often indignant or sardonic, frequently sentimental, and unfailingly intelligent, forthright, and humane. Laurin liked her work, and when the opportunity arose he gave her a regular weekly fashion column in *Tribuna*, notwithstanding the fact that (as she later warned her readers) "clothes don't interest me at all, what entices me is the culture of the individual."[37] Milena continued to provide the paper with translations (from Franz Werfel, Gustav Meyrink, Claire Goll, Maxim Gorky, Henri Barbusse, André Gide, and Heinrich Mann, among others) as well as stand-alone articles on cinema, children, handicrafts, advertisements, railway stations, Viennese markets, Christmas gifts, the "new big city type," and much else. She translated more of Kafka's writings for *Tribuna*, *Cesta* (The path), and S. K. Neumann's magazines *Kmen* and *Červen* (June), even though, as she told Max Brod, "it was ghastly to be so forlorn, working on his books."[38] During one of her visits to Prague in 1921 her aunt Růžena gave her an introduction at *Národní listy*, which, despite its conservatism and nationalism, became Milena's principal outlet from 1923 to 1929. By the time she finally left Vienna—and Pollak—in 1924, she had published nearly five hundred articles and translations.[39] The "last straw," she explained in a remarkably candid letter to Karel Hoch, the editor of *Národní listy*, was the fact that "there is still another girl who is expecting a baby by him [Pollak]."[40] Her divorce was finalized on 30 May 1925. After ten months living with communist friends in Dresden, Milena returned to Prague that summer with Franz Schaffgotsch in tow. She was twenty-eight.

She rented an apartment, probably with Schaffgotsch, in the House of the Two Devils on Maltézské Square in the Lesser Town, which was (and still is) one of the prettiest parts of Prague, with its quaint little plazas and narrow streets winding their way up the hill from the river to the castle. Milena focused on the neighborhood in an article for *Národní listy* in March 1926. It was a reckoning, of sorts, of how far she had traveled since leaving the city eight years earlier. She begins by evoking the Lesser Town she loved as a girl—the corners and lanes, the red tiled roofs, the towers, the bells, the old palace gardens flowering in spring, the lights on the riverbank, the orange glow of the town below, first love. But then, she writes, "I went abroad and I learned to see cities through different eyes . . . everything in the foreign city suddenly spoke another language; the city ceased to be a fairy tale shrouded in mists, a backdrop for dreams, and began to be what it is: a place where people live":

> And now after these years and with these well-founded experiences I chanced upon a flat in the Lesser Town. In an old house on the arcade of a small, strangely crooked square, and my joy knew no bounds. You know, I quite forgot for a moment what a city is and what a house is and it was as if I had plunged straight back into childhood. . . . But then it so happened that I needed coalmen and locksmiths and floor polishers and carpenters—and I suddenly began to see the Lesser Town through eyes that were altogether different. I saw a lot of small houses that are frankly awful. From the front door the toilets smell throughout the building, the house is full of balconies and galleries, full of dark, dirty ratholes, of damp, cold walls, of small windows into the courtyard, no light, no air, no space, adults, teenagers, children crammed in everywhere, several people to a bed and the rest on the floor, stoves that reek of bad goulash and cabbage, passages that stink of beer and cheap liquor, foul-smelling corridors, murderous dark staircases—and from this, living people spring out all over, children, women from the laundry and women from the kitchen. When you go out into the street and look back at such a house, you will be amazed at what squalor and fetid air such a charming façade from years gone by is covering up.

"We have a Club for Old Prague," she continues, "that watches out that nothing happens to these façades, stucco angels, corners and towers. I would like to suggest the founding of a club for the people who live in Old Prague . . . who are condemned to live in historic monuments with the needs of a modern individual"—like running water, flushing toilets, "a window here and there," and proper lighting for "that terrible staircase with five Virgin Marys but just one kerosene lamp."[41]

With her reputation as a journalist established by her dispatches from Vienna, Milena had little difficulty easing back into the cultural life of her native city. She continued to contribute prolifically to *Národní listy* and published a cookbook of recipes submitted by readers under the title *Mileniny recepty* (Milena's recipes, 1925) "because who couldn't do with enriching the old, domestic repertoire?"[42] She edited a book series called *Žena* (Woman) for the Topič publishing house, which also brought out a collection of her articles under the title *Cesta k jednoduchosti* (The road to simplicity), which she dedicated to her "Dear Father." A second anthology, *Člověk dělá šaty* (The person makes the clothes, 1927), soon followed. In November 1926 Milena launched "a completely new type of magazine" with the veteran cartoonist V. H. Brunner and the writer and caricaturist Adolf Hoffmeister. *Pestrý týden* (Weekly variety) aimed to be not just a "more or less entertaining weekly that can be read in half an hour and that provides you with a few charming little pictures" but a publication that coupled "journalistically significant photographs" with texts by "first-class experts" to keep its readers informed on "all the important events happening at home and abroad," as well as providing up-to-date coverage of "radio, amateur photography, sport, fashion, health, theater and film."[43] Soon the team was joined by Milena's friends Slávka Vondráčková, who was now a leading textile designer for the craft workshop Artěl, and Staša Jílovská, who took over editorship for volume 2. The contributors listed in a 1927 appeal for subscriptions represented a cross section of contemporary Czech arts and letters: Karel Čapek; František Langer; poets Konstantin Biebl, Vítězslav Nezval, and Jaroslav Seifert; architects Pavel Janák, Vlastislav Hofman, Josef Havlíček, Karel Honzík, and Jaromír Krejcar; critics F. X. Šalda, Antonín Matějček, and V. V. Štech; illustrators Otakar Mrkvička and Josef Lada; theater director E. F. Burian; dancer Milča (Milada) Mayerová; journalists Julius Fučík and Ma-Fa (Marie Fantová); and Karel Teige, leader of the Devětsil Artistic Union, which dominated Prague's avant-garde scene throughout the 1920s.[44] Unfortunately, Milena was fired by the publisher in the spring of 1928 for using the magazine to disseminate "propaganda in favor of the Soviet Union."[45] Staša resigned in solidarity. *Pestrý týden* went on to become one of the most popular publications of its day, producing 963 weekly issues before expiring in April 1945.

Franz Schaffgotsch soon faded out of the picture and was supplanted in Milena's affections by Devětsil architect Jaromír Krejcar, a star pupil of Jan Kotěra's. Milena and Jaromír met on a boat trip upriver hosted by the Spolek výtvarných umělců Mánes (Mánes Fine Artists' Society, or SVU Mánes) in the summer of 1926, and they were married in a civil ceremony on 30 April 1927. The witnesses at the wedding were Adolf Hoffmeister and Karel Teige, both of whom had been pupils not many years before at the Czech *realné*

FIGURE 2.2. Vratislav Hugo Brunner's advertising poster for *Pestrý týden*, 1926.
From Josef Kroutvor, *Poselství ulice*, Prague, 1991.

gymnasium (technical high school) founded in 1871 on Křemencova Street in
the New Town. Their fellow pupils included two other founding members of
Devětsil—the painter Alois Wachsmann and the writer Vladislav Vančura—as
well as Jiří Voskovec and Jan Werich (V + W), whose Osvobozené divadlo
(Liberated Theater), which started life under Jindřich Honzl and Jiří Frejka as
Devětsil's theatrical section in 1926, entertained thousand-strong audiences in
the U Nováků arcade from 1929 to 1938 with its montage of jazz, political satire,
inventive stagecraft, and Joe Jenčík's Girls. Hoffmeister later wrote that
Devětsil was born "under the desks and while skipping class."[46] Křemencova
Street is just a couple blocks from Vojtěšská Street, where the Minerva girls'
gymnasium was located. The "Czech college boys" who teased the *dívky z
Minervy* turned out to be more sophisticated than Mary Hockaday, and possibly Milena and her pals, had assumed.[47] Teige, who was four years younger
than Milena, was writing for *Kmen*, *Čas* (Time), and *Revoluce* (Revolution)
and the newspapers *Právo lidu* (People's right) and *Lidové noviny* (People's
news) before he graduated from high school in June 1919, six months before
she published her first piece in *Tribuna*.

   These Czech boys (and some Czech girls, like the painter Toyen) turned
Prague into one of the most exciting environments for avant-garde writers,

artists, and architects in interwar Europe. Two anthologies published in rapid succession in the fall of 1922, *Revoluční sborník Devětsil* (Devětsil revolutionary miscellany, edited by Jaroslav Seifert and Karel Teige) and *Život II* (Life II, edited by Jaromír Krejcar), caused ructions in Czech cultural circles—including some who saw themselves as bastions of progressive modernity. The word *devětsil* is the name of a flower, the butterbur, but it also puns the Czech term for nine forces or powers (*devět sil*), a possible allusion to the nine muses of antiquity. "This new revolutionary art is neither new, nor revolutionary, nor art," exploded Josef Kodíček in *Tribuna*, while Ferdinand Peroutka warned against "a situation in which a token allegiance to Marxism . . . [and] the legitimacy of the communist party, and frequent use of the words 'worker' and 'factory' . . . qualifies something as having artistic value and novelty."[48] "Poetism [as the Devětsil artists baptized their movement] is nothing but lyrical and visual excitement over the spectacle of the modern world," proclaimed Teige, "love for life and its events, a passion for modernity."[49] Devětsil was as keen to rid Czechoslovakia of stale air as Milena was to modernize the "foul-smelling corridors" and "murderous staircases" behind the charming façades of the Lesser Town. Prague, wrote Teige in 1928, was a place "whose gates we wanted to throw open to all the healthy breezes of the world and the gulf streams of worldwide creative activity . . . it was time to abandon provincial and regional horizons and nationality."[50]

Karel Konrád penned a tongue-in-cheek portrait of the company Milena was now keeping in the 1927–1928 volume of *Rozpravy Aventina* (Aventinum debates), a monthly arts magazine put out by one of the leading publishing houses of the day. "The Devětsil Union of Modern Culture" (as the group renamed itself in 1925), he wrote, "has two league teams. One is composed of professionals, luxuriating in a rather literary combination. Their offense is made up of five poets. At center-forward is the experienced regular *Vítězslav Nezval*, who towers over his surroundings with his brilliant footwork . . . it is a pity that his extravagance often gets him into an offside position. . . . Beside this prima donna, at inside left, is the quiet player *Jaroslav Seifert*. He works the ball decently. . . . The Javanese Leander *Konstantin Biebl*"—the reference is to Biebl's collection *S lodí, jež dováží čáj a kávu* (With the ship that imports tea and coffee), the product of his 1927–1928 travels to Algeria, Tunisia, Java, Sumatra, and Sri Lanka—"gets well-deserved attention at inside right. Beside the noisy Nezval, who has all the merits of the most modern tractor, Biebl is a more meditative player. . . . *František Halas* has worked out well at left wing."

At center-half is *Karel Teige* . . . the backbone of the whole team. He is everywhere: he holds onto every ball, helps the defense, drives the offensive line forward; he is always sharp. His international knowledge equips him to direct all offensive plays and deal with the most dangerous situations. His headers are flawless. With his direct, uncompromising passes he pushes the front line forward in the most literal sense of the term, never giving them a moment's rest, not even taking his pipe out of his mouth. . . . Fair play [the phrase is in English], pinpoint ball control, scientific tactics, and a sense of the whole action quite rightly make Teige the most popular player.

At left half is "*Julius Fučík* . . . an indispensable fighter, without whom it is impossible to win. Julius Fučík is a rare type of team player." The full backs are Jindřich Honzl and "the veteran international *Vladislav Vančura*." In goal is Konrád himself, chosen by Karel Teige, "who had seen my *Robinsonade* in a bookstore when we were out dancing together in Chuchle."[51]

Devětsil's second team "is overwhelmingly composed of architects and artists, centered on the captain . . . *Jaromír Krejcar*," whose "energetic style is without any kind of cornices, balustrades, or façades. . . . On the right wing is [Josef] *Šíma*, a simple and noble gymnast. What a delight it is to watch his graceful game. . . . This acrobatics is applauded even in Paris." Left half "*Jiří Weil* introduces Russian archetypes into his game . . . which of course assumes a knowledge of Soviet poets. . . . [Bedřich] *Feuerstein* plays left back. His current international class is unknown to us, since he is in Tokyo. . . . *Jindřich Štyrský* excels in goal," with his "artistic leaps and elastic still-lifes." Despite the fact that Toyen "spoke only in the masculine gender,"[52] Štyrský's longtime artistic collaborator doesn't make the team. It is a curious omission, given Toyen's prominence in Devětsil. Maybe Konrád was embarrassed by the thought of mixed-sex locker rooms. Toyen likely would not have been fazed: the exuberant couplings in her audacious *Polštář* (The pillow, 1922), painted when she was just twenty, inaugurated a lifetime of artistic engagement with all manners of sexuality.[53] Devětsil's clubhouse, Konrád goes on, is at the Odeon publishers, where "snapshots of thrilling moments as well as overviews of the individual players can be obtained from *Adolf Hoffmeister*." Team training sessions take place daily at the Café Slavia. And that young woman cheering so enthusiastically on the touchline? "Why, that's Ms. [*paní*] *Milena*."[54]

With her copious writings on what would now be called lifestyle, from practical interior design to comfortable clothing, healthy exercise, and nutritious food, Milena fit right into this brave new world. She popularized the purist outlook with a messianic fervor. Simplicity for her was not just an aesthetic credo but an ethical imperative. "The modern individual has a direct and immediate relationship toward life," she wrote in a 1926 article on modern living, "but already has a much less direct and immediate relationship toward possessions. He spends money on a trip to the sea, because he loves sun, sand, water, being abroad, his own suntanned body; but he will hardly spend money to pile up costly collections of things in his flat. . . . The private museum has lost its charm. Our walls are bare, smooth, light, simple, they are the walls of a residential flat, not the fortresses of past centuries. The sun draws pictures on them, the light of the lamp splatters them with shadows." Like Virginia Woolf writing three years later, Milena firmly believed in a room of her own.[55] "The modern person," she continues, "is above all an independent person. A woman works like a man, she has her independent social and civil position and also has a need for her own space, study, bedroom . . . here is my room and there is your room, there are doors between them, so that we can both pass through freely and as appropriate."[56] Milena wrote four reports for *Národní listy* on the celebrated Werkbund housing exhibition at Stuttgart-Weissenhof, which she visited with Jaromír in October 1927.[57] Describing the exhibition as "a realized town of modern buildings that up until now could be seen only as drawings in avant-garde magazines," she hails Le Corbusier as "a genius of infinite grace, spirit, and power" who is "the discoverer of the culture of modern living, just as Baudelaire is the discoverer of modern lyric poetry."[58]

After their marriage the Krejcars left the Lesser Town for a small downtown apartment above Jaromír's mother's confectionery shop in an old house at 35 Spálená Street in the New Town. Across the street stood the new glass-fronted Olympic department store, which was designed by Jaromír and completed in 1928. With its upper terraces receding like the decks of an ocean liner, the building (which still stands) was a classic example of the Devětsil architects' "emotional functionalism."[59] If Karel Teige had been converted to the severe utilitarian doctrines of Hannes Meyer's Dessau Bauhaus (where he taught at Meyer's personal invitation in 1930) by then, Krejcar saw no reason why the principles of the "easy-going, mischievous, fantastic, playful, non-heroic, and erotic art" championed in Teige's 1924 manifesto "Poetismus" (Poetism) should not be extended to architecture.[60] In an avant-garde counterpoint to the Friday Men's meetings at the Čapek brothers' Vinohrady villa, Milena and Jaromír hosted Saturday gatherings where "sausages were heated up, café au lait brewed, rolls devoured, and the gramophone played."[61] "There was no

FIGURE 2.3. Adolf Hoffmeister, *Avantgarda 1930*, ink drawing. Caricatured from left to right are Karel Teige, Vítězslav Nezval, Jindřich Honzl, Jan Werich, and Jiří Voskovec. From Karel Srp, ed., *Adolf Hoffmeister*, Prague, 2004. Courtesy of Martin and Ivan Hoffmeister, © Adolf Hoffmeister heirs.

money for any more," explains Milena's biographer Alena Wagnerová, "but the sausages were served on a large cut-glass platter."[62] The company was varied. Jiří Weil, who started but never finished a novel based on Jaromír and Milena called *Zlatý bengál* (Golden pandemonium), recalled that "often . . . visitors divided into two groups, one talking about the union movement and the other about makes of car."[63] It is a sharp observation that illustrates the wide compass of the notion of progressiveness in Prague in the Roaring Twenties. Once the flat was honored by a visit from F. X. Šalda,[64] whose "Česká moderna" (Manifesto of Czech modernism), coauthored with F. V. Krejčí and others back in 1895, had fired the opening salvos in Czech modernists' battle against the "imitation national songs [and] versified folkloristic baubles" of the national revival.[65] The veteran critic had taken up the cudgels on behalf of "the youngest generation" against Ferdinand Peroutka's 1922 attacks on Devětsil in *Tribuna*, proclaiming, "Well then I am going to start to *learn* from the young, whether it offends people or not, and from the young above all."[66]

Moscow—The Border

"For the first time, after fifteen years of a really bad life," Milena wrote to Adolf Hoffmeister in the fall of 1927, she was happy in her "equal relationship with my beautiful, noble, excellent husband."[67] Her happiness was crowned with a much-longed-for pregnancy, but the idyll was about to turn sour. Milena broke her leg on a skiing holiday with Jaromír, and though she seemed at first to be making a good recovery, she collapsed with a high fever and a paralyzed knee in July 1928. Accounts differ as to the cause, whether septicemia or gonorrhea caught from her "smiling, agreeable, irresistible-to-women Jaromír,"[68] but the consequence was that Milena was hospitalized for the rest of her pregnancy. Jana Krejcarová (later Černá) was born on 14 August 1928. Jana later claimed that her mother "spent the entire thirty-two hours [of labor] wishing for a boy and gripping her thumbs for luck."[69] In the absence of a son, Milena nicknamed the girl Honza (Jack), a Czech diminutive of Jan (John) by way of the German Hans—the name of her father and late brother. She spent most of the next year in sanatoriums in search of a cure for her crippled knee, first in Vinohrady and later at Piešťany in southwestern Slovakia, a spa town renowned for its mud baths and sulfur springs. "I was at death's door," she told the visiting Slávka, and confided, "Dad does everything for me, but I wouldn't give him the girl. Am I supposed to set up the same kind of future for her as he did for me? I'd rather drown her." She did not return home to Spálená 33 until the late summer of 1929, and when she did, it was on crutches. "All that remained of her was pain and little Honza," says Vondráčková.[70] Milena was left with a permanent limp, chronic pain, and an addiction to the morphine she had been given to relieve it.

Milena's illness took a considerable toll on the Krejcars' marriage as well as impacting her work. Afraid that her condition would jeopardize her employment at *Národní listy*, she contacted the newspaper *Lidové noviny* while still in Piešt'any. Her application was supported by Ferdinand Peroutka, the former editor-in-chief of *Tribuna* who was now *Lidové noviny*'s chief political correspondent and editor of the influential political and cultural review *Přítomnost*, which he founded in 1924 with the help of a donation from Tomáš Masaryk. Peroutka respected Milena's writing even though he disagreed with her politics. She worked for *Lidovky* (as it is colloquially known) from April 1929 to June 1931, editing and contributing to its Home—Fashion—Society page. Her last column for *Národní listy* appeared on 31 March 1929. Closely associated with the Čapek brothers, *Lidové noviny* was a far more liberal organ. One of Jesenská's best-known *Lidovky* articles, titled "Civilized Woman?" was published in December 1929 in connection with a Brno exhibition and bilingual Czech-German book of the same title.[71] The topic was the latest Paris fashions, but Milena had more on her mind than clothes. "Do I have to repeat everything that we have said ad nauseam about the modern woman?" she asked her readers:

> She is sporty, economical, clever, and astute. She is educated and resourceful, she knows how to handle weapons, machinery, work, and her own life freely, according to her own autonomous decisions. She is direct and simple, she is clear and brave, and above all: *she is independent.* I am not sure that we have yet really come to terms with the significance of this fact. Independent—that means capable of supporting herself. It literally means that the twilight has fallen on the times when we looked at the prostitute with sentimental pity and sympathized with the suffering of misunderstood women in degrading marriages. Even if it is still very difficult, it is all the same possible: to support herself.

"*Die neue Sachlichkeit,*" the article begins, "is not only the motto of the modern age. It is the creed of a generation and the magic formula that should liberate us. . . . For three years," Milena continues, "it seemed as if woman would also change on the outside; her dress stopped being a lure [*volavka*] and became just clothing." She conjures up a bright modernist vision of female emancipation, shimmering with light, air, and clarity:

A new life was beginning for young girls. . . . During the day they worked, studied, and learned. For this they needed simple and durable clothing. They got it. Never had a young girl so many pleasures to choose from, never could she spend her free time so happily. Thousands of leisure activities awaited her when she was done with work: gymnastics, weekends, scouting, dancing, motoring, winter swimming pools, winter tennis courts, kayaking, camping under the open skies, skiing, the mountains, water, snow, the whole wide world opened itself up to healthy people. Never had the world offered so many wonders to lovers, never had such festivals of bodily joy been celebrated, never did life mean so many beautiful things. . . . Our new dwellings are full of light and sunshine. Our new relationships are full of honesty and dependability. Our new age overflows with abundance just because we have thrown away the ballast binding us like chains.

But now Paris has decreed that it is time to turn the clock back, resurrecting "expensive, useless and ugly" clothes "laden with pretty and gratuitous trinkets" that "impede our progress" and "again make us sedate matrons." "We will walk around our liberated homes with trains on our dresses, lipstick on our lips and a permanent wave in our hair," Milena mocks, "not because it is what we like. But because it is modern." Small things turn out not to be trivial at all: "When we stand today in a social arena and look at the silhouettes of the young women that we know to be clever women, and we look at how they are dressed, we have to admit that the three years of liberation, the austerity and beautiful, simple, elegant line of our dresses, the love of quality material and good things, were not progress, as we mistakenly assumed—but they too were merely a fashion."[72]

In the spring of 1931 the Krejcars moved into a spacious, ultramodern penthouse above a functionalist office block Jaromír had designed for the Jednota soukromných úředníků (Association of Private Office Workers) on Francouzská Street in Vinohrady. The apartment had a living room "almost as big as the nave of a church," a wraparound balcony where Milena tended her admired "hanging gardens," a roof terrace with a magnificent view of Prague—and no marital bedroom. Milena's room of her own was empty except for a wide folding bed, with a black cross hanging at its head and a huge reproduction of Van Gogh's *Sunflowers* on the opposite wall.[73] The cross, which went everywhere with her, had belonged to her mother.[74] Jaromír was often away from home; one of his most renowned buildings, the Machnáč Sanatorium in Trenčianske Teplice in Slovakia, was built in 1930–1932. Around this time—the exact date is unknown because no documentary evidence survives—Milena joined the KSČ. "I joined the communist party after my illness and after my paralysis out of a great longing to be able to do something still that was needed in the world," she told the actress and writer Olga Scheinpflugová.[75]

It was a time of hard choices for everyone on the Czechoslovak Left. The economic growth of the late 1920s had come to a halt and the Great Depression was beginning to bite. By 1933 more than a million people were unemployed, and shantytowns sprang up on the outskirts of Prague. The German-speaking industrial areas of the northern borderlands were especially hard hit, fueling old national resentments. Out of 846,000 unemployed in 1935, some 525,000 were Germans.[76] Lyrical and visual excitement over the spectacle of the modern world didn't cut it anymore. Klement Gottwald and his Karlín Boys (*karlínští kluci*, so called from the location of the Prague KSČ headquarters) had captured control of the KSČ at its Fifth Congress in February 1929 and set about Bolshevizing the party. "We go to Moscow," Gottwald told members in his maiden speech to parliament, "to learn from the Russian Bolsheviks how to wring your necks."[77] Seven communist writers—S. K. Neumann, Vladislav Vančura, Jaroslav Seifert, Ivan Olbracht, Marie Majerová, Helena Malířová, and Josef Hora—challenged the "suicidal politics" of Gottwald's "incompetent" leadership, which, they claimed, "has in common with Leninist doctrine only the word, but which is completely foreign to the true Leninist spirit."[78] The Seven, as they became known, were soon kicked out of the KSČ. Most would later mend fences with the party. It says much about the changing climate that Karel Teige, Vítězslav Nezval, Konstantin Biebl, František Halas, and Jiří Weil were among those who condemned the writers' stance, and Seifert was expelled from Devětsil on Julius Fučík's suggestion.[79]

In 1932–1933 Milena worked as an editor at *Žijeme* (We live), the organ of Svaz Československého díla (SČD; Union of Czechoslovak Crafts). A Czechoslovak equivalent of the German Werkbund, SČD was responsible for the model housing estate exhibitions at Brno in 1928 and Baba in Prague in 1932, which showcased modern Czech architecture.[80] *Žijeme* gave Milena the opportunity to revisit some long-standing interests with new eyes. "Is it at all possible to raise a child well at home?" she asked in one article, challenging her readers to picture instead "a large and spacious house full of light, cleanliness, tidiness, and order. Somewhere outside the city or at least surrounded by gardens. A house, where we would drop off the children in the morning and pick them up in the evening," and the kids could spend their days away from "domestic anxieties, problems, sensitivities, and emotions. . . . Under the supervision of trained qualified people. Under the supervision of good doctors and good teachers."[81] Nowadays we call it a day care. What might have become a mutually productive association with SČD and *Žijeme* did not last. Once again Milena lost her job because her writings were deemed too left wing. For the next three years she worked almost entirely for KSČ outlets, publishing in the party's theoretical and cultural journal *Tvorba* (Creation)—working in its editorial collective with Julius Fučík, Jiří Weil, and Záviš Kalandra—as well as in the illustrated magazine *Svět práce* (The world of labor). *Tvorba* was founded by F. X. Šalda in 1925, but the critic became so incensed with repression of the KSČ press that he put his periodical at the party's disposal in June 1928. *Přitomnost* was soon ridiculing it as "a propagandist magazine of the first order."[82]

Milena grew close to "that beautiful boy, that Jula Fučík" (as Slávka Vondráčková described him)—so close, in fact, that they embarked on an affair. "He would rush up with an enormous bunch of flowers," Slávka relates. "He kneeled before Mistress Milena and laughed. And we had to go out with Honza to Petřín hill."[83] Fučík left Prague in August 1934 for a two-year stint in the Soviet Union as a correspondent for *Tvorba* and the KSČ daily *Rudé právo* (Red right). That same month Milena hid Klement Gottwald in her penthouse; the KSČ leader was on his way to Moscow, where he remained in exile until February 1936. The government had revoked Gottwald's parliamentary immunity and issued a warrant for his arrest for treason after he described Tomáš Masaryk (against whom he was running for the Czechoslovak presidency) as "the figurehead of the bourgeoisie, whose authority was being used for the establishment of an open fascist dictatorship."[84] By then Jaromír Krejcar was living in Moscow too. Like Milena, he had moved further to the left as the Roaring Twenties gave way to the Dirty Thirties. When the Marxist Bauhaus director Hannes Meyer was dismissed in 1930, Jaromír employed two of Meyer's former students, Antonín Urban and Nusim Nesis, in his practice.[85] He founded the architectural section of Levá fronta (Left Front), a forum created in November 1929 "to mobilize the cultural left" and "defend modern views and interests against conservatism and reaction."[86] Its first president was Karel Teige. The Left Front soon took over from Devětsil (which disbanded in 1931) as the center of Prague's avant-garde cultural life. Like a totemic incantation, the word *modern* is repeated no fewer than seventeen times in the two and a half pages of its founding proclamation. Whatever their views on Gottwald's Bolshevization of the KSČ, many on the Czech Left still believed that, as Vladislav Vančura put it in his foreword to Seifert's *Město v slzách* (City in *Tears*, 1921), "New, new, new is the star of communism . . . and outside it there is no modernity."[87]

Political commitments aside, the invitation to work as a foreign specialist in the workers' state was extremely tempting for a young architect whose commissions were collapsing due to the disastrous economy at home and whose many creditors were hounding him to pay off a mountain of debt. Though the Krejcars considered the advantages of educating Honza in the Soviet Union, Milena eventually decided that she and the child should stay behind in Prague. Jaromír left for Moscow in January 1934 to work at the Giprogor state urban planning institute under the constructivist architect Moses Ginzburg. Within months Sergei Kirov's assassination triggered Stalin's terror. Foreign specialists did not escape the purges. Jaromír was billeted at the rat-infested three-hundred-room Hotel Lux on Gorky Avenue, from which people soon started to disappear in the night.[88] Other guests included not only Klement Gottwald but also Ho Chi Minh, Zhou Enlai, Antonio Gramsci, Walter Ulbricht, and Milena Jesenská's future biographer Margarete Buber-Neumann. Krejcar was lucky to get back to Prague alive. So was Jiří Weil, who had been working in the Soviet Union as a translator since 1933. Weil drew on his experiences, which included some months "attached" to a labor camp in Soviet Central Asia, in what would be the first Western novels set in the world of Stalin's gulag. *Moskva—hranice* (Moscow—the border) came out in 1937. Julius Fučík trashed it in *Tvorba*. The sequel, *Dřevěná lžíce* (The wooden spoon), was written in 1938 but wasn't published legally in Czech until 1992. The young Czech architect Antonín Urban, one of seven ex-Bauhaus students who moved to the USSR as part of Hannes Meyer's Red Front Brigade in October 1930, was less fortunate than Krejcar and Weil. "After many years of working within the capitalist system," explained Meyer at the time, "I am convinced that working under such conditions is quite senseless . . . I am leaving for the USSR to work among people who are forging a true revolutionary culture, who are achieving socialism, and who are living in that form of society for which we have been fighting here under the conditions of capitalism."[89] Meyer was permitted to return to Switzerland in 1936. Urban was executed for espionage in June 1938.

While he was in Moscow, Jaromír fell in love with a Latvian translator, Riva Holcova. Milena agreed to a divorce, which came through in October 1934. In the meantime, she had taken up with Evžen Klinger, a Hungarian Jew and former secretary of the Slovak Communist Party. Klinger had started out as another KSČ fugitive hiding in her Vinohrady penthouse and ended up as her lover. After Jaromír returned to Prague with Riva in 1935, Milena, Evžen, and

FIGURE 2.4. Jaromír Krejcar's Czechoslovak pavilion (right, beneath the Eiffel Tower) at the Paris World's Fair, 1937. The Swedish pavilion is on the left. Photographer unknown. Wikimedia Commons.

Honza left the Francouzská Street apartment for more modest accommodations in Kouřimská Street, near the Olšany cemeteries. Jaromír was profoundly shaken by his Soviet experiences. "Whoever has spent three weeks in the [Soviet] Union," he reportedly said, "has material for a three-volume work on the subject. Whoever has spent three months there, will be more likely to come up with a small thirty-page pamphlet. Whoever has spent three years there, will not write a single word."[90] Even so, he did find the courage to publicly appeal in *Přítomnost* on behalf of the German communist actress and singer Carola Neher, for whom Bertolt Brecht (her former lover) had written the role of Polly Peachum in *The Threepenny Opera*. Krejcar was responding to reports that Neher had been condemned to death and executed in the USSR "for political reasons."[91] The actress had fled Germany in 1933 for Prague (where she performed at the New German Theater in Shakespeare's *Taming of the Shrew*) before moving to the Soviet Union in 1934. After her husband Anatol Becker was executed for alleged involvement in a plot to assassinate Stalin in 1937, Carola was sentenced to ten years in prison for Trotskyism. She died of typhus in the Sol-Ilezk transit camp near Orenburg, on the Kazakhstan border, in

June 1942 at the age of forty-one.[92] Ironically, in 1933 Milena had written an angry article in *Tvorba* attacking the Czechoslovak censor's refusal to allow the public release of G. W. Pabst's 1931 film version of *The Threepenny Opera*.[93] Guess who played the part of Polly Peachum?

Jaromír's most effective riposte to Joseph Stalin's socialism in one country was probably "the delicate glass poem on the banks of the Seine,"[94] which he created for the 1937 *Exposition internationale des arts et techniques de la vie moderne*. This was the same World's Fair where the Spanish republican government first exhibited *Guernica*, Picasso's painting protesting the bombing of the Basque city by German warplanes on 26 April 1937. Albert Speer's German pavilion and Boris Iofan's Soviet pavilion faced off in totalitarian stupidity and splendor on opposite sides of the central mall that led across the Pont d'Iéna to the Eiffel Tower. Krejcar's Czechoslovak pavilion survives only in photographs; plans to dismantle and reerect it in Prague on the banks of the Vltava came to nothing. Situated on the Quai d'Orsay directly across the river from Iofan's pomposity, the simple cube, elevated on four slender steel pillars, seemed almost to float. Its walls were constructed entirely of opaque Thermolux glass, hung from a gossamer-thin steel frame. The corners were gently curved, not just for poetic effect but with the object of "demonstrating the production possibilities of Czechoslovak industry." "Doubtless, angular corners would have been just as functional as rounded ones," Jaromír explained, but Thermolux glass plates of this size "were produced for the first time in the world."[95] The exhibits included an illuminated fountain by Zdeněk Pešánek. The pavilion was a poignant reminder of a modernity that seemed to be on the verge of passing beyond recall—a moment in history that turned out to be not progress, as people had mistakenly assumed, but merely a fashion.

Milena's final contribution to *Tvorba*, a translation of an article by the Prague-German communist writer F. C. Weiskopf ("A day in the summer camp of the 1st proletarian regiment"), appeared in September 1935. Her last articles for *Svět práce* came out in May 1936. Milena, too, had grown disillusioned with both the Soviet Union and the KSČ. She remained good friends with Jaromír, but his accounts of life in the USSR were not the only thing that weighed on her. The breach with *Svět práce* was caused by her refusal to comply with the editor's demand that she dump Evžen Klinger after he was kicked out of the party for Trotskyism.[96] It was not an unlikely diktat at the time, when the political was always expected to trump the personal. In January 1936 a campaign against "formalism and naturalism" began in Moscow, catching up Dmitry Shostakovich, Boris Pasternak, and Sergei Eisenstein, among others, and culminating in the closure of Vsevolod Meyerhold's avant-garde theater in January 1938. The sixty-five-year-old Meyerhold would be arrested, tortured, and executed in 1940. Hard on the heels of the antiformalism campaign came the trial and execution in August 1936 of Lenin's October Revolution comrades Lev Kamenev and Grigory Zinoviev and fourteen other old Bolsheviks. Sometime that year Milena left—or was perhaps expelled from—the Communist Party. So was her *Tvorba* colleague Záviš Kalandra, who responded by launching a left-opposition journal called *Proletář* (The proletarian). They were far from alone in their dissent.

Some of the sharpest criticism of the Stalinist turn came from the Czechoslovak Surrealist Group—though not from its instigator Vítězslav Nezval, who remained faithful to the KSČ. Karel Teige, who joined the group soon after its founding in 1934 and went on to become its principal spokesman alongside Nezval, did not mince his words. In an article written for the fiftieth birthday of the Mánes Fine Artists' Society in March 1937, he warned:

> In a time in which in the Third Reich art has been subjugated by reactionary racist and nationalist ideologies and a once vibrant artistic center has been changed into a cultural jailhouse, and in which artistic policies in the USSR have anathematized the remarkable avant-garde originating in LEF (the Left Front) and returned to old-fashioned academic Russian realism, we must be all the more grateful for the activity of Czech modernism . . . which transformed Prague, which was then on the periphery of artistic events, into one of the most intense hotbeds of international poetic and artistic modern ideas.

Teige hardly needed to remind his readers that Czechoslovakia was by then the only democracy left standing in central and eastern Europe. "The Paris school, which is to say the international artistic avant-garde," he continued, "has in today's Europe only two powerful concentric points of support beside Paris: Prague and Barcelona."[97]

After a stormy meeting at the U Locha wine bar in the Topič building at 9 Národní Avenue, during which Jindřich Štyrský threw some punches, Nezval announced the dissolution of the Czechoslovak Surrealist Group in the communist press on 9 March 1938. Refusing to be disbanded, the rest of the group—Štyrský, Toyen, Konstantin Biebl, Jindřich Honzl, Bohuslav Brouk, and Liberated Theater composer Jaroslav Ježek—united behind Teige's "Surrealismus proti proudu" (Surrealism against the current), published in May 1938. Here, Teige again emphasized that "in the USSR as well as the Third

FIGURE 2.5. Adolf Hoffmeister, *I Like the Spanish Land So Much*, 1937. Illustration from
10 let Osvobozeného divadla V + W, Prague, 1937. Courtesy of Martin and Ivan Hoffmeister,
© Adolf Hoffmeister heirs.

Reich an anathema has been imposed against *the same* new art," but his concerns were not only artistic.[98] He trenchantly condemned the Moscow trials and recent Soviet decrees "banning abortion, limiting divorce, and consolidating the family."[99] At an exhibition of works by Štyrský and Toyen in Brno the previous month, "a broader coalition" had "coalesced to take a stand against the Stalinist conformists and fight for avant-garde art's freedom," involving, among others, Teige, Štyrský, Toyen, Ježek, the surrealist group's "collaborators" František Halas, E. F. Burian, Roman Jakobson, and Jan Mukařovský, as well as Vladislav Vančura, Adolf Hoffmeister, Jiří Weil, and architect Jiří Kroha.[100] Whatever their misgivings about what was happening in the USSR, "Surrealism against the Current" went too far for many on the Czech Left. Vítězslav Nezval ("to toss Berlin and Moscow into one basket . . . testifies not only to a moral, but also— and above all—to an intellectual mistake"), Julius Fučík ("Nezval's action resolutely helps toward liquidating a fifth column among the intelligentsia"), and S. K. Neumann ("the Soviet proletariat rid itself of saboteurs") all doubled down on their support for the first workers' state.[101] It was not an incomprehensible stance. Prague had been full of refugees from Hitler since 1933.

Barcelona fell to General Franco's forces on 26 January 1939. Writing in *Přítomnost* a little over a month later, Milena Jesenská left readers no doubt where she now stood on the Soviet Union. The context was Comintern criticism of Czechoslovakia's alleged "fascist and malevolent cruelty . . . toward refugees, political and economic emigrants and our own nationals of the Jewish faith." Things were not simple, Milena wrote, now that the country had lost a third of its territory and population to Germany and Hungary because of the Munich Agreement, leaving hundreds of thousands of Czechoslovaks stranded on the other side of the border. If Czechoslovakia failed to maintain good relations with Germany, she warned, "more blows will fall upon us." She would be proved right sooner than she knew—the article was published on 8 March 1939, a week before Slovakia seceded and the Wehrmacht occupied Bohemia and Moravia. Milena dismisses Radio Moscow's propaganda as "paper sentences, unreal words, and bombastic phrases," a trite analysis that is "black-and-white, silently ignoring all inconsistent, complicated and apparently inexplicable social phenomena." She contrasts the reception of German, Hungarian, and Polish refugees who were given asylum in Tomáš Masaryk's liberal first republic with émigrés' treatment in the USSR. Many of the Schutzbund (Social Democratic Defense League) workers who fled Austria after the failure of the February Uprising in 1934, she notes, "were put in jail, many were sent beyond the Arctic Circle or to the great construction projects." After 1934 the Soviet Union closed its borders to refugees and shipped off most of those it had previously taken in to fight in the Spanish Civil War, while "only select functionaries remained in Moscow":

> Try to ascertain what remains of the German émigrés who fled to the Soviet Union and you will discover that the bones of the German communists lie mostly beneath Madrid. The same fate befell the Hungarian, Yugoslav, and Polish communist émigrés.... Would Moscow Radio not like to tell us ... what became of the many Czecho-Slovak [sic] communists and simple Czech workers who went to the Soviet Union years ago, fleeing from punishment or looking for work? Would we not discover, for example, that the majority of them are sitting in GPU prisons?

"It is interesting," she adds, "to reflect on who really built the gigantic Soviet constructions, canals, dams and dikes."[102]

The Refuse of the Past

Alexander Rodchenko's images of the construction of the White Sea Canal (Belomorkanal) in 1931–1933 display all the innovations that made him a legend in the history of photography—startling camera angles, dizzying perspectives, strong geometries, stark contrasts—all of which enhance his photographs' affective punch. A selection from upward of two thousand images Rodchenko shot during three lengthy visits to the site in the Karelia region on the Finnish border was published in December 1933 as a special issue of the magazine USSR in Construction, displayed in a montage format that mimicked a newsreel. Some might think they give grim pertinence to Roland Barthes's observation that "the photograph tells me death in the future.... Whether or not the subject is already dead, every photograph is this catastrophe."[103] But that was not how the photographer saw it, and if we are to begin to understand these images and their era, it is important to grasp why. Rodchenko captions one of the most famous photographs, that of the camp orchestra framed against the bed of the canal, with these words: "For twenty months, [the camp] has trained around 20,000 skilled workers in forty specialties. These are all former thieves, kulaks, vermin, and murderers. For the first time they come to learn about the poetry of labor, and the romance of construction. They worked to the music of their own orchestras."[104] It was not that Rodchenko was indifferent to the sufferings to which his Leica bore eloquent witness. They moved him deeply. The opportunity to photograph Belomorkanal, he wrote in *Soviet Photo*, "was my salvation; it was a new start in life." He was not just referring to the fact that the commission helped salvage his faltering career. The subject itself had a redemptive quality. "A gigantic will gathered the refuse of the past there to make the canal," he explained. "People were burning, sacrificing themselves, heroically overcoming all difficulties . . . I was bewildered, astonished. I was gripped by that enthusiasm."[105]

The American art critic Clement Greenberg oversimplified when he counterposed the avant-garde and kitsch in his famous 1939 essay. By kitsch, Greenberg meant "the debased and academicized simulacra of genuine culture . . . vicarious experience and faked sensations . . . the epitome of all that is spurious in the life of our times." He exemplifies the works of the Russian realist painter Ilya Yefimovich Repin, while making the acid comment that "it is lucky, however, for Repin that the [Soviet] peasant is protected from the products of American capitalism, for he would not stand a chance next to a *Saturday Evening Post* cover by Norman Rockwell."[106] But there is such a thing as modernist kitsch too, and nowhere is it better displayed than in these Belomorkanal images—unless, perhaps, in Leni Riefenstahl's notorious films *Triumph des Willens* (*Triumph of the Will*, 1935) and *Olympia* (1938), which employ a no less modernist visual vocabulary to glorify the 1934 Nuremberg rally and the 1936 Berlin Olympics, respectively. For Milan Kundera, kitsch is not just an aesthetic category but an attitude, a behavior, and a need. Rodchenko's enthusiasm is a textbook example of what Kundera sees as the defining feature of kitsch, "the need to gaze into the mirror of the beautifying lie and to be moved to tears at one's own reflection."[107] He elaborates in a well-known passage in *The Unbearable Lightness of Being*, which applies equally to Repin, Rockwell, and Rodchenko:

When the heart speaks, the mind finds it indecent to object. In the realm of kitsch, the dictatorship of the heart reigns supreme.

The feeling induced by kitsch must be a kind the multitudes can share. Kitsch may not, therefore, depend on an unusual situation; it must derive from the basic images people have engraved on their memories: the ungrateful daughter, the neglected father, children running on the grass, the motherland betrayed, first love.

Kitsch causes two tears to flow in quick succession. The first tear says: How nice to see children running on the grass!

The second tear says: How nice to be moved, together with all mankind, by children running on the grass!

It is the second tear that makes kitsch kitsch.

More simply: "Kitsch is the absolute denial of shit." Not the denial of death, because death can be sentimentalized. Kitsch is the denial of "everything . . . which is essentially unacceptable in human existence."[108] No wonder Kundera likes Kafka.

Enthusiasm was the watchword of the day. Jaroslav Seifert was equally moved when he visited the Soviet Union in October–November 1925 as part of a delegation from the Společnost pro kulturní a hospodářské sblížení s novým Ruskem (Society for Cultural and Economic Rapprochement with the New Russia), founded in 1924 by the musicologist Zdeněk Nejedlý. "When I was in Moscow, on the day of the anniversary of the revolution," he recorded, "I found myself caught up in the current of the enthusiastic crowd, which was rolling toward Red Square. In that moment I was dying with longing to become the poet of this people."[109] Karel Teige, Jindřich Honzl, and the poet Josef Hora were among his fellow pilgrims. Apart from bemoaning the absence of cafés, Teige liked what he saw. "The Bolsheviks are the greatest people on earth," he wrote to his mother. "Vote for the communists," he added, "because here it is evident just how beautiful communism is in reality. Love and kisses from your enthusiastic Karel."[110] That enthusiasm infects the studies of art, film, book production, and architecture that Teige wrote over the next two years and collected in *Sovětská kultura* (Soviet culture, 1927), one of the first Western publications to address the novelty of the Russian avant-garde. "To speak of modern Russian art," he insisted in *Tvorba* in January 1926, "necessarily and implicitly means to speak of Soviet life and of the conditions provided by the October Revolution." Constructivism "is not just some trendy new *ism*, the *dernier cri* of ateliers and exhibitions: Constructivism is rooted in a new and liberated labor, in the creation of functionally perfect values in the service of life, in the scientific and fair organization of production."[111] All the same, Teige never joined the Communist Party.

In 1934 Rodchenko helped design a commemorative volume on Belomorkanal, produced by a team of thirty-six writers headed by icon of Soviet literature Maxim Gorky. *Belomorsko–Baltiiskii kanal imeni Stalina: Istoriia stroitel'stva* (*The White Sea–Baltic Canal Named after Stalin: A History of the Construction*) went through four domestic editions with a total print run of 144,000 copies and was even translated into English. Whether and in what sense the prison labor that built the canal could be considered "liberated" is moot—but it is not a stupid question. The book was *intended* to highlight, in its own words:

The story of the construction of the White Sea–Baltic Canal named after Stalin, realized on the initiative of Comrade Stalin under the direction of the OGPU [All-Union State Political Administration, or secret police], using a workforce of former enemies of the proletariat. Vivid examples of the corrective labor policy of the Soviet authorities that has converted thousands of socially dangerous people into conscientious builders of Socialism. The heroic victory of human energy organized in a collective manner over the elemental forces of grim northern nature, the implementation of a tremendous hydrotechnical project. Its leaders are Chekists [members of Cheka, predecessor of OGPU], engineers, workers and also former counterrevolutionaries, wreckers, kulaks, thieves, prostitutes and speculators, who have been re-educated through labor, have obtained industrial skills and returned to a life of honest labor.[112]

Like some surrealist mash-up of Max Weber's *Protestant Ethic* and Michel Foucault's *Discipline and Punish* (with an anticipatory dash of Mao Zedong's Great Proletarian Cultural Revolution and Pol Pot's Year Zero thrown in), *The White Sea–Baltic Canal Named after Stalin* tells a tale of modernist mastery achieved on the backs of modern slaves. Around 100,000 prisoners worked on Belomorkanal at any one time, digging their way through thirty miles of solid granite by hand. No machines, no explosives. Official Soviet figures acknowledge some twelve thousand deaths during the construction. Other estimates are considerably higher.[113] When you chop wood, as Stalin was fond of saying, the chips fly. But another twelve thousand prisoners were released on completion of the project, living testimony to Marx's transformation of circumstances and selves—though many were subsequently rearrested.[114] They had "reforged" (the camp newspaper was called *Perekovka* [Reforging]) not only the arctic landscape but also their very souls in the crucible of revolutionary practice.[115]

Today the memory of the canal named after Stalin lingers in the pungent fumes of Belomorkanal, a popular brand of Russian cigarettes. Critics have suggested that this is rather like naming the leading brand of German cigarettes Dachau or Auschwitz (the gates of both these places, lest we forget, bore the words *Arbeit macht frei*). It was the cigarettes that gave Nicolas Rothwell the title of his 2013 novel *Belomor*, which he describes as "a book of narratives and remembrances."[116] Rothwell's books blur the border between fiction and nonfiction, often recalling the novels, if they can be called that, of W. G. Sebald. The first of the four narratives that make up *Belomor* segues from the carpet bombing of Dresden in February 1945 by way of "the strongest [cigarettes] in

FIGURE 2.6. Alexander Rodchenko's *White Sea Canal (Orchestra)*, spring 1933, gelatin silver print, 15.2 by 22.2 cm, printed 1994. Museum of Fine Arts, Houston; purchase funded by Brown Foundation Accessions Endowment Fund, 95.325.22. © Estate of Alexander Rodchenko/UPRAVIS, Moscow/ARS, New York.

the world" to Solovki—the Ur-camp in the Soviet gulag, established under Lenin in 1923 on the Solovetski Islands in the White Sea. Solovki furnished much of the labor for the White Sea Canal. "In the dark hours of actually existing socialism," Rothwell's character Stephan Haffner, an East German dissident, recalls a journey north to retrace the steps of his mentor Dmitry Sergeyevich Likhachev. Dmitry is not a fictional creation but a renowned linguist who, as a young man, spent five years in Solovki and took part in the building of Belomorkanal:

> We anchored close by the entrance to the canal. . . . The canal the convicts built, with pick and spade. Nineteen locks with their gates: one hundred thousand workers, ten thousand dead. I had no idea then, beyond hints and whispers; now I know: there was a dead man, a spirit, for every step. They might as well have mixed the concrete for the banks with human ash! There it was, the canal basin, wide before us, gleaming in the light. All was still—a

wondrous silence. It was as if no one was living any longer, in that settlement—and that was close, in fact, to truth. In the evening I walked out, alone, to the tip of the northern breakwater: from there you looked back, and saw the town stretched out beneath the thin bands of haze and the looming sky. You saw wide bridge spans, powerlines: there were coastal cutters and transport barges, listing, rusting away; empty loading docks, cantilevers, all motionless. Over everything there was that sense of beauty and desolation you come on at old, decaying industrial sites. So it was all for this, I whispered to myself: all for this, those years of effort: for this, that secret, hidden world of pain.

But that was not the epiphany. *This* was: Suddenly blinded by the "pure, blazing white, white like a fire's heart" as the setting sun slipped beneath the clouds, Haffner for the first time understood why it was called the White Sea. "As I was looking, what was before me had vanished. It melted away. It became whiteness—not waves, and beams of light, and sky. It was the whiteness behind the world . . . the void at the core of things. . . . Since that day it has been clear to me that there are moments in our lives when the world becomes unstable, when our visual field gives way: things break before us; they burst into fragments, disappear."[117]

Since we are trading in metaphors, it seems worth taking a detour down another signifying chain, if only in passing (I made much more of it in *Prague, Capital of the Twentieth Century*).[118] More than half a century after his visit to Moscow, deep in the dark hours of actually existing socialism, an older and wiser Jaroslav Seifert also reflected on how dark the light can sometimes be. "I am already an old man, and I don't like winter," he wrote in *All the Beauties of the World*. "I don't like snow anymore either. When there's a snowstorm, when outside the window it darkens with that familiar white darkness."[119] *Belomor*, writes Rothwell, "depicts a world in fragments, and the paths in life taken by its set of characters: individuals who find themselves drawn to seek affinities between the events and accidents that punctuate their lives. Their task—as for all of us, writers, readers—is to make order from what lies about them, to find beauty in the pattern of their experiences, to compose a world."[120]

Hundreds of Thousands Seeking No-Man's-Land

Banished from KSČ company, in bad health, and without a steady source of income, Milena Jesenská hit rock bottom in the winter of 1936–1937. She survived by doing translations from Hungarian with Evžen Klinger,[121] while (according to Alena Wagnerová) Miloš Vaněk helped her slip pseudonymous work into *Právo lidu* and Záviš Kalandra set her up with a small fashion column in *Světozor* (World outlook).[122] Her father helped her out financially, even though she was cohabiting with another Jew he didn't much like.[123] "Since August," Milena wrote to Olga Scheinpflugová in January 1937, "I have been struggling with unemployment, with illness—I have inflammation of the kidneys. . . . And I am standing here without a penny, truly, Olga, I don't have enough for tonight's dinner . . . *I must* get some regular work again, or else it will turn out with me like it did with Frycek [Bedřich] Feuerstein."[124] Along with Jaromír Krejcar, Karel Teige, and Josef Šíma, Feuerstein was one of the four coauthors of the celebrated photomontage cover of Devětsil's anthology *Život II*,[125] which stages the chance meeting of a Praga automobile wheel and a Doric column on the operating table of the open sea. He had committed suicide a few months earlier by emulating Max Brod's Pepí Vlková and jumping into the Vltava from Troja Bridge. There is no need to rehearse the abject details of Milena's struggles with morphine addiction here.[126] It suffices to note that on 2 February 1937 her teenage first love Jiří Foustka drove her to the mental hospital in what was then the little village of Bohnice (today it is a gigantic highrise housing estate) on the northern edge of Prague, where Milena checked herself in for a ten-day cold-turkey cure. She had work to do. When Honza visited, she found that her mother "could scarcely walk, her hands shook and her voice and face were strained beyond recognition."[127] But Milena came out clean. According to her doctors "she conducted herself heroically."[128] Now that she had parted ways with the KSČ, Ferdinand Peroutka invited her to join the editorial team at *Přítomnost* and gave her ample space in the paper for her own writing. The immediate crisis was over. Everything else soon got worse.

Between 29 September 1937 and 5 July 1939 Milena published more than fifty pieces in *Přítomnost*, many of them long essays of reportage in the Egon Erwin Kisch mold.[129] They are among her best work. Covering some of the most consequential events of the twentieth century, they provide a window on modernities in the making that democratic Western societies have pushed to the margins of their narratives of progress, even if, as a matter of historical fact, they loomed over much of the rest of the century and are still alive and kicking in the new millennium. Take, for example, "the so familiar image that stubbornly refuses to retreat from the life of our generation—somewhere in the world there is always a road full of carts with canvas covers, an old woman, children, chickens, a goat, eiderdowns."[130] Several generations have passed since Milena Jesenská wrote these words, but that image has not

disappeared—though it might have been supplanted by the more contemporary picture of a three-year-old Syrian boy in blue shorts and red top
lying facedown, dead, on a Greek beach. His name was Alan Kurdi, and he
drowned in the Mediterranean off the island of Kos on 2 September 2015 as he
and his family were trying to reach relatives in Vancouver, Canada. Milena
devoted her second article for *Přítomnost*, published on 27 October 1937, to
German refugees in Prague, whose numbers she estimated at thirty-five hundred. "They are foreign people, speaking foreign languages, coming from a
foreign land," she writes. "But we have one thing in common: at the word
swastika, our hearts are seized with the same feelings. This little handful of
exiles can teach us what the swastika is: they are living witnesses to great violence and powerful lies. They carry their testimony on their own skins, here
among us, and any one of us who is like doubting Thomas, who did not believe
until he could convince himself, can go and touch them with his finger."[131]

Written after the Austrian *Anschluss* of 13 March 1938, when Adolf Hitler
annexed Austria to the German Reich, "Judge Lynch in Europe?" begins by
locating the "political life of the little guy [*malý člověk*]" within the narrow
compass in which ordinary lives are lived—"across the square and down three
more streets, the journey to work, the journey home, the pub on the corner,
the tobacconist's opposite and the eight square meters called home." This is
where, Milena argues, "what is known as a pogrom arises. A pogrom is apart
from anything else the revenge of the little guy on the little guy," when "long
pent-up anger—whipped up and taken advantage of by some propaganda or
other—converges in a certain idea, crystalizes, and explodes." In more peace-
ful times the different people who occupy the typical Prague tenement block
managed to get along. But today, she warns, "politics has entered into the
homes of the little guys, the two-room flats with a kitchen and bathroom, sat
down at the tables with crocheted tablecloths, and it jangles from the radio
that used to play only songs." Identities harden.

> Today, Mr Novotný is above all a Czech and a good neighbor, Mr Kohn is
> a Jew, and the tenant Keller's son is a strapping lad, a very sporty youth in
> white Bavarian knee-socks—in the middle of peaceful Smíchov, where
> there is not a mountain to be seen from far and wide. Mr Svoboda, the tailor
> in the basement, is a social democrat. There are also two émigrés down
> there in the basement, German socialists, living on a registration card,
> without work, without papers, and all the tenants in the building—Czech,
> German, Jewish—are put out by their presence, even if they are a little

shamefaced about it. Because an emigrant—an emigrant is a black man [*černoch*] and moreover, he is a black man among white people, who is living where he does not belong.

"Today in Europe it is not necessary for people to have colored skin to become blacks," Milena explains. She draws an extended analogy between fascist Europe and Jim Crow America that is definitely not the country whose feats of architecture and engineering Jaromír Krejcar eulogized in *Život II*. "As everyone knows," she says, black men are not allowed to touch white women, black people must live in ghettos, and blacks are not the masters. Today, the blacks in Vienna are the "Jews, socialists, former Austrian nationalists, monarchists, Czechs here and there and often Catholics as well." But there is one distinction between "the centuries-old traditions" of European culture and the rough-and-ready ways of "a tad recent and a tad noisy" America. "In America, it sometimes happens that a mob, crazed with racial pride, hangs a black youth from the nearest tree—because he was black." But "in Vienna they do not hang anyone from trees." Oh no:

> Today, in Vienna there are a good half-million blacks. No one has done them much harm for the moment. They were "only" forbidden to work. Doctors are not allowed to practice; lawyers are not allowed to do their job; nobody is allowed to listen to writers or musicians. Their property has also "only" been confiscated and they have been given to understand that they should leave—uselessly, because those who could, have left already. *Otherwise*, however, they may live. Bizarre, horrible, *legal* Judge Lynch!

"These events abroad," Milena continues, "have given some people among us a lot of self-confidence. Vigorous youthful calves in white knee-socks strut over the Prague cobblestones with unprecedented resolution. . . . The constant flurry of classification of people has reached us too. In Vinohrady, Smíchov, Karlín, Holešovice, Libeň and other suburban streets"—the streets where Reiner Stach saw only the blank slate of a Czech future devoid of a past—"a quiet breeze of mutual tension is blowing from person to person." In the pubs people worry what France will do, what England will do, what Hitler will do. She has a different concern: "above all we have to know . . . what we are going to do ourselves. Not in the big international arena but in just that private compass whose radius is three and a half streets, the journey home and the two-room flat with a kitchen." "The greatest illness of the European individual," she concludes, "is the easy willingness to retreat, not to put up a fight, to cave in and fall into line 'because, after all, you have to live!'"[132]

"Hundreds of Thousands Seeking No Man's Land" begins with a chance encounter "in the center of Prague, in the center of Europe, on a quiet, sunny afternoon in the year 1938," which Jesenská subtitles "Ahasuerus on Vinohrad-ská Street." Vinohradská is a long and unremarkable road that begins at the back of the National Museum and makes its way up through Vinohrady, past the Olšany cemeteries, out to the edge of the city. Milan Kundera turned its endlessly revolving names (Černokostelecká Road, Marshal Foch Street, Marshal Schwerin Street, Marshal Stalin Street, Vinohrady Street) into a meta-phor for the century's merry-go-round of political regimes in his novel *Kniha smíchu a zapomnění* (*The Book of Laughter and Forgetting*, 1979).[133] Milena's Wandering Jew "had knocked-out teeth and bloody gums, he had rags instead of clothes, he didn't have a cent and hadn't eaten in many hours. . . . He just walked and walked and walked," she writes, "from fear they would send him back." She quotes two Jews she has interviewed, who are "as different from one another as two worlds." One is "Hungarian, a writer, a cultivated man," who tells her he "would like to write the handbook: *How to Emigrate*," having al-ready done so five times. The other is "a peasant from Slovakia, a Bohunk from somewhere in Poland . . . a man employed on the land and focused on the soil," who asks: "What is a house to a Jew? He will flee sometime anyway." "*This* is what they all have in common," Milena goes on, "the awareness that someday they will flee." But while Jewish history is full of pogroms—including the "horrific, cruel, and bloody" events in Germany in 1933—in post-*Anschluss* Austria she detects the emergence of "something quite new. Something of a purely German character—which is unique in history in its crudity, its consis-tent inhumanity, and its legal nonsensicality: *a cold pogrom* . . . a program-matic, smooth imposition by the state of regulations that do not deprive the Jews of life but deprive them of any possibility of living."[134]

There is nothing on Vinohradská now to recall Milena's strange meeting, but if you step off the main drag into the New Jewish Cemetery on Israelská Street, you will find plaque after plaque on the boundary wall listing people who are not buried there. One of them reads: "In memoriam Zikmund Kohn, rabbi and teacher in Vlašim, Emilie Kohnová, née Rezková, wife, Marta Kohnová, daughter, Bedřich Kohn, son, Gertruda Kohnová, daughter, Elsa Kohnová, daughter, deported by the Germans to the concentration camps of Treblinka, Majdanek and Malý Trostinec, where they were gassed, honor their memory." Another remembers "my Mom Elly Schorngast and 27 members of our family who were killed in the concentration camps." Janka Hoffmannová, née Blumová, was born on 5 March 1896 in Mukačevo and perished in Bergen-Belsen on 5 May 1945—less than a week before the end of the war. She was "one in a million" (*jedna z milionu*).[135] Intentionally or otherwise, the grim double entendre captures the enormity of these deaths better than any pieties of the "thoughts and prayers" ilk could. Mukačevo is in Podkarpatská Rus (Sub-Carpathian Ruthenia), which began the war as part of Czechoslovakia and ended it as part of the Soviet Union. The town is now in Ukraine, though, like Kundera's Avenue of the Marshals, it hasn't moved an inch. Not only do people wander across borders; borders wander across people too.

On 20 August 1938 Adolf Eichmann, whom future protector of Bohemia and Moravia Reinhard Heydrich had sent from Berlin to organize the "forced emigration" of *all* Austrian Jews, systematized Milena's cold pogrom under a single Central Agency for Jewish Emigration in Vienna. "When everything was ready and the assembly line was doing its work smoothly and quickly," relates Hannah Arendt, "Eichmann 'invited' the Jewish functionaries from Berlin to inspect it":

> They were appalled: "This is like an automatic factory, like a flour mill connected with some bakery. At one end you put in a Jew who still has some property, a factory, or a shop, or a bank account, and he goes through the building from counter to counter, from office to office, and comes out at the other end without any money, without any rights, with only a passport on which it says: 'You must leave the country within a fortnight. Otherwise you will go to a concentration camp.'"[136]

Eichmann would subsequently set up a similar office in Prague, where he was posted in July 1939. He settled his family in a villa confiscated from Jews in Střešovice for the duration of the war, "providing his wife and sons with stability and pleasant company while he traveled frequently for work"—if that's the right word for it. When in Berlin, Eichmann stayed "in rented rooms, in his office's guest residence, or, as everyone knew, with various lady friends."[137] He remembered his year in Vienna as "the happiest and most successful period" of his life. "His success was spectacular," Arendt records; "in eight months, forty-five thousand Jews left Austria."[138] But even the hostile environment of the cold pogrom didn't do the job fast enough.[139] On 9–10 November *Kristallnacht* (the night of broken glass) "was particularly brutal in Vienna." Mobs burned down most of the city's synagogues and prayer houses and ransacked Jewish shops and businesses. Firefighters intervened only when adjacent buildings were at risk (which was what saved the city's largest synagogue, the Stadttempl). Twenty-seven Jews were killed and many more injured. More than six thousand Jews were arrested and deported to Dachau, leaving two thousand apartments suddenly vacant.[140]

Youthful Calves in White Kneesocks

"There Will Be No *Anschluss*!" Milena Jesenská defiantly titled a two-part article written during a visit to the Sudetenland for the local elections in May 1938.[141] Pulling no punches in describing the stark economic misery of the region, she pleaded with Czechs not to lump all Germans together but "to support those people in the German camp who resisted fascism."[142] But a Sudeten *Anschluss* there was. Konrad Henlein's Sudetendeutsche Partei (Sudeten German Party; SdP), which campaigned for unity with the Third Reich, won 90 percent of the Sudetenland vote, and Hitler made what he claimed was his last territorial demand in Europe. There was plenty of evidence that Czechs were willing to defend their borders; on 22 September a quarter million people massed outside the Rudolfinum, which served as the seat of the Czechoslovak parliament during the first republic. Klement Gottwald was among the speakers (this was before the Molotov-Ribbentrop pact brought Hitler's Germany and Stalin's Russia into a temporary détente). A week later British prime minister Neville Chamberlain and French prime minister Edouard Daladier sat down with Hitler and Benito Mussolini in Munich and signed the agreement that Chamberlain believed would secure "peace for our time." The Czechoslovak government took no part in the talks. Abandoned by his Western allies, Edvard Beneš acquiesced to the Munich diktat (as Czechs call it) on 30 September. German troops began to move into the Sudetenland the next day, creating tens of thousands of new refugees overnight.[143] More fled or were forcibly expelled in November in the wake of *Kristallnacht*, when synagogues were torched in Liberec, Most, Opava, Sokolov, Nový Jičín, Karlovy Vary, and other Sudetenland towns.[144]

Beneš resigned on 5 October and fled to England on 22 October. Before leaving he told his presidential staff: "Do try to keep the spirit here, which I used to uphold and defend. I am leaving with the awareness that I have tried, with all my strength, to fulfil a superhuman task ... and I am leaving with a clear and proud conscience. I believe that we shall succeed in preserving the foundations of our national revolution, so that on the basis of this heritage we can take on our next struggle."[145] What followed was not the most edifying

FIGURE 2.7. Sudeten German demonstration, 1938. Photographer unknown. © ČTK.

period in Czech history. The noncommunist political parties merged in November and December into two groups: the right-wing Strana národní jednoty (National Unity Party) and the (relatively) left-wing Národní strana práce (National Party of Labor). The government of the second republic, led by conservative lawyer and president Emil Hácha and (from 1 December) prime minister and former Agrarian Party leader Rudolf Beran, sought to appease not only Germany but also homegrown Czechoslovak fascists. Anti-Semites were encouraged to come out of the woodwork. Sokol expelled its Jewish members. The Czech Medical Chamber, along with professional associations representing lawyers, engineers, and notaries, began to purge Jews from their ranks. Jews were banned from working in the civil service in January 1939. Seventy-seven Jewish teachers were dismissed from the German University.[146] Max Brod "was suddenly not allowed to write on German theater, but only on Czech productions, even though [he] had been the *Prager Tagblatt* critic for Czech and German theater for a whole decade."[147] KSČ activities were suspended on 10 October. The party was dissolved on 27 December, leading Gottwald to flee to Moscow for a second time, along with his deputy, Rudolf Slánský. The Liberated Theater was closed on 10 November, and Jiří Voskovec, Jan Werich, and Jaroslav Ježek left for New York. Czech institutions were not the only ones unable to survive in the new climate of intolerance: the liberal German newspapers *Bohemia* and *Prager Presse* both ceased publication on 31 December 1938. *Bohemia* had been published continually for 111 years. "The flag that we must lay down with honor today will be taken up by others," a final editorial assured its readers, but it was a requiem for old German Prague.[148]

Milena ended 1938 with an article focusing on the plight of the thousands trapped between barbed wire fences dividing the territories occupied by Germany, Hungary, and Poland as a result of the Munich Agreement from the rump of what was now hyphenated as Czecho-Slovakia, which had closed its borders to additional refugees. She recalls a German film she saw many years ago in Prague, a beautiful film, she writes, in which four characters—an Englishman, a German, a black man, and a Russian Jew—"four human frightened animals from the most varied corners of the world, from different social layers, with different languages and fates," found themselves caught between the barbed wire fences separating the combatants' trenches during World War I. It was called *Niemandsland* (*No Man's Land*, 1931, directed by Victor Trivas). In the film the Russian Jew, played by "the most marvelous actor in Europe today," Vladimir Sokoloff, is mute. For Milena, his figure "will remain forever as if prophetic . . . a mute among speakers, marked out even among deportees with a smile and eyes that express the sorrow of hundreds of thousands who move from century to century. They have reason, heart, and soul, they do not have a land, they do not have a home, they do not have a language. They really are mute." She explains what she means by telling a story that brings us back to the *kafkárna* of languages and identities with which we began:

I have heard talk of a rabbi who today lives in Palestine and speaks only Hebrew; he does not allow anyone around him to speak another language, he instils in young people love for this mother tongue of the Jews, a little artificially. But sometimes at home, in the corner, when it is getting dark, he murmurs to himself—Russian songs. Palestine is his home and Hebrew is his mother tongue. But Russia—it is his native land, and Russian songs are songs of that native land, his mother sang them, women in the village, children in school, men in the fields. The native land with thousands of sounds, customs, colors, and forms shaped the soul of this man. The man is grateful to it, for he shapes his thoughts and his words with this native language. Then someone comes and says: you don't belong here, get out! The Jew wanders and wanders, wanders to his promised land, and thereafter speaks only Hebrew, toiling away with all his strength, with his proud humility, with all his will in a land that again does not belong to him. But in the evening, in the corner of a room when it is getting dark—he quietly sings Russian songs. This is the muteness of the Jew in No-Man's-Land.[149]

Once upon a time now long gone, Milena had cast herself as a creature of light. She wanted to illuminate the dark staircases of the old houses in the Lesser Town; strip apartments of their clutter and expose their bare, smooth, light, simple walls to the sun; raise a new generation of carefree children in spacious halls full of light. She loved the simple, clean functionality of modern architecture for the same reasons she loved the sea, sun, snow, swimming, skiing, tennis, and camping and tramping in the open air. One of her favorite adjectives was *sportovní*. She believed in a healthy mind in a healthy body, and she believed that human relationships should be open and honest too. She thought youth was on the side of modernity and modernity was on the side of youth. But whether it was because her own body undid her, leaving her "old and lame" before her time,[150] or because one after another her relationships broke down, or—more likely—because her hopes and dreams kept foundering on gulags and concentration camps and eternally wandering Jews, by the late 1930s this bundle of associations was coming apart.

A white darkness was falling. The image of those youthful calves in white kneesocks tramples its vigorous way through these articles of 1938–1939, giving more sinister connotations to sporting, healthy, young white bodies celebrating festivals of joy in the open air. The first of Jesenská's "There Will Be No Anschluss" articles on the Sudetenland is titled "The Castles of the SdP." The castles in question are the "large brick buildings, which tower up in solitude in the blooming countryside near every city, near every small town, near every village"—*die deutsche Turnhalle*, the German gymnasium or sports hall. The *Turnhalle*, Milena says, is "a form of building entirely unknown to us," with high windows and broad interior spaces. This was not quite true: the Czech Sokol movement, in which her father had enrolled Milena in her youth, had long possessed its custom-built gymnasiums that were separate from schools, and it was no less nationalist than its Sudeten German counterpart. But the Sokols were not Nazis. The out-of-town locations of the *Turnhallen* meant that "German children march from schools to the gymnasium in serried ranks, singing German—which is to say, Nazi—songs. . . . You see columns of girls and boys striding along the road, singing and raising their arms in the German—which is to say, the Nazi—salute. And this march, these songs, this military step and the gatherings in gymnasiums and the spirit in which they educate the youth: all this is powerful support for the Henlein movement." Konrad Henlein was himself a gym instructor who became leader of the German Gymnastics Movement (Deutsche Turnbewegung) in Czechoslovakia in 1931.

Henlein established the Sudetendeutsche Heimatfront (Sudeten German Homeland Front) after the government banned the Czechoslovak branch of the Nazi Party in 1933. On 19 April 1935 the Heimatfront was renamed the Sudeten German Party. In the parliamentary election of May 1935 the SdP received 15.2 percent of the total votes cast—the highest for any single party in interwar Czechoslovak elections after 1920—and won 67.4 percent of the ethnic German vote. The ban on the Nazi Party, Milena points out, "did not forbid the Germans from training their youth. And in the gymnasiums the Germans trained young people to raise their right arms, to hate Germans who were not Nazis, to hate all Czechs wholesale, and to despise the Jews." Boys and girls came out to play, acting as the eyes and ears of the SdP. Come 1 May, when the German Social Democrats and the SdP organized their rival processions, an important role was played by "these cadres [*důvěrníci*]—most of them youths and children, twelve- to eighteen-year-old boys, the spitting image of those who on 13 March 'took over' the Vienna enterprises, editorial offices, stations. Boys from the German *Turnhalle*, boys in white kneesocks, boys making the Nazi salute. These lads—in twos and threes—led grown men from the factories—their fathers, uncles, brothers, neighbors, friends—to the [SdP] parade. These children noted down on a 'blacklist' the names of everyone who took part in the democratic procession." Milena watched the same "fourteen-year-old nasty pieces of work" in their white kneesocks stand guard outside Jewish shops and "note down or photograph everyone who enters."[151]

Unlike Kafka, Milena allowed herself an occasional respite from this world "full of invisible demons, tearing apart and destroying defenseless humans."[152] According to Jana Černá, "the tenser the world situation became and the more hazardous and precarious her own existence, the more jealously and frantically did Milena guard these brief escapes from the reality around her." She may have been less inclined than she once was to take refuge in a lie, blindness, enthusiasm, optimism, conviction, pessimism, the fallacies of reason, or the fantasies of the unconscious, but she did have three great escapist passions. All were of their time, which is to say, quintessentially modern. The first was German detective novels, of which Milena devoured "an incredible quantity." The second was the radio. Milena "felt hemmed in and longed to travel," but her health and finances made foreign trips impossible. So she "roamed the world in her imagination," switching the dial "from station to station until the early hours, and it mattered little whether it was speech or music . . . even when the speaker was emitting a stream of words in a language which she did not understand." The third was "the cinema . . . she did not miss a single film in those days. . . . She was quite capable of sitting through four films in one afternoon." Czechoslovakia had a thriving film industry centered on Barrandov Studios in the south of the city, and downtown Prague was well equipped with cinemas that screened foreign as well as domestic films.[153]

Milena must have seen the Czech director Gustav Machatý's scandalous *Extase* (*Ecstasy*, 1932), which starred eighteen-year-old Hedy Lamarr in what is often claimed to be the first nude scene in commercial cinema. It premièred in Prague in January 1933—by chance, the same month Hitler was sworn in as German chancellor. *Ecstasy* received a standing ovation at the Venice Film Festival and lavish praise from critics, but it was condemned by the Vatican and banned in Germany (and the United States). Too close to the bone. More shocking than Hedy's nudity was her frank portrayal of female orgasm, which likely *was* a first outside of pornography—although Ita Rina's marginally less explicit performance in Machatý's earlier silent film *Erotikon* (1929), based on a screenplay by Vítězslav Nezval, might challenge for that title:

Here, we follow the story of Andrea (Ita Rina) who lives in a small house with her father. When a handsome stranger named George Sydney turns up late at night, she is quickly seduced—and the day after he arrives, he gains entry into her bedroom. There follows what could be argued to be the first *Female Point of View* sex shot, with the camera pointing straight up towards George, who lurches unromantically above her for a few seconds, before the camera swings into a wide and dizzying circle and ends up pointing down at Andrea. The camera performs even more nauseating tilts and turns while she lies on her back in rapture. Continuing around the room the camera pauses to focus on a hooded virgin Mary in a frame on her wall, a golden gramophone—at once phallic and gaping—, and finally, once again, Andrea's head tilting back in uncontrolled pleasure. The wide loops are reminiscent of a merry-go-round; the slightly menacing music sounds like something you'd hear in a fun house.[154]

The scene culminates with the camera cutting away to two raindrops sliding down the windowpane before they finally merge into one.

Jana recalls that when "we went on an outing to the pictures in wintertime, the streets would already be dark when we came out of the cinema at six o'clock. The streetlamps and neon signs would be alight and the sign on the Melantrich publishing house would be writing the title of the evening edition of *České slovo* [The Czech word, organ of the National Socialist Party] over and over in a line of light. Milena never rushed me home. She knew how much I loved the night-time streets, and anyway it was an attraction she shared." As mother and daughter trailed through Wenceslas Square "from one chestnut seller to the next, warming our hands on the hot chestnuts . . . Milena patiently answered every possible and impossible question I might ask":

> After the Soviet film *Journey into Life*, for instance, I wanted to know what deprived children were and how they came to be deprived. After the American film *I Was Lynched*, I wanted to know what a mob was and what was so terrible and dangerous about it. How was it possible that people in a mob could be so different from when they were on their own? After *La grande illusion* I had to know what war was, what honor was, what human decency was and why it was all just an illusion.

These may seem like precocious questions for a ten- or eleven-year-old to ask, but Honza's mother was taking her to some pretty grown-up films. Milena did not always have the answers the girl sought. She could not explain, for instance, "how a normal man could become a murderer in the name of obedience."[155]

"Sometimes when I look at Honza I'm desperate," Milena wrote to Willi Schlamm in August 1938. "When I look at other children, I have sometimes

FIGURE 2.8. Willi Weigelt's film poster for Gustav Machatý's *Erotikon*, 1929.
From Marta Sylvestrová, ed., *Český filmový plakát 20. století*, Prague, 2004.

had enough of life. Right now in the cinema you can see an advert for gas masks for children—I cannot tell you just how terrifying the bad taste of this advert is. We are all going to die without knowing why."[156] In an eerie reprise of her correspondence with Franz Kafka, Milena wrote to Willi almost every other day. This letter was in German, although she often wrote to him in Czech. A former communist Jewish journalist from Vienna, Schlamm had arrived in Prague as a refugee with his wife Steffi in the mid-1930s. He met Milena in March 1937. She introduced him to *Přítomnost*, for which he wrote articles and she translated them. They grew close. "I love you very much, I don't know exactly *how* I love you, I only know that I love you very much," she once told him,[157] even though, as with Kafka, it is doubtful their relationship was ever physically consummated. As if it mattered, anyway. The times put things in perspective. Young as she was, Jana Černá is probably not exaggerating when she remembers her last prewar summer camp in Medlov in western Moravia in 1939, where she shared a hut with Milena, Jaromír, and Riva, as a place full of "actors, musicians, photographers, journalists, poets, students, musicians and goodness knows who else," where "friendships were made at incredible speed. . . . Couples would make love in the noonday sun in forest glades, returning to camp at twilight still in each other's embrace. Everyone knew about everyone else's intimacies. There was no keeping anything secret: not that anyone tried." After all, "we weren't holiday-makers, we were just terrified individuals uncertain whether the morrow would bring a new dawn or the end of the world."[158]

With Milena's help, the Schlamms had wandered off again, senselessly being drawn along, senselessly wandering through a senselessly obscene world. Willi was now in Brussels, another temporary refuge. They eventually washed up in New York on 16 November 1938, so much flotsam on the tide of history.

3

Love and Theft

Under the cap of the bell of night
O tomorrow full of despair
It is winter
And it falls to no one to give us comfort

—VÍTĚZSLAV NEZVAL, "TROJA BRIDGE
(IN MEMORY OF BEDŘICH FEUERSTEIN)"[1]

Poldi Kladno

In the afterword to Jaroslav Seifert's poetry collection *Samá láska* (*Sheer Love*) in 1923, Karel Teige claimed that the bard of Žižkov "has the romanticism of this great century in his poetry. In his poems lives Kladno, lives New York—lives Paris, lives Jičín, Prague, the whole world."[2] Jičín, the setting of Seifert's ballad "Verses about Love, Murder, and the Gallows," is a pretty little town in the scenic Český ráj (Bohemian paradise) in northern Bohemia. It was the hometown of the poet's girlfriend Marie Ulrychová, whom Jaroslav went on to marry in 1928. Kladno is an altogether grittier coal-mining and iron and steel town sixteen miles northwest of Prague. At the time Seifert was writing, it was a stronghold of the KSČ. One of the "Kladno personalities" highlighted on the town's website is Anton Cermak,[3] who served as mayor of Chicago from 1931 until he was shot dead during a failed assassination attempt on Franklin D. Roosevelt in 1933. Born Antonín Čermák in Kladno in 1873, he established the Democratic dynasty that has held Chicago City Hall ever since. The poet, dissident, and collagist Jiří Kolář, who was born in Protivín in southern Bohemia but raised in Kladno, also makes the list. Curiously, Marie Majerová, Jiří

Dienstbier, and Petr Pithart do not, even though they were all born or raised in Kladno. One of the seven writers expelled from the KSČ in 1929, Majerová rejoined the party after World War II and received many honors, including the title of National Artist in 1947. Dienstbier and Pithart were both signatories of the 1977 dissident manifesto Charter 77, which challenged the Czechoslovak government to live up to its human rights obligations under the Helsinki Accords. They subsequently became leading figures in the Velvet Revolution of 1989. Pithart served as prime minister and Dienstbier as foreign minister in the first postcommunist Czechoslovak government in 1990–1992. Dienstbier was elected senator for the Kladno region in 2008. Another puzzling absentee is the legendary theater director, scenographer, playwright, poet, composer, musician, and actor E. F. (Emil František) Burian, who was a major figure in the interwar avant-garde cultural landscape. A KSČ member since 1923 but no yes-man, Burian served as Kladno's representative in the national assembly from 1948 to 1954. The quiet forgetting of Czechoslovakia's second communist president Antonín Zápotocký, who was born in the nearby village of Záko-lany in 1884 and whose exploits as a labor organizer in Kladno in 1918–1920 were celebrated in classic socialist-realist fashion in Vladimír Vlček's 1955 film *Rudá záře nad Kladnem* (Red blaze over Kladno), may perhaps be more comprehensible.

The onetime Pittsburgh Penguins captain Jaromír Jágr also hails from Kladno, as do a raft of other National Hockey League players. In 1990 Jágr became the first Czechoslovak player to be drafted without having to defect. He went on to have a twenty-four-season NHL career in which his team won two Stanley Cups and he picked up five Art Ross trophies for top scorer. He remains the league's second all-time points scorer behind Wayne Gretzky. In 2018, at age forty-six, Jágr returned home to play for the Rytíři Kladno (Kladno Knights), the team with which he began his career. Back then the club was called Poldi Kladno, after its principal sponsor the Poldi iron and steel works. Poldi was founded in 1889 by Karl Wittgenstein, father of the philosopher Ludwig Wittgenstein. Karl named the firm for his wife Leopoldine, "the Jewish girl"who, writes Bohumil Hrabal, he "loved so strongly he had the image of her little head stamped into the steel, and still today that beloved face goes out into the world aboard every beam."[4] In unconscious anticipation of the communist future, Poldi's head was surmounted by a five-pointed star, which was intended to symbolize the five continents on which the company plied its wares. In 1946 the plant was nationalized and merged with Vojtěšská Iron Works, once the biggest iron ore smelting plant in the Austrian Empire. The

ČESKÝ FILM
PODLE STEJNOJMENNÉHO ROMÁNU
ANTONÍNA ZÁPOTOCKÉHO

RUDÁ ZÁŘE
NAD KLADNEM

SCÉNÁŘ A REŽIE: VLADIMÍR VLČEK, LAUREÁT
STALINOVY A ČS. STÁTNÍ CENY. KAMERA:
ZASLOUŽILÝ UMĚLEC JAN STALLICH. HUDBA:
LUDVÍK PODÉŠŤ. HRAJÍ: JOSEF BEK, VLASTA
CHRAMOSTOVÁ, NÁRODNÍ UMĚLEC JAROSLAV
PRŮCHA, LAUREÁT STÁTNÍ CENY, MARIE
JEŽKOVÁ, VLASTA FABIÁNOVÁ, ZASLOUŽILÝ
UMĚLEC JAROSLAV VOJTA, MÍLA BESSER,
EVA JIROUŠKOVÁ A JINÍ.

F-024526 GT 03

FIGURE 3.1. Film poster for Vladimír Vlček's *Red Blaze over Kladno*, 1955. Artist unknown. From Marta Sylvestrová, ed., *Český filmový plakát 20. století*, Prague, 2004.

conglomerate was broken up and privatized after 1989. Jágr's father acquired the Poldi Kladno hockey club (which his son now owns) in 1995. "We had a huge steel company—almost everybody was working for that company," explained Jaromír in a 2018 interview. "After the [1989] revolution, that company went bankrupt, so there was a lot of people moving out of the city. This is the only kind of sport in our city. A lot of families are involved with the hockey, and there's a lot of kids involved with the hockey. So it's our responsibility to keep going."[5] Whatever team he played for, Jágr always wore the number 68. It honors the Prague Spring.[6]

We should not be too surprised to find Bohumil Hrabal on the Kladno website, even if he was born in Brno, raised in Nymburk, and spent most of his adult life in Prague. One of the army of lawyers, military officers, small businessmen, academics, and other class enemies drafted into industry in the *77.000 do výroby!* (77,000 into production!) campaign launched in 1948, Hrabal worked as a manual laborer in the Poldi steel mill from 1949 to 1954. The speed of industrialization under the First Five-Year Plan had created serious labor shortages, but—as at Belomorkanal—the aim of the campaign was not only to boost the national economy but also "to form a completely different, new person."[7] In Hrabal's case the reforging worked, though perhaps not in the way the communists intended. "A crane fell on top of me in Kladno in 1952, after which my writing got better," he recalled.[8]

> I had borrowed a little from Rimbaud, a little from Baudelaire, a little from Éluard, and again from Céline. I used artificial clusters of words as though they were natural linguistic signs, and so I invented more and more impossible metaphors—until Kladno, in the steelworks, where my whole, pseudo-artistic, second-hand world collapsed, and for an entire year I merely looked around me and saw and heard fundamental things and fundamental words. It was some time before I realized that I had to start again from the ground up, give up trying to escape and begin to write as if I were writing for the newspapers, reporting on people and their conversations, their work, and in general, their lives.[9]

If anything, Hrabal's newfound "total realism," a concept he took from his young friend the poet Egon Bondy, made his work more surrealist—or, at any rate, more surreal—*because* of its firm roots in the communist everyday. One of the first fruits of Hrabal's new approach was the collection *Inzerát na dům, ve kterém už nechci bydlet* (An advertisement for a house I don't want to live in anymore, translated into English as *Mr. Kafka and Other Tales from the Time of the Cult*),[10] which was written mostly in the early 1950s but not published until 1965. Several of the stories are set in the Poldi works. The cast of characters negotiating the runaway cranes, bubbling vats of acid, and poisonous vapors in "Strange People" could have walked straight out of Bob Dylan's *Highway 61 Revisited*, which was released in August of the same year: the Dairyman, the Frenchman (who "had to leave home because I got mixed up in antigovernment politics"), the State Prosecutor, the Sergeant Major, the Priest, the curly-haired Cop, the Judge (whom everyone still calls "Your Honor"), and his daughter (whom everyone thought was "one of them defectors"). "The whole damn factory—all of Poldi Kladno—was full of people from professions and jobs and trades of all kinds, and the whole working-class character of the steelworks had gone down the drain," complains one old-time worker.[11] People discuss the poetry of Jaroslav Vrchlický and Vítězslav Nezval during their lunch breaks for Christ's sake. The story is a jewel of black comedy. But "anyone seeking to find in this book mere condemnation ... would be mistaken," Hrabal warns readers in his preface. On the contrary, he says, the people he lived with in Kladno during "the period referred to as 'the time of the cult of personality'" were "heroes if only because they had not succumbed to semantic confusion, but were able to call things and events by their real names and recognize them for what they were."[12]

From Taliesin to Tokyo

Jaromír Jágr played for the New York Rangers from 2004 to 2008, and Jiří Kolář lived in exile in Paris from 1980 to 1989, but if anybody connects Kladno to the whole world it has to be Antonín Raymond, who remains relatively little known in the land of his birth but is widely recognized as a key figure in the development of Japanese modern architecture before and after World War II.[13] Raymond is also responsible for two other unlikely Czech distinctions to set beside the first female orgasm on the silver screen: his Golconde dormitory for the Sri Aurobindo ashram in Pondicherry (1937–1945) was "the first concrete and modernist building in India, prefiguring Le Corbusier's later postwar work in Chandigarh and Ahmedabad,"[14] and his Church of the Angry Christ, aka Saint Joseph the Worker Church in Victorias City, Negros Occidental (1948–1950), was "the first ever sample of modern sacral architecture in the Philippines."[15] Antonín Reimann (as his school spelled his surname) or Rajman (as he spells it in his autobiography) was born in Kladno in 1888. His parents Alois Reimann and Růžena Taussigová, who owned a textile shop on

the town's main square, "belonged among people of the new, modern persua-
sion, who counted themselves as Czechs of the Jewish faith."[16] Antonín later
converted to Protestantism, likely at the urging of his wife. Though Alois Reimann was of German Jewish origin, Antonín was raised to think of himself as
Czech. He entered the Kladno *realné gymnasium* in 1900. After his mother's
death the family moved to Prague in 1905, where Antonín finished high school.
He enrolled in 1906 in the Czech Polytechnic (since 1920 the Czech Institute
of Technology, or ČVUT).[17] In the manner of the time, he got into fistfights
with students at the school's German counterpart.[18]

The simple buildings on his maternal grandparents' farm at Řenčov (now
Řevničov) in central Bohemia left a lasting impression.[19] He had little time for
the historicist architecture that was then the dominant idiom in the capital.
"My generation was brought up in the most appalling setting the world had
ever known," he relates, "the world of imitation marble, of three-tiered fringed
curtains, of respectable drabness and false luxury resulting from the discoveries of industry and the machine. Yet just outside our door stood the wonders
of the Romanesque, Gothic, Renaissance, baroque and other architectures."
On his way to school Antonín "passed a small plaza [Malé náměstí, the Small
Square] where there was a very beautiful fourteenth-century stone well with
a wrought-iron grille, and then the famous clock on the City Hall and the twin
towers of the Týn Cathedral with its ancient side entrance of half-decayed
sandstone sculpture on a narrow street. This daily walk past those wonders
and past the Gothic, Renaissance and Baroque houses and their covered sidewalks exerted a powerful influence over me for the rest of my life." He also
recalled the apartment the family rented in Josefov in "a very ancient building,
with a small open courtyard overhung with balconies featuring plain iron railings, and toilets, each serving more than one apartment. It was very romantic
and also very smelly. Six children and their father were cramped into three
rooms, uncomfortably hot and cold according to the season."[20]

Antonín's teachers at the polytechnic included Josef Schulz and Jan Koula,
architects of the National Museum (1890) and the art nouveau Svatopluk Čech
Bridge (1906–1908), respectively. But encountering the work of Frank Lloyd
Wright, in the shape of the portfolio published by Ernst Wasmuth in Berlin in
1910,[21] changed the course of his life. "Wright had restated the principles of
building," he wrote; "he had overcome the cell, liberated the plan, made space
flow, given buildings a human scale and blended them with nature, all in a
romantic, sensual and original way which left us breathless. He was what we
had been longing for, a real revolutionary."[22] The discovery led Antonín to the

United States. He never graduated from Prague Polytechnic. Bored, impatient, and in search of more than his homeland could offer, he absconded with the funds of the Czech Architectural Students' Club and sailed from Trieste on 10 July 1910 on the SS *Atlanta* bound for New York, leaving behind a warrant for his arrest. The sum involved was considerable—equivalent to around US$1,000, which today would have the purchasing power of more than $26,000.[23] The theft severely damaged the club, which had to discontinue funding scholarships for poor students. Though Antonín paid back much more than he had "borrowed" many years later, the episode left an enduring sour taste among his contemporaries.[24] No matter. Antonín Reimann had made it to the New World, where he morphed into Antonín (or, as his American friends called him, Tony) Raymond.[25]

Through contacts in the local Czech community Raymond got a job as a draftsman in the architectural practice of Cass Gilbert. He remained with the firm for three years. He provided the drawings for the bas-reliefs for the Woolworth Building—which, on its completion in 1912, became the tallest building in the world at 792 feet, a title it retained until 1930. Perhaps more important for his subsequent development was the experience of building with reinforced concrete, a skill he acquired when working on the Austin Nichols and Company warehouse in Brooklyn in 1913. Raymond considered abandoning architecture for painting, and after leaving Cass Gilbert he spent some time at an artists' community in a hill town outside Rome in the summer of 1914. The reverie was interrupted by the imminent outbreak of World War I, and he hastily booked passage on the last passenger ship bound for the United States. On board he met and fell in love with the French American graphic artist and designer Noémi Pernessin. Originally from Cannes, she moved to New York when she was twelve, attended the exclusive Horace Mann School in Morningside Heights, and studied under John Dewey at Columbia University. Antonín and Noémi married in New York on 15 December 1915.

Working in a variety of media, including iron, glass, wood, ceramics, and textiles, Noémi would become Antonín's design collaborator as well as his domestic partner for the next six decades. It was through her connections that Antonín finally got to meet Frank Lloyd Wright, who invited the Raymonds to work at Taliesin, his estate in Spring Green, Wisconsin. They arrived in May 1916. Frank was not the easiest person to live with (as Antonín delicately put it, "his nervous energy did not allow things to flow smoothly"),[26] and the couple returned to New York that December. Antonín enlisted in the American Expeditionary Force the following year and was posted to Europe, where he

served as a military intelligence officer. After he returned to the States, Wright
invited him to work as his chief assistant on the Hotel Imperial, which he was
building in Tokyo. When Raymond met with Wright in Chicago to finalize
arrangements in November 1919, he recognized "that feverish hammersledge
[*sic*] activity" the moment Frank stepped off the train. But he was also powerfully reminded of what had drawn him to the American architect in the first
place. Frank showed him some of his buildings in Oak Park. Antonín was blown
away. "The Unity church—Coonley house and all the houses—but especially
the monolithic concrete church," he wrote to Noémi, "made a deep impression
on me and you must see them. They are more beautiful than I thought. The
church certainly is the finest piece of modern architecture existing."[27]

The Raymonds and Wright arrived in Japan on 31 December 1919. Work
progressed slowly on the Hotel Imperial. Noémi contributed interior designs,
including for the mural in the celebrated Peacock Room. A year later Antonín
expressed a desire to open his own Tokyo practice while continuing to collaborate with Wright. In response, Frank fired him. "You have deserted your
post under circumstances particularly treacherous and for which under military rules a man would be stood up against a wall and shot," Frank wrote. He
warned Raymond that he took strong exception to "having anything resembling my own individual work planted ad nauseam, ad libitum in Japan at this
time by you or anybody else . . . the matter will not rest there, I assure you, if
you violate my confidence by taking a deliberately mean and dishonest advantage of your association with my work by selling what you can of it for what
you can get for it in Tokyo."[28] Raymond established the American Architectural Engineering Company with Leon Whittaker Slack in February 1921 in
Tokyo's Marunouchi business district. The Hotel Imperial withstood the city's
worst earthquake in fifty-two years on 26 April 1922. Wright, who was staying
in the hotel at the time, left Japan shortly afterward. On the day the Imperial
was due to officially open, another earthquake struck. The great Kantō earthquake of 1 September 1923 turned out to be Japan's worst natural disaster of the
twentieth century, killing 140,000 people and leaving much of Tokyo and Yokohama a smoldering ruin. Once again, the Hotel Imperial stood intact—
though it was more severely damaged than Wright later claimed. It served as
a refugee center that fed thousands and became the temporary home of the
US embassy. "What a glory it is to see the Imperial standing amidst the ashes
of the whole city . . . she stands like the sun, glory to you lieber-meister," wrote
Wright's assistant Arata Endo.[29] The building's survival was a triumph for
Wright. It did no harm to Raymond's reputation either.

After Wright left Japan the Raymonds remained in Tokyo. Antonín's practice became an incubator for a generation of modern Japanese architects, among them Kunio Maekawa and Junzō Yoshimura. By 1935 Raymond's team of more than twenty was almost entirely Japanese, even if the lingua franca of the office remained English.[30] Though Antonín had been an American citizen since 1916, the Czechoslovak government (having resolved the little difficulty of the "borrowed" architectural club funds) named him honorary consul in 1925. Edvard Beneš awarded Raymond the Order of the White Lion for his services in 1928. This appointment gave him an entrée into diplomatic circles that was not at all bad for business: from 1928 to 1930 he worked on the American, French, and Soviet embassies as well as the Canadian legation and the Italian embassy's summer villa in Nikkō. Other commissions included the Tokyo Woman's Christian College (1921–1937), housing for Standard Oil (1927–1928) and Rising Sun Petroleum Company (1929), gas stations for Shell Oil (1930), and the clubhouse for the Tokyo Golf Club (1933). Much of the firm's work involved private residences for Japanese and expatriate clients. Between 1921 and 1938 Raymond designed sixty-six such houses, many of which needed to meet the spatial challenges of accommodating both Western and Japanese lifestyles. The interior details of the Goto house, built for the mayor of Tokyo in 1924, suggest a lingering influence of Czech cubism.

Antonín employed what became his trademark reinforced concrete not only for its earthquake-resistant properties but also for its aesthetic qualities. The Raymonds' own Reinanzaka house in Tokyo (built in 1926) was "the first raw concrete finish house designed by Antonín Raymond and one of the first of its kind in the world."[31] Here, anticipating the brutalism that swept the world after World War II,[32] Antonín had his builders impress the grain of the Japanese cedar shuttering onto the surface of the concrete exterior. In his and Noémi's summer house in the mountains at Karuizawa (built in 1933), Raymond's craftsmen polished the exposed concrete foundation with sand and straw to reveal the texture of the local lava stone used as an aggregate. As was traditional in Japanese building, Antonín made extensive use of wood, preferably left in its natural state. He summarized his "lasting values in design" as honesty, simplicity, economy, and directness.[33] Echoes of Milena Jesenská are no doubt coincidental. Antonín was none too fussy about provenance. "Should we be too afraid of precedent or influence," he wrote in a letter to *Architectural Forum*, "we could do nothing at all. It does not matter from where we take anything but what we do with it."[34] The context for this statement was a review of his first book *Antonín Raymond: His Work in Japan, 1920–1935*, which criticized

FIGURE 3.2. Antonín Raymond's Reinanzaka House, Tokyo, 1923–1926.
Photographer unknown. From Helena Čapková and Kóiči Kitazawa, eds.,
Antonín Raymond v Japonsku, Prague, 2019.

his Karuizawa house for plagiarizing Le Corbusier's unrealized 1920 design for
the Errázuriz house at Zapallar in Chile. The Errázuriz house is most famous
for its anticipation of the butterfly roof introduced to America in 1945 by Marcel
Breuer in his Geller house in Lawrence, Long Island, and popularized by
William Krissel's houses for the Alexander Construction Company in Palm
Springs, California, in 1957.[35] This gives Raymond another unexpected first.
Since the Errázuriz house was never built, the expatriate Czech was the first
modern architect to employ a wildly popular roof genre that has since become
emblematic of neither Chile nor Japan but of Southern California.

Though the line between love and theft may sometimes be difficult to draw,
there is a world of difference between a copy and an interpretation. Yola Gloaguen's comparison of the Errázuriz and Karuizawa houses demonstrates that
Raymond's creation was very far from the simple rip-off some have suggested.

Among other things, Raymond adapted Le Corbusier's original plan to a Japanese proportion system based on tatami mats, replaced Le Corbusier's load-bearing masonry walls with wooden posts and beams, included multiple references to traditional Japanese architecture in details such as windowsills and removable doors and windows, and made extensive use of local timbers and other materials.[36] There is more of interest in this saga than just who took what from whom—and it bears upon more than just the history of architecture (and the national or stylistic frameworks within which we usually write about it, where someone like Antonín Raymond falls between all possible cracks). Karel Teige's *Moderní architektura v Československu* (*Modern Architecture in Czechoslovakia*, 1930) devotes just one line to Raymond ("a Czech architect naturalized in Japan and a one-time pupil of F. L. Wright"), which is not unreasonable, given the book's title.[37] But there's the rub. The boy from Kladno found his very personal identity, architectural and otherwise, not in Czechoslovakia but over the hills and far away, somewhere between Taliesin and Tokyo. What could better illustrate the "romanticism of this great century"?

The Sorrows of Poor Fricek

Japan was an object of considerable interest in Prague's interwar avant-garde circles. In June 1927 *Pestrý týden* (which was still at that time being edited by Milena Jesenská and friends) carried a piece on Japanese theater by the choreographer and dancer Milča Mayerová.[38] Trained under Rudolf Laban in Hamburg, Mayerová was a well-known performer at the Divadlo Dada (Dada Theater) and the Liberated Theater. She was featured on an early cover of *Pestrý týden* looking lithe and sprightly.[39] She is best remembered today for her role in *Abeceda* (*Alphabet*, 1926), which has been widely exhibited abroad in recent years and has been hailed as "a consummate Czech contribution to European modernism" and "a unique distillation of the spirit of the 1920s."[40] *Alphabet* began as a series of poems by Vítězslav Nezval inspired by the letters of the alphabet; it was published in Devětsil's magazine *Disk* in 1923 and later included in Nezval's collection *Pantomima* (Pantomime, 1924). Milča choreographed and danced to Nezval's verses at the Liberated Theater in 1926. The production proved so popular that *Alphabet* was republished as a book in which each stanza was paired with a "typo-photomontage" by Karel Teige in which "the elastic body of the dancer," photographed in a suitably athletic pose by Karel Paspa, was framed by an abstract rendition of the relevant letter of the alphabet.[41] It is not gratuitous, in the present context, to record that

Mayerová was married to the architect Jaroslav Fragner, one of the self-styled Purist Four (the others were Karel Honzík, Vít Obrtel, and Evžen Linhart) who, with Jaromír Krejcar, Josef Chochol, and Bedřich Feuerstein, founded Devětsil's architectural section ARDEV in 1923.

Pestrý týden ran an illustrated feature on Raymond's Reinanzaka house in May 1927. "Raymond," Jaromír Krejcar wrote, "is one of those few people who possess the courage for success. It isn't simple. Fifteen years ago he left for America, without having any idea what comes next." Raymond's latest works, Jaromír contended, "have a purity of architectonic form that ranks them among the best contemporary architecture in the world. This perfection of architectonic form, coupled with the absolute perfection of American industry, lends his oeuvre a magic ... that only work of the ultimate refinement of conception and execution can boast. The magic of simplicity. It isn't simple."[42] A month later the magazine featured the Japanese calligrapher Matsuko Katō. One photograph shows Katō poring over the latest issue with several female friends, with the caption: "*Pestrý týden* is read throughout the whole world; even people who don't understand the text are enthused by the beautiful illustrations of faraway countries." In another photo she is attending a dinner in Tokyo organized by the Czechoslovak ambassador. Sitting beside her is "the architect F[ricek] Feuerstein, a contributor to our paper," who was then a member of Raymond's team.[43] Helena Čapková has convincingly argued that Feuerstein, more than anyone else, nudged Raymond toward that magic of simplicity. But it wasn't simple. It seldom is.

Born in 1892 (and thus a few years older than most Devětsil members), Bedřich "Fricek" Feuerstein attended Prague Polytechnic from 1910 to 1917, after which he entered the Austrian army, serving as an engineer and later as an inspector of military graves. He also studied privately for a year with the Slovenian architect Jože Plečnik at Prague's Academy of Arts, Architecture, and Design, popularly known as UMPRUM.[44] In 1920 he won a stipend from the French government to study in Paris. He arrived in the City of Light the following year with his close friend Josef Šíma—the "simple and noble" acrobatic winger on Karel Konrád's second Devětsil soccer team—who stayed in France, married a French girl, and became a French citizen in 1926. For the next few years Fricek divided his time between Paris and Prague. Besides taking courses in architecture at L'École du Louvre and the Trocadéro he interned at the Théâtre des Champs-Élysées and the Comédie Montaigne. The former was the scene of the riotous première of Stravinsky's *Rite of Spring*, danced by Vaslav Nijinsky and Serge Diaghilev's Ballets Russes, on 29 May 1913. A landmark building whose ultimate creator is disputed, the theater was built by Auguste and Gustave Perret. It is notable not only for being the first art deco building in Paris but also for its reinforced concrete construction. Fricek began to publish in Czech journals—in a 1921 article in *Musaion* he noted the Japanese influence on Frank Lloyd Wright. With Teige, Krejcar, and Šíma, Feuerstein was one of the "Group of Four" that formed "a kind of embryonic nucleus of Devětsil's new artistic formation" in 1922–1923.[45] Their embrace of "the folklore of big-city streets" was spectacularly manifested in *Život II*.[46] This modernist departure from Devětsil's original program of primitivism, magic realism, and "proletarian art" led several early members of the group, including Adolf Hoffmeister, Alois Wachsmann, and the poet Jiří Wolker, to leave. Though Feuerstein completed only two architectural projects during this period, the crematorium in Nymburk (1924) is counted as one of the earliest purist buildings in Czechoslovakia.[47]

Fricek had greater initial success as a stage designer. He made his debut creating the sets for Karel Čapek's *R.U.R.* (*Rossum's Universal Robots*) at the National Theater on 25 January 1921. One of the best-known and most widely translated works of modern Czech literature, this play introduced the word *robot* to the world. It derives from the Czech *robota*, the term for the labor services Bohemian peasants once owed their lords. Karel's brother Josef was the first to give a name to this deeply unsettling phantasm, which has since come to symbolize all the promises and fears of modernity. Robots, one of Čapek's characters explains, "are mechanically more perfect than we are, they have an astounding intellectual capacity, but they have no soul. . . . They learn to speak, write, and do arithmetic. They have a phenomenal memory . . . but they never think up anything original. They'd make fine university professors."[48] *R.U.R.* was staged at the Tsukiji Shogekijo theater in Tokyo—Japan's first modern theater—in December 1924, but as Feuerstein later noted, "the bourgeoisie remained faithful to Kabuki," and the theater soon closed.[49] A Japanese edition of Čapek's text (translated from the English) was published the same year.[50] Fricek also designed the sets for the 1924 National Theater première of Bohuslav Martinů's ballet *Istar*, whose "perfection of color and form" drew on "elements of purist architecture."[51] His "scenographic architecture" was a refreshing change in an era when (as Jiří Voskovec complained) "above a battle scene from the Hussite Wars it was unavoidably necessary to suspend badly-painted purple clouds."[52] Over the course of his career Feuerstein would design the sets for more than fifty theatrical productions.

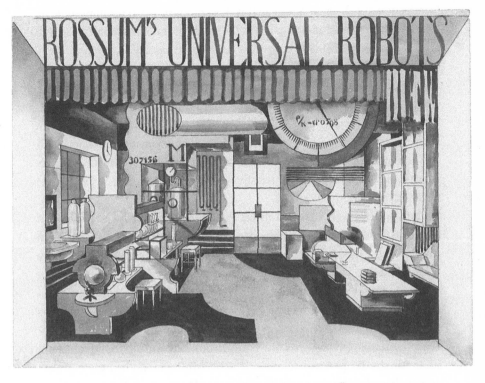

FIGURE 3.3. Bedřich Feuerstein's set design for première of Karel Čapek's *R. U. R.* at the National Theater, Prague, 25 January 1921. Pen-and-ink drawing and watercolor, 30 by 22 cm. H6D-25831, Collection of the National Museum, Prague, Czech Republic.

In 1922 Šíma introduced Feuerstein to Auguste Perret (whose portrait he had just painted). Le Corbusier had cut his teeth as a draftsman in Perret's practice in 1908–1910. Fricek worked in Perret's Paris office, without a regular wage, from 1923 to 1925. His most important assignment for Perret was the theater at the 1925 *Exposition internationale des Arts décoratifs et industriels modernes*, for which he designed a movable three-part stage. Of all the national pavilions at the exhibition, Fricek liked the "nicely insane Russian-Bolshevik" pavilion by Konstantin Melnikov best, followed by Josef Gočár's Czech pavilion (though he called Pavel Janák's interior "a horrible thing"). The Japanese pavilion, he wrote to his friend Josef Havlíček, was "pretty, but it is folklore."[53] Čapková emphasizes that the Japan Feuerstein was interested in "was dramatically different from the one created by preceding generations of Japonistes. In his image Japan was a country where people were not afraid to be modern."[54]

Fricek soon got the chance to see this new, modern Japan for himself. Josef Gočár offered him an assistantship in his studio at the Akademie výtvarných umění (Academy of Fine Arts, or AVU) in Prague, which Feuerstein certainly would have accepted had he not been invited to collaborate with Antonín Raymond. Raymond was in Prague lobbying to build a new Czechoslovak embassy in Tokyo and seeking a replacement for his partner Alec Sykes, who had just left the firm. Antonín's brother Viktor recommended Feuerstein. Havlíček, himself an architect (and ARDEV member), met with Raymond to size him up. "I have to say that the guy impressed me, everything he has built is first-rate . . . and far more modern than we are accustomed to in Prague," he reported to Fricek in Paris.[55]

"So I've finally just arrived in Japan," Feuerstein wrote to Havlíček in May 1926. "It doesn't seem kitschy here. Japan is altogether surprising. It is a country where there is very little *mauvais goût*. . . . All in all, it's perhaps a more artistic land than France. . . . In France there is always something to divert you: houses, trees, the girls' outfits, etc. etc. Here even more so. What misery, monotony, and boredom by contrast in Central Europe! With us everything is ersatz monumental, *y compér* supreme chief Mr Gočár. . . . They do not fear being modern in Japan—girls drive cars in kimonos, modern buildings stand alongside the Ter [*o-tera*—temples]."[56] Though Raymond had some private doubts about Feuerstein, his first impressions of his young colleague were very positive. "Feuerstein does me a lot of good," he told Noémi. "Perret speaks through him, when he criticizes my work; the crystal clear logic, together with spiritualized sensuality, of the French. He makes me realize the necessity of discipline in design. . . . He is fresh, with [a] lot of knowledge from his recent experiences with Perret, I have the feeling, that Perret came to help me and push me a little further, and on the right road."[57]

Feuerstein worked in Japan for four years and would have stayed longer if he could. He developed a keen interest in Japanese theater. In 1927 he published his book *Theatre Settings by Bedřich Feuerstein, Architect, Tokyo* in English and Japanese, funded by the sociologist Tadaichi Okada (who also translated Robespierre, Lenin, and Karl Liebknecht). *Národní listy* commended it as "the first Japanese writing on Czech art as well as the first serious recognition of Czech theater in the world."[58] Together with the Raymonds, Fricek joined the Garakutashū circle of the collector Heibonji Mita, a "unique, liberal forum where collectors, intellectuals, and artists from all over Japan gathered to exchange collectibles, and discuss a wide range of topics such as tradition versus modernity, history, religion and spirituality . . . that served as a multilevel contact zone between East and West in the interwar period."[59] "Mita loved new things, and when roller skates were introduced to Japan at the end of the 19th century he purchased a pair immediately, and . . . turned the second floor of his house into a roller-skating rink," according to the website of his home-town Minato City, now a ward in Tokyo.[60] Fricek also became close friends with architects and furniture designers Kameki and Nobuko Tsuchiura. The couple, who had worked under Frank Lloyd Wright on the Hotel Imperial, followed him back to the United States and stayed for two years in Los Angeles and Taliesin.[61] Nobuko Tsuchiura is generally considered the first woman ar-chitect in Japan, even though the firm bore the name of her husband alone. Feuerstein and the Tsuchiuras were neighbors in 1927–1928 in the Bunka apart-ments in the Ochanomizu area of Tokyo, built in 1925. They exchanged ideas on a project for the Soviet embassy (the commission eventually went to Ray-mond's office) and collaborated on competition entries for the Chikatetsu building in Tokyo and the Saito Kaikan cultural center in Sendai (both built in 1929).[62] The former bore a marked resemblance to Jaromír Krejcar's Olym-pic department store in Prague. The house the Tsuchiuras designed for them-selves, a miniature of modernist good taste erected in 1935 in the Shinagawa ward in Tokyo, still stands.

Helena Čapková maintains that Feuerstein's role in the Raymond firm's work has been "marginalized and distorted" in both English and Japanese lit-erature.[63] She shows that Fricek was a major contributor in his own right to several of the firm's most significant projects, including the Italian embassy villa, the Rising Sun Petroleum Company's office and residences, the Sacred Heart Girls' School (1928), the French embassy (1933), and, above all, the Soviet embassy and St. Luke's International Hospital (both 1933). In an unsent letter to Feuerstein, Raymond acknowledged that he "entrusted" Fricek with several projects, including the "Russian Emb. [and] St. Luke's," which caused him financial losses.[64] Writing to *Architectural Review* a quarter century later, he credited Fricek with "far-reaching and definite influence on my design, re-sulting in the St Luke's International Medical Center in Tokyo early in my career, which I believe has the earmarks of his influence."[65] I suspect there was more than a twinge of guilty conscience here. In the end Raymond and Feuer-stein parted company on terms as acrimonious as Raymond's rift with Frank Lloyd Wright (or Wright's earlier breach with his mentor Louis Sullivan). On returning in January 1930 from a study trip to Beijing, Fricek was summarily dismissed. Raymond berated him as a "thiev [*sic*] and criminal" and "pres-sured" him to sign an agreement that included a promise to leave Japan by "the beginning of March 1930." The reason Feuerstein gives for his dismissal was his "indiscretion" in talking with the wife of a Czechoslovak consular official about Antonín's theft of student club funds in Prague twenty years earlier.[66] Beneath this lay other differences that had been festering for some time. In the afore-mentioned draft letter, Antonín complained to Feuerstein: "You are convinced that the only correct way to do design is yours. Your approach to things is totally uncompromising. You are a purist, who will not accept that anybody who does not work according to your methods can be any good . . . you are experimenting and working on your artistic accomplishment at my expense."[67]

Another reason Antonín may have wanted Fricek out of Japan was to stop him from opening a rival firm with his colleague Jan Josef Švagr, at a time when commissions were beginning to dry up. After graduating from Prague Poly-technic, Švagr avoided military service during World War I on religious grounds (he was a staunch Catholic) and made his way to Russia, where he met his wife Elisabeth. The Bolsheviks exiled the couple to Siberia, but they succeeded in bribing their way into China. Švagr met Raymond in Shanghai in 1922 and followed him to Tokyo, where he joined the practice as an assistant. Jan quit shortly after Feuerstein's departure in 1930 and set up his own firm with his brother Prokop Bořivoj. They completed more than twenty projects, one of which was the first mosque built in Japan, at Kobe in 1935—another unexpected Czech first. The Kobe Muslim Mosque, as it is known, was one of the few structures in the city to survive both the American bombing in World War II and the great Hanshin earthquake of 1995. It is disconcerting to come face-to-face with the Czech saint Jan Nepomucký (John of Nepomuk) and the panorama of the Charles Bridge and Prague Castle in the stained-glass win-dows at Švagr's Cathedral of the Sacred Heart, aka the Yamate Catholic Church, in Yokohama (built in 1933). Švagr's architecture is nothing if not eclectic. While the Kobe mosque is built in a Moorish style that would fit in anywhere from Casablanca to Jakarta, the neogothic Yamate Church would not look out of place in Smíchov or Karlín. The English-style villa Švagr built in Yokohama for the merchant E. V. Bernard might be described as mock Tudor (David Vávra calls it "Tudor-Gothic").[68] Elisabeth Švagrová died in the late 1930s, and Jan left Japan in April 1941 for Chile; he later moved to Argentina. At age seventy-one he was ordained a priest. He died in 1969 and is buried at Claypole near Buenos Aires. *Kde domov můj?* (Where is my home?), we might ask, in the wistful words of the opening line of the Czech national anthem. But there they all are, Švagr, Raymond, and Feuerstein, photographed at the Czechoslovak embassy in Tokyo at the founding of the

Japan-Czechoslovak Society in December 1927, frozen in perpetual amity in the pages of *Pestrý týden*.[69]

Země česká, domov můj (the Czech land, my home), the anthem goes on.[70] But without Japan, Feuerstein was lost. A three-week trip to Moscow in 1931 with Adolf Hoffmeister (they stayed with Hannes Meyer) disappointed him. Fricek had been considering working in the Soviet Union, but what he saw there convinced him that the prospect offered much to sociologists and politicians but little to architects. "I believe, one day I shall come back [to Japan]," he wrote to Kameki Tsuchiura in October 1931. "Very often I feel homesick for Japan. It is the nicest country I have lived in."[71] Back in Prague Feuerstein redesigned the interiors for the Borový bookstore on Národní Avenue and (together with Josef Šíma) the Aventinum publishing house and gallery on Purkyňova Street. He lectured to the Mánes Fine Artists' Society on Japanese architecture, Japanese theater, and the Great Wall of China. He designed the stage sets for more than twenty productions at the National Theater, the Estates Theater, and elsewhere and was the scenographer for seven Liberated Theater productions in 1933–1935, including Béla Bartók's ballet *The Wooden Prince*, choreographed by Milča Mayerová, and Voskovec and Werich's *Osel a stín* (The ass and the shadow). A satire inspired by the Reichstag fire, the latter led to protests from the German embassy and demands from Czech fascists that the theater be closed.[72] Fricek also collaborated on a trio of films directed by Vladislav Vančura. *Na sluneční straně* (*On the Sunny Side*, 1933) was a "highly experimental film . . . [in which] Vančura draws on a wide range of styles, from the Surrealist-inflected stylization of René Clair to the frenzied montage of Dziga Vertov."[73] Vítězslav Nezval and Roman Jakobson wrote the screenplay.

But Feuerstein's architectural ambitions once again went unfulfilled. He set up a practice with Jaroslav Fragner, but although their competition entries won prizes, none of the projects were ever realized. His plans for monuments (with Otakar Švec), the Czechoslovak pavilion at the 1935 Brussels *Exposition universelle et internationale* (with Alois Wachsmann), and a tuberculosis sanatorium in Vyšné Hágy in Slovakia (with Josef Chochol) were no more successful. "I made some competitions and had some small jobs, but nothing of interest," Fricek wrote to Kameki Tsuchiura in February 1933. "There is not to [*sic*] much work here now in architecture proper. The people is [*sic*] afraid to spend money in building and the State has no money."[74] In the years after his return from Japan, Feuerstein managed to build just one project, a summer house for a family in Sázava in central Bohemia (and even his authorship of this is uncertain). The last straw was his failure to obtain a professorship at the Technical

University of Brno. In declining physical health and deeply depressed, he took his own life on 10 May 1936. The specter of Fricek throwing himself into the cold waters of the Vltava may have helped Milena Jesenská steel herself for the rigors of rehab in the asylum in Bohnice a few months later. Certainly his death was on her mind.

That morning, before making his way to the Troja Bridge, Fricek dropped a last letter into the mailbox of his friend Jaromír Čihař, who worked in the presidential office at Prague Castle, urging him "to endure and trust in socialism and the society it aims to produce."[75] It seems incongruous in the circumstances, but who is to say? Vítězslav Nezval penned a sad elegy on the architect's untimely end.[76] Karel Čapek wrote a brief but heartfelt tribute for *Lidové noviny*:

POOR FRICEK

Fricek, that's who Bedřich Feuerstein was to his friends and acquaintances. . . . Nobody would ever have expected his life to be cut short so tragically; he was gifted, everyone liked him and he always had good fortune. People believed in him even before he began to create; few of our architects and artists had such consistently good press, so warm a reception, and so many expectations as were directed toward him with hope from the very beginning. Everybody would have expected Fricek to have success in life; and it is absolutely terrible how it all came to nothing. Good reviews didn't help, friendship didn't help, Feuerstein's tasteful and inventive work didn't help; in a time when enough was still being built and multitudes of skilled bricklayers were working their fingers to the bone, there was no longer any decent work for poor Fricek. He was condemned to remain ever hopeful, until the moment when it all finished in despair. His death is a further and very painful proof of how strangely and wretchedly we look after talent here [*u nás*].[77]

Czechs would have picked up on the allusion to Mikoláš Aleš's 1883 drawing "The Fate of Talent in Bohemia," which the artist subtitled "the bitterest poem without words." It portrayed a young man about to depart on horseback as his lover vainly pleads with him to stay home.[78]

An Ashram in Pondicherry

"The façades of the 'superblock' by architect František Sammer in the Plzeň housing estate of Slovany are accentuated with relief-formed two-story porticos, ornamented with channeled pilasters and Ionic capitals topped with triangular pediments," observes a recent history titled *The Paneláks*—the Czech term for the apartment blocks made of prefabricated concrete panels that became synonymous with urban development in socialist Czechoslovakia.[79] A companion volume dismisses Sammer's porticos as "a dense symmetrical configuration of pseudo-renaissance architectonic links and folkloristic ornaments."[80] This gives us a flavor of the socialist realist (or, as it was known, *sorela*) architectural style that was briefly imposed on Czechoslovakia under Soviet pressure in the 1950s, especially in "provincial cities that received state favor for their heavy industry." As a "relatively well-equipped and relatively modern metropolis, and moreover not entirely politically positive-minded or reliable," Prague was not prioritized for such developments.[81] Happily, some might say—although it is perhaps not a bad thing that the Hotel International in Dejvice (František Jeřábek, 1953–1957) survives as a proud memorial to the *sorela* style, reminding us that once upon a time, and not so very long ago, Czechoslovakia stood "With the Soviet Union for All Eternity" (*Se Sovětským svazem na věčné časy*), a universal slogan of the 1950s. If František Sammer is remembered at all in the Czech Republic today, it is as the creator of one of the earliest *sídliště* (housing estates), built before the use of prefabricated panels became the ubiquitous method of construction. But Slovany, which he planned and built in 1954–1957, is a misleading monument to his ideals, which were modernist to the core.

Sammer may have been forgotten by history, but his progress through the margins of other people's stories has a disruptive coherence all its own.[82] Born in Plzeň in 1907, he dropped out of ČVUT in 1928 after completing less than a year's study. He left Czechoslovakia in 1931 for Paris with the intention, as he wrote to his parents, of studying architecture not in school "but by working in an office, JOINING theory with practice."[83] The young man talked his way into Le Corbusier's studio, where he impressed enough to remain on the staff for almost two years and to be rewarded with a regular monthly wage— unusual among Le Corbusier's assistants. He worked closely with Pierre Jeanneret and Charlotte Perriand, producing scores of drawings, some of which Le Corbusier selected for publication in magazines. He contributed significantly to some important projects, including the Swiss pavilion at the Cité Internationale Universitaire de Paris, the Plan Obus and L'Oued Ouchaia residential quarter for Algiers, and Le Corbusier's apartment building in Boulogne. During his time in Paris, František's political opinions moved sharply to the left. With the help of Le Corbusier, the Russian architect Nicolai Kolli, and others he scouted out the possibilities of working in the Soviet Union. In fall 1931 he worked on the design for Le Corbusier's entry in the competition for the Palace of the Soviets in Moscow. Much as Sammer revered the master, he found himself increasingly dismayed by Le Corbusier's politics (or lack thereof). "You know, I feel sorry about [Le Corbusier's] intelligence, of which he has too much for an ordinary bourgeois," he confided to Karel Teige toward the end of his time in Paris.[84] He referred to Teige's recent public spat with Le Corbusier over the latter's plans for Paul Otlet's Mundaneum, a proposed museum of world culture in Geneva. He had no doubt also read Teige's denunciation of Le Corbusier's villas in *Nejmenší byt* (*The Minimum Dwelling*, 1932) as "command performances for his wealthy clients," whose "flat roofs, terraces, horizontal windows, concrete furniture, chrome chairs, plate glass and so on have become a modernistic fetish."[85]

Together with Charlotte Perriand, František attempted to establish a working group of architects who would move to Russia, like Hannes Meyer's Red Front Brigade. "We are like a sect, we have common interests," he wrote to his parents in November 1931.[86] Despite the support of Kolli and the Vesnin brothers, who were among the leading avant-garde Soviet architects of the day, nothing materialized out of Perriand's exploratory visit to Moscow in the spring of 1932. František traveled to Moscow under his own steam in July 1933, where he found employment in Kolli's studio while also supervising work on Le Corbusier's Centrosoyuz (Central Cooperative Alliance) building. Sammer's time in Russia was far more productive than Jaromír Krejcar's. His work with Kolli included designs for a sports stadium, a trade unions' theater, a large apartment building, a bridge over the Moskva River, and several self-service gas stations. The best-known building with which he was associated was the constructivist Kirovskaya metro station (1935), which still stands today. Initially named after the assassinated Leningrad party boss Sergei Kirov, the station has been known since 1990 as Chistye Prudy. But the political tide was turning against modernism even as Sammer arrived in Moscow. "And we here—we are doing the work of the builders of the pyramids," he wrote to Charlotte Perriand in January 1935. He still hoped to persuade her to move to the Soviet Union. But as the strictures of socialist realism tightened their grip, doubts were beginning to set in. In the same letter, František let slip his feelings on seeing the newly published second volume of Le Corbusier's *Oeuvre complète*: "It was quite a sentimental day—JUST ONE DAY—to experience the good things that we have long been missing— good architecture. This is why I can't write Corbu.—I could not.—What is there to write about—architecture? Why?! We are doing valuable things here.

Which, other than their size, do not seem interesting in and of themselves in any way."[87]

František left Kolli's office in October 1936 for the Narkomzdrav (People's Commissariat of Public Health) design studio, which was headed by Moses Ginzburg in conjunction with Viktor and Alexander Vesnin. There he worked on a zoning plan for the Crimean coast and designs for sanatoria at Gagra in Georgia and Kislovodsk in the northern Caucasus. He traveled to Paris early in 1937 to prepare for the *Exposition internationale des arts et techniques de la vie moderne.* I have no idea what he thought of Jaromír Krejcar's Czechoslovak pavilion or whether, by that time, he shared Krejcar's wider disillusionment with Soviet politics. If so, he didn't let on. On 18 April he wrote to his parents that he was expecting to attend the All-Union Congress of Soviet Architects in Moscow in June (which put the last socialist realist nails in the constructivist coffin). Frank Lloyd Wright was an honored guest at the congress, where he reputedly pronounced that "if Stalin has betrayed the Revolution, he has betrayed it into the hands of the Russian people."[88] František never made it to the congress. Instead, he took a job with Antonín Raymond's practice in Tokyo.

Sammer and Raymond had first met during František's visit to Japan in 1935, when he traveled from Moscow on the Trans-Siberian Railway. It was likely Kunio Maekawa, whom Sammer knew from his time in Paris with Le Corbusier, who introduced him to Antonín. František and his wife Agnes Larsson "had a fantastic time" with "Mr Raymond and his wife and their young son," spending "many lovely days with them in Tokyo, and especially at their house in Hayama, on the seashore, where we were guests for several days.—We were invited for a longer stay in Karuizawa—Raymond's second home in the mountains."[89] "As both M. Raymond and M. Sammer were Czechs and had the same profession they were very friendly," Agnes said in 1974.[90] When František inquired about openings in Raymond's practice in 1937, Antonín urged him to "come at once."[91] František boarded the steamer SS *Hakozaki* in Marseille on 9 August. But when he arrived, he found Antonín on the verge of closing up shop, despite having recently signed articles of association for a new firm with Junzō Yoshimura and others. Japan's increasing militarism and growing closeness with Nazi Germany had led the Raymonds to the reluctant decision to return to the United States. They took a roundabout route. "I arrived at the end of Raymond's eighteen years in Tokyo," Sammer wrote to his parents, who were by now thoroughly confused by his peregrinations. "We are going to Pondicherry, probably in the first half of January."[92] Located on the Bay of

Bengal in southern India, Pondicherry (today called Puducherry) was a French colony. What brought them there was the project that Raymond later described as "the best architecture of my career"—the Golconde dormitory for the Sri Aurobindo ashram.[93]

The origins of what is now hailed as "one of the earliest works of sustainable modern architecture in the world" are as implausibly tangled as anything else in this tale of itinerant architects and interbreeding cultures.[94] Born to a wealthy Indian family in Calcutta and educated at St. Paul's School in London and King's College, Cambridge, Sri Aurobindo Ghosh was an early advocate of Indian independence. The British colonial authorities prosecuted him twice for sedition and once for conspiracy. In 1910 he withdrew from politics and "went to Pondicherry in order to devote himself entirely to his inner spiritual life and work."[95] There he developed the spiritual discipline he called integral yoga. With Mirra Alfassa, a French citizen of Egyptian-Turkish parentage known as the Mother, he established the Sri Aurobindo ashram in 1926. As the community grew, Raymond relates, "Sri Aurobindo Ghosh intended to build ... a truly up-to-date modern dormitory for his disciples." In 1935 Philippe B. St. Hilaire (aka Pavitra), a French engineer and ashram member whom Antonín had met in Japan, approached Raymond about the project. Raymond criticized Pondicherry's eighteenth-century French colonial architecture as "unsuitable in this day and age of advanced techniques. . . . This point of view and an unexplainable confidence in me from Sri Aurobindo brought about his request for my photograph upon the receipt of which he apparently formed a judgment of my character and sent me a considerable sum of money for expenses to cover the transportation of my wife, son and myself to India."[96] The Japanese American architect and furniture designer George Nakashima, who was then an assistant in Raymond's Tokyo office, made a site visit in 1936. Plans were drawn up the same year.

Construction began in 1937. No outside labor was used. Golconde was built entirely by the ashram members themselves. Contrasting sharply with its colonial surroundings, the four-story, two-wing structure made out of raw concrete, stone, and wood "brought to India an entirely new architectural vocabulary and construction technologies."[97] As described by Pankaj Vir Gupta and Christine Mueller, the exterior of the building "has a surreal, abstract quality." It was designed to encourage meditation, with the hot and humid climate in mind. The main frame was made of reinforced concrete. The roof used bowed concrete shell tiles to create an insulating layer above the flat concrete roof deck. No glass was employed anywhere. The exterior façades consisted of adjustable asbestos-cement louvers set in custom-made brass fittings (the brass was melted down from cooking pots donated by followers), allowing air and light to pass through while keeping out rain and direct sunlight. The gardens and reflecting pools, with sparse ground cover to the north and dense tree plantings to the south, not only brought the dormitory close to nature but also created cooling convection currents through the building. Communal dining and laundry facilities were on the ground floor, and the staircase and bathrooms were in a central tower that separated the two wings. The individual living cells on the three upper floors were shielded from the sun by a corridor that ran the length of the southern side of each wing, and each unit had slatted teak sliding doors designed by Noémi Raymond, which permitted the passage of air while maintaining privacy. The rooms had simple, handcrafted teak furnishings designed by Nakashima (and later by Sammer). Each cell contained a bed with a mosquito net, a cupboard, bookshelves, a writing desk and chair, a folding screen, a mirror, an armchair, and a ceramic vessel for filtered water, which was replenished twice daily. "The crushed seashell plaster walls and black stone floors of each room provide a luminous canvas for the mélange of breeze and light entering through the louvers and sliders," write Gupta and Mueller. Milena Jesenská would have loved it. "Golconde remains architecturally vital," they continue, "as a living testament to the original modernist credo—architecture as the manifest union of technology, aesthetics, and social reform. Within Pondicherry's unique cultural setting, Golconde offers an undiluted view of a wholly triumphant Modernism."[98] If this is not where we would expect to find such a paradigm of modernist vision, maybe it is our expectations that are awry.

The Raymonds arrived in Pondicherry in February 1938 and left eight months later. Nakashima and Sammer remained to supervise the construction, but no longer as Raymond's employees. Both became full members of the ashram community, working without payment in exchange for food and board. As at Belomorkanal (though in this case, voluntarily), work within the collective took on spiritual significance. It was at Golconde that George Nakashima made his first furniture. "Work for him was a spiritual calling, a linking of his strength to a transcendental force, a surrender to the divine, a form of prayer," relates his daughter Mira.[99] George was given the Sanskrit name Sundarananda (One who delights in beauty) and remained a practitioner of integral yoga for the rest of his life. "When a group of people concentrate with absolute sincerity and devotion on the common objective of a divine life," he later wrote apropos Golconde, "a creative spirit permeates the group's whole

FIGURE 3.4. Antonín Raymond's Golconde dormitory, Pondicherry, India, 1948. Photographer unknown. From Helena Čapková and Kóiči Kitazawa, eds., *Antonín Raymond v Japonsku*, Prague, 2019.

existence. . . . Everything becomes the handmaiden of a deeper search for consciousness; all fades into an awesome light."[100] František Sammer was no less
blinded by that light. "It is coming along splendidly, the way we are getting to
know the world—first in Russia and now in India," he wrote to his parents.
"With his intensive spiritual evolution, Sri Aurobindo, who today avoids public life, provides an example of remarkable energy for all youths and dominates
the whole India (which is very religious) with his great ideals. For him, the
reforms that were carried out in the USSR after the revolution . . . and also
all the reforms that Europe must now carry out, are the basis of a person's
spiritual development."[101] The conjunction of Lenin's October Revolution
and Sri Aurobindo's integral yoga may seem surreal today, but it made perfect
sense to Sammer at the time.

Nakashima left India in October 1939 and "finally made it back to Tokyo on
a Japanese refugee ship from Shanghai to Nagasaki."[102] The Second Sino-
Japanese War, the precursor of World War II in Asia, had started two years
earlier. George worked for six months in Kunio Maekawa's newly established
firm before returning to the United States. During this time he met his
American-born wife-to-be Marion Okajima, who joined him in Seattle in 1940.
Sammer stayed in Pondicherry for nearly four years. He finally left in 1942.
Concerned with the fate of his occupied homeland, he first tried to join the
Soviet Red Army, but when this proved too difficult he enlisted in the British
army, where he served in the East Yorkshire Regiment. He was seriously
wounded in the fighting in Burma and evacuated to England early in 1946.
During his convalescence he reestablished contact with his first wife Agnes,
who had left Pondicherry for her native Hawaii in 1939 (though she kept in
touch with the ashram for the rest of her life). František designed a beach
house for her in Honolulu—a third variant of the Le Corbusier design that
was first realized in Raymond's Karuizawa house—but like Le Corbusier's
Errázuriz house, it was never built.[103] František and Agnes had "spent several
lovely days in Karuizawa together" with the Raymonds in October 1937.[104]
Despite invitations from Raymond in the United States, Le Corbusier in Paris,
and Golconde, where construction was continuing, Sammer decided it was
time to return to Czechoslovakia. "I need to settle down at home to find serious work and stop traveling," he told Noémi Raymond in January 1947.[105]
When Antonín Raymond finally heard from his old assistant again in 1966, he
wrote, "this is a veritable 'resurrection.' We thought after all these years that
you weren't in our world anymore. Man, why didn't you write? You knew
where we were."[106] It showed how out of touch with his homeland Raymond

had become. "It was, in short, a period of terror. . . . What suffered most of all was the integrity of the creative process," František explained.[107] That is how a favorite pupil of Le Corbusier and Charlotte Perriand, coauthor of the Kirovskaya constructivist station on the Moscow metro and collaborator on the first modernist building in India, morphed into "the most active propagator of conservative socialist realist architecture in Plzeň."[108] Because, after all, you have to live.

Back in the United States the Raymonds bought a 150-acre farm and 1740s fieldstone Quaker farmhouse in New Hope, Pennsylvania, where they established a Taliesin of their own. "I am buying a big farm in Pennsylvania and I will start a modern architecture school there. . . . There are many young architects that want to work with me," Antonín informed the Tokyo office in March 1939. "If all goes well [New Hope] should develop into an 'art' center, the marvelous old barn being used for studios and work shop and the cows kept in the stables below," Noémi added the following month.[109] They remodeled the farmhouse, aiming for a "blending [of] the Bucks County Quaker vernacular architecture with Japanese design in accordance with their own modernist principles."[110] "What drew me to Pennsylvania," Antonín wrote in 1940, "was the charm of the reposeful, well settled country side with strong stone barns and houses that looked as though they had existed for hundreds of years and as though they would last forever. There was an atmosphere of peace and serenity that worked like a balm in this overwrought world where all the great realities seem forgotten."[111] Safe on the banks of the Delaware River, Antonín was the sole member of his family to survive the Holocaust. His brother Viktor, who had acted as go-between in the hiring of Bedřich Feuerstein, died on 31 July 1942 in Mauthausen. His brother Frank died on 26 January 1943 in Auschwitz. His brother Egon died on 25 October 1944 in Terezín. His sisters Ella and Irma were also killed in German camps; Irma died in Poland, place and date unknown.[112] After the United States entered World War II, Raymond undertook commissions for the military, including prefabricated houses for Camp Kilmer, New Jersey, and Camp Shanks, New York, and housing and an airport expansion at Fort Dix, New Jersey.

In 1943 the Raymonds sponsored the release of George Nakashima, his wife Marion, and their baby daughter Mira from Camp Minidoka in the high desert of southern Idaho, where the young family had been interned after Japan's attack on Pearl Harbor in December 1941. "This [internment of Japanese Americans] I felt at the time was a stupid, insensitive act, one by which my country could only hurt itself," George wrote later. "It was a policy of unthinking racism. Even

Eskimos with only a small percentage of Japanese blood were sent to the West-ern desert to die."[113] Born of immigrant parents in Spokane, Washington, in 1905, Nakashima was an all-American boy. He was educated at the University of Wash-ington, the École Americaine des Beaux-Arts in Fontainebleau outside Paris, and MIT, where he graduated with an MA in architecture in 1930. After a spell as a mural painter in New York State—his work included murals for the capitol in Albany—he lost his job to the Great Depression, sold his beloved 1929 Ford touring car, and bought a second-class around-the-world steamship ticket. He made it to France, where Chartres Cathedral and Le Corbusier's Swiss pavilion—on which Sammer also worked—equally affected his sensibilities. He "found a tiny room for eight dollars a month in Alésia on the outskirts of Montparnasse," where "polite starvation was a way of life, especially for the artists at the center of the creative movement. I was happy to be living in this electric atmosphere," he wrote in his memoir *The Soul of a Tree*, "to be part of the international creativ-ity evident on all sides." The talk in the cafés "had a strong undercurrent of ex-hilaration, a fervid conviction that new concepts were being born, old forms torn asunder." But "for me . . . there was a persistent nagging that this was not the whole truth." After a year in Paris "it was time to move on, and I would leave the whole modern art movement with its egotism and lack of beauty. Now, I felt, it was my destiny to make the long sea voyage to Japan, home of my ancestors."[114] He signed on with Raymond in Tokyo in 1934.

George first tried his hand at joinery at Golconde, but it was at Camp Mini-doka that he learned traditional Japanese carpentry skills from an older in-ternee, Gentaro Hikogawa. After their release the Nakashimas lived on the Raymonds' farm from May 1943 to March 1944. When their freedom was fully restored George established a furniture-making workshop in New Hope, which eventually became a legend in the American craft movement and is still operating today. "My father integrated life and work by not tying into the big-corporation mindset of mass production and making money,"[115] says Mira Nakashima (who now runs the workshop), but money flooded in all the same. In 1973 Nelson Rockefeller commissioned George to produce more than two hundred individual pieces for his New York estate. "If you had to name one artist collected by Steven Spielberg, Brad Pitt, Steve Jobs, Julianne Moore and Narciso Rodriguez, you probably would not guess George Nakashima," began a 2004 *Chicago Tribune* article. Diane von Furstenberg forked out $130,500 at a 2003 auction for a fourteen-foot Nakashima dining table.[116] The highest price paid for a Nakashima work is $822,400 for Arthur and Evelyn Krosnick's Arlyn dining table in redwood burl and black walnut, bought at Sotheby's in

New York in 2006.[117] On a more modest level, a simple Nakashima tray, manufactured under license by Knoll, will set you back $430.[118]

One of Nakashima's last projects was his peace tables. The first was installed by George himself in the Cathedral of Saint John the Divine in New York on New Year's Eve in 1986. Others followed at the Hall of Peace in Auroville, South India—an offshoot of the Sri Aurobindo ashram—in 1996 and at the Russian Academy of Arts in Moscow in 2001. "A while back there appeared a great bole of a tree, a Walnut," George explained in 1984:

> In a small but firm voice the bole asked to be realized; two adjoining slabs opened to make an extraordinary table, roughly twelve feet (3.6 meters) long by the same dimension wide, weighing almost 1 ton. Gradually a few people became interested in the project and suggested we make six Altars— one for each Continent. It will be a symbol, a token of man's aspirations for a creative and beautiful peace, free of political overtones; an expression of love for his fellow man. We have become so basically disoriented with our blind faith in science and technology without spirituality, it brought us to our pit of madness.[119]

Dugway Proving Ground, Utah

Were we to seek a geographic location for George Nakashima's pit of modern madness, the Dugway Proving Ground in Utah would be a strong candidate. It is not the easiest place to get to. DPG, as the military likes to call it, is "a US Army post roughly 90 miles southwest of Salt Lake City . . . between the Salt Lake Desert and Dugway Valley in Tooele County. The gas station–less road from Salt Lake City to the army post . . . is unfenced open range filled with wildlife, cattle, blind curves, and vision-impeding hillsides."[120] Despite occupying "over 1300 square miles of high mountain desert, a land area greater in size than the state of Rhode Island," DPG is "a closed Post with no public access." The US Army warns incoming personnel: "Use extreme caution when traveling at night as roadways are not lighted . . . be watchful for cattle and abundant wildlife on roadways. Cellular service is unreliable until DPG is reached, ensure vehicle is fueled and maintained prior to starting trip to DPG." Dugway's "primary mission," the US Department of Defense's website informs us, "is testing U.S. and Allied chemical and biological (CB) defense systems and performing nuclear, biological and chemical (NBC) survivability testing of defense materiel using CB agents and stimulants."

The DPG facility was established on 12 February 1942 in response to the Japanese attack on Pearl Harbor two months earlier. Initial experiments included "testing incendiary bombs, chemical weapons, and modified agents as spray disseminated from aircraft."[121] Since then the mission has crept onward and outward. Like the better-known Area 51 in Nevada, DPG has spawned plentiful horror stories and a rich vein of conspiracy theories.[122] "It was like a movie version of 'death and destruction'—you know, like after the bomb goes off. Sheep laying all over. All of them down—patches of white as far as you could see," Tooele County sheriff Fay Gillette told a reporter after a test spraying of VX nerve gas went wrong in March 1968, leaving thousands of dead livestock strewn across the landscape.[123] This is the same chemical that killed Kim Jong-nam, the brother of North Korean leader Kim Jong-un, in February 2017. Revelations that Dugway "had mistakenly sent live anthrax spores over a 12-year period to 194 laboratories in 50 states, the District of Columbia, three U.S. territories and nine foreign countries" caused a major scandal in 2015.[124] What is perhaps more disturbing is what happens when things at DPG are going right.

David Maisel, whose specialty is photographing what he calls "compromised landscapes," was first inspired to document "this deliberately obscured region of the American atlas" in 2003.[125] That was when he stumbled across "a site in the Tooele Valley, near the western slope of the Oquirrh Mountains. Positioned along the desert floor in uniform rows were hundreds of small buildings. What Maisel eventually learned about this gridded array was extraordinary—the buildings comprise the Tooele Army Depot, and they hold thirty million pounds of aging chemical weapons, including mustard gas and nerve agents such as sarin and tabun."[126] It is no doubt a coincidence that the project Maisel was working on when he discovered these nine hundred storage "igloos" was called *Terminal Mirage*, so named because the Great Salt Lake, whose "surreal, apocalyptic, and strangely beautiful" landscapes he was surveying, is a terminal lake, that is, one that has no natural outlets.[127] "From the air," he told an interviewer later, the igloos "resembled a Donald Judd installation or perhaps a prototype of some kind of suburban housing. But the notion of chemical weapons and nerve agents sitting in the landscape set off alarm bells for me. Why were they here? Where were they from?"[128]

They were from DPG, awaiting disposal. After much pulling of strings, the Pentagon finally granted Maisel permission to photograph within Dugway Proving Ground in 2014. Every site he was allowed to photograph was "highly vetted by layers of military personnel," and he was "accompanied at all times by a military representative."[129] The safety gloves that hang soft and limp through the portholes in Maisel's photograph *Whole System Live Agent Test Chamber* have a touch of Salvador Dalí about them, and the grain-elevator architecture depicted in *Air Force Target Grid Building 4*, silhouetted against the stark backdrop of the Utah desert, would have brought a lump to Le Corbusier's throat.[130] But Maisel's most compelling images are his aerial photographs. "It is a site of dark creativity," he says. "Looking down from above reveals colossal weapons testing sites that are carved into the land, nested circles and crosshatched grids, as though the abstract drawings of Agnes Martin or Sol Lewitt have been taken to a poisonous extreme. The gridded landscape becomes a measuring device against which dispersal rates, toxicity levels, and threats to the human body are measured."[131] This "hidden, walled-off, and secret site," Maisel believes, "offers the opportunity to reflect on who and what we are collectively, as a society."[132] His conclusions are not reassuring. "Whether in the form of abstracted test-grids through which clouds of chlorine gas will drift, the nested circles of chemical-release platforms, or uncanny laboratories built for neutralizing biological threats and decontaminating battlefield toxins," he writes, "the spaces of Dugway suggest an encounter with substances better left undisturbed, with dormant materials we shouldn't awaken."[133] You get the feeling he is not just talking about chemicals. "The proving ground is a disturbing place. The need for such a place is itself disturbing. . . . One can't help but feel the heart of darkness at the core of its mission."[134]

In March 1943 a series of meetings among the National Defense Research Committee, the Chemical Warfare Service, a team of Harvard scientists led by Louis Fieser (who invented napalm), and executives of the Standard Oil Company (which manufactured the new napalm-filled M-69 incendiary bomb) resulted in a decision to engage leading architects to design a "German village" and a "Japanese village" at Dugway Proving Ground on which incendiary bombs could be tested. Antonín Raymond had a long-standing connection with Standard Oil (for which he had built housing in Yokohama), and his deep knowledge of traditional Japanese building techniques made him the obvious candidate for the job. Construction of the Japanese village began on 28 March. Thanks to the use of inmate labor from Utah jails, the work was completed in just forty-four days, on 11 May 1943. Every care was taken to ensure authenticity:

> The "usual American stud-frame type" construction was done away with in favor of the traditional and "complicated keyed or mortised joints" of

typical Japanese structures. . . . Authentic *shoji* and *fusuma* screens and panels were also produced. Appropriately comparable wood was carefully selected and even dried to represent typical moisture content in Japan. The cultural "sensitivity" of this project did not end there. According to the official Standard Oil report, for the purpose of accurately measuring flammability, furnishings provided included: *tansu* (storage chests), *futon* (bedding), *zabuton* (sitting cushions), *hibachi* (stoves/braziers), low tables, and radios. The report further reflects such cultural nuances as the placement of shoe storage in the hallways since shoes are not worn in the house in Japan, and recognition that *futon* are stored in the closets during the daytime. Additionally, tests were conducted with the *amado* shutters open (in daytime) and closed (at night) to measure the different effects. . . . *Tatami* mats were considered vital, because *tatami*, more than any other element of furnishings, affected the way bombs penetrated the floors. At Standard Oil's insistence a factory was set up to produce facsimile mats; further, "without military orders and without any evidence," a tremendous surplus of *tatami* were "acquired" from Japanese-American homes, temples, stores, and clubs in Hawaii.[135]

Testing commenced on 17 May and ended on 16 July. Further tests were conducted into 1944 to transform the M-69s into cluster bombs. A variety of other bombs were dropped in addition to M-69s, including M-50 and M-52 thermite-based bombs. Different altitudes were tested, with the most effective being low-altitude strikes from five thousand to ten thousand feet. Reviewing the Dugway test results, British military intelligence concluded that although the M-69 was unlikely to be effective on housing in the European theater, "for attack in Japanese and other Far Eastern targets the M-69 bomb in a satisfactory projectile cluster would be more suitable than the 4-lb. incendiary bomb."[136] In the course of testing, Raymond's "representative structures" were destroyed and rebuilt several times.

After the war ended the Japanese village was reused as "an artillery range, machinery storage, a pigeon roost (for testing nerve gas), mannequin storage, and even as a small-scale laboratory" before "it burned down so fast and so hot that . . . they couldn't contain it," likely in 1952. Nothing is left of it today other than a few beams that were salvaged and redeployed in two buildings that are still standing in what used to be the German village. One observer who was stationed at DPG in 1943 likened the two villages to "abandoned movie sets picturing the aftermath of a devastating plague. Dust-devils swirled through the powdery lanes, curling high into the blue sky, and tumbleweeds rolled past the empty doors—as if the art director had made a mistake and built an old western ghost town with the wrong kind of houses."[137] There was no mistake. These were absolutely the right kind of structures for the purpose, and Antonín Raymond was absolutely the right architect to design them. But no, it wasn't simple. "It certainly was not an easy task for me and my wife to be instrumental in devising means of defeating Japan," Antonín wrote later. But "in spite of my love for Japan, I came to the conclusion that the quickest way to terminate this war was to defeat Germany and Japan as quickly and as effectively as possible."[138]

On the night of 9–10 March 1945, 279 Boeing B-29 bombers dropped more than two thousand tons of the M-59 cluster bombs tested at DPG on Tokyo. The flames could be seen from 150 miles away as 267,000 buildings burned fast and hot, leaving upward of 83,000 civilians dead (the most conservative estimate) and a million homeless.[139] By way of comparison, the Allied bombing raids on Dresden on 13–15 February 1945, which many have argued constituted a war crime, killed between 22,700 and 25,000 people, while the cumulative death toll from the Luftwaffe's Blitz on British towns and cities in 1940–1941, including successive raids on London for fifty-six out of fifty-seven days, was around 40,000.[140] Incendiary raids on other Japanese cities followed. Years later the tragic figure of "a gifted architect who helped modernize Tokyo's prewar skyline but is now charged with destroying it" inspired Jennifer Cody Epstein to make one "Anton Reynolds" a central character in *The Gods of Heavenly Punishment*, an "evocative and thrilling epic novel" whose heroine, "fifteen-year-old Yoshi Kobayashi, child of Japan's New Empire . . . is on her way home on a March night when American bombers shower her city with napalm."[141] Epstein "showcases war's bitter ironies," gushed *Vogue*, "as well as its romantic serendipities."[142]

At the start of *The Gods of Heavenly Punishment* the author warns us that although her book is "based on a true event" and "contains characters who are based on or inspired by true historical figures, it is in the end a work of fiction."[143] We first meet Anton and his Franco-American wife Béryl at their summer house in Karuizawa in 1935. Among the guests are George and Mary Yamashita, thinly disguised versions of George and Marion Nakashima,[144] and Yoshi's parents Kenji and Hana Kobayashi. Anton had met Kenji when "they'd worked together on Frank Wright's Imperial project," and Kenji had been "his favorite building contractor" ever since. He was one of "Japan's legendary master carpenters: strong, honest and simple, with an almost spiritual connection to the wood he'd learned to work from his own father." "Staunchly nationalist," Kenji "sometimes referred to his *tsuma* [wife] as a 'modern woman' and 'very western,' shaking his head as though repeating a fatal diagnosis." Hana was teaching Yoshi (who slips in Anton's thoughts from "this tiny East/West wonder" to "a little trilingual monkey" in the space of a paragraph) to be fluent in French, English, and Japanese. Hana, educated in England from the age of eight, had been brought back to Japan by her parents "to become a proper Japanese wife" after her high school graduation. "Did you *want* to come home?" asks Anton:

> "Home," she said thoughtfully. "Well, I suppose not. You see, I'd wanted to go on to study English literature at university, or perhaps theater." . . .
>
> The contractor—who didn't speak English—nevertheless nodded congenially. "*Or-u-do Japan*," he said, pointing to himself with his beer glass. Old Japan. "New Japan." He indicated his wife.
>
> "*So desu nee*," said Mary Yamashita in Japanese. "I wonder where that puts me and George [who were both Japanese Americans born in the United States]."
>
> "You? You're neither," said Kenji simply. He pointed to his round red cheek. "Japanese face only."
>
> An uncomfortable pause followed. Anton cleared his throat. "Well," he asked, packing and lighting his pipe, "it seems to have turned out very well for the both of you. Will you send your daughter to English boarding school as well?"[145]

A later chapter finds Anton at Dugway Proving Ground, waiting to see his Japanese village put to the test. Studying the "porcelain [roof] tiles that unfurled gracefully like gray waves in the winter sunlight," he "had a fleeting image of his wife's eighteenth-century Ibaraki serving plate, set squarely in the path of stampeding cattle. It was an odd thought. Also an embarrassingly transparent one. Like those dreams he kept having of their country house in Nagano turning to ash before his eyes." Ironically, the Japanese village was "the first exclusively Japanese structure he'd attempted. . . . No intellectual melding of East and West here; no Cubist windows or International-styled galleries or subtle Moorish touches to window arches or doorframes. From foundation to chimney, the whole thing was to be built just as traditional Japanese builders would have built it. The government would contribute whatever was needed." If the US government had known that George Yamashita, "a real 'Jap' (at least by their definition of real) had had a hand in Jap Village," Anton muses, "they would have locked them both up for good." This *is* the product of Epstein's imagination: George Nakashima could not have worked on the Dugway project because he was not released from internment until May 1943, by which time Raymond's Japanese village was completed. For the initial construction work in New Jersey, Anton had ended up with "an outfit of foul-mouthed but dependable Italians," none of whom, "so far as Anton knew, had been locked up as enemy aliens after Italy joined the Axis." This is likely another fiction, although the racism called out by Epstein was not. Neither Italian Americans nor German Americans were interned en masse during World War II. For Japanese Americans, including those born and raised in the United States, having a Japanese face sufficed.

Wandering through his Japanese village, Anton "was filled with the kind of reverence for his profession that up until that point he had felt only in the Orient. It was almost like a small homecoming, though he had to remind himself it was not. For wasn't that the whole point of this grim exercise in the first place? Putting his 'suspect' admiration of Japanese style to good use? Showing the damn Americans his damn Americanism?" Epstein gives the great American melting pot a final vicious stir, as the team toasts the successful completion of the project "with the last of Anton's Tengumai sake":

> "*Kampai*," he said, lifting his *sake* cup. "To the most Japanese project of our careers."
>
> "And," George [Yamashita] added—to his credit, without an ounce of discernible irony—"to good American labor."[146]

The Atomic Bomb Dome

After the war was over Raymond wrote to General Douglas MacArthur, "telling him I would like to return to Japan and help in my capacity as an architect-engineer."[147] Antonín was the first American civilian allowed into the occupied country. "One tries so hard to remember the landmarks," he wrote to Noémi on 22 October 1948. "The Shinagawa Bridge, the Yokohama Station, the Sakurugicho etc.—It is a real desolation, covered with shanties—once in a while part of it untouched, just to emphasize the destruction." He goes to the seashore in search of *temps perdu* and finds everything exactly as it was, yet somehow not:

> Along the sea to Hayama—The roads seemed narrower and crookeder than ever, so strange so romantic so run down. The sand of the beaches seemed

darker and everywhere they were drying sliced vegetables on straw mats—Very little change in anything—I had a hard time to find the lane leading to our house, it seemed so narrow—not the slightest change—the smoke, the vegetable gardens, the huts—Kawasaki's house burnt and only the walls are standing—blessing—and then the beach before our wall, littered as always with things sundrying, nets on poles, the pier running out, the pines, larger, the bay bushes much larger, the steps up, the gate with only one door, sagging on one hinge and the house, dilapidated, the garden neglected, but still there—it seemed so small and so shabby—and we had such glorious times there. . . . It is late, tired. *Je t'embrasse et Claude* [their son] *mille fois.*[148]

Antonín opened a New York practice in 1945 with the Slovak architect Ladislav Leland Rado. Another Prague Polytechnic graduate, Rado came to the United States at the invitation of Walter Gropius in 1939 and received an MA from Harvard in 1940. The Raymonds reopened their Tokyo office in 1949 and made it their main base, leaving Rado in charge of the New York side of the business. Rado and Raymond's Perry House (1950–1952), a six-story, sixty-unit apartment block for American diplomatic staff in Tokyo, was the first multistory reinforced concrete building in the city (and had considerable influence on younger Japanese architects).[149] Noémi Raymond designed the furniture.[150] Some of Antonín's most important larger commissions date from this postwar period, helping to define the style we now call midcentury modern. The Reader's Digest Building in Tokyo (with Rado, 1949–1951; demolished 1962) was inspired by Le Corbusier's *ville radieuse* and surrounded by gardens with sculptures by Isamu Noguchi, who took the remarkable step of voluntarily joining his fellow Japanese Americans in an internment camp in Arizona during the war.[151] Raymond's other notable postwar buildings include the Saint Anselm Meguro Church in Tokyo (1954), whose folded-plate concrete makes brilliant use of natural light; the brutalist Gunma Music Center in Takasaki, whose bare concrete walls are relieved by Noémi Raymond's bold abstract colored murals (1955–1961); and Nanzan University in Nagoya, with its curvaceous Divine Word Seminary Chapel (1964–1966).[152] Antonín died in 1976 at age eighty-eight. In all, he spent forty-three years of his life in Japan. Noémi died four years later, at age ninety-one. Both are buried in Pennsylvania.

Let me end this chapter with one more peripatetic Czech architect, whose legacy in Japan is perhaps the most poignant testimony of all to George Nakashima's pit of madness. Born in Náchod in 1880, Jan Letzel trained under

Jan Kotěra at UMPRUM and began his career with the Prague builder Quido Bělský in 1904–1905. Bělský's firm was responsible for two of the city's most notable secession-style landmarks: the Hotel Central on Hybernská Street (1899–1901) and the Grand Hotel Evropa on Wenceslas Square (as reconstructed by Alois Dryák and Bedřich Bendelmayer, 1906). Originally called the Archduke Štěpán Hotel, the Evropa was bought by the restaurateur Karel Šroubek and renamed the Grand Hotel Šroubek in 1924. It was here that Franz Kafka had his only public reading in Prague, in the Mirror Hall in 1912. The hotel was nationalized and renamed the Hotel Evropa in 1951. Russian cosmonaut Yuri Gagarin and the shah of Iran were among those who stayed there during the communist period. Restituted after the Velvet Revolution and sold in 1996, the Evropa is currently undergoing renovations and is due to reopen as the Prague W Hotel, operated by the Marriott hotel group. Jan Letzel was responsible for the building's grilles, railings, and exterior metal fittings. Together with Bohumil Hubschmann and Ladislav Šaloun, he also designed the Evropa's café, which has more claims to fame than just its impressive art nouveau interior decorations.

It was in this café that Nicholas Winton, alarmed by the imminent prospect of Hitler swallowing up what was left of Czechoslovakia after Munich, met with anguished Jewish parents in the winter of 1938–1939 and arranged to spirit their children to safety in Great Britain on *Kindertransport* trains. The young English stockbroker was not a lone white savior, as later accounts sometimes imply. He was responding to a call by Marie Schmolková, a Czech Jew who was president of the National Coordinating Committee for Refugees in Czechoslovakia. According to Milena Jesenská, who wrote about Schmolková with undisguised admiration in *Přítomnost* on 29 December 1938, "this woman personally knows every individual who has crossed the border in the last five years. . . . She perpetually moves between illness, life and death, between the London, Paris and Prague authorities; she has passed through no-man's-land, refugee camps, the ship that was on the Danube near Bratislava for two months after the annexation of Austria."[153] The first of Winton's children's transports left Prague on 14 March 1939—the day before the city was occupied—and the German authorities permitted another seven trains to depart over the summer, carrying 669 children to safety. A ninth train with 250 children on board was due to leave on 3 September, the day Great Britain declared war on Germany. It never arrived. There is (or used to be) a plaque commemorating Winton's "unique rescue mission . . . which has no parallel in modern history" in the café of the Grand Hotel Evropa, which somehow contrives not to mention the fact that the huge majority of the children Winton rescued were Jewish.[154] Marie Schmolková also escaped to London in 1939, where she died of a heart attack less than a year later at the age of forty-six. Tomáš Masaryk's son Jan delivered the eulogy at her funeral at Golders Green Crematorium.[155]

After working for two years in Fabricio Pascha's architectural office in Cairo, Jan Letzel took a position in 1907 in Yokohama as an employee of the German architect George de Lalande. He opened his own practice in Tokyo in partnership with Karel Jan Hora two years later. When Hora returned home to Bohemia in February 1913, Letzel dissolved the partnership and carried on the business alone. He designed at least fifteen completed buildings during his time in Japan, including Sophia University, the German embassy, schools, churches, and hotels, but he was forced to close his architectural office at the end of 1915.[156] Bohemia was still part of Austria-Hungary, with which Japan was at war. Despite being an enemy alien, Jan was able to stay in Tokyo throughout the war, returning to Prague in March 1920. He spent another year in Tokyo in 1922–1923. When he died in Prague on Boxing Day 1925, he was only forty-five years old. Gossip has it that he succumbed to the ravages of syphilis "in the same room in Prague's Institution for the mentally ill [the Bohnice psychiatric hospital] where Czech composer Bedřich Smetana passed away in 1884," allegedly from the same malady.[157] I won't vouch for the accuracy of either claim. Letzel built only one building in Bohemia, the Dvorana pavilion at Mšené-lázně (1905), a spa town twenty-five miles north of Prague. Zdeněk Lukeš describes it as "very much influenced by Oriental architecture . . . a beautiful example of art nouveau."[158] It still stands today.

The same cannot be said for Letzel's work in Japan, little of which survived the great Kanto earthquake and World War II—with one major exception. At 8:15 on the morning of 6 August 1945 the crew of a Boeing B-29 Superfortress bomber, sentimentally named *Enola Gay* after the pilot's mother, dropped Little Boy, the first atomic bomb used in warfare, on the city of Hiroshima. The explosion killed some sixty thousand to eighty thousand people instantly. When those who died later of their injuries or of radiation sickness are included, the final death toll was likely around 135,000. In the city center the empty shell of just one building, the Hiroshima Prefectural Industrial Promotion Hall, withstood the blast, although the 120 people working inside perished immediately. Completed in April 1915, Jan Letzel's three-story brick structure was steel framed with an outer wall of stone and mortar, topped with an oval copper dome. According to Zdeněk Lukeš, it was "designed in the

FIGURE 3.5. Ruins of Jan Letzel's Hiroshima Prefectural Industrial Promotion Hall (1915), known as the Atomic Bomb Dome (Genbaku) after the bombing of Hiroshima on 6 August 1945. Photographer unknown. Creative Commons Attribution—Share Alike 2.0 Generic license.

Viennese style, perhaps influenced by Otto Wagner's Steinhof Church in Vienna."[159] The skeleton remained intact because the bomb detonated almost directly above it, so the force of the blast went straight down. "The relics of this building remained like a ghost that symbolized the catastrophe of that day," said Shinzo Hamai, mayor of Hiroshima from 1947 to 1967.[160] There were long debates over what to do with Genbaku, or the Atomic Bomb Dome, as Letzel's building was popularly known. In 1966 the Hiroshima city assembly decided to preserve the ruin as a monument and a reminder. With supreme irony, Peace Memorial Park was built by clearing out the residents of what was "notoriously labeled the 'Genbaku (atom bomb) slum,' [which] existed . . . in the 1950s and the early 1960s. This slum district, shaped by illegal and temporary housing," writes Tomoko Ichitani, "was inhabited by people who were the economically disadvantaged, those who had lost their houses and land due to the atomic bomb and had been excluded from the city's housing projects." Many were Koreans who had moved to Hiroshima under Japan's colonial rule.[161] Sanitized and shorn of its human connections with the 1945 disaster, Genbaku was declared a UNESCO World Heritage Site in December 1996.

Everyone knows what Genbaku looks like. Far fewer are aware of its Czech connection. The last trace of the last act of a world war that claimed the lives of between sixty million and eighty-five million people—figures are always a little uncertain in such matters—the Atomic Bomb Dome seems an appropriate image to keep in mind as we return to Prague on the night of 14–15 March 1939. That was when, for the Czechs, World War II began. The first non-German-speaking European capital to be occupied by Hitler's armies, Prague would also be the last to be liberated from Nazi rule, a day after America celebrated VE Day, on 9 May 1945.

4

But Miss, We Can't Help It

The question needs to be asked over and over again: what follows from, and happens by order of, orders and proscriptions? How does the community, and how does the individual, deal with the predicament at hand?

—H. G. ADLER[1]

The Last Train Out

At the end of 1938 Tomáš Masaryk's son Jan was exiled in London, where he had served as Czechoslovak ambassador until resigning in protest at his country's being "subjected to what someone called the other day an experiment in vivisection." He gave a number of talks on American radio. "You will see things happening in my little country diametrically opposed to everything my father stood for and I humbly but proudly stand for today," he warned. "And I beg of you to understand it. My people were terribly hurt. They were suddenly told, with very little ceremony, that they must shut up and give up. Otherwise—it was a terrible otherwise. . . . This is another job for the historians. I am not really complaining. I am just trying to explain in simple words what went on in the heart of the simple Czech and Slovak, man and woman, who trusted their allies and their friends and quite suddenly found themselves alone, bereft and destitute in a blizzard of harshness."[2] The tawdry little Munich Agreement, touted as ensuring "peace for our time" at Czechoslovakia's expense, opened the door to the abyss, the void at the core of things.

For Max Brod and his wife Elsa, Munich was the last straw. That was when they decided to move to Palestine (which was administered by Britain under a League of Nations mandate), along with several friends. They saw no need to hurry because they were still "naïve enough" to believe Hitler's assurances that once the Sudetenland question was settled, the Führer had no desire to extend his rule over "a single Czech." Though Prague Jews were already subjected to "absurd anomalies," such as Brod being banned from reviewing German plays, "not one of us believed we were in any immediate danger."[3] A surviving letter to Albert Einstein dated 30 November 1938 suggests that whatever Max may have remembered two decades later, Palestine was not his preferred destination at the time. Brod knew Einstein from gatherings at Berta Fanta's salon back in 1911. "My position here becomes more intolerable from day to day," Max wrote to the physicist, who was safely ensconced at the Institute for Advanced Study in Princeton. "I can no longer write what I think . . . I also feel myself immediately threatened. . . . So, e.g., yesterday the *Völkischer Beobachter* carried a large open attack on me, with a photograph. The occasion was offered by certain erotic passages from my youthful works written decades ago." Of course. "I have decided to emigrate to America while there is still time," he continued. "I would bring all of the still unpublished manuscripts of Franz Kafka with me, edit them there, and establish a Kafka archive."[4] There is no record of any response on Einstein's part.

Max and Elsa applied to the Czecho-Slovak government for permission to emigrate and to the British authorities for visas allowing them to enter Palestine. "Exactly as in Kafka's *Castle*," Max says, "the world was an unending series of obstacles. We had to complete very long, accurate inventories in five or ten copies; questionnaires containing a host of important and less important questions; the investigating officials took particular interest, for example, in the amount of silver cutlery applicants had and wanted to take with them. Only the amount? Also the exact weight. Finally I had to submit confirmation, stamped by such and such an office, that I didn't owe any taxes for dogs. I never had a dog." Brod's reference to *The Castle* is not gratuitous; this was the typical experience of European Jews seeking to emigrate at a time when (in the words of H. G. Adler's monumental study of the Terezín concentration camp) "cumbersome state bureaucracies, as well as public and private institutions, no longer dealt with actual people but treated individuals as inventoried items represented by file cards."[5] In the end, Max managed to assemble the requisite Czech documentation. The British authorities proved a harder nut to crack. After much procrastination, an embassy official left for London and returned with "an expensive piece of paper" that, despite a last-minute hitch, finally found its way to the Brods. It arrived just in time. "On the night when the Germans occupied the remnant of Czechoslovakia," Max continues, "we miraculously fled our old country on the last train to depart from a free territory."[6]

Max and Elsa arrived at Wilson Station (until 1919, Francis Joseph Station and now Prague Main Station) at nine o'clock on the evening of 14 March 1939, a Tuesday. Kafka's manuscripts accompanied them: "journals, travel diaries, rough drafts, fair copies, sketches, hundreds of letters, and thin black notebooks in which Kafka earnestly practiced his Hebrew."[7] Many of the friends who came to see them off at the station expected to follow in the coming days and weeks, and they all looked forward to a reunion in Palestine. On the train were 160 Jewish families, mostly refugees from the Sudetenland, including many children. The Brods shared a compartment with Felix Weltch and his wife Irma. Everyone knew by then that Slovakia had declared independence earlier in the day and that Czecho-Slovak president Emil Hácha was in Berlin, but they expected Hitler to demand no more than the firing of the remaining liberal members of Rudolf Beran's government or, at worst, its replacement by an administration of Czech fascists. A rumor that the Germans were already in Ostrava was met with outright disbelief. The train left the station at eleven o'clock. It was a five-hour journey to the border. Max was sufficiently at ease (or should we say in denial?) to sleep all the way.

In Ostrava the Brods had to move from their sleeping car to a regular coach. As they climbed the steps of the railcar, a young lad emerged, looking like "some sort of scout." He wore a swastika armband. Max, who "had seen more than enough swastikas in Prague the previous Sunday" at a pro-German demonstration, thought little of it. Once he was seated in his compartment, he looked out the window into the station:

> Ten steps from me stood a soldier with a swastika in full combat gear, a helmet on his head, a rifle with a bayonet at his side. Astonishingly, even this didn't strike me as in any way catastrophic. That Ostrava or at least the station was already in the hands of the German army didn't occur to me even in my dreams.—The soldier stood and didn't move. Like a statue of a Roman legionary, very handsome when all is said and done. Young, energetic, eager features in a face that brought to mind Julius Caesar's troops in Gaul or the warriors on Trajan columns.
>
> In the station hall, along the tracks—groups of similar armed men. Even at this moment I still had not grasped the gravity of the situation.
>
> It is hard to explain why this sight did not fill me with horror. Maybe it was because I was so tired and daydreaming, half-asleep—or perhaps it was

because this young soldier a few steps away from me was such a fine human specimen. It is my old mistake: beauty in every form always cast a spell on me and many times in my life it brought me to the brink of ruin.[8]

This surely qualifies as one of Humphrey Jennings's small images that contain a whole world. Multiple pasts came together with the here and now in this strange encounter between a German soldier and a Jewish refugee on the Moravian-Polish border at four o'clock on a Wednesday morning in March 1939, crystalizing in a moment of extreme danger.[9]

The "distant love" Brod felt for German culture was deep. Its roots went back generations, at least to Joseph II's emancipation of the Jews in the 1780s. But from the Nazis' point of view, Max was a doubly poor human specimen. In addition to being Jewish, a racial *Untermensch*, he was a *cripple*, having suffered severe curvature of the spine (kyphosis) in childhood.[10] Yet here Max was, his wife by his side, fleeing the city where his family had lived for generations with nothing more than the clothes on his back and a suitcase full of Franz Kafka's manuscripts, captivated by the Aryan beauty of a young German soldier. The supposed link between classical antiquity and the Third Reich was, of course, a staple of Nazi ideology. This utterly specious genealogy is beautifully constructed (I choose my words advisedly) in the opening scenes of Leni Riefenstahl's *Olympia*, in which perfect young, white, athletic bodies carry the Olympic torch from ancient Olympia to modern Berlin—a film that would have its ceremonial première on 14 April 1939 at one of Prague's oldest movie houses, the cinema in the Lucerna Palace built by Václav Havel's grandfather in 1911. The torch relay, which has since become a familiar feature of every modern Olympics, originated at the 1936 Berlin Olympic Games as an exercise in Nazi racist propaganda. "Beauty is truth, truth beauty,—that is all / Ye know on earth, and all ye need to know," wrote John Keats in a youthful flush of romantic enthusiasm in 1819.[11] Brod, who was well acquainted with Prague's whorehouses, should have known better.

Czech customs officers woke him from the spell. Hurrying through the train, they weren't bothering to inspect the passengers' documents or luggage, despite the detailed inventories émigrés had been required to provide the authorities in Prague. "This unaccustomed official liberality," Max writes, "contributed in no small measure to our salvation. A few minutes later the train started rolling with a hiss, a few minutes after that we left Czech territory, which was already now German-occupied, and sped through free Poland." An hour later they pulled into Krakow. That morning the Gestapo raided the

Prague offices of the Jewish weekly *Selbstwehr*, in which Brod and Felix Weltsch, the paper's chief editor, had published "many articles against the new barbarism in Germany," only to be told that both men had left the night before. From then on, Max says, he looked at life as a gift: "By rights, I shouldn't be living any longer. By rights, I was executed long ago." He lived another thirty years. From Poland the Brods traveled across Galicia to Constanța in Romania, where they embarked on a long sea voyage through the Dardanelles to Piraeus and along the southern coast of Crete to Tel Aviv. Fittingly, perhaps, they said their farewells to "a shattered and devastated Europe" at the Acropolis in Athens, the supposed cradle of Western democracy.[12] Elsa died in 1942. Max spent the rest of his days in Israel, returning to Prague only once for the publication of his book *Der Prager Kreis* (The Prague circle) in 1966. He died in Tel Aviv on 20 December 1968, living just long enough to watch on TV as the tanks of another occupying army rumbled into his beloved but long-abandoned hometown.

In Israel Brod made his living as a critic and a dramaturg at the Habima Theater, originally founded by Nachum Zemach and the actors Hannah Rovina and Menachem Gnessin in Moscow in 1917. The company left the Soviet Union in 1926 because of the Communist Party's increasing hostility toward Zionism and toured in Europe and North America before settling in Tel Aviv in 1931. Habima became the National Theater of Israel in 1958.[13] One of Habima's early productions (1924), when the theater was still based in Moscow, was H. Leivick's *The Golem*, a "dramatic poem in eight scenes" based on the legend of Rabbi Löw, the Maharal of Prague, who constructed a clay servant to protect the Jewish community during the time of Emperor Rudolf II. One night the golem went berserk, rampaging through the ghetto. The Austrian writer Gustav Meyrink, who moved to Prague as a teenager in 1883 and lived there for the next twenty years, tackled the same subject in his popular 1914 novel of the same title, which prompted Franz Kafka's ruminations on "the ghetto within us" quoted earlier.[14] H. Leivick was the pseudonym of Leivick Halpern, a Belorussian Yiddish writer and member of the Jewish Social-Democratic Bund who was arrested for distributing revolutionary literature in 1906. After serving four years in tsarist prisons and labor camps, Leivick was exiled to Siberia, whence he eventually escaped and sailed to America in 1913. He wrote *The Golem* in 1921 while working as a wallpaper hanger in New York. Members of the Habima company, writes Alisa Solomon, "saw the play as an allegory addressing their own dilemma in newly Soviet Russia: Was the revolution a promising new beginning or an apocalypse? Had the Bolsheviks created a monster?" For Solomon, the play's "central concern is the self-destructive consequence of Jews resorting to violence to defend themselves."[15]

The ethical challenge posed by the legend of the Prague golem is hardly just a Jewish dilemma. The specter of humanity's awesome creations escaping human control and turning on their makers has haunted the literature of modernity from Mary Shelley's *Frankenstein*—written in 1818, a year before Keats's juvenile coupling of beauty and truth in his "Ode on a Grecian Urn"— to Karel Čapek's *R.U.R.* and beyond. Perhaps not surprisingly, some of the best later contributions to the genre have come from Japan. Rintaro's 2002 anime film *Metropolis*, a "wild elaboration" of Fritz Lang's 1926 expressionist classic, not only "asks whether a machine can love" but also stages the debate "within Tima [the movie's heroine] herself, between her human and robotic natures."[16] When Leivick's *The Golem* was staged at the New York Shakespeare Festival in 1984, another novelist writing in Yiddish hailed it as "a myth for our time." Memories of how World War II had ended were likely fresher then. "The resemblance of this golem to the golems of our nuclear age," wrote Nobel Prize winner Isaac Bashevis Singer, "staggers the imagination":

> While we attempt to surpass our enemies and to create new and more destructive golems, the awful possibility is lurking that they may develop a volition of their own, become spiteful, treacherous, mad golems. Like the Jews of Prague in the sixteenth century we are frightened by our golems. We would like to be in a position to erase the uncanny power we have given them, hide them in some monstrous attic and wait for the time when they too will become fiction and folklore.
>
> Can we actually do it? Do we possess enough free will to make a decision of this immensity? Will Satan and his host of devils and demons let it happen? This is the golem drama of our epoch.[17]

15 March 1939

When sixty-seven-year-old Emil Hácha arrived in Berlin shortly before midnight on 14 March 1939, he was kept waiting for over an hour before being ushered into Hitler's presence at the Reich Chancellery. Threatened with the annihilation of Prague by the Luftwaffe ("It would pain me enormously to have to destroy that beautiful city," purred Hermann Göring), Hácha signed a document affirming that he "confidently placed the fate of the Czech people and country in the hands of the Führer and the German Reich." "The nation didn't sign it," he told the writer Karel Horký a month later, "only, understand me, an unfortunate individual, only this unhappy Hácha. And so it happens, that this isn't for us a blemish of historic proportions. . . . [It is] only a personal blemish." "And still, as you know," he went on, "Saint Wenceslas is still standing in its place, Charles Bridge is standing, too, the Castle district was not blown 'into the air' and hundreds of thousands of our young people are still breathing and living."[18] The same fear of sacrificing his capital city and his nation in a war he could not possibly win had weighed heavily on Edvard Beneš six months earlier. "It became clear to me that France and England had decided, literally, to sacrifice us and that we were, from that moment, standing alone," he wrote. "War under these circumstances (we cannot fight alone), with greater probability, will bring about more destruction . . . than the postponement of the conflict to another more propitious time."[19] "Look, isn't she beautiful, the only unspoiled city in Central Europe, and all my doing," the restored president boasted to A. J. P. Taylor when the British historian visited him in Hradčany in 1946. "By accepting the Munich settlement," Beneš explained, "I saved Prague and my people from destruction."[20] Though it is not popular to say so, both men were probably right. But their capitulation came with costs.

After telephoning orders to Czech troops not to resist the German advance, Hácha spoke on Czech Radio at 4:30 a.m., appealing to the population to remain calm. The Wehrmacht took over Bohemia and Moravia, firing hardly a shot. The Gestapo got busy from day one, taking more than forty-six hundred communists, German refugees, and other enemies of the Reich into custody. They even arrested seventy-eight-year-old painter Alfons Mucha, though he was soon released. Mucha is best known in the West for the art nouveau posters he created in fin de siècle Paris.[21] The ordeal did nothing for the old man's health. He died within months and was buried in Vyšehrad Cemetery on 19 July 1939, alongside Božena Němcová, Bedřich Smetana, Antonín Dvořák, Karel Čapek, and other great Czech writers, artists, and musicians.[22] Čapek passed away on Christmas Day 1938 at age forty-eight. To the cosmopolitan author of *Francouzská poesie nové doby* (Modern French poetry, 1920), an anthology of his own translations of French poets from Baudelaire to Soupault,[23] not to mention the affectionate *Anglické listy* (*Letters from England*, 1924),[24] the Munich Agreement represented a betrayal of everything the West stood for. Poor Karel was condemned to remain hopeful until the moment it all finished in despair. It was not a good omen for the new year. "Outside it began to snow, and a bluish-white shadow settled into [Čapek's] room," reported Milena Jesenská. "He didn't fight. He didn't wrestle. He didn't struggle. He just stopped breathing and he just stopped living. If you want, you can believe that he died of bronchitis and pneumonia."[25]

"How do the greatest events occur?" Milena asks at the start of "Prague, the Morning of 15 March 1939," which was published in *Přítomnost* on 22 March, a week after the invasion. "Unexpectedly and suddenly," she answers. "Yet when they are here, we always find that *we are not* surprised. There is always some presentiment and knowledge within us of things to come, which is only drowned out by reason, will, desire, fear, hurry, and work. As soon as the soul of a person is left naked for a moment and freed of everything outside its uncanny feelings, it suddenly realizes: I knew it." Around the time Max Brod's train was pulling into Ostrava, news of the invasion began to percolate through Prague. "When the telephone rang at four in the morning, when friends and acquaintances called, when Czech Radio began to broadcast, the city beneath our windows looked like any other night. . . . Only, from 3.00 a.m. lights gradually began to come on: at the neighbors, opposite, down, up, then along the entire street. . . . That bleary daybreak over the roofs, the pale moon under the clouds, people's sleepless faces, mugs of hot coffee and the regular announcements on the radio. That's how great events come to people: quietly and out of the blue." These are the moments that make the situation of humanity suddenly and unexpectedly clear. Parting the veils of normality, they expose the void at the core of things, leaving us to make order out of the fragments that lie about us and find in them such beauty as we may.

"As always when great events are happening, the Czechs comported themselves superbly," Milena continues. Maybe so. But what she describes might have come straight out of a Samuel Beckett play. When the world around you loses its moorings and everything turns unreal overnight, what else is there to do but carry on as if nothing out of the ordinary had happened? "The German army is progressing from the borders to Prague," the radio reported, updating its bulletins every five minutes. "Keep calm. Go to work. Send the children to school."

At 7.30 in the morning a horde of children set off for school, as always. Workers and clerks left for work, as always. The trams were full, as always. Only the people were different. They stood and remained silent. I never heard so many people remain silent. Nobody was gathering in the streets. People weren't discussing things at all. In the offices they didn't even raise their heads from their desks. I don't know where this unified and unanimous behavior of thousands came from, whence this identical rhythm of so many souls unknown to one another sprang: at 9.35 in the morning on 15 March 1939 the army of the German Reich reached Národní Avenue. On the sidewalks there were throngs of people, as always. Nobody gaped, nobody turned to look. The German population of Prague welcomed the Reich soldiers.

Jesenská's first report from the occupied city is a series of brief, incoherent, disconnected vignettes. A German soldier comforts a crying Czech girl with the words "*Aber Fräulein, wir können doch nichts dafür . . . !*" (But Miss, we can't help it). "And in this simple, horribly ordinary sentence," Milena comments, "lies the key to everything." A German officer berates a Czech youth *in Czech* for his lack of national pride in wearing a swastika armband. Other Czechs fall over themselves to greet German officials with a hearty "Heil Hitler!" A Czech playwright can't wait to see his plays staged in Berlin.

A day or two later people begin to lay bunches of snowdrops at the Tomb of the Unknown Soldier in the Old Town Hall on the Old Town Square. Women, children, even grown men have tears running down their cheeks. A German soldier passes behind the crowd, stops, and salutes. "He looked at the eyes red with crying, the teardrops, the snow-covered mountains of snowdrops, he saw the crying people, people who were crying because he was here. And he saluted. Evidently he understood why we were sad," Milena continues. A film leapt into her mind—a film directed by Jean Renoir she had seen with her daughter Honza, prompting the girl to ask what war was, what honor was, what human decency was, and why it was all an illusion. "Watching him as he went," Milena says, "I thought about *La grande illusion*: will we ever really someday live side by side—German, Czech, French, Russian, English— without injuring one another, without having to hate one another, without inflicting mutual injustices upon one another? Will states really someday understand one another as individuals do? Will the borders between countries one day fall as they do in people's relationships? How beautiful it would be to live to see it!"[26] She didn't, of course. Nobody ever has. But in its own rational, modernist way, this is as eloquent an image as Max Brod's unsettling encounter with Aryan beauty in the Ostrava station. It is difficult to say which is more absurd: the German soldier saluting the weeping Czechs at the Tomb of the Unknown Soldier—which belongs in the grand pantheon of kitsch beside the legendary football game between British and German troops in no-man's-land on Christmas Day 1914 (after which they resumed slaughtering each other)— or the idea that peace on earth and goodwill toward all men could ever be

FIGURE 4.1. Poster by KNR (Miroslav Kouřil, Jiří Novotný, and Josef Raban),
for E. F. Burian's production of Jaroslav Hašek's *The Good Soldier Švejk* at
D 35 Theater, 1935. From Josef Kroutvor, *Poselství ulice*, Prague, 1991.

more than a grand illusion, fit only for small children and contestants in beauty
pageants. All the same, it is difficult *not* to be moved, as Milena was, by the
pathos of the situation. Nothing fuels the longing for kitsch quite like the di-
sasters of war.

The Czechs were less susceptible than many to the blandishments of what
Wilfred Owen, writing in the killing fields of World War I, called "The old Lie:
Dulce et decorum est / Pro patria mori."[27] Neither their geography—an exposed
Slavic promontory in a Germanic sea—nor their history, which since 1526 had
consisted largely of being ruled by others, encouraged a romantic view of war.
This is the homeland of the good soldier Švejk, the *malý český člověk* (little
Czech guy) whose main objective in life is to keep his head down and survive
whatever latest absurdities history sends his way long enough to sink a few
more beers. This is not meant to malign Czechs as a nation of cowards: we shall
see some extraordinary acts of courage in the pages that follow. Rather, the
point is to highlight the existential situation out of which Švejk can emerge as
a national antihero in the first place. Jaroslav Hašek's less-than-flattering

portrait of his fictitious countryman scandalized nationalistic Czechs when the first volume of *The Good Soldier Švejk* appeared in 1921.[28] "This is a literature only for communists and not for the *český člověk*," thundered the bookseller E. Weinfurter, who would not sully his firm's good name by carrying such "scurrilous literature."[29] Ivan Olbracht, by contrast, hailed Hašek's satire as "one of the best books ever written in Czech. . . . Švejk is a quite new type in world literature," he argued—"a clever idiot, perhaps a genius idiot, who through his stupid but crafty good nature must always win, since it's not possible for him to lose. That's Švejk." We would not find Švejk so funny, he added, "if Švejkery [*švejkovina*] were not a part—bigger, smaller, it doesn't matter—of us all, just as Don Quixote, Hamlet, Faust, Oblomov, and [the brothers] Karamazov are."[30] Posterity has sided with Olbracht. That *The Good Soldier Švejk* has been translated into more than fifty languages suggests its themes have more than merely local relevance. It is one of the great antiwar novels, right up there with *All Quiet on the Western Front, Catch-22,* and *Slaughterhouse-Five,* and like Franz Kafka's writings, it was a harbinger of the theater of the absurd. As it happens, the first translation was by Max Brod into German: an extract from chapter 1 appeared in *Prager Tagblatt* on 5 January 1923, two days after Hašek's death.[31] Brod's later dramatization of the novel, staged by Erwin Piscator in Berlin in January 1928, led to an infamous blasphemy trial. At issue were three woodcuts by Dadaist George Grosz in a publicity brochure for the production published by Wieland Herzfelde's firm Malik-Verlag. One depicted Christ on the cross wearing a gas mask. The trial ended in November 1931 with Grosz's and Herzfelde's acquittal.[32] A little over a year later, both would flee Germany, Grosz to New York and Herzfelde to Prague, where Malik-Verlag resumed operations in exile, publishing not only books but also the émigré version of *Arbeiter-Illustrierte-Zeitung* (Workers' illustrated news) edited by F. C. Weiskopf.[33]

Half a century and another invasion later, Milan Kundera reflected on the same Czech existential situation. His subject was not Švejk but Leoš Janáček. By then, Janáček had found worldwide acclaim as perhaps the greatest operatic composer of the twentieth century, but he was little understood by his compatriots during his lifetime. Janáček, too, owed his international fame in no small measure to Max Brod, who translated his librettos into German. Milan's father Ludvík Kundera was a well-known pianist, musicologist, and rector of Janáčkova akademie múzických umění (JAMU), the Brno music academy that bears Janáček's name. "Knowing no other musical gods but Smetana, nor other laws than the Smetanesque, the national ideologues were irritated by

[Janáček's] otherness," Kundera sneers. "A small nation resembles a big family and likes to describe itself that way," and "everything and everyone (critics, historians, compatriots as well as foreigners) hooks the art onto the great national family portrait and will not let it get away." In Janáček's case, years of being ostracized for his modernist dissonance grudgingly gave way to a "maternal indulgence" that "tears him out of the context of modern music and immures him in local concerns: passion for folklore, Moravian patriotism, admiration for Woman, for Nature, for Russia, for Slavitude, and other nonsense." Kundera's own artistic loyalties lie squarely with Janáček's modernism. But he understands exactly where the circling of the wagons comes from:

> Small nations. The concept is not quantitative; it describes a situation; a destiny: small nations haven't the comfortable sense of being there always, past and future; they have all, at some point or another in their history, passed through the antechamber of death; always faced with the arrogant ignorance of the large nations, they see their existence perpetually threatened or called into question; for their very existence *is* a question.[34]

Smetanesque

Adolf Hitler arrived at Prague Castle, where the swastika was already fluttering, at 7:15 on the evening of 15 March 1939. He had traveled by car from Česká Lípa. Hácha arrived home later on the train from Berlin. Accompanying Hitler were SS-Obergruppenführer Reinhard Heydrich, second only to Heinrich Himmler in the hierarchy of the Reich's state security apparatus, and Karl Hermann Frank, a Sudeten German who had been deputy leader of Konrad Henlein's SdP and was now Henlein's deputy as gauleiter of the Sudetenland. Both men would become key players in the Nazis' rule of Czech territories. That night, in the thousand-year-old seat of Bohemian governance, Hitler met with Nazi leaders, including Heydrich, Himmler, foreign minister Joachim von Ribbentrop, and Wilhelm Stuckart, state secretary of the Interior Ministry (and author of the Nazi program of euthanizing "defective" children at birth). The establishment of the Protectorate of Bohemia and Moravia was proclaimed at 11:00 a.m. the next day. In the afternoon delirious crowds of Bohemian Germans flocked to Hradčany to salute Hitler, and the Führer greeted uniformed German students assembled in the courtyard in the presence of Heydrich and Himmler.[35] Hitler left the city for Vienna soon after, parading through Olomouc and Brno en route. It was his only visit to the Bohemian capital. Before he departed, Hitler had himself photographed gazing out a window of the castle overlooking the Lesser Town. It found its way onto a protectorate postage stamp marking his fifty-fourth birthday in 1943.

The proclamation of 16 March 1939 began by asserting that Bohemia and Moravia had "belonged to the living space of the German nation for a thousand years" before being "ripped out of their ancient historical surroundings" and incorporated into "the artificial configuration of Czecho-Slovakia."[36] Unlike the nominally independent Slovakia, the protectorate would be an integral part of the German Reich. Bohemian Germans became German citizens. "Other inhabitants of Bohemia and Moravia" became subjects of the protectorate, which was nominally an "autonomous and self-governing" jurisdiction with its own "organs, offices, and officials." The Reich could nevertheless legislate for the protectorate and take over any area of administration that was deemed to be in the "common interest." Defense and foreign policy were matters for Berlin, and officials answered directly to Germany on issues involving transportation, posts, and telecommunications. War industries fell under the authority of Hermann Göring's Economic Ministry. The security services were a law unto themselves, reporting to state secretary (his new title) Karl Hermann Frank in Prague and through him to Reinhard Heydrich in Berlin. Supreme authority within the protectorate lay with the Reich protector for Bohemia and Moravia, who had the power to approve (or revoke) all laws and appointments made by the protectorate government, as well as to override court judgments and legislate by decree where necessary. The first protector was former German foreign minister Konstantin von Neurath, who was by Nazi standards (and in Joseph Goebbels's words) a "soft-pedaler."[37] Though Prague Castle remained the official seat of "state president" Emil Hácha, Neurath also had quarters there. The Reich Protectorate Office was located just up the road in Černín Palace on Loretánské Square, formerly the seat of the Czechoslovak Foreign Ministry. The Czechs continued to run their own police, courts, and other services, but every Czech department was supervised by its counterpart within the Protectorate Office.

The Czechs retained a space for political representation, even though it was largely symbolic, far from democratic, and thoroughly compromised by the requirement that the protectorate government operate "in accordance with the political, military, and economic needs of the Reich."[38] On 17 March Hácha persuaded Rudolf Beran and Antonín Hampl, leaders of the National Unity Party and the National Party of Labor, to merge their parties into Národní souručenství (National Solidarity, or NS),[39] which became the only Czech political organization permitted within the protectorate. NS was closely modeled on Nazi ideology, with Hácha as its "Führer" (*vůdce* in Czech)—a somewhat improbable role for the scholarly old jurist (and translator of Rudyard Kipling's "If" and Jerome K. Jerome's *Three Men in a Boat*). Hácha had stumbled into the presidency not out of political ambition but because, in the post-Munich chaos, he was widely seen as being above politics. The national assembly and the Senate were dissolved on 21 March 1939, and NS had its first meeting the same day. A week later Beran's government resigned, and a new administration was established under former army general Alois Eliáš. Hácha and Eliáš successfully rebuffed Czech fascist leader Radola Gayda's demands for the creation of a Czech fascist government and "Čestapo" secret police. Both men would try to intercede with the German authorities on numerous issues over the next two years, mostly in vain. Eliáš continued to maintain clandestine contact with the exiled Edvard Beneš and the Czechoslovak resistance abroad. Although these institutions allowed for some articulation of Czech interests, the price was de facto collaboration with Germany. To most people it seemed there was no choice.

National Solidarity was open to all Czech males—women and Jews were excluded—over the age of twenty-one, and a mass recruitment drive was launched. An astonishing 97.5 percent of those eligible, more than two million men, joined. At the end of April a member of the Politické ústředí (political center) resistance group, formed by Beneš's secretary Prokop Drtina and other first republic politicians, informed Czechoslovak exiles in London: "While the German authorities at the beginning supported National Solidarity and even publicized it . . . [they] have now turned sharply against the NS. What provoked this about-face was the fact that . . . [in] the cities with a large Czech majority . . . Czechs unanimously and spontaneously signed up under the NS banner to manifest their Czech national feeling [*češství*]. Everybody there joined up, even those who had ideological or other reservations about NS."[40] Emblazoned above the letters *NS* on National Solidarity's badge was the motto *Vlasti zdar!* (Success to the homeland!). The slogan echoed Sokol's greeting *Nazdar!* whose origins lay in the nineteenth-century campaign to establish a Czech National Theater (*Na zdar Národního divadla!*). Some brave souls, it is said, wore their badges upside-down to read *SN*, signifying *smrt Němcům*—death to Germans. Or maybe that is just retrospective wishful thinking.

The times made for some unlikely bedfellows. Notwithstanding Ferdinand Peroutka's blunt assessment that "in place of the former democratic Czech system a Czech totalitarian regime has been enthroned," *Přítomnost* threw its

FIGURE 4.2. Adolf Hitler looking out the window of Prague
Castle, 16 March 1939. Photographer unknown. © ČTK.

liberal weight behind National Solidarity.[41] Peroutka was arrested immediately
after the invasion but was released a few days later. Thereafter Milena Jesenská
became the magazine's de facto editor, even though Peroutka's name stayed
on the masthead.[42] Maintaining (not unreasonably) that "the situation of the
Czech nation changed more fundamentally on 15 March 1929 than it did on
29 October 1918," an editorial in the first postinvasion issue argued that "the
interests of the Czech nation must be represented, defended—and as far as
possible decided—by a single representative, a single party, a single organization . . . to preserve the unity of the nation, to strengthen it politically,

economically, culturally, and morally."[43] Multiparty democracy, Peroutka contended in his *Lidové noviny* column a month later, was a "luxurious bonus of a comfortable and secure life.... Hardly anyone among us," he warned, "can think they live in a time in which the heritage we have received from our ancestors is not at risk ... the point of National Solidarity is **to establish a Czech national organization alongside the German national organization.**"[44]

The title of the article, "Jsme Češi" (We are Czechs), immediately brought to mind Peroutka's 1924 book *Jací jsme?* (What are we like?), while sharply departing from its content. How better to signify how much times had changed? *What Are We Like?* began life as a series of *Tribuna* articles in 1922–1924 debunking popular myths about the Czech national character. "We have always contented ourselves," Peroutka wrote back then, "with the adage that we are the nation of Hus and Komenský [Comenius]. If we want to show some visiting foreigner what we are like, we show him the museum or take him to Slovakia or Chodsko, where we show him national costumes that people only nowadays wear for festivals and dances to the sound of bagpipes that are no less peculiar to us than they are to our guest. If we start to talk about manifestations of the Czech spirit in art, we always speak only of Božena Němcová, [Josef] Mánes, Aleš and Smetana. To the outside observer, it could appear from this that the Czech spirit in its entirety is already lying in Vyšehrad Cemetery." But "a modern sociologist ... who has already stopped imagining Bohemia, even when he is sitting under a rustling lime-tree, must look at the living, present nation around him, how it flows through the streets, works in the factories, buys, sells, and enjoys itself. We must get used to seeking the nation in ourselves and not in Smetana's operas."[45]

That was then. This was now. Taking issue with *Der neue Tag* (The new day) in May 1939 over the "fake pathos" the new German daily claimed Czech politicians were whipping up in the wake of the invasion,[46] Peroutka argues that German national socialists, of all people, should recognize that "nations, like individuals, cannot live by bread alone ... for although national socialist teaching has plenty to say about national bread, it always talks a lot more about national spirit and national feeling." Is it any wonder, he asks, "that at this crossroads of our history we act with a little solemnity? That taking the thread of national life into our hands more anxiously now than ever, we assiduously cultivate everything that links us to past generations, wanting it to be more timeless and enduring than a swarm of flies in autumn? That we bury our dead poets with great pomp and circumstance and tenderly lay flowers at the monuments of our great dead?"[47] Peroutka's reference to burying dead poets was

literal. After Munich the remains of Karel Hynek Mácha, author of the romantic epic *Máj* (May, 1836), were exhumed from Litoměřice in the Sudetenland,
where the poet had been buried in a pauper's grave in 1836, and brought back
to Prague. An estimated seventy thousand people filed by Mácha's coffin as he
lay in state in the pantheon of the National Museum on 6 May 1939, after which
his relics were taken in procession to Vyšehrad Cemetery. Thousands lined the
streets. Mácha's second funeral took place the next day. "Perhaps half Prague
came to Vyšehrad on Sunday to pay their respects at the poet's simple oak
coffin," reported *Lidové noviny*.[48]

The problem with this line of argument is that the conception of nationality
invoked by Peroutka was dangerously close to the Nazis' own. The Czech nation of which he speaks is not the "living, present nation" whose "national
character," he argued back in 1922, embraced the whole panoply of "our most
modern political history, with the difficulties of our exports and the helpless-
ness of our parliament, with our half-million-strong communist party, with
our nationalism and our pacifists . . . with the adventures of our foreign representatives abroad and the adventures of foreigners in our hotels." When the
chips are down Peroutka falls back on exactly the same "mystical nation" he
derided in *What Are We Like?*—the community of the dead, the living, and
the unborn that is timelessly rooted in blood, soil, and language.[49] The
imagined community around which the wagons were circling in the spring and
summer of 1939 was not the multiethnic Czechoslovakia championed by
Tomáš Masaryk or the Čapek brothers—and indeed, by Peroutka himself.[50]
Still less did the nation coalesce around the bright modernist visions of Milena
Jesenská and her avant-garde Prague friends. Milena herself hit peak sentimentality in her 1939 articles, conjuring up image after clichéd image of down-
home Czechness.[51] "People are returning with self-respect and pride to everything that is Czech," she assured *Přítomnost*'s readers. "They wander the streets
of Prague, Hradčany, the old gardens, they look at the city and sketch the curve
of the roofs in their mind's eye with different feelings than they did a month
ago. They strew flowers over the graves of our luminaries, they carry a Czech
book in their hand, they discuss Czech history with one another. Yesterday
this love was a quiet, steady fire, undisturbed by the wind. But today its flame
begins to grow. Our task is to make sure it doesn't weaken."[52] A more jaundiced
observer might detect a nightmare of eternal return, in which the dream of
modernity is just another fashion.

People decorated their houses with red, white, and blue—the colors of the
Czechoslovak flag—and sang patriotic songs in restaurants, pubs, and wine

bars, a practice the German authorities soon banned. Smetana's *Má vlast* (*My Homeland*, 1874–1879), Dvořák's *Slavonic Dances*, and other Czech classics played to full houses over nine evenings at the Prague Musical May Festival (all of which were broadcast), organized by the conductor Václav Talich at the National Theater. This would later give rise to a new tradition: *My Homeland* has opened the Prague Spring International Music Festival every year since 1952. Palacký's *History*, Němcová's *The Grandmother*, Neruda's *Prague Tales*, and other literary totems of Czechness were reprinted in large editions and prominently displayed in booksellers' windows. "Literature," wrote Peroutka, "is almost as much for us now as the Siegfried or Maginot Lines are for other nations. We have old national experience in this sort of work: a hundred years ago Jungmann's dictionary meant as much to us as a victorious battle."[53] Contemporary writers stepped up to the plate. Vladislav Vančura put his modernist literary skills to new use in his *Obrazy z dějin národa českého* (Pictures from the history of the Czech nation), creating "a unique epic world."[54] Though his medium remained modernist, his subject matter was anything but: the first president of Devětsil followed in the footsteps of Palacký's *History* and Alois Jirásek's historical novels,[55] tracing the nation's odyssey from its mythical "Old Slav" beginnings to the death of Přemysl Otakar II, the medieval "king of iron and gold" who extended the sway of the Bohemian crown to the shores of the Adriatic. Then Vančura was shot by the Nazis, leaving the story hanging in midsentence. Two new poetry collections, Jaroslav Seifert's *Vějíř Boženy Němcové* (Božena Němcová's fan) and František Halas's *Naše paní Božena Němcová* (Our Lady Božena Němcová), marked the 120th anniversary of Němcová's birth in 1940. Both had strong patriotic overtones and were written in plain everyday Czech. Even Julius Fučík got in on the act with his *Božena Němcová bojující* (Božena Němcová the fighter).

The epitome of hooking art onto the great national family portrait and not letting it get away was the exhibition *Národ svým výtvarným umělcům* (The nation to its artists), which opened on 12 November 1939 at the Municipal House, the Mánes Gallery, and three other Prague venues. Organized by the National Solidarity cultural committee and involving all the major Czech artists' societies, the show lasted a month. Six hundred sixty-two works were on display, and proceeds from the exhibition went to a fund to support the needs of Czech artists. Simultaneous exhibitions took place in eighteen towns and cities across the protectorate, including Brno, Ostrava, Plzeň, Olomouc, and Hradec Králové. In all, 828 artists participated in these events. Miloslav Hýsek, a conservative historian of Moravian literature and Charles University professor who chaired the NS cultural committee throughout the occupation,[56] supplied the preface for the catalog. Hýsek's academic forte was the work of the poet Petr Bezruč, author of *Slezské písně* (Silesian songs, 1899–1909), another Czech classic. Though Bezruč is celebrated in Czech literary history as a social realist, his collection contains a rich seam of anti-Semitism. The two have often gone together in these parts. "A girl, a man, a village, the Jew will buy," runs a line in "*Papírový Mojšl*" (Paper Meuschl). The poem begins with a Jewish beggar arriving in Silesia from Poland. Five years later he owns the village and insists on enjoying his *ius primae noctis* with the local brides. In "*Z Ostravy do Těšína*" (From Ostrava to Těšín), Bezruč runs a gauntlet of "villages full of Jews / foreign tracks, foreign mines . . . foreign churches, foreign schools."[57] Alois Ludvík Salač's grotesque anti-Semitic caricatures in *Slezské jařmo* (The Silesian yoke, 1925), an album of forty illustrations based on motifs in *Silesian Songs*, leave no doubt about how Bezruč's verses were read by his Czech contemporaries.[58]

"The most enduring manifestation of national existence is the national culture," Hýsek explains. "We all know what the fine arts meant in our national development, whose classical representatives Mánes, Myslbek, and Aleš belong among the names most loved by the Czech people; and we know that there are masters among our present-day artists whom the nation long ago took to its heart." It is the public's duty to support them. But now comes the quid pro quo. Everybody smile for the family portrait:

> And it is all the more our duty that everybody presents themselves in this exhibition as part of a united whole, as nothing more and nothing less than purely Czech artists. There is no barrier between them of artistic directions or ideological opinions, such as divided them in the past . . . all are imbued with the awareness that they belong together and go by different routes to a single end, which likewise illuminated Mánes and Smetana and Neruda and which is forever embodied in the name of Smetana's apotheosis *My Homeland*.[59]

And yes, opening the festivities in the Municipal House on 12 November 1939, Professor Hýsek did tell his audience that "the whole of our nation is one big family."[60] Really? Every family has its black sheep, but this show of unity in the service of the homeland was achieved by excluding much that had been central to Czech art over the previous four decades. The majority of the works shown in *The Nation to Its Artists* exemplified "realistic" art, with a preponderance of landscapes, flowers, and portraits of girls—just the kind of healthy, comprehensible stuff the Führer liked. Not a single Devětsil or Czechoslovak Surrealist

FIGURE 4.3. Josef Čapek, *Fire*, 1939, India ink drawing, 44 by 30 cm.
From Jaroslav Slavík, *Josef Čapek*, Prague, 1996.

Group artist participated in the event. One living artist that few would dispute *had* been taken to the nation's heart was conspicuously absent from the national roll call. Josef Čapek was in Buchenwald by then. So was the Osma veteran Emil Filla, though his *Village Lane* and *Landscape* somehow slipped in anyway. That oversight would be rectified by the omission of Filla's name from the list of participating artists in the commemorative catalog published by NS the following year.[61] Dominated by angry or sorrowful female figures, Čapek's powerful series of paintings *Oheň* (Fire) and *Touha* (Longing), completed in 1938–1939, are lamentations for the lost borderlands.

What is most striking about both this exhibition and the "apolitical politics" (as *Přítomnost* called it) of the postinvasion period in general is the sudden disappearance of the progressive modernism that had been such a characteristic feature of the first republic across so many cultural domains. "Horribly much of what we did with such passion during these twenty years was for nothing," wrote Peroutka; "we must reach down and begin again."[62] The reimagining of the national community as it passed through its latest antechamber of death was that of the nineteenth-century national revival—Havlíček's and Neruda's anti-Semitism included. "The bearers [of Czech culture] began to feel like representatives of some suffering Slavic-national [*slovanskonárodní*] cultural folklore of the southeastern corner of the Greater German Reich," wrote the literary critic Václav Černý.[63] This is what prompted Milena Jesenská's sharp cautionary comment quoted earlier: "I am *self-evidently* a Czech, but I try *above all* to be a decent human being." She needed that moral compass. One day Emanuel Moravec, a former legionnaire who would later become a collaborationist minister of education in the protectorate government, showed up at her Kouřimská Street flat, encouraging her to edit an "activist"— that is, pro-Nazi—periodical. "With your capabilities," he told her, "we will put whatever current magazine you want at your disposal! We will make you our new Božena Němcová!"[64] Milena showed him the door.

The Age of the Concentration Camp

Many Czechs viewed the incorporation of Bohemia and Moravia into the Third Reich as a situation their long experience as a minority within the Habsburg Empire had equipped them to deal with, but the reality proved harsher. Austria-Hungary was not a nation-state. On the eve of World War I only 23 percent of the empire's inhabitants identified their language of everyday use as German, and Czechs made up 12.5 percent of its population.[65] By contrast, the population of the German Reich in 1939 was 79.7 million, the great majority of whom were ethnic Germans, and the Czech minority was a mere 7.25 million.[66] More important, the Nazi state was based on theories of Aryan racial superiority that defined Slavic peoples as racial inferiors and regarded their lands as *Lebensraum* (living space) for the German *Herrenvolk* (master race). Habsburg rule was not always gentle. But the Habsburgs never set out to kill or expel half the Czech population, replace them with settlers from the Reich, and Germanize the rest, which was the proposal drawn up by Konstantin von Neurath and Karl Hermann Frank and approved by Adolf

Hitler in October 1940. This is where Peroutka's historical analogy breaks down. We are no longer in the nineteenth century—or at least not in Europe's nineteenth century. Enslavement and forced labor, land theft, ethnic cleansing, exemplary massacres, and cultural and physical genocide were not Nazi inventions. They had been the standard means of carving out Spanish, Portuguese, British, French, Dutch, German, Belgian, Russian, American, and Italian—in short, white—*Lebensraum* in Africa, Asia, Australasia, and the Americas since time out of mind. And they had been justified by scientific racism long before Hitler sat down to write *Mein Kampf*.[67]

After Germany invaded Poland on 1 September 1939 and officially triggered World War II, Hitler no longer had any interest in appeasing Britain and France and the gloves came off. Billboards and newspapers announced that acts of resistance to the Reich would be punished by death. The final issue of *Přítomnost* appeared on 30 August 1939. Two days later the Gestapo launched Action Albrecht I, detaining 1,247 intellectuals, politicians, clergy, Sokol functionaries, ex-legionnaires, communists, and other potential troublemakers.[68] The protectorate government neither took part in nor was informed of the action. This time Ferdinand Peroutka was not released. After spells in Prague's Pankrác prison and Dachau he was sent to Buchenwald. The Germans brought him back to Prague in April 1943 with an offer to edit a collaborationist version of *Přítomnost*, but he refused and was jailed again in Pankrác for over a year before being returned to the camp. Emil Filla and Josef Čapek were among those arrested, as was Milena Jesenská's *Tvorba* colleague Záviš Kalandra, who would spend most of the war in Sachsenhausen. Čapek and Filla had taken very public anti-Nazi positions in the 1930s. Peroutka, Filla, and Kalandra survived the camps. Čapek did not. After almost three years in Buchenwald, he was moved to Sachsenhausen in June 1942. There he wrote dozens of poems (and made a handful of translations, including from Rupert Brooke and James Joyce), which were published as *Básně z koncentračního tábora* (Verses from the concentration camp) in 1946. One of the earliest poems was a lament for his brother Karel, which, Josef wrote to his wife Jarmila on 1 January 1943, "found its pretty definitive wording on the day of his death, the 25th [December]." Josef was transported to Bergen-Belsen on 25 February 1945. He was alive on 4 April.[69] He died sometime in the next two weeks, likely in the typhus epidemic sweeping the camp, either soon before or just after British forces liberated Bergen-Belsen. On 23 June, Jarmila Čapková and Rudolf Margolius, a survivor of the Łódź ghetto, Auschwitz, and Dachau, made the difficult trip from Prague to Bergen-Belsen in a borrowed car to try to find out more. The journey proved fruitless.[70] Josef's body was never found.

Whatever Milena Jesenská may have publicly advised her compatriots to do in *Přítomnost* (where she always had to battle the censor), she herself joined the illegal resistance. After the invasion she worked with Joachim von Zedtwitz, a twenty-nine-year-old Bohemian-German medical student, as part of a network that helped people escape the country. "'Jochi,' as he was known, was the ideal underground activist," writes Jana Černá, "a blond, blue-eyed German, who spoke his mother-tongue so beautifully and authentically that he only just escaped lynching on Národní Avenue after the war."[71] Czech soldiers and airmen hoping to carry on the fight abroad, German antifascist refugees, communists, and desperate Jews assembled in Milena's flat at 6 Kouřimská Street in Vinohrady. There, they waited for Jochi to drive them in his two-seater Aero 30 to Moravská Ostrava, where they were met by other members of the resistance who guided them over the Polish border to Katowice. One of the earliest to make the journey was Rudolf Keller, chief editor of *Prager Tagblatt*. Milena's partner Evžen Klinger, who was doubly at risk as a Jew and a former communist functionary, soon followed. Milena promised to join Evžen in a few weeks with Honza, but she kept putting it off. "For the small Czech land there is only one solution," she proclaimed in July in what turned out to be her last *Přítomnost* article; "cleave to each other like limpets and stick together like a herd. Remain on our land and remain in our homes."[72] Jana Černá recalls that prior to Evžen's departure, her grandfather gruffly gave her a packet and a foreign banknote ("Give him [Evžen] that to be going on with, so at least he can get himself a square meal there"). "When Milena unwrapped the packet at home she burst into tears like a little girl. Apart from some pieces of dental gold, it contained the gold watch Professor Jesenský had once received for gaining his school certificate."[73] Evžen made it to London, where he survived the war. All hope of Milena and Honza following disappeared with the German invasion of Poland.

Milena wrote for and helped distribute *V boj!* (Into combat!), the most important of the sixty-six illegal newspapers and magazines that existed in Bohemia and Moravia during Neurath's tenure as protector. It was published by Družstvo v prvním sledu (Vanguard Squad), a resistance group founded on the day of the invasion by retired police inspector Josef Škalda and some of his former legionnaire comrades in Škalda's Vinohrady apartment. The group produced twenty-seven weekly issues of *V boj!* between May and November 1939, with print runs that eventually reached five thousand. The distribution network covered the Czech Lands. One of the key members of the Družstvo was the painter, typographer, and illustrator Vojtěch Preissig, an UMPRUM graduate who lived in the United States from 1910 to 1930, where he taught at Columbia University and the Wentworth Institute in Boston. During World War I Preissig was active in the Czechoslovak foreign resistance. By the time he and his family took up cudgels for the nation again in 1939, he was in his late sixties. Despite a ban on any celebrations of the anniversary of Czechoslovak independence on 28 October, anti-German demonstrations took place throughout the day. Protesters fought with security forces on Wenceslas Square, which was finally cleared by Czech and German police early in the evening after shots were fired outside the National Museum. A twenty-two-year-old apprentice baker, Václav Sedláček, was killed, and medical student Jan Opletal was seriously wounded by gunfire in separate incidents on Žitná Street. According to police reports, around four hundred mostly young people were arrested, of whom twenty-two were students.[74] *V boj!* prepared an issue covering the events, but its printer was betrayed by informers and arrested on 8 November.

Two days later Josef Škalda and other members of the Družstvo were apprehended as they left a meeting at the Zlatá husa Hotel (Golden Goose; today, the Ambassador) on Wenceslas Square, which led to a gunfight with Gestapo agents in the Alfa Arcade. Škalda was executed as an enemy of the Reich in Plötzensee prison in Berlin on 23 January 1942. He was one of 677 Czechs who met their end there. The arrests effectively put an end to Vanguard Squad, but Preissig's daughter Inka (Irena) Bernášková, who had just delivered some of her father's cover designs to the hotel, managed to escape the Gestapo net. Having spent her teenage years in the United States (she was a keen Girl Scout), Inka had returned to Prague with her two sisters in 1921. She now went into hiding under a false name and was soon producing issues of *V boj!* from her flat in Spořilov. "If she was previously an anonymous coworker, pushed to the back of many others, she now became the leading figure. She was the responsible editor, the publisher, the printer, the administrator, the sender, and the delivery girl," her colleague Arnošt Polavský wrote later.[75] Inka was arrested on Na Poříčí on 21 September 1940 for carrying false papers and was condemned to death by a German court in March 1942. She was the first Czech woman to be guillotined at Plötzensee, where she died on 26 August 1942. Forty other members of the Spořilov *V boj!* group were arrested in the fall of 1940, including Vojtěch Preissig, who was sentenced to three years' imprisonment. He died in Dachau in 1944, aged seventy.

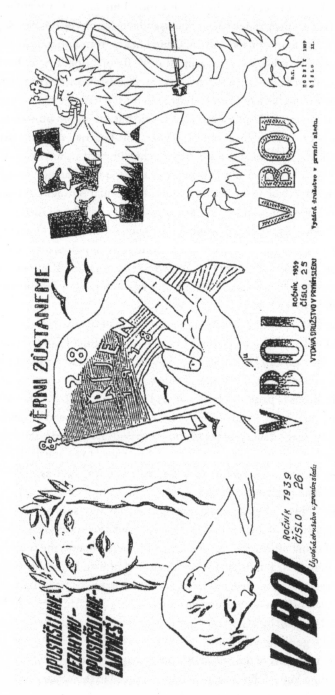

FIGURE 4.4. Vojtěch Preissig, *Into Combat!* cyclostyled covers, 1939. Wikimedia Commons.

Two days after the arrests of Škalda and his comrades at the Golden Goose, *The Nation to Its Artists* exhibition opened in the Municipal House. It was a Sunday, 12 November 1939. That morning Milena Jesenská sent Honza to pick up copies of *V boj!* as usual from Škalda's flat at 14 Budečská Street in Vinohrady. The door was opened by Jaroslav (aka Jaroslaus) Nachtmann, a Gestapo informer, who telephoned for police reinforcements. The police drove Honza home to Kouřimská Street, where they arrested Milena, leaving the eleven-year-old girl alone with a recently acquired black kitten.[76] They searched the flat but miraculously overlooked the copies of *V boj!* stacked under the linen chest. Honza had the good sense to burn them as soon as the police left. Milena was driven to Gestapo headquarters in the Petschek Palace (Petschkův palác) on Bredovská Street, which was renamed the Street of the Political Prisoners (Politických vězňů) in 1946; during the occupation Max Spielmann's imposing neoclassical building, built as a bank headquarters in 1926–1929, became infamous for its brutal and often fatal interrogations.[77] The Jewish owners had had the foresight (and good luck) to sell and move to Britain before the invasion. After initial questioning Milena was moved to Pankrác prison, where she was kept for three months before being transported to Dresden and tried for treason in March 1940. She conducted her own defense (in German), claiming that she had no prior contact with Škalda's group or knowledge of *V boj!* She testified that she had sent Honza to Budečská Street in response to a phone call to the *Přítomnost* offices from a Mr. Bělka, who said he had some "brochures" that might interest her "that are named similarly to Hitler's *Mein Kampf*, only without the word '*mein*'" (in Czech, *Kampf* translates into *boj*).[78] Milena was acquitted for want of evidence and returned to police custody in Prague, but the Gestapo were unwilling to release her and kept her in detention.

Jan Opletal, the medical student shot on 28 October, died of his injuries on 11 November 1939, the day before Milena's arrest. His funeral took place on 15 November on the Albertov campus of Charles University. After the service was over, under the watchful eye of the Czech police, about four thousand students peacefully followed the hearse carrying Opletal's coffin to Hybernské (now Masaryk) station, where it was put on a train headed back to his family in the little Moravian village of Lhota nad Moravou. Afterward a large crowd of students gathered in front of the ČVUT building on Charles Square, where they sang the banned national anthem. Czech police broke up the assembly. Skirmishes continued into the evening as groups of students roamed through the city center chanting anti-German slogans, destroying bilingual tram maps,

and allegedly molesting German civilians. K. H. Frank's car was attacked on
the corner of Národní Avenue and Spálená Street, leaving his driver Anton Uhl
with a broken nose. Students clashed with members of the Czech fascist
organization Vlájka (Flag), who were meeting in the Lucerna Palace off Wenceslas Square. Others fought running battles with police outside the Rudolfinum and at the Law Faculty further down the embankment by the Svatopluk
Čech Bridge. Neurath and Frank flew to Berlin the next morning to update
Hitler on the disturbances. The Führer summoned protectorate ambassador
František Chvalkovský and gave him a dressing-down in front of Himmler,
Martin Bormann, and other senior Nazis. "March 15," he declared, "was my big
mistake . . . I should have dealt with the Czechs like the Poles, but it doesn't
matter, that can still be done . . . I will disperse the Czechs and move Germans
there."[79] Neurath left after lunch, intending to stay overnight in his Berlin villa.
Frank flew back to Prague later in the afternoon, where he met with SS and
Gestapo officials at the Petschek Palace to coordinate *Sonderaktion* (special
action) *Prag vom 17. November 1939.*

In the predawn hours of 17 November German security forces raided
student dormitories in Prague, Brno, and Příbram, detaining more than
twelve hundred students. On Frank's orders nine individuals, chosen on the
basis of their prominence as officeholders in the National Union of Czech
Students rather than any evidence of personal involvement in the protests,
were summarily shot in Ruzyně barracks. Several of them had belonged to
right-of-center parties during the first republic and were active in National
Solidarity.[80] The rest of the students were transported to Sachsenhausen concentration camp on 18 November. Ten institutions of higher education were
closed, including Charles University, ČVUT, and AVU in Prague and Masaryk University and the Technical University in Brno. They did not reopen
until after the war. Over twelve hundred Czech faculty lost their jobs and
more than 17,500 students were deprived of an education. Most of the students detained in Sachsenhausen were released at the end of 1942, but not
before thirty-five of their colleagues had died.[81] At a rally at Caxton Hall in
London on 16 November 1941 the International Students' Council, which had
many refugee members, declared 17 November the International Day of the
Students. The poet Louis MacNeice scripted and narrated a BBC program
marking the anniversary of the *Sonderaktion* in 1943, in which he reminded
listeners that "the darkness that spread from Germany fell first on Prague."
Titled "The Fifth Freedom," the broadcast began with a stark, unaccompanied
choir singing the Czech folk song "*Ach, synku, synku*" (Oh, son, son!) and

ended with the Hussite chorale "*Ktož jsú boží bojovníci*" (Ye who are the soldiers of God).[82]

After her return from Dresden Milena Jesenská was again detained in Pankrác prison. She had her last meeting with her father and daughter at the
Petschek Palace in October 1940. "When at last she appeared, escorted by a
Gestapo officer, I couldn't recognize her," relates Jana Černá. "This gaunt figure
with its shoulder-length hair, prominent cheek-bones and huge blue eyes more
closely resembled the Milča [Millie] her father had once known than the
Milena I remembered, but even he did not immediately realize that it was his
daughter." Honza proudly told her mother that she and her friends were refusing to learn German at school, "but Milena only laughed and told me I was a
silly little donkey, that German was one of the most beautiful of languages and
it couldn't be held responsible for those who spoke it."[83] Shortly afterward
Milena was transported to Ravensbrück concentration camp for women in
Brandenburg.[84] There she struck up a close friendship, which would have been
conducted entirely in German, with Margarete (Greta) Buber-Neumann,
author of *Kafkas Freundin Milena*. Milena and Greta had much in common.
Both were journalists. Greta's first husband was the son of the Zionist Martin
Buber, whose 1909 Prague lectures had had such an impact on Max Brod.
Greta and her second husband, Heinz Neumann, spent years as activists in the
German Communist Party, in Heinz's case as editor of the party paper *Rote
Fahne* (Red flag), Comintern functionary, and communist member of the
Reichstag parliament. When Stalin's purges began the Neumanns were living
in exile at the Hotel Lux in Moscow, where Jaromír Krejcar was billeted during
his time in the Soviet Union. Heinz was arrested on 27 April 1937 and executed
on 26 November. Greta was arrested on 19 June 1938 and imprisoned in various
labor camps in Kazakhstan. Following the Molotov-Ribbentrop pact the Soviets returned her to Germany in 1940. The friendship with Greta got Milena
into hot water with the Czech communist women in the camp, and (according
to a letter from another former Ravensbrück inmate to Jana Černá) "pots of
jam were confiscated, she was rationed to just a small portion of bread, and
she was ostracized."[85]

The two women never got to write the book they were planning, which had
the working title "the age of the concentration camp."[86] Milena died of kidney
failure on 17 May 1944. She was forty-seven. The camp doctor wrote to Professor Jesenský and invited him to collect his daughter's remains, but the old man
was too crushed by the news to make the journey. Milena's ashes were sprin-
kled on Lake Fürstenberg, a long way from home. After her death, says Jana

Černá, Jesenský "insisted on addressing me as '*Milčo*.' He was fully aware that I was his grandchild and not his daughter and the confusion never went further than the name. But I never heard him say my own name again."[87] Jan Jesenský died in Prague in 1947. "Poor, poor Milena Jesenská!" wrote onetime editor of *Der Montag* Walter Tschuppik that same year to Joachim von Zedtwitz, glad to discover that one of those who had spirited him out of the protectorate in 1939 had survived the war. "What a great, brave person she was! It was she who put me in touch with you. As you know I spent the last night before you came to collect me in her flat."[88] What Jan Jesenský would have made of his wayward daughter being recognized in 1995 by the World Holocaust Remembrance Center Yad Vashem as Righteous among the Nations— that is, "non-Jews who took great risks to save Jews during the Holocaust"—is anyone's guess.[89] I like to think he would have been extremely proud.

5

The Void at the Core of Things

It has been characteristic of our history-conscious century that its worst
crimes have been committed in the name of some kind of necessity or in the
name—and this amounts to the same thing—of the "wave of the future."
For people who submit to this, who renounce their freedom and their right
of action, even though they may pay the price of death for their delusion,
anything more charitable can hardly be said than the words with which Kafka
concludes *The Trial*: "It was as if he meant the shame of it to outlive him."

—HANNAH ARENDT[1]

Mendelssohn Is on the Roof

By most measures Czechoslovakia had it easy during World War II compared
with many other countries. The Czechoslovak death toll was around 360,000
people, approximately 2.4 percent of the prewar population[2]—of which, it is
necessary to add, upward of 250,000 were Czechoslovak Jews murdered in the
Holocaust.[3] Czech cities escaped the infernos of Rotterdam, Coventry, Dresden, and Tokyo. Though the Allies bombed industrial areas of Plzeň, Brno,
Ostrava, Zlín, and elsewhere in the latter stages of the war, most Czech towns
survived with their historic cores intact. The largest American raid on Brno,
on 20 November 1944, left 578 dead and more than 6,000 homeless.[4] Prague
suffered only one serious bombing, when American B-17 Flying Fortresses
dropped their payloads over the New Town and Vinohrady on 14 February 1945,
leaving 701 dead, 1,184 seriously wounded, and 10,000 homeless. The pilots
thought they were over Dresden. More than three hundred buildings were
destroyed or badly damaged, including the Emmaus Monastery, the Palacký

Bridge, the Faust House and General Hospital on Charles Square, and the Jewish synagogue on Sázavská Street, at the time one of the largest in the world.[5] Another raid hit industrial targets in Libeň, Kbely, and Vysočany on 25 March,[6] but the center was spared any more assaults. The Prague Uprising of 5–8 May 1945 caused further destruction, damaging the Old Town Hall and other landmarks in and around the Old Town Square and reducing the city archives to ashes. Much of the physical damage was repaired after the war, but the spiritual corrosion of living under occupation for more than six years was more difficult to deal with. Abjection eats into the soul. In such circumstances it was impossible for most people *not* to be complicit in sustaining the regime to some degree. Once again parallels with other colonial situations are not out of place. If we want to understand the explosion of cathartic violence (and the ubiquitous language of cleansing) that followed the liberation of Czechoslovakia in 1945, we could do worse than to read Aimé Césaire's *Discourse on Colonialism* or Frantz Fanon's *The Wretched of the Earth*.[7]

Hitler did not follow through on his threat to "disperse the Czechs and move the Germans" into Bohemia and Moravia, but the prospect of ejection from a homeland that had been redefined as German *Lebensraum* forever was always there.[8] The only safeguard the Czechs had was a short-term one: prewar Czechoslovakia was the world's tenth largest per capita producer of industrial goods and its seventh largest armaments manufacturer, and most Czechoslovak industry was situated in Bohemia and Moravia. Czech factories and skilled workers were essential to the war effort, especially when German men were needed for the front. Hermann Göring brought a raft of Czech companies under the umbrella of his Göring Works, among them the Škoda plant in Plzeň and the Československá zbrojovka (Czechoslovak armaments works) in Brno, as well as the Vítkovice Iron and Steel Works in Ostrava and Poldi Kladno.[9] Zyklon B, the toxin used in the gas chambers of Auschwitz and other extermination camps, was manufactured by Kaliwerke AG in Kolín. Workers in key industries were paid above-average wages and given increased rations. The ranks of the industrial working class swelled from 730,000 in 1939 to 880,000 at the end of 1944, with a pronounced increase in employment in the metalworking and chemical industries.[10] Czechs also provided a substantial amount of labor in Germany itself, much of it forced. Estimates of the numbers of Czech men and women compelled to work in Germany between 1939 and 1945 range from 400,000 to 600,000.[11] One of them was Zdeněk Tmej, a young photojournalist who smuggled in Rolleiflex and Contax cameras to document his time as a *Zwangsarbeiter* in Breslau during 1942–1944. The images were

FIGURE 5.1. Zdeněk Tmej, *Eintopf for a Czech Student*, 1942–1944. From Vladimír Birgus and Jan Mlčoch, *Czech Photography of the 20th Century*, Prague, 2010.

published after the war in his photo book *Abeceda duševního prázdna* (Alphabet of spiritual emptiness, 1946).[12] Tmej's minimalist aesthetic was well suited to his subject matter; in the words of Vladimír Birgus and Jan Mlčoch, he "managed to make a personal, profoundly involved, and yet universalizing documentary, in which the grainy, high-contrast photographs accent the bleak atmosphere of the milieu."[13] They show meager meals (one is titled "*Eintopf for a Czech Student*"), men playing cards, men sleeping on bunk beds. Some of the photos were taken in the brothel staffed by foreign women located next door to the huge dance hall where Tmej was billeted with around a hundred other young Czech men. A sign at the entrance read "*Nur für Ausländer*" (For foreigners only). Beneath one photo Tmej wrote: "A Czech woman, she had the choice of a concentration camp or a brothel."[14] The boys' needs obviously had to be catered to, but you can't be too careful when it comes to safeguarding the purity of German blood.

Although the Nazis were clear that in the long term the protectorate was destined to be Germanized, there were disagreements over what this entailed.

When Hitler approved Neurath's and Frank's plans for Germanization in October 1940, it was assumed that an estimated 50 percent of Czechs could "join the *Volk*" once they had undergone "screening and sifting."[15] It was tacitly accepted that physical removal of the remainder was not in the cards until after the war. The assimilation policy was opposed by hard-line Nazi ideologists who believed that any mixing with racial inferiors "weakened German blood," but their objections were overruled. A report on the racial complexion of the protectorate population commissioned by Reinhard Heydrich from the SS "racial expert" Dr. Walter König-Beyer in 1940 concluded that, based on their physical characteristics, "most Czechs were no more than Germans who spoke another language."[16] Similar views were advanced by Karl Valentin Müller, who headed the Department of Social Anthropology and National Biology at the German University of Prague. K. H. Frank quoted Müller to the effect that Czechs and Germans were "racially on the same level," while Neurath noted that "one is continually amazed at the number of blond-haired people with intelligent faces and pleasing bodies."[17] When it came to ascertaining individuals' race for the purpose of determining entitlement to Reich or protectorate citizenship, we are once again in a *kafkárna*. Chad Bryant's *Prague in Black* does an excellent job of documenting the absurdities of the criteria used and the wildly inconsistent results of testing across different towns and regions within the protectorate. Not only "blue eyes, pleasing bodies, height, girth, or well-shaped heads" but also "clean houses, spinning wheels, class, virility, sexual morality, and social behavior" became de facto criteria for acceptance into the German *Volk*.[18]

Vigorous steps were taken to privilege the German language, German culture, and German institutions. In July 1940 Neurath required all government correspondence to be bilingual or in German alone, and he gave state employees until March 1942 to prove their competence in German. The next month German became the official working language of the Prague city administration. All signage, including shop and street signs in Czech areas, had to be bilingual, with the German text first. A *Volkstumsfond* (nationality fund) supported everything from German libraries and swimming pools to the Nazi daily newspaper. The New German Theater, which went bankrupt during the second republic, was revived as the Deutsches Opernhaus. The Estates Theater, which the mob had reclaimed for the Czech nation during the riots of November 1920, was taken over and renamed the Deutsches Schauspielhaus. On 4 November 1939—two weeks before all Czech institutions of higher education were closed—Neurath oversaw a ceremony there to transfer all the

German institutions of higher education in the protectorate to Reich jurisdiction. On 29 October 1941 the old theater hosted a gala performance of *Don Giovanni* to celebrate the 150th anniversary of Mozart's death. The square in front of the Rudolfinum concert hall, which had been called Smetana Square since 1919, was concurrently renamed Mozartplatz. The Rudolfinum itself, which served as the Czechoslovak parliament building throughout the first republic, became the seat of National Solidarity from the spring of 1939 until the summer of 1940. Thereafter it was used for German propaganda events and exhibitions until 17 October 1941, when the Berlin Philharmonic played Beethoven's Ninth Symphony as Neurath's successor as protector, Reinhard Heydrich, ceremonially "returned this place to German art."[19]

The American diplomat George F. Kennan, who was stationed in Prague from August 1938 until September 1939 (when he was transferred to the Berlin embassy), informed his superiors in October 1940 that "Bohemia has retained its muddy villages, its geese, its beer, its earthy fertility. And the city of Prague, to which Italian and Austrian architects long ago gave a grace and harmony unrivalled in central or northern Europe, has not lost its charm.... Under the surface, on the other hand, the changes have been profound." Kennan estimated that 120,000 Reich Germans had moved into Prague, excluding military personnel. This would have quadrupled the city's prewar German-speaking population. Many were bureaucrats paid at least double the salaries of Czechs in comparable positions, while "carpetbaggers of the occupation" were drawn by the prospect of acquiring looted Jewish (or Czechoslovak state) property. Due to the closure of Czech universities, "almost no young Czech can prepare to become a doctor, a lawyer, a professor, an engineer, or a minister of the gospel," leaving "little choice ... but to become an industrial or farm laborer, go into domestic service, learn some handicraft, or seek employment in the Reich."[20] The decades-long decline in the number of German schools was reversed. In part this was due to an influx of Czech pupils, although applicants were vetted for "racial" suitability. Czech schools were starved of teachers and textbooks. The middle schools, which offered a humanistic education that included Czech history and literature, were run down in favor of technical and vocational schools: 60,284 boys and 34,900 girls were studying in Czech middle schools in 1938–1939, but the comparable figures for 1943–1944 were only 29,051 and 13,787.[21] Kuratorium pro výchovu mládeže (Board for the upbringing of youth), founded on 26 May 1942, had the same Germanizing objectives. The Kuratorium, which was Heydrich's brainchild, was modeled on the Hitler Youth. All Czech children between the ages of ten and eighteen were enrolled in the organization, whose weekly activities included exercises and singing along the lines pioneered in Henlein's *Turnhallen*. Kuratorium also ran festivals, sporting events, and summer camps.

Two days after the invasion Czechs were ordered to drive on the right side of the road instead of the left. Prague was given until 26 March to relocate road signs and tram stops. Street names, too, were changed in ways that better projected Bohemia's thousand-year location within the German *Lebensraum*. Working with a team from the German University, the Reich Protectorate Office produced a report in April 1940 that led to the adoption of a new bilingual street directory for the capital.[22] Among the names that disappeared were Republic Square, Revolutionary Avenue, Masaryk Embankment, and Bridge of the Legions, which mutated into Hybernské Square, Berlin Avenue, Vltava Embankment, and Smetana Bridge, respectively. The Jirásek Bridge was renamed the Dientzenhofer Bridge, after the baroque architect Kilián Ignác Dientzenhofer. Charlotte G. Masaryk (today Mickiewiczova) Street vanished from Hradčany. So did Štefánik Street and Štefánik Square (today náměstí Kinských, the Square of the Kinskýs) from Smíchov; Milan Rastislav Štefánik, the Slovak who had worked with Masaryk and Beneš in the foreign resistance during World War I and died in a plane crash in 1919, was Czechoslovakia's first minister of war. Pštross Street in the New Town, named for Prague mayor František Václav Pštross, whose tenure from 1861 to 1863 saw the adoption of Czech as the official language of the Prague City Council, was renamed after his predecessor Václav Vaňka z Rodlova, who held office during the "Bach Absolutism" that followed the defeat of the 1848 revolution. English Avenue became Irish Avenue, French Avenue became Bismarck Avenue, and Paris Avenue became Nuremberg Avenue. London, Washington, Kyiv, and the Ural Mountains vanished from Praguers' horizons. The World War I battlefields of the Marne, Verdun, and Bakhmach were also wiped from the local map as Marshal Foch, supreme commander of the Allied forces on the western front, made way for Marshal Schwerin, who was killed leading Prussian troops against Austria at the Battle of Prague in 1757. The new directory also took the opportunity to eliminate duplicate street names, coining new names that "symbolized the centuries-old cohabitation of Czechs and Germans in the Prague region."[23]

As a result of Joseph Goebbels's attempt to hijack Winston Churchill's "V for Victory" campaign in 1941, Národní Avenue, where Czechs used to promenade on Sunday mornings during the last years of the Austro-Hungarian monarchy, became Victoria Avenue. Churchill launched his action, inspired by Belgian refugee Victor de Laveleye, via a BBC radio broadcast on 18 July. "Splash the V from one end of Europe to another!" urged the announcer.[24] Faced with the prospect of endless unruly iterations of the letter *V*—or its sonic equivalent, three dots and a dash in Morse code, which also happen to be the first four notes of Beethoven's Fifth Symphony—all over the continent, Goebbels decided to appropriate the symbol for the Nazi cause. The only problem was that the word for *victory* in German, unlike in English, French, and Czech (*vítězství*), begins with an *S* (*Sieg*, as in *Sieg heil!*). No matter. Classical antiquity rode to the Reich's rescue in the shape of the Roman goddess of victory, Victoria. Goebbels festooned occupied Europe with "V for Victoria" signs large and small, including a gigantic *V* on the Eiffel Tower above the legend "*Deutschland siegt auf allen Fronten*" (Germany is winning on all fronts). In Prague a massive letter *V* was painted onto the cobblestones of the Old Town Square, enormous banners bearing the letter *V* hung from the lampposts in Wenceslas Square, and the illuminated letter *V* was mounted on two structures visible from miles around, the National Monument on Vítkov hill and the observation tower on Petřín hill. Imitation is the highest form of flattery: the Petřín "Eiffelovka" is a sixty-meter-high, small-nation, *malý, ale naše* (it's little, but it's ours) homage to its grander Parisian cousin built for the Jubilee Exhibition of 1891. Both illuminations were exempted from the obligatory blackout.[25]

Instead of observing Masaryk's birthday (7 March) and the day of Czecho-slovak independence (28 October), public holidays now celebrated Hitler's birthday (20 April), Hácha's birthday (12 July), and the founding of the protectorate (16 March). Monuments to Havlíček, Palacký, the writer Svatopluk Čech, the nineteenth-century Czech politician František Ladislav Rieger, and the French historian of Bohemia Ernest Denis were stripped from Prague's streets and squares. All were restored after the war except, tellingly, the memorial to Denis, which had been installed in the upper part of the Lesser Town Square in celebration of the tenth anniversary of the Czechoslovak Republic in October 1928.[26] The memory of the betrayal at Munich festered long after 1945, becoming an essential building block in the postwar edifice of communist legitimacy. Soon after the United States entered the war the Germans destroyed Albín Polášek's statue of American president Woodrow Wilson, which had stood outside Prague's main station since 1928. It was replaced only in 2011.[27] The Nazis also removed the statues of Jan Hus and Tomáš Masaryk from the pantheon of the National Museum. The museum itself was renamed the Land Museum (Zemské muzeum) and used for spectacles like the *Deutsche*

FIGURE 5.2. Letter *V* for "Victory" painted on
cobblestones of the Old Town Square, 1941.
Photographer unknown. From Jan Kaplan and
Krystyna Nosarzewska, *Praha Prag Prague:
The Turbulent Century*, Cologne, 1997.

Größe (German greatness) exhibition that ceremonially opened on 15 March
1941, the second anniversary on the invasion, with the enforced participation
of Emil Hácha and Alois Eliáš. Emblems of Czech sovereignty were surgically
excised from protectorate insignia, stamps, and banknotes. In a grotesque act
of ritual self-abasement, on 19 November 1941, in the Saint Václav Chapel of

Saint Vitus's Cathedral, Emil Hácha presented Reinhard Heydrich with the seven keys to the chamber where the Bohemian crown jewels were kept. Whether there is any truth to the widespread Czech belief that the protector secretly tried on Saint Václav's crown and thereby fell afoul of the ancient prophecy that anyone who did so would die within the year, I cannot say.

Most insultingly of all, perhaps—remembering Milena Jesenská's description of the tearful crowds laying snowdrops at the Tomb of the Unknown Soldier in the Old Town Hall—one night in October 1941, on the personal orders of K. H. Frank, the tomb was broken into, the soldier's coffin opened, and his remains removed. Julius Klein, an SS man who took part in the operation, testified during his postwar interrogation that he personally drove the contents of the coffin to Troja and threw them in the Vltava.[28] Other accounts claim that the soldier's bones were taken to Gestapo headquarters in the Petschek Palace and cremated; the ashes were than shipped to Terezín concentration camp in April 1945, after which they disappeared.[29] The vandalizing of the tomb finds its way into the darkly comic opening scenes of Jiří Weil's novel *Na střeše je Mendelssohn* (*Mendelssohn Is on the Roof*, 1960). Though the Nazis classified Weil as a Jew, an identity he had never previously embraced, his marriage to his Aryan lover Olga Frenclová on 4 March 1942 initially protected him from transportation to the camps.[30] Jiří worked in the Jewish Museum from July 1943, where his job was to catalog on individual index cards thousands of artifacts looted from Holocaust victims as they were shipped to the camps.[31] In January 1945 Nazi policy toward those they considered halfbreeds (*Mischlinge*) hardened; first Jewish and then non-Jewish partners in mixed marriages started being transported to the camps too. When Weil's inevitable summons arrived the next month, he faked suicide from the Hlávka Bridge with the help of his wife and friends. He and Olga spent the rest of the war in hiding.[32]

Mendelssohn Is on the Roof begins the day after the concert at which Reinhard Heydrich reconsecrated the Rudolfinum to German art. The protector's evening ended on a sour note. After the music finished Heydrich was outside getting some air when he glanced up at the statues on the balustrade. "Suddenly his face twisted with fury and hatred. What? This was unbelievable! How could he have given a speech in a building with a statue of that disgusting composer on its roof. . . . 'Giesse,' he barked, and pointed at the balustrade. 'See to it that that statue is torn down immediately.'"[33] Robert Gies (as the name is correctly spelled) was the personal secretary to K. H. Frank. The next morning Julius Schlesinger, a municipal official and candidate for the SS, finds himself reluctantly supervising two Czech workmen who are doing their Švejkish best to carry out Heydrich's order. Unlike Heydrich, who was a cultured man and a classical music lover, Schlesinger has no clue which statue represents the Jewish composer Felix Mendelssohn. But "he, Schlesinger, had to carry out the order. It came directly from the Acting Reich Protector and he was even more ruthless than Frank. To disobey an order—everybody knew what that meant. . . . To disobey an order means death. *Even if the order is unintelligible.*" Employing knowledge gleaned from a Nazi lecture course on racial science, Schlesinger instructs the workmen to "go around the statues again and look carefully at their noses. Whichever one has the biggest nose, that's the Jew." The Czechs do as they are told, but to Schlesinger's horror, they put a rope around the neck of the one composer he *does* recognize: "Jesus Christ! Stop! I'm telling you, stop! . . . My God, it was Wagner, the greatest composer; not just an ordinary musician, but one of the greats who had helped build the Third Reich."[34] Schlesinger reluctantly retreats to find someone who can tell a Jewish composer from an Aryan. He fearfully reports his failure to his superior Josef Krug, the man who, on Frank's instructions, had organized the raid on the Tomb of the Unknown Soldier. "But Krug is silent. He's in trouble, too. Of course, he's responsible to Giesse, and Giesse to Frank, and Frank to Heydrich, and if the order isn't carried out, Heydrich and Frank will have them all arrested."[35] We may be getting closer to answering eleven-year-old Jana Krejcarová's question about how a normal man could become a murderer in the name of obedience.

Hitler's Hangman

Thousands of resistance suspects were rounded up over the spring and summer of 1940. One of them was Prague mayor Otakar Klapka, who was arrested on 9 July 1940 at a reception for Danish journalists at the Černín Palace, to which he had been personally invited by K. H. Frank. Hácha's and Eliáš's appeals for his release fell on deaf ears. In November the Gestapo raided premises in Troja where the KSČ had been illegally printing *Rudé právo*, and on the night of 12–13 February 1941 they arrested all but one member of the (first) illegal KSČ Central Committee. Resistance continued, fueled by food shortages caused by the diversion of supplies to the eastern front. The summer of 1941 saw an increase in sabotage, with attacks on railroad tracks, telephone lines, and fuel depots. In Prague strikes broke out at the Praga, Avia, and ČKD works, and two thousand workers laid down their tools at the Walter aircraft engine factory, leading to sixty-nine arrests. A boycott of newspapers in mid-September under the 1890s slogan "Each to his own!" was successful, with 70 percent of copies going unsold in Prague.[36] Something had to be done. Frank met with Hitler and Himmler in Berlin on 22 September. Neurath was put on sick leave the next day. On 24 September 1941 Heydrich was appointed acting protector of Bohemia and Moravia. "A tall blond with blue eyes who was a ladies' man as well as a skilled sportsman, musician and pilot," Hitler's hangman (as Thomas Mann called him) was a Nazi wet dream.[37]

Historians generally dislike what-ifs, but they can remind us of the contingencies on which the course of history sometimes turns. In his Goncourt Prize–winning 2009 novel *HHhH* (short for *Himmlers Hirn heißt Heydrich*, or Himmler's brain is called Heydrich) Laurent Binet dangles the thought that had the future protector not spent an illicit night with a young woman in Kiel eleven years earlier, "everything would have been very different . . . for thousands of Czechs and, perhaps, hundreds of thousands of Jews":

> In 1931 Heydrich is a navy lieutenant with the promise of a brilliant military career. He is engaged to a young aristocrat and his future is bright. But he is also an inveterate pussy-hound, making endless sexual conquests and visits to brothels. One evening he brings home a young girl he'd met at a ball in Potsdam and who'd come to Kiel to pay him a visit. I don't know for sure if she became pregnant, but in any case her parents demanded that he did his duty by her. Heydrich didn't respond, given that he was already engaged to Lina von Osten. . . . Unfortunately for him, the father of this young girl was Admiral [Erich] Raeder himself, commander in chief of the navy. Raeder kicked up a huge fuss. Heydrich . . . was court-martialed, disgraced, and finally booted out of the armed services.[38]

No records of Heydrich's court-martial survive and many details of the event, including the name of the jilted woman and whether or not she was pregnant, remain murky. She was certainly not Raeder's daughter, but she may have been the daughter of the director of the Kiel naval dockyard, who was the admiral's close friend. Raeder was old school in matters of sexual propriety. What is not in dispute is that after unexpectedly finding himself without a job in the depths of the Great Depression, the cashiered Oberleutnant zur See had an interview with Heinrich Himmler in Munich. The meeting was arranged by friends of Heydrich's fiancée Lina, who was an ardent National Socialist. Himmler liked the cut of Reinhard's jib and hired him to create a new intelligence agency, the SD (Sicherheitsdienst, or Security Service), within the SS (Schutzstaffel, or

Protection Squad). Heydrich's radicalization, which came *after* he joined the Nazi Party, was thus a roundabout outcome of his philandering.[39]

By the time Heydrich was assigned the task of sorting out the protectorate, he held the rank of SS-Obergruppenführer and police general and was director of the Reich Security Main Office (Reichssicherheitshauptamt, or RSHA), which controlled the SS, the SD, and the Gestapo. This made him one of the most powerful men in Germany. He had built up an impressive resumé. He played a leading part in the Night of the Long Knives, in which Himmler's SS broke the power of the SA (Sturmabteilung, or Storm Detachment) Brownshirts by murdering Ernst Röhm and other SA leaders in 1934. He helped Goebbels organize *Kristallnacht* and established the Central Agency for Jewish Emigration under Adolf Eichmann in Vienna. If any individual other than Hitler deserves the title architect of the Holocaust, it is Heydrich. On 24 January 1939 he was charged with "finding as convenient a solution as possible to the Jewish question."[40] When Germany invaded Poland he instigated the policy of ghettoizing Jews, Sinti, and Roma in "only a few cities of concentration" as "the first prerequisite for the final aim."[41] He formed the Einsatzgruppen (special task force) units for the "fundamental cleansing" of "Jews, intelligentsia, clergy, [and] nobles" in the Polish territories,[42] a euphemism for mass executions that were often carried out publicly. After Germany attacked the Soviet Union on 22 June 1941 the Einsatzgruppen left a trail of atrocities across not only Poland but also the Baltic states, Belarus, Russia, Ukraine, and Moldova—the swath of European territory Timothy Snyder aptly calls the bloodlands.[43] Two days after Heydrich arrived in Prague, forces under the command of Einsatzgruppe C murdered at least 33,771 Kyiv Jews in the (first) Babi Yar massacre of 29–30 September 1941.[44] Between 1941 and 1944 more than two million Soviet Jews were killed in mass shootings, and about 40 percent of Jewish Holocaust victims died in this way rather than in the camps:

> By late summer 1941 . . . wherever the Einsatzgruppen went, they shot Jewish men, women, and children without regard for age or sex, and buried them in mass graves. Often with the help of local informants and interpreters, Jews in a given locality were identified and taken to collection points. Thereafter they were marched or transported by truck to the execution site, where trenches had been prepared. In some cases the captive victims had to dig their own graves. After the victims had handed over their valuables and undressed, men, women, and children were shot, either standing before the open trench, or lying face down in the prepared pit.[45]

It is important to keep this image in mind when considering what Czechs have baptized the Heydrichiáda. Heydrich himself never lost sight of it. Pacifying the protectorate was but one step toward realizing the end of history that was the thousand-year *judenfrei* Greater German Reich.

After arriving in Prague around noon on 27 September 1941, Heydrich met with Frank at the Černín Palace. His first act as protector was to issue an order for the arrest of prime minister Alois Eliáš. Later that afternoon Heydrich ordered special courts to be set up at the Gestapo headquarters in Prague and Brno. He proclaimed martial law the next day. Ninety-two people were sentenced to death during the first three days of the emergency.[46] By the time martial law was lifted (on 19 January 1942), the Prague court in the Petschek Palace had imposed 247 death sentences and sent 1,344 people to concentration camps. Several resistance leaders were tried in its first session on 28 September, among them generals Josef Bilý and Hugo Vojta, who were promptly shot in Ruzyně barracks. Another eleven members of the resistance were executed on 1 October. Eliáš was sentenced to death the same day, but the sentence was not carried out. For the moment he remained a useful hostage. Prague mayor Otakar Klapka, who had been in custody for over a year, was tried on 2 October and executed on 4 October. Imprisoned members of the illegal KSČ Central Committee were among those who died along with the Sokol leader Augustin Pechát. Hundreds of Sokol members were arrested on the night of 7–8 October and sent to the camps.[47] The next day Heydrich signed an order dissolving Sokol and seizing its assets, valued at 1.12 billion Czech crowns.

Heydrich made sure to display the names of the executed on red-edged posters across the protectorate. At the same time he fanned the flames of class resentment, seeking to drive a wedge between the proletariat and the Czech intelligentsia. He increased industrial workers' food rations; provided them with new shoes, hot lunches, cigarettes, and holidays in Luhačovice spa; and used confiscated Sokol facilities to put on sporting events, movies, and other popular entertainments—while ostentatiously executing black marketeers, some of whom were ethnic Germans, alongside Czech political prisoners and partisans.[48] The mixture of brutality and bribery worked. There were no more strikes or sabotage. Jaroslav Krejčí, the minister of justice during the second republic, succeeded Eliáš as prime minister, and a new government was belatedly sworn in on 19 January 1942. Frank handpicked the minister of education and national enlightenment: Emanuel Moravec, the ex-legionnaire who had once promised to make Milena Jesenská the new Božena Němcová. Moravec's ministerial responsibilities included oversight of not only schools and the Kuratorium youth organization but also the press, theater, art, literature, and film.

A second illegal KSČ Central Committee was broken up in April–June 1942. One of the first members arrested, on 21 April, was Julius Fučík. After spending more than a year in Pankrác prison, the beautiful boy, as Slávka Vondráčková called him, was taken to Berlin, tried for treason, and hanged at Plötzensee prison on 8 September 1943. Fučík's personality cult reached monstrous proportions in the 1950s. "Written clandestinely in prison, then published after the war in a million copies, broadcast over the radio, studied in schools as required reading," his *Reportáž psaná na oprátce* (*Report from the Gallows*, 1947) "was the sacred text of the era." I quote Ludvík Jahn, the protagonist of Milan Kundera's novel *Žert* (*The Joke*, 1967), who goes on to tell how the KSČ commissioned the veteran art nouveau painter Max Švabinský to draw a posthumous portrait of the martyred journalist from a photograph. "Fučík's handsome face hung on the wall as it hung in a thousand other public places in our country, and it was so handsome, with the radiant expression of a young girl in love, that when I looked at it I felt inferior not just because of my guilt but because of my appearance as well."[49] Once again beauty was mistaken for truth, for when the unexpurgated text of *Report from the Gallows* was published for the first time in 1995, it became clear that Fučík had talked to the Gestapo under torture.[50] Who wouldn't? Kundera makes no mention of his own epic poem *Poslední máj* (The last May, 1955), published twelve years before *The Joke*, whose mawkish stanzas ("And it seems to him, that he is walking in a vast comradely crowd / And it seems to him, that they are spreading far across the land") contributed as much to the Fučík myth as any literary product of the era.[51]

When George Kennan published his reports from wartime Prague in 1968, he expressed the hope that they might "serve to shed some light on one of humanity's oldest and most recalcitrant dilemmas: the dilemma of a limited collaboration with evil, in the interests of its ultimate mitigation, as opposed to an uncompromising, heroic but suicidal resistance to it, at the expense of the ultimate weakening of the forces capable of acting against it. Everyone involved in the drama of post-Munich Czechoslovakia was tossed, one way or another, on the horns of this dilemma."[52] Nowhere was that dilemma more brutally illustrated than by Operation Anthropoid, whose objective, known to only a handful of top British and Czechoslovak government-in-exile officials, was to assassinate Reichsprotektor Reinhard Heydrich. Following Heydrich's crackdown, the government in exile became increasingly jittery about

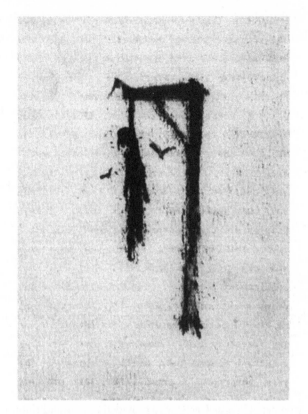

FIGURE 5.3. Jan Reegen, untitled drawing, 1948, Galerie
Ztichlá klika v Praze. From Jan Placák, ed., *Dopisy Hanese
Reegena Vladimíru Boudníkovi a Reegenova literární pozůstalost*,
Prague, 2014.

the lack of resistance at home, which threatened Beneš's ambitions to have
the Allies commit to reestablishing Czechoslovakia on its old borders. He was
also worried about losing the domestic initiative to the KSČ, now that the
noncommunist resistance had been crippled. Moscow was starting to drop its
own parachutists into the protectorate. As soon as the remnants of the domestic resistance realized what was being planned, they pleaded with Beneš
to call off the operation, arguing that "this assassination . . . would not only
endanger our hostages and political prisoners, but also cost thousands of
other lives."[53] "An act of violence . . . might be imperative or even necessary
in our country," Beneš responded. "This would save the nation internationally,
and even great sacrifices would be worth it."[54]

Jozef Gabčík (a Slovak) and Jan Kubiš (a Czech) parachuted into Bohemia on 28 December 1941. Their plane went astray and dropped them in a frozen field in the village of Nehvizdy, eighteen kilometers east of Prague, instead of near Plzeň as planned. Other parachutist teams—code-named Silver A, Silver B, Out Distance, Bioscope, and Tin—had separate tasks. Gabčík and Kubiš were fortunate to be found by local Sokol members who had contacts in the resistance. Equipped with false names and papers, the pair made their way to the capital, where friends of the resistance hid them at huge risk to the families involved. They never stayed more than a few days in one place. Their rendezvous point was the flat of Marie and Alois Moravec on Biskupcova Street in Žižkov, where they liaised with Josef Valčík of the Silver A group. Valčík stayed in the Moravecs' apartment for ten days in April 1942, and Karel Čurda and Adolf Opálka of Out Distance holed up there for shorter periods. It was Gabčík, not Kubiš, as Binet says in *HHhH*, who had an affair with "the beautiful Anna Malinová, with her raspberry lips," a young widow with a three-year-old daughter whom Jozef met on a tram in January.[55] Malinová in turn introduced Kubiš to Marie Kovárníková, the younger sister of her coworker Ludmila Soukupová, and Jan and Marie were soon on more than comradely terms too. Or so the romantic version has it. All three women were members of the resistance, so their affairs with the Operation Anthropoid parachutists may have been a front.[56] The sisters shared a ground-floor flat in Letenská Street in the Lesser Town that doubled as a dead-letter drop for František Šafařík, a carpenter at Prague Castle who provided Gabčík and Kubiš with information about Heydrich's movements. The protector had moved his family to a leafy estate confiscated from Jews in Panenské Břežany, a quiet village outside the city. He was driven to Hradčany every day in an open-topped Mercedes-Benz, often without an armed escort. Gabčík and Kubiš carefully scouted the route, looking for a suitable place for an ambush. Whatever their relationship, Anna's raspberry lips did not stop Gabčík from getting engaged on 24 May to Liběna (Liboslava) Fafková, the younger daughter of the Fafek family, in whose apartment he and Kubiš stayed in the week before the attack on Heydrich.[57]

The assassins' hand was forced three days later when they received intelligence from Šafařík that Heydrich was about to be recalled to Berlin and might be transferred to Paris. It was now or never. At 10:35 on the morning of 27 May Valčík flashed his shaving mirror from one hundred meters up the hill to signal the approach of Heydrich's car. Gabčík and Kubiš were lying in wait at the hairpin bend between V Holešovičkách and Zenklova Streets in Libeň,[58] where the vehicle would have to slow down. As Gabčík stepped out to open fire, his Sten gun jammed. Heydrich ordered his driver to stop and rose in his seat, brandishing a pistol. Kubiš threw an antitank grenade at the Mercedes; it exploded near the rear fender, leaving Heydrich with a collapsed lung, broken rib, torn diaphragm, ruptured spleen, and fragments of shrapnel and upholstery in his body. Gabčík, Kubiš, and Valčík escaped in the confusion, and Heydrich was rushed to nearby Bulovka Hospital and operated on the same day. Within an hour of the attack Hitler instructed Frank to execute ten thousand Czechs, but Frank flew to Berlin and persuaded him to hold off until more was known about the assailants. Frank reimposed martial law and threatened that anyone helping the assassins or with-holding information about the attack would be shot along with their families. A reward of ten million Czech crowns (which the protectorate government prom-ised to double) was offered for information leading to the arrest of the perpetra-tors. Items found at the crime scene—an overcoat, a hat, a briefcase, and a woman's bicycle—were displayed in the window of the Baťa store on Wenceslas Square in the hope of jogging Czech memories.[59] The next night the Germans sealed off the city and twelve thousand police, SS, and Wehrmacht troops con-ducted a house-to-house search that turned up nothing. Kubiš hid with the Fafeks in Kolínská Street in Žižkov before spending a last night at Marie Kovárníková's. Meanwhile, Anna Malinová concealed Gabčík in her Pankrác flat. Both men then moved to a hiding place prepared by the resistance in the crypt of the Orthodox Cathedral of Saint Cyril and Saint Methodius on Resslova Street in the New Town, where they joined Valčík and Opálka, as well as Jan Hrubý and Josef Bublík of Bioscope and Jaroslav Švarc of Tin, whose (now abandoned) mission had been to assassinate minister of education Emanuel Moravec.

In the early morning hours of 4 June Heydrich succumbed to his wounds. The autopsy gave the cause of death as septicemia. Heydrich's coffin was on display all day on 7 June in the first courtyard of Prague Castle, accompanied by the sound of "sad chorales and national songs."[60] His remains were then taken in procession to Hybernské Station and loaded on a train to Berlin. Prague's streets were (of course) lined with thousands of mourners. Heydrich's state funeral took place two days later in the Mosaic Hall of the Reich Chancel-lery. The Berlin Staatskapelle played Siegfried's funeral march from Wagner's *Götterdämmerung*,[61] Hitler eulogized his fallen comrade as "one of the stron-gest defenders of the German Reich idea, one of the biggest enemies of all the enemies of the Reich," and Himmler reminded the mourners that "Heydrich solved all problems from a racial point of view."[62] Emil Hácha was present, along with the entire protectorate government. They probably didn't need to be told that (in the words of an unsigned article in the next day's *Lidové noviny*) "the Czech nation is now in the gravest period of its thousand-year history."

They were well aware of Hitler's long-term ambitions for Bohemia and Moravia. They also likely knew that in his "secret" inaugural speech at Prague Castle on 2 October 1941 Heydrich had assured German officials that "this space must become German and in the end a Czech will no longer have any business being in it."[63] "Today every Czech man and woman stands before a critical question of whether to opt for the Reich or against it, for Hácha or against him, for Beneš or against him," the *Lidovky* article continued. "On one side stands the Czech nation with its responsible men, millions of working people in the homeland—on the other side are 23 mediocre political agitators and intriguers, who play games with the fate of the nation." "These gentlemen did not remain here to take responsibility before the nation for their actions," the anonymous author added. "No way! They preferred to flee abroad by night and in the mists and leave the nation in the lurch."[64] This is a refrain that would be heard time and again over the next half century.

Once again thousands of people were arrested. Between 28 May and 4 July the papers published (and the radio broadcast) daily lists of the names of people convicted by the Prague and Brno special courts and executed—in total, 1,381 Czech men and women.[65] One of the earliest casualties was Devětsil's first president Vladislav Vančura, who was shot at the Kobylisy military firing range in the northern suburbs of Prague on 1 June. Alois Eliáš met his end at Kobylisy on 19 June. They were among 538 people killed there during the second period of martial law.[66] The manhunt for Heydrich's assassins continued until Karel Čurda of the Out Distance team walked into the Petschek Palace on 16 June and told the Gestapo everything he knew. The next night the Gestapo sealed off the apartment block in Biskupcova Street in Žižkov where the Moravec family lived and stormed their flat. Someone made the mistake of letting Marie Moravcová go to the bathroom, where she swallowed a cyanide pill. Her husband Alois and sixteen-year-old son At'a were taken to the Petschek Palace and brutally interrogated. The boy finally cracked and betrayed the assassins' hiding place when his tormentors showed him his mother's head floating in a fish tank. In the early hours of 18 June more than seven hundred SS and Gestapo troops surrounded the Church of Saint Cyril and Saint Methodius on Resslova Street. All seven parachutists were killed or took their own lives in the ensuing battle, which lasted for more than six hours. The bullet holes can still be seen in the church walls. Bishop Goradz (Matěj Pavlík), chaplain Vladimír Petřek, and other members of the church community were arrested, tortured, and shot at Kobylisy in September. Alois and At'a Moravec were among 262 supporters and relatives of the parachutists executed in Mauthausen on 24 October.[67] So were Gabčík's fiancée Liběna Fafková (along with her father, mother, and older sister Rela), Marie Kovárníková, Ludmila Soukupová, and Anna Malinová. The Moravec family's sacrifice for the nation was completed when Aťa's older brother Miroslav Moravec, a pilot in RAF (Czechoslovak) Squadron 313, crashed his Spitfire on 7 June 1944 in Birdham Pool near Apuldram airport in Sussex shortly after taking off in support of the Allied troops who had landed on the Normandy beaches the day before.[68]

"America was my foreground, familiar and known: the crowds, the voices, Captain Kangaroo and Mr Magoo, the great, westbound trains that clattered and tilted past the crossing as my father and I sat waiting in the car on Orchard Road," writes Mark Slouka in his novel *The Visible World* (2007). "Behind it, though, for as long as I can remember, was the Old World, its shape and feel and smell, like the pattern of wallpaper coming through the paint. . . . When I think back on that close little apartment with the Kubilius sketches in the hallway and the bust of Masaryk by the door and the plastic slipcovers on the new sofa, it seems to me that even when the living room was full of people eating *meruňkové koláče* [apricot tarts] and drinking they were somewhere else as well. I don't quite know how to put it. They seemed to be listening to something . . . that had already passed." The visitor Slouka remembered best was Mr. Chalupa, who would "show up at our door every Friday, carrying his violin case and a bottle of wine in a kind of wicker net and a white paper bag with a loaf of the Irish soda bread my father liked . . . and my parents would smile for some reason and take the things from him and my mother would say, 'Say hello to Mr Chalupa, what's the matter with you?' and he'd say, 'How are the Beatles, young man? How are the fab four, eh?'—in English, as though he didn't know I spoke Czech."

Chalupa escaped Czechoslovakia in 1948 "like most of them, then spent some years in Salzburg, some more in Toronto, another in Chicago, before coming to a temporary rest in our apartment in Queens." Years later, when Slouka was living in Prague, Chalupa's name came up during a conversation in a café in Vinohrady:

"Miloš Chalupa?" the old man asked.

"You knew him?"

"Everyone knew him," he said. "Or of him. He was some kind of accountant before the war, though I'm not sure what he accounted for, or to whom. During the war he was an interpreter for the Gestapo." . . .

"You're saying Chalupa was a collaborator?" I said.

"Who knows?" the old man said. "They say he was approached by the Resistance some time in 1941, around the time the RAF dropped those paratroopers who were to assassinate Heydrich into the Protectorate. He told them he couldn't help them."

"So he was a collaborator," I said.

"Listen," the old man said, "if only the heroes were left in Prague after '45—or in Warsaw or Leningrad for that matter—there would be fifty people left between here and Moscow." . . .

"You see, it wasn't always easy," he said. "To tell. To know who was who. Now, take the boys who assassinated Heydrich in '42. A heroic act, a just act, and eight thousand people died because of it. Entire towns were erased from the map."

It turns out—at least in Slouka's novel—that Chalupa was the interpreter attached to the Gestapo unit that raided the Moravecs' flat on 17 June 1942. The old man continues with his "ugly story":

So there you have the basic situation. A wrecked room. Three people lined up against a wall. A single guard. "Please, I have to go [to the bathroom]," Madame Moravcová is pleading, over and over again. "Please." Perhaps she realizes that their lives are over, that life is simply done. Perhaps not. Suddenly someone is yelling from the hallway outside—Stop! Stop!—*Zastavte! Zastavte!*—though maybe it's just *Václave! Václave!*—the name. Who can tell? They sound alike; anyone could confuse them. And Chalupa—here's the thing—supposedly translates the first and the bastards run out, thinking the paratroopers have been flushed into the open, and in the five or six seconds before the guard remembers himself and rushes back in, Moravcová sees her chance and takes it, and by the time they push past her fallen body blocking the bathroom door from inside it's too late for the water they pour down her throat to do them any good. So . . . *Zastavte* or *Václave*—take your pick.

"I remembered Mr Chalupa," Slouka ends. "He'd slept in my room. I could see that irritated look, the way he would lift his violin out of its case with three fingers, the way he would sink into my father's chair. 'How are the Beatles, young man?' I could hear him say. 'How are the fab four, eh?'"[69]

But Lidice Is in Europe

In "the unending streams of those who came to . . . Prague Castle on Sunday [7 June] to pay their last respects at the catafalque with the remains of acting Reich protector SS-Obergruppenführer and police general Reinhard Heydrich," reported *Lidové noviny* on 10 June 1942, "delegations of workers and farmers stood out." Pride of place went to "a delegation of metalworkers and miners from Kladno, who came wearing their historic costumes and miners' lamps."[70] I do not know whether any of the Kladno delegates came from the village of Lidice, seven kilometers out of town, but most of Lidice's menfolk worked in Kladno's mines and foundries. The reporter could not have known that on the night of 9 June German troops and police had descended on Lidice and sealed the village off from the outside world. From midnight onward they raided every house and separated the men (and boys older than fifteen) from the women and children, who were kept in the village school overnight before being driven to the gymnasium of the high school in Kladno. All farm animals, agricultural implements, and other items of value were impounded and carted off to the nearby town of Buštěhrad. The Germans kept detailed inventories of the confiscated property; "a so far unascertained quantity of chickens and rabbits," reads one Kafkaesque entry.[71]

K. H. Frank arrived on the morning of the tenth to personally supervise the vengeance the Führer had personally ordered. Hitler's instructions were detailed and specific, and they were carried out to the letter. The Nazis broadcast the proclamation around the world:

During the search for the murderers of Obergruppenführer Heydrich it was conclusively proven that the inhabitants of the community of Lidice by Kladno provided support and help to a network who are likely to have perpetrated this crime. The relevant evidence was obtained without the help of the local population. The attitude toward the assassination shown by this is underlined by further actions hostile to the Reich, such as discoveries of anti-state printed matter, stores of arms and ammunition, illegal transmitters and an extraordinary quantity of rationed goods, and the fact that citizens of this settlement are in active enemy service abroad. Because the citizens of this community by their actions and support of the murderers of SS-Obergruppenführer Heydrich broke proclaimed laws in the grossest manner the adult men were put to death by shooting, the women were transported to concentration camps, and the children were taken to be appropriately brought up. The buildings in the village were razed to the ground and the name of the village was erased.[72]

There was no evidence whatsoever linking Lidice to Operation Anthropoid. This was a reprisal, pure and simple—collective punishment as spectacle, designed to deter through terror.

From 7:00 on the morning of 10 June, 173 males (the oldest was eighty-four, the youngest fourteen) were shot in groups of five to ten in the garden behind the Horák family barn. The wall was lined with mattresses to prevent ricocheting bullets. Twenty-six more villagers were shot at Kobylisy on 16 June. Of these, seven women and nine men were already in custody because they had relatives fighting with the Czechoslovak forces abroad, and ten men were at work or otherwise absent from Lidice on the night of 9 June. The children were taken from their mothers in Kladno. Of the 205 women deported to Ravensbrück, only 143 returned. Just ten of Lidice's children were considered suitable for Germanization; eighty-eight others were transported to the Łódź ghetto, of whom eighty-one were gassed in Chelmno on 2 July. They are commemorated today in Marie Uchytilová-Kučová's memorial. Only seventeen children survived the war. One of them, Václav Zelenka, would later become mayor of the rebuilt village. He was three years old when he was taken to Germany and given a new name. Zelenka's adoptive father "treated me like his own son. . . . I was scared to go back to Lidice," he told an interviewer in August 2004. "I did not want to leave. I was told that my mother was back and that she wanted me back, also. Mr. Wagner cried when I left to go back to Czechoslovakia. . . . When I came back I remembered nothing of my former life . . . I only spoke German and the Czech children thought of me as being German because of this. . . . They would not speak to me. It was very lonely."[73]

The troops doused the buildings with gasoline and set them on fire. Thirty Jewish prisoners were trucked in from Terezín. When they arrived in the burning village at 4:00 in the afternoon they were given pickaxes, shovels, 350 grams of bread, and 30 grams of margarine; taken to the place where the men's bodies were heaped up; and told to dig a mass grave twelve meters long, nine meters wide, and three meters deep by six the next morning "or else they can quietly lay down with the others."[74] One of them, the journalist and broadcaster František R. Kraus, wrote a powerful account of his experience soon

FIGURE 5.4. Lidice massacre, 10 June 1942. Photographer unknown. From Jan Kaplan and Krystyna Nosarzewska, *Praha Prag Prague: The Turbulent Century*, Cologne, 1997.

after the war ended. It was a Czech Jew who sang a requiem over the bodies of Lidice's Christian dead:

Suddenly the church breaks apart: a new metallic thundering breaks up the walls, the ringing of the bells resounds clearly, there is a thumping in the tower, flames roar up again, then suddenly the ringing stops, torn away from the roof the bell hurtles down, breaks through the wooden floor and ends with huge clattering on the stone floor, white smoke rolls out of the fallen nave. . . . Next to me stands Karl Langendorf, young, beautiful, the composer, he stands there like a marble statue, his mouth wide open, he raises and lowers his fists. . . . Then low singing sounds from his lips, it is Antonín Dvořák's *Requiem* . . . *Requiem aeternam dona eis domine et lux perpetua luceat eis* [Eternal rest grant them, O Lord, and let perpetual light shine upon them] . . . *Dies irae, dies illa* [Day of wrath, that day] . . . a windy morning rises from the blood-drenched east and Karl Langendorf sings *Sanctus, Sanctus, Sanctus* . . . *Dominus Deus Sabaoth* [Holy, holy, holy . . . Lord God of the Sabbath] . . . bricks drop onto the empty church benches, jump high again and dance to and fro as if it were a festive church holiday, then the beams clatter down and break the roof, walls and vaultings shake, pictures of saints in gold frames fall from the old walls, and thunder to the ground . . . mass is being celebrated for the last time here.

The grave diggers arrived back in Terezín to find candles burning at the heads of their bunks, "just as at that time, when the first of our comrades were hanged. Comrades are singing the monotonous melody of the Kadish [sic], stop, smother their joy." "I sink back. My eyes pass over the barred windows. Outside the night is of the deepest black. And beneath me, on the lower bunk, Karl Langendorf sings quietly: 'Requiem aeternam dona eis, Domine, et lux perpetua luceat eis. . . .' Then he adds in a low voice: 'But Lidice is in Europe!'"[75] Kraus survived the war to write one of the earliest Holocaust memoirs, titled Plyn, plyn . . . , pak oheň: vězeň č. B 11632 (Gas, gas . . . , then fire: Prisoner #B 11632), published in Havlíčkův Brod in 1945. Karel Langendorf, as he is named in Czech sources, was transported to Auschwitz on 18 May 1944. He did not survive.

Over the following weeks the ruins were blown up with plastic explosives and bulldozed to the ground. The trees were cut down, the carp pond drained, the stream that ran through the village diverted, the cemetery destroyed. By 7 July one hundred workers had put in "perhaps 20,000 man-hours" to obliterate all traces of the settlement.[76] A cameraman brought in from Prague filmed everything for posterity (the film became an exhibit in the Nuremberg trials of 1945).[77] The same fate befell the hamlet of Ležáky in the Pardubice region following the discovery of a radio transmitter belonging to the Silver A team. On 24 June the Nazis shot all thirty-two of Ležáky's adult inhabitants, both men and women, and sent eleven of its thirteen children to Chelmno to be gassed. Two infant sisters, Jarmila and Marie Šťulíková, were selected for Germanization. They were the only survivors. Ležáky had just eight houses. Unlike Lidice, it was not rebuilt after the war.

The Lidice massacre provoked international outcry, which, among other things, led the British and (Free) French governments to repudiate the Munich Agreement—exactly as Beneš had hoped. British foreign secretary Anthony Eden privately assured Beneš that the Allies would support the expulsion of Sudeten Germans from Czechoslovakia after the war was over.[78] The town of Stern Park Gardens, Illinois, renamed itself Lidice in solidarity, as did communities or districts in Mexico (San Jerónimo Lídice, now part of Mexico City), Brazil, Panama, Peru, Venezuela, Ecuador, and what is now Israel.[79] "Lidice, the little village, did more to keep alive the Freedom of Europe by being wiped out," opined the *New York Times*, "than the great city of Paris did, in 1940, by a surrender that kept its buildings intact. . . . We need tanks, planes and guns. We need symbols, too."[80] US secretary of state William Franklin Knox promised "15,000 persons at a United Nations rally in Boston Garden" that "the Allies would fight until 'the Nazi butchers' were swept from the face of the earth 'even as they obliterated Lidice.'"[81] The *Washington Post* described the massacre as "this most savage single act of repression in the history of the German occupation of continental Europe."[82] In fact, it was not, at least in terms of numbers; Babi Yar was. The *Post* should have known better, since the events in Kyiv had been reported in the *New York Times* three months earlier under the headline "50,000 Kiev Deaths Charged to Nazis."[83] But as Jonathan Harrison uncomfortably points out, "Lidice was an important moment of escalation. It signified the boundaries the Nazis were prepared to cross. It was one thing for the Third Reich to murder eastern European Jews secretly in enclosed camps or under cover of partisan warfare; it was another thing entirely to brazenly massacre a village full of Christians and leave photographic evidence of the carnage in full view."[84] Conceptually speaking, Babi Yar was not in Europe.

In Britain a Jewish doctor and councilor in the industrial town of Stoke-on-Trent began a "Lidice Shall Live" campaign. Barnett Stross was elected a Labour Party member of Parliament in the 1945 general election and rose to become minister of health in Harold Wilson's 1964 government, but he was born in Pabianice near Łódź in 1899. His parents immigrated to the United Kingdom in 1902 and settled in Leeds, where Barnett went to university and qualified in medicine in 1926. He was a member of the Socialist Medical Association and a campaigner for miners who suffered from pneumoconiosis; in the days before the National Health Service, he treated his poorer patients for free. There was a significant Czech immigrant population in Stoke at the time, and several of Nicholas Winton's rescued Czechoslovak children were fostered there.[85] Stross launched "Lidice Shall Live" before a crowd of three thousand people in the Victoria Hall in the presence of Edvard Beneš and the president of the Miners' Federation, Will Lawther. The British miners felt a bond with their Czech brethren, especially in the wake of the Sneyd pit disaster in Stoke on 1 January 1942, which killed fifty-six boys and men. The campaign raised £32,000, which would have a purchasing power of almost £1.5 million at 2019 values—an astonishing sum to be donated by ordinary working people under conditions of strict wartime rationing. After the war the money helped fund the building of new Lidice. Construction started in 1948. Linking the new village to the site of the old is the largest rose garden in the world, which was also Stross's idea.[86]

One of the earliest literary responses to the destruction of Lidice came from the Czech poet and diplomat Viktor Fischl, who may be better known as Avigdor Dagan, the name he adopted after abandoning Czechoslovakia for Israel in 1948. For Fischl, like many others, this was his second emigration; he first fled Czechoslovakia for London in 1939, where he headed the cultural division of Jan Masaryk's Ministry of Foreign Affairs in the Czechoslovak government in exile. "It is no more; it is no more / the tongueless bells no longer ring / only the smoking walls remain / and one stray dog who walks alone / searching in vain from stone to stone," he laments in *"Mrtvá ves"* (1942),[87] which Laurie Lee (of *Cider with Rosie* fame) rendered into English as *The Dead Village*.[88] In 1944 the Czechoslovak branch of the International PEN Club, which had been reestablished in London with Fischl as its secretary, published an anthology in tribute to Lidice.[89] "Cry to us, murdered village," writes Cecil Day Lewis:

> While your grave
> Aches raw on history, make us understand
> What freedom asks of us. Strengthen our hand
> Against the arrogant dogmas that deprave
> And have no proof but death at their command.[90]

"The Nazis are stupid beasts," wrote 1929 Nobel Prize winner Thomas Mann in the same volume. "They wanted to consign the name of Lidice to eternal oblivion, and they have engraved it forever into the memory of man by their atrocious deed."[91] Thomas's older brother Heinrich Mann, who was living in California by then, took Lidice as the subject of an eponymous novel published in 1943. After fleeing Germany in 1933, both brothers were granted Czechoslovak citizenship in 1935–1936. Rudolf Fleischmann, the Czech Jewish businessman who helped them obtain their passports, made it to Britain in March 1939; his daughters Milena and Eva followed on one of Nicholas Winton's trains.[92]

Fritz Lang and Bertolt Brecht, who were both exiled in America, somewhat uneasily cooperated on a Hollywood film (loosely) based on Heydrich's assassination, *Hangmen Also Die* (1943). Edna St. Vincent Millay's "The Murder of Lidice" was commissioned by the Writers' War Board and began life as a radio drama broadcast by NBC on 19 October 1942. According to Franklin W. Adams, the intent was "to make clear to all citizens of the United Nations the meaning of the word 'Lidice.' When that meaning is understood by every American, we never will stop short of total victory."[93] "In all frankness," wrote *Kirkus Reviews*, "were this not by a poet whose name means fame sales, the poetic drama written as straight good propaganda would hardly merit a place on the shelves with her creative work . . . as poetry, it is not exceptional."[94] Composed in exile in Manhattan in 1943, Bohuslav Martinů's *Památník Lidicím* (*Memorial to Lidice*) is of an altogether different artistic caliber.[95] So is Humphrey Jennings's remarkable 1943 film *The Silent Village*. The idea for the film was Viktor Fischl's. "The way from the poem to the film was not so long," he told an interviewer in 2000 (by which time he was eighty-nine). "I had this idea of trying to replace what happened in Lidice to a village in Wales, and I knew of course that there were differences between a Czech village and a Welsh village, but there were also many similarities."[96] Fischl pitched his idea to the Crown Film Unit, a branch of the UK government's wartime Ministry of Information. Jennings saw Fischl's draft and "said immediately that I thought it was really one of the most brilliant ideas for a short film that we'd ever come across."[97]

As might be expected of a leading member of the British surrealist group, *The Silent Village* was no ordinary documentary. Jennings sat on the organizing committee for the 1936 *International Surrealist Exhibition* in London, served as deputy editor of the British surrealist journal *London Bulletin* (1938–1940), and helped mount *The Impact of Machines* exhibition at the surrealists' London Gallery in April 1938.[98] He was also a cofounder with Charles Madge and Tom Harrisson of the pioneering social research organization Mass-Observation, which drew on the talents and testimonies of "coalminers, factory hands, shopkeepers, salesmen, housewives, hospital nurses, bank clerks, businessmen, doctors and schoolmasters, scientists and technicians"[99] to generate "that anthropological study of our own civilization of which we stand in such desperate need."[100] Here are a few lines of his poetry, responding to the Blitz:

> I see a thousand strange sights in the streets of London
> I see the clock on Bow Church burning in daytime
> I see a one-legged man crossing the fire on crutches
> I see three negroes and a woman with white face-powder reading
>   music at half-past three in the morning
> I see an ambulance girl with her arms full of roses
> I see the burnt drums of the Philharmonic
> I see the green leaves of Lincolnshire carried through London on the
>   wrecked body of an aircraft[101]

With the help of Arthur Horner, president of the South Wales Miners' Federation, Jennings went in search of a suitable Welsh mining village to play the part of Lidice. They settled on Cwmgiedd, "up in a narrow little valley . . . with a little straight street that goes up into the hills and on each side charming little stone houses, and down the middle, parallel to the street, is a mountain stream. . . . And halfway up is a grocer's shop on the right—Tom Powell, Family Grocer—and on the left, a beautiful white Methodist Chapel" against whose wall the men of the village would be lined up and shot. There were no professional actors: the people of Cwmgiedd "were playing themselves and themselves as the people of Lidice—that's to say, making an imaginary trans-formation of themselves. . . . We were using Cwmgiedd and the country round it as a country under the 'protection' of the greater German Reich, and this meant we had to take the story and the incidents of the Nazis in Czechoslova-kia and in Lidice and find the equivalents to them in Wales," explains Jennings. He instances the use of the Welsh language in the film, which would not be comprehensible to most of its intended audience but, like Czech in the pro-tectorate, becomes "the language of the underground movement." The soundtrack makes moving use of unaccompanied Welsh male choirs. It also employs Siegfried's funeral music from *Götterdämmerung*—first, as back-ground to the radio announcement of Heydrich's death, and later, with swell-ing crescendo and to devastating effect, as the soundtrack to extended shots of Cwmgiedd burning.[102]

Lidice rightly became a byword for Nazi inhumanity, and the response around the globe was truly heartwarming. But bearing in mind that it is Milan Kundera's second tear—the tear that says, "How nice to be moved, together with all mankind, by children running on the grass!"—that makes kitsch kitsch, we might ask how singular these events really were. After all, a year later, in June 1943, the US military was carrying out bombing runs at Dugway Prov-ing Ground, Utah, on a replica of a Japanese village designed by a Czech ar-chitect who, by the most petrifying of coincidences, was born and raised in Kladno, just down the road from Lidice. Those tests paved the way for the massacre of *more than eighty-three thousand civilians* and the destruction of *267,171 buildings in a single night*. I know there are differences between a Czech village and a Japanese city, but there are also many similarities. Except that Tokyo, of course, is not in Europe.

Back in the protectorate, Czechs set about demonstrating their loyalty to Hácha and the Reich with Švejkish zeal. On the evening of 24 June 1942 around eighteen hundred actors, musicians, and artists filled the National The-ater for a collective *Slib věrnosti Říši* (Promise of fidelity to the Reich). The stage was dominated by a large bust of Hitler. Prime minister Jaroslav Krejčí

FIGURE 5.5. Cover of *Pražský ilustrovaný zpravodaj*
magazine showing demonstration of loyalty to the Reich,
Wenceslas Square, 3 July 1942. Photographer unknown. From
Jan Kaplan and Krystyna Nosarzewska, *Praha Prag Prague:
The Turbulent Century*, Cologne, 1997.

was there. So was the lovely young Czech film star Lída Baarová, among many
other celebrities of stage and screen. Lída had returned to Prague after Hitler
forced Goebbels to end their scandalous two-year affair in August 1938. Emanuel Moravec expressed his immense gratitude at the turn of events that "led
Dr Hácha to Berlin three years ago" to join "the group of nations that are going
toward a great future under the banner of national socialism."[103] The SS report
for the day likely caught the mood better:

After the overture from *Lohengrin* the director of the National Theater
[Ladislav] Šíp said a few opening words in which he emphasized the inter-
connectedness of German and Czech art. . . . It was rewarded with

applause, but not at all spontaneous or convincing. The actor [Rudolf] Deyl's speech suffered from excessive pathos that bordered on the unendurable. At the hailing of the Führer and the Reich with which this speech culminated those present rose from their seats and silently saluted with a raised right arm. A lone voice called out "*zdar*" [success]. . . . Only a few parts of Moravec's speech aroused any interest or reaction. Those present visibly took their participation to be a necessary duty.[104]

Moravec spoke again on 3 July at a huge demonstration in Wenceslas Square at which, according to *Lidové noviny*, "more than 200,000 people spontaneously and unanimously expressed their loyalty to the Reich and the Führer."[105] His address has gone down in Czech memory as "one of the worst collaborationist speeches" of the occupation.[106] President Hácha took his place on the podium at seven o'clock in the evening to the accompaniment of the fanfare from Smetana's *Libuše* (which the composer wrote as "a festive work for special commemorative days") amid a forest of Nazi salutes.[107] At that same moment martial law was lifted. Because, after all, you have to live.

Monumental Details

In July 1939, on Reinhard Heydrich's instructions, Adolf Eichmann established a Central Office for Jewish Emigration in Bohemia and Moravia modeled on his "assembly line" in Vienna. An appreciable number of Czech Jews (19,016 by the end of 1939) did manage to emigrate,[108] but options became more restricted as the war went on, and emigration officially ceased across the entire Reich as of 1 October 1941. Hermann Göring wrote to Heydrich on 31 July 1941 "amending" his 1939 mandate in light of the "time constraints" on "emigration or evacuation" and authorizing him "to take all necessary preparatory measures, from an organizational, concrete and material point of view, for a total solution of the Jewish question in the German sphere of influence in Europe."[109] It was to this end that Heydrich convened the infamous Wannsee Conference on 20 January 1942 in an SS villa outside Berlin; it was attended by fifteen top Nazi officials, including Adolf Eichmann and Wilhelm Stuckart. The agenda was devoted to discussing not whether Europe's eleven million Jews (including those in Britain and neutral countries) would be murdered but how. Himmler and Heydrich were worried about the impact of Einsatzgruppen mass shootings on the morale of German soldiers. Gunning down naked men, women, and children by the truckload proved hard on the Aryan psyche. More distance was needed between killer and victim. Killing by carbon monoxide exhaust fumes in mobile "gas vans" had been trialed at Chelmno in Poland, where the first dedicated extermination camp had opened the previous month, and experiments with cyanide-based Zyklon B poison gas were already under way at Auschwitz.

By then, Milena Jesenská's cold pogrom had prepared the ground for the extermination of the Jewish community that had been such an integral part of Prague life—and especially of Prague-German life—by systematically extruding Jews from society. The young poet Jiří Orten, a protégé of František Halas's, mapped the contours of the city's latest spatial and temporal apartheid in his diary on 27 October 1940. The lines don't rhyme. But they do have an insistent rhythm, even in translation:

> I am not permitted to leave the house after eight in the evening.
> I am not permitted to rent an independent apartment.
> I am not permitted to move anywhere other than to Prague I or V [the Old Town and Josefov], and then only as a sub-tenant.
> I am not permitted to frequent wine bars, cafés, pubs, cinemas, theaters, or concerts, apart from one or two cafés that are reserved for me.
> I am not permitted to go to parks and gardens.
> I am not permitted to go to the municipal woods.
> I am not permitted to venture beyond the periphery of Prague.
> I am not permitted (therefore) to go home, to Kutná Hora, or anywhere else, without special permission from the Gestapo.
> I am not permitted to travel in motorized vehicles, and [I am allowed] only in the rear half of the last car on trams.
> I am not permitted to shop in any kind of stores except between 11.00 and 1.00 and 3.00 and 5.00 [in fact, it was 4:30].
> I am not permitted to perform in theaters or be publicly active in any other way.
> I am not permitted to be a member of any societies.
> I am not permitted to attend any kind of school.
> I am not permitted to mix socially with members of National Solidarity, and they are not allowed to socialize with me, they are not allowed to talk with me, to stop and speak about anything that is not necessary (e.g., when shopping).[110]

Orten's list could have been a lot longer. By the time he wrote those words, Jews were also banned from swimming pools, hotels, sports grounds, libraries, steamboats, taxis, dining and sleeping cars on trains (beginning in October 1941, they were allowed only in third-class compartments), and specified streets in the city center. They were not permitted to work in public institutions, courts of law, schools, or health facilities and could not share hospital rooms with Aryans or send their children to German (from July 1939) or Czech (from August 1940) elementary and middle schools. They were forbidden to own radios or breed pigeons. Jewish doctors were not permitted to treat non-Jewish patients. Jewish employees could be dismissed from their jobs without notice or compensation, and they were obligated to take on any work assigned by labor offices (including road building, railroad construction, factory work, and coal mining). Jewish real estate, stocks and shares, jewelry, works of art, bank accounts, insurance policies, and even items of furniture had to be exhaustively inventoried and were ruthlessly plundered. Trustees were appointed to run Jewish businesses, all of which would be closed or expropriated by 31 March 1941. Payments to Jews, including rents and pensions, had to be made into blocked accounts with strict weekly limits on withdrawals. From March 1940 Jews' identity cards were marked with a large letter *J*. In October 1940 the Prague municipal government required Jews to return their clothing ration coupons and to buy their clothes in junk shops. Over the course of the next year, additional edicts deprived Jews of their furs, telephones, typewriters, gramophones and gramophone records, cameras, and musical instruments; revoked their driving and fishing licenses; banned them from using buses, trolley buses, and public phone booths; and confined their visits to barbers and hairdressers to the hours of 8:00–10:00 a.m.

On 30 August 1941, as Jiří Orten crossed over what is now the Rašín Embankment to buy a pack of cigarettes, he was struck by a German ambulance. It was his twenty-second birthday. He was rushed to the hospital on Charles Square, only to be refused treatment. By the time he was transported to a Jewish-only facility, he was in a coma. He died two days later.[111] A month later the Vltava embankments were closed to Jews from the Smíchov railway bridge to the Hlávka Bridge, and Jews were banned from buying tobacco products. Either of these measures might have saved the poet's life, but perhaps Jiří too, like Franz Kafka, was better off out of it. A week after Orten's death a police decree on the identification of Jews required Czech Jews over the age of six to wear a yellow Star of David whenever they appeared in public. On 29 September Heydrich closed all synagogues. On 6 October he ordered the protectorate government to fire "Jewish half-breeds and public officials with Jewish relatives."[112] On 23 October the Ministry of Agriculture prohibited Jews from acquiring "fruit of any sort, fresh, dried, or otherwise preserved, including dried fruits and nuts, also marmalade, jam, cheese, sweets, fish and fish products, poultry and game."[113] The ban was later extended to onions (8 November), wines and spirits (21 November), coffee (Christmas 1941), and garlic (15 January 1942). By 12 December 1942 Jewish children were forbidden to receive honey. The number of places that were off-limits to Jews grew as laundries, dyeing works, cleaning agencies, museums, art galleries, Prague Castle, the Christmas Fair on Charles Square, Wenceslas Square between 3:00 p.m. Saturday and 8:00 a.m. Monday, and all post offices in the city except one in the New Town (accessible between 2:30 and 5:00 p.m. only) were added to the list. Beginning in January 1942 it was forbidden to sell newspapers to Jews. On 24 July 1942 the Central Office for the Regulation of the Jewish Question in Bohemia and Moravia (as Eichmann's Central Office for Jewish Emigration had been renamed) decreed that "all Jewish schools are to be closed, with immediate effect. All schooling of Jewish children, including in private, is forbidden. Violations will be dealt with by the police."[114]

From 15 March 1940 all persons in the protectorate considered to be Jews under the Nuremberg Laws were required to register with the Jewish community, whether they were of the Jewish faith or not. While the Nazis had great difficulty finding reliable criteria to distinguish Germans from Czechs, their procedures for identifying Jews were crystal clear. The arbitrariness of these classifications, on which lives and deaths turned, is terrifying. In the protectorate a Jew was anyone "descended by race from at least three wholly Jewish grandparents"—and a Jewish grandparent was defined *not* by any supposed "racial" characteristics but by membership in a Jewish religious community. Individuals of "mixed blood" (*míšenec/Mischling*) were "considered Jewish" if they had two Jewish grandparents who belonged to the Jewish religious community on 15 September 1935 or had been accepted into it afterward, and if they were either married to a Jew on or after that date or born of marriage with a Jew on or after that date.[115] The basis on which wartime Slovakia decided who to hand over to the Reich for extermination in exchange for a bounty of five hundred reichmarks per head was quite different.[116] According to the relevant law passed in April 1939, a Jew was anybody of the Jewish faith, even if they had converted to Christianity after 30 October 1918; anybody of no religion but with at least one parent of the Jewish faith; anybody descended from a Jew, with the exception of descendants who had joined a Christian denomination before 30 October 1918; and anybody who had married a person of the Jewish faith after the April 1939 law went into effect. In the last case, a person's Jewishness would expire when the marriage ended.[117] Franz Kafka's nieces Věra and Helena Davidová, the daughters of his sister Ottla and her Czech Christian husband Josef David, were not deemed Jewish in the protectorate. Had the David family lived in Slovakia, it would have been a different story.

Heydrich met with Slovak prime minister Vojtech Lazár Tuka in Bratislava on 10 April 1942, and Tuka agreed to deport all of Slovakia's Jews, more than seventy thousand people in total. Transports officially began the next day. However, Heather Dune Macadam recently established that the first trainload of Jews to Auschwitz had already left Slovakia two weeks earlier on 25 March. On board were nearly a thousand unmarried Jewish girls (some as young as fifteen) and young women whose parents had been told they would be away for only a few months while working in Germany. "Town criers announced that Jewish teenage girls and unmarried women up to age 36 must report to central locations such as schools and firehouses to register for government work service. The girls were shocked when they were locked inside these buildings and forced to strip in front of Slovakian and Nazi officials."[118] Between March and October 1942 around fifty-seven thousand Slovak Jews were concentrated in the Slovak camps at Sered', Nováky, and Vyhne before being turned over to German SS and police units. Most perished in Auschwitz, Majdanek, Sobibor, and other camps; only about three hundred survived the war. Another 12,600 Slovak Jews were deported by Einsatzgruppe H and SD units in the wake of the Slovak National Rising in September 1944, about half of whom survived.[119]

Kafka's sister Ottla divorced her husband in April 1942, registered as a Jew, and was transported to Terezín on 3 August. When Věra and Helena, then aged twenty-one and nineteen, found out what had happened to their mother, they demanded to be allowed to join her but were refused because they did not satisfy the "required conditions." On 5 October 1943 Ottla volunteered to accompany a transport of orphaned Polish children to Auschwitz and was gassed with them on arrival.[120] Kafka's other sisters, Elli and Valli, had been among the first wave of Jews deported from Prague two years earlier. On Heydrich's orders the first transport of protectorate Jews left for the Łódź ghetto on 16 October 1941. A second pulled out of Bubny Station on 21 October, with Elli Herrmann and her family aboard; Valli and her husband Josef Pollak followed ten days later on the fourth transport. They all reached Łódź, but Elli, Valli, and their entire families vanished from the historical record after September 1942. They may have died in the gas vans of Chelmno. The Kafka family's housekeeper Marie Wernerová was transported to Terezín in December 1941 and then to the Riga ghetto in January 1942, where she too disappeared.[121] In 2015, under the auspices of Památník šoa Praha (Prague Shoah Memorial), a timely transformation of Bubny Station into a Memorial of Silence began, intended "to remember not only the victims of deportation, but to also focus on the stigma of those who organized the Final Solution and to remember the role of the passive silent majority that did nothing to stop them," and to "call attention to the face of prejudice, xenophobia, racial enmity, and discrimination on the basis of 'otherness' in the world today."[122] In front of the station building stands Aleš Veselý's sculpture *Brána nenávratna* (Gate of the hereafter), twenty meters of railroad track ascending into the sky.

At a press conference at Prague Castle on 5 October 1941 Heydrich told journalists that although the Reich's objective was "not only to eliminate the influence of Judaism within the people of Europe but, to the extent to which this is possible, to resettle [the Jews] outside of Europe," in the protectorate "the first step in the immediate future will be the concentration of Jewry in a town or in part of a town . . . as a collection point and transitional solution for the already initiated evacuation."[123] This option was further discussed at a meeting with Eichmann and other SS top brass on 10 October. Heydrich officially designated Terezín, a fortress town established by Joseph II (and named after his mother Empress Maria Theresa, who had tried to expel the Jews from Bohemia in 1744), a "Jewish Resettlement District" on 17 October. A transport of 340 protectorate Jews arrived on 24 November, after which Terezín became the first destination for all deported Bohemian and Moravian Jews. It was initially intended to do double duty as an "old-age ghetto" for Jews older than sixty-five. By 4 December the ghetto had 4,365 inmates, all housed in one barracks.[124] By autumn 1944 almost 74,000 protectorate Jews had been deported to Terezín.[125] In all, more than 141,000 people—Jews from Slovakia, Germany, Austria, and all over occupied Europe, as well as from the protectorate—had passed through Heydrich's "collection point" by the end of the war, of whom 33,456 died in Terezín and 88,202 were transported to Auschwitz-Birkenau, Majdanek, Treblinka, Sobibór, Bełżec, Malý Trostinec, and other extermination camps.[126] Of these, "at most 3500 people, among them 2971 Czech Jews, which is hardly 4% of the total number," survived.[127]

The largest slaughter of civilians in Czech history took place at Auschwitz-Birkenau on 8 March 1944, when 3,792 inmates of the "family camp" were gassed in a single night.[128] Jiří Weil claims they went to their deaths singing the Czech national anthem "Where Is My Home?"[129] Of the 118,310 inhabitants

FIGURE 5.6. Aleš Veselý, *Gate of the Hereafter*. Holocaust memorial outside
Bubny Station, Prague, installed 2015. Photograph by author, 2018.

of the protectorate considered to be of the "Jewish race" at the outset of the occupation, nearly 26,000 had emigrated by the time Heydrich arrived in Prague. Of the 88,105 Jews still living in the protectorate, around 78,000 have a grave far away (*hrob v dáli*)—as the inscription on Josef Čapek's "symbolic grave" in Vyšehrad Cemetery reads—which is to say they have no grave at all.[130] After the war the names of 77,297 known Holocaust victims from Bohemia and Moravia were recorded on the walls of Prague's Pinkas Synagogue, "arranged alphabetically and by place" so that "every family steps forward anew here as a whole, [and] every individual remains alone. Those who during the war were degraded into numbers and transports again received a home and a human face." The words are those of Hana Volavková, the Jewish Museum's first director after the war and one of the few museum workers to survive the camps. She conceived of the memorial in the Pinkas Synagogue (1954–1959), which was designed by Václav Boštík and Jiří John.[131] Heydrich's propensity to solve all problems from a racial point of view also targeted the Roma, whose identification cards had to be marked with a *Z* (for *Zigeuner*, the German word for Gypsy) from the spring of 1942. Out of an estimated sixty-five hundred people in the protectorate classified as Gypsies, at least three thousand were killed at Auschwitz-Birkenau. Another 533 died in Gypsy camps at Lety in southern Bohemia and Hodonín in Moravia.[132]

Among Elli Herrmann's companions on the second transport to Łódź were Rudolf and Heda Margolius, a young couple who had married at the Vinohrady Synagogue in April 1939. Sixty years later, in a book aptly titled *Hitler, Stalin and I*, Heda described the bedlam at the assembly point in the precinct of Veletržní palác (Trade Fair Palace) in Holešovice, just up the road from Bubny Station. There were "ill people there who were carried in on stretchers, babies, and small children who cried incessantly . . . in the middle of it, in that biggest uproar, a small man sat on his suitcase playing his violin. Perhaps he hadn't observed what was happening around him, for he continued to practice Beethoven's Violin Concerto. Again and again." Other little details stuck in Heda's mind, disintegrating any standpoint from which she might begin to make sense of it all:

> During the transport, in the middle of the night, the train stopped at a small station to collect drinking water into barrels located in each wagon. With excessive yelling they chased us out of the train—one from each wagon. I was chosen and ran out terrified, tripping along the rails, and there on top of a pile of ballast illuminated by the station lamp grew a beautiful violet

flower. I can see it clearly even today. It looked like a wild iris. Why is it that one remembers comparatively trivial events while the most dramatic moments fade totally with time? Maybe it is my strangely developed sense for "monumental detail" that causes events to crumble into sharp impressions of the smallest elements, and at the same time, I miss the overall perspective.[133]

Things break before us; they burst into fragments, disappear.

"After the transports started," relates Peter Demetz, "acquaintances and friends disappeared without a word or with only a few," and "encounters to say goodbye were limited." A *Mischling* who was not yet subject to deportation, Demetz said farewell to his Jewish mother in the Trade Fair Palace compound; she later died in Terezín. Fortunate enough to survive the war, he fled Czechoslovakia "through the woods and across the border to Bavaria" with his girl-friend Hanna in late 1949, "and so it happened that we went through the refugee camps in West Germany, briefly worked for Radio Free Europe, and about two years later safely arrived at Idlewild Airport, New York, USA, with big rucksacks on our backs and a few pennies in our pockets."[134] Demetz published *Prague in Danger*, his history-cum-memoir of the war years, more than sixty years later in 2008, by which time he had turned eighty-five and was Sterling Professor Emeritus of Germanic Language and Literature at Yale University. "I do not remember much, if anything," he confesses; "the dark brown color of the sturdy valise, my mother's hair streaked with a little gray, a few children running around, and some old people, all alone." Memory is a tricky thing. Demetz places this farewell in "the main hall of the Prague Trade Fair . . . the great hall, nearly as big as a football field." H. G. Adler, however, is correct that "for a long time, the assembly point in Prague was situated *on the grounds* of the trade fair hall in a wooden exhibition shack that was unsuitable spatially and otherwise. It was not waterproof, was unheatable and thus bitterly cold in winter, and was neglected and dark, as there was only a small skylight. This miserable place had the euphemistic name 'exhibition palace.'"[135] The assembly point was not the Great Hall of the Trade Fair Palace, which had been inaugurated with the triumphant exhibition of Alfons Mucha's gargantuan series of twenty pan-Slavist paintings *Slovanská epopej* (Slavic epic) in September 1928, but the so-called Radiotrh (Radiomarket) across Veletržní Street from the palace, where the Park Hotel was later built.[136]

The minutiae of another parting lodged deeper in Demetz's mind. This, too, is one of those monumental details that deranges—another of Humphrey

FIGURE 5.7. Jan Lukas, *Before the Transport (Vendulka)*, 1942. Vendulka
survived Terezín, Auschwitz, and two death marches. In 1948 she moved with her
mother to Canada and then to the United States. Courtesy of Helena Lukas,
© Jan Lukas heirs.

Jennings's knots in the great tangled web of space and time that can symbolize
the whole inexpressible, uncapturable process:

> One day my colleague in the bookshop Mr. Glass, half Jewish as was I, in-
> vited me to say adieu to Eva L., who had received her transport order to
> Terezín. We all knew her melancholy and complicated story. Eva was the
> daughter of a well-known Prague journalist and writer who had escaped to

England in time, but she had refused to go because she was in love with a young Austrian who promised to take care of her. They tried to escape together, but it was too late. Eva was briefly imprisoned, and he was sent to Dachau; after she had been released, she tried again to leave, but nothing worked. Now she invited us to her little place for a last evening before she had to go to the transport center.

My colleague acted as host, and two other young men and I sat and sipped glasses of white wine until he announced that Eva had invited us each to make love to her before she left. It was not a gang-bang (whatever that word means and which I learned only fifty years later) but a strangely decorous affair, and so it happened that I was asked to enter the small bedroom, where I found Eva, after my predecessor had left, her body warm and clad in a chemise dating from better times. She was a little older than I, her ash blond hair cut short. She embraced me right away, and though I responded as I should have (I assumed), I still felt or thought I felt that I disappointed her, because I wanted to be as tender as I could while she expected a gust of passion, wordless and strong. Then I left the bedroom, drank another glass, my successor had his moment, and finally Eva came out of her room, clasped us all one after the other, and we left. We never saw her again. It is believed she died in Bergen-Belsen in the last year of the war.[137]

But Miss, we can't help it.

6

Avant-garde and Kitsch

You will not depart with the evening. The wide-open bed, the nakedness of the snow, and the spotlights of a fiery forgetting will deny nothing of what has been and what will be, what persists, what sings, what cries, what wonders, what suffers, what lies, what rears up and what does not find an answer.

—KAREL TEIGE[1]

The He and the She of It

And there she was, Anna Livia, she darent catch a winkle of sleep, purling around like a chit of a child, Wendawanda, a finger-thick, in a Lapsummer skirt and damazon cheeks. . . . She was just a young thin pale soft shy slim slip of a thing then, sauntering, by silvamoonlake . . . oso sweet and so cool and so limber she looked, Nance the Nixie, Nanon L'Escaut, in the silence, of the sycamores, all listening, the kindling curves you simply can't stop feeling.[2]

Reading such descriptions, I am not at all surprised that when Adolf Hoffmeister met with James Joyce in the latter's Paris flat in August 1929 to discuss a Czech translation of *Anna Livia Plurabelle*—a part of *Finnegans Wake* that appeared in *Le Navire d'Argent* in October 1925 and was published as an independent volume in New York in 1928—his thoughts momentarily strayed into the pastures of the erotic. Maybe he was enticed down this particular primrose path by the motherly reminiscences of the luscious Anna Livia herself: "She can't remember half of the cradlenames she smacked on them by the grace of her boxing bishop's infallible slipper, the cane for Kund and abbles for Eyolf and ayther nayther for Yakov Yea."[3] Whatever sparked his imagination, Ada (as Hoffmeister's friends called him) took off on a flight of flagellatory fancy in which one signifier conjured up another, as they do:

> Mr L[éon], Joyce's secretary, a Russian Jew, arrived and we talked more about the possibilities of translating *Work in Progress* [as *Finnegans Wake* was then called] into another language. It was a team meeting, but I felt more like a pupil about to take an end-of-year exam. Joyce stood up and went into the neighboring room. He returned with the slim volume of *Anna Livia Plurabelle* in his long fingers, a strict schoolmaster of tall stature, hidden behind the magnifying lenses of his glasses. His thin clenched lips puckered into a smile, perhaps from amusement at the peculiar suffering that the image of school arouses in us all. School, where you are punished with a cane. In a deserted old chateau, tense with dissolute terror. I remembered the Humming-Bird Garden boarding school in Robert Desnos' confiscated book *L'amour et la liberté* [sic]—*la scène de correction commença*. Léon and I sat silently on the edge of our chairs with the books in our hands.
>
> Who is going to translate it?
> We simultaneously answered:

Mrs Waterhallová	Leon Paul Fargue
Dr Vladimír Procházka	Eugène Jolas
Vítězslav Nezval	Phillippe [Philippe] Soupault
and I.	Valèry [Valéry] Larbaud
	Iwan [Ivan] and Claire Goll

> And you know it is impossible to translate.
> We know.[4]

André Breton claimed that Robert Desnos, "more than any of us, has perhaps got closest to the Surrealist truth" and "speaks Surrealist at will" because of "his extraordinary agility in orally following his thought."[5] The literary scene of correction that flitted across Hoffmeister's inner field of vision as he contemplated Joyce's thin-lipped smile takes up several pages of lovingly detailed chastisement, ending up "in a quiet plain surrounded by woods in the county of Kent," where "thirty young girls whip each other day and night and in the morning, when they are washing themselves, count the scars with which they are marked with an inexpressible pride."[6] Joyce himself harbored similar desires; he once wrote to his "sweet naughty little fuckbird" Nora Barnacle that he longed "to hear you call me into your room and then to find you sitting in an armchair with your fat thighs far apart and your face deep red with anger and a cane in your hand."[7] Perhaps Ada hoped for a similar masochistic frisson from translating the untranslatable. When he questions Joyce on the role of the erotic in *Ulysses*, the master reassures him that "obscenity fills the pages of life as well, and if any book is complete, it cannot spinelessly avoid the reality of what thoughts or actions are but are not allowed to be written about."[8]

This conversation, which Hoffmeister recounted in *Rozpravy Aventina* in 1930, strikes reverberant chords with Milan Kundera's essay on Leoš Janáček and the claustrophobic intimacy of small nations, discussed earlier. Prompted by Hoffmeister's observation that "your nationality is very evident in your work," Joyce emphasized that "every one of my books is a book about Dublin. Dublin is a city that has hardly 300,000 inhabitants and it has become the universal city of my work."[9] This may remind us of Max Brod—another eventual exile—speaking of his hometown of Prague. And yet, Ada tells his Czech readers, "Dublin, which [Joyce] celebrates so many times in his works of incontestably Irish temperament and moral sensibility, drove him out. After *Dubliners* was published Joyce abandoned Ireland, probably forever. The scandalizing of some philistines from the city expelled him from Ireland, likely for good. Nowadays he seldom travels even to England and goes almost incognito. Society is horrified [the word is in English] and in Ireland his name is anathema."[10] Joyce lived in Trieste and Zürich from 1904 to 1920, in Paris from 1920 to 1939, and in Zürich, where he died and is buried, from 1940 to 1941. He last set foot on Irish soil in 1912. Mikoláš Aleš's *Fate of Talent in Bohemia* again leaps to mind. But in this instance, it wasn't only Kundera's small nations that were small-minded—or only the Nazis who burned books. Serialized in *The Little Review* starting in 1918 and first published in book form by Sylvia Beach's Shakespeare and Company bookstore in Paris in 1922, *Ulysses* was banned in the United States until 1934 and in Britain until 1936. Five hundred copies of the second edition of the novel "were seized by His Majesty's Customs and Excise at Folkestone . . . [and] burned with conscientious gusto" in January 1923.[11]

Kevin Birmingham has pointed out the irony that "while [*Ulysses*] was banned to protect the delicate sensibilities of female readers, the book owes its existence to several women. It was inspired, in part, by one woman [Joyce's wife, Nora Barnacle], funded by another [Harriet Shaw Weaver], serialized by two more [Margaret Anderson and Jane Heap, editors of *The Little Review*] and published by yet another [Sylvia Beach]."[12] But then as now, men knew best, especially when it came to knowing what is best for women. On reading

"Nausicaa," an extract from *Ulysses* published in the July–August 1920 issue of *The Little Review*, John Sumner, head of the New York Society for the Suppression of Vice, brought an action for obscenity. In the offending text, "Leopold Bloom, his hand in his pocket, watches a young woman reclining on a beach. Thrilling to his gaze, she lets her skirt fall above her garter belt and he brings himself to orgasm." And so:

> In February 1921, at the Court of Special Sessions, three literary experts were called to testify in front of three judges that "Nausicaa" was art, not pornography. When the British novelist John Cowper Powys declared it a work of beauty that posed no threat to young girls, Heap restrained herself from saying that a young girl's mind frightened her more than anyone's. In one farcical moment, the prosecutor asked that the court hear some offending passages. A snoozing white-haired judge perked up, contemplated Anderson in her pearls and silk blouse, and forbade that obscenities be read out in her presence. Told she was the publisher, his honor said with paternal solicitude: "I am sure she didn't know the significance of what she was publishing."[13]

"The society for which Mr. Sumner is agent, I am told, was founded to protect the public from corruption," wrote Heap. "When asked what public? its defenders spring to the rock on which America was founded: the cream-puff of sentimentality, and answer chivalrously 'Our young girls.'" "I do not understand Obscenity," she goes on. "I have never studied it nor had it, but I know that it must be a terrible and peculiar menace to the United States. I know that there is an expensive department maintained in Washington with a chief and fifty assistants to prevent its spread—and in and for New York we have the Sumner vigilanti. To a mind somewhat used to life Mr. Joyce's chapter seems to be a record of the simplest, most unpreventable, most unfocused sex thoughts possible in a rightly-constructed, unashamed human being. Mr. Joyce is not teaching early Egyptian perversions nor inventing new ones. Girls lean back everywhere, showing lace and silk stockings; wear low cut sleeveless gowns, breathless bathing suits; men think thoughts and have emotions about these things everywhere—seldom as delicately and imaginatively as Mr. Bloom—and no one is corrupted. Can merely reading about the thoughts he thinks corrupt a man when his thoughts do not? All power to the artist, but this is not his function."[14]

To return to Adolf Hoffmeister's interview with James Joyce. "The stance of the Anglo-American public toward *Ulysses* is unwarranted and reflects

FIGURE 6.1. Jindřich Štyrský, *Emily Comes to Me in a Dream*, 1933, collage, plate 10.
From his *Emilie přichází ke mně ve snu*, Prague, 1933.

neither their real interest nor their real outrage," the expatriate Irish writer goes on. "The realistic form of following a day in a rhythm that fills the book with general truths or general symbols narrows into a focus on a few places where there is unconventional language about things and thoughts that are usually hushed up. I think the nakedness of animal human nature in *Ulysses* is faithful and temperate enough."[15] It surely is. Above all in Molly Bloom's soliloquy with which the book ends, one of the most honest attempts to trace what Breton calls "the actual functioning of thought . . . in the absence of any control exercised by reason, exempt from any aesthetic or moral concern" in world literature.[16] "What else were we given all those desires for Id like to know I cant help it if Im young still can I," Molly asks.[17] *Way* too close to the bone. "All the secret sewers of vice are canalized in [*Ulysses's*] flood of unimaginable thoughts, images, and pornographic words," spluttered James Douglas in the London *Sunday Express*. "The greater the artist the greater is his moral responsibility. If he debases and perverts and degrades the noble gift of imagination and wit and lordship of language in the service of Priapus, in the worship of Libitina, and in the adoration of Libido, let him die the death, and let his works perish with him."[18] Meanwhile, the sister rag in Lord Beaverbrook's right-wing populist stable, the *Daily Express*, reported the international boycott of German goods organized by critics of Nazi policies in 1933 under the headline "Judea Declares War on Germany."[19] By a strange set of circumstances that led via the French resistance through Auschwitz, Buchenwald, and Flöha to the small fortress where political prisoners were kept in Terezín, Robert Desnos died of typhoid in the Bohemian concentration camp on 8 June 1945. He had arrived there a day before the Red Army, severely weakened by the twenty-five lashes he had recently received in Flöha for fighting with a fellow prisoner.[20] That is true obscenity, but the censors of social morality would rather have us eternally gaze into the looking glass of kitsch than let pornographic thoughts cloud our minds.

Jan Fromek, whose firm Odeon had been Devětsil's house publisher through the 1920s,[21] brought out the translation of *Anna Livia Plurabelle* by Hoffmeister, Vladimír Procházka, and Marie Weatherall (not Waterhall) in 1932. It was the book's first full translation into any language.[22] This was not the Irish writer's first outing in Czech, however: as a result of an earlier meeting between Joyce and Hoffmeister in Paris in 1928, Václav Petr had published *Ulysses* and *Portrait of the Artist as a Young Man* in 1930, the latter translated by Milena Jesenská's friend Staša Jílovská. This was still four years before *Ulysses* was allowed into Prohibition-era America and only its third full-length translation into any language (it was preceded by French and German). A Czech translation of *Dubliners* came out in 1933. Hoffmeister's interview uncovers some additional Czech connections that are as unexpected as a French surrealist poet dying in Terezín, muddling the boundaries of language and nationality that frame literary histories, much as the careers of Antonín Raymond and his assistants disorder the genealogies of architectural modernism. Floored when Joyce utters the words "*České Budějovice*" and "*Živnostenská banka*" out of the blue "in clear Czech with a flawless accent," Ada asks the Irishman whether he has learned Czech since their last meeting and whether he was ever in Prague. Joyce replies, "No. But my brother-in-law was Czech. My sister Eileen met a man in Trieste, whom she married. He was called František Schaurek and he was a teller in the Trieste branch of the Živnostenská bank. We were all living together then at my brother Stanny's, a language teacher. Schaurek was Czech, maybe his family still lives in Prague (in Žižkov). . . . After the war the Schaureks moved to Prague. František Schaurek later shot himself and my sister is now living in Dublin. . . . It's only a family matter, which I don't like to talk about."[23]

"Hundreds of river names are woven into the text" of *Anna Livia Plurabelle*, Joyce wrote to Harriet Weaver in October 1927.[24] Anna is supposed to be both a woman and a river, Dublin's river Liffey, upon whose banks the chapter begins with two washerwomen gossiping. One of Anna's "fluvial maids of honour from all ends of the earth" is Prague's Vltava,[25] who enters the story as her Germanic avatar the Moldau ("My wrists are wrusty rubbing the mouldaw stains. And the dneepers of wet and the gangres of sin in it!").[26] Joyce urges Hoffmeister to "put your rivers in there: the Vltava, the Váh, the Úslava and the Nežárka. . . . Create a language for your country in my image." Curiously, he asks for a copy of the translation, when it is done, to give to Eileen. "I doubt she read the English original," he explains, "but maybe she'll be able to catch the meaning of the sentences in Czech."[27] And why not? For the original is written less in English as conventionally understood than in "a jetsam litterage of convolvuli of times lost or strayed, of lands derelict and of tongues laggin too."[28] Meaning is a shifty thing at the best of times, whatever language we believe we are communicating in.

"Well, you know or don't you kennet or haven't I told you every telling has a taling and that's the he and the she of it," writes Joyce in *Anna Livia Plurabelle*.[29] In the earliest versions of the text, instead of "every telling has a taling" he wrote "every story has an ending."[30] Evidently he had second thoughts. Contrasting the structure of *Ulysses*, whose action unfolds hour by hour over the course of a single day, he tells Hoffmeister that in *Finnegans Wake*, "wherever is the beginning, there the book also ends."[31] And indeed, if we join the unfinished sentence ("A way a lone a last a loved a long the") with which *Finnegans Wake* ends to the fragment with which it begins ("riverrun, past Eve and Adam's, from swerve of shore to bend of bay, brings us by a commodius vicus of recirculation back to Howth Castle and Environs"), the circle is unbroken.[32] Joyce's experimentation with language proliferates meaning rather than pinning it down. "*Work in Progress* may satisfy more readers than any other book," he tells Ada in response to a question about the difficulty of the text, "because it gives them the possibility of filling up the reading with their own ideas."[33] His tongue may have been in his cheek, but he had a point. The phrase "every telling has a taling," for instance, *may* mean every story has an ending. But it may also conjure up images of private eyes like Philip Marlowe—or perhaps, in the Prague context, secret policemen—furtively tailing their prey. Or it could bring to mind tailings ponds, where the toxic residues from mining are collected after the pure metals have been extracted from the ore, alerting us to what any narrative in its striving for coherence necessarily leaves out. For me, the pun on *tail* (end?) and (tall?) *tale* can also be read as a warning that only through narrative emplotment do events become *history* at all. Of course, Joyce's wordplay might be taken more vulgarly as a sly reminder that obscenity fills the pages of life as well.

A Used Bookstore of Dead Styles

"Seven years of a soulless, repellant masquerade that called itself cultural life," wrote Karel Teige, "simulated by sold-out theaters, large print runs for all sorts of books and countless exhibitions, of which the most taxing festival of the imbecility of Nazi-Protectorate culture was that indigestible grab bag first presented to the public under the slogan *The Nation to Its Artists*." Miloslav Hýsek, whose bromides of a small nation as one big happy family I discussed earlier, certainly would have seconded James Douglas's view that "the greater the artist the greater is his moral responsibility." But for Teige, *The Nation to Its Artists* showed exactly what happens to a culture when the James Joyces of this world are sacrificed on the altars of middlebrow morality:

> Empty-headed, bloodless academicism and the most banal kitsch, slops of
> stale naturalism and schmaltzy secondhand romanticism, a used bookstore
> of dead styles, a necrophilia of senile traditionalism, shallow virtuosity and

eclectic charlatanism, and on top of this a half-hearted, superficial, pussy-footing and parasitic pseudo-modernism—such were the ingredients of the turbid swill that was officially permitted art. . . . All living and progressive creativity . . . was persecuted by the Nazi censor as degenerate art, as snob-bish ivory tower culture, as perverted decadence. The artistic avant-garde was silenced almost without exception. Several of the artists whose work had been the vanguard and driving force of development perished in the war; others were imprisoned or lived on the other side of the battle lines, while those who remained were denied the possibility of showing in public. Some were completely prevented from working, others worked under the most precarious conditions, often without any mutual contact. . . . Several of those who had been or wanted, rightly or wrongly, to be regarded as avant-garde artists contrived to accommodate in one way or another to the requirements of reactionary fashions and popularizing slogans; they enthu-siastically brought to market their wares, which grew shabbier by the season.[34]

The brutal alternatives of exile, imprisonment, excommunication, or accom-modation to the regime undoubtedly defined the broad horizons for avant-garde artists throughout the occupation. They would continue to do so, to varying degrees, for large parts of the next half century, presenting Czech art-ists and writers with very different dilemmas from those faced by their West-ern counterparts long after World War II ended. But the Nazis' cultural polic-ing was not always consistent or effective, and many writers and artists continued to work underground. No less important was the "gray zone" be-tween what was permitted and what was banned, and it was on this borderline that others explored the limits of the possible.[35] In so doing they muddied the boundaries not only between resistance and collaboration but also between avant-garde and kitsch.

It is unlikely that Teige read Clement Greenberg's "Avant-garde and Kitsch," since it first appeared in the fall issue of *Partisan Review* in 1939, but he echoes the American critic's view of kitsch as "the debased and academicized simula-cra of genuine culture" almost word for word. Founded in "emigration from bourgeois society to bohemia," the avant-garde, Greenberg argues, gravitated toward "art for art's sake"; that is, "content is to be dissolved so completely into form that the work of art or literature cannot be reduced in whole or in part to anything not itself." The excitement of modern art "seems to lie most of all in its pure preoccupation with the invention and arrangement of spaces, surfaces, shapes, colors, etc., to the exclusion of whatever is not necessarily implicated in these factors," while "the attention of poets like Rimbaud, Mallarmé, Valéry, Éluard, Pound, Hart Crane, Stevens, even Rilke and Yeats, appears to be centered on the effort to create poetry . . . rather than on experience to be converted into poetry." It is above all this artistic *disengagement* from the world of common sense that alienates "the common man," who finds modern art, literature, or music incomprehensible and correspondingly threatening to his peace of mind. Consider the reputation of *Finnegans Wake*. "Every man, from the Tammany alderman to the Austrian house-painter, finds that he is entitled to his opinion. Most often this resentment toward culture is to be found where the dissatisfaction with society is a reactionary dissatisfaction which expresses itself in revivalism and puritanism, and latest of all, in fascism. Here revolvers and torches begin to be mentioned in the same breath as culture. In the name of godliness or the blood's health, in the name of simple ways and solid virtues, the statue-smashing commences."[36]

Prague's theaters were sold out during the war because (as Peter Demetz drily puts it) the wartime economy was one in which "people had more money to spend on theater and movie tickets than on other discretionary purchases."[37] The principal arenas for Czech performances were the National Theater, the Hudební divadlo Karlín (Karlín Musical Theater), and the Divadlo na Vinohradech (Vinohrady Theater) on what was then Reichsplatz/Říšské náměstí (Reich Square) but is now náměstí Míru (Peace Square). Karel Čapek was the Vinohrady Theater's resident dramaturg from 1921 to 1923, when he personally directed eight plays there. One of them was the première of his *Věc Makropulos* (*The Makropulos Case*), in which his girlfriend (and later wife) Olga Scheinpflugová played the role of Kristina. Leoš Janáček turned *The Makropulos Case* into an opera, which was first performed at the National Theater in Brno in 1926. The Moravian composer was unfailingly imaginative in his sources of inspiration, which ranged from Svatopluk Čech's satires on the little Czech guy (for *Výlety páně Broučkovy*, or *The Excursions of Mr. Brouček to the Moon and the Fifteenth Century*) through Rudolf Těsnohlídek's cartoons in *Lidové noviny* (for *Příhody lišky Bystroušky*, or *The Cunning Little Vixen*) to Dostoyevsky's *Z mrtvého domu* (for *From the House of the Dead*). "There are no fewer than three great artistic monuments in this century that my country has built," claimed Milan Kundera in 1985, "which are the three panels of a triptych portraying the hell that was to come: the bureaucratic maze in Kafka, the military idiocy of Hašek, the concentration camp despair of Janáček. Indeed, between the creating of *The Trial* in 1917 and *The House of the Dead* in 1928 everything had already been said in Prague, and History had only to make its entrance in order to mime what fiction had already imagined." He describes Janáček's "most beautiful and astonishing" opera as "violently modern," which sums it up nicely.[38] *From the House of the Dead* must be unique in the operatic literature for having not one female character (the lone mezzo-soprano plays the part of an adolescent Tartar boy, Alyeya).

That the first production at the revamped Karlín Musical Theater (which replaced the Estates Theater as the second stage of the National Theater) on 6 September 1939 was *The Bartered Bride* was symptomatic of the times. The folk costumes of Smetana's "national opera" were dusted off again at the National Theater for a gala performance on 7 November 1940 in honor of Joseph Goebbels's visit to the city. Though it may have reassured some Czechs that their culture was alive and well, this version of Czechness did not threaten the Reich. Even as the works of the exiled Bohuslav Martinů and Jaroslav Ježek were banned, musical manifestations of *češství* embellished the façades of protectorate autonomy. Not all was kitsch. In 1941 the National Theater mounted the first new production of Janáček's *Jenůfa* (known in Czech as *Její pastorkyňa*, or Her stepdaughter) on 27 February with Gabriela Preissová, the author of the play from which Janáček adapted the libretto, in the audience. Preissová's bleak story of unwed pregnancy and infanticide shows the seamier side of a peasant world where brides are bartered. A Dvořák Year culminated on 22 November 1941, by which time Heydrich's crackdown was in full swing, with Václav Talich's production of *Armida*. But there were limits to German indulgence. Karel Kovařovic's *Psohlavci* (The Dogheads, 1898), an opera based on Alois Jirásek's novel about the 1692–1693 peasant uprising in Domažlice against the German landowner Laminger von Albenreuth, had its last wartime performance on 30 September 1939. Smetana's *Braniboři v Čechách* (The Brandenburgers in Bohemia, 1863), an opera set during Otto of Brandenburg's occupation of Prague in 1278–1305, was not staged for the duration of the war. *Libuše* was dropped from the repertoire after a performance on 2 June 1939 in which Marie Podvalová's impersonation of the mythical Czech princess and founder of Prague was too enthusiastically encored. Smetana's "festive opera for special commemorative days" was performed, however, at the National Theater on 23 September 1943—by the Kuratorium youth organization during its *Umění mládeži* (Art for youth) campaign.[39] The Nazis were happy to mobilize symbols of Czechness when it suited them.

In 1942, at the Barrandov studios, filming began of *Kníže Václav* (Duke Wenceslas), an epic retelling of the story of Saint Wenceslas with the Czech patron saint reborn as a loyal German vassal. František Čáp was the director. The budget was an unheard of twenty-one million crowns, which would have made *Duke Wenceslas* the most expensive Czech film ever. A cast was assembled and outdoor crowd scenes were shot in various locations, but the Czechs deliberately dragged their heels, and after many delays and extensions the venture was abandoned "for financial reasons."[40] *Duke Wenceslas* was the only film to be directly commissioned by the German authorities during the protectorate's existence, but this does not mean the Nazis did not keep a tight rein on what was shown in movie theaters. Cinema was the most widespread form of popular entertainment, and the Nazis were keenly aware of the value of film as a propaganda vehicle. The Barrandov film studios, built by Václav Havel's developer father Václav Maria Havel and run by his uncle Miloš Havel, were among the largest and most advanced in Europe. On 28 June 1939 Miloš was summoned to the Černín Palace and told that because the studios were "Jewish property" (one of the minority shareholders in his A-B Film Company, founded in 1921, was Jewish), they would henceforth be administered by a *Treuhand* (trustee). Havel sold a controlling interest in A-B Film to the Cautio Treuhand in April 1940. He finally gave up his own residual 20 percent stake in June 1941. In November 1941 A-B's name was changed to Prag-Film. Joseph Goebbels toured the studios the same month, on the same day he was treated to a performance of *The Bartered Bride*.

A replica of the interior of Prague's Old-New Synagogue was built at Barrandov studios in June 1940 for one of the most notorious anti-Semitic films ever made, Veit Harlan's *Jud Süß* (*Jew Süss*). František Čáp inserted new scenes befitting the times into his 1941 film of Jindřich Šimon Baar's 1908 novel *Jan Cimbura*. Honest Czech farmers sink deeper and deeper into debt at the village pub, whose Jewish owner is more than happy to let them run up tabs at exorbitant rates of interest until one day their wives march on the pub, ransack the premises, burn their men's IOUs, and drive the Jew out of the village. "The camera dwells rather lovingly on the faces of the peasant women when they whip the waitress, skirts up, with sting nettles," notes Peter Demetz.[41] The contemporary message would have been obvious to all. From January 1941 Prague Jews were forcibly conscripted for construction work to expand the studios. Scenes from Leni Riefenstahl's *Tiefland* (*Lowlands*), a film adaptation of Eugen d'Albert's 1903 opera of the same title, were shot at Barrandov in the fall of 1944. The extras playing Pyrenean mountain folk were Roma from the concentration camps, personally selected by Riefenstahl. D'Albert's opera was a favorite of the Führer's, portraying the "contrast between the clean and unspoiled life in the mountains and the moral degeneration of the lowlands,"[42] in which, then as now, populist critics of "urban cultural elites" like to trade. Only three Czech films were made at the Barrandov studios in 1942, two in 1943, and three in 1944. In 1938 forty-one Czech films and forty-six German films played in Czechoslovak cinemas; in 1939 the Czech numbers held steady at forty-one while the German numbers doubled to ninety-two. By 1941 the totals were eleven Czech and sixty-nine German films; in 1944 they were nine and fifty-eight, respectively.[43]

Nineteenth-century Czech classics were staple fare in protectorate theaters, along with new works by pro-regime playwrights. Historical dramas were particularly favored. František Zavřel, a sometime member of the Czech fascist organizations Vlájka (the flag) and Národní obec fašistická (National Fascist Community), saw his *Valdštýn* (Wallenstein) and *Caesar* performed on both stages of the National Theater. Briefly imprisoned as a collaborator after the war, Zavřel was found destitute and homeless on a bench on Letná Plain in November 1947 and died in a hospital a month later. Olga Scheinpflugová described him as "a great tragicomic figure of authorial ambition" who "did not write a single decent play" but "was willing to sacrifice everything, honor and in the end his life as well, in order to hear his pointless words on the stage."[44] Scheinpflugová chose the opposite course. On 4 October 1941—a week after Heydrich's arrival in the city—Karel Čapek's plays were banned from Czech theaters. Soon afterward Emanuel Moravec summoned Čapek's widow to his office and gave her the choice of publicly proclaiming her loyalty to the regime or "forgetting that she ever performed on the stage or wrote plays."[45] Olga opted for the latter, and on 25 February 1942 her books and plays joined Karel's in the memory hole. What was forbidden during the occupation was generally far more interesting than what was performed,[46] although the censor's valiant struggles to create a world of alternative facts possess a grim entertainment value of their own. "On the stage . . . even the names of nations at war with the Reich cannot be mentioned, so heroes go to Madrid and Stockholm instead of London and Moscow [and] drink slivovice and beer instead of gin and whisky," writes Jiří Doležal.[47] No character could be named Adolf for fear of casting a shadow on the Führer,[48] and the line *"Vůdce zhynul! Vůdce zhynul!"* (The leader has perished! The leader has perished!) had to be excised from Karel Hynek Mácha's *May*. *Vůdce* is the Czech equivalent of Führer.[49] After 17 November 1939 university students (or at least Czech university students) no longer trod the boards. When Vilém Mrštík's *Pohádka Máje* (A May fairy tale, 1897) was dramatized at the National Theater in August 1942, the censor truncated "I am Peka and I study with your son in Prague at the Law Faculty" to "I am Peka and I study with your son in Prague." "He doesn't go to lectures [*do přednášek*]" became "He doesn't go to school [*do školy*]."[50] By then, the Law Faculty was closed and there were no university lectures for Czech boys and girls to skip.

Manon the Sinner

One of Prague's most famous prewar theaters was Emil František Burian's D 34, founded in May 1933. The *D*, said Burian, stood not only for *Divadlo* (theater) but also for "*dějiny* [history], *dnešek* [today], *dělník* [worker], *dav* [crowd, multitude, mass], *dělba* [division], *dílo* [product, work, publication], *duch* [spirit], etc." The number that followed it (D 35, D 36, and so on) changed with each season to underline the theater's contemporaneity. Together with Jindřich Honzl and Jiří Frejka, Burian was Czechoslovakia's leading avant-garde director as well as a composer, singer, actor, scenographer, dramaturg, and author. Emil cut his teeth at the Liberated Theater (1926–1927), the Dada Theater (1928–1929), and the Moderní studio (Modern Studio, 1929–1930) before briefly serving as director of the National Theater in Brno (1929–1930) and the Czech Theater in Olomouc (1930–1931). On his return to Prague he worked for a year with the Červené eso (Red Ace) political cabaret, where he directed a jazz chorus. A member of the KSČ since the age of nineteen, Burian made it clear from the outset that D 34 would be "a political theater . . . primarily against fascism and cultural reaction. . . . For a dramaturgic foundation, derived from a philosophic position of dialectical materialism, I plan a repertoire with an exclusively class meaning."[51] The repertoire was more entertaining than this mission statement might suggest. Between 1933 and 1941 Déčko (as the theater was affectionately known, from the colloquial Czech word for the letter *D*) mounted about seventy-five different productions ranging from contemporary Czech dramas like Božena Benešová's *Věra Lukášová* (1938, which Burian filmed in 1939) to "an antiracist and antifascist interpretation of Shakespeare's *Merchant of Venice*" (1934).[52] The theater staged Molière's *Miser* (in Burian's own Czech transcription, 1934), Brecht and Weil's *Beggar's Opera* (1934), Hašek's *Good Soldier Švejk* (1935), Pushkin's *Eugene Onegin* (1937), and Goethe's *Sorrows of Young Werther* (1938). Vsevolod Meyerhold was impressed with Burian's adaptation of Beaumarchais's *Barber of Seville* on his visit to Prague in October 1936. Despite his inability to speak Czech, he said, it was clear from the performance that he and Burian shared the same theatrical vision.[53]

FIGURE 6.2. Karel Šourek's cover for E. F. Burian's
Jazz, Prague, 1928.

Burian's agitprop ambitions did not prevent him from making major contributions to avant-garde stagecraft. *Co je to Voice-Band?* (What is voice-
band?), his April 1927 production at Jiří Frejka's Dada Theater, introduced "a
choral rendition of poetry based on the harmonic and rhythmic syncopations
of jazz, a wedding of poetic text and musical expression . . . including hissing,
whistling, and other nontraditional vocalization, with percussion accompaniment."[54] The voice-band performed works by Karel Hynek Mácha, Jan Neruda,
and the nineteenth-century folklorist and poet Karel Jaromír Erben, as well as
selections from contemporary writers Konstantin Biebl, Jaroslav Seifert,
Jindřich Hořejší, Karel Schulz, and Adolf Hoffmeister. A concert in Umělecká
beseda the next month added Apollinaire to the menu.[55] Burian later gave the
voice-band treatment to several D Theater productions, among them the Old

Testament *Song of Songs* (as rendered by Max Brod, 1935) and two separate adaptations of Mácha's *May* (1935, 1936). *Vojna* (Military service, 1935), whose text was based on Czech folk verses, "constructed a montage of scenes from village life dealing with such traditional rites as carnival, a wedding, army recruitment, and the parting of loved ones" to make an affecting antiwar protest. Though Déčko's sets were minimalist, Burian's innovative theatergraph system—a precursor of Prague's renowned Laterna magika—combined lighting with static and filmed projections to create a space where "you could not tell whether the actors were in front of, behind, or simply part of the projected image, enveloped in it."[56]

Seeking to be an all-around "center for modern culture," Déčko became a venue for poetry evenings, contemporary music concerts, and artists' exhibitions as well as theatrical performances. In March 1937 the first exhibition at the theater introduced a new generation of Czech surrealists: the painters František Gross, František Hudeček, Bohdan Lacina, and Václav Zykmund; the sculptor Ladislav Zívr; and the photographer Miroslav Hák. Karel Teige welcomed the youngsters to "a friendly rendezvous in the foyer of an avant-garde theater, which is one of the few oases in Prague . . . in which avant-garde poetic thoughts may be expressed without concern and without compromise."[57] Burian collaborated with the Czechoslovak Surrealist Group throughout the late 1930s. Déčko's second production of *May* was part of the group's attempt to reclaim "the great revolutionary romantic and the real founder of Czech poetry Karel Hynek Mácha" on the centennial of the poet's death.[58] Burian contributed an essay to their *festschrift Ani labut' ani Lůna* (Neither the swan nor the moon, 1936). The other contributors were Nezval, Teige, Hoffmeister, Bohuslav Brouk, Konstantin Biebl, Záviš Kalandra, the linguist Jan Mukařovský, and the Slovak poet and journalist Laco Novomeský. Burian's essay, titled "Mácha's Theater," savages naturalist dogma. "While on an empty stage without backdrops or the necessary requisites Shakespeare played night scenes in full sunshine in such suggestive monologue or dialogue that the spectator lived a night full of bliss and sorrow," he argues, "long after him and up to the present day the theater was unable to discover a technical replacement for this poet's fantasy that so admirably matched the fantasies of the spectator . . . we have to consider all the conditions of the life of the poetic work on the stage from the standpoint of the imagination of the spectator, and in no way from the mimetic realist standpoint of those who even today mistake natural signs for nature."[59]

D 40 opened the 1939–1940 season with Jindřich Hořejší's farce *Haló děvče!* (Hey, girl!). Hořejší was a working-class Žižkov boy and former Devětsil member best known for his commitment to proletarian poetry, to which he stayed faithful long after Teige and Seifert were seduced into poetism by Vítězslav Nezval's dazzling way with words.[60] This time he was constrained to adopt a subtler mode of resistance—one that took a leaf out of James Joyce's book, communicating all the more effectively in its refusal to have its meaning pinned down. Maybe Hořejší's work as an interlocutor between Prague and Paris helped. Having lived in Paris and Dijon from 1905 to 1914, he worked from 1922 to the end of his life as a translator in the state statistical office. He translated into Czech the poetry of Apollinaire, Robert Desnos, and Paul Éluard— not to mention the Comte de Lautréamont's *Songs of Maldoror*, which was published by Odeon in 1929 with illustrations by Jindřich Štyrský and promptly confiscated by the censor.[61] He also translated Jaroslav Hašek's *Good Soldier Švejk* into French. Hořejší must have imbibed some of the atmosphere of Georges Neveux's play *Juliette, ou La clé des songes* (Juliette, or the key of dreams), which he translated for Jiří Frejka's production at the National Theater in 1932, with stage sets by Bedřich Feuerstein. Set in a small seaside town where everyone has lost their memories and everyday life is correspondingly filled with absurdities, this was the surrealist drama on which Bohuslav Martinů based his opera *Julietta*, which premièred at the National Theater in the presence of president Edvard Beneš a year to the day before the Nazi invasion.[62]

Hey, Girl! was a very long way from proletarian poetry, as its lead actor Vladimír Šmeral explains:

> Just as the title itself was in nonsensical contradiction to the seriousness of the time, the whole play was filled with nonsensical absurdity. And yet in this absurdity to the point of the fantastic there was a meaning: opposition to the occupiers. Storyline, surprising situations, characters, dialog—there were allegories and symbols in everything. I played the lead role. This character had a pretty strange name: Grandpa Cowboy [*Dědeček Kovboj*]. At one rehearsal Jindřich Hořejší came up behind me during a break. He took me aside and explained to me in confidence all the allegories: what the characters mean, what is Slovakia, what is Hitler, what are the concentration camps, that the termites in the kitchen are the occupiers, etc. When he had disclosed everything and thoroughly clarified it for me, he took my hand and said: "Now you know everything, but for God's sake play it so that nobody can recognize it."

"Of course, this fantastic absurdity of the play has since caused audiences to find in it more allegories against the occupiers than were really there," Šmeral adds.[63] Who knows down what primrose paths a signifier on the lam may lead?

FIGURE 6.3. Scene from E. F. Burian's production of Karel Hynek Mácha's *Máj* at D 35 Theater, 1935. Photographer unknown. From Věra Ptáčková, *Česká scenografie xx. století*, Prague, 1982.

Hey, Girl! preceded Samuel Beckett's *Waiting for Godot* (1953) by more than a decade, and the world had yet to hear of Jean-Paul Sartre, Simone de Beauvoir, and existentialism. But Grandpa Cowboy would not be out of place in the postwar theater of the absurd. He hails, after all, from the land of Gregor Samsa, Josef K., and the good soldier Švejk, who knew the ways of Absurdistan long before Vladimir and Estragon discovered them. Soon the Nazis had enough of such nonsense and took out their revolvers. The Gestapo closed D 41 in March 1941. Burian spent the rest of the war in the small fortress at Terezín and in Dachau and Neuengamme concentration camps. Surviving a death march to the North Sea and the RAF bombing of a prison ship where he was being held with other evacuated prisoners in the Bay of Lübeck on 3 May 1945, he lived to see the postwar world.

D Theater's most popular wartime production was Vítězslav Nezval's *Manon Lescaut*, an adaptation of Abbé Antoine François Prévost's 1731 novel that premièred on 7 May 1940. "This Manon is my old love," Burian wrote to Nezval on 7 November 1939, "and I would be happy if I could direct and set her to music in your verses."[64] *Manon* was performed 128 times and is widely considered one of the most important works of Czech literature from the occupation. "The young, attractive and irresponsible heroine (played by Marie Burešová) and de Grieux (Vladimír Šmeral) . . . painfully in love, ready to forgive, easily duped, and blindly passionate," were the perfect antidote to the straightlaced miserablism of the time. "For years young people on evening walks through Prague recited Nezval's verse '*ach Manon Manon hříšnice*' [Ah Manon Manon the sinner]," relates Peter Demetz, "as if the lines were magic incantations. I know, I was there."[65] According to Adolf Hoffmeister, Nezval had been in love with Manon since he was fifteen. "It can even be said with certainty that Nezval wanted to meet his childhood Manon again. I think it went further than a longing for a meeting. He wanted to *have* Manon."[66] But Nezval's Manon—who was not quite the same girl, Ada says, as Prévost's heroine—also spoke to the needs of the time. The novel ends with Manon dying in the Louisiana wilderness after being transported to New Orleans as a prostitute. "How not to see in the procession of deported women, shackled with chains, the shock of the heart-rending news of the transports?" asks Hoffmeister. It was unlikely that many in the audience would have seen any such thing, for the first Jewish transports did not leave Prague for the Łódź ghetto until October 1941, six months after D 41 was closed. Ada wrote these words in 1965, by which time memory had had plenty of opportunity to reorder and give meaning to the past. "But none of this was in the text of the play," he continues. "It was in the audience. . . . The director [Burian] and actress [Burešová] gave the dying Manon a smile on her lips. A smile of hope. So it did not correspond to the text? So it did not correspond to the plot of the novel? So what? It answered to the moment . . . and the play entered political history." [67]

" . . . oso sweet and so cool and so limber she looked, Nance the Nixie, Nanon L'Escaut," rhapsodized James Joyce in *Anna Livia Plurabelle*.[68] "Burian knew," Ada goes on, "that he is not staging Prévost, but not just first and foremost but completely and only Nezval, the poet of the beauty of our language. . . . There is not an empty phrase in the play. There are no political pronouncements. There is no pity for the nation. There is not even a call for social justice." But "purity of language was in and of itself a patriotic act. The poetic beauty of Czech was regarded as something forbidden, banned, because the beauty of the language carried within it pride and contempt. Pride of a nation. Contempt for the occupiers."[69] "Create a language for your country in my image," Joyce had urged Hoffmeister, which is exactly what Nezval did with his reinvention of Prévost's heroine. "In my memory I can still see Nezval, with his wild red face, as he keeps repeating the word concrete, an adjective that for him embodied the basic quality of modern imagination, that he wanted charged as fully as possible with feelings, felt life and recollections," writes Milan Kundera. "Nezval hated the 'ideologues of art,' who did their best to reduce poetry or painting to the clichés of meaning, the poverty of message."[70] Fifteen years earlier, "at a time when factions for or against so-called proletarian poetry confronted one another," the poet had introduced his collaboration with Milča Mayerová and Karel Teige in *Alphabet* as an attempt "to react against the ideological approach . . . replacing the usual abstract ideology with the materiality of concrete images."[71] Nezval's flirty, dirty Manon is just such a concrete image, a very material girl who is much, much too real to be detained for long in the corsets of ideological abstraction. Who could resist the kindling curves of her beautiful Czech?

Jindřich Štyrský could. The painter had a history with Nezval, who had once been among his closest friends but with whom he had come to blows in the U Locha wine bar during the surrealists' split in 1938. As the occupation began to redefine the terms of cultural engagement, Nezval became the focus of a wider disgust that Štyrský had first voiced a decade earlier in his article "*Koutek generace*" (The Generation's Corner, 1929). Back then, the painter had accused his Devětsil colleagues of selling out and equating "the moon with the electric light bulb, love with sex, and poetry with cash."[72] Now his target was the wave of patriotic kitsch unleashed by the occupation. In an undated, untitled, unpublished rant from 1940 he again laid into his peers:

> Poets fill their purses with patriotism. . . . And my generation! They will be writing their slave songs until they die. František Halas, in your poetic biography of Božena Němcová you failed to mention when she had her first period! And Seifert too has commercialized his love of country in the stupidest way. Konstantin Biebl is only the baby of the family alongside them both and not worth bothering with. And Vítězslav Nezval? *Business is business!* [English in original]. . . . The glutton is celebrating his fortieth birthday. For this occasion, he hatched up a reworking of Abbé Prévost's *Manon*

Lescaut, stripping it of its genius. And E. F. Burian, another moron, crook, and professional fraudster is staging it as "Nezval's Manon." It is the stupidest thing imaginable. And the mob, that is to say the Czech nation, cheers, screams, and grunts with pleasure. MANON rhymes with MAMMON. Prévost overcooked twice over. A genius fucked by two illustrious saucemakers. Cretinous versifying, wretched direction . . . I fled at the second intermission.

"I have the right to be merciless, and I consider it a duty to nail to the pillory the names of the deserters, the names of those who betrayed," Štyrský insists. He did not subscribe to the view that, after all, you have to live. "I lived through death once before [when he had a heart attack during a visit to Paris with Nezval in 1935] and do not fear it. Death is only falling asleep."[73]

Noble as this refusal to accommodate artistic principle to the tawdry realities of the day may sound, there was more at stake than just art for art's sake. Štyrský had a history with Marie Burešová too, and he was less engaged by the kindling curves of her Czech than by her "miraculous summer body!"[74] After seeing Burian's star perform in the première of Alfred de Musset's play *Les Caprices de Marianne* (Marianne's moods, 1833) on 12 April 1939, Štyrský sat up all the next night penning a love letter. "Marianne," he writes—not Mlle. Burešová or even Marie—"everything good as well as evil in life has its source in a dream." "I say to myself, Marianne is clad in white satin. What a shame it isn't flecked with rowanberries. She is beautiful. I saw her at the front of the stage, smiling and happy. She reaps the applause. She's a success. Marianne is a real actress of very high quality. Like Rachel, Sarah Bernhardt, and Nazim once were."[75] They became lovers, but Štyrský wanted a muse. In the early days of their relationship he made a manuscript book out of one of Jindřich Hořejší's translations of a Robert Desnos poem just for her.[76] Under the headline "Artist Inspired by Actress," *Lidové noviny* announced that "Jindřich Štyrský is working on a cycle of twelve paintings titled *Marianne's Moods* after Alfred de Musset's play of the same name, which was staged by D 40 with Marie Burešová, the inspiration for Štyrský's series, in the leading role."[77] Štyrský completed only four of the canvases, one of which, *Majakovského vesta* (Mayakovsky's vest), is among his best-known works. It features a man and a woman whose upper torsos and faces are hidden by curtains and a red vest hanging from a tree with a blackened hole over the heart—a likely allusion to Mayakovsky's suicide. The man is fully clothed while the woman wears frilly lace knickers, stockings, and high-heeled shoes. Štyrský had originally intended the whole cycle to bear this inscription: "This heaviest weight and most beautiful part of my life I dedicate to the actress Marie Burešová." However, the legend on *Mayakovsky's Vest*, dated December 1939, reads "This PIECE of my life I dedicate to Toyen."[78]

By then, his relationship with Burešová was over. "This muse has exhausted me," he wrote in another unpublished diatribe (there is no reason to believe Marie ever saw it). "Love brings only heartache and memories. . . . The only reliable feeling is friendship." He accuses the actress of pursuing "cheap success . . . not immortality, popularity, not glory"—the celebrity of a Lída Baarová when "I wanted you to be my Sarah Bernhardt." The cruelty of *his* response to *her* refusal to live out his dreams is remarkable—though not, perhaps, entirely out of the ordinary when it comes to the he and the she of it:

> I had other girls too. They were office workers, dancers, philosophers, models, mannequins, married women, and many others. These occasional lovers were not evil, they helped me bear my human misery. I remember one woman, similar to you, who I knew before we met. . . . She didn't know how to clasp her hands so devotedly behind my neck and grunt on my shoulder in the moment of orgasm like you. She did not know as you do how to soar straight to the moon like Nike of Samothrace. A great individual needs and always finds in life another great individual. Yesenin had Duncan, Maeterlinck had Leblanc, Degas had Sarah Bernhardt, Delacroix had Rachel, Bakst had Gzovska, only I had a cow who confessed everything in *Pražanka* [*Pražanka: list paní a dívek*, or Prague woman: a paper for women and girls]. Evidently I am not a great individual. I will never forget how after a hot session in the sack at my place you told me that I write you only clichés. You wanted me to write to you: "I shall give you a monthly allowance of 3000 crowns."[79]

The Strongholds of Sleep

No members of the Czechoslovak Surrealist Group were killed in the war or imprisoned, but they did not have an easy time of it. Jaroslav Ježek left for New York with his Liberated Theater colleagues Jiří Voskovec and Jan Werich at the end of 1938. Jindřich Honzl took a day job as a clerk at city hall. Excluded from the large public theaters, he ran the tiny Divadélko pro 99 (Little Theater for 99) in the basement of the Topič building on Národní Avenue from the spring of 1940 until the authorities pressured the Borový publishing house to cancel his lease in the fall of 1941. Honzl intended, he said, to turn his back on "non-poets" and "paper simulations" in favor of "great poets" and "the drama of real life."[80] He spent the last years of the war living in seclusion in a basement flat on Klárov Street in the Lesser Town. Bohuslav Brouk was more fortunate, working as an "aesthetic adviser" at the Bílá labut' (White Swan) department store on Na Poříčí, a glass-fronted icon of functionalist architecture completed in 1939 and owned by his father. Honzl, Brouk, and Konstantin Biebl gradually became disconnected from the other Prague surrealists. Biebl spent much of the war living in the country. He was unable to publish anything of consequence during these years. Nor was Karel Teige.[81] After a spell hiding out in Bulovka Hospital at the start of the occupation, Teige worked as a freelance book designer for Melantrich and Práce. His contributions provided an income but were seldom credited.

Štyrský and Toyen were not permitted to exhibit their paintings. Toyen made a living creating covers and other artwork for more than sixty book titles between 1940 and 1944. Among them were photomontage jackets for several detective fiction series whose "most common motifs became the faces of terrified victims and the menacing shadows of approaching murderers"—shadows that would become much more than a clichéd trope of pulp fiction in her 1946 painting *Mýtus světla* (The myth of light), one of her best-known works.[82] The male shadow in the painting is Jindřich Heisler, who became the youngest member of the Czechoslovak Surrealist Group when he joined in 1938 (he was twenty-five).[83] Štyrský designed books for ELK (Evropský literární klub, or European Literary Club) publications, two of which were certainly as deserving of the label patriotic kitsch as anything by Halas, Seifert, or Nezval. *Co daly naše země Evropě a lidstvu* (What our lands have given to Europe and humanity, 1939) is a celebration of Czech culture edited by the linguist Vilém Mathesius, and it delivers exactly what it says.[84] František Kožík's perennially popular novel *Největší z Pierotů* (The greatest mime, published in English as *The Great Debureau*),[85] a fictionalized biography of the French pantomime player Jean-Gaspard Deboreau, sold fifty thousand copies upon its appearance in late 1939 and has gone through many editions since then. Deboreau was born of a Czech father and a French mother in Kolín in 1796 as Jan Kašpar Dvořák. Though critics panned *The Great Debureau* for pandering to "success, popularity and advertising," Kožík "entertained his reader with stories of suffering and success, theatrical revolutions, plucky Parisian street girls and vampiric courtesans, and a good deal of sentimental nostalgia for Bohemia, which Debureau-Dvořák had to leave behind when he was

FIGURE 6.4. Jindřich Štyrský, *Emily Comes to Me in a Dream*, 1933, collage, plate 9. From his *Emilie přichází ke mně ve snu*, Prague, 1933.

a boy."[86] Štyrský was not forced to compromise his artistic ideals for very long. He died of natural causes—in a manner of speaking—on 21 March 1942, aged forty-three. He might have lived longer had the war not ended the import of the medicines on which the treatment of his heart condition depended.

The Nazis' proscription of surrealism as "degenerate art" stopped more than just publication and exhibition by individual surrealists. Collective activities lay at the heart of surrealist practice: not only group exhibitions but also evening meetings in cafés and bars, discussions and debates, questionnaires, games, *dérives*, provocations, and collaborations on magazines and anthologies. Plans to publish a new surrealist magazine called *Lykantrop* were abandoned. The galleries and publishing houses were off-limits, and the downtown cafés and bars the Prague surrealists had patronized before the war were crawling with informers. During the early years of the occupation, it was probably the half-Jewish Heisler, who had the most to lose, who made the greatest effort to maintain the creative cohesion of what was left of the group. As the darkness descended, Heisler, Štyrský, and Toyen reached new heights in coupling poetic texts and visual images. Twelve of Toyen's 1936–1937 drawings of figures in a desert landscape accompany Heisler's poems in *Les spectres du désert* (*Specters of the Desert*, 1939). Heisler's imagery—including a reference to the Ku Klux Klan—is unremittingly violent.[87] Though *Specters* was printed in Prague, it carried the imprint of Éditions Albert Skira, Paris, publisher of the legendary surrealist art magazine *Minotaure*, to evade the censor. The text was in French, translated by Jindřich Hořejší. Toyen's drawings also complemented (it would be wrong to say illustrated) Heisler's poems in *Jen poštolky chčí klidně na desatero* (Only kestrels piss calmly on the Ten Commandments), which was privately printed later that year—fifteen copies in Czech and forty in German. Heisler rather quixotically intended to distribute it to occupying troops. "This book originated in the suffocating atmosphere of military commands as a document of Surrealist activity that none of the reactionary powers of mobilized Europe can destroy," declared the colophon.[88]

Heisler and Toyen's *Z kasemat spánku* (*From the Strongholds of Sleep*, 1940) was privately published in an edition of just seventeen copies sometime before 23 July 1940. Startlingly original in conception, it consists of seven "materialized poems" (*realizované básně*) in which Heisler's words were cut out and arranged in an imaginary landscape furnished with objects—dollhouse furniture, toy soldiers, marbles, a police booth, a flaming candelabra, trees, rabbits, cotton-wool clouds, cutouts of human figures, and more. The whole was then photographed and the images printed in black and white on glossy

photographic paper. Several scenes bring to mind nineteenth-century diora-
mas, while others gesture to window displays, movie posters, and magazine
advertisements. Matthew Witkovsky suggests that "*Strongholds* engages play-
fully and subversively with this history of modern spectatorship," as well as
"confronting . . . issues of disciplinary violence and control."[89] As with all
works of art, the meaning of this assemblage is always subject to interpretation.[90] Discussing surrealist "illustration that is not illustration," Heisler looked
forward to a "not too distant future [in which] books will be executed that
enclose a unique *and multidirectional* movement between word and image."[91]
"*Strongholds* . . . remains today the most remarkable product of Czech wartime
surrealism, both in concept and execution," argues Jindřich Toman.[92] Remarkable as *From the Strongholds of Sleep* may be as a surrealist work of art, it is still
relatively little known.[93]

 Na jehlách těchto dní (*On the Needles of These Days*, 1941), which pairs a prose
poem by Heisler with thirty photographs taken by Štyrský in Prague and Paris
in 1934–1935 for his series *Muž s klapkami na očích* (The man with blinkers on
his eyes) and *Žabí muž* (Frog man), has fared better. The book was initially
produced as a single copy in which Heisler's text on the left-hand pages faced
Štyrský's photographs, "sealed into plastic sheets using Band-Aids," on the
right. Embodying "a brutal aesthetics of poverty, a bulky block entombed in
plastic and bandages,"[94] this surrealist collaboration foreshadowed the multitude of works whose first editions were clandestinely produced in samizdat
during Czechoslovakia's forty-two years of communist rule.[95] *Needles* was
published by František Borový in 1945 as a regular book, designed by Karel
Teige. It has since been translated into German (1980), French (1984), and
English (1984, 1988).[96] "Any discussion of artistic photobooks in Czechoslovakia in the second half of the 1940s must begin with the most significant work
of its time, the magnificent surrealist volume *Na jehlách těchto dní*," says James
Steerman in Manfred Heiting's *Czech and Slovak Photo Publications 1918–1989*,
while Martin Parr and Gerry Badger are no less effusive in *The Photobook: A
History*, writing, "This remains a haunting photobook, 50 years after the war."[97]

 Heisler provided a handwritten dedication to Teige in the original copy of
Needles, which read: "For Karel, at a moment when the constellation has
brightened above the gardens of HOPE, which dictated these poems to me."[98]
By then, hope was in dwindling supply. The Heydrichiáda came and went. The
most poignant of the Czechoslovak Surrealist Group's wartime productions
may be the delightful handmade album of poems and collages titled *Život
začíná ve čtyřiceti* (Life begins at forty) that Heisler, Teige, and Honzl made for

Toyen's fortieth birthday on 21 September 1942. "Perhaps more important than issues of form," writes Jindřich Toman—who is Heisler's nephew as well as a distinguished scholar of the Czech avant-garde—"is the overall spirit of this collective attempt to respond to everyday circumstances, which were now unambiguously murderous. Much hope—and irony—is embedded already in the title; the Surrealist Group, now under heavy pressure, assured Toyen (and themselves) that friendship still existed and life lay ahead."[99] By the time Toyen turned forty, Štyrský, who had been her artistic partner since they met on holiday in Yugoslavia in 1922 when Marie was just nineteen, was six months dead and Heisler was in hiding, much of the time in her studio flat on Krásova Street in Žižkov. As Jan Mukařovský wrote, it was a time when "surreality [*nad-realita*] became the official reality. The ruler on the writing desk changed into a revolver, if that was what the Gestapo needed for a conviction."[100]

Heisler and his younger sister Anna had tried to escape to South America with Toyen in the summer of 1939, but they were swindled by the visa agent. While Anna was protected from deportation by her marriage to a non-Jew, Jindřich was not. Sometime in late 1941 or early 1942 he went underground. "It isn't necessary to explain how complicated everything was," Anna relates. "Everything was a problem: food, doctor, contact with friends . . . Jindra obviously didn't have food coupons."[101] For the next three years Heisler holed up either at Toyen's or in Anna's attic flat in Vršovice, venturing out only briefly with false identity papers and mostly at night. Teige helped conceal him. After the war Jindra gave Teige an album for his forty-sixth birthday containing six hand-colored photographs from his series *Ze stejného těsta* (Cut from the same cloth, 1944), dedicated "To Teige, who I will not forget hid me during the war in the smoke of his pipe."[102] Heisler had two close calls during the hunt for Heydrich's assassins. Upon hearing the lower floors of the building on Krásova Street being searched, he left the flat, went down the stairs, and boldly walked out the front door past the guard, who must have assumed that his apartment had already been cleared. He arrived exhausted at Anna's place in Vršovice and stayed the night. Judging it unsafe to return to Toyen's, he stayed the next night too—and the Gestapo showed up again. "The two siblings moved to the balcony, holding each other's hand, determined to jump if the knock at the door came. The search inexplicably stopped a floor below," recounts Toman.[103]

And yet, marvels Anna:

In the terrible time of the Protectorate these most beautiful paintings and drawings came into being in Toyen's studio flat. I remember her pictures from the cycles *Střelnice* [The shooting range, 1939–1940] and *Schovej se, válko!* [Hide yourself, war, 1944], Jindra's collages and photo-graphics [*fotografiky*]. . . . Certain pictures, for example Toyen's *Nebezpečná hodina* [The dangerous hour, 1942], were particularly realistic above all because of the way they perfectly expressed the atmosphere of the protectorate. Others matter to me because of their chance associations—so for instance whenever I look at the paper bag in *Po představení* [After the performance, 1943] . . . I cannot forget that this is the same bag in which I brought plums "from outside" and which we then threw on the floor. This is also a "history" of Czech surrealism.[104]

In *The Dangerous Hour* an eagle with folded human hands sits on a fence topped with shards of glass. *After the Performance* portrays a ballerina dressed in white suspended upside down from an exercise rail, her legs disappearing into (or emerging from) the wall behind her. Her skirt hangs down over her upper body and face, exposing her midriff and underwear. Propped up against the wall beside her is a large fly swatter. Anna's paper bag lies open on the floor. Though everything is meticulously rendered, neither of these paintings is remotely "realistic" in any conventional sense of the word. They are pure products of the imagination—"the realistic depiction of a world, which for a positivistic realist is unreal [*ireálné*] and non-existent," as Teige put it.[105] Heisler too spent his time in the small Krásova Street apartment realistically depicting imagined landscapes, creating objects, assemblages, and photomontages that he then photographed.[106] In *Filosofie v budoáru* (Philosophy in the boudoir, c. 1943) an ornate metal frame houses a portrait of a young blonde woman whose face is entirely covered by chains. *Hrábě* (Rake, 1944) shows a garden rake whose tines have been replaced with burning candles. "*Rake* . . . sparkled with contradictions," writes Toman; "the titular object lies amid wood shavings. To use it for its proper function would be to cause devastation—and liberation—through fire."[107]

Teige had no hesitation in declaring *The Shooting Range* "a *Desastres de la Guerra* of our age." But whereas "Goya's work is monothematic, it is reportage and a chronicle of war events ending in several allegorical compositions," there is hardly any overt depiction of war in Toyen's cycle. "All the things that are drawn here belong to the repertoire of children's memories and games; just one motif—fence posts with barbed wire—recalls those years of terror and massacres, but this motif is sufficiently powerful to give a double meaning to the series' title and bury childhood memories, whose ruined toys are scattered

FIGURE 6.5. Jindřich Heisler, *Rake*, 1944, gelatin silver print, image 16.4 by 23.3 cm,
paper 17.1 by 24 cm. From Jindřich Heisler, *Z kasemat spánku*, Prague, 1999.
Courtesy of Jindřich Toman. © Jindřich Heisler heirs.

through the drawings, under the shadow of images of wartime horrors in the
viewers' minds even if these are nowhere directly expressed." *The Shooting
Range* operates on "two contradictory levels: the world of childhood is confronted with the world of war." In this interplay "a symbol is never completely
identical with its meaning." "The emotional power of an artistic work," Teige
explains, "lies in exactly this disconcerting darkness of internal tension between separate spheres of meaning, whose coming together strikes sparks: in
this discharge of lyrical electricity between the poles of a thing and a symbol,
and life and dream. The polysemous cryptogram of picture and poem is never
completely or definitively deciphered." Toyen's drawings "guard their secrets and
leave their magnetic effectiveness intact."[108] We are back to Milan Kundera's
density of unexpected encounters. We are also back to James Joyce, spattering
meanings like the cradle names Anna Livia Plurabelle smacked on her children
with her boxing bishop's infallible slipper.

Theodor Adorno once said that "to write poetry after Auschwitz is barbaric."[109] Teige begged to differ. He believed the world needed poetry more
than ever, not as a retreat from reality but as an indispensable means of

penetrating the simulacra of official culture. He has no doubt that *The Shooting Range* is "an anti-war and anti-Nazi protest." But Toyen's drawings

> in no way regress to the methods of descriptive and schematic realism, they are not casual flyers for ideological propaganda, and they do not abandon but rather authenticate the prerequisites that surrealism has recognized and acknowledged as essential conditions for poetry, which is to say free choice of a theme that is independent of external circumstances and heterogeneous demands, the right to complete license, and absolute freedom for fantasy. The drawings in *The Shooting Range* do not fall into line with contemporary directives to draw their subject matter from historical facts: they do not have any a priori topics at all but create their subject and theme in the process of crystallizing and concretizing imaginative ideas. They do not portray, illustrate or allegorize rational slogans, rather they draw upon the innermost fantasized images. They do not serve pacifist, anti-military and anti-imperialist tendencies, and their magically bewitching revolutionary power and effectiveness consists in their latent content.

The series is proof that "poetic thought ... didn't grow in a greenhouse and didn't faint when confronted with today's traumas."[110] These works were created under conditions of extreme hardship, oppression, and danger; of constant fear. Perhaps that is what gives them their edge. All the Prague surrealists needed, as André Breton urged in the *Manifesto of Surrealism*, was to be "simple receptacles of so many echoes, modest recording instruments" soaking up the feel of the time and allowing it to express itself in whatever images came spontaneously to mind.[111]

And what of Teige himself? Forcibly disengaged from public life for the duration of the occupation, this most public of intellectuals poured his creative energies into the most private of passions. Between 1935 and 1951 he produced a total of 374 collages, very few of which he titled. They were not primarily intended for exhibition or publication. Karel made them for his own pleasure and for that of his inner circle, sometimes giving them as gifts. Apart from members of the Czechoslovak Surrealist Group, he gave collages to his companion Jožka (Josefina) Nevařilová and his lover Eva Ebertová, his friends Marie Pospíšilová and Lída Nováková, and members of Skupina Ra, a group of younger artists and writers with whom he maintained close contact during the later years of the war. While Teige had often used photomontage in his designs for book covers, nothing in his previous output prepares us for these images. They do not illustrate or advertise a text but are self-contained works of art, speaking an oneiric language of their own. They are notable for the range of sources on which they draw (Dürer, Rembrandt, Goya, David, Ingres, and the Czech painters Karel Škréta and Jaroslav Čermák, among many others, as well as Duchamp, Magritte, and Toyen) and for their frequent use of work by contemporary avant-garde photographers. It is likely no coincidence that three-fifths of the collages date from 1939 to 1942, but they were not commentaries on current events. Rea Michalová is closer to the mark when, quoting Teige himself, she argues that "the main impulse for his collage work was 'the tension that has emerged from desire's renunciation of unbearable reality.'"[112]

Taken together, Teige's collages might be seen as staging an unending Freudian contest between Eros and Thanatos, but that, too, is for the viewer to decide. "We are all aware that all art is nothing more than transposed eroticism," Karel wrote to Marie Pospíšilová in January 1944.[113] Threading its way through all but a small handful of his collages is a single obsessive motif—the female body, disordering all the settings in which Teige places it. The mood of these compositions is sometimes melancholic, sometimes humorous, sometimes lyrical, frequently grotesque. Women's torsos, legs, breasts, hands, heads, eyes, and lips interject themselves into antique and modern landscapes, interiors and exteriors, fields and woods, mountains and seashores, imposing animal human nakedness on the National Theater, the restaurant at the Barrandov Terraces, the Lesser Town rooftops overlooking Charles Bridge, the Dzerzhinsky Station in the Moscow metro, persistently reminding us that whether or not we are permitted to write about it, obscenity fills the pages of life as well. I am content to leave it to others to debate whether such images are misogynistic, though my personal view is that they are anything but. Teige might well have responded by quoting the closing sentence of André Breton's *Nadja* (1928): "Beauty will be CONVULSIVE, or will not be at all."[114]

The World in which We Live

As the remnants of the prewar Czechoslovak Surrealist Group mounted their assault on the official culture of the protectorate from the strongholds of sleep, the younger artists of Skupina 42 (Group 42) planted their standard in the supposedly more solid ground of the everyday. The members of Group 42 have often been described as "neorealists" (Teige eventually dismissed them as a disappointing replay of *neue Sachlichkeit*),[115] but there was more to it than that—in their own eyes, anyway. The group sought to ground their art, wrote Jindřich Chalupecký, in the concrete world of *things*:

Things. *These* things. Not the anaesthetized, standardized, typifying confections of abstracted memories, but living, undeniable, existing, singular things, unquestionable in their obstinate strangeness, in their irreducible reality . . . not artistic things, polished and tidied up to be beautiful, pleasant, palatable; hard, evil, uncanny things, persistently asserting themselves in their impenetrable consistency and forcefully impressing themselves on the tender skin of the living organism, the "air, rocks, coal, iron" after which Rimbaud's famous verse ["*Fêtes de la faim*," c. 1872] hungered.

"How many times," Chalupecký asks, "did art look for an example in a dream; and yet human timidity mistook the dream for dreaming, for the pleasing assembly of simple, safe, cozy, made-up artifacts, not daring to learn from the power of the dream, which puts before us just these things that we constantly encounter and is indifferent to what rational or esthetic qualities we take it into our heads to assign or deny them?"[116] I quote from his influential essay "*Svět v němž žijeme*" (The world in which we live), which was published in February 1940 in conjunction with an exhibition of the works of František Gross, František Hudeček, Ladislav Zívr, Miroslav Hák, and Jan Kotík at Emil Burian's D 40 Theater.

Group 42 brought together painters (Gross, Hudeček, Kotík, Kamil Lhoták, Jan Smetana, and Karel Souček), poets (Ivan Blatný, Jan Hanč, Jiřina Hauková, and Jiří Kolář), a sculptor (Zívr), a photographer (Hák), and the theorists Jindřich Chalupecký and Jiří Kotalík. Gross, Hudeček, Zívr, and Hák were among the six "younger surrealists" who exhibited at Burian's D 37 Theater in March 1937, but they had since moved on to pastures new. The group's first unofficial meeting took place in Jan Smetana's atelier on 27 November 1942.[117] Several future members exhibited jointly in Prague and elsewhere in 1940–1942,[118] but they first showed as a collective in March 1943 at the Aula High School in the small town of Nová Paka, the hometown of Gross, Zívr, and Hák; they followed this up with an exhibition in Topič Salon from 30 August to 19 September of the same year. Both these shows were only semilegal, and the first was closed down. The Prague show was the group's last collective exhibition during the occupation. Their first exhibition under the name Skupina 42 opened at the Pošova Gallery in Prague on 30 August 1945 and traveled to Bratislava and Brno early in 1946. Group 42 artists were prominently represented in *Art tchécoslovaque 1938–1946*, which was held at the Galerie La Boëtie in Paris in June–July 1946 before traveling to Brussels, Antwerp, Liège, and (in 1947) Lucerne.[119] This was part of an official postwar international cultural offensive designed to show the world that, as Adolf Hoffmeister (who ran the campaign on behalf of the Ministry of Information) put it, "The motto '*Malý, ale naše*' [it's little, but it's ours] must disappear once and for all from the lexicon of the textbooks of our national character."[120] Josef Šíma and Paul Éluard selected the exhibits.

Group 42 members were less confident in adopting an avant-garde posture than the Young Turks of the Devětsil generation; indeed, it might be argued that their sensibility was postmodern *avant la lettre*. Chalupecký begins his 1946 article "*Konec moderní doby*" (The end of the modern era) with an endorsement of Václav Navrátil's proclamation six years earlier that "the modern age is already over" (Navrátil believed modernity lasted perhaps a hundred years and ended with the 1929 Wall Street crash). The seminal achievements of modernism in the arts, says Chalupecký—"Joyce's *Ulysses* 1914–1921, Eliot's *Waste Land* 1922, analytical cubism 1910, Chirico 1912, Stravinský's *Soldier's Tale* 1918, atonal music 1921–1922"—were completed in a single decade. "The only original and significant action between the wars was surrealism," which had now exhausted its potential (and whose first manifesto was written in 1924). But "modern science, modern philosophy, modern art not only work themselves out as *theory*; they are also realized as fascism, as the atomic bomb. . . . The old world, which went on its predictable and controllable way, is lost, never to return; and nothing can help us avoid the astonishing, impassable, beautiful and evil landscape of the future stretching out before us."[121]

> We are continually in a single history, to which everything necessarily belongs: surrealism and the atom bomb, Mauthausen and depth psychology, Stakhanovites and existentialism, mathematical physics and Negro spirituals, the Marx brothers and Karl Marx, soldiers dying in the deserts and at sea and soldiers walking thousands of kilometers through foreign lands, Trotsky and Christian Science, revolution and poetry, everything, everything, everything, and me and you, readers, faith, mistakes, betrayals, courage, ruins, enthusiasm, weakness and strength; everything, that the individual and society ceaselessly learn about themselves and with which they ceaselessly create one another.[122]

We might summarize by saying that (post)modernity will be CONVULSIVE or will not be at all, but that is my formulation rather than Chalupecký's.

For Chalupecký, the demand that artists "situate themselves in the world of their real existence," rather than "some special aesthetic universe,"[123] meant that "the reality of the modern painter and poet is in practice the city; its people, its cobblestones, its lampposts, the placards on its shops, its houses, staircases, flats."[124] The city that interested him was not the "magic Prague" tourists come to see but the ordinary suburban landscapes that Franz Kafka described as "the miserable dark edge of the city" and Reiner Stach saw as dominated by "a present devoid of history"—the landscapes in which most people live but that usually pass beneath the radar of the fine arts. Hudeček, Gross, Lhoták, and Smetana all painted canvases whose titles played on the word *periferie* (outskirts, periphery). Hák titled one photo *Z periferie* (From the periphery) and another, a desolate image of a couple walking along a deserted highway, *Okraj Prahy* (The edge of Prague).[125] Kamil Lhoták struck a more lyrical note:

> The Prague suburbs, particularly Holešovice, a landscape where dilapidated walls and the tarred fences of factory buildings take the place of tree-lined avenues. Scrawny little locust trees gather round telephone boxes. Flowers only grow on the roofs of modern apartment blocks, in artificial gardens thirty meters above the ground. It is a magnificent spectacle, which here and there brings to mind the civilization of old silent-film comedies. Asphalt streets, reinforced concrete, bricks, lampposts, board fences, wind, rain, smoke, fog. Holešovice, Nusle, Michle, Žižkov. An immense park in immediate proximity to factories: Stromovka.[126]

Miroslav Hák's photograph *Holešovice* captures the feel of the periphery perfectly: a man in a cloth cap sits on the plinth between two gas pumps. In front of him a scrubby grass island with a lamppost divides the gas station from the road. Behind the pumps are a ramshackle kiosk for the attendant; a high board fence bearing the legend "E. PORGES," other lettering too faded to read, and a peeling winged horse logo; four factory chimneys. It is an image that is at once comforting, familiar, and a little bleak. It is not remotely pretty, but you can imagine having played there as a child (one of František Hudeček's drawings is titled *A Street Where Children Play*).[127]

František Gross painted a chair with a broken seat on a wooden deck in a backyard in Košíře, the factories of Vysočany, and (again and again) the gasholders and smokestacks of Libeň. Jan Smetana painted the factories of Michle and Karlín. Kamil Lhoták painted circuses and summer evenings and an 1899 murder in Holešovice (where he was born in 1912), Stromovka Park with a baby carriage, Stromovka Park with the chimneys of Holešovice power station, the Hlubočepský Viadukt, and the nicely titled *Předměstí (Za Vinohrady)* (A suburb [beyond Vinohrady]).[128] The anonymous suburban road in Lhoták's

Krajina 20. století (Twentieth-century landscape)[129] became emblematic of Group 42—even if it is not entirely typical of his work, whose whimsicality (as Otakar Mrkvička told *Lidové noviny* readers in April 1939) appeals to those who like "oddity and peculiarity as many of us do but are ashamed to admit it."[130] More often than not, Group 42's subjects are identified only by anonymous titles, easing their transition into metaphors for the modern condition: city, suburb, street, embankment, three houses, a station, an automobile graveyard, a park at night, brickyard landscape, smoke, a yard, roofs, a fence, two streetlamps, a shack, an arcade, a newsstand in the evening, a swimming pool, a cyclist, motorcyclist, radiologist, a figure at a desk, a woman in the street, an interior, in the waiting room, at the hairdresser's, in the automat, tram, office, bistro, pub, telephone booth. All become elements of Chalupecký's "mythology of the modern individual or the world, in which we live," whose essence is summed up in the title of the 1947 painting by the group's postwar recruit Bohumír Matal: *Člověk ve městě, město v člověku* (The individual in the city, the city in the individual).[131]

Group 42's work may be seen as a deliberate counter to the rural and historicist emphases of such official manifestations of Czech identity as *The Nation to Its Artists*, but it was no less a response to what Chalupecký saw as people's more general alienation from their surroundings in the modern world.[132] Magical realism is a better description of this art than neorealism; the surrealist phase through which many in the group passed in the 1930s left a lasting impression on their work. Lhoták furnishes his suburban vistas with vintage cars, motorcycles, biplanes, and hot-air balloons rendered with the hyperrealism of an Andrew Wyeth (or Salvador Dalí), transporting us well beyond *neue Sachlichkeit*. So does the *Noční chodec* (Nightwalker) that František Hudeček drew and painted in multiple incarnations during the war years. Hudeček's title echoes Vítězslav Nezval's book *Pražský chodec* (*A Prague Flâneur*, 1938), a *dérive* through the streets of Prague that evokes an earlier urban *passant*, Monsieur G. in Baudelaire's 1863 essay "The Painter of Modern Times."[133] But Hudeček's nightwalker is no Parisian flâneur. In this neck of the woods, he is more likely to bring to mind Rabbi Löw's golem. A shadowy, faceless figure, sometimes fracturing into near geometric abstraction, sometimes looming as tall as the tenements between which he walks and at other times hunched and dwarfed as they tower menacingly over him, he is always alone and the streets he wanders are always empty. Often the scene is dark, but in *Noční chodec II* (1941) both city and sky are spangled with cold but brilliant stars, as if in parody of Van Gogh's *Starry Night*.[134] There *is* realism here

FIGURE 6.6. František Hudeček, *Nightwalker*, 1944, etching, 24 by
17.3 cm. Photograph © East Bohemian Gallery in Pardubice
(Východočeská galerie v Pardubicích).

(the stars do look brighter in a blackout), but as Chalupecký remarks, "His
[Hudeček's] city is a hallucination; his reality is a dream."[135]

The wartime blackout nourished urban legends of "a 'Razorman' [*Žiletkář*]
who reputedly pursued women through the dark streets of the city or a 'Springman' [*Pérák*] who frightened passers-by and unexpectedly leapt in their path,"
writes Vojtěch Lahoda. Jiří Trnka made an animated short film in 1946 titled
Pérák a SS (Springman and the SS, released in English as *The Chimney Sweep*),
in which Springman is a little Czech superhero who uses his prodigious jumps
to taunt the Nazis and help their victims escape. "At first sight the world around
looked normal," Lahoda continues, "but all the same something oppressive

and threatening lay within it ('Razorman,' 'Springman,' German soldier, informer, collaborator, Gestapo, stool pigeon ...). Under the Protectorate Chalupecký's 'world, in which we live' was wrapped up in a layer of strangeness, secrecy, and without any doubt also of horror. It was something foreign, at the same time well known and yet strange, to which the Freudian term *unheimlichkeit* [uncanny] can be applied."[136] A sense of the uncanny permeates much of Group 42's work, in which something often seems to be ever so slightly off. What *are* so many bright yellow hot-air balloons doing in Lhoták's Prague periphery, anyway? And what induced him—in 1948—to give the subtitle *Vstříc osudu* (Toward fate) to his painting *Nádraží* (The station), which shows a line of people innocently waiting to board a departing train heading into an indeterminate horizon?[137]

Nowhere is this sense of vague unease better conveyed than in some of Miroslav Hák's images. Susan Sontag once observed that photography "is the one art that has managed to carry out the grandiose, century-old threats of a Surrealist takeover of the modern sensibility" in its capturing of "concrete, particular, anecdotal ... moments of lost time."[138] The camera can almost be defined as an apparatus for petrifying coincidences, freezing the ephemera of the moment into images that can haunt us for eternity. Hák's *Ve dvoře* (In the courtyard, 1943) and *Konečná v Dejvicích* (Terminus in Dejvice, 1944) provoke that familiar shudder when someone walks over your grave. *In the Courtyard* shows a dress hanging from a chain strung between the handles of an upended handcart in the corner of a courtyard deep in shadow. The photo could be one of Atget's images of Paris, but we know this is occupied Prague, and context changes everything. Empty clothing was a common enough surrealist trope (used by Toyen, among others), but at this date, Lahoda suggests, "A dress without a body evokes death."[139] *Terminus in Dejvice* depicts a stationary train carriage with the doors open on both sides so that we can see through to a broken wall, a small human figure, and tall factory chimneys on the other side of the tracks.[140] Interpret the image how you will, but the title is double-edged.

ACT 2

Verso 1938–1989

It was like the climax of a Gothic novel: You were standing naked on the stairs with bound hands, looking at the carpet where the setting sun was painting an arabesque of bird-eating fish. It was an immensely fanciful and cruel vision. The trees shook hands and the houses opened their windows in welcome. This truly is not how we imagined liberation. The photographic camera has stood itself on its three legs in the way of all hope. The incriminating document burned in the fireplace in the corner of the room, and above the doorway a Chinese dragon rocked gently in a hammock. The cone-shaped volcano on the horizon exploded in fireworks of spectral colors, and the phantoms living in the outskirts of bombed cities sang miserere. Perhaps it might still be possible to lay the table, prepare a meager dinner, and deal cards to all the angels, but we have long known that a throw of the dice will never abolish chance.

—KAREL TEIGE, WRITING FRAGMENT, CIRCA 1937–1945

7

As Time Goes By

After all, my dear Prokop, what difference does it make? So you *have* lost
everything. Does it really matter? Did you ever care whether you had things or
not? You have lost love and home and fatherland. But didn't you dream, even
when you were a schoolboy, of world-citizenship, of the free life of the
vagabond, of exotic loves?

—ADOLF HOFFMEISTER[1]

A Citizen of the World

Born with a silver spoon in his mouth and blessed with nine lives and the luck
of the devil, Adolf "Ada" Hoffmeister was a fixture of Prague's cultural scene
for five decades—a remarkable feat of survival, considering the fickleness of
the location and the treachery of the times. We first met him as Milena Jesenská's
colleague at *Pestrý týden* and a witness at her wedding with Jaromír Krejcar.
We learned that he went to school with Karel Teige, Vladislav Vančura, and
Voskovec and Werich at the Křemencova Street *realné gymnasium* and was
one of Devětsil's founders. Still in school and just eighteen years old, Ada was
the group's youngest member. He exhibited his magic realist–style paintings
at the Devětsil Spring Exhibition in April 1922,[2] and he remained on good
terms with the group despite leaving later that year to join the Nová skupina
(New Group), which was dedicated to preserving Devětsil's original primitiv-
ist and *proletkult* ideals. Karel Konrád happily cast him as a hawker of Team
Devětsil merchandise at the Odeon clubhouse in his 1928 soccer satire in
Rozpravy Aventina. Ada turned up again with Bedřich Feuerstein in Hannes
Meyer's apartment in Moscow; then we ran into him in Paris fantasizing

scenes of correction in English girls' boarding schools *chez* James Joyce. A prodigious traveler and an indefatigable networker, Hoffmeister was personally acquainted with many of the leading international cultural figures of his day. The lengthy entry in the Czech Wikipedia describes him as "a Czech writer, publicist, dramatist, painter, illustrator, scenographer, caricaturist, translator, diplomat, lawyer, professor, and traveler" (to which the French Wikipedia adds "radio commentator") and credits him with forty-three books of poetry, prose, and essays; fourteen works for the stage; seven collections of drawings and caricatures; and contributions to five films.[3] But although he has been described as "without any doubt one of the greatest caricaturists of the last century,"[4] Ada did not make the English-language Wikipedia until 2021, with a brief entry that the editors warn "needs additional citations for verification." The omission says more about Anglo-American insularity than it does about Hoffmeister.

After graduating high school, Ada trained at the Law Faculty of Charles University, obtaining the title doctor of laws in December 1925. He worked in the family's law practice until 1939, which gave him the time and money needed to support his literary and artistic activities. He spent the summer term of 1924 studying Egyptology at Cambridge University (he would visit Egypt and Palestine in 1932). *Cambridge—Praha* (Cambridge—Prague), published in 1926, is a lighthearted souvenir of his English adventure. "No. 9 Baker Street in London has been pulled down," he informs his compatriots "across the salty sea" with mock horror. "Don't you understand? Don't you remember? No. 9 Baker Street, where Sherlock Holmes lived with his friend Dr. Watson, has disappeared from the earth."[5] Ada visited England again in 1926, at which time he met and became friends with G. K. Chesterton and George Bernard Shaw. Besides helping Milena Jesenská launch *Pestrý týden*, Hoffmeister was a sometime editor at *Lidové noviny* (1928–1930) and *Literární noviny* (Literary news, 1930–1932). He had a long association with Otakar Štorch-Marien's Aventinum publishing house beginning in 1925, when he drew more than fifty caricatures for the first volume of *Rozpravy Aventina*.[6] His *České podoby* (Czech portraits), caricaturing prominent Czech cultural figures, were featured on the covers of *Rozpravy Aventina*'s fifth volume (1929–1930). For the sixth volume, Štorch-Marien dispatched Ada across Europe to draw and interview Tristan Tzara, Le Corbusier, André Gide, Paul Valéry, Jean Cocteau, George Grosz, Hannes Meyer, Erich Maria Remarque, Stefan Zweig, and Anatoly Lunacharsky, among others.[7] Hoffmeister also contributed to the annual almanacs issued by the progressive publishers' association Kmen,[8] which provided a sampling of the best in contemporary Czech and world literature, and he designed covers and illustrated books for most of the leading Prague publishing houses of the day.[9]

A month after Voskovec and Werich's *Vest Pocket Review* catapulted them into the limelight, Ada's "American comedy" *Nevěsta* (The bride) premièred at the Liberated Theater under Jindřich Honzl's direction on 25 May 1927. His ballet *Park* debuted the same month, with music by Jaroslav Ježek. Mira (or Míra) Holzbachová, one of Devětsil's few female members, danced the lead role. Voskovec and Werich took over the Liberated Theater soon after, and Ada worked closely with his former schoolmates on posters, flyers, programs, and scenery for more than a decade. He coauthored V + W's review *Svět za mřížemi* (A world behind bars), which premièred on 12 January 1933—a work into which, claims Václav Holzknecht, Hoffmeister introduced "a grotesque and derisive merriment . . . that didn't used to be in the comedians' humor."[10] The bawdy map of Europe Ada drew for V + W's 1932 revue *Caesar* and updated in 1936 for their *Rub a líc* (The pros and the cons) became famous. Though Ada never formally joined the Czechoslovak Surrealist Group, he was an enthusiastic collaborator from its beginnings. He contributed translations of Tristan Tzara and Robert Desnos's poetry and news reports from Paris and Berlin to Vítězslav Nezval's *Zvěrokruh* (Zodiac, 1930);[11] helped organize *Poesie 1932* at the Mánes Gallery, the largest exhibition of surrealist works mounted anywhere in the world at the time;[12] defended surrealism in the Mánes Artists' Society journal *Volné směry* (New directions) against Ilya Ehrenburg's charge that the surrealists were "too busy studying pederasty and dreams" to do an honest day's work;[13] and contributed an essay and a drawing to the surrealists' centennial tribute to Karel Hynek Mácha, *Neither the Swan nor the Moon*.

Ada made no bones about his disagreements with Soviet cultural policy, but unlike the signatories of "Surrealism against the Current," he stopped short of extending his criticisms to the Soviet regime more generally. He was active in the Left Front and PEN club, as well as the Klub českoněmeckých divadelních pracovníků (Czech-German Theatrical Workers' Club), founded in 1935. Together with Vítězslav Nezval he was a delegate to the First Congress of Soviet Writers in Moscow in August 1934, and he served on the Committee for Aid to Democratic Spain during the Spanish Civil War. Following his trip to the Soviet Union in 1931, where he met with Anatoly Lunacharsky, Vladimir Tatlin, and the theater directors Alexander Tairov and Erwin Piscator in Moscow and hooked up with Aldous Huxley and George Bernard Shaw in Leningrad, Ada published a slim volume of reportage under the title *Povrch pětiletky*

(The surface of the Five-Year Plan). "Dear readers," he begins, "a journey to the USSR is a journey to the workers. Travelogues usually write about ancient cathedrals, picturesque landscapes, sunsets, about monuments to the great past.... In the USSR history is in ruins. Everything there is to see is new."[14] The book, which begins with a letter appealing to Ferdinand Peroutka to visit the USSR and see the future for himself, is made up largely of letters to friends on various aspects of Soviet life, including housing (to Karel Honzík), food, bathrooms (to Jan Werich), fashion, transportation, the army, prisoners (to Julius Fučík), and advertisements (to Karel Teige). The most touching addressee is Ada's goddaughter "Miss Honza Krejcarová, Prague XII, Francouzská Street 5"—Milena Jesenská's daughter Jana, who was then approaching her third birthday. To Jana Hoffmeister extols the delights of a Soviet childhood.[15] All the same, Ada did not join the KSČ.

"He had an amazing ability to connect with people," says Hoffmeister's son Martin, who opened the luxury Hotel Hoffmeister in Prague's Lesser Town in the 1990s, complete with an Ada Restaurant hung with his father's drawings.[16] When Vladimir Mayakovsky visited Prague in April 1927 he stayed at Ada's apartment in Spálená Street, just down the road from the Krejcars. Hoffmeister was also the perfect host when Philippe Soupault passed through town a month later: "I know of few people who so unselfishly acquaint artists from abroad with our magical city as Adolf Hoffmeister," wrote Vítězslav Nezval in his memoir Z mého života (From my life, 1957–1958). "I don't know how we hunted down or dreamed up that Apollinaire stayed in the old Hotel Bavaria on Na Poříčí, that his Ahasuerus danced at the U Rozvařilů pub."[17] Le Corbusier had dinner at Ada's during his third visit to Prague in 1928.[18] Hoffmeister met Alfred Barr, the founding director of New York's Museum of Modern Art, on his first trip to the United States in the fall of 1936. When Barr passed through Prague a year or two later, Ada relates, "He stayed at my place for several days. Whether his money ran out or what I don't know. We were both young.... We sat up whole nights talking about questions that were ahead of their time and grew larger the longer we spoke about them."[19] The apartment in which Hoffmeister lived for most of his life was in one of Prague's first cubist buildings, Emil Králíček's Diamant House (1912–1913), which was owned by Ada's father.

Soupault wrote the catalog text for Visages par Adolf Hoffmeister, which opened at the Galerie d'art contemporain in Paris on 3 November 1928. It was Ada's first foreign exhibition. Mayakovsky showed up out of the blue on opening night. In Ada's words:

Suddenly a great stamping on the staircase, as if a herd of horses was galloping up. It's Mayakovsky, Ehrenburg, Altman, Volovik and maybe ten
Russians. They make a racket, run hither and thither, make fun of one another and are terribly merry. Mayakovsky bangs his head against the ceiling.
He brandishes a bottle of whiskey. White Horse. He assures me that it is a
top-shelf brand. For the first time in my life I think I like Russians. More
people arrive.... I'm so glad that Alois Wachsmann arrived from Prague,
straight off the train. Suddenly there are so many people, I don't believe it.
I speak with them like they are phantoms. Perret, the Berges, Ivan Goll,
Joseph Deltiel, Enrico Prampolini, Ribemont-Dessaignes, Roger Vailland,
Jean Cassou, Jean Girardoux, Osip Zadkine, Le Corbusier, James Joyce,
Goncharova, Larionov, Tristan Tzara, Léon Pierre-Quint, Lucien Romier
arrive. Minister Osuský arrives with his wife, Dr. Nebeský, B. Martinů,
Mrs. Pellé; Richard Weiner from Lidovky, Klein from *Tribuna*, G. Winter
from *Právo lidu*, the communists from *Monde*, the Grand Jeu group, the
youngest of the youngest ... altogether 600 people came.[20]

"A caricature is something completely up-to-date," Hoffmeister wrote in
1927. "A portrait is superseded by superior photography. When all is said and
done a portrait is vain, but a caricature retains its modernity because it draws
the subject not as it appears but as it is."[21] "The less, the better," he added in a
Miesian vein. "A line is enough, but many lines are a little."[22] Ada drew his
avant-garde Prague friends with a touch of affectionate malice. Teige is seldom
without stubble on his chin and a pipe clamped between his teeth, and Nezval's head is invariably in the clouds. The rotund poet often has a beatific expression on his face and sometimes walks among flowers.[23] The proletarian
Seifert, by contrast, may be ascending to the heavens in a balloon, but it is
through a pea-soup smog belched out by factory smokestacks.[24] In *Avantgarda
1930* Teige (who carries a book in his hand with the French title *Je sais tous*—
I know everything), Nezval (with a harp), a serious-looking Honzl, and a jolly
Voskovec and Werich stride forward into the future under a red banner. *Ten-
Ta-Toyen* (1930) depicts Marie Čermínová wearing masculine coveralls but
casting a shadow wearing a dress. Elsewhere a dapper Emil Burian sits behind
a drum kit marked "JAZZ." Among the vignettes in *Letos v létě* (This summer,
August 1927) is a drawing with the legend: "The editorial office of *Pestrý týden*
is the only place where hard work went on. Professor V. H. Brunner carved 718
baskets out of peach stones, Ms. Milena read 27 detective novels and Ms. Staša
progressively had a toothache in 33 teeth." For several years Staša Jílovská was

Hoffmeister's girlfriend. In *13 obrázků z Paříže* (13 little pictures from Paris), published in *Pestrý týden* in December 1927, Ada gently mocked "the painter Josef Šíma, a Frenchman who speaks perfect Czech."[25]

As we move into the 1930s, Ada's cartoons get darker. "Merriment, innocent merriment has been almost eliminated from the caricaturists today," he wrote in 1934, "because the times are rapidly changing."[26] In these circumstances a caricature becomes "a shorthand capturing of the atmosphere of the time in its most concise and eloquent form."[27] *Tichá práce* (Quiet work, 1933) shows Adolf Hitler standing on the prow of a liner giving the Nazi salute as swordfish spear the hull below the waterline. *Umění ve Třetí říši* (Art in the Third Reich, 1934) portrays spectators in a vast gallery surrounded by endless identical paintings and sculptures of the Führer; the cartoon is captioned "Germany— the most artistic country in the world." In *Španělskou zemi mám tak rád . . .* (I like the Spanish land so much . . . , 1937) Ada draws Voskovec and Werich singing in front of his map of Europe, only now blood pours from his bare- breasted tart's head (Spain).[28] Hoffmeister saved his most potent venom for fascists, but he still found time to skewer the apostles of socialist realism. In *S. K. Neumann* (1938) the onetime editor of *Červen* and *Kmen* and member of the Seven, who had long since converted to the Stalinist party line on art, towers triumphant above the severed heads and hands of Josef Čapek, Vítězslav Nezval, Josef Šíma, Jindřich Štyrský, E. F. Burian, and other Czech modernist and avant-garde figures. Neumann's infamous 1937 *Tvorba* article "Dnešní Mánes" (Today's Mánes) ridiculed Václav Špála and František Muzi- ka's "postimpressionist artistic wandering," savaged Emil Filla's "cruel defor- mation of the human body," and denounced Štyrský and Toyen's use of "sexually pathological literature and erotic photography" in terms every bit as sanctimonious as those of James Joyce's persecutors.[29] Ada had used the same motif four years earlier in a composition titled *Umrlčí hlavy týdne* (Dead heads of the week), where the executioner was Adolf Hitler, the occasion was the Night of the Long Knives, and the heads belonged to Ernst Röhm and his SA comrades.[30]

Some of Hoffmeister's most acerbic cartoons appeared in the bilingual anti- Nazi satirical weekly *Simplicus*,[31] whose first issue appeared on Prague news- stands on 25 January 1934. Ada's caricatures were outnumbered only by those of Antonín Pelc and the magazine's editor František Bidlo; other contributors included Josef Čapek and Josef Lada. Later that spring Ada organized the *First International Exhibition of Caricatures and Humor* at the Mánes Gallery with Emil Filla and Alois Wachsmann. The exhibition drew protests from the

FIGURE 7.1. Adolf Hoffmeister, *S. K. Neumann*, 1938. From Karel Srp, ed., *Adolf Hoffmeister*, Prague, 2004. Courtesy of Martin and Ivan Hoffmeister, © Adolf Hoffmeister heirs.

German, Austrian, Italian, and Polish governments, not to mention that eternal censor of social morality the Vatican. The Czechoslovak government ordered several works to be removed; the ensuing brouhaha ensured that the show had sixty thousand visitors by the time it closed. All the leading Czech caricaturists of the time were represented. The most eminent foreign participants were George Grosz, Otto Dix, John Heartfield, Thomas Theodor Heine, and Erich Godal. By then, Grosz was already in America, and Dix had been fired from his position at the Dresden Academy (he would later be forbidden to paint anything but landscapes). Heartfield, Heine, and Godal had arrived in Prague as refugees in 1933.

Heartfield and Heine moved on again in 1938—Heartfield to England (where he was soon interned on the Isle of Man)[32] and Heine to Oslo and then (in 1942) Stockholm. Godal made it to the United States, where he became a political cartoonist for *Ken* magazine and the New York newspaper *PM*. His widowed mother Anna Marien-Goldbaum, whom Godal had been forced to leave behind, was less fortunate. Finally given an exit visa from Germany in 1939, she was one of more than nine hundred Jewish passengers on the MS *St. Louis*, which sailed from Hamburg to Havana on 13 May. The ship was turned away from Cuba and was then refused permission to dock in the United States (by president Franklin D. Roosevelt) and Canada (by prime minister William Lyon Mackenzie King). A US State Department telegram sent while the ship was close enough to the coast to see the lights of Miami stated that the passengers must "await their turns on the waiting list and qualify for and obtain immigration visas before they may be admissible into the United States."[33] The *New York Daily Mirror* published two letters "from an aged mother on the wandering steamship to her son, an artist, in New York" on 6 June 1939. "It is so strange how near, and yet how much cut off we really are," Mrs. Goldbaum wrote.[34] The *St. Louis* turned back to Europe the same day. Anna Goldbaum was marooned in Belgium. She was deported to the death camps within a year.

Plus ça change, plus c'est la même chose. As the Western world faced another "refugee crisis" in 2015, the Nigerian American writer and photographer Teju Cole remembered Walter Benjamin—"not so much Benjamin the scholar of surrealism as Benjamin the despairing refugee. The Benjamin who fled, like millions of others, for fear of his life"—who committed suicide in 1940 in the little town of Port Bou on the Franco-Spanish border rather than be sent back to occupied France. "The receipt made out to the dead man, the difunto Benjamin Walter, by the Hotel de Francia, for the four-day stay . . . include[d] five sodas with lemon, four telephone calls, dressing of the corpse, plus disinfection of his room and the washing and whitening of the mattress." "The itemization reminds me of two things," writes Cole. "Less, of the usual little list of what I drank or ate (mineral water, Toblerone), what I spent, when I check out of these frequent hotels of my life. More, of the little plastic bags I saw at the public morgue in Tucson, containing the last few personal effects of unknown travelers recovered from the Sonora desert in Arizona. A few dollars, a few pesos, photograph of a family, a mother's passport to remember her by." These are the rags and the refuse, the dialectical images that condense the terrible recurrences of the past in the present, blowing Benjamin's "phantasmagoria of history" to smithereens.[35] "Every refugee is alike, but each generation fails refugees in its own special way," explains Teju Cole.[36]

The Usual Suspects

In June 1938 Louis Aragon organized an exhibition of Hoffmeister's caricatures at the Maison de la Culture in Paris with the aim of educating the French public on the political crisis about to engulf Czechoslovakia. A founder of surrealism along with André Breton and Philippe Soupault, Aragon broke with Breton in 1932 and went on to become one of the leading intellectuals of the Parti communiste français (PCF). "Perhaps it won't be unpleasant for you to visit Paris in May, when the sun shines, the leaves are on the trees and the terraces open up in front of the cafés," he wrote to Ada.[37] Recognizing that he was being invited not because of his artistic celebrity but because "I was available, I know a lot of people, and I speak French,"[38] Hoffmeister arrived (direct from Italy) on 1 June. The next evening the Association Internationale des Écrivains pour la Défense de la Culture (International Association of Writers for the Defense of Culture) staged a concert at the Salle Chopin on the rue du Faubourg Saint-Honoré "in honor of the journey to Paris of the famous graphic artist ADOLF HOFFMEISTER" titled "Paris—Prague."[39] The brilliant young Moravian composer Vítězslava Kaprálová, who had been studying in Paris with Bohuslav Martinů since October 1937, conducted music by Smetana, Janáček, Dvořák, Martinů, Novák, and Suk; Josef Páleníček played the piano; and the editor of Ce Soir invited Hoffmeister, Martinů, and the raging reporter Egon Erwin Kisch to the podium to speak during the intervals. From Paris Ada went to London, where he addressed a crowd of three thousand at an antifascist rally in Queens Hall. Kaprálová followed him across the English Channel and conducted the BBC Symphony Orchestra in the same concert hall on

17 June in a performance of her *Vojenská symfonieta* (Military sinfonietta), which opened the sixteenth annual festival of the International Society of Contemporary Music. The *Military Sinfonietta*, Kaprálová explained in her program notes, was "not an appeal for war, but an appeal for ... the preservation of national independence."[40] The work was well received, and the "little girl conductor," as the British newspapers dubbed her, was a huge hit, receiving eight encores.[41]

When Ada next set foot in Paris, it was as a refugee. He left Bohemia shortly after the Nazi invasion on the pretext of staging one of his children's plays in Germany,[42] and he was admitted to France on an emergency visa obtained for him by Louis Aragon. His apartment in Spálená Street was subsequently confiscated and given to Jaroslav Nachtmann,[43] the boxer–turned–Gestapo informer who arrested Milena Jesenská and left Ada's goddaughter Honza alone with her kitten in the Vinohrady flat. After arriving at the Gare de l'Est on 24 April, Ada went straight to Josef Šíma's, dumped his luggage, and headed for the Left Bank. He met up with André Breton and Yves Tanguy at Les Deux Magots café on the place Saint-Germain and spent the evening with his old friend Tristan Tzara. He moved into the nearby Hotel Jacob, cheap digs that had sentimental associations for Czechs ever since Tomáš Masaryk lived there during World War I. A week later Ada was joined by his fellow cartoonist Antonín Pelc, with whom, he wrote to his future wife Lilly Rohne, he shared "a smelly and damp basement room."[44] Pelc had managed to get out of the protectorate thanks to a telegram accrediting him as illustrator for the magazine *Le Jardin de la Mode* (The garden of fashion). A Jewish, Sudeten German actress who performed at the New German Theater, Rohne escaped to London in March 1939. Martin Hoffmeister says his parents first met through Ada's efforts to help Jewish refugees from the Sudetenland after the Munich diktat.[45] Lilly's five siblings died in Terezín and Treblinka.[46]

Among the other Czechs staying at the Hotel Jacob were the journalist Ivo Ducháček, the painter Rudolf Kundera, and Alfons Mucha's son Jiří, a medical student who kept the wolf from the door by penning theatrical reviews for *Lidové noviny*. The young German-Czech Jewish writer Lenka Reinerová, whom Hoffmeister and Pelc took under their wing, ate with them in cheap local establishments (which Ada knew well) almost every evening.[47] "They treated me tenderly," she writes, "so to speak [as] an abandoned Prague flower, the only solitary girl among celebrities who were for the most part already internationally renowned."[48] "My first home was in Prague," Lenka relates in her memoir *Bez adresy* (Without an address, 2000). "I didn't choose it, my mother gave birth to me there: in the suburb of Karlín, in a very long suburban street [then Královská, since 1948 Sokolovská] bordering on the industrial districts of Libeň and Vysočany. We were a bourgeois family, all those around us were too. By contrast mostly workers lived in Libeň and Vysočany. When they were spoken of, they were often called proletarians. I couldn't really imagine what this word—in German, *Proletarier*—meant, but I found it strangely beautiful." As a child Lenka remembered watching from the window as "side by side, shoulder to shoulder, people from the proletarian quarters marched past our house" on the First of May.[49] She got her first job in 1936 as a journalist working for Wieland Herzfelde's *Arbeiter-Illustrierte-Zeitung* under F. C. Weiskopf, from whom she learned much. She was on a journalistic assignment in Romania when the Wehrmacht entered Prague. When she called home, her younger sister warned her that the Gestapo had already come to the house searching for her. A colleague from the *Baltimore Sun* helped her get a French visa by declaring that she was his secretary.[50] Forbidden to live in Paris, Lenka stayed at the Hotel Moderne in Versailles along with Egon Erwin Kisch and his wife Gisl, both of whom she "knew very well" from Prague.[51] In the mid-1930s Lenka had rented an attic room at 7 Melantrichova Street, just off the Old Town Square; number 14 was the Kisch family seat at the House of the Two Golden Bears, where Egon's mother served cakes and coffee to "literati, anti-fascist émigrés from Hitler's Reich, and Egon Erwin's Prague friends."[52] At some later date the Bear House (as Kisch called it) passed into the ownership of the Museum of the City of Prague and housed the library where I did much of my research for *The Coasts of Bohemia*.

Paris had been a magnet for Czech artists since the late nineteenth century. Some Czech artistic expatriates like František Kupka, Josef Šíma, Bohuslav Martinů, and the painters Alén Diviš, Jiří Kars, and Maxim Kopf made it their permanent home—or so they thought. Others, like Vítězslava Kaprálová, found themselves stranded in the City of Light by the German invasion.[53] Hoffmeister helped support Pelc, Diviš, Kaprálová, and other Czech exiles out of his own pocket, as well as raising funds through his French contacts.[54] His mother spirited money to him through London via Ralph Parker, the Prague correspondent for the London *Times* and *New York Times*—the same Ralph Parker who later broke the story of the Babi Yar massacre from Moscow. "Several Czech artists used to spend their time at the Café Bonaparte near the boulevard Saint-Germain," recounts Maxim Kopf, "and there I met A. Hoffmeister, the caricaturist Pelc, [Vlado] Clementis, [Hubert] Ripka and various Czech intellectuals in exile—with General [Sergey] Ingr, Mucha, Martinů and so on."[55] Clementis was a KSČ journalist, and Ripka was a correspondent for *Lidové noviny*. Both Ripka and Ingr later served in Edvard Beneš's Czechoslovak government in exile in London, and Ripka became minister of foreign trade in the postwar National Front governments from 1945 to 1948.[56] We will meet Vlado Clementis again later as a victim in Czechoslovakia's most spectacular communist show trial. It was at the Café Bonaparte that Jiří Mucha first met Vítězslava Kaprálová on 27 April 1939. They ended the evening in Jiří's garret in the Hotel Jacob, stared through the skylight at the stars, and (in Jiří's words) "that night Vítka didn't go home."[57] They married in April 1940. Two months later, on the day the Germans entered Paris, Vítka died of tuberculosis in a Montpellier hospital—a huge loss to modern music. Jiří made it to England, where he became a pilot in the RAF and a BBC war correspondent in North Africa, Italy, the Middle East, Burma, and China.[58]

Longtime expatriates and recent refugees alike threw themselves into patriotic activities. Czech painters living in France—including an unusual number of women artists—took part in the *Hommage à la Tchéco–Slovaquie* exhibition at the Galerie Contemporaine from 15 December 1938 to 5 January 1939.[59] Kupka, Kaprálová, and Pelc contributed to *Československý boj* (The Czechoslovak struggle), an émigré newspaper started in April 1939 by Ivo Ducháček, Jiří Mucha, and others. On 1 August Hoffmeister supplied an appreciation of Jiří's father Alfons Mucha, who had died two weeks earlier in Prague, for *Světový rozhled* (World view),[60] another émigré organ that was edited by former *Rudé právo* editor in chief Jan Šverma, one of Klement Gottwald's Karlín Boys. The magazine was soon suppressed by the French authorities. Anticipating arrest, Šverma fled Paris in October and made it to Yugoslavia; from there he eventually escaped via Bulgaria to Moscow. He died of exposure in the Tatra Mountains in November 1944 during the Slovak National Rising. Štefánik Bridge (Štefánikův most) in Prague bore his name (Švermův most) from 1947 to 1997, as did what is now Jinonice metro station on Line B. All memories have their day. After 1989, history ended differently again, and the names of the city's landmarks had to be changed too. But Jan Šverma's traces obstinately linger in the old KSČ strongholds, refusing to be erased from the map. When the mining villages of Motyčín and Hnidousy in the Kladno coalfield merged in 1949, neither would accept the other's name, so the new town of Švermov was born. Švermov kept its name when it was incorporated as a district of Kladno in 1980. Hockey legend Jaromír Jágr may describe himself as a son of Hnidousy rather than of Švermov, and he may joke that he will take his next girlfriend not to the Seychelles but to the field that was once upon a time the family farm,[61] but postcommunist attempts to change the name have so far been unsuccessful.[62]

Largely through Hoffmeister's efforts,[63] during the summer of 1939 the International Association of Writers for the Defense of Culture succeeded in renting a large three-story villa in the sixth arrondisement near the Luxembourg Gardens to serve as a House of Czechoslovak Culture. The building was intended to provide accommodations for impoverished Czechoslovak artists as well as be a cultural center for Czechoslovak resistance. It "looked romantic," writes Lenka Reinerová, "but not perhaps enticing."[64] From time to time, Czechoslovak airmen "en route to their future units in England" would stay overnight.[65] Among the exiles who moved into the house were Hoffmeister, Pelc, Reinerová, Maxim Kopf, Jiři Kars, the Catholic journalist Rudolf Šturm, and the young violinist Jan Šedivka. Alén Diviš and Egon Erwin Kisch were constant visitors, while Ingr, Ripka, Ducháček, Clementis, the painters František Matoušek and Imro Weiner, and the writers František Langer and Egon Hostovský shared many "merry evenings at the Maison de la Culture" debating "politics, culture, and the complicated life in exile."[66] "As the only female inhabitant of the house," says Reinerová, "it fell to me to act as housekeeper, which of course I could not have managed even in the smallest details without Ada's efficient help."[67] She describes Hoffmeister as "an affable, restless soul, full of joie de vivre and fantasy."[68] "Nowadays we sit at home every evening and drink wine—picture to yourself first-rate Bordeaux at 4 francs a bottle—we chat, and we go to bed at two-thirty in the morning," Ada wrote to Lilly Rohne on 30 August 1939, adding, "Our house is simply fabulous and the only thing I'm lacking is a fine girl."[69] Four days later France and Britain declared war on Germany. "Paris became another city," Max Kopf recorded. "Everything was disrupted—food, theater, whores; Paris lost its charm."[70] Inhabited by suspicious foreigners speaking an incomprehensible language, the house on the rue Notre-Dame des Champs did not escape the general paranoia.

Police commandos raided the villa while the Czechs were eating breakfast on Monday, 18 September, and carted away twenty people in paddy wagons. Smetana's "My Homeland" was playing on the radio, recalled Reinerová.[71] She was among those detained alongside Hoffmeister, Pelc, Ducháček, and Kopf; Diviš and Šturm were picked up later. Ducháček thought they were being arrested because the locals had mistaken their nighttime revels for celebrations of the German victories in Poland. The police report gave the real reason for the raid: "the seat of the association 'House of Czechoslovak Culture' . . . is in

FIGURE 7.2. Adolf Hoffmeister, illustration from *Unwilling Tourist*, London, 1942.
Courtesy of Martin and Ivan Hoffmeister, © Adolf Hoffmeister heirs.

reality nothing but the new seat of the recently reorganized central committee of the Communist Party of Czechoslovakia."[72] It was not: the only KSČ members who had any link to the house were Clementis, Kisch, and F. C. Weiskopf, and Weiskopf had left for America before it even opened. Adding insult to injury, the report accused Hoffmeister, Reinerová, and others of being Gestapo agents. Both accusations were nonsensical but—as always— they made perfect sense in the circumstances. After Joachim von Ribbentrop and Vyacheslav Molotov signed the Treaty of Non-Aggression between Germany and the USSR on 23 August, the French government closed the communist paper *L'Humanité* and imposed strict restrictions on the press. The PCF was dissolved on 26 September, and its parliamentary representatives were detained on 8 November. Not for the last time in modern history, the émigrés' foreignness trumped whatever reasons they had for fleeing their native land. They were aliens—which was quite enough to make them undesirables.

And so Ada and his friends found themselves in La Santé prison in Montparnasse, charged with espionage. Reinerová spent six months in La Petite Roquette women's prison. When the cell door closed behind him that first night in La Santé, Hoffmeister was struck by the absurdity of his situation above all. "I tried to think myself into the seriousness of my predicament . . . but I acknowledged the truth: my first emotions were not at all despondent. I was amused," he writes. His description of his new accommodations is suitably surreal:

> The wall, in which there is a window, is bare. Opposite the window is a door maybe two meters high, in whose center is a bracket on which the guard puts a can of soup through a small opening. . . . The peephole above the opening resembles the profane eye of God. On the left of the door in the corner is a toilet. Above it is a water faucet. Instead of a cover a clay washbasin teeters above the hole. Beside the toilet is a rusty central heating grate. It covers up a thick decade-old layer of dust. To the right of the door are two empty shelves. Beneath them three wooden hooks for towels and a gas mask. By the wall on the left . . . is an iron folding bed with a pallet, two sheets, a cylindrical bolster and two blankets. By the wall on the right is a hinged oak table and a chair chained to the floor. Pasted on the right-hand wall are the disciplinary regulations, an announcement from the prison bookstore, a handwritten list of canteen prices and instructions on how to write requests to the canteen and keep receipts. The tin cup is almost new. The wooden spoon is bitten. The handle is all that remains of the toilet brush. In this bare space the black broom has a very bourgeois look about it. It wasn't even a month before I was robbed of my last joy—sunlight. They painted the outside of the window an iridescent transparent blue.[73]

Describing himself as "a person disengaged from life, standing outside time and history,"[74] Ada did some heavy reading during the seven months he spent in La Santé. He purchased the books at the prison bookstore. Descartes's *Discourse on Method*, he said, was "the most expensive book I ever bought. It meant a week without smokes and not supplementing my food ration."[75]

I quote here from Hoffmeister's *Vězení* (Prison), which he wrote in La Santé and smuggled out via his lawyer. The text is illustrated with six tracings he made of the graffiti on the walls of his cell. "The vast wall diary of the prisoners speaks a sensitive, poetic language, full of mistakes in grammar, telling their large and small miseries," he writes in *Unwilling Tourist* (1942), a fictionalized version of his wartime odyssey that was first published in 1941 in New York under the title *The Animals Are in Cages*. The hero Jan Prokop, "an odd little man with a big moustache," is a thinly disguised version of Ada himself. Hoffmeister introduces Jan as "not very important. A writer and cartoonist. 5 1/2 feet tall, weight 170 lb., age 37, Catholic, bachelor," whose political record comprises "satirical verses, books, and utterances, mostly of an anti-fascist nature."[76] "With Freudian drawings," he goes on, "the prisoners adorn the record of their most intimate adventures":

> Prisoners know different districts of Dreamland better than do people sleeping in towns and villages, people lying tired by the freedom of work and movement.... On the burlesque runway of Dreamland, lovely young girls, huge of bosom and backside, dance wonderfully and undress with well-calculated slowness. In spite of the doses of bromide in the prisoners' daily soup, they bend warmly over the sleeper and then race away into the distant blue when he reaches out for them. They have the beautiful names of all the unconsummated loves of the past and inject a pleasantly indecent note into the night's proceedings.[77]

The walls of La Santé were more than a Freudian document for Alén Diviš. In the words of art historian Anna Pravdová, "the cell walls became a tool of work, a source of inspiration, a sheet of paper or a canvas. Diviš devoted himself to them the most intensively, and they left a permanent scar on his imagination,"[78] recurring again and again in his subsequent work. "The walls of the cell are dirty and faded," Alén later wrote, "flaking, covered in stains and mildew. I contemplated them for whole hours, whole days and nights. When you gaze on them for a long time they come alive, they change into figures, clouds, landscapes, cliffs and waterfalls, wrestling giants, sailing monsters, dancing sprites. The stains formed whole images, which I made more comprehensible by incising and scratching forms and outlines with a piece of plaster or stone chipped from the wall, so that the stains would assume more solid forms of people, animals, and landscapes ... I learned from them the stories of many prisoners who had been in the cell before me."[79] Art, indelibly rooted in the real, yet as disengaged from what we prefer to believe is reality as it can get.

FIGURE 7.3. Alén Diviš, *Guillotine—Prison Wall*, 1941,
gouache, pencil, paper, 59.5 by 43 cm.
Photograph © National Gallery Prague, 2021.

Transit

On his 1939 New Year's card for Jiří Voskovec, Jan Werich, and Jaroslav Ježek, Hoffmeister drew the Liberated Theater's three musketeers waiting at the dockside to embark for New York. Bundled up in scarves and thick winter coats, Jiří and Jan carry bags plastered with souvenir stickers, while Jarka tinkles the ivories on a suitcase that has metamorphosed into an upright piano.[80] Beneath the drawing are a few bars of music from one of the trio's biggest hits, a jaunty little number from V + W's 1931 film *Pudr a Benzin* (Powder and petrol). In Czech it alliterates and rhymes. "Nobody should ever take anything as definitive [*Nikdy nic nikdo nemá míti za definitivní*]," the two clowns sing, "nobody ever knows what may happen [*nikdy nikdo neví co se může státi*]."[81] It was an apt enough caution for uncertain times. The three men were unknowns in the United States. According to Werich, Ježek's first concern when he got off the boat in New York was not food or lodging but "Where is Benny Goodman playing?"[82] And why not? Catch the music while you still can. Nearly blind like James Joyce, speaking little English, and barred from working by immigration laws, the Czech Gershwin (as Ježek was known back home) had little else in which to place his trust. "Pears don't ripen in Kamchatka," he wrote to his friend Gustav Janouch shortly after his arrival. "My music was planted here [Czechoslovakia], in this land, in this soil. It's something you can't take with you. We can't just pop our homeland into a suitcase. A homeland—that is air, pavement, language, people—that is what you must leave behind. . . . Maybe I'm fleeing from one death to another."[83] As it turned out, he was, but not before he had written what Michael Beckerman describes as his "exquisite, blues-inflected" Piano Sonata.[84] Ježek died of kidney failure in New York on New Year's Day 1942, three days after marrying Frances (née Františka) Bečáková, an earlier Moravian immigrant who kept house for him in Manhattan.

Ada reached American soil by a more circuitous route. The charges against the Czechs were dismissed in March 1940. But instead of being set free, the men were taken to Roland-Garros stadium, then as now the home of the French Open tennis tournament. From September 1939 it served as a transit point to around a hundred internment camps for foreign nationals spread across France. Conditions at the stadium were less than salubrious, but at least Ada was able to write to Lilly Rohne for the first time in six months. He had nothing definitive to tell her. "I don't know what awaits me," he wrote, "maybe I'll become a soldier, maybe I'll be transferred to another camp, maybe in a few weeks I'll be set free."[85] A week later Hoffmeister, Pelc, Diviš, Kopf, Šturm, and Šedivka were transported to the Damigny labor camp near Alençon in Normandy. Reinerová had meantime been shipped to the Rieucros camp in the Lozère, where she shared a wooden hut with thirty or forty other "suspicious and undesirable foreign women," among them "shoplifters, prostitutes, a forger, [and] a pimp who procured unsuspecting servant girls for her customers."[86] Less fortunate than her male comrades, Lenka would be imprisoned there until 1941. On 29 May, as the German armies closed on Paris, the Damigny prisoners were evacuated to the

Bassens camp near Bordeaux. On 20 June, as the Germans bombarded Bordeaux, the guards opened the gates and the inmates fled. Hoffmeister, Pelc, Diviš, and Kopf reached the Atlantic port of Bayonne on 22 June, the day France surrendered.

The next day the Czechs boarded the SS *Divona*, a coal boat bound for what was then French Morocco. According to Hoffmeister's account in *Unwilling Tourist* (in which the *Divona* becomes the SS *Lorient* and carries a cargo of torpedoes rather than coal), when they entered Casablanca harbor five days later, "the refugees argued cynically over just what a refugee was." Whether or not any such conversation took place, the dialogue is worth reproducing in full. The humor is quintessentially Czech:

"The refugee is a homeless man who searches everywhere he goes for that which he has lost in some far-distant place. And the officers keep saying: 'Now you're warm. Warmer. Still warmer. Hot! No . . . colder . . . still colder. . . .'"

"The refugee is the one honest man whose papers can never be in order, and, therefore, the police constantly demand that he show them."

"A refugee is a man who embarrasses only those who have not yet been refugees."

"A refugee is an unwilling tourist."

"Being a refugee is the occupation of the patriot, for the time being."

"A refugee is one who runs from country to country with but one desire—to sit quietly at home."

"A refugee is one who runs away because he has done something good. So each port he enters suspects, a priori, that he will do something bad."

"A refugee is the poor relative who likes to tell over and over how rich he was."

"The refugee is the man forever on his way home."

"The refugee is the too-faithful lover, who, fleeing through the world, loses each new love when he calls her by the name of his beloved wife."

"The refugee is a man with a center of gravity outside his body."

"The refugee is a being without money or fatherland, but with, alas, a body."

"A refugee is a lover who abandons his love, wanting her only the way she used to be."

"The refugee is the man who cannot stay at home because he belongs sometimes to yesterday, sometimes to tomorrow, but never to today."[87]

When they were finally given permission to land, the Czechs were detained on a hospital ship before being "stuffed into buses and rocketed inland to a concentration camp at Ain-Chock on the edge of the desert."[88] At this point Ada's story melts into the movie *Casablanca*, though without Rick, Ilsa, or Sam. The 1942 movie, which to the filmmakers' surprise won Academy Awards for best director, best film, and best adapted screenplay, revolves around the fictional Czech resistance leader Victor Laszlo's attempts to escape Vichy-controlled Morocco to neutral Portugal and continue the fight against fascism from America. Laszlo may have been fictional, but the actor who played him, Paul Henreid, was a flesh-and-blood refugee who fled Austria in 1935. He once described himself as "naked in four countries."[89] Conrad Veidt (Major Strasser), who appeared in *The Cabinet of Dr. Caligari* (1920); Peter Lorre (Signor Ugarte), who starred as the serial child murderer in Fritz Lang's *M* (1931); Curt Bois (the pickpocket); and S. Z. Sakall (Carl the waiter) all fled Germany after Hitler's rise in 1933. Marcel Dalio (Rick's croupier), who fled France for Lisbon in June 1940, played the Jewish prisoner of war Lieutenant Rosenthal in Jean Renoir's *La Grande Illusion* (1937). The Nazis used his face on posters to show "a typical Jew." "A dozen other refugees cast adrift," writes Aljean Harmetz, "brought to a dozen small roles in *Casablanca* an understanding and a desperation that could never have come from Central Casting."[90] The devil is in the details: professors as waiters, bankers as bellhops, the endless procession of pretty young women through the office of Claude Rains's charmingly (and chillingly) cynical chief of police, willing to trade sex for exit visas. The Czechs were released from Aïn-Chock after two weeks, but like Victor Laszlo, they were not yet free to continue their struggle. "The crucial point of our difficulties," Ada wrote to Lilly from Casablanca on 26 August 1940, "is that it is absolutely impossible to leave this country. . . . I will never succeed in getting an exit visa from Morocco even if I have all the visas, papers, and other requisites to go anywhere else. . . . We are in a cage, a beautiful, hospitable, and gracious cage, but all the same a cage. . . . I've already had this beautiful white city up to here. Fruit, swimming in the ocean, starry nights and deserts with camels—I've had it up to here."[91]

Lenka Reinerová, who was released from Rieucros early in 1941 with the help of the Dutch consulate in Marseille, would soon find herself in limbo in French Morocco too. "Nowadays you just go to some travel agency to buy a ticket and you are God knows where," she told a Radio Prague interviewer in 2005, "but to this day I am sure that I was the very first ever girl from Prague who ever walked through Casablanca." The experience was unexpectedly liberating:

It was involuntary also—I was on my way to Mexico from France, and the boat I was on stopped there and didn't continue. So I was stuck there. First I was in some camp and then I somehow I managed to get a "laissez-passer" for 48 hours, and of course I never came back to this camp.

And then I was half a year—a full six months—living in Casablanca, and that is to this day one of my greatest adventures in life. I was completely alone. I had almost no money. I had to make some money even just to be there, and somehow, I managed. Not only did I manage, but I am—if it is possible—kind of grateful to myself that even in this very complicated situation, I enjoyed being there. I somehow felt—this is an adventure and take it![92]

Lenka's months in Morocco were far from easy, she writes, "but I was in Africa, the white city of Casablanca, and that was already, more than half a century ago, an extraordinary adventure and a fantastic experience. Those colors, smells, sounds, the vibrant atmosphere of a crowded city, the strange nature, completely different human behavior—it was all forever written into me, remains with me, and fills me with joy whenever I remember it." She adds: "When Hitler with his millions of followers came to power in Germany and then the war broke out, somebody dreamed up a bitter joke: Join the Jews and see the world."[93]

Ada's luck held and he managed to obtain travel documents just three days after writing his despairing letter to Lilly Rohne. He slipped away on a Breton lobster boat bound for Portugal with a cargo of almonds and twenty-four refugees. He had a brief scare when the vessel was detained by General Franco's troops "for four days without food and water" in that "nest of international bloodsuckers" Tangier, but the passengers were eventually allowed to leave on a motorized Spanish skiff.[94] The weather was fine, and they arrived safely in Lisbon as it was bathing in the warm gold of sunset. As night fell the city lit up, a sight Hoffmeister had not seen since the outbreak of war. "'Over a year ago the lights of my Paris went off,' he [Jan Prokop] thought," writes Ada in *Unwilling Tourist*, "'and tonight Lisbon turns hers on.'"[95] "We arrived without money and once again without luggage, exhausted and deadly tired, but on the other hand to a land where there is peace and prosperity. We checked into the best hotel and waited (a young Spaniard, J. Gráf and I) for money from America," Ada wrote to Voskovec and Werich in New York from the Hotel Metropole on 8 September. He was trying to get to the States, he went on, but everything remained uncertain; his Canadian visa had expired, and all passages on ships

FIGURE 7.4. Adolf Hoffmeister's New Year's card for Voskovec, Werich, and Ježek, 1939. From Karel Srp, ed., *Adolf Hoffmeister*, Prague, 2004. Courtesy of Martin and Ivan Hoffmeister, © Adolf Hoffmeister heirs.

were booked until October. "*Nikdo nic nikdy nemá míti za definitivní*," he jokes. "I'd love to read a word or two from you. For a year I haven't received even a line from anyone. All the best to everyone and till we maybe meet again. Ada."[96] Jan, Jiří, and Jan's wife Zdena had been active on behalf of Ada and his companions since their arrest in 1939, enlisting Eleanor Roosevelt's help to locate them in Morocco and paying for Ada's passage to America on a Greek steamer from Lisbon (which he was unable to take because he was still stuck in Casablanca).[97] But Hoffmeister wasn't to know that.

Lisbon's café life was not what Ada had been used to at Les Deux Magots and the Café Bonaparte, or even at the Unionka and Metro back in the day in Prague. "He [Jan Prokop] sat with the Portuguese in tiny side-street bars, afraid of the main thoroughfares crowded with foreigners. Each passer-by, it seemed to Jan, had evil intentions. And he was nearly right. The big cafés on the Rossio echoed with the tongues of every conquered nation, German dominating them all. When Jan sat down at his table in the Café Chaave d'Ouro he could be sure that with him sat a British agent, a Nazi spy, a Portuguese Secret Service man, and at least one refugee. Worn out by the everlasting hiding, the endless waiting for overseas visas, the mass of the refugees became shapeless, formless things, no longer men."[98]

> "Not even a year ago," remembered Jan, "I used to face the sardonic smile of the great French painter Fernand Léger in the Café de Flore on the Boulevard Saint-Germain. Today the sweet wines of Portugal taste bitter to both of us."
>
> Then would come Jean Renoir, *grand illusioniste* of the French screen, walking in thought, passing but not noticing Josephine Baker, the coffee-tan star of countless Paris musicals. . . .
>
> In the Café Chaave d'Ouro Prokop met his countrymen. Jan knew most of those who gathered on the terrace for their daily chat—the emotional and disheveled Franz Werfel, the skinny poet-pessimist Egon Hostovsky, the easy-going sceptic Friedrich Torberg (all of them writers), and the heavy, melancholy eyelids of the great comedian Hugo Haas. Caricaturists [Ivan] Sors and Adolf Hoffmeister doodled on the tablecloths.

And so, as the "last echoes of Europeanism" died away "in this last little light of peace on the westernmost fringe of Europe," Ada continues, "a whole section of cultural Europe . . . from almost every nation on the continent . . . reluctantly recognized their fellow-delegates to this unsummoned convention of genius. All of them had to pass through this halfway halt on the road to salvation. All of them had to sit in one of the pastry shops on Rossio Square and enviously read the shipping news. . . . In the inns and bars of fair Lisbon they bade a last farewell to the old Madam, the girl for sale, the gypsy who could always charm again. And how she could love! And dress! And undress! And drink! And kiss! They sat till dawn in the smoky half-dark, with heads on the table, and whispered like unhappy lovers: 'Her name was Europe.'"[99]

While Ada was kicking his heels in Lisbon, Pelc, Kopf, and Diviš killed time and made a little money painting watercolors in Casablanca. In November 1940 the Czechs were arrested again and imprisoned in a camp at Sidi el Ayachi in the south of Morocco. Released after four months, they returned to Casablanca. This time they succeeded in obtaining American visas. On 5 April 1941 they boarded the SS *Capitaine Paul-Lemerle*, which had sailed from Marseille on 25 March bound for Martinique. The old cargo ship carried some 350 men, women, and children "who were scarcely still connected to Europe, except by this ship's deck; at least, to today's Europe with all its fury and havoc! Germans, Austrians, Czechs, Spaniards, and a handful of French; those not fleeing barbaric racial prejudice were just paying for the crime of holding noble ideals under the noses of their present masters."[100] The words are those of André Breton, who was one of the refugees traveling on the overcrowded freighter with his wife Jacqueline Lamba and their little daughter Aube. The Bretons were accompanied by the Russian French writer Victor Serge and his twenty-year-old son Vlady (Vladimir Kibalchich), who had been living with them in the Villa Air Bel on the outskirts of Marseille along with Varian Fry, organizer for the Emergency Rescue Committee (ERC) established in New York after the fall of France. Using funds from the Rockefeller Foundation and lists compiled with the help of Thomas Mann and Alfred Barr, the ERC helped more than two thousand artists and intellectuals escape Europe before Fry was expelled by the Vichy authorities in August 1941 for "being pro-Jewish and anti-Nazi and for having sent help to a known Communist in a camp in Morocco."[101] "Happy that Vlady is here, tall and solid; happy for him that he'll discover the world," Victor Serge recorded in his notebook as they set out from Marseille. "I would like to stay. You."[102] *You* was his companion Laurette Séjourné, who had been unable to get a visa. It would be almost a year before Victor and Laurette saw each other again.

Also traveling on the *Capitaine Paul-Lemerle* was Germaine Krull, whose 1928 portfolio of images *Métal* had made her "the most prominent avant-garde photographer in Paris."[103] Krull recorded the voyage (including the obligatory King Neptune baptism as they crossed the equator) in words and images. "Almost without exception," she writes, "the passengers were cultivated people, educated and having enjoyed high social positions: doctors, lawyers, a professor of philosophy, writers . . . the son of an ambassador to Mexico . . . a former Catalan minister with his wife and children; a French film director—Jacques Rémy . . . a German ex-banker and his wife, a former factory owner from Bavaria; and a series of young people of all nationalities." Germaine's own voyages would take her first to Brazil and then back across the ocean to Brazzaville, where she worked for France Libre. "It was a time," she observed, when "no obstacle was too large, no voyage too long—the fact of passing through Hong Kong to get to New York seemed completely natural—no sacrifice too great."[104] Other notable passengers included the German communist writer Anna Seghers, author of the novel *Transit* (1944), about a group of refugees engaged in a desperate Kafkaesque search for the right set of documents to leave Marseille; the Cuban surrealist painter Wifredo Lam and his German-born chemist wife Helena Holzer; and the thirty-three-year-old anthropologist Claude Lévi-Strauss, who was on his way to take up a teaching position at the New School for Social Research in New York, where the émigré University in Exile (founded in 1933) and École Libre des Hautes Études (founded in 1941) kept German and French intellectual life alive in the New World.

Lévi-Strauss later related how he and Breton became "firm friends in the course of an exchange of letters which we kept up throughout our interminable journey; their subject was the relation between aesthetic beauty and absolute originality."[105] But of course. "With Lévi-Strauss . . . we discuss homelands (I have several and feel that I am tearing myself away from all of them) and the goal of the voyage," wrote Serge. "We're going 'somewhere in the other hemisphere,' L.-S. says softly, 'Nowhere.' He doesn't expect to return. Return where? And why? He has no attachments anywhere."[106] In another conversation the anthropologist hypothesizes that South America was "inappropriate for the higher forms of life—up till now." Victor objects "that one shouldn't divert social causes toward geographical hypotheses . . . the Nahuas of Mexico, like the Incas of Peru, didn't die a natural death: they were purely and simply killed, the way people are being killed in Poland today."[107] Serge's memories of Europe's bloodlands were fresh and raw. "Five years ago today I left Russia, torn apart," he wrote on 17 April. "Behind me captivity, the captives: my comrades. . . . All of them have perished since, shortly afterwards, because they were incapable of renouncing the truth."[108] By then he had no illusions about modernity's capacity for barbarism. "Our civilization; mighty and impoverished," he remarks on seeing the "pile of modern buildings of no interest" with which the French colonizers had littered Oran.[109]

"This was not the solitary adventure I had had in mind," wrote Lévi-Strauss in his memoir *Tristes Tropiques* (1955); "it was more like the departure of a convict-ship." There were only two passenger cabins on the *Capitaine Paul-Lemerle*, with seven sleeping berths between them. World-famous artists and intellectuals got no privileges: Lévi-Strauss secured one of the berths only because he had sailed with the company on his previous ethnographic trips across the Atlantic, and the official in Marseille "felt that it was out of the question for one of his former first-class passengers to be quartered like a cow or a pig."[110] The Bretons were quartered with the rest of the refugees in the lightless and airless hold, sleeping on straw pallets on a scaffold rigged up by the ship's carpenter. "The sanitary installations (if one can use the term)," wrote Germaine Krull, "are three small wooden shacks on the deck. The first a sea-water shower; the other two men's and women's toilets, installed for four people at a time in the most rudimentary manner."[111] Lévi-Strauss recalled the state of the toilets vividly: "The unventilated huts were made of planks of green and resinous fir-wood; these planks, impregnated with filthy water, urine, and sea air, would ferment in the sun and give off a warm, sweet, and altogether nauseating smell, which, when mingled with other smells, soon became intolerable, more especially if a swell was running."[112] Prevented from going ashore in Oran (only French passengers were permitted to disembark), Serge recorded his "feeling of captivity on this floating concentration camp, with its stinking hold."[113] Despite the refugees' common plight, this turned out to be a highly stratified little society:

> March 31, 1941—The *Wirtschaftsemigranten* [economic refugees], on the lookout for the best places, have installed themselves between the central deck and the boiler Jews with money. They rent the cabins of the crew, stuff themselves, hang out with the staff, mingle only with each other, distrust everyone, play cards, read *Clochemerle*. We call this corner the Champs-Élysées and invade it in part because it is sheltered from the wind and the sun. They give us dirty looks. Shit.
>
> The forward section is more densely populated but maintains a chic tone because of a group of filmmakers and well-dressed emigrants with cash who put on airs as if they were at a café on the Left Bank. (There are no banks anywhere.)
>
> The upper deck, which is not really a deck but a kind of roof encumbered by lifeboats, is occupied by the Lams, the Bretons, and Vlady. Jacqueline sunbathes almost completely nude and scorns the universe which, by ignoring her, vexes her. Helene Lam takes care of Wilfredo [*sic*], who is ill, the ganglia of his throat swollen; he's sad, stretched out on a blanket with his head on his wife's lap. His eyes of an aged Sino-Negro child are full of animal desolation. But he's doing better. I sometimes climb up, and from there you can see the whole ship, the whole sea. It's Montparnasse.[114]

In Marseille the passengers had told themselves that "Martinique the marvelous isle must be a free country, already American," relates Krull, but instead they found "the marvelous isle transformed into a Gestapo outpost." When the *Capitaine Paul-Lemerle* docked in Fort-de-France on 20 April, the passengers were detained again, in this case at Lazaret concentration camp, so named because it was a former leper colony, across the bay at Pointe Rouge. There was next to no food and little water, and conditions were generally atrocious. Germaine thought it worth noting that "we were not only under the control of Vichy and the yoke of the Gestapo, but moreover whites guarded by Negroes."[115] The Bretons were released after five days and allowed to live in a hotel in town, but they were kept under close surveillance. There were some unexpected consolations. By chance André stumbled across a copy of the review *Tropiques* in a shop window, which led to a meeting with "the great black poet" Aimé Césaire and his wife Suzanne, "beautiful as the flames playing on rum punch."[116] Césaire's "appearance in his own element—and I do not mean only on that day," Breton wrote, "takes on the significance of a sign of the times." He described Césaire as "a black man who handles the French language as no white man today is capable of handling it. And it is a black man who is the one guiding us today into the unexplored, seeming to play as he goes, throwing ignition switches that lead us forward from spark to spark. And it is a black man who, not only for blacks but for all humankind, expresses all the questions, all the anguish, all the hopes and all the ecstasy and who becomes more and more crucial as the supreme example of dignity."[117] For his part, the author of *Discourse on Colonialism* and *Cahier du retour au pays natal* (*Return to My Native Land*, 1939), a work Breton declared to be "nothing less than the greatest lyrical monument of our times," considered the surprise encounter "utterly crucial and decisive. . . . If I am who I am today, I believe that much of it is due to my meeting with André Breton."[118]

Antonín Pelc was much taken with the tropical landscape. "Martinique, that is—Gauguin," he wrote, explaining: "It is impossible not to see it through Gauguin's eyes, in warm and glowing and blinding colors."[119] Perhaps that is why one of his drawings, captioned "5. V. Martinique 1941," depicts a slender young Martiniquaise sitting naked under a sombrero and cradling a rooster in her lap—not a common sight, I would guess, in the streets of wartime Fort-de-France, but who is to gainsay the inner model of the artistic imagination? The Gauguinesque colors of Pelc's *Boy from Martinique* would brighten up the dreary vistas of normalization on a Czechoslovak postage stamp in 1973.[120] Breton, too, says he was "wildly seduced" by "the magnetic force of this ideal and real place," but "at the same time . . . we were wounded and indignant" at the circumstances that took him and his family there.[121] His little book *Martinique: charmeuse de serpents* (*Martinique: Snake Charmer*, published in 1948), reflects this tension. The volume, a mixture of prose poems, essays, and drawings, was a collaboration with the painter André Masson, who arrived with his (Jewish) wife Rose from Marseille on the SS *Carimare* a week after the Bretons. Masson apparently vomited when he heard the Vichy racial laws announced on the radio.[122] In his illustrations for *Martinique* the landscape and vegetation of the island keep mutating into bodies of women.

The book's juxtaposition of "lyrical language" and "the language of simple information," writes Breton, reassures us that "it is less important to view this

FIGURE 7.5. Antonín Pelc, *Martinique*, 1941, watercolor.
From Anna Pravdová, *Zastihla je noc*, Prague, 2009.

world as artists than to respond to it as human beings."[123] His prose poem
"Map of the Island," which is composed entirely of local place names, obliter-
ates any distinction between the two: it begins "Pocketknife, Sweetheart, Trap
Door, Rose Point, Noble Bearing Beacon, Wisp-of-Love, Carefree Pass."[124]
But in the end, another image lingers for me—and, perhaps, for Breton. "One
previous morning, at the same spot [on the deck of the *Capitaine Paul-
Lemerle*]," he writes, "I was struck by the appearance of three objects lined up
in a row and intertwining their flames—a disemboweled cow hanging from
the day before, the cabins on the afterdeck, and the rising sun. In April 1941,
their rather hermetic assemblage took on deeper significance."[125] The scene
also left an impression on Victor Serge:

On board: the cooks kill a steer and bleed it on the deck, in the middle of a circle of children, between the men's and women's toilets (which are obviously no longer either gentlemen's or ladies'). A mother takes her little girl to see this. A sailor drinks the animal's hot blood and wipes his face with the back of his hand. "It makes you strong." He has a small head and a large mouth. His eyes are dark as nail heads. The steer's hide remains on the deck, a strange sight: the skin, its head emptied of its contents, alongside a small heap of viscera of strange, dark colors. In the evening the gutted animal is hung among the stars in the moonlight.

Thought about the remains of men on battlefields and that prayers for the dead were a generous, exalting invention.[126]

The Strip Street

Hoffmeister languished for four months in Lisbon before obtaining an American visa thanks again to the Emergency Rescue Committee, which interceded on his behalf with the American consul.[127] After his Canadian plans fell through, Ada intended to travel from New York to Mexico with Egon Hostovský, but their American transit visas were changed to residents' visas at the last moment.[128] *Nikdy nikdo neví*. They left Lisbon on Christmas Day 1940 and arrived in New York City via Havana on 28 January 1941 on the Spanish liner SS *Magallanes*, two years to the month after Voskovec, Werich, and Ježek disembarked from the SS *Acquitania*. Hostovský wrote his psychological novel *Úkryt* (*The Hideout*, 1943) in New York while working for the Czechoslovak consulate; the narrator is a Czech engineer on the run from the Germans, confronting both himself and his memories while holed up in a dark, lonely cellar in northern France.[129] Lévi-Strauss made it to Manhattan and the New School in April by way of Puerto Rico, where, he wrote in *Tristes Tropiques*, "The American police, when faced with my load of anthropological material, had their full share of the suspicions which I had feared to meet with in Martinique. In Fort de France I had been treated as a Jew and a Freemason who was probably in the pay of the Americans. Here, in Porto Rico, I was taken for an emissary of Vichy if not, indeed, of the Germans." He was detained for weeks "in an austere hotel in the Spanish style, where I was fed on boiled beef and chick-peas, while two filthy and ill-shaven native policemen took it in turns, night and day, to guard my door," before he was permitted to proceed on his journey.[130] Pelc, Kopf, Diviš, and the Massons left Martinique on the SS *Duc Daumale* in April and reached New York on 29 May 1941; Kopf stayed on after the war, married the journalist Dorothy Thompson, and died in New York in 1958. The Bretons followed on 16 May and arrived on the SS *Presidente Trujillo* in mid-July via Guadeloupe and the Dominican Republic.

Senselessly being drawn along, senselessly wandering through a senselessly obscene world, around 250,000 refugees from Germany or Nazi-occupied states were admitted to the United States between 1933 and 1943. They included more than 5,000 doctors, 1,682 university professors, some 2,000 lawyers, 2,000 psychologists, 500 other scientific researchers, 717 painters and sculptors, around 1,900 writers and journalists, and over 2,000 theater and film actors, directors, and musicians.[131] Marc Chagall, Salvador Dalí, Marcel Duchamp, Max Ernst, George Grosz, Fernand Léger, Piet Mondrian, and Yves Tanguy were among the painters; Bertolt Brecht, Alfred Döblin, Ivan and Claire Goll, Lion Feuchtwanger, Heinrich and Thomas Mann, André Maurois, and Franz Werfel among the writers; Arnold Schoenberg, Igor Stravinsky, Béla Bartók, Paul Hindemith, and Darius Milhaud among the composers. The Drama Workshop founded by the exiled Erwin Piscator at the New School in 1940 nursed the theatrical talents of Tennessee Williams, Marlon Brando, Tony Curtis, Walter Matthau, Elaine Stritch, Harry Belafonte, and Judith Malina, among others. The humanities and social science scholars Theodor Adorno, Hannah Arendt, Ernst Bloch, Rudolf Carnap, Erich Fromm, Max Horkheimer, Siegfried Kracauer, Leo Löwenthal, Herbert Marcuse, Leo Strauss, and Karl Wittfogel all found refuge in the United States, as did the first and last Bauhaus directors Walter Gropius and Ludwig Mies van der Rohe and faculty members Marcel Breuer, László Moholy-Nagy, and Josef and Anni Albers. Another refugee architect, Erich Mendelsohn, designed the German village at Dugway Proving Ground, whose remnants were left by the army to crumble "out of bounds, out of place, out of time and 90 miles from Salt Lake City."[132] Mendelsohn's village was the testing site for the firebombing of Dresden and other German cities, just as Antonín Raymond's Japanese village was for the napalming of Tokyo. I won't attempt to list the scientists in this European diaspora, but this may be an appropriate place to remind ourselves that the atom bomb that left Jan Letzel's Genbaku Dome standing in Hiroshima "was born in . . . American university laboratories with the aid of refugees from fascism,"[133] including Albert Einstein, Leo Szilard, Hans Bethe, and Enrico Fermi.

Many of the exiles chose to remain in the United States after the war ended, and many of those who did not left their enduring mark on American society anyway. Some of them had close connections with Prague. The composer Bohuslav Martinů left Paris for Aix-en-Provence in 1940 and reached New York via Spain and Portugal in January 1941. He taught at the Berkshire Music Center, the Mannes School of Music, and Princeton University and became an American citizen in 1952. He spent his last years in France, Italy, and Switzerland, where he died in 1958.[134] The Czech soprano Jarmila Novotná, whose ship docked in New York on the day Prague fell to Hitler, made her debut at the Metropolitan Opera on 5 January 1940 as Mimi in *La Bohéme*, a role she sang (according to *New York Times* critic Olin Downes) "with charming simplicity, feeling and high artistic intelligence."[135] In 1942 she recorded an album of Czech folk songs for RCA Victor under the title *Songs of Lidice*, with Jan Masaryk at the piano. Novotná performed at the Met for seventeen seasons, retiring in 1956. She returned home in 1945 but chose to go into a second exile in 1948.[136] The Devětsil dancer and choreographer Mira Holzbachová also found her way to New York in January 1939. At Eleanor Roosevelt's invitation she performed the dances "Women in Bondage" and "Woman Liberated" at Rockefeller Center on 15 June 1942 for the National Council of Women of the United States. Holzbachová had danced in *Rudý prapor a hold revoluci* (The red flag and tribute to the revolution) in celebration of the Russian Revolution in Prague's Municipal House on 7 November 1926 and had been a KSČ member since 1931.[137] Happier with the postwar order than Novotná, Mira returned to Czechoslovakia after the war, where she played an important role in cultural politics and published several popular books on Native American life and legends.[138]

One of Lévi-Strauss's New School colleagues was Roman Jakobson, whose structuralist linguistics would have a profound influence on the anthropologist's work. The Russian-born Jakobson, who was also Jewish, first came to Prague as a translator for the Soviet Red Cross in 1920. A cofounder of the Prague Linguistic Circle with Vilém Mathesius and Jan Mukařovský, he was a member of Devětsil and a close collaborator with the Czechoslovak Surrealist Group. He taught at Masaryk University in Brno from 1933 to 1939 and took Czechoslovak citizenship in 1937. Roman and his wife Svatava fled Brno after the German invasion and hid out in Prague while waiting for visas. They arrived in Denmark in April 1939 and moved on to Norway on 1 September, the day World War II officially broke out. On hearing of the German ultimatum to Norway on 9 April 1940, they dropped everything and took the first train north. Two weeks later they walked across the mountains into Sweden. By current American standards, the couple were spectacularly undocumented and decidedly illegal,[139] but Swedish colleagues vouched for Roman and he was given a visiting professorship at the University of Uppsala. The Jakobsons remained in Sweden for more than a year before they found passage on a cargo boat from Gothenburg to New York, arriving on 4 June 1941.[140] It was the last ship the Germans allowed to sail from Sweden to the United States.[141] Roman went on to teach at Columbia, Harvard, and MIT. By the end of his career he had accumulated twenty-five honorary doctorates and was a member of nine national academies of sciences.[142] He did not return home in 1945 because, he said, he "did not expect the coalition government to last."[143] Jakobson's work was condemned for formalism in the early 1950s, and his Brno chair was revoked. After 1956 he was able to attend professional meetings again in Moscow, Leningrad, Warsaw, Sofia, Bucharest, and other Soviet bloc cities, but he did not revisit Czechoslovakia until August 1968, when he participated in the Sixth International Congress of Slavists in Prague. Charles University and what had now been renamed Purkyně University in Brno awarded him honorary degrees. On 21 August the Slovak Academy of Sciences gave him its Gold Medal.[144] The Warsaw Pact forces invaded the same day, bringing us by a *commodius vicus* of recirculation back to the events of three decades earlier that had triggered what Roman described as "the years of homeless wandering from one country to another."[145]

Jaroslav Josef Polívka engineered the most spectacular feature of one of the best-known buildings in New York City: the curved ramp gallery that spirals upward without visible means of support around the walls of Frank Lloyd Wright's Solomon R. Guggenheim Museum, completed in 1959. Born in Prague in 1886, Polívka graduated with a doctorate in structural engineering from ČVUT in 1917. After finishing his military service, he established his own architectural and engineering consultancy and made a name for himself specializing in reinforced concrete, steel, and glass. He worked with Devětsil's Josef Havlíček on two of the earliest functionalist buildings in Prague—the Chicago Palace on Národní Avenue and the Habich Palace on Štěpánská Street (both built in 1927–1928).[146] Havlíček and Polívka submitted a daring entry for the first of several competitions for a viaduct across the Nusle Valley in 1927: each of the pillars supporting the bridge would house elevator shafts and stairwells for a multistory apartment block, and the cost of the bridge's construction would be defrayed by sales of the resulting nine hundred flats. The supporting pillars were to be separated from the rest of the development by expansion joints with flexible inserts to prevent the spread of vibrations from the bridge deck into the apartments. Though it was never realized, the design is famous in Czech architectural circles.[147] A more orthodox but still magnificent bridge across the valley was finally built in 1967–1973. When it opened it was called the Klement Gottwald Bridge (most Klementa

Gottwalda), but nowadays it is just the Nusle Bridge (Nuselský most). Polívka was responsible for the steel frame of the Czechoslovak pavilion at the 1937 Paris World's Fair. Without his technical expertise, Jaromír Krejcar's "delicate glass poem on the banks of the Seine" never would have floated as it did.

Polívka's collaboration with the architect Kamil Roškot on the corresponding pavilion for the 1939–1940 World's Fair was what brought him to New York early in 1939.[148] By the time the fair had its grand opening on 30 April 1939 at Flushing Meadows–Corona Park in Queens, the Czechoslovak pavilion represented a state that no longer existed. It would be the first of several pavilions to be orphaned by the time the fair closed on 27 October 1940. This did not stop exiled president Edvard Beneš from ceremonially inaugurating the pavilion on 31 May in the presence of New York mayor Fiorello La Guardia and other dignitaries. Mira Holzbachová played a part in the proceedings; she may have been one of the "Czech folk dancers in traditional dress, with a gas mask," caught in a contemporary press photograph.[149] The plain concrete exterior was adorned with the Czechoslovak coat of arms and emblazoned (in English) at the last minute with the words of a prayer by an earlier Czech exile, the seventeenth-century pedagogue Comenius: "After the tempest of wrath has passed the rule of thy country will return to thee, O Czech people." The same words are written on the Jan Hus monument in Prague's Old Town Square, erected in 1915 on the quincentenary of Hus's death, when Bohemia was still ruled from Vienna. It was a message that sat uneasily with the fair's modernist imagery of the Perisphere, Trylon, and Democracity and its comically optimistic slogan, given the year: "Dawn of a New Day!"

Inside the pavilion was an exhibition whose aim, according to its creator Ladislav Sutnar, was "to show the remarkable links and significant contributions of the Czech and Slovak nations to Western Civilization by a few historical and contemporary highlights."[150] Sutnar was probably the most outstanding Czech product and graphic designer of the interwar period. He was artistic director of the Krásná jizba (Beautiful Room) furniture chain, a precursor of Terence Conran's Habitat and Ingvar Kamprad's IKEA, as well as its associated publishing house Družstevní práce (Cooperative Work), for which he coedited the influential lifestyle magazine Žijeme (on which Milena Jesenská worked in 1932–1933).[151] Sutnar arrived in New York on 14 April with $10,000 in cash, tasked with dismantling the installation at the fair. Instead, he set about completing it, at considerable risk to his family back in Prague. The Nazis prevented about half the material for the exhibitions in the pavilion from leaving Europe; Sutnar highlighted the vacancy with a statement at the entrance reading: "The young Republic became the victim of a ruthless inva-sion which strangled the liberty of her people. More eloquently than words could express it, the emptiness that surrounds you tells the story." The remain-ing exhibits were dominated by a Baťa company display of five large glass panels by Cyril Bouda, depicting scenes from the life of the company's founder Tomáš Baťa (titled "Hymn of Work"), and a large-scale model of the company town of Zlín crafted out of rare woods from around the globe. The Baťa display an-nounced that it was "intended to show the world a state progressing toward an industrialized, rationally planned society,"[152] a tad ironically, under the circum-stances. Sutnar worked with Czechoslovak relief organizations throughout the war. In 1942 he cooperated with Adolf Hoffmeister and Antonín Pelc on a float titled "Czechoslovakia Fights On" for the New York at War parade, as well as designing a traveling exhibition on Lidice, which was never realized.

Ladislav remained in New York after the war, and his wife and sons joined him in 1946. He made significant contributions to Western civilization in a field that he was one of the first to dub "information design."[153] Among other proj-ects he redesigned the American telephone directory, introducing the conven-tion of putting area codes in parentheses. The sexy, colorful "Joy-Art" nudes of Sutnar's later years speak to a time and place where the nakedness of animal human nature momentarily got loose from the corsets of kitsch. "In the days of its glory, I lived on Fifty-second Street, in the block between the Fifth and Sixth Avenues," he reminisced in his introduction to *The Strip Street: Posters without Words* (1963), "the famous strip street known far and wide as the sexiest place in town." "To live in the midst of nightlife madness, heightened by the advent of World War II, cast memorable spells that haunted me for a long time to come." He relishes the street's "tawdry physical vulgarity, obscene language and a close low view of human behavior unmasked in a quest for a variety of tempta-tions," the "stream of week-end crowds [that] flowed constantly, dammed only that one Pearl Harbor Sunday, then rushing on again the following weeks, never ending, virulent, sometimes violent in its wartime complexities." Above all he celebrates "the shapely disrobing ladies who were so essential a part of the strip street scenery . . . the dim, murky, aphrodisiac atmosphere of female bodies in movement. . . . Or, maybe just an arm loosening the hair."[154] It was wartime, after all. Sutnar died in New York City in 1976.

Polívka, too, settled permanently in the United States, eventually becoming a professor at the University of California at Berkeley. In 1946, after reading an article in *Architectural Forum* in which Frank Lloyd Wright was quoted as call-ing engineers "complete damn fools!" he wrote to Wright describing himself

FIGURE 7.6. Ladislav Sutnar, *Venus*, 1963–1964,
acrylic, Masonite, 181 by 109 cm. From Iva Knobloch,
ed., *Ladislav Sutnar: Americké Venuše (U.S. Venus)*,
Prague, 2011.

as "an old admirer of you and your work." "You may be right," he told Frank,
"since the engineers in their structural conceptions are very seldom guided by
eternal laws of Nature. Take for example cobwebs of a spider which definitely
should be studied by an engineer whose specialty is to build suspension
bridges. . . . The average engineer knows only beams, girders, columns, and any
deviation from these every day tools is considered as unusual, crazy, or dangerous."[155] Wright invited Jaroslav to Taliesin, and another collaboration between
the American architectural maestro and a former ČVUT student was born.
Over the next thirteen years Polívka and Wright worked together on seven
projects, one of which was a stunning design for a reinforced concrete "butterfly wing bridge" in San Francisco based on the cantilever beam principle,

with main spans of five hundred and one thousand feet. The idea was Jaro's, as Polívka was known to his friends.[156]

Only two of these projects were ever realized: the Guggenheim Museum in New York and the fifteen-story Johnson's Wax Research Tower in Racine, Wisconsin (1947–1950). Wright's original design for the Guggenheim had envisaged supporting posts on every floor of the ramp, but "Polívka, an expert in experimental stress analysis and photo-elasticity, offered to help with the design and eliminate the columns. After a number of experiments," writes Ivan Margolius, Jaro "suggested replacing the trigonometric spiral with a spirally warped ramp, which offered much greater stiffness. Polívka tried to obtain payment for his services but without result and later conceded, realizing that it was a real honor to work for such a genius."[157] The Johnson's Wax Research Tower—one of only two high-rise structures in Wright's entire portfolio—is equally unorthodox. The tower is anchored by a "taproot" central vertical core, off which the floors are cantilevered. The exterior walls are made of fifty-eight hundred Pyrex glass tubes, lined with bands of Cherokee red bricks. When the tower was renovated and opened for public tours in 2014, a columnist for the *Chicago Tribune* marveled, "The glass tubes transform daylight into a series of curving horizontal bands that range in color from white to blue. The ghost-like silhouettes of nearby brick buildings can be glimpsed through the translucent glass, adding faint red tones to its ethereal mix of light."[158] Though the scale of the structure is very different, the imprint of Jaromír Krejcar's delicate glass poem on the Seine, down to the curved opaque Thermolux glass corners, is palpable. It's that Old World pattern of wallpaper bleeding through the New World paint again, haunting the future with its shape and its feel and its smell.

Here's Looking at You, Kid!

Not all the refugees who crossed the Atlantic on the SS *Capitaine Paul-Lemerle* were welcome in the land of the free. After being denied temporary entry at the Port of New York on 16 June 1941, Anna Seghers and her family eventually found their way to Mexico City,[159] where Anna wrote her masterpiece *Transit*. Victor Serge's onward voyage from Martinique took him through the Dominican Republic, Haiti, and Cuba to Mérida in the Yucatán, where he disembarked on 4 September and traveled on to Mexico City the next day. He recorded some vivid impressions during his stay in Ciudad Trujillo (now Santo Domingo), the capital of the Dominican Republic. Who could forget the multicultural humanity of the street where the rent girls live?

The road: puddles, mud, ruts, garbage. Tall soldiers in wide felt hats stroll, blacks and Chinese wander or gather, animation around the hairdressers and the bars; small, noisy café, Dios y Trujillo [God and (President) Trujillo], back room with lanterns and billiards. Hookers everywhere, they make you think of those beautiful, pearly- or blue-winged flies you see swarming around rotting objects—or of flowers growing out of a swamp. . . .

The vigorous Chinese woman with a flat face, big eyes, a long black chignon, a debauched look, a beautiful female, walks back and forth dressed in electric blue. The Malayan girl (that's what I call them; they're products of unknown mixtures) is astonishingly slender in a short, striped dress, fine-featured triangular face, slanted eyes, lovely, sharp, smile; she clings caressingly to a black man who is taking her to the billiard room in Dios y Trujillo. She's nothing but a human stem of perfect loveliness. There are broad-faced Polynesian women, their skin the gold of peaches; black women with magnificent teeth; a few young white girls, lovely.[160]

We are a long way from Prague, but maybe not. Franz Kafka likely would have been as much at home here (remember his closely observed girls in the U Šuhů brothel?) as he was anywhere. The café's name, by the way, was the Dominican Republic's official state motto at the time.

On 9 September, less than a week after their arrival in Mexico City, Serge and his son Vlady visited the home of Leon Trotsky, who had been murdered a year previously by a Spanish Stalinist assassin named Ramón Mercader. The government of president Lázaro Cárdenas granted Trotsky asylum on 6 December 1936, and Frida Kahlo and Diego Rivera met the exiled Russian revolutionary and his wife Natalia Sedova at Tampico Harbor in January 1937. The Trotskys lived with Frida and Diego at their home, the Casa Azul (Blue House), in the suburban district of Coyoacán for two years before moving to the villa on the nearby Calle Viena in April 1939. "Tall trees, wide deserted avenue, pure air, all is green, we arrive in the rain," Victor's notebook entry begins. He had last seen "the Old Man" in 1928 or 1929 "on the eve of his arrest (exile to Alma-Ata) . . . at the home of Beloborodov (executed)." In Trotsky's office were "a large table without drawers, notes on India, bloodstains. Plank bookshelves, bare walls. Map of Mexico. The laboratory, a work cell for a mind. It curiously resembles my own place," Serge observes, "with far greater means: it's truly Russian and revolutionary, the style of several generations characterized by the stripping away of individualism, the search for objectivity." The entry ends on a note that puts things in perspective: "In that fortress in Coyoacán, two armed young men are guarding shadows, a deserted intellectual laboratory, a devastated woman-child of sixty-five. Citadel of ghosts, haunted tomb, absolute distress. Around it rich vegetation, blue mountains, the great, radiant sky."[161] In a surreal footnote to Trotsky's story, the Czechoslovak embassy in Mexico granted Mercader Czechoslovak citizenship after the assassin completed his prison sentence in 1960, and he spent some time in Prague before moving on to Moscow.[162] Legend has it that an embassy car was waiting for him outside the jail on his release.

Under Cárdenas and (to a lesser degree) his successor Manuel Ávila Camacho, Mexico was unusually hospitable to left-wing refugees. Had Adolf Hoffmeister not changed his plans and stayed in the United States, he would have renewed some old acquaintances and made some interesting new ones in Mexico, as he always loved to do. Egon and Gisl Kisch found themselves in Mexico City at the end of November 1940 after spending nearly a year in New York, which they had to leave when their transit visas expired. They rented a small apartment on the corner of Avenida Amsterdam and Calle Michoacán in the art deco Colonia Condesa district,[163] where Egon wrote *Sensation Fair*. The memoir of Prague appeared in July 1942 as the first title published by Das Freie Buch/El Libro Libre (The Free Book), an association of exiled antifascist writers whose members included Bruno Frei, Ludwig Renn, Bodo Uhse, and André Simone, as well as Seghers and Kisch. Founded in November 1941, their journal *Freies Deutschland* (Free Germany), which was edited by Frei and Uhse, boasted at least twenty thousand readers by 1943.[164] Seghers was president and Kisch vice president of the Heinrich Heine Club, which staged readings, lectures, concerts, and plays and became a social and cultural center for German-speaking émigrés. Renn and Uhse were communist writers who had fought in the International Brigades during the Spanish Civil War. Frei was an Austrian communist journalist who knew Kisch from Berlin. Fleeing to Prague in March 1933, he created the émigré paper *Der Gegen-Angriff* (Counterattack) with F. C. Weiskopf and Wieland Herzfelde before moving on to Paris in 1936. The journalist and Comintern agent André Simone—born Otto Katz in Jistebnice in southern Bohemia and raised in Prague—had been a close friend of Kisch's since 1920. He was well known in liberal Hollywood circles due to his fund-raising in California for anti-Nazi organizations and counted Lillian Hellman, Dorothy Parker, and Charlie Chaplin among his admirers. Some believe Simone was the model for Victor Laszlo in *Casablanca*.[165] If so, this gives the film's ending a savage twist. It seems that Rick gave up Ilsa for nothing, since "the nonchalant impresario and idea-man of the great Comintern variety show" (as Arthur Koestler called Simone)[166] would meet his end on a gallows in Pankrác prison in Prague a decade later, at the hands not of the Nazis but of the KSČ. Like Vlado Clementis, Simone was one of the victims of the Slánský trial, about which I have much more to say later.

Another of Ada's old contacts, the former Bauhaus director Hannes Meyer, arrived in June 1939 with his wife Lena Bergner and their daughter Lilo. A textile designer trained under Josef Albers and Wassily Kandinsky, Lena was one of the Bauhaus students who accompanied Hannes to the Soviet Union in 1931. She created more than forty fabric designs for the Decorativtkan textile factory during her years in Moscow, including the remarkable "Metro."[167] Lena and Hannes returned from the Soviet Union in 1936 and married the next year. For a time Lena was the family's main breadwinner: Hannes was unable to find regular work in Switzerland because of his political views. He came to Mexico to head the newly created Institute of Planning and Urbanism at the National Polytechnic Institute. Unfortunately, he lost his new job in 1941, after Diego Rivera accused pro-Soviet communists of involvement in Trotsky's assassination. He was subsequently employed as technical director of projects for the Ministry of Labor, where he oversaw planning for several (mostly unbuilt) housing estates.[168] The family remained in Mexico City until 1949, when they returned to Switzerland. During their time in Mexico, Lena contributed designs to the magazine *Arquitectura y Decoración*, and she and Hannes were both heavily involved with the Taller de Gráfica Popular (People's Graphic Workshop). Hannes lectured on Mexican urbanism at the Heinrich Heine Club and designed covers for *Freies Deutschland*. He also edited *El Libro Negro del Terror Nazi en Europa* (The black book of Hitler's terror in Europe), published by El Libro Libre in a print run of ten thousand copies in 1943. It contains fifty-six essays by Kisch, Seghers, Uhse, Simone, Heinrich Mann, Lion Feuchtwanger, and other prominent German émigrés and is notable for including "perhaps the earliest print related to the Holocaust and the death camps"—the Mexican printmaker Leopoldo Méndez's *Deportación a la muerte* (Deportation to death: death train).[169] Kisch, Simone, Renn, and the Italian-born American communist photographer Tina Modotti were regular guests at the "three-times weekly lunch table of emigrant friends" in Hannes and Lena's Cuauhtémoc apartment.[170] Modotti died suddenly and unexpectedly in the back of a taxi while returning from a party at the Meyers' residence in January 1941. Ada Hoffmeister would not have been out of place in this company, though he likely would have had private doubts about their orthodox pro-Soviet politics.

On a four-month visit to Mexico in 1938—his first venture outside Europe—André Breton had hailed it as "the Surrealist place *par excellence.*"[171] During World War II Mexico City became a surrealist refuge second only to New York. In the fall of 1939 the painter Wolfgang Paalen moved into a house in the suburb of San Ángel with his wife, the poet and painter Alice Rahon, and the photographer Eva Sulzer. Paalen and the Peruvian poet César Moro organized a large *Exposición Internacional del surrealismo* in January 1940 at the Galeria de Arte Mexicano, showing works by Diego Rivera, Frida Kahlo, and other Mexican painters, photographs by Manuel Alvarez Bravo, and indigenous artifacts side by side with the usual European suspects. The French poet Benjamin Péret arrived with his painter partner Remedios Varo in mid-December 1941 on the SS *Serpa Pinto* (which ferried an estimated 110,000 refugees to the Americas during the war). Leonora Carrington, Esteban Francés, and the Hungarian photographer Kati Horna also found refuge in the Mexican metropolis. Horna settled in the Colonia Roma with her Spanish husband José, whom she met while photographing the Spanish Civil War.[172] In 1944 Jacqueline Lamba (who had left André Breton by then) visited for seven months with daughter Aube, staying with Gordon Onslow Ford and his wife in the remote village of Eronguaricuaro as well as with Frida Kahlo in Mexico City.[173] Wolfgang Paalen's review *DYN*, whose first issue appeared in the spring of 1942, extended surrealism's horizons (and challenged Bretonian orthodoxy) through a simultaneous engagement with pre-Columbian art and modern physics.[174]

Carrington spent the rest of her long life in Mexico. So did Remedios Varo, Alice Rahon, Kati Horna, and Victor Serge's companion Laurette Séjourné, who arrived in March 1942 with Victor's daughter Jeannine and went on to become one of Mexico's best-known archaeologists.[175] Leonora and her future husband Emerico "Chiki" Weisz, a Hungarian photographer who had also found his way to Mexico via Casablanca, lived for a time with Varo and Péret in their run-down apartment on Gabino Barreda Street in the working-class area of San Rafael. Gunther Gerzso's *Los días de la calle de Gabino Barreda* (The days of Gabino Barreda Street), a "portrait of Leonora Carrington, Remedios Varo, Benjamin Péret, Esteban Francés, and Self-Portrait" (1944), is a fitting souvenir. "Gerzso's painting," writes Alexxa Gotthardt, "is chock-full of disembodied forms, hybrid creatures, and windows and doors cracked open into other realms. But it is also rooted in reality. While Péret's head floats in the middle of a strange pyramid-vortex, Gerzso also shows his bald spot—an accurate reflection of the living, breathing artist. Varo, for her part, is depicted crouching, shrouded in a mask, and surrounded by a brood of glaring cats. . . . Around them, allusions to both Mexico and Europe mingle. Behind adobe structures and across an ocean, smoke billows into the sky—a symbol of war in Europe."[176] Carrington sits naked on the floor meshed in vines while holding another female nude full-frontally aloft. The house was infested with rats that Péret tried to poison while Varo fed them with cheese, "an indefatigable duel."[177] Ada likely would have found Gabino Barreda Street a congenial place to hang out, too.

Continuing to grab adventure with both hands, Lenka Reinerová boarded the SS *Serpa Pinto* in Casablanca in November 1941 and arrived in Veracruz in December on the same crossing as Péret and Varo.[178] Her old boss F. C. Weiskopf arranged for her ticket in New York.[179] She made her way to Mexico City, where she found employment with the embassy of the Czechoslovak government in exile. She became an active member of the Heinrich Heine Club and a regular contributor to *Freies Deutschland*, but she took something of a backseat in the émigré community, she says, not only because of her youth but also because, "as integrated as I was within the group of German communists, I was and remained 'the Czech girl.'"[180] This did not deter her from editing *El Checoslovaco en México* (Czechoslovakia in Mexico) on behalf of the Czechoslovak-Mexican Association from the end of 1942 to 1945, with Kisch and Simone as her editorial staff.[181] The two men were witnesses at her 1943 wedding to the Yugoslav journalist and writer Theodor Balk, whom she had first met in Prague.[182] The idea for *El Checoslovaco en México*, which would "explain to the local people what Czechoslovakia is, how the fascists are now ruling there and how the people are fighting against this," was born one evening in the Kisches' Condesa flat.[183] "In Mexico Kisch suffered horribly from the fact that Prague was occupied," Lenka told a Czech TV interviewer in 2001. "When we were alone, Egon spoke in Czech with me in Mexico—out of nostalgia and homesickness."[184]

Nostalgia and homesickness did not blunt the raging reporter's insatiable curiosity. Egon's *Entdeckungen in Mexiko* (Discoveries in Mexico, 1945) contained twenty-four essays on a wide range of topics, including sports among the ancient Maya, how to make tortillas, the hallucinogenic properties of peyote, and the cultural history of the cactus.[185] He attends a Sabbath service in the village of Venta Prieta, whose thirty-seven Jewish inhabitants, "in no way distinguishable from other Indians or Mestizos," were descended from Spanish Jews who fled the Inquisition in the sixteenth century. And he recites the Kaddish:

DIE ARBEITER-JLLUSTRIERTE ZEITUNG ALLER LÄNDER

FIGURE 7.7. Upton Sinclair, Charlie Chaplin, and Egon Erwin
Kisch, Germany, late 1920s. Photographer unknown. © ČTK.

My father and mother were born in Prague, lived there, and are buried there.
It never could have occurred to them that one day one of their sons would
be reciting the prayer for the dead for them amid a group of Indians, in the
shadow of the silver-laden mountains of Pachuca. My parents, who lived
their entire lives in the Bear House of Prague's Old Town, never dreamt that
their sons would sometime be driven out of the Bear House, one of them to
Mexico, another to India, and the two who were unable to escape the Hitler
terror, to unknown places of unimaginable horror. My thoughts roamed
farther—to relatives, friends, acquaintances, and enemies, sacrifices of
Hitler, all entitled to be remembered in the prayer for the dead.[186]

Looking back on her life from an imaginary café located "in the mysterious
blue-gray mists above the verdigris-covered domes and stern church towers"

of Prague in *Das Traumcafé einer Pragerin* (The dream café of a Prague woman, 1996),[187] Lenka relates how half a century earlier in Mexico City Kisch got the news that the Nazis had killed his brothers Arnold and Paul. "Immediately after Gisl told me on the phone," she writes, "I rushed to their place."

"I don't know whether Egonek will let you in. He doesn't want to see anyone," [Gisl] told me as she opened the door.

"I'll try." I knocked on the door of his room. "Egonek, let me in, please!"

After a minute we heard shuffling steps. He opened the door in his pajamas—it was the afternoon—and unshaven. His hand, holding a cigarette, was trembling.

"Do you have any coffee?" he asked, when he saw Gisl. "Come in, dope [*blbá*], you are from Melantrich Street too and the same thing awaits you. They murdered them."

He was in deep shock but all the same that day we talked together for hours and hours. He told stories about his mother, about his brothers, about Prague and the wild years of his youth, about his regular visits home. "That's all gone now," he ended with a sigh.

When I left the Kisches that day with my husband, Egon accompanied us to the door, still in his pajamas, with dark stubble on his face and a cigarette in the corner of his mouth. There he said to Balk: "Come and get me, when your wife receives the same news from Prague as I did today. It is inevitable and I promise her that I will immediately come running to her too."

He promised nothing like that to me. But when I learned that the Nazis had murdered my parents and both my sisters, altogether eleven of my relatives, he came to our place immediately without needing to be asked. He sat beside me and said:

"That's the way it is. Do you know how many people are now receiving news like this?"

"What are we going to do, Egonek?" I repeated the question that I had so often heard from him.

"What are we going to do? Carry on."[188]

Egon and Gisl left Mexico on 17 February 1946, nine months after the war in Europe ended. Both had been eager to go home sooner, but transit visas for the United States were still not easy to come by for those the FBI was calling premature antifascists. Kisch remained under the bureau's surveillance as "a well-known Communist whose opinions are greatly respected by the

Communists of Mexico."[189] His FBI dossier was 169 pages long (that on Anna Seghers ran to more than a thousand pages).[190] The Kisches spent a few days in New York before crossing the Atlantic on the *Queen Elizabeth* and then flew from London to Prague. They landed at Ruzyně airport on 21 March. "For various reasons," says Reinerová, Egon and Gisl were unable to move into the House of the Two Golden Bears on Melantrichova Street. Instead, they stayed at the Hotel Alcron on Štěpánská Street off Wenceslas Square. One day Egon ran into an old school friend, Rudolf Fischer, who owned a villa in U laboratoře Street in Střešovice that was too big for him because his wife and two children had perished during the occupation. Lenka doesn't say how or why they died. No need. Fischer offered the Kisches a three-room flat on the second floor of his villa, and Egon and Gisl gratefully moved in. The house was surrounded by a well-kept garden, but in one place two huge tree stumps protruded from the grass. "What barbarian had those magnificent trees cut down?" asked Kisch one day. The response was a bombshell. "Barbarian!" exclaims Lenka. "During the Protectorate, the Jew Fischer was expelled from the villa and the mass murderer Adolf Eichmann lived there during his residence in Prague. On the first [i.e., American second] floor. Maybe those two trees obstructed his view of Prague from the terrace, who knows. . . . Kisch never wrote about this unreal meeting, about the monstrous predecessor in the flat. Maybe he couldn't face dealing with so terrible a theme anymore. Maybe. . . ."[191]

The raging reporter wrote only six articles after returning to Czechoslovakia, one of which was on the May 1946 execution of Karl Hermann Frank. The last was on Karl Marx's visits in the 1870s to take the waters in Karlovy Vary or, as Marx would have called it, Karlsbad. Egon suffered a stroke in November 1947. He had a second stroke on 24 March 1948 and died in the hospital on 31 March, just weeks after the Victorious February coup. He was sixty-two. The KSČ gave him a "party funeral" (*stranický pohřeb*) on 5 April. His coffin lay in state in the Central Committee building on Na Příkopě in a ceremony attended by deputy prime minister Antonín Zápotocký, mayor of Prague Václav Vacek, and Václav Kopecký, Václav Nosek, and other government ministers, not to mention Rudolf Slánský, general secretary of the KSČ. Thousands of people turned out along Na Příkopě and in Wenceslas Square to watch the funeral procession, just as they had a few years earlier for Karel Hynek Mácha and Reinhard Heydrich. The next day *Rudé právo* carried a report on the front page headlined "Parting with E. E. Kisch. 'You were the people's writer—and the people loved you.'" These latter words were spoken at the end of the eulogy by "Kisch's closest coworker André Simone." A minute's silence followed, and then the *Internationale* was played.[192] "Kisch—perhaps thank God—didn't live to see the tragic end of his friend," writes Lenka Reinerová.[193] Indeed. Had Egon survived another four years, there is every reason to think he would have ended his life on the same Pankrác scaffold as Simone and Slánský.

Lenka (who was five months pregnant) and Theodor returned to Europe in 1945 on a Yugoslav freighter from Montreal and spent three years in Belgrade before moving to Prague in 1948. "When I finally returned to my hometown," she writes in *Without an Address*, "it was not a joyful reunion. Was I still at home here at all?"[194] "I used to walk through Prague and remember," she told an interviewer in 2008. "For years I couldn't go to Karlín, where I was born and raised, at all. Prague finished for me at the Powder Tower. Then one time I overcame it and went there. And you keep asking yourself one question: why was I spared?"[195] Imprisoned for fifteen months in Ruzyně jail in 1952–1953, Lenka spent a year in solitary before being released without charge. The "socialist prison" was "incomparably worse," she says, than the "bourgeois prison" of La Petite Roquette, but the worst thing of all was being separated from her little daughter Anna. When asked why she was arrested, Lenka responded: "I was a Jew, an exile, I lived in France, in Mexico, in Yugoslavia, my husband fought in Spain, I knew a lot of people who were not to the taste of the new regime. . . . They had plenty of reasons to take me into custody."[196] Of course. She endured "the darkness of the fifties. Then the hope of the Prague Spring— and the tragedy of the 'fraternal' occupation, followed by the period of the absurdly named 'normalization.'"[197] But still, she said in 2004, "I go with the tram somewhere in Prague, and I come home, and I am full of adventures. I saw many things and I liked things, or I found things funny, and I prefer to laugh than to weep."[198] Lenka fell and broke her hip three years later in her daughter's flat in London and was unable to walk normally again, but she still insisted that "so long as I see, hear, and think, it's worth it."[199] She died in 2008, the last of the Prague-German writers.

Every telling has a taling, but it would be a mistake to think the story ends here. History doesn't do closures. The psychotherapist Anna Fodorova writes, "The first generation [of Holocaust survivors] remained heroically, manically positive and active into their advanced age, while the generation after them, to which 'nothing' has happened, tend to flounder, climbing on and off the therapist's couches. . . . In my own family," she goes on, "an expression of anger was rarely allowed. . . . To feel depressed was out of the question. Our lives were not directly threatened, we have experienced no deprivations, no reason seemed serious enough to feel down."

If an occasional spillage of denied rage, of triumph or fear of persecution escaped, the next generation was there to introject it. The parents' unprocessed feelings were internalized by their children; they became their own murderous hatred, their own triumph. The second generation's "normal" developmental depressive defenses during the various stages of separation and mourning were hijacked and intensified by the hatred and despair that didn't belong to them and to which they had no entitlement. They became their "illegitimate" bearers. After all, nothing has ever happened to them to provoke their aggression, their persecutory fears or their sorrow. As inheritors of these raw, unworked through, disavowed feelings the next generation often felt overwhelmed by their intensity and yet, at the same time, as if lacking authenticity in their own lives.

Of all the first-person testimonies I have read in researching this book, this is one of the saddest. The article, aptly titled "Mourning by Proxy," is by Lenka Reinerová's daughter Anna, writing in London in 2005.[200]

A Première in Terezín

Jaroslav Ježek's ashes were brought home from New York to Prague in 1947 and laid to rest in Olšany Cemetery. Nearby is the shared tomb of Jiří Voskovec and Jan Werich. The smile into which both their names are carved on the headstone covers up rather a lot. The erstwhile stars of the Liberated Theater spent the first two years of their American exile doing the rounds of Czech American clubs in New York, Binghamton, Baltimore, and Chicago while struggling to improve their English enough to perform in English versions of their reviews *Těžká Barbora* (Heavy Barbara, 1937) and *Osel a stín* (The ass and the shadow, 1933) in Cleveland, Ohio.[201] After an unsuccessful trip to California, where they hoped to break into the Hollywood movies, the duo returned to New York in 1941 and worked for the Office of War Information, regularly broadcasting on the Czechoslovak service of Voice of America. They made their Broadway debut in January 1945 not as V + W but as Trinculo and Stephano in Shakespeare's *The Tempest*. Werich returned to Prague in October 1945, but Voskovec—who in the meantime had married the American actress Anne Gerlette—delayed his return for another year. By 1948 the two comedians were coming under increasing pressure from the KSČ because of their perceived pro-Western leanings. Werich weathered the storm and went on to have a successful career on stage and screen in Czechoslovakia. Voskovec managed to get himself posted to UNESCO in Paris, but he resigned soon afterward and sailed for New York in 1950. It should not come as a surprise that he was detained for eleven months on Ellis Island as a suspected communist sympathizer. When he was finally readmitted to the United States, Jiří changed his name to George Voskovec and played parts that required strong Slavic accents in movies such as *The Spy Who Came in from the Cold*. His best-known film role was as juror 11 in *Twelve Angry Men*. He acted in scores of stage productions on and off Broadway, the last in 1979 as Willie in Samuel Beckett's *Happy Days*. He died in Pearblossom, California, in 1981. His remains were repatriated to Prague in 1990.

And Hoffmeister? After a brief stay with Ježek in New York, Ada spent several months with Werich in Cleveland before accompanying V + W on their trip to Hollywood. Five months later he returned to New York City. He got the only thing he had been lacking in Paris—a fine girl—when Lilly Rohne joined him from London in 1942. He threw himself into anti-Nazi activities with his usual gusto. As well as *Unwilling Tourist*, he wrote the play *Slepcova píšťalka aneb Lidice* (The blind man's whistle or Lidice, 1942), which was staged for the exiled Czech community under Voskovec's direction, with sets by Antonín Pelc. He lectured, wrote articles, and drew caricatures for American, British, and émigré Czech newspapers and magazines, among them the *New York Times* and the *Nation*. He became a broadcaster with the Czechoslovak section of the Voice of America and its director in 1944. He exhibited in *Art in Exile* at the New York Public Library and *Cartoons by Hoffmeister, Pelc, Stephen and Z.K.* in London. Opening on 12 May 1943, *War Caricatures by Hoffmeister and Peel* (as Pelc had taken to calling himself) was the Museum of Modern Art's first exhibition of Czech art. Ada's contributions included *Wanted in Prague, Never Mind the Corpses*, and *Herr Goebbels Has Requested All Women of Germany to Give Their Furs to the German Army in Russia*, while "Antoine T. Peel" offered *The German Dove of Peace, The Ailing World Order*, and a large gouache titled *Lidice*.[202] The caricatures, proclaimed the MoMA press release, "constitute a savagely brilliant attack on the Axis partners, principally the Nazis, impaling them on barbs of ridicule."[203] What made the exhibition possible were those late-night discussions with Alfred Barr about issues that were ahead of their time and grew larger the longer the two men spoke about them in Ada's flat on Spálená Street before the war.

Three months after *War Caricatures by Hoffmeister and Peel* closed in New York, Hans Krása's children's opera *Brundibár* began its astonishing run of fifty-five performances in the Terezín ghetto. Terezín was home to a remarkable cultural life, albeit one to which the prisoners there had unequal access. The camp was as stratified as the SS *Capitaine Paul-Lemerle*, with younger Czech Jews of both sexes ruling the roost. "Inmate society," writes Anna Hájková, "was based on inequality; although everyone was a prisoner, even the smallest differences became extremely important."[204] The ghetto hosted not only operatic productions, including *The Bartered Bride*, Mozart's *Marriage of Figaro* and *Magic Flute*, Verdi's *Rigoletto*, and Puccini's *Tosca*—all of which were accompanied only by piano—but also the Carousel cabaret and a jazz band that, with grim humor, billed itself as the Ghetto Swingers.[205] This suited the Nazis, who used Terezín not only as a holding pen for transports to the death camps but also for propaganda purposes. Hoffmeister was *Brundibár*'s librettist. Hans and Ada had first met at the Czech-German Theatrical Workers' Club. This was their second collaboration: Krása wrote the music for Ada's *Mladí ve hře* (Youth in the play), which premièred at D 35 in February 1935. Written for a competition in 1938, *Brundibár* was first performed—totally illegally, since by then Jews were not permitted to perform at all—under Rafael Schächter in July 1941 in the dining hall of the Jewish orphanage in Belgická Street in Vinohrady. After Schächter was deported to Terezín in November, rehearsals continued under the young conductor Rudolf Freudenfeld. The Devětsil architect, designer, and scenographer František Zelenka built "a simple set of three large fences made up of several boards with three posters stuck on them. The posters had a sparrow, cat and dog wittily presented, and the animal characters would stick their heads through the poster when they first appeared in the action."[206] In such contexts E. F. Burian's injunction to "consider all the conditions of the life of the poetic work on the stage from the standpoint of the imagination of the spectator" takes on added poignancy. In happier times Zelenka had created many stage sets and advertisements for the Liberated Theater, including the poster for *Powder and Petrol*, the musical in which Voskovec and Werich first sang their ever-popular hit "Nobody should ever take anything as definitive [*Nikdy nikdo neví co se může stati*]."

By the time *Brundibár* had its second (and last) performance at the Vinohrady orphanage in the winter of 1942–1943, Krása and Zelenka had been transported to Terezín too. Zelenka designed sets and costumes for twenty-five plays and operas in Terezín, not all of which were allowed to be staged. When Rudi Freudenfeld arrived in the camp in July 1943, he brought the piano score of *Brundibár* with him. Krása reorchestrated the work for the instruments available (a flute, a clarinet, a trumpet, a guitar, an accordion, a piano, a side drum and bass drum, four violins, a cello, and a double bass), and Zelenka bricolaged a new stage set out of odds and ends. The opera had its triumphant Terezín première in the Magdeburg barracks on 23 September 1943. Of course, *Brundibár* was performed when the Red Cross inspected the hastily tarted-up ghetto a year later on 22 September 1944 and gave the camp a clean bill of health. Parts of the children's performance were included in the Nazis' infamous propaganda film *Theresienstadt: Ein Dokumentarfilm aus dem jüdischen Siedlungsgebiet* (Terezín: a documentary film from the Jewish settlement area). It turned out to be *Brundibár*'s final Terezín production. In the words of Joža Karas, "Once the committee of the International Red Cross departed, and scenes from the opera have been immortalized on a celluloid strip . . . [Krása] received from the Nazis their customary reward in Auschwitz."[207] Hans left Terezín on 16 October on the same transport as the composers Pavel Haas, Viktor Ullmann, and Gideon Klein. Krása, Haas, and Ullman were all murdered on arrival. Klein died on 27 January 1945, less than two months after his twenty-fifth birthday, possibly during a death march as the camp was evacuated in the face of the advancing Red Army.[208]

The members of the Ghetto Swingers, too, were transported to Auschwitz soon after the Red Cross concluded its whitewash, as were Rafael Schächter, Rudolf Freudenfeld, František Zelenka, and most of the children in the *Brundibár* cast. The date of Zelenka's death is unknown, but he perished in the gas chambers along with his wife Gertruda and their eight-year-old son Martin.[209] Schächter died on a death march. Only three of the sixteen Ghetto Swingers survived the war. One was the guitarist Coco Schumann, who, on arrival at the camp, was ordered to start a band along with two of his colleagues. "He spent his first evening in Auschwitz jamming popular tunes from the Hamburg red-light district. . . . 'The music,' Coco keeps repeating, 'saved our lives. . . . What we saw in those days was unbearable, and yet we bore it. We played the tunes to it, for the sake of our bare survival. We played music in hell.'"[210] Ela Weissberger, who sang the part of the cat in *Brundibár*, was another of the lucky ones—if that is the right word for it. To understand why I hesitate, read Arnošt Lustig's heartbreaking novel *Díta Saxová* (1962).[211] Ela was almost fifteen when the Russian tanks liberated Terezín. A year later she was amazed to hear someone whistling the *Brundibár* finale in the crowds celebrating a year of liberation on Wenceslas Square. It was Rudi Freudenfeld. "As the opera drew to a close and we sang the victory march 'Brundibár is defeated,'" Ela related later, "there was—each time—thunderous applause. . . . We all wanted to completely exhaust that moment of freedom. When we were onstage, it was the only time we were allowed to remove our yellow stars."[212]

FIGURE 7.8. František Zelenka's film poster for Voskovec and Werich's *Powder and Petrol*, 1931. From Josef Kroutvor, *Poselství ulice*, Prague, 1991.

Pavel Haas was a star pupil of Leoš Janáček's. His opera *Šarlatán* (Charlatan) shared the Smetana Foundation's annual award with Vítězslava Kaprálová's *Military Sinfonietta* in 1938.[213] His father Zikmund also perished in Auschwitz. His brother, the actor and director Hugo Haas, took different trains. During the 1930s Hugo played eighty-five different roles at the National Theater in dramas ranging from Shakespeare's *Merchant of Venice* to Nezval's *Milenci z kiosku* (Lovers from the newsstand, 1932, directed by Jiří Frejka with stage sets by Bedřich Feuerstein). Karel Čapek wrote the part of Dr. Galén for Hugo in his antifascist play *Bílá nemoc* (*The White Disease*, 1937), which Haas filmed, writing his own screenplay, the same year. His last role before he was let go "for racial reasons" in April 1939 was in Čapek's *R.U.R.*[214] Hugo fled Prague with his wife Maria (Bibi) soon after the invasion. Hoffmeister's Jan Prokop recalled "the heavy, melancholy eyelids of the great comedian" from their daily chats on the terrace of the Café Chaave d'Ouro in Lisbon in *Unwilling Tourist*. Hugo and Bibi reached the United States in the fall of 1940. In 1942 Hugo directed a Czech poetry reading for which Ladislav Sutnar designed the set. By then Haas was sufficiently fluent in English to play Pierre Bezukhof in Tolstoy's *War and Peace* under Erwin Piscator in New York. He later created the role of Cardinal Barberini alongside Charles Laughton in Brecht's *Galileo* at the Coronet Theater in Los Angeles in August 1947. Like Bohuslav Martinů, Roman Jakobson, Ladislav Sutnar, and Jaroslav Polívka, Haas remained in the United States after the war. Nostalgia brought him back to Europe at the end of the 1950s, and he settled in Vienna in 1961. "A tentative visit" to Czechoslovakia in 1963 led nowhere, but he planned "a final and definitive homecoming" after the Prague Spring erupted in 1968. "But the tanks were faster," writes Josef Škvorecký. "He died, broken-hearted, on December first, 1968. Only his ashes returned to Prague; they were buried near the remains of Franz Kafka."[215]

Hugo Haas's most enduring American legacy turned out to be low-budget noir movies in which bad girls lure lonely older men to their downfall. He wrote, directed, produced, and played the male lead in more than a few. Those melancholic eyelids served him well, as did his sweet sad smile. Hugo's costars Beverly Michaels and Cleo Moore (with whom he made six films) were cut from a mold that is well described by Dave Kehr: "It's easy to recognize the Bad Girl. She's usually a bottle blonde, stuffed into a tight sweater that outlines her oddly conical breasts. Her mouth is wide, painted and clamped on a cigarette. Her eyes burn a little too brightly, and her legs, planted in a pair of high-rise pumps, go on forever."[216] The garish Hollywood posters for Haas's movies give ample promise of a perilous pneumatic bliss: "You can 'pick up' this girl ... but you won't if you know what's good for you! ... The low-down on a come-on girl!" (*Pickup*, 1951). "Another shocker from the maker of 'PICKUP.' ... Wait till <u>you</u> feel her STRANGE FASCINATION" (*Strange Fascination*, 1952). "Men and money and me ... go together!" (*One Girl's Confession*, 1953). Martin Scorsese, who is evidently a fan, conceded in a 2019 interview that although Haas's movies are "maybe not good films" they are "good art" that "stayed with me." He likes their "palpative [*sic*—a nicely Joycean neologism] sense of sexuality," which is "lurid ... its own truth, part of human nature ... genuine, real ... anything on the seamy side."[217]

But there is more to Haas's work than the he and the she of it. "I don't care <u>what</u> she is. ... She's mine!" declared the poster for *Night of the Quarter Moon* (1959), a "racial love story" in which "a beautiful quadroon enter[s] a distinguished, if skeptical, San Francisco family on the arm of her proud new husband."[218] Hugo directed this movie almost a decade before Stanley Kramer's taboo-breaking *Guess Who's Coming to Dinner* (1967). Hollywood was not fond of rocking the racial boat: it was only in 1967 that the US Supreme Court

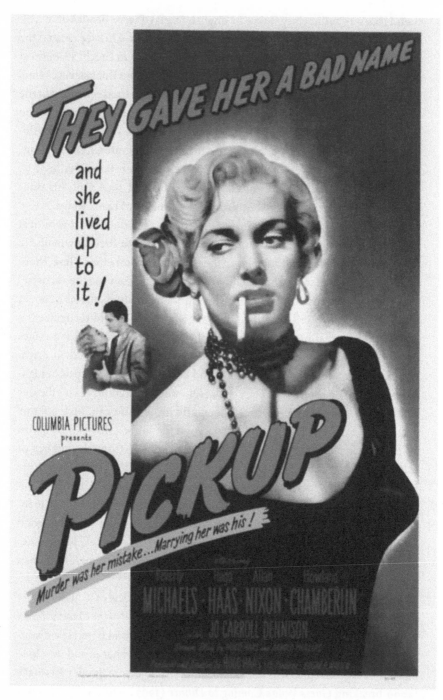

FIGURE 7.9. Advertising postcard for Hugo Haas's *Pickup*, 1951. Artist unknown.
© 1952 Columbia Pictures Corp.

struck down all state laws banning interracial marriage in the landmark case *Loving v. Virginia.* "She's man bait . . . and murder!" screamed the publicity for *The Girl on the Bridge* (1951), adding, "That PICKUP girl is back!" Well, she wasn't, even though she was played by the same actress, Beverly Michaels. The triangle in *The Girl on the Bridge*—David Toman, a middle-aged watchmaker; Clara, a single mother with a murky past; and Mario, a nightclub piano player— is standard Haas fare, but this is no generic B movie. Toman is a refugee from the Nazis, and Clara turns out not to be a bad girl at all. There are only two di- rect allusions to the Holocaust in the film—one near the beginning, when David tells Clara that his wife and two boys were killed by the Nazis, and the other near the film's climax, when he exclaims, "I'm trying desperately not to lose everything again." Like the lone strand of barbed wire fence in Toyen's *Shooting Range,* this backstory colors everything, transforming what could have been a trite two-bit melodrama into something much darker. Haas's haunted, frightened, desperate watchmaker is a difficult figure to forget. But the real kicker is of another order, as Michael Beckerman relates:

> Their [David and Clara's] domestic life is shattered when Clara's former lover, Mario and Mario's cousin Harry appear. Harry, the cousin, tries to blackmail David and the old watchmaker kills him unintentionally during a fight. . . . Mario, Clara's former boyfriend is blamed for the crime and put in jail. . . . In the following scene the two discuss the matter. Clara says, "You know David, I can't help thinking about it all the time," and after a pause, "How desperate he must feel sitting there hopelessly." The watchmaker, seemingly without explanation, loses his temper in a vicious manner shout- ing: "Don't talk about him like that." Of course in the context of the film it is David's guilt speaking, since he's responsible for the imprisonment of an innocent man, but even that does not account for the volcanic nature of his outburst. In a moment that certainly escapes most of the original viewers who saw it, or more recent audiences on YouTube, and was probably meant to escape them, there's another kind of cinema going on. If one looks closely on the piano as David passes by there is a small photo of Pavel Haas with a black band across the frame.[219]

How many viewers of *The Girl on the Bridge,* suckered in by the lurid posters, would recognize Hugo's composer brother, murdered in Auschwitz? *How des- perate he must feel sitting there hopelessly.* That Old World peeps through again.

Less than a month after the liberation of Czechoslovakia, the new com- munist minister of information Václav Kopecký urged Adolf Hoffmeister to return to Prague as quickly as possible. Ada arrived on 28 August. He prudently joined the KSČ the next month. In November Kopecký put him in charge of Czechoslovakia's cultural activities abroad. Ada married Lilly Rohne in January 1946, and their son Martin was born in January 1947. Hoffmeister's job at the Ministry of Information gave him plenty of opportunities for travel. Besides France, where he was responsible for the *Art tchécoslovaque 1938–1946* exhibition at which Group 42 made its international debut, he visited Poland, Romania, the Soviet Union, and Yugoslavia. He made it to Mexico in 1947 with the Czechoslovak delegation to the second UNESCO conference. Extending his stay, he met Frida Kahlo and Diego Rivera and toured the country with the Czech Jewish writer Norbert Frýd—a survivor of Terezín, Auschwitz, and Dachau and the only person, says Lenka Reinerová, who had the courage to speak up in her defense when she was arrested and imprisoned in 1952.[220] When Rivera passed through Prague on his way home from receiving medical treatment in the Soviet Union in March 1956, he made sure to stop by the Diamant House in Spálená Street.[221] Ada had always been an excellent host.

After his experiences in La Santé, it must have given the caricaturist considerable satisfaction to be made an officer of the Légion d'honneur by the French government in 1946. Better yet, in June 1948 he was appointed Czechoslovak ambassador to France. Ada's luck was continuing to hold. For the time being, anyway.

8

The Cleansing of the Homeland

There is almost no kind of outrage ... which does not change its moral colour when it is committed by "our" side. ... Whether such deeds were reprehensible, or even whether they happened, was always decided according to political predilection.

—GEORGE ORWELL[1]

Why Should We Not Rejoice?

On 5 April 1945 a new Czechoslovak government was proclaimed in Košice in eastern Slovakia, which had been liberated by the Soviet Red Army on 19 January. Among those who helped free the city were Leonid Brezhnev, the chief political commissar for the Fourth Ukrainian Front who, as Soviet leader, would launch the Warsaw Pact invasion of Czechoslovakia on the night of 20–21 August 1968, and Sergei Gorbachev, the father of Mikhail Gorbachev, whose *perestroika* and *glasnost* would open the door to the Velvet Revolution of November 1989.[2] In an improbable realization of the dreams of nineteenth-century pan-Slavist awakeners and twentieth-century avant-garde writers and artists alike, Czech history and Russian history were about to get intimate in a way they never had before. After the French and British betrayal at Munich and six years of German occupation, many Czechs looked forward to the prospect. The new government's composition was agreed in Moscow on 22–29 March in talks between Edvard Beneš (representing the London government in exile) and the KSČ. The opening paragraphs of the Košice Government Program set the tone for much of Czechoslovakia's next half century:

After more than six years of foreign subjection the time has come when the sun of freedom rises over our sorely tested homeland. On its glorious victorious journey to the west the Red Army has liberated the first part of the Czechoslovak Republic. Thanks to our great ally the Soviet Union it has been made possible for the president of the republic to return to liberated territory and a new Czechoslovak government has been formed here, once again on home soil.

The new government has to be a government of a broad National Front of Czechs and Slovaks, made up of representatives of all social strata and political persuasions who led the national liberation struggle for release from German and Hungarian tyranny at home and abroad.[3]

"Expressing the infinite gratitude of the Czech and Slovak Nation to the Soviet Union," the text stated, "the government will take as the unshakeable leading principle of Czechoslovak foreign policy the closest possible alliance with the victorious Slavic great power to the east. The Czechoslovak-Soviet treaty of 12 December 1943 ... will determine the foreign policy position of our state for the whole future."[4] It continued: "The Slavic orientation in our cultural politics will be strengthened in accordance with the new significance of Slavism in international politics as well as in our Czechoslovak homeland," and it promised a thoroughgoing overhaul of school syllabuses, "as well as the cultural orientation of our scientific and artistic institutes. ... Not only will everything that was anti-Soviet be expunged from our textbooks and teaching aids, but the youth will be properly educated about the USSR. For that reason, Russian will take first place among foreign languages in the new syllabus."[5]

Much more was going on here than just a radical reorientation of Czechoslovakia's foreign policy—though it was that, too. This was a profound cultural revolution. The Košice Program defined Czechoslovakia as first and foremost an ethnically Slavic nation-state located within an imagined community of kindred Slavic nations (*Slovanstvo*) centered on Russia. This marked a return to nineteenth-century conceptions of Czech identity that had been widely rejected by progressive opinion after 1918, not least within the ranks of the KSČ itself (which was the only major political party *not* organized along ethnic lines in the first republic). Indeed, such uncritical pan-Slavism would have raised the eyebrows of both Karel Havlíček Borovský, whose experiences as a tutor in Russia led him to write in 1846 that "Russian frosts and other Russian things extinguished in me the last spark of pan-Slav love,"[6] and František Palacký, who warned in his famous letter to the Frankfurt parliament in

April 1848 that "the breakup of the Austrian Empire into many republics and mini-republics" would offer "a fine foundation for universal Russian monarchy."[7] We have come a long way from Ferdinand Peroutka's gentle mockery of Bohemia as seen from under a rustling lime tree in *What Are We Like?* let alone the ridicule of "Hey Slav-ing" (*hejslovanství*) and "Where is my home-ing" (*kdedomování*) in the *Manifesto of Czech Modernism*.[8] This is another reminder, if any is still needed, that in this corner of the globe, history is just as inclined to go round and round in circles as to progress forward, backward not a step (*Kupředu, zpátky ni krok*)—to paraphrase a ubiquitous slogan in communist Czechoslovakia.

Events moved swiftly in the coming weeks. Hitler committed suicide on 30 April. Berlin fell to the Red Army on 2 May. Germany surrendered to the Allies on 7 May. The last fighting of the war on European soil took place in Prague. Soon after noon on 5 May, Czech police took over the radio station on Schwerin (today Vinohradská) Avenue and broadcast appeals for rebellion. Barricades were built, and fighting spread across the city. Almost three thousand Czechs were killed in the Prague Uprising,[9] and substantial damage was inflicted on parts of the historic city center. There was abundant brutality on both sides. Fifty-eight Czech captives were massacred in Masaryk Station; German soldiers were hung head-down from an arch on the corner of Vodičkova Street and Wenceslas Square, drenched in gasoline, and set on fire.[10] This was far from the only example of "living torches," and they would later become a recurrent image in fiction set during the uprising.[11] A cease-fire was agreed at around midnight on 8 May. As the German forces retreated, Red Army troops entered the northern suburbs in the early-morning hours of 9 May. The first Soviet tank arrived in Wenceslas Square at 8:10 a.m.[12] The Košice government flew into the military airport at Prague-Kbely the next day.

Introducing the Košice Program in his 5 April speech to the Slovak National Council, Beneš emphasized, "We are all fully aware that the renewed republic should not be a simple return to what existed before Munich." "Our new democracy [*demokracie*]," he explained, "should be a new genuine *people's government* [*lidovláda*]."[13] "Those political parties that so gravely damaged the interests of the nation and the republic" in the years before the war were banned.[14] The Agrarian Party, the National Democrats, and the Slovak People's Party were the main targets here.[15] Only six parties were represented in the National Front government: the Social Democrats (Československá sociální demokracie); the National Socialists (Československá strana národně socialistická); the People's Party (Československá strana lidová); the (Slovak) Democratic

Party (Demokratická strana); the KSČ; and the Communist Party of Slovakia (Komunistická strana Slovenska, KSS). This arrangement recalls the Pětka,[16] an informal cabal of five party leaders that kept the same political elites in power (and the communists out of it) throughout the first republic, but now the shoe was on the other foot. The difference between *demokracie* as understood in Czechoslovakia before the war and *lidovláda* is graphically illustrated by the fact that the right-wing parties outlawed in 1945 had received more than half the total votes cast in the last national election ten years earlier.[17]

Each of the National Front parties was allotted three ministerial portfolios, which gave the communists control of six ministries. Two out of five deputy prime ministers, Klement Gottwald for the KSČ and Viliam Široký for the KSS, were also communists. The KSČ and KSS together contributed eight government members, the Democratic Party four, and the Social Democrats, National Socialists, and People's Party three each. There were four nonparty ministers, including Jan Masaryk at foreign affairs and Ludvík Svoboda at defense. The ministers of the interior (Václav Nosek), information (Václav Kopecký), education (Zdeněk Nejedlý), agriculture (Július Ďuriš), and labor and social affairs (Jozef Šoltész) were all communists, giving the party control over the police, the radio and the press, universities and schools, agrarian reform, and relations with trade unions and other civil organizations. The KSČ also wielded influence in the Foreign Ministry, where Vladimír Clementis was state secretary, and at the Ministry of Defense, where General Ludvík Svoboda was a KSČ sympathizer. Prime minister Zdeněk Fierlinger was a pro-Moscow Social Democrat who worked closely with the communists during this period. The Košice Program promised "universal, secret and direct elections" as soon as practicable to a constituent assembly.[18] In the meantime, the government legislated by presidential decree. Ninety-eight "Beneš decrees" (*Benešovy dekrety*), as they are known, were issued from May to October 1945, all of which were retrospectively ratified when the provisional national assembly met in Prague on 28 October.[19]

"In contrast to the former bureaucratic apparatus, distant from the people," the Košice Program boasted, new national committees (*národní výbory*) responsible for public administration and security at the municipal, district, and regional levels would be "elected by the people, under the constant control of the people, and recallable by the people" (except in areas with "unreliable, non-Slavic populations," where other arrangements would be made).[20] Members of these committees, which were modeled on Russian soviets, were chosen at public meetings on 18–23 May from candidates put forward by the

National Front. In the months after liberation, the national committees were often the real power on the ground. In the Prague committees, the KSČ had 108 members, the National Socialists 92, the Social Democrats 89, the People's Party 54, and nonparty candidates 23.[21] Another important organ of *lidovláda*, the extraordinary people's courts (*mimořádné lidové soudy*), were established by the so-called Great Retribution Decree of 19 June 1945 to bring to justice "all war criminals, all traitors, all conscious and active helpers of German and Hungarian repression." These tribunals operated throughout the country until the end of 1948. Each court had a five-member bench made up of a professional judge and four lay members who were selected—as were public prosecutors—from lists drawn up by the national committees. The courts worked under the rules of martial law, and trials had to be concluded within three days. There was no right of appeal, and death sentences were usually carried out within two hours. Two national courts in the Czech Lands and Slovakia heard the most egregious cases; each had a seven-member bench consisting of a majority of laypeople. By May 1947 the people's courts had sentenced 713 people to death, 741 to life imprisonment, and 19,888 to prison terms of ten years or more.[22] Among those executed were K. H. Frank (in front of sixty-three hundred spectators at Pankrác prison),[23] deputy protector Kurt Daluege, and deputy Prague mayor Josef Pfitzner. Karel Čurda, the betrayer of the Anthropoid parachutists, was captured on 19 May and eventually hanged on 29 April 1947. Konstantin von Neurath was tried for war crimes at Nuremberg and sentenced to fifteen years. Emanuel Moravec shot himself to avoid capture on 5 May. Konrad Henlein slashed his wrists in American captivity in Plzeň on 10 May. Emil Hácha was arrested on 13 May and died in Pankrác prison hospital on 27 June. He was buried in Vinohrady Cemetery three days later in an unmarked grave, on the orders of interior minister Václav Nosek. The lovely Lída Baarová was held in Pankrác for sixteen months on suspicion of collaboration, but the charges were eventually dropped. The film star fled to Austria with her second husband, the puppeteer Jan Kopecký—nephew of information minister Václav Kopecký—shortly after Victorious February.[24]

President Beneš and his wife Hana returned to Prague on 16 May 1945. In a nice counterpoint to Max Brod's hurried departure to Moravská Ostrava six years previously, the presidential locomotive left Blansko in southern Moravia at 8:36 a.m. festooned with Czechoslovak and Soviet flags and portraits of Beneš and Stalin. The journey took nearly seven hours as the train crawled through the crowds lining the tracks at each station, stopping several times

FIGURE 8.1. President Beneš's homecoming, Old Town Square,
16 May 1945. Photographer unknown. From Jan Kaplan, Václav
Ledvinka, and Viktor Šlajchrt, *Praha 1900–2000: Sto roků stověžatého
města*, Prague, 1999.

along the way. Every station was decorated with "Czechoslovak, Soviet, American, and English [*sic*] flags and pictures of presidents Masaryk, Beneš, and
Marshal Stalin." As the train pulled into what was once again (Woodrow) Wilson Station at 3:15 p.m., the fanfare from Smetana's *Libuše* rang out. The welcoming party included the entire cabinet, representatives of the Czechoslovak
and Soviet armed forces, the Soviet ambassador, KSČ general secretary Rudolf
Slánský and other senior party officials, Tomáš Masaryk's granddaughter Anna
Masaryková, and "comrade Marie Švermová, whose husband, member of parliament [Jan] Šverma"—whom we met earlier as an exiled journalist in Paris—
"perished in the struggles for the liberation of Slovakia."[25] A motorcade took
the president through Wenceslas Square, down Národní Avenue, along the

riverbank, and up Pařížská Street to the Old Town Square, where prime minister Zdeněk Fierlinger and mayor of Prague Václav Vacek publicly welcomed
the exile home. The twelve hundred barricades built during the uprising had
by now been cleared, but burnt-out buildings and shattered windows afforded
plentiful evidence of the recent fighting. It was the first time Beneš had seen
the city in more than six years. He spoke at length. "We are returning to the
homeland—the government and I—after one of the most terrible wars in
history," he began. "We were to a great extent the bearer, the symbol as well
as the victim of this terrible war. The war began in Prague and in Prague it
ended."[26] After the speeches were over the motorcade continued back along
the riverside to Charles Bridge and across the river to the castle, where the president "once again stood in the seat of the head of the Czechoslovak state to take
charge of managing our national affairs and the work of renewing the national life."[27]

The next day's edition of *Rudé právo*, which had just resumed legal publication, devoted its entire front page to Beneš's homecoming. Under the
headline "President Dr. E. Beneš in Prague. Hundreds of Thousands of
Praguers Welcome the Head of State" were two photographs. On the left,
Beneš shook hands with Russian and Czech officers at Wilson Station. On
the right, two girls in national costume greeted the president "according to
the old Czech custom" with bread and salt. Beneath the left-hand picture,
under the headline "Stalin to President Beneš. Greetings to Liberated
Prague," was a message from the Soviet leader in bold type assuring Beneš
that "the free road to development and blossoming is opened to the Czechoslovak Republic."[28] The entrance to the Old Town Square from Pařížská
Street—beneath the Oppelt House, where the Kafka family used to live—
was lined with "units of the Red Army, the Czechoslovak Army, groups of
partisans, Revolutionary Guards, police and gendarmes," the paper reported.
"Opposite the main podium, facing the silent indictment of the burnt-out
Old Town Hall, stood workers from Prague factories carrying banners with
inscriptions welcoming the president. The Hus monument was completely
covered with girls in Czech and Moravian costume, whose throats not even
the relentless heat of a beautiful May afternoon could dry out and prevent
from singing our beautiful folk songs" as everybody waited for the president
to arrive. The recital concluded with a lively rendition of the chorus "*Proč
bychom se netěšili?* [Why should we not rejoice?] from our *Bartered Bride*."[29]
The semiotics speak as eloquently as anything that was said, but much was
said all the same.

This Sweet Apocalypse

"It will be necessary," the president continued, "to liquidate [*vylikvidovat*] the Germans out of the Czech Lands and the Hungarians from Slovakia especially uncompromisingly.... Let our motto be: to definitively de-Germanize [*odgermanisovat*] our homeland, culturally, economically, politically."[30] In the coming days and weeks politicians across the spectrum outbid one another in retributive zeal. "Our new republic cannot be built as anything other than a purely national state, a state of Czechs and Slovaks and nobody but Czechs and Slovaks," thundered Prokop Drtina at the National Socialist congress in the Lucerna Palace on 17 May. "We must begin to expel the Germans from our lands at once, immediately, by all methods.... Every one of us must help in the cleansing of the homeland."[31] The Lucerna complex was built by Václav Havel's grandfather Vácslav Havel in 1911; it was the first building in Prague to use reinforced concrete in its construction. Drtina, who was Beneš's personal secretary from 1936 to 1938, was well known to Czechs from his wartime broadcasts from London under the pseudonym Pavel Svatý (Paul Saint); he would join the government as minister of justice in November 1945. Speaking in Brno on 23 June, Klement Gottwald castigated "the mistakes of our Czech kings, the Přemyslids, who invited the German colonizers here" back in the thirteenth century, and he demanded the removal "once and for ever beyond the borders of our land of an element hostile to us" and resettlement of the borderlands by Czechs and Slovaks.[32] Similar sentiments were expressed by many other leading Czech political figures.[33]

A raft of anti-German decrees quickly followed. A 19 May decree put all property of "Germans, Hungarians, traitors, and collaborators" under state administration. A 21 June decree confiscated agricultural lands belonging to "Germans, Hungarians, traitors and enemies of the Czech and Slovak nations." A 20 July decree authorized subdivision of the confiscated estates and set out procedures for their resettlement by Czechs and Slovaks. Following the Allies' agreement to the "transfer" of 2.5 million Bohemian Germans to occupied Germany at the Potsdam Conference (held 17 July to 2 August), a 2 August decree stripped all Germans and Hungarians of their Czechoslovak citizenship unless they could demonstrate to their local national committees that they "had remained faithful to the Czechoslovak Republic, had never committed offenses against the Czech and Slovak nations, and either actively participated in struggles for its freedom or were victims of Nazi or fascist terror." A 19 September decree made those who had lost their citizenship subject to compulsory labor to repair war damage and rebuild the economy. Decrees of 18 October dissolved the German University of Prague and the German Technical Universities in Prague and Brno, transferring their property to the equivalent Czech institutions. A final decree of 25 October expropriated Germans' and Hungarians' remaining real and movable property. Bohemian Germans were anathematized in ways that mimicked the Nazis' own treatment of Jews: they were excluded from pubs, restaurants, and cinemas; banned from sitting on park benches or taking trains; restricted from shopping outside specified hours; and required to wear white patches or armbands with a large letter N (for Němec, German).[34] The 2 August decree furnished the legal basis for their expulsion from the country. The rest of the decrees ensured that they would take nothing of value with them when they left. Grotesquely, but not entirely surprisingly, given the history of Czech anti-Semitism, "persons of Jewish descent" were exempted from the confiscations of land and property only in September 1946. Even then, "national committees often ignored the new directive," and "Czechs still refused to vacate apartments and houses once owned by Jews."[35]

By the time of the 2 August decree, some 600,000 Germans had already been hounded out of Bohemia and Moravia in the so-called wild expulsion (divoký odsun). The Czech word divoký also translates as "savage": Drtina's "by all methods" included beating, torture, rape, and murder.[36] To call these expulsions wild in any other sense is misleading. These were not the actions of undisciplined mobs: Tomáš Staněk, the leading Czech historian of the expulsion, argues that although "at this stage the displacement operations often really were inspired 'from below' . . . their preparation and realization always required some degree of participation of various rungs of the state authorities. . . . We cannot really speak of 'spontaneity' as such."[37] On the evening of 30 May national committee security forces in Brno evicted twenty thousand German men, women, and children from their homes and marched them toward the Austrian border, picking up another eight thousand Germans in villages along the way. By the time orders arrived from Prague to halt the operation, two-thirds of the column had already crossed into Austria; the remaining captives were dispersed to epidemic-ridden internment camps. More than seventeen hundred people died during what became known as the Brno Death March.[38] Between 3 and 7 June at least 763 Germans—this being the number of bodies later exhumed from mass graves—were rounded up, tortured, and shot by Czechoslovak troops in Postoloprty in the Sudetenland. In 1947 a parliamentary commission recommended that the bodies be dug up and burned so that "Germans should have no memorials to which they could point as a source of suffering by their people." Nobody was charged or punished, and the existence of the massacre was hushed up until two Czech reporters broke the story in the regional press in the 1990s. Many of Postoloprty's current inhabitants opposed a proposed monument in 2007.[39] During the night of 18–19 June 1945 troops under the command of a Slovak officer named Karol Pazúr hauled 267 Carpathian Germans (120 women, 72 men, and 75 children) off a train near Přerov in Moravia and slaughtered them by firing squad. Sentenced to twenty years imprisonment by the Supreme Military Court in Prague in 1949, Pazúr was amnestied by Klement Gottwald in 1951, having spent just a little over a year behind bars.[40]

When an explosion destroyed a sugar refinery used to store munitions in Ústí nad Labem on 31 July 1945, soldiers from the Twenty-Eighth Infantry Regiment, revolutionary guards, and Czech civilians attacked Germans in several locations across the city. "They tossed women with baby carriages into the Elbe, and these became targets for soldiers, who fired on the women until they no longer came to the surface. They also threw Germans into the water reservoir at the market square and pressed them under with poles whenever they came up," related one eyewitness.[41] The authorities did nothing to stop the carnage; in the end it was Russian soldiers who restored order. Even the head of the local office of the Ministry of Information admitted that "a section of the troops intensified the chaos and whipped up the population into bloody violence."[42] Václav Nosek and Ludvík Svoboda visited the scene the next day, and the cabinet discussed the events on 3 August. Blame was squarely laid on the victims. Foreign trade minister Hubert Ripka, whom we last encountered partying with Ada Hoffmeister, Lenka Reinerová, and other assorted Czech émigrés at the House of Czechoslovak Culture in Paris in 1939, argued that "if there is not a quick decision from the Allies on the smooth progress of the expulsion, the Czechs must refuse all responsibility for the excesses and lawlessness associated with this wild transfer." General Svoboda added, "We are all responsible for what happened because so far we have not yet managed to free ourselves of the greatest criminals—the Germans."[43] Rudé právo reported the Ústí explosion on its front page on 1 August under the headline "New Crimes of Germans in the Borderlands." There was no mention of the massacre. Instead, the article called for "merciless punishment of the Nazi traitors and incendiaries and their accomplices and an equally uncompromising and thorough cleansing of our border region from German influence, which was and is a hotbed of crimes against our republic and our people today just as before the war."[44]

Bohumil Hrabal catches the thrill as well as the horror of the time in *Svatby v domě* (*In-house Weddings*, 1986), the first volume of an autobiographical trilogy of novels in which he portrays himself through the eyes of his wife Pipsi (née Eliška Plevová). His bitterness may owe something to the fact that Eliška was a sixteen-year-old Sudeten German girl when her parents were deported in 1945. She was allowed to stay behind because she had been educated in a Czech school.

> Such a happening [*hepenink*] we went through in forty-five! Revolution, revolution, yes a revolution too, but [it was] mainly about property and defenseless people, when does it ever happen that a regular guy can have whatever he can take from Germans' flats, take whatever cattle he wants out of the barn, the shops of all the German firms in Prague and Jihlava and Brno were left unguarded and beautiful German girls in dirndls, and beautiful nurses in field hospitals, everything was offered up for the historic moment when the last German soldier pulls out and then heaven help the defeated! And anyone that people thought was a collaborator, they could kill with impunity, Hieronymus Bosch and his hell risen from the dead, Pieter Breughel's slaughtered innocents come to life, all in the name of recompense for what the Germans had done to us and those other nations, but all like a happening, because there can be nothing more beautiful for a person when he gets angry, when he may commit evil in the name of this great history . . . and what beauty, when a person may do whatever he will, whatever he feels, when nobody is keeping guard over heaven, when you can watch the castles and old furniture of the German bourgeoisie and nobility burn, when you can be the creator of this sweet apocalypse of fires and blood and fornication, which is permitted.[45]

In *Obsluhoval jsem anglického krále* (*I Served the King of England*, 1982), which is probably Hrabal's best-known novel in the English-speaking world, the antihero Ditie is sent to the former Sudetenland after 1948 to work as a solitary road builder. "Just before winter set in," he relates, "when I couldn't take it anymore and began to long for someone to be with, I bought some big old mirrors in the village, and some of them I got for nothing. People were glad to be rid of them, because when they looked into them, they said, Germans would appear."[46]

How should we weigh the "excesses" of the expulsion against the Nazi atrocities at Lidice and Ležaky, which live on in the international annals of infamy while the atrocities committed by Czechs at Postoloprty, Přerov, and

FIGURE 8.2. Bohemian Germans awaiting expulsion, Prague,
May 1945. Photographer unknown. © ČTK.

Ústí nad Labem have been largely forgotten? To the authorities at the time
(and to most Czechs since then), there was a world of moral difference
between what outsiders, looking back with hindsight seventy years later,
might see as equally heinous acts of collective vengeance. It was Sudeten
German support for Henlein's SdP before the war, they argued, that gave
Hitler the excuse to dismember Czechoslovakia. The sequence of events
that led to the Munich diktat and thence to the longest European occupation of World War II must never be repeated. The nation's very survival had
been in question *and could be again* if the "German problem" were not

solved once and for all. This made perfect sense in the circumstances of the time. It invariably does. There is *always* some standpoint from which a *kafkárna* can be made rational: that is the very essence of the beast. "I know there were individual Germans who were aware of these horrors," Edvard Beneš explained at Lidice on the third anniversary of the massacre. "But it is a question of the direct guilt of the overwhelming majority of Germans, and that is why the Germans as a whole are responsible."[47] In accordance with this logic, the provisional national assembly approved an amnesty in May 1946 for all "acts carried out between 30 September 1938 and 28 October 1945 whose objective was to aid the struggle for reclaiming the freedom of Czechs and Slovaks or which aimed toward just recompense for actions of the occupiers and their accomplices . . . *even if such acts would otherwise be punishable by law.*"[48]

This Manichaean construction of all Germans as Nazi monsters and all Czechs (other than out-and-out collaborators) as innocent victims continues to this day, undisturbed by anything as mundane as new factual evidence. This is sacred ground, not to be profaned by shades of gray. In 2020 the Czech Republic's minister of culture, Lubomír Zaorálek, fired the director of the Lidice Memorial (Památník Lidice), Martina Lehmannová, for supporting *research into* claims that one of the women deported to Ravensbrück had denounced her Jewish subtenant to the authorities a week before the massacre. Ten of the sixteen managerial and technical staff at the memorial resigned in solidarity with Lehmannová, objecting that "this symbol [the Památník] will be taken back to the normalization version of history."[49] The minister stood his ground, insisting that "to work in the Lidice Memorial is not only to study the past but rather to recall that the past is always with us. . . . I would wish the next director of the Memorial to be someone who appreciates the whole lingering weight of the Lidice tragedy and that here the past is not simply something that just once was but is somehow always with us and threatens to return."[50] Knowingly or otherwise, Zaorálek was echoing Zdeněk Nejedlý, the aged musicologist and biographer of Bedřich Smetana who served as Czechoslovak minister of education in 1945–1946 and 1948–1954 and had enormous influence over KSČ cultural policy until his death in 1962. "To us, history is not the dead past," Nejedlý wrote, "indeed it is not the past at all. It is an ever-living part of the present too." He was introducing a large exhibition of historical documents in Prague Castle in 1958, whose subtitle said all the Czechs needed to know about the trajectory of their history: *From the Heroic Past toward the Victory of Socialism.*[51]

The wild expulsion served the Czechoslovak government's strategic aims: faced with ongoing "spontaneous" violence in the borderlands, the Allied leaders in Potsdam had little choice but to accept its proposal to remove the remaining Germans from Bohemia and Moravia in an "orderly and humane" manner. A quota of 2.5 million deportees was set (1.75 million to the American occupation zone, 750,000 to the Soviet zone), and Germans were rounded up and kept in labor camps across the country—one of them a repurposed Terezín—while awaiting removal. One camp in České Budějovice had a sign at the entrance that read "An Eye for an Eye—a Tooth for a Tooth." The detainees were treated accordingly.[52] Staněk estimates that between six thousand and seven thousand Germans perished in these camps, mostly from disease but sometimes from violence.[53] The wagons started to roll at the end of January 1946. At the height of the evacuation, twelve trains, each carrying twelve hundred deportees in forty cattle cars, left for Germany each day. Estimates of casualties during the expulsion differ widely, and the facts remain bitterly contested.[54] Reviewing the evidence in 1996, a joint commission of Czech and German historians arrived at a figure of between nineteen thousand and thirty thousand deaths (including five thousand suicides).[55] That number could be much higher if deaths from starvation, illness, and exposure were included.

On 24 October 1946 Václav Nosek informed the Czechoslovak parliament that "in the coming hours the historic undertaking that our National Front government took upon itself will be completed: the expulsion of the Germans." Of the 2.5 million Germans still living in the country at the time of the Potsdam Conference, 2,165,135 had been deported. The 300,000 Germans remaining in the republic were mostly essential workers in industry or mining and individuals married to Czechs. Having thanked all those (beginning with the Soviet Union) who made possible "the fulfilment of this age-old dream of our ancestors"—a telling phrase, suggesting that more was going on than just payback for recent events—Nosek ended his speech to "loud and prolonged applause."[56] German antifascists, communists, social democrats, and their families were transferred to the Soviet zone, despite the provisions for their exemption in the Beneš decrees. "We do not have progressive Germans and we do not know them," sneered Zdeněk Nejedlý.[57] Czechoslovakia expelled about three million of its German-speaking citizens between May 1945 and October 1946—or almost a third of the prewar population of the territory that is now the Czech Republic. In the last prewar census in 1930, people who declared their nationality as German made up 29.5 percent of the inhabitants of the Czech Lands. In the 1950 census, that figure had fallen to 1.5 percent—just 165,117 people.[58]

In the words of Czech writer Pavel Tigrid, the expulsion of Bohemian Germans from Czechoslovakia ranks as "one of the most extensive ethnic cleansings of modern European history."[59] At best, it might be seen as a catharsis whose explosive violence was integral to cleansing the soul of a people who had been forced to live for years in a state of corrosive and humiliating abjection. Much as the United States (which has no such excuse) continues to bear the scars of its original sins—genocide of the indigenous population and enslavement of Africans[60]—so ethnic cleansing was the foundation on which the postwar Czechoslovak state was built. It was, above all, the Holocaust and the expulsion of the Germans that transformed the ethnic and cultural potpourri of interwar Czechoslovakia into Prokop Drtina's purely national state of Czechs and Slovaks. Another source of ethnic and cultural diversity was eliminated when Sub-Carpathian Ruthenia was quietly ceded to the Soviet Ukraine in 1945. These events made the so-called Czech Lands (*české země*) of Bohemia and Moravia *Czech* for the first time in their long history. These years cast a long shadow. Today's Czech Republic is one of the most ethnically homogeneous states in Europe, where *multikulti* has become a term of derision.

Hand in hand with the expulsion of Bohemian-German bodies from the Czech Lands went wholesale cultural de-Germanization. German speakers had been an integral part of Bohemian society for centuries, but mere historical fact doesn't stand a chance against the timelessness of imagined community. Traces of the German presence were wiped from the land. Sixty-four municipalities dumped the prefix *Německý* (German) from their names.[61] Egon Erwin Kisch's "German Prague!"—which was also in large part Kisch's, Kafka's, and Brod's Jewish Prague—was again reclaimed for the Czech nation. Back in 1882 mayor Tomáš Černý had caused outrage (and provoked the resignation of the last German members of the Prague City Council) when he described the Bohemian capital as "our historic city, our hundred-towered, our ancient, our beloved, *golden Slavic Prague*."[62] Golden or not, from now on, Prague would be proudly, indisputably, and exclusively Slavic. No more morning and evening editions of *Bohemia* or *Prager Tagblatt* on the newsstands, no more Karl-Ferdinand University or German Polytechnic. No more bilingual anything. The New German Theater metamorphosed into the Smetana Theater (Smetanovo divadlo). The Estates Theater (Stavovské divadlo) lost both its German and its aristocratic associations when it was renamed the Tylovo divadlo in 1949 in honor of Josef Kajetán Tyl, author of the words to the Czech

FIGURE 8.3. Bilingual street sign: Berg Gasse/Vrchová ulice, 2016. Photograph by author.

national anthem. Today it is once again the Stavovské divadlo. The German Casino on Na Příkopě, long the hub of Prague-German social life, was reborn as the Slavic House (Slovanský dům). The Czech Philharmonic took back the Rudolfinum for Czech art.

And yet, and yet. Mendelssohn, whose statue was restored to its rightful place after the war, remains on the Rudolfinum roof. So do Bach, Handel, Haydn, Gluck, Mozart, Beethoven, Weber, Schubert, and Schumann, all of them mute witnesses to which of Prague's ethnic communities the building had belonged to before it became the seat of the Czechoslovak parliament in

1919. Wagner was never there in the first place; Jiří Weil was using poetic license to get at deeper truths. When the Rudolfinum first opened on 7 February 1885 the Czech press complained that "few Czech artists participated in the ceremonies and few Czech compositions were heard." National animosities grew so intense thereafter that Czech painters boycotted a competition to decorate the Rudolfinum's concert hall in 1891.[63] When Antonín Dvořák conducted his *New World Symphony* there at the Czech Philharmonic's first concert on 4 January 1896, ten of the sixteen composers on the roof were German. None were Czech—and that remains the case to this day. Prague's Germans and Jews may be long gone, but reminders of their absence are ever-present *puncta*, to use Roland Barthes's term, spattered across the fabric of the city to quietly but repeatedly pierce the *studium* of eternal Czechness in which its history has been steeped. A German inscription on a weathered gravestone in Olšany Cemetery marks the resting place of soldiers fallen in the revolutionary "June Days" of 1848, when the forces of Field Marshal Alfred I, prince of Windischgrätz, shelled the Old Town from Hradčany to restore imperial order. If you walk down Břetislavova Street in the Lesser Town—once upon a time the most shameful street in Prague, where Jaroslav Seifert fled in panic at his first sight of a girl's naked breasts—you can see, high up on a wall, the trace of a bilingual street sign, predating the City Council's purge of German street names in 1893. Painted directly onto the stucco is the legend "Berg Gasse / Vrchová ulice," which is what the street was called from 1839 to 1870. Prague is a palimpsest on which many scripts, modern as well as ancient, have been written and erased. A *punctum*, says Barthes, is "this element which rises from the scene, shoots out of it like an arrow, and pierces me . . . a photographer's *punctum* is that accident that pricks me."[64] However hard we try to cover up their traces, old worlds keep bleeding into the new.

Forward, Backward Not a Step!

Side by side with de-Germanization of the homeland, the National Front government launched a fierce assault on Czechoslovakia's propertied classes. The two campaigns fed off each other: national liberation was presented as a class war and class war as a patriotic duty. This identification of the nation (*národ*) with the ordinary people (*lid*) did not come out of nowhere; there had been a strong populist strand in modern Czech nationalism from the outset. Tomáš Masaryk, for one, argued in *The Czech Question* that "younger writers and poets . . . are seeking a more concrete Czech human being, and they are naturally discovering him in the Czech countryside and in those classes of the people who were least touched by cultural development . . . nationality is perceived as the popular. In the popular [*lidovost*], Czechness [*českost*] and Slavness [*slovanskost*] are definite, concrete, living."[65] A year later Masaryk wrote, "Among us the *idea of nationality* gradually through the development of the revival *altered* in such a way that the nation always more and more came democratically to understand itself as *the people* [*lid*], that it comprehended itself in popular terms."[66] Svatopluk Čech's rotund Prague landlord Mr. Brouček, who just wants to eat pork sausages when the effete inhabitants of the moon offer him the scents of exquisite flowers, is a satirical take on the same phenomenon, as is Jaroslav Hašek's infamously coarse good soldier Švejk. The unspoken corollary was that whatever services the Bohemian nobility may have rendered the country in the past—aristocratic "land patriots"[67] had, after all, founded the Estates Theater (1783), Royal Society of Bohemia (1790), Academy of Fine Arts (AVU, 1799), Prague Polytechnic (ČVUT, 1806), Prague Musical Conservatory (1811), and National Museum (1818)—they did not belong to the Czech *nation*. The epitome of an out-of-touch urban cultural elite, they were so far removed from the everyday world of ordinary people that *they literally spoke a different language*—German, which at that date was still a badge of class distinction rather than national identity. The aristocracy paid the price in 1919–1920 when their titles were abolished and their estates were confiscated and redistributed among Czech and Slovak smallholders.

After World War II the historical entanglements of language, ethnicity, and class took on renewed salience. Following the confiscations of 1945–1946 around 28 percent of the agricultural land in Bohemia and Moravia changed hands. Roughly three million hectares were seized from "Germans, Hungarians, traitors and collaborators" and given to "Czech, Slovak, and other Slavic farmers,"[68] of which 2,400,449 hectares lay in the Czech Lands.[69] This was a much greater economic and social upheaval than the reform of 1919–1920, which had resulted in 1.8 million hectares of aristocratic land changing ownership over a period of ten years. The main beneficiaries of the 1945–1946 reform were agricultural workers and small farmers (with priority being given to those who "distinguished themselves and served in the national liberation struggle").[70] Workers, small traders, and "socially disadvantaged" persons could also apply for up to half a hectare of land on which to build their own homes. There was a clear link between the 1919–1920 and the 1945–1946 land reforms, as the KSČ lost no opportunity to point out. Commending the land reform bill in the national assembly in April 1919, social democrat deputy František

Modráček explained, "Today we are ridding ourselves once and for all of that aristocracy that played such an infamous role in the history of our nation, and the especially sad role after the Battle of White Mountain up to the present."[71] "The historical roots of the denationalization of Czech land lead 300 years back, all the way to the catastrophe at White Mountain, where the majority of our soil came into the hands of a foreign nobility," minister of agriculture Július Ďuriš told *Rudé právo* in June 1945.[72]

It was not difficult to tar the commercial and industrial bourgeoisie with the same brush. The Košice Program had given due warning to "traitors from the ranks of financial, industrial and agricultural magnates."[73] Many of prewar Czechoslovakia's larger enterprises had been owned by Bohemian Germans, and these came under state administration as a result of the decree of 19 May 1945. The Czech bourgeoisie was no less suspect, at least in the eyes of the KSČ. Jan Antonín Baťa, whose Zlín-based concern employed sixty-seven thousand people worldwide on the eve of World War II, had dreamed in 1937 of building a Czechoslovak state for forty million people that would be "culturally and economically the healthiest, strongest, and richest state in Europe."[74] After the Austrian *Anschluss* Jan saved the lives of many of the firm's Jewish employees by transferring them to Baťa enterprises abroad. One was the father of British playwright Tom Stoppard (né Tomáš Straüssler in Zlín in July 1937), whom Baťa posted to Singapore together with other Jewish families on 14 March 1938.[75] Jan fled to the United States in June 1939 and thence to Brazil in 1941, while Baťa factories in the protectorate became important cogs in the Nazi war machine. Despite his exile (and financial support for the overseas resistance), he was tried in absentia in 1947 as an alleged collaborator and sentenced to fifteen years imprisonment. The conviction was quashed on 15 November 2007, to the delight of Jan's granddaughter Dolores Bata Arambasic, who was born in Batatuba in Brazil and grew up speaking Czech, Serbian (from her father), and Portuguese.[76] "When I go to Zlín," Dolores told a Radio Prague interviewer in 2017, "something happens ... I feel like I've come back home. And it's very interesting, because I'm Brazilian. I was not born here."[77] Miloš Havel was also fingered for collaboration, though he was acquitted for lack of evidence in December 1947. But as with the Bohemian Germans, the real settling of scores was collective. The bourgeoisie were liquidated as a class.

In one of the National Front government's last acts before the provisional national assembly met, decrees of 24 October 1946 nationalized all mines, ironworks, steelworks, energy producers, banks, and insurance companies; key chemical, pharmaceutical, and armaments manufacturers; all enterprises of any kind employing more than 500 workers; and all firms with more than 150 workers in food processing and light industry. These decrees went further than anything that had been promised in the Košice Program, but they were unanimously approved by the National Front cabinet. In all, 2,119 firms were affected, which employed 62 percent of industrial workers and produced 75 percent of all manufacturing output.[78] "We are making good our domestic Munich in the economic field," proclaimed Klement Gottwald, again appropriating a powerful signifier of national humiliation for the domestic class struggle.[79] President Beneš was photographed signing the decrees in Prague Castle in the presence of "prime minister Fierlinger, deputy prime ministers Gottwald, David and Ursiny, ministers Laušman, Šrobár, Majer and Šoltész . . . as well as deputies A. Zápotocký and Evžen Erban for the Ústřední rada odborů [ÚRO, Central Trades Union Council] and representatives of the Prague working class, who came directly from factories in their working clothes."[80] The next day hundreds of thousands of cheering people filled Wenceslas Square for a demonstration organized by ÚRO in support of the decrees—one of 120 such meetings taking place in towns and cities across the country. Beneš, Fierlinger, Gottwald, Zápotocký and others addressed the crowd, and the speeches were broadcast live on Czechoslovak Radio.[81]

Rudé právo devoted four of its six pages on 25 October to the nationalization decrees, leading with a banner headline in red type: "A Historic Work Achieved." An entire page was given over to congratulations from E. F. Burian, Emil Filla, Jaroslav Fragner, Jiří Frejka, František Halas, Adolf Hoffmeister, Jindřich Honzl, Marie Majerová, Jan Mukařovský, Ivan Olbracht, Václav Špála, and other literary and artistic figures. Burian hailed the nationalization as "one of the first steps toward the fairer organization of society, which has enormous significance especially for culture."[82] Gottwald left no doubt as to who was who, what was what, and where the nationalization decrees fit into the progressive unfolding of the national destiny:

> This nationalization is the consistent continuation of our national and democratic revolution. We are conclusively liquidating the position of German and Hungarian capital in our national economy, we are significantly weakening the economic power of the Czech and Slovak large bourgeoisie who betrayed the nation and the state, we are liberating our economic life from direct foreign influences, we are transferring a certain part of our economy into state ownership and putting it directly at the service of the whole nation.

It is remarkable that we have already arrived at this hugely significant action in the first six months of our national liberation and that it was carried out unanimously by the whole of our National Front of Czechs and Slovaks, representing the various social and political components of our population. It is further proof that the national unity that was forged in the struggle against foreign occupiers and traitors has also fully proven its worth in the period of building the new republic. . . . The nationalization decrees are thus a great work, but they are only **the beginning**.[83]

Gottwald was right. In this respect as in others, much of the groundwork for the subsequent forty-two years of communist rule in Czechoslovakia was laid by the Beneš decrees. This is not always sufficiently acknowledged, particularly by Czechs who would rather portray communism as an alien imposition. Suffice it to say that by 1947 "nationalized industries and confiscated companies employed approximately 80 per cent of all workers and disposed of over two-thirds of Czechoslovakia's production capacity."[84]

The general election of 26 May 1946—the first since 1935—delivered a thumping endorsement of the government's policies. Only candidates from the National Front parties were allowed to run,[85] but they represented a wide range of views on the future direction of the country. There is no reason to think the election was otherwise anything but free and fair. Campaigning was vigorous, and turnout was a massive 93.9 percent. The communists were the clear victors, capturing 38.12 percent of the vote nationwide and 134 of 300 seats in the national assembly. Along with the Social Democrats, who took 12.3 percent of the vote and won thirty-seven seats, the Left had a comfortable majority in the new parliament. The communists received more than twice as many votes as their nearest rivals the National Socialists, who got 18.37 percent. The KSČ was far and away the most popular party in the Czech Lands, winning 43.25 percent of the vote in Bohemia and 34.46 percent in Moravia. The KSS came in second in Slovakia but still captured 30.4 percent of the vote (to the Democratic Party's 62.3 percent). The communists did predictably well in their old industrial heartlands like Plzeň (44.8 percent) and Kladno (53.6 percent), but some of their most impressive tallies came in the resettled Sudetenland (Karlovy Vary, 52.3 percent; Liberec, 48.3 percent; Ústí nad Labem, 56.5 percent). The party's championing of the expulsions and land reforms had paid handsome dividends, giving it a solid rural base for the first time in its history. In Prague the KSČ took 36 percent of the vote, ahead of the National Socialists' 33.3 percent, but it achieved much higher totals in

FIGURE 8.4. KSČ election poster, 1946. Artist unknown. From Tomáš Bojar, Jan Třeštík, and Jakub Zelníček, *Moc obrazů, obrazy moci/Power of Images, Images of Power*, exh. cat., Prague, 2005.

working-class districts such as Libeň and Vysočany. This was the party's worst showing in any electoral region in Bohemia. In Moravia the KSČ took 33.8 percent of the vote in the Brno region, 37.9 percent in Moravská Ostrava, and 38.6 percent in Jihlava. Zlín was the only region anywhere in the Czech Lands where the KSČ (winning 30.9 percent of the vote to the National Socialists' 36.4 percent) was not the largest party.[86] After the elections the KSČ controlled the chairmanships of all regional national committees, 78 percent of district national committees, and half of all local national committees.[87]

The new government that took office on 2 July 1946 was still a National Front coalition, but the KSČ's position was greatly strengthened. Communists held nine of twenty-seven ministerial posts. Klement Gottwald replaced Zdeněk Fierlinger as prime minister. Václav Nosek (interior), Václav Kopecký (information), Július Ďuriš (agriculture), Viliam Široký (one of five deputy prime ministers), and Vlado Clementis (state secretary at foreign affairs) all kept their jobs. Zdeněk Nejedlý took over from Jozef Šoltész at labor and social affairs (the KSČ relinquished the Ministry of Education to the National Socialist Jaroslav Stránský), and the communists gained control of the key economic ministries of finance and domestic trade. The People's Party had five portfolios, the National Socialists and the Slovak Democrats four each, and the Social Democrats three. Jan Masaryk remained minister of foreign affairs, and Ludvík Svoboda stayed at defense. This may be the only occasion in history when a communist-led coalition won a plurality of the popular vote in a "free and fair" national election anywhere in the world and went on to form a democratic government. It was a remarkable achievement for the KSČ.

Victorious February

Speaking at Westminster College in Fulton, Missouri, on 5 March 1946, two months before the Czechoslovak elections, Winston Churchill warned:

> From Stettin in the Baltic to Trieste in the Adriatic, an iron curtain has descended across the Continent. Behind that line lie all the capitals of the ancient states of Central and Eastern Europe. Warsaw, Berlin, Prague, Vienna, Budapest, Belgrade, Bucharest and Sofia, all these famous cities and the populations around them lie in what I must call the Soviet sphere, and all are subject in one form or another, not only to Soviet influence but to a very high and, in many cases, increasing measure of control from Moscow. . . . The Communist parties, which were very small in all these Eastern States of Europe, have been raised to pre-eminence and power far beyond their numbers and are seeking everywhere to obtain totalitarian control. Police governments are prevailing in nearly every case, and so far, *except in Czechoslovakia*, there is no true democracy.[88]

We should pay attention to Churchill's caveat. Whatever happened later, Czechoslovakia did not yet belong to the "Soviet sphere" of "police governments." To be sure, Prague was subject—by no means unwillingly, as we have seen—to Soviet influence, and the KSČ enjoyed preeminence and power far exceeding anything in its prewar existence. But this revolution was emphatically homegrown. The 1946 elections *were* democratic, and the plurality gained by the communists was as accurate an expression of the will of the people as any democratic election can deliver. The KSČ had never been a small party: it came in second in the 1925 general election with 13.2 percent of the vote (behind the Agrarians with 13.7 percent) and polled above 10 percent in the 1929 and 1935 elections (in which no Czech party gained more than 14 percent). It had 150,000 members in 1928, before Gottwald's Bolshevization purges reduced its membership to maybe 75,000 by 1934.[89] This still made it one of the largest communist parties in the world, with strong support among the industrial working class and key sections of the intelligentsia. By the time of the 1946 elections the KSČ boasted more than a million members out of a population of around twelve million.[90]

Events in Czechoslovakia were not out of line with what was happening across western Europe. After the war communist parties joined coalition governments in France and Italy too, and not just as junior partners. The French Communist Party (PCF) attracted 5,005,336 votes, 26.1 percent of the total, in the constituent assembly elections of October 1945 and 28.26 percent in the national assembly elections of November 1946—its best performance ever.[91] It emerged from both elections as the largest single party in the parliament, and the left-wing tripartite alliance of which the PCF was part gained well over 70 percent of the vote. The Italian Communist Party (PCI) served in every government from June 1944 through May 1947, winning 19 percent of the vote in the 1946 elections. France nationalized its major banks and the Renault car company in 1945, followed by mines, gas, and electricity in 1946. Churchill exempted "the British Commonwealth and . . . the United States" from the dangers he believed "Communist parties or fifth columns" posed to "Christian civilization," but Britain did not escape the wave of postwar radicalism either.[92] Having defeated Churchill's conservatives by a landslide in the July 1945 election, Clement Attlee's Labour government nationalized the Bank of England, coal mines, iron and steel, railways and long-distance road haulage, electricity and gas, telecommunications, the Thomas Cook travel firm, and all the country's hospitals, which became part of the National Health Service.

Like the PCF and the PCI, the KSČ advocated a distinctive national road to socialism, advancing a vision of the country as a bridge between East and West rather than a Soviet satellite. But as in 1938–1939—or, come to that, as in 1918, 1968, and 1989—the fate of the Czechs became entangled with international geopolitics, leaving only a faint memory of democratic socialist might-have-beens. Addressing a joint session of Congress on 12 March 1947, US president Harry S. Truman promised "to help free peoples to maintain their free institutions and their national integrity against aggressive movements that seek to impose upon them totalitarian regimes."[93] This put the Czechoslovak government in a bind, since the Czechoslovak-Soviet friendship treaty was the cornerstone of its foreign policy. One expression of the Truman Doctrine was the European Recovery Program, aka the Marshall Plan, whose establishment was publicly announced in June 1947. American officials privately made it clear that receipt of American aid would be conditional upon accepting Truman's anticommunist agenda. Despite the ensuing expulsion of communists from the French and Italian coalition governments in May 1947, the Czechoslovak government *unanimously* accepted the joint British-French invitation to attend the upcoming conference of European states in Paris to discuss implementation of the Marshall Plan. Stalin summoned Gottwald and Masaryk to Moscow on 9 July and informed them that he would consider Czechoslovak participation in the Economic Recovery Program a breach of the friendship treaty. Czechoslovakia obediently pulled out of the Paris conference. Lines were hardening, forcing the Czechs to make choices that, left to their own devices, they might not have made. But since when have small nations been left to their own devices when the interests of the world's great powers are at issue?

The next elections were scheduled for the spring of 1948. Tensions were rising within the National Front over additional nationalization proposals, economic policy, agriculture, Slovak autonomy, a "millionaire's tax," and the KSČ's use of its position in government to advance its power and undermine other parties. In the summer of 1947 parcel bombs were sent to Jan Masaryk, Prokop Drtina, and the National Socialist Party leader Petr Zenkl, which Drtina's Ministry of Justice traced back to communists in Olomouc. In retaliation, Nosek's Ministry of the Interior arrested several national socialists in Duchcov and accused them of espionage.[94] The crisis came to a head in February 1948. Hoping to bring extraparliamentary pressure to bear on the other parties, the KSČ called for a congress of workers' councils in Prague on 22 February, followed by a congress of peasants' organizations on 29 February. As the mobilization neared, Nosek transferred all noncommunist police commanders out of Prague, intensifying fears that a putsch was in the offing. When Nosek refused to rescind his order, twelve ministers from the National Socialist, People's, and Democratic Parties tendered their resignations, hoping to force President Beneš to call new elections. It was a catastrophic miscalculation. Neither Jan Masaryk nor the Social Democrats followed the lead of the bourgeois ministers (as the KSČ referred to them). The KSČ pressured Beneš to accept the resignations and allow Gottwald to appoint new ministers.

Beneš hesitated in the face of a decision as momentous as the one he had confronted in September 1938. He was well aware of the stakes. The KSČ flexed its muscles with a 250,000-strong demonstration on 21 February in the Old Town Square. "We want to resolve this crisis constitutionally, democratically, and by parliamentary means," Gottwald told the crowd from the Kinský Palace balcony, but the point was the massive display of extraparliamentary force. He called for the establishment of action committees in all walks of economic, political, and social life, and over the next few weeks they became key instruments for consolidating the KSČ's power.[95] The following day the congress of workers' councils met in the Industrial Palace at the Výstaviště exhibition grounds in Stromovka Park. The Ministry of Information's illustrated weekly *Svět v obrazech* (The world in pictures) hailed the congress as "the most important event in our political life since the liberation." Assembled beneath an enormous banner carrying the Czechoslovak state coat of arms (the two-tailed

Czech lion and the Slovak cross), the eight thousand delegates called for a one-hour general strike on 24 February.[96] The strike was a huge success. The next morning's *Rudé právo* claimed that 196,000 people took part in Prague, 49,000 in Plzeň, 220,000 in the Ostrava region, and 60,000 in the Kladno region.[97] Under the heading "Forward, Backward Not a Step!" the same issue carried a proclamation by 170 "progressive cultural workers" supporting "development toward the new higher form of national and popular freedom." The signatories included Marie Burešová, E. F. Burian, Jiří Frejka, Adolf Hoffmeister, Mira Holzbachová, Jindřich Honzl, Marie Majerová, Vítězslav Nezval, and Ivan Olbracht.[98] The trade unions made sure that factories stopped supplying the noncommunist papers with newsprint, and the KSČ controlled what was broadcast on the radio. Opposition student demonstrations were suppressed by the police. The People's Militia, fifteen thousand men armed with guns brought from Brno armaments factories in a convoy of thirty-three vehicles, was waiting in the wings just in case.

At 4:30 on the afternoon of 25 February Beneš accepted the bourgeois ministers' resignations and approved all Gottwald's nominations for a new government. The new cabinet contained eleven representatives of the KSČ or KSS, three Social Democrats, two members of the People's Party, two National Socialists, and two representatives of the trade union council ÚRO—one of whom was the communist Antonín Zápotocký. Rounding out the team were a Slovak Democrat and a member of the Slovak Freedom Party, together with Ludvík Svoboda, who would formally join the KSČ in September or October, and Jan Masaryk. Unlike in earlier National Front coalitions, the non-KSČ ministers were handpicked by Gottwald rather than delegated by their own parties. To fully savor the jubilation of the historic day, we must turn to *Rudé právo*. "Soon after noon on Wednesday," the communist daily reported,

> tens of thousands of workers from all Prague enterprises poured out of the suburbs into the center of Prague and completely packed Wenceslas Square, where they stormily demonstrated for the immediate establishment of Gottwald's government. All of a sudden, the sirens of SNB [Sbor národní bezpečnosti, or National Security Corps, the national police] motorcyclists rang out and the prime minister's familiar ZIS car [a Soviet-made limousine] came to a stop in front of the podium. To the rapturous cheering of the crowds, comrade Gottwald stepped out with KSČ general secretary comrade Slánský, followed by minister of the interior comrade Nosek and parliamentary deputy comrade Švermová.

The prime minister immediately went to the microphone and announced to the working people of Prague that the president of the republic has just signed the document authorizing the new government.

And the whole of inner Prague resounded to the thunderous shout: "Long live Gottwald's new government!"

It was not easy for Beneš to make this decision, Gottwald told his delirious compatriots, but he did so because "he saw that it was the wish, the will, and the voice of the people."[99] It may well have been. The putsch did not lack popular support, but we will never know how much, as the people would not have their say in free elections again until June 1990.

"Czechoslovakia always got by and is getting by today," said Jan Masaryk in response to what was swiftly christened Victorious February. "The people of Czechoslovakia have spoken. I always went with the people and will go with them today too."[100] Three weeks later, during the night of 9–10 March, Jan's lifeless body was found in the courtyard beneath the bathroom window of his service apartment in the Černín Palace, which was once again the headquarters of the Czechoslovak Foreign Ministry. An StB (Státní bezpečnost, the communist secret police) investigation concluded on 12 March that the foreign minister had committed suicide. He was given a lavish state funeral the next day. It was insinuated that Masaryk's mind had been momentarily unbalanced by imperialist accusations of treachery: "his onetime friends in the West," sneered Rudolf Slánský, "pronounced an anathema over him only because he refused to help in the preparation of a new Munich."[101] Arguments still rage over whether Masaryk's death was accident, suicide, or murder. The case was reopened during the 1968 Prague Spring, but after the Soviet invasion the investigation was suspended, leaving an open verdict of accident or suicide but definitely not foul play. A new investigation in 1993–1996 suggested that Jan fell while trying to escape an assailant who had broken into the flat. An investigation in 2001–2003 concluded, based on new forensic evidence, that he *was* murdered by persons unknown. The state prosecutor ordered the case reopened yet again as recently as October 2019, but the inquiry was shelved in March 2021 with the statement, "We can neither confirm nor exclude an active involvement of other people in the event."[102] Whatever the cause of Masaryk's demise, it recalled a long and doleful tradition of Prague defenestrations. The first, of city councilors from the upper-story windows of the New Town's town hall on 30 July 1419, precipitated the ruinous Hussite Wars. The second, of two of emperor Ferdinand II's officials and a hapless secretary from a window in

Hradčany Castle on 23 May 1618, launched the Rising of the Bohemian Estates, which catastrophically ended at the Battle of the White Mountain. Such precedents were not reassuring. Another of Jan Masaryk's blizzards of harshness was on its way.

After Victorious February all pretense of a national road to socialism disappeared and Czechoslovakia was rapidly integrated into the Soviet bloc. One of the first actions of the KSČ central committee was to ban the import of "reactionary" foreign newspapers and periodicals and install a regime of press control that relied on self-censorship by compliant editors to ensure their adherence to the party line. Action committees purged the civil service, replacing officials at all levels of government with worker loyalists. The same happened in the army, factories, offices, and schools. By January 1949 Czech institutions of advanced education had lost a fifth of their students through political screening.[103] The "leading role of the communist party" later became enshrined in the *nomenklatura* system, in which the central committee had to ratify appointments to more than a quarter million posts,[104] guaranteeing that power in all significant political, economic, social, and cultural institutions remained in the hands of reliable cadres at both the local and the national level. It also sent the clear message that personal advancement in any occupation depended on playing ball with the KSČ. Emulating National Solidarity under the protectorate, between 29 February and 11 July 1948 KSČ membership ballooned from 1.4 million to 2.5 million, with 856,657 new recruits signing up in the Czech Lands and 192,928 in Slovakia.[105] It was mainly the middle class—professors, physicians, lawyers, engineers, technicians, teachers, nurses—that swelled the party's ranks, in Muriel Blaive's words "taking the side of the victors as long as there was still time."[106] Purges reduced membership to 1,677,433 by 1951.[107] Nevertheless Czechoslovakia retained the dubious distinction of having the largest communist party in the world relative to the size of its population.

Leading figures from noncommunist political parties were arrested (like Prokop Drtina) or went into exile (like Hubert Ripka and Jaroslav Stránský). Ivo Ducháček, who had roomed at the Hotel Jacob in Paris with Adolf Hoffmeister, Antonín Pelc, and Jiří Mucha back in 1939, fled through the forests of Bavaria to become an émigré for a second time after serving as a People's Party representative and chair of the foreign relations committee in the Czechoslovak parliament. He ended up a professor of political science at City University of New York, where he broadcast his *"Zápisník o USA"* (American diary) on Voice of America every week for thirty-eight years under the pseudonym Martin Čermák.[108] The National Front provided the fig leaf behind which the KSČ

FIGURE 8.5. Adolf Zábranský's poster for the anniversary of
Victorious February 1948. © ČTK.

ruled for the next four decades. The freely elected 1946 parliament unanimously endorsed Gottwald's new government after only nine representatives
resigned in protest against the coup.[109] One of them was National Socialist
deputy Milada Horáková, a leading women's rights campaigner who was active
in the Czech resistance until she was arrested by the Gestapo in July 1940; she
spent the rest of the war in captivity. In the next elections, which took place
on 30 May 1948, voters were presented with a single list of candidates. Few
people were rash enough to advertise their dissent by exercising their right to
request a blank ballot. The National Front won every seat in parliament with
89.2 percent of the vote, after which the Social Democrats merged with the
KSČ. Refusing to sign the Soviet-style constitution approved by the new national assembly, Edvard Beneš resigned the presidency for a second time on 7
June and was succeeded by Klement Gottwald. Antonín Zápotocký became
prime minister. Beneš died at his villa in Sezimovo Ústí three months later on
3 September 1948, leaving future historians to argue the rights and wrongs of
choices they were fortunate never to have had to make.

Nationalization was extended to construction, wholesale trade, import-export, typesetting, travel, and all enterprises employing more than fifty workers; it was later expanded to include private traders and craftsmen. By the end of 1949 more than 95 percent of workers in industry were employed by the state.[110] The first Five-Year Plan was introduced in 1949, with a strong emphasis on heavy industry. Farmers began to be herded into agricultural collectives the same year. The trade unions were absorbed into the National Front, where they effectively became transmission belts for the KSČ. The "77,000 into Production" campaign that took Bohumil Hrabal to the Poldi steelworks was not the only attempt to address labor shortages created by the Five-Year Plan. In 1950–1954 upward of twenty-five thousand men were drafted into the so-called Auxiliary Technical Battalions (Pomocné technické prapory, or PTP) of the Czechoslovak army. They were not allowed to carry weapons: the PTP "were set up exclusively to carry out . . . 'correctional work.' So conditions were dreadful, particularly for those battalions involved in underground mining. The accommodation and food were bad, while quotas were very high," explains the historian Milan Bárta. "There were former mine owners, former private farmers, priests. But it turned out that to fulfil the ambitious plans set for the battalions, they needed more people. So as well as the so-called politicals, others were also sent. Those included the physically unsound, Romanies, the illiterate, and inadaptable and problematic people. The mix of soldiers who served there was very strange."[111]

Czechoslovakia soon acquired its own apparatus of secret police and informers, torture chambers, labor camps, and show trials. In another eternal return of the never-quite-the-same, Jaroslav Nachtmann, the Gestapo informer responsible for Milena Jesenská's arrest, put his talents at the disposal of the StB after spending years in and out of Soviet and Czech prisons. So did other members of his wartime network.[112] Jiří Mucha's wartime adventures in the West caught up with him when he was sentenced to six years imprisonment for espionage in 1951. He tells the story in his prison diary *Studené slunce* (Cold sun, 1967, published in English as *Living and Partly Living*),[113] which was written between shifts in a coal mine and smuggled out by a sympathetic miner. Mucha was amnestied after Gottwald's death in 1953. He would later be outed as a "social agent" who cooperated with the StB after his release, informing on the American, British, French, Italian, and Canadian diplomats who were frequent guests at his parties.[114] His cooperation seems to have been less than full-hearted. An StB report from April 1962 recommended dispensing with his services on the grounds that "he informs superficially, is unreliable and indulges in a bohemian, dissolute lifestyle. . . . The results of his work don't live up to its potential."[115] Nevertheless, Jiří was able to maintain a highly privileged lifestyle for the rest of the communist period, entertaining in his palatial house on Hradčanské Square and spending considerable time abroad in France and Britain. From 1989 to 1990 he served as president of the Czech PEN Club. Mucha was far from the only one who faced such dilemmas. The ambiguities and duplicities were those of the era.

Every self-respecting modern revolution needs its tumbrils and its *tricoteuses*, and the KSČ did not shrink from its duty to history. Záviš Kalandra—Milena Jesenská's former editorial colleague at *Tvorba*, who started the Trotskyist paper *Proletář* after being expelled from the KSČ in 1936—was arrested in November 1949 and indicted for treason and espionage as an alleged coconspirator with Milada Horáková in the country's first great political show trial. Horáková had been under arrest since 27 September 1949. Kalandra and Horáková had never previously met, but that was no obstacle to their conviction. They were hanged in Pankrác prison on 27 June 1950.[116] Pankrác was the execution site for 1,176 people guillotined by the Gestapo in 1943–1945, 147 "traitors and collaborators" hanged by the extraordinary people's courts in 1945–1948, and most of the political prisoners executed during the communist period.[117] Between October 1948 and December 1952, Czechoslovak courts imposed 233 death sentences for political offenses, of which 178 were carried out.[118] Drawing on a range of sources and taking the most conservative estimates, Robert K. Evanson arrives at "a minimum total of 132,770 political prisoners" in Czechoslovakia between 1948 and 1967, including 35,770 sentenced for serious antistate offenses, 50,000 for lesser antistate offenses, 22,000 confined to labor camps without trial, and 25,000 in the PTP. If we add to these numbers the victims of politically inspired prosecutions who were imprisoned under other pretenses (such as economic speculation or unemployment without a valid reason) and temporary detentions without trial by the StB (such as Lenka Reinerová's fifteen months in Ruzyně), "several hundred thousand persons in a population that varied between 12 and 14 million in the pre-1968 period were direct victims of political repression."[119]

The jewel in the crown of the Czechoslovak gulag was the uranium mines at Jáchymov near Karlovy Vary, where political prisoners labored to supply fissile material for the Soviet nuclear arsenal. Jáchymov is celebrated as the "Cradle of the Atomic Era" on a 1966 postage stamp bearing František Hudeček's "symbolic representation of glowing uranium red and a model of the atom."[120] This is the same František Hudeček whose nightwalker prowled the streets of wartime Prague. With nary a political prisoner in sight and no hint of what became known as Jáchymov miners' disease—carcinoma of the lung—to darken the bright white vistas of the socialist future, the stamp is as good an image as any for this age of beautiful denial.

Sentence First, Verdict Afterwards

Returning from a dinner party at Antonín Zápotocký's in the early-morning hours of 24 November 1951, KSČ general secretary Rudolf Slánský was arrested at his villa and taken to Ruzyně prison.[121] The politburo was informed the next day. At the central committee plenum on 6 December, Klement Gottwald denounced his old comrade as a traitor and an enemy agent. More arrests followed, and several party and state functionaries who were already in custody were retrospectively roped into the plot. One of them was Vladimír Clementis, who had succeeded his boss Jan Masaryk as foreign minister in March 1948. Adolf Hoffmeister took Vlado for a walk in Central Park when they were both in New York for a United Nations session in October 1949 and handed him a letter from a journalist warning that he was in danger—an extraordinarily courageous action in the circumstances, even if the two men were old friends. But Clementis, Ada said later, "trivialized the warnings and made fun of the persons who submitted them."[122] Gottwald and the Karlín Boys did all they could to set Vlado's mind at rest, even allowing his wife Lída to join him in New York. According to Lída, Gottwald personally telephoned Vlado to assure him of his safety.[123] The couple returned to Prague in time for Christmas. Clementis was stripped of his post the following March and given a job in a bank. He was arrested in January 1951 with a view to being tried for "bourgeois Slovak nationalism" with the surrealists' collaborator Laco Novomeský and future Czechoslovak president Gustáv Husák, but plans changed at the last minute. Novomeský and Husák were eventually tried in April 1954 and sentenced to long terms in prison, but by then Vlado was dead.

The trial of the leadership of the antistate conspiratorial center headed by Rudolf Slánský, as the spectacle was officially styled, opened on 20 November 1952. Orchestrated from Moscow and modeled on the Soviet purges, similar show trials were taking place across the communist bloc. "In the front of the courtroom at Pankrác stand three benches," wrote the poet Ivan Skála in Rudé právo. "Simple, firmly screwed, made of oak. But even benches sometimes have a history. On one of them here a few years ago sat the traitor to the Czech nation K. H. Frank. On these benches sat war criminals, answering here before our people. These benches remember Horáková and Kalandra, the whole former band of onetime fabricators, social fascists, Trotskyists, spies, they remember treacherous agents of the Vatican in bishops' garb, they remember the agrarian and clerical-fascist vermin of the so-called Green International. Today these benches are again occupied. This time on them sit the biggest, most dangerous band of agents and henchmen of imperialism."[124] The fourteen accused were described in the indictment as follows:

> Rudolf Slánský . . . of Jewish origin, from a businessman's family . . . former general secretary of the KSČ, before his arrest deputy prime minister of the government of the Czechoslovak Republic.
>
> Bedřich Geminder . . . of Jewish origin, son of a businessman and innkeeper . . . former head of the international division of the central committee of the KSČ.
>
> Ludvík Frejka . . . of Jewish origin, son of a doctor . . . former head of the national-economic section of the chancellery of the president of the Czechoslovak Republic.
>
> Josef Frank . . . Czech, from a working-class family . . . former representative of the general secretary of the KSČ.
>
> Vladimír Clementis . . . Slovak, from a bourgeois family . . . former minister of foreign affairs.
>
> Bedřich Reicin . . . of Jewish origin from a bourgeois family . . . former deputy minister of national defense.
>
> Karel Šváb . . . Czech, from a working-class family . . . former deputy minister of national security.
>
> Artur London . . . of Jewish origin, son of a businessman . . . former deputy minister of foreign affairs.
>
> Vavro Hajdů . . . of Jewish origin, son of the owner of the Smrdáky spa . . . former deputy minister of foreign affairs.
>
> Evžen Löbl . . . of Jewish origin, son of a wholesale business owner . . . former deputy minister of foreign trade.
>
> Rudolf Margolius . . . of Jewish origin, son of a wholesale business owner . . . former deputy minister of foreign trade.
>
> Otto Fischl . . . of Jewish origin . . . son of a businessman . . . former deputy minister of finance.
>
> Otto Schling [Šling] . . . of Jewish origin, son of a factory owner . . . former chief secretary of the regional committee of the KSČ in Brno.
>
> André Simone . . . of Jewish origin, son of a factory owner . . . former editor of *Rudé právo*.[125]

The lines don't rhyme. But they do have an insistent rhythm, even in translation. We have been here before. The constant classification of people that Milena Jesenská remarked upon in 1938, wafting on a quiet breeze of mutual tension into the suburban streets of Vinohrady, Smíchov, Karlín, Holešovice, and Libeň, did not end with the Nazi occupation.

Highlighting the fact that eleven of the fourteen defendants were "of Jewish origin" was not unrelated to the Soviet campaigns against "rootless cosmopolitanism" that began in 1949 and peaked with the so-called Doctors' Plot of 1953. But not all the blame can be laid at Russia's door. Václav Kopecký reassured his compatriots in November 1945 that "the Jewish super-rich who . . . succeeded in escaping the country before the critical period of the republic's defensive struggle, who were able to abandon their property, hand it over voluntarily [sic] to the Germans, who were able to forsake their Czechoslovak citizenship and assume foreign citizenship, such Jewish super-rich panickers may never return to the republic!"[126] Then as now, "cosmopolitanism" was an anti-Semitic dog whistle—though the label was not pinned only on Jews. By 1951 very few Jews were left in the Czech Lands since most Holocaust survivors had emigrated to Israel or the United States.[127] But the specter of the Wandering Jew whose loyalties lie *elsewhere* remained a *point de capiton* of the Czech imagination, anchoring the era's updated intersections of nationality, ethnicity, and class. The Jew was the eternal citizen of nowhere whose rootlessness underlined what made Czechs citizens of somewhere and what made that somewhere eternally Czech.[128] Such imagery had a pedigree stretching back through Bezruč to Neruda and Havlíček. Even Tomáš Masaryk, who had publicly lamented his compatriots' anti-Semitism during the Hilsner affair, admitted to Karel Čapek: "When did I overcome in myself this popular anti-Semitism? Sir, in feeling perhaps never, only intellectually."[129]

Rudolf Slánský did much to create the apparatus that swallowed him up. He inaugurated the arrests of noncommunists after Victorious February. He proposed the establishment of labor camps modeled on the Soviet gulag. He drafted the telegram signed by Klement Gottwald on 16 September 1949 requesting that Soviet advisers be sent to help the StB search for "enemies" within the KSČ. These "advisers" assisted the Czechs at every level in instigating and orchestrating the show trials under the direct orders of Stalin. With the cooperation of Bedřich Reicin at defense and Karel Šváb at state security, Slánský oversaw the construction of what was by the time of his trial a well-oiled machine. Its operations have been documented in state files as well as survivors' accounts.[130] After the victims were selected, their crimes were

FIGURE 8.6. Klement Gottwald (right) addressing the masses from the Kinský Palace balcony in the Old Town Square, 21 February 1948. Vlado Clementis is on the left. Photographer unknown. © ČTK.

FIGURE 8.7. The preceding photograph of Gottwald addressing the masses was subsequently altered to exclude Vlado Clementis after his execution in December 1952 at the end of the Slánský trial. © ČTK.

minutely fabricated. Evidence was manufactured through surveillance, bug-
ging of offices and apartments, and wiretapping of phones. Take the case of
Rudolf Margolius. We left him boarding the second Jewish transport from
Bubny Station with Franz Kafka's sister Elli, her family, and his young wife
Heda, who stumbled across a wild iris. We had come across him previously,
driving Jarmila Čapková to Bergen-Belsen in June 1945 on a fruitless search for
the body of her husband Josef Čapek. In a nice piece of Prague grotesquerie,
StB agents gained entry to the Margoliuses' apartment on Veverkova Street in
Letná on the evening of 6 December 1951 by impersonating Saint Nicholas
(aka Santa Claus) and his helpers the angel and the devil, who traditionally go
from house to house distributing fruits, nuts, candies, and small gifts to good
Czech children and lumps of coal to bad ones on the saint's feast day. As the
nearly five-year-old Ivan Margolius recited a rhyme he had learned from a
book by Josef Lada, they scouted out the flat. A few days later, after ensuring
that Rudolf and Heda were held up at work, an StB team broke into the apartment using copies of keys they had stolen from the Margoliuses' nanny Marie
Bednářová and installed listening devices.[131]

While most of the accused in the Slánský trial were veteran communists,
Margolius joined the party because of his experiences during the war—which
he spent in the Łódź ghetto before he and Heda were transported to Auschwitz in August 1944. Heda's parents were gassed on arrival, and she and
Rudolf were separated. He was subsequently moved to other camps and ended
up in Dachau. Heda escaped from a death march to Bergen-Belsen and made
her way back to Prague, where—after being turned away by several Czech
friends and acquaintances—she was hidden by partisans. Rudolf was likely
roped into the Slánský trial because scapegoats were needed for Czechoslovakia's poor economic performance, but his true crime was his otherness. A
street commune report sent to minister of state security Ladislav Kopřiva on
28 November 1951 went to the heart of the matter:

> We've been asked to report on families that do not fit into our community.
> We believe that the Margolius family is such a case. Neither Comrade Mar-
> golius nor Comrade Margoliusová attends the Commune meetings. They
> have a thoroughly unproletarian attitude. They don't greet their fellow com-
> rades in the street in the prescribed Communist manner or dress appropri-
> ately to conform to other comrades. They don't participate in the brigades
> organized by the Commune to clean the park and street and improve our
> environment. They don't decorate their apartment windows with flags of

the beloved Soviet Union, our saviors from Fascism, and the Czechoslovak Republic as required on all state occasions and the birthdays of our greatest leaders, Comrades Stalin and Gottwald. Their little boy refuses to play with our children in the street.

They never queue for food and send their domestic help (please note, they have domestic help!) to do all the citizens' work for them. They have a number of foreign visitors who visit them often and who are entertained into the small hours. They listen to broadcasts from abroad, buy large quantities of books and often go to the theater or cinema. Comrade Margoliusová even has time to go to the hairdresser. They also own a car and none of the other families we know has one. We've heard that both Margoliusová's and Margolius's fathers were Jewish capitalists who exploited the workforce. Their general bourgeois pre-revolution attitude appears as though they are superior to our ruling proletarian class and we recommend that proceedings be taken against them.[132]

On 10 January 1952 Rudolf was working late at the office. He and Heda had had a rare argument the night before about where the country was going. After trying to cheer herself up with *The Good Soldier Švejk*, Heda took an aspirin and went to bed. Soon afterward the StB sealed off and floodlit the street, and "men in leather coats swarmed along the street making as much noise as possible . . . the scene was set for maximum impact on the neighborhood."[133] "The whole street was lit up by car headlights," Heda recalled in a 1968 interview, "it was staged, a bit like in a film."[134] When Rudolf got out of his ministry car he was "heroically and theatrically" arrested and taken to Ruzyně prison. Five StB men knocked on the apartment door around midnight. Heda lit one cigarette after another while "they searched everything—even all of our books, everything."[135]

Arrests were followed by detention in solitary confinement, the duration of which depended on how long it took to extract a confession. Prisoners were interrogated for fourteen to sixteen hours a day, with the interrogators working in shifts. Otto Šling was once questioned nonstop for twenty-two hours.[136] The StB's enhanced interrogation techniques (as the CIA now terms them)[137] included beating, burning with cigarettes, electric shocks, hooding, sleep deprivation, forced standing for long periods, subjection to extreme cold, withholding of food and medical attention, drugging, sexual humiliation (especially of women), and forcing prisoners' heads into buckets of their own excrement. Interrogators also used psychological torture such as mock executions and threats to harm or arrest family members.[138] Margolius was told, "Your whore who was arrested a few days ago tried to commit suicide" and "your delinquent brat is in a Slovak orphanage, where he belonged from day one."[139] Heda believed it was fear for her and Ivan's fate that finally led Rudolf to confess.[140] Sooner or later everyone broke. Once prisoners agreed to cooperate, they spent weeks memorizing the scripts for their testimony, which were written by prosecutors and on which they were repeatedly tested. During this phase, conditions were eased and they were allowed some contact with other inmates. For the Slánský trial, which was broadcast live on Czechoslovak Radio, a full dress rehearsal was taped so that the recording could be switched on should the defendants fluff their lines on the big stage. None of them did.

The former general secretary and his alleged coconspirators confessed to multiple crimes of high treason, espionage, military treason, and sabotage, all plotted and carried out through a web of intrigue worthy of a John Le Carré novel. Slánský admitted to "a grave crime in connection with the death of Jan Šverma. . . . It happened on November 10, 1944, during a march from the Chabenec Mountain in the low Tatras. . . . When the snowstorm rose, Šverma fell behind and I did not arrange for assistance for him. I feel, therefore, that I am responsible for Šverma's death and I admit this responsibility."[141] Jan's wife Marie Švermová—the same comrade Švermová who greeted the returning President Beneš at Wilson Station on 16 May 1945 and stepped out of the limousine on 25 February 1948 with Gottwald, Slánský, and Nosek to announce Beneš's acceptance of KSČ demands to the jubilant masses in Wenceslas Square—was fortunate not to be in the dock herself. Pilloried during the trial as "a Czech bourgeois nationalist" who collaborated with Milada Horáková, Marie was arrested in February 1951. She told the court, "I helped Slánský in carrying out his hostile policy, above all by placing hostile cadres in the Party machinery. This enabled the conspirators to gradually dominate key positions in the state. . . . We had ideas about a particular Czechoslovak road to socialism," she explained, "dispensing with the dictatorship of the proletariat and adopting a conciliatory attitude toward the bourgeoisie."[142] Many Czechs believed the true reason for Švermová's persecution was her rejection of Václav Kopecký's marriage proposal after Šverma's death.[143] Released in 1956 and rehabilitated in 1963, Švermová fell foul of the authorities again after 1968 and ended up as a signatory of the dissident manifesto Charter 77 in January 1977.

André Simone, the supposed inspiration for Victor Laszlo in *Casablanca*, was introduced as "a cunning globe trotter, a spy without backbone, who as a son of a wealthy manufacturer, obstinately hated the working class."[144] Vlado Clementis testified that he "became personally acquainted with Simone in Paris in 1938. . . . I learned about his vast connections with the representatives of the world capitalist press and of his connections with the West. After the war, his entire orientation can be described as typically cosmopolitan."[145] Simone confessed to becoming a Trotskyist in 1926 when he met with "Erwin Piscator, a theatrical director in Berlin." Then "in September 1939," he said, "I pledged myself to the French Minister Mandel in Paris." He was recruited to British intelligence by Paul Willert, whom he met in New York in April 1939 as the director of the American office of Oxford University Press, and by "his chief, Noel Coward, who at that time held an important position in the British Intelligence Service. I lunched with Noel Coward in Willert's presence in a private room in a Paris restaurant." The deal was sealed over another lunch at the Café Marino, after which "Noel Coward welcomed me as the new member of the British Intelligence Service." Throughout his time in Mexico City, Simone testified, he reported to London on "activities of exiles, including communist organizations, and plans of the Mexican government." In February 1946, when he was passing through New York on his way back to Europe, "the Jewish Nationalist and U.S. Intelligence Agent David Schoenbrunn" blackmailed him into cooperating with the American Secret Service by threatening to expose his work for Mandel to the communists. The French minister, Schoenbrunn told him, "had rendered splendid service to Capitalist Jewry." André met Willert again in April in London and agreed "to write to Willert, by letters addressed to Hamish Hamilton, Publishers, as soon as he knew his, Simone's, address in Europe. A few days after that conversation with Willert, he left by air for Czechoslovakia where he continued his cooperation with the intelligence service." Simone thus returned to Czechoslovakia in 1946 as a "triple agent of the British, U.S., and French Intelligence Services."[146]

Many of these details ring true. Rudolf Margolius did negotiate trade agreements to sell *slivovice* to the United States and TV tubes to Great Britain, but not with a view to harming the Czechoslovak economy or strengthening the British military potential.[147] The combination of gentlemanly amateurism and mindless bureaucracy (André had to sign his pledge as a secret agent *in triplicate*) in Simone's story of being recruited by British intelligence is bang on. The playwright and theatrical impresario Noel Coward really was one of the Secret Service's Baker Street Irregulars, as they called themselves, along with Ian Fleming and Roald Dahl.[148] It was all jolly good fun. "Paris is beautifully war-gay. Nobody dresses and everybody collects at Maxim's," Coward wrote to his set designer Gladys Calthrop in September 1939.[149] But the transcript fails to mention that Paul Willert was a member of the British Communist Party who put up agents of the Soviet secret police in his New York apartment—or that he quit the party over the Molotov-Ribbentrop pact. Willert served in 1939–1940 with the Special Operations Executive in France before joining the Royal Air Force, where he rose to the rank of group captain.[150] Britain, France, and the United States were allies with Czechoslovakia (as represented by Beneš's London government) and the Soviet Union at the time, so Simone's espionage activities were neither treasonous nor anti-Soviet. But so what? As the future changed, so did the significance of the past.

"Sentence first—verdict afterwards," demands the Queen of Hearts at the trial that climaxes Lewis Carroll's *Alice's Adventures in Wonderland*, before Alice wakes up and realizes it was all a dream.[151] There was no awakening from the Slánský trial. In his closing address state prosecutor Josef Urválek called for punishment to the fullest extent allowed by law:

> Citizen judges,
>
> in the name of our nations, against whose freedom and happiness the criminals rose up, in the name of peace, against which they shamefully conspired together, I request the sentence of death for all the accused. Let your judgment fall like an iron fist without the slightest mercy. Let it be a fire, which burns to the roots this shameful cancer of treachery. Let it be a bell, calling through the whole of our beautiful homeland for new victories on the march toward the sun of socialism.[152]

The next day Slánský, Geminder, Frejka, Frank, Clementis, Reicin, Šváb, Margolius, Fischl, Šling, and Simone were sentenced to death; London, Hajdú, and Löbl received life imprisonment. The death sentences were carried out at Pankrác prison in the early morning of 3 December 1952. The last of the eleven to be executed, Rudolf Slánský was hanged at 5:37 and his death was confirmed at 5:45. "He did not pronounce any last words," recorded the official report signed by Dr. Milan Cícha, but "after the sentence was announced he said quietly: 'I have what I deserve.'"[153] Many Czechs would doubtless agree. "During the trial we saw how the sympathies with people of Jewish origin that our working people had after the time of Hitler's racial purges were criminally misused," Václav Kopecký told delegates at a KSČ conference later that month.[154] The condemned were "typical cosmopolitans, people without feeling, without character, without country, without any kind of friendly relations toward the Czech and Slovak nation and its people," wrote Ivan Olbracht in

FIGURE 8.8. "To Vlado Clementis from his Šíma" (*Vladovi Klementisovi jeho Šíma*).
Dedication carved into the frame of Josef Šíma's painting *The Sun of Other Worlds*, 1934,
oil on canvas, 81 by 100 cm. This painting hangs in the National Gallery's permanent collection
in the Trade Fair Palace. The gallery purchased it in 1975. Photograph by author.

Rudé právo. "This is how all must end who betray the interests of the working
class, the nation and the revolution."[155]

In a convulsively beautiful Benjaminian image, Ivan Margolius relates that,
after they had agreed to confess to crimes neither of them had committed,
"Rudolf [Margolius] was allowed to be with Vladimír Clementis for a time.
They recreated Dvořák's Cello Concerto in B minor, Op. 104, whistling the
whole score—all three movements, *Allegro, Adagio ma non troppo* and *Allegro
moderato*—with one replacing the solo instrument and the other filling in the
orchestral support, for its full extent of over forty minutes."[156] Rudolf is commemorated by a plaque on the Margolius family tomb in the New Jewish Cemetery at Olšany, together with multiple relatives murdered by Germans in the
Shoah. Like them, he is not buried there. Security police disposed of the ashes
of all eleven hanged men on an icy road outside Prague, scattering them under
the wheels of their Tatraplan to provide traction after it skidded and got stuck
in a snowdrift. Never, they joked, had the car been so full.[157] "That's Prague!

That's Czecho—absurdity happens all the time," Ivan told a Czech Radio interviewer in 2020.[158]

Heda was taken to see Rudolf for the last time on the night before his execution. "It was a moment . . . terrible . . . one of the worst of my life," she said later. "At this last conversation we were divided by a thick double screen, far from one another, we couldn't even see each other properly, we were not allowed to hold hands, I had brought him the latest photos of our child to look at but was not allowed to give them to him." She did not receive Rudolf's death certificate until 1955. "It was another one of those cruelties, because, you know . . . I, I came to the conclusion that he was still alive. I told myself that perhaps this whole affair was too horrible to be real, so I told myself that maybe it was only some sort of a performance, a comedy, that was necessary for some political aim and maybe they didn't execute these people, maybe they were only imprisoned or interned somewhere, that perhaps they are still alive."[159] Shortly after the executions Heda was thrown out of the family's Letná apartment and stripped of her possessions. Denied employment (and thus at risk of being jailed as a "social parasite") and treated as a pariah, she lived with Ivan for two years in a single room in a "dreadful shack" in Žižkov, unheated and crawling with cockroaches. She subsisted by weaving carpets and providing book illustrations under the names of artist friends with whom she split the fees.

Heda remarried in 1955 and found work as a translator from English and German through her second husband Pavel Kovály. Among those whose works she translated—the translations were initially published under Pavel's name—were Arnold Zweig, Heinrich Böll, Philip Roth, Arthur Miller, John Steinbeck, Raymond Chandler, and Saul Bellow. The marriage cost Pavel his job as a philosophy professor at the Czechoslovak Academy of Sciences, and he took up a new career as a plumber's mate. Ivan defected to the United Kingdom in 1966, where he trained as an architect; he was allowed to leave, he thinks, because by then he was an embarrassment to the authorities. He was "quite thrown" by the lack of central heating but "overwhelmed by the freedom of swinging London at that time. The Beatles, Carnaby Street, Flower Power, Twiggy and miniskirts."[160] Pavel Kovály left Czechoslovakia in 1967 and took up a position at Northeastern University in Boston in 1970. Heda finally abandoned Prague and joined him after the Soviet invasion in 1968. The Toronto-based Sixty-Eight Publishers put out her memoir *Na vlastní kůži* (translated as *Under a Cruel Star*) in 1973. The literal translation of the original Czech title is "on my own skin." Heda's novel *Nevina, aneb Vražda v Příkré ulici* (*Innocence;*

or, Murder on Steep Street), a Chandleresque detective story set amid the everyday terrors of 1950s Prague, followed in 1985; it was published under a pseudonym in Cologne by Index, another émigré outfit. An English translation appeared under Heda's own name in 2015.[161] Her oral history *Hitler, Stalin and I*, which was first recorded for a documentary film by Helena Třeštiková in 2000–2001, was translated into English by Ivan Margolius and published in 2018. The Koválys returned to Prague in 1996, where Heda died in 2010. She is buried in the Margolius family tomb in the New Jewish Cemetery. It seems more than fitting that the Margolius plot backs directly onto the grave of Franz Kafka.

Regarded as theater of the absurd, the Slánský trial outdoes anything written by Samuel Beckett, Eugène Ionesco, or Harold Pinter, but Kafka came uncannily close in *The Trial*. He may have come closer still in his short story "In the Penal Colony" (1919), with its disturbingly erotic undertones. "It's a remarkable piece of apparatus," the story begins. Kafka proceeds to describe an execution machine that slowly kills its victims by writing their crimes—of which they were previously unaware—on their naked bodies. As the needles penetrate the skin, jets of water wash away the blood, revealing the text to the eager spectators gathered around. "The first six hours the condemned man stays alive almost as before, he feels only pain. . . . But how quiet he grows at just about the sixth hour! Enlightenment comes even to the most dull-witted. It begins around the eyes. From there it radiates. A moment that might tempt one to get under the Harrow oneself. Nothing more happens than that the man begins to understand the inscription," which takes up to another six hours for him to fully decipher. At the end of the story the officer who operates the machine, fearing that its days are numbered with the appointment of a liberal new commandant, strips naked and lays under the Harrow. The script he programs the machine to write is: "Be just!" But something goes wrong. "The Harrow was not writing, it was only jabbing, and the bed was not turning the body over but only bringing it up quivering against the needles. . . . This was no exquisite torture such as the officer desired," writes Kafka, "this was plain murder."[162]

9

The Lyrical Age

What actually remains of that distant time? Nowadays everyone regards it as
an era of political trials, persecution, forbidden books, and judicial murder.
But we who remember must bear witness: that was not only a time of terror
but also a time of lyricism! The poet reigned along with the hangman. The wall
behind which people were imprisoned was made entirely of verse and in front
of the wall there was dancing. No, not a *danse macabre*. Here innocence
danced. Innocence with its bloody smile.

—MILAN KUNDERA[1]

A Dream of Meissen Breasts

On the night of 4–5 May 1942—three weeks before Reinhard Heydrich's assassination, though there is (of course) no rational connection between the
two—Karel Teige had a dream:

> Into the shop of an antiquarian, who is a good friend of mine and where I
> was standing, leaning against a cabinet in the background, a beautiful young
> woman entered in a quick and swaying step. I recognize her; it is E. I am
> very surprised and dumbstruck. She does not notice me; apparently she
> does not see me.
> —How may I help you? Says the antiquarian. What have you brought
> me?
> When he sees that she is not carrying any package, he assumed that she
> is one of those who will pull from her handbag or sleeve a small, none too
> expensive antique, perhaps a fan inherited from her grandmother, an

antique handheld fan whose fandangos glitter in the gloomy shop when it is unfolded. . . .

But Eva approaches the antiquarian, leans across the counter and says in a quiet voice:

—I've brought you authentic Meissen breasts.

—Ah, that is another matter, answers the antiquarian. Come, then. And he leads her into a small office behind the shop where he has a writing table and where he purchases more valuable jewels and more outstanding works of art.

Not seeing me, Eva enters calmly, with the decisive expression of a person who is determined to do anything, and she shows the antiquarian her breasts.

—Meissen? . . . Meissen? whispers the antiquarian, turning the breasts every which way in his hands, the way we turn a vase when we are looking for the brand.

—Look at the brand. And Eva, who has offered her breasts from the finest Meissen porcelain and who knew where the factory mark is, engraved like a scar or birthmark, shows the antiquarian: Look, here it is.

The antiquarian looks with a magnifying glass: he is amazed at this authenticity. Then he sits at his table and counts out a large number of bank notes.

And Eva, a woman with the finest authentic Meissen breasts, leaves the store, now with a slim boyish figure and the sad face of a girl who has sold her last family jewelry.[2]

I will not presume to interpret Teige's dream. But in the interest of casting (in the words of André Breton's *Communicating Vessels*) "a *conduction wire* between the far too distant worlds of waking and sleep, exterior and interior reality, reason and madness," it may be helpful to say a little about the context in which Karel's antiquarian friend had this encounter with the marvelous. After all, says Breton, there is "a door half-opened, beyond which there is only a step to be taken in order, upon leaving the vacillating house of poets, to find oneself fully in life."[3]

The beautiful young woman invading Teige's sleep was Eva Ebertová, whom he had met nine months earlier. Eva was then twenty-six. They soon became lovers, initiating an uneasy threesome with Karel's longtime partner Josefina (Jožka) Nevařilová that lasted until all their lives ended in October 1951. A pioneering social worker who established Prague's first children's clubs as well as a translator of Baudelaire, Nevařilová had been Teige's companion and collaborator since 1924. Jaroslav Seifert, who knew Jožka from his youth, describes her as "a serious, gracious, and noble woman."[4] Marie Bieblová, the wife of the poet Konstantin Biebl and later of the architect Vít Obrtel, recalled Nevařilová as having "none of the ostentatious, uniform look of Prague's women intellectuals. She was simple, did not wear make-up, was more boyish."[5] Though Karel assured Jožka back in 1926, "I cannot be alone, I absolutely could not manage to live without your company,"[6] they never married, considering it a bourgeois institution. Their homes in Černá Street in the New Town (designed by Jaromír Krejcar in 1927) and U Šalamounky Street in Smíchov (designed by Jan Gillar in 1937) consisted of separate studio apartments with entrances off a common stairwell and a shared kitchenette, which was located in Jožka's quarters. Teige was no philanderer: there can be little doubt that he loved both women and that both women loved him. "He didn't want to be and of course was incapable of being an actor in a banal marital triangle," writes Seifert. It was a matter, rather, of "a tragedy of a man and two female hearts."[7] Everything was open and aboveboard, which didn't make it any easier for any of the three people involved.

Ebertová has remained a good deal more marginal in the literature on Teige than she was to Karel himself, both as a research assistant and as a lover. After the war Karel lunched and spent his afternoons in her apartment on Štefánikova Street in Smíchov almost daily, where Eva helped him assemble material for his unfinished ten-volume *Fenomenologie moderního umění* (The phenomenology of modern art). The one thing we invariably *are* told about Eva is that she was the illegitimate daughter of Josef Svatopluk Machar, a founder of modern Czech poetry and a signatory of the *Manifesto of Czech Modernism*. Eva's mother Ida Janowitz hailed from a German-speaking Jewish family that owned a distillery in Brandýs nad Labem in central Bohemia. Hans Janowitz, coauthor of the screenplay for the expressionist horror film *The Cabinet of Dr. Caligari*, was a relative. Ida reputedly learned Czech in order to be able to read Machar's poetry in the original and was sufficiently infatuated with her idol to move to Vienna with the object of hunting him down. Before long a marriage was arranged with the Jewish distiller Emil Ebert, who promised to invest in Ida's father's business in exchange for his daughter's hand. Ida agreed on two conditions: that Ebert would touch her only with her permission, and that she could have a child by Machar (who was already married with two daughters and in no position to legalize his relationship with her). Eva was born in Vienna on 27 January 1915, fathered by Machar but raised as Emil Ebert's child.[8]

However convenient this arrangement may have been for all parties at the time, Eva's biological parentage took on new significance in the fall of 1941. Teige met Eva that September, the same month Heydrich arrived in Prague and a month before the first transports left Bubny Station for the Łódź ghetto. As the daughter of Emil Ebert, Eva faced certain deportation; but as the daughter of J. S. Machar, she would be a *Mischling* and therefore safe (for the moment) from the transports. Emil Ebert was happy for the truth to be revealed "if an Aryan father saves Eva from deportation," but J. S. Machar, who by then was "old, sick, and embittered," refused to publicly acknowledge that Eva was his child. The journalist and writer Michal Mareš therefore decided that he would admit to Eva's paternity himself. Drawing on Mareš's posthumously published *Ze vzpomínek anarchisty, reportéra a válečného zločince* (Memoirs of an anarchist, reporter and war criminal), Jiří Kamen tells the story, which takes us places the art-historical literature does not venture.[9] If Mareš is to be believed—and he was undeniably prone to embellishment—he "took to the appropriate office of the protectorate Ministry of the Interior, which determines who is a Jew, a half-breed or an Aryan, his friend Karel Teige. . . . In the office a scene played out that rivals for surreality Max Ernst's painting in which the poets Éluard and Breton watch through a peephole as Mary spanks the infant Jesus on his bare bottom: Teige, the theoretician of so-called—according to Nazi criteria—degenerate art, tells the officials seeking purity of Aryan race how as a boy he watched through a keyhole in his parents' apartment (!) as the Aryan Mareš seduced the beautiful Jew Ida Janowitz, the mother of his future coworker and lover."[10] True or not, the story is vintage Absurdistan. So is everything that followed for Ebertová, Mareš, and Teige.

After Machar died in March 1942 Eva advanced her case based on her real parentage. Heads were duly measured in the time-honored Viennese fashion. Eva was deported to Terezín on 10 August 1942, but the ongoing investigation into her paternity temporarily shielded her from being sent to the death camps. Of the 1,460 people on her transport (designated Ba), only 165 (plus eight of unknown fate) survived the war.[11] Eva's own dream of the night of 6–7 February 1944—that is to say, while she was still in Terezín—is recorded in a typescript that survived among Teige's papers. "I find myself on a sidewalk from which a set of stairs leads steeply upward," she relates. "I run up along them and all at once am standing in a garden where Jožka is seated in a summer dress at a table set for mealtime. I sit down next to her, she offers me something to eat and all at once we are talking about you [Teige], and I confess my desire

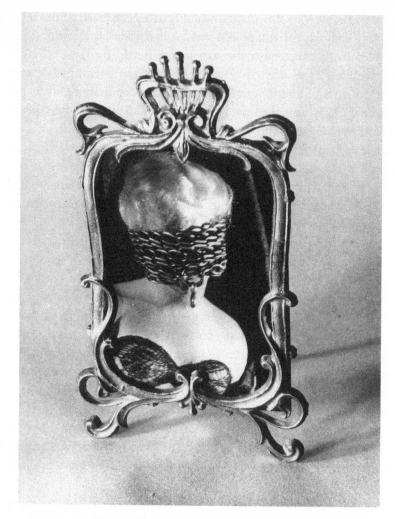

FIGURE 9.1. Jindřich Heisler, *Philosophy in the Boudoir*, c. 1943, gelatin silver print, image 22.9 by 17.1 cm, paper 24 by 18 cm. From Jindřich Heisler, *Z kasemat spánku*, Prague, 1999. Courtesy of Jindřich Toman. © Jindřich Heisler heirs.

for you in such an exquisitely intimate manner (no dilemmas at all—simply like a beautiful dream). J. listens with a smile, somewhat patronizingly (as I always find her to be), but she gradually opens up and soon is completely engrossed in conversation, in our sharing of intimate feelings. Now you arrive—it is all so terribly normal—to tell us something about the political situat., and you prophesy (of course) that the war will soon end, and I speak briefly about

Terez. and add that, from my bidding my leave of you two, the present company has rightly deduced the end of the war."[12] Eva had to wait another fifteen months for liberation, but she survived the conflict. Her mother and stepfather did not. Emil and Ida Ebert were transported to Terezín three months before their daughter, on 7 May 1942, and three days after Teige dreamed of Eva's Meissen breasts. Ida died there on 22 January 1943. Emil was put on a train to Auschwitz on 17 May 1944, where he perished on a date unknown.[13]

Michal (né Josef) Mareš was a colorful figure who was well known in both Czech and German Prague literary circles in his day. An anarchist in his youth, Michal adopted his nom de plume from Mikhail Bakunin. During the 1911 Imperial Reichsrat election, eighteen-year-old Mareš took the minutes at the electoral meetings of Jaroslav Hašek's Party for Moderate Progress within the Limits of the Law (Strana mírného pokroku v mezích zákona), which were held mostly in the U zlatého litru (Golden Liter) and Kravín (Cowshed) pubs in Vinohrady. Members included the anarchist František Gellner, the writer František Langer, and the illustrator Josef Lada, who would later entertain the world with his inimitable drawings of Hašek's good soldier Švejk. As its name suggests, the party's program was (as the British say) to take the piss. After World War I ended, Mareš published a volume of poetry, Přicházím z periferie (I come from the periphery, 1920), a book of prose sketches, Policejní šťára (Police raid, 1922), and a novella about a backstreet abortionist, Andělíčkářka (The Angel Maker, 1922), about which he wrote, "From this wretched land I greet all THOSE WHO SUFFER, who live everywhere, even in prosperous countries, everywhere where the sun of God shines down on womankind."[14] Several longer fictions followed, including Oasa (Oasis, 1924, "an African novel of suffering and love" set in the phosphate mines of Tunisia), Zelená garda (The green guard, 1927, "a revolutionary novel" that drew on Mareš's experiences with a band of deserters on the Bohemia-Moravia border in 1918), and Pan Václav: Český trhan v cizině (Mr Václav: a Czech tramp abroad, 1925) and its follow-up Internacionální patriot: pan Václav doma (The international patriot: Mr Václav at home, 1931). Sing-Sing (1928), a play inspired by the 1927 execution of Nicola Sacco and Bartolomeo Vanzetti in the United States, showed that despite becoming a founding member of the KSČ in 1921, Mareš never lost his sympathy for anarchism. He also wrote the screenplay for the first full-length Czech sound film, Fridrich Fehér's Když struny lkají (When the strings moan), which premièred at the Alfa cinema on Wenceslas Square on 19 September 1930. Mareš was fully bilingual, and his journalism appeared in Tribuna, Rudé právo, Lidové noviny, Prager Mittag, and Prager Tagblatt, among other outlets.

During the occupation Mareš helped run an underground postal service to Terezín, possibly with Eva Ebertová as his internal contact.[15] Arrested by the Soviet secret police in May 1945 in a case of mistaken identity, he was lucky to keep his life—or possibly not, considering what followed. Expelled from the KSČ in 1947, he was the first writer to be arrested after Victorious February.[16] He was sentenced to seven years' hard labor on trumped-up charges that he had received 400,000 crowns for hiding a Gestapo agent during the 1945 Prague Uprising.[17] What damned him was the series of articles documenting the horrors of the expulsion of the Bohemian Germans he wrote in 1946–1947 for Ferdinand Peroutka's successor to *Přítomnost*, *Dnešek* (Today, 1946–1948), under the title *Přicházím z periferie republiky* (I come from the periphery of the republic). These reports bear comparison with Milena Jesenská's prewar dispatches from the Sudetenland, except that the evil no longer came in white kneesocks but in Czech national costume. "How to continue with this reportage?" Michal asked himself in the second piece in the series; "above all as a witness under cross-examination: I promise to tell the truth and nothing but the truth."[18] Mareš's articles were finally republished in 2009.[19] In describing the "depopulated region where crops stand in the fields with no-one to harvest them and mad cows run around in the rain at night with no-one to milk them," wrote one reviewer, "Mareš was suddenly the one who on account of the cows and the crops spoiled the great work of the revolution."[20] Michal pulled no punches in describing the vile conditions in internment camps or detailing the torture and killing carried out with the complicity of the Czechoslovak authorities. He served his full sentence in the KSČ gulag. After his release he worked as an artist's model at AVU for the sculptor Vincenc Makovský, a founding member of the Czechoslovak Surrealist Group who had been expelled in 1936 (for his role in decorating a triumphal arch for King Carol II of Romania's visit to Prague) and had since turned to socialist monumentalism. Mareš died in obscurity in 1971. It took until 1991 for him to belatedly be acquitted of his "war crimes."

It happens that Mareš left us with the only record of Franz Kafka's final days in Prague before he left for the Wienerwald Sanatorium in Austria, where he died in 1924. Or so says Reiner Stach in what has been universally hailed as a model of scholarship and the definitive Kafka biography. "We have no information about [Franz's] departure from Prague and from his family," Stach writes. "It was his final departure; he would never again see his parents or his hometown. One little scene, recorded by the journalist and poet Michal Mareš, is all that remains for posterity":

Mareš had known Kafka for many years, and ran into him on the street on a lovely spring day shortly before Kafka left. Kafka was holding a big, colorful ball in his hands, which he threw to his niece Věra. Ottla was standing nearby and watching the game. "Would you like to have lunch with us?" Kafka asked with a smile. But Mareš had other plans, and he left. This scene was on Altstädter Ring [the Old Town Square], at the entrance to a funeral home.[21]

The Czech Kafka scholar Josef Čermák insists that "this story of the ball on the Old Town Square is pure invention."[22] In my view his grounds for this conclusion are flimsy at best, but Čermák had other reasons for wanting to discredit Mareš as a source—namely, Mareš's attempts to link Kafka to Prague anarchist circles. Kafka scholarship has seldom been a disinterested academic pursuit in these parts. A perennial survivor who adroitly trimmed his sails to the prevailing political wind, Čermák wielded huge influence at the flagship arts publishing house SNKLHU/Odeon throughout most of the communist period. He has since made a career out of rescuing the true Kafka from the recollections of those who knew him, including not only Michal Mareš but also Gustav Janouch. Which does not, of course, necessarily make him wrong.

Since in this case there were no independent witnesses, the facts will forever remain moot. As to the *truth*, that is another matter. Is there not a door half opened beyond which there is only a step to be taken, upon leaving the vacillating house of poets, to find oneself fully in life? Bearing in mind the scenes that played out on the same square when Edvard Beneš addressed the nation upon his return from exile on 16 May 1945, was not Michal Mareš's chance encounter with one of the greatest writers of the twentieth century and a little girl playing with a big colorful ball outside a funeral home on what Kafka once called "the most beautiful set in all the world and of all time" a remarkably sharp *image* for the times?[23] And even more so if Mareš's wayward memory, as prone to revising the past as anyone else's, conjured up this scene *after* the war, *after* the Holocaust, *after* Ottla's murder, and *after* the cleansing of the homeland, in 1946?

Torn Dolls

As František Hudeček, František Gross, Ladislav Zívr, and Miroslav Hák abandoned surrealism to explore the obstinate strangeness and irreducible reality of *things* with Group 42, the two remaining "young surrealists" who exhibited at Emil Burian's D 37 theater in March 1937, Bohdan Lacina and Václav Zykmund, stayed faithful to the surrealist cause. Other young writers and artists, writes František Šmejkal, also found in surrealism "one of the most appropriate means for expressing the terrors and deep traumas the war had brought into people's lives."[24] During the protectorate, underground surrealist groups sprang up in the Prague districts of Žižkov, Michle, and Spořilov (the writers Zbyněk Havlíček, Robert Kalivoda, Rudolf Altschul, and František Jůzek and the painter Libor Fára), as well as in Brno, Bratislava, Louny, and Zlín.[25] In the summer of 1942 one of these groups assembled a samizdat collection of texts by Otta Mizera, Zdeněk Lorenc, and Ludvík Kundera with drawings by Mizera, Josef Istler, and Miroslava Miškovská titled *Roztrhané panenky* (Torn dolls). Mizera and Miškovská subsequently left to further their own explorations of the theme of monstrosity. Karel Teige introduced Lorenc and Istler to Václav Tikal,[26] who joined the group the next year, and met with these and other young supporters of surrealism in the Westend Café in Smíchov throughout 1943. In January 1944 Karel introduced Tikal, Lorenc, and Istler to Václav Zykmund and put Ludvík Kundera in touch with Zykmund and Lacina in Brno. These six became the core of the Ra group. The photographers Miloš Koreček and Vilém Reichmann joined later.

After the war ended Teige threw himself back into the public arena from which he had so long been excluded. In the three years between liberation and the communist coup he introduced exhibitions by Toyen, František Muzika, Václav Tikal, and Josef Istler. He published several important theoretical articles.[27] He coorganized a posthumous retrospective of Štyrský's work at the Mánes Gallery with Toyen and designed Borový's edition of *On the Needles of These Days*. He and Jaromír Krejcar helped revive the Czechoslovak section of CIAM (Congrès Internationaux d'Architecture Moderne), which had been one of the organization's most radical chapters between the wars. He designed covers for dozens of books, including the collected works of F. X. Šalda, poetry anthologies by Paul Verlaine and Paul Éluard, and the first Czech edition of Adolf Hoffmeister's *Unwilling Tourist* (*Turistou proti své vůli*, 1946). His *Moderní česká fotografie* (Modern Czech photography), an album of photographs by Josef Ehm, Jaromír Funke, Miroslav Hák, Karel Plicka, and Josef Sudek first published in 1943 in a bibliophile edition of fifty copies, was reissued and Karel was finally credited as its editor in Eva Ebertová's German translation in 1947.[28] He also tried to expand what was left of the Czechoslovak Surrealist Group to include members of Ra, but the generation gap proved too great to overcome.

Ludvík Kundera later wrote that by 1944, "to most of us—manifestly or implicitly, consciously or unconsciously—the erstwhile avant-garde nature of surrealism began to appear problematic."[29] Josef Istler concurred, writing to Kundera in January 1945 that, "in view of the situation in which Teige and his Surrealist group, if there is such a thing, currently find themselves ... I think that any closer collaboration on our part is completely impossible."[30] In the summer of 1946 Kundera and Zdeněk Lorenc described Ra as "surrealists 'cum grano salis.'"[31] The group's first exhibition in Brno in 1947 was accompanied by a manifesto that distanced them from Teige, Toyen, and Heisler. "It is more than certain that we do not completely identify with them. ... This is natural," they explained: "the terrible years of cultural isolation during the Protectorate and the total break from foreign avant-gardes brought about this state of affairs. ... The question of whether we are or are not surrealists remains unresolved." Although Ra's manifesto criticized Group 42 and "Chalupecký's very far from clear theorizing,"[32] there was considerable overlap between the work of the two groups. Vilém Reichmann's *Osidla* (Snares, 1941) shows the naked torso of a female statue ensnared in vines. The photo is "an ambiguous expression of the conflict between Eros and Thanatos," says Antonín Dufek, "which, even in an international context, stands as an unrivaled manifesto of Surrealist photography. That, however, does not exhaust the meaning of the image. If we take into account the time at which it is taken, it will necessarily change, before our eyes, into a symbol of the threat of war."[33] The same obviously goes for Reichmann's series *Raněné město* (Wounded city, 1946), which explores the convulsive beauties of bomb damage in Brno. Any of these images might have been shot by Group 42's Miroslav Hák.

Toyen and Heisler left for Paris in March 1947 for the first postwar international surrealist exhibition *Le Surréalisme en 1947*, which opened on 7 July at the Galerie Maeght. The two Czechs played a significant part in the spectacle, each contributing one of the twelve "pagan altars" that formed the centerpiece of the show. Seeing which way the political wind was blowing back home, they decided to stay in the French capital and joined André Breton's surrealist group. During his years in Paris Heisler launched the surrealist magazine *Néon* (five issues, 1948–1949); produced more "book-objects" for Breton, Benjamin Péret, and Toyen; and created a remarkable *Alphabet* of twenty-five wooden letters faced with xylographic collages.[34] He had a heart attack on 3 January 1953, at age thirty-eight, and died on the fourth. It was pure coincidence that the most famous of all absurdist dramas, Samuel Beckett's "tragicomedy in two acts" *En attendant Godot* (*Waiting for Godot*), had its world première the next day at the nearby Théâtre de Babylone.[35] Toyen continued to explore landscapes of sexual desire in her new surroundings. In contrast to Breton's prewar Paris surrealist group, many core members of its postwar successor were women.[36] According to her friend Annie Le Brun, "for her entire life Toyen never stopped indefinitely considering this 'act of no importance'"—referring to sex, in all its infinite variety—and collected "naive erotic objects, series of pornographic photos, but also thousands of mouths, legs, breasts, eyes cut out at random from magazines" to the end of her days.[37] She died in 1980. Toyen and Heisler are both buried near André Breton (who died in 1966) in the Batignolles Cemetery in Paris, an unprepossessing location on the edge of town, bisected by the Boulevard Périphérique.

The Paris surrealists split over various issues in 1946–1947, and Christian Dotrement and Noël Arnaud led a breakaway faction called the Revolutionary Surrealists. The rebels were dismayed by what they saw as Breton's retreat into mysticism—a shift in outlook expressed in his rhapsodic *Arcane 17* (*Arcanum 17*), written in the summer of 1944 on the Gaspé Peninsula in Quebec, where André was "playing hooky" with his soon-to-be third wife Elisa Claro[38]—as well as by his final break with the French Communist Party in his June 1947 text *Rupture inaugurale*. What was now being demanded of left-wing artists and intellectuals was *engagement* as preached by Jean-Paul Sartre. It is difficult not to sympathize with the rebels. Behind the rift lay a chasm of wartime experiences. While Breton had been collecting indigenous artifacts, swooning over the beauties of the Canadian wilderness, and reading the collected works of the utopian socialist Charles Fourier in his North American exile, Arnaud and Dotrement were survivors of the surrealist collective La Main à plume, which had been formed in Paris after Breton's departure in 1940. The first, undated issue of the group's eponymous journal declared, "We still refuse to flee reality for poetry. We will stay."[39] They had to face the irreducible reality of hard, evil, uncanny things: eight of their members were shot by the Germans or died in the camps. One of them was the "extraordinarily beautiful and talented" Czech painter Edita Hirschová,[40] who was known to her friends as Tita (that was how she signed her work) and is hardly known to art history at all. Hirschová was likely gassed immediately after she got off the train in Auschwitz on 16 September 1942. In addition to the crimes of being Jewish and a degenerate artist, she was stone deaf.

Ra declined an invitation to participate in *Le Surréalisme en 1947*. Instead, Josef Istler and Zdeněk Lorenc attended the International Conference of Revolutionary Surrealists in Brussels and a congress of communist artists and

FIGURE 9.2. Tita (Edita Hirschová), illustration for Marc Patin's *Femme magique*, 1941. From Anna Pravdová, *Zastihla je noc*, Prague, 2009.

writers in Antwerp on the group's behalf in October 1947. The Revolutionary Surrealists "condemned surrealism, as it has been more or less identified with André Breton," and recognized "on the national plane . . . the Communist Party as the only revolutionary force."[41] On 8 November 1948 Christian Dotrement and Joseph Noiret would join the Dutch and Danish artists Karel Appel, Constant (Constant Anton Nieuwenhuys), Corneille (Cornelius Guillaume Van Beverloo), and Asger Jorn in the Café Notre-Dame in Paris to form the short-lived but influential COBRA movement, whose manifesto *La cause était entendue* (The case has been heard) argued for a spontaneous, experimental art based on "desire unbound." Dotrement saw the three main threats to the development of COBRA as "surrealism, abstract art, and social realism."[42] The name COBRA, which comes from the artists' hometowns of Copenhagen, Brussels, and Amsterdam, was chosen, he says, as "a tribute to the geographic passion which filled us in our re-found freedom."[43] Although some of Istler's graphics were shown at COBRA exhibitions in Brussels and Amsterdam in 1949, the Ra artists were unable to participate in the new movement as a group. The KSČ made its revolution on the national plane, Europe's geography shifted yet again, and refound freedom was no longer on the menu in Prague.

A small-scale reprise of *Le Surréalisme en 1947* opened in November 1947 at the Topič Salon under the title *Mezinárodní surrealismus* (International surrealism). Ludvík Kundera later wrote that "Prague was whirling with surrealism."[44] "When I was 17, so maybe in mid-April 1947," relates the poet Egon Bondy,

> instead of being in school I was sitting, as had become my custom, on the Mánes terrace and had just eaten meatloaf. At 50 grams it was the biggest portion on the menu, it was the cheapest, and best of all it was served with gherkins and bread (in 25-gram slices) on three or four plates, which seemed to me particularly elegant. I sat in my legendary fashionable clothes, made-to-measure from expensive fabric, in my legendary white made-to-measure shoes, and in my legendary expensive American cravat and expensive sunglasses. I ostentatiously topped all this off with a small elegant five-pointed red star in my lapel, of the kind party members and sympathizers wore.

The boy was approached by a young couple he didn't know. "He had a full beard, which was then quite exceptional, and she had a large ponytail and a very long skirt, which was then very chic. All the same it was plain to see that they were poor students." Vladimír Šmerda and Libuše Strouhalová had come in search of Bondy after hearing about him at the D Theater, which Emil

Burian had revived after the war. "In the first few sentences," Egon continues, "we immediately agreed that we were surrealists. That was then still constantly a magical and bewitching word, like few in history. It meant everything—art as well as political conviction, as well as a way of life. André Breton was progress and Vítězslav Nezval was a poet of genius. And the word UMPRUM, where they were both planning to go after the summer vacation, was scarcely less magical. . . . It was a world of freedom and a ground on which it really was possible to prepare for the world revolution, which was not far off. . . . For it was self-evident that we were Marxists, and perhaps Šmerda was even already in the party."[45] I will not belabor the multiple ironies of this encounter. It is an exquisite miniature of its time and place. Bondy joined the youth wing of the KSČ soon afterward, though he would be expelled within a year.

Ludvík Kundera had wanted to print Karel Teige's speech at the *International Surrealism* vernissage in *Blok*, but "experts" blocked its publication: "Too radical, they said, defamatory toward several individuals, a fad." He notes: "That was an early symptom."[46] Breton and Teige wrote essays for the catalog, which was edited by the Group 42 theorist Jiří Kotalík. Proclaiming that "ART MUST NEVER TAKE ORDERS, WHATEVER HAPPENS!" Breton reminded his readers that "the offensive against free art, during the years immediately preceding the war, was launched concurrently by regimes claiming to have opposite ideological objectives." "The despicable word *engagement*, which has caught on since the war," he added, "exudes a servility that is abhorrent to art and poetry."[47] His forebodings were amply justified. A discussion evening on 2 December, organized in connection with the exhibition, proved so popular that it had to be moved from Topič Salon to the large dance hall in the Žofín Palace on Slovanský ostrov (Slavic Island), where six hundred people heard Karel Teige, Jindřich Chalupecký, Zdeněk Lorenc, and others debate the place of surrealism in the postwar era. It was, says Lenka Bydžovská, "the last public manifestation of the avant-garde in Czechoslovakia."[48]

Prague was about to enter an era of peak cliché of meaning and poverty of message. Švejkishly or otherwise, large numbers of Czechs seemed happy to trade their recent glimpses into the void at the core of things for the comforts of kitsch. Sitting in one of the dives on Ladislav Sutnar's Fifty-Second Street on 1 September 1939, W. H. Auden had looked back on the Dirty Thirties as a "low, dishonest decade."[49] What is most striking, in retrospect, about the 1950s is a no less dishonest and willful ingenuousness—on both sides of the Iron Curtain. The Czechs were not so very different from their counterparts playing happy families in pre–Betty Friedan suburbs on the other side of the Atlantic, while senator Joseph McCarthy and J. Edgar Hoover kept the free world safe from the red menace. This might charitably be seen as a kind of collective cultural PTSD whose most visible symptom was a determination to live in a Disneyland of Pollyannaish denial. Denial of the midnight madness of the Strip Street, with its tawdry physical vulgarity, obscene language, and never-ending quests for a variety of low temptations whipped into a frenzy by the dirty excitement of war. Denial of what human beings like to do to one another's bodies not only in the bedroom but also in the concentration camps, the torture chambers, and the firestorms of napalm so painstakingly rehearsed at Dugway Proving Ground before being unleashed on Dresden and Tokyo. Denial of the unpalatable truths that Milena Jesenská instantly *knew* when reason, will, desire, fear, hurry, and work momentarily ceased to drown things out and left her soul naked before the void in the wee small hours of 15 March 1939. Denial of shit. As the author of *The Waste Land* once put it, "human kind / Cannot bear very much reality."[50]

It says a lot that between 1949 and 1956 "no nude photograph appeared in a periodical in Czechoslovakia."[51]

Danse Macabre in Smíchov

"The situation in Prague is perhaps not quite so desperate, at least for now, and it is still possible to work here," Karel Teige wrote to Marie Pospíšilová in Zurich a few days before Victorious February. "But I am terrified by the thought and the feeling that I am now quite alone. Everyone from my generation has more or less gone stupid or sold out ... I feel like an outsider."[52] "I see a very dark future ahead," he told Lída Nováková the same day. "I feel quite alone in my work, and everything strikes me as useless and futile. Ever since Manka [Toyen] moved to Paris, I have nobody with whom to talk about these things." His angst was not just personal: "And when you read in the news, all in one day, about a Soviet Communist Party resolution on modern music, about how [Sergei] Eisenstein suddenly (and apparently just in time) has died, and thirdly, how the Soviet constitution was changed to add a ban on marriages with foreign citizens, including those of allied and Slavic countries—tell me, how can anyone still breathe in this world? Perhaps in the stratosphere, but soon there will be V5 rockets with atom bombs flying through there. Nice, right?"[53]

The action committees Gottwald had called for in his speech in the Old Town Square rapidly moved to cleanse institutions and organizations in all walks of life. A Central Action Committee of the National Front (Ústřední akční výbor Národní fronty) was set up on 23 February 1948 to coordinate the purges; its cultural section included Ivan Olbracht, Marie Majerová, and Emil Burian. Three days later an action committee was formed in the Syndicate of Czech Writers, of whom twelve members (including Majerová, Jan Mukařovský, and Vítězslav Nezval) were communists, three were social democrats, and one was from the People's Party. At the end of the month this cabal succeeded in getting Ferdinand Peroutka replaced as editor of *Svobodné noviny* (Free news) by the communist writer Jan Drda, whose editorials were soon being popularly ridiculed as *rudé prdy Jana Drdy* (the red farts of Jan Drda).[54] Peroutka fled the country, first to Britain and then to the United States. From 1951 to 1961 he was director of the Czechoslovak section of Radio Free Europe in Munich. In one of his broadcasts he sourly noted the parallels between the atrocities of the expulsion that Michal Mareš had documented in *Dnešek*— whose last issue appeared on 19 February 1948—and what happened to the KSČ's political enemies after the coup: "If it is possible to condemn a person for the fact that he belongs to a certain nation," he argued, "then it is also possible that he will later be condemned for belonging to a certain social class or political party."[55] By the beginning of March the action committee had purged more than thirty writers from the syndicate, including Mareš, Prokop Drtina, and Nezval's onetime surrealist group comrade Bohuslav Brouk.[56] Mareš was soon arrested and jailed. Brouk escaped via Germany to Paris, Melbourne, and finally London, where he died in 1978. Drtina was less fortunate. Having unsuccessfully attempted his own suicide by defenestration just a few days after Jan Masaryk, the seriously injured former minister of justice was taken to Bulovka Hospital. He was detained without trial until 1953, at which time he was sentenced to fifteen years. He was amnestied in 1960 and later became a signatory of Charter 77.

"The summer after February 1948," writes Alena Nádvorníková, "fell on Czech culture with the full weight of its victorious and dangerous stupidity."[57] Satirical cabarets like Haló kabaret, Alhambra, the Satire Theater (Divadlo satiry), and Rokoko were gradually closed down, as were numerous magazines, including *Obzory* (Horizons), *Akord*, *Archa* (Ark), *Divadelní zápisník* (Theatrical diary), and *Kritický měsíčník* (Critical monthly).[58] On 10–11 April the KSČ held a congress of national culture in the Lucerna Palace addressed by Klement Gottwald, Václav Kopecký, Zdeněk Nejedlý, and party ideologist Ladislav Štoll. Tristan Tzara, Louis Aragon, and Aragon's wife Elsa Triolet were among the foreign guests. Born in Moscow as Elsa Kagan, Triolet was the sister of Mayakovský's lover Lilya Brik. She was a well-known writer and a prominent figure in the French Communist Party; after Nikita Khrushchev denounced the "cult of personality" at the Twentieth Congress of the CPSU, the story of Otakar Švec, the unfortunate sculptor responsible for creating Prague's Stalin monument, would inspire Triolet's best-known novel *Le monument* (1957).[59] Stressing the need to popularize the visual arts as the radio did music, Kopecký announced that preparations were under way for a multivolume encyclopedia of Czech art "from the earliest beginnings to the present day"; its authors would include Karel Teige and Jindřich Chalupecký.[60] Teige worked on this project throughout 1948, as well as a monograph on Štyrský for Melantrich and a planned exhibition of the Czech cubist painter Bohumil Kubišta. But he held out little hope for the future. "To lose an entire life, to fail in your life's work, has become quite an everyday tragedy in this great, overwhelming, and odious time," he wrote to Marie Pospíšilová. "The world is drowning in idiocy."[61]

By the end of the year all these contracts had been canceled. In the case of the Štyrský monograph, this happened months after the text had been typeset and the plates for the illustrations had been prepared. "So from now on, I will be writing my posthumous treatises," Teige told Pospíšilová in January 1949.[62] By then Marie had decided to remain in Zurich, where her husband had been Czechoslovak consul general. "It is a wasteland here, and it will be so for a long time to come. I do not believe that we will live to see better times," Karel wrote to Lída Nováková two weeks later.[63] The last text Teige was permitted to publish was a version of his essay for the unrealized Kubišta show, which appeared in Vít Obrtel's *Kvart: Sborník poezie a vědy* (Quarto: an anthology of poetry and science) in July 1949, the last issue before the magazine was shut down. Chalupecký too would be prevented from publishing throughout the 1950s. Václav Kopecký spelled out the new order for the arts at the Ninth Congress of the KSČ in May 1949: "The method of socialist realism means: To create realistic art in a socialist spirit."[64] This was straight out of Andrei Zhdanov's Soviet copybook for engineering human souls. "The method of socialist realism," Zhdanov told the First Congress of Soviet Writers in Moscow in 1934, involved "knowing life so as to be able to depict it truthfully in works of art, not to depict it in a dead, scholastic way, not simply as 'objective reality,' but to depict reality in its revolutionary development. In addition to this, the truthfulness and historical concreteness of the artistic portrayal should be combined with the ideological remolding and education of the toiling people in the spirit of socialism."[65]

In January 1950 Ladislav Štoll gave a two-hour speech to the Czechoslovak Writers' Union that was later published under the title *Třicet let bojů za českou socialistickou poezii* (Thirty years of struggles for Czech socialist poetry). It was a watershed in Czechoslovak cultural politics. Teige and Štoll, who became a close adviser of Kopecký's and went on to serve as minister of education (1953–1954) and culture (1954–1960), were old adversaries: they had argued the respective merits of socialist realism and surrealism along with Vítězslav Nezval, Jindřich Honzl, and Záviš Kalandra before an audience of over a thousand people in a celebrated Left Front debate at the Prague City Library back in 1934.[66] The difference now was that the KSČ controlled the press, the publishing houses, and all writers' and artists' organizations, and Štoll's dividing lines between progressive and petit bourgeois literary tendencies set the agenda for what could and could not be published. After 1948 the number of voluntary associations permitted to exist in Czechoslovakia was cut from over 60,000 to just 683.[67] Independent cultural associations like the Mánes Artists' Society were dissolved and their assets transferred to new bodies like the Union of Czechoslovak Writers (Svaz československých spisovatelů [SČSS]), the Union of Czechoslovak Fine Artists (Svaz československých výtvarných umělců [SČSVU]), and the Union of Czechoslovak Composers (Svaz československých skladatelů). These organizations acted as gatekeepers to the public realm. SČSS controlled the Československý spisovatel (Czechoslovak Writer) publishing house and several magazines, including *Literární noviny*, while SČSVU ran the Orbis publishing house, the magazines *Výtvarné umění* (Fine art) and *Výtvarná práce* (Artistic work), and the main galleries.

Konstantin Biebl, the recently deceased František Halas,[68] and Jaroslav Seifert all failed Štoll's ideological test. Seifert's *Píseň o Viktorce* (Song about Viktorka, 1950), which embroiders on the story of a young girl driven to madness by a sinister lover in Božena Němcová's *Babička*, was viciously attacked as "a mockery of our working people.'" "Today, when our whole land has turned into a true workshop of human happiness," charged Ivan Skála in *Tvorba*, "the poet, who in the time of the cruelest economic crisis, unemployment, hardships, and police repression wrote verses full of idealistic brightness ... writes verses of ruin, of misty daydreams, of resignation, of disintegration. ... In the sunniest moment of our history he chose from the sunniest book in our literature the tale of an unhappy mad girl as the most contemporary subject for poetry."[69] *Thirty Years of Struggles* devotes considerable space to Karel Teige, ridiculing him as a "little Czech cosmopolitan" who "in [his] role as cultural counterfeiter aimed to lead Czech poetry astray towards Parisian cultural commerce."[70] Štoll hails S. K. Neumann (who died in 1947) and Jiří Wolker as models of socialist realism. Wolker, who quit Devětsil when it abandoned proletarian poetry for modernism in 1922, was the ideal poster boy for this age of faux innocence. Like Keats, Shelley, Pushkin, and Lermontov he died young (in January 1924, aged twenty-three), "a student and a socialist / Believing in myself, in steel inventions, and in the good Jesus Christ." I quote from his "Svatý Kopeček" (The little holy hill, 1921), a poetic meditation on a popular site of Catholic pilgrimage outside Olomouc.[71] The fiftieth anniversary of Wolker's birth later that spring brought further attacks on Teige in *Tvorba*.

Soon afterward, recalled Anna Marie Effenbergerová, "The political trials and executions began. And again I can see Teige sitting at our home, horrified at the mechanical confessions to everything that the prosecutor presented to the accused. Among the executed was Záviš Kalandra. We were all horrified, not just at the fabricated trials, but at the clear anti-Semitism that emanated from them. Nazism had ended only recently! And the skies darkened over Teige as well."[72] Emil Burian helpfully wrote and directed a new play titled *Pařeniště* (The hotbed), dealing with "loyalty and betrayals among the Czech intelligentsia after 1948,"[73] which premiered at D 51 on 15 September, barely three months after the executions of Kalandra and Horáková. Teige had every reason to fear the StB would be coming for him next. He wrote a last will and a last letter to his partner Jožka Nevařilová in December 1950.[74] Rea Michalová suggests that Vítězslav Nezval and the architect Jiří Kroha, both of whom had pull with the KSČ, may have "managed to hold back State Security while [Teige] was still alive."[75] Nezval spoke up (privately) in Teige's defense, arguing, "Karel Teige is not even remotely any of the things that he has been called. I will never forget what he did for us and what he discovered for us."[76] Nezval would also paint a positive picture of Teige in *From My Life*, at a time when his former artistic comrade in arms was still officially persona non grata.[77] But Karel was right: he was increasingly alone, even if he was now meeting every Tuesday at the Westend Café or in Josef Istler's studio in Karlín or in the Effenbergers' Smíchov apartment with a group of younger friends brought together less by "a clearly shared ideological foundation" than by "the inability to publish."[78] Anna Fárová insists that these were "get-togethers as friends"; "what linked us was mutual friendship and trust more than unanimity of opinion."[79] Teige celebrated his fiftieth birthday at the Istlers'. The evening was "unforgettable," says Anna Marie Effenbergerová, "because Teige suggested we be on a first-name basis. When he saw the embarrassment of this young being terrified by the idea that she might address such a personage by his first name, he calmed my fears. I could call him by his surname, and he would address me as Mrs. And so we drank to our friendship."[80] It is a bittersweet anecdote.

Just as they had in the dark years of the protectorate, the surrealists again disengaged their art from the public sphere and retreated into the samizdat shadows. A second incarnation of the Czechoslovak Surrealist Group came together around Teige in 1950. It consisted of the poet, playwright, and literary theoretician Vratislav Effenberger; Josef Istler and Václav Tikal, who, according to the critic Václav Černý, "wanted more to adhere to surrealism than not"[81] when the majority of their Ra Group comrades went over to the regime; Jan Kotík from Group 42; the Spořilov surrealist painter and photographer Libor Fára and his girlfriend Anna Šafránková, who went on to achieve fame as the photographer, art historian, and Charter 77 signatory Anna Fárová; and the poet Karel Hynek, who died in 1953. They were joined in the spring of 1951 by the photographer Emila Tláskalová (later Medková) and her painter boyfriend (later husband) Mikuláš Medek, son of the distinguished legionnaire, army general, and playwright Rudolf Medek.[82] This group remained active through the 1950s, acquiring new members along the way. Among them were Stanislav Dvorský, Roman Erben, Zbyněk Havlíček, Zdena Holubová, Petr Král, Jindřich Kurz, Věra Linhartová, Milan Nápravník, Alois Nožička, Ludvík Šváb, and Prokop Voskovec.[83] They conducted inquiries on surrealism and creative work, held poetry readings in one another's apartments, wrote plays and pantomimes that were never publicly performed, and tape-recorded anthologies. Their first collective work, *Znamení zvěrokruhu* (Signs of the zodiac), took the form of ten collections of typewritten texts and images (drawings, photographs, original prints) that were "published" in a single monthly copy from January to October 1951. Miraculously, all have survived. These were followed by five collections entitled *Objekt* (Object, 1953–1962), each of which also consisted of just one copy.[84] In the 1960s the group baptized themselves Okruh pětí Objektů (Circle of Five Objects).

The final *Signs of the Zodiac* was headed "Karel Teige in Memoriam." It opens with a photograph of Karel surrounded by his books and smoking his pipe, taken by his niece Olga Hilmerová. Teige died from a heart attack on 1 October 1951 at a tram stop near Arbes Square on his daily visit to Eva Ebertová's. He was fifty-one. His onetime "sweetheart" Emy Linhartová (née Emy Häuslerová),[85] to whom Karel used to recite Verlaine poems as they strolled through the Luxembourg Gardens in Paris and Letná Park in Prague in the summer of 1922, recounts how Eva "found him pale-faced, leaning against a post, and with great difficulty helped him home before running to get a doctor. But by the time she returned, he was gone."[86] On learning of Karel's death, Jožka Nevařilová, who had shared his life, home, and work for over a quarter century, put her head in a gas oven; ten days later, having sorted through Teige's manuscripts and given some to Effenberger, Eva Ebertová followed suit. Effenberger recorded that he and Istler could not talk Ebertová out of killing herself, despite trying desperately to do so. "It is an experience whose smallest details we will carry in our memories for the rest of our lives," he goes on. "In this circle of death, logical arguments have no value."[87] But were the women's decisions so illogical? It seems to occur to no one to interpret their suicides as anything other than the ultimate romantic dénouement of Seifert's "tragedy of a man and two female hearts," but Jožka and Eva's futures were no more secure than Karel's had been. Milada Horáková was, after all, the first woman to be executed in Czechoslovakia in peacetime (the Nazis had no scruples about the sex of their victims), and plenty of women were incarcerated in communist prisons and labor camps by then.

This *danse macabre* in Smíchov (as Jaroslav Seifert calls it)[88] would have made a fine plot for a twentieth-century opera in the vein of Alban Berg's *Lulu* or *Wozzeck*. The final act takes place after the principal players have departed the stage. For scene 1, the curtain rises on the "almost empty . . . ceremonial hall at Teige's funeral." "There were only a few of his young friends there," records Seifert, "who at that time I still didn't know. From friends and acquaintances of our generation—the generation of Teige and not at all that of Wolker, as it was already being called—nobody was there. I stood alone with the faithful painter Muzika behind the empty chairs."[89] Scene 2 is set in StB headquarters in Bartolomějská (Bartholomew) Street in the Old Town, a location that had served the same grim function under successive political regimes since long before Jan Neruda introduced it as a "run-down, destitute, gloomy place" in his *Obrázky policejní* (Police tableaux, 1868).[90] The StB ransacked Karel and Evá's apartments after their deaths, confiscating carloads of books, magazines, cuttings, paintings, photographs, correspondence, and manuscripts. On the stage lascivious cops are going through the evidence against Teige with a fine-tooth comb, preparing a posthumous conviction. A prurient note in the police file records that Karel's library "consists almost exclusively of degenerate bourgeois books of a pornographic and erotic nature."[91]

Scene 3 shifts to the Philosophical Faculty of Charles University, where young Mojmír Grygar is preparing a PhD thesis on *Neruda bojovník za pravé vlastenectví české literatury* (Neruda, fighter for the true patriotism of

Czech literature). Mojmír had originally wanted to develop a stylistic analysis of Vladislav Vančura's *Pictures from the History of the Czech Nation*, but his adviser Jan Mukařovský warned him, "Today is not the time for structuralist analysis."[92] The cofounder of the Prague Linguistic Circle with Vilém Mathesius and Roman Jakobson and longtime collaborator with the Czechoslovak Surrealist Group would soon publish an abject self-criticism in *Tvorba*. Mukařovský prudently begins by quoting Joseph Stalin on economic bases and ideological superstructures.[93] Grygar will later become one of the leading Slavic scholars of his generation. He will leave Czechoslovakia and, starting in 1969, teach at the University of Amsterdam, where he will organize symposia on Václav Havel (1980), Jaroslav Hašek (1983), Jaroslav Seifert (1985), and Bohumil Hrabal (1987). But that is music of the future. Right now, he is putting the finishing touches on a three-part demolition job for *Tvorba* titled "*Teigovština—trockistická agentura v naší kultuře*" (Teigeism—a Trotskyist agency in our culture).

Once again, middlebrow morality gets down and, in this case, very dirty with middlebrow aesthetics. Teige's *Poetist Manifesto*, Mojmír splutters, "is not just an exemplary expression of cosmopolitanism, formalism, anti-realism, etc., but it also promotes Freudianism," providing "an absolutely clear 'theoretical justification' of pornography." Wallowing in the populist gutter, he castigates Teige's "shameless" praise for French cuisine "at a time when, during the First Republic, our workingmen and proletarians often lacked even dry bread to eat" and berates Teige's "abundant use of foreign words," which "is aimed toward the systematic destruction of our national language." Do we hear a distant echo of the Hussites denouncing Pope Paul II in 1469 for seeking to "destroy, wipe out, and utterly suppress the Czech language"?[94] Possibly. "Today, Hus would be the head of a political party and his platform would not be the pulpit but Prague's Lucerna or Wenceslas Square," claimed Zdeněk Nejedlý in his essay *Komunisté, dědici velkých tradic českého národa* (The communists, heirs to the great traditions of the Czech nation, 1946), "and his party would be very close—of this we can be quite sure—to us communists."[95] The Hussites were everywhere in these years, born again on stamps and banknotes, in statues and street names, and in the long-demolished Bethlehem Chapel in Prague, where Jan Hus preached in plain, honest Czech. Jaroslav Fragner—who in a former life had been one of Devětsil's "Purist Four"—"restored" the latter as a "cradle of the Czech people's movement under the government of the people and by its will in the years 1948–1954."[96]

"Karel Teige," Grygar continues,

was the leading promoter of cosmopolitanism in our art and culture for
nearly a quarter of a century. His kowtowing to the bourgeois West went
hand in hand with his disdain for the cultural heritage of our nation. Starting in the early 1920s, Teige very persistently and without missing a single
opportunity infected our intelligentsia with a lack of appreciation and dis-
regard for all the healthy roots of the national culture, hiding his cosmopolitan propaganda behind pseudo-internationalist slogans.

As early as in the 1922 "Devětsil" anthology, he wildly attacked our cultural heritage, including the national classics beloved by any Czech patriot,
calling Alois Jirásek, K. V. Rais, Svatopluk Čech and others . . . ordinary
kitsch, repulsive and sentimental.[97]

We have been here before, too, even if this time the cocktail comes with a
splash of communist bitters. Each time is different, and all of them are the
same. Once again, the wagons circle. Once again, all come together in national
solidarity. Once again, artists stand as part of a united whole, as nothing more
and nothing less than purely Czech artists. And once again, in the name of
simple ways and solid virtues—in this case, in Mojmír Grygar's words, "the
veracity, straightforwardness, and manly comradeship that so distinctly char-
acterize the workingman's mentality"[98]—the statue smashing commences.

A month later Konstantin Biebl killed himself in the time-honored Prague
fashion, jumping from a fifth-floor window on Na výtoni Street in Podskalí on
11 November 1951. He had burned most of his unpublished poems the week
before out of fear they might be used against him in court. "I am afraid to go
home, to see the leather coats on the stairs," he wrote.[99] Ironically, Biebl's first
collection of poetry in twelve years, published a few months earlier, was titled
Bez obav (Unafraid). Jiří Peňás calls it "perhaps the most paradoxical title in
Czech literature. After the publication of the collection in which he demon-
stratively expressed his loyalty to the regime, Biebl's anxiety and fears only
grew, and were compounded by his bad state of health. Three whole months
he waited for the first review—Rudé právo, the weekly Tvorba, as well as Lidové
noviny all keep silent, each waiting on the other. Then on 1 October Teige dies
of a heart attack, fourteen days later the first part of [Grygar's] anti-Teigeism
attack appears in Tvorba, a week later finally the review, basically positive but
graphically damaged by the second anti-Teigeism demagoguery. Biebl . . . in-
terprets it as a message to himself." A distraught Vítězslav Nezval was left to
express his grief in another anguished poem on the suicide of an old friend,

"*Kosťo, proč nezdvihs aspoň telefon?*" (Kosťa, why didn't you at least pick up the phone?).[100] Earlier that year Sláva (as his friends called him) had written to Biebl: "You know well, dear Kosťa, that we two are silently on the same wavelength regarding everything that connects us, that often connects only us."[101]

Country Music

Emil Filla did his best to adjust to the new order and produce art that was comprehensible to the masses while remaining true to himself. The veteran of the pre–World War I avant-garde groups the Eight and the Skupina výtvarných umělců (Group of Fine Artists) spent a good deal of his time in the central Bohemian highlands, rendering the landscape in a series of large-format ink and watercolor drawings that were influenced by Chinese art (*Krajiny českého středohoří* [Landscapes of the central Bohemian highlands], 1950–1952).[102] Vojtěch Lahoda describes their style as "a peculiar syncretism, mixing cubist artificial techniques of spraying and dispersing colors with expressionist abbreviation and Chinese brushstroke painting."[103] Filla was not only one of the founders of Czech modern art but also an active antifascist. He helped organize the *First International Exhibition of Caricatures and Humor* with Adolf Hoffmeister at the Mánes Gallery in 1934. His 1937 cycles *Boje a zápasy* (Fights and struggles) and *Balady, národní písně a říkadla* (Ballads, folk songs and rhymes) were patriotic responses to the darkening prewar political situation. The *Ballads* were inspired by Karel Jaromír Erben's *Kytice z pověstí národních* (A bouquet from national legends, 1853), a collection of poems based on folklore that stands alongside Mácha's *May* and Němcová's *Grandmother* as a cornerstone of Czech national revival literature. Arrested on 1 September 1939, Filla spent the entire war in Dachau and Buchenwald. In 1947 he introduced his collection of writings *O svobodě* (On freedom), with the words: "This is not a book. It's no diary. I wrote it in Buchenwald so as not to perish."[104] It was his experiences in Buchenwald that led Filla to join the KSČ.

On 21 June 1951 members of the third regional center of SČSVU met in the Mánes building to discuss Emil's request to include works from his latest series *Písně* (Songs, 1950–1951) in his upcoming seventieth birthday exhibition of *Landscapes of the Central Bohemian Highlands*.[105] At issue was whether (in the words of the painter Richard Wiesner, who chaired the meeting) these were "a contribution to finding the communal artistic expression of our new socialist era." Twenty-five artists, art historians, and theoreticians took part in the discussion, which began at 8:30 in the evening and finished at 2:30 the next morning. Wiesner began by asking Filla to provide an explanation of his latest works, to which Filla retorted: "What sort of explanation? Everyone can see that these are Moravian-Slovak and Slovak folk songs.[106] They are not conceived as illustrations but rather as equivalents of what a poem and a song are." The sculptor Miloš Axman accused Emil of mixing up his Moravian-Slovak and Slovak sources, snorting, "With [Mikoláš] Aleš nobody can be in any doubt that these songs are from Bohemia." Libuše Halasová, an art historian (and František Halas's widow), answered, "It is not a question here of a topographical description but an artistic work. Filla created an artistic work, inspired by songs." Later in the discussion Axman accused her of having "cosmopolitan views." Axman would go on to become rector of AVU from 1976 to 1985.

Axman's invocation of Mikoláš Aleš might seem bizarre, but it was par for the course by then. When V. V. Štech introduced the catalog of Aleš's eightieth jubilee exhibition at the Myslbek Artists' Society in 1932, he characterized him as "a patriarch outside time, a representative of times that are irrevocably gone."[107] But here as elsewhere, the irrevocably gone came roaring back, and the Czech equivalent of Mother Goose became the measuring rod of all that was healthy and wholesome in contemporary art.[108] The centenary of the patriarch's birth—Aleš died in July 1913—was celebrated in the Aleš Year of 1952 with the largest art exhibition Prague had ever seen. Aleš's works colonized the Riding School of Prague Castle, Slavic Island, the National Museum, and the Kinský Palace for six months. This time, Štech's catalog essay adopted a more prudent tone. His survey of Aleš's oeuvre—under the headings juvenilia, oils, cycles, illustrations, frescoes and sgraffiti, history, songs—ends with the claim that Aleš was "at his most Czech" in the songs, which were published under the title *Špalíček národních písní a říkadel* (A chapbook of national songs and rhymes) in two volumes in 1907 and 1912. Štech does not mention that these were the years, coincidentally, of the first exhibitions of the Eight and the Group of Fine Artists, both of which young Emil Filla participated in. In the *Chapbook*, he says, Aleš "returned to youth, to nature, for the sources of life, poetry, popular character [*lidovost*]" to create "an artistic parallel to the music of Smetana and Dvořák" that remains "living and valid up to the present."[109]

Jan Slavíček, son of the impressionist painter Antonín Slavíček, called Filla's *Songs* "hideous." When Slavíček complains that "the expression of this woman is demented," Emil replies, "But after all this woman has spring fever." Vojtěch Tittelbach questions "why comrade Filla chose this means of paraphrasing these songs by the Chinese method. . . . Why did he not choose according to our traditions?" The art critic Lubor Kára observes, "The only certainty is that we are fighting for an art with a socialist content and a national form," parroting the official Soviet line of the time. "Cosmopolitanism is in conflict with all our nineteenth-century national classics," he notes with a frown. He goes on to criticize Filla's choice of folk songs, in which "there is no evident popular heroism, no popular valor, but sentiment, anxiety, depression." Konstantin Biebl was clearly out of joint with the time when he admitted, "I like Filla's pictures. They are beautiful." But then Kost'a wasn't long for this earth. The comedy was worthy of Samuel Beckett:

> PROCHÁZKA: It's not just about the costumes, but the anatomy of the body. For example, this figure has deformed hands.
>
> UIBERLAY: What are we to do about Picasso's dove, who flies with her head sitting on her shoulder? In actual fact, she can't fly.
>
> FILLA: I propose this meeting resolve that Picasso received the peace prize by mistake.
>
> WIESNER: Picasso's dove arose out of different political conditions. His action for world peace, which is expressed by his flying dove, has nothing to do with today's discussion.
>
> JOSEF NĚMEC: There's a whole legend about Picasso's dove. He did it from a dead dove.[110]

Emil was not permitted to exhibit *Songs*.[111] *Landscapes of the Central Bohemian Highlands* were shown at the Práce Gallery in 1952. Vítězslav Nezval wrote the preface to the catalog.

Filla died on 2 October 1953. Speaking over his coffin at UMPRUM, Jaromír Pečírka addressed the "artist, painter, martyr for the freedom of the Czechoslovak people." "There in the concentration camp," he said, "you dreamed of freedom. . . . At every second you had to assure yourself that you are you, a person, and not a number":

> On one page of your Buchenwald book you compiled a superabundance of art: a Rembrandt drawing, passionately loved, a Chinese landscape from the 12th century, a head of Princess Nefertiti, a sweet gothic Czech Madonna, a Van de Velde still life, a Goya landscape and a Seurat beach scene, a Persian miniature and a woodcut from the Gold Coast, a relief from Selinunte and a torso study of John the Baptist by Rodin, Mácha's *May* and the *Iliad*, Byzantine mosaics as well as Rembrandt's self-portrait and Caravaggio's *Flight into Egypt* and Rousseau's *Snake Charmer* and El Greco's *Annunciation* and Picasso's *Guernica*. . . . You invited all these artists to come

to rescue you. You created an environment that in that moment was more real to you than the whole of Buchenwald.[112]

It is difficult to think of a better riposte to the SČSVU *kafkárna*. Or, indeed, to the century.

When Filla's *Landscapes of the Central Bohemian Highlands* were shown again in a posthumous exhibition in 1954, they got short shrift from *Výtvarná práce*:

> Why so much sophistication, when the reality of nature is so simple? Think of Lada. . . . Why is the color flecked, why are colors aniline sharp, why the arty labyrinth and tangle of lines? (The obvious influence of cubism is always still here, most of all in surfaces processed into variegated structures, often improvised on a certain theme in reality, simply as an end in itself.) Before these landscapes we can admire Filla's artistic ability and his high culture and intelligence, but certainly in many places we lose Czech nature.[113]

The comparison with Josef Lada, who was awarded the title National Artist in 1947, is instructive. Explaining Lada's continuing popularity a half century after his death, Jan Třeštík suggests, "He is so popular because everybody understands his visual style. It is clear to everyone. Children like it, parents like it, everybody likes it. There is no abstraction, there is no expressionism, and there is no cubism."[114] Actually, there are elements of all three. As Jaromír Krejcar said of Antonín Raymond's architecture, the magic of simplicity isn't simple. The beloved illustrator of Hašek's *Good Soldier Švejk* was not a realist painter, socialist or otherwise. Lada's visual style, which he perfected early in his career and never altered, was a deliberate primitivism whose most distinctive element is his use of strong black outlines. But Lada's subject matter—the Czech countryside, the village square, the brass band, the church on the hill, pub brawls, children, animals, the morose Czech *vodník* (water sprite), dancing Czech *rusalky* (freshwater mermaids), pig-killing time, Saint Nicholas with his Angel and Devil, hand-painted Czech Easter eggs and the plaited pussy-willow switches (*pomlázky*) Czech boys use to warm up Czech girls' behinds on Easter Mondays to keep them young and fertile—is as folksy as you can get.[115] Lada loved Czech Christmases, with their nativities and vats of live carp; he relished "the sparkling brightness of the white snow and the whistles of children on sleighs, as the warm rosy glow of the dying day gives way to the blue of the night, which for me always ended with the trumpet call of the night watchman, and the dogs barking in the neighboring villages." These are Kundera's "basic images people have engraved on their memories" on which kitsch depends. What Lada portrays is the nation as it exists in Smetana's operas. "In Lada's paintings there is no sex, no violence, no death," writes Pavla Pečínková. "In his pictures it is eternal spring, there is harmony, children are playing. It's a world of positive values."[116] Just like Norman Rockwell's covers for the *Saturday Evening Post*.[117]

Karel Svolinský, who was awarded the title National Artist in 1961, drew on the same repertoire of nostalgic archetypes. Born in 1896 in Svatý Kopeček by Olomouc—the same place of pilgrimage where Jiří Wolker coupled "great Russia and the brave Lenin" with the Blessed Virgin Mary—Svolinský first made his name in 1929 with his stained-glass window in Saint Vitus's Cathedral in Prague, which shows Abraham preparing to sacrifice his son Isaac. He drew over a thousand illustrations for the monumental four-volume *Český rok v pohádkách, písních, hrách a tancích, říkadlech a hádankách* (The Czech year in fairy tales, songs, games and dances, rhymes and riddles); the first volume *Jaro* (Spring) came out in 1944, followed by *Léto* (Summer) in 1950, *Podzim* (Fall) in 1954, and *Zima* (Winter) in 1960.[118] Svolinský designed over two hundred Czechoslovak postage stamps between 1947 and 1986, on three occasions winning prizes for the most beautiful stamp in the world.[119] His "national costumes" (1955, 1956, 1957) and "Czech and Slovak popular art" (1963) sets are exquisite. The 1966 first-day cover marking the centenary of Smetana's *Bartered Bride*, which (of course) features "a girl in national costume" above a few bars of "Why should we not rejoice?" is also his handiwork.[120] The young woman in a head scarf who graced Svolinský's hundred-crown 1951 banknote was intended to be "a typical portrait of a Czech woman of the people"; "with her focused and resolute expression," explained Mirko Valina of the National Bank of Czechoslovakia, she "embodies the creative, energetic labors of the people in the building of socialism."[121] She cuts a pretty figure in a down-to-earth, straightforward, *Anna proletářka* kind of way.[122] Behind her is the silhouette of Říp mountain, where, according to Alois Jirásek's endlessly reprinted *Staré pověsti české* (*Old Czech Legends*, 1894), Forefather Čech, the mythical founder of the Czech nation, looked out and "rejoiced over this pleasant and lovely land, and meditated as he looked upon it how the gods had granted it to his people, and how the future generations of his tribe would make their home there."[123] In the straight line of descent from Josef Mánes and Mikoláš Aleš, and about as far away as one can get from anything that might reasonably be considered twentieth-century reality, these vapid but charming idealizations were perfectly attuned to the ersatz ingenuousness of the time.

FIGURE 9.3. Karel Svolinský designed this 100-crown banknote, 1951. From Roman Musil and Eduard Burget, eds., *Karel Svolinský 1896–1986*, Olomouc, 2001.

After the war Svolinský was commissioned to reconstruct the sixteenth-century astronomical clock in the north wall of Olomouc Town Hall, which had been destroyed in the fighting in 1945. The replacement was unveiled on the tenth anniversary of liberation, 9 May 1955. Its symbolism blends popular customs like the Ride of the Kings, a traditional Moravian Whitsuntide procession portrayed in the upper section of the alcove, with more overtly ideological signifiers like the worker and the chemist at the base of the clock, "who both strive to create a new, more perfect life."[124] Important dates like the birth and death of Lenin, Stalin, and Gottwald appear in red on the lower calendar dial. Medallions in the sides of the alcove depict work during the different months of the year, and a blacksmith strikes the hour on an anvil. In place of Catholic saints, sixteen revolving figures of a weaver, a butcher, a mother and child, an office worker, an athlete, a countrywoman, and other representatives of the working people crafted by Karel's wife Marie Svolinská appear at noon to the sound of folk songs played on a carillon.[125] "I do not doubt that in years to come the Olomouc astronomical clock will become as dear to the Czech nation as the one in Prague," wrote the local folklore expert Jan R. Bečák in 1949.[126] Instead, argues Pavel Zatloukal, Svolinský's creation (which he describes as "one of the greatest pieces of kitsch ever produced here") "gradually changed into a symbol of the whole era of its birth. . . . In the words of Jiří Šetlík, it became a symbolic 'monument to the happy-looking tragedies of a dishonest age.'"[127]

The clock's noon shenanigans open Jaromil Jireš's 1969 film of Milan Kundera's *The Joke*, which is set in the author's native Moravia. The joke in question is a postcard reading "Optimism is the opium of the people! A healthy atmosphere stinks of stupidity! Long live Trotsky!"[128] Ludvík Jahn sends this postcard to his hot but humorless nineteen-year-old girlfriend Markéta in 1949 because he cannot stand her being happy at a communist summer camp while he's missing her so much. The personal soon becomes political, and Ludvík loses his girlfriend, his party card, and his place at the university and winds up in a PTP brigade working in a coal mine. Kundera savages the "grave joy that proudly called itself 'the historical optimism of the victorious class,' a solemn and ascetic joy, in short, Joy with a capital J" that "could tolerate neither pranks nor irony."[129] But there is more to the novel than politics. When *The Joke* was first translated into English, the publishers cut out an entire chapter on Moravian folklore, which they regarded as of little interest to Anglophone readers. A livid Kundera protested the mutilation of his text in a letter to the *Times Literary Supplement*.[130] "From childhood," he explains elsewhere, "I have been fascinated by the folk tradition called 'The Ride of the Kings': a singularly beautiful ceremony whose meaning has long been lost and which survives only as a string of obscure gestures. This rite frames the action of the novel; it is a frame of forgetting. Yesterday's action is obscured by today, and the strongest link binding us to a life constantly eaten away by forgetting is nostalgia. Remorseful nostalgia and remorseless skepticism are the two pans of the scales that give the novel its equilibrium."[131]

The excised chapter (part 4) is set in 1966. Ludvík's boyhood friend Jaroslav, "a dyed-in-the-wool Moravian patriot and a folklore expert," is trying to convince his fifteen-year-old son Vladimír that "songs, fairy tales, ancient rites and customs, proverbs and sayings" still matter. The boy has been chosen to play the king in the Ride of the Kings but would rather watch the motorcycle races in Brno. This "modest culture, completely hidden from the eyes of Europe," Jaroslav explains, was "the only narrow footbridge across the two-hundred-year gap" between the Battle of the White Mountain and the national revival when "the Czech nation almost ceased to exist. . . . That is why the first Czech poets and musicians spent so much time collecting tales and songs" on which they "grafted" a reborn Czech literature. Karel Jaromír Erben's *Bouquet from National Legends*, the inspiration for Emil Filla's *Ballads*, was one of those grafts. By coincidence, or maybe not, Alén Diviš, who returned home from New York in April 1947, illustrated *A Bouquet* in

1948–1949. He first had the idea for the series in 1940–1941 while lying ill on his bunk in the Sidi el Ayachi internment camp in Morocco.[132] Diviš's water sprites and dancing skeletons, scratched through almost monochromatic oil paint on canvas, are far darker than Svolinský's or Lada's creations—and therefore that much closer, I suspect, to the specters of the folk imagination whose origins have been lost to time out of mind. It is surely no accident that many folk songs exhibit sentiment, anxiety, and depression rather than popular heroism and popular valor. Isn't that the reality of peasant life? Czech water sprites (*vodníci*) are not cute and cuddly: they drown unwary humans who stray into their domain and keep their souls under mugs on the riverbed. You can almost smell the dank cell walls in La Santé, covered in stains and mildew.[133]

Jaroslav's love of folk art, he tells Vladimír, dates from the war, when "they tried to make us believe we were nothing but Czech-speaking Germans. We needed to prove to ourselves we'd existed before and still did exist. We all made a pilgrimage to the sources." "In the last year of the Nazi occupation," he reminisces, "the Ride of the Kings was staged in our village," and "The Ride turned into a demonstration. A host of colorful young men on horseback, with sabers. An invincible Czech horde. A deputation from the depths of history." Jaroslav, fifteen years old at the time himself, was chosen to play the part of the king. Ludvík's old friend was no communist: "For us," he says, "the February coup meant a reign of terror." But the communist government generously funded new folk ensembles. "Folk music, fiddle and cimbalom, resounded daily from the radio. Moravian folk songs inundated the universities, May Day celebrations, youth festivities, and dances. Jazz not only disappeared from the face of our country but became a symbol of Western capitalism and decadence. Young people stopped dancing the tango and the boogie-woogie. They grabbed one another's shoulders and danced circle dances."[134] And Jaroslav joined the KSČ.

The day after being kicked out of school seventeen years earlier, Ludvík had returned to his hometown, where Jaroslav cajoled him into being best man at his wedding. The nuptials were celebrated in traditional fashion (regional dress, a cimbalom band, carrying the bride over the threshold, songs). Only one thing was missing: "a traditional wedding was unthinkable without a priest and God's blessing." The signifiers remained constant, but the signified had changed beyond recognition. Jaroslav asks Ludvík to join the band for old times' sake. He refuses. "I was unable to take the clarinet, and all this folkloric din filled me with disgust, disgust, disgust."[135]

The Tender Barbarians

Vladimír Vlček's film *Zítra se bude tančit všude* (Tomorrow there will be dancing everywhere, 1952) epitomizes Kundera's *Joy* with a capital *J*. According to
a publicity blurb, this tale of a Moravian folk music band promised "to fight
through folk song and dance for a joyful life, for a new human being, for amity
and friendship of all nations, for peace. It conducts us around our beautiful
homeland; with song and dance our young people get to Berlin, which for
fourteen days in 1951 becomes the city of world youth and shows the whole
world that song, dance and joy are fighting too for a better world, for peace."[136]
The title song—whose lyrics were penned by the twenty-four-year-old novelist, playwright, and poet Pavel Kohout—is much more certain of what the
future has in store than Voskovec and Werich's *"Nikdy nic nikdo nemá míti"*:

> With a song and a happy smile
> we greet a new dawn;
> our homeland is already beautiful today
> but it will be even lovelier tomorrow![137]

Kohout went on to become a prominent dissident. "What the great Slovak
writer Dominik Tatarka called 'the demon of conformity' suited those of us
who in those days were emerging from both puberty and the bloody tunnel of
history," he explained decades later. "It was wonderful to be part of a collective
which together remolded history. The driving force was enthusiasm."[138]

"We were the children of war who, not having actually fought against anyone, brought our wartime mentality with us into those first postwar years,
when the opportunity to fight for something presented itself at last," writes
Zdeněk Mlynář, a leading reform communist and architect of the 1968 Prague
Spring.[139] "We were bewitched by history," concurs Milan Kundera; "we were
drunk with the thought of jumping on its back and feeling it beneath us . . .
there was still (and especially, perhaps, in us, the young), an altogether idealistic illusion that we were inaugurating an era in which man (all men) would
be neither *outside* history, nor *under the heel of history*, but would create and
direct it."[140] Like Kohout and Kundera, the novelist Ivan Klíma was a member
of the KSČ in his youth but later became a critic of the communist regime.
Trying to comprehend "why so many people from my generation succumbed
to an ideology that had its roots deep in the thinking, in the social situation
and societal atmosphere, of the turn of the nineteenth and twentieth centuries," he argues that

it is less ideology than the need of people, especially the young, to rebel against a societal order they did not create themselves and do not consider their own. Besides, people need to have some kind of faith or goal they consider higher than themselves, and they are inclined to see the world and its contradictions in unexpected, apparently simple relationships, which appear to explain everything that is important, everything they are going through, or everything with which they do not agree. And for these often deceptive goals they are willing to sacrifice even their lives.[141]

And, he might have added, the lives of others.

Not all young Czechs were content to live in a conformist bubble of wholesome kitsch. *Doslov aneb Abdikace* (*Epilogue or Abdication*), a manifesto read out in the company of Bohumil Hrabal, Vladimír Boudník, Egon Bondy, Jana Krejcarová, Mikuláš Medek, and Zbyněk Sekal sometime in 1950, "renounced a happy future in socialism."[142] With the exception of Hrabal (born in 1914) and Boudník (born in 1924), the members of the group were all around twenty years old.[143] Still children during the war, they "never belonged to the past system. But please," they insisted, "we do not belong to the future either." "We want to go on our own path," they went on, "which we still hardly know. We don't want to resemble the rest of the people, whose faces more and more resemble the faces of idiots. . . . We don't want to be happy in the ways they do. If any among us find it difficult to continue down this path they are not lost yet. A happy future in socialism is open to them. The gate is wide open."[144] "This tract was read almost twenty-three years ago in Libeň, at 24, The Levee of Eternity Street," wrote Bondy in 1973. "It was delivered by a young man in the company of other young folk, some of whom had already started on their path while others were just at the beginning. . . . Who wrote 'Abdication' and who read it out? I cannot say for sure, and it's not important. Maybe it was Egon Bondy, maybe Zbyněk Sekal, maybe Jana Krejcarová, maybe Mikuláš Medek. Besides, the important thing is not the signature but what is universal, anonymous, even if signed."[145]

It was at this time, says Hrabal, that "Bondy superseded surrealism with total realism."[146] Although he was still only twenty, Egon had come a long way since that encounter with a bearded young man and a girl with a ponytail while eating meatloaf and gherkins on the Mánes terrace. In Hrabal's words, "Bondy the poet says that real poetry must hurt, as if you'd forgotten you wrapped a razor blade in your handkerchief and you blow your nose, no book worth its salt is meant to put you to sleep."[147] Rejecting all aesthetic embellishment, the verses in Egon's collection *Ich und Es: Totální realismus* (The ego and the id: total realism, published in his own samizdat Edice Půlnoc in 1951) employed

FIGURE 9.4. First Czechoslovak All-State Spartakiáda, 1955.
Photographer unknown. © ČTK.

"documentary, direct, sometimes raw methods" that exposed the surreality of
the real in all its prosaic glory.[148] The matter-of-factness of these poems, if they
can still be called that, cuts like a knife. Take this:

I was just reading the report about the trial of the traitors
when you arrived
In a bit you undressed
and when I lay down with you
you were sweet as ever

When you left
I finished reading the report on their execution

Or this:

. . . in Ruzyně they shot somebody again
in the factory they arrested somebody again
and I can't take it in
because I'm dreaming of you kissing me

"The loudspeakers in the streets announce the exact time / of power outages / the results of the latest show trials / and sporting events," reads another poem in *The Ego and the Id*—in its entirety.[149] The group's aim was to "look reality squarely in the face ... to record it as accurately as possible, to grasp everything in its true connections."[150] There is a strong echo here not only of Jindřich Chalupecký's insistence on engaging with "living, undeniable, existing, singular *things*" but also of André Breton's view of surrealists as "modest *recording instruments*." Hrabal once compared himself to a pair of bellows: "I simply breathe in a certain amount of information, and as I write I'm exhaling it." "I have never described myself as a writer," he told László Szigeti during their 1984–1985 dialogues. "I have always said I am a recorder, or minute-taker." *I Served the King of England* "was written *alla prima*. I wrote it up on the roof; for eighteen days no one came and I just wrote down everything I knew, and because I live in pubs it was things I knew from others ... I got the opening from the publican at the Blue Star in Sadská."[151]

Hrabal is widely regarded as the greatest Czech writer of the second half of the twentieth century. His style is what Czechs call *pábení* or *pábitelství*, an untranslatable term often rendered in English as "palavering" or "rambling on," which Hrabal—quoting one of his readers—defines as "the capacity to be humanely garrulous, to enmesh oneself and others in a fabric of beautiful words and deeds."[152] Elsewhere he likens his writing to "one of those Prague courtyards, with their sections of scaffolding scattered about, and their overflowing trash cans ... the forgotten and discarded remains of old material, spare parts, wiring, ducts, all the junk that got carted away on scrap metal Sundays."[153] *Taneční hodiny pro starší a pokročilé* (*Dancing Lessons for the Advanced in Age*, 1964), in which "an old man, a shoemaker who once wore a pince-nez and carried a stick with a silver mounting because he wanted to look like a composer tells the story of his life to six young, beautiful women basking in the sun," rambles on for 117 pages without a single period—including at the end.[154] In its resolute fidelity to the hesitations and digressions, non sequiturs and hiatuses, the constant fracturing of coherence in the flow and ebb of everyday speech, not to mention its gleeful relish of the obscenity and profanity of everyday life, Hrabal's prose recalls James Joyce—"whose morning monologue of Mrs Molly Bloom," he observes in the second volume of his autobiography *Vita nuova* (1986), "was written without punctuation a sort of *Schlummerlied* an inner monologue that like Earth Gaia neither knows nor needs to know punctuation or grammar."[155] "Then suddenly, during the Fifties," Hrabal told Szigeti, "I found my way to what Whitman, Sandberg, Eliot in *The*

Wasteland, and of course Joyce wrote about. For me Joyce was a real giant, and I am still reading him today. His *Ulysses* is another pinnacle for me; everything's there really. The whole of modern art is in *Ulysses,* which was written somewhere between 1912 and 1921, so all the art-forms—I mean Dadaism, Realism, Surrealism, the psychoanalytical, they all run through it; that current is even in Molly Bloom, it's the border area between the subconscious and consciousness, just about visible."[156]

Hrabal and Boudník met when they were both working in the Poldi Steel Works in Kladno. Bohouš soon moved in with Vladimírek (as they affectionately called each other) at 24 Na hrázi Street, sharing the workshop of a former smithy. The name Levee of Eternity Street was their conceit; Na hrázi simply means on the dike or levee, in this case, of a former fishpond. "Where I lived in Libeň, in the Fifties, people . . . lived like [the beatniks lived]," Hrabal told Szigeti. "Vladimír Boudník was there, Egon Bondy; [Mikuláš] Medek would come, and Zbyněk Sekal, the Suprasectdadaists [*sic*] were there. . . . They lived there a year or two, or even longer. They had their groups—the Surrealists, Total Realists, Suprasexdadaists—those were the Fifties. So what you had in America, I reckon came earlier in Prague."[157] Bondy, Boudník, and Hrabal became fast friends. If Hrabal is to be believed, the three "brash beer dudes" spent most of their time discussing art, football, "the essence of Surrealism, who Dostoyevsky really was, the basis of Existentialism . . . Kafka as well" in a prodigious assortment of Prague pubs.[158] Hrabal's book *Něžný barbar (Pedagogické texty)* (*The Tender Barbarian: Pedagogic Texts,* 1974) began life as a short tribute to Boudník on what would have been the artist's fiftieth birthday, but "so many memories came flooding back to me of those years spent with tender barbarians Vladimír and Egon Bondy that I just had to keep writing." The immensely talented Boudník didn't make it past forty-four, dying by his own hand in 1968. "Vladimír generally worked in the buff when making prints," Hrabal confides; "he approached the etching press or the copper plate exactly as if he were making love. As he gradually put himself in a state of erotic, and therefore creative, arousal, he would calculate the time between the scratching and biting of the plate so that it would span the same magnificent arc between erection and ejaculation. He always anointed his prints with semen when rolling them through the press, all his prints were mottled with this delicate carnal viscosity."[159]

One of the "ballads" in Hrabal's *Morytáty a legendy* (*Murder Ballads and Other Legends*), a collection of stories published during the Prague Spring of 1968 but most of which were written much earlier, follows Bohouš, Vladimírek,

Egon, and friends on a hilarious walk from Kampa Island through the Lesser Town. Two "postscripts" Hrabal added in 1968 are four times longer than the original story. In the first, Boudník explains his "explosionalist" method,[160] in which stains on walls act like Rorschach blots, stimulating the imagination. "When I'm drawing on the street, people begin giving of themselves—I unleash something within them, the very thing each one of the Surrealists was reaching after." "On the Lesser Town Square he unfolded a stepladder," Hrabal relates. "Then a board with a white quarto sheet. Paints."

> "This section here," said Vladimírek, and he approached a supporting column and pointed. "This section here, what do you suppose it is?" "A moonscape," I said, "a lake by a pasture with a bull grazing." Vladimírek was mixing turpentine. Along came a beautiful girl on stiletto heels. "What's that man drawing?" she said after a while. I said: "Do you see this bull here, grazing in a meadow by the lake?" But the girl declared: "What I see is—Do you see it? A black huntsman." Vladimírek said: "Fine. We'll make a black huntsman." And into the moonscape with the grazing bull he added a black huntsman. "I see something completely different there," said a little man with a newsboy cap pulled down over his forehead, "I see a map of Europe," and his finger traced what he saw in the crack in the wall. And Vladimírek drew a map of Europe over the grazing bull standing in the moonscape. And then onlookers began to step out from the crowd to trace their visions with their fingers, and Vladimírek began to draw them one over the other on the quarto. Owls and peacocks, lava flowing at the foot of Vesuvius, slop pouring from a bucket and frozen in midair, two freshly milked goats.

There is another whiff of La Santé here, of the figures, clouds, landscapes, cliffs and waterfalls, the wrestling giants, sailing monsters, and dancing sprites Alén Diviš saw in the walls of his prison cell. And sure enough, "A traffic warden approached from the intersection, raised his white glove like a priest, and said: 'Don't block the street!' An intelligent man wearing glasses cried: 'But that's not art! Art should be beautiful and sophisticated, something transcendent. . . . That's nothing but scribbles.'" Three men in duffle coats step forward and one of them asks: "'What, pray, is the maestro painting?' 'Nothing,' said Vladimírek. 'Well, well,' said the man, 'Listen, citizens!! While the nation builds its five-year plan, this man is creating NOTHING.' . . . 'This is a fascist provocation! A provocation of the working people. Someone should call the police.'" They often did. "I just want again to emphasize that the development of abstraction in Prague over several years (1949–1955)," Boudník later wrote, "rested on a foundation of hundreds and hundreds of experiments, of personal polemics with people in the Prague streets" during which he endured "many hours of opposition and every degree of insult."[161]

In Hrabal's second postscript, Egon Bondy recalls "that time in the Vienna lockup, what a heap of swill, I tear a newspaper to roll a cig and as I tear, I read: Záviš executed." He is referring to the unfortunate Záviš Kalandra. "You know," he goes on, "when they let Záviš have a last meeting with his wife, they spoke as if they were meeting one another for the first time and fell in love at first sight. He confessed his love for her and she swore to be faithful to him, and then they talked about their future together."[162] Bondy first met Kalandra when Jana Krejcarová introduced them on New Year's Eve 1948, before she and Egon headed out to the country "in an empty and icy train . . . with just two bottles of champagne." Egon was blown away by "finally seeing a real genuine Trotskyist from the old times," and they became good if rather improbable friends.[163] His poem *Pražský život* (Prague life, November 1950–January 1951), published in samizdat in 1951, carries the dedication: "In memoriam comrade Záviš Kalandra, member of the 4th International, executed in Prague in July 1950."[164] It was an extraordinarily brave—not to say foolhardy—gesture under the circumstances of the time.

The other visual artists associated with the Libeň group were equally remote from Andrei Zhdanov's socialist simulacra. Jan (Hanes) Reegen's *Rita* (1950) is painted in tempera on a canvas consisting of "pages from a Protectorate newspaper and a poster from the Svaz české mládeže [Union of Czech Youth]," whose words peep through like the wallpaper pattern coming through the paint in Mark Slouka's description of his childhood in Queens. Bondy wrote of Reegen, an occasional student at the State Graphic School, "although we were all poor, Hanes was the poorest . . . because he truly lived like Diogenes."[165] Reegen painted on "wrapping paper, the backs of school drawings, old newspapers, blank pages from magazines, old advertisements, cardboard and various packaging materials."[166] He died of tuberculosis in 1952. *Rita* is "a brutal, aggressively red, intentionally crude drawing of a naked woman with a skull and coffins. A naked, contented member of the communist youth organization [*mládežnice*] from the year 1950, surrounded by nothing but death and death alone," comments Jan Placák.[167] If Reegen's paintings are often reminiscent of Robert Rauschenberg's "combines," the polished execution and quietly violent imagery of Mikuláš Medek's paintings from the turn of the 1950s— eyes, animals' heads with wide-open jaws, birds' heads with sharp beaks, knives, razors, arrows, vast, empty desert landscapes—bring to mind the dreamscapes of René Magritte or Salvador Dalí.[168] Although these paintings look nothing like Boudník's explosionalist creations, Medek too likened them to "walls, on which certain situations are exposed."[169] He imagines that "some walls are alive, blood flows in them, red warm blood pulsates under the thin layer of plaster in the stones. . . . Sometimes when I walk around some wall, I remember the wall that lives in my fantasy, and I am fearful, I'm afraid the plaster will fall off and expose the flesh of the walls."[170] Mikuláš's "magical realist" phase, as he called it, did not last long. "Perhaps I laid surrealism to rest," he wrote in 1951, "because I painted bad surrealist pictures. It's possible. But still in this a little recognition of the real mess that surreal[ism] was in, and that's enough."[171]

Surrealist or not, *Imperialistická snídaně (Emila a mouchy)* (Imperialist breakfast: Emila and flies, 1952), one of Medek's best-known images, straddles Hrabal's border between the subconscious and consciousness. Mikuláš's wife Emila sits at a kitchen table with her back to us; her body looks deformed, almost hunchbacked—the crew down at SČSVU certainly would not have approved. On the table is an egg in an eggcup, around which black flies are swarming. It is an extraordinarily compelling image, especially when set against the chocolate-box banality of the official art of the time, like Jan Čumpelík's *Na úsvitu únorového dne* (At the dawn of a February day, 1950), in which three militiamen stand on guard as the new era dawns, or the formulaic folk who inhabit the 3.2-meter by 150-meter fresco *Československý lid v životě, práci a výstavbě socialismu* (The Czechoslovak people in life, work, and the building of socialism, 1952–1953), with which Richard Wiesner decorated the ticket hall of Prague-Smíchov Station.[172] Which is more surreal, *Imperialist Breakfast* or these cookie-cutter products of the socialist realist imagination, I wouldn't venture to say. The eggcup returns in Medková's photograph *Vodoplad vlasů* (Waterfall of hair, from her cycle *Stínohry* [Shadow plays], 1949–1950), in which hair cascades out of a faucet.[173] As with Toyen's wartime paintings and drawings, it is impossible to pin down what these images *mean*, but they exude an aura of fear and menace.[174] They are documents of their time and place, fraught with its traces.

The Medeks, too, were in search of "a dialectical, rough and scientific realism." "I don't paint, I vomit definitions out of myself, i.e., with the aid of artistic means I try to define those subjective and objective situations that I consider very interesting," Mikuláš responded to an "Inquiry on Surrealism" included in the first *Signs of the Zodiac* anthology in January 1951. "I photograph to record objective and subjective situations that I consider to be fundamental," said

FIGURE 9.5. Mikuláš Medek, *Imperialist Breakfast (Emila and Flies)*,
1952, tempera and oil, canvas pasted onto chipboard, 110 by 82 cm.
From Lenka Bydžovská and Karel Srp, *Mikuláš Medek:
Nahý v trní/Naked in the Thorns*, exh. cat., Prague, 2020.

Emila. "We think that the inner model is not an autonomous product of our subconscious," they went on, "but it is the projection of the movement of objective reality within us . . . which is not a rigid and dead set of facts surrounding our unsteady subjects, but reality seen through the whole of our body, the reality of existence, of nothingness, the reality of consciousness."[175] They elaborated in their answers to a second questionnaire on surrealism in the spring of 1953:

We think that concrete irrationality and the irrational concrete are fundamental preconditions of modern authentic poetry and a modern feeling of life. This principle of the life of the contemporary modern individual is an objective category of objective reality in the year 1953. This reality is a space in which the whole systematized chaos of this world is mirrored, and this reality is non-negotiable. But are these realities truly objective categories of life and poetry? 15 million political prisoners in the USSR, who are deprived of the benefits of atomic fog and rain, several million Jews gassed in German laboratories who did not have the pleasure either of seeing the delirium of Stalin heads on parade or of participating in the "run for peace" [klus míru], the restoration of God and mustachioed angels in the Kremlin, atomic energy and forced labor, peace-loving militarism, an unending train of deathly mythology, subjective civilized poverty and so on ad infinitum, all this is the reality that modern individuals live and into which they project their poetry.

"Black humor," the Medeks added, "is a reaction to the lethal stupidity and peace-loving debility of optimism."[176]

A Pearl at the Bottom of a Chasm

Born in Prague in 1930 as Zbyněk Fišer—the name under which he would later publish many books on philosophy—Egon Bondy was, "above all, a remarkable eccentric. He's been a part of our scene for 60 years," explained Václav Havel in an interview with the *Independent* in 2006. "He was a Maoist, a Trotskyist, an emigrant, a police informer—a phenomenon unto himself."[177] Zbyněk Fišer became Egon Bondy when he and Jana Krejcarová published what was likely the first samizdat book of the communist period, *Židovská jmena* (Jewish names), at the beginning of 1949. Together with his school friend Ivo Vodseďálek, Egon went on to found Edice Půlnoc (Midnight Editions), which brought out forty-eight illegal books between 1949 and 1954, mostly in typed editions of no more than four copies.[178] *Jewish Names* was a collection of surrealist writings in a cyclostyled edition of one hundred copies; its most memorable feature, according to Bondy, was that "everyone chose brazenly Jewish pseudonyms, as a protest against the resurgent anti-Semitism. The rest forgot their pseudonyms—I began to use mine."[179] The immediate impetus for the volume was an anti-Semitic speech to cultural workers by Zdeněk Nejedlý in Lucerna in May 1949.[180] Among the authors were

Krejcarová herself (alias Sarah Silberstein and Gala Mallarmé), Karel Hynek (alias Nathan Illinger), and Vratislav Effenberger (alias Pavel Ungar). The book opened with a text by Tristan Tzara translated by Szatmar Neméthyová, aka Anna Marie Effenbergerová.

We met Jana Krejcarová earlier as Milena Jesenská's daughter (and Adolf Hoffmeister's goddaughter) Jana Černá—the married name under which she published her biography of her mother. Natascha Drubek argues that Honza, as Jana had been known since childhood, "played a pivotal role . . . in this unique project [Jewish Names]," not only as the link between Karel Teige's postwar surrealist group and Bondy's circle but also because of her childhood experience helping her mother distribute V boj![181] She had known Teige, who was her other godfather, all her life. It was Honza who introduced Egon and his friends to Salvador Dalí's texts, which she had read in the Spořilov surrealist Zbyněk Havlíček's translations. Vodseďálek recalls his first meeting with Honza. Bondy, he says, "called me again. To come to Slavia immediately. He was sitting in the empty cafe with a scruffy young woman in a tight sweater and men's pants, which was quite incomprehensible back then. The slightly squinting Jana Krejcarová."[182] In one of his later poems Zbyněk Havlíček wrote: "I went again . . . / Through the street where I practiced psychiatry on a stepladder / Continuously for thirty-six hours / With poor squint-eyed Honza whose mother / Is the arresting treasure addressed in / Briefe an Milena [Letters to Milena]."[183] Honza wryly described herself in her novella Clarissa (1951): "The tragedy lay in the fact that my nails are too long for making revolution and I have few abilities and many inclinations toward the realization of bourgeois dreams. I think that if I was born in the role of Marie Antoinette the French Revolution would have broken out several years earlier. As the daughter of a progressive journalist and a surrealist architect I can only give everything that even sniffs of revolution a miss."[184] Egon and Honza soon parted ways with Teige's surrealists, whose "Bretonian discipline" they had no time for. "I was of course a sufficiently ungovernable element," Bondy explained, "and when I met Honza Krejcarová, who for the Effenbergerites was the embodiment of scandal, I became impossible to assimilate to the surrealist group and before long our aesthetic criteria went in different directions too."[185]

We left Jana at the age of twelve, seeing her mother for the last time in October 1940 at Gestapo headquarters in the Petschek Palace. After Milena's arrest Honza lived for a while with her grandfather Jan Jesenský, but she soon ran away. Through her teenage years she roomed in girls' hostels or stayed with family friends before being taken in by Mikuláš Medek's mother Eva Medková in the fall of 1944.[186] Honza never stayed more than a few weeks with her father Jaromír Krejcar and his wife Riva, who were then living in a top-floor flat above the Louvre Café on Národní Avenue. Jaromír survived the occupation, though not without a heart attack (he suffered a second in 1947). He was one of three winners of the competition to rebuild Lidice in 1945 with a project titled (in English) *Lidice Shall Live!* It promised to create "not a community of a few rich kulaks and their retainers and smallholders, but a socially liberated community, a community of worker and farmer equals, working in a common endeavor."[187] In 1947 Krejcar was given a chair at Brno Technical University, where his old friend Jiří Kroha was now dean of the architecture faculty, but he and Riva fled to England after Victorious February. "Dad was afraid to stay here," Honza told Slávka Vondráčková. "He didn't like Soviet architecture and he didn't like the bizarre and unbelievable system he had experienced in the USSR either."[188] Jaromír became a professor at the Architectural Association School in London, where he died of another heart attack on 5 October 1949.

"When I was eighteen and still penning little surrealist stupidities at Karel Teige's," Bondy wrote in 1976, "Honza Krejcarová had already written the jewel of the second half of our century."[189] He was referring to Jana's cycle *V zahrádce otce mého* (In my father's garden), which she dated 21 December 1948, a few days before she and Egon met and more than a year before Bondy coined the concept of total realism. The last of the four poems foreshadows both the physical and the intellectual incandescence of their relationship: "Not in the ass today / it hurts / Besides I'd like to chat with you first / because I admire your intellect / It can be assumed that / this will be sufficient / to fuck into the stratosphere." When the poems were first published in the samizdat *Revolver Revue* nearly forty years later, they astonished Krejcarová's contemporaries. "It was the first time in Czech literature," says Bondy, "that poetry of this type was written by a female hand. However Czech poetry, especially the poetry of the underground, may have developed since then toward unprecedented positions, to this day Honza Krejcarová's collection remains pretty shocking."[190] He claims that the title, taken from a French folk song, was intended "to recall [Jana's] incest with her father,"[191] an interpretation that might be supported by the lines "We will go on the hobbyhorse / like when we were little / like when we were big / Flying in the airplane / Flying in bed."[192] There is no evidence of any such incestuous relationship. Honza told her psychiatrist, "One night I slept at [Krejcar's] and there was a double bed and we slept beside one another. . . . Father told me he would not hesitate to have sex with me. For me it was a big shock . . . but nothing happened." Ivo Vodseďálek was more skeptical than Bondy, pointing out that Honza was given to "mystification" and "perhaps felt a need to project the taboo into her own life and really definitively dissolve it."[193] She sometimes claimed to be Franz Kafka's daughter too, which was an impossibility, since Kafka died four years before Jana was born.

There is an unsettling sense of déja vu about Jana's life—the weight of a mother's past that the daughter seemed condemned to relive but could never live up to. Milena had lost her own mother at sixteen. Honza was a year younger when Jan Jesenský received the news of Milena's death in Ravensbrück, and forever after called his granddaughter Milčo. Honza got pregnant at sixteen and again at eighteen. Both pregnancies ended in abortions—the first in her grandfather's house, just like her mom's. After a year of study at Prague Musical Conservatory, Honza dropped out, just as Milena had. When Jesenský died in 1947 he left the eighteen-year-old Honza a considerable inheritance, but she went through it "in record time ... as a result of which I am still told that I take after my mother."[194] According to Bondy, they blew the last forty thousand crowns in a three-day binge, drinking champagne at Mánes.[195] Honza's garret at 6 V Horní Stromce Street in Vinohrady—just around the corner from the apartment where her mother had been arrested in Kouřimská Street—became a center of bohemian life, just as Milena and Jaromír's golden pandemonium at Spálená Street had been during the late 1920s. Honza didn't get to keep the flat for long. Determined to make her living by writing, she shunned regular employment. Her first articles appeared in 1946–1947 in Ferdinand Peroutka's *Svobodné noviny* (Free news) and Emil Burian's *Kulturní politika* (Cultural politics), but after Victorious February she was unable to publish. Honza got by taking occasional jobs like tram conductor, cleaner, and kitchen maid, along with begging and thieving—just as Milena had thirty years earlier in Vienna. Bondy writes that *Clarissa* came into being "in the unimaginably hard living conditions of a social outlaw without a flat, without food coupons, without employment and without money, who pretty much moved between individuals in short-term relationships and sleeping rough (and if need be, in beds for an appropriate remuneration)."[196]

Honza married young, unhappily, and often. Like Milena, she also had many lovers—in Jana's case, of both sexes.[197] Her first marriage, to Pavel Fischl, an actor at E. F. Burian's D Theater, lasted from December 1947 to sometime in 1948. A survivor of Terezín and Auschwitz and the younger brother of Viktor Fischl, the poet who inspired Humphrey Jennings's *The Silent Village*, Pavel decided to immigrate to Israel. "I spent three years in a concentration camp," he said, "and had no wish to repeat the experience."[198] Honza met Bondy on Christmas Day 1948. Two days later he declared his love in the back of a taxi on Wenceslas Square. "As soon as I sat down beside her there was no more testing or thinking about it," says Egon. "Everything had gone to fuck again, and such a season was about to start, by comparison with which Rimbaud's [*A Season in Hell*] was an idyll." Egon was the love of Honza's life, and she of his, but they proved incapable of living together or of keeping away from each other. "I followed her," he writes, "like a calf to the slaughter."[199] Repeating the desperate measures Jan Jesenský had taken to separate his daughter from Ernst Pollak, in March 1949 Bondy's father had his son committed to Bohnice psychiatric hospital—the institution where Milena finally broke her morphine habit—citing the boy's obsession with "a twenty-year-old divorced female student" as grounds for commitment.[200]

The treatment was not successful: "The two who meant most for me were Lenin and Honza," Egon wrote ten years later in his autobiographical poem "*Kádrový dotazník*" (Personnel questionnaire). "What I live without Honza / is indeed very gripping very taxing and very important / but for me it is not life."[201] By then he had acquired a wife and an infant son. Jana first sought psychiatric help in the summer of 1948. The only time she ever set foot outside Czechoslovakia as an adult was when she and Egon crossed the Austrian border illegally in August 1950 and were jailed for ten days in (of all places) Gmünd, the little town where Kafka and Milena had their last tryst thirty years earlier to the month. Austria returned the runaways to Czechoslovakia, where their psychiatric records kept them out of jail—a remarkable stroke of luck. Honza spent another two months in the hospital. Despite Egon's entreaties, in January 1951 she married her second husband Miloš Černý, a student who had been part of her bohemian entourage at V Horní Stromce Street. The next month she gave birth to Bondy's son, whom she named Jan in the Jesenský family tradition. She was later hospitalized several more times for depression or—just like her mother—drug addiction.

Honza had three more husbands and five children in all, two of them by men who were not her husbands. As Martin Černý explained in 2010, "I am the second son of Jana Krejcarová-Černá, my older brother by a year, Jan Černý, is the son of my mother and Bondy. Then I have a younger brother, he is the son of my mother and Mikuláš Medek."[202] Beginning in 1957 Honza was once again able to publish stories and sketches in magazines as well as the books *Hrdinství je povinné* (Heroism is obligatory, 1964) and *Nebyly to moje děti* (They were not my children, 1966), but she was unable to keep her chaotic

FIGURE 9.6. Jan Reegen, *Egon Bondy*, 1949, ink drawing, Galerie Ztichlá
klika v Praze. From Jan Placák, ed., *Dopisy Hanese Reegena Vladimíru
Boudníkovi a Reegenova literární pozůstalost*, Prague, 2014.

and poverty-stricken life together. "Jana wasn't a bad mother," explained Jan
Černý in 1993, "but she was a bad housekeeper."[203] As Honza slipped in and
out of marriages and mental hospitals, her children made the rounds of
children's homes. Jan and Martin spent two years with their mother in the
early 1960s "in a small Holešovice flat that for Jana and her sons became a
symbol of a family idyll," but things soon fell apart again.[204] In 1965 Honza was

committed under a court order to Bohnice, where she spent three months. The following year she was charged with child neglect and sentenced to a year in prison. Her fourth husband, Ladislav Lipanský, got off with a seven-month suspended sentence; socialist pieties about equality of the sexes notwithstanding, children were assumed to be primarily a woman's responsibility. Jaroslav Němeček, an old court reporter who had once worked with Milena Jesenská for *Svět práce*, warned Jana against her neighbors: "You don't fit into your surroundings, into the environment in which you live, this is not forgiven. In short you have no feel for life at no. 47 [Jankovcova Street]."[205] Remember the street commune report on the Margolius family in Letná?

After a suicide attempt (and another month in Bohnice), Jana was transferred to the women's prison in Pardubice, or what she described as the "stereotyped monotony that paralyzes." I quote from her essay "*Otisky duši*" (Printouts of souls), which was published in the Klub Mladá poesie (Young Poetry Club) magazine *Divoké víno* (Wild wine) in 1968. Honza writes about her fellow inmates with a clear-eyed compassion that is equally devoid of moralizing and sentimentality. In the front row of a prisoners' performance of J. K. Tyl's *Tvrdohlavá žena* (The obstinate woman), "two inseparable girlfriends are sitting together. One of them raped her foster daughter, a five-year-old little girl, and injured her so badly that the kid had to be taken to hospital. The other is here for a drunken fight in which she almost killed her daughter-in-law. Now they are holding hands and scarcely breathing," caught up in the action on the stage. As "the fairy-tale is nearing its end, good and evil get what each deserves," and "the two of them, with tears in their eyes, go out into the courtyard of the block. Everything turned out well. . . . Moved and crying, they lead each other by the hand back to their quarters." The essay is divided into five sections headed Astonishment, Fear, Sadness, Joy, and Hope. "There are things here," Honza writes, "that arouse astonishment. There are many more of those that arouse fear or sadness. And fewer of those that arouse hope or joy. . . . Truly it is difficult to distinguish hope from fear."[206] The quality of Krejcarová's prose is outstanding, but the times were against her. *Kafka's Milena* was scheduled to come out in 1969 but never reached bookstores. Neither the author nor her subject was deemed a suitable role model for normalization. *Divoké víno*, founded in 1964 during the brief thaw of the 1960s, was suppressed in 1971.

Sometime in the spring of 1962, when Honza was in her early thirties, she sat down to write to Egon Bondy. He had asked her for five or six lines, but she gave him twenty close-typed pages. By any standard, this is a remarkable text. Honza's outpourings are at once an artistic credo and a passionate love letter.

"I never had much inclination to hold onto common sense [*zdravý rozum*]," she warns Egon near the start, "perhaps simply because I don't have any common sense, or maybe because I have an antipathy toward healthy [*zdravým*] and sensible [*rozumným*] things that is almost physical . . . common sense destroys everything in me that has some meaning for me, common sense strips potency away from me, any kind of potency whatsoever, from erotic to intellectual." Turning to Bondy's writing, she tells him, "If there is a real and true hope that you will yield fertile fruit (and there is), it will only be when you put your whole self into it, socks, resistance to libraries, whiskers, beer, fantasies, intellect, cock, the whole lot. Nothing excites me so much as the hope of a work that comes from a direct relation with all of these things, the hope of a work from which nothing will be eliminated, the hope of a work that is uncensored, raw, brutal, and monstrous, but absolute . . . of a work that will not have limits and will not allow limits to be imposed on it anytime or anywhere."

Honza certainly put *her* whole self into what follows. "Understand me well, my love, it's all inextricably linked, that I love you and want to sleep with you with how I cling to your work, it's hard to say what part your body, which I know so intimately, plays in what excites me, and what part is played by our debates, truly it's hard to say, I can talk philosophy with you in bed and when we're talking about it at the table my cunt is standing at attention, there's no way the one can be divided or abstracted from the other." Later in the letter she asks, "Please, what is this nonsense, that you aren't here?" Molly Bloom's imagination had nothing on Jana's, but then, when all is said and done, Molly was the fantasy of a man:

What is this fuckery, that I can't kiss you right now, that I can't lie with you, that I can't fondle you, arouse you and arouse myself with you, that I can't bring you to orgasm with my mouth. . . . That I can't give you my whole body to plunder from tits to cunt to ass. . . . Why don't I have your tongue in my cunt when I so horribly strongly want it, why am I not feeling the ticklish pain of your biting the soles of my feet, why can't I stick out my ass for you to fuck, bite, spank, and sprinkle with sperm, why can't I lie beside you after and talk about whatever, from philosophy to the immortality of the June bug, in the obvious intimacy in which we belong beside one another while I casually play with your cock out of a surfeit of high spirits? Why can't I lie down with you with joyful, almost asexual tenderness and chat with you during intercourse about what we had for dinner or how was the weather? Why can't I lay you down on your stomach and fuck your ass with my hands, breasts, tongue, slaver it with my cunt, which is wet at the mere thought of it. . . . Why can't I then turn you on your back and nibble your nipples, lick your navel and take your balls into my mouth one by one until you groan and fart with excitement. . . . Why can't I put my legs on your shoulders and let you look at my hole and examine my cunt with cold shamelessness, so close to its lips and hair that I feel your breath. . . . Why aren't you here to turn me over on my stomach so you can paint my ass like a decorated Easter egg until tiny droplets of blood flow from it? Droplets from which little scabs would form, that I would feel on my ass for many days after?[207]

Honza's wish list is adult, it is honest, and it really *is* joyful, the antithesis of Kundera's saccharine *Joy* with a capital *J*. In a Prague twist on the madwoman in the attic, "an unhappy mad girl," a modern Viktorka, speaks truth to power.[208] An authentic child of a monstrous time, Milena's grown-up daughter undermines the superhuman fantasies of the era, exposing its rationalist airs and social pretensions for the childish delusions they are.

Shortly afterward Bondy met his second wife Julia Nováková; they fell in love, and Egon and Jana's on-again, off-again affair finally came to an end. They remained good friends until the end of her life. Jana's last marriage, to the graphic artist Daniel Ladman in 1973, seems to have been her happiest. She was killed when their car collided with a truck and a bus at Bořanovice on the eastern outskirts of Prague on 5 January 1981. The funeral was in Olšany Cemetery. "Before we say a last goodbye to Honza, Milena's daughter," Jiří Žantovský began his oration, "let us remember the bottomless loneliness and immeasurable longing for life that linked them both, just like their unconventional literary talents."[209] Julia Nováková was among the mourners.[210] Bondy was away in Hlinsko, an "icy town" near Pardubice, working on a book about Indian philosophy. At 2:45 in the afternoon, he wrote in an untitled poem, "I put down the pencil / Glory to her What I suffered with her / . . . nobody knows / that she was the greatest / that a human being can achieve."[211]

Bohumil Hrabal heard the news in his favorite pub, U zlatého tygra (The Golden Tiger) on Husova Street in the Old Town. "Flashy life, flashy death" (*frajerský život, frajerská smrt*), he supposedly said.[212] When Honza's letter to Bondy was first published in 1990 alongside *Clarissa* and "In My Father's Garden," Hrabal penned a tribute titled "*Černá lyra*" (The black lyre). "Although [Anna] Akhmatova used to say of herself that she was a black swan," he wrote, "Honza was a white swan with a wounded wing, but with beautiful big and sad eyes and the heart of a *poète maudit*. In noisy company she used to sit like a pearl at the bottom of a chasm, staring with a squinting eye where the wise rabbis who had survived several pogroms were looking." It is a striking choice of metaphor, but we are in Prague, after all, where even though most of the Jews are long gone, their presence still lingers. Was it a memory of Honza that crossed Bohouš's mind, I wonder, when he told László Szigeti that, in Antonín Dvořák's opera *Rusalka*, it was "as if there was a girl lurking in his [Dvořák's] soul, a young woman with one eye slightly displaced towards the Garden of Eden, like a rabbi's daughter gazing into the very heart of human infinity and human eternity"?[213] "With her," Hrabal continues in "The Black Lyre," "it was as if a sentence from Joyce had risen from the dead . . . in her life and her poems and texts, Honza is a *poète maudit* and Prague should be proud that her Fate, the fate of Honza Krejcarová, is linked with the heart of Europe, Prague."[214]

10

Midcentury Modern

At the turn of the 1950s and '60s of the last century I condemned the terrible, to me utterly incomprehensible so-called political trials, completely shocked but still captive to their ideology. I mainly wanted to prove to my persecutors, but to myself as well, that I was completely "innocent." Only, was this really so? Did I not have a share in these unforgivable events, be it only to the smallest extent, too?

—LENKA REINEROVÁ[1]

National Artists

A photograph snapped sometime in the 1930s catches Vítězslav Nezval, Karel Teige, and Roman Jakobson horsing around in the swimming pool of the modernist villa Jiří Kroha designed for himself in Brno. The image gains its weight, as photographs often do, from what happened afterward. We already know Jakobson's and Teige's postwar fates. Kroha and Nezval were headed in the opposite direction. So were plenty of others who had been critical of KSČ cultural policy before the war, including Jakobson's Prague Linguistic Circle colleague Jan Mukařovský (rector of Charles University from 1948 to 1954) and Nezval's old pal Emil Burian (director of the Czechoslovak Army Theater, as the revived D Theater became from 1951 to 1955, as well as a parliamentary representative for Kladno). Ra was not the only wartime avant-garde group whose members parted ways after Victorious February. Group 42 also split in 1948. Jindřich Chalupecký and Jan Kotík strongly opposed socialist realism. "Paintings and sculptures created out of political oppression and under pressure do not even have value as artifacts," wrote Kotík later. "They are only a document of organized lies and testimony to the truth of the saying that 'where art is oppressed, people are oppressed too.'"[2] But František Hudeček, František Gross, Karel Souček, and Jan Smetana all found ways to accommodate the new regime. So did Jiří Kotalík, who wound up as director of the National Gallery from 1967 to 1990. A consummate survivor, Kotalík did his best to champion the modernist cause whenever he could and kept his head down when he couldn't.[3] We encountered Hudeček's "Jáchymov—Cradle of the Atomic Age" postage stamp earlier. It was one of many he designed. Marie Judlová describes Gross, who had no problem adapting his favored industrial motifs to socialist realist demands, as "the most tragic example" of artists who "gave up their internal freedom too lightly."[4] He became a leading functionary in the Artists' Union SČSVU. When the painter Jiří Načeradský smiled at the idea of a socialist art, Gross reportedly responded: "Do you have something against peace?"[5]

Jiří Kroha was one of interwar Czechoslovakia's leading modern architects and a well-known figure in the interwar Prague and Brno avant-garde. As a young man he painted the cubist murals for the Montmartre Café, where Jaroslav Hašek and Egon Erwin Kisch partied. In 1921 he was elected to the committee of Socialistická scéna (Socialist stage), whose eponymous magazine he also edited. Josef Hora, Marie Majerová, Helena Malířová, Ivan Olbracht, and S. K. Neumann—all part of the Seven, those writers expelled from the KSČ in 1929 for criticizing Gottwald's "Bolshevization" of the party—were colleagues in the same organization, whose objective was to create "a new, modern theatrical art . . . a new truly popular theater, in the spirit and truth of our times . . . that would provide a warm and sunny home to all working people in the evenings."[6] Jiří and his wife spent six weeks in the Soviet Union in 1930, where they met Vladimir Tatlin, the Vesnin brothers, and other avant-garde Soviet architects. "From this time," recalled Karel Honzík, "his intensive political activity began. I see him in my memory, lecturing in the Metro Café in his famously excited way. He points to the east so suggestively that the audience almost graphically see how the socialist land is rising to the skies."[7] A lecture called "Today's Russia," together with some injudicious remarks at a KSČ meeting where Kroha "publicly incited against the democratic-republican state form,"[8] landed him with a three-month jail sentence, and he lost his post at Brno Technical University in 1934. Le Corbusier and Auguste Perret were among those who signed a petition for his reinstatement, and Jiří was allowed to return to teaching in 1937.

Before his suspension Kroha worked with his students on the *Sociologický fragment bydlení* (Sociological fragment of living),[9] which was exhibited in

FIGURE 10.1. Vítězslav Nezval, Karel Teige, and Roman
Jakobson (left to right) in the swimming pool at Jiří Kroha's
Brno villa, 1933. Photographer unknown. From Rea
Michalová, *Karel Teige: Captain of the Avant-garde*,
Prague, 2018.

Brno in 1933 and at the Clam-Gallas Palace in Prague the next year. It was a
masterpiece of agitprop sociology. How time was spent in the household by
men and women, distance to work, men's and women's social circles, bodily
hygiene, infant mortality, "sexual function," and leisure, art, and entertainment
in the home, were among the elements compared and contrasted according to
social class and presented on large colorful panels montaged with images from
Pestrý týden, Žijeme, Hvězda (Star), and other popular magazines.[10] Stripped of
his professorship again under the second republic, Kroha was arrested by the
Gestapo on 1 September 1939 and spent a little over a year in Dachau and Buchenwald. Red Cross pressure helped secure his release on health grounds, and for
the rest of the occupation he lived under close police surveillance in Brno.

Before the war Jiří had somewhat hyperbolically described the "mortification of the free creative and critical intellect" in the USSR as "the greatest spiritual degradation of the individual in history" and condemned S. K. Neumann's polemics against modern art in *Tvorba* as "the naivest kowtowing any Czech intellectual has ever performed."[11] But when liberation came, he had no doubt where his loyalties lay. He coordinated cultural activities for the Brno national committee before being appointed dean of the architecture faculty of Brno Technical University in October 1945. In November 1948 he was named the university's rector. He became only the second architect to be given the title of National Artist the same year.

Kroha directed one of the first large public cultural events to take place after Victorious February, the *Slovanská zemědělská výstava* (Slavic Agricultural Exhibition), which opened at the Výstaviště exhibition grounds in Prague in April 1948. The choice of venue was a significant one: Bedřich Münzberger's Industrial Palace had been built for the Jubilee Exhibition of 1891 and used again in the Czechoslavic [*sic*] Ethnographic Exhibition (*Národopisná výstava českoslovanská*) of 1895, both milestones of national self-assertion.[12] One of the major attractions at the Czechoslavic Ethnographic Exhibition was a reenactment of the Moravian Ride of the Kings through the streets of Prague. The Slavic Agricultural Exhibition was intended to be no ordinary agricultural show but (in Jiří's words) "an exhibition of the new agricultural politics, an exhibition of the great transformations in life and work in our new republic in connection with political and economic changes and with a view to new active Slavic, socialistically motivated cooperation."[13] "Executed in a flamboyant and optimistic style," writes Kimberly Elman Zarecor, "the exhibition evoked not only the figural qualities of Soviet socialist realism, with its romanticization of workers' muscular bodies and quaint peasant garb, but also the fluid lines, bright colors, and amorphous shapes of interwar expressionism and Kroha's own early work."[14] At this point, but not for much longer, it was still possible to exhibit "avant-garde art together with realistic works of the Stalinist type."[15] *Rudé právo* hailed the spectacle as "A Rebirth of Art" in which "two hundred artists portrayed our people from the times of serfdom to the joyful life of today in a comprehensible and contemporary way, mostly to a high artistic standard."[16] Outside the Industrial Palace, in an echo of Jaromír Krejcar's delicate glass poem on the banks of the Seine, stood a new illuminated fountain by Zdeněk Pešánek. This one threw sheer walls of water thirty to fifty meters in the air, and images were projected on them to synchronize with music and poetry readings. The following year Jiří staged the exhibition *Sovětský svaz, náš učitel, náš bratr* (The Soviet Union, Our Teacher, Our Brother) at the Mánes building and gave the Industrial Palace at Výstaviště another spectacular makeover for the Ninth Congress of the KSČ.

Over the next decade Kroha became Czechoslovakia's most visible architect. His ANU (Ateliér národního umělce Jiřího Krohy, or Studio of National Artist Jiří Kroha) designed not only exhibition installations, public buildings, and monuments but also the new town of Nová Dubnica in Slovakia and the Stalingrad housing development in Ostrava. Though Jiří had been a cubist, constructivist, and functionalist in the 1920s and 1930s, in the 1950s he built in a modified neoclassical style that avoided the excesses of Stalinist monumentalism while (he argued) embodying "the humanist character of realistic architectural forms and orders."[17] In this he anticipated later Western postmodernist criticisms of the alleged soullessness of high modernism. ANU was responsible for the renovation of Prague's Strahov Stadium for the 1955 Spartakiáda games. Originally built in 1926 for Sokol's mass gymnastic displays, Strahov had once been the largest sports stadium in the world. In 1945–1946 it was used as a holding pen for Bohemian Germans, just as the Roland-Garros stadium had been for aliens in France in 1939. At the eleventh Sokol jamboree in 1948, the opening parade turned into an anticommunist demonstration. Dozens were arrested, and 15,000 Sokols were purged. During the Nazi occupation 1,135 Sokol members had been executed, 1,979 perished in concentration camps, and 589 died in the Prague Uprising, but what of it?[18] The old patriotic society lost the last vestiges of its independence in December 1952, when it was subsumed under the State Committee for Physical Education and Sport. Beginning in 1955 mass calisthenic displays again took place every five years at Kroha's renovated Strahov Stadium, but they were now named after Spartacus, and their aim was to show "the joyful life in building socialism."[19]

There is a metaphor here for the KSČ's wider program of reducing, reusing, and recycling older symbols, routines, and rituals of Czech identity, especially those of the nineteenth-century national revival. "The entire period of the 1950s was oriented toward maximal semantic reduction to a specific register of themes and methods of arrangement," argues the semiotician Vladimír Macura. But "Spartakiad was exceptional in its monumentality. It became an exercise in which the inhabitants of the country metamorphosed into signs . . . they cast away their uniqueness and non-substitutability and were transformed into mutually exchangeable stones in the overall mosaic."[20] Evidently the message got through, at least to impressionable outsiders in search of something on which to pin their hopes and hang their dreams. Among the guests at the 1955 Spartakiáda was Adolf Hoffmeister's Lisbon drinking companion Fernand Léger, who told Czechoslovak Radio, "My God, I have found a land of people well fed and full of joy."[21] Another celebrity spectator, onetime Dadaist Tristan Tzara, was equally caught up in the spectacle, enthusing, "I feel I am in the very center of a free and joyful people who are conscious of their marvelous prospects."[22]

Otakar Švec's Stalin monument was unveiled on Letná Plain that same year. Jiří Kroha had a hand in that too. Six years earlier, on 19 October 1949, Czech and Slovak artists had gathered in the Old Town Hall to discuss the competition for the monument. "On behalf of Czechoslovak artists," reported *Obrana lidu* (Defense of the people), "rector Ing. Arch. Kroha . . . said that the artists are aware of the magnitude of the assigned task and will spare no effort to fulfil it properly." At the end of the discussion, "Vítězslav Nezval recited his lyrical-epic poem in seven stanzas dedicated to J. V. Stalin on his seventieth birthday."[23] Like Kroha, Nezval—who had been a loyal KSČ member since 1924—became a star in Czechoslovakia's postwar cultural firmament. The poet was recruited "to the service of the state" by Václav Kopecký in 1945, along with Adolf Hoffmeister, František Halas, Ivan Olbracht, and Marie Majerová.[24] Kopecký made him director of the film division of the Ministry of Information, a post he held until 1951. According to Jiří Voskovec, Nezval was "important, affable, very warm toward me" in his new role, "but also full of lavish lies. He obviously enjoyed his power. . . . He played the film magnate and lyrically exhorted: 'You, boys, must do great, beaoooootiful [*krrrrásný*] things. . . . Today everything can be done! It's not like before. It will be beaoooootiful.'"[25] As we saw earlier, in February 1948 Nezval became a member of the action committee in the Syndicate of Czech Writers. He went on to serve on the presidium of the central committee of the Union of Czechoslovak Writers, which replaced the syndicate, until his death. He too was made a National Artist by Klement Gottwald in 1953, a title that was not just honorific but came with a lifetime pension.

Nezval's postwar poetry toed the socialist realist line in much the same way that Sláva, who had several affairs and fathered an illegitimate son by the dancer Olga Jungová in 1954, remained faithful to Františka (aka Fáfinka) Řepová, the woman he married at the party's insistence in 1948 after twenty-two years of unwed cohabitation. His 1948 collection *Velký orloj* (The great astronomical clock) contained paeans not only to Stalin, Gottwald, Kopecký, and Neumann but also to Apollinaire and the Catholic writer Jakub Deml, whose *Zapomenuté světlo* (Forgotten light, 1934) Bohumil Hrabal considered "the very acme of twentieth-century prose."[26] When Deml was put on trial later that year, Nezval's intervention kept him out of prison. "With the lightness typical of him," says Ivan Klíma, Sláva next published "a long servile poem in praise of one of the bloodiest tyrants in history,"[27] the previously mentioned lyrical-epic *Ode to Stalin* (1949). This was followed by *Zpěv míru* (A song of peace, 1950), a celebration of "the happy life of our children, the joyful free work of our adults and the beauty of our nature."[28] Nezval reputedly said of this work, "Well, they wanted it, so I puked it up for them for two hundred thousand crowns."[29] *Z domoviny* (From the homeland, 1951), which takes its title from two duets for violin and piano written by Bedřich Smetana in 1880, was billed as "a poetic expression of the author's memories of a childhood spent in a Moravian village."[30] *Křídla* (Wings, 1952) was advertised as "inspired by the life of the homeland, the building of socialism, [and] the struggle of all progressive people for world peace," but the blurb also promised "a cycle of lyrical, personal confessions by the author, his enthusiastic celebration of the beauties of his native region, a farewell ballad to his dead mother and greetings to his dead fellow-poets (K. Biebl and F. Halas)."[31] It fails to mention that the "greeting" to Biebl, first published in *Lidové noviny*, was "Kost'a, why didn't you at least pick up the phone?"—Nezval's anguished response to his friend's suicide to escape his fear of the leather coats on the stairs.

The aged Petr Bezruč, the fiery social poet we first encountered in the context of *The Nation to Its Artists* exhibition, thought the verses devoted to Biebl and Halas "exquisite."[32] After 1918 Bezruč's *Silesian Songs* was frequently reprinted, but the author withdrew into reclusive retreat in the small town of Kostelec na Hané near Přerov in Moravia. Bezruč was named National Artist in 1945, the first living (and second ever) recipient of the newly created title.[33] Nezval visited him in Kostelec in March 1952, and the two men struck up a warm relationship. The ancient P. B., as Bezruč signed himself, was glad to see that Sláva's "Moravian skin still hasn't fallen off . . . after you have lived for so many years on the Vltava." He read the seven books of poetry Nezval brought him three times, "as is the wont of a hundred-year-old man if he wants to understand a book well."[34] He considered *Manon* "excellent"—he knew Abbé Prévost's original—but that didn't stop him from suggesting improvements.[35] When Nezval's father died in the summer of 1957, Bezruč sent him a brief but tender note of condolence:

† Bohumil Nezval.
Choc jsem starečka neznal,
sdílím s Vámi tichý žal.

FIGURE 10.2. Otakar Švec's Stalin monument under construction, 1954. The banner translates: "Our task must be fulfilled by 28 October 1954." Photographer unknown. From Hana Píchová, *The Case of the Missing Statue*, Prague, 2014.

The couplet translates as: "Though I didn't know the old man, I share with you a quiet grief."[36] Bezruč died in the hospital in Olomouc less than a year later on 17 February 1958. He was ninety. Nezval followed him shortly before midnight on 6 April 1958. He was fifty-seven.

It was an untimely death, and tributes poured in from, among many others, Ladislav Štoll ("It was like lightning from a blue sky, when the news came on Easter Monday. The poet of our people, the poet immensely close to us, had died"), Jan Mukařovský ("One of the greatest Czech lyricists of this century has gone. And also one of the greatest lyricists of our time, whose name was pronounced in the same breath as the names of Pablo Neruda and Nazim Hikmet"), and Milan Kundera ("I cannot shake off the feeling that with him has gone an entire monumental epoch in Czech culture").[37] Jiří Kotalík recalled Nezval's closeness to art and artists since his Devětsil days, citing Sláva's friendships with Štyrský, Toyen, Josef Šíma, and Emil Filla. Kotalík was also careful to emphasize the poet's "longstanding, ceaselessly renewed relationship to the painting of Jan Slavíček—the still lifes, landscapes, and Prague views," and his admiration for "the sunny artistic work of Ludvík Kuba," an older folk song collector and landscape painter favored by the regime.[38] The socialist realist grip was beginning to slacken by then. But not too much: the biography in the same obituary issue of *Literární noviny* discusses Nezval's Devětsil years and "close friendships" with "Jiří Wolker, Konstantin Biebl, Vladislav Vančura and others," without mentioning Štyrský and Toyen or, most significantly, Karel Teige, and it (preposterously) omits the name of André Breton when listing Nezval's Parisian friends "Paul Éluard, Pablo Picasso, Tristan Tzara, [and] later [Louis] Aragon." Surrealism, which Nezval did more to introduce to the Czech Lands than anybody else, merits just one sentence: "In the year 1934 Nezval founded and led the Group of Czech Surrealists, which he dissolved in 1938."[39]

Nezval's body lay in state in the House of Artists (Dům umělců), as the Rudolfinum had been renamed, from 9:00 on the morning of 10 April 1958 until 1:00 in the afternoon. There was an unseasonal blanket of snow on the Rudolfinum roof, but the sun was shining. The coffin was guarded by "pioneers, members of the people's militia, artists and representatives of the people" as solemn music filled the concert hall.[40] Vladimír Šmeral (Grandpa Cowboy/De Grieux) and Marie Burešová (Manon) recited Nezval's poems. Václav Kopecký led off the orations at 3:00 p.m., after which the national anthem rang out and the funeral procession set off along the embankment to the Mánes building and thence to Vyšehrad Cemetery.[41] "The whole nation moans with grief over this heavy, irreplaceable loss," said Kopecký.[42] Not Jiří Kolář. The poet had seen his book *Roky ve dnech* (Years in days) pulped in 1949 and spent nine months in prison in 1952 after the StB discovered the manuscript of his "collage-diary" *Prometheova játra* (Prometheus's liver, 1950) during a search of Václav Černý's house. The police offered not to prosecute if Jiří agreed to become an informer, but he refused.[43] He was not allowed to publish for much of the 1950s. That afternoon Kolář was sitting at his usual table in the Café Slavia on the corner of Národní Avenue and Smetana Embankment with his old Group 42 buddy Kamil Lhoták, the writer Josef Hiršal, and the young translator Jan Zábrana. In his diary Zábrana recalled:

> When the beginning of the procession with the coffin began to pass under the windows . . . I got up to go and watch the funeral. Kolář said to me: "Are you going to have a look, kid, at how they bury this carrion? This informer rat, who made a career when other poets were sitting in jail or unable to publish, this self-regarding asshole who called the cops on the young guys?

Yeah, off you go." . . . At the time Kolář's anger, this abusing of the dead, did not seem at all improper or distasteful. At the time of his passing the dead man was universally despised, he betrayed solidarity with everyone, he saved only his own skin in a time of arrests, imprisonment, and executions, he was willing to pay any price for his own salvation, he removed the names of former friends who had fallen into disfavor from his books (Teige, Jakobson, tens of others).[44]

Kolář later denied saying any such thing, adding, "Don't forget, I remembered that Nezval had after all defended Deml."[45] Zábrana recorded the conversation in his diary in 1976, eighteen years after the event, so his memory might well have misled him. But such sentiments were widely held at the time and persist in some quarters to this day.

Ivan Klíma, whose dissident credentials are impeccable, offers a more nuanced view. With his "unexpectedly degraded poetry," he argues, Nezval "forged for himself a solid shield: none of the Party ideologists could any longer attack the man who had sung the praises of the ruling dictator and fighter for peace." Sláva "probably had no illusions about this work," which was a "tactical maneuver to preserve himself and the whole of his past work." Uniquely, "during the period of the Stalinist darkness he published his entire prewar oeuvre." Klíma recalls, "On that desert that had spread over the Czech book market and engulfed it with socialist-realist literary refuse, Nezval's prewar poetry had the effect of living water, of an unexpected and unbelievable oasis." After Stalin's death, "Nezval did whatever he could to cleanse his dead or rejected friends and once more called for freedom of the artist as an indispensable prerequisite of creative work."[46] There is plentiful evidence that the poet used his position to protect Teige, Seifert, Halas, and others—including Jiří Kolář—whenever he could. When the film mogul Miloš Havel was put on trial after an unsuccessful attempt to flee to Austria in 1949, Nezval testified in his defense.[47] The future president's uncle finally escaped to Munich on a forged passport in 1952, where he opened a restaurant called Zur Stadt Prag.

Zábrana goes on to say that "this feeling of contempt for the dead man in no way altered the fact that the majority of those who pronounced judgment over him were aware that this was one of the greatest Czech poets of the twentieth century."[48] For Petr Král, "not only was Nezval the greatest Czech poet of the interwar years; he also incarnated many of the contradictions of his time, if not of the modern individual in general."[49] Beauty is not necessarily truth, nor truth beauty. Because, after all, you have to live.

An Age-Old Checkerboard of Modernity

We left Adolf Hoffmeister at the point of taking up his post as Czechoslovak ambassador to France in June 1948. The appointment, for which Ada lobbied hard, was right up his alley.[50] He had first visited Paris with his mother as a twenty-year-old in 1922 and liked it so much that he returned once or twice a year until the outbreak of World War II. "Hoffmeister belonged to the great generation of Czech avant-garde artists, he was the most cosmopolitan among them," wrote Milan Kundera in 2016; "he was, so to speak, their foreign minister; and at the same time European culture's ambassador to us."[51] The early 1950s was not the best of times for cosmopolitans. Ada used up another of his nine lives when he was abruptly recalled to Prague in the spring of 1951 and dismissed from the service of the Foreign Ministry. He escaped the show trials, he told the art historian Jiří Šetlík, "by the skin of his teeth."[52] Ada's dismissal was an episode in the ongoing power struggle between the prewar avant-gardists employed in Kopecký's Ministry of Information and the mostly younger, hard-line champions of Soviet-style socialist realism based in the culture and propaganda division of the KSČ's central committee. Kultprop, as it was popularly known, was headed by the journalist Gustav Bareš, who instigated the campaign against Jaroslav Seifert's *Song about Viktorka*. Fortunately for Hoffmeister, Kultprop got caught up in the purge that followed Rudolf Slánský's arrest in November 1951, which (somewhat ironically) resulted in "the removal of the entire radical Stalinist wing led by Gustav Bareš from Czechoslovak cultural politics."[53] Ada kept the chair he had been given in May 1951 in the newly created division of animated and puppet film at UMPRUM and remained Czechoslovakia's delegate to UNESCO and the International PEN Club. Two weeks before Slánský's arrest he entertained the Chilean poet Pablo Neruda and the Mexican muralist David Alfaro Siqueiros (an orthodox communist who once led an armed attack on Trotsky's villa in Mexico City) in the Diamant House on their way home from Moscow, just as he had Vladimir Mayakovsky, Alfred Barr, and Le Corbusier in days past.[54]

Over the next few years Hoffmeister did what was necessary to prove his undying loyalty to the socialist camp, of which he remained a leading international cultural ambassador; his caricatures from 1952 include a tight-faced John D. Rockefeller conspiring with a figure of death at the New York Stock Exchange on Black Friday 1929, a bloated John P. Morgan taking a stroll over the bodies of the poor, and blood-red profits from the Korean War raining down on Wall Street.[55] But at home Ada began to probe the limits of the possible. In January 1952 he published an article in *Lidové noviny* titled "*Kritika výtvarné kritiky*" (A critique of art criticism), which provoked a six-month-long debate in *Literární noviny* involving Antonín Pelc, Otakar Mrkvička, and Ladislav Štoll, among others. Ada made sure that he never questioned socialist realism as "an artistically and politically binding program of creation," but he condemned "the authoritarian, vulgarizing, and sectarian attitude" of "unscientific and un-concrete art criticism" that "lashes out with mere ideological programs and phrases, can't tell quality work from kitsch . . . and doesn't know how to distinguish between monumentality and the snares of phony pathos." He went on to defend "the traditions of Czech modern art during the first half of the twentieth century," praising Rudolf Kremlička's representations of washerwomen and the *češství* (Czech national feeling) of Václav Špála's paintings and drawing attention to the "social art produced under the direct influence of [Jiří] Wolker" by Alois Wachsmann and František Muzika.[56]

While genuflecting to the ideological powers that be ("art criticism limps far behind literary criticism and awaits its Štoll"),[57] Ada was defending specifically *artistic* values against crude politicization. A pithy epigram he published on 30 April 1953 in *Výtvarná práce* went to the heart of the matter:

I know that time changes tomorrow into yesterday,
Art, however, never changes into non-art.
But it's not clear to quite a few critics up till now
That non-art doesn't change into art any sooner.[58]

Štoll supported Hoffmeister's critique of "sectarianism" while continuing to warn against the dangers of "liberalism."[59] In July 1952 SČSVU elected a new central committee that distanced itself from the "vulgarization and undemocratic coercive methods" of the previous leadership,[60] which (it was now universally acknowledged) represented exactly the kind of "left-wing communism" Lenin had characterized as an "infantile disorder."[61] Having expunged "the so-called second center, which tried to undermine our art with sectarian and doctrinaire methods," the ranks closed again into "a broad front of creative artists."[62] It was an important—if limited—victory. Cubism and surrealism remained officially off-limits. But a range of what Vojtěch Lahoda calls "creeping modernisms" was able to shelter under the realist umbrella.[63] At the Tenth KSČ Congress in June 1954 Václav Kopecký criticized "schematism in art without poetic beauty," defended the right of artists to their individual differences, and went so far as to argue that "nobody has a patent on socialist realism, for socialist realism is a creative method." Articles in *Výtvarná práce* began to cautiously reconsider the relation of form and content with reference to the work of Filla, Kremlička, the sculptor Otto Gutfreund, and other earlier Czech modernists.[64]

On 5 March 1953 Joseph Stalin died in the Kremlin. Klement Gottwald followed him to the grave nine days later. Czechs joked that the "first workers' president" succumbed to the Moscow flu caught at the generalissimo's funeral, but the cause of death was a ruptured aorta resulting from untreated syphilis aggravated by alcoholism. The hysteria of the moment is frozen in Jan Lukas's *Obálky (Zemřel Stalin a Gottwald)* (Covers: Stalin and Gottwald died, 1953), a closely cropped photograph of a Prague newsstand displaying magazines, every single one of which carries a black-edged portrait of Stalin or Gottwald on its cover. Not only *Socialist World* but also *Boating Sports, Innovator and Inventor, Reader, Equestrian Shooting and Fencing, Healing, National Insurance, Basketball and Volleyball, Work of the Pioneers, Airplane Modeler, Cycling, Tennis, Skittles, Handball, Sphere of the Stars, Christian Woman, Musical Views,* and the women's magazine *Vlasta*—among many others—were united in grief. It is hard to think of a better image of what Czechs call *totalita,* a political regime distinguished by its attempt to control all aspects of social life. Lukas, says Marie Klimešová, conceived *Covers* as a "subversive found collage, capturing the absurdity of the cult of personality by documentary means."[65] The same deadpan surreality is exhibited in his *Pětiletka—fasada* (Five Year Plan—façade, 1953), a close-up of the exterior of a building festooned with portraits of party functionaries, hammers and sickles, and other communist bling. These are the kinds of "symptomatic details" that Egon Bondy believed "amplified the absolute debility" and condensed "the deformed mythology" of the era.[66]

Antonín Zápotocký succeeded Gottwald as Czechoslovak president, and the Slovak party leader Viliam Široký replaced Zápotocký as prime minister. The position of KSČ president, which Gottwald had held since 1945, was abolished, and Antonín Novotný became the party's first secretary. While Zápotocký had some mildly liberal leanings, Novotný was a Stalinist hard-liner. The son of a poor bricklayer and a mechanic by trade, he had been a member of the KSČ since 1921. He worked in the resistance in Prague until he was arrested in September 1941 and spent the rest of the war in Mauthausen. The new leadership went ahead with a planned currency devaluation in May 1953, which wiped out most people's savings and provoked the first public protests since 1948. Under pressure from Moscow the KSČ adopted a "new course" in October 1953 that included less emphasis on heavy industry, price cuts on many consumer goods, and a promise that all those who wished to leave collective farms could do so.

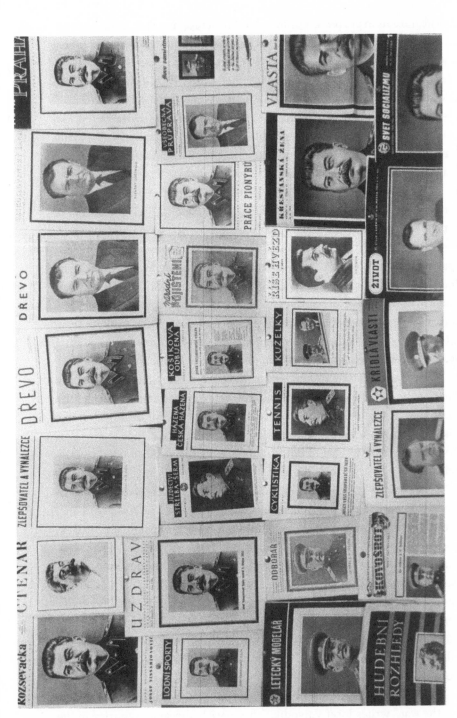

FIGURE 10.3. Jan Lukas, *Covers: Stalin and Gottwald Died*, 1953. From Marie Klimešová, *Roky ve dnech: české umění 1945–1957*, Prague, 2010. Courtesy of Helena Lukas, © Jan Lukas heirs.

The liberalization proved to be limited. In April 1954 members of the "subversive group of bourgeois nationalists in Slovakia" were belatedly brought to trial and received prison sentences ranging from ten years (Laco Novomeský) to life (Gustáv Husák). Collectivization resumed in 1955. Khrushchev's denunciation of Stalin's "cult of personality" in his secret speech to the Twentieth Congress of the CPSU in February 1956—which was soon leaked, translated, and broadcast by Radio Free Europe and other Western radio stations—could not have come at a more awkward moment. The Stalin monument had been officially unveiled on Letná less than a year earlier, on May Day 1955.

At the Second Congress of the Czechoslovak Writers' Union in April 1956, Jaroslav Seifert and his fellow poet František Hrubín called for freedom of artistic expression and the release of imprisoned writers. Prague students assembled at Albertov the same month and drafted a lengthy list of demands that included not only an end to compulsory lectures on Marxism-Leninism but also "a public review of the Slánský trial and other political trials," "a guarantee of rightful political punishment for persons who tolerated illegal procedures during interrogations," and "amnesty for convicted persons."[67] In an effort to defuse tensions, the traditional *majáles* student carnival, banned since 1948, was reinstated, providing an opportunity for satirical cosplay in both Bratislava (where students heaved a coffin labeled "academic freedom" into the Danube) and Prague.[68] A few students were expelled, and the revolt soon fizzled out. At a central committee meeting in June, Novotný made it clear that discussion of Khrushchev's revelations was over and it was time to move on. The October riots in Poland (which brought the previously purged and imprisoned Władysław Gomułka back to power) and the Hungarian Uprising (which was crushed by a Soviet invasion in November) were warnings of what could happen if things were allowed to get out of hand. The KSČ weathered the storm much more easily than its counterparts in Budapest and Warsaw, possibly because—though many Czechs would consider it heresy to say so— Victorious February was more of a popular revolution to begin with and the party still enjoyed substantial support, especially among the working class. As late as 1962, 17.8 percent of the adult population remained KSČ members, compared with 7.6 percent in Poland and 7.1 percent in Hungary.[69] When Zápotocký died in November 1957, Novotný became president, reuniting the offices of head of state and head of party. Stalin continued to gaze over Prague from his perch on Letná.

And what of Ada? "Though Hoffmeister was 'a tourist against his will' during the war," writes Josef Vojvodík, "after 1948 he became 'a tourist' in the service of the new regime, one of the chosen ones who were able to travel abroad and cross the otherwise impassible borders of socialist reality and acquaint the reader with his experiences of foreign cultures."[70] Despite popular perceptions, the Iron Curtain never succeeded in hermetically sealing the country from the outside world, but for the overwhelming majority of Czechs, it might as well have: the border was guarded not only by barbed wire fences and machine gun towers but also by difficult-to-obtain exit visas; censorship of newspapers, magazines, and books; jamming of foreign radio broadcasts; and a nonconvertible currency. Travel restrictions eased significantly only in the 1960s. Hoffmeister belonged to a highly privileged minority. Together with Marie Majerová, Marie Burešová, and Pavel Kohout, he traveled to Mongolia and China from September to December 1953 as part of a Czechoslovak cultural delegation that participated in National Day celebrations led by Mao Zedong, met Chinese writers and artists, and toured in a "friendship train" that made stops in Shanghai, Nanjing, Guangzhou, and other cities. He returned to Beijing and Shanghai for a two-month "study visit" in 1955. His *Pohlednice z Číny* (Postcards from China) and *Kuo-cha*, "a travel reportage on Chinese painting," came out in 1954. The "beautiful stones from the viewpoint of form" that Chinese people place in their gardens, Ada innocently remarks in *Kuo-cha*, "could be sculptures by Hans Arp, Brancusi, Henry Moore, Alexander Calder, Giacometti, Lipchitz, or others. But I ask myself, is nature formalistic? No chisel worked on these stones. The artist didn't touch them."[71] The dig would not have been missed by those accustomed to reading between the lines, but the censors let it pass. In May 1956, a few months before Gamal Abdel Nasser nationalized the Suez Canal and provoked the Suez crisis, Hoffmeister took part in another cultural delegation, this time to Egypt, which was an old passion of his. His *Vyhlídka z pyramid* (A view from the pyramids), "about the new youth of the oldest culture in the world," came out the next year. In December 1956 the road show moved to India, where Ada made sure not to miss Le Corbusier's modernist Chandigarh.

Fresh from organizing an exhibition of Czech medieval art at the Musée des Arts Décoratifs in Paris, Ada flew to Tokyo in September 1957 to take part in the Twenty-Ninth International PEN Club Congress, where he renewed his friendship with John Steinbeck and made the acquaintance of Alberto Moravia and John Dos Passos. Where else would he stay but at Frank Lloyd Wright's Imperial Hotel?[72] *Made in Japan: cestopisná reportáž o zemi, kde vybuchla první atomová puma* (Travel reportage from the land where the first atomic bomb exploded) appeared the next year, with illustrations whose geometric style came close to op art. They formed the core of Hoffmeister's extensive solo exhibition at the Československý spisovatel gallery in November–December 1958. "When I illustrated *Made in Japan*," Ada said, "I had in mind the architecture of the black-and-white Japanese type. A sort of age-old checkerboard of modernity."[73] It is a strikingly oxymoronic formulation, confounding Western conceptions and cartographies of the modern. How much Hoffmeister was influenced by his friend Bedřich Feuerstein's love of girls driving cars in kimonos I don't know, but while he was in the land where Little Boy and Fat Man had so recently upended the age-old checkerboard, Ada had an unexpected brush with his avant-garde past. "The world is small and coincidences like to play games with people," he observes. Hoffmeister and friends had just ordered lunch at a hotel by a lake in Hakone, a beautiful spot near Mount Fuji, when into the dining room strode "a tall, conspicuously erect, burly man and two ladies, who sat down at the table next to us":

> It was the architect Antonín Raymond. The self-assured, world-renowned seventy-year-old with his French wife. . . . He asked after names, the names of my friends, my generation.
>
> Karel Teige, Josef Havlíček, Karel Honzík, Jaromír Krejcar, Bohuslav Fuchs, Evžen Linhart, Jaroslav Fragner etc. . . . In Tokyo he has a Japanese house that he designed himself. Simple and modern. A wooden house. Japanese ingenuity, American practicality and Czech artistic sensibility all come together here. . . . He himself—and this is his American modesty— believes he is the only global Czech architect.[74]

It is doubtful that even Hoffmeister could have gotten away with publishing these words just two or three years earlier—for all sorts of reasons. In the words of Vojtěch Lahoda, "A time of thaw, pre-spring, perhaps just an echo of melting had arrived: it was projected into some artistic activities. The terminally ill patient was reviving."[75]

Art of Another Kind

In 1955 *Výtvarná práce* published open letters from sixty-nine young artists and 179 UMPRUM students criticizing the official SČSVU line on socialist realism and modern art.[76] The ensuing debates led to the establishment of a Galerie mladých (Gallery of Youth). The following year the SČSVU statutes were revised, and for the first time since 1949, "creative groups" were allowed to form under the umbrella of the union. The Šmidrové, a coterie of art and music students, mounted an unofficial *Exhibition for One Evening* on Prague's Střelecký ostrov (Shooter's Island) in the Vltava on 5 April 1957, and the entertainment included a poetry reading by a young Václav Havel.[77] Taking their name from a staple character in Czech puppet theater—a stupid policeman—they refused to wear "the servile hat of prefabricated norms," preferring "Dadaistic performances of practical jokes and slapstick comedy."[78] Máj 57 (May 57), whose members included Richard Fremund, Libor Fára, Robert Piesen, Stanislav Podhrázský, and Zbyněk Sekal, was the first creative group officially allowed to publicly exhibit its work, which was shown in the Municipal House in June 1957 under the title *Mladé umění* (Young art). František Dvořák and Ladislav Dydek wrote that the group's work "arises out of free and purely artistic impulses and in opposition to art that is determined by extra-artistic literary dogmatism."[79] "After ten years," Dvořák proclaimed in the exhibition catalog, this was "our first collective exhibition selected solely from the point of view of fine art," and its object was to make an impact "by autonomous visual means."[80] Podhrázský's sculpture *Nohy* (Legs, 1948) was vandalized on the opening day.

Exhibitions of the creative groups Trasa 54 (Route 54) and Pět (The Five) followed. Other groups like Brno 57, Skupina G, Proměna (Change), UB 12, and Etapa (Stage) emerged over the next few years. Not all were artistic rebels or critics of the regime. Adolf Hoffmeister, Vincenc Makovský, Antonín Pelc, Karel Svolinský, and Jiří Trnka were among the artists who got together in 1960 as the Mánes Creative Group (not to be confused with the old Mánes Artists' Society, which ceased activities after 1949 and was formally dissolved in 1956), while Group 42 veterans František Gross, František Hudeček, and Ladislav Zívr were the best-known members of Skupina Radar, which practiced what some Czech critics have cruelly characterized as a "tamed modernism."[81] The Radar Group refused to join the Blok tvůrčích skupin (Bloc of Creative Groups) formed in the early 1960s to defend creative groups' interests against the SČSVU bureaucracy. Some significant artists who had been unable to show their work earlier in the decade were now able to do so: Richard Fremund, Robert Piesen, Jan Kotík, and Libor Fára all had solo shows in 1956–1957. Václav Tikal, who, like Kotík and Fára, was a member of the semilegal surrealist Circle of Five Objects, exhibited his paintings and drawings created from 1941 to 1957 at the Československý spisovatel gallery in January 1958. The catalog was the first text Vratislav Effenberger had been able to legally publish for ten years. A few months earlier Effenberger had included his poem *"Přízrak třetí války"* (The phantom of World War III), illustrated with photographs by Emila Medková, in the third of the surrealists' samizdat *Object* anthologies.

One of the most important artistic events of the late 1950s was the exhibition *Zakladatelé moderního českého umění* (Founders of Modern Czech Art), curated by the young art historians Miroslav Lamač and Jiří Padrta at the House of Art in Brno in October 1957; it was reprised the following spring at the Riding School of Prague Castle. This was the first time most of these early twentieth-century works by members of the Eight and the Group of Fine Artists had been seen by anybody much younger than thirty. The exhibition had an enormous impact on young artists. The curators' disclaimer, "We don't have to agree with this history today, but we must comprehend it,"[82] did not protect the exhibit from being savaged in the popular magazine *Květy* (Blooms), which juxtaposed reproductions of paintings from the show with familiar nineteenth-century Czech paintings by Josef Mánes and others alongside quotations from Lenin, Gottwald, Neumann, and Zdeněk Nejedlý.[83] The Nazis had used a similar technique in the catalog for the notorious *Degenerate Art* exhibition of 1937.[84] Although most other reviews of *Founders of Modern Czech Art* were more positive, they were careful to emphasize that the works displayed should not be seen as "a program for the younger generation because our societal life today is different from that in which The Eight were working."[85] To his credit, Jiří Kotalík was not afraid to suggest that the exhibition had "extraordinary current relevance."[86] Despite the brouhaha, the sky didn't fall, and a standing exhibition of the National Gallery's collection of modern art opened in Prague City Library in April 1959. The first photographic nude to be seen in many years made her appearance in the January 1957 issue of *Československá fotografie* (Czechoslovak photography).[87]

Later that year Franz Kafka's writings resurfaced for the first time since 1948 when *Světová literatura* (World literature), a magazine founded in 1956 and edited by Josef Škvorecký, carried Kafka's story "The Burrow," along with an introductory essay by its translator Pavel Eisner. Eisner's translation of *The Trial*—the first into Czech—was published the next year. Czech translations of *Amerika* and Franz's "Letter to His Father" had to wait until 1962. Kafka may have slipped past the KSČ watchdogs, but Škvorecký's *Zbabělci* (*The Cowards*) did not. Written in 1948 when Josef was twenty-four, it had been lying in his desk drawer for a decade. His debut novel presents a distinctly antiheroic picture of the uprising against the Germans during the last week of the war. Škvorecký recalls, "under the impression that I was an avant-garde author of the same kind as Jirka [Jiří] Kolář, [Jan] Hanč, or Hrabal," Jindřich Chalupecký asked him to provide a typescript of *The Cowards* (which existed only as a handwritten text in thirty-five school exercise books). "And the result? Pitiful. *I'm sorry I made you do such pointless work. The Cowards is not literature.*"[88] Posterity has begged to differ. Ivan Klíma catches what made *The Cowards* a bombshell when it was finally published in 1958 by Československý spisovatel:

> Škvorecký, like Salinger [in *Catcher in the Rye*], chose a teenager to be the narrator, a keen jazz fan. His hero, if for no other than for generational reasons, sees the entire attempt at an uprising against the already essentially defeated German army as an incompetent farce, an escapade. Although he takes part in the revolution and is even taken prisoner, then liberated, whereupon he destroys a German tank, his unfulfilled longing for love is more important for him. Events which were officially or in general presented as being among the principal moments in modern Czech history thus lose all their glory. This vision of the young hero deprives these events of their pathos by giving priority to his amorous longing. An ironic distance, long, jabbering enamored dialogues, and a seemingly cynical view of all that is sacrosanct, helped Škvorecký use dramatic historic events in the fiber of the novel in such a way as to avoid cliché.[89]

"And so it exploded," recounts Škvorecký. "For two whole weeks, day after day, I was pummeled by a succession of reviewers; some indicated sinister connections with Tito's Yugoslavia, and Radio Free Europe. One day the President himself spoke about me at a private meeting of Private Secretaries." Josef lost his job at *Světová literatura*. So did "the director, the editor-in-chief, and a few other editors" at Českoskoslovenský spisovatel, "as well as Jiří Lederer, a reviewer for an evening paper, who dared support my book in a short review."[90] *The Cowards* was withdrawn from the market and was not reissued until 1964. Škvorecký feared arrest. "Obviously others shared that fear. There were the classic phenomena of people crossing to the other side of the street or developing a sudden interest in the noticeboard of the Union of Friends of the USSR and the like. . . . On New Year 1958, when they were beginning to speak of me in Prague as an interesting new author, I received almost 300 New Year cards. On New Year 1959 just seventeen."[91]

In the visual arts, party ideologues fought a rearguard action that lasted well into the 1960s. Lamač and Padrta planned follow-up shows to *Founders of Modern Czech Art* on the art of the 1920s and 1930s, but in the event, only the second exhibition took place in Brno, and it was stopped from traveling to Prague.

That their catalog essay contrived to discuss Devětsil at length without once mentioning Karel Teige or Toyen speaks volumes.[92] A major exhibition titled *Umění mladých výtvarníků Československa 1958* (The Art of Young Artists of Czechoslovakia 1958) took place in Brno, but once again the Prague reprise was canceled and the catalog was withheld from publication. The larger exhibition spaces continued to show only officially approved art. Sympathetic discussions of the work of "the young" appeared in *Výtvarná práce*, *Výtvarné umění*, and *Květen* (May), a new monthly magazine launched by the Writers' Union in September 1956,[93] but commentary as a whole remained largely negative, especially in the popular press. Ludmila Vachtová was able to introduce the work of Fremund, Piesen, Kotík, Istler, and Medek to Czech audiences in 1956 in *Tvar* (Form),[94] but only because, she told an interviewer in 1999, "it was a magazine for applied art, and therefore in those days nobody paid it much attention and none of the comrades complained about anything."[95] May 57's *Young Art* exhibition at the Municipal House met with a much rougher press reception. *Tvorba* ridiculed the "surrealist hemorrhages" of Podhrázský's and Sekal's "lifeless, stylized canvases."[96] Otakar Mrkvička— whose 1923 montaging of skyscrapers, ocean liners, airplanes, and a red star onto Wenceslas Square for the cover of Jaroslav Seifert's *Sheer Love* was a classic of poetist design—acknowledged that the May 57 artists were "neglected and silenced" during the period of "dogmatism." He nevertheless complained that the exhibition had been mounted "out of spite, in defiance of everything that has happened here."[97] Only a visit by President Zápotocký saved the May 57 show from being taken down.[98] *Květen* was suppressed in June 1959, a casualty of a campaign against "revisionism."

Jiří Padrta considered Vladimír Boudník "one of our most original creators," ranking him alongside Jackson Pollock, while Zdenek Primus believes "the uncompromising visual quality" and "absence of content [*bezobsahovost*]" of Boudník's prints "is without parallel in Bohemia or the world."[99] But at the time when Vladimír was "unlock[ing] the metaphysical from the banal,"[100] hardly anybody knew of the existence of his works apart from his friends and his coworkers at the ČKD factory in Vysočany, where he had been employed as a toolmaker and draftsman since the early 1950s. It was there that he developed what he called his "structural graphics," pulling the delicately colored abstract compositions from metal plate matrices into which he had welded, hammered, or glued broken files, nuts and bolts, sand, and other debris from the factory floor. "Vladimír would become excited over a cement mixer and its bowels, a pot of hot tar, a jackhammer, an acetylene tank with hose and torch quietly purring and glowing blue, a metalworker's solder, a blowtorch, the white ice covering a fish counter, a housepainter and the splatters of paint on newspaper, dried come stains on his boxers, bloodstains on the sheets," reminisces Bohumil Hrabal. "His prints are the apotheosis of his materialistic worldview."[101] As a reward for being named best worker, Boudník was permitted to exhibit his prints at the ČKD works in 1959—his first independent exhibition. The show was closed a week later because it "lured people away from realism."[102] Here as elsewhere, the undisciplined real has a nasty habit of undercutting the carefully curated simulacra we prefer to believe are reality.

Mikuláš Medek, who had become a hugely respected figure among younger artists, was left out of *The Art of Young Artists of Czechoslovakia 1958*, and his requests to exhibit at the Československý spisovatel gallery were repeatedly turned down.[103] His work was first shown on 21–22 March 1958 in a private exhibition at the Philosophical Faculty of Charles University organized by František Šmejkal and other young art critics, alongside the work of Jan Kotík, Josef Istler, Libor Fára, and others. Medek's first independent exhibition (jointly with Jan Koblasa) took place in August 1963 not in Prague but in Teplice in northwestern Bohemia. Emila Medková had made her solo debut three years earlier in Hradec Králové. When Kotík exhibited at Umělecká beseda's Aleš Hall in 1960, the catalog was banned from publication, and reviews were prohibited. Exhibitions by Jiří Balcar and Robert Piesen were stopped in 1961; Piesen, who was one of only three members of his Jewish family to survive the Holocaust, took the opportunity to slip away during an international exhibition in Zurich in 1965 and immigrated first to Vienna and then to Israel. The Galerie Krzywe Kolo in Warsaw staged a collective exhibition of Polish and Czech abstract art in 1962 under the title *Argumenty 1962* (Arguments 1962) featuring Balcar, Boudník, Istler, Medek, Piesen, Jan Koblasa, and Aleš Veselý, but Istler's first domestic exhibition since 1947, which was scheduled for later that year at the regional museum in Písek, was canceled, even though the catalog had already been printed. When Ludmila Vachtová published an article on Medek, Istler, Koblasa, Kotík, and Zdeněk Sklenář in the Italian magazine *La Biennale di Venezia* in 1961, she was investigated by the StB and fired from *Výtvarné umění*. She got her editorial job back after numerous appeals but was no longer allowed to publish in the magazine.[104]

Jan Koblasa was the initiator of two landmark exhibitions in March and October 1960, both of which were officially invisible at the time. Vladimír Boudník was an invited participant, but all the other artists were a generation

EXPLOSIONALISMVS 1956

Vladimír Boudník

FIGURE 10.4. Vladimír Boudník, *Explosionalism*, 1956, collage, active
graphic, paper, 18.2 by 12 cm, Galerie Ztichlá klika v Praze. From Marie Klimešová,
Roky ve dnech: české umění 1945–1957, Prague, 2010.

younger. *Konfrontace* (Confrontations) *I* and *II*, as the events were called, were privately staged in Jiří Valenta and Aleš Veselý's Libeň and Žížkov studios, respectively, to the accompaniment of records of concrete music by Karlheinz Stockhausen. The works on exhibit emphasized "a new conception of artistic language, which through heavy, almost monochromatic coloring and the raw substance of non-traditional materials and techniques exposed existential feelings of anxiety, skepticism and uncertainty."[105] To anyone expecting art to be representational, these exhibitions were as incomprehensible as *Finnegans Wake*. In the (unpublished) catalog for *Confrontations I*, František Šmejkal described the group's art as "a specifically Czech version of European *informel*"—as Michel Tapié had baptized the formless styles of abstraction prevalent on both sides of the Atlantic in the 1940s and 1950s in *Un art autre* (Art of another kind, 1952).[106] On 17 October 1961 Boudník, Istler, Kotík, Medek, Medková, and Piesen joined forces in Medek's studio with Balcar, Koblasa, Valenta, Veselý, and other younger artists to found a creative group dedicated to abstract art, which they also named Konfrontace. The group's guests included Richard Fremund, Jiří Kolář—who had his small debut exhibition as a visual artist at the Mánes Gallery in June 1962—Zbyněk Sekal, and Václav Tikal. This is verging on a who's who of the leading Czech artists of the day. Yet while 1962 saw a large joint exhibition of the Mánes Creative Group and the Bloc of Creative Groups at the Mánes building initiated by Adolf Hoffmeister and prepared by Jindřich Chalupecký under the title *Jaro 62* (Spring 1962),[107] the Konfrontace group was still not recognized by the SČSVU or permitted to exhibit as a collective.

These inconsistent official responses to "young art" in the 1956–1963 period prefigured the wider political tensions that would eventually explode in the 1968 Prague Spring. But we might stop to ask why *art informel* in particular continued to be anathematized. Part of the answer might lie in the Joycean threat posed by the dissolute aesthetics of the *formless* (*informe*) to any regime that depends on Kundera's clichés of meaning and poverty of message—to any social order, in other words, based on adherence to ideology. Like Jindřich Hořejší's *Hey, Girl!* or Toyen's wartime drawings, the subversiveness of these works lies less in what they *say* than in their refusal to be imprisoned in the corsets of Macura's semantic reduction and mobilized as signs in the first place. They remain singular *things*, unquestionable in their obstinate strangeness, in their irreducible reality, open to infinite interpretations or none at all. Georges Bataille, "surrealism's old enemy from within" (as he called himself), put it this way in "Critical Dictionary," published in his magazine *Documents* in 1929:

FORMLESS. A dictionary would begin starting from the moment when it no longer provided the meanings of words but their jobs. Thus *formless* [*informe*] is not only an adjective having a specific meaning but a term serving to un-class [*déclasser*], requiring in general that every thing has its form. . . . For academics to be satisfied, it would indeed be necessary for the universe to take form. The whole of philosophy has no other aim; it is a question of putting a frockcoat on what exists, a mathematical frockcoat. To affirm on the contrary that the universe resembles nothing at all and is only *formless*, amounts to saying that the universe is something like a spider or a gob of spit.[108]

The Brussels Style

On 17 April 1958, a week after Vítězslav Nezval's funeral in Prague, the first world's fair since World War II opened in Brussels; earlier efforts had been stymied by the Cold War. By the time Expo 58 closed on 19 October, it had drawn eighteen million visitors, eleven million of them foreigners.[109] Among the fairgoers were around six thousand Czechs who had been allowed out for the occasion. Drawing on some of the world's foremost museum collections, the multinational exhibition *Fifty Years of Modern Art* gave younger Czech artists the opportunity to see key works of modern and contemporary Western art, including examples of abstract expressionism and *art informel*. Brussels left its impression on youthful Czech visitors in other ways too. Miroslav Řepa, who later designed the Czechoslovak pavilion for Expo 67 in Montreal but was then in his final year of study at AVU, remembers, "I bought *France-Soir* and Coca-Cola, sat myself down on the square and felt great. We saw the half-naked Brigitte Bardot in the film . . . *And God Created Woman*. We were also in a bar called The Wolf on the Roof, where a Czech emigrant was working, and we saw a striptease for the first time. A visit to a department store filled us with despair. There were an awful lot of such experiences."[110] Modern and forward-looking, Expo 58 picked up the baton dropped by its 1939 predecessor in New York and projected "a message of limitless optimism and a reflection of a society confident in its future and enthusiastic about the future of humanity." Outdoing the Perisphere and Trylon at Flushing Meadows was the Atomium, a 102-meter-high model of atoms in an iron crystal magnified 165 billion times, symbolizing "*a world for a better life for mankind* where this *new world* of never-ending growth was based on faith in technical and scientific progress."[111] The nine stainless-steel spheres linked by tubular walkways became a totem of the city. The Atomium's space-age design has a quaintly dated feel today, like something out of *The Jetsons*. Lucien de Roeck's jaunty anthropomorphic star logo admirably caught the spirit of the fair, whose official slogan was "A balance sheet of the world for a more human world" (*Bilan du monde pour un monde plus humain*).

Even though the Cold War had temporarily quieted after Khrushchev's secret speech, Hiroshima still cast a long shadow. "Developments in science and technique have deeply disturbed the structure of economic and social relations, filling mankind with uneasiness," warned the Expo's organizers.[112] As Bruno Zevi suggested at the time ("Germany pretends to have forgotten the gas chambers and shows us a distinguished face as if to say that technology justifies everything, whether tanks or electric razors") and David Crowley has argued since ("the exhibition grounds at Brussels—organized in the name of progress—only materialized irrational Cold War anxieties"), Expo 58's feelgood, all-lives-matter humanism covered up a multitude of sins.[113] Crowley reminds us of Roland Barthes's critique of another iconic exhibition of that era, the Museum of Modern Art's *Family of Man*, which opened in New York in January 1955 and toured the world for the next eight years. "The Family of Man," explained Edward Steichen in the press release announcing the project, "is planned as an exhibition of photography portraying the universal elements and emotions and the oneness of human beings throughout the world":

> This exhibition will require photographs, made in all parts of the world, of the gamut of life from birth to death with emphasis on the everyday relationships of man to himself, to his family, to the community and to the world we live in: subject matter ranging from babies to philosophers, from the kindergarten to the university, from the child's home-made toys to scientific research, from tribal councils of primitive peoples to the councils of the United Nations. It will require photographs of lovers and marriage and child bearing, of the family unit with its joys, trials and tribulations, its deep rooted devotions and its antagonisms, photographs that reveal the selflessness of mother love.

When the MoMA show hit the Musée National d'Art Moderne in Paris in January 1956, Barthes refused to be swept along by Steichen's "moralized and sentimentalized" narrative. "Everything here," he wrote, "the content and appeal of the pictures, the discourse which justifies them, aims to suppress the determining weight of History: we are held back at the surface of an identity, prevented precisely by sentimentality from penetrating into this ulterior zone of human behavior where historical alienation introduces some 'differences' which we shall here quite simply call 'injustices' ... why not ask the parents of Emmett Till, the young Negro assassinated by the Whites what they think of The Great Family of Man?"[114] You can almost hear Milan Kundera sneering, "The brotherhood of man on earth will be possible only on a basis of kitsch."[115]

The Atomium stood where the Avenue de Belgique met the Avenue du Congo and the Avenue de L'Atomium met the Avenue de L'Urundi. Near its base, occupying a seventeen-acre site dubbed the Congorama, were the Palais du Congo Belge and several pavilions dedicated to mining, agriculture, and other facets of Belgium's activities in its African colonies. Despite the rising tide of anticolonial movements—the Mau Mau revolt (and its brutal British suppression) had convulsed Kenya since 1952, the Algerian war had been raging since 1954, French Morocco had ceased to be French in 1956, and Ghana had become the first black African state to recover its independence from European colonizers just a year earlier in March 1957—the Expo magazine wrote that Belgium would use its displays to advertise its "good work in the vast field of civilizing the African continent ... industrializing native conditions and furthering social development."[116] Part of the spectacle was an "indigenous village" in which Congolese people who had been brought to the fair as part of a cultural exchange "found themselves standing behind a bamboo fence, on live display for Europeans, some of whom made monkey noises to get their attention."[117] This was disturbingly reminiscent of the "human zoo" King Leopold II created for the 1897 Brussels International Exposition in the Palace of the Colonies (now called the Africa Palace) in nearby Tervuren, where 267 Congolese men, women, and children were among the fair's "*fêtes diverses et attractions.*"[118] The Republic of the Congo gained its independence less than two years after Expo 58 closed, on 30 June 1960.

Now that the Third Reich was no more, it was the United States and the Soviet Union that stared each other down on adjacent sites at the eastern end of the Avenue des Nations. Theirs were the largest and most visited pavilions at the fair.[119] Each country played to its strengths. The centerpiece of the Soviet pavilion was a replica of the *Sputnik* satellite launched on 4 October 1957, one field in which the USSR was clearly ahead of the United States. Around half the displays highlighted Soviet prowess in science and technology, industry, and agriculture. Other exhibits showcased free public education, health care, and childcare. All this was ponderously documented in charts and graphs. The American pavilion was more seductive, relying on the power of images rather than the weight of information. The State Department's brief was to convey the "democratic vitality and romance" of American capitalism.[120] On entering, spectators encountered "a huge map of the United States hanging from the ceiling, under which were a variety of objects . . . an antique model-T automobile, the first Edison lightbulb, early images of Mickey Mouse, a saddle and pair of cowboy boots, a section of a redwood tree, a tumbleweed, a gold nugget, an Idaho potato, and automobile license plates from every state."[121] Visitors could wander a Main Street with "shopfronts, traffic signs, postboxes, a newsstand above which flashed news bulletins, and a drugstore with a soda fountain selling ice cream and soft drinks"; play bridge against a computer; listen to hi-fis in soundproofed rooms; watch color TV; dig into hamburgers, hot dogs, and clam chowder at the Brass Rail restaurant; and marvel at the thickness of the Sunday edition of the New York Times. Models clad in ready-to-wear fashions sauntered among the appliances in the "Islands of Living" that purported to show "the living habits of Americans through the furnishings and appurtenances of their daily surroundings" before descending the catwalk to the pool below.

Be it "out of admiration or envy," reported Jan Werich in Literární noviny, viewers were always impressed by the Soviet pavilion, whereas "people came out of the American pavilion puzzled and confused. In all languages they asked themselves: what do they actually want to show us?"[122] Given the years he spent in the States, the comic should have known better (and likely did). They were advertising the American dream. Outside the main building, Disney's Circarama offered "a 360-degree film tour across the United States from the New York harbor to the Golden Gate Bridge," and a display titled "Unfinished Business" addressed racial inequality, housing shortages, and other unresolved social problems. Opposition from southern congressmen led to closure of the latter display—the crisis that had erupted when Arkansas governor Orval Faubus mobilized the National Guard to prevent nine African American students from enrolling in Little Rock Central High School in September 1957 was still rumbling. The US and USSR pavilions put on a mouthwatering program of live cultural events. The Soviets brought in the Bolshoi Ballet with its star ballerina Galina Ulanova, the Red Army Choir, and the Moscow State Circus, while the Americans offered Benny Goodman, the Philadelphia Symphony Orchestra, and the Harlem Globetrotters.

But it was "These Czechs!" gushed the Dutch newspaper De Geldelander, that were "the surprise of the exhibition. . . . Their excellent pavilion is a dream of artistic fantasy, of incomparable beauty, taste, and talent."[123] The organizers agreed, awarding Czechoslovakia the Gold Star for the best pavilion as well as fifty-six grand prix, forty-seven honorary diplomas, and thirty-six gold, seventeen silver, and fourteen bronze medals—the most prizes won by any nation.[124] Adolf Hoffmeister was a member of the jury, but that was no doubt coincidence. Although the original concept and script for the pavilion's exhibition *One Day in Czechoslovakia* were Hoffmeister's, Jindřich Santar, the section chief for exhibitions at the Ministry of Information (and son-in-law of the executed Devětsil writer Vladislav Vančura), was in charge of its realization. Ada illustrated and designed the cover for the accompanying brochure, 500,000 copies of which were printed in Czech, German, and English. Santar took a pragmatic view of his task, putting politics to one side and choosing his collaborators and exhibitors with a view to creating "a modern scenographic-exhibitory whole that would be able to hold its own in a foreign competition."[125] "We managed to put together a team of people who knew what was going on and stupid socialist realism didn't interest them," he told an interviewer fifty years later. Not everyone approved. "After the first week in Brussels I returned home and heard the president of the architects speaking on the radio. He said that our exhibition was a great disappointment because it had no ideological content. A week later I was summoned by the head of the cultural division of the KSČ central committee. In the office the tables were covered in foreign newspapers. So look at that, he said, the enemy speaks highly of you, examine your conscience. At that time it was touch and go for all of us and even if today it will sound like a celebration of the previous regime it was minister Kopecký who saved the day. It was he who recommended us for a state prize. We got it and after that everything was fine."[126]

František Cubr, Josef Hrubý, and Zdeněk Pokorný designed the Czechoslovak pavilion in the light, bright style that characterized the architecture of Expo 58 as a whole. Before the war Hrubý had been one of the architects of the iconic Bílá labuť department store on Na Poříčí. Santar's intention was to deliver a *Gesamtkunstwerk* in which the building and its contents would make an integrated statement. "We wanted to create a complex work," wrote the three architects, "arising out of the broadest possible cooperation with painters, sculptors, and graphic artists . . . We tried to ensure that the architecture itself would be an appropriate frame for the artistic works that were to be its contents."[127] František Tröster and Josef Svoboda drew on their scenographic experience to treat the interior displays as theater sets, using both natural and artificial lighting and music to create an immersive dramatic experience for visitors. Texts were minimal: the exhibition communicated primarily by visual means, including large-scale blown-up photographs by leading Czechoslovak photographers and striking photomontage panels. Ladislav Guderna's "stylized technical motifs with a [nude] girl's figure and an animal or plant motif" in the engineering section managed to make even heavy industry look sexy.[128] We are light years away from the pitheads, smokestacks, and square-jawed proletarians on the posters and postage stamps of the heroic period of socialist construction.

The Praha Restaurant, an elegant semicircular two-story steel-and-glass structure supported on slender columns in the courtyard outside the main pavilion, served four thousand customers a day with roast pork, sauerkraut, and dumplings (*vepřo-knedlo-zelo*, the Czech Sunday roast) and other Czech delicacies washed down with good Pilsner beer. It employed 140 staff.[129] The restaurant was run by Miroslav Hříbek, manager of the Hotel Alcron, where Egon and Gisl Kisch had bedded down on their return to Prague in 1946; he brought his chef Florián Zimmermann and other subordinates with him. "Almost all of the employees posted to Expo had families at home, which was an insurance policy against [their] emigration," remembered one of the waiters.[130] The restaurant building was dismantled after the world's fair and reconstructed in Letná Park, where it still stands. The main pavilion was also shipped back to Prague and rebuilt in the exhibition grounds at Výstaviště, which were at that time officially known as the Julius Fučík Cultural Park and colloquially ridiculed as "Julda Fulda" or "Fučíkárna."[131] The pavilion was destroyed by fire in 1991. Nowadays there is nothing to recall the once ubiquitous martyred KSČ journalist at Výstaviště either.

Alongside the vases, ornaments, drinking glasses, and tea and coffee services displayed in the vitrines, the glass and ceramics section of the pavilion showcased large freestanding sculptural compositions whose style ranged from Josef Kaplický's figurative *Hold sklu* (Tribute to glass) to René Roubíček's abstract *Sklo—hmota, tvar, výraz* (Glass—material, form, expression). The backstory of Jan Kotík's six-meter-tall iron and glass sculpture *Slunce, vzduch, voda* (Sun, air, water) says much about the absurdities of the cultural politics of the era. Kotík was unexpectedly permitted to participate in the First World Congress of Liberated Artists at Alba in September 1956 (where he contributed to the collective painting *Untitled*, along with the COBRA artists Constant and Asger Jorn).[132] The platform of the congress, of which Jan was a signatory, became a foundational document of the Situationist International established by Guy Debord the next year. "The Alba Congress," it proclaimed, "will probably one day be seen as a key moment, one of the difficult stages in the struggle for a new sensibility and a new culture, a struggle which is itself

FIGURE 10.5. František Cubr, Josef Hrubý, and Zdeněk Pokorný's Brussels Expo 58 Praha restaurant, 1956–1958, as reconstructed on Letná Plain. Photograph by author, 2016.

part of the general revolutionary resurgence characterizing the year 1956, visible in the upsurge of the masses in the USSR, Poland and Hungary . . . in the successes of the Algerian revolt, and in the major strikes in Spain. These developments allow us the greatest hopes for the near future."[133] Like many Czechoslovak painters who were seldom permitted to exhibit their work, Jan made a living in the applied arts, working with glass foundries in northern Bohemia. He was awarded the Expo commission without having to submit a detailed plan for his project in advance. On seeing the result, the Ministry of Culture's bureaucrats concluded that *Sun, Air, Water* was "not representative of the leading ideological principles of our contemporary art." But deadlines were looming, so "after explaining that it was not a matter of an artistic work with a pictorial thematic conception but of a decorative exhibit without any kind of pictorial intent, created only as an effective composition of the colored glass of our new manufacture, comrade minister [of culture, František Kahuda] decided: a) that the exhibit would be accepted, b) to recommend to the organizers that they situate the exhibit in such a way that ensures it is not the centerpiece of glass production."[134]

Abstraction was running riot in the applied arts from fabrics to fashion to book jackets—all of which were on display in the pavilion's "taste" exhibit curated by Antonín Kybal, whose eye-catching geometric carpets had been best sellers at Ladislav Sutnar's Krásná jizba stores before the war.[135] Many artists who were unable to show their paintings in public left their mark on book design, a field in which the Czechs had long excelled and where they reached many more people than they would have in the galleries. Jiří Balcar, Libor Fára, Josef Istler, and Jan Kotík designed covers for the SNKLHU (State Publishing House for Belles-Lettres, Music and Art, renamed Odeon in 1966) Contemporary World Prose library, a prestigious imprint from the leading arts publisher of the communist era. Most books in this series had print runs of several thousand copies; Harper Lee's *To Kill a Mockingbird*, with a cover by Adolf Born, was translated in 1966 in an edition of thirty-two thousand.[136] Vladimír Boudník, Jiří Kolář, Mikuláš Medek, Zbyněk Sekal, Václav Tikal, Jiří Valenta, and Aleš Vesely were all well represented on book covers of the day.[137] The fiction was that since the applied arts were not "pictorial" but merely "decorative," they need have no ideological content. The reality was that the "Brussels style" became a powerful visual signifier of an alternative modernity in its own right. *One Day in Czechoslovakia* depicted a dreamworld, a landscape of desires that contrasted sharply with the overcrowded housing, restricted consumer goods, surly services, recurrent shortages, and endless queuing of actually existing socialism. In retrospect, it was the most poignant of memorials to Czech might-have-beens.

The Magician's Lantern

The greatest draw in the Czechoslovak pavilion—and one of the biggest attractions at Expo 58—was the multimedia shows in the cultural hall, which seated 139 spectators and hosted several performances every day.[138] Created by Josef Svoboda, perhaps the most famous postwar Czech theater designer and head of artistic and technical operations at the National Theater from 1950 to 1992, the Polyekran (the word literally translates as "multiscreen") combined simultaneous film projections onto eight screens suspended from the ceiling at various angles with stereophonic sound. *Pražské jaro* (Prague spring), a ten-minute "musical pictorial composition" portraying Prague's annual music festival directed by Alfréd Radok, was shown 2,230 times. "Images of real objects and people are projected," explained Svoboda, "but the relationships among them are not realistic, but rather supra-realistic, perhaps surrealistic. Essentially, it's the principle of abstract and pure collage." The Laterna magika (Magician's Lantern) shows, which were repeated three times daily, took the principle of collage one step further, combining static and film projections on multiple screens with live actors, dancers, and musicians. "Above all, Laterna magika has the capacity of seeing reality from several aspects," Radok emphasized. "Of 'extracting' a situation or individual from the routine context of time and place and apprehending it in some other fashion, perhaps by confronting it with a chronologically distinct event."[139] Alfréd was given a free hand with Laterna magika in Brussels, with one hilarious proviso: "that I would use already prepared and finished film material about factory work, chicken hatcheries, and the beauties of Slovak vacation lands."[140]

Like the Czechoslovak pavilion itself, Laterna magika was the product of teamwork. Svoboda was the scenographer, ably assisted by Radok's younger brother Emil; Alfréd was the director, Jan Grossman the dramaturg, and twenty-six-year-old Miloš Forman the scriptwriter. There is a distinguished lineage here. The coupling of screen projections with live performance was pioneered at Emil Burian's D Theater, where Alfréd learned his trade as assistant director in 1940–1941. After Burian was arrested by the Gestapo, Radok moved on to the Městské divadlo na Poříčí, for which he prepared a production of Jiří Mahen's *Mezi dvěma bouřkami* (Between two storms) combining live actors and film projections. It was never staged because (in his own words) "the Nazi occupation came. My father became a Jew."[141] Alfréd kept photographs and rolls of negatives from the rehearsals, which he filed in his archive under the heading "The first Laterna magika."[142] Thereafter, he explains, "I worked under various pseudonyms, the last time was in Pilsen [Plzeň]; and then Jiří Plachta hid me for a while in the Vinohrady Theater in Prague. Then came a work camp for Jewish *Mischlings*, half-breeds. My father was arrested; he died in cell #3 in the Little Fortress at Terezín. Other members of my family perished in other concentration camps."[143] Svoboda and Radok met in 1946 when they worked together on Offenbach's *Tales of Hoffman* at the Divadlo 5. května (5 May Theater), which took over the former New German Theater in 1945 and staged plays and operas there until the company was dissolved in July 1948. Jan Grossman joined Burian's Czechoslovak Army Theater as dramaturg in 1953. Rating Alfréd Radok "the best director of the Czech theater," Josef Škvorecký describes him as "the immediate, highly influential, predecessor of the [Czechoslovak] New Wave," of which Forman's *Černý Petr* (*Black Peter*, 1964), *Lásky jedné plavovlásky* (*Loves of a Blonde*, 1965), and *Hoří, má panenko* (*The Firemen's Ball*, 1967) were standout films.

DALEKÁ CESTA   REŽIE: A. RADOK — NÁMĚT: E. KOLÁR — KAMERA: J. STŘECHA
HRAJÍ: B. WALESKÁ, O. KREJČA, V. OČÁSEK, Z. BALDOVÁ, E. KOHOUT,
A. VAŇKOVÁ, S. RAŠILOV, J. PLACHÝ — Československý státní film

FIGURE 10.6. Film still from Alfréd Radok's *Distant Journey*, 1949. US Holocaust Memorial
Museum Collection. Gift of Ken Sutak and Sherri Venokur.

Radok's first film *Daleká cesta* (*Distant Journey*, 1949), says Škvorecký, "was
as much of a revelation to all of us as were the films of Věra Chytilová, Miloš
Forman or Jan Němec fourteen years later. It was a tragically premature and
anachronistic work of art."[144] The *New York Times* film critic Bosley Crowther
described it as "the most brilliant, the most powerful and horrifying film on
the Nazis' persecution of Jews that this reviewer has yet seen," adding that "the
faint of heart, however curious, are advised to see it at their own risk." Beginning in Prague under the second republic, the plot—"the slow destruction of
a family, ripped asunder in agonizing bits, with the daughter, a graduate physi-
cian, and her 'Aryan' husband the last to go"—is straightforward enough, the
cinematography much less so.[145] From the opening sequences in which the
shadows of Jewish prisoners shuffling along a wall are juxtaposed with a procession of torch-bearing Nazi Brownshirts and marching Wehrmacht soldiers,

Radok employs a battery of avant-garde techniques, montaging newsreel, still images from concentration camps, and clips from Leni Riefenstahl's *Triumph of the Will* into Hana and Toník's story. Radok's visual vocabulary owes much to German expressionist cinema (the communist writer Marie Pujmanová complained that "expressionism follows the talented Radok like a curse").[146] In one of the most haunting scenes, a jazz band plays what sounds like a wildly discordant cross between Schoenberg and a New Orleans funeral march at night in the pouring rain as a column of Terezín prisoners trudges past through the mud on the way to their transports. *Distant Journey*, says Škvorecký, "possessed as little 'class approach' as the Nuremberg Laws. . . . The appropriate official places exploded: the film was labelled 'existential' and 'formalistic.' After a very brief run, the film was withdrawn from public showing and for almost two decades was locked away in the Barrandov vault."[147]

Radok was acutely aware of the capacity of "realistic" images to mislead. Verisimilitude, he believed, is not the same thing as truth. "What I wanted to say on film, and later in the theater," he told the Czech journalist and film critic A. J. (Antonín Jaroslav) Liehm in 1972, "probably has its origins with Hitler."

> My father was a Jew. I think that is important; it played an important role in my life. The name "Hitler" evokes a picture in my mind: A little girl, all sugar and spice, is handing Hitler a bunch of wildflowers. Hitler bends over her and smiles a benevolent smile. To me this image is linked with the awareness of what National Socialism meant, just because the image conceals something. I can't imagine how it would be possible to describe the war, Hitler, National Socialism, and concentration camps, without this image. . . . The picture of Hitler with the girl, the hyperemotional parades— all that was interconnected. Things were gradually adding up. And when you had their sum total, they were suddenly true; they showed the whole truth—arranged in a certain order, of course, with the right cuts: the parades, the little girls, plus the concentration camps, all in that order.

"I wanted to stress the paradox that so many people—and this was true later of many in Communist Czechoslovakia—simply don't see things," Radok says, "don't want to see them, or see only the picture of Hitler with the little girl. And that is the horror of it. . . . If you really want to get a picture of that period, you have to see the one and the other, not one but two, both sides. And that is what I call matter-of-factness [*věcnost*]." "This is something like the effect of Laterna Magica," he continues. "What is it, this matter-of-factness that

I am talking about? The Germans call it *Sachlichkeit*. In my mind, it means the ability to see things truly, to be able to reproduce the realities of life in a factual manner—that is, to see in each phenomenon the tension of at least two opposite poles. If I love, I simultaneously hate. I see this paradox everywhere I look. That is, if one knows how to view things as an artist does." Instead, says Radok, "They turned *Laterna* into a carnival attraction for foreigners and foreign countries, and it ceased to interest me after that."[148]

Laterna magika was established as a division of the National Theater in May 1959, performing in the former basement cinema at Pavel Janák's Adria Palace on the corner of Národní Avenue and Jungmannova Street. Since 1992 it has had a permanent home in Karel Prager's Nová scéna (New Stage), one of Prague's most distinctive brutalist buildings, where it is a major tourist attraction.[149] Radok was the first director. His tenure did not last long. He was fired in 1960 after he was stopped from including his rendition of Bohuslav Martinů's cantata *Otvírání studánek* (*Opening of the Wells*, 1955) in a Laterna magika touring program. Martinů had recently died an unrepentant exile in Basel, and besides, complained Václav Kopecký to Ladislav Štoll at the preview, "This here is your Jewish expressionism, Láďa!"[150] The film component of the performance has survived; with cinematography by Jaroslav Kučera, it is eighteen minutes of pure visual poetry and one of the glories of Czech cinema.[151] For the next five years Alfréd worked for Městská divadla pražská (Prague Municipal Theaters). Václav Havel was the assistant director in 1961–1962 for his productions of Chekhov's *The Swedish Match* and Georges Neveux's *La Voleuse de Londres* (The woman thief of London). Introducing the French première of the latter in 1960, Neveux—who also wrote the play Martinů adapted for *Julietta*—confides that "throughout my childhood I was haunted by a figure who strolled through the silent films and pulp fiction of the era: the female thief." The curtain opens on the kleptomaniac heroine Pamela meeting with a prefect of police in a brothel. According to Neveux, he set the action in a London located "at the crossroads between fantasy and reality."[152] Where better to stage it, then, than Prague?

Alfréd got his Laterna magika job back in 1966, only to have his ambitions crushed two years later by Soviet tanks. On 28 August 1968, a week after the invasion, he fled with his wife and children to Sweden, where he was appointed director of the Folkteatern in Gothenburg. Since the Folkteatern was a socialist collective, things didn't work out so well. Josef Škvorecký recalls that when he was ostracized in Prague following party attacks on *The Cowards* in 1958, he received "an invitation from a man who I didn't even know personally. . . . Mrs Radoková cooked a pheasant, and because I was tight-lipped, because I was scared shitless, for the whole evening Alfréd Radok spoke by turns about the beauties of *The Cowards*—very concretely, not at all in general—and still more concretely about the idiocies of the Stalinistas [*stalinčíků*]. . . . In the end they ran down the poor guy in exile in Sweden. He went there never expecting that in the seventies intelligent people in the West would still believe in socialist realism."[153] "A person can live the life of a human being here," Alfréd told Liehm, "though not really a life of culture, although one can't measure culture simply by the theater and film. And there's not a sign of a Pankrác prison and court in Sweden. The last time they burned a witch here was ages ago."[154] Radok was sentenced in absentia to fifteen months in prison and stripped of his title of National Artist. He died in Vienna in 1976, directing Václav Havel's plays *Zahradní slavnost* (*The Garden Party*, 1963) and *Audience* (1975) at the Burgtheater. "He was an artist," wrote Havel in a combative obituary, "endowed with abilities that were inescapably denied to his opponents: to see all the tragic as well as the grotesque paradoxes of life, to rejoice in its beauty as well as lay bare its wretchedness, to feel the fifth dimension of things—the dimension of mystery."[155]

There is one film Alfréd Radok didn't get to make. We can only guess what his "'big dream' for a film" might have looked like:

> I am sorry that I never got around to filming something that I have been getting ready to do ever since: a documentary about how everyone who had anything to do with preparing those trials—beginning with the guard at the gate to the Pankrác prison and ending with the state prosecutor Urválek—was innocent. The camera would interview all of these "innocents" about the details of their lives and "work." The camera would try to prove, through its questions, that they did everything simply because they were "ordered to." The comrades from the prisons at Pankrác and Koloděje would show how none of them could help it. And after that I wanted to do a dry and factual reconstruction of the reality of the "interrogations" and the "preparations" for interrogation. I wouldn't try to conceal the fact that it would only be a reconstruction, prepared by actors and for the movie camera. The commentary to the film would have been an authentic record of the trials and interrogations, supplemented by photographs and, where possible, by documentary film shots that have survived (e.g., the Slánský trial, the speeches of members of the Party's Central Committee and of the government). . . . It is the only way that the unbelievable, inconceivable reality that we experienced could have been conceived for film.[156]

But Miss, we can't help it.

If a Thousand Clarinets

On 11 July 1960 the Czechoslovak national assembly met in the Vladislav Hall in Prague Castle to adopt a new constitution. "Socialism has triumphed in our country!" proclaimed the preamble. If not quite at hand, the end of history was indisputably on the horizon: "While completing the socialist construction of our country, we are proceeding towards the construction of an advanced socialist society and gathering strength for the transition to communism."[157] "This unwavering strength and durability of our socialist regime—as well as its humanism"—enabled Antonín Novotný to announce the largest amnesty since 1948, which gave 5,601 political prisoners "the opportunity to atone for their guilt before the people by honest work."[158] Former justice minister Prokop Drtina, the alleged Slánský "conspirator" Evžen Löbl, and the "bourgeois Slovak nationalist" Gustáv Husák were among those released (though not rehabilitated). But behind this façade the pressures for reform were becoming irresistible. The economy was stagnating, despite measures adopted in 1958 to counter the rigidities of central planning. The Third Five-Year Plan had to be abandoned in the summer of 1962, and output fell in 1963–1964. Slovakia was growing restless, artists and intellectuals were demanding greater freedom, and a younger generation of party activists, untainted by involvement in the purges of the 1950s, was stepping onto the stage. When Nikita Khrushchev doubled down on his criticisms of Stalin at the Twenty-Second Congress of the CPSU in October 1961, the KSČ leadership had little choice but to fall into line. The Stalin monument was demolished in 1962.

The following year a commission under Drahomír Kolder concluded that *all* the political trials between 1949 and 1954 had been rigged. Novotný saved his own skin by throwing the KSČ old guard under the bus. Jozef Lenárt replaced Viliam Široký as prime minister, and Alexander Dubček replaced Karol Bacílek as first secretary of the Slovak Communist Party. Josef Urválek, the chief prosecutor in the Horáková and Slánský trials, resigned as president of the Czechoslovak Supreme Court. By the end of 1963, half the KSČ presidium elected in 1958 was gone. The somewhat ironic upshot was that (in the words of Zdeněk Mlynář) "the height of Novotny's power coincided with his eliminating the old Gottwald-Stalinist clique. . . . Now he had his own leadership, composed not of people who had brought him to power but whom he himself had appointed." The new presidium "consisted of a majority of people who were not closed to the idea that further development required changes and reforms."[159] During the remaining years of Novotný's tenure, recognition of the need for reform jostled with fear of its consequences. Ota Šik's new system of economic management, to take the most glaring example, was approved by the KSČ central committee in 1965. Had the reforms been properly implemented, they would have represented the most radical attempt to combine planning with market mechanisms anywhere in the Soviet bloc—or anywhere else. Instead, the center repeatedly interfered with enterprise autonomy, compounding the paralysis Šik's reforms were intended to resolve.

This was a time of mixed messages for the arts. The thaw that began in 1963 went well beyond earlier moves toward liberalization, but from time to time the censors still showed their claws. *Umění 1900–1963: Obrazy, plastika, grafika* (Art 1900–1963: paintings, sculpture, graphic art), a major exhibition at the Aleš South Bohemian Gallery in Hluboká nad Vltavou in the summer of 1963, was "the first in a long time to present the development of Czech modern art without ideological limitations." Although the show went on as planned, distribution of its catalog was stopped, and the texts by František Šmejkal and others remained unpublished until the 1990s.[160] *Rychnov 63: Současná výtvarná tvorba* (Rychnov 63: current artistic creation), which Jiří Padrta curated a couple months later at the château in Rychnov nad Kněžnou, featured eighty-five artists ranging from members of wartime avant-garde groups to Křižovatka (Crossroads), a new group founded in 1963 by Jiří Kolář, Richard Fremund, and others. Křižovatka had a show in March 1964 at the Galerie Václava Špály (Václav Špála Gallery). The Konfrontace abstractionists were finally permitted to exhibit as a group at Nová síň (New hall) the same month under the title *Výstava D* (Exhibition D).[161] But once again press reviews were forbidden and the catalog was banned, underlining the continuing pertinence of Bohumír Mráz's point in its preface: "Here no sooner had modern art, which was persecuted during the [German] occupation as 'degenerate art,' begun to actively flower again and re-establish severed international contacts after 1945 than it found itself on the Index again."[162] Together with the Galerie na Karlově náměstí (Charles Square Gallery) and the Galerie Vincence Kramáře (Vincenc Kramář Gallery), the Špála Gallery and Nová síň became Prague's principal exhibition spaces for contemporary art.[163]

The Artists' Union SČSVU chose Adolf Hoffmeister as its president at its Second Congress in December 1964 and elected a slate of other candidates supported by the Bloc of Creative Groups into leading positions. The congress agreed to give more control to gallery managers and to foster contacts with foreign artists.[164] Jindřich Chalupecký became director of the Špála Gallery, Ludmila Vachtová director of the Charles Square Gallery, and the UB 12 painter Alois Vitík director of Nová síň. Each was backed up by reform-minded advisory boards. All delivered ambitious exhibition programs. Mikuláš Medek made his official (and much belated) Prague debut in April 1965 at Nová síň, showing thirty-nine paintings dating from 1947 to 1965. There is symbolism, as well as irony, in the fact that on 1 May 1966 Medek took over the spacious studio in Letná that had once been occupied by Jan Čumpelík, creator of *At the Dawn of a February Day*, who had died the previous October.[165] Over the next four years Mikuláš traveled and exhibited widely across Europe, but his work was proscribed again after 1970. He died of diabetes at the age of forty-seven in 1974. Josef Istler and Vladimír Boudník had solo exhibitions at the Charles Square Gallery in September 1965 and January 1966, respectively. The Špála Gallery staged retrospectives like *Mistři 20. století* (Twentieth-century masters, 1966; thirty-four foreign artists, including De Chirico, Ernst, Kokoschka, Munch, and Schiele) and "confrontations" like *Fotografie 7 + 7* (fourteen photographers, including Josef Sudek, Miroslav Hák, Emila Medková, and Josef Kouldelka, curated by Anna Fárová, 1967). Chalupecký and his assistant Eva Petrová put together some notable thematic exhibitions, including *Objekt* (The object, 1965), *Obraz a písmo* (Image and writing, curated by Jiří Padrta, 1966), and *Aktuální tendence českého umění, obrazy, sochy, grafika* (Current trends in Czech art: paintings, sculptures, graphics, 1966). Organized in conjunction with the International Association of Art Critics and spread over four major exhibition spaces, the latter was one of the most ambitious surveys of contemporary Czechoslovak art yet attempted. Václav Tikal, who died in 1965, was given a posthumous retrospective at Mánes in 1967. All this represented a sea change in the kind of art that could be publicly seen and written about.

Surrealism gradually resurfaced after fifteen years in the shadows. Vratislav Effenberger lectured to the Mánes Group in 1963–1965 on Karel Teige, the Circle of Five Objects, Dadaism and absurdity, and Salvador Dalí. The Prague surrealists renamed themselves UDS ("an absurdly enigmatic acronym, the meaning of which was never defined")[166] in 1964 and reestablished contact with the Paris surrealists in 1966. Věra Linhartová and František Šmejkal curated the first post-1948 retrospective of Czech surrealist and related art, *Imaginativní malířství 1930–1950* (Imaginative painting 1930–1950), at the Aleš South Bohemian Gallery in March–April 1964. After much flip-flopping by the authorities, the exhibition was closed to the public and the catalog suppressed.[167] A smaller version of the show, which excluded all post-1945 works, was reprised by the National Gallery at UMPRUM in July–August with a bare minimum of publicity. The documentation stressed that this was a "working exhibition . . . above all of a study character," intended to provide "a real foundation for discussion, resting on recognition of facts and scientific treatment" of an "extremely complicated" era in Czech art.[168] Several artists who appeared in Konfrontace's *Exhibition D* also exhibited in another Špála Gallery show, Šmejkal's *Fantasijní aspekty současného českého umění* (Fantasy aspects of contemporary Czech art, 1967), whose object was to "draw attention to the existence of 'imaginative constants' and attempt to define the emergence of a new fantasy wave in Czech art."[169] Abstraction was not the only game in town.

Karel Teige's writings began to see the light of day again, beginning with *Jarmark umění* (The art fair, 1933–1936) in 1964. In 1966 Československý spisovatel published the first of three volumes of Teige's *Selected Works*, containing essays and articles from the 1920s. His collages were exhibited for the first time at the Vincenc Kramář Gallery; Vratislav Effenberger's catalog was the longest the gallery produced before 1972.[170] Another Teige exhibition titled *From Poetism to Surrealism* was held at the House of Art in Brno and the Aleš South Bohemian Gallery in 1967. Šmejkal curated a Štyrský and Toyen exhibition for the Moravian Gallery in Brno in November 1966, which traveled to Mánes the following January. Effenberger, Stanislav Dvorský, and Petr Král prepared a UDS exhibition at Galerie D in September–October 1966 to show surrealism's contemporary relevance. *Symboly obludnosti* (Symbols of monstrosity) was "a more or less conscious protest," they wrote, which "opposes, through imagination, the daily, almost self-understood monstrosity opening more and more widely the abyss between the miracles of technology and the stupefying emptiness of the spirit."[171] This was a step too far for the authorities: the show was closed, and the catalog was pulped. But Effenberger, Dvorský, and Král were still able to lecture on Teige in 1967 and make a radio series, "The Avant-Garde without Legends and Myths," featuring Adolf Hoffmeister, Josef Šíma, and Jan Zrzavý, among others. The trio's anthology of Czech surrealist texts *Surrealistické východisko 1938–1968* (*The Surrealist Point of Departure 1938–1968*) came out in 1969, slipping under the wire before the full rigor mortis of normalization set in.[172]

On 5 April 1966 Prague experienced its first happening under the title "*nehudba nedivadlo neliteratura* **neumění**" (not music not theater not literature **not art**), courtesy of Fluxus members Eric Andersen, Arthur "Addie" Køpcke, and Tomas Schmit, at Reduta on Národní Avenue.[173] Reduta is one of Europe's oldest surviving jazz clubs. Located in the same building as the Louvre Café, it opened its doors in 1957, two years before Ronnie Scott's in London.

The club's website makes much of Bill Clinton's jamming with local performers on the tenor sax when Václav Havel took him there during the US president's visit to Prague in 1994.[174] In the early days Reduta offered not just jazz but also skiffle, American folk music, and rock and roll; in 1958 František Sodoma sang Jiří Suchý's lyrics "Rok co rok se měníme" (year by year we change) to the melody of Bill Haley's "Rock around the Clock."[175] The club is known as "the cradle of small theater" because of its role in fostering one of the most important cultural phenomena of the 1960s thaw. "The last promise of our spiritual renewal through liberation of culture came in the sixties from our young theater in the flowering of so-called 'small forms,'" wrote Václav Černý, which "worked through a cabaret stage, suited to song, through pantomime, musicals, grotesque 'black theater,' theatrical experiment; humor and satire was a popular type of inspiration, a range of genre that extends from farce through socially critical comedy."[176] Jiří Suchý, Jiří Šlitr, and Ivan Vyskočil performed what they called "text-appeals," a kind of literary cabaret combining stories, sketches, and songs, at Reduta in 1957–1958. Suchý, a graphic designer by trade, played bass and wrote the words; Šlitr, a lawyer, played piano and composed the music. Šlitr cut his musical teeth in 1948 with the Czechoslovak Dixieland Jazz Band at Emil Burian's theater and was one of the Laterna magika musicians at Expo 58. Vyskočil, who coauthored the first text-appeals with Suchý, was a psychologist, writer, and actor.

When an unused hall with room to seat 150 people became vacant on Anenské Square in the Old Town, Suchý and Vyskočil started the Divadlo Na zábradlí (Theater on the Balustrade). The opening production, which premièred on 9 December 1958, was a musical fantasy titled Kdyby tisíc klarinetů: leporelo o 36 obrazech (If a thousand clarinets: a pop-up book in 36 pictures) that starred Suchý, Šlitr, and the singer Ljuba Hermanová. The musical was made into a film in 1965 with a cast that included film director Jiří Menzel, actress Jana Brejchová, and the popular singers Hana Hegerová, Waldemar Matuška, and Karel Gott. Suchý left in October 1959 to establish the Semafor Theater with Šlitr. Ivan Vyskočil stayed until 1962; in 1964 he founded the Nedivadlo Ivana Vyskočila (Ivan Vyskočil's Nontheater), a text-appeal ensemble that was once again based in Reduta. After Jan Grossman, Laterna magika's dramaturg at Expo 58, was appointed as the Theater on the Balustrade's chief director in 1962, it developed into a renowned center of absurdist drama. Eugène Ionesco's The Bald Soprano and Samuel Beckett's Waiting for Godot and Act without Words had their Czechoslovak premières there in 1964. Alfred Jarry's Ubu roi was staged the same year, followed in 1966 by Grossman's celebrated production of Franz Kafka's *Trial*. The resident dramaturg was Václav Havel, whose own absurdist plays took their final form in rehearsals. *The Garden Party* premièred on 3 December 1963 and played 203 times before its last performance on 27 July 1968, followed by *Vyrozumění* (*The Memorandum*) in 1965 and *Ztížená možnost soustředění* (*The Increased Difficulty of Concentration*) in 1968.[177]

One of the most artistically innovative of the 1960s theaters was Otomar Krejča's Divadlo za branou (Theater beyond the Gate), which opened in 1965 and shared premises in the Adria Palace with Laterna magika. Libor Fára, Jan Koblasa, Mikuláš Medek, and Josef Šíma were among its set designers. Suchý and Šlitr's Semafor Theater also started out with high artistic ambitions, aiming to provide a multimedia venue for musical comedy, poetry, jazz, film, the visual arts, dance, and puppet theater; its name was an acronym for "seven small forms" (*SEdm MAlých FORem*). Jan Lukas showed his photographs under its auspices, and the young Jan Švankmajer, who would go on to become one of the world's greatest animated filmmakers, exhibited his artwork in the foyer. Švankmajer's adaptation of Vítězslav Nezval's *Škrobené hlavy: Příběh řadového vojáka* (Papier-maché heads: the tale of a rank-and-file soldier, 1960) was the first of a series of productions for Semafor by his Divadlo masek (Theater of Masks), but the "mixture of 'popular and traditional' marionette theater, pantomime, black light theater, and resolutely avant-garde experiment" didn't go down well with audiences, and the troupe was let go in 1962.[178] The Theater of Masks moved to Laterna magika, where Švankmajer renewed his collaboration with Emil Radok, who had remained as technical director after his brother Alfréd was fired. The two men had previously worked together in 1958 on Emil's animated film *Johanes Doktor Faust*, which Švankmajer revived as a stage performance at Semafor in 1961. Following Suchý and Šlitr's wildly successful debut as a cabaret duo in *Jonáš a tingl-tangl* (Jonah and the tingle-tangle, 1962), Semafor became a vehicle for their performances as S + Š, in the same way the Liberated Theater had for V + W in the 1930s—with one crucial difference. As Josef Škvorecký sardonically puts it, Suchý and Šlitr's songs "helped to form the emotional world of the young generation of the 1960's in a truly revolutionary fashion. Their revolution—perhaps for the first time in history—lay in the separation of their songs from any political involvement."[179] We are at the opposite pole from Sartrean *engagement*.

The second of the two short films that make up Miloš Forman's *Konkurs* (*Audition*, 1963), one of the first films of the Czechoslovak New Wave, was shot at the Semafor Theater on Forman's personal 16mm Pentaflex movie camera, with the sound recorded on a Grundig tape recorder.[180] "Semafor announced sham auditions for a female singer and crowds of unsuspecting misses flocked to be captured on the malicious sixteen," relates Škvorecký. "Cruelty mercilessly joined with the grotesque" as the pitiless camera recorded "the grotesqueness of a life that has illusions of its own beauty."[181] "The stars were favorable," says Forman: "Khrushchev proclaimed somewhere that young people should be given a chance, and immediately Novotný said the same thing."[182] The New Wave soon attracted international attention. In June 1967 the Museum of Modern Art in New York sponsored a Festival of New Czechoslovak Cinema and an accompanying exhibition of eight-five stills to "focus attention on the achievements of the young cinema of Czechoslovakia, which runs the gamut from neo-realist, cinema-vérité to Kafkaesque and highly avant-garde works." MoMA rated Sedmikrásky (Daisies) "the most original film from Europe this year. The director, Věra Chytilová, and her cameraman husband, Jaroslav Kučera"—who also shot Alfréd Radok's Opening of the Wells—"have fashioned a work filled with visual delights and mordant humor."[183] Described by Chytilová as a "philosophical documentary in the form of a farce,"[184] Daisies follows the anarchic adventures of two young women, both named Marie, who decide to "go bad" because the world around them is doing the same. Ján Kadár and Elmar Klos's Obchod na korze (The Shop on Main Street, 1965), a Holocaust drama set in Slovakia, won an Academy Award for the best foreign-language film in 1965, as did Jiří Menzel's Ostře sledované vlaky (Closely Watched Trains, 1966) in 1967. Forman's Loves of a Blonde and Firemen's Ball were nominated for the same award in 1966 and 1968, respectively. The Czechs were in distinguished company. Other 1960s Oscar winners in this category included Ingmar Bergman's Through a Glass Darkly, Federico Fellini's 8½, Claude Lelouch's A Man and a Woman, and Sergei Bondarchuk's War and Peace.

Asked to explain this sudden upsurge in Czech cinematic creativity, Ivan Passer, the director of Intimní osvětlení (Intimate Lighting, 1965), put it down to the serendipities of time and place. The New Wave was launched by graduates of FAMU (Filmová a televizní fakulta Akademie múzických umění v Praze [Film and Television Faculty of the Academy of Performing Arts in Prague]), who saw themselves as part of a "conspiracy against stupidity." "We were very young," he says. They began their careers when "the communist regime was slowly melting." This situation was "absolutely unique," in that "everyone understood that success for one was an opportunity for the others" that "opens the door for everybody."[185] Notwithstanding Forman's Firemen's Ball ("I didn't intend to shoot a political allegory—I don't like it in movies—but in this story of the looted raffle, the guiding lights of the Communist Party perceived a satirical swipe at them," Miloš said later)[186] and Jan Němec's *O slavnosti a hostech* (*A Report on the Party and the Guests*, 1966, a Kafkaesque romp that Antonín Novotný took personally and promptly banned),[187] outright political satire was rare; but artistic subversion of the norms of socialist realism was everywhere. Location shooting in ordinary settings using cinema vérité techniques, casting of amateur actors, surrealistic experimentation, and a nose for absurd humor all ate away at the simulacra of the socialist Disneyland. *Perličky na dně* (*Pearls of the Deep*, 1966) was, in effect, a New Wave manifesto. Five directors,[188] all FAMU graduates, each take on a story from Bohumil Hrabal's first legally published book, *Perlička na dně*, which came out in 1963.[189] Vladimír Boudník plays himself in Věra Chytilová's contribution, the marvelously if darkly imaginative "*Automat Svět*" (World café). It is a poignant memento of a life cut short. In the early-morning hours of 5 December 1968, after a spat with his new young wife, Boudník tied a noose around his neck "assuming that someone would come and untie him, as they had countless times before"— says Bohumil Hrabal—but nobody did. It was a huge loss for Czech art.[190]

Jiří Menzel's *Closely Watched Trains* and *Skřivánci na niti* (*Larks on a String*, 1969, which was "shelved" and not released until 1990) are also based on Hrabal's work.[191] *Closely Watched Trains* is a tender, cruel, comical, and ultimately tragic tale set in a small-town railroad station in occupied Bohemia early in 1945. Hrabal worked closely with Menzel on the screenplay. Miloš Hrma, an apprentice train dispatcher, is another little Czech antihero. Like Josef Škvorecký's alter ego Danny Smiřický in *The Cowards*, he is far more concerned with his love life than the war. Unfortunately, Hrma is afflicted with *ejaculatio praecox*, a condition that leads him to slash his wrists after he is unable to satisfy his conductor girlfriend Máša. As we might expect of anything coming from Hrabal's pen, the film is saturated with Czech bawdy, from the stationmaster's wife massaging the long neck of the goose she is force-feeding as the tongue-tied Miloš explains his sad predicament (which he hopes she might help him remedy) to the rakish dispatcher Ladislav Hubička livening up the night shift by imprinting the station's rubber stamps one by one on the naked bottom of the pretty young telegraphist Zdenička Svatá. "Lamplight caresses the bodies of the performers, highlighting the soft, goose-bumped textures of Zdenka's skin; the room's clock, scale and ever-active tape-machine become sentient little contraptions, mysterious and beautiful in chiaroscuro," writes Jonathan Owen, relishing the scene.[192] But there is more to Hubička, we slowly learn, than meets the eye, and more to the movie than a salacious

FIGURE 10.7. František Zálešák's film poster for Jiří Menzel's *Closely Watched Trains*, 1966.
From Marta Sylvestrová, ed., *Český filmový plakát 20. století*, Prague, 2004.

coming-of-age rom-com. "Good comedy should be about serious things," Menzel told an interviewer in 2008. "If you start to talk about serious things too seriously, you end up being ridiculous."[193]

Miloš loses his virginity to Viktoria Freie, an improbably code-named trapeze artist turned resistance fighter who shows up late one night carrying a gift-wrapped package for Hubička. "And then she touched me, and drew me with her to the station-master's couch, and dropped onto it and drew me down upon her," Miloš relates (in Hrabal's original text), "and then all in an instant I was glued to Viktoria . . . and I was overwhelmed by a flood of light growing ever more brilliant, I was marching, marching uphill, the whole earth shook, and there was the rolling of thunder and storm, and I had the impression that it didn't come from me or from Viktoria's body, but from somewhere outside, that the whole building was shaking to its foundations, and the windows rattling. I could hear even the telephones ringing in honor of this my glorious and successful entry into life, and the telegraphs began to play Morse signals of their own accord, as sometimes happened during storms . . . and at last the very horizon soared and blazed with the colors of fire, and the station building shook again, and shifted on its foundations." In this instance the earth really did move:

> Viktoria Freie sat up and listened. She smoothed her hair, and said:
> "There's a terrible air-raid somewhere."
> I opened the window and tugged at the blind, which rushed upwards with a sucking sound. Far away beyond the hill burst out more and more fires, the entire horizon was red and frayed over there beyond the hill, towards the center of some distant disaster.
> "That could well be Dresden," she said.[194]

The movie ends as Hubička faces a disciplinary commission for "abuse and disgrace of the German language" owing to his amorous game with the rubber stamps. While the commission is riveted by the smiling Zdenička's explanation of how her backside came to be festooned with the insignia of the protectorate, Miloš quietly enters and removes Viktoria's package from the drawer where Hubička stashed it. It is a time bomb intended for one of the closely watched munitions trains of the film's title. The train is seven minutes away from the station. In a juxtaposition worthy of Shakespeare, the camera pans between the approaching train, the increasingly farcical scenes taking place in the stationmaster's office, and Miloš making his way along the platform. Encountering Máša, he tells her to wait, he'll be back in a minute. He climbs the ladder to the signal and lies down on the gantry. As the train passes beneath him, he sets the timer and drops the package. A burst of gunfire comes from the train and Miloš falls onto the roof of one of the cars. After the train has passed through the station the bomb goes off, unleashing a chain of massive explosions. Hubička is laughing hysterically on the platform. The blast sends Miloš's cap bowling along the ground into the uncomprehending Máša's arms.

11

The Prague Spring

I think our task today is not to ascertain who was or wasn't a scoundrel, our task is to ascertain what causes led to these things, what circumstances permitted them, and which people did them; whether they were scoundrels or not will only be shown during honest and thorough investigation of all of these things.

—HEDA MARGOLIUS KOVÁLY[1]

The King of May

"Prague is absolutely beautiful," wrote Allen Ginsberg to his father sometime in March 1965. "Old medieval town, the Golem synagogue, weird castles and cathedrals, Kafka's homes—Kafka just published here this past few years after 15 years blackout—by that you can measure the winds of political change. . . . Everyone here official & non-official complaints [sic] about the Horror of the '50s as if it were a nightmare. They're slowly working out of it."[2] As Ginsberg's biographer and editor Michael Schumacher points out, the well-traveled Beat poet may not have been an "ugly American," but he "was still, in essence, an American poet writing as an American . . . seeing the world through the filter of his own experience."[3] Kafka's writings were indeed prohibited in Czechoslovakia from 1948 to 1957, as they would be again (with the exception of a 1983 reissue of a collection of short stories) from 1969 to 1989.[4] But this was not only a question of totalitarian repression—though it was that too. Kafka's shorter writings were quite widely disseminated in Czech between the wars, and Pavel Eisner's translation of *The Castle* was issued by Mánes in 1935.[5] Not even Toyen's cover, which looked like a still from a film noir, helped the book sell. Regardless of how much Kafka's work may have appealed to surrealists, Prague's most celebrated writer in postwar Western eyes had never been a significant figure in mainstream *Czech* culture.[6] Eisner commented in 1950 that, "in the eyes of the Czechs, the German Jew was a stranger in three senses: as a Jew, either owing to creed or to unmixed blood; as a generally comfortable, prosperous and, often enough, rich citizen, in the midst of a crowd of proletarians and small bourgeois; and thirdly, as a 'German.'"[7] At the very moment Kafka was being discovered and lionized in the West, he became a posthumous casualty of the Holocaust, the expulsion of Bohemian Germans, and the class war in his homeland. The effects still linger. "In contemporary Prague, Kafka remains peculiarly absent," writes Veronika Tuckerová. "Czechs did not appropriate Kafka's works in constructing their new, post-communist, European identity. The Czech authors to be published in massive print runs after 1989 were the former exile and samizdat authors: Václav Havel, Ivan Klíma, Pavel Tigrid, or Josef Škvorecký. . . . Kafka was relegated to the status of a tourist attraction."[8]

Yet it was this cohort of Czech writers that Kafka most profoundly affected. "For young, non-conforming Prague intellectuals of the 1950s who hung around literature or who wrote themselves, it was typical that almost all of them had a couple of Franz Kafka's short stories at home which they had translated and which they lent or read out at meetings with friends and acquaintances," recalled Jan Zábrana.[9] Tuckerová suggests that "rather than finding in Kafka an abstract notion of totalitarianism," as Western readers did, eastern Europeans "seemed to recognize in Kafka's fiction their everyday life, especially in the 1970s and 1980s."[10] Czech intellectuals were drawn to Kafka for the same reasons they were drawn to Beckett or Ionesco. Bohumil Hrabal, Milan Kundera, Václav Havel, Ivan Klíma, Josef Topol, Věra Linhartová, and Ivan Martin Jirous were all deeply influenced by Kafka's work. In the early 1960s Jirous, who would later become a leading figure in the post-1968 Czech underground, "copied practically the whole of Kafka's works from the dispersed translations—apart from *The Trial*, which came out in 1958," publishing them in the samizdat edition *Opsáno na Brancourově* (Copied in Brancourov).[11] Adolf Hoffmeister, too, had Kafka on his mind. Between 1963 and 1968 Ada produced a series of Kafka collages that "thematized the traumas of the twentieth-century artist. He evoked the situations and emotions familiar from Kafka's texts, he captured his perception of space and time."[12] Franz returns in the morning to his flat in Celetná Street; Franz stumbles through the Hebrew inscriptions in the Old Jewish Cemetery; Franz cowers beside his towering, self-satisfied father; Franz gets lost in a labyrinth, is besieged by text, is assaulted by multiple television screens.[13] Jiří Kolář's later series *Kafkova Praha* (Kafka's Prague, 1977–1978) consists of thirty-one photographs of Prague landmarks—the Castle, Saint Vitus's Cathedral, the National Theater, the Powder Tower, Golden Lane—paired with brief excerpts from Kafka's writings. The images have been crumpled then pressed flat, a technique Kolář called *froissage* ("crumplage"). The buildings appear to be disintegrating, as if in the midst of an earthquake. *Froissages* "offer analogies for life," explains Kolář, "analogies with the events and explosions of destiny which *crumple* human beings with such suddenness and so profoundly that they are never able to smooth themselves out again."[14] The process, he says, was inspired by Vladimír Boudník's explosionalism and structural graphics.[15]

One who shared Ginsberg's sense that Kafka's reemergence was a measure of the winds of political change was future president Gustáv Husák, who reportedly said that "the Prague Spring began with Kafka and it ended with counterrevolution."[16] He was referring to the Franz Kafka International Conference that took place on 27–28 May 1963 at Liblice, a castle north of Prague owned by the Czechoslovak Academy of Sciences, ostensibly to mark the eightieth anniversary of Kafka's birth. Organized by Eduard Goldstücker, the Liblice conference has been widely hailed as "a key intellectual precursor of the political upheaval in Czechoslovakia that culminated in the Prague Spring in 1968."[17] Marek Nekula rightly criticized the "teleology" of claims that "the election of Eduard Goldstücker as Chairman of the Czechoslovak Writers' Guild [in 1968] seems to complete an arc which began with the Liblice conference and ended with the Prague Spring."[18] The reality was murkier. The conference was in part prompted by a speech at the 1962 World Peace Conference in Moscow in which Jean-Paul Sartre denounced the West's use of Kafka as a "weapon" against communism. More than twenty speakers from Czechoslovakia, the German Democratic Republic (GDR), Poland, Hungary, Yugoslavia, France (Roger Garaudy), and Austria (Ernst Fischer) took part. As Josef Škvorecký emphasizes, "it was a conference of Marxists, some of them with pretty awful Stalinist pasts and with equally awful neo-Stalinist futures. Dr Jiří Hájek, for instance."[19] He is referring to the editor of the magazine *Plamen* (Flame), who took the helm of a revived *Tvorba* in the service of normalization from 1969 to 1976, not his namesake, the foreign minister in the 1968 Prague Spring government and founding signatory of Charter 77.

The intent of the conference was to counter Western views of Kafka from what Goldstücker called "the Prague perspective." For Hannah Arendt, Kafka's significance was universal: "The generation of the forties and especially those who have the doubtful advantage of having lived under the most terrible regime history has so far produced know that the terror of Kafka adequately represents the true nature of the thing called bureaucracy—the replacing of government by administration and of laws by arbitrary decrees. . . . Kafka's so-called prophecies were but a sober analysis of underlying structures which today have come into the open."[20] But according to Goldstücker, "the first precondition of Marxist research into Kafka, so to speak in order to ground Kafka, is to study his life and work in connection with all the sociohistorical contexts in which he lived and out of which he created. This will show that a serious word on the range of Kafka problems may only legitimately be uttered from Prague."[21] Having spun elements of Franz's biography to transmute him from a "representative of the 'Prague German-Jewish bourgeoisie' into a son of the 'Czech-Jewish rural proletariat,'"[22] Goldstücker, Marie Majerová, Pavel Reiman, Klaus Wagenbach, and other speakers at Liblice then read his work through the prism of Karl Marx's concept of alienation. The latter was a major point of contention in the 1960s between Marxist humanists, who regarded the young Marx's analysis of alienation as fundamental to his overall world-view, and Soviet Marxists, who dismissed the texts in which Marx developed the concept as juvenilia. The debate mattered because the idea of alienation provided a theoretical basis for developing a critique of "actually existing socialism" while remaining a card-carrying Marxist. Goldstücker was clear that his aim was to co-opt Kafka, whom he described as a "victim . . . of the cult of personality," for a reform communist agenda.[23] "Although the controversy about Kafka is only a small part of the struggle to extricate Marxism from its Stalinist captivity and deformation," he wrote ten years later, "it reflects what it was all about and what methods were used."[24]

The critic Václav Černý summed up the "largely unsuccessful international conference on Kafka in Liblice" with this ambivalent comment: "Goldstücker was quite clumsy in his endeavors at the conference to bang Kafka into the size and shape of the social, if not socialist, poet. . . . Yet Kafka had been sanctioned—a sign of the changing times!"[25] Černý was conspicuously not invited to Liblice, even though he had been writing on Kafka, whom he saw as a precursor of existentialism, since the 1940s. Nor was Gustav Janouch, the author of Conversations with Kafka, who by 1962 was probably "the only man living in Prague who had known Kafka personally."[26] It was not an oversight. Alexej Kusák confronted Goldstücker on what seemed to be an astonishing omission:

Why did you cut Janouch from the list of participants on three occasions?

He has nothing to say on Kafka.

But he is one of the few, if not the last one, who demonstrably knew Kafka. And he wrote a book, which all foreign Kafka scholars have read.

It contains only fabrications. Janouch has no business at a scientific conference.

Others judge otherwise. What was the real reason why you banned him from participating in the conference?

I already said. What more do you want?

I know that Janouch has many disgusting things on his conscience, I comprehend that as a person who doesn't have the best memories of the police, you don't want to invite Janouch as a person who is tied up with the police, but why do you prevent others from inviting him, like the television? Why do you want it to be only you who decides who is credible and who is not?

The conversation ended with Kusák, who was Goldstücker's former student, complaining that "this conference, which should have been from the outset a settling of accounts with Stalinism, is unfortunately from the outset marked by the methods that prevailed under Stalinism."[27]

Gustav Janouch, whom we met near the start of this book as the shy young poet who worshipped Kafka, grew up to be a jazz pianist and a writer of jazz instruction manuals. He may or may not have collaborated with the Nazis, depending on how one defines collaboration. He performed in Germany during World War II and his 1944 article "The Magic of Jazz" rehearses stock Nazi racist clichés ("unbridled animalistic sound") while at the same time praising Czech jazz. Škvorecký, who was sympathetic to "an old jazzman who, as a young greenhorn, had had the dubious good fortune of briefly knowing one of the great intellectuals of our century," judged it "an attempt to make jazz acceptable for surveillance, through political compromises . . . which, to my mind, exceed[ed] the necessity."[28] In January 1946 Janouch was arrested and accused of collaboration, extortion, bribery, kidnapping, and killing a Red Army officer—crimes that normally would have netted him the death penalty. He was released in February 1947 and acquitted in March 1948, a month after Victorious February. *Conversations with Kafka* was first published in West Germany in 1951 and subsequently translated into Swedish, English, Spanish, Italian, Japanese, and other languages—though not into Czech until 2009. Josef Čermák, who also participated in the Liblice conference, claims that Janouch was an StB informer from 1951 to 1954. He provides no evidence of this, but Veronika Tuckerová is no doubt right that Janouch's "acquittal in a judicial system where arrest equaled conviction, his apparently free ability to correspond about Kafka with Zionist émigrés [Max Brod], his ability to publish abroad, and the implausible absence of as much as a mention in the secret police files, implies with a very high likelihood that somebody powerful was protecting him. The most likely explanation is that he was working in some capacity for the secret police."[29]

Enough said, we might think. Except that Goldstücker had a backstory too. It has many parallels with Janouch's, only the jazzman was small fry and the professor moved in high party and state circles. A member of the KSČ since 1936, Goldstücker spent World War II in Britain working for Beneš's government in exile. In 1949 he was appointed Czechoslovakia's first ambassador to Israel. Recalled from his post like Adolf Hoffmeister, he was arrested in December 1951, tried for espionage and treason in May 1953, and sentenced to life in prison. Unusually, he was released in 1955 and fully rehabilitated when the Supreme Court annulled the 1953 verdicts soon afterward. His KSČ membership was restored and (at his request) he was given a position lecturing in German literature at Charles University, where he rose to become head of the German Department and was promoted to full professor in 1964. What made Goldstücker's dealings with the police so painful to remember, as Alexej Kusák and everyone else very well knew, was the part he played as a prosecution witness in the Slánský trial, where—in the words of the official transcript—he "described his role of go between [linking] Slánský and 'the agent of the British Intelligence Service, Konni Zilliacus.' His relations with Slánský, he explained, went back to 1946 when Slánský's attention had been drawn to Goldstücker's 'Jewish bourgeois origin' and his 'connections with various enemy elements in the west.'"[30] Goldstücker's testimony, which also incriminated Bedřich Geminder, Ludvík Frejka, and Vlado Clementis, was undoubtedly coerced.[31] But there is every reason to believe that Gustav Janouch's collaboration with the StB was not entirely voluntary either. As for Čermák, we encountered him earlier doing a similar hatchet job on Michal Mareš's reminiscences of Kafka. Škvorecký characterizes him as "an ambitious and rather vainglorious man" who enjoyed "a very influential position at Odeon Publishers, the respectable place to sell yourself," where he had worked since its beginning (as SNKLHU) in 1952.[32] Čermák was appointed Odeon's chief editor in April 1972. He stepped down in 1977 but retained effective control over the Odeon list in the newly created position of chief reader (lektor) until 1990.[33] Twentieth-century Prague is not the best place to take the moral high horse.

Many years later Lenka Reinerová was glad to see an old friend show up in her dream café above the verdigris-covered domes and stern church towers of Prague. "'Eda,' I call, because the new arrival was none other than the restless spirit, Germanist, diplomat, prisoner, president of the Czechoslovak Writers' Union, exile, pro-rector of Charles University, honorary president of the Czech Goethe Society (only how can so much contradiction, good and evil, fit into one life?)—Professor Eduard Goldstücker."[34] Eda and Lenka first met back in 1936 in the poky office of the League for Human Rights, of which Goldstücker was then secretary, on Žitná Street in the New Town. Lenka arrived to fill in for a friend, a young lawyer who had decided to join the International Brigades. "My friend fell on the Spanish front. My friendship with Eduard lasted until his recent death [in October 2000]," she wrote in a 2003 afterword to Goldstücker's memoirs. Sometime after Eda's release in 1955 they met by chance in a Prague street. "I was waiting in a throng of people at a crosswalk when somebody lightly tapped me on the shoulder. I turned around and behind me stood Eda . . . he said quietly: 'Do you still know me? You have behind you a criminal.' 'Me too,' I responded, 'admittedly less, but equally. We are alive!'"[35] Lenka was at Liblice too, sitting in the front row. "Thanks to the 'negation of everything positive,'" she records, "they say the counterrevolution began right then at the Kafka conference."[36]

Allen Ginsberg knew nothing of this *kafkárna*. "My visit seems to have done some good," he wrote to his father:

Everybody here adores the Beatniks, & there's a whole generation of Prague teenagers who listen to jazz & wear long hair & say shit on communism & read *Howl*. I gave a reading at Charles Univ. (on the banks of Die Moddau [*sic*] river) with big audience & answered all sorts of sex and brainwash questions. Food good middleeuropean soups & pork & knaedlich—I live in expensive Ambassador Hotel at Writer's Union with expense & my picture's in all the literary supplements with long strange explanations about marijuana & LSD and Hari Om Namo Shiva Indian mantras—and I run around with teenage gangs and have orgies & then rush up to Writer's Union & give lectures on the glories of U.S. pornography Henry Miller etc. All very happy—Love to you—

I'll send you a card from Moscow.[37]

Allen's Prague adventure began with his expulsion from Cuba, ostensibly for smoking pot but more likely because of his outspokenness over gay rights, the legalization of marijuana, and Che Guevara's sexiness during his visit to Fidel

Castro's "island of freedom" in January–February 1965.[38] As a result of the American blockade, there were no direct flights to the United States, so the Cubans put him on a flight to New York via Prague and London. Ginsberg landed at Ruzyně airport on 18 February. He had two acquaintances in Prague: Josef Škvorecký, whom he phoned from Ruzyně, and Jan Zábrana, who had translated parts of Howl (1956) for Světová literatura in 1959.[39] They contacted the Writers' Union, which obtained a visa for Ginsberg, gave him a two-week work grant, and accommodated him at "the most elegant hotel on that big street, the Hotel Ambassador"—formerly the Golden Goose Hotel on Wenceslas Square, where members of the Vanguard Squad had been arrested by the Gestapo back in 1939. Royalties and fees that had accumulated from earlier recitals of his work in the Viola "poetry café" (now the Viola Theater) at 7 Národní Avenue enabled Ginsberg to extend his stay for another two weeks. The Vinárna Viola was another of Prague's small stages, offering jazz every evening and theater once a week.

"So every intellectual student would have at one time or another taken his date out to the Vinárna Viola," Ginsberg reminisced in a 1986 conversation with Andrew Lass, the son of an American defector who grew up in Prague and acted as Allen's guide to the city. "And once a week for many years they had one evening of actors reading Beat poetry translated by Zábrana. Ferlinghetti, Corso and myself . . . they had a large chunk of Kaddish in excellent translation. Somebody giving a dramatic recitation of Howl, maybe Sunflower Sutra. . . . So when I arrived in Prague every student that was awake knew my poetry."[40] Allen gave readings at Viola and a recital at the U Fleků pub, where (according to the StB report) "over 50 young artists and university students chanted long live Ginsberg, etc."[41] His recital at the university, where he read in English and Zábrana followed him in Czech, attracted several hundred people. Though Ginsberg was kept under surveillance throughout his visit, he stayed out of trouble and received favorable (if slightly puzzled) coverage in Literární noviny, Kulturní tvorba (Cultural creation), and even Rudé právo. "They let me loose, I talked freely, the walls of the State didn't fall, everybody was happy, sex relations with anyone male or female is legal over age of 18," he wrote to a friend.[42]

On 18 March Ginsberg traveled by train to the Soviet Union ("late afternoon in compartment with Czech military attaches, travelling rocking thru sunlight by the river Elbe"),[43] where he got drunk with Yevgeny Yevtushenko and Andrei Voznesensky, met Anna Akhmatova and Evgenia Ginzburg ("a little old Jewish lady cooking soup for her son and her friends and his friends"),[44] and spent an evening at Lilya Brik's, where they "ate caviar and raisins and blue cheese and talked French." "Mayakovsky very sexy—very tender as lover—very gentle," Lilya confided.[45] Allen returned to Prague six weeks later by way of Warsaw and Krakow, arriving on 30 April. His second visit turned out to be very different from his first.

> I called Jan Zábrana, my translator, to reconnect with him and to meet with Škvorecký again. Of course, Škvorecký was for me one of the most interesting people there. He was a real writer and he was also a jazz clarinetist and he edited a jazz magazine and knew all about Charlie Parker and Bebop and he completely understood Kerouac's prose from that point of view so he was totally right on as far as understanding what was going on with American prosody and was himself considered sort of like the new, almost Kerouac of Czechoslovakia. So I called him up . . . we got together and then he called me up the next day and said that the students from the Polytechnic Institute [ČVUT] had approached them about the May Day parade to ask if he would be their candidate for the King of May. But he had the flu. So he said "I suggested to them they recruit you."

In hopes of avoiding the confrontations between police and students gathering at Karel Hynek Mácha's statue on Petřín hill that had broken out every May Day since 1962, the Novotný regime permitted the *majáles* students' festival to take place again for the first time since 1956. The afternoon parade wended its way through the city from the Old Town Square to the Julius Fučík Park of Culture at the Výstaviště exhibition grounds. "[They] put me on the float, we got down to the park of culture . . . and there were a hundred thousand people there," Allen relates. "What I had expected was this little May Day ceremony with a few hundred or a thousand scraggly, scruffy students in the park, but instead it's this sea of faces." In lieu of a speech he chanted Buddhist mantras that he thought appropriate to "a society slowly thawing and moving towards some kind of open mind. . . . Actually I was using that [mantras] as a way of undercutting the rigidly hyper rationalistic Marxist dogmatism that I was hearing both from Cuba and not so much from the Czechs who were sophisticated but from their official voices," he told Andrew Lass.[46] The American poet was duly acclaimed Král majáles (King of May). Lass says the election was fixed, but Ginsberg didn't know that. After midnight Allen went with a group of students to the ČVUT Hlávkova dorms, where he spent two hours discussing the situation in Czechoslovakia and answering their questions. According to an StB report he ended the discussion by saying that the *májales*

FIGURE 11.1. Allen Ginsberg as the King of May, Prague, 1965.
The photo was taken with Ginsberg's camera by an unknown
photographer. Courtesy of the Allen Ginsberg Project,
© Allen Ginsberg LLC.

festival "was for him a spectacle like nothing he'd seen—a combination of the
political courage to protest and to organize the entire environment with maximum eroticism."[47]

A few days later Allen was lunching in a restaurant when "suddenly two big,
the Kafkian fat men, big bulky guys, came up to the table and said: 'Mister
Ginsberg,' and I said 'Yes.' 'Did you lose a notebook?' And I said 'yes, I did,'
and he said, 'well, we have found it, somebody has turned it in to the lost-and-
found, and if you'll come down with us to the station you can sign for it and
you'll have it back.'" At the station "they took me up to the third floor where
there was a clerk. Sort of a small room, in an office, a prosecutor or somebody

or the assistant district attorney, small room, big desk, lots of papers, my book on the desk. And he said 'Is this your book?' and I said 'Yes.' 'Well, if you'll sign for it we'll give it to you.' So I signed for it and he said 'You're under arrest' and I said 'What for?' . . . He said, 'You'll have to ask yourself that.'" Eduard Goldstücker got the same Kafkaesque response when he asked the same question in December 1951: "I asked why I was arrested, and the answer was a smile, an ironic smile, and [he] said . . . that is what you will tell us and not we tell you."[48] The notebook was Ginsberg's personal journal, which he had "lost" a couple days earlier in the Vinárna Viola. "I saw Ginsberg there every night. I found him unlikable. He drank a lot and was horribly dirty to boot," relates the film director Pavel Juráček, who is best known for *Případ pro začínajícího kata* (*The Case for a Rookie Hangman*, 1969), an absurdist satire loosely based on Jonathan Swift's *Gulliver's Travels* and one of the last films of the Czechoslovak New Wave. "I saw him in the odd company of three men who ordered Georgian cognac by the bottle," Pavel continues. "Ginsberg could barely stand. . . . He staggered about the Viola confusedly as if he were looking for something. I was sitting with Vašek [Václav] Havel and we watched him with some abhorrence. Three days later I read that some citizen found an English notebook on the street, in which the StB then discovered Ginsberg's notes about his homosexual episodes with Prague boys. Then it came to me who those three in the Viola were and what Ginsberg had been looking for."[49] Among other things, says Allen, the notebook contained "some really interesting notation about jacking off in the Hotel Ambassador with a broom stick up my ass, which I'm sure must of [sic] blown their mind."[50] He never did get it back.

The next day, 7 May 1965, Ginsberg was driven to Ruzyně airport and put on a plane to London. He wrote one of his best-known poems on the flight, titled "Kral Majales":

> and I am the King of May, in a giant jetplane touching Albion's airfield trembling in fear
> as the plane roars to a landing on the gray concrete, shakes & expels air,
> and rolls slowly to a stop under the clouds with part of blue heaven still visible.[51]

Allen need not have feared. A message was waiting for him from Bob Dylan: "Can you come over immediately to the hotel near Charing Cross?" The next day, Ginsberg told Lass, "We went downstairs on the Thames embankment while he sang 'Subterranean Homesick Blues.' This was like 24 or 36 hours after being arrested and booted out of Prague. So it was like going from this very amazing scene in Prague to an even more amazing scene, just the opposite, the breakthrough of personal emotion and youth culture in England just at its crest. The next night I wound up escorting Marianne Faithfull to Dylan's concert and then going back to the hotel for the after-concert party and winding up that night at midnight in a room with Dylan and all of the Beatles talking about William Blake. So that was the end of that."[52] Just a reminder, as we approach the *annus mirabilis, annus horribilis* 1968, that the 1960s were in Prague and Prague was in the 1960s, and both were located at the crossroads between fantasy and reality.

We Want Light, We Want More Light!

On 24 January 1968 Eduard Goldstücker became president of the Union of Czechoslovak Writers (SČSS). Eda accepted the position after months of hesitation, he explained in a TV interview, in order to help "normalize relations between the union and our society." He wished to "preserve the unity of the community of writers that . . . has somewhat surprisingly manifested itself in recent months since the Fourth Congress," where "discontent was expressed . . . with the unhealthy relationship of a part of our society toward the intelligentsia." The KSČ, he went on, "is one of the few revolutionary workers' parties that from the beginning of its existence had huge support" from "the flower of the national intelligentsia," an intelligentsia that "has played a huge role in the national life in comparison with other nations" ever since the national revival. "This intelligentsia came mostly from the lowest social strata," he added, "and it always enjoyed great respect within the nation for its origin as well as its role . . . the hostility, suspicion toward the intelligentsia that has recently manifested itself is in my view artificially introduced into our society."[53] He was right on all counts. Antonín Novotný was eventually brought down by an ad hoc coalition of Slovaks seeking greater autonomy within a federalized Czechoslovakia, economic reformers like Ota Šik, and communist believers in "socialism with a human face." But it was above all the intelligentsia that took the lead during the Prague Spring. The first salvos were fired at the Fourth Writers' Union Congress, which met in Vinohrady on 27–29 June 1967.

"We got together at Saša [Alexandr] Kliment's, I can't now say for sure how many of us were there (but certainly Ludvík Vaculík and Karel Pecka were, and our friends from the editorial staff of Československý spisovatel, Zdeněk Prokop and Jaroslav Smetana) and we worked out who would say what at the upcoming Fourth Writers' Congress. For it provided the opportunity to present forbidden ideas about freedom of expression in a public forum," Ivan Klíma told *Lidové noviny* fifty years later. Such opportunities were few and far between: "public speeches could be delivered only at the forums of permitted organizations, which were all controlled by party functionaries. The only occasional and reluctantly tolerated exceptions were the artists' unions, and especially the Writers' Union, where mainly younger writers (even if some were party members) refused to submit to control by higher party functionaries."[54] Milan Kundera opened the first day's discussion of a text prepared by the union's central committee with input from "Laco Novomeský, Jaroslav Seifert . . . and many others," which, he told the delegates, had already "provoked very sharp criticism at a plenum of the ideological division of the KSČ central committee." The document insisted that "conditions of cultural tolerance, conditions of the free clash of values on the field of socialist democracy, are the only conditions in which the most authentic values of the free individual can find their genuine—not at all fictitious—realization."[55] Kundera argued that "any kind of infringement upon the freedom of thoughts and words . . . is a scandal in the twentieth century and a fetter on the many-sided development of our literature."[56] After Kliment mentioned *Le Monde*'s recent publication of Alexander Solzhenitsyn's letter to the Fourth Congress of Soviet Writers calling for an end to all censorship, Pavel Kohout rose from the floor. "I have here a Czech translation of Solzhenitsyn's letter. Would the congress like to hear it?" As Kohout began to read Solzhenitsyn's text, the KSČ central committee secretary Jiří Hendrych, a close associate of Novotný's (they had been imprisoned together in Mauthausen during World War II) and a member of the KSČ presidium since 1958, stormed out of the hall, telling the delegates, "You have lost everything!"[57]

Things got worse on the second day. Reminding his audience that Czech history did not begin in February 1948, Ivan Klíma unfavorably compared the new Czechoslovak press law that had taken effect in January 1967 with the Austrian Imperial Patent of 4 March 1849, which stipulated that "everyone has the right to freely express their opinions by speech, writing, printing, or visual means" and "the press cannot be subjected to censorship." The requirement to submit writings to the censor for advance clearance prior to publication had been reimposed on Bohemia in 1851–1852, only to be quashed again in the December Constitution of 1867. "Those who have chosen the year 1967 to promulgate a press law renewing advance censorship on the exact hundredth anniversary of its abolition," Klíma drily commented, "are not lacking in a certain type of absurd humor."[58] Recalling that the journals *Květen* and *Tvář*

(Face, 1964–1965), established by the Second and Third Writers' Union Congresses, respectively, had both been shut down by the authorities, Václav Havel warned against the more recent past repeating itself. He then read an open letter to the minister of culture from "representatives of the youngest generation of Czechoslovak film directors" signed by Věra Chytilová, Miloš Forman, Jaromil Jireš, Pavel Juráček, Jiří Menzel, Jan Němec, Ivan Passer, Evald Schorm, and others protesting an attack by parliamentary deputies on five New Wave films, among them Chytilová's *Daisies* and Němec's *A Report on the Party and the Guests*.[59]

But it was Ludvík Vaculík, whose novel *Sekyra* (*The Axe*) came out in 1966, who delivered "the sharpest criticism of the communist regime publicly uttered at that time in any such official assembly."[60] "I speak here as a citizen of a state that I never want to abandon, but in which I cannot contentedly live," Vaculík told the congress. "I am ... a member of the communist party and I am therefore not supposed to and don't want to speak about party matters. But things turned out in such a way in our country that there is nowadays almost nothing that would not at some stage of debate become a party matter. ... When I stand here and speak I don't at all have that free feeling that a person ought to have when he freely says what he likes." The privileges enjoyed by writers were double-edged: "Because what do these words mean, that we have received the union, we have received a literary fund and a publishing house and a newspaper? A threat that they will take them away from us if we don't behave." Vaculík moved well beyond the pale of Czech literature. "It is necessary to acknowledge that after twenty years not a single human problem has been solved among us," he went on, "from basic needs like housing, schools, and economic prosperity to subtler needs that the undemocratic systems of the world are unable to meet—like the sense of full legality in society, the subordination of political decision-making to ethical criteria, faith in the meaningfulness of even humble work, the need for trust between people, better education for the masses."[61] The congress's final resolution, which demanded the abolition of censorship, among other reforms, was adopted with only one abstention.[62] President-elect Jan Procházka ended his closing address with an echo of an old song by Voskovec and Werich: "The congress is over, the search continues, it is literature's good fortune that nothing is definitive."[63]

For the next six months the fate of the Writers' Union hung in the balance. Hendrych was unable to bully it into packing its newly elected central committee with KSČ-approved nominees, but he did succeed in getting Pavel Kohout, Ivan Klíma, Ludvík Vaculík, and Václav Havel removed from the list approved by the congress. Rather than carry a laundered version of the proceedings, *Literární noviny* refused to cover the congress beyond publishing the opening and closing speeches and the final resolution, together with an anodyne summary of the discussions ("Ludvík Vaculík took the floor with an extensive contribution on the relation of the citizen and power, power and culture") and a short extract from Kundera's speech.[64] Meantime, the secret police were getting busy. An StB report of 2 August mapped out the contours of "The Operative Situation in the Field of Culture." "The most important foreign center for ideological-diversionary activities among the Czechoslovak intelligentsia," it advised, was Pavel Tigrid's Paris-based journal *Svědectví*. Václav Černý was "the chief initiator and organizer of antisocial and anti-party activities both internally and in links with abroad"; he "mediated relations with Václav Havel, [the Marxist-humanist philosopher] Ivan Sviták, and [the Catholic literary critic and former political prisoner] Bedřich Fučík" and "indirectly influenced the formation of other opposition groups" such as those "made up of Jiří Kolář, Josef Hiršal, Jiří Padrta, Miroslav Lamač . . . and others." Havel had played a significant part in *Tvář*, "a tribune for the spreading of negative opinions about the cultural politics of the communist party," which had also infected Věra Linhartová and Jan Němec. The report pinned responsibility for "reviving liberal and opportunistic opinions and activating negative elements" on the Writers' Union journals *Literární noviny*, *Host do domu* (Guest in the house), and *Kulturní život* (Cultural life, the journal of the Slovak Writers' Union); "artists of the Bloc group (Lamač, Padrta, Šmejkal . . . Chalupecký, etc.), with the support of Adolf Hoffmeister"; and "representatives of 'New Wave' film (Jan Němec, Věra Chytilová, Evald Schorm, Ester Krumbachová and others)" who "refuse open engagement of their work" and display "a very problematic relation to socialism."[65]

When the KSČ presidium discussed the congress three days later, Jiří Hendrych took the lead in calling for a crackdown. Everyone agreed that steps had to be taken, but there was disagreement as to what they should be. Warning that overly repressive measures might backfire, Alexander Dubček and Oldřich Černík, the most liberal members of the party's top body, opposed any public campaign against writers and intellectuals. Novotný saw the congress "as an attempt at a political platform that would end up in an opposition movement against the party and install bourgeois democracy" and relished the prospect of a showdown. "Obviously I regard Kundera as the chief 'whizz kid,'" he said. "I consider Kundera to be one of the principal ideological architects of the whole opposition line." Although a majority of members rejected Hendrych's proposal to undermine the "material basis" of the Writers' Union and other cultural unions by transferring their publishing activities and funds to the Ministry of Culture, the presidium unanimously agreed that *Literární noviny* should be put under ministry control immediately. Only Dubček voiced his "very grave concerns" that depriving the Writers' Union of its weekly paper "could be met with incomprehension."[66] This recommendation was accepted at the central committee plenum on 26–27 September, together with resolutions to expel Ludvík Vaculík, Ivan Klíma, and Antonín J. Liehm from the party; strip Jan Procházka of his positions as candidate member of the KSČ central committee and president-elect of the Writers' Union; and begin disciplinary proceedings against Milan Kundera (who was still a party member, having been expelled in 1950 and readmitted in 1956). Pavel Kohout escaped with a reprimand.[67]

A string of StB reports from November and December 1967 confirmed that, despite these measures, the intellectuals' revolt was not dying down. The Union of Film and TV Artists (Svaz filmových a televizních umělců, FITES) strongly opposed the removal of *Literární noviny* from the Writers' Union and condemned plans to censor film screenplays; the "terrifying atmosphere" had already led to Elmar Klos and Jaromil Jireš resigning their positions in the union and Jan Němec quitting the film studio.[68] Further dissent was expressed at the congress of the Union of Czechoslovak Composers in the first week of December. The StB reported on 14 December that the Writers' Union congress was still being discussed among writers and artists, in the theaters, in newspaper and radio newsrooms, in institutions of higher education, and especially among students. There was "continual interest in Vaculík's speech," which was being spread in an ever-increasing number of samizdat copies. Anonymous letters criticizing Novotný and Hendrych had been sent to party and state offices, and flyers were circulating among students deriding the "Hendrychiáda." Preparations for the upcoming SČSVU congress, warned another StB report, involved "efforts to eliminate undemocratic conditions in the union, to deal with the legitimacy of interventions by the communist headquarters in the life of the union, to take action on new organization of creative artistic groups," and "to fill the union's presidium with representatives of modern artistic trends."[69] As for the Writers' Union, the effect of the September measures was the opposite of what Hendrych had hoped it would be. The writers were not cowed into submission and the dissidents were not isolated from their colleagues. *Literární noviny* defiantly published a revised version of Kundera's speech at the congress in the penultimate issue before its ministry takeover.[70]

The union organized a successful boycott of the "new" *Literární noviny*, to which few of its members contributed, whatever their political leanings. Not a single member of the eighteen-person editorial board and none of the nine editorial staff remained with the journal, which changed its name to *Kulturní noviny* (Cultural news) in February 1968.[71] The ministry was unable to recruit editorial or technical staff, and by December, sales had collapsed from 150,000 to 60,000 copies per week.[72]

Under normal circumstances the dissent probably would have petered out, as it had after the Second Writers' Union Congress in 1956. These were not normal circumstances. Novotný was now under fire from several directions, and the party leadership was deeply split. Not for the first or the last time in Prague's history, the violent suppression of an unauthorized student demonstration proved to be a harbinger of change. The immediate cause of the so-called Strahov events (*Strahovské události*) was dissatisfaction with the living conditions of ČVUT and other students at the Strahov dormitories, which had been built in 1964–1965 on the site of demolished Sokol changing rooms and were still used to accommodate participants in the Spartakiáda meets held every five years. The buildings suffered repeated power outages and regular interruptions in heat and loss of hot water. When the electricity went off at around nine o'clock on the evening of 31 October, "students began to assemble in front of the dormitories and in the end with the ambiguous slogan 'We want light, we want more light!' and lighted candles in their hands set off on a protest march for the city center."[73] Where Neruda Street (Nerudova ulice) enters the upper part of the Lesser Town Square (Malostranské náměstí), the protesters were confronted by SNB riot police, who pushed them back toward Strahov with truncheons and tear gas, pursued them into the dormitory buildings, and beat them savagely, the girls as well as the boys. Five students were seriously injured, and several others required medical attention. As the news percolated out, Charles University rector Oldřich Starý and the *Mladá fronta* (Young front) newspaper questioned the need for SNB intervention,[74] and ČVUT rector Josef Kořoušek and the universities committee of the Prague KSČ deplored the police brutality.[75] Students at the Philosophical Faculty of Charles University passed a resolution on 9 November that "indignantly condemned the brutal action of representatives of the security police toward the Strahov students." Demanding an inquiry into the events, they scheduled another demonstration for 17 November—International Students' Day—which they eventually called off for fear of provoking more police violence.[76]

The proletarian Novotný had never had much time for pointy-headed intellectuals, who made him feel insecure. Speaking to the KSČ presidium on 28 November, he put the latest disturbances into historical perspective:

> Comrades, before I address these questions, I would like to state that as regional secretary I have faced student demonstrations in Prague before and I led a counterdemonstration against the reactionary students with the help of working-class youth and the workers' militia. . . . It was in the time of February 1948 on Wenceslas Square, after which the demonstrators tried to get to the Castle and there was a clash in the same places as now when security forces stood up against the students. Back then they petitioned Beneš to investigate police actions and so on.
>
> Unfortunately, I see no great difference politically between that demonstration and the aims it pursued and the political situation among part of the university student body today, as well as the recent student demonstration, which at the end of the day equally culminated in political events . . . this is not about economic matters or deficiencies in the Strahov dormitories but about political affairs.[77]

But this was not 1948, and Novotný was increasingly out of touch. Just a few hours before the students set off from Strahov with their ambiguous chants and their candles, Alexander Dubček had launched an open attack on Novotný's leadership at the closing session of the KSČ central committee plenum of 30–31 October. "The new phase and new tasks basically require new, more precise, and more appropriate methods of political leadership and management methods," he urged. There must be "less ordering about and more practical work with communists whom the party has entrusted with jobs in any sector of its activity." Novotný responded by accusing Dubček of being "in the grip of certain narrow national interests," a tactic that did little to improve his standing among disaffected Slovaks in the party.[78] It is perhaps symbolic that while anger was growing in Prague over the mistreatment of the Strahov students, Novotný spent the next nine days in Moscow celebrating the fiftieth anniversary of the Great October Socialist Revolution. Dubček, who had spent his childhood in the Soviet Union, was conspicuously missing from the Czechoslovak delegation. Novotný sought Leonid Brezhnev's support in the escalating inner-party struggle, but after a visit to Prague on 8–9 December, during which the Soviet leader had one-on-one discussions with Dubček (for four and a half hours) and others, Brezhnev decided to remain on the sidelines with the apocryphal comment, "*Eto vashe delo*" (It's your affair).[79] He told the

Hungarian leader János Kádár that "Novotný is himself to blame for all these problems because he does not know what collective leadership is and how to handle people."[80]

The arguments continued at an extraordinary meeting of the presidium on 11–14 December. A week later, at the central committee plenum of 19–21 December, Ota Šik proposed separating the functions of KSČ first secretary and state president, offices that Novotný had held since 1957.[81] There was no consensus, and the meeting was adjourned. When the plenum resumed on 3–5 January 1968, a resolution "to separate the post of president of the republic from that of first secretary of the KSČ and entrust these posts to two different persons" passed with no opposition and only two abstentions. Clearly the Christmas break had focused minds. The central committee approved "Antonín Novotný's personal request as president of the ČSSR to be released from the post of first secretary," thanked him for his "worthy and dedicated work . . . at the head of the KSČ during this complicated and challenging period," and appointed his nemesis Alexander Dubček to replace him.[82] The politburo of the CPSU sent Dubček a congratulatory telegram wishing him success in his work "from the bottom of its heart."[83] The Prague Spring was under way.

It Starts with the Arts

Among the first public signs that there was more afoot than the usual game of musical chairs at the top were two articles by Josef Smrkovský in *Práce* (Work) on 21 January and *Rudé právo* on 9 February titled "*Oč dnes jde?*" (What's going on today?) and "*Jak nyní dál?*" (What lies ahead?). One of the most popular politicians of the Prague Spring, Smrkovský had been a member of the KSČ's fourth illegal central committee during the Nazi occupation. As vice president of the Czech National Committee, he had negotiated the withdrawal of German troops from Prague in May 1945. This did not endear him to the Soviets, who would have preferred to take the city by force than allow the Germans to surrender to the Americans, but it saved many Czech lives. Three years later Smrkovský played an important part in the Victorious February coup as deputy commander of the people's militia. That did not stop him from being arrested in 1951 and sentenced to life imprisonment for aiding the Slánský conspiracy. He was released in 1955 and chaired a collective farm for several years before resuming his political career in 1963. At the beginning of 1968 Smrkovský was minister of forestry and water management in Jozef Lenárt's government.

The January plenum, he wrote, was not just "a personal quarrel and a rotation of individuals":

> The personnel changes were in fact motivated by considerations that are of far greater urgency and importance to the party: the imperative to remove the obstacles that for some time have been obstructing the party's progressive efforts. . . . I am referring to a series of tasks that should have been performed a long time ago, as well as to topical and pressing matters in the social and economic system. It is also essential to eliminate everything that has been distorting socialism, damaging people's spirits, causing pain, and depriving people of their faith and enthusiasm. . . . There is a conviction growing that everything we have achieved in transforming the structure of our society will facilitate—indeed will absolutely necessitate—a basic change of course. Such a change must be aimed at the democratization of the party and society as a whole.[84]

In the interest of fostering transparency, on 6 February the presidium agreed to publish reports of all its future meetings in the media.

On 1 February the Writers' Union fired Jiří Hájek as editor of *Plamen* and appointed a new editorial board headed by Josef Škvorecký. Later in the month the union named new editors for *Plamen* and *Literární listy* (Literary pages), its replacement for *Literární noviny*, without the prior approval of the KSČ central committee, even though these were *nomenklatura* positions. The first issue of *Literární listy* appeared on 1 March with Ludvík Vaculík's article "*Toleranční patent*" (The toleration patent) on the front page. Ludvík clearly did not intend his allegorical piece to be read as referring only to Joseph II's measure of 1781, which had ended "the harsh struggle in Austria against confessions other than state Catholicism."[85] *Literární listy*'s editorial board (including Ivan Klíma, Milan Kundera, and Jan Procházka) and staff (including A. J. Liehm and Ludvík Vaculík) were identical to those of *Literární noviny* at the time the ministry took it from the union. So was the paper's graphic design, with the familiar large letter *L* now doubled in the masthead. On 4 March, in what might have been the single most consequential decision of the Prague Spring, the KSČ presidium ended advance censorship. This was formalized when the national assembly amended the 1967 press law to abolish the Central Publication Administration (Ústřední publikační správa, ÚPS) on 26 June,[86] but by then, journalists, writers, and broadcasters had taken full advantage of the new latitude. Over the following months *Literární listy* became a key organ of free discussion, and by the end of June it had an astonishing weekly circulation of

300,000 copies (among a population of fourteen million), a figure comparable with daily newspapers like *Práce*.[87]

On 13 March the first of two public meetings under the banner "*Mladí se ptají*" (Young people ask) was held in Slovanský dům, the old German casino on Na Příkopě. The hall was packed and the atmosphere was electric.[88] Josef Smrkovský, Jan Procházka, Jiří Kroha, Marie Švermová, Pavel Kohout, and other political and cultural personalities responded to unscripted questions from the floor on formerly taboo topics. Asked about her experience during the 1950s purges, Marie Švermová assured the audience that, "despite it all, never, not even in the cruelest moments, did I cease to believe that truth will prevail, that thoughts and ideals cannot be destroyed, that it may be possible to deform and disfigure the ideas of socialism for a time but they can never be erased from the minds of the people and especially of the Czech nation, which is linked with the idea of socialism like few others."[89] *Rudé právo* failed to mention that Švermová also said: "I am convinced the communist party does not need to have its leading role inscribed in the constitution. If this is needed it testifies not to its strength but its weakness."[90] The second meeting on 20 March drew twenty thousand people to the Industrial Palace at Výstaviště. This time the panel also included Gustáv Husák, Ota Šik, and Eduard Goldstücker. "In the course of the discussion," it was agreed to send a letter "to A. Novotný with a request that he step down," reported *Rudé právo* the next day.[91] Both "Young People Ask" discussions were broadcast live on the radio. The first public call for Novotný to resign as president had appeared on 6 March, just two days after the suspension of censorship.[92] Thereafter demands that the president go came thick and fast: from the Slovak cultural organization Matica Slovenská, which accused him of "insulting national feeling"; from speakers at regional and district KSČ meetings; from university students in Bratislava; from the trade union council ÚRO; and from the teaching staff of the KSČ's party school (Vysoká škola politická ÚV KSČ). On 21 March the presidium "agreed to Antonín Novotný's request" to be relieved of his presidential duties, and his resignation was announced in the press the next day.[93] He was succeeded by the seventy-two-year-old war hero and former defense minister Ludvík Svoboda, whom the national assembly elected president on 30 March by a vote of 282 to 6.

During the week of 14–21 March, Michal Chudík was dismissed as president of the Slovak national assembly, Josef Kudrna and Jan Bartuška were fired as minister of the interior and general procurator, and Miroslav Pastyřík resigned the presidency of ÚRO. The poet Ivan Skála, whose musings on the sturdy oak benches in the Pankrác courtroom and attacks on Jaroslav Seifert's *Song about Viktorka* entertained us earlier, was replaced as director of the Mladá fronta publishing house. *Kulturní tvorba* and the daily *Večerní Praha* (Evening Prague) got new editors. Miroslav Zavadil quit as president of the Czechoslovak Union of Youth (Československý svaz mládeže, ČSM), as did two of the union's secretaries. The next week Vilém Nový stepped down as director of the KSČ party school and was replaced by the reformer Milan Hübl. Under pressure from his staff, Josef Kořoušek retired as rector of ČVUT "for health reasons." Helena Leflerová bowed out as president of the Czechoslovak Union of Women (Československý svaz žen), and the Union of Czechoslovak Journalists (Svaz československých novinářů) relieved Luděk Kapitola of his responsibilities as editor in chief of *Svobodné slovo* (The free word). By the end of the month KSČ functionaries had resigned from regional party committees in central, eastern, and southern Bohemia, Plzeň, Ostrava, Ústí nad Labem, Bánská Bystrica, and elsewhere. On 3 April defense minister Bohumír Lomský "asked to be relieved of his function," and he was.[94] In an especially piquant twist, six members of the KSČ's Central Control and Audit Commission (Ústřední kontrolní a revizní komise, ÚKRK), including chairman Pavel Hron, resigned at its 22–24 March meeting, after which the commission voted to reinstate Ivan Klíma, A. J. Liehm, and Ludvik Vaculík as KSČ members; annul Pavel Kohout's reprimand; and drop disciplinary proceedings against Milan Kundera. The next day the presidium accepted these recommendations and rescinded its negative evaluation of the Fourth Writers' Union Congress and the transfer of *Literární noviny* to the Ministry of Culture.

The KSČ central committee plenum of 1–5 April 1968 was extraordinary in more ways than one. Antonín Novotný and Michal Chudík were removed from the presidium. Novotný's associates Jiří Hendrych, Jaromír Dolanský, Bohuslav Laštovička, and Otakar Šimůnek stood down, as did presidium candidate member Miroslav Pastyřík. Hendrych also lost his membership in the KSČ secretariat and his post as president of its ideological commission, whence he had waged his culture wars. Jozef Lenárt, who was replaced as prime minister by Oldřich Černík, was demoted from a full member to a candidate member of the presidium. The new presidium, which was elected by secret ballot, contained a finely balanced mix of reformers (Dubček, Černík, Smrkovský, František Kriegel, Josef Špaček, and František Barbírek) and conservatives (Vasil Biľak, who had replaced Dubček as KSS first secretary; Drahomír Kolder, who initially supported the reformers but later changed sides; and Jan Piller, Emil Rigo, and Oldřich Švestka). Reformers Čestmír Císař,

Zdeněk Mlynář, Štefan Sádovský, and Václav Slavík joined the party secretariat, as did the conservative Alois Indra. Oldřich Černík's new government, which was sworn in on 8 April, had a decidedly reformist cast. Jiří Hájek (the diplomat, not the editor of *Plamen*) replaced Václav David at foreign affairs, and Josef Pavel replaced Josef Kudrna as minister of the interior. Ota Šik became a deputy prime minister, along with Peter Colotka and Gustáv Husák. Although his name would later become synonymous with normalization, Husák was then seen as being in the reformist camp. Ladislav Štoll, author of *Thirty Years of Struggles for Czech Socialist Poetry*, lost his job as director of the Institute for Czech Literature of the Czechoslovak Academy of Sciences, and František Kriegel was elected chairman of the National Front the same day. On 18 April Josef Smrkovský was elected speaker of the national assembly.

The plenum adopted the Akční program KSČ (Action program of the Communist Party of Czechoslovakia), which had been in preparation since January and in many ways embraced a breathtaking agenda of reform. The sections dealing with reforms in the political system were written by Zdeněk Mlynář.[95] The program committed the KSČ to fighting for a new constitution that would "provide firm guarantees against a return to the old methods of subjectivism and highhandedness." These guarantees included "freedom of speech of minority interests and opinions," "constitutional freedom of movement, particularly the traveling of our citizens abroad," and "better and more consistent" protection of "the personal rights and property of citizens." "Constitutional freedoms of assembly and association" would be furthered by ensuring that "the possibility of setting up voluntary organizations, special-interest associations, societies, etc. is guaranteed by law . . . without bureaucratic interference and without monopoly of any individual organization."[96] Economic reform was a central plank of the program, which envisaged an economy based on "independence of enterprises and enterprise groupings and their relative independence from state bodies, a full and real implementation of the right of the consumer to determine his consumption and his style of life, [and] the right to a free choice of working activity."[97] The Slovaks were promised "a socialist federal arrangement . . . of two equal nations in a common socialist state."[98] The economic reforms would fall by the wayside in the wake of the impending Soviet invasion, along with the freedom of speech, movement, and assembly. The federalization of Czechoslovakia, which was legislated by the national assembly on 24–28 June and set up separate Czech and Slovak national councils for the two new federated republics, outlasted the Prague

Spring, slaking what had been a powerful source of discontent throughout the Novotný years.

The Action Program acknowledged that "the rehabilitation of people—both communists and non-communists—who were the victims of legal violation in previous years, has not always been carried out in all its political and civic consequences."[99] On 21 March the presidium set up a commission under Jan Piller to reinvestigate the 1950s trials (this would also become a casualty of the invasion). Without waiting for the commission's report, ÚKRK voted at its 22–24 March session to fully rehabilitate Rudolf Slánský, Otto Šling, Bedřich Geminder, Marie Švermová, Josef Smrkovský, and several other party members. These rehabilitations were ratified by the central committee at the April plenum. Meanwhile, the newspaper *Student* had launched a series titled "Women with a Similar Fate: A Series of Conversations of Students with the Widows of Those Executed in the 1952 Trial." The first to be interviewed was Heda Margolius Kovály. "To my mind," she said, "the cause of everything was too much power in too few hands." Notwithstanding Heda's view that the issue was not whether the men who framed, tried, and hanged her husband Rudolf were scoundrels (*lumpové*) but the conditions that allowed them to do so, she was quite clear that this did not absolve them from personal responsibility: "a person who inflicts harm and is even responsible for the death of innocent people, should at the least be removed from their position, this is completely obvious."[100] She knew, as did the editors and readers of *Student*, that many of those complicit in the trials still held office. On 27 March an organization called K-231 was established in Prague to get justice for *all* citizens persecuted in the 1950s, communist or otherwise. "Facing the truth of history" did not stop with the 1950s trials.[101] On 10 March the press devoted considerable attention to the twentieth anniversary of Jan Masaryk's death as over two thousand Prague students visited his grave at the presidential retreat at Lány Castle near Kladno.[102] That same day Ivan Sviták wrote to the general procurator demanding "an investigation into whether twenty years ago the foreign minister in Gottwald's post-February government, Jan Masaryk, was murdered as the first victim on the road to totalitarian dictatorship."[103] His letter was published on the front page of *Student* on 3 April. An inquiry into Masaryk's death was set up a week later.

Between March and May *Student*, which had previously acted as a compliant mouthpiece of the ČSM, carried interviews with the widows of Vlado Clementis and Otto Šling, not to mention František Antel, the procurator in the Slánský trial; articles by Sviták, Václav Černý, and the former editor of *Tvář*

Emanuel Mandler; reports of the student disturbances in Poland and France; a letter in which the exiled archbishop of Prague, cardinal Josef Beran, discussed his house arrest and internment from 19 June 1949 to 4 October 1963; the transcript of Emil Filla's 1951 "trial" at the hands of his fellow artists in SČSVU; interviews with Pavel Juráček, Jan Němec, Evald Schurm, and others on political interference in the film industry; translations of Isaac Deutscher on Stalin and Leszek Kolakowski on Marxism; and features on Sokol, the Czechoslovak Legions in Russia, Tomáš Masaryk, Ferdinand Peroutka, Tomáš Baťa, prison labor in the uranium mines at Jáchymov, and the deportation of Allen Ginsberg. The paper also reported on German student leader "Red Rudi" (rudé Rudi) Dutschke's visit to Prague for the Third Christian Peace Conference and interviewed the French poet Jean Schuster, who was in town for Princip slasti (The Pleasure Principle), the first international surrealist exhibition to take place in Czechoslovakia since 1947.[104] One scoop was a four-part exchange between Pavel Kohout and the German novelist Günter Grass on democratization in Czechoslovakia, in which the Czech playwright insisted that "there are many ways to resolve social conflicts," among which "performative [manifestační] flight abroad and performative appeals to the conscience of the world are among the least successful." "The only police of whom I am currently afraid," Pavel joked, "are the traffic cops in the free Hanseatic city of Hamburg," where he had recently arrived to direct a theatrical adaptation of The Good Soldier Švejk.[105] The sense of liberation in these pages is palpable. For the previous twenty years such freedom of discussion had been unthinkable.

The events in Prague sent shock waves across the Soviet bloc. On 22 February GDR leader Walter Ulbricht compared the Czechoslovak situation to Hungary in 1956 and warned that Ota Šik's economic reforms paved the way for a return to capitalism.[106] On 23 March the leaders of Bulgaria, Czechoslovakia, East Germany, Hungary, Poland, and the Soviet Union met in Dresden to consider "the Czechoslovak question," although the Czechoslovaks were not told in advance that this would be the agenda. Instead of the discussion of economic cooperation they had been expecting, they got what delegate Drahomír Kolder described as a cold shower. "We see a danger, and we want to talk about it," began Leonid Brezhnev. "A wave of public and political activities of an entire group or of entire centers has come into existence which has brought the entire public life of Czechoslovakia to counterrevolution." "Why not draw conclusions from what happened in Hungary?" demanded the Polish leader Władysław Gomułka. "In our country and in Hungary everything began

FIGURE 11.2. Adolf Hoffmeister, *Franz Kafka—Constantly Threatened Prague*, 1968. Collage. From František Šmejkal, Hoffmeisterova ironická kronika doby, Litoměřice, 2016. Courtesy of Martin and Ivan Hoffmeister, © Adolf Hoffmeister heirs.

with the writers. . . . It starts with the arts." Ulbricht concurred: "Five years ago the capitalist world press had already written that Czechoslovakia was the most advantageous point from which to penetrate the socialist camp. Why? Because within your intelligentsia—I am speaking now of writers and artists—the Western oriented forces are the strongest. . . . There was the discussion about Kafka, then other issues."[107] As if to prove his point, two days later 134 Czechoslovak writers and artists published an open letter to the KSČ central committee welcoming Novotný's resignation as a sign that "the current democratization process . . . will lead to permanent democracy."[108] Among the signatories were Jaroslav Seifert, Adolf Hoffmeister, and Eduard Goldstücker.

Dubček and his comrades were caught on the horns of an impossible dilemma. Even as the pressure mounted from other members of the Warsaw Pact, the reformers were coming under increasing fire at home for not going far or fast enough. Bohuslav Blažek expressed a widespread skepticism when, at the beginning of June, he opened an article in *Student* titled "Democracy Our Destination?" with this cutting sentence: "After twenty years of its rule the Czechoslovak Communist Party has for certain reasons decided that under its leadership, we will be allowed to engage in a battle for something it took away from us twenty years ago, i.e., democracy."[109] Two months earlier Alexandr Kramer had asked an equally pointed question: "What Kind of Democracy?" Rejecting Josef Smrkovský's contention that "no party or organization can exist among us that does not have the building and development of a socialist society in its program," Kramer maintained that "democracy is indivisible. Simply—democracy. And without it there cannot be socialism either." Any KSČ-led democratization, he argued, will fall foul of "sacred, inviolable principles.—The leading role of the communist party. Friendship and alliance with the Soviet Union. A socialist system.—These are our axioms. We can't touch them. The moment somebody brushes up against them discussion ends, we stop using arguments. Emotions enter, tears in the eyes, beating of breasts and—what is worse—banging of tables."[110]

The Action Program tried valiantly to square this circle. It acknowledged, "In the past, the leading role of the Party was often conceived as a monopolistic concentration of power in the hands of Party bodies." Its proposed remedies included a clear institutional separation of party and state; a greater role in state policymaking for other political parties within the National Front, as well as for trade unions and voluntary organizations; and the strengthening of democratic norms within the KSČ itself. Conceding that "at present it is most important that the Party practices a policy fully justifying its leading role in society," the program sought to redefine the party's role as one of leading by example rather than by direction. "The Communist Party," it proclaimed, "enjoys the voluntary support of the people; it does not practice its leading role by ruling the society but by most devotedly serving its free, progressive socialist development. The Party cannot enforce its authority but this must be won again and again by Party activity. It cannot force its line through directives but by the work of its members, by the veracity of its ideals." The one thing the Action Program did not envision was the existence of genuine opposition parties ("The Communist Party of Czechoslovakia considers the National Front to be a political platform which does not separate the political parties into the government and the opposition"), because the one thing the program refused to contemplate was that the KSČ could ever be voted out of power.[111]

Unlike many future dissidents, such as Milan Kundera, Pavel Kohout, Ludvík Vaculík, and Ivan Klíma, Václav Havel had never been a member of the Communist Party, and he called out the elephant in the room. "The halfheartedness of all these conceptions," he argued in Literární listy on 4 April, "has a common cause: none of them make possible a real *choice*. Really: democracy can properly be spoken of only when the people have the opportunity—once in a while—to freely choose who will govern them. Which presupposes the existence of at least two commensurable alternatives. Thus, of two competent, equal and mutually independent political forces, both of which have the same chance of becoming the leading power in the state if the people so decide."[112] The playwright was not the only one unconvinced by the communist reformers' attempts to reconcile democratization with the leading role of the KSČ. On 3 May around four thousand people gathered in the Old Town Square to discuss establishing an opposition party. On 13 May the newly formed Klub angažovaných nestraníků (Club of Committed Non-Party Members, KAN) issued a manifesto denouncing "the abnormal situation of the past twenty years when a sharp divide was created between communists and non-communists" that "virtually prevented non-communists from holding any higher economic, political, and, hence, social position."[113] Attempts were made to resurrect the Social Democratic Party, whose absorption into the KSČ in 1948 had no legal basis in the first place, argued Zdeněk Karl in an open letter to Dubček, Svoboda, Smrkovský, and František Kriegel on 22 May.[114]

The most significant manifestation of the will to press forward, backward not a step, was the "*Dva tisíce slov*" (Two thousand words) manifesto published in Literární listy, Mladá fronta, Práce, and Zemědělské noviny (Agricultural news) on 27 June. Written by Ludvík Vaculík in response to a request from a group of concerned scientists, the text carried nearly seventy signatures. Among them were Josef Hiršal, Miroslav Holub, Ivan Klíma, Pavel Kohout, Milan Kundera, A. J. Liehm, Jan Procházka, Jaroslav Seifert, Josef Škvorecký, Josef Topol, and many other writers; Jiří Hanzelka, whose articles, books, radio broadcasts, and films of his travels in a Tatraplan car with Miroslav Zykmund through eighty-three countries in the 1940s and 1950s had made him a celebrity throughout the Soviet bloc; film directors Jaromil Jireš, Jiří Menzel, Alfréd Radok, Emil Radok, Jan Švankmajer, and Jiří Trnka; painter and glassmaker Jan Kotík; Olympic medalists Věra Čáslavská, Jiří Raška, Emil Zátopek, and Dana Zátopková; National Artist Jan Werich; entertainers Jiří Suchý and Jiří Šlitr; National Theater tenor Beno Blachut; pop singers Yvonne Přenosilová and Karel Gott; director of the Czechoslovak Radio Dance Orchestra Karel Krautgartner; theater director Otomar Krejča; and actors Rudolf Hrušínský, Iva Janžurová, Jiřina Jirásková, Jan Kačer, Marie Tomášová, and Jan Tříska. Scientists and scholars in fields ranging from literary theory (Felix Vodička) and philosophy (Karel Kosík) to geology and medicine lent their names, along with twenty-five workers and technicians from the ČKD engineering works in Prague. So did Martin Vaculík, first secretary of the KSČ's Prague city committee, and Oldřich Starý, rector of Charles University, both of whom were members of the KSČ central committee; indeed, every third signatory of "Two Thousand Words" was a KSČ member. Vlado Kašpar, president of the Svaz českých novinářů (Union of Czech Journalists),[115] and Ludvík Pacovský, secretary of FITES, also signed the manifesto, but this time, SČSVU president Adolf Hoffmeister and SČSS president Eduard Goldstücker kept their powder dry. Subsequently, at least 120,000 other citizens from all walks of life wrote to the newspapers and added their signatures.[116]

Vaculík neither pulled his punches nor minced his words. "The Communist Party, which after the war enjoyed great popular trust," he charged, "gradually bartered this trust for offices, until it had all the offices and nothing else":

> The mistaken line of the leadership transformed a political party and union based on ideas into an organization for exerting power.... Parliament unlearned how to debate, government how to govern, and managers how to manage. Elections had no significance, and the law carried no weight. We could not trust our representatives on any committee or, if we could, requesting anything from them was pointless because they were unable to accomplish anything. Worse, we could hardly trust one another. Personal

and collective honor deteriorated. Honesty counted for nothing, and all talk of evaluation according to capability was in vain. So most people lost their interest in public affairs.

"Let us demand the departure of people who abused their power, damaged public property, and acted dishonorably or cruelly," Vaculík urged, and engage in "public criticism, resolutions, demonstrations, demonstrative work brigades, collections for gifts for their retirement, strikes, and picketing at their doors. . . . Let us revive the activity of the National Front. Let us demand public sessions of national committees. For questions that nobody else wants to know about, let us set up our own civic committees and commissions. . . . Let us convert the district and local press, which has mostly degenerated into an official mouthpiece, into a tribune for all positive political forces . . . let us start new papers. Let us form committees for the defense of free speech."

Noting that "there has been great disquiet recently over the possibility that foreign forces will intervene in our development"—a threat that would soon be spelled out by the communist parties of Bulgaria, East Germany, Hungary, Poland, and the Soviet Union in the so-called Warsaw letter of 14–15 July—"Two Thousand Words" ends on a note of quiet defiance. Some might detect an echo of Milena Jesenská's dispatches in *Přítomnost*. "In the face of whatever superior forces, we can only stick to our guns with decency and not start anything ourselves," writes Vaculík. "We can show our government that we will stand behind it, if necessary with weapons, so long as it does what we give it a mandate to do . . . this spring just finished and will never return. By winter we will know all."[117] Later that day the KSČ presidium met in emergency session. While acknowledging that "we have no reason to doubt [the signatories'] good intentions," it unanimously condemned the publication of "Two Thousand Words" as "an act that in its objective consequences could extraordinarily impede, and indeed even endanger the further development of the KSČ Action Program, the policies of the National Front as well as of the government of our republic."[118] Josef Smrkovský was blunter: "Comrade Dubček, if we don't put an end to this now, it will be settled by tanks."[119]

The Odium of Treason

"I saw what was being said and done around me as in a movie," writes Zdeněk Mlynář. "It was like absurd theater. Here were people anxiously wondering what would happen in the next hour, both to the nation and to themselves personally, who, without ever admitting it aloud, were worried about possible arrest and deportation; and beside them, people who would have much preferred to be in the Soviet embassy by now forming a new government. And here these two camps were, sitting silently together, each preoccupied with their own thoughts while the words of the man who had set the whole calamity in motion were droning on in stammered phrases."[120] After a long and heated discussion, the KSČ presidium voted by a majority of seven to four to issue an immediate public proclamation, which had been drafted on the spot at Dubček's request by Čestmír Císař and Zdeněk Mlynář. It was nearly 1:30 a.m. on Wednesday, 21 August.

To All the People of the Czechoslovak Socialist Republic
Yesterday, 20 August 1968, at around 11:00 p.m., the armies of the USSR, the Polish People's Republic, the German Democratic Republic, the Hungarian People's Republic, and the Bulgarian People's Republic crossed the state borders of the ČSSR. This took place without the knowledge of the president of the republic, the executive of the national assembly, the prime minister's office, and the first secretary of the KSČ central committee and without the knowledge of these organs. At this time the KSČ central committee presidium was in session and preparing for the Fourteenth Congress of the party. The KSČ central committee presidium calls upon all citizens of the republic to keep calm and not resist the advancing troops, because the defense of our borders is now impossible.

This is why neither our army, nor our security services nor our people's militia have received orders to defend our land. The KSČ central committee presidium considers this act as contrary not only to the fundamental principles of relations between socialist states, but also as a violation of the fundamental norms of international law.

All leading officials of the party and the National Front remain in their functions, to which they were chosen as representatives of the people and members of their organs according to the laws and other regulations valid in the ČSSR. Immediate meetings of the national assembly and the government of the republic have been convened by the constitutionally authorized officials [*ústavními činiteli*] and the KSČ central committee presidium is convening a plenum of the party central committee to discuss the emerging situation.[121]

Dubček, Černík, Smrkovský, Kriegel, Špaček, Barbírek, and Piller voted in favor of the proclamation; Biľak, Kolder, Rigo, and Švestka against. According to Mlynář's memoirs, among the candidate members of the presidium and members of the KSČ secretariat who participated in the meeting but did not have voting rights, Bohumil Šimon, Čestmír Císař, Václav Slavík, Štefan Sádovský, and Mlynář himself backed the resolution, while Alois Indra, Antonín Kapek, and Miloš Jakeš opposed it; Mlynář could not remember what position Jozef Lenárt took, but he did not recall Lenárt supporting Bil'ak's group.[122]

The Soviets and their internal collaborators had not bargained for a repudiation of their intervention. The plan had been for a palace coup to take place at the presidium meeting, immediately *followed by* a request for "fraternal aid." However, the Warsaw Pact forces crossed the borders before a vote could be taken on a report by Indra and Kolder on the internal political situation, which had been intended to precipitate the putsch. Barbírek and Piller had promised to support a motion of nonconfidence in Dubček, but they were not prepared to publicly endorse an unsolicited invasion of the country.[123] Over the next twenty-four hours the KSS presidium,[124] Prague city KSČ committee and several other regional and local KSČ committees, national assembly, Czechoslovak government, Czech national council, central committee of the National Front, ÚRO, Svaz protifašistických bojovníků (Union of Antifascist Fighters), Czechoslovak Academy of Sciences, Charles University, and creative unions all denounced the occupation.[125] This made it far more difficult to install a credible puppet regime than the Soviets had anticipated.

It emerged later that Bil'ak, Kolder, Švestka, Indra, and Kapek were the authors of a secret "Letter of Invitation" requesting "support and assistance with all the means at your disposal . . . as an urgent request and plea for your intervention." Bil'ak had handed this letter to Soviet politburo member Pyotr Shelest in the men's washroom during talks between Czechoslovakia and the Soviet Union, East Germany, Poland, Hungary, and Bulgaria in Bratislava on 3 August.[126] The Bratislava meeting had been called to ratify agreements reached in negotiations between the KSČ presidium and the Soviet politburo at Čierna nad Tisou on the Slovak-Ukrainian border on 29 July–1 August, ending a tense month of military posturing and diplomatic skirmishing. The pretext for the invasion was the failure of the Czechoslovak leadership to implement measures agreed at Čierna, "which required that all the mass media—the press, radio, and television—be placed under the supervision of the Central Committee and the government, and that all anti-socialist and anti-Soviet publications be stopped." Dubček, the Soviets charged, had not instituted "effective measures against periodicals such as *Literární listy*, *Mladá fronta*, *Reportér*, and *Práce*."[127] Nor had he removed "Pelikán, Císař, Kriegel, and other scoundrels" from their posts. I quote Leonid Brezhnev, who saw the dismissal of Czechoslovak Television director Jiří Pelikán as "the first step needed to restore order in the mass media."[128] Čestmír Císař headed the KSČ central committee's section for education and science and was elected the first president of the Czech national council on 10 July. Dubček had hoped to temporize until the Extraordinary Fourteenth KSČ Congress scheduled for 9 September, which he was confident would consolidate the reform wing's hold over the party leadership. For the same reason, Bil'ak, Indra, and their fellow conservatives were determined to prevent the congress from taking place. Another major figure in the conspiracy, deputy interior minister and de facto StB head Viliam Šalgovič, liaised closely with Soviet intelligence in laying the groundwork for the invasion and coordinating the arrests of reformers afterward.

As soon as the presidium meeting was over, the struggle to establish alternative facts began. Kolder, Bil'ak, and Indra left for the Soviet embassy. Černík set out for the prime minister's office, and Švestka headed for the offices of *Rudé právo*, where he was editor in chief. Císař went home. Dubček, Smrkovský, and other members of the party leadership remained in the central committee building. The text of "To All the People of the Czechoslovak Socialist Republic" was telephoned to Czechoslovak Radio soon after 1:00 a.m., but Karel Hoffmann, director of Ústřední správy spojů (the Central Communications Authority), cut off broadcasting of the proclamation midway through the first sentence, and Oldřich Švestka stopped its publication in *Rudé právo*. In both instances staff phoned Josef Smrkovský at the central committee building, who countermanded those orders. As the previously unknown Radio Vltava began to spew pro-invasion propaganda in bad Czech,[129] Czechoslovak Radio repeatedly broadcast the proclamation once it resumed normal service at 4:30 a.m. Tanks arrived at the station's headquarters on Vinohradská Street at around 7:30, where they were met with barricades. At 8:00 a.m. Czechoslovak TV refused to broadcast a statement from "a group of Czechoslovak state and party functionaries asking the Soviet Union for help."[130] The radio building was occupied soon after 9:00. So were the stations in Ostrava and Bratislava, but Czechoslovak Radio managed to stay on the air, using local and army transmitters, for another two weeks. On 21 August every Prague daily carried the presidium's proclamation. In a special edition of *Rudé právo* the editorial board stated that it "firmly stands behind Dubček's leadership of the Communist Party of Czechoslovakia, behind president of the Czechoslovak Socialist Republic Ludvík Svoboda, behind Černík's government of the republic," and it advised readers to stay calm, avoid provocations, and treat the occupying forces "neither as enemies, nor as friends."[131] By early afternoon Soviet troops had occupied and evacuated the *Rudé právo* offices and print shop too. The ČTV building was occupied on the afternoon of the twenty-second.

While the best-laid political plans were going awry, the military operation proceeded like clockwork. During the night of 20–21 August at least 200,000 Warsaw Pact troops entered the country from the GDR, Poland, and Hungary with some five thousand tanks and eight hundred aircraft.[132] At around 1:30 a.m. two Soviet military aircraft landed at Ruzyně with several dozen soldiers aboard, who seized the main airport building. During the night 120 Antonov AN-12 and AN-24 planes followed at one-minute intervals, transporting an entire airborne division. Soviet paratroopers arrested Oldřich Černík at bayonet point in the prime minister's office at around 3:00 a.m. Led by a limousine from the Soviet embassy, a convoy of tanks and armored cars surrounded the KSČ central committee building at around 4:30. By 5:00 a.m. troops had occupied the premises and cut off the phones. Soldiers entered Dubček's office and detained him at gunpoint for several hours, along with Smrkovský, Kriegel, Špaček, Šimon, Mlynář, and other senior officials and aides. At around 9:00 a group of StB and KGB men arrived and arrested Dubček, Smrkovský, Kriegel, and Špaček in the name of the "revolutionary government led by comrade Indra."[133] After several hours, during which they were confined in the absent Císař's office, they were driven to Ruzyně airport, as were Černík and Šimon. In the meantime, Císař had been arrested at home, escaped, and gone into hiding. In the evening the Czechoslovak leaders were flown to Poland and then taken by train to a KGB barracks at Uzhgorod, in what used to be Sub-Carpathian Ruthenia but was now part of Soviet Ukraine. Their guards did not treat them kindly.[134]

A reporter for *Mladá fronta* filed an update of an old story, describing the situation at 4:30 a.m. on 21 August 1968 outside the KSČ central committee building on the Embankment of the Kiev Brigade (today, Ludvík Svoboda Embankment):

On Prague's streets, the streets of my proud city, I lived through the Munich humiliation, on Na Příkopě on 15 March 1939 we threatened the Nazis, on 28 October 1939 we demonstrated for freedom, in May 1945 we welcomed the new freedom with the first issues of *Mladá fronta*, after January 1968 we opened the road to a new life.

Our history is studded with tragedies. We have often been crushed. But we always lived to see freedom. And this time too freedom will arise in our land.

"Journalists show up as well as young people from various strata. They discuss, they disagree with the occupation, some of the girls are crying."[135] As day broke, hundreds of Praguers began to gather in the Old Town Square around the Hus memorial, above which the Czech flag flew. *Práce* reported that "directly under the tower of the Old Town Hall meritorious artist [*zasloužilá umělkyně*, an honorific title] Vlasta Chramostová is talking with a Soviet captain: 'Why did you come? After all you are our friends. And friends don't come for a visit bearing weapons. We want calm, freedom, sovereignty, and friendship.'" The actress would pay for her bravery. After 1968 she was banned from film, TV, and radio. She worked at Otomar Krejča's Theater beyond the Gate until it was closed by the authorities in 1972; after she signed Charter 77 she was banned from the stage too, so she confined herself to invitation-only performances in her Bytové divadlo (Apartment Theater), held at her own and friends' private homes. "There are tears in the eyes of many people," *Práce* continued. "If the Soviet soldiers and commanders knew how to read them, they would understand."[136] Some did. At the occupied provisional parliament building on Senovážné Square (then Maxim Gorky Square), one of the representatives, a "typical broad in the beam Slovak mama," gave a Russian soldier a piece of her mind. "I've got two boys as old as him, their whole lives they have heard the nicest things possible about them [Russians] . . . I asked him, how am I supposed to explain all this to my sons? He understood and he's crying. Now he wants to be alone to pull himself together before his commander arrives."[137] "People crying in the streets," wrote another journalist in *Svobodné slovo*. "These scenes are like press clippings from the weekly magazines of 15 March 1939."[138] Every time is different. And every time is the same.

Recent research has identified a total of 137 Czech and Slovak civilians killed during the invasion, of whom fifty were shot dead on the first day.[139] During the fighting at Czechoslovak Radio three people were killed and fifty-two wounded by gunfire, twelve lost their lives when a munitions truck exploded, and two died jumping from the windows of a burning building. The façade of the National Museum and other nearby structures were damaged by shelling, and several vehicles were destroyed.[140] The symbolism of this violation of the cradle of the national revival was missed by no one. Jan Drda—he of the red farts, who replaced Ferdinand Peroutka as editor of *Svobodné noviny* back in the glory days of February 1948—wrote with bitter fury:

My pen trembles in my hand, my voice tightens in my throat. For twenty-five years I have taught my children to love the Soviet Union, to see

Moscow as the lodestar of our security, the guarantor of our national and state independence. Now it is all in ruins. These faces, these uniforms . . . that I taught them to revere as the faces of our liberators, my children now see with their own eyes with horrible associations. They see them spill Czech blood, shell our national monuments, they are witnesses to how with unparalleled cynicism they abduct Dubček and Černík—the representatives of our sovereignty—to God knows where. The count of the crimes committed in Prague streets during these days calls to the heavens. . . . Whoever wrote [these words] on a Prague wall was a hundred times right: "Don't bend to them even a hair, don't give them even a drop of water."[141]

Young people in particular thronged the streets, surrounding the tanks and remonstrating with the invaders in the Russian they had all learned in school. Road signs were turned around and street names obliterated, along with nameplates on apartment doorbells. Anti-Soviet graffiti and posters sprang up everywhere. Many showed that "well-known Czech humor, that always and everywhere helped us," said one report, giving the example: "Ivan, come home quick, Natasha's dating Kolja!"[142] Even some StB units refused to obey orders from collaborators.[143] A two-minute strike hastily organized by the creative unions at noon on 21 August brought the city to a standstill. One-hour general strikes followed on the twenty-second and twenty-third. From 9:00 to 9:15 a.m. on the twenty-sixth the entire country was filled with the din of sirens, church bells, and car horns. Josef Václav Myslbek's Saint Wenceslas statue on Wenceslas Square was covered with Czechoslovak flags, flyers demanding that the occupiers go home, and the ubiquitous slogan "Dubček—Svoboda," a play on words, as *svoboda* is Czech for "freedom." "The inscription on the statue, which normally we wouldn't even notice," commented *Rudé právo*, "today takes on living significance."[144] That inscription reads "*Nedej zahynout nám, ni budoucím*" (Don't let us perish, nor our descendants), a line from the Saint Václav Chorale, the second-oldest song in the Czech language. "It was the picture of a city whose inhabitants were absolutely united in unarmed, passive resistance against alien interlopers," writes Zdeněk Mlynář. He adds: "It was something that could not have taken place with the Nazi armies when they arrived in March 1939."[145] In many ways that made it so much worse.

On the afternoon of 21 August around a third of the KSČ central committee members met at the party's private Hotel Praha (today the Grand Hotel Bohemia) on Králodvorská Street in the Old Town, just behind the Municipal House. Kolder, Indra, Biľak, and Barbírek showed up in the evening with an

FIGURE 11.3. Soviet-led Warsaw Pact invasion of Czechoslovakia, Prague, August 1968. Photographer unknown. Central Intelligence Agency.

armed guard of Soviet soldiers whose presence, reported Martin Vaculík, caused several members to "change their previous positions"—he does not say in which direction. Indra, Kolder, Piller, Vilém Nový, and future KSČ first secretary Miloš Jakeš were "unequivocal collaborators."[146] But the attendees came to no conclusion as to what should happen next. The following day Indra, Bil'ak, Kolder, Barbírek, Rigo, Piller, Švestka, Šalgovič, Lenárt, Jakeš, and others met at the Soviet embassy to discuss forming a "Provisional Revolutionary Workers' and Peasants' Government." Though no one present—including Zdeněk Mlynář—opposed the idea, everyone knew that (as Indra bluntly put it) "the odium of treason will be left on everyone who takes over." There were no volunteers to usurp Dubček's position as KSČ first secretary, and President Svoboda, the group's favored candidate to lead such a provisional government, refused point-blank to do so because, he said, "ninety-five percent of the population are behind Dubček and Černík." At a meeting at Prague Castle later that night with Bil'ak, Piller, Kolder, Soviet ambassador Stepan Chervonenko, and others, Svoboda proposed that Dubček and Černík should be released and restored to their posts, with the understanding that they would immediately step down. He asked to go to Moscow for talks. "If we proceed in this tactical way," he pleaded, "the people will accept it ... and it will be done without bloodshed. Otherwise, 15 million people will curse the president and all members of the government and the Central Committee presidium."[147] Edvard Beneš and Emil Hácha might be forgiven a wry smile at their communist successor's predicament.

While Bil'ak, Indra, and company were arguing at the Soviet embassy over the composition of a quisling government, the party held its Extraordinary Fourteenth Congress in a works canteen of the ČKD plant in Vysočany. At the suggestion of Bohumil Šimon, Dubček had acted to schedule the congress and summon delegates to Prague immediately after the presidium meeting ended on 21 August. Despite the circumstances, 1,192 out of 1,543 elected delegates from regional and city KSČ organizations made it to Vysočany. The Slovak delegation led by Gustáv Husák, Laco Novomeský, and Peter Colotka was stopped and arrested at Břeclav in southern Moravia. As a result, only five Slovaks were present at the start of the meeting, although some fifty more arrived later. Even though the KSS central committee met on 25 August and endorsed the results of the Vysočany congress, this would subsequently be used as a pretext for declaring it illegal.[148] Sitting from 11:00 a.m. to 9:15 p.m., the delegates adopted several documents condemning the invasion as well as electing a new central committee, which, they insisted, "will be the only legal representative of the party."[149] The first eight names chosen were of "the comrades who were prevented from coming to the congress . . . Svoboda, Dubček, Černík, Smrkovský, Císař, Šimon, Špaček, Kriegel."[150] Others elected included foreign minister Jiří Hájek, Ota Šik, Eduard Goldstücker, Oldřich Starý, Karel Kosík, Martin Vaculík, Zdeněk Mlynář, Jiří Pelikán, Laco Novomeský, and Gustáv Husák. There was no place on the 144-member body for Bil'ak, Kolder, Rigo, Švestka, Barbírek, Piller, Indra, Kapek, Lenárt, Jakeš, or Šalgovič; the congress made it clear that "it does not recognize even as members of the party those members of the former central committee who failed to pass muster in this difficult test."[151] Later that evening the new central committee chose a twenty-eight-member presidium that was also dominated by reformers and unanimously reelected Alexander Dubček as first secretary of the KSČ.[152]

Having failed in their original plan, the Soviets went back to the drawing board. Sometime on the morning of 23 August (he had "lost sense of the time"), Dubček was taken from his cell in Uzhgorod to an upstairs office. "After a short while the phone rang," he related later, "and it was [Nikolai] Podgorny speaking. He talked to me very cordially, and then said that we needed to negotiate. I said to him: 'Where?' He replied: 'How about Moscow?' And I said into the telephone: 'Well, fine, but in what capacity will I be brought there? As a prisoner? You see, I demand to know where the others are who were arrested with me are. I am unwilling to discuss anything until we're all together.'" Dubček was flown to Moscow, where he and Černík were reunited with Svoboda, who had arrived at 2:15 p.m. together with Bil'ak, Indra, Piller, Husák, minister of defense Martin Dzúr, and justice minister and Socialist Party leader Bohuslav Kučera. Dubček felt there was something odd in Svoboda's demeanor: "I sensed in his face a certain stiffness. . . . He was tense the whole time, as if he were doing something he didn't really want to do."[153] Brezhnev claimed Svoboda had privately told Soviet leaders "he did not trust Dubček and would do his utmost to have him dismissed from office after normalization," but "for now if he were to return home without Dubček, it would be Dubček, not he, who would be the hero."[154]

Over the next three days Zdeněk Mlynář's theater of the absurd was reprised in Moscow as Dubček, Černík, Smrkovský, Špaček, Šimon, Czechoslovak ambassador Vladimír Koucký, and the members of Svoboda's delegation had several meetings with Brezhnev, Kosygin, and other Soviet leaders. Barbírek, Rigo, Švestka, Jakeš, Lenárt, and Mlynář flew in to join the talks on 25 August. Only František Kriegel refused to play his part in the pantomime and asked to be returned to his place of detention. The "Jew from Halič [Galicia]," as Pyotr Shelest contemptuously called him, was the only representative of the prewar communist generation left in Dubček's leadership apart from Josef Smrkovský. Kriegel had served in both the Spanish and the Chinese civil wars as a medical doctor.[155] Brezhnev offered to release Dubček, Černík, and Smrkovský, "provided that guarantees are given that Dubček and Černík will fulfill the pledges made at Čierna nad Tisou and that the so-called congress is declared illegal." He also demanded "minor changes" of personnel: "For example, the anti-Leninist Císař, let him be chairman of the Czech National Council, but he cannot be in the leadership of the party."[156] On the night of 26 August all the Czechoslovaks except for Kriegel signed the so-called Moscow Protocol. Dubček (who had suffered a mild heart attack when Podgorny raised the specter of civil war) held out until the last moment—his remarks caused Brezhnev to walk out at one point—but he finally capitulated.[157] "I didn't feel justified in risking a confrontation between a morally courageous but unarmed populace, on the one hand, and the military machinery of a superpower, on the other," he explained many years later.[158] The echo was unmistakable. In the words of Petr Král, "They signed the new Munich accords."[159]

The Moscow Protocol declared the Vysočany congress illegal and its resolutions invalid; undertook to dismiss "persons whose activities were not in keeping with the interests of ensuring the leading role of the working class and the communist party" from party and state organizations; guaranteed there would be no reprisals against "individuals . . . because of their friendly attitude toward the Soviet Union"; and promised to institute "immediate measures . . . to reinforce the regime of the working masses and the positions of socialism." The latter included "prohibition of anti-socialist and anti-Soviet measures in the press, on radio, and on television; a ban on activities by various groups and organizations advocating anti-socialist positions; and a ban on activities by the anti-Marxist Social Democratic Party." Only when "the threat to the gains of socialism in Czechoslovakia and the threat to the security of the countries of the socialist commonwealth have been eliminated" would "the allied troops . . . be withdrawn in stages from the ČSSR's territory."[160] The Czechoslovak leaders returned to Prague early in the morning on 27 August. Feeling there had been no alternative but to compromise, Smrkovský told the nation, "we were aware of the consequences, above all the moral and historical consequences that such a solution could have." Though he was nearly sixty and "had not experienced little in life," the previous few days "were the most difficult of my life, and I also know that the days to come will not be easy."[161]

Alexander Dubček addressed his compatriots on the radio at around 5:00 p.m. on the twenty-seventh. "He was so devastated after his six-day detention," writes Milan Kundera, "he could hardly talk; he kept stuttering and gasping for breath, making long pauses between sentences, pauses lasting nearly thirty seconds." It was another one of those images that contain in little a whole world:

> The compromise saved the country from the worst: the executions and mass deportations to Siberia that had terrified everyone. But one thing was clear: the country would have to bow to the conqueror. For ever and ever, it will stutter, stammer, gasp for air like Alexander Dubček. The carnival was over. Workaday humiliation had begun.[162]

The First Torch

One of the documents adopted at the Vysočany congress was a letter to Dubček that ended with the words: "The congress has again elected you to the new central committee and we see in you our foremost representative for the future. We firmly believe that the government of the affairs of the Czech and Slovak nation will return to its hands and that you will return among us."[163] The letter addresses Dubček by the familiar *Ty* form used among family and close friends rather than the more formal *Vy*. This is not the only way the language used conveys far more than the text explicitly states. The words "the government of the affairs of the Czech and Slovak nation will return to its hands" echoed the exiled Comenius's prayer following the defeat of Bohemian Protestantism (and the extinction of Bohemian independence) in the Thirty Years' War—*"vláda věcí tvých k tobě se zase navrátí, ó lide český"* (the government of your affairs will return to you again, O Czech people).[164] These are the same words (translated into English) Ladislav Sutnar plastered across the front of the Czechoslovak pavilion after the German invasion left it stranded at the New York World's Fair in 1939. Tomáš Masaryk, too, had begun his first speech to the national assembly as Czechoslovak president by quoting these words on 22 December 1918.[165] Dubček did return to his people. He even managed to retain his position as first secretary of the KSČ for a time. The government of the affairs of the nation was another matter.

The KSČ central committee was informed of the contents of the Moscow Protocol—whose text was not made public—at a plenary session on 31 August, where a new presidium was also chosen. Dubček, Černík, Smrkovský, Špaček,

Bil'ak, and Piller were reelected; Kolder, Rigo, Švestka, and candidate member Kapek were not. Nor was František Kriegel. Čestmír Císař was relieved of his duties as secretary to the central committee. New presidium members included Gustáv Husák, Zdeněk Mlynář, Václav Slavík, Štefan Sádovský, Bohumil Šimon, Evžen Erban, and Ludvík Svoboda. Husák had also been elected first secretary of the KSS at its Fourteenth Extraordinary Congress in Bratislava on 26–29 August in place of Vasil Bil'ak. Although the plenum formally annulled the decisions of the Vysočany congress, Dubček co-opted eighty of those elected at Vysočany to the central committee. Notwithstanding the departure of Kriegel and Císař, the overall effect of these changes, in appearance at least, was to reduce the representation of the pro-Soviet faction in the KSČ's central organs while strengthening that of the reformers. But the other "personnel changes" demanded by the Soviets came soon enough. Interior minister Josef Pavel was dismissed on 31 August, followed by deputy prime minister Ota Šik (who was shipped off to be an adviser to the Czechoslovak embassy in Belgrade) on 2 September. Šik fled to Switzerland six weeks later, where he ended up teaching at the University of St. Gallen for twenty years.[166] František Kriegel resigned as chairman of the National Front on 6 September, and Jiří Hájek stepped down as foreign minister on 14 September. On 30 August a new Office for Press and Information (Úřad pro tisk a informace, ÚTI) was established to "bring into line the news and journalism of the Czechoslovak press, radio and television," and on 13 September the national assembly formally restored censorship. Jiří Pelikán was replaced as director of Czechoslovak Television shortly thereafter, as was Zdeněk Hejzlar as director of Czechoslovak Radio. The media firings were not entirely one-sided: Oldřich Švestka also lost his job as chief editor of Rudé právo, and Karel Hoffmann was dismissed as director of the Central Communications Authority. The nonparty organizations K-231 and KAN were banned on 5 September. On 16 October Černík and Kosygin signed a treaty on the "Temporary Presence of Soviet Troops in the ČSSR." As it turned out, temporary meant twenty-three years; the last Soviet soldier left Czechoslovakia on 22 June 1991.[167]

Hundreds of young people demonstrated against normalization in the capital on 28 October and again in Prague (where 176 people were arrested), Bratislava, Brno, and several other cities on 7 November. The Union of University Students published a ten-point proclamation calling for the end of censorship after six months and guarantees of freedom of assembly and association, academic and cultural freedom, and the right to travel abroad.[168] On 13 November Ludvík Vaculík, Martin Vaculík, Emil Zátopek, chess grand master Luděk Pachman, and other critics of the occupation participated in a meeting on Slavic Island reminiscent of the "Young People Ask" sessions back in March. Ludvík Vaculík told the students, "The threat facing young people again and again in every generation is our own fanaticism, which is the very thing that happened to our socialism."[169] I doubt it was what they wanted to hear. When the students were denied permission to organize a procession for the International Day of the Students, they responded with a three-day occupation of university buildings in Prague, Bratislava, Brno, Liberec, and elsewhere. Journalists were concurrently up in arms over a one-month ban on publication of *Reportér*. The last issue of *Literární listy*, a two-page leaflet, had appeared on 28 August. On 7 November the Writers' Union launched *Listy*, whose first issue contained articles by Karel Kosík, A. J. Liehm, and Jaroslav Seifert. The poet had just been elected to succeed Eduard Goldstücker as the union's president. Eda, who was vacationing in the Tatras at the time of the invasion, had fled to Vienna with his "toothbrush and pajamas" on 4 September. He got a telephone call the next day offering him a position as visiting professor at Sussex University in England, where he ended up teaching comparative literature until his retirement.[170] Dozens of writers participated in *Listy*'s questionnaire "On the Meaning of Our Actions." Václav Havel's answer was memorable: "We proclaim! We demand! We stand! We don't slacken off! We challenge! We promise! We don't betray! We refuse! We don't allow! We reject! We condemn! We endure! We don't disappoint! We won't retreat! We won't sign on!"[171]

It was against this background that the KSČ central committee, meeting in plenary session on 14–17 November, once again fine-tuned the party leadership. Zdeněk Mlynář was relieved of all his party positions at his own request, although he remained an ordinary member of the central committee. By then, he says, he had given up all hope of salvaging any reforms. Disillusioned with the postinvasion leadership, he would rather go back to his academic research as an entomologist. After seeing his colleagues sit down in October with Alois Indra, the erstwhile intended head of the Revolutionary Workers' and Peasants' Government "freshly delivered from Moscow . . . as though nothing had happened," he asked himself, "How could I have ever believed that the Prague Spring represented such people's sincere political attitudes? Hadn't I known for more than ten years that Antonín Zápotocký was both a judicious tactician and a man who raised his hand for the death sentence for long-time friends and comrades? These people were no different. In this society," he reflected, "I suppose such behavior really is normal."[172] This wasn't Mlynář's first encounter with the banality of evil. After the execution of the defendants in the Slánský trial," he tells us, "their property was sold off cheap to surviving high-level functionaries, and on this occasion the Novotný family (Mrs Božena Novotná personally) bought the bedclothes and china tea service belonging to Vlado Clementis!"

> The thought that the first secretary of the ruling party and the head of state slept between bedsheets belonging to a man whom he had helped send to the gallows is something quite incredible in twentieth-century Europe. Nevertheless it was true. And it is not as if the Novotnýs did not know what they were doing. I talked about this matter to Lída Clementisová in 1956, and I learned that Božena Novotná had admired the Clementis's china tea service when she and her husband had been for a visit back in the days when Clementis was foreign minister.[173]

Mlynář was replaced by deputy prime minister Lubomír Štrougal, a minister of the interior in the Novotný era. A new executive committee comprising Dubček, Černík, Erban, Husák, Sádovský, Smrkovský, Svoboda, and Štrougal was concurrently established within the nineteen-member presidium. The effect was to reduce the influence of the more radical reformers elected on 31 August.

Three weeks later Dubček, Svoboda, Černík, Husák, and Štrougal met with Brezhnev, Kosygin, Podgorny, and Shelest in Kyiv. Brezhnev again brought up personnel matters, fingering Kriegel ("clearly anti-Soviet and a right-winger"), who was still a member of the central committee, and the "virulently anti-Soviet" Milan Hübl, who had succeeded the conservative Vilém Nový as director of the party school. Kriegel would be expelled from the party five months later at the central committee plenum of 29–30 May 1969. But the Soviet leader's main target—and a conspicuous absentee from the Kyiv meeting—was Josef Smrkovský. "It's very important who serves as head of the National Assembly," Brezhnev complained, and "we don't hide our consternation about the way Smrkovský acts, and yet no one has found enough strength to take him to task."[174] The onetime political prisoner Gustáv Husák stepped into the breach. At a KSS central committee meeting in Bratislava on 22 December he demanded that, since two of the three top state offices—president and prime minister—were held by Czechs, the speaker of the national assembly (or, as it was called from 1 January 1969, the federal assembly) should be a Slovak. In the context of federalization, this was an argument that could not be dismissed. Despite massive public support and threats of a general strike,

Smrkovský agreed to stand down and was replaced by Peter Colotka, whose deputy he now became. This sidelining of one of the best-loved "men of January" was ratified by the central committee on 16 January 1969.

That same afternoon Jan Palach, a twenty-year-old student of history and political economy at the Philosophy Faculty of Charles University, doused himself in gasoline and set himself on fire on the ramp of the National Museum on Wenceslas Square. He died from his injuries three days later. A letter was found in his briefcase:

> Because our nations find themselves on the brink of hopelessness, we have decided to express our protest and awaken the people of this land by the following means. Our group is composed of volunteers who are determined to let themselves burn for our cause. I had the honor of drawing the first lot and so have gained the right to write the first letters and step up as the first torch. Our demands are:
>
> Immediate ending of censorship.
>
> A ban on the circulation of *Zprávy* [the newspaper published by the occupying forces from 30 August 1968].
>
> If our demands are not met within five days, i.e., by 21 January 1969, and if the people do not come out in sufficient support (i.e., an indefinite strike), more torches will ignite.
>
> Torch no. 1
>
> P.S. Remember August. A space has
been freed up for the ČSSR, use it.[175]

Palach's death unleashed a national outpouring of grief. His coffin was displayed on 24 January in the Karolinum, the ancient seat of Prague University. Tens of thousands of people lined up for hours to say their farewells. The funeral ceremonies commenced the next morning with eulogies in the Karolinum courtyard. "In deep emotion, with pain and pride the academic community of Charles University bows before the dead Jan Palach, a student of the Philosophical Faculty," began rector Oldřich Starý. "His heroic and tragic act is the expression of a pure heart, of the highest love for the homeland, truth, freedom and democracy." Starý too alluded to Comenius's seventeenth-century prayer, assuring the mourners that the governance of their affairs would return to them, even if the path would be thorny.[176] After the orations were over, the coffin was placed on a hearse, behind which Palach's mother Libuše, older brother Jiří, and sister-in-law Ilona led "an

FIGURE 11.4. Czechoslovak citizens lining up to pay their respects at Jan Palach's coffin as he lies in state at the Karolinum, 24 January 1969. Photographer unknown. © ČTK.

immense procession, which snaked like a river through the Fruit Market (Ovocný trh), Celetná Street, and the Old Town Square and stopped in front of the Philosophical Faculty building on the square that was spontaneously renamed Jan Palach Square in honor of the immolated young man on 20 January 1969."[177] The square did not officially become náměstí Jana Palacha until 20 December 1989; until then it was called Red Army Square (náměstí Krasnoarmějců) in remembrance of the Soviet soldiers who died in the liberation of Prague in 1945.

An estimated 200,000 mourners filled Prague's streets for Palach's funeral. Minister of education Vilibald Bezdíček and minister of sport Emanuel Bosák were the only government representatives. Both were newly appointed and little known to the public. Dubček, Černík, Smrkovský, and Svoboda signed a telegram of condolence to Palach's mother on the day of Jan's death, but neither they nor any other senior KSČ official came to pay their respects. It is a stark illustration of how far apart the nation and those entrusted with its governance had already grown. Jan's sacrifice did not galvanize the people to political resistance, as he had hoped. It was too late for that. Instead, the dead student took his place in a long line of national martyrs running from Jan Hus—whose fiery example of dying in truth after refusing to recant before the Council of Constance in 1415 inspired Palach's action as much as the Buddhist monks of Vietnam—through Comenius and Karel Havlíček Borovský to Jan Opletal. After the authorities turned down a Student Union request to inter Palach in the Slavín (Pantheon) mausoleum in Vyšehrad, he was buried in Olšany Cemetery, where his grave became a pilgrimage site. Tired of the endless visitors with their candles and their flowers, the StB bribed two grave diggers with a couple bottles of cognac to exhume Jan's remains one night in July 1973. His body was cremated and returned to his family in Všetaty, a small town in central Bohemia. The pilgrims still came, but there were fewer of them, and at least it wasn't Prague.[178]

"Nobody is allowed to remain alone," wrote Jaroslav Seifert in Listy on behalf of all the creative unions. "Not even you, students who have resolved upon the most despairing act, can be allowed to have the feeling that there is no other path than the one you have chosen. I beg you, do not think in your despair that our cause can only be solved now and that it will be solved only here."[179] He was right. It would take another twenty years before the government of their affairs was returned to Czech hands, and that it happened all depended more on events in Moscow than on anything anyone said or did in Prague. Such is the fate of small nations whose existence is a perpetual question mark. Knowingly or otherwise, the student motto from November 1989, *Kdo, když ne my, kdy, když ne teď!* (Who, if not us, when, if not now!), echoed Seifert's words and took up their implicit challenge. The slogan is credited to Květoslava Morávková, a geobotany student in her final year at Charles University.[180] But Seifert's plea did not sway Jan Zajíc, an eighteen-year-old high school student from Šumperk in northern Moravia, who chose the anniversary of the 1948 KSČ coup, 25 February, to go up in flames as "Torch no. 2" in the doorway of a building on Wenceslas Square. Zajíc penned the following poem—one of two he dedicated to Palach—a few days before his own immolation. It is titled *"Poslední"* (The last):

I hear your cowardice,
it cries in the fields,
it bawls in the cities,
it whimpers at the crossroads,
it stammers with fear of death
and does not feel how death alerts and entices

From the church towers tolls
the death knell of the nation and the land
In the name of life
yours
I burn

Jan[181]

It is no doubt the height of bad taste to mention Jaromil, the nineteen-year-old hero of Milan Kundera's *Život je jinde* (*Life Is Elsewhere*, completed in Bohemia in 1969 and published in Paris in 1973) in this context, but I can't keep him from flitting across my mind. "Jaromil is a talented poet, with great imagination and feeling. And he is a sensitive young man," Kundera tells us. "Of course, he is also a monster."[182] The novel climaxes in Jaromil's ecstatic betrayal to the police of his girlfriend's brother's plans to flee the country in the heady revolutionary days following Victorious February. As a result, the girl is arrested and Jaromil realizes that "through his decisive act he had *entered the realm of tragedy*."[183] "Of course, it was terrible to sacrifice an actual woman (redheaded, nice, delicate, talkative) for the sake of the future world," he reflects, "but it was probably the only tragedy of our time that was worthy of beautiful verse, worthy of a great poem!" He fondly fantasizes her being abused and humiliated by the prison guards, one of whom "watched her through the peephole while she was sitting on a bucket, urinating."[184] There is a disturbing resemblance between events in *Life Is Elsewhere* and the accusations the magazine *Respekt* leveled against Kundera in 2008, but maybe that is just coincidence.[185] "I did not choose those years because I wanted to draw their portrait," he explains, "but only because they seemed to me to be a matchless trap to set for Rimbaud and Lermontov, a matchless trap to set for poetry and youth."[186] Ludvík Vaculík had a point when he warned young people to beware their fanaticism. Kundera's Jaromíl too dreamed of dying by fire.

"*What are we going to do? Carry on*," Egon Erwin Kisch told Lenka Reinerová the day she learned her entire family had been murdered in the Holocaust.

Reinerová concludes *Dream Café of a Prague Woman* with glimpses of the raging reporter "in the shadow beneath the arch of the portal with the bears, in the smile of a girl, in a lighted cigarette" as she walks down Melantrichova Street, where they both used to live way back when. But on the last page of the book is a photograph of the author, who was by that time an imperious old lady, standing in front of the family home in Karlín, where she couldn't bear to set foot for years. Beneath it she writes:

> After Jan Palach's death I received a letter at the editorial office [of the magazine *Im Herzen Europas*, of which she was editor in chief from 1958 to 1970]. It had no return address, but its author was a girl from Berlin. She was the same age as Jan and said she had decided to die the same death. What now? I rushed to the print works, removed an article from the new issue and in its place wrote an open letter on how one must live and want to do something and that my unknown girl shouldn't do it. Sometime at the end of summer someone knocked at the door and a girl entered the editorial office. She shyly introduced herself and said in German: "I am your suicide." So she survived it. Today she is already a mature woman, and her daughter is called Maria-Lenka. It was my most successful article.[187]

As for the Prague Spring, it was all over bar the shouting. The final act began with what has gone down in history as the Czechoslovak Hockey Riots. On 21 March 1969, at the World Ice Hockey Championships in Sweden, the Czechoslovak national team beat the Soviet Union 2–0. On 28 March they made it back-to-back victories with a score of 4–3. Nobody could mistake this for a sporting event: some of the Czechoslovak players had put black tape over the red star on their jerseys, and the entire team refused to shake hands with their opponents at the end of the game. Czechoslovak TV anchor Milena Vostřáková described the result as a "moral victory" and was immediately fired. She was banned from the media for the next twenty years. "Hundreds of thousands of fans have come to Wenceslas Square to celebrate our victory," the radio announced. "Wenceslas Square has never seen such a celebration before. Unfortunately, there was also vandalism—and not only in Prague."[188] Half a million people poured into the streets across the country, and the celebrations soon escalated into anti-Soviet protests. The Aeroflot office on Wenceslas Square was trashed, almost certainly by StB provocateurs. The violence provided the pretext for Leonid Brezhnev's coup de grâce. On 31 March Soviet defense minister Andrei Grechko arrived unannounced in Prague and threatened a renewed military crackdown if the Czechoslovaks did not quickly snuff out the "counterrevolution." This time he found receptive ears in the KSČ leadership, with Černík, Svoboda, and Husák at the fore.

At its plenary session of 17 April 1969 the KSČ central committee accepted Alexander Dubček's resignation as general secretary and elected Gustáv Husák in his stead. The executive committee of the presidium was abolished. Its last act was a proclamation clearing Vasil Bil'ak, Drahomír Kolder, Miloš Jakeš, Alois Indra, Jan Piller, František Barbírek, Emil Rigo, Oldřich Švestka, Jozef Lenárt, and Antonín Kapek of any wrongdoing in connection with the 1968 invasion. The presidium shrank from twenty-two to eleven members: Bil'ak, Černík, Colotka, Dubček, Erban, Husák, Piller, Sádovský, Svoboda, Štrougal, and Karel Poláček, who took Smrkovský's place. Dubček replaced Peter Colotka as speaker of the federal assembly. Husák, Svoboda, and Indra went for a two-week vacation to the Crimea in early August, where they met with Brezhnev. Soon after their return, student demonstrations on Wenceslas Square were put down on 19–20 August and over five hundred people arrested. On 21 August—the first anniversary of the invasion—protests in Prague, Brno, Bratislava, Liberec, and elsewhere were brutally suppressed. In Prague three demonstrators were killed, nineteen wounded, and 649 taken in for questioning, 80 percent of whom were younger than twenty-five years of age. The next day Svoboda, Černík, and Dubček signed the so-called Baton Act (*pendrekový zákon*), on the basis of which 1,526 people were convicted for participating in the August demonstrations.[189]

Dubček was relieved of his position as speaker of the federal assembly a month later and was appointed ambassador to Turkey in December. He was voted off the KSČ presidium at the central committee plenum of 25–26 September, which undertook further housecleaning of the party's central organs. Among others, Josef Smrkovský, Zdeněk Mlynář, Jiří Hájek, and Milan Hübl were removed from the central committee, and Josef Špaček, Bohumil Šimon, and Martin Vaculík resigned, supposedly of their own volition. Václav Slavík was expelled from the party. The same meeting repudiated the presidium's proclamation of 21 August 1968 and confirmed that the Vysočany congress was "illegal and anti-party." From now on the Warsaw Pact invasion would officially be described as "fraternal and international aid." The presidium accepted Dubček's resignation from the central committees of the

KSČ and KSS on 19 January 1970. Oldřich Černík resigned as prime minister nine days later and was succeeded by Lubomír Štrougal, who would head the Czechoslovak federal government for the next eighteen years. That same day the KSČ central committee approved the resignations of Černík, Sádovský, and Poláček from the presidium. Their replacements included Jozef Lenárt and Antonín Kapek. Jan Piller resigned in February 1971 and was replaced by Alois Indra, and Karel Hoffmann was added to the presidium in May 1971. Only one member of the presidium remained from the night of the 1968 invasion: Vasil Bil'ak.[190]

Comenius's prayer had one more echo in this period. Two days after the invasion twenty-five-year-old pop singer Marta Kubišová recorded a song called "*Modlitba pro Martu*" (A prayer for Marta). Songwriters Jindřich Brabec and Petr Rada originally intended it to be an uplifting ending for the TV serial *Píseň pro Rudolfa III* (Song for Rudolf III, 1967–1969), a musical comedy about a Prague butcher and his resourceful teenage daughter Šárka, but "A Prayer for Marta" metamorphosed into a protest song against the Soviet occupation. "It never occurred to me where it would lead," Marta said later. "I was firmly convinced that they would never be able to ban me just because I sang some song." Kubišová was then at the peak of her popularity, winning the national *Zlatý slavík* (Golden Nightingale) award for best female singer in 1966, 1968, and 1969. She was dating the film director Jan Němec; they made a glittering couple. The Beatles' "Hey Jude" sounds stunning in her deep, smoky contralto; apart from the Fab Four, her favorite singers were Dionne Warwick, Nancy Wilson, and Tom Jones.[191] Her miniskirts and mascara would not have been out of place in London's Carnaby Street. Issued as a single by Supraphon in October 1968, "A Prayer for Marta" was included on Kubišová's first LP *Songy a balady* (Songs and ballads), which was released in the summer of 1969 and rapidly sold out. A second pressing at the beginning of 1970 omitted "A Prayer" at the insistence of the censor, and the record disappeared from stores soon after.[192] Marta was presented with her third Golden Nightingale award in the editorial offices of *Mladý svět* (Young world) with no publicity. As the screws of normalization tightened, the authorities pressured the Pragoconcert agency, which had a monopoly of bookings, to drop her from its roster. Her last public appearance (until twenty years later) was in Ostrava on 27 January 1970 with her trio the Golden Kids.

A month later, forged pornographic photographs provided the pretext to ban Kubišová from recording or performing publicly. The StB offered her a chance to sing again if she signed a statement supporting normalization, but

FIGURE 11.5. Marta Kubišová (on the right) and the Golden Kids in the Netherlands, July 1969. Photographer unknown. Nationaal Archief, licensed under Creative Commons Attribution—Share Alike 3.0 Unported.

Marta refused. Despite winning a lawsuit over the obscenity allegations, she was not allowed to resume her musical career. Supraphon's director admitted in court that the photographs were not of Marta, but "in the meantime they had canceled everything—work contracts, fees, recordings, I lost them all in eight months . . . I was completely done for."[193] These were the offending lyrics of "A Prayer for Marta":

> Let peace long remain with this land,
> Malice, envy, hate, fear, and strife,
> Let them pass away, let them pass already.
> Now, when the lost government of your affairs
> returns to you, people, returns.[194]

12

Normalization and Its Discontents

Všude dobře, doma nejlíp [Everywhere's good, but home's best].

—OLD CZECH SAYING

Our Věra

Postage stamps can reveal much about an era. In Czechoslovakia after Victorious February, the youthful athletic body took its place alongside Lenin, Stalin, tractors, smokestacks, Hussites, national costumes, and space exploration as a philatelic emblem of socialist construction. Youth symbolized the new world coming into being, and sport was seen as a means of glorifying the nation while cultivating the new individual. The cult of healthy minds in healthy bodies plucked a resonant string in the Czech Lands: remember Milena Jesenská's advocacy of gymnastics, tennis, and swimming as essential activities for the modern, liberated young woman? Spartakiáda originated in 1921 as a working-class alternative to the nationalistic Sokol, which had disciplined Czech bodies for the nation since 1862.[1] In addition to commemorating the Spartakiáda meets (1955, 1960, 1965) and the summer and winter Olympic Games (1960, 1963, 1964, 1968), Czechoslovak postage stamps celebrated "Physical Education" (1952–1954), "Sport" (1956–1959, 1961–1963), and "Sporting Events" (1965–1967). Amid the endless anonymous running, jumping, skiing, swimming, discus-throwing, and javelin-hurling bodies in motion, individual achievements were occasionally recognized. The athletes featured in the "Czechoslovak Olympic Victories" set of stamps issued in 1965 included Emil Zátopek, the army captain who took gold in the 5,000 meters, 10,000 meters, and marathon at the 1952 Helsinki

Games—a feat nobody has matched before or since—and the gymnast Věra Čáslavská, who won three gold medals at the Tokyo Olympics in 1964.[2] These were household names in Czechoslovakia as well as international sporting celebrities.

It was embarrassing for the normalization regime that Zátopek and Čáslavská had both signed "Two Thousand Words." So did Jiří Raška, the gold medalist in the ski jump in the 1968 Grenoble Winter Olympics, and Dana Zátopková, who won gold in the javelin in Helsinki an hour after her husband Emil won the 5,000 meters. In the immediate aftermath of the invasion, Zátopek became a vocal critic of normalization. He was discharged from the army, thrown out of the KSČ and all sporting organizations, and reduced to working as a laborer. He eventually found a job with a geological enterprise. A month after Jan Palach's suicide Vilém Nový, the former head of the KSČ party school, floated a ludicrous conspiracy theory that the student's immolation had been an attempted fraud using fake fire that had gone tragically wrong; he claimed that Zátopek, Pavel Kohout, chess grand master Luděk Pachman, journalist Vladimír Škutina, and student leader Luboš Holeček were all implicated. Zátopek, Kohout, Pachman, and Škutina sued Nový for defamation, but Zátopek pulled out of the litigation at the last minute in July 1970, apologizing in court for "besmirching the honor of a respected communist" and "insulting the Communist Party of Czechoslovakia during the difficult hours of its existence." Kohout was livid. "It was Emil who suggested we go to court," he complained, but "after a sordid agreement with power he launched into two decades of nauseating normalization."[3] Zátopek went on to condemn the signatories of Charter 77 as "anti-state elements," and he denounced the 1984 Los Angeles Olympics, which the Soviet bloc boycotted, as "imperialist." "Emil wasn't interested in politics," explained Dana Zátopková in his defense. "It's easy to spit on someone. We were famous, and so the regime abused us. There were many such moments."[4]

Jiří Raška withdrew his signature from "Two Thousand Words" in May 1970.[5] Despite the incomprehension of friends (who urged her, "Věra, when you recant you'll have peace and quiet, you'll travel all over the world, you'll be able to train youth, you'll live fabulously"), Čáslavská refused to do the same.[6] At the Tokyo Olympics a Japanese admirer, Ryuzo Otsuka, had presented her with a samurai sword that had been in his family since the seventeenth century—not for her victories but for the fighting spirit she showed after falling from the uneven bars in the final:

I had an element on the uneven bars that amazed the Japanese. It was the so-called double turn from one hanging position to another, which the Japanese gymnasts Takashi Ono and Yukio Endo were the first in the world to demonstrate on the horizontal bar. Up until then no woman had done such a combination, so the Japanese called it Ultra-C. The public were really looking forward to it. In the final I could have done an average exercise because I had already accumulated enough points from the compulsory and free elements to win the gold medal. . . . But that way I would have disappointed the public. So I did the exercise with the Ultra-C. . . .

When a crash like that happens in the final there is an unwritten rule that ordinarily the competitor does not complete the exercise and returns to the dressing room. But I had in my head "their" Ultra-C. I jumped back on the bars and I nailed the exercise like never before. It was a sort of gift to the Japanese.[7]

Had she succumbed to the pressure and retracted her signature on "Two Thousand Words," Věra said, she never could have looked at the sword again.[8]

I said earlier that the 1960s were in Prague and Prague was in the 1960s, a decade of cultural challenge and political protest across the world from Paris to Tokyo to Chicago. Hundreds of people were killed in Mexico City when government forces opened fire on student demonstrators just ten days before the opening of the 1968 Olympic Games. The Mexico Olympics is indelibly associated with Tommie Smith's and John Carlos's defiant black power salutes at the medal ceremony for the 200 meters—"the nasty demonstration against the American flag by negroes," as (white) International Olympics Committee (IOC) president Avery Brundage described it; fifty years later Donald Trump hurled the same willfully misleading accusation at "that son of a bitch" Colin Kaepernick when the San Francisco 49ers' quarterback kneeled during the playing of the US national anthem as a protest against racial injustice.[9] This was not the only podium protest at the 1968 games. When the Soviet tanks rolled into Czechoslovakia, Čáslavská was at a training camp in Šumperk, the home of "Torch no. 2" Jan Zajíc. The mountain rescue service spirited her away to a cottage in the nearby Jeseník Mountains, afraid that she would be arrested because of her support for the Prague Spring. "I was totally isolated for three weeks, but I continued to train," she told the Los Angeles Times in 1990. "While the Soviet gymnasts were already in Mexico City, adjusting to the altitude and the climate, I was hanging from trees, practicing my floor exercise in the meadow in front of the cottage and building callouses on my hands by

FIGURE 12.1. Věra Čáslavská performing on the uneven bars, 1966.
Photographer unknown. Nationaal Archief, made available under Creative
Commons CC0 1.0 Universal Public Domain Dedication.

shoveling coal."[10] It was uncertain whether the Czechoslovak team would be permitted to compete at all, and they were only cleared to fly to Mexico at the last minute. "If we weren't allowed," Věra concluded, "it would have amplified the fact that it was an occupation, and not their [the Soviets'] fraternal help."[11] Mexican spectators gave the Czechoslovak athletes a standing ovation as they entered the stadium during the opening ceremony. They adopted Čáslavská as one of their own.

"It was a big mistake that Mr Brezhnev let me go," laughs Věra in Olga Sommerová's 2012 film *Věra 68*. Čáslavská took gold in the vault, uneven bars, and floor exercise, as well as silver on the balance beam, and she successfully defended her all-around title won at Tokyo, one of only two women gymnasts ever to do so. That record still stands, and she remains the only competitor, male or female, to win Olympic gold medals in every gymnastics discipline. But Věra's athletic performance was not the only reason millions of Czechs— and Mexicans—took her to their hearts. Twice she stood on the podium as a Soviet competitor was awarded the gold: as the silver medalist behind Natalia

Kuchinskaya on the balance beam (a result the crowd noisily booed), and as a joint gold medalist in the floor exercise with Larisa Petrik (whose scores had been raised by the judges after Věra was declared the winner). Both times Čáslavská cast her eyes down and turned her head away from the ascending flags as soon as the Soviet anthem started to play. When the music stopped, she told Petrik, "I congratulate you on your gymnastics and as a gymnast but not for what your country has done and the invasion of our country."[12] The next day Věra married her teammate, the runner Josef Odložil, at the Metropolitan Cathedral on Mexico City's Zócalo, the Plaza de la Constitución. The couple were besieged by thousands of spectators inside the building (where a bodyguard of weightlifters had to clear enough space for the priest to administer the vows) and out.[13] "I have the most valuable medal, the man of my dreams, and my wish to have the wedding in this beautiful country has been fulfilled," Věra told Mexican journalists. "But the greatest happiness of my life was to receive the gold medal for my country."[14]

On 31 October, four days after the games ended, President Svoboda welcomed the Olympic team to Prague Castle. The nation had rare cause to celebrate. Punching well above its weight, Czechoslovakia finished eighth in the overall medals table.[15] In the presence of Alexander Dubček, Oldřich Černík, Josef Smrkovský, and Evžen Erban, representing the KSČ, the government, the national assembly, and the National Front, respectively, Svoboda congratulated the team before conferring the Order of the Republic (*Řád republiky*), the country's highest civilian honor, on Čáslavská. The twenty-six-year-old was single-handedly responsible for four of Czechoslovakia's seven gold medals and five of its total thirteen medals in Mexico, as well as sharing in the silver for the all-around women's gymnastics team's performance. "I would like to say a few words to you, Věruška," the president began, using the familiar, diminutive form of her name. "I know that abroad they have given you tens of names and titles. For us at home you are simply '**our Věra**.' And we love you. Not only for your excellent successes, but for your modesty. What you have accomplished is the fruit of huge perseverance and tenacity, but also of that modesty and love for our socialist homeland. . . . Your example is especially significant in this respect for our youth. . . . And so you have every right to the Order of the Republic I am conferring upon you and for which I congratulate you with my whole heart." In return, Věra gave each of her Prague Spring heroes Dubček, Svoboda, Černík, and Smrkovský a miniature replica of one of her gold medals. The ceremony was the lead story in next day's *Rudé právo*.[16]

FIGURE 12.2. Věra Čáslavská receiving her Order of the Republic from president Ludvík Svoboda at Prague Castle, 31 October 1968. Alexander Dubček stands behind Svoboda, and Josef Smrkovský stands to the president's left. Photographer unknown. © ČTK.

"In the beginning it was great glory, we brought medals and then it began, and I was unemployed for five years," Věra told the oral history archive *Pamět' národa* (Memory of the nation) in 2014. There were four things the normalization regime would not forgive her: "I refused to revoke my signature on 'Two Thousand Words,' I beat the representatives of the occupiers in Mexico, I got married in church, and I turned my head away from the occupiers' flag on the victory podium during the Soviet anthem."[17] Contrary to some accounts, Věra was not banned from competing after the Mexico games. She retired from competition to lead a "normal life" and have children. But the Prague gymnastics club Rudá hvězda Strašnice (Red Star Strašnice) expelled her in 1971 for "insufficient cooperation," and she was not allowed to coach.[18] She was stopped from traveling abroad, and journalists were forbidden to write about her. An appeal to Svoboda fell on deaf ears. Věra's "fan" (her sardonic description) sent out his chief of staff with this message: "The president is sorry, but you must do something about your signature on 'Two Thousand Words.' To err is human, but to refuse to correct an error is diabolical." When Mladá fronta published Čáslavská's memoir *Cesta na Olymp* (The road to Olympus) in 1972, all passages relating to the Soviet invasion and her protest at the Mexico Olympics were deleted by the censor. After several years spent cleaning houses "in disguise," beginning in 1975 Věra was permitted to advise the national gymnastics team's coaches but not to coach the athletes directly. It took another decade (and sustained pressure from IOC president Juan Antonio Samaranch, who visited Prague in 1985 to award Čáslavská and Zátopek the Olympic Order) before she was appointed a full-time coach for the national team in preparation for the 1988 Seoul Olympics.

Čáslavská was one of the individuals who appeared beside Václav Havel on the Melantrich publishing house balcony overlooking Wenceslas Square during the nightly demonstrations of November 1989. When the playwright became president, she returned to Prague Castle as his adviser on sports, education, and youth. She recalled it as a period of incredibly hard work in which "there was no time to take in those unique life moments," such as when she met Barbara Bush, when Pope John Paul II wagged his finger and told her to be a good girl, and when she was photographed with the Rolling Stones. She served as president of the Czechoslovak Olympic Committee from 1990 to 1996. But there was to be no Hollywood ending. Though Věra loved her husband Josef, the man of her dreams "had a temper." She ended the relationship after he abused her parents and her children Radka and Martin. Josef and Věra divorced in 1987. In 1993 the site of Věra's unorthodox training for the Mexico Olympics acquired new associations when Martin tried to stop a fight between his father and another man at a dance club in Bělá pod Pradědem in the Jeseník Mountains. Martin pushed (or some say hit) Josef, who fell to the floor, struck his head, and died in the hospital a month later. The Šumperk district court sentenced Martin to four years in prison in 1996. He was pardoned by Václav Havel, but in her own words, Věra "fell to pieces. For sixteen years." At one point she made her way to Nusle Bridge in a sweatshirt in the rain, sizing up the mesh barriers intended to prevent suicides. By a miracle, she says, she overcame her depression and resumed coaching and public life in 2009. She was awarded Japan's Order of the Rising Sun for her "extraordinary contribution to the mutual understanding of two such distant cultures" and helped organize aid to Japan after the earthquake and tsunami of March 2011.[19] Revisiting Tokyo later that year, she tracked down the family of Ryuzo Otsuka, whose samurai sword had steeled her during her long conflict with the communist authorities.[20] She died of pancreatic cancer on 30 August 2016.

Čáslavská may have been officially forgotten in Czechoslovakia during the decades of normalization, but she was fondly remembered in Mexico. When coal supplies from the Soviet Union to Cuba were interrupted in 1979, Mexican president Jose Lopez Portillo offered to replace them on the condition that the Czechoslovak government allow Věra to take up a coaching position in Mexico. Čáslavská returned to Mexico City with Josef and the children in tow in May 1979 to coach 150 young gymnasts. She lived there for two years, became fluent in Spanish, and had her own TV program, *Exercising with Věra*. A sequence in *Věra 68* splices footage of the Czech national anthem "*Kde domov můj?*" playing as the young Čáslavská proudly receives one of her gold medals in 1968—the commentator cannot help but sing along and chokes up at the words "*a to jest ta krásná země, země česká, domov můj*" (and this is that beautiful land, the Czech land, my home)—with images shot in 2012 of Věra visiting the pyramids at Teotihuacán, less than an hour's drive from Mexico City and one of the most awe-inspiring sights on this planet. "I am glad I am here," she says, "on my old knees. And I have to say that today, these pyramids, I have stroked these pyramids with my eyes, I have touched them with my eyes, and it almost made me cry." Now a stout and stately woman, her face deeply lined and wrinkled, she smiles as the film jump-cuts to grainy black-and-white footage of her stretching her limbs in the same spot, just a young thin pale soft shy slim slip of a thing then, over forty years before.

Liquidation of a Person

Normalization was not a simple reprise of the Stalinist terror that followed Victorious February. Though the odd playwright, journalist, or rock musician was thrown in jail from time to time *pour encourager les autres*, the KSČ did not restore its authority by spectacular show trials, exemplary executions, and a gulag full of inmates serving sentences of ten years to life.[21] The machinery of normalization was more mundane and more insidious than that: purging the party; reestablishing control over economic, social, and cultural institutions through the *nomenklatura*; banning independent organizations; censoring publications, radio, TV, performances, and exhibitions; denying employment and educational opportunities to dissidents and their families, who were sometimes hounded into emigration and deprived of their Czechoslovak citizenship. Watching over everyone and everything required a monstrous surveillance apparatus in which large segments of the population were bribed, blackmailed, or coerced into snitching on their coworkers, friends, and neighbors.[22] The regime dangled carrots as it threatened with sticks, delivering higher living standards and going a long way toward solving Czechoslovakia's perennial housing problem. Though Václav Havel may have derided the high-rise *paneláky* estates that mushroomed around Prague and other Czechoslovak towns and cities in the 1970s and 1980s as "rabbit hutches,"[23] they hugely improved many families' quality of life (and are nowadays enjoying a renaissance in the private housing market). The watchword of the day was *klid* (peace and quiet); its foundation was a happy family life, and its emblem was the weekend country cottage. Writing in 1978, Zdeněk Mlynář savored the ironies of the new normal. "After 1956," he wrote, "Communist intellectuals were . . . occasionally prohibited from publishing or working in cultural or academic institutions. But even that, for the most part, was only temporary. . . . Although limited by censorship, *Literární noviny* and other magazines whose political line was unequivocally critical of the regime and in favor of reform communism came out." And now? "Now, when former associates—reform Communists who are now window-washers, laborers, and invalid pensioners—meet [Jiří] Hendrych in the streets of Prague, he stops to chat amiably with them but never fails to end the conversation with some little dig, such as, 'Still cursing the sixties?'"[24] Since his ouster from the presidium in April 1968, the scourge of the Writers' Union had settled into a cozy retirement.

In the months following Husák's takeover in April 1969, nine regional and fifty-nine district KSČ secretaries were replaced, and more than a third of the elected members of the central, regional, and district party committees resigned or were expelled from the party.[25] In January 1970 the presidium formally launched the most extensive purge in the history of the KSČ. All 1.5 million members were required to "renew their membership cards" in a process that involved interviews by 70,217 committees.[26] On 21 March 1970 Smrkovský, Císař, Špaček, Mlynář, Šimon, Jiří Hájek, Oldřich Starý, and several other leading reformers were thrown out of the party. Alexander Dubček was recalled from the embassy in Ankara on 24 June and relieved of his party card two days later. Stalin would have had him shot, but this was the post-totalitarian era (as Václav Havel dubbed it),[27] and in September the presidium gave the former first secretary a menial job in the state forests in Krasňany in western Slovakia. Oldřich Černík was expelled from the party in December. Such high-profile casualties were only the tip of the iceberg. In November 1970 Husák reported to the presidium that 67,147 party members had been expelled (*vyloučeno*) and another 259,760 had had their membership canceled (*vyškrtnuto*).[28] By the time the official Fourteenth Congress of the KSČ opened on 25 May 1971—Vysočany having disappeared down the memory hole—membership had shrunk from 1,535,537 on 1 January 1970 to 1,194,151.[29]

On 13 February 1970 all divisions of the central committee were instructed to identify individuals who should be removed from *nomenklatura* positions "as a consequence of their right-wing opportunistic opinions and who must continue to be kept under surveillance . . . and have their future employment monitored."[30] The presidium discussed preliminary results of the clean-outs at government ministries on 6 March. The Ministry of Culture had by then dismissed two deputy ministers, eight division directors, and five department heads, and six other senior officials had quit. The Ministry of the Interior had fired 245 senior police officers and 263 other members of the SNB and demoted scores more. All deputy ministers had been replaced at the Ministry of Education, and twenty-one staff members had been dismissed from other managerial positions. In the universities 167 faculty and staff had been fired and an additional 263 faculty and 38 staff members remained under investigation, while 9 professors, 49 associate professors, 247 other teaching staff, 27 PhD students, and 1,036 other students remained abroad. In May the Československá akademie věd (Czechoslovak Academy of Sciences, ČSAV) reported that all signatories of "Two Thousand Words" had been removed from senior positions. Thirteen members of the ČSAV presidium and eleven directors of research institutes had been let go, as had 322 employees who had emigrated. By the end of the year 1,200 scholars at ČSAV, 900 university professors, and one-quarter of the country's elementary and secondary school teachers would lose their jobs.[31] Twenty members of the ÚRO trade union council were replaced at its June plenum. In July it was confirmed that 15,692 people had been dismissed or resigned from national committees. In September minister of defense Martin Dzúr reported that 25 percent of generals and officers had lost their positions at the Ministry of Defense, along with 66 percent of military district commanders, 50 percent of division and brigade commanders, and 17 percent of regimental commanders.

The media were hit especially hard. Fifteen hundred Czechoslovak Radio employees were fired in Prague alone.[32] Jan Zelenka, who was appointed director of Czechoslovak TV in August 1969 and remained at the helm for the next twenty years, presided over several waves of "cleansing" between 1970 and 1973, one of which was prompted by "Two Thousand Words" signatory Zdeněk Servít quoting Allen Ginsberg's poetry on the air.[33] In April 1969 the KSČ presidium banned the magazine *Politika*. The following month the Czech Office for Press and Information (ČÚTI) fired the editors in chief of *Práce, Mladá fronta*, and *Květy* and halted publication of *Listy, Reportér, MY 69, Plamen*, and the student union newspaper *Studentské listy.*[34] *Svět práce, Tvář,*[35] and *Host do domu* followed later. *Literární život* was banned in July, and the license for *Filmové a televizní noviny* (Film and television news) was revoked in November. In January 1970 ČÚTI closed *Analogon*, a surrealist magazine edited by Vratislav Effenberger. Among the offensive contents of its one and only issue was a feature titled "The Laughter of History," which demonstrated the eternal return of Absurdistan by juxtaposing cartoons from the 1937 April Fools' Day edition of *Světozor*, satirizing the "Trotskyist-terrorist-nihilist bandit" Záviš Kalandra and the "Bucharinist-fascist Karel Teige," with quotations from Josef Urválek's closing speech in the Horáková trial ("in this moment Záviš Kalandra stands before this state court exposed in all his nakedness as a traitor") and Mojmír Grygar's "Teigeism—A Trotskyist Agency."[36] *Divadelní noviny* (Theater news), the magazine of the Union of Czech Theatrical Artists, was suppressed in March 1970.

The normalizers did not publicly burn books, but they might as well have. Published works were recalled from bookstores or removed from warehouses and destroyed. Books in press were abandoned, and forthcoming lists were "cleansed." The second volume of Karel Teige's *Selected Works*,[37] which contained "Surrealism against the Current" and other studies from the 1930s, was printed but withheld from distribution in 1969 and pulped in 1971. As was often the case when the authorities ordered books to be destroyed, some copies were squirreled away and survived. Bohumil Hrabal, who worked at a paper recycling plant in Spálená Street from 1954 to 1958, hilariously describes one such rescue operation in the third novel in his autobiographical trilogy, *Proluky* (*Gaps*, 1986).[38] Hrabal's experiences at the pulping plant inspired his novella *Příliš hlučná samota* (*Too Loud a Solitude*, 1966), which is as comically chilling a tale as any in his repertoire. He puts the communists' latest attempts to control the printed word in historical perspective. This is the land of eternal returns.

"For thirty-five years now I've been compacting old paper and books, living as I do in a land that has known how to read and write for fifteen generations; living in a onetime kingdom where it was and still is a custom, an obsession, to compact thoughts and images patiently in the heads of the population, thereby bringing them ineffable joy and even greater woe;

living among people who will lay down their lives for a bale of compacted thoughts," relates the narrator Haňťa. "And now it is all recurring in me."[39]

The third volume of Teige's *Selected Works*, containing writings from the 1940s, was ready for the press in 1970 but remained unpublished until 1994. Miroslav Lamač's *Osma a Skupina výtvarných umělců 1907–1917* (The Eight and the Group of Fine Artists 1907–1917), a landmark study of the early-twentieth-century Czech expressionist and cubist avant-garde, was on the verge of being printed at the start of the 1970s but was not published until 1988.[40] By the end of September 1970 more than 130 titles had been withdrawn from the market. The next month the Ministry of Culture issued a list of "writers in liquidation," as Hrabal called them, that was updated frequently. Martina Spáčilová has identified 209 "disappeared books" from 1969–1972.[41] On 31 March 1972 the KSČ central committee turned its attention to libraries, issuing a directive establishing restricted "special collections"; this was accompanied by a list of 142 authors whose works were to be removed from public access and 160 whose writings were to be selectively culled.[42] The first attempt to map these "white spaces" in postwar Czech literary history, the *Slovník zakázaných autorů 1948–1980* (Dictionary of prohibited authors 1948–1980), was published in samizdat by Ludvík Vaculík's Edice Petlice (Padlock Editions) in 1979 and listed more than four hundred individual authors.[43]

Czechoslovak writers were not the only ones whose work was suppressed. Jan Zábrana's edition of selected poems by Allen Ginsberg was rejected by Odeon in 1970 and not published until 1990 (under the title *Kvílení*, or *Howl*).[44] Odeon published Aloys Skoumal's new translation of James Joyce's *Ulysses* in an edition of seven thousand copies in 1976, only to have it "reserved for sale only to Party members and/or medical experts in the field of psychiatry" and made available in libraries "only with special permission."[45] If the censors did not succeed in wholly reducing Bohemia to a "cemetery of culture," as Heinrich Böll charged, it was not for lack of trying.[46] Fortunately, works by proscribed authors were published by émigré houses or circulated in samizdat typescripts in what became a substantial cottage industry, and the continuity of Czech literature was largely preserved.[47] Padlock Editions alone had published 200 titles by 1980 and more than 360 by the end of the 1980s.[48] But what mattered politically was that authors who had once reached 300,000 people a week through *Literární listy* were now writing mostly in and for a literary ghetto.

Independent voluntary organizations—whose right to exist the KSČ Action Program had promised to enshrine in law—were either banned altogether (beginning with KAN, K-231, and the resurgent Social Democrats) or dissolved and replaced by more pliable alternatives. In June 1969 the Ministry of the Interior revoked the registration of the Svaz vysokoškolského studentstva Čech a Moravy (Union of University Students of Bohemia and Moravia, SVSČM), founded on 25 May 1968. Eighteen months later Gustáv Husák addressed a new Socialistický svaz mládeže (Socialist Union of Youth, SSM) at its first all-state conference in November 1970 in Prague. SSM's membership of 300,000 was one-third the size of its pre-1968 predecessor, the Czechoslovak Union of Youth (ČSM).[49] The journalists' union presidium was replaced in September 1969, and purges of the rank and file began in December. A. J. Liehm was one of those expelled in February 1970. A couple weeks earlier his *Generace* (Generations), a "self-portrait of those who prepared the 'Prague Spring,'" was published in a French translation by Gallimard in Paris under the title *Trois générations* (Three generations). Adolf Hoffmeister illustrated the book with caricatures of Liehm's interviewees, who included Milan Kundera, Josef Škvorecký, Václav Havel, Ludvík Vaculík, Ivan Klíma, Karel Kosík, Eduard Goldstücker, Laco Novomeský, and Jiří Mucha. Jean-Paul Sartre supplied a preface with the cute title "The Socialism that Came in from the Cold." "We are tempted to compare them to the lights that come to us from dead stars, as they used to be, before the country was plunged back into silence, carrying a message that was not addressed to us," he wrote. "Yet it is today that we *must* listen to them."[50] Though *Generace* was translated into several languages, it was not available in Czech until 1988 (from the émigré publishing house Index in Cologne). Československý spisovatel, to whom the book was contracted back in 1969, published the first domestic edition in 1990.

On 20 May 1969 the KSČ presidium decreed that the Koordinační výbor českých tvůrčích svazů (Coordinating Committee of Czech Creative Unions, KOO TS) established a year earlier would no longer be recognized by the National Front and was therefore an illegal organization. Henceforth only individual unions could negotiate with the Ministry of Culture and other state bodies on behalf of writers and other creative artists. Meeting in the Film Club on Národní Avenue two days later, 350 KOO TS members declared, "We can be silenced, but we cannot be forced into saying anything we do not think. . . . The cultural community is faithful to its language, to its national traditions, to its people despite the adversity of the time."[51] Conflicts flared up again in November when the cinematic union FITES gave one of its annual awards to Vlastimil Vávra's *Na pomoc generální prokuratuře* (To help the general procurator), a documentary film challenging official accounts of Jan Masaryk's death.

At a gathering of cultural workers at Slovanský dům on 8 December, Czech minister of culture Miloslav Brůžek condemned "the passive resistance that is still being carried on by some representatives of the cultural front, especially by certain forces in the leadership of the creative unions."[52] FITES was expelled from the National Front on 7 January 1970, and the other creative unions were warned that their continued membership (and their legal existence) would require "critical reevaluation of their past standpoints," "public cancelation of illegal resolutions and decisions," "distancing from right-wing elements, including political émigrés," "personnel restructuring in the unions' leadership," and "practical support for measures implementing National Front and government policy in the cultural field."[53]

Federalization provided further opportunities to bring the creative unions to heel. The Czech successor to SČSS, the Svaz českých spisovatelů (Union of Czech Writers, SČS), had its founding congress on 10 June 1969 in Prague. Its five hundred members chose to retain Jaroslav Seifert as president. Despite several revisions, its statutes were not accepted by the authorities, and Seifert found himself having to defend the union against attacks in *Tvorba* and elsewhere. In November 1969 SČS lost its right to handle its members' passport affairs, and in December it was forbidden to maintain relations with foreign organizations. In March 1970 it was banned from publishing books, and in April its assets were transferred to the Czech Literary Fund. On 20 April the Ministry of Culture forbade SČS from accepting any new members, and in June ÚTI closed down its internal bulletin. The union's bank account was frozen, leaving it no choice but to gradually lay off its employees. Its last activities took place in December 1970.[54] The story was similar at the Svaz českých výtvarných umělců (Union of Czech Fine Artists, SČVU), the Czech successor to SČSVU established at the latter's Third Congress on 24–25 March 1969. Outgoing SČSVU president Adolf Hoffmeister, who had been one of the animating spirits of KOO TS, announced that he would not be a candidate for the SČVU presidency; he was tired, he said, of getting nowhere in discussions with state bodies. He stressed the need to keep fighting for artistic freedom. In December the new SČVU leadership prepared a report for Husák and Brůžek that agreed to support the political positions of the party and the government. It fell far short of what was required because it lacked any explicit critique of SČSVU's activity in 1968. The union was told that it would be admitted to the National Front only if it carried out a purge of members and publicly distanced itself from the previous leadership under Hoffmeister. Further negotiations got nowhere.

On 18 December 1970 an all-state caucus of communist writers, composers, artists, and theatrical performers met at the Valdštejn Palace in Prague to affirm "the necessity publicly, before the eyes of our nations, to distance ourselves from the activities of the former leadership of the artistic unions."[55] Six weeks later, all the remaining creative unions were dissolved by order of the federal Ministry of the Interior, to be replaced by organizations that were no longer part of the National Front but subordinate to the Ministry of Culture. At the end of the year the ministry approved a set of statutes for a new Union of Czech Writers, which was still called SČS and was still based in the old SČSS building on Národní Avenue. Most writers of any worth either were excluded from or boycotted the new union. All SČVU employees were dismissed on 1 March 1971. It was eighteen months before the founding congress of the new Union of Czech Fine Artists took place on 20 December 1972. The union's statutes defined it as "a selective and ideologically creative" body whose "membership is an expression of conscious determination to actively participate under the leadership of the Communist Party ... to build a socialist society and its artistic culture."[56] The creative groups were not renewed. Jindřich Chalupecký lost his job at the Špála Gallery. By December 1972 membership of the Writers' Union had fallen from 492 to 124, and that of the Artists' Union had dropped from 3,687 to 294.[57]

And what of Hoffmeister? For the first year after the invasion, Ada's life didn't change too much. Jean-Paul Sartre and Simone de Beauvoir visited him in Spálená Street on 30 November 1968, and he hosted Graham Greene on 8 February 1969; the following month he met with Max Ernst in Paris, chatted with Arthur Miller on the plane to a PEN Club international executive committee meeting in London, and had a major exhibition at the Palais des Beaux-Arts in Brussels. He returned to Paris to give a series of lectures in April at the Centre Universitaire Expérimental de Vincennes. Established in response to the May 1968 student protests, Vincennes was every 1960s academic progressive's dream; Michel Foucault headed the Philosophy Department, whose members included Hélène Cixous, Judith Miller, Gilles Deleuze, Jean-François Lyotard, and Alain Badiou. The authorities were happy, since trouble had been relocated from the Quartier Latin to a leafy campus on the city's far eastern periphery. Ada was offered a two-year appointment but was unwilling to abandon Prague, so he accepted a visiting position instead. He was in Paris again in October for an exhibition of Czech and Slovak culture at the Grand Palais that never took place, hanging out with Ernst, Marc Chagall, André Malraux, and Louis Aragon (who, to his credit, had vocally opposed the Soviet invasion).

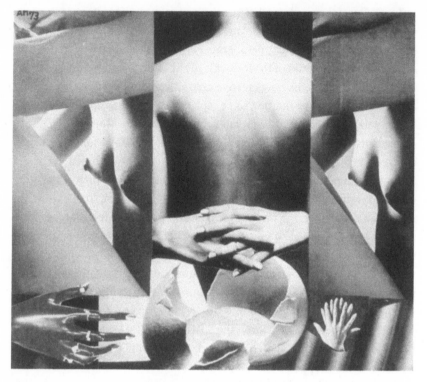

FIGURE 12.3. Adolf Hoffmeister, *Broken Life II*, 1973, collage.
From Karel Srp, ed., *Adolf Hoffmeister*, Prague, 2004. Courtesy of Martin
and Ivan Hoffmeister, © Adolf Hoffmeister heirs.

The previous month Gallimard had published a French translation of Ada's
1940 prison diary from La Santé. Československý spisovatel brought out the
Czech original of *Prison* at the end of 1969. Ironically, it was the last book
Hoffmeister was permitted to publish in Czechoslovakia. His extraordinary
run of luck was about to come to an end, and the history whose thunderous
waves he had been surfing for the last fifty years finally sucked him under.

When Ada next set foot in Paris, it was not as a refugee but to give a second
series of lectures at Vincennes in April–June 1970. He had no stomach for a
second exile at his age. "He foresaw that it was the last time" he would visit the
City of Light, says Karel Srp. "From the middle of the year there are an increasing number of entries in his diary about bans, rejections, deaths."[58] Ada's request for a two-year extension of his tenure at UMPRUM was turned down
by the Ministry of Education, and he was facing enforced retirement at the end
of August. His screening with the KSČ central committee was set for 28 July.

"3½-hour meeting . . . after 2½ hours they began to put unanswerable questions," he recorded in his diary. "I was expelled from the party. Basically, it is the liquidation of a person." The next day he wrote: "I am becoming aware of all the consequences of yesterday's expulsion. It seems to me that I have died but fortunately or unfortunately I still remain alive. I worry about the children." He said farewell to his UMPRUM colleagues at a reception on 2 October: "Such a sad colorless get-together. Svolinský and [Hedvika] Vlková were offended and didn't come. Everyone is more despairing than they should be and they are becoming more and more powerless. Today the school is a ruin of everything we have built over 25 years. It is on the threshold of insignificance."[59]

After Ada retired, he spent much of his time at his cottage in Říčky in the Orlické Mountains in eastern Bohemia, though he still visited and met with a small circle of close friends in Prague. He was forbidden to publish or exhibit and knew very well that the three plays he wrote in 1970–1973 would "not be staged in any theater here or abroad or be printed in the foreseeable future."[60] The plays were *Řecká tragedie* (A Greek tragedy, 1970), *Poprava* (The execution, 1971), and *Pissoir* (The urinal, 1973). *The Execution* is set entirely in a prison cell in which the hero, a political prisoner the same age as Hoffmeister, has a series of conversations: with his twenty-five-year-old self, with a prison warder, with a cardinal, with a murderer, with his girlfriend, and finally with death. "We go along with it, even if personally we think that everything is and should be quite different," he tells the warder. "How many times in life have I consented even though inside I deeply disagreed? I know that it was all a mistake, you know. As a citizen I was in favor, but for myself I was against."[61] *The Urinal* is "an absurd farce about survival in a world tossed about by fighting," which some might think an apt summation of Ada's life.[62] Hoffmeister's visual output in his last years was no less impressive. Apart from illustrations for his *Alenčina překvapení* (Alice's surprise), a series of short stories inspired by Lewis Carroll, he made many collages. The Alice illustrations, in which a little girl wanders through a desolate landscape, are reminiscent of Toyen's *Shooting Range* and *Hide Yourself, War!* The collages are often bright and colorful and exhibit an abundance of grotesque humor, but innocent merriment is not on the menu. Their titles speak for themselves: *Death Lies in Wait Everywhere for Children* (1970); *The Last Man* (1971); *Murder, Spring Slaughter, A Memory of Hospital* (1972); *A Sick Woman, The End of the Earth, The Last Child, Radioactive Fish, Relics from the Time of People, A Butcher's Shop with Human Innards, Broken Life, Life and Death, The Last Color Will Be Red* (1973).[63] It is not a sentimental view of the human condition. *Homage to the Beatles* (1973), a psychedelic variation on a baroque theme, momentarily relieves the gloom. The collage incorporates the English words *strange, mysterious, humorous, startling, ironic, frightening, incredible, ghostly, fascinating, delightful, bizarre,* and *provocative.*[64]

Ada was near death, and he knew it. His heart was failing, and he was hospitalized on several occasions. "I sometimes get the impression that it's high time I died," he wrote in his diary in March 1971. From the beginning of 1973 he suffered increasing bouts of depression. "I have some unpleasant forebodings. It's that old persecution mania that I have carried with me from prison and the concentration camp," he recorded on 31 January. "Lunch in the Architects' Club with [Jan] Werich, [Ota] Janeček, [Jiří] Brdečka, [Eduard] Hofman," he wrote nine days later. "Werich in good spirits. He said to me: 'Take care of yourself' [English in the original]. Why?" At the end of April Ada planned a final show. "I miss Paris terribly. It's tough to realize that I will never walk through Paris again. Yesterday I spoke for a long time with [Miroslav] Lamač and then with Martin [Hoffmeister] about an exhibition that I want to stage here at home in the studio and summer house for invited guests. If I make it to June. It will be my last exhibition."[65] Martin helped install his father's 1971–1973 collages in the Spálená Street apartment, and the exhibition was open to Ada's friends from 11 to 22 June. This time there was no herd of drunken Russians galloping up the stairs or laudatory reviews in the press. Ada carefully recorded the names of those who came to say farewell in his diary. He died of a heart attack in Říčky a month later, on 24 July 1973.

Splinters of Dreams

Miloš Forman first encountered theater as a boy during the war when his elder brother Pavel worked as a painter for the itinerant East Bohemian Operetta. He was then living with relatives in Josef Škvorecký's hometown of Náchod. "The backstage of the operetta company smelled nicely of a mixture of voluptuous femininity, cheap scents, violets, sweating bodies, roses, make-up, stiff laces being ironed, moth balls, alcoholic drinks, cookies, ballet shoes with sweaty tights and little skirts with a light scent of urine," he said later, "and I immediately decided that this is the world I belong to."[66] Miloš's father Rudolf was arrested for resistance activities in 1940, when the future film director was eight. His mother Anna followed when he was ten. Anna died in Auschwitz on 1 March 1943; Rudolf died of scarlet fever in Buchenwald in May 1944.[67]

After the war Miloš was enrolled in the Jiří z Poděbrad boarding school for wartime orphans in Poděbrady, which, owing to its generous funding and excellent teaching, doubled as a school for the sons of Czechoslovak elites. Ivan Passer and "a roly-poly kid with an air of intelligence" named Václav Havel were among his fellow students, and Forman formed lifelong friendships with both.[68] Miloš and Ivan hooked up again a decade later at FAMU. Passer worked on all of Forman's Czech films and cowrote *Loves of a Blonde* and *The Firemen's Ball*. It was Ivan who introduced Miloš to Miroslav Ondříček, the cameraman for *Audition, Loves of a Blonde*, and *The Firemen's Ball*, as well as for his later American movies *Amadeus, Ragtime*, and *Valmont*. Ondříček was also the cinematographer for Lindsay Anderson's quintessentially 1960s fantasy of insurrection at an English public (i.e., exclusively and expensively private) school *if...* (1968), which took the Palme d'Or at Cannes in 1969.

In the spring of 1968 Forman was in New York with his friend the French director Jean-Claude Carrière. They planned to work on a film adaptation of the musical *Hair*—Miloš had seen the first off-Broadway public preview the previous summer—but they were unable to obtain the rights. Instead, they started writing the script for *Taking Off*, an affectionately malicious comedy about teenage dropouts and their confused suburban middle-class parents inspired by the hippies of the East Village. The two directors roomed (where else?) at the Chelsea Hotel on West Twenty-Third Street, where Dylan Thomas drank himself to death, William Burroughs wrote most of *The Naked Lunch*, and Janis Joplin gave Leonard Cohen head on an unmade bed while the limousines waited in the street. The Chelsea had been home at one time or another to Mark Twain, O. Henry, Tennessee Williams, Brendan Behan, Allen Ginsberg, Jack Kerouac, and Jackson Pollock. Arthur C. Clarke wrote *2001: A Space Odyssey* there with Stanley Kubrick, Bob Dylan stayed up for days writing "Sad-Eyed Lady of the Lowlands" for his wife Sara, and Andy Warhol shot *Chelsea Girls* (1966). Arthur Miller, who moved into the Chelsea in 1960 after his breakup with Marilyn Monroe, called it "a house of infinite toleration":

> You could get high in the elevators on the residue of marijuana smoke. "What smoke?" Mr Bard [the manager] would ask indignantly. Allen Ginsberg was hawking his new *Fuck You* magazine in the lobby sometimes, Warhol was shooting film in one of the suites, and a young woman with eyes so crazy that one remembered them as being above one another, would show up in the lobby now and then, distributing a ream of mimeographed curses on male people whom she accused of destroying her life and everything

good, and threatening to shoot a man one of these days . . . she shot Warhol two days later as he was entering the lobby from 23rd Street, aiming for his balls. But this only momentarily disturbed the even tenor of the Chelsea day, what with everything else going on.[69]

Warhol was born in Pittsburgh in 1928, but his parents were immigrants from the village of Miková in what is now eastern Slovakia. Valerie Solanas actually shot him not in the Chelsea Hotel but in his office at 33 Union Square West on 3 June 1968, but why spoil the poetics of a good story with minor quibbles of fact? It is pure coincidence that one of the earliest literary works associated with the hotel was William Dean Howells's 1892 novel *The Coast of Bohemia*.

Václav Havel also happened to be in New York that spring, staying with Jiří Voskovec at 63 West Sixty-Ninth Street. *The Memorandum* had its American première on 23 April 1968 under Joseph Papp's direction at the Public Theater, where *Hair* had opened the season a few months earlier. Miloš showed Vašek around. Both of them were fascinated by the hippie counterculture. "They were just all over the place—stoned guitar players and chanters and so forth," remembers Papp's wife Gail. "There was musical variety then. It was just absolutely incredible, it was wonderful, and [Havel] liked that . . . he bought a lot of those crazy psychedelic posters and brought them home." The audience for *The Memorandum* appreciated its "craziness . . . they were the same people that had just barnstormed us to see Hair [laughs], so they were a special kind of audience. It wasn't a Broadway audience, it was a different kind. A lot of young people."[70] At the time, the Beatles (and the Bee Gees' "Massachusetts") were more up Havel's alley than "Venus in Furs" or "Heroin," but the playwright also took home a copy of *The Velvet Underground & Nico*. He did not meet Lou Reed until 1990, and they became good friends. Havel later told Salman Rushdie that "it was impossible to overstate the importance of rock music for the Czech resistance during the years of darkness between the Prague Spring and the collapse of communism. . . . 'Why,' he asked me, with a straight face, 'do you think we called it the Velvet Revolution?'"[71]

Martin Luther King's assassination in Memphis on 4 April led to "an outburst of racial and student disturbances. Reality was much more fascinating and exciting than art," says Forman. "And it was all on TV—live, with instant replays in slow motion. It was impossible to concentrate. We went back to France for some peace and quiet, so we could finish our script," only to get caught up in *les évènements* of May 1968. "And it was the same old story all over again—students killed and wounded in the Latin Quarter, a general strike, and all on TV."[72] After a farcical visit to the Cannes Film Festival, which Jean-Luc Godard, François Truffaut, and Claude Lelouch succeeded in shutting down in solidarity with the protesting Paris students, Forman and Carrière decided to finish the script in Czechoslovakia. *The Firemen's Ball* had been a strong candidate to take the Palme d'Or, but it was not to be. "Everybody was taking films out of the festival, so out of emulation and solidarity with the French film-makers, I withdrew my film, too," Miloš explained. "It was basically a kind of Marxist-based upheaval. The absurdity was that the likes of me and [Jan] Němec were hoping that the red flag in our country would come down. It was a totally absurd situation, but I guess we accepted the contradictions."[73] Unfortunately, in Prague too "the reality of life outstripped the fiction," and Forman and Carrière returned to Paris, which General de Gaulle had managed to subdue, in August.

On the night of 21 August 1968 Miloš was in a seedy corner bar in Pigalle "getting drunk and talking with a shady, beautiful Israeli named Eva. We were young and did nothing in moderation," he explains. At 2:30 he was woken by a phone call informing him that the Russians had invaded Czechoslovakia. The film director Claude Berri and producer Jean-Pierre Rassam borrowed François Truffaut's Citroen, drove to Prague, and brought Forman's second wife Věra Křesadlová and their young twins Matěj and Petr back to Paris. Miloš didn't dare make the trip himself. An actress and singer, Křesadlová played the female leads in *Audition* and Ivan Passer's *Intimate Lighting* and a supporting role in Jaromil Jireš's *The Joke*. Berri and Rassam got into Czechoslovakia easily enough, only to find themselves "in a vast maze. . . . There were no road signs, no streets signs, no numbers on any doors, no nameplates anywhere."[74] Forman's Parisian friends found the family a flat near the Bois de Boulogne, where, in a reprise of scenes at the House of Czechoslovak Culture thirty years earlier, an assortment of displaced Czechs, including Passer, Jireš, Pavel Juráček, Jan Němec, and Josef Škvorecký, passed through. "There were nights when we had nine guests sleeping over, a virtual *Who's Who* of the Czech New Wave," recalled Miloš.[75] Not quite. Věra Chytilová, Jiří Menzel, and Evald Schorm all stayed home in Prague, where they would have checkered careers over the next two decades.

After the invasion the Czechoslovak border remained open, and those who had left (or remained abroad) had a few months to make up their minds whether to cut the umbilical cord or return. It was seldom an easy choice. Unhappy in Paris and tempted by Jiří Šlitr's offer of a new contract at the Semafor Theater, Věra Křesadlová returned to Prague, taking the twins with her.

"Being in a foreign country means walking a tightrope high above the ground without the net afforded a person by the country where he has his family, colleagues, and friends, and where he can easily say what he has to say in a language he has known from childhood," explains Milan Kundera when his heroine Tereza returns to "the land of the weak" in *The Unbearable Lightness of Being*. "In Prague she was dependent on [her husband] Tomáš only when it came to the heart; here [Zurich] she was dependent on him for everything."[76] Věra "missed her parents, her world, her language," says Miloš.[77] Šlitr also persuaded his stage partner Jiří Suchý to come home from London, where Suchý had fled after the invasion stranded him and his family in Yugoslavia. "I have never regretted it," Suchý said fifty years later, even if he refused to revoke his signature on "Two Thousand Words" and was kept off radio and TV and out of the bookstores for many years. Šlitr died unexpectedly at Christmas 1969. Although Semafor was closed down for a few weeks in 1971, the theater survived under Suchý's management, and his performances with new partner Jitka Molavcová proved extremely popular. Audiences, he says, "began to look between the lines. On several occasions they started to laugh and cheer, and we didn't know why. In many ways the people were much smarter than us."[78] Praguers had plenty of practice in detecting double meanings, including those that weren't intended. Remember Jindřich Hořejší's *Hey, Girl*?

In Paris Pavel Juráček and Ivan Passer signed three-month screenwriting contracts with Paramount Pictures, which paid them a weekly wage of $200. Though Pavel wrote a sketch of a documentary about the Russians in Czechoslovakia in 1945 (as "liberators"), in 1948 (as "advisers"), and in 1968 (as "defenders from counterrevolution"), he reckoned "it was lost time." Invited to serve on the jury at the Mannheim International Film Festival, he issued a strong statement against the invasion ("Every action and every word of ours has been distorted. The indignity went so far that they asked us to accuse and condemn ourselves and spit into our own faces") but promised he would "neither ignore nor judge unjustly" films from the Warsaw Pact countries. At a hotel in Heidelberg, he relates, "I lay on my stomach and cried and Hanka [Ťukalová, his girlfriend] just kept on saying nothing." Pavel and Hana returned to Prague on 30 October. "The world is different than it was before 21 August," he recorded in his diary on 3 November, "and it will never be like it was again. . . . What will happen tomorrow? What will happen in a week's time? What will happen in a year's time? There are fourteen million of us and we are all asking in vain."[79] It was his first entry since 22 August. Pavel completed *The Case for a Rookie Hangman* in 1969, but the film was withdrawn from cinemas after just two months. "The time in which we live baffles any logic, and reason has lost its meaning in it," he wrote by way of explanation of the film's nonsensicalness.[80] Pavel and Hana married in the Old Town Hall in 1970, with Václav Havel and the actor and playwright Pavel Landovský as witnesses; Marta Kubišová and Jan Němec were among the guests.[81] Juráček was fired from Barrandov Studios in November 1971 and never made another film. Jaromil Jireš also decided against remaining abroad, despite the obvious risks he was running as a signatory of "Two Thousand Words," not to mention as director of *The Joke*. "If one has to be unhappy," he reasoned, "it's better to be unhappy in my own country. Exile is never a pleasure even for someone like Milan Kundera, who has always known success."[82] Back in Czechoslovakia, Jireš filmed Vítězslav Nezval's surrealist novel *Valerie a týden divů* (*Valerie and Her Week of Wonders*, 1970), one of the last flourishes of the New Wave.

The sixth annual New York Film Festival closed on 28 September 1968 with a double bill of Forman's *Firemen's Ball* and Jan Němec's *Oratorium pro Prahu* (*Oratorio for Prague*), at which Němec was present. "It was by far the finest movie program showing at that moment anywhere in New York," wrote Renata Adler in the *New York Times*, praising *The Firemen's Ball* as "a hilarious shaggy dog story, with the pessimism of the exquisite logic that leads nowhere."[83] "*Oratorio for Prague* is a film so moving that one is near tears from the first moment after the credits appear. The movie was begun as a documentary about the liberalization of Czechoslovakia, and then simply continued when the Russian tanks moved in. . . . Nothing sensational, no scoops or extreme violence, only a bloodstain on the pavement, burning tanks, two corpses, young faces mouthing 'Fascist,' a gesture to block the camera, a Russian soldier reassembling a torn Czechoslovak tract in a private moment, Němec himself driving toward the invading forces, quiet Czechoslovak humor, a few verses of 'We Shall Overcome,' which, far from seeming trite or jaded, gave one chills."[84] The final version was assembled in Paris with support from François Truffaut and Claude Berri after Němec smuggled the raw footage out via Vienna. "I wrote the [original] commentary," says Josef Škvorecký. "We edited it on the 19th of August, 1968, at the laboratories in Vodičkova Street. On the twentieth I left for a vacation in France." Then the film got one of Jiří Kolář's *froissages*, which *crumple* human beings so profoundly and with such suddenness that they are never able to smooth themselves out again. "I saw the film in Paris in October" Škvorecký continues.

It had changed and was then called *Oratorio for Prague* (1968). Tanks smashed into the idyllic counterpoints. Next to the dancing Smrkovský, lay a boy shot by a machine-gun. Next to a priest raising a chalice, stood two boys with a bloodied flag. Next to Dubček waving to the crowds, a Soviet political officer waved his revolver at the crowds from a tank turret. One of the cameramen who made the film was, at that time, lying in a hospital with his jaw shot off. I met with Honza [Němec] in a hotel in the Latin Quarter; he seemed to be deranged. We got desperately drunk on pastis, and Honza left for a film festival in West Germany, where the progressive German students booed *Oratorio for Prague*. The film contains a shot of Czech people who, for the first time since 1948, were permitted to decorate the graves of the American soldiers who had died on Czechoslovakian soil while driving out the fathers of the booing youths.[85]

From New York Němec traveled to Houston, where *Oratorio for Prague* was reprised on 15 November in a series called "The Film Revolution," in which Andy Warhol made his first public appearance since being shot.[86] Then Honza flew home.

Perhaps Marta Kubišová should have seen trouble ahead when Němec fired six bullets into the window of her Vinohrady apartment late one night in March 1969. The singer had an autograph session scheduled the next morning and had refused to spend the night with her boyfriend when he telephoned her drunk sometime after 11:00 p.m., after a trying day in the studio. "He claimed he just wanted to shoot his heart into my window," she said later. "It seemed comical to me then. Nobody died, so what?"[87] They married in October, but things soon began to fall apart. Unable to earn money after she was prevented from singing in February 1970, Marta was "glad that I found any work at all—I glued paper bags for the Směr cooperative. Otherwise I would have been threatened with parasitism and the police would have been after me."[88] She lost a baby in the seventh month of pregnancy in 1971; she clinically died and had to be revived twice during the ordeal. Němec was little help. He was banned from filming altogether after 1969. "He drank incessantly," Marta relates. "In the morning he began with a double in the kitchen, in the afternoon he'd take another shot and by four he was already under the table. Once he gave me the keys to the closet and implored me: don't give me any, even if for instance I take an axe to you! Only one day he really did come after me with an axe, so I gave him the keys. I said to myself, I'm still not crazy enough to let myself be killed."[89] They divorced in 1973. Kubišová later became the first female spokesperson for Charter 77. Her appearance on the Melantrich balcony on 21 November 1989 to sing an unaccompanied version of "A Prayer for Marta" remains one of the enduring images of the Velvet Revolution. She "managed to get a few verses out," she said, even though she hadn't sung in public for twenty years. "I didn't cry, I was overcome by the sheer sight of the whole square jammed with people. I said to myself, no singer ever had a comeback like this! Foreign film crews told me people were in tears and when they asked what are you crying for, they said, it's that woman."[90]

Němec left Czechoslovakia in 1974. "I have never emigrated," he insisted to an interviewer in 2001. "I was an exile. There is a very big difference. An emigrant is somebody who decides to leave the country, while an exile is chased away, like J. A. Komenský [Comenius]. In 1974, they wanted to put me in prison, but they gave me a choice, as with Milan Kundera. We were told that the criminal prosecution would be canceled if we applied for a legal departure motivated not by political protest but by a working contract. I took this offer and left the country legally. . . . After two years they stripped me of my citizenship." After spending fifteen years in Germany (where his 1975 slapstick adaptation of Kafka's "Metamorphosis" for German TV led one critic to fume that "it was incomprehensible how a Czechoslovak film director could make fun of classics from German literature") and America (where he became an unlikely pioneer of wedding videos), Jan returned to Czechoslovakia on 26 December 1989.[91] He remained on good enough terms with Kubišová to make a short movie about her life for Czechoslovak TV in 1996.[92] His film *Toyen* (2005) tackles the relationship between Toyen and Jindřich Heisler in occupied Prague and postwar Paris. "Němec makes it clear in the film's subtitle, *Splinters of Dreams*, a quotation from Toyen, that it will be no ordinary work," writes the film historian Peter Hames. "Němec works by association, forging links between the real world and that of the imagination, which emerges as a higher form of reality."[93] Not unlike Lindsay Anderson's *if.* . . .

Miloš Forman did not emulate Kundera's Tomáš, who followed Tereza home out of love and compassion, refused to retract his signature from a document he no longer gave a damn about, and traded his position as a doctor in a hospital in Zurich for cleaning windows in Prague (which at least gave him ample opportunity for philandering). Nor did Passer and Škvorecký. All returned briefly to Czechoslovakia later in 1968, but none of them stayed. "I was in Paris with my wife when the Soviets entered Prague," Škvorecký told an interviewer in 1985, "and when I heard the news I didn't want to return, because I knew this was the end. Zdena [Salivarová] was a student at the Academy

[FAMU] and wanted to continue her studies. She convinced me to return in October, 1968, but after three months, she realized how terrible things were, so we left. . . . [It] was just after the funeral of Jan Palach . . . Prague was dreary and gloomy, and there was a foreboding of bad tidings to come."[94] After a short spell in the United States the Škvoreckýs settled in Canada, where Josef taught American literature at Erindale College of the University of Toronto. Zdena—not Josef—founded and ran Sixty-Eight Publishers, the most important of the Czech émigré publishing houses. "That's why I'm sorry," Josef wrote, "when from time to time, pretty often, I read praise, certainly well-intentioned, that Škvorecký founded, that Škvorecký is publishing, that Škvorecký from the time of Karel Čapek did for Czech literature . . . because it was all Honzlová [Salivarová]. That girl, who I met in Prague, who smooth-talked me (not into marrying her, that was the other way around). Perhaps there really exists a subconscious *male chauvinism* [English in the original]." Škvorecký's pet name for his wife comes from the heroine of her novel *Honzlová*, which Zdena wrote in three months in 1969 in Berkeley, "cut off from the New World, sheared off from home but always in it, as if I wanted to stamp Prague back on that paper."[95]

It is only to be expected of Absurdistan that Sixty-Eight Publishers' last book would be Salivarová's *Osočení—Dopisy lidí ze seznamu* (Smears—letters of people on the list, 1993), in which she and dozens of other former dissidents and émigrés fought back against accusations of collaborating with the StB.[96] Salivarová's name appeared in an extremely problematic list of 200,000 people named as informers in StB files that was published by the Charter 77 signatory Petr Cibulka in 1992. In Škvorecký's novel *Two Murders in My Double Life*, written in 1996 and first published in Canada in 1999, Danny Smiřický, the teenage narrator of *The Cowards*, is now a professor of American literature at "Edenvale College" in Toronto. It cannot be accidental that Škvorecký gives his alter ego's wife a nom de plume (Sidonia) that brings to mind another archetype of male chauvinist fantasy, the biblical Jezebel.[97] "Sidonia was on the List," he tells us, "and despite her wisdom succumbed to a deadly depression. The trumped-up charges came shortly after the world-renowned playwright, who was now president of the country, had awarded her the Order of the White Lion, for her twenty-five years of publishing drudgery in Toronto."

> Due to historical events, however, Sidonia's publishing activities eventually became redundant. Then Mr. Mrkvicka [i.e., Petr Cibulka] subjected them to an unexpected interpretation . . . she had been a lifelong agent of the StB; in fact, she had married me on orders from her StB bosses, to keep me under

round-the-clock surveillance . . . on orders from above, Sidonia drew me
with her into exile in Canada, where she launched her publishing business:
a front, of course, so that the StB would have control over émigré publications. Her publishing lists were always submitted to the Central Committee
of the Communist Party for their okay. The article further revealed that Sidonia flew regularly and secretly to Prague, to report to her StB bosses.[98]

Forman and Passer abandoned Czechoslovakia three weeks before the
Škvoreckýs. *The Firemen's Ball* and *Intimate Light* had been banned by then, the
latter (according to Ivan) not because it criticized the communists but because
it totally ignored them.[99] On the night of 9 January 1969 Passer saw a column
of Soviet tanks on the move in a military barracks outside Prague. He called
Forman. "Miloš said, 'Pick me up in an hour. We'll go.'" They had their passports and a few hundred American dollars but no exit visas, "a yellow piece of
paper," explains Ivan, "that nobody got."[100] They arrived at the Austrian border
at around 4:00 a.m. Patches of snow, no one there. A border guard comes out
of his shack with a Kalashnikov slung over his shoulder. He chats with Miloš
while Ivan rummages in back in search of the nonexistent yellow papers:

> "You know, I have seen all your movies" . . .
>   "And I bet you didn't like any of them!"
>   "Are you kidding?" says the officer. "You remember in *Loves of a Blonde*,
> the ring and it's rolling on the floor, under the table?" He proceeds to de-
> scribe other favorite scenes from Miloš's films.
>   After more banter, the guard leans into the window and says, "Don't look
> for the exit visas." Waving his arm, he adds, "OK, gentlemen," and opens
> the red-and-white crossing gate.
>   In parting, the guard says goodbye to the two travelers, but instead of
> the common phrase, he says, "*Sbohem*"—God be with you—which one
> Czech says to another whom he knows he'll never see again.[101]

Though Passer told this tale on several occasions, Forman says nothing
about the episode in his memoir *Turnaround* or in interviews. He always remained vague about when and how he left his homeland. In A. J. Liehm's *The
Miloš Forman Stories*, Miloš says he and Carrière finished the script for *Taking
Off* "in early winter of 1968" and flew back to America, "where Robert Kennedy
had been murdered and where the National Guard had been called out to keep
order at the Democratic Convention in Chicago," arriving "on a Friday night
sometime in November."[102] He makes no mention of any subsequent return

FIGURE 12.4. Publicity still for Miloš Forman's *Loves of a Blonde*, 1965.

to Prague. In *Turnaround* he implies that he flew to the States direct from Paris sometime after Věra left, airily adding, "the rest was details": "I flew to New York with Ivan, who had decided to emigrate outright. I didn't have to burn my bridges to Czechoslovakia yet because I was still under my official Filmexport contract with Paramount. I entered the country with my Czech passport, on a visa that gave me the right to work in America." He adds: "I still didn't want to emigrate from the old country as Ivan had done."[103] After following up with Věra Křesadlová, Miloš's son Petr Forman, and Ivan Passer in 2019, the *Los Angeles Times* staff writer John Penner confirmed Passer's story. He speculates that Miloš "didn't want trouble for Věra and the kids back home; and, given his international fame, neither he nor Czech authorities wanted to convey the kind of break that 'defection' connotes."[104] The ambiguity served Forman well when he was allowed to go back to Prague fifteen years later to film *Amadeus* (1984), even though he had acquired US citizenship by then. His most successful film, *Amadeus* won eight Academy Awards (including for best director and best picture), four BAFTA Awards, four Golden Globe Awards, and a Directors Guild of America award.

However they got there, in the winter of 1968–1969 Miloš and Ivan were back in New York. Jiří Voskovec found them a "wonderful cheap little house to rent" on Leroy Street in Greenwich Village, where (says Miloš), every time the playwright John Guare entered the house, "he had the sensation of leaving America and entering a colony of refugees and foreign artists, where only books and alcohol mattered: an embassy of avant-garde Bohemia."[105] *Taking Off* (1971) was awarded the Jury Special Grand Prix at Cannes, but flopped at the box office and left Forman broke. Miloš moved back into the Chelsea Hotel and lived on a dollar a day, spending half on a bottle of beer and half on a can of chili con carne. He stayed there until 1973. "I was waiting for an offer which could change my life," he relates, "but in the meantime I jumped for anything that promised at least a free lunch."[106] The life-changing offer came from actor Michael Douglas and producer Saul Zaentz in 1974. *One Flew over the Cuckoo's Nest* scooped the 1975 Oscars, winning the awards for best picture, best director, best actor, best actress, and best adapted screenplay. Miloš finally got to shoot *Hair* (with Mirek Ondříček as director of photography) in 1979. By then, he says, it "had become a period piece. . . . By the late seventies the 'sixties' were over and hadn't yet begun to provoke nostalgia. Nostalgia implies distance. . . . Nostalgia happens only when the era stops threatening you with its messiness, contradictions, anarchy, and choices."[107]

By the early 1980s Forman had put his money worries behind him and settled into a converted barn in rural Connecticut, where it was warm in summer and snowed in winter and the woods reminded him of the forests between Poděbrady, Kolín, and Čáslav, where he was born. "When we were writing *Amadeus* together in Connecticut," reminisces the Czech writer Zdeněk Mahler (who is billed as "Special Music and Historical Consultant" in the *Amadeus* credits), "he had dogs, and his favorite was a setter named Mandy. Only Mandy got lost." What follows is another of those indelible images in which whole worlds are condensed:

And one day Miloš came in and said: "Maybe I'm going crazy, but I saw Mandy. Come with me." We stood on the bank of a frozen lake; in the depths lay Mandy, who must have run along the bank, slipped, and the ice gave way beneath her. We dragged her out with pitchforks and that day we didn't do any more work. The next morning, I wake up and see that Miloš has got hold of a lime tree somewhere (in America they are rare and expensive), planted it and buried Mandy underneath. I heard him singing the anthem and tears were pouring down his face. That dog and that lime tree and *Kde domov můj*. But you know that these things are horribly complicated, and they maybe emerge in the middle of the night and on the opposite side of the globe—and only there do they get their clear meaning.[108]

Home and Away

It is impossible to say how many people left Czechoslovakia after August 1968. Perhaps 100,000 Czechs and Slovaks were outside the country when the Soviets invaded, and a significant number never came back.[109] Tens of thousands more left in the immediate aftermath, but not all of them remained abroad. Karl Petrlik, who later served as Austrian ambassador to Czechoslovakia, recalls that embassy officials in Prague were handing out three thousand visas a day through the ground-floor window because the lines to get into the building were so long. "Between July and September," he says, "we issued perhaps 100,000 visas."[110] According to Václav Chyský, "180,000 people fled in panic to Austria but after weeks and months of vacillation many of them returned."[111] Jan Werich had the requisite papers to travel to Austria legally but feared being arrested at the border because of his signature on "Two Thousand Words." The comedian and his wife Zdena escaped through the woods to Bavaria with the help of Czech border guards on 25 August and made their way to Vienna.[112] From there they contacted Jiří Voskovec in New York, who set about publicizing Werich's plight and trying to find work and money for his old Liberated Theater partner in America. Jan became "childish" in exile, Zdena wrote to Jiří. She was contemplating divorce and a return to Prague, where, she hoped, "the unfortunate political situation at home will help me resolve my situation without effect and emotions." The Werichs returned to their home on Kampa Island together at the end of October. "Go fuck yourselves," the furious Voskovec told the "Flying Bohemians [*Fliegender Boehmen*]," complaining that the Werichs "fly back and forth like dirty laundry." He was nonetheless delighted when President Svoboda invited Werich to represent the Czech film industry in the United States. Jan arrived in New York in November but returned to Prague at the end of the year, having nearly died of emphysema.[113] Despite his legendary status, Werich was banned from the stage, TV, and film for most of the 1970s. His last public appearance was at a concert with Jiří Suchý at Lucerna Palace in 1977, celebrating the fiftieth anniversary of *Vest*

Pocket Review—a reward, perhaps, for his cooperation with the authorities' "Anticharta" campaign against Charter 77. He died in 1980.

According to official Ministry of the Interior figures, 70,130 people "illegally deserted the country" between August 1968 and the end of 1969.[114] Estimates based on demographic data for the same period are higher, ranging from 100,000 to 138,000.[115] Comparing population numbers for 1 January 1968 and 31 December 1971 and adjusting for a natural increase, Vladimir Kusin arrives at a total of 171,376 emigrants over those four years, a figure he is "reluctant to accept."[116] Travel to the West was restricted from November 1968 and the border was officially closed on 8 October 1969. Thousands still contrived to leave, and by 1971 the official count of "deserters" had risen to 88,005.[117] Thereafter emigration fell dramatically but rose again in the late 1970s after the KSČ leadership decided that it made more sense to permit—or in some cases, force— malcontents to emigrate and charge them for the privilege. Beginning in 1977 exiles were allowed to regularize living abroad, so long as they obtained a pardon from the president and paid an (individually assessed) sum to "compensate" for the costs of their education. This offered the state a useful source of hard currency and gave the secret police a valuable channel of information on émigrés' domestic contacts.[118] According to the Ministry of the Interior, around 50,000 people left between 1977 and 1987.[119] Overall estimates for the entire 1968–1989 period range from a low of 140,000 to 150,000 to a high of 250,000 to 300,000. Official sources give a total of 146,462 émigrés, of whom 106,837 were sentenced in absentia for deserting the republic.[120]

The loss to the nation—and the gain to others—can be compared with Germany's hemorrhaging of talent after Hitler's rise to power in 1933. A. J. Liehm, who had been a representative of Czechoslovak State Film in Paris since the fall of 1968, decided to stay when his term expired the following year. Over the next two decades he taught at universities in France, Switzerland, and the United States and edited various periodicals. Vladimír Vlček, director of the socialist realist films *Red Blaze over Kladno* and *Tomorrow There Will Be Dancing Everywhere*, was perhaps a more surprising émigré. He left for France soon after the invasion and subsequently worked in Italy, China, and Japan. He died in London in 1977 and is buried in Munich.[121] The Marxist-humanist philosopher Ivan Sviták fled to Austria in August 1968 and was stripped of his Czechoslovak citizenship in 1970. By the time he was sentenced to eight years in prison in 1971 he was ensconced at Cal State in Chico, where he taught until 1990. In 1969 the painter Jan Kotík accepted a fellowship from the German government to work in Berlin, and he and his wife were deprived of Czecho-slovak citizenship in 1970. Czechoslovak Radio director Zdeněk Hejzlar fled to Sweden in 1969. Czechoslovak TV director Jiří Pelikán asked for political asylum in Rome the same year and later became a Socialist Party member of the European parliament for Italy. Karel Ančerl, the artistic director of the Czech Philharmonic Orchestra, left Prague after the invasion and served as music director of the Toronto Symphony Orchestra until his death in 1973. Slovak soprano Edita Gruberová stayed on at the Vienna State Opera after making her foreign debut there as Mozart's Queen of the Night in 1969. The ballerina and choreographer Zora Šemberová, who created the role of Juliet in Prokofiev's *Romeo and Juliet* at the Mahen Theater in Brno on 30 December 1938, had been teaching at the Prague Conservatory while maintaining a long-distance relationship with her husband Rainer Radok, a professor of mathematics at Flinders University in Australia. She flew out to join him after the invasion and went on to teach at Flinders and to found the Australian Mime Theater in Adelaide.[122]

Josef Škvorecký and Zdena Salivarová were far from the only Czech writers to desert the homeland for the Bohemia of the soul. Fired from FAMU and banned from publishing, Milan Kundera stuck it out for a few years before taking a position at the University of Rennes in 1975. He moved to L'École des hautes études en sciences sociales in Paris (where he still lives) in 1979, and was relieved of his Czechoslovak citizenship the same year. He became a French citizen in 1981. His two best known novels, *The Book of Laughter and Forgetting* and *The Unbearable Lightness of Being* were written in exile and first published in French translations in 1976–1978 and 1982. Kundera is the most internationally famous of all Czech postwar authors, but beginning with *Le lenteur* (*Slowness*, 1995) he has written entirely in French. He seldom visits the land of his birth, and when he does so, like James Joyce in England, he goes almost incognito. Arnošt Lustig, whose *Dita Saxová* (1962), *Modlitba pro Kateřinu Horovitzovou* (*A Prayer for Kateřina Horovitzová*, 1962), and other novels are classics of Holocaust literature, was in Italy with his wife Věra Weis-litzová and their two children on the day of the invasion. Jan Němec's breakout film *Démanty noci* (*Diamonds of the Night*, 1964) is based on Lustig's story "*Tma nemá stín*" (Darkness casts no shadow, 1958). After spending a year in Israel, the Lustigs immigrated to the United States, where Arnošt taught at the American University in Washington from 1973 to 2004.

Lustig's work is well known to Anglophone readers; Weislitzová's less so. Her collection of poems *Dcera Olgy a Lea/The Daughter of Olga and Leo* powerfully evokes her experiences as a teenager, beginning with the Nazi invasion ("March 14, 1939 in Ostrava / The night is deep as it intoxicates / It smells of hangman's sweat, open wounds"). The poems progress through Milena Jesenská's cold pogrom ("There was a sign at the door . . . To Gypsies, Jews and dogs / It is forbidden to enter the shop"), deportation ("My new address, no, I don't know / They say, we'll go East"), Terezín ("In Maria Theresa's Fortress / Behind the Wall / I am sixteen / The age of the first ball"), and the transports ("We live just for this while / never knowing when we'll have to go"). She mourns the deaths of her grandmother Bertha ("You were seventy-seven / When you with your sisters, Rosa, Hermeena and Jenie / Unloaded / Face to face to the gas chambers in Auschwitz"), her mother Olga ("Through the world I go . . . I cannot find the aroma / Of your hands"), and her father Leo, over whose grave she would like to intone the Kaddish and lay a rose but can't ("There are enough roses here / only you don't have a grave"). Věra and her sister survived the Shoah, but 120 members of their extended family did not. The sanctuary the Lustigs found in the United States in 1970 did not make her forgive or forget. "Why should I reconcile," she asks, "While your sisters dug their own graves / You went to beauty parlors, decorated wedding cakes . . . Why can't I understand / While you charmed and ragtimed in the light of Liberty / You turned away my sinking boat?"[123] Despite spending more than three decades in the New World, the Lustigs returned to Prague after Arnošt's retirement.

"Like his friend the architect Eva Jiřičná," Jan Kaplický "made his way to London, but not before he had painted, in careful Russian cyrillic a sign on the National Museum inviting the neighbors to go back where they had come from, and checking with his mother that he had got the grammar right."[124] "On the evening of 12 September," writes Kaplický's fellow architect and émigré Ivan Margolius, "[Jan] alighted at Victoria Station with a portfolio, 100 dollars in his pocket, two pairs of socks, and nothing more."[125] After gaining a foothold at Piano and Rogers, he helped prepare drawings for the team that won the competition to design the Centre Pompidou in Paris. In 1979 Kaplický cofounded the visionary Future Systems architectural firm, whose realized designs include the Media Centre at Lord's Cricket Ground in London (1994), the Selfridges department store in Birmingham, England (1999), and Comme des Garçons stores in Paris, Tokyo, and New York (1997–1998). When a Future Systems' design won the international competition for a new National Library on Letná Plain in 2007, Jan described it as "the most momentous moment of my life," which he hoped would "close the circle from the time in 1955 when they refused to accept me at Prague Technical University [ČVUT] as an un-reliable pupil." Despite support from Richard Rogers, Norman Foster, Dominique Perrault, Zaha Hadid, and other world-renowned architects, the project fell foul of political opposition led by Czech president Václav Klaus. "Why in Bohemia do politics, football and beer triumph over culture?" Kaplický lamented.[126] He collapsed and died while visiting Prague in January 2009. Jan's onetime girlfriend Eva Jiřičná founded her own firm in 1982; her commissions in the United Kingdom included the Canada Water Bus Station (1998), the Bollinger Jewellery Gallery for the Victoria and Albert Museum (2008), and the Miles Stair at Somerset House (2016). The Architektura Interiér Design (AI Design) studio she established with Petr Vagner in Prague in 1999 is responsible for the trendy Hotel Josef in Rybná Street in the Old Town (2002). Jiřičná won the 2013 Jane Drew Prize for her outstanding contribution to the status of women in architecture, and judges Zaha Hadid and Rafael Vinoly described her work as "incredibly influential."[127]

Czech popular music lost several of its stars to exile. Yvonne Přenosilová began her career as one of the unsuspecting misses who flocked to the Semafor Theater for the competition Miloš Forman filmed for *Audition*, where she caught the eye of composer Karel Mareš. She was just sixteen and still in school when she had her first hit in 1964 with a Czech version of Brenda Lee's "I'm Sorry."[128] Later she covered Nancy Sinatra's "These Boots Are Made for Walkin'." Yvonne was a week shy of her twenty-first birthday when she signed "Two Thousand Words." Soon after the invasion she left for England, where she appeared on the TV show *Ready Steady Go!* alongside the Rolling Stones. She subsequently moved to Munich, where her parents joined her. Flight was in their blood. Before the war the singer's Viennese mother Markéta and her Jewish first husband escaped the Nazis and fled to Palestine, where Markéta met Yvonne's father Jiří, a refugee from Moravia who was serving with the British army. Markéta and Jiří married in Jerusalem and returned to Prague in 1945. Because of postwar Czech hostility toward anyone and anything German, Markéta pretended to be English, and the family spoke English at their home in Troja. It didn't save them. "Father was a soldier body and soul, fighting the enemy under a 'bad' flag," Yvonne later related. "They came to arrest him at night, and without the family being given any news he finished up in the notorious *domeček* near the Castle."[129] Jiří Přenosil spent a year in prison. Despite Yvonne's fluency in English and German, her attempts to renew her singing career abroad were unsuccessful, and she wound up working as a British Airways flight attendant throughout the 1970s. She married one of her passengers (and became an unlikely baroness) in 1978 but divorced in 1985. After that, the poet and singer-songwriter Karel Kryl helped her get a job as a presenter on Radio Free Europe playing mostly American country music.

Kryl supposedly wrote his song "Bratříčku, zavírej vrátka" (Little brother, shut the gate) on the night of 21 August 1968. The powerful acoustic lament entered Czechoslovak Radio's top forty at number 2 on 8 December and topped the chart the following week. Supraphon was unwilling to take the risk of producing Kryl's first album, of which "Bratříčku" was the title track, but Panton did so in January 1969.

> It's raining and outside it's getting dark
> This night will not be short
> The wolf is lusting for the lamb
> Little brother shut the gate!
> Shut the gate![130]

"Little Brother" remained at number 1 until both the song and the radio program were banned on 30 March 1969. Karel traveled to West Germany for a music festival on 9 September and did not return for twenty years. He recorded his second album *Rakovina* (Cancer) in the studio of Radio Free Europe in October. His records were smuggled into Czechoslovakia and became part of the underground culture. Kryl continued to work throughout the next two decades with Radio Free Europe, which in 1983 gave him a full-time position as a music commentator.

On the cover of the *Bratříčku* LP a small boy sits on a Prague sidewalk with a target on his back. The photograph is by another world-famous émigré, Josef Koudelka. An aeronautical engineer by trade, Josef began his photographic career in 1961 with an exhibition at the Semafor Theater. He was allowed to move around the stage freely during rehearsals at the Theater beyond the Gate and the Theater on the Balustrade, where he captured some remarkable souvenirs of Jan Grossman's 1966 production of Alfred Jarry's *Père Ubu*. These images won him an SČSVU prize in 1967. His exhibition *Cikání* [*Gypsies*], *1961–1966* was presented at the Theater beyond the Gate the same year, and thereafter Koudelka devoted himself full time to photography. When *Gypsies* was published in 1975 by Aperture in New York, it "sealed his reputation as one of the finest photographers still using the humanist documentary mode in the last quarter of the twentieth century."[131] Koudelka returned to Prague from Romania, where he had been shooting more photographs of Roma, the day before the Soviet invasion. The British photojournalist Ian Berry, who was the only Western photographer in Prague that week, recalled Koudelka as "an absolute maniac who had a couple of old-fashioned cameras on string round his neck and a cardboard box over his shoulders, who was actually just going up to the Russians, clambering over their tanks and photographing them openly. . . . I felt either this guy was the bravest man around or he is the biggest lunatic around."[132] Josef felt he had no alternative. "I wasn't a reporter. I had never photographed anything that you would call 'news.' Suddenly, for the first time in my life, I was confronted with that kind of situation. I responded to it. I knew it was important to photograph, so I photographed. I didn't think much about what I was doing."[133]

Through the efforts of Anna Fárová and Eugene Ostroff, the curator of photography at the Smithsonian Institution, Josef's photographs found their way to Elliott Erwitt, president of the Magnum photographic agency in New York. Magnum arranged for the photos to be published in major newspapers and magazines around the world on the first anniversary of the invasion. The images were credited to an anonymous "Prague Photographer," in which guise Koudelka won the Overseas Press Club's Robert Capa Award. Funded by a grant from Magnum, he left Czechoslovakia in May 1970 "to see all the places where gypsies gather." His trip started with the annual Roma pilgrimage at Saintes-Maries-de-la-Mer in the Camargue—one of the inspirations for Bob Dylan's 1976 album *Desire*—before taking him to horse races and fairs in England, Scotland, and Ireland. "When I passed through Paris, I visited the Magnum office, . . . They advised me not to return to Prague. I decided to stay in England. In order to avoid reprisals against my family Magnum continued to distribute my photographs of the 1968 invasion without mentioning my name. Only after the death of my father did I admit that they were mine."[134] Koudelka has been on the move ever since. "To be in exile," he told a *Le Monde* interviewer in 2015, "is simply to have left one's country and to be unable to return. Every exile is a different, personal experience. Myself, I wanted to see the world and photograph it. That's forty-five years I've been traveling. I've never stayed anywhere more than three months. When I found no more to photograph, it was time to go."[135] Jan Lukas, author of the "found collage" of magazine covers on a newsstand mourning the deaths of Joseph Stalin and Klement Gottwald, beat him to it. The fifty-year-old photographer fled Czechoslovakia with his family in 1965 because, he said, "I didn't want my children to live in a country without the rule of law."[136] After ten months in an Italian refugee camp, they settled permanently in New York in 1966. Jan

FIGURE 12.5. Jan Lukas, *Free at Last*, 1965. The photograph was taken with
Lukas's camera by a friend and published as the penultimate image in his *Pražský
deník/Prague Diary 1938–1965*, Prague, 1995 (from which it is reproduced here).
Courtesy of Helena Lukas.

captioned a photograph of the four of them: "Behind the fence of a refugee
camp in Italy—free at last!"[137]

Some of those who emigrated in the 1970s were still children when the
tanks rolled in. "Miss Navratilova Asks U.S. Asylum," announced the *New York
Times* on 7 September 1975. The eighteen-year-old tennis prodigy walked into
the Manhattan office of the Immigration and Naturalization Service (INS)
after losing the US Open women's singles semifinal to her friend and doubles
partner Chris Evert two days earlier. Her request was "very routine," said an
INS spokesman. "She's from a Communist country. If she wants to stay here
she'll be permitted to stay." The *Times* went on to inform readers that "Miss

Navratilova, an exuberant personality given to gesturing, screaming and glaring while on the court, is a very free-spirited, free-thinking individual whose tastes range from a love of American hamburgers to off-beat outfits."[138] "I wanted my freedom," the teenager told a packed press conference. She decided to defect after being informed that she would have to return home and finish high school after the US Open, rather than playing in tournaments that fall. The Czechoslovak Sports Federation issued a statement saying, "Navrátilová had all the possibilities in Czechoslovakia to develop her talent, but she preferred a professional career and a fat bank account."[139] Martina later became an outspoken defender of gay rights. Billie Jean King rated her "the greatest singles, doubles, and mixed doubles player who ever lived."[140] Since the beginning of the open era in 1968, no male or female tennis player has won more singles tournaments (167), doubles events (177), or matches (2,189) than Navrátilová. They include eighteen major singles championships, nine of them at Wimbledon.

Navrátilová next set foot in her hometown of Prague in 1986 as a proud member of the US Federation Cup team. A couple weeks earlier, after winning her fifth straight Wimbledon singles title, a reporter asked how it felt to be going home after so long:

> "Yeah, sure," she said. "I've been gone a long time. I can't wait to see my house again. See my dogs and my cats. I've been gone now for, oh, 2½ months, so I'm anxious to. . . ."
>
> And she kept on gabbing like that, about absence making the heart grow fonder and such, and it suddenly hit you like a forehand smash: *She was talking about Texas. Fort Worth bloody Texas.*[141]

Notes from Underground

On 21 August 1969 Ludvík Vaculík, Václav Havel, and eight others signed an open letter to Czechoslovak authorities titled *"Deset bodů"* (Ten points). Among other things, they condemned the continuing presence of Warsaw Pact troops on Czechoslovak soil and demanded an end to censorship.[142] It was an utterly quixotic gesture by then. Three of the authors, KAN founder Rudolf Battěk, historian Jan Tešar, and chess maestro Luděk Pachman, were quickly arrested. Along with five other signatories, including Havel and Vaculík, they were charged on 29 June 1970 with "preparing a criminal act to subvert the republic."[143] No further action was taken, although the charges were not dropped. Battěk and Tešar were released soon after. "Ten Points" was Pachman's idea, and he spent the longest time in jail.[144] Typical of his generation, Luděk joined the KSČ at age twenty-one in 1945 and worked for the education department at ÚRO. From 1952 he devoted himself to chess full time. As Václav Kopecký explained to the central committee, "We have dozens of dumb trade unionists, but only one chess player like Pachman."[145] Few have bettered Luděk's lifetime record of two wins, two losses, and four draws against Bobby Fischer. Awarded the title of grand master in 1954, Pachman was the Czechoslovak champion seven times between 1946 and 1966. From 1959 he wrote for and then headed the foreign section of the magazine *Československý sport*. Luděk first attracted political attention when he and Arnošt Lustig wrote to the KSČ central committee protesting Czechoslovak policy toward Israel. Jiří Hendrych sharply criticized Pachman and Lustig's letter at the Fourth Writers' Union Congress in 1967, and the delegates, who had previously been unaware of its existence, demanded that it be read out loud—which it was, to widespread applause. Luděk was promptly given six months' unpaid leave from *Československý sport*, which he spent teaching chess in Puerto Rico. When he returned to Prague in May 1968, he threw himself into the reform movement.

Pachman was arrested at half past midnight on 22 August 1969. Refusing to cooperate with his interrogators, he went on a hunger strike and at one point attempted suicide. The experience turned the once fervent Marxist into a lifelong Catholic ("You always have to be in some party," Vaculík chided him).[146] A little over a year later another signatory of "Ten Points," the Czechoslovak Radio correspondent Karel Kyncl, apologized to his colleagues at the Union of Czech Journalists for Luděk's absence from a meeting called to ratify the latest expulsions from the union. Kyncl was glad his friend couldn't be there. "After a year's isolation from the development of our absurdity—sorry, I wanted to say reality," he explained, Pachman might have found it difficult to comprehend why earning twelve hundred crowns a month from journalistic activities was now a prerequisite for membership when a majority of journalists were prevented from publishing "even an essay on raindrops in spring. . . . Luděk Pachman would perhaps not appreciate that this isn't at all a matter of political persecution, that it has nothing to do with the existential destruction of people—on the contrary, it is simply a matter of the professional cleansing of a journalists' union in which non-journalists have no place." Pachman "was released a few days ago," Kyncl goes on. "Released, but not into freedom. Right now, he is lying in pavilion number 2 in the psychiatric clinic in Prague-Bohnice and nobody except his wife is allowed to visit him . . . after almost fourteen months in Ruzyně and Pankrác prisons in Prague a previously healthy person is a human ruin."[147] Pachman was allowed to leave the country on 29 November 1972 with his wife Evženie, the former head of figure-skating coverage at Czechoslovak TV. He won the West German chess championship in 1978. Following a spell in prison, Kyncl was permitted to immigrate to Britain in 1983.

Looking back on the events of 1969–1970 from the vantage point of 1990, Vaculík saw nothing heroic about "Ten Points." Even at the time, he says, "I felt clearly that it was a nonsensical action that would have no effect. . . . When it led to prosecution and legal action, I considered it a just punishment for myself—a punishment for stupidity!"

> Since then the main question for me has been how to hold up under pressure, what kind of counterpressure to bring to bear to find an appropriate stance. . . . But above all: the time has come of individuals and small strong groups; the nation is done for. I could better comprehend, for example, those who assassinated the Reichsprotektor than those who wanted to summon the nation anew to an uprising. Palach's action was appropriate and accurate! Petlice [Padlock Editions, Vaculík's samizdat press], discovered by accident, was also one of the means to gather new strength. . . . Charter 77 was a further step. Until the time of "Několik vět" [A few sentences, a proclamation issued by Charter 77 in the summer of 1989] "Ten Points" was simply nonsense—To be more accurate: it made sense as a proclamation of the standpoint of those who signed it. Nothing more.[148]

As had happened many times before in Czech history, the opposition was forced underground. Vaculík presents this withdrawal from active politics as a tactical retreat until circumstances changed. For others, disengagement itself became a form of resistance in which isolation from official politics, society, and culture was transformed into something close to a moral imperative.

"The Platform of Prague," a text jointly issued by the Prague and Paris surrealist groups following the latter's visit to the Czech capital in April 1968, hailed "the authentic emergence of the union of revolutionary dynamism of the spirit and objective freeing of the conditions of life. Today," it exulted, "we see in Cuba and Czechoslovakia two places in the world where the first conditions have come together in which a new human awareness against the repression of right and left can take shape, through direct contact and by the union of the working class and the intelligentsia, without the intermediary of any party apparatus, which always brings with it the danger of a new Stalinism."[149]

A year later Czechoslovakia was back in the hands of the party apparatus, Fidel Castro's "island of freedom" had thrown its support behind the Soviet invasion, and the Paris surrealist group had fractured in the wake of the defeats of 1968. In "*Možné proti skutečnému*" ("The Possible against the Real," September 1969), the Prague surrealists insisted that surrealism had a future. Changing the world through political action no longer seemed to be a part of it. Foremost among their priorities were liberating "the grandiosity and lust, existing in the unconscious, potentially and virtually critical and inspiring in man's fight against the numbing effects of civilization's mechanisms" and "strengthening the ludic forms of life at the expense of the instrumental ones."[150] This was a retreat to positions Effenberger had articulated in his 1966–1967 essay "*Varianty, konstanty a dominanty surrealismu*" (Variants, constants, and dominants of surrealism). Whereas the prewar surrealists had dreamed of a revolution that would "transform the world and change life," he argued, "later political developments" had shown the orgasmic union of Marx and Rimbaud to be "in its maximalist presuppositions only a romantic ideal."[151]

The Prague surrealists were just as traumatized by the collapse of the mirages of 1968 as their Parisian comrades, and soon UDS splintered too. Petr Král fled to Paris in 1968, where he became a regular correspondent for *Le Monde* and *L'Express*. Zbyněk Havlíček died in January 1969. Stanislav Dvorský, Roman Erben, and Prokop Voskovec all quit UDS in 1969–1970. In 1971 a new Group of Surrealists in Czechoslovakia (they deliberately adopted their prewar predecessor's name) coalesced around Effenberger.[152] Alena Nádvorníková, who joined the following year, recalls that surrealist games, "one of the few possible and justifiable ways of existence in a totalitarian reality, though certainly by no means only there," were a central feature of the group's "regular weekly meetings with very irregular outcomes."[153] Unable to publish or exhibit in Czechoslovakia, they compiled several collections of texts and images in single copies, as well as contributing to the French journals *BLS* (*Bulletin de liaison surréaliste*) and *Surréalisme* and producing a joint anthology with Vincent Bounoure's reconstituted Paris surrealist group titled *La civilisation surréaliste* (1976).[154] "That we were isolated from any possibility of public engagement . . . is generally known," they wrote in 1987. "But it is less generally known that by the nature of our beliefs we necessarily distanced ourselves from the conglomerate of forces that were considered and considered themselves to be representative of the opposition to the totalitarian regime of the time. . . . We chose to remain a party outside all power and market coalitions." They were no less dismissive of the "mystico-folkloric underground pirouetting in happenings between rock and marijuana."[155] Unfairly so, I would say, since the long-haired rabble they were mocking shared their contempt for "power and market coalitions" and were no less wary of what they derided as the official opposition.

Ivan Martin Jirous, who together with Egon Bondy was the leading figure in the post-1968 Czechoslovak underground, begins his *"Zpráva o třetím českém hudebním obrození"* ("Report on the Third Czech Musical Revival," 1975) with a confrontation between "the underground" and "the establishment." Tellingly, he uses the English words for both throughout.

> At the end of 1974, a day before New Year's Eve, we went by train to a concert in Líšnice, a small village west of Prague. We got out at the nearest station and went the remaining few kilometers on foot, though the dusky, half-frozen muddy fields. There were about forty-five of us: we knew that another crowd of our friends were approaching Líšnice from the bus stop on the other side, and that many more were coming by car. Our mood was one of sheer joy. There was a tangible hope that we would be celebrating the end of the year with music: we were going to the first concert of a group called Umělá Hmota (Artificial Material), and after that the Plastics and DG 307 were to play. As we walked through the bleak countryside, many of us experienced an intense feeling, which some expressed in words. It reminded us of the pilgrimages of the first Hussites into the mountains.... As soon as we came to Líšnice ... we were told to disperse at once, or else force would be used.... Today people who want to listen to the music they like (just like the people in the days of Hus who went to the hills to listen to words they wanted to hear) have no other recourse for the time being but to retreat from violence.[156]

Why does this scene bring to mind an earlier New Year's Eve when Jana Krejcarová introduced Egon Bondy to the old-time Trotskyist Záviš Kalandra before she and Egon headed to the country in an empty and icy train with just two bottles of champagne?

Jirous's text, which is the nearest the underground came to a manifesto, is in large part a history of Czech rock music since the 1960s, profiling the leading underground bands of that era—the Primitives, the Plastic People of the Universe, Aktual, the Midsummer Night's Dream Band, DG 307, Umělá Hmota—and the singer-songwriters Charlie (Karel) Soukup and Svatopluk Karásek, an evangelical pastor whose spiritual "Say No to the Devil, Say No!" became an underground anthem. Jirous, who was universally known to Czechs by his

FIGURE 12.6. Jan Kaspar's photograph of Ivan Martin Jirous
("Magor"), no date. © ČTK/Kaspar Jan.

nickname Magor, the "Madman," was artistic director of the Plastic People, for whom he played a role akin to Andy Warhol's part in the Velvet Underground. Before that he was artistic director for the Primitives, "a rough-hewn group, miles away from the artificial smoothness of other bands," that split up in April 1969.[157] Canadian translator Paul Wilson, who sang with the Plastics from 1970 to 1972, remembers Jirous as "a bright, energetic and very determined young man whose first loves were literature and art. Then he heard the Beatles. And, as the Lou Reed song goes, his life was changed by rock 'n' roll. He came to Prague, studied art history, hung around the nascent rock scene, grew his curly chestnut hair long, and wrote inflammatory articles."[158] It was Jirous's older cousin Jiří Padrta—the co-organizer with Miroslav Lamač of the landmark *Founders of Modern Czech Art* exhibition in Brno in 1957—who encouraged Magor to study art history at Charles University after it became clear that he would not get into FAMU to study film. As we saw earlier, the young Jirous also copied reams of Czech translations of Franz Kafka and circulated them in samizdat. Martin (as he was known to his family and friends) graduated in 1969, writing his master's thesis on the visual poetry of Jiří Kolář and Henri Michaux, and he published articles in *Výtvarná práce* and *Vytvarné umění* until he was stopped in 1971.[159]

While Jirous was a dyed-in-the-wool intellectual, the underground bands and their fans were mostly working-class youth, many of whom never finished high school. "The 'rock 'n' roll revolution," writes Martin Machovec, "was a 'revolt of the barbarians,' no longer very tender or holy, rather than being the result of some intellectual, ideological-aesthetic discourse."[160] Four teenagers from the Prague district of Břevnov formed the Plastic People in September 1968. They took their name from a song by Frank Zappa. Aside from original compositions by their seventeen-year-old founder Milan Hlavsa, the band introduced Czech audiences to the music of the Velvet Underground and the Fugs, which they sang in English. Hlavsa set texts by Shakespeare, William Blake, Jiři Kolář, and Magor's first wife, the poet and art historian Věra Jirousová (née Vačilová) to music. One of Jirousová's lyrics tells of a virgin whose "pale cunt is a magnolia / that catches the morning dew"; she joyfully deflowers herself with the "bright white horn" of a unicorn, "smooth and marvelous"—more shades of Molly Bloom.[161] After 1969, "groups were forbidden to have repertoires sung in English, bands with English names were forced to change them, and many top rock musicians deplorably became back-up musicians for the stars of commercial pop music." Because the Plastics refused to compromise, they lost their status as professional musicians, along with their instruments (which their agency Akord had lent them) and their practice space (in the Kinský Palace) in May 1970, and the band members had to get regular jobs. Thereafter they were legally allowed to play only at private functions. Some members left the band and new ones joined. By 1973 a core had coalesced around Milan Hlavsa on bass, Josef Janíček on guitar, Jiří Kabeš on violin and viola, and Vratislav Brabenec on sax.[162] "The mythological underground," says Jirous, had now become "a genuine sociological and cultural underground, in the sense proclaimed in the early sixties by Ed Sanders, Allen Ginsberg, Jeff Nuttall, Timothy Leary, and many other pioneers of this movement."

"The final impulse that the Plastic People needed to become troubadours," Magor continues, "was an encounter with the work of the poet Egon Bondy."

Jirous saw Bondy's total realism as the incarnation of the categorical imperative set out in Jeff Nuttall's *Bomb Culture*: "To uproot absolutely, and once for
all, the Pauline lie which silently assumes, in Christian convention, that people
do not shit, do not piss, and do not fuck."[163] Bondy and Jirous first met in the
psychiatric ward at Bohnice hospital.[164] It was a location Egon knew well,
having first been confined there back in 1949 when his father sought to keep
him away from Milena Jesenská's daughter. The Madman introduced the Poet
to the band when the Plastics played at the ČKD Polovodiče works in the Krč
district of Prague on 29 June 1972.[165] Bondy's poems furnished the lyrics for
the Plastic People's first album, which was illegally recorded in the unheated
halls of Houska Castle north of Prague in December 1974 and released in
France in 1978 under the punning English title *Egon Bondy's Happy Hearts Club
Banned*. Bondy had long ago lost hope that the system could be reformed from
within. "When I was twenty they executed Záviš Kalandra / who was then
more to me than my own father / A couple years later they nearly executed me
/ and now convicted and on their way to Jáchymov / are Petr Uhl and thirteen
other comrades," he wrote in his "*Březnová báseň 1971*" (March poem 1971).
Uhl was a Marxist journalist who founded the short-lived Hnutí revoluční
mládeže (Revolutionary Youth Movement) in December 1968, for which he
was arrested a year later and spent four years in prison. Bondy goes on: "Don't
ever again allow yourselves to be pushed around like in 1968 by those professional apparatchiks / the Svobodas the Dubčeks the Černíks / who under-
standably have no interest in really changing the regime that created them and
from which they live."[166]

Jirous ends his "Report" with a call not to overthrow the system but to
stand outside it and "live in truth"—a phrase both he and Bondy used before
Václav Havel took it up and reworked it for his own ends in his celebrated 1978
essay "The Power of the Powerless."[167] Magor doesn't directly quote Timothy
Leary, but he might as well have: his message is to turn on, tune in, and drop
out. "In Bohemia," he maintains, "the situation is essentially different, and far
better than in the West, because we live in an atmosphere of total agreement:
the first culture doesn't want anything to do with us and we don't want anything to do with the first culture":

> The aim of the underground in the West is the destruction of the establish-
> ment. The aim of the underground here in Bohemia is the creation of a
> second culture: a culture that will not be dependent on official channels of
> communication, social recognition, and the hierarchy of values laid down

by the establishment; a culture that cannot have the destruction of the establishment as its aim because in doing so, it would drive itself into the establishment's embrace; a culture which helps those who wish to join it to rid themselves of the skepticism which says that nothing can be done and shows them that much can be done when those who make the culture desire little for themselves and much for others. This is the only way to live on in dignity through the years that are left to us and to all those who agree with the words of the Taborite chiliast Martin Húska who said: "A person who keeps the faith is more valuable than any sacrament."[168]

Maybe. But between the fixed poles of the establishment and the underground, Magor's first and second cultures, lies an indeterminate region that was neither one nor the other. This gray zone, argues Josef Škvorecký, provided a space for "the conspiracy of normal people who stand between the fanaticism of the orthodox and the cynicism of the pragmatic on the one side, and the abnormal moral courage of the dissidents on the other. The overt solidarity of these men and women is to Caesar, but their covert sympathies belong to God. They hang portraits of the consecutive Big Brothers over their desks but right under their eyes they read Orwell and listen to Charlie Byrd."[169] He exemplifies the creative publishing activities of the Jazz Section (Jazzová sekce) of the Musicians' Union (Svaz hudebníků ČSR), which issued a bulletin for members titled *Jazz* starting in 1972 and organized annual Prague Jazz Day festivals beginning in 1974. Under the editorship of its chairman Karel Srp, father of the art historian of the same name, the Jazz Section started two series in 1979 called Jazzpetit and Situace. Nominally these were supplements to *Jazz*, though many were substantial books. Crucially, because these were internal union publications and not for sale to the public, they were not subject to advance censorship.

The first Jazzpetit, titled *Rocková poezie 1* (Rock poetry 1), contained Czech translations of lyrics by Captain Beefheart, the Mothers of Invention, and other Western rock bands; later titles included *Český rock'n'roll 1956–1969* (Czech rock and roll 1956–1969), *John Ono Lennon*, and the three-volume encyclopedia *Rock 2000*. The series also embraced other musical genres (Ludmila Vrkočová's *Music of the Terezín Ghetto*, Zdeněk Justoň's *Music of Primitive Peoples*) and—more dangerously—ventured into realms that were not musical at all. Srp published Bohumil Hrabal's *I Served the King of England* as Jazzpetit #9 in 1982, when none of the official publishers dared touch it. When Joska Skalník, the book's artistic designer, was challenged to explain why the Jazz Section was publishing a work that had nothing to do with jazz, he retorted,

FIGURE 12.7. Jazzpetit edition of Bohumil Hrabal's *I Served the King of England*, 1982. From Vladimír Kouřil, *Jazzová sekce v čase a nečase*, Prague, 1999.

"We regard Hrabal's method of writing as jazz."[170] Jazzpetit #2 was Jindřich Chalupecký's *O Dada, surrealismu a českém umění* (Dada, surrealism and Czech art), which, among other things, contained the first complete published text of "The World in Which We Live." Later Jazzpetit titles included Karel Srp Jr.'s anthology on the contemporary American art scene *Minimal & Earth & Concept Art*, Ludvík Kundera's *Dada*, and Anna Fárová's *Jindřich Štyrský: fotografické dílo 1934–1935* (Jindřich Štyrský: photographic work 1934–1935). Fárová wrote under the pseudonym Annette Moussu because she had signed Charter 77, and "chairman Karel Srp did not want to draw attention to our relations with people from the political opposition."[171] The twenty-sixth and last Jazzpetit, Chalupecký's *Marcel Duchamp*, was ready for publication in 1984 but was confiscated by the police before it could be printed.

The fifteen Situace publications, each comprising two pages of text by Karel Srp Jr. and eighteen pages of black-and-white reproductions, were devoted to "artists standing outside the official scene, exhibiting only sporadically or by chance or only abroad"—as Emila Medková, Libor Fára, and Václav Boštík, among others, had once again become.[172] The Jazz Section published Jaroslav Seifert's Nobel Prize acceptance speech in 1984, which was delivered in Stockholm on the poet's behalf by his daughter Jana and resolutely ignored in the official media. The Musicians' Union was eventually dissolved by the Ministry of the Interior in October of that year, but the episode shows how porous the walls of the apparent *totalita* could be. Such people, concludes Škvorecký, are "the Grey Zone which makes really-existing socialism livable. In fact, they make it work."[173]

Largo Desolato

What Martin Machovec calls the "under-the-ground" intelligentsia of "dismissed Czech university professors" and the self-proclaimed "underground" of "admirers of the music played by bands like The Velvet Underground, The Fugs, The Mothers of Invention, and Captain Beefheart's Magic Band" were hardly natural allies;[174] the first time Martin Jirous met Václav Havel he told him, "You were essentially a paid agent of the regime."[175] It was shared persecution that brought them together. It likely helped that Vašek was a Velvet Underground fan and Magor was an unusually cultured rocker. Jirous was jailed for ten months in July 1973 after an altercation with a retired StB major in a restaurant in the Podskalí district of Prague. Following numerous sporadic clashes between music fans and the police over the next couple years, the authorities launched a concerted crackdown. It is unclear exactly what threat the longhairs posed to the socialist order, given that they were so resolutely apolitical, but their greatest offense was probably precisely this refusal of politics. The trigger was the Second Festival of the Second Culture held on 21 February 1976 in Bojanovice, a village west of Prague. This was ostensibly a private celebration of the wedding of Jirous and his second wife Juliana Stritzková, where, among other acts, Egon Bondy sang with Uměla hmota. Beginning on 17 March, twenty-two members of the underground were arrested, including Jirous, Svatopluk Karásek, Charlie Soukup, and Milan Hlavsa, Vratislav Brabenec, Josef Janíček, and Jiří Kabeš of the Plastic People. Most were released between April and August, but three young laborers were prosecuted in Plzeň for organizing an event in December 1975 at which Jirous spoke and Karásek and Soukup performed. They were given sentences of fifteen, nine, and four months. On 23 September the "Trial of the Plastic People of the Universe," as it soon became internationally (if inaccurately) known, opened in Prague.[176] In the dock were Ivan Martin Jirous, Vratislav Brabenec, Svatopluk Karásek, and DG 307 member Pavel Zajíček. All were found guilty of hooliganism. Karásek and Brabenec were each sentenced to eight months, Zajíček twelve months, and Jirous eighteen months.

Václav Havel had contacted Jirous soon after the Bojanovice festival, and he took the lead in organizing support for the musicians. At the time, Jirous's brother-in-law, the photographer Jan Ságl, told Magor, "You are a complete moron. Now in front of the house his informers have met with our informers and now it's a question of days before they begin to pick us up."[177] On 9 April Jiří Kolář, Jindřich Chalupecký, Josef Hiršal, the philosopher Jan Patočka, and the writer Zdeněk Urbánek wrote to Gustáv Husák protesting the arrests. On 12 June Václav Černý, Václav Havel, Ivan Klíma, Pavel Kohout, and Ludvík Vaculík issued a statement arguing, "If young people with long hair are going to be condemned for their unconventional music as criminal delinquents today . . . then it will be all the easier tomorrow to condemn any other artists for their novels, poems, essays, and pictures."[178] The following month Černý, Havel, Klíma, Kohout, Patočka, Karel Kosík, and Jaroslav Seifert appealed to Nobel Prize laureate Heinrich Böll for help in publicizing the plight of "young people [who] will stand before the court, not for their political opinions, activity, or ambitions, but for . . . the 'crime' of attempting with their compositions to sing out their revulsion for the established values of the world they live in, to its hypocritical morality, the uniformity of its life, to bureaucratic insensitivity and to the consumerist way of life." "Naturally, all of this is not written in the indictment," they went on; "that speaks only of alleged 'mischief,' which consisted of some of their texts containing so-called indecent words, which were supposed to have shocked someone."[179] Of course. Obscenity is a terrible and peculiar menace to decent people always and everywhere. We are back in the Court of Special Sessions in New York in 1921 with James Joyce, Jane Heap, and the Sumner vigilanti.

The trial provided the catalyst for the first open political opposition in Czechoslovakia since 1969. Charter 77, whose text was officially dated 1 January 1977, was drafted during a series of meetings in December 1976 involving Havel, Zdeněk Mlynář, Pavel Kohout, Ludvík Vaculík, former foreign minister Jiří Hájek, Petr Uhl, and Jiří Němec. A cousin of the film director Jan Němec, Jiří Němec was a Catholic philosopher and clinical psychologist. He and his wife Dana Němcová, also a psychologist, formed an important link with the youthful underground; its members frequently crashed at their flat at 7 Ječná Street in the New Town, where the couple held a permanent open house.[180] The name Charta 77 was coined by Kohout. The stated aim was to hold the Czechoslovak state responsible for living up to the human rights commitments it made when it signed the Helsinki Accords, which regularized the political status quo in Europe, on 1 August 1975. However, the true intent, according to Mlynář, was to create a "broader movement that would constantly add new members."[181] The charter brought together writers and artists, scientists and academics—historians and sociologists were especially well represented—reform communists expelled from the KSČ, former political prisoners, Catholic and evangelical religious believers, Trotskyists and Maoists, members of the underground, and even a sprinkling of workers. Jirous was unable to sign because he was in jail; he did so after his release.[182] Egon Bondy signed in December 1976, but at a meeting at Václav Havel's, "Jiří Němec tore up the paper with Bondy's signature, explaining that he did not regard him as legally competent. Uhl therefore created a duplicate and made a note that it was to be held on deposit."[183] By the end of 1979, 1,018 people had signed the charter.[184] Though their numbers remained minuscule, over the next decade the chartists would become a constant thorn in the KSČ's side, relentlessly documenting and publicizing the regime's human rights abuses through their extensive network of émigré and foreign contacts.[185]

Following a Keystone Cops car chase through Prague on 6 January 1977, Václav Havel, Ludvík Vaculík, and Pavel Landovský were arrested while trying to mail the Charter 77 text and signatures to members of the federal assembly. When *Le Monde*, the *Frankfurter Allgemeine Zeitung*, the *Times*, and the *New York Times* published (and Radio Free Europe and Voice of America broadcast) the text, the authorities had no hope of keeping the charter under wraps. Instead, they unleashed a vehement public campaign of denunciation. The StB concurrently began Operation *Asanace*—the same term that had been used to describe the Prague slum clearance at the turn of the twentieth century—with the aim of decontaminating the body politic by forcing dissidents to leave the country. Chartists were subjected to what Ludvík Vaculík called "meticulously conceived mental terror,"[186] whose techniques included around-the-clock surveillance, tapping of telephones and bugging of apartments, lengthy and repeated police interrogations, and occasional physical assaults. Seventy-year-old Jan Patočka—who, with Václav Havel and Jiří Hájek, was one of the first three official spokespersons for Charter 77—was hospitalized with chest pains after spending ten hours in StB custody on 3 March 1977. He died ten days later. Whether the interrogation contributed to his heart attack is immaterial: the philosopher instantly joined the honor roll of Czech martyrs for truth. "He stepped into the arena two months before his death," recorded Jan Zábrana in his diary, "and now, already now—a couple hours after his death—he has stepped into Czech history, for as long as there will be a Czech history. The succession is clear: Hus, Comenius, both Masaryks, the boy Palach, now Patočka."[187] Another charter spokesperson, the novelist Zdena Tominová, was attacked by a man wearing a balaclava at the entrance to her apartment building on 5 June 1979. She was left with concussion; things could have been much worse if not for the intervention of a "lady with an umbrella, which she was not afraid to use."[188]

StB torments large and small are matter-of-factly documented amid the mundane details of gardening at the cottage and the nuts and bolts of running a samizdat press in Ludvík Vaculík's *Český snář* (*A Czech Dreambook*), a diary (of sorts) covering 22 January 1979 through 2 February 1980. Dissidents could routinely expect months of delay in renewing their driver's licenses and more than their fair share of parking tickets. In Vaculík's case, the StB's dirty tricks included releasing to the press nude photographs Ludvík and Zdena Erteltová, a copyist for Petlice with whom he had a long-running extramarital affair, had taken of each other lying on gravestones in a cemetery. The police had confiscated the photos during a house search in 1975. The newspaper *Ahoj na sobotu* (Hello on Saturday) published two of these images on 21 January 1977, at the height of the campaign against the charter, under the prurient headline: "Terrible? Unbelievable? But true! This is also 'freedom of speech.'"[189] The *Dreambook* records, "The police offensive against Padlock [Edice Petlice] ... culminated last August in an original form of terror: they interned Zdena in the V.D. clinic and forcibly examined her for venereal infection. She was kept there for three weeks, banned from using the phone, writing letters or receiving mail."[190] The persecution of Pavel Kohout and his wife Jelena Mašínová, which Kohout relates in his "memoir-novel" *Kde je zakopán pes* (Where the dog is buried, 1987), culminated in cutting the brake cables in Jelena's car and poisoning their dog.[191] Kohout was permitted to spend a year working at the Burgtheater in Vienna in 1978. When he and Jelena tried to return in October 1979, they were refused entry at the Czechoslovak border and had their citizenships revoked. The same thing happened to Pavel Landovský after he was allowed out of the country to work at the Burgtheater for two years in 1979. The Café Slavia lost one of its most famous regulars when Jiří Kolář was deprived of his citizenship

ČTENÁŘI AHOJI
AHOJ ČTENÁŘŮM

Otřesné?
Neuvěřitelné?
Ale
pravdivé!

To je také
„svoboda
projevu"

Náš časopis je určený především na víkend, aby pomáhal vytvářet dobrou pohodu při zaslouženém odpočinku našich pracujících. Tím více námi otřáslo, když jsme dostali do redakce snímky, jak jeden představitel „elity", autor kontrarevolučního pamfletu z roku 1968 „Dva tisíce slov", tráví své víkendové dny takovým způsobem, jak ukazují fotografie. Nyní se tento pán znovu objevuje mezi hlavními iniciátory a autory tzv. Charty 77. Jaké hodnoty uznává a vyznává, to dokumentují tyto snímky: hřbitov a hroby, místo, kam se všichni slušní lidé chodí poklonit památce zesnulých, zneuctil L. V. způsobem, který svědčí o jeho morálce, o jeho kulturní úrovni.

Na hřbitově osady Strašice, obec Drahobuzy (Severní kraj), se L. V. spolu se svou milenkou fotografoval na hrobce rodiny Strachových-Halofských a na hrobce rodiny Schneider-Jahnel. Morální zvrácenost, exhibicionismus, perverze, to jsou ty „hodnoty", jejichž vrcholným vyznavačem se L. V. stal. A to jsou také jediné „zbraně", které mu zbyly. Podle autorových informací L. V., který se v poslední době specializoval na vydávání ilegálních tiskovin, dal do oběhu sérii pornografických obrázků, prý na podporu „boje za lidská práva". Uveřejněné snímky jsou dvě nejméně závadné ukázky z tohoto seriálu.

FIGURE 12.8. *Ahoj na sobotu!* exposes Ludvík Vaculík and Eva Erteltová, 21 January 1977. Photographs taken by the couple were leaked to the newspaper after being seized in a police raid. From Petr Blažek and Radek Schovánek, *Prvních 100 dnů Charty 77*, Prague, 2018.

while in West Germany on a fellowship in 1977. The poet and collagist settled in Paris in 1980.

Many of the dissidents who had refused to emigrate earlier now cut their losses. Pavel Juráček departed for Munich in 1977. Zdeněk Mlynář fled to Vienna the same year. After being kidnapped by StB thugs, beaten up, and dumped in the woods outside Prague, Mikuláš Medek's brother Ivan, a music critic, left for Vienna in 1978, where he became a broadcaster for Radio Free Europe and a correspondent for Voice of America. Zdena Tominová was stripped of her citizenship after immigrating to England with her husband, the philosopher Julius Tomin, and their two children in 1980. Written in English but set in dissident Prague, her novel *The Coast of Bohemia: A Winter's Tale*, came out in 1987.[192] Others who threw in the towel under the pressure of Operation *Asanace* included journalist Jiří Lederer; writers Jiří Gruša, who had been a mainstay of Edice Petlice, and Karel Trinkewitz; playwright Karol Sidon; surrealist poet Prokop Voskovec; singer-songwriters Jaroslav Hutka, Svatopluk Karásek, Charlie Soukup, and Vlastimil Třešňák; and the Plastics' saxophonist Vratislav Brabenec. Jiří Němec left in 1983. "Jiří wanted to support publication of Patočka's writings in Vienna," Dana Němcová explained later. "He wanted us to go together, but at that time I had things I had already embarked upon here."[193] She went on to become a Charter 77 spokesperson.

"When someone leaves here, they are gone," Vaculík bitterly complained in *A Czech*

Dreambook. "The shortcoming of these people is not that they emigrate, but that they started fighting as if intending to keep it up. Courage has to be rationed like water in the desert or bread during a siege."[194] Even if they enjoyed the support of such international celebrities as Samuel Beckett, Ingmar Bergman, Harold Pinter, Tom Stoppard, and Arthur Miller, the dissidents who remained in the country needed all the courage they could muster. Vaculík managed to stay out of jail, but many others did not. On 29 May 1979 Václav Havel was arrested with sixteen other members of Výbor na obranu nespravedlivě stíhaných (Committee for the Defense of the Unjustly Persecuted), an offshoot of Charter 77 formed in April 1978 that is commonly known by its acronym VONS. Having broken down the door of his Dejvice flat and found nobody at home, the police picked him up in the apartment of "Anna Kohoutová, the beautiful, Yugoslav-born brunette ex-wife of Pavel Kohout," with whom Havel had been carrying on a passionate affair "for quite some time." This not only testifies to the persistence of Swinging Sixties mores in the dissident world but also underlines just how closeted that world was. "If it resembled a libertine wife-swapping community," writes Havel's friend, press secretary, and adviser Michael Žantovský, "this was dictated by sheer necessity, the result of severely limited contact with the outside world and its sexual opportunities. Havel's girlfriend was Kohout's ex-wife, just as Ivan Havel's wife Květa was the future wife of Jiří Dienstbier, and Věra Jirousová, the ex-wife of Magor, became a girlfriend to Jiří Němec."[195]

Vaculík's *Czech Dreambook* exposes another tight little tangle of infidelities that left Madla (Marie) Vaculíková in the same predicament as Olga Havlová. On 24 November 1979 Ludvík peeks into his wife's diary and reads: "Dad is off somewhere. He says he's going to Brno to see [Milan] Šimečka but I don't believe him. He never tells the truth, so even when he does, it's not the truth for me anymore. It's odd how everyone thinks of him as a fighter for truth." Vaculík responds to Madla's complaint with the comment, "It's not my fault they're all stupid . . . I have never, I hope, proclaimed myself to be anybody but me. My lies are as much mine as the truth, and I don't know which will prove the most reprehensible."[196] It is a sharp observation that applies as much to the political as to the personal. The two did not always neatly align, as Milan Kundera delighted in pointing out:

"The struggle of man against power is the struggle of memory against forgetting." That remark by Mirek, a character in *The Book of Laughter and Forgetting*, is often cited as the book's message. This is because the first thing a reader recognizes in a novel is the "already known." The "already known" in that novel is Orwell's famous theme: the forgetting that a totalitarian regime imposes. But to me the originality of Mirek's story lay somewhere else entirely. This Mirek who is struggling with all his might to make sure he is not forgotten (he and his friends and their political battle) is at the same time doing his utmost to forget another person (his ex-mistress, whom he's ashamed of).[197]

Havel, Petr Uhl, Jiří Dienstbier, the journalist Otka Bednářová, and the Catholic philosopher Václav Benda were given prison sentences ranging from three to five years for their activities in VONS. Dana Němcová escaped with a two-year suspended sentence. Before the trial started, the authorities had encouraged Havel to take up Miloš Forman's invitation to visit the United States on a one-year "theatrical fellowship" sponsored by Joseph Papp at the Public Theater, where *The Memorandum* had played in 1968. After considerable hesitation and a long discussion with his wife Olga during her prison visit of 5 September, the playwright refused.[198] While in jail, Havel made a sterling contribution to that branch of (very) twentieth-century meditative literature that includes Rosa Luxemburg's *Letters from Prison*, Antonio Gramsci's *Prison Notebooks*, Martin Luther King Jr.'s *Letters from a Birmingham Jail*, and Nelson Mandela's *Conversations with Myself*. His *Dopisy Olze* (*Letters to Olga*), mailed from jails in Prague (Ruzyně), Ostrava (Heřmanice), and Plzeň (Bory), were published in 1990.[199] Jirous characterized the composition of prison letters as an absurdist catch-22 "literary task when you had to write something but were not able to" due to the restrictions of censorship.[200] He too added to the prison lit genre, with letters to his second wife Juliana and the poems smuggled out of Valdice maximum security prison near Jičín that were published in samizdat in 1985 as *Magorovy labutí písně* (Magor's swan song).[201] Jirous spent a total of eight and a half years behind bars between 1973 and 1989.

Having nearly died of pneumonia, Havel was released from jail early, in February 1983. He spent a good deal of time at his country home in Hrádeček, near Trutnov in northeastern Bohemia, beside which the StB built a watchtower in the shape of a miniature Swiss chalet to keep their quarry under permanent observation. Visiting in 1986, the journalist and author Samuel G. Freedman noticed "the collection of posters on the wall of Mr. Havel's study. One is the original advertisement for 'Hair.' Several others, with their Day-Glo colors and wavy lettering, look like relics from a Janis Joplin concert at Winterland. It is as if time has not existed since 1968 for Vaclav Havel. And, in a sense, it has not."[202] Freedman was right; for a while, normalization succeeded in freezing time. But not forever. Faced with the liberalizing wind that started blowing strongly from the east after Mikhail Gorbachev became general secretary of the CPSU in 1985, the KSČ leaders initially tried to dig in their heels. In May 1987 Karel Srp and four other former members of the Jazz Section's committee were put on trial for continuing the "illegal production, distribution, and sale" of publications. It was the biggest repressive action since the 1979 VONS trial, and it sent a clear message as to how far *glasnost* and *perestroika* would be permitted to go in Husák's Czechoslovakia. Srp got sixteen months in prison, his assistant Vladimír Kouřil got ten months, and the others received suspended sentences. On 21 August 1988—the twentieth anniversary of the Soviet invasion—riot police used tear gas to disperse more than ten thousand young people who were chanting support for Gorbachev's reforms on Wenceslas Square. During "Palach Week" the following January, marking the twentieth anniversary of the student's self-immolation, police broke up daily demonstrations with tear gas, batons, water cannon, and dogs. Václav Havel, Dana Němcová, Jiří Hájek, Rudolf Battěk, and the writer Eva Kantůrková were among those arrested.[203] This time Havel was sentenced to nine months for incitement. He was released from Pankrác prison on 17 May 1989, halfway through his sentence, in response to protests at home and abroad. The times were changing, even in Prague. During his earlier incarceration, the playwright told a Reuters correspondent, he had been treated as "an outcast among outcasts, a pariah among pariahs . . . whereas this year I was a privileged inmate with conditions other prisoners can only dream about."[204]

After his release Havel set about organizing a Charter 77 petition calling for the freeing of political prisoners, freedom of assembly, freedom of religion, the end of censorship, action to protect the environment (which had been badly damaged by the communists' fetishization of heavy industry), and open discussion "not only of the fifties, but also of the Prague Spring, the invasion of the five Warsaw Pact states, and the ensuing normalization." The text of the petition (thanks to Ivan Medek in Vienna) was broadcast by Radio Free Europe, Voice of America, and the BBC on 29 June. "It is sad," the document observed, "that while in several countries whose armies then intervened in Czechoslovak development this topic is already beginning to be seriously discussed, here it still remains a great taboo—only so that people would not have to resign from political and state leadership who are responsible for the twenty-year decline in all regions of our social life."[205] In a deliberate nod to Vaculík's "Two Thousand Words," the document was titled "A Few Sentences." Unlike the "Ten Points," this time the skeptical Ludvík thought the action worthwhile. His instincts were correct. By 10 November the petition had

FIGURE 12.9. Alexander Dubček, Marta Kubišová, and Václav Havel
on the Melantrich balcony during a demonstration in Wenceslas Square,
24 November 1989. Photographer unknown. © ČTK.

garnered 38,250 signatures, including those of Jiří Suchý, Jiří Menzel, the popular singer Hana Zagorová, and other prominent cultural figures who had previously kept a cautious distance from the dissidents.[206] Charter 77, by contrast,
managed to attract only 1,889 signatures over its entire existence.[207] For the
first time since 1968, a broad opposition movement was in the cards.

And so, by swerve of shore and bend of bay, we return to where we began.
When the people finally came out in the streets in the hundreds of thousands
following the events of 17 November 1989, it was the dissidents who had the
political experience and the moral authority to provide leadership for what
might otherwise have been an inchoate mass revolt. Havel and others hur-
riedly set up Občanské forum (Civic Forum) on 19 November to speak for
"that part of the Czechoslovak public which is constantly more critical toward
the policies of the current Czechoslovak leadership and which has been deeply
shocked during these days by the brutal massacre of the peacefully demonstrating students."[208] Against a background of nightly demonstrations in
Wenceslas Square (which had to be moved to Letná Plain on 25 November
because they grew too large for the downtown space) and a two-hour general

strike on 27 November, Civic Forum representatives sat down with KSČ leaders in the Municipal House—where Czechoslovak independence had been proclaimed on 28 October 1918—to negotiate the formation of a government of national unity pending free and fair elections. On 10 December Gustáv Husák swore in the first Czechoslovak government with a noncommunist majority since 1948. He resigned as president later that day. On 28 December Alexander Dubček was restored to his post of speaker of the federal assembly. The next day the assembly met in Vladislav Hall of Prague Castle and unanimously elected Václav Havel president of the Czechoslovak Federal Republic. The playwright concluded his first New Year's address to his compatriots with a nod to Tomáš Masaryk—and an echo of Marta Kubišová's forbidden song from 1968. "My most illustrious predecessor began his first speech with a quotation from Comenius," he told his audience. "Permit me to end my first speech with my own paraphrase of the same utterance": "Your government, people, has returned to you."[209]

Fittingly, Civic Forum had its impromptu headquarters in the Laterna magika theater in the basement of Pavel Janák's Adria Palace on Národní Avenue, an extravagant rondocubist building Karel Teige once condemned as "a despicable and monstrous Miramare furnished with bizarre battlements, giving it from afar the impression of a *bonbonnière*."[210] Michal Horeček, a reporter with *Mladý svět*, describes the scene:

> That Laterna magika—that was it. All those famous reporters from all over the world came here, they barged in with equipment nobody here had ever seen, we looked at it in complete panic. Tom Brokow, Dan Rather were here—all those star reporters from the American CBS and NBC television networks. Also I remember the young Christiane Amanpour. This was where it was all happening. On the one hand there was the foreign media, but I have to say that above all a program went out every day from here that actually only reacted to the growing radicalism of the people in the streets with misery.[211]

Somewhere in the fifth dimension Alfréd Radok, who saw all the tragic and grotesque paradoxes of life, rejoicing in its beauty as well as laying bare its wretchedness, gave a wry chuckle. For a moment, situations and individuals were extracted from the routine context of time and space and apprehended in another fashion entirely. It wasn't the end of history. But it was the end of another of modernity's great failed experiments in living in the future.

Coda

LIVING IN TRUTH

The truth! Of course people know what it is, broadly speaking ... In Prague nowadays people are extremely careful with their truth, and from time to time, at moments of increased danger, they stuff it deep into their suitcase among the dirty clothes, like contraband at a customs post. It is necessary—or so they say—to be two-faced.

JAN LUKAS[1]

TEMPTING AS IT WOULD BE to end this book with the triumph of truth and love over lies and hatred,[2] the trace of an earlier theatrical production peeps through the shiny new paint. And despite the many coats that have been applied to the Absurdistan polity since the *annus mirabilis* 1989, it is an image that refuses to go away. On 28 January 1977 hundreds of Czechoslovakia's leading film and theater personalities gathered at the National Theater in Prague, one of the most sacred Czech *lieux de mémoire*, to publicly demonstrate their support for the communist regime. On the stage of the "cathedral of Czech art" (as Alois Jirásek described it)[3] sat three rows of party and state functionaries. The TV cameras paid as much attention to the auditorium as they did to the stage, dwelling on the better-known faces in the audience. They repeatedly returned to Jan Werich, who sat in the front row but looked like he would have preferred to be almost anywhere else. Those with long enough memories might have recalled Czech artists' "Promise of fidelity to the Reich," organized in the same venue on 24 June 1942. If so, they likely shrugged off any feeling of déjà vu; after all, they told themselves, they were only going through the motions. "Everybody knew it was a scam. It was a Potemkin's village. That's exactly why I laugh at it," explained the musician František "Ringo" Čech forty years later. Čech acknowledged that "nobody disputed it would help the regime" but rejected the easy condemnations of posterity. "Values and truth exist for you. It existed for us too," he insisted, "but there was no other option. It's as if you would want to let everyone burn like Hus. In Constance you would know how many people would recant."[4]

Jan Kozák, president of the Czech Writers' Union (SČS), opened the proceedings. He was followed by Jiřina Švorcová, secretary of the Svaz českých dramatických umělců (Union of Czech Dramatic Artists), who read a statement on behalf of the creative unions titled "*Za nové tvůrčí činy ve jménu socialismu a míru*" (For new creative actions in the name of socialism and peace). After paying homage to the Great October Socialist Revolution (which "illuminates . . . the road of progress, the road to a happy future") and invoking Bedřich Smetana, Mikoláš Aleš, and "Bezruč's furious anti-landlord protests," the actress got down to business: "We despise those anywhere in the world— and groups of such apostates and traitors can be found among us too—who, out of unbridled pride of vain superiority, selfish interest, or even for filthy lucre, turn away and isolate themselves from their own people, its life and real interests and with inexorable logic become the tool of the anti-humanist forces of imperialism. . . . We are convinced that the coming years will be filled with new creative activities linked with the interests of our working people, the humanistic aims of our socialist society, and the policies of our leading force—the Communist Party of Czechoslovakia."[5] No names were named, and Charter 77 was never mentioned. No need. All those present were invited to sign a paper affirming their support for Anticharta, as "For New Creative Actions in the Name of Socialism and Peace" soon became known. On 4 February another rally was held at the Divadlo hudby (Music Theater), where Karel Gott, the most popular singer of the day, played the male lead. In the following weeks similar events took place across the country. Writers, visual artists, and other members of the "cultural front" signed Anticharta in the offices of newspapers, radio and TV stations, publishing houses, and the creative unions, and their names were published in *Rudé právo* daily from 29 January to 12 February.

A handful of brave—or, as many saw it, stupid—souls refused to partake in the charade. One of them was Ivan Vyskočil, whose text-appeals with Jiří Suchý and Jiří Šlitr at the Reduta jazz club instigated the "small forms" of theater that were so integral to the 1960s thaw.[6] Jiří Suchý signed. So did 76 National Artists, 360 meritorious artists, and over 7,000 other writers, artists, composers, and performers.[7] Anticharta was probably the largest collective action by Czech and Slovak creative artists in history. Jiří Menzel and Bohumil Hrabal both put their names to the document. Like the watchmaker David in Hugo Haas's movie *The Girl on the Bridge*, the director of *Closely Watched Trains* was desperately trying not to lose everything again. "They hunted me, I hid," Menzel explained later. "They summoned me to the head office and said: sign here, and you'll be OK. . . . When the Russians came I wasn't allowed to do anything, that lasted a while then gradually I got work again. And suddenly it looked like I was losing it again." "People were always having to humiliate themselves in one way or another," he said, "so those who signed Anticharta often did so with a light heart, because they said to themselves: they won't hassle me, I'll be left alone, and so it didn't bother them too much."[8] Hrabal's signature would have been no surprise to anyone. "All these people in liquidation," he wrote later, "suffered not from guilt, but from terror."[9] After seeing his books *Poupata* (Buds) and *Domácí úkoly* (Homework) pulped in 1970, being banned from publishing, and enduring repeated harassment by the StB in Prague and at his country cottage in Kersko for the next five years, the author of *Closely Watched Trains* agreed to give an interview to *Tvorba* to set the record straight. He "could not imagine a present or future without socialism," Bohouš was quoted as saying. For "honest Czech writers," the most important thing was "what their work says to our readers, not to some foreign broadcaster."[10] This passage was inserted by *Tvorba*'s editor in chief Jiří Hájek, but Hrabal never disowned it.

Hrabal's work was allowed to appear again, albeit with very close scrutiny by the censor. *I Served the King of England*, which was written in Kersko in 1971, remained in a desk drawer until its publication in 1982 by the Jazz Section. Despite StB demands, Hrabal refused to say that it had been published without his permission. After Československý spisovatel rejected *In-house Weddings* in 1986, Hrabal again confined his writing to samizdat. When Bill Clinton asked Václav Havel whether he could meet the now world-famous writer during his visit to Prague in 1994, Bohouš said, "You know where to find me," and the two presidents and UN ambassador Madeleine Albright headed downtown to the Golden Tiger. Hrabal died three years later when he fell out of a fifth-floor window at Bulovka Hospital in Libeň, allegedly while trying to feed the pigeons. It was another dubious Prague defenestration; many of his friends thought it was suicide. Had Bohouš not written, "How many times I've felt like jumping from the fifth floor . . . but always at the last moment my guardian angel saves me"?[11] Jiří Menzel got to film *I Served the King of England* in 2006.

Describing it as "filled with wicked satire and sex both joyful and pitiful," *Chicago Sun-Times* film critic Roger Ebert suggested, "We will not soon see a comedy like this made in the United States. Even if it were entirely translated into American characters and terms, audiences would wonder what it was about."[12] Quite.

The legions of Czechs who lined up to buy Hrabal's books after his *Tvorba* interview were grateful for his accommodation to the realities of normalization. But some former fans saw only betrayal. Here is another image for the ages—to my mind, a rather chilling one, and not only because of the historical antecedents:

> Thirteen of them came to Prague's Kampa Island. They stood in a circle, their long hair falling on their shoulders over the raised collars of their coats. From their bags and backpacks they took out all the books by Hrabal that they found at home and threw them in a heap. Then Ivan Jirous, nicknamed Magor, struck a match. It was April 1975, and in the center of Prague a peculiar protest began: under the touch of the flame the pages blackened of books that all these long-haired young men around the fire loved and read with passion and admiration—*Closely Watched Trains, Murder Ballads and Other Legends, An Advertisement for a House I Don't Want to Live in Any More.*

"Bohumil Hrabal didn't distance himself from the text," explains Ondřej Nezbeda, "and that alone, that he accepted [*Tvorba's*] offer to demonstrate his switch toward the normalizers, for them meant treachery. In their eyes Bohumil Hrabal changed into one of the advertising faces of the regime, an intellectually more attractive Karel Gott."[13] Hrabal never asked to be a standard-bearer for dissent, but so what? Marie Burešová never asked to be Jindřich Štyrský's Sarah Bernhardt either.

"Do you know who Gustáv Husák was?" went the joke. "An insignificant president in the era of Karel Gott."[14] Over the course of six decades, the Divine Kája (Božský Kája), the "Sinatra of the East" who starred in the Anticharta rally at the Music Theater on 4 February 1977, won an astonishing forty-two Golden (from 1996 Czech) Nightingale awards for best male singer as voted by the Czech public, and sold over fifty million records. Karel described himself as "a tenor who likes to sing romantic songs because they are melodic and profess love"; the Polish journalist Mariusz Szczygieł called him "the Czech Presley and Pavarotti rolled into one."[15] Husák awarded Gott the title of National Artist in 1985, telling him, "This is from the people"—a claim that (for once) might have been accurate. Not to be outdone, Václav Havel's right-wing successor as Czech president Václav Klaus added the Medal of Merit (*Za zásluhy*) First Class in 2009. Kája's popularity transcended political differences and extended throughout *Mitteleuropa*, the place, Milan Kundera reminds us, where "the word 'kitsch' was born."[16] The singer's death from leukemia on 1 October 2019 was front-page news in Austria and Germany, where *Bild* announced that "one of the biggest stars in the world of popular music [*Schlagerwelt*] . . . the 'golden voice from Prague' died shortly before midnight on Tuesday evening at the age of 80."[17] Slovak Republic prime minister Peter Pellegrini hailed Gott as "a phenomenon, who through all his activities helped detach people from their everyday life problems and offered them an art they could understand and with which they could identify. *Sbohem*, maestro, let your voice remain forever in the hearts of the people it has rightly enchanted."[18]

Karel got his start at the Semafor Theater in 1962 and made his film debut two years later in *If a Thousand Clarinets*. He won his first Golden Nightingale in 1963 with the Šlitr-Suchý song "*Oči sněhem zaváté*" (Eyes closed with snow). He was one of the original signatories of "Two Thousand Words" but, unlike many others, he was allowed to quietly forget it. After the invasion he remained loyal to the regime, with the exception of a brief "trial emigration" to Germany. Kundera tells the story—or at least a version of it—in *The Book of Laughter and Forgetting*:

> When Karel Gott, the Czech pop singer, went abroad in 1972, Husák got scared. He sat right down and wrote him a personal letter (it was August 1972 and Gott was in Frankfurt). The following is a verbatim quote from it. I have invented nothing.
>
> > *Dear Karel,*
> > *We are not angry with you. Please come back. We will do everything you ask. We will help you if you help us . . .*
>
> Think it over. Without batting an eyelid Husák let doctors, scholars, astronomers, athletes, directors, cameramen, workers, engineers, architects, historians, journalists, writers, and painters go into emigration, but he could not stand the thought of Karel Gott leaving the country. Because Karel Gott represents music minus memory, the music in which the bones of Beethoven and Ellington, the dust of Palestrina and Schönberg, lie buried.
>
> The president of forgetting and the idiot of music deserve one another. They are working for the same cause. "We will help you if you help us." You can't have one without the other.

A few pages later Husák gives a speech to children that begins with the words "Children, you are the future!" "The reason children are the future," Kundera sourly comments, "is not that they will one day be grownups. No, the reason is that mankind is moving more and more in the direction of infancy, and childhood is the image of the future."

> Karel Gott came out onto the podium and sang. Husák was so moved that the tears streamed down his cheeks, and the sunny smiles shining up at him blended with his tears, and a great miracle of a rainbow arched up at that moment over Prague.
>
> The children looked up, saw the rainbow, and began laughing and clapping.
>
> The idiot of music finished his song, and the president of forgetting spread his arms and cried, "Children, life is happiness!"[19]

Here Kundera seamlessly elides Clement Greenberg's concept of kitsch ("the debased simulacra of genuine culture") with his own ("the mirror of the beautifying lie") to make Karel Gott's music, which might best be filed under "easy listening," a metaphor for the normalization regime. But every telling has a taling, and in this case, there is much of interest in what Kundera leaves out.

At the beginning of May 1971—not 1972—Gott was permitted to tour West Germany so long as he returned home by the end of June. When he failed to do so, he was considered an illegal emigrant, and the StB questioned his friends and associates and searched his parents' house, confiscating books and records.[20] Having written to minister of culture Miloslav Brůžek without response, on 21 July Karel wrote to Husák directly. "I am not a politician, but a singer," he explains, "who should at all times bring people joy."

> Although in 1969 and 1970 I stood with all my colleagues in the ranks of those who sincerely wished for the normalization of civic and cultural life in our country, at home I encountered insurmountable difficulties at every step. It was me and my orchestra who were the first to visit the Soviet Union at a time when such acts were viewed as collaboration. It was our group that flew to Cuba, almost without demanding a fee, and it was I who signed a contract with Pragokoncert for an extensive tour of the socialist countries even though this didn't make me at all popular with my colleagues. In response to this attempt—to normalize cultural relations between socialist lands, at home we received only bans and nonsensical censors' interference in the mass media. Although my songs never engaged with any political

tendency or group, some of the lyrics I sang were banned from Czechoslovak radio and TV. My appearances were cut from TV programs and the film
I made in Moscow has still not been shown. My concert activity has often
been obstructed by the inflexible and bureaucratic apparatus of Pragokon-
cert. Recording has become a protracted and unpleasant process, because
officials repeatedly return straightforward lyrics with incomprehensible
demands for revision.

"We want to return before our public," the letter concludes, "provided we are
convinced that the interference I have spoken of in this letter was just a part of
a complicated consolidation process."[21]

It was *in response* to this plea that Husák asked the singer to return to
Czechoslovakia, but not in any "personal letter" that Kundera could have seen.
"Husák summoned us, Kundera was right about that," says Gott. "Not by letter,
but through the trade mission . . . in Frankfurt, where they invited us and told
us that there is an offer here from the top boss of a sort that it's not good to
discuss by phone or letters. He also guaranteed that everything will be explained and there will be no persecution, that no-one will harm us. We went
back to negotiate this agreement and then continued our tour."[22] "Instead of
positively evaluating the fact that I remained at home in Prague, where people
needed me, and didn't emigrate," Karel complains, "I was sometimes blamed.
Not a lot of people criticized me, but it was most often heard in the new period.
I felt this to be unjust in that according to them I made a mistake in coming
back. And with this I got labeled as the singer of the system that was here. If I
had stayed in western Europe and went there like several others to better myself
and then returned from emigration with a victorious gesture, I would likely
have gotten a better welcome." Gott accepted that it had been "a mistake" to
front Anticharta and admitted that "some people masterfully manipulated me,
and I didn't face up to this strongly enough."[23] But he maintained that, "in concrete terms, I did not directly serve any regime at all. If I served anyone, then it
was rather in signing 'Two Thousand Words.'"[24] He tactfully omits his refusal,
in the summer of 1989, to sign "A Few Sentences."[25]

In later English editions of *The Book of Laughter and Forgetting* Kundera
altered Karel Gott's name to the fictitious Karel Klos,[26] and when he finally
allowed the book to be published in the Czech Republic in 2017, he cut that
chapter altogether. "Was he perhaps afraid that Gott would sue him," asks Jan
Čulík, "or did he no longer wish to interfere with the popularity of the people's
singer in a land heading for Babišism [a reference to the populist billionaire

Andrej Babiš, who was prime minister of the Czech Republic from 2017 to 2021]?"[27] I don't have an answer. Nor do I know how to reconcile this airbrushing with Kundera's outrage when others dared to "mutilate" the text of *The Joke*, and I cannot explain why he deprived his compatriots of *The Book of Laughter and Forgetting* many years longer than the communist censors did. To be clear, my complaint is not that Kundera plays fast and loose with historical truth. He is a writer of fiction and has as much right to bend the facts for dramatic effect as, say, Jennifer Cody Epstein in *The Gods of Heavenly Punishment*, Laurent Binet in *HHhH*, or Jiří Weil in his tale of Reinhard Heydrich and the statues on the Rudolfinum roof. But it is a fine irony that Kundera should retrospectively purge the text of a novel that is globally celebrated for the immortal line: "The struggle of man against power is the struggle of memory against forgetting."[28] And it is no less ironic that an author who has repeatedly berated Western commentators for treating "the literature of the so-called East European countries as if it were indeed nothing more than a propaganda instrument, be it pro- or anti-communist," treats Gott's music as *exactly that*.[29] I suspect Kundera would be less censorious if he didn't find the Divine Kája's crooning so aesthetically wanting. But the art adorning the totalitarian façades has not always been inferior. It is Mayakovsky and Rodchenko, Leni Riefenstahl and Vítězslav Nezval, Richard Wagner and Ezra Pound who are the hard cases. Go listen to the ethereal divided violins that open the overture to *Lohengrin*, as Czech artists displaying their loyalty to the Thousand-Year Reich did in the National Theater on 24 June 1942. It is sublime. Kundera of all people should know better than to equate beauty with truth.

The novelist's disdain for Gott's music was clearly not shared by the forty-nine thousand people who lined up for hours on Friday, 11 October 2019, to pay their respects as the singer's body lay in state in Žofín Palace on Slavic Island.[30] The next day Kája was given a send-off with full state honors at Prague Castle, beginning with a requiem mass at Saint Vitus's Cathedral celebrated by Václav Havel's onetime fellow inmate in Plzeň-Bory prison, cardinal Dominik Duka, the archbishop of Prague. The service was broadcast live on three Czech television channels in its entirety. In the congregation sat president Miloš Zeman, prime minister Andrej Babiš, parliamentary speaker Radek Vondráček, and a raft of government ministers. Minister of culture Lubomír Zaorálek—the same minister who fired the director of the Lidice Memorial for countenancing the suggestion that one of the martyred Czech villagers might have outed her Jewish neighbor to the Nazis—told television reporters, "Thanks to him [Gott] it was better here for us. Of whom else can that be said?"[31] Jiří Suchý, Jaromír Jágr, and Václav Havel's second wife Dagmar—who, in her earlier life as the actress Dagmar Veškrnová, had been present at the Anticharta rally—were among the invited guests in the audience, along with many other celebrities. Lucie Bílá, who won the Czech Nightingale award for best female singer every year from 2007 to 2017, performed Schubert's "Ave Maria," one of the maestro's best-loved (and most syrupy) recordings. After-ward Karel was cremated at the Motol crematorium. There was much specula-tion in the press over his final resting place. Though fans had agitated for his ashes to be interred in the Slavín mausoleum at Vyšehrad, his family chose the Malvazinky Cemetery in Smíchov, where, his widow Ivana explained, Kája "spent the greater part of his life, loved, and felt at home."[32]

If anybody had a right to criticize Karel Gott, it was Marta Kubišová, but she did not. Asked why people had traveled to Prague from all corners of the republic to attend his funeral, she responded simply: "Because the people love him. . . . It's not enough just to watch it on TV, they want to be there in person." "I liked him," she added, "he was always so kind, sweet." They stayed in touch after her excommunication and even went out drinking in Prague: Kubišová, Jan Němec, Pavel Juráček, Pavel Landovský, and Kája. Later Marta discovered that "in appropriate places [Gott] always raised the question, why can't Kubišová sing?" She sympathized with his predicament. "Through the whole time I truly felt sorry for almost all of them. I said to myself: you [artists who were permitted to perform under normalization] are walking through a mine-field and you don't know when it will explode and when you will follow me." After the regime fell, "Kája wanted to explain it to me. More than one time. I think it tormented him that back then we stood on opposite sides, that this regime divided us."[33] "It was obvious that he was dealing with it and looking back, it hurt him," she told another reporter. "When not long after the revolu-tion I flew to Tokyo with the Luboš Andršt Orchestra, the boys in the band discussed this with me. I told them: 'If I looked at everything as strictly as you, I'd have nobody to talk to in Prague at all.'"[34] Remember that apartment in Queens, with the bust of Masaryk by the door and the plastic slipcovers on the sofa? "Listen," the old man said, "if only the heroes were left in Prague in '45—or in Warsaw or Leningrad for that matter—there would be fifty people left between here and Moscow."

Commenting on "the hysteria that broke out in the Czech Republic" after Karel Gott's death, the Glasgow-based Czech scholar and journalist Jan Čulík found it depressing that, "for many people, an individual of the middle to lower cultural stream remarkably became a symbol of the Czech nation and Czech

FIGURE 13.1. Jovan Dezort's photograph of Karel Gott and Marta Kubišová
at the Golden Nightingale awards, 1967. © ČTK/Dezort Jovan.

culture."[35] Was it so remarkable? Unlike the émigrés, Kája turned his back on
what almost certainly would have been a successful career abroad and stuck it
out with the Czech nation through thick and thin; and unlike the dissidents,
he shared in the nation's abjection, making the same shabby moral compromises, big and small, that almost everyone else did. He was cowardly, fallible,
and human, *just like them*. He comforted them with the kind of music they
liked—undemanding sentimental music that kept the void at the core of
things at bay. And the people loved him for it. Who can blame them? Normalization lasted a full twenty years. This was as long as Tomáš Masaryk and Edvard Beneš's first republic; as long as Gottwald's, Zápotocký's, and Novotný's
combined terms as president; and more than three times as long as the Protectorate of Bohemia and Moravia. After 1970, little seemed to happen and
nothing seemed to change in the upper echelons of power. Gustáv Husák replaced the senile Ludvík Svoboda as president in 1975, reuniting the top state
and party posts until December 1987, when Miloš Jakeš succeeded Husák as
KSČ general secretary. The presidium appointed at the Fourteenth KSČ Congress in May 1971 remained virtually unchanged until 1989.[36] Lubomír Štrougal
served as prime minister in six successive governments before resigning in

October 1988. There was no opposition outside of the tiny dissident ghetto, and the dissidents were not even remotely representative of the Czechoslovak people. "As the term 'normalization' implies, the 1970s and 1980s were intended to be without events, stagnant," writes Paulina Bren. She asks: "As historians, how do we begin to write a history of nothingness when we are trained to look for defining moments, to uncover change, transition, transformation?"—a question that might lead us, once again, to ponder what exactly we understand by a history.[37] But while history seemed to have stopped, everyday life went on. When it came to politics, sensible folks kept their heads down, their noses clean, and their thoughts to themselves.

This was no longer Milan Kundera's lyrical age of the poet and the hangman. Nor was it the dreamworld of the 1960s, hovering at the crossroads between fantasy and reality. The post-totalitarian age was a more prosaic era, best represented by the Prague greengrocer in Václav Havel's "The Power of the Powerless," who "places in his window, among the onions and carrots, the slogan: 'Workers of the world, unite!'" The greengrocer displays the slogan, says Havel, not because he gives a damn about the fate of the global proletariat but "because it has been done that way for years, because everyone does it, and because that is the way it has to be. If he were to refuse, there could be trouble. . . . He does it because these things must be done if one is to get along in life. It is one of the thousands of details that guarantee him a relatively tranquil life." The greengrocer's indifference to what the slogan says, Havel argues, does not make his action meaningless. Quite the contrary. "The slogan is really a sign, and as such it contains a subliminal but very definite message. Verbally, it might be expressed this way: 'I, the greengrocer XY, live here and I know what I must do. I behave in the manner expected of me. I can be depended upon and am beyond reproach. I am obedient and therefore I have the right to be left in peace.'"

Normalization depended neither on brute force—even if the specter of the leather coats on the staircase was always there, lurking in the background—nor on ideological commitment. It did not demand belief, only performance. It *relied on* the knowing complicity of its subjects, the cynical awareness that they were merely going through the motions to safeguard what really mattered—the job, the apartment, the cottage, the car, the holiday in Bulgaria, their kids' chances of going to university—and therefore would not rock the boat. "For by this very fact," Havel goes on, "individuals confirm the system, fulfill the system, make the system, are the system." They are "objects in a system of control, but at the same time they are its subjects as well. They are both victims of the system and its instruments."[38] "The Power of the Powerless" is a brilliant analysis of how power worked under late communism—and, I suggest, not only there. Is there not, as Ivan Olbracht said of Hašek's Švejk, something of Havel's greengrocer in all of us? Is this not *exactly* how power relations are sustained in Western societies too, from the corporation to the university—neither by coercion, nor by commitment, but by complicity and collaboration? But as a program for action in post-1969 Czechoslovakia, "The Power of the Powerless" had little to offer. Because, after all, you have to live. Havel called on his greengrocer to take the sign out of the window and start "living in truth." The greengrocer—and every one of the signatories of Anticharta—might very well reply: But I *am* living in truth. It is you who are living in a cloud cuckoo land where truth and love triumph over lies and hatred. I know exactly what I'm doing and why. And yes, it hurts. Just not as much as the alternatives.

Havel's greengrocer is a worthy denizen of twentieth-century Prague, a good soldier Švejk for normalized times, who does what the little Czech guy has to do to get by when faced with the *kafkárna* of an irredeemably absurd world. Ludvík Vaculík had his measure. At the end of 1978, when the chartists were reeling under the assault of Operation *Asanace*, the author of "Two Thousand Words" upset many of his fellow dissidents (and elicited a sharp response from Mr. Václav, as he called Havel) with his feuilleton "Remarks on Courage," in which he "raised the matter of what it is worth going to prison for." "The purpose of my article," Vaculík recorded in *A Czech Dreambook*, "was not entirely confined to what I wrote: it was to break out of the 'dissident' circle":

> I wanted it to get through to the people who somehow manage to put up with the times, but were disgusted by them: the ones who had a bad conscience, but suppressed it. What earthly good would it be to have a brilliant handful of indomitable warriors on one side, while on the other, society as a whole went to rack and ruin. Our survival depended upon what would be preserved in the community's consciousness and morality, not on what would be preserved in literature. How many people had the strength to be dragged downstairs by their feet? Unattainable models increase the depression of the rest. Someone should give the millions absolution—for not having burned themselves to death like Palach, for not having gone on strike, for having taken part in the elections, for not having signed Charter 77 and for not having the capacity to resist violence of various kinds. But at the same time they should be told that all their other duties remain.[39]

NOTES

Preface

1. Milan Kundera, Speech at Fourth Congress of Czechoslovak Writers' Union, 27 June 1967, in *IV. sjezd Svazu československých spisovatelů /protokol/*, ed. Otakar Mohyla, Prague: Československý spisovatel, 1968, p. 27.

2. Derek Sayer, *The Coasts of Bohemia: A Czech History*, Princeton, NJ: Princeton University Press, 1998. Hereafter cited as *CB*.

3. "To designate my characters' country," writes Kundera, "I always use the old world 'Bohemia.' From the standpoint of political geography, it's not correct . . . but from the standpoint of poetry, it is the only possible name." Milan Kundera, "Sixty-Three Words," in *The Art of the Novel*, trans. Linda Asher, New York: Grove Press, 1988, p. 126. Bohemia (*Čechy*) is the westernmost of the three provinces of the Czech Republic—Bohemia, Moravia (*Morava*), and the rump of Silesia (*Slezsko*)—that constituted the core of the medieval Kingdom of Bohemia. Collectively these are known as the Czech Lands (*české země*). I use the term *Bohemia* in Kundera's sense unless I am specifically referring to the province. The meaning should be clear from the context.

4. Derek Sayer, *Prague, Capital of the Twentieth Century: A Surrealist History*, Princeton, NJ: Princeton University Press, 2013. Hereafter cited as *PC*.

5. André Breton and Paul Éluard, *Dictionnaire abrégé du surréalisme*, facsimile reprint, Paris: José Corti, 2005, p. 17.

6. *PC*, pp. 10–11.

7. *PC*, p. 7; Walter Benjamin, *The Arcades Project*, trans. Howard Eiland and Kevin McLaughlin, Cambridge, MA: Harvard University Press, 1999, pp. 460–61. I discuss my intellectual debts to Benjamin more fully in the introduction to *PC*, pp. 1–7, and elaborate in Derek Sayer, *Making Trouble: Surrealism and the Human Sciences*, Chicago: Prickly Paradigm Press, 2017.

8. Jean-François Lyotard, *The Postmodern Condition: A Report on Knowledge*, trans. Geoff Bennington and Brian Massumi, Manchester, UK: Manchester University Press, 1994.

9. Humphrey Jennings, *Pandaemonium 1660–1886: The Coming of the Machine as Seen by Contemporary Observers*, London: Icon Books, 2012, pp. xiii–xiv; emphasis added.

10. Benjamin, *Arcades Project*, pp. 462–64.

11. Josef Škvorecký, "Bohemia of the Soul," *Daedalus*, Vol. 119, No. 1, 1990.

12. Mimi Sheller and John Urry, "The New Mobilities Paradigm," *Environment and Planning A*, Vol. 38, 2006, pp. 207–26.

13. I am alluding to British prime minister Neville Chamberlain's notorious BBC radio broadcast of 27 September 1938, available at https://www.bbc.co.uk/archive/chamberlain-addresses-the-nation-on-his-negotiations-for-peace/zjrjgwx.

Prelude

1. Arthur Miller, "The Year It Came Apart," *New York Magazine*, 30 December 1974–6 January 1975, pp. 30, 32. (Thanks to Andrea Orzoff.) An earlier version of this introduction was published as "Prague at the End of History (The Prague Address)," *New Perspectives*, Vol. 27, No. 2, 2019, pp. 149–60.

2. See, for example, "Žádný Mezinárodní den studentstva, 17. listopad se přejmenovávat nebude," Novinky.cz, 19 April 2016.

3. Quoted in "Připomeňte si události 17. listopadu 1989 minutu po minutě," iDNES.cz, 17 November 2009.

4. Quoted in "Miloš Zeman se vtipně loučil," Slovácký deník.cz, 16 October 2015.

5. "Projev Miloše Zemana na Albertově k 17. listopadu," iDNES.cz, 17 November 2015.

6. "Vánoční poselství prezidenta republiky Miloše Zemana (2015)," at https://cs.wikisource.org/wiki/Vánočn%C3%AD_poselstv%C3%AD_prezidenta_republiky_Miloše_Zemana_(2015) (accessed 22 August 2018).

7. Quoted in "Umělec osadil památník 17. listopadu hajlujícíma rukama," Lidovky.cz, 22 November 2009.

8. Francis Fukuyama, "The End of History," *National Interest*, Summer 1989.

9. See David Černý et al., *David Černý*, Prague: Meetfactory, 2017, pp. 50–57. Many examples of Černý's work can be viewed on his official website at http://www.davidcerny.cz/startEN.html.

10. Petr Král, *Prague*, Seyssel: Editions du Champ Vallon, 1987, pp. 114–15.

11. See *PC*, pp. 120–21.

12. Vladimír Just, "Divadlo Járy Cimrmana," in *Česká divadelní encyklopedie*. See also Zdeněk Svěrák a kolegové, *Půlstoletí s Cimrmanem*, Prague: Paseka, 2016.

13. Kundera, *Art of the Novel*, p. 135.

14. André Breton, *Anthology of Black Humor*, trans. Mark Polizzotti, San Francisco: City Lights, 1997, pp. vi–vii.

15. Milan Kundera, *Testaments Betrayed*, trans. Linda Asher, New York: HarperCollins, 1995, pp. 32–33.

16. Kundera has vigorously denied this charge. See Jana Prikryl, "The Kundera Conundrum: Kundera, Respekt and Contempt," *Nation*, 20 May 2009.

17. Anthony Giddens, *Conversations with Anthony Giddens: Making Sense of Modernity*, Stanford, CA: Stanford University Press, 1998, p. 94.

18. Václav Havel, "The Power of the Powerless," International Center on Nonviolent Conflict, at https://www.nonviolent-conflict.org/resource/the-power-of-the-powerless/ (accessed 4 May 2021).

19. Max Weber, "Politics as a Vocation," in *From Max Weber*, ed. Hans Gerth and C. Wright Mills, London: Routledge, 1970; Hannah Arendt, *The Origins of Totalitarianism*, Boston:

Mariner Books, 2001; Zygmunt Bauman, *Modernity and the Holocaust,* Ithaca, NY: Cornell University Press, 2002.

20. Arthur Rimbaud, letter to Georges Izambard, 13 May 1871, in *Rimbaud: Complete Works, Selected Letters,* ed. and trans. Wallace Fowlie, Chicago: University of Chicago Press, 1966, p. 304.

Chapter 1: *Kafkárna*

1. Milena Jesenská, "Letters of Notable People," *Tribuna,* 15 August 1920, in Franz Kafka, *Letters to Milena,* trans. Philip Boehm, New York: Schocken, 1990, p. 262.

2. Letter to Max Brod, beginning of May 1920, in Franz Kafka, *Letters to Friends, Family, and Editors,* trans. Richard Winston and Clara Winston, New York: Schocken, 1977, p. 237.

3. Jana Černá, *Kafka's Milena,* trans. A. G. Brain, Evanston, IL: Northwestern University Press, 1993, p. 72. For criticisms of the reliability of Černá's memoir, see Marta Marková-Kotyková, *Mýtus Milena,* Prague: Primus, 1993.

4. Margarete Buber-Neumann, *Mistress to Kafka: The Life and Death of Milena,* London: Secker and Warburg, 1966; Margarete Buber-Neumann, *Milena: The Tragic Story of Kafka's Great Love,* trans. Ralph Manheim, New York: Arcade, 2014; Jana Černá, *Adresát Milena Jesenská,* Prague: Concordia, 1991; Mary Hockaday, *Kafka, Love and Courage: The Life of Milena Jesenská,* Woodstock, NY: Overlook, 1997 (quote from inside cover blurb). An excellent selection of Jesenská's writing can be found in Milena Jesenská, *The Journalism of Milena Jesenská: A Critical Voice in Interwar Central Europe,* ed. and trans. Kathleen Hayes, New York: Berghahn, 2003.

5. Černá, *Kafka's Milena,* p. 86.

6. Letter to Brod, May 1920, in Kafka, *Letters to Friends,* p. 237.

7. Černá, *Kafka's Milena,* pp. 65–66. Alena Wagnerová, *Milena Jesenská,* Prague: Prostor, 1994, p. 78, confirms that Milena from time to time accepted "living in threes," without naming Beer.

8. In *Červen,* Vol. 4, Nos. 17–20, 1921. The letters were to Sophie Liebknecht, whose husband Karl Liebknecht was murdered in 1919, along with Rosa Luxemburg.

9. Letter to Milena Jesenská, 15 July 1920, in Kafka, *Letters to Milena,* p. 88.

10. Letter to Milena Jesenská, November 1920, in Kafka, *Letters to Milena,* pp. 221–22.

11. For Milena's state of mind at the time, see her letter to Max Brod, beginning of January 1921, in Kafka, *Letters to Milena,* pp. 146–47.

12. Kafka's letter has not survived. Milena quotes it in her undated letter to Max Brod, presumably written in early January 1921, in Kafka, *Letters to Milena,* p. 246.

13. Franz Kafka, *The Diaries of Franz Kafka 1910–23,* ed. Max Brod, trans. Martin Greenberg and Hannah Arendt, London: Penguin, 1964, p. 401 (entry for January 1922).

14. Letter to Milena Jesenská, end of March 1922, in Kafka, *Letters to Milena,* p. 223.

15. Letter to Milena Jesenská, end of April 1920, in Kafka, *Letters to Milena,* p. 8.

16. Letter to Willi Schlamm, undated [1938], quoted in Wagnerová, *Milena Jesenská,* p. 71. On Schaffgotsch, see pp. 74–75. Milena was twenty-one when she moved to Vienna in March 1918 and twenty-three when she started corresponding with Kafka.

17. Max Brod, *Franz Kafka: A Biography,* New York: Schocken, 1963, p. 222.

18. Letter to Willi Schlamm, probably after 12 August 1938, in Milena Jesenská, *De Prague à Ravensbrück: Lettres de Milena Jesenská 1938–1944,* ed. Hélène Belletto Sussel and Alena Wagnerová, Villeneuve d'Ascq, France: Presses Universitaires de Septentrion, 2016, p. 55.

19. Ludwig Wittgenstein, *Tractatus Logico-Philosophicus*, trans. C. K. Ogden, London: Kegan Paul, Trench, Trubner, 1922, p. 74. Kafka was born in 1883, Wittgenstein in 1889.

20. Letter to Milena Jesenská, 8–9 August 1920, in Kafka, *Letters to Milena*, p. 148.

21. Letter to Max Brod, 8 April 1920, in Kafka, *Letters to Friends*, p. 233.

22. Bohumil Kvasil et al., eds., *Malá československá encyklopedie*, Vol. 3, Prague: Academia, 1986, p. 256.

23. Brod, *Franz Kafka*, p. 217.

24. Gustav Janouch, *Conversations with Kafka: Notes and Reminiscences*, 2nd rev. and enl. ed., trans. Goronwy Rhys, New York: New Directions, 1971, p. 80. Janouch first met Kafka in March 1920, around the same time Franz began his relationship with Milena. Max Brod and Kafka's last companion, Dora Diamant, both regarded Janouch's *Conversations* as truthful testimony, but Eduard Goldstücker (see Alexej Kusák, ed., *Tance kolem Kafky, Liblická konference 1963, vzpomínky a dokumenty po 40 letech*, Prague: Akropolis, 2003, pp. 79–88, 110–16) and Josef Čermák (*Franz Kafka: Výmysly a mystifikace*, Prague: Gutenberg, 2005) have argued that much of it is fiction. For a more sympathetic view (and more about Janouch), see Josef Škvorecký, "Franz Kafka, Jazz, and the Anti-Semitic Reader," in *Talkin' Moscow Blues*, Toronto: Lester and Orpen Denys, 1988, pp. 157–62.

25. The former ghetto was renamed Josefov (after Emperor Joseph II) and incorporated into the city as Prague V (hence the Fifth Quarter) in 1850.

26. Karel Ladislav Kukla, *Pražské bahno: historie nemravností*, Prague: XYZ, 2017 (reprint), p. 108. This establishment is also discussed in Radim Kopáč and Josef Schwarz, *Nevěstince a nevěstky: obrázky z erotického života Pražanů*, Prague: Paseka, 2013, p. 35. This book contains many contemporary photographs of the Fifth Quarter before the *asanace*.

27. Karel Ladislav Kukla, *Konec bahna Prahy: Ilustrovaná revue skutečných příběhů, dramat i humoresek z nejtemnějších i nejskvělejších útulků mravní bídy, zoufalství, tmy, šibeničního humoru, prostituce i zločinů v salonech, barech, uličkách, krčmách, špitálech, blázincích, brlozích i stokách Velké Prahy*, Prague: Švec, 1927.

28. The phrase "ratcatcher's beauty" is Leppin's own. Both Leppin and Brod's description of him are quoted in the blurb to Paul Leppin, *Severin's Journey into the Dark: A Prague Ghost Story*, trans. Kevin Blahut, Prague: Twisted Spoon Press, 2012.

29. Paul Leppin, *Others' Paradise: Tales of Old Prague*, trans. Stephanie Howard and Amy R. Nestor, Prague: Twisted Spoon Press, 2016, pp. 46–47.

30. Leppin, *Others' Paradise*, pp. 51–52.

31. Kafka, *Diaries*, p. 12 (undated entry, but from before 17 May 1910).

32. See Kafka, *Diaries*, pp. 444, 458–59.

33. Reiner Stach, *Kafka: The Decisive Years*, trans. Shelley Frisch, Princeton, NJ: Princeton University Press, 2013, p. 330. See also Kopáč and Schwarz, *Nevěstince a nevěstky*, p. 120; Radko Pytlík, *Pražské kuriosity*, Žďár nad Sázavou: Impresso Plus, 1993, pp. 169–70; Soňa Brunner, "Vyhlášený pražský nevěstinec navštívil i Franz Kafka," *Náš region.cz*, 24 February 2018, at http://nasregion.cz/praha/vyhlaseny-prazsky-nevestinec-salon-gogo-lakal-umelce-i-habsburky (accessed 30 July 2018).

34. Letter to Max Brod, 9 June 1908, in Kafka, *Letters to Friends*, p. 43; Max Brod, *Über Kafka*, quoted in Reiner Stach, *Kafka: The Early Years*, trans. Shelley Frisch, Princeton, NJ: Princeton University Press, 2017, p. 328. The photograph of Kafka and Hansi is reproduced as plate 42 in the latter.

35. Letter to Max Brod, 29–30 July 1908, in Reiner Stach, *Is That Kafka? 99 Finds*, trans. Kurt Beals, New York: New Directions, 2016, p. 57.

36. Kafka, *Diaries*, p. 238 (entry for 19 November 1913).

37. Stach's *Is That Kafka?* shows a more human side of Kafka than the usual stereotypes. James Hawes, *Excavating Kafka*, London: Quercus, 2008, is an entertaining takedown of the more common Kafka myths. This revisionism was anticipated in Milan Kundera's essay "The Castrating Shadow of Saint Garta," in *Testaments Betrayed*, pp. 35–54.

38. Column in the Hebrew paper *Davar*, 1941, quoted in Elif Batuman, "Kafka's Last Trial," *New York Times Magazine*, 22 September 2010.

39. Kafka, *Diaries*, p. 489.

40. See Kafka, *Diaries*, p. 59 (entry for 1 October 1911).

41. Franz Kafka, diary entry for 1 October 1911, as quoted in Stach, *Kafka: The Early Years*, p. 330. Kukla discusses this brothel (under the Czech name U Šuhů) in *Pražské bahno*, p. 112.

42. Kundera, "Castrating Shadow of Saint Garta," pp. 44–51.

43. Breton, *Anthology of Black Humor*, pp. 261–73.

44. Bohuslav Brouk, afterword to Jindřich Štyrský, *Emily Comes to Me in a Dream*, in Vítězslav Nezval and Jindřich Štyrský, *Edition 69*, trans. Jed Slast, Prague: Twisted Spoon Press, 2004, pp. 109–10. This volume contains full English translations of Nezval's *Sexual Nocturne* and Štyrský's *Emily*.

45. Flyer introducing *Edice 69* in 1931, in Nezval and Štyrský, *Edition 69*, p. 128. I discuss *Edice 69* more fully in *PC*, pp. 261–70.

46. Karel Srp, "Osvobozené libido," afterword to Jindřich Štyrský, *Emilie přichází ke mně ve snu*, Prague: Torst, 2001 (facsimile reprint), p. 39.

47. Brouk, afterword to Štyrský, *Emily*, in Nezval and Štyrský, *Edition 69*, pp. 109–10.

48. Stach, *Kafka: The Decisive Years*, p. 42.

49. "Wenn Du Dich davor fürchtest, werde ich selbst mit Dir hingehn." Franz Kafka, *Letter to the Father*, bilingual ed., trans. Ernst Kaiser and Eithne Wilkins, New York: Schocken, 2015, pp. 102–3. Hermann is clearly referring to the brothel ("other options") here, not, as Kaiser and Wilkins translate it, to "go with you to see her" (Julie Wohryzek). I follow Stach (*Kafka: The Decisive Years*, pp. 277–78) in this interpretation.

50. "Osek," in *Ottův slovník naučný*, Vol. 18, Prague: Jan Otto, 1902, p. 906.

51. Anthony Northey, *Kafka's Relatives: Their Lives and His Writing*, New Haven, CT: Yale University Press, 1991, p. 4.

52. Kafka, *Letter to the Father*, pp. 7, 9.

53. Prague Trade Directory, quoted in Jiří Gruša, *Franz Kafka of Prague*, trans. Eric Mosbacher, New York: Schocken, 1983, p. 18.

54. The letterhead is illustrated in Stach, *Kafka: The Decisive Years*, plate 8.

55. This information is from Hermann Kafka's census return for 1890. See Marek Nekula, *Franz Kafka and His Prague Contexts*, Prague: Karolinum, 2015, pp. 54–55.

56. Letter to Felice Bauer, 19–20 December 1912, in Franz Kafka, *Letters to Felice*, trans. James Stern and Elisabeth Duckworth, New York: Schocken, 1973, p. 213.

57. Letter to Milena Jesenská, 21 June 1920, in Kafka, *Letters to Milena*, p. 53.

58. The editors of Kafka's *Letters to Friends* state that "she spoke only Czech" (p. 465); Nekula (*Franz Kafka and His Prague Contexts*, p. 55) says that Czech was Wernerová's "dominant language," noting that both Kafka and his mother wrote to her in Czech rather than German.

59. See his letter to Ottla Davidová during the first week of January 1924, in Franz Kafka, *Letters to Ottla and the Family*, ed. N. N. Glaser, trans. Richard Winston and Clara Winston, New York: Schocken, 1982, p. 89.

60. See Kafka's 20 February 1924 letter to his parents, in Franz Kafka, *Dopisy rodičům z let 1922–24*, ed. Josef Čermák and Martin Svatoš, Prague: Odeon, 1990, p. 93. Wernerová was a year younger than Franz and did not join the Kafka household until he was in his twenties. See Alena Wagnerová, *La famille Kafka de Prague*, Paris: Bernard Grasset, 1997, p. 103.

61. Kafka, *Diaries*, p. 127 (entry for 28 November 1911). For a thorough discussion of Kafka's ability in Czech, see Nekula, *Franz Kafka and His Prague Contexts*.

62. Letter to Milena Jesenská, 19 May 1920, in Kafka, *Letters to Milena*, p. 17.

63. Letter to Max Brod, 11 March 1921, in Kafka, *Letters to Friends*, p. 266.

64. By the 1890s all educational institutions in Bohemia were segregated by language. See *CB*, pp. 89–91.

65. Letter to Milena Jesenská, May 1920, in Kafka, *Letters to Milena*, p. 14.

66. Letter to Milena Jesenská, 30 May 1920, in Kafka, *Letters to Milena*, p. 21.

67. Letter to Ottla Davidová, 20 February 1919, in Kafka, *Letters to Ottla*, p. 36.

68. Kafka, *Diaries*, p. 88 (entry for 24 October 1911).

69. Kafka, *Diaries*, p. 444 (travel diary, entry for 4 September 1911).

70. Letter to Max Brod, June 1921, in Kafka, *Letters to Friends*, p. 268.

71. I am alluding here to Sigmund Freud, "The Uncanny" (1919), trans. Alix Strachey, in *The Standard Edition of the Complete Psychological Works of Sigmund Freud*, Vol. 17 (1917–1919), *An Infantile Neurosis and Other Works*, ed. James Strachey, London: Hogarth Press, 1955, pp. 218–252.

72. Letter to Milena Jesenská, 24 June 1920, in Kafka, *Letters to Milena*, p. 58.

73. Barbora Procházková, "Když se řekne kafkárna," *Naše řeč*, Vol. 92, No. 4, 2009, pp. 220–23.

74. Joseph II, "Edict of Toleration for the Jews of Lower Austria," 2 January 1782, at http://germanhistorydocs.ghi-dc.org/sub_document_s.cfm?document_id=3648 (accessed 23 July 2018). Joseph's edict initially applied only to Lower Austria, but its provisions were gradually extended across the imperial lands, including Bohemia and Moravia.

75. Franz Kafka, "An Introductory Talk on the Yiddish Language," in *Dearest Father: Stories and Other Writings*, trans. Ernest Kaiser and Eithne Wilkins, New York: Schocken, 1954, p. 382.

76. For details, see Guido Massino, "Franz Kafka's Vagabond Stars," Digital Yiddish Theater Project, 24 October 2016, at https://yiddishstage.org/franz-kafkas-vagabond-stars (accessed 23 July 2018); Evelyn Torton Beck, *Kafka and the Yiddish Theater: Its Impact on His Work*, Madison: University of Wisconsin Press, 1971, pp. 12–30. The café in question is not the present Café Savoy on Vítězná Street; it was situated at 859/9 Vězeňská Street in Josefov.

77. Letter to Kurt Pinthus, 8 April 1913, quoted in Stach, *Kafka: The Decisive Years*, p. 60.

78. Letter to Felice Bauer, 16 January 1913, in Kafka, *Letters to Felice*, p. 157.

79. Letter to Max Brod, 16 September 1913, in Kafka, *Letters to Friends*, p. 100. Chapter 4 of Benjamin Balint, *Kafka's Last Trial: The Case of a Literary Legacy*, New York: Norton, 2018, titled "Flirting with the Promised Land" (pp. 49–69), is a detailed, sensitive, and nuanced discussion of Kafka's ambivalent relationship with Zionism.

80. Kafka, *Diaries*, p. 252 (entry for 8 January 1914).

81. Letter to Milena Jesenská, November 1920, in Kafka, *Letters to Milena*, p. 217.

82. The National Theater opened in 1881, was severely damaged by fire after only twelve performances, and reopened in 1883. See *CB*, pp. 102, 142.

83. Letter to Milena Jesenská, mid-November 1920, in Kafka, *Letters to Milena*, pp. 212–13 (translation modified).

84. Franz Kafka, "The Metamorphosis," in *Selected Short Stories of Franz Kafka*, trans. Willa Muir and Edwin Muir, New York: Modern Library, 1993, p. 20.

85. See Hawes, *Excavating Kafka*, pp. 88–91.

86. Letter to Max Brod, beginning of August 1920, in Kafka, *Letters to Milena*, p. 245. Milena called him Frank based on the scrawled signature on his letters: Franz K. See facsimile in Kafka, *Letters to Milena*, p. 7; Stach, *Is That Kafka?* p. 259.

87. Letter of April 1920, in Kafka, *Letters to Milena*, p. 6.

88. "Milena Jesenská's Obituary for Franz Kafka," *Národní listy*, 6 June 1924, in Kafka, *Letters to Milena*, pp. 271–72.

89. Max Brod, *Život plný bojů*, Prague: Nakladatelství Franze Kafky, 1994, p. 7 (translation of his *Streitbares Leben: Autobiographie 1884–1968*, Frankfurt: Insel, 1979).

90. I discuss this more fully in *CB*, pp. 39–41.

91. Gary B. Cohen, *The Politics of Ethnic Survival: Germans in Prague 1861–1914*, Princeton, NJ: Princeton University Press, 1981, p. 274. See also Hillel J. Kieval, *The Making of Czech Jewry: National Conflict and Jewish Society in Bohemia 1870–1918*, New York: Oxford University Press, 1988.

92. See *CB*, chs. 2 and 3 (pp. 53–153).

93. *Ottův slovník naučný*, Vol. 20, Prague: Jan Otto, 1903, p. 488.

94. František Palacký, *Dějiny české v stručném přehledu*, Prague: Alois Hynek, 1898, p. 41.

95. *Ottův slovník naučný*, Vol. 20, p. 488.

96. *Ottův slovník naučný*, Vol. 20, p. 488.

97. Nekula, *Franz Kafka and His Prague Contexts*, p. 39.

98. Josef Erben, ed., *Statistika královského hlavního města Prahy*, Vol. 1, Prague: Obecní statistická komisse královského hlavního města Prahy, 1871, pp. 124–28.

99. Gary B. Cohen, *The Politics of Ethnic Survival: Germans in Prague, 1861–1914*, 2nd ed., West Lafayette, IN: Purdue University Press, 2006, pp. 70–71. Ten years later the percentages of German speakers had shrunk to 10.4 in the Old Town, 12.5 in the New Town, 8.6 in the Lesser Town, 6.9 in Hradčany, and 7.7 in Josefov.

100. Josef Šiška, "Populační a bytové poměry," in *Praha v obnoveném státě československém*, ed. Václav Vojtíšek, Prague: Rada hlavního města Prahy, 1936, p. 74. The figures for 1900 and 1921 are standardized according to the 1922 boundaries of Greater Prague.

101. Egon Erwin Kisch, "Germans and Czechs," in *Egon Erwin Kisch, the Raging Reporter: A Bio-anthology*, ed. Harold B. Segel, West Lafayette, IN: Purdue University Press, 1997, pp. 95–96. The full *Marktplatz der Sensationen* has since been translated into English as *Sensation Fair: Tales of Prague*, trans. Guy Endore, Lexington, MA: Plunkett Lake Press, 2012 (unpaginated e-book).

102. Letters to Hans Tanner, 24 April 1911, and Willem Julius, 15 November 1911, as translated in Michael P. Gordin, *Einstein in Bohemia*, Princeton, NJ: Princeton University Press, 2020, pp. 88, 77.

103. Kisch, "Germans and Czechs," p. 95.

104. Gary Cohen has shown that in 1910 one-third of Prague's German speakers "fell into the laboring or lowest lower-middle-class strata." Cohen, *Politics of Ethnic Survival*, 1981 ed., p. 122.

105. Egon Erwin Kisch, "The Leopold Hilsner Case," in *Sensation Fair*.

106. Letter to Milena Jesenská, 20 June 1920, in Kafka, *Letters to Milena*, p. 51.

107. Jan Neruda, *Prague Tales*, trans. Michael Henry Heim, London: Chatto and Windus, 1993; Jan Neruda, "Pro strach židovský," in *Studie krátké a kratší*, Prague: L. Mazač, 1928, p. 248. For a fuller discussion, see Michal Frankl and Jindřich Toman, eds., *Jan Neruda a Židé: texty a kontexty*, Prague: Akropolis, 2012. Havlíček is quoted from Tomáš Masaryk, *Karel Havlíček*, 3rd ed., Prague: Jan Laichter, 1920, pp. 446–47. A translation of part of Havlíček's text (including this passage) can be found in Wilma Abeles Iggers, ed., *The Jews of Bohemia and Moravia: A Historical Reader*, Detroit: Wayne State University Press, 1992, pp. 134–35.

108. The census recorded 31,751 people in Prague who were adherents of the Jewish faith, or 4.7 percent of the city's population. Of these, 5,900 stated their nationality as Jewish, 7,426 as German, and 16,342 as Czechoslovak. In the same census, a total of 30,429 people recorded their nationality as German. Figures from Šiška, "Populační a bytové poměry," pp. 71–78.

109. Letter to Carl Stumpf, 1914, quoted in Gordin, *Einstein in Bohemia*, p. 193.

110. Max Brod, "Jews, Germans, Czechs," quoted in Nekula, *Franz Kafka and His Prague Contexts*, p. 39.

111. Max Brod, "Praha a já," *Literární noviny*, Vol. 5, No. 1, 10 December 1930, p. 4.

112. See Miroslav Lamač, *Osma a Skupina výtvarných umělců 1907–1917*, Prague: Odeon, 1988; Jiří Padrta, ed., *Osma a Skupina výtvarných umělců 1907–1917, teorie, kritika, polemika*, Prague: Odeon, 1992. The Eight were rare among art groups of the time, having both Czech and Bohemian-German members.

113. F. X. Šalda, "Židovský román staropražský," in *Soubor díla F. X. Šaldy*, Vol. 19, *Kritické projevy 10, 1917–18*, Prague: Československý spisovatel, 1957, pp. 286–87.

114. The title of Kisch's collection is *Der rasende Reporter*, Berlin: Erich Reiss, 1925.

115. Jiří Kroha quoted in Marcela Macharáčková, "Životopis," in *Jiří Kroha v proměnách umění 20. století (1893–1974), Architekt · Malíř · Designér · Teoretik*, exh. cat., ed. Marcela Macharáčková and Jindřich Chatrný, Brno: Muzeum města Brna, 2007, p. 387. This book reproduces some of Kroha's sketches for the murals and a photograph of the Montmartre interior (which no longer survives) (pp. 36–39). See also Kateřina Piorecká and Karel Piorecký, *Praha avantgardní: literární průvodce metropolí v letech 1918–1938*, Prague: Academia, 2015, pp. 292–95.

116. Kisch, "Germans and Czechs," pp. 94–96.

117. Hawes, *Excavating Kafka*, pp. 79–80; George Gibian, in Černá, *Kafka's Milena*, p. 5.

118. Hawes, *Excavating Kafka*, pp. 79–80.

119. Quoted in Stach, *Kafka: The Early Years*, p. 378.

120. Jiří Karásek ze Lvovic, "Z německé literatury," *Moderní revue*, Vol. 21, No. 7, 1909, p. 361.

121. Letter to Milena Jesenská, 8–9 August 1920, in Kafka, *Letters to Milena*, pp. 146–48. Kafka does not record the girl's nationality or name.

122. See Kafka, *Diaries*, pp. 155–56 (entry for 28 December 1911).

123. Kafka, *Diaries*, p. 179 (entry for 7 February 1912).

124. Jaroslav Seifert, "Píseň o dívkách," in *Dílo Jaroslava Seiferta*, Vol. 1, Prague: Akropolis, 2001, p. 96. Translations are available in Ewald Osers, ed. and trans., *The Selected Poetry of Jaroslav Seifert*, New York: Collier, 1986; Dana Loewy, ed. and trans., *The Early Poetry of Jaroslav Seifert*, Evanston, IL: Northwestern University Press, 1997.

125. Jaroslav Seifert, *Všecky krásy světa*, Prague: Československý spisovatel, 1992, pp. 166–67. See also *PC*, pp. 80–82.

126. Kukla, *Pražské bahno*, p. 112.

127. Kafka, *Diaries*, p. 119 (entry for 18 November 1911).

128. *Ottův slovník naučný*, Vol. 27, Prague: Otto, 1908, pp. 877–79.

Chapter 2: A Modern Woman

1. "US Devětsil," *Pražské pondělí*, 6 December 1920, in *Avantgarda známá a neznámá*, Vol. 1, ed. Štěpán Vlašín, Prague: Svoboda, 1971, p. 81.

2. Stach, *Kafka: The Early Years*, p. 15.

3. Tomáš Masaryk, *Česká otázka*, Prague: Svoboda, 1990, p. 124.

4. Klub za starou Prahu website, at http://www.zastarouprahu.cz/menu-horni/o-klubu/kategorie-3/ (accessed 23 August 2018).

5. The writer Vilém Mrštík published an anti-*asanace* pamphlet titled *Bestia Triumphans* in 1897. He was a signatory of the Manifesto of Czech Modernism, discussed later.

6. Unless otherwise indicated, information on Prague's streets and other place names is from Marek Lašťovka et al., *Pražský uličník: Encyklopedie názvů pražských veřejných prostranství*, 2 vols., Prague: Libri, 1997–1998.

7. "Praha zamítla obnovu mariánského sloupu na Staroměstském náměstí," Novinky.cz, 14 September 2017. This reversed an earlier decision to replicate the column in 2013.

8. Quoted in Masha Volynsky, "Controversial Marian Column to Return to Old Town Square," Radio Praha, 27 March 2013.

9. "Marian Column Replica May Return to Old Town Square, *Prague Morning*, 23 January 2020.

10. Hannah Brockhaus, "Prague Catholics Rejoice at Restoration of Marian Statue Toppled by Angry Mob," Catholic News Agency, 15 June 2020.

11. *Svému osvoboditeli československý lid*, Prague: Orbis, 1955, p. 10. I discuss Švec and the Stalin monument at greater length in *CB*, pp. 271–74; *PC*, pp. 102–3, 111–12. See also Hana Píchová, *The Case of the Missing Statue: A Historical and Literary Study of the Stalin Monument in Prague*, Prague: Arbor Vitae, 2014.

12. Paulina Bren, *The Greengrocer and His TV: The Culture of Communism after the 1968 Prague Spring*, Ithaca, NY: Cornell University Press, 2011, p. 2.

13. Černá, *Kafka's Milena*, p. 58.

14. Jiří Karásek and Arnošt Procházka, proclamation dated 1 September 1894, reproduced as inside front cover of Otto M. Orban, ed., *Moderní revue 1894–1925*, Prague: Torst, 1994.

15. Letter to Milena Jesenská, 4 July 1920, in Kafka, *Letters to Milena*, p. 62.

16. Brod, *Franz Kafka*, p. 222.

17. Wagnerová, *Milena Jesenská*, p. 10.

18. "O umění zůstat stát," *Přítomnost*, 5 April 1939, in Milena Jesenská, *Křižovatky (Výbor z díla)*, ed. Marie Jirásková, Prague: Torst, 2016, pp. 705–7.

19. "Jsem především Češka?" *Přítomnost*, 10 May 1939, in Jesenská, *Křižovatky*, pp. 722–23.

20. Černá, *Kafka's Milena*, p. 46.

21. Jaroslava Vondráčková, *Kolem Mileny Jesenské*, Prague: Torst, 1991, pp. 12, 14.

22. Vondráčková, *Kolem Mileny Jesenské*, p. 20.

23. Josef Kodíček, Radio Free Europe broadcast, Munich, 2 June 1953, quoted in Hockaday, *Kafka, Love and Courage*, p. 20.

24. Several commentators make a point of mentioning Milena's dress as an indication of her free spirit. See, for example, Hockaday, *Kafka, Love and Courage*, pp. 19–20; Peter Demetz, *Prague in Danger*, New York: Farrar, Straus and Giroux, 2008, pp. 128–29.

25. Max Brod, "Frühling in Prag," *Die Gegenwart*, 1907, in Lamač, *Osma a Skupina*, p. 32.

26. Reiner Stach, *Kafka: The Years of Insight*, trans. Shelley Frisch, Princeton, NJ: Princeton University Press, 2013, p. 320.

27. Letter to Max Brod, beginning of August 1920, in Kafka, *Letters to Milena*, p. 245.

28. Wagnerová, *Milena Jesenská*, p. 65.

29. Vondráčková, *Kolem Mileny Jesenské*, p. 23.

30. Letter to Max Brod, 21 July 1920, in Kafka, *Letters to Milena*, p. 241.

31. Letter to Willi Haas, 20 June 1917, quoted in Wagnerová, *Milena Jesenská*, p. 65.

32. Letter to Max Brod, beginning of August 1920, in Kafka, *Letters to Milena*, p. 245.

33. Not to be confused with the distinguished novelist Arnošt Lustig (1926–2011), author of many works on the Holocaust, who is discussed later.

34. Kundera, "Castrating Shadow of Saint Garta," p. 50.

35. "Vídeň," *Tribuna*, 30 December 1919, in Jesenská, *Křižovatky*, pp. 5–7.

36. "Kavárna," *Tribuna*, 18 August 1920, in Jesenská, *Křižovatky*, pp. 29–31.

37. "Dorůstající dívky," *Národní listy*, Vol. 64, No. 343, 14 December 1924, p. 14.

38. Letter to Max Brod, January–February 1921, in Kafka, *Letters to Milena*, p. 250.

39. These are listed in the relatively complete bibliography in Jesenská, *Křižovatky*, pp. 817–65.

40. Letter to Karel Hoch, 20 March 1924, reproduced in Černá, *Kafka's Milena*, pp. 181–82.

41. "Malá Strana z druhého hlediska," *Národní listy*, 11 March 1926, in Jesenská, *Křižovatky*, pp. 353–54.

42. Milena Jesenská, *Mileniny recepty*, Prague: Nakladatelství Franze Kafky, 1995 (facsimile reprint), p. 3.

43. In "Nejužitečnější vánoční dárek," *Pestrý týden*, Vol. 2, No. 50, 1927, p. 17. The contributors mentioned below are from the same source. Many others are also listed.

44. See Rea Michalová, *Karel Teige: Captain of the Avant-garde*, Prague: Torst, 2018. This is the most comprehensive study of Teige to date, which I have drawn on extensively in this book.

45. Hockaday, *Kafka, Love and Courage*, p. 136.

46. Adolf Hoffmeister, *Podoby a předobrazy*, Prague: Československý spisovatel, 1988, p. 21, quoted in Michalová, *Karel Teige*, p. 64. On the Liberated Theater, see *PC*, pp.107–9.

47. See Hockaday, *Kafka, Love and Courage*, pp. 20, 25. On the role of the Křemencova Street gymnasium in the foundation of Devětsil, see Michalová, *Karel Teige*, pp. 64–65.

48. Josef Kodíček, "Devěthnid: in margine Revolučního sborníku Devětsil," *Tribuna*, Vol. 4, 31 December 1922, in Vlašin, *Avantgarda*, Vol. 1, p. 383; Ferdinand Peroutka, "O té avantgarrda rrevolutionairre," *Tribuna*, 6 and 9 January 1923, as quoted in Michalová, *Karel Teige*, p. 121.

49. Karel Teige, "Poetism," in *Between Worlds: A Sourcebook of Central European Avant-gardes, 1910–1930*, ed. Timothy O. Benson and Eva Forgacs, Los Angeles: Los Angeles County Museum of Art, 2002, pp. 580–81.

50. Karel Teige, "Poetism Manifesto," in Benson and Forgacs, *Between Worlds*, p. 593.

51. Karel Konrád, *Robinsonáda: Zabili všechny mládence na rozkaz krále Heroda*, Prague: Hyperion, 1926.

52. Seifert, *Všecky krásy světa*, p. 175.

53. See Karla Huebner, *Magnetic Woman: Toyen and the Surrealist Erotic*, Pittsburgh, PA: Pittsburgh University Press, 2021. I discuss Toyen's eroticism in *PC*, pp. 215–16, 245–47, 263–64, 399–400.

54. Karel Konrád, "S. M. K. Devětsil," *Rozpravy Aventina*, Vol. 3, Nos. 11–12, 1927–1928, p. 140.

55. Virginia Woolf, *A Room of One's Own*, London: Penguin, 2014.

56. "Moderní bydlení," *Národní listy*, 21 February 1926, pp. 348–49, in Jesenská, *Křižovatky*, pp. 348–49.

57. In *Národní listy*, Vol. 67, No. 292, 1927, p. 13; Vol. 67, No. 299, 1927, p. 10 ("Moderní materiál"); Vol. 67, No. 306, 1927, p. 10 ("Moderní kuchyně"); Vol. 67, No. 320, 1927, p. 10.

58. Milena Jesenská, "Mezinárodní výstava Werkbundu 'Die Wohnung' ve Stuttgartu," *Národní listy*, Vol. 67, No. 292, 1927, p. 13.

59. See Rostislav Švácha, ed., *Jaromír Krejcar 1895–1949*, exh. cat., Prague: Galerie Jaroslava Fragnera, 1995, pp. 69–73.

60. Karel Teige, "Poetismus," in *Svět stavby a básně: studie z 20. let, Výbor z díla*, Vol. 1, Prague: Československý spisovatel, 1966, p. 123.

61. Vondráčková, *Kolem Mileny Jesenské*, p. 94.

62. Wagnerová, *Milena Jesenská*, p. 123.

63. Quoted in Švácha, *Jaromír Krejcar*, p. 79.

64. Vondráčková, *Kolem Mileny Jesenské*, p. 94.

65. F. X. Salda, "Česká moderna," in *Soubor díla F. X. Šaldy*, Vol. 11, *Kritické projevy—2, 1894–1895*, Prague: Melantrich, 1950, pp. 361–63.

66. F. X. Šalda, "O úpadku literatury . . . i mnohých věcí jiných . . . ," *Tribuna*, 26 December 1922, in *Soubor díla F. X. Šaldy*, Vol. 21, *Kritické projevy—12, 1922–1924*, Prague: Československý spisovatel, 1959, p. 120.

67. Letter to Adolf Hoffmeister, 2 September 1927, quoted in Wagnerová, *Milena Jesenská*, p. 123. Wagnerová points out that fifteen years takes Milena back to the death of her mother.

68. Vondráčková, *Kolem Mileny Jesenské*, p. 94. See also Hockaday, *Kafka, Love and Courage*, p. 136; Wagnerová, *Milena Jesenská*, pp. 124–27.

69. Černá, *Kafka's Milena*, p. 112.

70. Vondráčková, *Kolem Mileny Jesenské*, pp. 101–2.

71. Božena Horneková, Jan Vaněk, and Zdeněk Rossmann, eds., *Civilisovaná žena: Jak se má kultivovaná žena oblékati/Zivilisierte Frau: Wie sich eine kultivierte Frau ankleiden soll*, Brno: J. Vaněk, 1929. The cover, by Zdeněk Rossmann, is famous. Milena contributed an essay to the volume entitled "She Has Free Will, but She Doesn't Have Clothes."

72. "Civilizovaná žena?" *Lidové noviny*, 1 December 1929, in Jesenská, *Křižovatky*, pp. 488–89. See also "Jak žije samostatná žena?" *Lidové noviny*, 3 November 1929, in Jesenská, *Křižovatky*, pp. 482–84.

73. Gusta Fučíková, *Život s Juliem Fučíkem*, Prague: Svoboda, 1971, p. 283. Julius Fučík's future wife was a tenant in the Krejcars' apartment for several months in 1931–1932. Švácha, *Jaromír Krejcar*, pp. 102–5, reproduces the apartment floor plans.

74. Wagnerová, *Milena Jesenská*, pp. 46–47; Černá, *Kafka's Milena*, p. 138.

75. Undated letter in the private archive of Marie Jirásková, quoted in Wagnerová, *Milena Jesenská*, pp. 134–35. Scheinpflugová married Karel Čapek in 1925.

76. As estimated by Rudolf Jaworski, cited in Chad Bryant, *Prague in Black: Nazi Rule and Czech Nationalism*, Cambridge, MA: Harvard University Press, 2009, p. 25.

77. Speech of 21 December 1929, in Klement Gottwald, *Spisy*, Vol. 1, Prague: Svoboda, 1950, p. 322.

78. "Spisovatelé komunisté komunistickým dělníkům," in *Avantgarda známá a neznámá*, Vol. 3, *Generační diskuse 1929–1931*, ed. Štěpán Vlašín, Prague: Svoboda, 1970, p. 48.

79. "Zásadní stanovisko k projevu 'Sedmi,'" in Vlašín, *Avantgarda*, Vol. 3, pp. 54–55; Seifert, *Všecky krásy světa*, p. 506.

80. I discuss Baba and its inhabitants at greater length in Derek Sayer, *Prague, Crossroads of Europe*, London: Reaktion Books, 2018, pp. 195–202. See Stephan Templ, *Baba: Die Werkbundsiedlung Prag/The Werkbund Housing Estate Prague*, Basel: Birkhäuser, 1999; Tomáš Šenberger, Vladimír Šlapeta, and Petr Urlich, *Osada Baba: Plány a modely/Baba Housing Estate: Plans and Models*, exh. cat., Prague: Czech Technical University, 2000. On the 1928 Brno Nový dům kolonie exhibition, see Zdeněk Kudělka and Jindřich Chatrný, *For New Brno: The Architecture of Brno 1919–1939*, exh. cat., Brno: Muzeum města Brna, 2000, Vol. 1, pp. 28–29, Vol. 2, pp. 1283–34 (plans and photos).

81. "Je vůbec možno vychovati dobře dítě doma?," *Žijeme*, December 1932, in Jesenská, *Křižovatky*, p. 503.

82. "O komunistické propagaci," *Přítomnost*, Vol. 7, No. 2, 16 January 1930, p. 20.

83. Vondráčková, *Kolem Mileny Jesenské*, pp. 107–8.

84. Quoted in H. Gordon Skilling, "Gottwald and the Bolshevization of the Communist Party of Czechoslovakia (1929–1939)," *Slavic Review*, Vol. 20, No. 4, 1961, p. 650.

85. Vondráčková, *Kolem Mileny Jesenské*, p. 88; Markéta Svobodová, *Bauhaus a Československo 1919–1938/The Bauhaus and Czechoslovakia 1919–1938: Students/Concepts/Contacts*, Prague: Kant, 2016, p. 216.

86. "Levá fronta," in Vlašín, *Avantgarda*, Vol. 3, pp. 119–21.

87. Seifert, *Dílo Jaroslava Seiferta*, Vol. 1, p. 12. The foreword is signed "US Devětsil," but it was written by Vančura. *City in Tears* is translated in full in Loewy, *The Early Poetry of Jaroslav Seifert*.

88. On the Hotel Lux, see Vondráčková, *Kolem Mileny Jesenské*, pp. 120–21; Artur London, *Doznání: v soukolí pražského procesu*, Prague: Československý spisovatel, 1990, pp. 227–28; Bedřich Utitz, ed., *Svědkové revoluce vypovídají*, Prague: Orbis, 1990, pp. 8–9.

89. Interview in *Pravda*, Berlin dispatch dated 10 October 1920, quoted in Anatole Kopp, "Foreign Architects in the Soviet Union during the First Two Five-Year Plans," 1988, at https://thecharnelhouse.org/2013/07/30/foreign-architects-in-the-soviet-union-during-the-first-two-five-year-plans/ (accessed 7 October 2018). Meyer made several visits to Prague between his dismissal from the Bauhaus and his move to the USSR, staying with the Krejcars, Slávka Vondráčková, or Karel Teige. See Michalová, *Karel Teige*, pp. 349–50.

90. Václav Šantrůček, "Architektura v SSSR," *Stavba*, Vol. 13, 1936–1937, p. 29, quoted in Švácha, *Jaromír Krejcar*, p. 146.

91. Jaromír Krejcar, "Neohrožená žena nesmí zemřít!" *Přítomnost*, Vol. 15, 9 February 1938, p. 84.

92. John Haag, "Neher, Carola (1900–1942)," in *Women in World History: A Biographical Encyclopedia*, ed. Anne Commire, at https://www.encyclopedia.com/women/encyclopedias-almanacs-transcripts-and-maps/neher-carola-1900-1942 (accessed 15 February 2021).

93. "O Žebrácké opeře," *Tvorba*, 30 March 1933, in Jesenská, *Křižovatky*, pp. 513–15.

94. Rostislav Švácha quotes this from the journal *Architekt SIA*, without giving a more precise reference, in *Jaromír Krejcar*, p. 138.

95. Jaromír Krejcar, "Czechoslovak Pavilion at the International Exhibition of Art and Technology in Modern Life, Paris 1937," in Švácha, *Jaromír Krejcar*, p. 174 (originally published in *Stavitel*, Vol. 16, 1937–1938, pp. 68–73).

96. Wagnerová, *Milena Jesenská*, p. 142; Černá, *Kafka's Milena*, p. 122.

97. Karel Teige, "Mezinárodní orientace českého umění. K jubileu SVU Mánes a výstavě moderního francouzského umění v Praze," in *Zápasy o smysl moderní tvorby: studie z 30. let. Výbor z díla*, Vol. 2, Prague: Československý spisovatel, 1969, pp. 397–98.

98. Karel Teige, "Surrealismus proti proudu," in *Zápasy o smysl moderní tvorby*, p. 491.

99. Teige, "Surrealismus proti proudu," p. 477.

100. Michalová, *Karel Teige*, p. 414; Karel Teige, "Schůze surrealistické skupiny v Praze 14.III. 1938," in *Zápasy o smysl moderní tvorby*, p. 662.

101. Vítězslav Nezval, "Řeč ke studentstvu o roztržce se skupinou surrealistů 24.3.1938," in *Tvorba*, Vol. 13, 1938, p. 150, quoted in Teige, "Surrealismus proti proudu," p. 485; Julius Fučík, in *Tvorba*, Vol. 13, No. 11, quoted in Teige, "Surrealismus proti proudu," p. 506; Stanislav Kostka Neumann, *Anti-Gide, neboli optimismus bez pověr a ilusí*, Prague: Svoboda, 1946, p. 102. I discuss the events summarized in this paragraph at greater length in *CB*, pp. 217–20, and *PC*, pp. 380–85. For a detailed account, see Ivan Pfaff, *Česká levice proti Moskvě 1936–1938*, Prague: Naše vojsko, 1993.

102. "Dobrá rada nad zlato," *Přítomnost*, 8 March 1939, in Jesenská, *Křižovatky*, pp. 694–97. The hyphen in Czecho-Slovak was inserted after the Munich Agreement.

103. Roland Barthes, *Camera Lucida: Reflections on Photography*, trans. Richard Howard, New York: Hill and Wang, 2000, p. 96.

104. Rodchenko, *USSR in Construction*, December 1933, quoted in Oleg Klimov, "'I Wanted to Be the Devil Myself': The Forgotten History of How a Soviet Photographer Glorified the Gulag's White Sea Canal," *Meduza*, 4 August 2015.

105. Alexander Rodchenko, "The Reconstruction of the Artist," *Sovetskoye Foto*, Nos. 5–6, 1936, quoted in Mikhail Karasik, *The Soviet Photobook 1920–1941*, ed. Manfred Heiting, trans. Paul Williams, Göttingen: Steidl, 2015, p. 344.

106. Clement Greenberg, "Avant-Garde and Kitsch," in *The Collected Essays and Criticism*, Vol. 1, *Perceptions and Judgments 1939–1944*, ed. John O'Brian, Chicago: Chicago University Press, 1988, pp. 12, 16.

107. Kundera, *Art of the Novel*, p. 135.

108. Milan Kundera, *The Unbearable Lightness of Being*, trans. Michael Henry Heim, New York: HarperCollins, 1991, pp. 248–51.

109. Quoted in *Reflex*, No. 39, 1992, p. 68.

110. Letter from Karel Teige to his mother, 18 October 1925, quoted in Michalová, *Karel Teige*, p. 231.

111. Karel Teige, "Z SSSR," *Tvorba*, Vol. 1, No. 5, 1 January 1926, pp. 85–86, quoted in Michalová, *Karel Teige*, p. 232.

112. M. Gor'kii, L. L. Averbakh, and S. G. Firin, eds., *Belomorsko-Baltiiskii kanal imeni Stalina: Istoriia stroitel'stva*, Moscow: Gosudarstvennoe izdatel'stvo "Istoriia fabrik i zavodov," 1934, quoted from a summary at the beginning of the book in Karasik, *Soviet Photobook 1920–1941*, pp. 342–43.

113. For example, in "'I Wanted to Be the Devil Myself,'" Oleg Klimov claims that "around 100,000 people had to go out to work every day (according to the archive of the Medvezhegorsk Municipal Museum). The monthly mortality rate of prisoners reached 14 percent (for the entire period of the canal's construction, between 100,000 and 200,000 people died or were shot)." Anne Applebaum gives a figure of 25,000 in *Gulag: A History*, London: Penguin, 2003, p. 79.

114. "The coincidence of the changing of circumstances and of human activity or self-change can be conceived and rationally understood only as revolutionary practice." Karl Marx, "Theses on Feuerbach," in Karl Marx and Friedrich Engels, *Collected Works*, Vol. 5, London: Lawrence and Wishart, 1976, p. 4.

115. On "reforging," see Julie Draskoczy, "The 'Put' of Perekovka': Transforming Lives at Stalin's White Sea–Baltic Canal," *Russian Review*, Vol. 71, No. 1, January 2012, p. 36.

116. "Belomor," at http://nicolasrothwell.com/2013/02/04/belomor/ (accessed 19 October 2013).

117. Nicolas Rothwell, *Belomor*, Melbourne: Text Publishing, 2013 (electronic ed., unpaginated), ch. 1, "Belomorkanal."

118. See *PC*, pp. 193, 419–25.

119. Seifert, *Všecky krásy světa*, pp. 37–38.

120. Nicolas Rothwell website, at http://nicolasrothwell.com (accessed 19 October 2018).

121. Evžen supplied literal translations, which Milena then transformed into good Czech. Černá, *Kafka's Milena*, pp. 126–27.

122. Wagnerová, *Milena Jesenská*, pp. 146–47. The bibliography in Jesenská, *Křižovatky*, lists no writings in *Světozor* or *Právo lidu* during this period.

123. See Černá, *Kafka's Milena*, p. 123.

124. Letter to Olga Scheinpflugová, January 1937, in Wagnerová, *Milena Jesenská*, p. 146 (from the personal archive of Marie Jirásková).

125. Helena Čapková believes that this was "preeminently" Feuerstein's work; see her *Bedřich Feuerstein: cesta do nejvýtvarnější země světa*, Prague: Kant, 2014, p. 21. The *Život II* cover is generally considered the first Czech photomontage cover. See Jindřich Toman, *Foto/montáž tiskem/ Photo/montage in Print*, Prague: Kant, 2009, pp. 80–81.

126. See Jana Černá's account in *Kafka's Milena*, pp. 123–26, which is substantially reproduced by both Hockaday and Wagnerová.

127. Černá, *Kafka's Milena*, p. 141.

128. Quoted in Wagnerová, *Milena Jesenská*, p. 147.

129. All Jesenská's *Přítomnost* articles are reproduced in full in *Křižovatky*. Twelve of the most important, including several discussed here, are translated in Hayes, *Journalism of Milena Jesenská*, and three are translated in Černá, *Kafka's Milena*.

130. "Dobrá rada nad zlato," p. 694.

131. "Lidé na výspě," *Přítomnost*, 27 October 1937, in Jesenská, *Křižovatky*, pp. 536–37, 541.

132. "Soudce Lynch v Evropě?" *Přítomnost*, 30 March 1938, in Jesenská, *Křižovatky*, pp. 564–68.

133. Milan Kundera, *The Book of Laughter and Forgetting*, trans. Michael Henry Heim, London: Penguin, 1986, p. 158.

134. "Statisíce hledají zemi nikoho," *Přítomnost*, 27 July 1938, in Jesenská, *Křižovatky*, pp. 602–8.

135. Personal observation, 1 May 2016.

136. Hannah Arendt, *Eichmann in Jerusalem: A Report on the Banality of Evil*, New York: Viking Press, 1964 (electronic ed., unpaginated), ch. 3.

137. Bettinga Stangneth, "Otto Adolf Eichmann: Reich Main Security Office. The RSHA's 'Jewish Expert,'" in *The Participants: The Men of the Wannsee Conference*, ed. Hans-Christian Jasch and Christoph Kreutzmülle, New York: Berghahn Books, 2017.

138. Arendt, *Eichmann in Jerusalem*, ch. 3.

139. I take this concept from the "hostile environment" policy introduced in the United Kingdom by home secretary (and later prime minister) Theresa May in 2012. See Jamie Grierson, "Hostile Environment: Anatomy of a Policy Disaster," *Guardian*, 27 August 2018.

140. US Holocaust Memorial Museum (hereafter USHMM), "Vienna," in *Holocaust Encyclopedia*, at https://encyclopedia.ushmm.org/content/en/article/vienna.

141. "Anšlus nebude, 1, Hrady SdP" and "Anšlus nebude, 2, Napříč rodinami," *Přítomnost*, 25 May and 1 June 1938, respectively, in Jesenská, *Křižovatky*, pp. 580–92.

142. "Anšlus nebude, 1," in Jesenská, *Křižovatky*, p. 585.

143. Václav Kural breaks down the refugee numbers as 160,000 Czechs, 20,000 to 30,000 mostly German-speaking Jews, and "thousands" of German antifascists in *Místo společenství—konflikt! Češi a Němci v velkoněmecké říši a cesta k odsunu (1938–1945)*, Prague: Karolinum, 1997, p. 44. Volker Zimmermann counts 151,997 refugees from the Sudetenland by December 1938, of which 125,425 were Czechs, 14,925 Jews, and 11,647 Germans; by the summer of 1939 the total had climbed to 200,000. Volker Zimmermann, *Sudetští Němci v nacistickém státě 1938–1945: Politika a nálady obyvatel říšské župy sudetské*, Prague: Prostor, 2001, p. 58.

144. For details, see https://www.holocaust.cz/zdroje/zidovske-komunity-v-cechach-a-na-morave/kristalova-noc-v-pohranici/ (accessed 2 March 2019).

145. Edvard Beneš, "A Message of November 1938 to a Czechoslovak Politician [Ladislav Rašín] in Prague," 18 November 1938, in Milan L. Hauner, "Edvard Benes' Undoing of Munich: A Message to a Czechoslovak Politician in Prague," *Journal of Contemporary History*, Vol. 38, No. 4, 2003, p. 574.

146. Demetz, *Prague in Danger*, p. 35.

147. Brod, *Život plný bojů*, p. 270.

148. "Zum Abschied," *Deutsche Zeitung Bohemia*, 31 December 1938, p. 1.

149. "V zemi nikoho," *Přítomnost*, 29 December 1938, in Jesenská, *Křižovatky*, pp. 671–72.

150. Milena's own description, as related by Jana Černá in *Kafka's Milena*, p. 137.

151. "Anšlus nebude, 1," pp. 580–83.

152. Milena Jesenská, "Obituary for Kafka," in Kafka, *Letters to Milena*, p. 271.

153. Quotations in this paragraph from Černá, *Kafka's Milena*, pp. 132–37.

154. Colette de Castro, "The Destruction of Bliss: Gustav Machatý's *Erotikon* (1929) and *Ecstasy* (*Ekstase*, 1933)," *East European Film Bulletin*, Vol. 78, October 2017.

155. Černá, *Kafka's Milena*, pp. 133–35.

156. Letter to Willi Schlamm, after 12 August 1938, in Jesenská, *De Prague à Ravensbrück*, pp. 56–57.

157. Letter to Willi Schlamm, July 1938, in Jesenská, *De Prague à Ravensbrück*, p. 36.

158. Černá, *Kafka's Milena*, p. 151.

Chapter 3: Love and Theft

1. Vítězslav Nezval, "Trojský most (Památce Bedřicha Feuersteina)," in *Praha s prsty deště*, Prague: Borový, 1936, p. 33.

2. Devětsil [Karel Teige], afterword to Jaroslav Seifert, *Samá láska*, in *Dílo Jaroslava Seiferta*, Vol. 1, pp. 128–29. The *Samá láska* collection is translated in full in Loewy, *The Early Poetry of Jaroslav Seifert*.

3. "Osobnosti Kladna," at https://mestokladno.cz/vismo/dokumenty2.asp?id_org=6506&id=1412963&p1=2100050451 (accessed 6 September 2021).

4. Bohumil Hrabal, *In-house Weddings*, trans. Tony Liman, Evanston, IL: Northwestern University Press, 2007, p. 56.

5. Tal Pinchevsky, "Back Home in Czech Republic, Jaromir Jagr Plots His Next Move," *New York Times*, 6 April 2018.

6. "The Kid from Kladno," *Sports Illustrated*, 12 October 1992.

7. Jaroslav Cuhra, speaking on Česká televize, "77.000 do výroby!" 17 February 2011.

8. Quoted in Nicholas Lezard, "The Very Czech (and Very Funny) Brilliance of Bohumil Hrabal," *Spectator*, 12 March 2016.

9. Bohumil Hrabal, *Be Kind Enough to Pull down the Blinds: A Selection of Love Letters*, quoted in Paul Wilson, translator's afterword to Bohumil Hrabal, *Mr Kafka and Other Tales from the Time of the Cult*, New York: New Directions Books, 2015, pp. 139–40.

10. Bohumil Hrabal, *Inzerát na dům, ve kterém už nechci bydlet*, Prague: Mladá fronta, 1965.

11. "Strange People," in Hrabal, *Mr Kafka and Other Tales*, pp. 17–44.

12. Hrabal, *Mr Kafka and Other Tales*, p. ix.

13. See Kurt G. F. Helfrich and William Whitaker, eds., *Crafting a Modern World: The Architecture and Design of Antonín and Noémi Raymond*, exh. cat., New York: Princeton Architectural Press, 2006; Ken Tadashi Oshima, *International Architecture in Interwar Japan: Constructing Kokusai Kenchiku*, Seattle: University of Washington Press, 2009.

14. Martina Hrabová, "Between Ideal and Ideology: The Parallel Worlds of František Sammer," *Umění/Art*, Vol. 64, No. 2, 2016, p. 147.

15. "Czech Architect's Negros Project Exhibited in Prague," *Manila Times*, 27 October 2015. See Dan Merta and Klára Pučerová, eds., *Antonín Raymond 7x*, exh. cat., Prague: Galerie Jaroslava Fragnera, 2015.

16. Irena Veverková, "Před 40 lety zemřel Antonín Raymond, zakladatel novodobé japonské architektury," *Židovské listy*, 21 November 2016.

17. ČVUT stands for České vysoké učení technické v Praze.

18. The schools had split in 1869–1870.

19. Antonín Raymond, *An Autobiography*, Rutland, VT: Charles E. Tuttle, 1973, p. 12.

20. Raymond, *Autobiography*, pp. 21–22.

21. *Ausgeführte Bauten and Entwürfe von Frank Lloyd Wright*, Berlin: Ernst Wasmuth, 1910. This is available in English as *Drawings and Plans of Frank Lloyd Wright: The Early Period (1893–1909)*, New York: Dover Books, 1984.

22. Raymond, *Autobiography*, p. 24.

23. The calculation is based on the US Bureau of Labor Statistics' consumer price index.

24. Čapková, *Bedřich Feuerstein*, pp. 46–47. Elsewhere Čapková says that Raymond "regretted the theft deeply and later would give back more than double its amount." Helena Čapková, "Influence of Spirit and Not of Form: Antonín Raymond, Le Corbusier, and Architectural Piracy in the Transwar Era," in *A Pirate's View of World History: A Reversed Perception of the Order of Things from a Global Perspective*, ed. Shigemi Inaga, Kyoto: International Research Center for Japanese Studies, 2016, p. 86.

25. "Now Tony's sporting a boater hat, a cane, and spats!" Frank Lloyd Wright quoted in Oshima, *International Architecture in Interwar Japan*, p. 38.

26. Quoted in Meryle Secrest, *Frank Lloyd Wright: A Biography*, Chicago: Chicago University Press, 1998, p. 247.

27. Letter to Noémi Raymond, 24 November 1919, in Helfrich and Whitaker, *Crafting a Modern World*, pp. 315–16.

28. Letter to Antonín Raymond, 5 January 1921, in Helfrich and Whitaker, *Crafting a Modern World*, pp. 316–17.

29. Arata Endo to Frank Lloyd Wright, 8 September 1923, quoted in Joseph M. Siry, "The Architecture of Earthquake Resistance: Julius Kahn's Truscon Company and Frank Lloyd Wright's Imperial Hotel," *Journal of the Society of Architectural Historians*, Vol. 67, No. 1, 2008, p. 96.

30. Yola Gloaguen, "Antonín Raymond, an Architectural Journey from Bohemia to Japan in the Early 20th Century," *Friends of Czech Heritage Newsletter*, No. 16, Winter 2016–2017; Čapková, *Bedřich Feuerstein*, p. 57.

31. Yola Gloaguen, "Towards a Definition of Antonín Raymond's 'Architectural Identity': A Study Based on the Architect's Way of Thinking and Way of Design," PhD diss., Kyoto University, 2008, unpaginated appendix, entry on Reinanzaka house.

32. The term *brutalism* comes from the French *béton brut*, meaning a raw concrete surface; it has nothing to do with brutality.

33. Antonín Raymond, "Lasting Values in Design" (1949), Kitazawa collection (private archive by Kitazawa Kōichi), pp. 7–11, quoted in Čapková, "Influence of Spirit," p. 90.

34. Letter to the editor of *Architectural Forum*, quoted in Helfrich and Whitaker, *Crafting a Modern World*, p. 26.

35. Marni Epstein-Mervis, "Le Corbusier's Forgotten Design: SoCal's Iconic Butterfly Roof," *Curbed Los Angeles*, 24 December 2014.

36. Gloaguen, "Towards a Definition of Antonín Raymond's 'Architectural Identity,'" p. 85.

37. Karel Teige, *Modern Architecture in Czechoslovakia and Other Writings*, trans. Irena Žantovská Murray and David Britt, Los Angeles: Getty Research Institute, 2000, p. 177.

38. Milča Mayerová, "Japonští herci," *Pestrý týden*, Vol. 2, No. 24, 15 June 1927, p. 23. Japanese theater was also featured in Vol. 2, No. 37, 1927, and Vol. 3, No. 1, 1928.

39. *Pestrý týden*, Vol. 1, No. 9, 29 December 1926.

40. Matthew S. Witkovsky, "Creating an Alphabet for the Modern World," in Vítězslav Nezval, *Alphabet*, trans. Jindřich Toman and Matthew S. Witkovsky, Ann Arbor: Michigan Slavic Publications, 2001. I discuss *Abeceda* further in *PC*, pp. 237–41.

41. Vítězslav Nezval, *Abeceda*, Prague: Torst, 1993, p. 22. This is a facsimile reprint of the first edition (Prague: Otto, 1926).

42. J. K. [Jaromír Krejcar], "Vila českého architekta Raymonda v Tokiu," *Pestrý týden*, Vol. 2, No. 18, 4 May 1927, p. 8.

43. Untitled photo spread, *Pestrý týden*, Vol. 2, No. 23, 8 June 1927, p. 3. Feuerstein's given name was Bedřich, but he was known to friends by the diminutive Fricek.

44. Founded in 1885 as the Uměleckoprůmyslová škola v Praze, the academy has officially been known since 1946 as the Vysoká škola uměleckoprůmyslová v Praze (VŠUP).

45. Michalová, *Karel Teige*, p. 93. This nucleus was expanded in 1923 to include Jindřich Štyrský, Toyen, Otakar Mrkvička, and Jiří Jelínek. Devětsil's founding is discussed in detail in Michalová, *Karel Teige*, pp. 64–74.

46. The phrase is Rostislav Švácha's, quoted in "Towards an Iconography of Czech Avant-Garde Architecture," in *The Art of the Avant-Garde in Czechoslovakia 1918–1938*, exh. cat., ed. Jaroslav Anděl, Valencia: IVAM Centre Julio Gonzalez, 1993, p. 121.

47. The other was the Military Geographical Institute in the Bubeneč district of Prague (Vojenský zeměpisný ústav, 1921–1925).

48. Karel Čapek, *R.U.R. (Rossum's Universal Robots)*, in *Toward the Radical Center: A Karel Čapek Reader*, ed. Peter Kussi, North Haven, CT: Catbird Press, 1990, pp. 41, 45.

49. Bedřich Feuerstein, "Japonské divadlo Nó," *Volné směry*, Vol. 30, No. 1, 1933–1934, p. 28. Čapek's play *Ze života hymzu* was also produced at Tsukiji Shogekijo in 1925.

50. *Ze života hymzu* (*The Insect Play*) followed in 1925. Jaroslav Hašek's *Good Soldier Švejk* and Ivan Olbracht's *Anna proletářka* (*Anna the Proletarian*) were translated in 1930.

51. Věra Ptáčková, *Česká scénografie XX. století*, Prague: Odeon, 1982, p. 43.

52. Jiří Voskovec, "Stavitel divadelních obrazů," quoted in Ptáčková, *Česká scénografie*, p. 41.

53. Letter to Josef Havlíček, 3 September 1925, quoted in Čapková, *Bedřich Feuerstein*, p. 33.

54. Čapková, *Bedřich Feuerstein*, p. 198.

55. Letter to Bedřich Feuerstein, 16 September 1925, quoted in Čapková, *Bedřich Feuerstein*, p. 36.

56. Letter to Josef Havlíček, 6 May 1926, quoted in Čapková, *Bedřich Feuerstein*, p. 37, and (at greater length) in Helena Čapková, "Transnational Correspondence: Tsuchiura Kameki, Tsuchiura Nobuko and Bedřich Feuerstein," *Design History*, Vol. 8, 2010, p. 121. This article also reproduces the correspondence between Feuerstein and the Tsuchiuras.

57. Letter to Noémi Raymond, 14 May 1926, in Helfrich and Whitaker, *Crafting a Modern World*, p. 327.

58. "Japonská monografie o českém jevištním výtvarnictví," *Národní listy*, 10 April 1927, p. 9. See Čapková, *Bedřich Feuerstein*, pp. 48–50.

59. "Garakutashu—A Network for Modern Craft and Design," exhibition brochure, Institute for Art Anthropology, Tamu Art University, 2021.

60. "Prominent People of Minato City: Heibonji Mita," at https://www.lib.city.minato.tokyo.jp/yukari/e/man-detail.cgi?id=91 (accessed 20 November 2018). See also Čapková, *Bedřich Feuerstein*, p. 52.

61. See Nicolai Kruger, "A Modern Marriage: Kameki and Nobuko Tsuchiura at Tatemono-en," *Artscape Japan/Focus*, 2 April 2014.

62. See letters in Čapková, "Transnational Correspondence."

63. Čapková, *Bedřich Feuerstein*, p. 45.

64. Undated draft of letter to Feuerstein, in Čapková, *Bedřich Feuerstein*, p. 118. The latter phrase is in English in the original.

65. Letter to the editors of *Architectural Review*, Vol. 115, No. 685, January 1954, pp. 1–2.

66. Undated letter from Feuerstein addressed to the Ministry of Foreign Affairs, reproduced in Čapková, *Bedřich Feuerstein*, p. 119. The phrase "thiev and criminal" is in English in the original. The agreement between Raymond and Feuerstein is reproduced on p. 121.

67. Undated draft of letter to Feuerstein, in Čapková, *Bedřich Feuerstein*, p. 118.

68. Information in this paragraph is taken from the Česká televize series "Šumné stopy," which consists of ten programs by the architect David Vávra on Czech architects in Japan and Bosnia. The program about Švágr was broadcast on 25 May 2011. Other programs are devoted to Jan Letzel, Antonín Raymond (and followers), and Bedřich Feuerstein.

69. "Ústavení Japonsko-Československé společnosti v Tokiu na československém vyslanectví v prosinci 1927," *Pestrý týden*, Vol. 3, No. 4, 28 January 1928, p. 3.

70. The anthem comes from the František Škroup (music) and Josef Kajetán Tyl (libretto) opera *Fidlovačka*, which premièred at the Estates Theater on 21 December 1834.

71. Letter to Kameki Tsuchiura, 21 October 1931, in Čapková, "Transnational Correspondence," p. 142.

72. The other five productions were all V & W reviews. Feuerstein also designed the sets for V & W's *Balada z hadrů* (A ballad of rags, 1935) at the Spoutané divadlo. On the political storm caused by *Osel a stín*, see Michal Schonberg, *Osvobozené*, Prague: Odeon, 1992, pp. 208–11.

73. "*Na sluneční straně* (On the Sunny Side). 1933. Directed by Vladislav Vančura," MoMA Exhibitions and Events, 18 April 2017.

74. Letter to Kameki Tsuchiura, 22 February 1933, in Čapková, "Transnational Correspondence," p. 147. The letter was written in English.

75. Quoted in Helena Čapková, "'Believe in Socialism . . .': Architect Bedřich Feuerstein and His Perspective on Modern Japan and Architecture," *Review of Japanese Culture and Society*, Vol. 28, 2016, p. 80.

76. Quoted as the epigraph to this chapter.

77. Karel Čapek, "Chudák Fricek," *Lidové noviny*, 12 May 1936, reprinted in *Spisy*, Vol. 19, *O umění a kultuře III*, Prague: Československý spisovatel, 1986, p. 696.

78. Mikoláš Aleš, *Osud talentu v Čechách—nejtrpčí báseň beze slov*, 1883.

79. Lucie Skřivánková, Rostislav Švácha, and Irena Lehkoživová, eds., *The Paneláks: Twenty-Five Housing Estates in the Czech Republic*, Prague: Museum of Decorative Arts, 2017, p. 35.

80. Lucie Skřivánková, Rostislav Švácha, Martina Koukalová, and Eva Novotná, eds., *Paneláci: Historie sídlišť v českých zemích 1945–1989*, Prague: Uměleckoprůmyslové muzeum, 2017, p. 68. Sammer's sketches for the façades and a photograph of the block can be seen in Radomíra Sedláková, *Sorela: česká architektura padesátých let*, Prague: Národní galerie, 1994, pp. 38–39.

81. Skřivánková et al., *Paneláks*, p. 35.

82. Little has been written on Sammer. *Bibliography of the History of the Czech Lands*, produced by the Historical Institute of the Czech Academy of Sciences, lists just one publication: Hrabová's "Between Ideal and Ideology." This is my main source for what follows.

83. Letter to his parents, 9 March 1932, quoted in Hrabová, "Between Ideal and Ideology," p. 138.

84. Letter to Karel Teige, 14 February 1933, quoted in Hrabová, "Between Ideal and Ideology," p. 140.

85. Karel Teige, *The Minimum Dwelling*, trans. Eric Dluhosch, Cambridge, MA: MIT Press, 2002, pp. 180–81. For the Mundaneum controversy, see *Oppositions*, No. 4, October 1974, which contains English translations of both Teige's "Mundaneum" and Le Corbusier's response.

86. Letter to his parents, 21 November 1931, quoted in Hrabová, "Between Ideal and Ideology," p. 139.

87. Letter to Charlotte Perriand, 19 January 1935, quoted in Hrabová, "Between Ideal and Ideology," p. 140.

88. Secrest, *Frank Lloyd Wright*, p. 459.

89. Letter to his parents, 27 July 1935, quoted in Hrabová, "Between Ideal and Ideology," p. 143.

90. Quoted in Hrabová, "Between Ideal and Ideology," p. 159, n. 95.

91. Hrabová, "Between Ideal and Ideology," p. 143. This is based on the recollections of Agnes Larsson.

92. Letter to his parents, 14 December 1937, quoted in Hrabová, "Between Ideal and Ideology," p. 143.

93. Antonín Raymond, "Autobiography," *Kenchiku*, October 1961, p. 21, quoted in Hrabová, "Between Ideal and Ideology," p. 145.

94. Pankaj Vir Gupta and Christine Mueller, *Golconde: The Introduction of Modernism in India*, AIA Report on University Research, Austin: University of Texas, 2005, p. 147.

95. "Sri Aurobindo," at https://www.sriaurobindoashram.org/sriaurobindo/ (accessed 10 December 2018).

96. Raymond, *Autobiography*, quoted in Gupta and Mueller, *Golconde*, p. 148.

97. Hrabová, "Between Ideal and Ideology," p. 145.

98. Gupta and Mueller, *Golconde*, pp. 152–53; Helena Čapková, "Dormitář Golconde," in *Bydlet spolu. Kolektivní domy v českých zemích a Evropě ve 20. století*, ed. Hubert Guzik, Prague: Arbor Vitae, 2017, p. 142.

99. Mira Nakashima, *Nature, Form and Spirit: The Life and Legacy of George Nakashima*, New York: Abrams, 2003, quoted in Wendy Moonan, "George Nakashima Believed Every Tree Has a Living Spirit," *Chicago Tribune*, January 25, 2004.

100. George Nakashima, *The Soul of a Tree: A Woodworker's Reflections*, New York: Kodansha, 2011, p. 64.

101. Letter to his parents, May 1938, quoted in Hrabová, "Between Ideal and Ideology," pp. 137, 148.

102. Nakashima, *Soul of a Tree*, p. 69.

103. The three designs are illustrated in Hrabová, "Between Ideal and Ideology," p. 149.

104. Letter to Antonín Raymond, 8 October 1972, quoted in Hrabová, "Between Ideal and Ideology," p. 161, n. 128.

105. Letter to Noémi Raymond, 16 January 1947, quoted in Hrabová, "Between Ideal and Ideology," p. 151.

106. Letter to František Sammer, 30 August 1966, quoted in Irena Veverková, "Poválečné kontakty Antonína Raymonda s rodnou zemí," in *Antonín Raymond v Japonsku 1948–1976: vzpomínky přátel*, ed. Helena Čapková and Kóiči Kitazawa, Prague: Aula, 2019, p. 231.

107. Letter to Antonín Raymond, 7 January 1967, quoted in Hrabová, "Between Ideal and Ideology," p. 151.

108. Petr Domanický, *Lesk, barvy a iluze: Architektura Plzně šedesátých let*, Plzeň: Západočeská galerie, 2013, p. 14, quoted in Hrabová, "Between Ideal and Ideology," p. 152.

109. Letters to Japan office, 19 March and 6 April 1939, quoted in Sara Gdula, "The New Hope Experiment: An Investigation and Conservation Plan for the Antonín and Noémi Raymond Farm," master's thesis, University of Pennsylvania, 2018, p. 33.

110. Gdula, "New Hope Experiment," p. 33.

111. Antonín Raymond, "The Common Ground of Pennsylvania Colonial and Modern Architecture" (1940), unpublished ms., quoted in Gdula, "New Hope Experiment," p. 19.

112. Irena Veverková, "Mladá léta světově známého architekta Antonína Raymonda," *Slanský Obzor: Ročenka Musejního spolku v Slaném*, No. 6, 1999, pp. 53–59.

113. Nakashima, *Soul of a Tree*, p. 69.

114. Nakashima, *Soul of a Tree*, pp. 49–53.

115. Mike McLeod, "The Life, Legacy and Furniture of George Nakashima and a Conversation with Mira Nakashima," *Southeastern Antiquing and Collecting Magazine*, August 2015.

116. Moonan, "George Nakashima Believed Every Tree Has a Living Spirit."

117. "New Life for the Noble Tree: The Krosnick Collection of Masterworks by George Nakashima," Sotheby's press release, at https://sothebys.gcs-web.com/static-files/b0511907 -c255-446c-9256-e3b53456f15a (accessed 21 March 2020).

118. Knoll website, https://www.knoll.com/product/nakashima-tray (accessed 12 December 2018).

119. George Nakashima, "Manifesto," at Nakashima Foundation for Peace website, https:// nakashimafoundation.org/manifesto/ (accessed 12 December 2018).

120. Dylan J. Plung, "The Japanese Village at Dugway Proving Ground: An Unexamined Context to the Firebombing of Japan," *Asia-Pacific Journal*, Vol. 16, Issue 8, No. 3, 15 April 2018.

121. US Department of Defense, Military Installations website, "In-depth Overview of Dugway Proving Ground," at https://installations.militaryonesource.mil/in-depth-overview /dugway-proving-ground (accessed 14 December 2018).

122. See Arvid Keeson, "Dugway Mysteries Revealed—The New Area 51," *Utah Stories*, 12 October 2012.

123. Lorraine Boissoneault, "How the Death of 6,000 Sheep Spurred the American Debate on Chemical Weapons," *Smithsonian Magazine*, 9 April 2018.

124. See Tom Vanden Brook, "Army Lashes General over Anthrax Debacle," *USA Today*, 24 November 2016.

125. Publisher's blurb for Geoff Manaugh, William L. Fox, and Tyler Green, *David Maisel: Proving Ground*, Göttingen: Steidl, 2019.

126. David Maisel, "Proving Ground," Story Institute, n.d.

127. "Terminal Mirage," at http://www.instituteartist.com/filter/david-maisel-feature /feature-Terminal-Mirage-David-Maisel (accessed 15 December 2018).

128. Glen Helfland, "Death from Above: How David Maisel Turned 'the New Area 51' into Land Art," *Guardian*, 5 May 2017.

129. Maisel, "Proving Ground."

130. Both these images are reproduced at http://davidmaisel.com/works/proving-ground-2/ (accessed 17 December 2018).

131. Maisel, "Proving Ground."

132. Maisel, quoted in publisher's blurb for Manaugh, Fox, and Green, *David Maisel*.

133. David Maisel, "Proving Ground," at http://davidmaisel.com/works/proving-ground-2/ (accessed 14 December 2018).

134. Maisel quoted in Helfland, "Death from Above."

135. Plung, "Japanese Village."

136. Military Intelligence Division, Great Britain, "Dropping Trials of Incendiary Bombs against Representative Structures at Dugway, U.S.A.," quoted in Plung, "Japanese Village."

137. Plung, "Japanese Village"; observer quoted in Jack Couffer, *Bat Bomb: World War II's Other Secret Weapon*, Austin: University of Texas Press, 1992, pp. 208–9.

138. Raymond, *Autobiography*, p. 188.

139. Figures from Plung, "Japanese Village."

140. Figures from Wikipedia, entries "Bombing of Dresden in World War II" and "The Blitz."

141. Review of Jennifer Cody Epstein, *The Gods of Heavenly Punishment*, at https://www.goodreads.com/book/show/17986422-the-gods-of-heavenly-punishment (accessed 16 December 2018)

142. *Vogue* review, quoted on the front cover of Jennifer Cody Epstein, *The Gods of Heavenly Punishment*, New York: Norton, 2014.

143. Epstein, *Gods of Heavenly Punishment*, unpaginated front matter.

144. The Nakashimas did not meet until later, after George returned to Tokyo in late 1939.

145. Epstein, *Gods of Heavenly Punishment*, pp. 48–51.

146. Epstein, *Gods of Heavenly Punishment*, pp. 150–57.

147. Raymond, *Autobiography*, p. 198.

148. Letter to Noémi Raymond, 22 October 1948, in Helfrich and Whitaker, *Crafting a Modern World*, pp. 338–39.

149. Jane C. Loeffler, *The Architecture of Diplomacy: Building America's Embassies*, Princeton, NJ: Princeton Architectural Press, 1998, pp. 85–86.

150. Helfrich and Whitaker, *Crafting a Modern World*, p. 19.

151. See Yoke-Sum Wong, "The Future Is Hybrid: Isamu Noguchi and the Mid-Century Modern," in *Feelings of Structure: Explorations in Affect*, ed. Karen Engle and Yoke-Sum Wong, Montreal and Kingston: McGill-Queen's University Press, 2018, pp. 117–38.

152. On Raymond's postwar work in Japan, see Čapková and Kitazawa, *Antonín Raymond v Japonsku*.

153. "V zemi nikoho," in Jesenská, *Křižovatky*, p. 671. For more on Schmolková, see Anna Hájková, "The Woman behind the Kindertransport," *History Today*, Vol. 68, No. 12, December 2018; on Winton, see Muriel Emanuel and Vera Gissing, *Nicholas Winton and the Rescued Generation*, London and Portland, OR: Vallentine Mitchell, 2003.

154. Personal observation, 2009. One of "Winton's children," the UK Labour Party politician Alfred (later Lord) Dubs, recalled in 2015 that "the difficulties were enormous, not the least of which was to persuade the Home Office to allow unaccompanied children to enter the country." Alfred Dubs, "Nicholas Winton Saved Me from the Nazis. I Only Found out 50 Years Later," *Guardian*, 3 July 2015. A few months after writing these words, Dubs found himself fighting

Theresa May's Home Office to allow unaccompanied children into Britain during another refugee crisis. He succeeded in getting Parliament to approve an amendment to the 2016 Immigration Act that would allow three thousand children from Syria and elsewhere into the United Kingdom. However, to Dubs's chagrin, after May became prime minister, her government reneged on the promise, having taken in only 350 children. Boris Johnson's government ended the practice entirely as part of its 2020 legislation to leave the European Union. Asked what he thought of the Czech Republic and Hungary refusing to accept Syrian refugees, Dubs said: "I am disappointed. I've talked to politicians from the Visegrad countries and what they've tended to say is that refugees are not their problem. And then they say, We are only interested in white Christians . . . I find that shocking." Ironically, Dubs let it slip that "I first met Theresa May at a birthday party of Nicky Winton's," who lived in Maidenhead, part of the prime minister's constituency. Ian Willoughby, "'Winton Child' Lord Alfred Dubs: I Was Luckier than Most—I Was Met by My Father in the UK," Radio Praha, 11 December 2017.

155. Anna Hájková and Martin Šmok, "Dějiny zapomínají na hrdinky: Nová iniciativa připomíná Marii Schmolkovou, ženu, která zachránila tisíce lidí před holokaustem," a2larm.cz, 13 November 2017.

156. Fifteen projects are listed on the Foreign Architects in Japan website, at https://japan-architect.jimdo.com/foreign-architects-in-japan/jan-letzel/ (accessed 17 December 2018).

157. "Fame Escapes Czech Who Gave Hiroshima Its Dome," Aktuálně.cz, 6 August 2008.

158. Quoted in Jan Velinger, "Look at the Czech Architect Who Built Hiroshima's Industrial Promotion Hall—Today's A-Bomb Dome," Radio Praha, 3 August 2005.

159. Quoted in Velinger, "Look at the Czech Architect."

160. Quoted in "103 Years Ago: 04-05 (1915) Hiroshima A-Bomb Dome Is Completed," at http://www.meijishowa.com/calendar/4656/04-05-1915-hiroshima-s-a-bomb-dome-is-completed (accessed 18 December 2018).

161. Tomoko Ichitani, "'Town of Evening Calm, Country of Cherry Blossoms': The Renarrativation of Hiroshima Memories," *Journal of Narrative Theory*, Vol. 40, No. 3, 2010, pp. 368–69.

Chapter 4: But Miss, We Can't Help It

1. H. G. Adler, *Theresienstadt 1941–1945: The Face of a Coerced Community*, trans. Belinda Cooper, Cambridge: Cambridge University Press, 2017, p. 812.

2. Jan Masaryk, radio broadcast, end of 1938, quoted in David Vaughan, "An Experiment in Vivisection: Czechoslovakia's Second Republic 1938–1939," Radio Prague, 23 November 2019.

3. Brod, *Život plný bojů*, pp. 269–70.

4. Letter to Albert Einstein, 30 November 1938, quoted in Gordin, *Einstein in Bohemia*, p. 172.

5. Adler, *Theresienstadt*, p. 4.

6. Brod, *Život plný bojů*, pp. 270–72.

7. Balint, *Kafka's Last Trial*, p. 144.

8. Brod, *Život plný bojů*, pp. 276–77.

9. See Benjamin, *Arcades Project*, p. 462.

10. Stach, *Kafka: The Early Years*, p. 218.

11. John Keats, "Ode on a Grecian Urn," at https://www.poetryfoundation.org/poems /44477/ode-on-a-grecian-urn (accessed 4 January 2019).

12. Brod, *Život plný bojů*, pp. 277–79.

13. Hani Seligsohn, "The Tale of Habima," Habima National Theater Archives, at http://archive.habima.co.il/media/1009/history_en.pdf (accessed 6 January 2019).

14. Gustav Meyrink, *The Golem*, trans. E. F. Bleiler, New York: Dover, 1976.

15. Alisa Solomon, "Theater; a Jewish Avenger, a Timely Legend," *New York Times*, 7 April 2002.

16. Roger Ebert, review of *Metropolis* (2002), 25 January 2002, at https://www.rogerebert .com/reviews/metropolis-2002 (accessed 15 January 2019).

17. Isaac Bashevis Singer, "The Golem Is a Myth for Our Time," *New York Times*, 12 August 1984.

18. Quoted in Bryant, *Prague in Black*, pp. 29, 42.

19. Beneš, "A Message of November 1938 to a Czechoslovak Politician in Prague," p. 573.

20. A. J. P. Taylor, *Politicians, Socialism, and Historians*, London: Hamish Hamilton, 1980, p. 211.

21. I discuss Mucha at length in *CB*; see especially pp. 18–21, 147–53, 249–52.

22. I discuss Vyšehrad Cemetery in *PC*, pp. 90–99.

23. Karel Čapek, *Francouzská poesie. Spisy*, Vol. 24, Prague: Český spisovatel, 1993.

24. Karel Čapek, *Letters from England*, trans. Geoffrey Newsome, London: Continuum, 2004. Capek's other travel writings included *Italské listy* (Italian letters, 1923), *Výlet do Španěl* (An excursion to Spain, 1930), *Obrázky z Holandska* (Pictures from Holland, 1932), and *Cesta na sever* (Journey to the north, 1936; covering Denmark, Sweden, and Norway).

25. "Poslední dny Karla Čapka," *Přítomnost*, 11 January 1939, in Jesenská, *Křižovatky*, p. 681.

26. "Praha, ráno 15. března 1939," *Přítomnost*, 22 March 1939, in Jesenská, *Křižovatky*, pp. 697–99. *La grande illusion* is a 1937 film by Jean Renoir.

27. Wilfred Owen, "Dulce et Decorum Est," Poetry Foundation, at https://www .poetryfoundation.org/poems/46560/dulce-et-decorum-est (accessed 15 January 2019).

28. Jaroslav Hašek, *The Good Soldier Švejk*, trans. Cecil Parrott, London: Penguin, 1974.

29. Quoted in Jiři Opelík, "Fučík jako kritický vykladač Haškova Švejka," *Česká literatura*, Vol. 2, No. 4, 1954, p. 354.

30. Ivan Olbracht, "Osudy Dobrého vojáka Švejka za světové války," *Rudé právo*, Vol. 2, No. 267, 15 November 1921, pp. 1–2.

31. Jar[oslav] Hašek, "Švejk greift in den Weltkrieg ein," *Prager Tagblatt*, Vol. 48, No. 3, 5 January 1923, pp. 3–4.

32. Ralph Jentsch, *George Grosz: Berlin–New York*, exh. cat., Milan: Skira, 2008, pp. 151–54.

33. See James Fraser, ed., *The Malik-Verlag: 1916–1947*, New York: Goethe House, 1984.

34. Milan Kundera, "The Unloved Child of the Family," in *Testaments Betrayed*, pp. 192–96.

35. Details in this paragraph are from Jiří Padevět, ed., *Průvodce protektorátní Prahou. Místa— události—lidé*, Prague: Academia/Archiv hlavního města Prahy, 2013, pp. 54–57.

36. "Výnos vůdce a říšského kancléře o Protektorátu Čechy a Morava ze dne 16. března 1939," at https://www.holocaust.cz/zdroje/dokumenty/protektorat-cechy-a-morava/vynos-vudce-a -risskeho-kanclere-o-protektoratu-cechy-a-morava-ze-dne-16-brezna-1939/ (accessed 19 January 2019). The decree was mostly the work of Wilhelm Stuckart.

37. Joseph Goebbels quoted in Bryant, *Prague in Black*, p. 33.

38. "Výnos vůdce a říšského kancléře o Protektorátu Čechy a Morava ze dne 16. března 1939."

39. The word *souručenství* can also be translated as "partnership" or "community spirit." The German name for the organization was Nationale Gemeinschaft, which conveys its *völkisch* overtones.

40. A. Pešl quoted in Vojtěch Šír, "Národní souručenství—odznak," at https://www.fronta .cz/dotaz/narodni-sourucenstvi-odznak (accessed 20 January 2019).

41. Ferdinand Peroutka, "Když všechno se mění . . . ," *Přítomnost*, Vol. 16, No. 21, 24 May 1939, p. 314.

42. See Marie Jirásková, *Stručná zpráva o trojí volbě: Milena Jesenská, Joachim von Zedtwitz a Jaroslav Nachtmann v roce 1939 a v čase následujícím*, Prague: Nakdadatelství Franze Kafky, 1996, pp. 26–27.

43. Cis, "Jediná česká politická strana," *Přítomnost*, Vol. 16, No. 12, 22 March 1939, p. 178.

44. Ferdinand Peroutka, "Jsme Češi," *Lidové noviny*, 23 April 1939, p. 1.

45. Ferdinand Peroutka, "Jací jsme," *Tribuna*, 21 June 1922. The lime or linden tree (*lípa*) is a Czech national symbol. Josef Mánes was a nineteenth-century painter.

46. *Prager Tagblatt* was dissolved on 4 April 1939 and its offices and printing presses were used to launch *Der neue Tag*, which became the official mouthpiece of the German authorities. See Demetz, *Prague in Danger*, pp. 37–39.

47. Ferdinand Peroutka, "Tvář českého čtenáře," *Přítomnost*, Vol. 16, No. 20, 17 May 1939, pp. 297–98.

48. "Májový pohřeb básníkův," *Lidové noviny*, Vol. 47, No. 229, 8 May 1939, p. 3. I give a much fuller account of the Vyšehrad funerals of Karel Čapek, Karel Hynek Mácha, and Alfons Mucha in *CB*, pp. 20–28. See also Vojtěch Lahoda, "Marné volání," in *Konec avantgardy? Od mnichovské dohody ke komunistickému převratu*, exh. cat., ed. Hana Rousová, Prague: Arbor vitae, 2011, pp. 245–53.

49. Peroutka, "Jací jsme."

50. See *Přítomnost*, Vol. 16, No. 14, 5 April 1939, pp. 206–7.

51. See especially "Česká maminka," *Přítomnost*, 19 April 1939, in Jesenská, *Křižovatky*, pp. 714–16. I discuss this article in *CB*, pp. 226–27.

52. "O střízlivosti a gestu," *Přítomnost*, 29 March 1939, in Jesenská, *Křižovatky*, p. 704.

53. Ferdinand Peroutka, "Národní umění se rodí stále znovu," *Přítomnost*, Vol. 16, No. 15, 12 April 1939, p. 224. Josef Jungmann's *Czech-German Dictionary*, which was published in five volumes in 1834–1839, was a key work of the national revival. See *CB*, pp. 108–11.

54. See Milan Jankovič, "Nad Vančurovými *Obrazy z dějin národa českého* (Podíl rytmičnosti na utváření smyslu)," *Česká literatura*, Vol. 48, No. 4, 2000.

55. I discuss Jirásek and his writings, which would play a key role in KSČ cultural politics after 1948, in more detail in *CB*, pp. 130–33.

56. Jan Chodějovský, "Miloslav Hýsek (1885–1957)," *Akademický bulletin*, 16 January 2012, at http://abicko.avcr.cz/2007/3/07/ (accessed 30 January 2019).

57. Petr Bezruč, *Slezské písně*, Prague: Orbis, 1950.

58. Alois Ludvík Salač, *Slezské jařmo*, Plzeň: Česká ročenka, 1925.

59. Miloslav Hýsek et al., *Výstava Národ svým výtvarným umělcům*, exh. cat., Prague: Kulturní rada ústředí pro kulturní a školskou práci Národního souručenství, 1939 (unpaginated). Josef

Václav Myslbek was the most famous Czech sculptor of the late nineteenth and early twentieth centuries. His best-known work is the Saint Václav statue on Wenceslas Square.

60. The speech is reproduced in František Kovárna, ed., *Národ svým výtvarným umělcům*, exh. cat., Prague: Kulturní rada, 1940, pp. 15–16.

61. Compare the list of exhibits in *Výstava Národ svým výtvarným umělcům* with the list of participating artists in Kovárna, *Národ svým výtvarným umělcům*, p. 27.

62. Ferdinand Peroutka, "Naše ústava," *Přítomnost*, Vol. 16, No. 14, 5 April 1939, p. 201. For a fuller discussion, see Z. Smetáček, "Nepolitická politika—naše metoda nynější," *Přítomnost*, Vol. 16, No. 15, 26 April 1939, pp. 217–20.

63. Quoted in Anděla Horová, "Doba protektorátu a poválečná léta," in Rostislav Švácha and Marie Platovská, *Dějiny českého výtvarného umění [V] 1939–1958*, Prague: Academia, 2005, p. 21.

64. This account is based on the testimony of Jesenská's next-door neighbor in Kouřimská Street, Mrs. Vilímovská, as quoted in Jirásková, *Stručná zpráva o trojí volbě*, p. 28.

65. Figures from census of 31 December 1910, in "Ethnic and Religious Composition of Austria-Hungary," Wikipedia (accessed 1 February 2019).

66. Chad Bryant, "Either German or Czech: Fixing Nationality in Bohemia and Moravia, 1939–1946," *Slavic Review*, Vol. 61, No. 4, 2002, p. 684.

67. A vast literature could be cited here, but this case is eloquently made in Sven Lindqvist, *"Exterminate All the Brutes,"* trans. Joan Tate, New York: New Press, 2007.

68. Jan Vajskebr and Radka Šustrová, "Německá bezpečnostní opatření v Protektorátu Čechy a Morava na začátku války," *Paměť a dějiny*, No. 3, 2009. The total number of people arrested might well be higher; this was the official figure given by the Ministry of the Interior.

69. These details are from Josef Čapek, *Oheň a touha: Básně z koncentračního tábora*, Prague: Odeon, 1980, pp. 271–73. The letter to Jarmila Čapková was written in (mandatory) German.

70. Jarmila Čapková, *Vzpomínky*, Prague: Torst, 1998, pp. 331–32. Unfortunately, several pages of the manuscript describing the trip are missing.

71. Černá, *Kafka's Milena*, pp. 145–47.

72. "S 'ubohým a holým,'" *Přítomnost*, 5 July 1939, in Jesenská, *Křížovatky*, p. 741.

73. Černá, *Kafka's Milena*, p. 144.

74. Tomáš Pasák, *17. listopad 1939 a Univerzita Karlova*, Prague: Karolinum, 1997, p. 45.

75. Quoted in Marek Mahdal, "Inka Bernášková—statečná žena ze Spořilova," *Spořilovské noviny*, 27 September 2005. This paragraph also draws on Jan B. Uhlíř, "Zapomenutý hrdina Josef Škalda," *Noviny Prahy 2*, 12 December 2012.

76. The fullest account of Milena's resistance work with Zedtwitz and *V boj!* and her arrest is Jirásková's *Stručná zpráva*.

77. See Padevět, *Průvodce protektorátní Prahou*, pp. 226–41, for a day-to-day chronology of events in this building throughout the war.

78. Milena Jesenská's court deposition, quoted in Jirásková, *Stručná zpráva*, p. 57.

79. Quoted in Petr Borl, "Chrámy vědění osiřely: Intervenční úsilí představitelů protektorátní správy o zmírnění následků německé akce vůči českému vysokému školství na podzim roku 1939," Diplomová práce, Univerzita Karlova, 2014, p. 24.

80. See Demetz, *Prague in Black*, p. 81.

81. This figure is widely given in Czech sources. Demetz, *Prague in Danger*, p. 82, gives a much lower figure of fifteen.

82. A version of the program broadcast in 1944 can be heard at David Vaughan, "Message of Student Solidarity Still Powerful after More than Seventy Years," Radio Praha, 1 August 2015.

83. Černá, *Kafka's Milena*, p. 160.

84. Not Bergen-Belsen, as Demetz says in *Prague in Danger*, p. 131.

85. Unnamed correspondent, letter to Jana Černá, quoted in Černá, *Kafka's Milena*, p. 167.

86. Hockaday, *Kafka, Love and Courage*, p. 209.

87. Černá, *Kafka's Milena*, pp. 171–72.

88. Letter to Joachim von Zedwitz, n.d., quoted in Jirásková, *Stručná zpráva*, p. 35.

89. Yad Vashem, "Milena Jesenská," at https://www.yadvashem.org/righteous/stories/jesenska.html (accessed 9 March 2019).

Chapter 5: The Void at the Core of Things

1. Hannah Arendt, "Franz Kafka: A Revaluation on the Occasion of the Twentieth Anniversary of His Death," in *Essays in Understanding 1930–1954*, trans. Jerome Kohn, New York: Harcourt Brace, 1994, p. 71.

2. Poland lost 6 million (17 percent of the population), the Soviet Union perhaps 26.6 million (13.5 percent), Lithuania 370,000 (14 percent), Latvia 250,000 (12.5 percent), Yugoslavia 1–1.7 million (7–11 percent), Greece 500,000–800,000 (7–11 percent), and Estonia 83,000 (7 percent). China lost 15–20 million (3–4 percent). France, Britain, and the United States lost 600,000, 450,900, and 419,400 (1.5, 1.0, and 0.5 percent), respectively. Germany lost 6.9–7.4 million (8–9 percent), and Japan lost 2.5–3.1 million (3.5–4.5 percent). Wikipedia, entry "World War II Casualties." Sources for the national figures are given in the Wikipedia article.

3. USHMM, *Holocaust Encyclopedia*, gives a figure of 263,000 for the territories of the prewar Czechoslovak Republic. Erich Kulka gives an overall figure for the ČSR of about 261,500 Jewish victims: 78,000 in the protectorate, 60,000 in Slovakia, 38,500 in Hungary, and 85,000 in Ruthenia. Erich Kulka, "The Annihilation of Czechoslovak Jewry," in *The Jews of Czechoslovakia*, Vol. 3, ed. Avigdor Dagan, Philadelphia: Jewish Publication Society of America, 1984. Livia Rothkirchen gives figures of 78,154 victims in the protectorate and 250,000 in the Czechoslovak Republic as a whole. Livia Rothkirchen, "Czechoslovakia," in *The World Reacts to the Holocaust*, ed. David S. Wyman, Baltimore: Johns Hopkins University Press, 1996, p. 190.

4. "II. americký nálet na Brno," *Internetová encyklopedie dějin Brna*, at https://encyklopedie.brna.cz/home-mmb/?acc=profil_udalosti&load=117 (accessed 9 October 2019). Bryant (*Prague in Black*, p. 227) claims that more than thirty thousand apartments were destroyed in Brno.

5. Vojtěch Lahoda, "Praha po bombardování 1945," in Rousová, *Konec avantgardy?* p. 122.

6. The official death toll was 235. Jan Uhlíř gives a higher figure of about 370. Christian Falvey, "The Bombing of Prague from a New Perspective," Radio Praha, 13 December 2011. Jan Adamec gives a figure of 245. Ian Willoughby, "Used to US Planes Overhead, Praguers Ignored Sirens," Radio Praha, 13 February 2015.

7. Aimé Césaire, *Discourse on Colonialism*, trans. Joan Pinkham, New York: Monthly Review Press, 2001; Frantz Fanon, *The Wretched of the Earth*, trans. Constance Farringdon, New York: Grove Weidenfeld, 1963.

8. The fullest English-language study is Bryant, *Prague in Black*. For an excellent summary, see Richard Gerwarth, *Hitler's Hangman: The Life of Heydrich*, New Haven, CT: Yale University Press, 2012, pp. 244–56.

9. See R. J. Overy, *War and Economy in the Third Reich*, Oxford: Oxford University Press, 1994, pp. 151–56, for fuller details.

10. Bryant, *Prague in Black*, p. 182.

11. Martin Hořák, "Vzpomínání a zapomínání na české oběti nuceného pracovního nasazení," in *Nucená práce 1939–1945: Příběhy pamětníků ve výuce*, p. 6, at https://nucenaprace.cz/prirucka -pro-ucitele.pdf (accessed 4 March 2019). Once again, figures differ widely among sources.

12. Alexandra Urbanová and Zdeněk Tmej, *Abeceda duševního prázdna*, Prague: Zádruha, 1946. This is discussed (and many images are reproduced) in Manfred Heiting, *Czech and Slovak Photo Publications 1918–1989*, Göttingen: Steidl, 2018, pp. 200, 240–41. See also Vladimír Birgus and Jan Mlčoch, *Czech Photography of the Twentieth Century*, Prague: Kant, 2010, pp. 126–31.

13. Birgus and Mlčoch, *Czech Photography of the Twentieth Century*, p. 127.

14. Vojtěch Lahoda, "Abeceda duševního prázdna," in Rousová, *Konec avantgardy?* p. 213. The photo is reproduced in Vladimír Birgus, *Hořká léta 1939–47/The Bitter Years 1939–47*, exh. cat., Opava: Slezská univerzita, 1995, p. 18.

15. The phrase is from Himmler's May 1940 memorandum "Some Thoughts on the Treatment of Alien Populations in the East," quoted in Bryant, *Prague in Black*, p. 113.

16. Bryant, *Prague in Black*, p. 126, summarizing König-Beyer's unpublished 1940 report.

17. Quoted in Bryant, *Prague in Black*, p. 119.

18. Bryant, *Prague in Black*, p. 158.

19. Quoted in Padevět, *Průvodce protektorátní Prahou*, p. 194.

20. George F. Kennan, "Report, Written October 1940, on 'A Year and a Half of the Protectorate of Bohemia and Moravia,'" in *From Prague after Munich: Diplomatic Papers, 1938–9*, Princeton, NJ: Princeton University Press, 1968, pp. 226–27, 232, 234. In the 1930 census 41,701 people in Prague identified themselves as being of German nationality (about eight thousand of them were Jewish).

21. Jiří Doležal, *Česká kultura za Protektorátu: školství, písemnictví, kinematografie*, Prague: Národní filmový archiv, 1996, p. 84.

22. *Amtliches Verzeichnis der Straßen, Plätze und Freiungen der Hauptstadt Prag—Úřední seznam ulic náměstí a sadů hlavního města Prahy*, Prague: Deutsche Druckerei, 1940.

23. Lašťovka et al., *Pražský uličník*, Vol. 1, p. 22.

24. Dwight John Zimmerman, "The 'V for Victory' Campaign," Defense Media Network, 24 July 2011.

25. See Lucie Zadražilová, "Světelné instalace," in Rousová, *Konec avantgardy?* p. 174.

26. Milan Krejčí, *Pražské sochy a pomníky*, Prague: Galerie hlavního města Prahy, 1979 (unpaginated).

27. "U.S. Embassy Participation in the President Wilson Monument Handover Ceremony," US Embassy Prague, 7 October 2011, at cz.usembassy.gov.

28. Klein's testimony is quoted in Vojtěch Drnev, "Zničení hrobu Neznámého vojína," in *Šest let okupace Prahy*, ed. Václav Buben, Prague: Orbis, 1946, pp. 25–27.

29. Zdeňka Kuchyňová, "Hrob Neznámého vojína vznikl na památku bezejmenných obětí," Radio Praha, 8 May 2018.

30. The date for the marriage given in earlier Czech sources, 19 March 1942 (which I followed in *CB*), is inaccurate.

31. See *The Precious Legacy: Judaic Treasures from the Czechoslovak State Collections*, exh. cat., ed. David Altshuler, New York: Summit Books, 1983. I discuss the wartime fate of the Jewish Museum in *PC*, pp. 138–40.

32. Jan Hrubeš and Miroslav Kryl, "Ještě jednou Jiří Weil (O jeho životě a díle)," *Terezínské listy*, Vol. 31, 2003, pp. 25–28. Weil's novel *Life with a Star* (trans. Rita Klimova and Roslyn Schloss, Evanston, IL: Northwestern University Press, 1998) is a thinly fictionalized account of his wartime experiences. On Weil, see also *CB*, pp. 229–31; *PC*, pp. 132–34.

33. Jiří Weil, *Mendelssohn Is on the Roof*, trans. Marie Winn, Evanston, IL: Northwestern University Press, 1998, p. 23.

34. Weil, *Mendelssohn Is on the Roof*, pp. 3–8; emphasis added. The truth of this incident is poetic rather than empirical. The Mendelssohn statue was laid down and removed from view during the war (it was restored to its proper place after 1945), but there was never a statue of Wagner on the Rudolfinum roof. See Jana Orlová, "Tajemství soch na střeše Rudolfina," *Magazín české filharmonie*, No. 4, 2019.

35. Weil, *Mendelssohn Is on the Roof*, p. 12.

36. Bryant, *Prague in Black*, pp. 88, 131–32; Zdeněk Míka et al., *Dějiny Prahy v datech*, Prague: Mladá fronta, 1999, pp. 229–31; Padevět, *Průvodce protektorátní Prahou*, p. 33.

37. Jacob Heilbrunn, "Himmler and Heydrich: Hitler's Lieutenants," *New York Times*, 6 January 2012, p. BR18.

38. Laurent Binet, *HHhH*, trans. Sam Taylor, New York: Farrar, Straus and Giroux, 2013, pp. 31–32.

39. This is also the argument of Gerwarth's biography *Hitler's Hangman*; see pp. xvii–xviii, 292–94. Gerwarth discusses the court-martial and the meeting with Himmler on pp. 43–49.

40. Letter from Hermann Göring to Reinhard Heydrich, 31 July 1941, in Adler, *Theresienstadt*, p. 14.

41. "The Einsatzgruppen: Heydrich's Instructions to Einsatzgruppen Chiefs (September 21, 1939)," in Jewish Virtual Library.

42. Heydrich quoted in Bryant, *Prague in Black*, p. 111.

43. Timothy Snyder, *Bloodlands: Europe between Hitler and Stalin*, New York: Basic Books, 2012.

44. "Kiev and Babi Yar," in USHMM, *Holocaust Encyclopedia*.

45. "Einsatzgruppen: Mass Shootings," in USHMM, *Holocaust Encyclopedia*.

46. Bryant, *Prague in Black*, p. 143; Gerwarth, *Hitler's Hangman*, p. 227.

47. For fuller details of the victims of Heydrich's martial law trials, see Padevět, *Průvodce protektorátní Prahou*, pp. 232–35. Demetz (*Prague in Danger*, p. 137) gives protectorate-wide figures of 486 death sentences and 2,242 people sent to concentration camps during the sixteen weeks of martial law. Five transports of political prisoners left the protectorate for Mauthausen concentration camp in Austria in the winter of 1941–1942; of 1,299 Czechs sent there, only 4 percent survived the war. Gerwarth, *Hitler's Hangman*, p. 227.

48. Bryant, *Prague in Black*, p. 144; Gerwarth, *Hitler's Hangman*, pp. 229–30, 236.

49. Milan Kundera, *The Joke*, 1993 edition, p. 190.

50. Julius Fučík, *Reportáž psaná na oprátce*, Prague: Torst, 1995. This edition identifies the passages the KSČ authorities cut out of earlier editions.

51. Milan Kundera, *Poslední máj*, 2nd rev. ed., Prague: Československý spisovatel, 1961, pp. 28–29.

52. Kennan, *From Prague after Munich*, p. x.

53. Radio transmission, 11 May 1942, quoted in Gerwarth, *Hitler's Hangman*, pp. 8–9.

54. Message of 15 May 1942, quoted in Gerwarth, *Hitler's Hangman*, p. 9.

55. Binet, *HHhH*, p. 231. Western accounts frequently describe Malinová as Kubiš's girlfriend. This is incorrect. See Jan Gazdík, "Matka pomohla Gabčíkovi. Nezlobím se, říká potrestaná dcera," Aktuálně.cz, 24 October 2014 (which draws on an interview with Malinová's daughter Alena); Miroslav Šiška, "Lásky československých parašutistů Gabčíka a Kubiše," Novinky.cz, 26 June 2015; Simona Fendrychová, "Role milenky byla jen zástěrka. Statečnost českých žen během heydrichiády zaskočila i ostré nacisty," Aktuálně.cz, 27 March 2017.

56. See Fendrychová, "Role milenky byla jen zástěrka."

57. See Demetz, *Prague in Danger*, p. 167.

58. Both Bryant (*Prague in Black*, p. 169) and Demetz (*Prague in Danger*, p. 169) mistakenly situate the attack in Holešovice itself.

59. Katrin Klingan, ed., *A Utopia of Modernity: Zlín*, Blumenthal: Jovis, 2010, p. 33.

60. "Rozloučení s hrdinou," *Lidové noviny*, Vol. 50, No. 290, 10 June 1942, p. 1.

61. Alex Ross, "Ghost Sonata. What Happened to German Music?" *New Yorker*, 24 March 2003.

62. "Heydrich Funeral Speeches, Berlin, 9 June 1942," at http://www.worldfuturefund.org /Reports/Heydrich/heydrichfuneral.htm (accessed 30 March 2019). See also Gerwarth, *Hitler's Hangman*, pp. 278–79.

63. Quoted in Padevět, *Průvodce protektorátní Prahou*, p. 62. See also Gerwarth, *Hitler's Hangman*, pp. 246–47.

64. "Česká osudová otázka. Kdo za kým stojí?" *Lidové noviny*, Vol. 50, No. 290, 10 June 1942, p. 3.

65. See Buben, *Šest let okupace Prahy*, pp. 173–207. Čestmír Amort, ed., *Heydrichiáda: dokumenty*, Prague: Naše vojsko, 1965, p. 59, gives a figure of 1,357 shot between 27 May and 3 July; Gerwarth, *Hitler's Hangman*, p. 285, gives a figure of 1,327 condemned to death by 24 June.

66. Padevět, *Průvodce protektorátní Prahou*, p. 677. These figures do not include those murdered in the reprisals at Lidice and Ležaky, discussed later, nor the two thousand Jews transported from Terezín to unknown destinations on 12 and 13 June, none of whom survived.

67. Jan Gazdík, "Před 75 lety začala nacistická pomsta za Heydricha. V Mauthausenu popravili stovky odbojářů i dětí," Aktuálně.cz, 24 October 2017.

68. Paul Kopecek, "The Czech Fighter Squadrons in West Sussex," Free Czechoslovak Air Force website (fcfa.com).

69. Mark Slouka, "The Little Museum of Memory," *Granta*, Vol. 96, 27 December 2006. This is chapter 6 of his *The Visible World: A Novel*, Boston and New York: Houghton Mifflin, 2007.

70. "Lidé práce u katafalku na Hradě," *Lidové noviny*, Vol. 50, No. 290, 10 June 1942, p. 3.

71. Letter from SS Standartenführer Horst Böhme to director of security police, 12 June 1942, in Amort, *Heydrichiáda*, pp. 212–14.

72. Buben, *Šest let okupace Prahy*, pp. 165–66.

73. Interview in Carmen T. Illichmann, "Lidice: Remembering the Women and Children," *UW-L Journal of Undergraduate Research*, No. 8, 2005, pp. 2–3. Figures are from Miroslav Moulis, *Lidice žije*, Prague: Středočeské nakladatelství, 1972, and Buben, *Šest let okupace Prahy*. Amort, *Heydrichiáda*, pp. 49, 288, and Gerwarth, *Hitler's Hangman*, pp. 280–81, give slightly different totals. Uchytilová-Kučová's memorial has eighty-two statues (forty-two girls and forty boys).

74. "Šanda, Jaroslav: terezínští vězni v Lidicích," DOCUMENT.JMP.SHOAH/T/3/343/080, Židovské muzeum v Praze, at https://collections.jewishmuseum.cz/index.php/Detail/Object /Show/object_id/2796 (accessed 22 February 2021).

75. František R. Kraus, "But Lidice Is in Europe," in *Art from the Ashes*, ed. Lawrence L. Langer, New York: Oxford University Press, 1995, pp. 67–69.

76. Report to K. H. Frank, 7 July 1942, in Amort, *Heydrichiáda*, p. 304.

77. "Nazis Filmed the Destruction of My Village," interview with Jaroslava Skleničková, BBC World Service program "Witness," at https://www.bbc.com/news/av/magazine-27924054 /nazis-filmed-the-destruction-of-my-village (accessed 4 April 2019).

78. Gerwarth, *Hitler's Hangman*, p. 283.

79. A full list is given at "Lidice ve světě," Památník Lidice website, at http://www.lidice -memorial.cz/pamatnik/pamatnik-a-pietni-uzemi/lidice-ve-svete/ (accessed 8 April 2019).

80. "Lidice, Illinois," *New York Times*, 30 June 1942, p. 36. The town is now called Crest Hill, but a Lidice monument still stands.

81. "Knox Pledges Nazi Doom. Says 'Butchers' Will Be Erased as Was Town of Lidice," *New York Times*, 15 June 1942, p. 5.

82. "Czech Town of 1200 Wiped out to Avenge Death of Heydrich," *Washington Post*, 11 June 1942, p. 1.

83. Ralph Parker, "50,000 Kiev Deaths Charged to Nazis," *New York Times*, 27 March 1942, p. 8.

84. Jonathan Harrison, "Murder at Lidice—Why Did This Forgotten Nazi Atrocity Create More Outrage in the West in 1942 than the Holocaust?" *Military History Now*, 16 June 2014.

85. Ian Willoughby, "A True Act of Solidarity: How Barnett Stross and the Miners of Stoke-on-Trent Helped Rebuild Lidice," Radio Praha, 9 June 2017.

86. On Barnett Stross and the "Lidice Shall Live" campaign, see the 2013 film sponsored by the Stoke City Council in 2013 and presented by Stross's successor in Parliament Tristram Hunt, *Lidice: A Light across the Sea*, at https://www.youtube.com/watch?v=7E_Jd2c61E8 (accessed 5 April 2019).

87. Quoted in David Vaughan, "The Literary Legacy of Lidice," Radio Praha, 9 June 2012.

88. Viktor Fischl, *The Dead Village*, trans. Laurie Lee, London: Young Czechoslovakia, 1943.

89. Harold Nicolson, ed., *Lidice: A Tribute by Members of the International P.E.N*, London: Allen and Unwin for the Czechoslovak P.E.N., 1944.

90. Cecil Day Lewis, "Lidice," quoted in Vaughan, "Literary Legacy of Lidice."

91. In Nicolson, *Lidice: A Tribute*, p. 90.

92. Anthony Grenville, "Thomas Mann's Czech Connection," *AJR: The Association of Jewish Refugees Journal*, Vol. 17, No. 2, 2017, pp. 1–2. On the Mann brothers' activities in Prague, including lectures at the Bertolt-Brecht-Klub, see Jean-Michel Palmier, *Weimar in Exile: The Antifascist Emigration in Europe and America*, trans. David Fernbach, New York: Verso, 2006, pp. 137–40.

93. Edna St. Vincent Millay, "The Murder of Lidice," introduction by Franklin W. Adams, *Saturday Review of Literature*, 17 October 1942, p. 3. Millay's text is in Nicolson, *Lidice: A Tribute*.

94. "The Murder of Lidice by Edna St Vincent Millay," *Kirkus Reviews*, n.d.

95. I describe it as "eight minutes of swelling melody assassinated by snatch squads of baying brass and persistent rumbles of tympani from the depths." *PC*, p. 339. I write about Martinů at length in *PC*, pp. 339–55.

96. Quoted in David Vaughan, "A Tale of Two Villages," 2000, Radio Praha archive, at http://old.radio.cz/en/article/91540 (accessed 7 April 2019).

97. Humphrey Jennings, "Radio Talk: The Silent Village," in *The Humphrey Jennings Film Reader*, ed. Kevin Jackson, Manchester, UK: Carcanet, 2004, p. 67.

98. See *London Bulletin*, Nos. 4–5, 1938, special double issue "The Impact of Machines."

99. Humphrey Jennings and Charles Madge with T. O. Beachcroft, Julian Blackburn, William Empson, Stuart Legg, and Kathleen Raine, eds., *May the Twelfth: Mass-Observation Day-Surveys 1937 by over Two Hundred Observers*, London: Faber and Faber, 1937, pp. ix–x.

100. Geoffrey Pyke, "King and Country," *New Statesman and Nation*, 12 December 1936, p. 974 (to which Charles Madge responded on the same page).

101. "I See London," May 1941, in Jackson, *Humphrey Jennings Film Reader*, p. 297.

102. All quotations in this paragraph from Jennings, "Radio Talk: The Silent Village," in Jackson, *Humphrey Jennings Film Reader*, pp. 67–75.

103. "Českým uměním dobudeme Říše, Evropy i světa," *Lidové noviny*, Vol. 50, No. 320, 26 June 1942, p. 4.

104. Quoted in Miloslav Turek and Rostislav Taud, "Bohéma nebyl jen Štěpánek. Osudový projev Rudolfa Deyla v Národním divadle před hajlujícími herci," Český rozhlas, 6 March 2017.

105. *Lidové noviny*, Vol. 50, No. 338, 6 July 1942, p. 1 (photo caption).

106. Padevět, *Průvodce protektorátní Prahou*, p. 295, on which I draw for this account.

107. Smetana quoted in Ladislav Šíp, *Česká opera a její tvůrci*, Prague: Supraphon, 1983, p. 40.

108. Adler, *Theresienstadt*, p. 4. The protectorate had 118,310 inhabitants classified as Jewish on 15 March 1939; that figure fell to 97,961 by 31 December 1939, to 90,041 by 31 December 1940, and to 88,686 by 30 June 1941. Adler attributes this reduction mainly to emigration.

109. Letter from Hermann Göring to Heydrich, 31 July 1941, in Adler, *Theresienstadt*, p. 14.

110. Quoted in Ctibor Rybár, *Židovská Praha: glosy k dějinám a kultuře. Průvodce památkami*, Prague: Akropolis, 1991, p. 156. The following discussion also draws on Demetz, *Prague in Danger*; Adler, *Theresienstadt*, pp. 3–12; and "Nazi Restrictions on the Jews of Prague" at http://www.holocaustresearchproject.org/ghettos/restrictions&roles.html (accessed 26 March 2019).

111. Demetz, *Prague in Danger*, pp. 122–23. The Rašínovo Embankment (formerly the Palackého Embankment, named after František Palacký, from 1876 to 1940; the Vltavské Embankment from 1940 to 1942; and, part of Reinhard-Heydrich-Ufer Embankment until 1945) is not in Smíchov, as Demetz says, but on the opposite side of the river.

112. Letter to Emil Hácha, 6 October 1941, quoted in Gerwarth, *Hitler's Hangman*, p. 257.

113. Quoted in Adler, *Theresienstadt*, p. 9. See also Demetz, *Prague in Danger*, pp. 97–98.

114. Quoted in Adler, *Theresienstadt*, p. 10.

115. In addition, anyone born of an extramarital relationship with a Jew after 31 July 1936 was considered a Jew. Zdeněk Tobolka, "Židovský majetek," in *Naučný slovník aktualit*, ed. Zdeněk

Tobolka, Prague: L. Mazáč, 1939, p. 608. The Nuremberg Laws were extended to the protectorate on 21 June 1939.

116. Rothkirchen, "Czechoslovakia," p. 169.

117. Jaroslav Hendrych, "Židé na Slovensku," in Tobolka, *Naučný slovník aktualit*, p. 607.

118. Renee Ghert Sand, "First Transport of Jews to Auschwitz Was 997 Young Slovak Women and Teens," *Times of Israel*, 2 January 2020, reviewing Heather Dune Macadam, *999: The Extraordinary Young Women of the First Official Jewish Transport to Auschwitz*, New York: Citadel Press, 2019.

119. "The Holocaust in Slovakia," USHMM, *Holocaust Encyclopedia*.

120. Wagnerová, *La famille Kafka de Prague*, pp. 256–60; Adler, *Theresienstadt*, p. 128.

121. Wagnerová, *La famille Kafka de Prague*, pp. 249–54.

122. "Bubny Memorial of Silence," at https://www.bubny.org/en/memorial-of-silence (accessed 16 October 2019).

123. Quoted in Gerwarth, *Hitler's Hangman*, p. 257.

124. Adler, *Theresienstadt*, p. 604.

125. Gerwarth, *Hitler's Hangman*, p. 258.

126. Hana Volavková, ed., *I Never Saw Another Butterfly: Children's Poems and Drawings from Terezín*, New York: Schocken, 1993, pp. xx–xxi. Adler, *Theresienstadt*, p. 38, gives a figure of 88,196 deportees to the east.

127. Adler, *Theresienstadt*, p. 45.

128. Toman Brod, Miroslav Kárný, and Margita Kárná, eds., *Terezinský rodinný tábor v Osvětimi-Birkenau*, Prague: Melantrich, 1994, p. 9.

129. Jiří Weil, *Žalozpěv za 77,297 obětí*, Prague: Československý spisovatel, 1958, p. 28.

130. Livia Rothkirchen, "Osud Židů v Čechách a na Moravě v letech 1938–45," in Livia Rothkirchen, Eva Schmidt Hartmann, Avigdor Dagan, and Milena Janišová, *Osud Židů v Protektorátu 1939–1945*, Prague: Trizonia, 1991, p. 68, gives a figure of 78,154.

131. Hana Volavková quoted in Rybár, *Židovská Praha*, p. 276. See *PC*, pp. 137–43.

132. Gerwarth, *Hitler's Hangman*, p. 258.

133. Heda Margolius Kovály and Helena Třeštíková, *Hitler, Stalin and I: An Oral History*, trans. Ivan Margolius, Los Angeles: DoppelHouse Press, 2018, pp. 33–34.

134. Demetz, *Prague in Danger*, p. x.

135. Demetz, *Prague in Danger*, p. 173; Adler, *Theresienstadt*, p. 59. Ferdinand Peroutka makes the same mistake in his *Oblak a valčík* (quoted in Radomíra Sedláková, *Jak fénix: minulost a přítomnost Veletržního paláce v Praze*, Prague: Národní galerie, 1995, p. 24), as does W. G. Sebald in his novel *Austerlitz*, New York: Knopf, 2001, pp. 178–80. See also *PC*, pp. 419–25.

136. Vojtěch Šír, "Transporty Židů do Terezína," Fronta.cz, 17 December 2017. On Mucha and the *Slovanská epopej*, see *CB*, pp. 147–53.

137. Demetz, *Prague in Danger*, pp. 143–44.

Chapter 6: Avant-garde and Kitsch

1. Karel Teige, reworked automatic writing fragment dating from sometime between 1937 and the mid-1940s, in Michalová, *Karel Teige*, p. 451.

2. James Joyce, *Finnegans Wake*, London: Faber and Faber, 1975, pp. 199, 202–3.

3. Joyce, *Finnegans Wake*, p. 201.

4. Adolf Hoffmeister, "Osobnost James Joyce (Dokončení)," *Rozpravy Aventina*, Vol. 6, No. 3, 1930–1931, p. 30. The full text of Hoffmeister's interviews with Joyce was translated into English by Michelle Woods in James Joyce, "The Game of Evenings," *Granta*, Vol. 89, April 2005. Hoffmeister perfectly captured Joyce-as-schoolmaster in his 1928 caricature "James Joyce, irský Odysseus," in *Adolf Hoffmeister (1902–1973)*, exh. cat., ed. Karel Srp, Prague: Gallery, 2004, p. 67.

5. André Breton, *Manifesto of Surrealism*, in *Manifestoes of Surrealism*, trans. Richard Seaver and Helen R. Lane, Ann Arbor: University of Michigan Press, 1972, p. 29.

6. "Le pensionnat de Humming-Bird Garden," excerpt from Robert Desnos, *La liberté ou l'amour*, at http://freaklit.blogspot.com/2011/09/le-pensionnat-de-humming-bird-garden .html (accessed 8 May 2019).

7. James Joyce to Nora Barnacle, letters of 9 and 13(?) December 1909, in *Selected Letters of James Joyce*, ed. Richard Ellman, London: Faber and Faber, 1992, pp. 185, 188.

8. Quoted in Adolf Hoffmeister, "Osobnost James Joyce," *Rozpravy Aventina*, Vol. 6, No. 2, 1930–1931, p. 14.

9. Hoffmeister, "Osobnost James Joyce," p. 14.

10. Hoffmeister, "Osobnost James Joyce (Dokončení)," p. 30.

11. David Bradshaw, "*Ulysses* and Obscenity," British Library, 25 May 2016.

12. Kevin Birmingham, *The Most Dangerous Book: The Battle for James Joyce's "Ulysses,"* London: Head of Zeus, 2014, p. 12, as quoted in Bradshaw, "*Ulysses* and Obscenity."

13. Emma Garman, "The Lesbian Partnership that Changed Literature," *Paris Review*, 22 October 2020.

14. jh [Jane Heap], "Art and the Law," *Little Review*, Vol. 7, No. 3, 1920, pp. 5–7.

15. Hoffmeister, "Osobnost James Joyce," p. 14.

16. Breton, *Manifesto of Surrealism*, p. 26.

17. James Joyce, *Ulysses*, Paris: Shakespeare, 1922; New York: Dover Books, 2010 (facsimile), pp. 726–27.

18. Quoted in Bradshaw, "*Ulysses* and Obscenity."

19. "Judea Declares War on Germany," *Daily Express*, 24 March 1933, p. 1.

20. See *PC*, pp. 130–31.

21. Other than the name, there is no connection between Fromek's firm and the Odeon publishing house established by the communist regime in 1966.

22. David Vichnar, "Plačky nad Finneganem osmdesátileté," *Bubínek Revolveru*, 8 May 2019. Substantial parts of the text were previously translated into French by Samuel Beckett, Alfred Péron, Ivan Goll, Eugène Jolas, Paul Léon, Adrienne Monnier, and Philippe Soupault, with Joyce's assistance, as "Anna Livie Plurabelle," *Nouvelle Revue Française*, No. 36, 1 May 1931, pp. 633–46.

23. Hoffmeister, "Osobnost James Joyce (Dokončení)," p. 30.

24. Letter to Harriet Weaver, 28 October 1927, quoted in Patrick O'Neill, *Trilingual Joyce: The Anna Livia Variations*, Toronto: University of Toronto Press, 2018, p. 6.

25. James Joyce to Valery Larbaud, mid-October 1927, quoted in O'Neill, *Trilingual Joyce*, p. 6.

26. Joyce, *Finnegans Wake*, p. 196. This is also quoted in Hoffmeister, "Osobnost James Joyce (Dokončení)," p. 31.

27. Hoffmeister, "Osobnost James Joyce (Dokončení)," p. 30.

28. Joyce, *Finnegans Wake*, p. 292.

29. Joyce, *Finnegans Wake*, p. 213.

30. James Joyce, "Continuation of a Work in Progress," *transition*, No. 8, November 1927, p. 33.

31. Hoffmeister, "Osobnost James Joyce," p. 14.

32. Joyce, *Finnegans Wake*, pp. 628, 3.

33. Hoffmeister, "Osobnost James Joyce," p. 1.

34. Karel Teige, *Nové obrazy Františka Muziky*, exh. cat., in *Osvobozování života a poezie: studie ze 40. let, Výbor z díla III*, ed. Jiří Brabec, Vratislav Effenberger, Květoslav Chvatík, and Roberta Kalivoda, Prague: Aurora, 1994, p. 508.

35. For a detailed discussion of this "gray zone," see Vojtěch Lahoda, "Moderní umění a cenzura v letech protektorátu," in Švácha and Platovská, *Dějiny českého výtvarného umění [V]*, pp. 115–30.

36. Greenberg, "Avant-Garde and Kitsch," in *Collected Essays and Criticism*, pp. 12, 7–9, 18–19.

37. Demetz, *Prague in Danger*, pp. 151, 193. Theaters were closed throughout the Reich from 1 September 1944 until the end of the war.

38. Milan Kundera, "Prague: A Disappearing Poem," *Granta*, Vol. 17, September 1985. *The Trial* was in fact written in 1914–1915.

39. Information on performances from Padevět, *Průvodce protektorátní Prahou*.

40. Jaroslav Lopour, "Protektorátní Kníže Václav," *Národní filmový archiv revue*, 20 April 2016, at https://www.filmovyprehled.cz/cs/revue/detail/protektoratni-knize-vaclav (accessed 14 June 2019).

41. Demetz, *Prague in Danger*, p. 203.

42. David Chaloupka, "Nížina—film Leni Riefenstahl podle opery Eugena d'Alberta," *Opera plus*, 8 December 2017.

43. Figures from Doležal, *Česká kultura za Protektorátu*, p. 238; other information in this paragraph from Padevět, *Průvodce protektorátní Prahou*, pp. 515–27.

44. Olga Scheinpflugová, *Byla jsem na světě*, Prague: Mladá fronta, 1988, pp. 312–13.

45. Bořivoj Srba, "K historii fašistické perzekuce českého divadla v letech 1939–1945," *Otázky divadla a filmu*, No. 1, 1969, p. 164.

46. For a detailed discussion of theatrical censorship under the protectorate, see Olga Kovaříková, "Cenzura a její vliv na divadelní život v Protektorátu Čechy a Morava," Disertační práce, Pedagogická fakulta, Univerzita Karlova v Praze, 2013.

47. Doležal, *Česká kultura za Protektorátu*, p. 20.

48. Kovaříková, "Cenzura a její vliv," p. 105.

49. It was replaced by the repeated line "Náš pán zhynul" (Our lord perished), which is taken from the next stanza of the poem. See Karel Hynek Mácha, *Výbor z díla*, ed. Luisa Kasalická, Prague: L. Mazáč, 1942, p. 312; *Živý třpyt: dílo Karla Hynka Máchy*, ed. Luisa Kasalická, Prague: L. Mazáč, 1944, p. 107. A Družstevní práce edition from May 1941 retains Mácha's original line, so the censorship was likely a consequence of Heydrich's arrival in Prague in September 1941. I owe this information to Jindřich Toman.

50. Kovaříková, "Cenzura a její vliv," p. 120.

51. Quoted in Jarka M. Burian, *Leading Creators of Twentieth-Century Czech Theatre*, London: Routledge, 2013, p. 44.

52. Bořivoj Srba, "Divadlo D 34," *Česká divadelní encyklopedie.*

53. Piorecká and Piorecký, *Praha avantgardní*, pp. 352–354.

54. Burian, *Leading Creators of Twentieth-Century Czech Theatre*, p. 41.

55. Srp, *Adolf Hoffmeister*, p. 334.

56. Burian, *Leading Creators of Twentieth-Century Czech Theatre*, pp. 49–51. The word *vojna* can also mean war.

57. Karel Teige, "První výstava v D 37," in *Zápasy o smysl moderní tvorby*, p. 385.

58. "Předmluva," in *Ani labuť ani Lůna: sborník k 100. výročí smrti K. H. Mácha*, ed. Vítězslav Nezval, Prague: Concordia, 1995 (facsimile reprint of 1936 ed.), p. 7.

59. E. F. Burian, "Máchovo divadlo," in Nezval, *Ani labuť ani Lůna*, pp. 63–64.

60. See Jindřich Hořejší,' *Hudba na náměstí* (Music on the square), Prague: CIN, 1921; Jindřich Hořejší, *Korálový náhrdelník* (The coral necklace, 1923), Prague: SNKLU, 1961 (reprint); Jindřich Hořejší, *Den a noc* (Day and night), Prague: Janská, 1931.

61. Jindřich Hořejší, *Překlady*, Prague: SNKLU, 1965. On *Maldoror*, see *PC*, p. 243.

62. I discuss Martinů's *Julietta* in more detail in *PC*, pp. 341–44.

63. Vladimír Šmeral, *Bez studu jíti pražskou ulicí*, quoted in Kovaříková, "Cenzura a její vliv," p. 175; emphasis added.

64. Letter to Vítězslav Nezval, 7 November 1939, in Vítězslav Nezval, *Korespondence Vítězslava Nezvala: depeše z konce tisíciletí*, Prague: Ceskoslovenský spisovatel, 1981, p. 102.

65. Demetz, *Prague in Danger*, p. 153.

66. Adolf Hoffmeister, *Čas se nevrací!* Prague: Československý spisovatel, 1965, p. 30; emphasis added.

67. Hoffmeister, *Čas se nevrací!* pp. 50–51.

68. Joyce, *Finnegans Wake*, pp. 202–3.

69. Hoffmeister, *Čas se nevrací!* pp. 51–52.

70. Kundera, "Prague: A Disappearing Poem."

71. Nezval, *Alphabet*, p. 9.

72. Štyrský, "The Generation's Corner," in Benson and Forgács, *Between Worlds*, p. 676.

73. "Fragmenty z pozůstalosti," in Jindřich Štyrský, *Texty*, Prague: Argo, 2007, pp. 191–94. Alternative translations of all these 1939–1940 text fragments can be found in Jindřich Štyrský, *Dreamverse*, trans. Jed Slast, Prague: Twisted Spoon Press, 2018, pp. 222–31.

74. Štyrský, *Texty*, p. 190.

75. Štyrský, *Texty*, p. 187.

76. This is reproduced in Lenka Bydžovská and Karel Srp, *Jindřich Štyrský*, exh. cat., Prague: Argo/Galerie hlavního města Prahy, 2007, p. 534.

77. Štyrský, *Texty*, p. 188. The announcement was carried in *Lidové noviny*, 24 November 1939, p. 7.

78. Štyrský, *Texty*, p. 189. *Mayakovsky's Vest* is reproduced in Bydžovská and Srp, *Jindřich Štyrský*, p. 453.

79. Štyrský, *Texty*, pp. 189–91.

80. Quoted in Vojtěch Lahoda, "Divadlo světa," in Rousová, *Konec avantgardy?* p. 146.

81. The main exceptions were the essay "Jan Zrzavý—předchůdce [predecessor]" and the album *Moderní česká fotografie* (Modern Czech photography).

82. Lenka Bydžovská and Karel Srp, *Knihy s Toyen,* Prague: Akropolis, 2003, p. 68. Petr Ladman lists all the known titles to which Toyen contributed in the same volume.

83. "O Heislerovi a Toyen. Rozhovor se sestrou Jindřicha Heislera zaznamenal Jindřich Toman," 1983, in Jindřich Heisler, *Z kasemat spánku,* comp. František Šmejkal, Karel Srp, and Jindřich Toman, Prague: Torst, 1999, p. 367.

84. Vilém Mathesius, ed., *Co daly naše země Evropě a lidstvu,* Prague: Evropský literární klub, 1939.

85. František Kožík, *Největší z Pierotů,* 2 vols., Prague: Evropský literární klub, 1939; Francis Kozik, *The Great Debureau,* trans. Dora Round, New York: Farrar and Rinehart, 1940.

86. Demetz, *Prague in Danger,* pp. 91–94.

87. Heisler, *Z kasemat spánku,* p. 15. There is an English edition of this work: Toyen, *Specters of the Desert,* trans. Stephen Schwartz, Chicago: Black Swan Press, 1974.

88. Quoted in Jindřich Toman, "The Hope of Fire, the Freedom of Dreams: Jindřich Heisler in Prague and Paris, 1938–1953," in Jindřich Toman and Matthew S. Witkovsky, *Jindřich Heisler: Surrealism under Pressure 1938–1953,* exh. cat., Chicago: Art Institute of Chicago, 2012, p. 12.

89. Matthew S. Witkovsky, "Night Rounds: On the Photo-Poem 'From the Strongholds of Sleep,'" in Toman and Witkovsky, *Jindřich Heisler,* pp. 28–29.

90. See Susan Sontag, "Against Interpretation," in *Essays of the 1960s and 70s,* ed. David Lieff, New York: Library of America, 2013, pp. 10–20.

91. Jindřich Heisler, "On Illustration that Is Not Illustration," 1946, translated in Toman and Witkovsky, *Jindřich Heisler,* pp. 131–32; emphasis added.

92. Toman, "Hope of Fire," p. 13.

93. Other than in its original edition, of which only six copies are known to have survived, it was not published until 1977 (Jindřich Heisler, *Aniž by nastal viditelný pohyb,* ed. Věra Linhartová, Toronto: Sixty-Eight Publishers, 1977). The first domestic publication was in *Analogon* in 1992. It took another twenty years for the first English translation to appear in the catalog of the exhibition *Jindřich Heisler: Surrealism under Pressure* at the Art Institute of Chicago.

94. Toman, "Hope of Fire," p. 24.

95. Imported into Czech from Russian, the literal meaning of the word is self-publication.

96. For details, see Heisler, *Z kasemat spánku,* p. 432.

97. Heiting, *Czech and Slovak Photo Publications 1918–1989,* p. 258; Martin Parr and Gerry Badger, *The Photobook: A History,* Vol. 1, New York: Phaidon, 2004, p. 197. See also Krzysztof Fijalkowski, Michael Richardson, and Ian Walker, *Surrealism and Photography in Czechoslovakia,* London: Ashgate, 2016, pp. 67–83 (on "Needles"), 84–87 (on "Strongholds").

98. Quoted in Toman, "Hope of Fire," p. 14.

99. Toman, "Hope of Fire," p. 17. The album is reproduced in Heisler, *Z kasemat spánku,* pp. 145–59.

100. Quoted in Lenka Bydžovská, "Realita nadreality," in Rousová, *Konec avantgardy?* p. 232.

101. "O Heislerovi a Toyen," p. 366. Other information in this paragraph is from the same source.

102. Quoted in Toman, "Hope of Fire," p. 15. *Ze stejného těsta* literally means "from the same dough."

103. Toman, "Hope of Fire," p. 15. Anna tells the same story, without the detail of the siblings holding hands on the balcony, in "O Heislerovi a Toyen," p. 367.

104. "O Heislerovi a Toyen," p. 366.

105. Karel Teige, "Střelnice," in *Osvobozování života a poezie*, p. 89. This text is available in English as "Střelnice (The Shooting Range)," trans. William Hollister, in *Analogon*, No. 37, 2003, supplement "Anthology of Czech and Slovak Surrealism I," pp. xiii–xxi; and as "The Shooting Gallery," trans. Kathleen Hayes, in Karel Srp and Lenka Bydžovská with Alison de Lima Greene and Jan Mergl, *New Formations: Czech Avant-Garde Art and Modern Glass from the Roy and Mary Cullen Collection*, exh. cat., Houston: Museum of Fine Arts, 2011, pp. 235–43.

106. See Toman and Witkovsky, *Jindřich Heisler*, pp. 70–83.

107. Toman, "Hope of Fire," p. 17.

108. Teige, "Střelnice," pp. 87–98.

109. Theodor W. Adorno, *Prisms*, trans. Samuel Weber and Shierry Weber, London: Spearman, 1967, p. 34.

110. Teige, "Střelnice," pp. 96–97.

111. Breton, *Manifesto of Surrealism*, pp. 27–28.

112. Michalová, *Karel Teige*, p. 429, quoting Teige's essay "K českému překladu Prokletých básníků" (1946). Michalová's chapter on the collages (pp. 425–40) is one of the most comprehensive discussions available in English. See also Toman, *Foto/montáž tiskem*, pp. 324–27; Vojtěch Lahoda, "Karel Teige's Collages, 1935–1951: The Erotic Object, the Social Object, and Surrealist Landscape Art," in *Karel Teige 1900–1951: L'Enfant Terrible of the Czech Modernist Avant-garde*, ed. Eric Dluhosch and Rostislav Švácha, Cambridge, MA: MIT Press, 1999; Vojtěch Lahoda, "Teige's Violation: The Collages of Karel Teige, the Visual Concepts of Avant-garde and René Magritte," in Rumjana Dačeva, Vojtěch Lahoda, and Karel Srp, *Karel Teige, Surrealistické koláže 1935–1951*, exh. cat., Prague: Středoevropská galerie, 1994; Vojtěch Lahoda, "The Architecture of the Fragment, On Collages (1935–1951)," in *Karel Teige: Architettura, Poesia: Praga 1900–1951*, exh. cat., ed. Manuela Castagnara Codeluppi, Milan: Elekta, 1996.

113. Quoted in Michalová, *Karel Teige*, p. 432.

114. André Breton, *Nadja*, trans. Richard Howard, New York: Grove Press, 1960, p. 160.

115. See the discussion of Skupina 42 in the manuscript version of Teige's 1946 article "Osud umělecké avantgardy v obou světových válkách," in his *Osvobozovaní života a poezie*, pp. 505–6.

116. Jindřich Chalupecký, "Svět v němž žijeme," in *Skupina 42: Antologie*, ed. Zdeněk Pešat and Eva Petrová, Brno: Atlantis, 2000, p. 85. This essay is also available in English as "The World We Live in," trans. Kathleen Hayes, in Srp et al., *New Formations*, pp. 226–31.

117. František Gross, diary entry, cited in Eva Petrová et al., *Skupina 42*, exh. cat., Prague: Akropolis/GHMP, 1998, p. 67.

118. For details, see Pešat and Petrová, *Skupina 42: Antologie*, pp. 463–64.

119. The catalog is reproduced in facsimile in Anna Pravdová, "Pokus o rekonstrukci výstavy," in Rousová, *Konec avantgardy?* pp. 310–16.

120. Adolf Hoffmeister, "Export kultury," *Kulturní politika*, Vol. 1, No. 21, 1946, p. 3, quoted in Anna Pravdová, "Organizovaný vývoz kulturních hodnot: Výstava Art tchécoslovaque 1938–1946 a české umění v Paříži v roce 1946," in Rousová, *Konec avantgardy?* p. 300.

121. Jindřich Chalupecký, "Konec moderní doby," in *České umění 1938–1989: programy/kritické texty/dokumenty*, ed. Jiří Ševčík, Pavlína Morganová, and Dagmar Dušková, Prague: Academia, 2001, pp. 71–72.

122. Chalupecký, "Konec moderní doby," p. 81.

123. Jindřich Chalupecký, "Teze," manuscript, 19 September 1943, in Pešat and Petrová, *Skupina 42: Antologie*, p. 23.

124. Chalupecký, "Svět v němž žijeme," pp. 85–86.

125. For reproductions, see Petrová et al., *Skupina 42*, pp. 48, 193; Marie Klimešová, *Věci umění, věci doby: Skupina 42*, exh. cat., Prague: Arbor vitae, 2011, pp. 60, 104, 68, 69, 166.

126. Kamil Lhoták, in *Praha a okolí v obrazek členů Umělecké besedy*, exh. cat., Prague: Umělecká beseda, 1943, quoted in Pešat and Petrová, *Skupina 42: Antologie*, p. 142.

127. Miroslav Hák, *Holešovice* (1943), and František Hudeček, *Ulice, kde si hrály děti* (1943), reproduced in Klimešová, *Věci umění, věci doby*, pp. 72, 54, respectively.

128. Reproduced in Anna Fulíková and Nina Machková, *Kamil Lhoták, sic itur ad astra: Obrazy, básně, přátelé/Paintings, Poems, Friends*, exh. cat., Prague: Retro Gallery, 2015, p. 54.

129. Reproduced in L. H. Augustin, *Kamil Lhoták*, Prague: Academia, 2000, pp. 22–23, 104.

130. Quoted in Fulíková and Machková, *Kamil Lhoták*, p. 35.

131. Chalupecký, "Svět v němž žijeme," p. 84; Bohumír Matal, *Člověk ve městě, město v člověku*, reproduced in Klimešová, *Věci umění, věci doby*, p. 149.

132. Vojtěch Lahoda develops his argument about the art of this period in his article "(Ne)přirozený svět," in Rousová, *Konec avantgardy?* pp. 201–22.

133. Vítězslav Nezval, *Pražský chodec*, Prague: Borový, 1938; Charles Baudelaire, *The Painter of Modern Life and Other Essays*, trans. Jonathan Mayne, New York: Phaidon, 2005.

134. *Noční chodec II* is reproduced in Petrová et al., *Skupina 42*, p. 57. This book contains other *Noční chodec* paintings or drawings on pp. 71–73, 115–16, 194, as do Klimešová, *Věci umění, věci doby*, pp. 48–49, 112, 115, 119, and Pešat and Petrová, *Skupina 42: Antologie*, pp. 21, 97, 162.

135. Unpublished text for František Hudeček exhibition catalog, 1944, in Pešat and Petrová, *Skupina 42: Antologie*, p. 161.

136. Lahoda, "(Ne)přirozený svět," pp. 203–4.

137. Reproduced in Augustin, *Kamil Lhoták*, p. 135. Trnka's *Perák a SS* is available at https://www.youtube.com/watch?v=P9xCsOpeCM4 (accessed 19 March 2020).

138. Susan Sontag, *On Photography*, New York: Picador, 1977, pp. 51–52.

139. Lahoda, "(Ne)přirozený svět," p. 205. The photograph is also reproduced in Petrová et al., *Skupina 42*, p. 149, and analyzed in Fijalkowski et al., *Surrealism and Photography*, pp. 103–7. For the motif of emptiness in Toyen, see Jindřich Toman, "The Woman Is Hollow: Toyen's Melancholy In-Sights," *Umění*, Vol. 66, No. 4, 2018, pp. 283–95.

140. Reproduced in Petrová et al., *Skupina 42*, p. 150.

Chapter 7: As Time Goes By

1. Adolf Hoffmeister, *Unwilling Tourist*, trans. Don Perris, London: John Lane the Bodley Head, 1942, p. 118.

2. Hoffmeister abandoned painting in 1923. He briefly resumed in the early 1930s but stopped again because, he said, "the strength of his talent lay elsewhere." Srp, *Adolf Hoffmeister*, p. 113.

3. See, respectively, https://cs.wikipedia.org/wiki/Adolf_Hoffmeister and https://fr.wikipedia.org/wiki/Adolf_Hoffmeister (both accessed 25 June 2019).

4. Justine Lacoste, "Adolf Hoffmeister, homme de plumes et d'encres," *l'Humanité*, 6 January 2007.

5. "Baker Street č. 9," in Adolf Hoffmeister, *Kaleidoskop*, Prague: Labyrint, 2004, p. 18 (from his book *Cambridge—Praha*, Prague: Alois Srdce, 1926).

6. Otakar Štorch-Marien, *Sladko je žít*, Prague: Aventinum, 1992, p. 303.

7. The interviews were subsequently published in book form as Adolf Hoffmeister, *Piš jak slyšíš, kniha interviewů*, Prague: Družstevní práce, 1931.

8. For a fuller discussion of Aventinum and Kmen, see *CB*, pp. 202–8.

9. A full list of the books to which Hoffmeister contributed as author, translator, illustrator, or designer can be found in Srp, *Adolf Hoffmeister*, pp. 362–75.

10. Václav Holzknecht, *Jaroslav Ježek a Osvobozené divadlo*, Prague: SNKLHU, 1957, quoted in Srp, *Adolf Hoffmeister*, p. 139.

11. Hoffmeister contributed to the only two issues, both of which are in *Zvěrokruh 1/ Zvěrokruh 2/Surrealismus v ČSR/Mezinárodní bulletin surrealismu/Surrealismus*, Prague: Torst, 2004. Hoffmeister's contributions are on pp. 36–37, 43, 79–81, and 83–86.

12. *Výstava Poesie 1932*, exh. cat., Prague: SVU Mánes, 1932. Hoffmeister was one of six members of the exhibition committee, alongside Toyen, Muzika, Makovský, Šíma, and Bedřich Stefan.

13. Ilya Ehrenburg, quoted in Mark Polizzotti, *Revolution of the Mind: The Life of André Breton*, New York: Da Capo, 1997, p. 418; Adolf Hoffmeister, "Milý příteli Iljo Ehrenburgu . . . ," *Volné směry*, Vol. 30, No. 6, December 1933.

14. Adolf Hoffmeister, *Povrch pětiletky*, Prague: Sfinx, 1931, pp. 5–6.

15. Hoffmeister, *Povrch pětiletky*, pp. 51–58.

16. Martin Hoffmeister, interviewed in Aviva Lori, "Meisterpiece," *Haaretz*, 13 August 2010.

17. Vítězslav Nezval, *Z mého života*, Prague: Československý spisovatel, 1961, p. 234. The references are to Apollinaire's story "Le passant de Prague," which I discuss in *PC*, pp. 33–43.

18. Piorecká and Piorecký, *Praha avantgardní*, p. 144 (quoting Karel Honzík, *Ze života avantgardy*, Prague: Československý spisovatel, 1963, who wrongly dates Le Corbusier's visit as 1929). Le Corbusier visited Prague in May 1911, January–February 1925, and October 1928. In spring 1935 he spent several weeks in Zlín (see *PC*, pp. 162–63).

19. Hoffmeister, *Čas se nevrací!* p. 188. He doesn't give the exact date of Barr's visit.

20. Hoffmeister, *Kalendář*, Prague: Aventinum, 1930, pp. 120–24, quoted in Srp, *Adolf Hoffmeister*, pp. 75, 82.

21. Adolf Hoffmeister, *Hors d'oeuvres: feuilletony, karikatury, epigramy*, Prague: Aventinum, 1927, p. 50, quoted in Srp, *Adolf Hoffmeister*, p. 60.

22. Hoffmeister, *Hors d'oeuvres*, quoted in Miroslav Lamač, *Výtvarné dílo Adolfa Hoffmeistera*, Prague: Nakladatelství československých výtvarných umělců, 1966 (unpaginated).

23. See, for example, *Náš Vítek (Vítězslav Nezval)* (1929), in Srp, *Adolf Hoffmeister*, p. 83.

24. *Jaroslav Seifert* (1930), reproduced in František Šmejkal, *Hoffmeisterova ironická kronika doby*, exh. cat., Litoměřice: Severočeská galerie výtvarného umění/Památník Terezín, 2016, p. 52.

25. These are reproduced in Srp, *Adolf Hoffmeister*, pp. 86 (*Avantgarda 1930*), 90 (*Ten-Ta-Toyen*), 61 (*E. F. Burian*), 62 (*Letos v létě*), and 63 (*13 obrázků z Paříže*).

26. Hoffmeister, *Karikaturisté a karikovaní* (1934), quoted in *V okovech smíchu: Karikatura a české umění 1900–1950*, exh. cat., ed. Ondřej Chrobák and Tomáš Winter, Prague: Gallery, 2006, p. 73.

27. Adolf Hoffmeister, speech at opening of exhibition of Hoffmeister and Antonín Pelc, Benešov, February 1935, quoted in Chrobák and Winter, *V okovech smíchu*, p. 73.

28. Reproduced in Šmejkal, *Hoffmeisterova ironická kronika*, pp. 80 (*Tichá práce*), 82 (*Umění ve Třetí říši*), and 78 (*Španělskou zemi mám tak rád*).

29. S. K. Neumann, "Dnešní Mánes," *Tvorba*, Vol. 12, No. 20, 1937.

30. Compare *S. K. Neumann* and *Umrlčí hlavy týdne*, in Srp, *Adolf Hoffmeister*, pp. 135 and 146, respectively. *Simplicus* ran Hoffmeister's cartoon *SA—SS—SOS* on the Night of the Long Knives instead (reproduced in Srp, p. 147). I discuss the context of the Neumann cartoon more fully in *CB*, pp. 217–20, and *PC*, pp. 381–83.

31. The name reflected that of the German magazine *Simplicissimus*, whose Jewish editor Thomas Theodor Heine fled to Prague in 1933. *Simplicus* became a German-only publication under the name *Simpl* in September 1934.

32. I discuss Heartfield at greater length in *PC*, pp. 230–31, 270–79, 285–86, 356–64.

33. Quoted in "Voyage of the St. Louis," USHMM, *Holocaust Encyclopedia*.

34. Quoted in "Godal, Eric," in *Encyclopedia of America's Response to the Holocaust*, David S. Wyman Institute for Holocaust Studies.

35. Benjamin, *Arcades Project*, pp. 25–26.

36. Teju Cole, "Go Down Moses," 5 September 2019, at https://www.facebook.com /Teju-Cole-200401352198/ (accessed 5 September 2019). He is quoting Michael Taussig, *Walter Benjamin's Grave*, Chicago: University of Chicago Press, 2006. See also *PC*, pp. 286–87.

37. Aragon to Hoffmeister, 29 April 1938, quoted in Anna Pravdová, *Zastihla je noc: čeští výtvarní umělci ve Francii 1938–1945*, Prague: Národní galerie/Opus, 2009, p. 43. I am much indebted to Pravdová's book for what follows. I discuss Aragon in *PC*, pp. 364–74.

38. Hoffmeister, "O Československu v Paříži a v Londýně," unidentified press cutting in Archiv Hoffmeister, Prague, quoted in Pravdová, *Zastihla je noc*, pp. 43–44.

39. Publicity flyer, reproduced in Pravdová, *Zastihla je noc*, p. 44.

40. 1938 ISCM festival brochure, p. 12, quoted in Eugene Gates and Karla Hartl, "Vítězslava Kaprálová: A Remarkable Voice in 20th-Century Czech Music," *Tempo*, New Series, No. 213, 2000, p. 23.

41. Bohuslav Martinů, "Mezinárodní festival v Londýně," *Lidové noviny*, Vol. 46, No. 322, 28 June 1938, p. 7; Jiří Mucha, *Au seuil de la nuit*, trans. Françoise Tabery and Karel Tabery, La Tour d'Aigues: Éditions de l'aube, 1991, p. 140.

42. Hoffmeister states this in a typescript autobiography in Archiv Hoffmeister, cited in Pravdová, *Zastihla je noc*, p. 22. This differs substantially from the account of his fictional counterpart Jan Prokop's struggles to exit the protectorate in *Unwilling Tourist*, pp. 9–22.

43. Padevět, *Průvodce Protektorátní Prahou*, p. 249. For more on Jaroslav/Jaroslaus Nachtmann, see Jirásková, *Stručná zpráva*, pp. 68–78.

44. Hoffmeister to Lilly Rohne, 16 July 1939, quoted in Pravdová, *Zastihla je noc*, p. 22. Other details in this paragraph are from the same source, which draws on Hoffmeister's unpublished diaries.

45. Martin Hoffmeister, in Lori, "Meisterpiece."

46. Shawn Clybor, "Laughter and Hatred Are Neighbors: Adolf Hoffmeister and E. F. Burian in Stalinist Czechoslovakia, 1948–1956," *East European Politics and Societies*, Vol. 26, No. 3, 2012, p. 595.

47. Lenka Reinerová, "La Maison," in Hoffmeister, *Kaleidoskop*, p. 286.

48. Lenka Reinerová, *Bez adresy: neskutečně skutečné příběhy*, Prague: Městká knihovna, 2019, p. 25. I draw on this work extensively in what follows.

49. Reinerová, *Bez adresy*, pp. 8–9.

50. Interview by Irena Jirků, "Lenka Reinerová: Život je nepochopitelný, někdy prapodivný," *Sanquis*, No. 46, 2006, p. 66. On Herzfelde and the *Arbeiter-Illustrierte-Zeitung*, see *PC*, pp. 270–73.

51. Reinerová, *Bez adresy*, pp. 16–22. See also interview by Jiří Hrabě, "Lenka Reinerová—Moje století," *Vital*, 15 June 2008; Lenka Reinerová, *Kavárna nad Prahou*, Prague: Labyrint, 2001, pp. 15–16, 40–48.

52. Reinerová, *Kavárna nad Prahou*, p. 15.

53. I discuss the history of Czech artists in Paris in more detail in *PC*, pp. 170–79.

54. See Pravdová, *Zastihla je noc*, pp. 28–29.

55. Quoted in Pravdová, *Zastihla je noc*, p. 28.

56. Ripka went into exile for a second time and died in London in 1958. Sergey Ingr was minister of national defense in Beneš's London government. He also went into a second exile after the 1948 KSČ coup and died in Paris in 1954.

57. Mucha, *Au seuil de la nuit*, p. 64.

58. I tell Jiří and Vítka's story in *PC*, pp. 339–55.

59. For more details, see Pravdová, *Zastihla je noc*, pp. 30–32.

60. Adolf Hoffmeister, "Malíř Alfons Mucha," *Světový rozhled*, No. 3, 1 August 1939, p. 74.

61. "Šprým zemědělce Jágra: Seychely? Příští slečnu vezmu na pole u Kladna," Blesk.cz, 4 August 2015.

62. "Švermov," Kladno_minulé, 15 July 2008.

63. The committee comprised Hoffmeister, F. C. Weiskopf, and Laco Novomeský. Weiskopf traveled to the United States in June 1939, intending to spend a month there raising funds, but he ended up staying. Novomeský never got to Paris. Lenka Reinerová called Hoffmeister the "soul of the whole project" (Jirků interview, "Lenka Reinerová").

64. Reinerová, *Bez adresy*, p. 26.

65. Reinerová, "La Maison," p. 286.

66. Ivo Ducháček, typescript diary 1939, quoted in Pravdová, *Zastihla je noc*, p. 50.

67. Reinerová, "La Maison," p. 287.

68. Reinerová, *Bez adresy*, p. 25.

69. Letter to Lilly Rohne, 30 August 1939, quoted in Pravdová, *Zastihla je noc*, p. 50.

70. Quoted in Pravdová, *Zastihla je noc*, p. 52.

71. Reinerová, *Bez adresy*, p. 32.

72. Police report, 18 September 1939. This and other details in the paragraph are from Pravdová, *Zastihla je noc*, pp. 53–56.

73. Adolf Hoffmeister, *Vězení*, Prague: Československý spisovatel, 1969, pp. 10–11. See also Hoffmeister, *Kaleidoskop*, pp. 76–79 (along with drawings of the cell).

74. Hoffmeister, *Vězení*, p. 75.

75. Hoffmeister, *Vězení*, p. 27.

76. Hoffmeister, *Unwilling Tourist*, pp. 5–7.

77. Hoffmeister, *Unwilling Tourist*, pp. 37–39.

78. Pravdová, *Zastihla je noc*, p. 64. See, for example, his *Gilotina (Zeď vězení)* and *Vzpomínka na zeď v cele*, reproduced in Lenka Bydžovská, Vojtěch Lahoda, and Karel Srp, *Černá slunce: Odvrácená strana modernity*, exh. cat., Prague: Arbor Vitae, 2012, pp. 290–91.

79. Alén Diviš, "Vzpomínky na pařížské vězení Santé," *Revolver Revue*, No. 17, August 1991, pp. 84–85.

80. "Novoročenka pro Voskovce, Wericha a Ježka na roce 1939," 1938, reproduced in Srp, *Adolf Hoffmeister*, p. 166.

81. Lyrics from http://www.velkyzpevnik.cz/zpevnik/werich-voskovec-jezek/nikdy-nic -nikdo-nema (accessed 11 July 2019).

82. Michael Beckerman, "The Dark Blue Exile of Jaroslav Ježek," *Music and Politics*, Vol. 2, No. 2, Summer 2008.

83. Letter to Gustav Janouch, January 1939, in František Cinger, *Šťastné blues aneb z deníku Jaroslava Ježka*, Prague: BVD, 2006, p. 147, as translated in Beckerman, "Dark Blue Exile."

84. Beckerman, "Dark Blue Exile."

85. Letter to Lilly Rohne, 12 March 1940, quoted in Pravdová, *Zastihla je noc*, p. 66.

86. Reinerová, *Bez adresy*, p. 38.

87. Hoffmeister, *Unwilling Tourist*, pp. 79–80.

88. Hoffmeister, *Unwilling Tourist*, p. 82. Hoffmeister fictionalized some place names: Damigny became Sanglière, and Bassens became Cresson.

89. Quoted in Aljean Harmetz, *Round up the Usual Suspects: The Making of Casablanca: Bogart, Bergman, and World War II*, New York: Hyperion, 1992, p. 210.

90. Harmetz, *Round up the Usual Suspects*, p. 214.

91. Letter to Lilly Rohne, 26 August 1940, quoted in Pravdová, *Zastihla je noc*, p. 70.

92. David Vaughan, interview with Lenka Reinerová, "'Here's Looking at You Kid . . .': A Czech Girl in Wartime Casablanca," Radio Prague, 21 April 2005.

93. Reinerová, *Bez adresy*, p. 52. "Join the Jews and see the world" is in English in the original.

94. Letter to Jiří Voskovec and Jan Werich, 8 September 1940, in Jan Werich, *Listování: úryvky z korespondence a článků*, Prague: Brána, 2003, p. 46.

95. Hoffmeister, *Unwilling Tourist*, p. 113.

96. Letter to Voskovec and Werich, 8 September 1940.

97. See correspondence in Werich, *Listování*, pp. 40–45.

98. Hoffmeister, *Unwilling Tourist*, pp. 113–14.

99. Hoffmeister, *Unwilling Tourist*, pp. 120–21.

100. André Breton, *Martinique: Snake Charmer*, trans. David W. Seaman, Austin: University of Texas Press, 2008, p. 66.

101. Varian Fry, *Surrender on Demand*, New York: Random House, 1945, quoted in Martica Sawin, *Surrealism in Exile and the Beginning of the New York School*, Cambridge, MA: MIT Press, 1997, p. 143. For more on the ERC and Fry, see Palmier, *Weimar in Exile*, pp. 474–76.

102. Victor Serge, *Notebooks 1936–1947*, trans. Mitchell Abidor and Richard Greeman, New York: New York Review Books, 2019, pp. 49, 52–53.

103. Michel Frizot, *Germaine Krull*, exh. cat., Paris: Hazan/Jeu de Paume, 2015, p. 256. See Germaine Krull, *Métal*, Paris: Calavas, 1928, reprint, Cologne: Ann and Jürgen Wilde, 2003; Kim Sichel, *Germaine Krull: Photographer of Modernity*, Cambridge, MA: MIT Press, 1999.

104. Germaine Krull and Jacques Rémy, *Un voyage: Marseille–Rio 1941*, Paris: Stock, 2019, pp. 126–30, 110.

105. Claude Lévi-Strauss, *Tristes Tropiques*, trans. John Russell, New York: Atheneum, 1964, p. 26. The letters are published in Claude Lévi-Strauss, *Look, Listen, Read*, trans. Brian C. J. Singer, New York: HarperCollins, 1997, pp. 143–51.

106. Serge, *Notebooks*, p. 64.

107. Serge, *Notebooks*, p. 66.

108. Serge, *Notebooks*, p. 70.

109. Serge, *Notebooks*, p. 52.

110. Lévi-Strauss, *Tristes Tropiques*, p. 25.

111. Krull and Rémy, *Un voyage*, pp. 117–19.

112. Lévi-Strauss, *Tristes Tropiques*, p. 27.

113. Serge, *Notebooks*, pp. 52–53.

114. Serge, *Notebooks*, pp. 55–56.

115. Krull and Rémy, *Un voyage*, pp. 134, 142, 151.

116. Breton, *Martinique*, p. 88.

117. Breton, *Martinique*, pp. 87–88.

118. Breton, *Martinique*, p. 90; Aimé Césaire, quoted in Polizzotti, *Revolution of the Mind*, p. 498.

119. Pelc, quoted in Pravdová, *Zastihla je noc*, p. 73.

120. The stamp is reproduced in Alois Dušek et al., *Příručka pro sběratele československých poštovních známek a celin*, Prague: Nakladatelství dopravy a spojů, 1988, p. 260. All information about postage stamps is from this source unless otherwise noted.

121. Breton, *Martinique*, p. 40.

122. Sawin, *Surrealism in Exile*, p. 132.

123. Breton, *Martinique*, p. 40.

124. Breton, *Martinique*, p. 62.

125. Breton, *Martinique*, p. 66.

126. Serge, *Notebooks*, p. 62.

127. Undated letter (early January 1942) to Lilly Rohne, cited in Pravdová, *Zastihla je noc*, p. 72.

128. Hoffmeister's letter to his mother, 2 January 1941, cited in Pravdová, *Zastihla je noc*, p. 72.

129. Egon Hostovský, *The Hideout*, trans. Fern Long, London: Pushkin Press, 2017.

130. Lévi-Strauss, *Tristes Tropiques*, p. 36.

131. Figures are from Maurice Davie's *Refugees in America*, an official US government report published in 1946, as summarized in Palmier, *Weimar in Exile*, p. 479.

132. Jonathan Glancey, "Goodbye to Berlin," *Guardian*, 12 May 2003. See also Sloan Schrage, "Dugway's German Village Shows How Far Allies Were Willing to Go to End WWII," KSL.com, 5 November 2015.

133. Palmier, *Weimar in Exile*, p. 481. Other information is from the same source.

134. I discuss Martinů in more detail in *PC*, 339–55.

135. Review by Olin Downes, *New York Times*, 6 January 1940.

136. I discuss Novotná more fully in *PC*, pp. 337–39.

137. "Holzbachová, Mira," in *Česká divadelní encyklopedie*.

138. *Amerika země Indiánů* (America, Land of the Indians, 1963), *Indiánské pohádky* (Indian Tales, 1971), and *Děti tropického slunce* (Children of the Tropical Sun, 1978).

139. See Bengt Jangfeldt, "Roman Jakobson in Sweden 1940–41," *Cahiers de l'ILSL*, No. 9, 1997, pp. 146–49.

140. Stephen Rudy, "Roman Jakobson: A Brief Chronology," at https://libraries.mit.edu /archives/research/collections/collections-mc/mc72.html#ref8425 (accessed 30 August 2019).

141. "Ernst Cassirer (1874–1945)," *Internet Encyclopedia of Philosophy*.

142. For details, see Henry Kučera, "Roman Jakobson," *Language*, Vol. 59, No. 4, 1983, p. 881.

143. Quoted in Kučera, "Roman Jakobson," p. 878.

144. Details from Rudy, "Roman Jakobson,"

145. Quoted in "Jakobson, Roman Osipovich," *YIVO Encyclopedia of Jews in Eastern Europe*. On Jakobson, see also Jindřich Toman, *The Magic of a Common Language: Jakobson, Mathesius, Trubetzkoy and the Prague Linguistic Circle*, Cambridge, MA: MIT Press, 1995.

146. The Habich Palace still stands, but the façade has been hugely disfigured by restorations after 2000. See "Byl jednou jeden dům," *Lidové noviny*, 26 May 2018.

147. See Josef Havlíček, *Návrhy a stavby*, Prague: Státní nakladatelství technické literatury, 1964, p. 120.

148. See *PC*, pp. 332–34, and the "War and the Czech Pavilion" section of the New York Public Library exhibition "The World of Tomorrow: Exploring the 1939–40 World's Fair Collection," at http://exhibitions.nypl.org/biblion/worldsfair/moment-time-brink-war/story /story-czech (accessed 18 January 2021).

149. "Holzbachová, Mira," in *Česká divadelní encyklopedie*; the photograph is reproduced in the New York Public Library "War and the Czech Pavilion" exhibition.

150. Ladislav Sutnar, *Visual Design in Action*, ed. Reto Caduff and Steven Heller, Zurich: Lars Müller Publishers, 2015 (facsimile reprint), p. c/14. On Sutnar, see Iva Janáková, ed., *Ladislav Sutnar—Praha—New York—Design in Action*, exh. cat., Prague: Argo, 2003. I discuss Sutnar's time in America more fully in *PC*, pp. 333–35.

151. See Marta Filipová, "Krásná Jizba: Design for Democracy, 1927–1948," *CRAACE*, 9 March 2019.

152. Zachary Doleshal, "Imagining Baťa in the World of Tomorrow: The Baťa Company, Czechoslovakia, and the 1939 New York World's Fair," in *Company Towns of the Baťa Concern: History—Cases—Architecture*, ed. Ondřej Ševeček and Martin Jemelka, Stuttgart: Franz Steiner Verlag, 2013, pp. 75–77. Other information in this paragraph is from the same source.

153. Ladislav Sutnar and Knud Löndberg Holm, *Designing Information*, New York: Whitney Publications, 1947.

154. In Iva Knobloch, ed., *Ladislav Sutnar: Americké Venuše (U.S. Venus)*, exh. cat., Prague: Arbor Vitae, 2011, pp. 197–98.

155. Quoted in Barry Muskat, "In Wright's Shadow: The Legacy of Jaroslav Polivka," *Buffalo Spree*, November–December 2000, at https://www.buffalospree.com/buffalospreemagazine /archives/2000_1112/111200architecture.html (accessed 18 January 2021).

156. Dave Weinstein, "Visionaries on the Wing," Eichler Network, n.d.

157. Ivan Margolius, *Architects + Engineers = Structures*, Chichester, UK: Wiley-Academy, 2002, p. 43.

158. Blair Kamin, "Frank Lloyd Wright's Tower Worthy of Debate, and a Trip," *Chicago Tribune*, 23 April 2014.

159. Christiane Zehl Romero, "Anna Seghers, 1900–1983," Jewish Women's Archive, *The Encyclopedia of Jewish Women*.

160. Serge, *Notebooks*, p. 83.

161. Serge, *Notebooks*, pp. 89–91.

162. Rubén Gallo, "Who Killed Leon Trotsky?" *Princeton University Library Chronicle*, Vol. 75, No. 1, Autumn 2013, pp. 109–18.

163. Segel, *Egon Erwin Kisch*, p. 62. They moved to the Avenida Tamaulipas, also in Condesa, in 1942.

164. Palmier, *Weimar in Exile*, pp. 578–79. I am grateful to Andrea Orzoff for information on Das Freie Buch and the Heinrich Heine Club.

165. See, for example, Miroslav Šiška, "Podivná cesta Andrého Simona k šibenici," Novinky. cz, 9 December 2018.

166. Arthur Koestler, *The Invisible Writing: An Autobiography*, Boston: Beacon Press, 1954, p. 333.

167. María Montserrat, Farías Barba, Marco Santiago Mondragón, and Viridiana Zavala Rivera, "Lena Bergner: From the Bauhaus to Mexico," *Bauhaus Imaginista Journal*, Issue 2, 2019, at http://www.bauhaus-imaginista.org/articles/2485/lena-bergner-from-the-bauhaus-to-mexico (accessed 15 September 2019). "Metro" is illustrated and discussed there.

168. For examples, see Pablo Lazo, "Dislocating Modernity: Two Projects by Hannes Meyer in Mexico," *AA Files*, No. 47, Summer 2002, pp. 57–63.

169. Art Institute of Chicago website, cited in Menachem Wecker, "Did Mexican Artists Produce the First Images of the Holocaust?" *Forward*, 12 November 2016.

170. Hannes Meyer to Käte Duncker, 16 November 1940, quoted in Georg Leidenberger, "'Alles z'Unterobsi': Hannes Meyer and German Communist Exiles in Mexico," p. 14, at https://www.academia.edu/37306841/Alles_zUnterobsi_._Hannes_Meyer_and_German_Communist_Exiles_in_Mexico (accessed 31 August 2019).

171. Quoted in Polizzotti, *Revolution of the Mind*, p. 454.

172. Péter Baki, Colin Ford, and George Szirtes, *Eyewitness: Hungarian Photography in the Twentieth Century*, exh. cat., London: Royal Academy of Arts, 2011, p. 229.

173. Salomon Grimberg, "Jacqueline Lamba: From Darkness, with Light," *Woman's Art Journal*, Vol. 22, No. 1, 2001, p. 10.

174. Sawin, *Surrealism in Exile*, discusses *DYN* at length.

175. Varo died in 1963, Rahon in 1987, Horna in 2000, Séjourné in 2003, and Carrington in 2011.

176. Alexxa Gotthardt, "When Mexico Became a Surrealist Mecca," *Artsy*, 25 June 2019. See also Susan L. Aberth, *Leonora Carrington: Surrealism, Alchemy and Art*, Burlington, VT: Lund Humphries, 2004, pp. 59–60.

177. Héctor Antonio Sánchez, "Un aire más puro: itinerario de Benjamin Péret," *Casa del Tiempo*, Vol. 2, Series 5, April 2015, p. 24.

178. Reinerová is listed on the SS *Serpa Pinto* passenger list as "Reiner, Helene, 26, Checa, Israelita, periodista." USHMM, Holocaust Survivors and Victims Database, at https://resources.ushmm.org/vlpnamelistimages/ReferenceCollection/AC0367/AC0367.PDF (accessed 18 September 2019).

179. Hrabě interview, "Lenka Reinerová—Moje století."

180. Lenka Reinerová, "Zweite Landung in Mexiko" (1996), quoted in Hélène Leclerc, "L'exil mexicain de Lenka Reinerová," *Études Germaniques*, Vol. 63, No. 4, 2008, p. 762.

181. Magdaléna Trojanová, "Časopis 'El Checoslovaco en México' v letech 1942–1945," Disertační práce, Univerzita Karlova v Praze, 2011.

182. Lenka Reinerová, *Čekárny mého života*, Prague: Labyrint, 2007, pp. 40–41.

183. Lenka Reinerová, *Hranice uzavřeny*, Prague: Mladá fronta, 1956, pp. 191–92, quoted in Trojanová, "Časopis 'El Checoslovaco en México,'" p. 71.

184. "Životní příběh Lenky Reinerové, poslední německy píšící pražské autorky," Česká televize, 2001, quoted in Trojanová, "Časopis 'El Checoslovaco en México,'" p. 70.

185. Egon Erwin Kisch, *Entdeckungen in Mexiko*, Mexico City: El Libro Libre, 1945. One of the sketches, "An Indian Village under the Star of David," is translated in Segel, *Egon Erwin Kisch*, pp. 365–72.

186. Kisch, "Indian Village under the Star of David," pp. 366, 371.

187. Reinerová, *Kavárna nad Prahou*, p. 11.

188. Reinerová, *Kavárna nad Prahou*, pp. 72–73.

189. See Segel, *Egon Erwin Kisch*, p. 88, nn. 64, 68.

190. Jennifer E. Michaels, "Migrations and Diasporas. German Writers in Mexican Exile. Egon Erwin Kisch's and Anna Seghers' Promotion of Cross-Cultural Understanding," *Studia Theodisca*, Vol. 19, 2012, p. 20.

191. Reinerová, *Kavárna nad Prahou*, pp. 73–74 (ellipses in original).

192. "Rozloučení s E. E. Kischem," *Rudé právo*, No. 81, 6 April 1948, p. 1.

193. Reinerová, *Kavárna nad Prahou*, p. 68.

194. Reinerová, *Bez adresy*, p. 75.

195. Hrabě interview, "Lenka Reinerová—Moje století."

196. Jirků interivew, "Lenka Reinerová."

197. Reinerová, *Kavárna nad Prahou*, p. 49.

198. Interview by David Vaughan, "Lenka Reinerova—A Writer Who Keeps the Rich Tradition of Prague German Literature Alive," Radio Prague, 22 August 2004.

199. Hrabě interview, "Lenka Reinerová—Moje století."

200. Anna Fodorová, "Mourning by Proxy: Notes on a Conference, Empty Graves and Silence," *Psychodynamic Practice*, Vol. 11, No. 3, 2005, pp. 301–10. Fodorová has since published a memoir about her mother: *Lenka*, Prague: Labyrint, 2020.

201. Schonberg, *Osvobozené*, p. 390.

202. "Exhibition 228: War Caricatures by Hoffmeister and Peel," at moma.org. See also Anna Pravdivá, "Anti-Fascist Caricatures by Adolf Hoffmeister and Antonín Pelc at MoMA in 1943," Parts 1 and 2, *MoMA Post*, 4 and 25 January 2017.

203. "Museum of Modern Art Opens Exhibition of War Caricatures by Czechoslovakian Artists," MoMA press release, 5 May 1943.

204. Anna Hájková, *The Last Ghetto: An Everyday History of Theresienstadt*, New York: Oxford University Press, 2021, p. 59.

205. See Harald Kisiedu, "Jazz and Popular Music in Terezín," Orel Foundation, 2021.

206. "Brundibár," Music and the Holocaust website, at http://holocaustmusic.ort.org/places /theresienstadt/brundibar/ (accessed 25 September 2019). I have discussed Zelenka at greater length in *PC*, pp. 424–25.

207. Joža Karas, *Music in Terezín 1941–1945*, Hillsdale, NY: Pendragon Press, 1990, p. 110.

208. David Bloch, "Gideon Klein," at https://holocaustmusic.ort.org/places/theresienstadt/klein-gideon/ (accessed 11 September 2021).

209. *František Zelenka: plakáty, architektura, divadlo*, exh. cat., ed. Josef Kroutvor, Prague: Uměleckoprůmyslové museum, 1991.

210. Michaela Haas, "The Ghetto Swinger: The Incredible Story of Jazz Star Coco Schumann Who Played in Auschwitz for His Life," *Huffpost*, 6 December 2017.

211. Arnošt Lustig, *Dita Saxova*, trans. Jeanne Němcová, Evanston, IL: Northwestern University Press, 1993.

212. Susan Goldman Rubin with Ela Weissberger, *The Cat with the Yellow Star: Coming of Age in Terezin*, New York: Holiday House, 2006, pp. 24, 29–30.

213. Karla Hartl and Erik Entwistle, eds., *The Kaprálová Companion*, Lanham, MD: Lexington Books, 2011, p. 149, n. 62. On Pavel Haas, see Karas, *Music in Terezín*, pp. 76–84.

214. "Hugo Haas," Národní divadlo archives, at http://archiv.narodni-divadlo.cz/default.aspx?jz=cs&dk=Umelec.aspx&ju=1881 (accessed 11 September 2019).

215. Josef Škvorecký, *All the Bright Young Men and Women: A Personal History of the Czechoslovak Cinema*, trans. Michael Schonberg, Toronto: Peter Martin, 1971, p. 22.

216. Dave Kehr, "Carnal, Gum-Crackin' and Dangerous to Know," *New York Times*, 5 February 2010.

217. "Martin Scorsese on Hereditary, Hugo Haas, and Joanna Hogg," interview with Kent Jones, 1 October 2019, New York 57th Film Festival, uploaded on YouTube by Lincoln Center.

218. Howard Thompson, "Racial Love Story," *New York Times*, 5 March 1959. For the posters, see Dennis Dermody, "Hugo Haas: The Skid Row Orson Welles," *Original Cinemaniac*, 11 July 2018.

219. Michael Beckerman, "How Desperate He Must Feel Sitting There Helplessly: Jews, Gypsies, Czechs . . . and the Chinese . . . from *Zápisník* to Terezín and Beyond," *Musicologica Brunensia*, Vol. 55, No. 2, 2019, p. 7. I am grateful to Mike for bringing this to my attention.

220. Jirků interview, "Lenka Reinerová."

221. Srp, *Adolf Hoffmeister*, 347.

Chapter 8: The Cleansing of the Homeland

1. George Orwell, "Notes on Nationalism," *Polemic*, October 1945.

2. Viera Bajtošová, "Košice Was Liberated by the Army of the Fourth Ukrainian Front 65 Years Ago," Košice website, 28 January 2010, at https://www.kosice.sk/article/kosice-was-liberated-by-the-army-of-the-fourth-ukrainian-front-65-years-ago- (accessed 3 October 2019).

3. "Košický vládní program text," p. 1, at http://www.totalita.cz/txt/txt_kvp.pdf (accessed 3 October 2019).

4. "Košický vládní program text," pp. 4–5. The Czechoslovak-Soviet treaty was signed during Beneš's visit to Moscow in December 1943.

5. "Košický vládní program text," pp. 13–14.

6. Karel Havlíček Borovský, "Slovan a Čech," in *Obrození národa: svědectví a dokumenty*, ed. Jan Novotný, Prague: Melantrich, 1979, p. 333.

7. František Palacký, "Psaní do Frankfurtu," in *Úvahy a projevy z české literatury, historie a politiky*, Prague: Melantrich, 1977, pp. 158–59.

8. "Česká moderna," in Šalda, *Kritické projevy*—2, p. 362.

9. Early postwar lists gave a figure of 1,691 dead (which is what I drew on in *CB*, p. 235); a revised count by historians at the Vojenský historický ústav (Military Historical Institute) in 2015 identifies 2,898 individual victims, which is the basis of my assertion here. See "Padli na barikádách: Historici zpřesnili počet obětí Pražského povstání," EuroZprávy.cz, 4 May 2015.

10. See the account by Zdeněk David quoted in Bryant, *Prague in Black*, p. 235.

11. Robert Pynsent, "Conclusory Essay: Activists, Jews, the Little Czech Man, and Germans," *Central Europe*, Vol. 5, No. 2, 2007, pp. 299–302.

12. Padevět, *Průvodce protektorátní Prahou*, p. 296.

13. Edvard Beneš, speech to Slovak National Council, 5 April 1945, in *Bojující Československo 1938–1945*, ed. V. Žižka, Košice: Žikeš, 1945, pp. 227, 230.

14. "Košický vládní program text," p. 8.

15. Antonín Švehla's Agrarian Party was established in 1922 through a merger of the Czech Agrarian Party and the Slovak National Republican and Peasant Party. Founded in 1918, Karel Kramář's National Democrats were the successors to the Young Czechs. In 1934 they merged with two smaller right-wing parties to form Národní sjednocení. The Slovak People's Party split from the Slovak National Party in 1913 under the leadership of Andrej Hlinka.

16. The original Pětka was made up of Antonín Švehla (Agrarian Party), Alois Rašín (National Democratic Party), Rudolf Bechyně (Social Democratic Party), Jiří Stříbrný (Socialist Party), and Jan Šrámek (People's Party). The name derives from the Czech word for five (*pět*).

17. Pavel Bělina, *Dějiny zemí koruny české*, Vol. 2, Prague: Paseka, 1992, p. 249.

18. "Košický vládní program text," pp. 1, 5.

19. The texts of all the Beneš decrees discussed here are available online under the relevant date in *Sbírka zákonů ČR* at https://www.zakonyprolidi.cz/cs/sbirka. This is my source for all subsequent quotations from the decrees unless otherwise indicated.

20. "Košický vládní program text," p. 5.

21. Míka et al., *Dějiny Prahy v datech*, p. 239.

22. Prokop Drtina, speech in Czechoslovak parliament, 29 May 1947, at http://www.psp.cz/eknih/1946uns/stenprot/055schuz/s055005.htm (accessed 4 October 2019).

23. Benjamin Frommer, *National Cleansing: Retribution against Nazi Collaborators in Postwar Czechoslovakia*, Cambridge: Cambridge University Press, 2004, p. 236.

24. Chris Johnstone, "Czech Film World Focuses on Traumatic Life of Lída Baarová," Radio Prague International, 23 January 2016.

25. "Po cestě do Prahy a Prahou," *Rudé právo*, No. 10, 17 May 1945, p. 1.

26. "Projev presidenta republiky Dr Edvarda Beneše na Staroměstském náměstí," *Rudé právo*, No. 10, 17 May 1945, pp. 2–3.

27. "Po cestě do Prahy a Prahou," p. 3.

28. "Stalin presidentu Benešovi," *Rudé právo*, No. 10, 17 May 1945, p. 1.

29. "Po cestě do Prahy a Prahou," p. 1.

30. "Projev presidenta republiky Dr Edvarda Beneše na Staroměstském náměstí."

31. This speech is reproduced in full in Prokop Drtina, *Československo můj osud*, Vol. 2, Bk. 1, Prague: Melantrich, 1992, pp. 63–64.

32. Quoted in Tomáš Staněk, *Odsun Němců z Československa 1945–1947*, Prague: Academia, 1991, p. 60.

33. I discuss and exemplify these sentiments further in *CB*, pp. 239–42.

34. Norman M. Naimark, *Fires of Hatred: Ethnic Cleansing in Twentieth-Century Europe*, Cambridge, MA: Harvard University Press, 1992, p. 119; Bryant, *Prague in Black*, p. 242.

35. See Bryant, *Prague in Black*, pp. 248–49, for examples.

36. I focus here only on the larger massacres. For examples of "routine" ill treatment, including the widespread use of rape as an instrument of intimidation, see Naimark, *Fires of Hatred*, pp. 117–19. The most extensive documentation of such "excesses" is Tomáš Staněk, *Poválečné 'excesy' v českých zemích v roce 1945 a jejich vyšetřování*, Prague: Ústav pro soudobé dějiny, 2005.

37. Petr Blažek and Pavel Zeman, "Nechat mluvit fakta," interview with Tomáš Staněk, *Paměť a dějiny*, No. 2, 2013, p. 70. For more details, see Staněk's three-part article with Adrian von Arburg, "Organizované divoké odsuny? Úloha ústředních státních orgánů při provádění 'evakuace' německého obyvatelstva (květen až září 1945)," *Soudobé dějiny*, Vol. 12, Nos. 3–4, 2005, pp. 465–533; Vol. 13, Nos. 1–2, 2006, pp. 13–49; Vol. 13, Nos. 3–4, 2006, pp. 321–76. According to R. M. Douglas, "the so-called 'wild expulsions' were in almost every case carried out by troops, police, and militia, acting under orders and more often than not executing policies laid down at the highest levels." R. M. Douglas, *Orderly and Humane: The Expulsion of the Germans after the Second World War*, New Haven, CT: Yale University Press, 2012, Ch. 4.

38. See Eagle Glassheim, "National Mythologies and Ethnic Cleansing: The Expulsion of Czechoslovak Germans in 1945," *Central European History*, Vol. 33, No. 4, 2000, pp. 475–79.

39. Hans-Ulrich Stoldt, "Revenge on Ethnic Germans. Czech Town Divided over How to Commemorate 1945 Massacre," *Spiegel Online*, 4 September 2009. Staněk (*Poválečné 'excesy,'* p. 127) believes the total death toll at Postoloprty was near eight hundred.

40. "Big Cross Near Přerov to Commemorate Germans Killed after WW2," *Prague Daily Monitor*, 12 February 2018.

41. German social democrat Alois Ullman, quoted in Bělina, *Dějiny zemí koruny české*, Vol. 2, p. 253.

42. Quoted in Franz Chocholatý-Gröger, "Výbuch v Krásném Březně 31. 7. 1945 a krvavé události v Ústí nad Labem," *CS magazín*, September 2010, at http://www.cs-magazin.com/index .php?a=a2010091031 (accessed 18 January 2021). Tomáš Staněk, *Perzekuce 1945: Perzekuce tzv. státně nespolehlivého obyvatelstva v českých zemích (mimo tábor a věznice) v květnu-srpnu 1945*, Prague: ISE, 1996, p. 136, gives a figure of between fifty and one hundred deaths. In his later *Poválečné 'excesy'* (pp. 151–53) he gives a figure of one hundred to two hundred.

43. Stenographic report of forty-third meeting of Košice government, quoted in Chocholatý-Gröger, "Výbuch v Krásném Březně 31. 7. 1945."

44. "Nové zločiny Němců v pohraničí," *Rudé právo*, No. 72, 1 August 1945, p. 1.

45. Bohumil Hrabal, *Svatby v domě*, Toronto: Sixty-Eight Publishers, 1987, pp. 113–14.

46. Bohumil Hrabal, *I Served the King of England*, trans. Paul Wilson, London: Picador, 1990, p. 230.

47. Quoted in Staněk, *Odsun Němců*, pp. 58–59.

48. "Zákon o právnosti jednání souvisících s bojem o znovunabytí svobody Čechů a Slováků," *Sbírka zákonů ČR*, 8 May 1946; emphasis added.

49. ČTK, "Deset pracovníků Památníku Lidice podalo výpověď kvůli odchodu ředitelky," *Seznam Zprávy*, 30 January 2020. See also Filip Petlička, "V Lidicích odehrává boj za nezávislost vědeckých organizací . . . ," *Literární noviny*, 22 January 2020.

50. Lubomír Zaorálek, "Tragédie Lidic je tu stále s námi," *Právo*, 24 January 2020.

51. Zdeněk Nejedlý, preface to *Celostátní výstava archivních dokumentů: od hrdinné minulosti k vítězství socialismu*, exh. cat., Prague: Ministerstvo vnitra, 1958, epigraph.

52. See Naimark, *Fires of Hatred*, p. 118, for details.

53. Tomáš Staněk, *Tábory v českých zemích 1945–1948*, Opava: Tilia, 1996, pp. 193–96.

54. See Chad Bryant, *The Thick Line at 1945: Czech and German Histories of the Nazi War Occupation and the Postwar Expulsion/Transfer*, Washington, DC: National Council for Eurasian and East European Research, 2006.

55. Iva Weidenhofferová, ed., *Konfliktní společenství, katastrofa, uvolnění: Náčrt vykladu německo-českých dějin od 19. století*, Prague: Ústav mezinárodních vztahů, 1996. Staněk (*Odsun Němců*, pp. 365–72) discusses differing estimates of those who "died prematurely as a result of the *odsun*"—up to a quarter million.

56. "V příštích hodinách skončí v podstatě odsun Němců," *Rudé právo*, No. 247, 25 October 1946, p. 1.

57. Quoted in Staněk, *Odsun Němců*, p. 59.

58. The Hungarian population of Slovakia fell from 17.6 to 10.3 percent during the same period. See Bělina, *Dějiny zemí koruny české*, Vol. 2, pp. 252–53.

59. Quoted in Arnold Suppan, "Austrians, Czechs, and Sudeten Germans as a Community of Conflict in the Twentieth Century," Working Paper 06-1, Center for Austrian Studies, University of Minnesota, October 2006. During his first exile from 1939 to 1945 Tigrid was director of radio programs for Beneš's London government; during his second exile from 1948 to 1989 he was program director for Radio Free Europe in Munich before moving to the United States in 1952 and then back to Paris in 1960. He edited *Svědectví* (Testimony) from 1956 to 1992. After returning to Prague in December 1989, Tigrid served as the Czech Republic's minister of culture from 1994 to 1996.

60. See Nikole Hannah-Jones, Caitlin Roper, Ilena Silverman, and Jake Silverstein, eds., *The 1619 Project: A New Origin Story*, New York: One World, 2021.

61. *Přehled obcí a částí v ČSR, jejichž názvy zanikly, byly změněny . . .*, Prague: Ústřední správa spojů, 1964.

62. Quoted in Jindřich Šolc, "Tomáš Černý," *Almanach královského hlavního města Prahy*, Vol. 13, 1910, p. 209; emphasis in original.

63. "Historie," at https://www.rudolfinum.cz/o-budove/historie/ (accessed 21 October 2019).

64. Barthes, *Camera Lucida*, pp. 26–27.

65. Masaryk, *Česká otázka*, pp. 115–16.

66. Tomáš Masaryk, "Naše nynější krise," in *Česká otázka*, p. 217.

67. I discuss the "land patriotism" of the Bohemian aristocracy in *CB*, pp. 53–63, and *Prague: Crossroads of Europe*, pp. 99–112.

68. "Dekret presidenta republiky o osídlení zemědělské půdy," *Sbírka zákonů ČR*, 26 July 1945.

69. Karel Kaplan, *Československo v letech 1945–1948*, Prague: Státní pedagogické nakladatelství, 1991, p. 23; Miroslav Buchvaldek et al., *Dějiny Československa v datech*, Prague: Svoboda, 1968, p. 363.

70. "Dekret presidenta republiky o osídlení zemědělské půdy."

71. Quoted in Glassheim, "National Mythologies and Ethnic Cleansing," pp. 469, 475. See also *CB*, pp. 243–48.

72. "Naše půda bude výrvána z cizáckých rukou," *Rudé právo*, No. 27, 7 June 1945, p. 2.

73. "Košický vládní program text," p. 8.

74. Jan A. Baťa, *Budujme stát pro 40,000,000 lidí*, Zlín: Tisk, 1937, p. 10.

75. See *PC*, pp. 164–66.

76. Daniela Lazarová, "Jan Antonin Bata's Name Cleared after Sixty Years," Radio Prague International, 16 November 2007.

77. Ian Willoughby, "Jan Antonín Baťa Always Said He Put His People First, Says Granddaughter Dolores Bata Arambasic," interview, Radio Prague International, 6 February 2017.

78. Buchvaldek et al., *Dějiny Československa v datech*, p. 363; Kaplan, *Československo v letech 1945–1948*, p. 22. The text of the decrees can be found at *Sbírka zákonů ČR*.

79. Quoted in H. Gordon Skilling, "The Break-up of the Czechoslovak Coalition, 1947–8," *Canadian Journal of Economics and Political Science*, Vol. 26, No. 3, 1960, p. 398.

80. "Dějinný okamžik na hradě v Praze," *Rudé právo*, No. 143, 25 October 1945, p. 1.

81. See coverage in *Rudé právo*, No. 144, 26 October 1945, pp. 1–3.

82. "Radostný ohlas v českém kulturním světě," *Rudé právo*, No. 143, 25 October 1945, p. 4.

83. Klement Gottwald, "Pevný kámen do základů nové republiky," *Rudé právo*, No. 143, 25 October 1945, p. 1.

84. Alice Teichova, *The Czechoslovak Economy 1918–1980*, London: Routledge, 1988, quoted in Filip Novokmet, *The Long-Run Evolution of Inequality in the Czech Lands, 1898–2015*, WID. world Working Paper Series No. 2018/06, 2018, p. 56.

85. In addition to the six parties already discussed, the National Front now included two small Slovak parties: the Slovenská strana slobody (Slovak Freedom Party) and the Strana práce (Labor Party). These parties received 4.2 and 3.1 percent of the 1946 vote and three and two seats in the national assembly, respectively.

86. Buchvaldek, *Dějiny Československa v datech*, 468; Bělina, *Dějiny zemí koruny české*, Vol. 2, pp. 256–57; Český statistický úřad, *Výsledky voleb do Poslanecké sněmovny 1920–2006*, 2008, pp. 85–87.

87. Skilling, "Break-up of the Czechoslovak Coalition," p. 402; Bryant, *Prague in Black*, p. 261.

88. Winston Churchill, "The Sinews of Peace," speech, 5 March 1946, Westminster College, Fulton, Missouri, at https://winstonchurchill.org/resources/speeches/1946-1963-elder -statesman/the-sinews-of-peace/ (accessed 30 October 2019); emphasis added.

89. Skilling, "Gottwald and the Bolshevization of the Communist Party of Czechoslovakia," p. 645. These are Comintern figures, which (Skilling cautions) may not be wholly reliable.

90. To be exact, 1,081,544 at the Eighth KSČ Congress in March 1946. Daniel Růžička, "Komunistická strana Československa (KSČ) odhad velikosti členské základny," at http://www .totalita.cz/vysvetlivky/s_ksc_clen_01.php (accessed 30 October 2019). By the time of the 1950 census, the population of Czechoslovakia was 12,338,000.

91. Figures from Wikipedia, entries on "1945 French legislative election" and "1946 French legislative election," drawing on Dieter Nohlen and Philip Stöver, *Elections in Europe: A Data Handbook*, Baden-Baden: Nomos, 2010.

92. Churchill, "Sinews of Peace."

93. "President Harry S. Truman's Address before a Joint Session of Congress, March 12, 1947," Yale Law School, Avalon Project, at https://avalon.law.yale.edu/20th_century/trudoc.asp (accessed 2 November 2019).

94. Ivo Duchacek, "The February Coup in Czechoslovakia," *World Politics*, Vol. 2, No. 4, 1950, pp. 518–19. This is the same Ivo Ducháček we met at the Hotel Jacob in Paris in 1939.

95. "Úplný text řeči předsedy vlády Klementa Gottwalda," *Rudé právo*, 22 February 1948, pp. 1–2.

96. Josef Pospíšil, "Kupředu, zpátky ni krok!" *Svět v obrazech*, Vol. 4, No. 9, 28 February 1948, p. 5. The date on the cover of this issue is 1947, an evident misprint.

97. "Miliony pracujících manifestovali," *Rudé právo*, 25 February 1948, p. 1.

98. "Kulturní pracovníci v rozhodující chvíli: Kupředu, zpátky ni krok!" *Rudé právo*, 25 February 1948, p. 1. More people signed over the coming days, including Olga Scheinpflugová.

99. "Nová Gottwaldova vláda jmenována," *Rudé právo*, 26 February 1948, p. 1.

100. Quoted in "Vždycky jsem šel s lidem," special supplement to *Svět v obrazech*, March 1948, p. 2.

101. "V historických dnech zůstal věren," excerpt from speech by Rudolf Slánský to constitutional national assembly, 11 March 1948, special supplement to *Svět v obrazech*, March 1948, p. 3.

102. Radim Vaculík, "Žalobce znovu otevřel případ smrti Jana Masaryka," *Právo*, 30 October 2019; Ruth Fraňková and Eva Kézrová, "Police Shelve Investigation into Mysterious Death of Jan Masaryk," Radio Prague International, 10 March 2021. For a wider sampling of the debates over Masaryk's death, see Ladislava Kremličková, ed., *Jan Masaryk (úvahy o jeho smrti)*, Prague: Úřad dokumentace a vyšetřování zločinů komunismu, 2005.

103. Josef Alan, ed., *Alternativní kultura: příběh české společnosti 1945–1989*, Prague: Lidové noviny, 2001, pp. 558–59.

104. For details of the posts, see Karel Kaplan, ed., *Kádrová nomenklatura KSČ 1948–1956: sborník dokumentů*, Prague: Ústav pro soubobé dějiny ČSAV, 1992.

105. Růžička, "Komunistická strana Československa."

106. Muriel Blaive, "The Czechs and Their Communism, Past and Present," in *Inquiries into Past and Present*, Vol. 17, ed. D. Gard, I. Main, M. Oliver, and J. Wood, Vienna: IWM Junior Visiting Fellows' Conferences, 2005.

107. Hugh Agnew, *The Czechs and the Lands of the Bohemian Crown*, Stanford, CA: Hoover Institution Press, 2004, p. 235.

108. Glenn Fowler, "Ivo Duchacek, 75, Broadcaster," obituary, *New York Times*, March 3, 1988.

109. Muriel Blaive, "The Danger of Over-Interpreting Dissident Writing in the West: Communist Terror in Czechoslovakia, 1948–1968," in *From Samizdat to Tamizdat: Transnational Media during and after Socialism*, ed. Friederike Kind-Kovács and Jessie Labov, New York: Berghahn, 2013, pp. 142–43.

110. Agnew, *The Czechs*, p. 241.

111. Quoted in Ian Willoughby, "1950s Forced Labour Conscripts Set to Receive Compensation," Radio Prague, 6 December 2012. Estimates of those conscripted into the PTP vary from 25,000 to 100,000; Barta (as quoted in Willoughby) gives a figure of 40,000–60,000.

112. See Jirásková, *Stručná zpráva*, pp. 95–97.

113. Jiří Mucha, *Living and Partly Living*, trans. Ewald Osers, London: Hogarth, 1967.

114. His widow Geraldine and family have vehemently denied this allegation. See Charles Laurence, *The Social Agent: A True Intrigue of Sex, Lies, and Heartbreak behind the Iron Curtain*, London: Ivan R. Dee, 2010.

115. Captain Kalandra, report of 2 April 1963, quoted by Doubravka Olšáková, "Jiří Mucha, agent, který zklamal," Český rozhlas, 19 August 2021.

116. Jan Buchal and Oldřich Pecl were also executed; nine other defendants received lengthy prison sentences. Hundreds more were caught up in local trials linked to the alleged conspiracy across the country. See PC, pp. 409–12.

117. Chris Johnstone, "The Inside Story of the History of Prague's Pankrác Prison," Radio Prague, 25 September 2012.

118. Robert K. Evanson, "Political Repression in Czechoslovakia, 1948–1984," Canadian Slavonic Papers, Vol. 28, No. 1, 1986, p. 3. This figure "does not include an unknown number of persons executed for political reasons without trial." Figures for political executions are disputed; see Pavel Baroch, "Communist era executions displayed online," Aktuálně.cz, 11 September 2008.

119. Evanson, "Political Repression," pp. 3–5. For 1948–1954, Kevin McDermott and Klára Pinerová give figures of just under ninety thousand citizens prosecuted for political crimes, more than twenty-two thousand incarcerated in labor camps, and around sixty thousand in the PTP. Kevin McDermott and Klára Pinerová, "The Rehabilitation Process in Czechoslovakia: Party and Popular Responses," in De-Stalinising Eastern Europe: The Rehabilitation of Stalin's Victims after 1953, ed. Kevin McDermott and Matthew Stibbe, Basingstoke, UK: Palgrave Macmillan, 2015, pp. 109–10. It should perhaps be said that however they are counted, the number of victims of forty-two years of communist rule was nevertheless infinitely smaller than the number of Czechoslovak citizens who were killed or incarcerated by the Nazis and their Slovak allies in the six years between 1939 and 1945. To adapt George Orwell, all evils are evil, but some evils are more evil than others.

120. Dušek et al., Příručka pro sběratele československých poštovních známek, p. 210.

121. Ivan Margolius, Reflections of Prague: Journeys through the Twentieth Century, Chichester, UK: Wiley, 2006, pp. 182–83. On the Slánský trial, see Karel Kaplan, Report on the Murder of the General Secretary, London: I. B. Tauris, 1990.

122. Adolf Hoffmeister, quoted in Josette Baer, "Spirits that I've Cited . . . ?" Vladimír Clementis (1902–1952): The Political Biography of a Czechoslovak Communist, New York: Columbia University Press, 2017, p. 277. Other information in this paragraph is from the same source.

123. See Lída Clementisová's interview with Jan Kavan and Alexandr Kramer, "Ženy s podobným osudem: seriál rozhovorů studenta s vdovami po popravených v procesu z roku 1952, 2. Hovoří Lída Clementisová," Student, Vol. 4, No. 13, 27 March 1968, p. 1.

124. Ivan Skála, "Tři lavice," Rudé právo, Vol. 33, No. 318, 28 November 1952, p. 2.

125. From Bedřich Utitz, ed., Neuzavřená kapitola: politické procesy padesátých let, Prague: Lidové nakladatelství, 1990, pp. 16–17. This work is a collection of excerpts from the trial transcript, which was originally published under the title Proces s vedením protistátního spikleneckého centra v čele s Rudolfem Slánským, Prague: Ministerstvo spravedlnosti, 1953.

126. Václav Kopecký, Antisemitismus poslední zbraní nacismu, November 1945, quoted in Pynsent, "Conclusory Essay," p. 326.

127. Israeli statistics show that 2,558 immigrants born in Czechoslovakia arrived in 1948 and 15,689 in 1949. Roughly fourteen thousand to eighteen thousand Jews remained in Czechoslovakia at the end of 1950. "Czechoslovakia," YIVO Encyclopedia of Jews in Central Europe.

128. "If you believe you're a citizen of the world, you're a citizen of nowhere." I quote from "Full Text: Theresa May's Conference Speech," *Spectator*, 4 October, 2016. Plus ça change.

129. Karel Čapek, *Hovory s T. G. Masarykem, Spisy*, Vol. 20, Prague: Československý spisovatel, 1990, p. 22.

130. Evžen Löbl, *Sentenced and Tried*, London: Elek, 1969; Artur London, *On Trial—L'Aveau*, London: Macdonald, 1970; Heda Margolius Kovály, *Under a Cruel Star: A Life in Prague 1941–1968*, London: Granta, 2012; Margolius Kovály and Třeštíková, *Hitler, Stalin and I*; Josefa Slánská, *Report on My Husband*, New York: Atheneum, 1969; Marian Šlingová, *Truth Will Prevail*, London: Merlin, 1968.

131. Margolius, *Reflections*, pp. 167–70.

132. "Draft Report on Margolius Family Living in 6 Veverkova Street, Prague 7, Letná," 21 November 1951, in Margolius, *Reflections*, pp. 162–63.

133. Margolius, *Reflections*, p. 185.

134. Interview with Jan Kavan and Alexandr Kramer, "Ženy s podobným osudem . . . 1. Vypráví Heda Ková́lyová-Margoliová," *Student*, Vol. 4, No. 12, 20 March 1968, p. 3.

135. Margolius Kovály and Třeštíková, *Hitler, Stalin and I*, pp. 114–15. In her 1968 *Student* interview Heda places Rudolf's arrest and the StB search at 1:00 a.m. on 11 January.

136. Margolius, *Reflections*, p. 200.

137. See US Senate, Select Committee on Intelligence, *Report of the Senate Select Committee on Intelligence Committee Study of the Central Intelligence Agency's Detention and Interrogation Program*, Washington, DC, December 9, 2014.

138. On methods of interrogation, see Antonín Kratochvíl, ed., *Žaluji*, Vol. 1, *Stalinská justice v Československu*, Prague: Česká expedice, 1990, pp. 73–84; Veronika Halamová, *Political Processes in Czechoslovakia 1949–1953: An Instrument of Legitimation of the Communist Regime*, Lublin: El-Press, 2014, pp. 63–73; Pynsent, "Conclusory Essay," p. 340; Margolius, *Reflections*; and the other firsthand accounts cited in note 130 of this chapter.

139. Margolius, *Reflections*, p. 212.

140. "Other Europe: Jacques Rupnik Interview with Heda Margolius-Kovály, New York, January 10, 1988." At https://www.youtube.com/watch?v=Chq939cXAfU (accessed 4 February 2022).

141. Quoted in *Proceedings of the Trials of Slansky, et al., in Prague, Czechoslovakia, November 20–27, 1952 as Broadcast by the Czechoslovak Home Service*, Prague: Czechoslovak Home Service, n.d. [1952 or 1953], pp. 6, 12–13.

142. *Proceedings of the Trials of Slansky*, pp. 14, 42, 158–59.

143. See Ivana Chmel Denčevová, "Z přesvědčené komunistky signatářka Charty 77. Osudové ženy: Marie Švermová," *Dvojka*, Český rozhlas, 12 May 2017.

144. *Proceedings of the Trials of Slansky*, p. 102.

145. *Proceedings of the Trials of Slansky*, pp. 73–74.

146. All of Simone's quoted testimony is from *Proceedings of the Trials of Slansky*, pp. 102–16.

147. See Margolius, *Reflections*, pp. 203–4, 223–24.

148. See Stephen Koch, "The Playboy Was a Spy," *New York Times*, Book Review, 13 April 2008; "Churchill's Dirty Tricks Squad," NPR, 2 November 2013.

149. Letter to Gladys Calthrop, September 1939, in Noël Coward, *The Letters of Noël Coward*, London: Knopf, 2007, p. 78.

150. W. Roger Louis, ed., *History of Oxford University Press*, Vol. 3, *1896 to 1970*, Oxford: Oxford University Press, 2014, p. 617.

151. Lewis Carroll, *Alice's Adventures in Wonderland*, New York: Appleton, 1866, p. 187.

152. Utitz, *Neuzavřená kapitola*, p. 114. The latter sentence is omitted from the English version of the radio transcript.

153. Enclosure in letter from Štefan Rais, minister of justice, to Klement Gottwald, 3 December 1952, in Margolius, *Reflections*, pp. 239–40.

154. Quoted in Margolius, *Reflections*, p. 227.

155. Ivan Olbracht, "Konec zrádcův," *Rudé právo*, Vol. 33, No. 318, 28 November 1952, p. 2.

156. Margolius, *Reflections*, p. 215. See also Margolius Kovály and Třeštíková, *Hitler, Stalin and I*, p. 120.

157. Margolius, *Reflections*, pp. 244–45; Margolius Kovály and Třeštíková, *Hitler, Stalin and I*, p. 127.

158. Ian Willoughby, "Author Ivan Margolius on a Chilling Personal Connection to Classic Tatra Cars," Radio Prague International, 3 October 2020.

159. Kavan and Kramer, "Ženy s pobobným osudem . . . 1. Vypráví Heda Kovályová-Margoliová," p. 3.

160. Margolius, *Reflections*, p. 279.

161. Heda Margolius Kovály, *Innocence; or, Murder on Steep Street*, trans. Alex Zucker, New York: Soho Press, 2015.

162. Franz Kafka, "In the Penal Colony," in *Selected Short Stories of Franz Kafka*, pp. 109–10, 132.

Chapter 9: The Lyrical Age

1. Milan Kundera, *Life Is Elsewhere*, trans. Aaron Asher, New York: HarperCollins, 2000, p. 363.

2. Karel Teige, dream record, text with revisions, dated 4.–5.V.42, in Michalová, *Karel Teige*, pp. 452–53.

3. André Breton, *Communicating Vessels*, trans. Mary Ann Caws and Geoffrey T. Harris, Lincoln: University of Nebraska Press, 1997, pp. 86, 5.

4. Seifert, *Všecky krásy světa*, p. 510.

5. "Vzpomínka na Karla Teigeho," *Umění*, Vol. 42, 1994, p. 90, quoted in Michalová, *Karel Teige*, p. 288. Teige and Jiří Voskovec were witnesses at Marie's wedding to Biebl in 1931.

6. Letter to Josefina Nevařilová, 18 July 1926, in Michalová, *Karel Teige*, p. 290.

7. Seifert, *Všecky krásy světa*, p. 510.

8. Jiří Kamen, *Češi patří k Vídni, aneb třicet dva výprav do Vídně v českých stopách*, Prague: Mladá fronta, 2019, unpaginated e-book, section "Josef, Ida, Eva."

9. Michal Mareš, *Ze vzpomínek anarchisty, reportéra a válečného zločince*, Prague: Prostor, 1999. Mareš's credibility has been severely damaged since Josef Čermák attacked his claims that Franz Kafka was a closet anarchist. But even Čermák warns that "we cannot, however, underestimate or wholly reject the value of his narratives . . . in his texts the borderline between reality

and invention is always blurred and difficult to locate." Josef Čermák, *Franz Kafka: Fables et Mystifications*, trans. Hélène Belletto-Sussel, Paris: Presses Universitaires de Septentrion, 2010, p. 36. This is a translation of his *Franz Kafka: Výmysly a mystifikace*, Prague: Gutenberg, 2005.

10. Kamen, *Češi patří k Vídni*, section "Klíčovou dírkou."

11. Miroslav Kárný et al., *Terezínská pamětní kniha: židovské oběti nacistických deportací z Čech a Moravy 1941–1945*, Prague: Melantrich, 1995, p. 865 (digitized at USHMM).

12. Eva Ebertová, dream record, 6–7 February 1944, typescript in Památník národního písemnictví, translated in Michalová, *Karel Teige*, p. 445.

13. Kamen, *Češi patří k Vídni*. The Holocaust.cz website has individual entries with information on Emil Ebert and Ida Ebertová. A list of dates of transports from the protectorate to Terezín can be found at Vojtěch Šir, "Transporty Židů do Terezína," Fronta.cz, 17 December 2017.

14. Michal Mareš, *Andělíčkářka—The Angel-Maker: A Czech-English Parallel-Text Concise Novel*, trans. David Short, London: Jantar Press, 2011 (quoted in publisher's blurb).

15. See Romana Nejdlová, *Amšel (syn Herrmanna Kafky)*, Prague: Galén, 2013, p. 64.

16. Pavel Janoušek et al., *Dějiny české literatury 1945–1989*, Vol. 2, *1948–1958*, Prague: Academia, 2007, p. 40.

17. "Michal Mareš odsouzen za 7 let," *Rudé právo*, Vol. 28, No. 265, 13 November 1948, p. 5.

18. Michal Mareš, "Přicházím z periferie republiky II.," *Dnešek*, Vol. 1, No. 15, 4 July 1946, p. 231. Mareš published these articles in *Dnešek* only after *Rudé právo* refused them. *Dnešek* was published weekly under Peroutka's editorship from 27 March 1946 to 19 February 1948.

19. Mareš's reports were republished as *Přicházím z periferie republiky*, Prague: Academia, 2009.

20. Jakub Vaníček, "Michal Mareš, hanebný sluha reakčních salonů," deníkreferendum.cz, 17 February 2010.

21. Michal Mareš, "Kafka und die Anarchisten," in *"Als Kafka mir entgegenkam…": Erinnerungen an Franz Kafka*, rev. ed., ed. Hans-Gerd Koch, Berlin: Klaus Wagenbach, 2005, p. 90, quoted in Stach, *Kafka: Years of Insight*, p. 551. This collection was first published in 1958. Mareš first related the story in "Setkání s Franzem Kafkou," *Literární noviny*, No. 15, 1946. For an alternative take on Mareš's relationship with Kafka, see Nejdlová, *Amšel*, pp. 61–82.

22. Čermák, *Franz Kafka: Fables et Mystifications*, p. 51. Stach's *Kafka: Years of Insight* was published in 2008, three years after Čermák's book.

23. Kafka, *Diaries*, entry for 9 November 1911, p. 112. This is another dream narrative whose setting is the Old Town Square. I discuss this dream in *PC*, pp. 115–17.

24. František Šmejkal, "Le groupe Ra," in František Šmejkal et al., *Skupina Ra*, exh. cat., Prague: Galerie hlavního města Prahy, 1988, p. 148.

25. On the Spořilov surrealists, see Anna Fárová, "Má setkání se Karlem Teigem," in *Dvě tváře*, Prague: Torst, 2016, pp. 714–15. For a survey of Czech surrealist groups in this period, see Lenka Bydžovská, "Surrealismus 1939–1947," in Švácha and Platovská, *Dějiny českého výtvarného umění [V]*, pp. 171–95.

26. Michalová, *Karel Teige*, p. 463 n. 53, quoting Zdeněk Lorenc.

27. In particular, "Entartete Kunst" (1945), "Vnitřní model" (1945; translated as "The Inner Model" in Dluhosch and Švácha, *Karel Teige*, pp. 338–47), "Osud umělecké avantgardy v obou světových válce" (1946), "K aktuálním otázkám kulturního života" (1946), and "Bohumil

Kubišta" (1949), all published in *Kvart*; and "Několik poznámek o moderní typografii" (1947) and "Malířka Toyen" (1947), published in *Blok*.

28. Rea Michalová describes the introduction as "the first . . . comprehensive overview of the history of Czech avant-garde photography." (*Karel Teige*, p. 568). Teige's text is in *Osvobozování života a poezie*, pp. 530–38.

29. Ludvík Kundera, "Ra memoáry," in Šmejkal et al., *Skupina Ra*, p. 42. This Ludvík Kundera is not to be confused with his uncle Ludvík Kundera, who was Milan Kundera's father.

30. Josef Istler to Ludvík Kundera, 10 January 1945, quoted in Kundera, "Ra memoáry," p. 44.

31. Ludvík Kundera and Zdeněk Lorenc, "Mladší surrealisté," quoted in Bydžovská, "Surrealismus 1939–1947," p. 193.

32. "Skupina (Ra)," in Šmejkal et al., *Skupina Ra*, p. 126. Although the text was signed by the whole group, the authors were Ludvík Kundera and Václav Zykmund.

33. Antonín Dufek, *Vilém Reichmann*, Prague: Foto Mida, 1994. "Osidla" is plate 53 (and is also reproduced on the front cover).

34. These are illustrated in Toman and Witkovsky, *Jindřich Heisler*, pp. 106–29.

35. Toman and Witkovsky, *Jindřich Heisler*, p. 31.

36. Among others, Elisa Breton, Nicole Espagnol, Annie Le Brun, Joyce Mansour, Nora Mitrani, Mimi Parent, and Gisèle Prassinos.

37. Annie Le Brun, "A l'instant du silence des lois," in *Štyrský, Toyen, Heisler*, exh. cat., ed. Jana Cleverie, Paris: Centre Georges Pompidou, 1982, pp. 57–58. See Le Brun's essay "Luxury in the Wild: Toyen and Eroticism," in *The Dreaming Rebel: Toyen 1902–1980*, exh. cat., ed. Anna Pravdová, Annie Le Brun, and Annabelle Görgen-Lammers, Prague: Národní galerie, 2021.

38. Breton dedicated the book to Elisa: "à toi ce cahier de grande école buisonnière, mon amour." André Breton, *Arcane 17*, Paris: Biro, 2008 (facsimile reprint) p. 35.

39. Quoted in Nathalie Aubert, "'Cobra after Cobra' and the Alba Congress," *Third Text*, Vol. 20, No. 2, 2006, p. 261.

40. Pravdová, *Zastihla je noc*, p. 106. Pravdová devotes a substantial section of her excellent book (pp. 104–23) to Tita's life and work and provides several reproductions.

41. "Déclaration Internationale," *Bulletin Internationale du Surréalisme Révolutionnaire*, January 1948, in *Le Surréalisme Révolutionnaire*, Brussels: Didier Devillez, 1999, p. 1.

42. Letter to Asger Jorn, n.d., quoted in David Hopkins, ed., *A Companion to Dada and Surrealism*, New York: Wiley, 2016, p. 421.

43. Christian Dotrement, "La Cause était entendue," quoted in "The CoBrA Story," at https://www.theartstory.org/movement/cobra-group/history-and-concepts/ (accessed 1 March 2020).

44. Kundera, "Ra memoáry," p. 57.

45. Egon Bondy, *Prvních deset let*, Prague: Maťa, 2002, pp. 15–17. Burian revived Déčko in 1945 as D 46 and it continued to exist (from October 1951 to the summer of 1955 under the name Czechoslovak Army Theater) until 1960. Burian died in August 1959.

46. Kundera, "Ra memoáry," p. 57.

47. André Breton, "Second Ark," in *Free Rein*, trans. Michael Parmentier and Jacqueline d'Amboise, Lincoln: University of Nebraska Press, 1997, pp. 99–101; originally published in *Mezinárodní surrealismus*, exh. cat., ed. Jiří Kotalík, Prague: Topičův salon, 1947.

48. Bydžovská, "Surrealismus 1939–1947," p. 194.

49. W. H. Auden, "September 1, 1939," poets.org website, at https://poets.org/poem/september-1-1939 (accessed 11 December 2019).

50. T. S. Eliot, "Burnt Norton," from *The Four Quartets*, in *Collected Poems 1909–1962*, London: Faber and Faber, 1974, p. 190.

51. Birgus and Mlčoch, *Czech Photography of the Twentieth Century*, p. 169.

52. Letter to Marie Pospíšilová, 15–16 February 1948, in Michalová, *Karel Teige*, p. 489.

53. Letter to Lída Nováková Bobrušková, 15 February 1948, in Michalová, *Karel Teige*, p. 489.

54. Jan Nejedlý and Jakub Šofar, *Po práci legraci: lexicon lidové tvořivosti z dob socialismu*, Prague: Albatross, 2016, p. 126.

55. 1956 Radio Free Europe broadcast, quoted in Milan Churaň, *Kdo byl kdo v našich dějinách v 20. století*, Vol. 2, Prague: Libri, 1998, p. 61.

56. Jiří Knapík, *Únor a kultura: Sovětizace české kultury 1948–1950*, Prague: Libri, 2004, pp. 23–25.

57. Alena Nádvorníková, "Poslední rok Karla Teigeho," in *K surrealismu*, Prague: Torst, 1998, p. 107.

58. Alan, *Alternativní kultura*, p. 558.

59. Elsa Triolet, *Le monument*, Paris: Gallimard, 1957.

60. Václav Kopecký, "Každy kout vlasti zkultivujeme," in Ševčík, *České umění 1938–1989*, p. 136.

61. Letter to Marie Pospíšilová, 7 September 1948, in Michalová, *Karel Teige*, pp. 493–94.

62. Letter to Marie Pospíšilová, 28 January 1949, in Michalová, *Karel Teige*, p. 482.

63. Letter to Lída Nováková Bobrušková, 13 February 1949, in Michalová, *Karel Teige*, p. 494.

64. Václav Kopecký, "Marxisticko-leninská výchova," in Ševčík, *České umění 1938–1989*, p. 138.

65. Andrei Zhdanov, "Soviet Literature: The Richest in Ideas, the Most Advanced Literature," in *Problems of Soviet Literature: Reports and Speeches at the First Soviet Writers' Congress*, ed. H. F. Scott, New York: International Publishers, 1935. Zhdanov's speech made socialist realism official Soviet cultural policy. The phrase "engineer of human souls" comes from Stalin.

66. The texts were published in Karel Teige and Ladislav Štoll, eds., *Surrealismus v diskusi*, Prague: Levá fronta, 1934.

67. Agnew, *The Czechs*, p. 236.

68. Halas died on 27 October 1949. His poem "Staré ženy" (Old women) came under particularly vicious attack.

69. Ivan Skála, "Cizí hlas," in *Z dějin českého myšlení o literatuře: antologie k dějinám české literatury 1945–1990*, Vol. 1, *1945–1948*, ed. Michal Přibáň, Prague: Ústav pro českou literaturu AV ČR, 2001, p. 40; originally published in *Tvorba*, Vol. 19, No. 12, 1950, pp. 285–86.

70. Štoll, *Třicet let bojů za českou socialistickou poezii*, quoted in Michalová, *Karel Teige*, p. 500.

71. Jiří Wolker, "Svatý Kopeček," in *Host do domu*, Prague: Městká knihovna, 2011, pp. 53–60.

72. Anna Marie Effenbergerová, "Moje vzpomínka na K. Teigeho," *Jarmark umění*, No. 9, 1994, p. 17, quoted in Michalová, *Karel Teige*, p. 505.

73. Quoted in Jana Machalická, "Pařeniště zůstalo agitkou," *Lidové noviny*, 21 February 2008.

74. Nádvorníková, "Poslední rok Karla Teigeho," p. 110.

75. Michalová, *Karel Teige*, p. 507.

76. Michalová, *Karel Teige*, pp. 503–4, quoting from Jiří Kolář, *Prométheova játra*.

77. See, for example, Nezval's account of his first meeting with Teige in *Z mého života*, pp. 122–24.

78. Vratislav Effenberger, "Přednáska o Karlu Teigovi v Klubu umělců 20.5.1963," typescript quoted in Michalová, *Karel Teige*, p. 504.

79. Fárová, "Má setkání se Karlem Teigem," p. 714.

80. Effenbergerová, "Moje vzpomínka na K. Teigeho," quoted in Michalová, *Karel Teige*, pp. 507–8.

81. Quoted in Nádvorníková, "Poslední rok Karla Teigeho," p. 111.

82. On Rudolf Medek, see *CB*, pp. 274–75.

83. Jiří Kolář was also close to the group. For selections of postwar Czechoslovak surrealist texts, see Stanislav Dvorský, Vratislav Effenberger, and Petr Král, eds., *Surréalistické východisko 1938–1968*, Prague: Československý spisovatel, 1969; Petr Král, ed., *Le Surréalisme en Tchécoslova-quie*, Paris: Gallimard, 1983; and (in English translation) "Anthology of Czech and Slovak Surrealism," *Analogon*, Issues 37–45, 2003–2005.

84. Stuart Inman details their contents in "Surrealism in Czechoslovakia 1951–63," in *Andre Breton: The Power of Language*, ed. Ramona Fotiade, Exeter, UK: Elm Bank, 2000, pp. 192–95.

85. Karel Teige to Jaroslav Seifert, August 1923, quoted in Michalová, *Karel Teige*, p. 95.

86. Emilie Linhartová Häuslerová, "Mé vzpomínky na Karla Teigeho," typescript, as quoted in Michalová, *Karel Teige*, p. 526. For the Verlaine anecdote, see Michalová, p. 95.

87. Michalová, *Karel Teige*, pp. 523–24, quoting Effenberger's diary.

88. Seifert, "Smíchovský danse macabre," in *Všecky krásy světa*, pp. 504–11.

89. Seifert, *Všecky krásy světa*, p. 511.

90. Quoted in Ivan Klíma's introduction to Neruda, *Prague Tales*, p. viii.

91. StB file, quoted in Michalová, *Karel Teige*, p. 533.

92. "Rozhovor s literárním teoretikem a historikem Mojmírem Grygarem," *Česká literatura*, Vol. 61, No. 3, 2013, pp. 371–72.

93. Jan Mukařovský, "Ke kritice strukturalismu v naší literární vědě," at https://is.muni.cz/el/1421/podzim2008/CJA011/um/4127428/mukarovsky-1.pdf (accessed 9 December 2019).

94. "Provolání k boji na obranu pravdy," in *Husitské manifesty*, ed. Amadeo Molnár, Prague: Odeon, 1986, pp. 29–40; for further discussion of this point, see *CB*, pp. 37–41.

95. Zdeněk Nejedlý, *Komunisté, dědici velkých tradic českého národa*, Prague: Československý spisovatel, 1953, p. 47.

96. Plaque in the Bethlehem Chapel, Betlémské náměstí, personal observation, 1990. On these and other examples of the KSČ's appropriation of the Hussites, see *CB*, pp. 274–80, 288–89.

97. Mojmír Grygar, "Teigovština—trockistická agentura v naší kultuře," *Tvorba*, Vol. 20, Nos. 42–44, 18 October, 25 October, 1 November 1920, pp. 1008–10, 1036–37, 1060–62; excerpts translated in Michalová, *Karel Teige*, pp. 527–32. I discuss Teige's 1922 article from which Grygar is quoting ("Umění dnes a zítra") in *PC*, pp. 199–200.

98. Grygar, "Teigovština," in Michalová, *Karel Teige*, p. 529.

99. Milena Šimsová, "Úzkost a strach Konstantina Biebla," *Listy*, No. 5, 2012.

100. Jiří Peňás, "Smrt Konstantina Biebla: bez obav a plný děsu," *Lidové noviny*, 15 December 2011. The poem was reprinted in 1952 in Nezval's collection *Křídla*, discussed below, p. 392.

101. Letter to Konstantin Biebl, 21 February 1951, in Nezval, *Korespondence*, pp. 42–43.

102. See his article "Krajina v čínském umění," *Volné směry*, Vol. 40, 1947–1948, extracts in Emil Filla, *Myšlenky*, Most: Severočeské nakladatelství, 1990, pp. 100–101.

103. Vojtěch Lahoda, *Emil Filla*, Prague: Academia, 2007, p. 627. Some of these works are reproduced in Marie Klimešová, *Roky ve dnech: české umění 1945–1957*, exh. cat., Prague: Arbor Vitae, 2010, pp. 230–31.

104. Emil Filla, *O svobodě*, Prague 1947, quoted in Jaromír Pečírka, "Rozloučení s Emilem Fillou (Projev nad rakví v Uměleckoprůmyslové škole)," *Výtvarná práce*, Vol. 1, No. 27, 1952–1953, reprinted in *Zajatec kubismu: dílo Emila Filly v zrcadle výtvarné kritiky (1907–1953)*, ed. Tomáš Winter, Prague: Artefactum, 2004, p. 250–51.

105. Several of the *Písně* drawings are reproduced in Klimešová, *Roky ve dnech*, pp. 216–21.

106. Moravian Slovakia (Slovácko) is a cultural region in southeastern Moravia, on the border with Austria and Slovakia, famous for its folklore. Its largest town is Uherské Hradiště.

107. *Seznam děl Jubilejní výstavy Mikoláše Alše*, exh. cat., 2 vols., Prague: SVU Myslbek, 1932–1933, vol. 1, pp. 13–14. See *CB*, pp. 294–98, for fuller discussion of the Aleš Year. My article "A Quintessential Czechness," *Common Knowledge*, Vol. 7, No. 2, 1998, pp. 136–64, discusses the contrasting Czech responses to Mikoláš Aleš and the novelist Alois Jirásek during their lifetimes, under the first republic, and after World War II as a case study in the politics of memory.

108. Mikoláš Aleš, *Špalíček národních písní a říkadel*, Prague: Orbis, 1950.

109. V. V. Štech, "Alšovým dílem," in *Výstava díla Mikoláše Alše 1852–1952*, exh. cat., Prague: Orbis, 1952, p. 44.

110. "Stenografický záznam tvůrči diskuse členů III. Krajského střediska SČSVU s Emilem Fillou," in Tereza Petišková, *Československý socialistický realismus, 1948–1958*, exh. cat., Prague: Gallery, 2002, pp. 88–93. This is an excerpt. A different selection is given in Ševčík, *České umění 1938–1989*, pp. 172–81; I quote Biebl from there (p. 180). The minutes were published in full in *Student*, No. 17, 27 March 1968.

111. See Anna Fárová, *Josef Sudek*, Prague: Torst, 1995, p. 81.

112. Pečírka, "Rozloučení s Emilem Fillou," p. 251.

113. "Krajiny Emila Filly," *Výtvarná práce*, Vol. 2, No. 7, 1954, p. 4, quoted in Vojtěch Lahoda, "Plíživý modernismus," in Švácha and Platovská, *Dějiny českého výtvarného umění [V]*, p. 383.

114. Quoted in Rosie Johnson, "Josef Lada—Landscape Painter and Švejk Illustrator," Radio Prague, 1 November 2011.

115. This is a folk ritual whose origins are lost in the mists of time that is still widely performed in the Czech Republic on Easter Monday. The word *pomlázka* has the same root as *mládež* (youth).

116. Lada and Pečinková both quoted in Johnson, "Josef Lada." Pečinková is the author of *Josef Lada*, exh. cat., Prague: Obecní dům, 2008.

117. I should perhaps add that there was more to Rockwell than these famous covers. He broke with the *Saturday Evening Post* in 1963 over its refusal to allow him to address political themes in his work. Rockwell was a strong advocate for racial integration and civil rights. His 1964 painting *The Problem We All Live With*, published in January 1964 as a centerfold in *Look* magazine, shows a six-year-old African American girl, Ruby Bridges, being escorted to school by four US marshals during the 1960 New Orleans school desegregation crisis.

118. Karel Plicka and František Volf, *Český rok v pohádkách, písních, hrách a tancích, říkadlech a hádankách*, 4 vols., Prague: Mladá fronta, 2010–2011.

119. See Alena Reichová, "Známková tvorba," in *Karel Svolinský 1896–1986*, exh. cat., ed. Roman Musil and Eduard Burget, Olomouc: Nadace Karla Švolinského a Vlasty Kubátové, 2001, pp. 227–49.

120. All of these are reproduced in Dušek, *Příručka pro sběratele československých poštovních známek*, under the relevant years.

121. Letter of 17 November 1949, quoted in Musil and Burget, *Karel Svolinský*, p. 217. The banknote is depicted on p. 215.

122. I refer to Karel Steklý's 1953 film *Anna proletářka* (Anna the proletarian), starring Marie Tomášová, adapted from Ivan Olbracht's 1928 novel of the same title.

123. Alois Jirásek, *Legends of Old Bohemia*, trans. Edith Pargeter, London: Hamlyn, 1963, p. 18.

124. Speech at unveiling of the astronomical clock on 9 May 1955, quoted in Pavel Zatloukal, "'Je to velké a šťastné Vaše dílo,' Olomoucký orloj Karla Svolinského," in Musil and Burget, *Karel Svolinský*, p. 204.

125. Magdalena Karelová, *Tajemná místa komunismu*, Prague: Albatros, 2018, p. 236.

126. Letter to Svolinský, 5 April 1949, quoted in Zatloukal, "'Je to velké a šťastné Vaše dílo,'" p. 200.

127. Zatloukal, "'Je to velké a šťastné Vaše dílo,'" p. 206.

128. Milan Kundera, *The Joke*, trans. Aaron Asher, New York: HarperCollins, 1993, p. 34.

129. Kundera, *The Joke*, 1993 ed., pp. 31–32.

130. Milan Kundera, "Letter to the Editor," *Times Literary Supplement*, 30 October 1969, p. 1259. See Kundera's Author's Note in *The Joke*, 1993 ed., pp. 319–22.

131. Preface to first (1967) edition of *The Joke*, trans. David Hamblyn and Oliver Stallybrass, London: Macdonald, 1967, as quoted in Brian Kenety, "Milan Kundera, Intangible Czech Heritage and the 'Ride of the Kings,'" *Česká posice*, 28 November 2011.

132. Pravdová, *Zastihla je noc*, p. 72.

133. See reproductions in Klimešová, *Roky ve dnech*, pp. 206–11.

134. Kundera, *The Joke*, 1993 ed., pp. 47, 128–29, 133, 138, 141.

135. Kundera, *The Joke*, 1993 ed., p. 47.

136. "Zítra se bude tančit všude," synopsis, Česko-Slovenská filmová databáze, at https://www.csfd.cz/tvurce/86208-bozena-sochova/ (accessed 10 February 2020).

137. "Zítra se bude tančit všude," at http://budovatel.cz/pisen.phtml/zitra_se_bude_tancit_vsude (accessed 10 February 2020).

138. Quoted in Ian Willoughby, "DVD Series Resurrects 1950s Czechoslovak Socialist Realist Films," Radio Prague International, 25 November 2011.

139. Zdeněk Mlynář, *Night Frost in Prague: The End of Humane Socialism*, trans. Paul Wilson, London: Hurst, 1980, pp. 1–2.

140. Kundera, *The Joke*, 1993 ed., p. 71.

141. Ivan Klíma, *My Crazy Century*, trans. Craig Cravens, New York: Grove Press, 2013.

142. Ševčík, *České umění 1938–1989*, p. 118.

143. Egon Bondy, "The Roots of the Czech Literary Underground in 1949–1953," in *Views from the Inside: Czech Underground Literature and Culture (1948–1989)*, ed. Martin Machovec, Prague: Karolinum, 2018, p. 58. See also Martin Pilař, *Underground, aneb Kapitoly o českém literárním undergroundu*, 2nd ed., Brno: Host, 2002.

144. Zbyněk Sekal, "Doslov aneb Abdikace," in Ševčík, *České umění 1938–1989*, pp. 118–19. The final text was written by Sekal. An English translation is available in Bohumil Hrabal, *The Tender Barbarian: Pedagogic Texts*, trans. Jed Slast, Prague: Twisted Spoon Press, 2020, pp. 88–95. Sekal was another of the Spořilov surrealists, who returned to Prague in 1945 from Mauthausen. See Fárová, "Má setkáni s Karlem Teigem," p. 715.

145. Bondy, preface to "Epilogue, or Abdication," in Hrabal, *Tender Barbarian*, p. 88.

146. Bohumil Hrabal, "Černá lyra," in Jana Krejcarová, *Clarissa a jiné texty*, Prague: Concordia, 1990, p. 67.

147. Bohumil Hrabal, *Dancing Lessons for the Advanced in Age*, trans. Michael Henry Heim, New York: Harcourt Brace, 1995, pp. 32–33.

148. Klimešová, *Roky ve dnech*, p. 277.

149. Untitled poems dated 31 October, 26 November, and 4 December 1950, in Egon Bondy, *Básnické spisy I 1947–1963*, ed. Martin Machovec, Prague: Argo, 2014, pp. 83, 84, 107.

150. Sekal, "Doslov aneb Abdikace," p. 119.

151. Bohumil Hrabal, *Pirouettes on a Postage Stamp: An Interview-Novel with Questions Asked and Answers Recorded by László Szigeti*, trans. David Short, Prague: Karolinum, 2008, pp. 33, 42, 68.

152. Bohumil Hrabal, "A Ballad Written by My Readers," in *Murder Ballads and Other Legends*, trans. Timothy West, Bloomington, IN: Three String Books, 2018, p. 4.

153. Bohumil Hrabal, *Gaps: A Novel*, trans. Tony Liman, Evanston, IL: Northwestern University Press, 2011, p. 43.

154. Hrabal, *Dancing Lessons*, jacket text.

155. Bohumil Hrabal, *Vita Nuova: A Novel*, trans. Tony Liman, Evanston, IL: Northwestern University Press, 2010, p. 3. This text also lacks paragraphs or punctuation.

156. Hrabal, *Pirouettes on a Postage Stamp*, pp. 57–58.

157. Hrabal, *Pirouettes on a Postage Stamp*, pp. 109–10. "Suprasectdadists" was a typo; Hrabal pronounced the error "superb" (p. 110 n. 125).

158. Hrabal, *Pirouettes on a Postage Stamp*, p. 97. Boudník later fell out with Bondy.

159. Hrabal, *Gaps*, pp. 85–86; Hrabal, *Tender Barbarian*, pp. 26–27, 82–83.

160. See Vladimír Boudník, "Manifest explosionalismu č. 2," in Ševčík, *České umění 1938–1989*, pp. 110–11. This is translated along with other explosionalist manifestos and texts by Boudník in Hrabal, *Tender Barbarian*, pp. 105–43. This volume contains some reproductions of Boudník's explosionalist work; see also Klimešová, *Roky ve dnech*, pp. 102–5, 341–45.

161. Boudník, letter to Eduard Ovčáček, 22 January 1961, reproduced in Vladislav Merhaut, "Urputná pouť Vladimíra Boudníka," Novinky.cz, 26 June 2004. Compare Boudník's account of another explosionalist expedition, "The Streets," in Hrabal, *Tender Barbarian*, pp. 127–33.

162. Bohumil Hrabal, "The Legend of Egon Bondy and Vladimírek," in *Murder Ballads*, pp. 5–12, my retranslation from Bohumil Hrabal, *Morytáty a legendy*, Prague: Mladá fronta, 2000, pp. 23–25.

163. Bondy, *Prvních deset let*, p. 37. I have drawn on this source extensively below.

164. Egon Bondy, "Pražský život [jeskyně divů aneb Prager Leben]," in *Básnické spisy I*, p. 115.

165. Egon Bondy, "Vzpomínka na Hanese Reegena," *Revolver Revue*, No. 26, 1994, p. 191.

166. Vladimír Boudník, *Vladimír Boudník a přátelé*, Vol. 2, *Dopisy Hanese Reegena Vladimíru Boudníkovi a Reegenova literární pozůstalost*, ed. Jan Placák, Prague: Ztichlá klika, 2014, p. 127.

167. Jan Placák, "Smrt je požár muzea," *Revolver Revue*, No. 26, 1994, p. 162. "Rita" is reproduced in full color in Klimešová, *Roky ve dnech*, p. 329.

168. Several of these are reproduced Klimešová, *Roky ve dnech*, pp. 143–45. See also Lenka Bydžovská's essay "Hluk ticha/The Noise of Silence," in *Mikuláš Medek: Nahý v trní/ Naked in the Thorns*, exh. cat., Prague: Národní galerie, 2020.

169. "Hovoří: Mikuláš Medek, 39 let, malíř" (interview, 1966), in Mikuláš Medek, *Texty*, Prague: Torst, 1995, p. 261.

170. Mikuláš Medek, diary entry, 13 April 1951, in *Texty*, p. 125. Walls were also a significant motif in Emila Medková's oeuvre. See Lenka Bydžovská and Karel Srp, *Emila Medková*, exh. cat, Prague: Kant, 2001.

171. Medek, *Texty*, p. 131.

172. Reproduced in Švácha and Platovská, *Dějiny českého výtvarného umění [V]*, pp. 348, 346, respectively. Tereza Petišková's chapter here contains many other examples, as does her *Československý socialistický realismus*. Kundera is quoted from *The Joke*, 1993 ed., p. 190.

173. *Imperialistická snídaně* and *Vodoplad vlasů* are reproduced in Klimešová, *Roky ve dnech*, pp. 148, 163, respectively. The *Stínohry* series is reproduced in Medek, *Texty*, pp. 58–71.

174. See Marie Klimešová's chapter "Imaginace strachu" in *Roky ve dnech*, pp. 140–71, which discusses Libor Fára, Václav Tikal, Josef Istler, Zbyněk Sekal, and others, as well as the Medeks.

175. Medek, *Texty*, pp. 91–94. This is available as "From the Inquiry on Surrealism (January 1951)," trans. Roman Dergam and William Hollister, *Analogon*, No. 37, 2003, pp. iii–xii.

176. "Odpovědi Mikuláše Medka a Emily Medkové na otázky jarní ankety o surrealismu, 1953," in Medek, *Texty*, pp. 102, 107. See also Mikuláš's draft responses, which are fuller (pp. 110–11).

177. Václav Havel quoted in John Walsh, "Vaclav Havel: Artist. Dissident. President. Icon," interview, *Independent*, 20 June 2006.

178. See Martin Machovec, "Několik poznámek k podzemní ediční řadě PŮLNOC," p. 71, at http://scriptum.cz/soubory/scriptum/bibliografie-z-kritickeho-sborniku/kriticky-sbornik _1993_03_pulnoc_bibliogr_zm_ocr.pdf (accessed 23 April 2020.)

179. Bondy, *Prvních deset let*, p. 34. See also Martin Machovec, "Židovská jména rediviva: Významný objev pro dějiny samizdatu," *A2 Sociální divadlo*, Nos. 51–52, 2007.

180. Marek Švehla, *Magor a jeho doba: život Ivana M. Jirouse*, Prague: Torst, 2017, p. 214.

181. Anna Militzová, *Ani víru ani ctnosti člověk nepotřebuje ke své spáse. Příběh Jany Černé*, Olomouc: Burian a Tichák, 2015, pp. 50–51; Natascha Drubek, "Sich (k)einen Namen machen: Die Židovská jména der Honza K.," *Slovo a Smysl*, Vol. 14, No. 28, 2017, pp. 51–73.

182. Ivo Vodseďálek, *Urbondy*, quoted in Militzová, *Ani víru ani ctnosti*, p. 50.

183. Zbyněk Havlíček, *Žiji život a píši báseň* (1961), quoted in Stanislav Dvorský, "Z podzemí do podzemí," in Alan, *Alternativní kultura*, p. 94.

184. Krejcarová, *Clarissa a jiné texty*, pp. 12–13.

185. Bondy quoted in Lenka Bydžovská, "Surrealismus, existencialismus, explozionalismus," in Švácha and Platovská, *Dějiny českého výtvarného umění [V]*, p. 388.

186. For details, see Militzová, *Ani víru ani ctnosti*, pp. 21–28, 39–44. I have drawn on this source, the only biography of Krejcarová to date, extensively in what follows.

187. Jaromír Krejcar, *Architekt ČSR*, Vol. 5, 1945–1946, p. 92, quoted in Švácha, *Jaromír Krejcar*, p. 149.

188. Letter to Jaroslava Vondráčková, 12 March 1972, quoted in Militzová, *Ani víru ani ctnosti*, p. 37.

189. Unpublished poem dated 15 February 1976, in Egon Bondy, *Básnické spisy III 1976–1994*, ed. Martin Machovec, Prague: Argo, 2016, p. 35.

190. Quoted in Militzová, *Ani víru ani ctnosti*, p. 53, citing from Dana Braunová, "Causa Jana Černá," *Reflex*, No. 25, 1995, p. 52.

191. Egon Bondy, "Předmluva," in Krejcarová, *Clarissa a jiné texty*, p. 8.

192. "V zahrádce otce mého," in Krejcarová, *Clarissa a jiné texty*, pp. 27–30.

193. Both quoted in Militzová, *Ani víru ani ctnosti*, pp. 41–42.

194. Černá, *Kafka's Milena*, p. 43. See also Militzová, *Ani víru ani ctnosti*, pp. 34–35.

195. "Kádrový dotazník," in Egon Bondy, *Básnické spisy II 1962–1975*, ed. Martin Machovec, Prague: Argo, 2015, p. 14.

196. Bondy, "Předmluva," p. 8. See Ivo Vodseďálek in Krejcarová, *Clarissa a jiné texty*, pp. 25–26, for more information.

197. For more details on Jana's personal relationships see Militzová, *Ani víru ani ctnosti*.

198. "Vzpomínka na Pavla Fischla," at https://www.holocaust.cz/zdroje/clanky-z-ros-chodese/ros-chodes-2008/kveten-13/vzpominka-na-pavla-fischla/ (accessed 24 April 2020).

199. Bondy, *Prvních deset let*, pp. 36, 38.

200. Jan Fišer, "Dopis Zemskému ústavu v Praze," *Haňťa Press*, No. 10, 1991, p. 112.

201. "Kádrový dotazník," pp. 15, 19.

202. Martin Černý quoted in Drubek, "Sich (k)einen Namen machen," p. 55. Jana's later husbands were Alois Krátký, Ladislav Lipanský, and Daniel Ladman.

203. Personal communication to Anna Militzová, quoted in *Ani víru ani ctnosti*, p. 75.

204. Militzová, *Ani víru ani ctnosti*, p. 89.

205. Letter cited in Jaroslava Vondráčková's unpublished memoir *Bez břehů a bez hranic*, quoted in Militzová, *Ani víru ani ctnosti*, p. 110.

206. Jana Černá, "Otisky duší," *Divoké víno*, Nos. 1–2, 1968.

207. Jana Krejcarová, "Dopis," in *Clarissa a jiné texty*, pp. 32–33, 41–42, 49–51.

208. See Sandra M. Gilbert and Susan Gubar, *The Madwoman in the Attic: The Woman Writer and the Nineteenth-Century Literary Imagination*, New Haven, CT: Yale University Press, 2020. I am alluding here to the character Viktorka in Božena's Němcová's *Grandmother* (see above, p. 353).

209. Jiří Žantovský, "Rozloučení s Janou Černou-Ladmanovou," ms. in Černý family archive, quoted in Militzová, *Ani víru ani ctnosti*, p. 130. Žantovský curated the exhibition *Franz Kafka: Life and Work* at the National Literary Museum in 1964, part of the reemergence of Kafka in the 1960s "thaw," discussed later.

210. Bondy, *Prvních deset let*, p. 36.

211. Untitled poem in Bondy, *Básnické spisy III*, p. 296.

212. Quoted in Radan Wagner, "Život mezi surrealismem, marxismem a obscénností," *Česká pozice*, *Lidové noviny*, 18 January 2017.

213. Hrabal, *Pirouettes on a Postage Stamp*, p. 172.

214. Hrabal, "Černá lyra," pp. 67–68. He is alluding to Paul Verlaine's *Les poètes maudits* (The cursed poets), published in 1884. Hrabal's title also puns on Honza's married name.

Chapter 10: Midcentury Modern

1. Lenka Reinerová, *Všechny barvy slunce a noci*, Prague: Městká knihovna, 2019, p. 7.

2. Jan Kotík, *Systhema* (typescript, 1974), quoted in Iva Mladičová, "Jan Kotík 1916–2002—monografie," Disertační práce, Univerzita Karlova v Praze, Ústav pro dějiny umění, 2012, p. 26.

3. In the catalog for *Deset let Československé lidově demokratické republiky ve výtvarném umění 1945–1955* [Ten years of the Czechoslovak people's democratic republic in art 1945–1955], Prague: Ministerstvo kultury, 1955, Kotalík wrote that monumental decorative painting "most eloquently testifies to the transformation our art has experienced in the decade since liberation. A range of successfully realized works exemplify how the art world responsibly understands its social mission and forges a new relationship with society," in which "heroization of significant events in the national history and contemporary life" achieves "an organic unity of content and form." One of his examples is the astronomical clock in Olomouc that "Karel Svolinský filled with the joyous rhythm and lively atmosphere of folk art" (p. 9). In May 1968, when Kotalík introduced *50 let československého malířství 1918–1968* [50 years of Czechoslovak painting 1918–1968], Prague: Národní galerie, 1969, the Prague Spring was well under way. This time he stressed "the diversity of conception and expressive breadth of our painting, in full agreement with the plurality and polarization, the polyphony and contrasts of modern art" (p. 7). "Not long after February 1948," he continued, "in a fallacious interpretation of realism imposed by decree, an autocracy of dogmatic and vulgarizing opinions broke the continuity of creative endeavors [and] distorted the mission and tasks of art. . . . Out of all the names and paintings that were officially favored at that time hardly any remain today" (p. 14). The only milestones from these years listed in the catalog's chronology are the formation of "the semi-illegal surrealist group around Karel Teige in 1950" and its "ten unpublished anthologies under the name *Signs of the Zodiac*" (p. 127). In 1984–1989 Kotalík risked a series of National Gallery shows titled *Czech Painting of the Twentieth Century*. There were no catalogs, only cyclostyled press releases. Devětsil and the Czechoslovak Surrealist Group were covered in the twelfth exhibition in April 1989, but even at this late date, Kotalík refrained from naming Karel Teige in his commentary. See *Cyklus výstav Sbírky moderního malířství, XII. část*, Prague: National Gallery, 25 April 1989.

4. "Úvod," in *Ohniska znovuzrození: České umění 1956–1963*, exh. cat., ed. Marie Judlová, Prague: Galerie hlavního města Prahy, 1994, p. 9.

5. Quoted in Jiří Machalický, "Pohnuté osudy: generace komunistické izolace. U malíře Františka Grosse nebylo nic černobílé," *Lidové noviny*, 7 November 2015.

6. Speech by Emil Pacovský, quoted in Marcela Macharáčková, "Životopis," in Macharáčková and Chatrný, *Jiří Kroha*, p. 389.

7. Quoted in Macharáčková, "Životopis," p. 401.

8. Brno Technical University disciplinary commission letter to Jiří Kroha, quoted in Macharáčková, "Životopis," p. 405.

9. The word *bydlení* may be translated as either "housing" or "living."

10. Several of the panels are reproduced in Klaus Spechtenhauser, "Sociologický functionalismus: k Sociologickému fragmentu bydlení Jiřího Krohy," in Macharáčková and Chatrný, *Jiří Kroha*, pp. 226–72. The whole cycle is published as Jiří Kroha, *Sociologický fragment bydlení*,

Brno: Krajské středisko státní památkové péče a ochrany přirody v Brně, 1973, but many of the black-and-white reproductions are of poor quality.

11. Jiří Kroha, "Přispěvek k diskuzi," *U-Blok*, Vol. 3, No. 1, 31 March 1938, quoted in Macharáčková, "Životopis," p. 407.

12. I discuss these exhibitions in *CB*, pp. 124–27, and *PC*, pp. 152–53.

13. Jiří Kroha, *K realizacím mých projektů*, quoted in Macharáčková, "Životopis," p. 410.

14. Kimberly Elman Zarecor, *Manufacturing a Socialist Modernity: Housing in Czechoslovakia, 1945–60*, Pittsburgh, PA: University of Pittsburgh Press, 2011, p. 184. Zarecor's chapter on Kroha gives more detail on his post-1948 projects. See Macharáčková and Chatrný, *Jiří Kroha*, pp. 306–15, for a fuller discussion of the Slavic Agricultural Exhibition with many illustrations.

15. Tereza Petišková, "Oficiální umění padesátých let," in Švácha and Platovská, *Dějiny českého výtvarného umění [V]*, p. 360.

16. Rudolf Martin, "Obrození výtvarného umění," *Rudé právo*, Vol. 28, No. 98, 25 April 1948, p. 4.

17. Jiří Kroha to Ostrava-Karviná Coal Mines Building Department, 2 February 1951, quoted in Zarecor, *Manufacturing a Socialist Modernity*, p. 197.

18. Frommer, *National Cleansing*, p. 26.

19. František Morkes, "Jak vzniklo slovo 'spartakiáda,'" Český rozhlas, 24 September 2010.

20. Vladimír Macura, *The Mystifications of a Nation: The "Potato Bug" and Other Essays on Czech Culture*, trans. Hana Píchová and Craig Cravens, Madison: University of Wisconsin Press, 2010, p. 103.

21. David Vaughan, "Calisthenics, Communist Style," Radio Prague International, 23 June 2012.

22. "Tristan Tzara v Československu," *Literární noviny*, Vol. 4, No. 28, 1955, p. 3, quoted in Macura, *Mystifications of a Nation*, p. 103.

23. "Stalinovou sochu bude vidět z celé Prahy," *Obrana lidu*, 20 October 1949, p. 2.

24. "Smuteční projev Václava Kopeckého v Domě umělců," *Literární noviny*, Vol. 7, No. 15, 12 April 1958, p. 2.

25. Quoted in Markéta Kořená and Petr Zídek, "Smrt krále básníků," *Lidové noviny*, 5 April 2008.

26. Hrabal, *Pirouettes on a Postage Stamp*, p. 28.

27. Ivan Klíma, foreword to Vítězslav Nezval, *Prague with Fingers of Rain*, trans. Ewald Osers, Tarset: Bloodaxe Books, 2009, p. 13.

28. Description from https://www.databazeknih.cz/knihy/zpev-miru-81582 (accessed 7 April 2020).

29. Quoted in Kořená and Zídek, "Smrt krále básníků."

30. Description from https://www.databazeknih.cz/knihy/z-domoviny-162850 (accessed 7 April 2020).

31. Description from https://www.databazeknih.cz/knihy/kridla-219874 (accessed 7 April 2020).

32. Petr Bezruč to Vítězslav Nezval, 14 November 1952, in Nezval, *Korespondence*, p. 32.

33. Josef Hora was the first to be awarded the title, posthumously, on the day after his death.

34. Petr Bezruč to Vítězslav Nezval, 10 May 1952, in Nezval, *Korespondence*, p. 27.

35. Petr Bezruč to Vítězslav Nezval, 22 March 1953, in Nezval, *Korespondence*, pp. 33–34.

36. Petr Bezruč to Vítězslav Nezval, 26 June 1957, in Nezval, *Korespondence*, p. 35.

37. Quoted in Alsen Hanson, ed., *Úmrtí Vítězslava Nezvala v dobovém tisku a ve vzpomínkách současníků*, 2018, pp. 33–38, e-book available at http://vitezslavnezval.cz/dokumenty/Umrti-Vitezslava-Nezvala-v-dobovem-tisku.pdf (accessed 9 April 2020).

38. Jiří Kotalík, "Přítel a kritik," *Literární noviny*, 12 April 1958, p. 9.

39. "Životopis Vítězslava Nezvala," *Literární noviny*, 12 April 1958, p. 12.

40. "Lid se rozloučil se svým básníkem," *Rudé právo*, 11 April 1958, p. 1.

41. Ministerstvo školství a kultury a Svaz československých spisovatelů announcement, reproduced in Hanson, *Úmrtí Vítězslava Nezvala*, p. 9.

42. "Smuteční projev Václava Kopeckého."

43. See Marek Suk, "'Jsem člověk, který se těžko podvoluje': Proces s Jiřím Kolářem v roce 1953," *Česká literatura*, Vol. 61, No. 4, 2013, pp. 547–59. *Prometheus's Liver* was published in samizdat in Václav Havel's Edice Expedice in 1979, by the émigré press Sixty-Eight Publisher's in 1985, and officially by Československý spisovatel in 1990.

44. Jan Zábrana, *Celý život: Výbor z deníků 1948–1984*, Prague: Torst, 2001, p. 483.

45. His words were "Já jsem tohle nikdy o Nezvalovi neřek"; quoted in Milan Blahynka, "Kdo co vlastně řekl," *Obrys-Kmen*, No. 23, 7 June 2008, p. 23.

46. Ivan Klíma, foreword to Nezval, *Prague with Fingers of Rain*, p. 13.

47. For more details of these cases and others, see Kořená and Zídek, "Smrt krále básníků."

48. Zábrana, *Celý život*, p. 484.

49. Petr Král, "Případ Nezval," in *Vlastizrady*, Prague: Torst, 2015, p. 206.

50. See *PC*, p. 407.

51. Milan Kundera, "Veliký Velvyslanec," in Šmejkal, *Hoffmeisterova ironická kronika doby*, p. 238.

52. Quoted in Lenka Bydžovská, "Ve službě míru," in Srp, *Adolf Hoffmeister*, p. 203.

53. Petišková, "Oficiální umění," p. 365. Clybor, "Laughter and Hatred Are Neighbors," gives a detailed analysis of these events, though it is marred by some chronological errors.

54. Srp, *Adolf Hoffmeister*, p. 346.

55. These three cartoons are reproduced in Srp, *Adolf Hoffmeister*, pp. 203–4. On this period in Hoffmeister's life and work, see Bydžovská, "Ve službě míru."

56. Adolf Hoffmeister, "Kritika výtvarné kritiky," *Lidové noviny*, 13 January 1952, quoted in Bydžovská, "Ve službě míru," p. 204.

57. Hoffmeister, "Kritika výtvarné kritiky," p. 204.

58. Quoted in Bydžovská, "Ve službě míru," p. 205.

59. See Ladislav Štoll, "Ke kritice výtvarné kritiky," *Literární noviny*, Vol. 1, No. 11, 19 April 1952; Ladislav Štoll and Jiří Taufer, "Proti sektářství a liberalismu—za rozkvět našeho umění," *Literární noviny*, Vol. 1, No. 19, 14 June 1952.

60. Antonín Pelc, "K práci svazu malířů, sochařů a grafiků," *Výtvarná práce*, Vol. 1, Nos. 1–2, 1952, p. 3, quoted in Petišková, "Oficiální umění," pp. 365–66.

61. See the unsigned editorial "Do nové etapy našeho výtvarného umění," *Literární noviny*, Vol. 1, No. 22, 5 July 1952; Otakar Mrkvička, "Nástup široké fronty výtvarných umělců," *Literární noviny*, Vol. 1, No. 23, 12 July 1952.

62. "Bdělě střežit odkaz našich klasiků," Dopis československých výtvarníků presidentu republiky Klementu Gottwaldovi, *Literární noviny*, Vol. 1, No. 23, 12 July 1952, p. 2.

63. See Lahoda, "Plíživý modernismus," in Švácha and Platovská, *Dějiny českého výtvarného umění [V]*.

64. Petišková, "Oficiální umění," pp. 365–66; Kopecký is quoted in the same source.

65. Klimešová, *Roky ve dnech*, p. 281. This photograph is reproduced on p. 283.

66. Quoted in Klimešová, *Roky ve dnech*, p. 281. *Pětiletka—fasáda* is reproduced on p. 314.

67. "Resolution Adopted by the School Organization of the Czechoslovak Youth Union, School of Mathematics and Physics, Charles University, Prague, April 26, 1956," in John P. C. Matthews, "Majales: The Abortive Student Revolt in Czechoslovakia in 1956," Working Paper No. 24, Washington, DC: Woodrow Wilson International Center for Scholars, 1999, appendix A.

68. See the photographs in Petr Blažek, "Majáles 1956: Pražská studentská slavnost ve fotografích Antonína Rozsypala," *Paměť a dějiny*, No. 1, 2016, pp. 108–13.

69. Blaive, "The Czechs and Their Communism," in *Inquiries into Past and Present*, ed. D. Gard et al., Vienna: IWM Junior Visiting Fellows' Conferences, Vol. 17, p. 376.

70. Josef Vojvodík, "Postavantgardní *Homo Viator* za hranicemi principu (socialistické) reality," in Srp, *Adolf Hoffmeister*, p. 224.

71. Adolf Hoffmeister, *Kuo-cha: Cestopisná reportáž o čínském malířství*, Prague: SNKLHU, 1954, quoted in Vojvodík, "Postavantgardní *Homo Viator*," p. 229 (which makes this same argument).

72. Wright's building was demolished in 1967 and replaced by the present high-rise hotel on the same site.

73. *Adolf Hoffmeister: Ilustrace*, exh. cat., Prague: Galerie Československého spisovatele, 1958, quoted in Srp, *Adolf Hoffmeister*, p. 218.

74. Adolf Hoffmeister, *Made in Japan*, Prague: Československý spisovatel, 1958, as quoted in Čapková, *Bedřich Feuerstein*, p. 44.

75. Vojtěch Lahoda, "Krotký modernismus," in Judlová, *Ohniska znovuzrození*, p. 17.

76. See Antonín Michalčík, "O umění XX. století," *Výtvarná práce*, No. 4, 1955; Antonín Michalčík, "Cesta našeho umění," *Výtvarná práce*, No. 20–21, 1955; "Hlas mladých" and "Připomínky posluchačů VŠUP," *Výtvarná práce*, No. 24, 1955.

77. Sevčík, *České umění 1938–1989*, p. 436.

78. J. Kříž quoted in Jiří Šetlík, "Počátky činnosti tvůrčích skupin a jejich význam," in *Česká kultura na přelomu 50. a 60. let*, ed. Marie Judlová, Prague: Galerie hlavního města Prahy, 1988, p. 5.

79. Letter to SČSVU, 1 December 1956, quoted in Šetlík, "Počátky činnosti tvůrčích skupin," p. 4.

80. František Dvořák, catalog essay, quoted in Lahoda, "Krotký modernismus," p. 20.

81. Lahoda, "Krotký modernismus." See also Kateřina Tučková, "Skupina RADAR," Diplomová práce, Univerzita Karlova v Praze, Filozofická fakulta, Ústav pro dějiny umění, 2014.

82. Miroslav Lamač, Jiři Padrta, and Jan Tomeš, *Zakladatelé moderního českého umění*, exh. cat., Brno: Dům uměni města Brna, 1957, p. 6.

83. Redakce, "Zakladatelé českého moderního umění," *Květy*, 24 April 1958, pp. 6–7. This was strongly criticized in Václav Formánek, "Ještě k Osmě," *Literární noviny*, 2 May 1958.

84. The catalog is reproduced in facsimile (with a translation) in Stephanie Barron, ed., *"Degenerate Art": The Fate of the Avant-garde in Nazi Germany*, Los Angeles: Los Angeles County Museum of Art, 1991, pp. 358–90. I discuss this exhibition in *PC*, pp. 251–61.

85. "Výstava moderního českého umění," *Obrana lidu*, 9 March 1958. Compare Prokop H. Toman, "Zakladatelé českého moderního umění," *Svět v obrazech*, 22 March 1958.

86. Jiří Kotalík, "O české moderní umění," *Literární noviny*, 15 March 1958, p. 1.

87. Zdenek Primus, *Umění je abstrakce: česká vizuální kultura 60. let*, Prague: Kant, 2003, p. 259. The photographer was Josef Nový.

88. Josef Škvorecký and Zdena Salivarová, *Samožerbuch: Autofestšrift*, Prague: Panorama, 1991, p. 118. Jan Hanč was a member of Skupina 42.

89. Ivan Klíma, *Fictions and Histories*, UC Berkeley Occasional Papers, 1998, p. 8, at https://escholarship.org/uc/item/8gx209mk (accessed 21 July 2020).

90. Škvorecký, *All the Bright Young Men and Women*, p. 58.

91. Škvorecký and Salivarová, *Samožerbuch*, pp. 129, 121.

92. Miroslav Lamač and Jiří Padrta, *Moderní české malířstvi II: léta dvacátá*, exh. cat., Brno: Dům uměni města Brna, 1958.

93. For a fuller discussion and examples, see Judlová, *Ohniska znovuzrození*, p. 9.

94. See Judlová, *Ohniska znovuzrození*, pp. 159–60. The English summary erroneously states that Vachtová's articles appeared in *Tvorba*.

95. "Každý máme svoje lobby (s historičkou umění Ludmilou Vachtovou hovoří Terezie Pokorná a Viktor Karlík)," *Revolver Revue*, No. 43, 2000.

96. Jiří Šmíd, "Slova a skutečnost," *Tvorba*, 4 July 1957, p. 11, quoted in Judlová, *Ohniska znovuzrození*, p. 92.

97. Otakar Mrkvička, "Mladí z Máje," *Literární noviny*, Vol. 6, No. 26, 29 June 1957, p. 5.

98. See Šetlík, "Počátky činnosti tvůrčích skupin," p. 4.

99. Jiří Padrta, "Vladimír Boudník," *Výtvarná práce*, Vol. 13, No. 22, 1965, p. 7 (quoted in Mahulena Nešlehová, "Odvrácená tvář modernismu," in Judlová, *Ohniska znovuzrození*, p. 166); Primus, *Umění je abstrakce*, p. 65.

100. Hrabal, *Vita Nuova*, p. 6.

101. Hrabal, *Tender Barbarian*, pp. 12–13.

102. Vladimír Boudník, conversation with Alois Kusák, 1967, quoted in Judlová, *Ohniska znovuzrození*, p. 302.

103. Antonín Hartmann, ed., *Mikuláš Medek*, exh. cat., Prague: Gema Art, 2002, p. 199.

104. "Každý máme svoje lobby."

105. Mahulena Nešlehová, "Konfrontace," in *Nová encyklopedie českého výtvarného umění*, 2 vols., ed. Anděla Horová, Prague: Academia, 1995, vol. 1, p. 377.

106. Quoted in Ševčík, *České umění 1938–1989*, p. 440, and Mahulena Nešlehová, "Poznámka ke Konfrontačním roku 1960," in Judlová, *Česká kultura*, p. 22. See also Mahulena Nešlehová, ed., *Český informel (Průkopníci abstrakce z let 1957–1964)*, exh. cat., Prague: Galerie hlavního města Prahy, 1991.

107. *Jaro 62: výstava tvůrčí skupiny Mánes, hostí a bloku tvůrčích skupin*, exh. cat., Prague: Mánes, 1962.

108. Georges Bataille, "On the Subject of Slumbers," in *The Absence of Myth: Writings on Surrealism*, ed. and trans. Michael Richardson, London: Verso, 2006, p. 49 ("old enemy from within"); "Informe," *Documents*, No. 7, December 1929, p. 382.

109. Valérie Piette and Gonzague Pluvinage, "Discovering the World: Visiting Expo 58," in *Expo 58: Between Utopia and Reality*, exh. cat., ed. Gonzague Pluvinage, Brussels: Lannoo Uitgeverij, 2008, p. 155–56.

110. Quoted in Krystyna Wanatowiczová, "Expo 58: když nám patřil svět," *MF Dnes*, 18 June 2008.

111. Quoted in "Expo 58," Atomium website, at https://atomium.be/expo58?lang=en (accessed 22 June 2020).

112. Expo 58, news release no. 2, n.d., quoted in David Crowley, "Humanity Rearranged: The Polish and Czechoslovak Pavilions at Expo 58," *West 86th: A Journal of Decorative Arts, Design History, and Material Culture*, Vol. 19, No. 1, 2012, p. 89.

113. Crowley, "Humanity Rearranged," pp. 88–89, quoting Zevi, "Bruxelles 1958: primi interrogative," *L'architettura*, May 1958, p. 4.

114. MoMA press release, 31 January 1954; Roland Barthes, "The Great Family of Man," in *Mythologies*, trans. Annette Lavers, New York: Farrar, Straus and Giroux, 1991, pp. 100–101. See Edward Steichen, *The Family of Man*, exh. cat., New York: Museum of Modern Art, 1983.

115. Kundera, *Unbearable Lightness of Being*, p. 251.

116. *Sight*, No. 1, 1956, p. 8, quoted in Crowley, "Humanity Rearranged," pp. 89–90.

117. David Emery, "Is This a Photograph of a 'Human Zoo' at the 1958 World's Fair?" Snopes Fact Checks, 4 March 2019.

118. This is how the display was depicted on an 1897 Belgian postage stamp commemorating the Brussels International Exposition. Leopold ruled the Congo Free State (as it was then named, without any conscious irony) as his personal property from 1885 to 1908 and enslaved its inhabitants to harvest ivory and rubber. Apart from millions of deaths from disease and hunger, his regime is remembered for its savage brutality, which included amputating the hands and feet of the children of workers who failed to meet their quotas. Leopold was forced to cede his private African fief (for a tidy sum) to the Belgian state in 1908. See Adam Hochschild, *King Leopold's Ghost: A Story of Greed, Terror, and Heroism in Colonial Africa*, 2nd ed., Boston: Mariner Books, 2020.

119. Daniela Kramerová and Vanda Skálová, "Realita bruselského snu," in *Bruselský sen: československá účast na světové výstavě EXPO 58 v Bruselu a životní styl 1. poloviny 50. let*, exh. cat., ed. Marie Bergmanová, Prague: Arbor Vitae, 2008, p. 32.

120. Quoted in Rika Devos and Mil de Kooning, "Architecture and Graphics at Expo 58: 'Not Modern . . . Twenty Years Ahead of Its Time,'" in Pluvinage, *Expo 58*, p. 150.

121. Quotations and details about the American pavilion in this and the next paragraph are from Anthony Swift, "Soviet-American Rivalry at Expo '58," in *World's Fairs in the Cold War: Science, Technology, and the Culture of Progress*, ed. Arthur P. Molella and Scott Gabriel Knowles, Pittsburgh, PA: University of Pittsburgh Press, 2019, pp. 38–40.

122. "Jan Werich a labyrint světa," *Literární noviny*, Vol. 8, No. 28, 1958, p. 12.

123. Quoted in Bergmanová, *Bruselský sen*, unpaginated front matter.

124. Petr Volf, "Volfův revír: Brusel 1958–1000x více než Nagano," *Víkend*, Ihned.cz, 20 April 2018.

125. Kramerová and Skálová, "Realita bruselského snu," p. 21.

126. Jindřich Santar, interviewed in Wanatowiczová, "Expo 58."

127. Quoted in Kramerová and Skálová, "Realita bruselského snu," p. 47. On the Czechoslovak pavilion, see Cathleen M. Giustino, "Industrial Design and the Czechoslovak Pavilion at Expo '58: Artistic Autonomy, Party Control and Cold War Common Ground," *Journal of Contemporary History*, Vol. 47, No. 1, 2012, pp. 185–212; Kimberly Elman Zarecor and Vladimir Kulić, "Czechoslovak and Yugoslav Pavilions at the 1958 Brussels World's Fair," in *Meet Me at the Fair:*

A World's Fair Reader, ed. Celia Pearce, Laura Hollengreen, Rebecca Rouse, and Bobby Schweizer, Pittsburgh, PA: ETC Press, 2014, pp. 225–40.

128. Kramerová and Skálová, "Realita bruselského snu," p. 55; this is illustrated on p. 62.

129. Martin Franc, "We're Good Enough to Host the World: Czech and Slovak Cuisine at World Fairs in 1958, 1967 and 1970," in *A Taste of Progress: Food at International and World Exhibitions in the Nineteenth and Twentieth Centuries*, ed. Nelleke Teughels and Peter Scholliers, London: Routledge, 2016, p. 135.

130. Ladislav Svatoš, quoted in Wanatowiczová, "Expo 58."

131. See Zdeněk Lukeš and Petr Kratochvíl, *Praha moderní IV: velký průvodce po architektuře 1950–2000*, Prague: Paseka, 2015, pp. 72–73; Lucie Zídková, "Julius Fučík, kdo to je?" Magazín Patek LN, *Lidové noviny*, 25 September 2020, pp. 13–16; *CB*, pp. 252–53.

132. "For an Imaginist Renewal of the World. The Alba Congress: 1956–2019," Castello di Rivoli Museum of Contemporary Art, at https://www.e-flux.com/announcements/280674/for-an-imaginist-renewal-of-the-world-the-alba-congress-1956-2019/ (accessed 1 October 2020).

133. Lettrist International, "The Alba Platform," in *The Situationist Anthology*, rev. and expanded ed., ed. Ken Knabb, Berkeley, CA: Bureau of Public Secrets, 2006, pp. 22–23.

134. *Zpráva o činnosti komise ministerstva školství a kultury pro přejímání uměleckých děl čsl. exposice na Světové výstavě Brusel 1958*, unpublished document, quoted in Kramerová and Skálová, "Realita bruselského snu," p. 28.

135. For a useful survey, see Mariana Kubištová, "Design padesátých let: východiska a podoby bruselského stylu," in *Design v českých zemích 1900–2000: instituce moderního designu*, ed. Iva Knobloch and Radim Vondráček, Prague: Academia/UMPRUM, 2016, pp. 341–72.

136. See Nikola Klímová, ed., *SNKLHU Odeon 1953–1995: České knižní obálky v edičních řadách*, Prague: UMPRUM, 2016, pp. 68–93.

137. See Klímová, *SNKLHU Odeon*, and Primus, *Umění je abstrakce*, for examples.

138. Unless otherwise stated, details are taken from Kramerová and Skálová, "Realita bruselského snu," pp. 72–74.

139. Svoboda and Radok are both quoted in "Josef Svoboda," at https://monoskop.org/Josef_Svoboda (accessed 1 July 2020). For a fuller account of the theory behind Laterna magika, see Jan Grossman, "Combining Theater and Film," in *Laterna Magika: Nouvelles technologies dans l'art tchéque du XXe siècle/New Technologies in Czech Art of the 20th Century*, exh. cat., ed. Marion Diez, Prague: Kant, 2002, pp. 129–36. See also Ivan Margolius, "Svoboda," *British Czech and Slovak Review*, February–March 2020, p. 10.

140. Interview with Antonin J. Liehm, "Alfred Radok," in *International Journal of Politics*, Vol. 3, No. 1/2, 1973, p. 38.

141. Liehm, "Alfred Radok," p. 25.

142. Helena Kresová, "Laterna magika," *Český dialog*, June 2017.

143. Liehm, "Alfred Radok," p. 25.

144. Škvorecký, *All the Bright Young Men and Women*, p. 40.

145. Bosley Crowther, "The Screen in Review: Two Arrivals; Powerful Film about the Nazi Persecution of Jews Comes from Czechoslovakia," *New York Times*, 28 August 1950, p. L13.

146. Quoted in Jonathan Owen, "Distant Journey (Daleká cesta)," booklet accompanying second-run DVD, 2020, p. 4.

147. Škvorecký, *All the Bright Young Men and Women*, p. 41. This is not strictly true. The film surfaced very occasionally at brief showings in suburban and rural cinemas in the late 1950s.

148. All quotations from Liehm, "Alfred Radok," pp. 29–39.

149. For the convoluted history of Laterna magika, the National Theater, and Nová scéna, see "The New Stage - history," at https://www.narodni-divadlo.cz/en/stages/the-new-stage/history (accessed 15 February 2022).

150. Quoted by Miloš Forman, who was present at the preview, in Miloš Forman and Jan Novák, *Turnaround: A Memoir*, London: Faber and Faber, 1994, p. 116. See also Eva Stehlíková, "The Laterna Magika of Josef Svoboda and Alfréd Radok," *Theatralia*, Vol. 14, No. 1, 2011, especially pp. 180–89.

151. Radok's film of *Otvírání studánek* is included with the second-run DVD of *Distant Journey*.

152. Georges Neveux, "Propos de l'Auteur," in unpaginated theater program, *La Voleuse de Londres*, Théâtre du Gymnase, Paris, 1960.

153. Škvorecký and Salivarová, *Samožerbuch*, p. 121.

154. Liehm, "Alfred Radok," p. 26.

155. Václav Havel, "Alfréd Radok: Nekrolog," 26 April 1976, Václav Havel Library.

156. Liehm, "Alfred Radok," p. 26. Koloděje Castle in Prague was used as an StB interrogation center during the 1950s; Otto Šling, Laco Novomeský, Gustáv Husák, and Marie Švermová were among those held there.

157. *Constitution of the Czechoslovak Socialist Republic*, Prague: Orbis, 1964, p. 225, at https://www.worldstatesmen.org/Czechoslovakia-Const1960.pdf (accessed 14 July 2020).

158. "Rozhodnutí presidenta republiky a vlády Republiky československé o amnestii," *Sbírka zákonů ČR*, 10 May 1960. I quote from the preamble. Figure from Jaroslav Rokoský, "Amnestie 1960," *Paměť a dějiny*, No. 1, 2011, p. 36.

159. Mlynář, *Night Frost in Prague*, pp. 69–70.

160. Ševčík, *České umění 1938–1989*, pp. 444–45.

161. Ševčík, *České umění 1938–1989*, p. 259. Šmejkal's catalog text is reproduced on pp. 259–62. The exhibitors were Jiří Balcar, Vladimír Boudník, Josef Istler, Čestmír Janošek, Jan Koblasa, Mikuláš Medek, Karel Nepraš, Robert Piesen, Zbyněk Sekal, Jiří Valenta, and Aleš Veselý.

162. Quoted in Alena Binarová, "Svaz výtvarných umělců v českých zemích v letech 1956–1972: oficiální výtvarná tvorba v proměnách komunistického režimu," Disertační práce, Univerzita Palackého v Olomouci, Filozofická fakulta, 2016, pp. 105–6.

163. On these galleries, see Alois Micka, "Umění mezi sjezdy," Disertační práce, Univerzita Karlova v Praze, Filozofická fakulta, Ústav pro dějiny umění, 2019.

164. See "Usnesení sjezdu SČSVU," in Ševčík, *České umění 1938–1989*, pp. 252–58.

165. Karel Srp, "Hosté bez hostitele/Guests without a Host," in *Mikuláš Medek: Náhý v trní*, p. 129.

166. František Dryje, "Editorial," in "Anthology of Czech and Slovak Surrealism III," *Analogon* 40, 2004 supplement, p. II.

167. František Šmejkal, *České imaginativní umění*, exh. cat., Prague: Galerie Rudolfinum, 1996, p. 617. Exhibitors included Štyrský, Toyen, Teige, Heisler, Tikal, Istler, Medek, and Medková.

168. *K výtvarné problematice třicátých let*, Prague: Narodní galerie, 1964, unpaginated.

169. Šmejkal, *České imaginativní umění*, p. 620. Istler, Janošek, Koblasa, Medek, Nepraš, Valenta, and Veselý exhibited in both shows. Other contributors to *Fantasijní aspekty* included Stanislav Podhrázský, Jan Švankmajer, and Eva Švankmajerová.

170. Micka, "Umění mezi sjezdy," p. 213.

171. Stanislav Dvorský, Vratislav Effenberger, and Petr Král, *Symboly obludnosti*, exh. cat., Prague: Galerie D, 1966; facsimile reproduction in Marie Langerová et al., *Symboly obludností: mýty, jazyk a tabu české postavantgardy 40.–60. let*. Prague: Malvern, 2009, p. 429. The English summary is in the original.

172. Dvorský, Effenberger, and Král, *Surrealistické východisko 1938–1968*. See also *Avantgarda bez legend a mýtů: rozhlasový cyklus o patnácti dílech*, Prague: Rozhlasový cyklus, 1967 (mimeographed transcript of radio broadcasts, private limited edition).

173. See Pavlína Morganová, *Procházka akční Prahou: akce performance happeningy 1949–1989*, Prague: Akademie výtvarných umění, 2014, pp. 241–43.

174. "Bill Clinton a Václav Havel v Redutě," at https://www.redutajazzclub.cz/bill-clinton-a-vaclav-havel-in-reduta (accessed 23 July 2020).

175. Ivan Poledňák, "Accord Club," in *Český hudební slovník osob a institucí*, ed. Petr Macek, Brno: Ústav hudební vědy Filosofická fakulta Masarykova univerzita, n.d.

176. Václav Černý, *Paměti III, 1945–1972*, Brno: Atlantis, 1992, pp. 476–77.

177. Premiéry DNz dle derniéry, at https://www.nazabradli.cz/cz/repertoar/archiv (accessed 13 July 2020).

178. See František Dryje and Bertrand Schmitt, eds., *Jan Švankmajer: Dimensions of Dialogue/ Between Film and Fine Art*, exh. cat., Prague: Arbor Vitae, 2012, pp. 68–74.

179. Škvorecký, *All the Bright Young Men and Women*, p. 57.

180. "Audition," Miloš Forman: Miloš Forman's Official Website, at https://milosforman .com/en/movies/konkurs (accessed 7 August 2020).

181. Škvorecký, *All the Bright Young Men and Women*, p. 75.

182. Antonín J. Liehm, ed., *The Miloš Forman Stories*, New York: Routledge, 2016, p. 36.

183. Museum of Modern Art, New York, press release no. 61, 14 June 1967. Kučera also worked on Jaromil Jireš's *The Cry*, Jan Němec's *Diamonds of the Night*, and *Pearls of the Deep*.

184. Quoted in Ronald Bergan, "Věra Chytilová obituary," *Guardian*, 14 March 2014.

185. "In-person: Q&A with Director Ivan Passer," Billy Wilder Theater, 14 September 2018, at https://www.cinema.ucla.edu/events/2018/09/14/closely-watched-trains-larks-on-string (accessed 5 August 2020).

186. "The Firemen's Ball," at https://milosforman.com/en/movies/the-firemens-ball (accessed 26 November 2020).

187. The translation is rather ambiguous because of the variety of meanings of the word *party* in English. In Czech, *slavnost* unambiguously means a celebration, not a political party.

188. The five were Věra Chytilová (dir. *O něčem jiném/Something Different*, 1963; *Sedmikrásky/Daisies*, 1966), Jaromil Jireš (dir. *Křik/The Cry*, 1963; *Žert/The Joke*, 1968), Jiří Menzel (dir. *Ostře sledované vlaky/Closely Watched Trains*, 1966; *Skřivánci na niti/Larks on a String*, 1969), Jan Němec (dir. *Démanty noci/Diamonds of the Night*, 1964; *O slavnosti a hostech/A Report on the Party and the Guests*, 1966), and Evald Schorm (dir. *Každý den odvahu/Courage for Everyday*, 1964; *Návrat ztraceného syna/Return of the Prodigal Son*, 1966).

189. Hrabal memorably describes the events surrounding the publication in *Gaps*, pp. 3–14.

190. For a detailed discussion of the circumstances of Boudník's death, see Vladimír Merhaut, *Grafik Vladimír Boudník*, Prague: Torst, 2009, pp. 362–64.

191. Menzel, interviewed in Steve Rose, "Irony Man," *Guardian*, 9 May 2008. Menzel later filmed Hrabal's *Postřižiny* (*Cutting It Short*, 1980), *Slavnosti sněženek* (*The Snowdrop Festival*, 1985), and *Obsluhoval jsem anglického krále* (*I Served the King of England*, 2008).

192. Jonathan L. Owen, *Avant-Garde to New Wave: Czechoslovak Cinema, Surrealism and the Sixties*, London: Berghan Books, 2011, p. 78.

193. Rose, "Irony Man."

194. Bohumil Hrabal, *Closely Watched Trains*, trans. Edith Pargeter, Evanston, IL: Northwestern University Press, 1990, pp. 68–69. Hrabal's description is a pastiche on Ernest Hemingway, *For Whom the Bell Tolls*, New York: Charles Scribner's Sons, 1940, p. 159.

Chapter 11: The Prague Spring

1. "Ženy s podobným osudem . . . Výpr áví Heda Kovályová-Margoliová," interview with Jan Kavan and Alexandr Kramer, *Student*, Vol. 4, No. 12, 20 March 1968, p. 3.

2. Letter to his father, March 1965, in Allen Ginsberg, *Iron Curtain Journals January–May 1965*, ed. Michael Schumacher, Minneapolis: University of Minnesota Press, 2018, p. 163.

3. Michael Schumacher, editor's introduction to Ginsberg, *Iron Curtain Journals*, p. xi.

4. Veronika Tuckerová, "Reading Kafka in Prague: The Reception of Franz Kafka between the East and the West during the Cold War," PhD diss., Columbia University, 2012, pp. 3–4.

5. Jiří Soukup, "České podoby Franze Kafky před druhou světovou válkou," Disertační práce, Filosofická fakulta, Univerzity Karlova, 2017, pp. 158–62, lists forty-five Czech publications of Kafka's writings (in addition to Eisner's translation of *The Castle*) up to 1938 in twenty-two different newspapers and magazines. For Toyen's cover, see Bydžovská and Srp, *Knihy s Toyen*, p. 47.

6. See Veronika Tuckerová, "Kafka—a Hanč? K českým překladům a literární recepci Franze Kafky 1948–1963 (ukázka)," *Bubínek revolveru*, 17 December 2018.

7. Pavel Eisner, *Kafka and Prague*, trans. Lowry Nelson and René Wellek, New York: Arts, 1950, p. 36.

8. Tuckerová, "Reading Kafka," p. 8. The first collection of Kafka's works in Czech was published by the Společnost Franze Kafky in Prague in thirteen volumes in 1997–2007.

9. Zábrana, *Celý život*, p. 833.

10. Tuckerová, "Reading Kafka," p. 13.

11. Ivan M. Jirous, *Magorův zápisník*, Prague: Torst, 1997, p. 612.

12. Lenka Bydžovská, "Dobrodružství koláže," in Srp, *Adolf Hoffmeister*, p. 270. Some of these collages are reproduced on pp. 276–77.

13. These are reproduced in Bydžovská, "Dobrodružství koláže," pp. 276–77, and Šmejkal, *Hoffmeisterova ironická kronika doby*, pp. 187–98.

14. Jiří Kolář, *Kafkova Praha/Kafkas Prag/Prague de Kafka 1977–1978*, Prague: Alea, 1994.

15. Jiří Kolář, *Dictionnaire des méthodes*, Paris: Revue K, 1991, p. 108.

16. Josef Čermák, interview in Avi Kempinski, "Just Wild about Franz Kafka," *Washington Post*, 4 October 1992. The GDR leader Walter Ulbricht made the same claim (see later).

17. "Kafka and Power. 1963–1968–2008. Zipp—German-Czech Cultural Projects—Conference," at https://www.kulturstiftung-des-bundes.de/en/programmes_projects

/sustainability_and_future/detail/kafka_und_die_macht_196319682008.html (accessed 23 January 2022).

18. Nekula, *Franz Kafka and His Prague Contexts*, pp. 14–15.

19. Škvorecký, "Franz Kafka, Jazz, and the Anti-Semitic Reader," in *Talkin' Moscow Blues*, Toronto: Lester and Orpen Denys, 1988, p. 161.

20. Arendt, "Franz Kafka: A Revaluation," in *Essays in Understanding 1930–1954*, trans. Jerome Kohn, New York: Harcourt Brace, 1994, pp. 73–74.

21. Eduard Goldstücker, "Jak je to s Franzem Kafkou?" *Literární noviny*, Vol. 12, No. 7, 16 February 1963, p. 5.

22. Nekula, *Franz Kafka and His Prague Contexts*, p. 25.

23. Goldstücker, "Jak je to s Franzem Kafkou?" p. 4.

24. Eduard Goldstücker, "Ten Years after the Kafka Symposium of Liblice," *European Judaism: A Journal for the New Europe*, Vol. 8, No. 2, 1974, p. 22.

25. Černý, *Paměti III*, p. 475 (as translated in Nekula, *Franz Kafka and His Prague Contexts*, p. 30).

26. Škvorecký, "Franz Kafka, Jazz, and the Anti-Semitic Reader," p. 161. Michal Mareš was also still alive in 1963 but living in obscurity.

27. Kusák, *Tance kolem Kafky*, pp. 48–49.

28. Škvorecký, "Franz Kafka, Jazz, and the Anti-Semitic Reader," p. 161; unpublished letter to Veronika Tuckerová, 28 February 2008, quoted in her "Reading Kafka," p. 104. Other details from Tuckerová's account are based on files in the Ministry of Security Forces Archive in Prague.

29. Tuckerová, "Reading Kafka," p. 109.

30. *Proceedings of the Trials of Slansky*, pp. 46–47.

31. See Tuckerová, "Reading Kafka," pp. 155–60, for more details.

32. Škvorecký, "Franz Kafka, Jazz, and the Anti-Semitic Reader," p. 161.

33. Klímová, *SNKLHU Odeon 1953–1995*, p. 240.

34. Reinerová, *Kavárna nad Prahou*, p. 27.

35. Lenka Reinerová, "Štěstí a hořkost jednoho života," in Eduard Goldstücker, *Vzpomínky 1913–1945*, Prague: G plus G, 2003, pp. 145, 147.

36. Reinerová, *Kavárna nad Prahou*, p. 29 (caption to photograph of Reinerová at Liblice).

37. Ginsberg, letter to his father, March 1965.

38. Ginsberg's description quoted in Petr Blažek, "The Deportation of the King of May: Allen Ginsberg and the State Security," *Behind the Iron Curtain*, No. 2, 2012, p. 35.

39. See Josef Škvorecký to Louis Armand, 12 September 2010, *Vlak*, No. 4, 2012, pp. 3–4.

40. "The King of May: A Conversation between Allen Ginsberg and Andrew Lass, March 23, 1986," *Massachusetts Review*, Vol. 39, No. 2, 1998, pp. 170–71.

41. Blažek, "Deportation of the King of May," p. 37.

42. Letter to Nicanor Parra, 29 August 1965, in Ginsberg, *Iron Curtain Journals*, p. 312.

43. Ginsberg, *Iron Curtain Journals*, p. 168.

44. "King of May: A Conversation," p. 174.

45. Ginsberg, *Iron Curtain Journals*, p. 244.

46. "King of May: A Conversation," pp. 172–78.

47. "Allen Ginsberg, American Poet—Beatnik—Report," Interior Ministry file, 3 May 1965, quoted in Blažek, "Deportation of the King of May," p. 43.

48. "Interview with Professor Eduard Goldstücker," National Security Archives, CNN broadcasts, episode 6, Reds, 1 November 1998, at https://nsarchive2.gwu.edu/coldwar /interviews/episode-6/goldstucker1.html (accessed 20 October 2020).

49. Pavel Juráček, *Deník III. 1959–1974*, Prague: Torst, 2018, p. 569. The article to which Juráček refers actually appeared in *Mladá fronta* on 16 May.

50. "King of May: A Conversation," pp. 177–82.

51. Allen Ginsberg, "Kral Majales," at https://www.poemhunter.com/poem/kral-majales -king-of-may/ (accessed 22 August 2020).

52. "King of May: A Conversation," p. 183.

53. "Záznam televizního rozhovoru šéfredaktora Televizních novin Československé televize Kamila Wintra s předsedou Svazu československých spisovatelů Eduardem Goldstückrem," 3 February 1968, *Pražské jaro 1968: dokumenty*, Ústav pro soudobé dějiny Akademie věd České republiky, at http://www.68.usd.cas.cz/cz/dokumenty-2.html (accessed 3 September 2020).

54. Ivan Klíma, "Po dlouhém mlčení pravda," *Lidové noviny*, 26 June 2017.

55. "Návrh. Stanoviska ÚV SČSS k některým otázkám československé literatury," in Mohyla, *IV. sjezd*, p. 12.

56. Milan Kundera, speech, 27 June 1967, in Mohyla, *IV. sjezd*, pp. 22–28. *Le Monde* published Solzhenitsyn's letter on 31 May.

57. Pavel Kohout, *Z deníku kontrarevolucionáře aneb Životy od tanku k tanku*, Prague: Mladá fronta, 1997, p. 235. For a blow-by-blow account of the congress that draws not only on the proceedings but also on the minutes of KSČ and ÚV SČSS private meetings, see Karel Kaplan, *"Všechno jste prohráli!" (Co prozrazují archivy o IV. sjezdu Svazu československých spisovatelů 1967)*, Prague: Ivo Železný, 1997.

58. Mohyla, *IV. sjezd*, p. 112.

59. Mohyla, *IV. sjezd*, pp. 132, 136–37.

60. Kaplan, *"Všechno jste prohráli!"* p. 112.

61. Mohyla, *IV. sjezd*, pp. 142, 146, 148, 150.

62. Mohyla, *IV. sjezd*, pp. 193–94.

63. Mohyla, *IV. sjezd*, p. 204.

64. "Přehled sjezdové diskuse," *Literární noviny*, Vol. 16, No. 27, 8 July 1967, pp. 4–5. The previous issue (No. 26, 1 July 1967) carried a report on the conference by Hendrych and the opening speeches by Vilém Závoda and Jiří Šotola. Jan Procházka's closing speech was carried in No. 30, 29 July 1967. The full proceedings were finally published in 1968.

65. "O operativní situaci na úseku kultury," supplement to StB report of 2 August 1967, quoted in Kaplan, *"Všechno jste prohráli!"* pp. 129–30. Bedřich Fučík was a Catholic literary critic and translator (of, among other works, Max Brod's autobiography *Streitbares Leben/Život plných bojů*). He was sentenced to fifteen years in 1952 in the trial of the "clerico-fascist vermin of the so-called Green International" (discussed earlier). He was amnestied in 1960.

66. Stenographic record of KSČ presidium meeting of 19 September 1967, quoted in Kaplan, *"Všechno jste prohráli!"* pp. 144–48.

67. "Resolution of the September 1967 CPCz [KSČ] Plenum," in *The Prague Spring: A National Security Archive Documents Reader*, ed. Jaromír Navrátil, Budapest: CEU Press, 1998, p. 12.

68. StB report of 9 November 1967, quoted in Kaplan, *"Všechno jste prohráli!"* p. 162.

69. StB report of 14 December 1967, quoted in Kaplan, *"Všechno jste prohráli!"* pp. 128, 160–61.

70. Milan Kundera, "Nesamozřejmost národa," *Literární noviny*, Vol. 16, No. 38, 22 September 1967, p. 3.

71. "Literární listy týdeník Svazu československých spisovatelů: kdo je kdo," *Literární listy*, Vol. 1, No. 0 [*sic*], 22 February 1968, p. 1.

72. Figure given in Galia Golan, *The Czechoslovak Reform Movement: Communism in Crisis 1962–1968*, Cambridge: Cambridge University Press, 1971, p. 250.

73. "Strahovské události v roce 1967 byly předzvěstí pražského jara," ČVUT zpravodajský servis, 29 October 2017.

74. "Slova o strahovských příčinách a následcích," *Mladá fronta*, 14 November 1967, pp. 1, 6. Jaromír Hořec criticized the press coverage of the events in *Rudé právo* and in "Logika nepravdy," *Universita Karlova*, Vol. 14, No. 7–8, 1967, pp. 1, 6.

75. These statements were published in *Student*, Vol. 3, No. 46, 1967, p. 3.

76. "Z rezoluce studentů Filozofické fakulty UK z 9. 11. 1967," reproduced in Jaroslav Pažout, "'Chceme světlo! Chceme studovat!' Demonstrace studentů z vysokoškolských kolejí v Praze na Strahově 31. října 1967," *Paměť a dějiny*, No. 1, 2008, p. 10.

77. Antonín Novotný, speech to KSČ presidium, 28 November 1967, excerpt in Pažout, "'Chceme světlo!" p. 11. On Novotný and intellectuals, see Mlynář, *Night Frost in Prague*, p. 72.

78. "Speeches by Alexander Dubček and Antonín Novotný at the CPCz [KSČ] CC Plenum, October 30–31, 1967," in Navrátil, *Prague Spring*, pp. 13–17.

79. See "Remarks by Leonid Brezhnev . . . December 9, 1967," in Navrátil, *Prague Spring*, pp. 18–19.

80. "János Kádár's Report to the HSWP Politburo of a Telephone Conversation with Leonid Brezhnev, December 13, 1967," in Navrátil, *Prague Spring*, pp. 20–22.

81. Šik's speech is reproduced in *Svědectví*, Vol. 9, Nos. 34, 35, 36, 1969, pp. 154–57.

82. "Resolution of the CPCz [KSČ] CC Plenum, Jan 5, 1968," in Navrátil, *Prague Spring*, pp. 34–36.

83. K. Urianek and M. Michálková, *Československo 1966–1971 Přehled událostí: Chronologie*, Prague: Komise vlády ČSSR pro analýzu událostí 1967–1970, 1991, pp. 31–32, 38.

84. Josef Smrkovský, "What Lies Ahead," in Navrátil, *Prague Spring*, p. 47; translation of "Jak nyní dál: Nad závěry lednového pléna ÚV KSČ," *Rudé právo*, 9 February 1968, p. 2.

85. Ludvík Vaculík, "Toleranční patent," *Literární listy*, Vol. 1, No. 1, 1 March 1968, pp. 1–2.

86. On the legal and bureaucratic complexities of the process of dismantling censorship, see Martina Šmídtová, "Pražské jaro 1968 v kulturních časopisech: Literární listy & Listy, Host do domu, Index," Diplomová práce, Masarykova univerzita, Brno, 2007, pp. 18–22.

87. Milan Jungmann, *Literárky—můj osud: kritické návraty ke kultuře padesátých a šedesátých let s aktuálními reflexemi*, Brno: Atlantis, 1999, p. 278, cited in Šmídtová, "Pražské jaro," p. 32.

88. See the ČTV video at https://www.facebook.com/archivct24/videos/1882042278475547 (accessed 18 September 2020).

89. Quoted in "Mladí se ptají na minulost, přítomnost a budoucnost," *Rudé právo*, Vol. 48, No. 73, 14 March 1968, pp. 1, 6.

90. Quoted in Alexandr Kramer, "Jaká demokracie," *Student*, Vol. 4, No. 14, 3 April 1968, p. 6.

91. "Mladi zastánci současné obrody," *Rudé právo*, Vol. 48, No. 80, 21 March 1968, p. 1.

92. In Jan Štern, "Dogmatici včera a dnes," *Práce*, Vol. 24, No. 65, 6 March 1968, p. 3.

93. See Urianek and Michálková, *Československo 1966–1971*, pp. 55–70.

94. Urianek and Michálková, *Československo 1966–1971*, pp. 58–84.

95. These are reproduced in Mlynář, *Night Frost in Prague*, pp. 268–81.

96. *The Action Programme of the Communist Party of Czechoslovakia*, Spokesman Pamphlet No. 8, Nottingham, UK: Bertrand Russell Peace Foundation, 1970, pp. 9–10; italics omitted.

97. *Action Programme*, p. 14; italics omitted.

98. *Action Programme*, p. 10; italics omitted.

99. *Action Programme*, p. 10; italics omitted.

100. "Ženy s podobným osudem . . . Výpráví Heda Kovályová-Margoliová," interview with Jan Kavan and Alexandr Kramer, p. 3. In the same series, see "Hovoří Lída Clementisová," *Student*, Vol. 4, No. 13, 27 March 1968, p. 1; "Hovoří Marian Vilbrová-Slingová, doplňuje Jan Šling," *Student*, Vol. 4, No. 15, 10 April 1968, p. 3.

101. Smrkovský, "What Lies Ahead," p. 47.

102. *Student*, Vol. 4, No. 12, 20 March 1968, p. 1.

103. Ivan Sviták, "Podnět generální prokuratuře," *Student*, Vol. 4, No. 14, 3 April 1968, p. 1.

104. I discuss *The Pleasure Principle* exhibition and the Paris surrealists' visit to Prague in 1968 in *PC*, pp. 433–39.

105. "Grass Kohout II. Dopis Pavla Kohouta Günteru Grassovi," *Student*, Vol. 4, No. 16, 1968, p. 3.

106. Urianek and Michálková, *Československo 1966–1971*, pp. 47–48.

107. "Stenographic Account of the Dresden Meeting, March 23, 1968," in Navrátil, *Prague Spring*, pp. 64–72. The Czechoslovak delegates were Dubček, Černík, Lenárt, Kolder, and Biľak.

108. "Open Letter from 134 Czechoslovak Writers and Cultural Figures to the CPCz [KSČ] Central Committee, March 25, 1968," in Navrátil, *Prague Spring*, pp. 76–77.

109. Bohuslav Blažek, "Demokracie náš cíl," *Student*, Vol. 4, No. 23, 5 June 1968, p. 1.

110. Kramer, "Jaká demokracie."

111. All quotations from *Action Programme*, pp. 6–9.

112. Václav Havel, "Na téma opozice," *Literární listy*, Vol. 1, No. 6, 4 April 1968, p. 4.

113. "Manifest Klubu angažovaných nestraníků," *Svobodné slovo*, 11 July 1968, translated in Navrátil, *Prague Spring*, pp. 156–57.

114. Zdeněk Karl, "Otevřený dopis," *Student*, Vol. 4, No. 21, 22 May 1968, p. 1.

115. Like other statewide organizations, the Union of Czechoslovak Journalists (SČSN) split into separate Czech and Slovak journalists' unions at its extraordinary congress of 21–23 June 1968.

116. "Text manifestu 2000 slov," at http://www.totalita.cz/txt/txt_2000slovt.php (accessed 30 September 2020).

117. "Text manifestu 2000 slov." An alternative English translation can be found in Navrátil, *Prague Spring*, pp. 177–81. The Warsaw letter is translated on pp. 234–38.

118. "Předsednictvo ústředního výboru KSČ československé veřejnosti. Zpráva ze schůze předsednictva ústředního výboru KSČ zabývající se manifestem Dva tisíce slov," 27 June 1968, at http://www.68.usd.cas.cz/files/dokumenty/edice/627_2.pdf (accessed 1 October 2020).

119. "Poznámky z diskuse na 81. schůzi předsednictva a sekretariátu ÚV KSČ k článku Dva tisíce slov," 27 June 1968, at http://www.68.usd.cas.cz/files/dokumenty/edice/627_1.pdf (accessed 1 October 2020).

120. Mlynář, *Night Frost in Prague*, pp. 146, 149–50.

121. "Všemu lidu Československé socialistické republiky," *Práce*, 21 August 1968, from *Sedm pražských dnů, 21.–27 srpna 1968: dokumentace*, Prague: Historický ústav ČSAV, September 1968, p. 6. For an alternative translation, see Navrátil, *Prague Spring*, pp. 414–15. President Ludvík Svoboda also attended this meeting from around midnight to 1:00 a.m.

122. Mlynář, *Night Frost in Prague*, pp. 150–51.

123. For a detailed account of the 20 August meeting by an anonymous participant, see "Informace o osudné noci," *Rudé právo*, 23 August 1968, reprinted in *Sedm pražských dnů*, pp. 8–13.

124. The KSS presidium initially supported the invasion by a six-to-four vote, based on a false report that, with the exception of Smrkovský and Kriegel, all members of the KSČ politburo, including Dubček, had signed the invitation letter. The presidium changed its position when the truth became known.

125. The relevant statements are reproduced in *Sedm pražských dnů*, ch. 2, "Středa—21. srpna."

126. "The 'Letter of Invitation' from the Anti-Reformist Faction of the CPCz [KSČ] Leadership, August 1968," in Navrátil, *Prague Spring*, pp. 324–25.

127. "CPSU CC Politburo Message to Alexander Dubček, August 13, 1968," in Navrátil, *Prague Spring*, pp. 343–44.

128. "Transcript of Leonid Brezhnev's Telephone Conversation with Alexander Dubček, August 13, 1968," in Navrátil, *Prague Spring*, pp. 345–56.

129. For examples, see *Sedm pražských dnů*, pp. 15–24. The template was the draft "Declaration of the CPCz [KSČ] Presidium and the Government of the Czechoslovak Socialist Republic" appended to the Soviet politburo's 17 August resolution to invade Czechoslovakia. The text is translated in Navrátil, *Prague Spring*, pp. 379–83.

130. Urianek and Michálková, *Československo 1966–1971*, p. 261.

131. "Provolání redakce Rudého práva," 21 August 1968, in *Sedm pražských dnů*, pp. 30–31.

132. Navrátil, *Prague Spring*, p. 313. The eventual total was closer to 500,000. Jiří Šedivý, "The Pull-out of Soviet Troops from Czechoslovakia," *Perspectives*, No. 2, 1993–1994, p. 21.

133. Navrátil, *Prague Spring*, pp. 416–19; *Sedm pražských dnů*, pp. 64–72.

134. "Alexander Dubček's Recollections of the Invasion and Its Immediate Aftermath," in Navrátil, *Prague Spring*, pp. 420–23.

135. "Zpráva o situaci v Praze. Noc na 21. srpna." *Mladá fronta*, 21 August 1968, in *Sedm pražských dnů*, pp. 13–15.

136. "Staroměstské náměstí v hodině dvanácté," *Práce*, special 2nd ed., 21 August 1968, in *Sedm pražských dnů*, p. 32.

137. "Parlamentní zpravodaj hlásí," *Mladý svět*, No. 35, 1968, in *Sedm pražských dnů*, p. 127.

138. "Zpráva o situace v Praze. Psáno horkým perem," *Svobodné slovo*, 22 August 1968, in *Sedm pražských dnů*, p. 36.

139. See Prokop Tomek and Ivo Pejčoch, *Okupace 1968 a její oběti*, Prague: Vojenský historický ústav, 2017.

140. Urianek and Michálková, *Československo 1966–1971*, p. 250.

141. Jan Drda, "Nekřivte jim ani vlas, nedejte nim ani kapku vody," *Rudé právo*, 27 August 1968, in *Sedm pražských dnů*, pp. 374–75.

142. "Lenine, probuď se!" *Mladá fronta*, 25 August 1968, in *Sedm pražských dnů*, pp. 310–11.

143. "Varování před zrádci," *Zemědělské noviny*, 24 August 1968, in *Sedm pražských dnů*, pp. 196–97.

144. "Zpráva o situaci v Praze," *Rudé právo*, 22 August 1968, in *Sedm pražských dnů*, pp. 52–53.

145. Mlynář, *Night Frost in Prague*, p. 199.

146. "Zpráva M. Vaculíka o průběhu zasedání části ÚV KSČ v Hotelu Praha," *Mladá fronta*, 23 August 1968, in *Sedm pražských dnů*, pp. 74–75.

147. "Discussions Involving Certain Members of the CPCz [KSČ] CC Presidium and Secretariat . . . August 22, 1968," in Navrátil, *Prague Spring*, pp. 460–64. See also Mlynář, *Night Frost in Prague*, pp. 187–98.

148. Urianek and Michálková, *Československo 1966–1971*, p. 301.

149. "Prohlášení mimořádného XIV. sjezdu KSČ občanům ČSSR," *Rudé právo*, 23 August 1968, in *Sedm pražských dnů*, pp. 94–97. See also *The Secret Vysocany Congress: Proceedings and Documents of the Extraordinary Fourteenth Congress of the Communist Party of Czechoslovakia, 22 August 1968*, ed. Jiří Pelikán, trans. George Theiner and Deryck Viney, London: Allen Lane, 1971.

150. "Nemožné se stalo skutkem," *Svoboda*, 24 August 1968, in *Sedm pražských dnů*, pp. 106–8.

151. "Prohlášení mimořádného XIV. sjezdu KSČ občanům ČSSR," p. 96.

152. "Komuniké z 1. zasedání nově zvoleného KSČ," *Rudé právo*, 24 August 1968, in *Sedm pražských dnů*, p. 173. Husák and Goldstücker were among the new presidium members.

153. "Alexander Dubček's Recollections of the Invasion," p. 422.

154. "Minutes of the First Post-Invasion Meeting of the 'Warsaw Five' in Moscow, August 24, 1968," in Navrátil, *Prague Spring*, p. 475.

155. Mlynář, *Night Frost in Prague*, pp. 180–81.

156. "Minutes of Soviet-Czechoslovak Talks in the Kremlin, August 23 and 26, 1968 (Excerpts)," in Navrátil, *Prague Spring*, pp. 469–73.

157. "Minutes of the First Post-Invasion Meeting of the 'Warsaw Five,'" p. 475.

158. Mlynář, *Night Frost in Prague*, p. 242; "Alexander Dubček's Recollections of the Invasion," pp. 481–83. For Dubček's speech, see Navrátil, *Prague Spring*, p. 472.

159. Petr Král, "Fin d'un printemps," in Josef Koudelka, *Prague, 1968: Photographies de Josef Koudelka*, Paris: Centre National de la Photographie, 1990, unpaginated.

160. "The Moscow Protocol, August 26, 1968," in Navrátil, *Prague Spring*, pp. 477–80.

161. "Josef Smrkovský's Address to the People after His Return from Moscow, August 29, 1968 (Excerpts)," in Navrátil, *Prague Spring*, p. 489.

162. Kundera, *Unbearable Lightness of Being*, p. 26.

163. "Dopis s. Dubčekovi," *Večerní Praha*, 24 August 1968, in *Sedm pražských dnů*, p. 102.

164. The words come from Comenius's *Kšaft umírající matky Jednoty Bratrské*, published in 1650 as a response to the Peace of Westphalia.

165. T. G. Masaryk, *Cesta demokracie: soubor projevů za republiky*, Vol. 1, *1918–1920*, Prague: ČIN, 1934, p. 10.

166. Šik and Goldstücker both returned for a brief visit in January 1969, but neither stayed. See "Ota Sik, Eduard Goldstuecker Return to Czechoslovakia, Plan to Leave Again," Jewish Telegraphic Agency, 24 January 1969.

167. Olga Szantová, "Ten Years Ago Last Russian Soldiers Left Czechoslovakia," Radio Prague International, 22 June 2001. The treaty is translated in Navrátil, *Prague Spring*, pp. 533–36.

168. Svaz vysokoškolského studentstva, "Deset bodů," at https://www.janpalach.cz/cs /default/indexovnik/vecny/idv/49. See also the documents collected in Pavel Kadrmas, "Studentské hnutí proti ústupkům a poraženectví," in *Proměny pražského jara 1968–1969: Sborník studií a dokumentů o nekapitulantských postojích v československé společnosti*, ed. Jindřich Pecka and Vilém Prečan, Brno: Doplněk, 1993, pp. 245–80.

169. Ludvík Vaculík, *A Czech Dreambook*, trans. Gerald Turner, Prague: Karolinum, 2019, p. 118. Vaculík is quoting from the minutes of the meeting. Ludvík and Martin Vaculík were not related.

170. "Interview with Professor Eduard Goldstücker," CNN broadcasts, episode 14, Red Spring (The Sixties), 17 January 1999, at https://nsarchive2.gwu.edu/coldwar/interviews /episode-14/goldstucker1.html (accessed 20 October 2020).

171. "O smyslu našeho konání," *Listy*, No. 1, 7 November 1968, quoted in "Kalendárium roku 1968," at http://www.totalita.cz/kalendar/kalend_1968_11.php (accessed 19 October 2020).

172. Mlynář, *Night Frost in Prague*, pp. 253–55. Indra remained in Moscow "to receive medical treatment" after the rest of the Czechoslovak delegation returned home on 27 August.

173. Mlynář, *Night Frost in Prague*, p. 66.

174. "Minutes of Soviet-Czechoslovak Negotiations in Kiev, 7–8 December 1968," in Navrátil, *Prague Spring*, pp. 555–60.

175. "Poslední Dopis Jana Palacha," at http://www.moderni-dejiny.cz/clanek/posledni -dopis-jana-palacha/ (accessed 20 October 2020).

176. Petr Mančal, "Pohřeb Jana Palacha," Český rozhlas, 22 January 2007.

177. Jan Hřídel, "Přechodový rituál k normalizaci. Při pohřbu Jana Palacha lidé vyšli do ulic, ale zůstali zticha," Česká televize, 25 January 2019.

178. Jan Gazdík, "Příběh Palachova hrobu vypovídá o stupňující se komunistické zvůli i teroru StB," Aktuálně.cz, 21 January 2020.

179. Quoted in Mančal, "Pohřeb Jana Palacha."

180. "Kdo, když ne my, kdy, když ne teď!" Pavel Kovář, interview with Květoslava Moravková, iForum, Online magazín Univerzity Karlovy, 4 November 2009.

181. Radim Kopáč, "Aj byl to ohniváček na nejtenčí větvi . . . ," *UNI Kulturní magazín*, January 2019. Both poems are reproduced here.

182. Preface to Milan Kundera, *Life Is Elsewhere*, trans. Peter Kussi, London: Penguin, 1986.

183. Kundera, *Life Is Elsewhere* (1986 ed.), p. 264.

184. Kundera, *Life Is Elsewhere* (2000 ed.), p. 356.

185. See Prikryl, "Kundera Conundrum."

186. Kundera, *Life Is Elsewhere* (2000 ed.), p. 364. Kundera draws an explicit parallel between Jaromil and Palach; see pp. 392–93.

187. Reinerová, *Kavárna nad Prahou*, pp. 75, 77.

188. Quoted in Brian Kenety, "How Czechoslovakia's 'Moral Victory' on Ice Triggered the Hockey Riots, Onset of 'Normalisation,'" Radio Prague International, 28 March 2019.

189. Figures from "Kalendárium roku 1969: srpnové události," at http://www.totalita.cz/kalendar/kalend_1969_08.php (accessed 29 October 2020).

190. For a fuller account, see Vladimir V. Kusin, *From Dubček to Charter 77: A Study of "Normalization" in Czechoslovakia, 1968–1978,* Edinburgh: Q Press, 1978, pp. 70–74.

191. Miroslav Brada, "Marta Kubišová: Tí, čo boli pri revolúcii, sa na nej stále vezú," interview, *Britské listy,* 18 August 2003. Kubišová's story, along with that of her fellow singers Helena Vondráčková and Karel Gott, is very well told in Mariusz Szczygieł, *Gottland: Mostly True Stories from Half of Czechoslovakia,* trans. Antonia Lloyd-Jones, Brooklyn, NY: Melville House, 2014, pp. 161–85. In my opinion, *Gottland,* a book of reportage in the Egon Erwin Kisch tradition by an eminent Polish journalist, is one of the best works ever written on Absurdistan.

192. "Modlitba pro Martu," at https://www.supraphon.cz/historie-spolecnosti/123-modlitba-pro-martu (accessed 13 November 2020).

193. Quotations in this and the previous paragraph are from Marta Kubišová, "Dokud tu byl Václav, byla jsem v klidu," in *Bytová revolta: Jak ženy dělaly disent,* ed. Marcela Linková and Naďa Straková, Prague: Academia, 2018, pp. 179–80.

194. "Lyrics: Modlitba pro Martu," at https://www.musixmatch.com/lyrics/Marta-Kubisova/Modlitba-pro-Martu (accessed 13 November 2020).

Chapter 12: Normalization and Its Discontents

1. See František Morkes, "Jak vzniklo slovo 'spartakiáda,'" *Český rozhlas,* 24 September 2010.

2. All these stamps are depicted in Dušek, *Příručka pro sběratele československých poštovních známek.*

3. Pavel Kohout, quoted in Tomáš Lánský, "Palach se upálit nechtěl, byl to 'omyl,' hlásal kovaný komunista Nový," iDNES.cz zpravodajství, 23 January 2019.

4. Both quoted in Jan Gazdík, "Pád běžecké legendy. Emil Zátopek se stal nechtěným symbolem nastupující normalizace," Aktuálně.cz, 26 March 2018.

5. Jiří Raška, "Vím, že jsem udělal chybu: Jiří Raška se distancuje od svého podpisu pod 2000 slov," *Rudé právo,* Vol. 50–51, No. 111, 12 May 1970, p. 2.

6. Quoted in Markéta Bernatt-Reszczyńská, "Nejstatečnější. Věra Čáslavská protestovala proti sovětské okupaci na stupních vítězů," *Paměť národa,* 19 October 2020.

7. Martin Hašek, "Legendární gymnastka Věra Čáslavská: Můj meč hlavy nestínal," interview with iSport.cz, 4 November 2011. At the time, the scoring system ran from A to C, with C being the most difficult—hence Ultra-C.

8. See Olga Sommerová's film *Věra 68* (2012).

9. Avery Brundage to Pedro Ramirez Vazquez, 19 August 1969, quoted in Eric Gomez, "Letters Reveal Olympic Organizers' Desire to Curb U.S. Protests in '68," ESPN, 16 October 2018; Bryan Armen Graham, "Donald Trump Blasts NFL Anthem Protesters: 'Get that Son of a Bitch off the Field,'" *Guardian,* 23 September 2017.

10. Quoted in Randy Harvey, "Blossoming in the Prague Spring: Gymnastics: Vera Caslavska Won Olympic Medals in 1964 and '68, Then Disappeared . . . ," *Los Angeles Times,* 5 April 1990. Callouses are needed to perform on the uneven bars.

11. Quoted in Bernatt-Reszczyńská, "Nejstatečnější."

12. As reported by the British gymnast Mary Prestidge, quoted in Tom Reynolds, "Vera Caslavska and the Forgotten Story of Her 1968 Olympics Protest," BBC Sport, 20 October 2018.

13. See the newsreel footage in *Věra 68*.

14. Quoted in Bernatt-Reszczyńská, "Nejstatečnější." ·

15. According to the method of calculation used by the IOC, whose ranking order is based first on the number of gold medals won, then silver and bronze. This is distinct from ranking by the total number of medals won.

16. "Za účasti soudruhů A. Dubčeka, J. Smrkovského, O. Černíka a E. Erbana president republiky přijal čs. olympijskou výpravu," *Rudé právo*, Vol. 49, No. 298, 1 November 1968, p. 1. Footage of the ceremony, including Svoboda's speech, is included in *Věra 68*.

17. Čáslavská, quoted in Bernatt-Reszczyńská, "Nejstatečnější." Unless otherwise indicated, everything quoted in this and the next two paragraphs is from Čáslavská in the film *Věra 68*.

18. For details, see Harvey, "Blossoming in the Prague Spring."

19. Chikahito Harada, Japanese ambassador to Czech Republic, quoted in "Čáslavská převzala Řád vycházejícího slunce," Sport.cz, 7 December 2010.

20. Hašek, "Legendární gymnastka Věra Čáslavská."

21. In 1969–1972, 653 people were sentenced to prison terms for political reasons in the Czech Lands. Jaroslav Cuhra, *Trestní represe odpůrců režimu v letech 1969–1972*, Prague: Ústav pro soudobé dějiny AV ČR, 1997, p. 75. The largest trial was that of Peter Uhl and other members of the Revolutionary Youth Movement in 1969–1970. Contrast figures given above (pp. 323–24) for the 1948–1967 period.

22. An official list of Czech citizens (including three thousand émigrés) who allegedly knowingly collaborated with the StB, based on information in StB files and published by the Ministry of the Interior in 2003, contained some seventy-five thousand names. See Dita Asiedu, "Czechs Wait Thirteen Years for Official Names of Secret Police Collaborators," Radio Prague International, 24 March 2003.

23. Quoted in Benjamin Tallis, "Panel Stories: Public Lies and Private Lives in Paneláks and Sídlištes," in *Abolishing Prague: Essays and Interpretations*, ed. Louis Armand, Prague: Literaria Pragensia, 2014, p. 126.

24. Mlynář, *Night Frost in Prague*, pp. 64–65, 76.

25. Kusin, *From Dubček to Charter 77*, p. 74.

26. Figures from Kusin, *From Dubček to Charter 77*, p. 81.

27. Havel, "Power of the Powerless."

28. Unless otherwise stated, all quotations and figures in this and the following paragraph are taken from "Kalendárium roku 1970," at http://totalita.cz (accessed 9 November 2020).

29. "Komunistická strana Československa (KSČ): odhad velikosti členské základny," at http://www.totalita.cz/vysvetlivky/s_ksc_clen_01.php (accessed 9 November 2020).

30. See also "Pravicoví oportunisté—zpráva o černé listině," *Lidové noviny*, 21 July 1992.

31. Agnew, *The Czechs*, p. 271. For fuller details of the purges in education and academia, see Kusin, *From Dubček to Charter 77*, pp. 95–99.

32. Agnew, *The Czechs*, p. 272.

33. See Bren, *The Greengrocer and His TV*, pp. 45–48.

34. Not to be confused with *Student*, which published its last legal issue on 21 August 1968. The *Student* editors decided to cease publication after the Moscow Protocol.

35. Banned in 1965, *Tvář* was revived in 1968.

36. "Smích dějin," *Analogon*, No. 1, 1969, illustrations between pp. 85 and 86. The issue also contained essays and poetry by Parisian and Czech surrealists; Ivan Sviták's "Krise vědomí" (Crisis of consciousness); interviews with Herbert Marcuse and Claude Lévi-Strauss; excerpts from the manifesto "For an Independent Revolutionary Art," written by André Breton and Leon Trotsky in Mexico City in 1938; extracts from Karel Teige's letters to Marie Pospíšilová; several pages of Záviš Kalandra's writings; and a Czech translation of André Breton's "Open Letter to Paul Éluard," appealing to his fellow poet to intercede to prevent Kalandra's execution in 1950. I discuss Breton's "Open Letter" and Éluard's response in *PC*, pp. 410–12. *Analogon* was revived in 1990 and is still being published several times a year.

37. Teige, *Zápasy o smysl moderní tvorby*. Some copies survived, with the imprint Československý spisovatel 1969.

38. Hrabal, *Gaps*, pp. 81–84.

39. Bohumil Hrabal, *Too Loud a Solitude*, trans. Michael Henry Heim, New York: Harcourt Brace Jovanovich, 1976, pp. 2–3.

40. Miroslav Lamač, "Předmluva," in *Osma a Skupina*, p. 7.

41. Hrabal, *Gaps*, p. 81; Martina Spáčilová, "Zmizelé knihy: Původní české beletristické knihy, které byly na přelomu šedesátých a sedmdesátých let dvacátého století cenzurou z ideologických důvodů "zastaveny" v různých fázích výroby či distribuce," Diplomová práce, Univerzita Karlova v Praze, Filozofická fakulta, 2014, pp. 27–36.

42. "Směrnice ministerstva kultury ČSR o zvláštních fondech tiskovin v knihovnách jednotné soustavy ČSR," quoted in Spáčilová, "Zmizelé knihy," p. 61. Figures from "Rok 1972: Seznam zakázaných knih aneb 'Jen pro vnitřní potřebu,'" Český rozhlas, 2 July 2018. For a fuller discussion of books banned from libraries in the normalization period, see *CB*, pp. 257–69.

43. Jiří Brabec et al., *Slovník zakázaných autorů 1948–1980*, Prague: Státní pedagogické nakladatelství, 1991. Among these authors were Ivan Blatný, Egon Bondy, Jana Černá, Václav Černý, Jindřich Chalupecký, Jiří Dienstbier, Vratislav Effenberger, Anna Fárová, Viktor Fischl, Bedřich Fučík, Eduard Goldstücker, Jan Grossman, Jiří Gruša, Jiří Hanzelka, Václav Havel, Josef Hiršal, Adolf Hoffmeister, Miroslav Holub, Egon Hostovský, Bohumil Hrabal, Ivan Martin Jirous, Robert Kalivoda, Eva Kantůrková, Ivan Klíma, Alexandr Kliment, Pavel Kohout, Jiří Kolář, Karel Kosík, Heda Margolius Kovály, Petr Král, Ludvík Kundera, Milan Kundera, Karel Kyncl, Miroslav Lamač, Jiří Lederer, A. J. Liehm, Věra Linhartová, Arnošt Lustig, Emanuel Mandler, Michal Mareš, Jiří Mucha, Jan Mukařovský, Karel Pecka, Ferdinand Peroutka, Petr Pithart, Jan Procházka, Lenka Procházková, Alfréd Radok, Lenka Reinerová, Zdena Salivarová, Jaroslav Seifert, Karol Sidon, Josef Škvorecký, Ivan Sviták, Pavel Tigrid, Josef Topol, Zdeněk Urbánek, Ludvík Vaculík, Jaroslava Vondráčková, Jiří Voskovec, Prokop Voskovec, Ivan Vyskočil, Jan Werich, and Jan Zábrana. I have confined this list to writers who were still living at the time and are mentioned or discussed elsewhere in this book.

44. Josef Škvorecký to Louis Armand, 12 September 2010, *Vlak*, No. 4, 2012, pp. 3–4.

45. David Vichnar, "The Fabulous Artificer, the Architect, and the Roadmender: On Retranslating Aloys Skoumal's Czech Ulysses," in *Retranslating Joyce for the 21st Century*, ed. Jolanta Wawrzycka and Erika Mihálycsa, Leiden: Brill Rodopi, 2020, pp. 151–52.

46. Böll was speaking at a press conference in Stockholm on 8 December 1972, quoted in A. Heneka et al., eds., *A Besieged Culture: Czechoslovakia Ten Years after Helsinki,* Stockholm: Charta 77 Foundation, 1985, p. 15.

47. See Jan Čulík, ed., *Knihy za ohradou: Česká literatura v exilových nakladatelstvích,* Prague: Trizonia, 1991.

48. Marketa Goetz-Stankiewicz, ed., *Good-bye Samizdat: Twenty Years of Czechoslovak Underground Writing,* Evanston, IL: Northwestern University Press, 1992, p. xxvii.

49. Agnew, *The Czechs,* p. 271.

50. Antonin Liehm, *Trois générations. Entretiens sur le phénomène culturel tchécoslovaque,* Paris: Gallimard, 1970, publisher's blurb.

51. Jarmila Cysařová, "Koordinační výbor tvůrčích svazů vznikl jako obrana proti represím," in *Souboj slova a obrazu s mocnými: Novináři a média v Pražském jaru´68,* ed. Jindřich Beránek, Prague: Klub novinářů Pražského jara, 1968, p. 151.

52. Quoted at http://www.totalita.cz/kalendar/kalend_1969_12.php (accessed 10 November 2020).

53. Central Committee of the National Front of the Czech Socialist Republic, "Zvláštní informace. Současná politická situace ve vedení uměleckých a tvůrčích svazů a návrhy na řešení neuspokojivých vztahů vůči politice NF ČSR," quoted in Jiří Mikeš, "Svaz českých výtvarných umělců v době normalizace," Magisterská diplomová práce, Masarykova univerzita, Filozofická fakulta, Brno, 2013, p. 6.

54. Kateřina Bláhová, "Svaz českých spisovatelů (1), 1969–1970," in *Slovník české literatury po roce 1945,* ed. Michal Přibáň, Prague: Ústav pro českou literaturu AV ČR, n.d.

55. "Stanovisko umělců a kulturních pracovníků," in Ševčík et al., *České umění 1938–1989,* p. 342; originally published in *Rudé právo,* Vol. 51, No. 301, 19 December 1970, p. 1.

56. "Návrh stanov Svazu českých výtvarných umělců," *Výtvarná práce,* No. 5, 2 March 1971, p. 1, quoted in Binarová, "Svaz výtvarných umělců," p. 192.

57. Binarová, "Svaz výtvarných umělců," p. 197.

58. Srp, *Adolf Hoffmeister,* p. 298. Other details are from pp. 356–60.

59. Adolf Hoffmeister, diary entries, quoted in Srp, *Adolf Hoffmeister,* pp. 298–99.

60. Adolf Hoffmeister, preface to *Poprava,* quoted in Srp, *Adolf Hoffmeister,* p. 300.

61. Adolf Hoffmeister, *Poprava—Pissoir,* Prague: Dilia, 1991, p. 12, quoted in Srp, *Adolf Hoffmeister,* p. 301.

62. Srp, *Adolf Hoffmeister,* p. 300.

63. These are all reproduced in Srp, *Adolf Hoffmeister,* pp. 299–329, or Šmejkal, *Hoffmeisterova ironická kronika,* pp. 201–30.

64. Reproduced in Šmejkal, *Hoffmeisterova ironická kronika,* p. 214.

65. Hoffmeister, diary entries, quoted in Srp, *Adolf Hoffmeister,* pp. 304, 308. Janeček was a painter and graphic artist; Brdečka a writer, artist, and film director; Hofman a director of animated films.

66. "Miloš Forman's Official Website," at https://milosforman.com/en/about/biography (accessed 26 November 2020). Compare Forman, *Turnaround,* pp. 35–36.

67. Forman and Novák, *Turnaround,* pp. 26, 28. Rudolf Forman was actually Miloš's stepfather, but Miloš only learned this as an adult. His biological father was the Jewish architect Otto Kohn.

68. Forman and Novák, *Turnaround*, p. 54.

69. Arthur Miller, "The Chelsea Affect," *Granta*, 28 June 2002.

70. Ian Willoughby, "Gail Papp on Václav Havel among New York's Hippies—and under House Arrest in Communist Czechoslovakia," Radio Prague International, 19 November 2018. Other details are from Michael Zantovsky, *Havel: A Life*, New York: Grove Press, 2014, pp. 110–11.

71. Salman Rushdie, "An Ageing Rocker," *Prospect Magazine*, May 1999. On "Massachusetts," see Jonathan Bolton, *Worlds of Dissent: Charter 77, the Plastic People of the Universe, and Czech Culture under Communism*, Cambridge, MA: Harvard University Press, 2012, p. 10.

72. Forman, *Miloš Forman Stories*, p. 102.

73. Donald Clarke, "May '68: When Revolution Came to the Cote d'Azur," *Irish Times*, 5 May 2018.

74. Forman and Novák, *Turnaround*, pp. 173–74. See also Věra Křesadlová, quoted in "Spolužáci mezi tanky," Ten okamžik, Český TV, 29 July 2018; Tomáš Koloc, "Miloš Forman— Osud viděný zblízka (3. část—proč a jak odchází umělci z vlasti)," *Kulturní noviny*, No. 11, 2017.

75. Forman and Novák, *Turnaround*, p. 175. See also Škvorecký, *All the Bright Young Men and Women*, pp. 180–81.

76. Kundera, *Unbearable Lightness of Being*, p. 75.

77. Forman and Novák, *Turnaround*, p. 175.

78. Jan Herget, "Místo emigrace zvolil v roce 1968 návrat do vlasti. 'Nikdy jsem nelitoval,' říká Jiří Suchý," interview, Český rozhlas, 8 August 2018.

79. Quoted in Juráček, *Deník III*, pp. 756–58. The Mannheim proclamation, a typescript written in English and headed "Statement by Pavel Juráček," is reproduced in Magdaléna Dvořáčková, "Pavel Juráček v kontextu šedesátých let," Diplomová práce, Univerzita Karlova v Praze, Fakulta Humanitních Studií, 2017, p. 119. Other details are from "Pavel Juráček," at https://www.filmovyprehled.cz/cs/person/8127/pavel-juracek (accessed 28 December 2020).

80. "The Case for Pavel Juráček," Berkeley Art Museum and Pacific Film Archive, 2013, at https://web.archive.org/web/20130925161339/http://www.bampfa.berkeley.edu/film/FN14925 (accessed 28 December 2020).

81. Oldřich Škácha, "Václav Havel as a Witness at the Wedding of Pavel Juráček," photograph in Václav Havel Library, at https://artsandculture.google.com/asset/v%C3%A1clav-havel-as-a-witness-at-the-wedding-of-pavel-jur%C3%A1%C4%8Dek/HAEXJ6ns3KjEBw (accessed 14 February 2022).

82. "Jaromil Jires: 'S'il faut être malheureux, autant l'être dans son pays,'" interview with Michèle Levieux, *L'Humanité*, 21 August 1999.

83. Renata Adler, "Film Festival: A Muted Comedy and a Deeply Moving Documentary from Czechoslovakia End Series: 'Firemen's Ball' and 'Oratorio for Prague,'" *New York Times*, 30 September 1968, p. 60.

84. Renata Adler, "Liberalization and Invasion: High Drama in Low Key," *New York Times*, 30 September 1968, p. 60.

85. Škvorecký, *All the Bright Young Men and Women*, pp. 136–37.

86. Gerald O'Grady, "Hallelujah for Prague: An American Orbis Picta," in *The Banned and the Beautiful: A Survey of Czech Filmmaking 1963–1990*, New York: Public Theatre, 1990, p. 60.

87. Quoted in Jiří Pánek, "Střelba do oken zpěvačky Kubišové. Pachatel se přiznal po třech dnech," iDNES.cz, 23 March 2019.

88. Marta Kubišová, "Dokud tu byl Václav," in Linková and Straková, *Bytová revolta*, p. 181.

89. Quoted in Pánek, "Střelba do oken."

90. Quoted in Ian Willoughby, "Prayer for Marta Singer Kubišová Recalls Dramatic Comeback during 1989's Velvet Revolution," Radio Prague International, 18 November 2009. Her performance can be viewed at https://www.youtube.com/watch?v=npMZ7UxwVgU (accessed 17 March 2021).

91. Ivana Košuličová, "Everything You Always Wanted to Know about My Heart . . . An Interview with Film Director Jan Němec," *Central Europe Review*, Vol. 3, No. 17, 14 May 2001.

92. "The Life of Singer Marta Kubišová through the Eyes of Jan Němec," at https://iffr.com/en/2017/films/the-life-of-singer-marta-kubišová-through-the-eyes-of-jan-němec (accessed 19 December 2020).

93. Peter Hames, "Jan Němec: Enfant Terrible," Czech Centre, London, n.d. [2017].

94. "Josef Skvorecky: The Art of Fiction No. 112," interview with John A. Glusman, *Paris Review*, No. 112, Winter 1989. They left Czechoslovakia on 31 January 1969.

95. Škvorecký and Salivarová, *Samožerbuch*, pp. 25, 181.

96. Zdena Salivarová-Škvorecká, ed., *Osočení—Dopisy lidí ze seznamu*, Toronto: Sixty-Eight Publishers, 1993. Sixty-Eight Publishers did print one more book, Škvorecký's *Povídky tenor-saxofonisty*, but this was a limited edition for "our most faithful readers" and not for sale to the public. *Osočení* was first published in the Czech Republic in 2000 by Atlantis.

97. "And as if it had been a light thing for him to walk in the sins of Jeroboam son of Nebat, he [Ahab] took as his wife Jezebel daughter of King Ethbaal of the Sidonians, and went and served Baal, and worshiped him." 1 Kings 16:31.

98. Josef Škvorecký, *Two Murders in My Double Life*, New York: Farrar, Straus, Giroux, 2001, ch. 1, as published in *New York Times*, 20 May 2001. The fictionalizing here is very thin: *cibulka* in Czech means a (small) onion, *mrkvička* a (young) carrot. See also Muriel Blaive, "L'ouverture des archives d'une police politique communiste: le cas tchèque, de Zdena Salivarová à Milan Kundera," in *Archives et histoire dans les sociétés postcommunistes*, ed. Sonia Combe, Paris: La Découverte, 2009, pp. 203–25.

99. Ivan Passer, interview by Olivier Père, "Eclairage intime de Ivan Passer," Arte.tv, 2 November 2016.

100. "In-person: Q&A with Director Ivan Passer," Billy Wilder Theater, 14 September 2018, at https://www.cinema.ucla.edu.

101. John Penner, "Milos Forman, Ivan Passer and Their 73-Year Friendship: Childhood, Escaping Czechoslovakia and Conquering Hollywood," *Los Angeles Times*, 13 December 2019.

102. Forman, *Miloš Forman Stories*, pp. 102–3.

103. Forman and Novák, *Turnaround*, pp. 175–76.

104. John Penner, "Behind the Story: Learning the Truth about Director Milos Forman's Escape from Czechoslovakia," *Los Angeles Times*, 13 December 2019.

105. Forman and Novák, *Turnaround*, p. 176.

106. Quoted on the Miloš Forman website; see also Forman and Novák, *Turnaround*, pp. 189–92.

107. Forman and Novák, *Turnaround*, pp. 230–31.

108. Zdeněk Mahler, quoted in Tomáš Koloc, "Miloš Forman, válka, domov a sen," *Kulturní noviny*, No. 16, 2018.

109. Vojtěch Jeřábek, *Českoslovenští uprchlíci ve studené válce*, Brno: Stilus, 2005, p. 150, quoted in Michaela Tvrdíková, "Proměny československé emigrace v letech 1948–1989," Diplomová práce, Masarykova Univerzita v Brně, Filozofická fakulta, 2007, p. 34.

110. Quoted in Zdeňka Kuchyňová, "Do dvou let odešlo po srpnu 1968 do emigrace 70 tisíc lidí," Radio Prague International, 25 August 2018.

111. Václav Chyský, "Exil jako důsledek totalitarismu," in *Český a Slovenský exil 20. století*, Vol. 1, exh. cat., ed. Jan Kratochvíl, Brno: Meadow Art, 2002, p. 44.

112. Jan Bohata, "Jan Werich v srpnu 1968 emigroval," *MF Dnes*, 22 August 2018.

113. Details and quotations from "Rok šedesát osm Jana Wericha: Před tanky utekl z Prahy do Vídně, málem přišel o ženu a skoro zemřel," Blesk.cz, 20 August 2018.

114. This figure is quoted in Tvrdíková, "Proměny československé emigrace," p. 34; Nikola Kleinová, "Emigrace z komunistického Československa a Češi v Dánsku," Diplomová práce, Universita Karlova v Praze, Fakulta Humanitních Studií, 2013, p. 36; "Emigrace aneb Století ztracených domovů," Český rozhlas, 24 November 2013.

115. Chyský gives a figure of 100,000 to 130,000; Tomáš Vilímek gives a figure of up to 138,000. Both cited in Kleinová, "Emigrace," p. 3.

116. Kusin, *From Dubček to Charter 77*, pp. 173–74.

117. Kleinová, "Emigrace," p. 36.

118. See Škvorecký, "Bohemia of the Soul."

119. Wikipedie.cz, entry "Emigrace."

120. Tvrdíková, "Proměny československé emigrace," p. 34; Kleinová, "Emigrace," p. 36.

121. "Vladimír Vlček, biografie," Česko-Slovenská filmová databáze.

122. Jill Sykes, "First Juliet a Historical Figure in Dance," *Sydney Morning Herald*, 19 February 2013.

123. Quotations from "The Lullaby," "In the Asmodeus Shadow," "Farewell," "Sweet Sixteen," "In the Teens in 1944," "Grandmother Bertha," "From Fragrances," "Růže a hrob," and "A Question to Mankind" (respectively), all in Věra Weislitzová, *Dcera Olgy a Lea/The Daughter of Olga and Leo*, Prague: Unitisk, 1994. The Czech and English texts are not always the same.

124. Deyan Sudjic, *Jan Kaplický—Vlastní cestou/His Own Way*, exh. cat., Prague: DOX Centre for Contemporary Art, 2010, unpaginated.

125. Ivan Margolius, *Jan Kaplický Drawings*, London: Circa, 2015, p. 18. See also Jan Kaplický, *Album*, Prague: Labyrint, 2010, p. 166.

126. Kaplický, *Album*, pp. 198, 202.

127. "About—AI Design," at https://www.aidesign.cz/about (accessed 13 January 2021). All these projects are discussed and pictured on this site.

128. "Roň slzy," interview on Czechoslovak TV, at https://www.youtube.com/watch?v=JE3TDwWlAJQ (accessed 22 December 2020).

129. Quoted in "Bolestivé dětství Yvonne Přenosilové (69): Doma slýchávala, že je pitomá . . . dokonce i kráva!" *Aha!* 24 July 2016. See also "Yvonne Přenosilová: zpěvačka, moderátorka," Česká televize, at https://www.ceskatelevize.cz/lide/yvonne-prenosilova/ (both accessed 21 December 2020).

130. "Bratříčku, zavírej vrátka," from https://genius.com/Karel-kryl-bratricku-zavirej-vratka-lyrics. Koudelka's cover is reproduced at https://www.allmusic.com/album/bratr%C3%ADcku-zav%C3%ADrej-vrátka-mw0001167282 (both accessed 22 December 2020).

131. Parr and Badger, *Photobook*, Vol. 1, p. 230.

132. Quoted in Melissa Harris, interview with Josef Koudelka, "Invasion 68: Prague Photographs by Josef Koudelka," *Aperture*, Issue 192, Fall 2008.

133. "Josef Koudelka: The 1968 Prague Invasion," at https://www.magnumphotos.com /newsroom/josef-koudelka-invasion-prague-68/ (accessed 22 December 2020).

134. "Josef Koudelka: The 1968 Prague Invasion." Koudelka admitted authorship in 1984. The most complete published collection of these images is Josef Koudelka, *Invasion 68: Prague*, New York: Aperture, 2008. See also "'The Maximum, That's What Always Interested Me,' Notes from Discussions between Josef Koudelka and Karel Hvížďala," in Anna Fárová et al., *Josef Koudelka*, Prague: Torst, 2002.

135. "Josef Koudelka: Exiles," at https://www.magnumphotos.com/newsroom/society /josef-koudelka-exiles/ (accessed 10 January 2021).

136. Jan Lukas, "Proč jsem volil exil až v roce 1966?" *Svědectví*, Vol. 8, No. 30, 1966, quoted in Josef Moucha, *Jan Lukas*, Prague: Torst, 2003, p. 6.

137. Jan Lukas, *Pražský deník 1938–1965*, Prague: Torst, 1995, unpaginated.

138. "Miss Navratilova Asks U.S. Asylum," *New York Times*, 7 September 1975, pp. 209, 213.

139. Quoted in Steve Tignor, "1975: Martina Navratilova Defects to U.S. while Playing the U.S. Open," Tennis.com, 7 May 2015 (accessed 8 January 2021).

140. "Martina Navrátilová: Biography," International Tennis Hall of Fame, at https://www .tennisfame.com/hall-of-famers/inductees/martina-navratilova (accessed 8 January 2021).

141. Mike Downey, "Navratilova Czechs in on Her Past," *Los Angeles Times*, 23 July 1986.

142. "Deset bodů adresovaných federální vládě, Federálnímu shromáždění ČSSR, České národní radě, vládě České socialistické republiky a ÚV KSČ," in Pecka and Prečan, *Proměny pražského jara*, pp. 282–89.

143. "Obžaloba z 29.6. uznesená Krajskou prokuraturou v Praze proti osmi signatářům petice Deset bodů a usnesení Městského soudu v Praze z 4.9.1970," in Pecka and Prečan, *Proměny pražského jara*, pp. 289–304.

144. See extracts from Pachman's memoir *Jak to bylo. Zpráva o činnosti šachového velmistra 1924–1972*, in Pecka and Prečan, *Proměny pražského jara*, pp. 305–9.

145. Quoted in Pavel Kovář, "Luděk Pachman," *Reflex*, 6 April 2003.

146. Quoted in Kovář, "Luděk Pachman."

147. "Diskuzní příspěvek Karla Kyncla," reproduced in Miroslav Sigl, "Počátky posrpnové perzekuce novinářů," at http://www.totalita.cz/norm/norm_07.php (accessed 23 November 2020).

148. Letter from Ludvík Vaculík to Ústav pro soudobé dějiny ČSAV, 8 August 1990, in Pecka and Prečan, *Proměny pražského jara*, pp. 309–10.

149. "The Platform of Prague," in "Anthology of Czech and Slovak Surrealism III," *Analogon*, No. 40, 2004, p. xxvii.

150. "The Possible against the Real," trans. Malgosia Turzanska, in "Anthology of Czech and Slovak Surrealism IV," *Analogon*, No. 41–42, 2004, pp. xi–xii.

151. Vratislav Effenberger, "Varianty, konstanty a dominanty surrealismu," in Dvorský, Effenberger, and Král, *Surrealistické východisko 1938–1968*, pp. 211–12. For an English translation of this text (in three parts), see "Anthology of Czech and Slovak Surrealism," *Analogon*, Nos. 38–39, 40, 41–42, 2003–2004.

152. The initial members were Karol Baron, Andrew Lass, Albert Marenčin, Juraj Mojžíš, Martin Stejskal, Ludvík Šváb, Jan Švankmajer, and Eva Švankmajerová. Alena Nádvorníková joined in 1972, and Emila Medková resumed her involvement after Mikuláš Medek's death in 1974. František Dryje and Jiří Koubek joined in the late 1970s.

153. Alena Nádvorníková, "Surrealistická skupina v Československu v 70. a 80. letech," in *K surrealismu*, p. 198. For details, see František Dryje, "Ludikativní experimentace Surrealistické skupiny v Československu v letech 1971–1985," *Analogon*, No. 6, 1992, pp. i–v.

154. Vincent Bounoure, ed., *La civilisation surréaliste*, Paris: Payot, 1976. For fuller details of the group's activities in this period, see Alena Nádvorníková, "Surrealistická skupina v Československu v 70. a 80. letech;" "Chronologický přehled," *Analogon*, No. 41–42, 2004, pp. i–xii.

155. "Dvacet let od Pražské platformy," *Analogon*, No. 3, 1990, pp. 83–84.

156. Ivan Martin Jirous, "Report on the Third Czech Musical Revival," trans. Paul Wilson and Ivan Hartel, in Machovec, *Views from the Inside*, pp. 9–10. The Czech original can be found in Jirous, *Magorův zápisník*, pp. 171–98.

157. Unless otherwise attributed, all quotations in this and the next two paragraphs are from Jirous, "Report on the Third Czech Musical Revival," pp. 12–21.

158. Paul Wilson, "What's It Like Making Rock'n'Roll in a Police State?" in Machovec, *Views from the Inside*, p. 41.

159. See Jirous's very interesting 1995 interview with Viktor Karlík and Jan Placák, "Ivan Martin Jirous: Když nejde o život, tak jde o hovno," in Jirous, *Magorův zápisník*, pp. 608–30.

160. Martin Machovec, "Underground and 'Under-the-Ground,'" in *Writing Underground: Reflections on Samizdat Literature in Totalitarian Czechoslovakia*, Prague: Karolinum Press, 2019, p. 29.

161. Věra Jirousová, "Jednorožec," in *The Plastic People of the Universe: Texty*, ed. Jaroslav Riedel, Prague: Maťa, 2001, p. 47.

162. Details from Jaroslav Riedel, "The Plastic People of the Universe v datech," in Riedel, *Plastic People*, pp. 15–29. The latter contains the lyrics of the songs referred to here, as well as those from *Egon Bondy's Happy Hearts Club Banned*.

163. Jirous, "Report on the Third Czech Musical Revival," p. 21; translation modified. The original is in Jirous, *Magorův zápisník*, p. 183.

164. Paul Wilson, quoted in Jonathan Bousfield, "Crucif*cked: The Extraordinary Career of Egon Bondy," *Satellite Review*, 16 March 2016.

165. Wilson, "What's It Like Making Rock'n'Roll," p. 46.

166. Egon Bondy, "Tzv. 'Březnová báseň 1971' čtená na veřejném shromáždění," in *Básnické spisy II*, pp. 346–48.

167. See Machovec, *Writing Underground*, pp. 210–11; Jonathan Bolton, "The Shaman, the Greengrocer, and 'Living in Truth,'" *East European Politics, Societies and Cultures*, Vol. 32, No. 2, 2018, pp. 255–65.

168. Jirous, "Report on the Third Czech Musical Revival," pp. 10, 33, 35–36.

169. Josef Škvorecký, "Hipness at Noon," in *Talkin' Moscow Blues*, p. 113.

170. Vladimír Kouřil, *Jazzová sekce v čase a nečase 1971–1987*, Prague: Torst, 1999, p. 260.

171. Kouřil, *Jazzová sekce*, p. 261. Fárová was born in Paris in 1928 to a Czech father (Miloš Šafránek) and a French mother (Anne Moussu) and was called Annette as a child. The text is reproduced in her *Dvě tváře*, pp. 614–43.

172. Kouřil, *Jazzová sekce*, p. 272.

173. Škvorecký, "Hipness at Noon," p. 113.

174. Machovec, "Underground and 'Under-the-Ground,'" p. 28. Bolton's *Worlds of Dissent* is an excellent study of the different strands of opposition in the normalization period.

175. Jirous, "Pravdivý příběh Plastic People," in *Magorův zápisník*, p. 345.

176. On the semiotic work done by this misnomer, see Bolton, *Worlds of Dissent*, pp. 115–18.

177. Quoted in František Stárek Čuňas and Martin Valenta, *Podzemní symfonie Plastic People*, Prague: Argo, 2018, p. 84.

178. Quoted in Bolton, *Worlds of Dissent*, p. 134.

179. Jaroslav Seifert et al., "A Letter to Heinrich Boll," 16 August 1976, in Heneka, *Besieged Culture*, p. 20.

180. See Dana Němcová's interview in Linková and Straková, *Bytová revolta*, pp. 245–59.

181. Quoted in Bolton, *Worlds of Dissent*, p. 144.

182. Petr Blažek and Radek Schovánek, *Prvních 100 dnů Charty 77*, Prague: Academia, 2018, p. 98. In addition to the organizers, the initial 242 signatories included Rudolf Battěk, Vratislav Brabenec, Václav Černý, Vlasta Chramostová, Jiří Dienstbier, Vratislav Effenberger (who signed with reservations and was the only member of the surrealist group to do so), Anna Fárová, Jiří Hanzelka, Josef Hiršal, Milan Hübl, Věra Jirousová, Pavel Juráček, Svatopluk Karásek, Alexander Kliment, Jiří Kolář, František Kriegel, Marta Kubišová, Karel Kyncl, Pavel Landovský, Jiří Lederer, Ivan Medek, Jan Patočka, Jaroslav Seifert, Karol Sidon, Josefa Slánská (Rudolf Slánský's wife), Rudolf Slánský Jr., Marie Švermová, Julius Tomin, and Josef Topol. A facsimile of the original "Prohlášení Charty 77," with the signatures, is on pp. 91–97.

183. Petr Blažek, quoted in Machovec, *Writing Underground*, p. 47.

184. Machovec, *Writing Underground*, pp. 49–50.

185. See Blanka Císařovská and Vilém Prečan, eds., *Charta 77: Dokumenty 1977–1989*, 3 vols., Prague: Ústav pro soudobé dějiny AV ČR, 2007.

186. Vaculík, *Czech Dreambook*, p. 87.

187. Zábrana, *Celý život*, p. 527.

188. Jonathan Bolton, "Afterword," in Vaculík, *Czech Dreambook*, p. 553; Kateřina Surmanová, "Zemřela mluvčí Charty 77 Zdena Tominová, disidentce a spisovatelce bylo 79 let," *Lidové noviny*, 24 May 2020.

189. Daniela Iwashita, "Vaculíkovy nové šaty," *Lidové noviny*, 30 May 2009, Orientace supplement, p. 22.

190. Vaculík, *Czech Dreambook*, pp. 58–59, 86–87.

191. Pavel Kohout, *Kde je zakopán pes*, Brno: Atlantis, 2000. See Bolton, *Worlds of Dissent*, p. 180.

192. Zdena Tomin, *The Coast of Bohemia: A Winter's Tale*, London: Hutchinson, 1987.

193. Dana Němcová, interview in Markéta Reszczyńská, "Sedminásobná matka Dana Němcová neúnavně bojovala proti bezpráví režimu," *Pražský deník*, 27 April 2019.

194. Vaculík, *Czech Dreambook*, pp. 127, 400.

195. Zantovsky, *Havel: A Life*, pp. 210–11.

196. Vaculík, *Czech Dreambook*, p. 454. Milan Šimečka, a dissident political writer, was imprisoned for thirteen months in 1981.

197. Kundera, *Art of the Novel*, p. 130.

198. Compare the accounts of this episode in Eda Kriseová, *Vaclav Havel: Životopis*, Brno: Atlantis, 1991, p. 106; Zantovsky, *Havel: A Life*, pp. 214–18.

199. Václav Havel, *Dopisy Olze*, Brno: Atlantis, 1990.

200. Petra Čáslavová, quoted in Chris Johnstone, "Prisoners' Letters: A Fragile Lifeline for Dissidents under Normalisation," Radio Prague International, 12 May 2015.

201. Juliana Jirousová and Ivan Martin Jirous, *Ahoj milý miláčku: vzájemná korespondence z let 1977–1989*, Prague: Torst, 2015; Ivan Martin Jirous, *My Itinerary Has Been Monotonous for Quite a While*, trans. Marek Tomin, London: Divus, 2017.

202. Samuel G. Freedman, "Portrait of a Playwright as an Enemy of the State," *New York Times*, 23 March 1986.

203. Tom McEnchrow, "This Was Something New," Radio Prague International, 14 January 2019.

204. Michael Wise, "Czech Dissident Havel Freed after Serving Half Jail Term," Reuters News, 17 May 1989, quoted in Zantovsky, *Havel: A Life*, p. 285.

205. "Dokument: Plné znění manifestu Několik vět," iDNES.cz, 23 June 2009.

206. Jiří Suk, *Politika jako absurdní drama: Václav Havel v letech 1975–1989*, Prague: Paseka, 2013, p. 295. See also Jiří Urban, "Několik vět: Posledních pět měsíců komunistické diktatury petiční optikou," *Paměť a dějiny*, No. 1, 2010, pp. 20–45.

207. These are listed in Císařovská and Prečan, *Charta 77*, Vol. 3, pp. 337–78.

208. "Ustavující prohlášení Občanského fóra," 19 November 1989, in *Občanské fórum, den první: vznik OF v dokumentech a fotografiích*, ed. Ivana Koutská, Vojtěch Ripka, and Pavel Žáček, Prague: Ústav pro studium totalitních režimů, 2009, p. 96.

209. "Novoroční projev prezidenta ČSSR Václava Havla," 1 January 1990, in Václav Havel, *Projevy leden-červen 1990*, Prague: Vyšehrad, 1990, p. 19.

210. Teige, *Modern Architecture in Czechoslovakia*, pp. 154–55.

211. Quoted in Eva Turečková, "Po stopách sametové revoluce 2. Laterna magika," Radio Prague International, 12 November 2019.

Coda

1. Jan Lukas, "Why I chose Exile," *Svědectví*, 1966, quoted in Ondřej Kundra, *Vendulka: Flight to Freedom*, trans. Gerald Turner, Prague: Karolinum, 2021, p. 116.

2. "Pravda a láska musí zvítězit nad lží a nenávistí!" (Truth and love must prevail over lies and hatred) was one of Václav Havel's favorite mottos.

3. "Řeč Al. Jiráska," in *Za právo a stát: sborník dokladů o československé společné vůli k svobodě 1848–1914*, Prague: Státní nakladatelství, 1928, pp. 298–300.

4. Quoted in "Před 40 lety podepsali Antichartu. Co říkají dnes? 'Všichni věděli, že je to podvod,'" Český rozhlas, 28 January 2017. Every Czech would understand Čech's allusion. Hus was burned at the stake by the Council of Constance in 1415 after refusing to recant his heretical views.

5. "Za nové tvůrčí činy ve jménu socialismu a míru," in Blažek and Schovánek, *Prvních 100 dnů Charty 77*, pp. 264–70.

6. Yvonne Pokorná, "Kteří umělci odmítli podepsat Antichartu a jak dopadli?" Extrastory. cz, 27 January 2017; "Petr Janda zaútočil na Gotta: Antichartu podepsal, aby mohl jezdit do Německa," Blesk.cz, 6 September 2018.

7. "Anticharta," Ústav pro studium totalitních režimů website, 2009. The signatures are listed in full in "Anticharta—necenzurovaný seznam podepsaných," at https://www.cd89.cz /anticharta (accessed 5 February 2021).

8. Quoted in "Před 40 lety podepsali Antichartu."

9. Hrabal, *Gaps*, p. 123.

10. "Rozhovor s Bohumilem Hrabalem," *Tvorba*, 8 January 1975, quoted in Ondřej Nezbeda, "Bohumil Hrabal: v osidlech cenzury," *Respekt*, 23 March 2014. On Hrabal's persecution in this period, see his *Gaps*, especially pp. 122–26.

11. Bohumil Hrabal, "The Magic Flute," in *Total Fears: Letters to Dubenka*, trans. James Naughton, Prague: Twisted Spoon Press, 1998, p. 12.

12. Roger Ebert, "But I Did Not Shoot My Deputy Down," 4 September 2008, at https://www.rogerebert.com/reviews/i-served-the-king-of-england-2008 (accessed 9 February 2021).

13. Nezbeda, "Bohumil Hrabal: v osidlech cenzury." See also Radim Kopáč, "Eugen Brikcius uvádí: Díl druhý/Bohumil Hrabal & Ivan Martin Jirous," *Kulturní magazin*, March 2019.

14. Anna Vančová, "V dobrém i ve zlém, skončila jedna epocha. Karel Gott odešel a milenky pláčou," *Krajské listy*, 2 October 2019.

15. Gott, interview with *Lidové noviny*, 8 June 2001, quoted in "Dnešní jubilant ve výrocích slavných: Gott jako národní totem i parodie," *Lidové noviny*, 14 July 2014; Szczygiel, *Gottland*, p. 175.

16. Kundera, *Art of the Novel*, p. 135.

17. Hartmut Kascha et al., "Karel Gott (80) ist tot," *Bild*, 2 October 2019.

18. Quoted in "Smrt Karla Gotta zasáhla Německo, Rakousko i Slovensko," Novinky.cz, 2 October 2019.

19. Kundera, *Book of Laughter and Forgetting*, 1986 ed., pp. 181, 186–87.

20. "Gott žádal při návratu z 'cvičné' emigrace Husáka o shovívavost," Česká televize, 28 July 2009.

21. Letter from Karel Gott to Gustáv Husák, cosigned by Jiří and Ladislav Štaidl, 21 July 1971, in Eliška Bártová, "Gott psal Husákovi: Upřímně jsem si přál normalizaci," Aktuálně.cz, 28 July 2009. This source provides a photographic copy of the letter, which was found in StB files.

22. Karel Gott, interview in Eliška Bártová, "Karel Gott exkluzivně o svém spise: Já s StB netančil," Aktuálně.cz, 29 July 2009.

23. Quoted in Luboš Procházka, "Gott poprvé otevřeně o svých chybách: Anticharta? Mistrně mě zmanipulovali!" interview, Blesk.cz, 13 October 2018.

24. Václav Pacina, "Do arény musím jít jako vítěz, říká Gott," iDNES.cz, 18 October 2001.

25. See Ondřej Šťastný and Jakub Pokorný, "Výročí Několika vět: osm svědectví o petici, která pomohla 'dobit' režim," iDNES.cz, 23 June 2009.

26. Milan Kundera, *The Book of Laughter and Forgetting*, trans. Aaron Asher, New York: HarperCollins, 1996, p. 249.

27. Jan Čulík, "Případ Karel Gott: 'Idiot hudby a prezident zapomnění,'" *Britské listy*, 4 October 2019.

28. Kundera, *Book of Laughter and Forgetting* (1996 ed.), p. 4.

29. "Kundera on the Novel," *New York Times*, 8 January 1978.

30. "S Karlem Gottem se na Žofín přišlo rozloučit 49 tisíc lidí," Novinky.cz, 11 October 2019.

31. Quoted in "Tělo Karla Gotta převezli do motolského krematoria," Novinky.cz, 12 October 2019. Other details are from the same source. The full service can be seen at https://www.youtube.com/watch?v=6H1ukxdYlXs&t=2791s (accessed 9 December 2020).

32. Statement reproduced in "Hrob Karla Gotta," at https://www.extra.cz/tema/hrob-karla-gotta (accessed 9 December 2020).

33. Jiří Kubík, "S Kubišovou o Gottovi: Umělce, kteří pracovali za totality, jsem spíš litovala," interview, seznamzpravy.cz, 11 October 2019.

34. "Trápil se tím léta! Kubišová přiznala pravdu o Gottovi a Antichartě," Blesk.cz, 5 October 2019.

35. Čulík, "Případ Karel Gott."

36. Václav Hůla was added in 1975, Ludvík Svoboda stepped down in 1976, and Miloš Jakeš was added in 1981; Antonín Kapek, Peter Colotka, and Lubomír Štrougal stepped down in 1988 and were replaced by Jan Fojtík, Ignác Janák, and František Pitra.

37. Bren, *The Greengrocer and His TV*, p. 4.

38. Havel, "Power of the Powerless."

39. Vaculík, *Czech Dreambook*, pp. 27–28.

SOURCES

This is a listing not of every individual text cited in this book but of the sources from which I obtained them. With the exception of the interviews in section 7B, items published in newspapers, periodicals, and websites included in sections 1–4 are not listed separately here. In the same way, works contained in edited collections and anthologies included in other sections of this bibliography are not listed individually. Full details are given in the relevant notes.

1. Newspapers, News Agencies, and Internet News Sites

A. Czech, Czechoslovak, Bohemian-German, and Czechoslovak Émigré Publications

Aha.cz
Ahoj v sobotu (supplement to *Svobodné slovo*)
Aktuálně.cz
Blesk.cz
Československý boj
Deník Referendum
Der neue Tag
Deutsche Zeitung Bohemia
Echo24.cz
EuroZprávy.cz
iDNES.cz
Ihned.cz
Krajské listy
Lidové noviny
Lidovky.cz
MF Dnes
Mladá fronta
Mladý svět
Národní listy
Novinky.cz
Noviny Prahy
Obrana lidu
Práce

Prager Tagblatt
Prague Daily Monitor
Prague Morning
Právo
Pražské pondělí
Pražský deník
Rudé právo
Seznam Zprávy.cz
Slovácký deník.cz
Spořilovské noviny
Světový rozhled
Svobodné slovo
Tribuna
V boj!
Večerní Praha
Zemědělské noviny
Židovské listy

B. International Publications

Bild
Catholic News Agency
Chicago Tribune
Daily Express
Defense Media Network
Guardian
Haaretz
Huffpost
l'Humanité
Independent
Irish Times
Jewish Telegraphic Agency
KSL.com
Los Angeles Times
Manila Times
Le Monde
New York Times
Pravda
Reuters News
Spiegel Online
Sunday Express
Sydney Morning Herald
Times
Times of Israel

USA Today
Washington Post

2. Magazines, Journals, and Yearbooks

A. Czech, Czechoslovak, and Émigré Publications

Akademický bulletin
Almanach královského hlavního města Prahy
Analogon
British Czech and Slovak Review
Britské listy
Bubínek Revolveru
Červen
Česká posice
Český dialog
CS magazín
Divoké víno
Dnešek
Extra.cz
Extrastory.cz
Haňťa Press
iForum
iSport.cz
Kulturní noviny
Květy
Listy
Literární listy
Literární noviny
Magazín České filharmonie
Mezinárodní bulletin surrealismu
Moderní revue
Obrys-Kmen
Paměť' národa
Pestrý týden
Přítomnost
ReD
Reflex
Revolver Revue
Rozpravy Aventina
Simplicus
Statistika královského hlavního města Prahy
Stavba
Stavitel
Student

Surrealismus
Surrealismus v ČSR
Svědectví
Svět v obrazech
Svoboda
Terezínské listy
Tvorba
UNI Kulturní magazín
Universita Karlova
Vlak
Volné směry
Výtvarná práce
Život
Zvěrokruh

B. International Publications

AJR [Association of Jewish Refugees] *Journal*
Aperture
Architectural Forum
Artforum
Buffalo Spree
Bulletin Internationale du Surréalisme Révolutionnaire
Granta
Kirkus Reviews
The Little Review
London Bulletin
Look
MoMA Post
New Statesman and Nation
New York Magazine
New Yorker
Paris Review
Prospect Magazine
Satellite Review
Saturday Evening Post
Saturday Review of Literature
Smithsonian Magazine
Spectator
Sports Illustrated
Times Literary Supplement
transition
USSR in Construction
Utah Stories

3. Radio and Television

Arte TV
BBC
Česká televize (ČTV)
Český rozhlas
CNN
Czechoslovak TV
ESPN
Radio Free Europe/Radio Liberty
Radio Prague
Radio Prague International
Radio Praha

4. Websites

Academia.edu (academia.edu)
AI Design (aidesign.cz)
Art Institute of Chicago (artic.edu)
The Art Story (theartstory.org)
Artsy (artsy.net)
Atomium (atomium.be)
The Avalon Project: Documents in Law, History and Diplomacy (avalon.law.yale.edu)
Berkeley Art Museum and Pacific Film Archive (bampfa.org)
British Library (bl.uk)
Bubny Memorial of Silence (bubny.org)
Budovatel: písně, statě a básně, které hrdinně budovaly socialistickou společnost (budovatel.cz)
Castello di Rivoli Museum of Contemporary Art (castellodirivoli.org)
Česko-Slovenská filmová databáze (csfd.cz)
Český statistický úřad (czso.cz)
The Charnel House: From Bauhaus to Beinhaus (thecharnelhouse.org)
Continuity/rupture: Art and Architecture in Central Europe 1918–1939 (craace.com)
Czech Centre, London (london.czechcentres.cz)
Czech Technical University in Prague (ČVUT) (cvut.cz)
Databazeknih.cz (databazeknih.cz)
David Černý (davidcerny.cz)
David Maisel (davidmaisel.com)
Digital Yiddish Theater Project (https://web.uwm.edu/yiddish-stage/)
Divadlo Na zábradlí/Theater on the Balustrade (nazabradli.cz)
Eichler Network (eichlernetwork.com)
Filmový přehled (filmovyprehled.cz)
Foreign Architects in Japan (japan-architect.jimdofree.com/foreign-architects-in-japan/)
Free Czechoslovak Air Force (fcafa.com)
Fronta.cz: Druhá světová válka (fronta.cz)

Genius (genius.com)
German History in Documents and Images (germanhistorydocs.ghi-dc.org)
Goodreads (goodreads.com)
Habima National Theater Archive (archive.habima.co.il)
Holocaust.cz: Institut Terezínské initiativy (holocaust.cz)
Holocaust Education and Archive Research Team (holocaustresearchproject.org)
Institute (instituteartist.com)
International Churchill Society (winstonchurchill.org)
International Film Festival Rotterdam (iffr.com)
International Tennis Hall of Fame (tennisfame.com)
Jan Palach: Multimediální projekt Univerzity Karlovy (janpalach.cz)
Jewish Virtual Library (jewishvirtuallibrary.org)
Kladno: město pro kvalitní život (mestokladno.cz)
Kladno_minulé (kladnominule.cz)
Klub za starou Prahu (zastarouprahu.cz)
Knoll (knoll.com)
Košice (kosice.sk)
Magnum Photos (magnumphotos.com)
Masaryk University, Brno (is.muni.cz)
Meijishowa (meijishowa.com)
Military History Now (militaryhistorynow.com)
Miloš Forman: Miloš Forman's Official Website (milosforman.com)
Minato City (lib.city.minato.tokyo.jp)
Miscelanea Bizarriensis (freaklit.blogspot.com)
MIT Libraries (libraries.mit.edu)
Moderní dějiny: vzdělávací portál pro učitele, studenty a žáky (moderni-dejiny.cz)
Museum of Modern Art, New York (moma.org)
Music and the Holocaust (holocaustmusic.ort.org)
Musixmatch (musixmatch.com)
Nakashima Foundation for Peace (nakashimafoundation.org)
Národní demokracie (narodnidemokracie.cz)
Národní divadlo/National Theater, Prague (narodni-divadlo.cz)
Národní galerie Praha/National Gallery Prague (ngprague.cz)
National Security Archive (nsarchive.gwu.edu)
Nicolas Rothwell (nicolasrothwell.com)
Nucená práce 1939–1945 (nucenaprace.cz)
Opera+ (operaplus.cz)
The Orel Foundation (orelfoundation.org)
Original Cinemaniac: Movie Reviews by Dennis Dermody (originalcinemaniac.com)
Památník Lidice (lidice-memorial.cz)
Poemhunter: poems, quotes, poetry (poemhunter.com)
Poetry Foundation (poetryfoundation.org)
Poets.org (poets.org)

Poslanecká sněmovna parlamentu České republiky digitální repozitář (psp.cz)

Pražské jaro 1968 (68.USD.cas.cz)

Reduta Jazz Club Prague (redutajazzclub.cz)

Roger Ebert.com (rogerebert.com)

Rudolfinum (rudolfinum.cz)

Scriptum.cz (scriptum.cz)

Snopes Fact Checks (snopes.com)

Sotheby's Auction House (sothebys.com)

Sport.cz (sport.cz)

Sri Aurobindo Ashram (sriaurobindoashram.org)

The Story Institute (thestoryinstitute.com)

Supraphon (supraphon.cz)

Teju Cole Writer and Photographer (facebook.com/people/Teju-Cole/100044361222793/)

Tennis (tennis.com)

Totalita.cz (totalita.cz)

United States Holocaust Memorial Museum (ushmm.org)

US Bureau of Labor Statistics (bls.gov)

US Department of Defense, Military Istallations (installations.militaryonesource.mil)

US Embassy Prague (cz.usembassy.gov)

US Senate, Select Committee on Intelligence (intelligence.senate.gov)

Ústav pro soudobé dějiny Akademie věd České Republiky (usd.cas.cz)

Ústav pro studium totalitních režimů (ustrcr.cz)

Václav Havel Library (vaclavhavel.cz)

Velký zpěvník (velkyzpevnik.cz)

Vítězslav Nezval (vitezslavnezval.cz)

Wikizdroje (cs.wikisource.org)

World Future Fund (worldfuturefund.org)

Yad Vashem (yadvashem.org)

YouTube (youtube.com)

Židovské muzeum v Praze (jewishmuseum.cz)

Zipp—German-Czech Cultural Projects—Conference (kulturstiftung-des-bundes.de)

5. Primary Documents: Texts and Anthologies

A. History and Politics

The Action Programme of the Communist Party of Czechoslovakia. Spokesman Pamphlet No. 8. Nottingham: Bertrand Russell Peace Foundation, 1970.

"Anticharta." Ústav pro studium totalitních režimů website, 2009.

A Besieged Culture: Czechoslovakia Ten Years after Helsinki. Ed. A. Heneka et al. Stockholm and Vienna: Charta 77 Foundation, 1986.

Bojující Československo 1938–1945. Ed. V. Žižka. Košice: Žikeš, 1945.

Charta 77: Dokumenty 1977–1989. Ed. Blanka Císařovská and Vilém Prečan. 3 vols. Prague: Ústav pro soudobé dějiny AV ČR, 2007.

Constitution of the Czechoslovak Socialist Republic. Prague: Orbis, 1964.

Heydrichiáda: dokumenty. Ed. Čestmír Amort. Prague: Naše vojsko, 1965.

Husitské manifesty. Ed. Amadeo Molnár. Prague: Odeon, 1986.

I Never Saw Another Butterfly: Children's Poems and Drawings from Terezín. Ed. Hana Volavková. New York: Schocken, 1993.

The Jews of Bohemia and Moravia: A Historical Reader. Ed. Wilma Abeles Iggers. Detroit: Wayne State University Press, 1992.

Kádrová nomenklatura KSČ 1948–1956: sborník dokumentů. Ed. Karel Kaplan. Prague: Ústav pro soubobé dějiny ČSAV, 1992.

Neuzavřená kapitola: politické procesy padesátých let. Ed. Bedřich Utitz. Prague: Lidové nakladatelství, 1990.

Občanské fórum, den první: vznik OF v dokumentech a fotografiích. Ed. Ivana Koutská, Vojtěch Ripka, and Pavel Žáček. Prague: Ústav pro studium totalitních režimů, 2009.

Obrození národa: svědectví a dokumenty. Ed. Jan Novotný. Prague: Melantrich, 1979.

The Prague Spring: A National Security Archive Documents Reader. Ed. Jaromír Navrátil. Budapest: CEU Press, 1998.

Praha v obnoveném státě československém. Ed. Václav Vojtíšek. Prague: Rada hlavního města Prahy, 1936.

Pražské jaro 1968: dokumenty, Ústav pro soudobé dějiny Akademie věd České republiky. At Pražské jaro 1968 website.

Proceedings of the Trials of Slansky, et al., in Prague, Czechoslovakia, November 20–27, 1952 as Broadcast by the Czechoslovak Home Service. Prague: Czechoslovak Home Service, n.d. [1952 or 1953].

Proces s vedením protistátního spikleneckého centra v čele s Rudolfem Slánským. Prague: Ministerstvo spravedlnosti, 1953.

Proměny pražského jara 1968–1969: Sborník studií a dokumentů o nekapitulantských postojích v československé společnosti. Ed. Jindřich Pecka and Vilém Prečan. Brno: Doplněk, 1993.

Sbírka zákonů ČR at https://www.zakonyprolidi.cz/cs/sbirka.

The Secret Vysocany Congress: Proceedings and Documents of the Extraordinary Fourteenth Congress of the Communist Party of Czechoslovakia, 22 August 1968. Ed. Jiří Pelikán, trans. George Theiner and Deryck Viney. London: Allen Lane, 1971.

Sedm pražských dnů, 21.–27 srpna 1968: dokumentace. Prague: Historický ústav ČSAV, September 1968.

Souboj slova a obrazu s mocnými: Novináři a média v Pražském jaru ʹ68. Ed. Jindřich Beránek. Prague: Klub novinářů Pražského jara, 1968.

Svědkové revoluce vypovídají. Ed. Bedřich Utitz. Prague: Orbis, 1990.

Svému osvoboditeli československý lid. Prague: Orbis, 1955.

Za právo a stát: sborník dokladů o československé společné vůli k svobodě 1848–1914. Prague: Státní nakladatelství, 1928.

Žaluji. Vol. 1. Stalinská justice v Československu. Ed. Antonín Kratochvíl. Prague: Česká expedice, 1990.

B. Culture and the Arts

Ani labut' ani Lůna: sborník k 100. výročí smrty K. H. Mácha. Ed. Vítězslav Nezval. Prague: Concordia, 1995 (facsimile reprint of 1936 ed.).

"Anthology of Czech and Slovak Surrealism." *Analogon*, Issues 37–45, 2003–2005.

Avantgarda bez legend a mýtů: rozhlasový cyklus o patnácti dílech. Prague: Rozhlasový cyklus, 1967.

Avantgarda známá a neznámá. Ed. Štěpán Vlašín. 3 vols. Prague: Svoboda, 1970–1972.

Between Worlds: A Sourcebook of Central European Avant-gardes, 1910–1930. Ed. Timothy O. Benson and Eva Forgacs. Los Angeles: Los Angeles County Museum of Art, 2002.

České umění 1938–1989: programy/kritické texty/dokumenty. Ed. Jiří Ševčík, Pavlína Morganová, and Dagmar Dušková. Prague: Academia, 2001.

La civilisation surréaliste. Ed. Vincent Bounoure. Paris: Payot, 1976.

Co daly naše země Evropě a lidstvu. Ed. Vilém Mathesius. Prague: Evropský literární klub, 1939.

Deset let Osvobozeného divadla 1927–1937. Ed. Josef Träger. Prague: Borový, 1937.

IV. sjezd Svazu československých spisovatelů /protokol/. Ed. Otakar Mohyla. Prague: Československý spisovatel, 1968.

Good-bye Samizdat: Twenty Years of Czechoslovak Underground Writing. Ed. Marketa Goetz-Stankiewicz. Evanston, IL: Northwestern University Press, 1992.

Lidice: A Tribute by Members of the International P.E.N. Ed. Harold Nicolson. London: Allen and Unwin for the Czechoslovak P.E.N., 1944.

Moderní revue 1894–1925. Ed. Otto M. Orban. Prague: Torst, 1994.

Osma a Skupina výtvarných umělců 1907–1917, teorie, kritika, polemika. Ed. Jiří Padtra. Prague: Odeon, 1992.

The Plastic People of the Universe: Texty. Ed. Jaroslav Riedel. Prague: Maťa, 2001.

Problems of Soviet Literature: Reports and Speeches at the First Soviet Writers' Congress. Ed. H. F. Scott. New York: International Publishers, 1935.

The Situationist Anthology. Ed. Ken Knabb. Rev. and expanded ed. Berkeley, CA: Bureau of Public Secrets, 2006.

Skupina 42: Antologie. Ed. Zdeněk Pešat and Eva Petrová. Brno: Atlantis, 2000.

Le Surréalisme en Tchécoslovaquie. Ed. Petr Král. Paris: Gallimard, 1983.

Le Surréalisme Révolutionnaire. Brussels: Didier Devillez, 1999.

Surrealismus v diskusi. Ed. Karel Teige and Ladislav Štoll. Prague: Levá fronta, 1934.

Surréalistické východisko 1938–1968. Ed. Stanislav Dvorský, Vratislav Effenberger, and Petr Král. Prague: Československý spisovatel, 1969.

Tance kolem Kafky: Liblická konference 1963, vzpomínky a dokumenty po 40 letech. Ed. Alexej Kusák. Prague: Akropolis, 2003.

Úmrtí Vítězslava Nezvala v dobovém tisku a ve vzpomínkách současníků. Ed. Alsen Hanson. 2018. E-book available at vitezslavnezval.cz.

Views from the Inside: Czech Underground Literature and Culture (1948–1989). Ed. Martin Machovec. Prague: Karolinum, 2018.

Z dějin českého myšlení o literatuře: antologie k dějinám české literatury, 1945–1990. Vol. 1. *1945–1948.* Ed. Michal Přibáň. Prague: Ústav pro českou literaturu AV ČR, 2001.

Zajatec kubismu: dílo Emila Filly v zrcadle výtvarné kritiky (1907–1953). Ed. Tomáš Winter. Prague: Artefactum, 2004.

Zvěrokruh 1/Zvěrokruh 2/Surrealismus v ČSR/Mezinárodní bulletin surrealismu/Surrealismus. Prague: Torst, 2004.

6. Primary Texts: Individual Authors

Baťa, Jan A. *Budujme stát pro 40,000,000 lidí*. Zlín: Tisk, 1937.

Baudelaire, Charles. *The Painter of Modern Life and Other Essays*. Trans. Jonathan Mayne. New York: Phaidon, 2005.

Beneš, Edvard. "A Message of November 1938 to a Czechoslovak Politician in Prague." In Milan L. Hauner, "Edvard Benes' Undoing of Munich: A Message to a Czechoslovak Politician in Prague." *Journal of Contemporary History*, Vol. 38, No. 4, 2003.

Breton, André. *Communicating Vessels*. Trans. Mary Ann Caws and Geoffrey T. Harris. Lincoln: University of Nebraska Press, 1997.

——. *Free Rein*. Trans. Michael Parmentier and Jacqueline d'Amboise. Lincoln: University of Nebraska Press, 1997.

——. *Manifestoes of Surrealism*. Trans. Richard Seaver and Helen R. Lane. Ann Arbor: University of Michigan Press, 1972.

Breton, André, and Paul Éluard. *Dictionnaire abrégé du surréalisme*. Paris: José Corti, 2005 (facsimile reprint).

Brod, Max. *Franz Kafka: A Biography*. New York: Schocken, 1963.

Čapek, Karel. *Spisy*. Vol. 19. *O umění a kultuře III*. Prague: Československý spisovatel, 1986.

——. *Toward the Radical Center: A Karel Čapek Reader*. Ed. Peter Kussi. North Haven, CT: Catbird Press, 1990.

Fárová, Anna. *Dvě tváře*. Prague: Torst, 2016.

Filla, Emil. *Myšlenky*. Most: Severočeské nakladatelství, 1990.

Goldstücker, Eduard. "Ten Years after the Kafka Symposium of Liblice." *European Judaism: A Journal for the New Europe*, Vol. 8, No. 2, 1974.

Gottwald, Klement. *Spisy*. Vol. 1. Prague: Svoboda, 1950.

Havel, Václav. "The Power of the Powerless." International Center on Nonviolent Conflict, at https://www.nonviolent-conflict.org/resource/the-power-of-the-powerless.

——. *Projevy leden-červen 1990*. Prague: Vyšehrad, 1990.

Havlíček, Josef. *Návrhy a stavby*. Prague: Státní nakladatelství technické literatury, 1964.

Heisler, Jindřich. *Z kasemat spánku*. Comp. František Šmejkal, Karel Srp, and Jindřich Toman. Prague: Torst, 1999.

Hoffmeister, Adolf. *Kaleidoskop*. Prague: Labyrint, 2004.

——. *Kuo-cha: Cestopisná reportáž o čínském malířství*. Prague: SNKLHU, 1954.

——. *Made in Japan*. Prague: Československý spisovatel, 1958.

——. *Podoby a předobrazy*. Prague: Československý spisovatel, 1988.

——. *Pohlednice z Číny*. Prague: Československý spisovatel, 1954.

——. *Povrch pětiletky*. Prague: Sfinx, 1931.

Jennings, Humphrey. *The Humphrey Jennings Film Reader*. Ed. Kevin Jackson. Manchester, UK: Carcanet, 2004.

———. *Pandaemonium 1660–1886: The Coming of the Machine as Seen by Contemporary Observers.* London: Icon Books, 2012.

Jennings, Humphrey, Charles Madge, et al., eds. *May the Twelfth: Mass-Observation Day-Surveys 1937 by over Two Hundred Observers.* London: Faber and Faber, 1937.

Jesenská, Milena. *The Journalism of Milena Jesenská: A Critical Voice in Interwar Central Europe.* Ed. and trans. Kathleen Hayes. New York: Berghahn, 2003.

———. *Křižovatky (Výbor z díla).* Ed. Marie Jirásková. Prague: Torst, 2016.

———. *Mileniny recepty.* Prague: Nakladatelství Franze Kafky, 1995 (facsimile reprint).

Jirous, Ivan M. *Magorův zápisník.* Prague: Torst, 1997.

Karásek ze Lvovic, Jiří. "Z německé literatury." *Moderní revue,* Vol. 21, No. 7, 1909.

Kennan, George F. *From Prague after Munich: Diplomatic Papers, 1938–9.* Princeton, NJ: Princeton University Press, 1968.

Kisch, Egon Erwin. *Der rasende Reporter.* Berlin: Erich Reiss, 1925.

———. *Egon Erwin Kisch, the Raging Reporter: A Bio-anthology.* Ed. Harold B. Segel. West Lafayette, IN: Purdue University Press, 1997.

———. *Entdeckungen in Mexiko.* Mexico City: El Libro Libre, 1945.

———. *Sensation Fair: Tales of Prague.* Trans. Guy Endore. Lexington, MA: Plunkett Lake Press, 2012.

Kolář, Jiří. *Dictionnaire des méthodes.* Paris: Revue K, 1991.

Král, Petr. *Prague.* Seyssel: Editions du Champ Vallon, 1987.

———. *Vlastizrady.* Prague: Torst, 2015.

Kroha, Jiří. *Sociologický fragment bydlení.* Brno: Krajské středisko státní památkové péče a ochrany přírody v Brně, 1973.

Kukla, Karel Ladislav. *Konec bahna Prahy: Ilustrovaná revue skutečných příběhů, dramat i humoresek z nejtemnějších i nejskvělejších útulků mravní bídy, zoufalství, tmy, šibeničního humoru, prostituce i zločinů v salonech, barech, uličkách, krčmách, špitálech, blázincích, brlozích i stokách Velké Prahy.* Prague: Švec, 1927.

———. *Pražské bahno: historie nemravností.* Prague: XYZ, 2017 (reprint).

Kundera, Milan. *The Art of the Novel.* Trans. Linda Asher. New York: Grove Press, 1988.

———. "Prague: A Disappearing Poem." *Granta,* Vol. 17, September 1985.

———. *Testaments Betrayed.* Trans. Linda Asher. New York: HarperCollins, 1995.

Lévi-Strauss, Claude. *Look, Listen, Read.* Trans. Brian C. J. Singer. New York: HarperCollins, 1997.

Mareš, Michal. *Přicházím z periferie republiky.* Prague: Academia, 2009.

Masaryk, Tomáš. *Česká otázka.* Prague: Svoboda, 1990.

———. *Cesta demokracie: soubor projevů za republiky.* Vol. 1. *1918–1920.* Prague: ČIN, 1934.

———. *Karel Havlíček.* 3rd ed. Prague: Jan Laichter, 1920.

Medek, Mikuláš. *Texty.* Prague: Torst, 1995.

Mukařovský, Jan. "Ke kritice strukturalismu v naší literární vědé." Brno: Masaryk University, 2008 (is.muni.cz).

Nádvorníková, Alena. *K surrealismu.* Prague: Torst, 1998.

Nejedlý, Zdeněk. *Komunisté, dědici velkých tradic českého národa.* Prague: Československý spisovatel, 1953.

Neruda, Jan. *Studie krátké a kratší.* Prague: L. Mazač, 1928.

Neumann, Stanislav Kostka. *Anti-Gide, neboli optimismus bez povĕr a ilusí*. Prague: Svoboda, 1946.

Palacký, František. *Dĕjiny české v stručném přehledu*. Prague: Alois Hynek, 1898.

——. *Úvahy a projevy z české literatury, historie a politiky*. Prague: Melantrich, 1977.

Šalda, F. X. *Soubor díla F. X. Šaldy*. Vol. 11. *Kritické projevy—2, 1894–1895*. Prague: Melantrich, 1950.

——. *Soubor díla F. X. Šaldy*. Vol. 19. *Kritické projevy—10, 1917–18*. Prague: Československý spisovatel, 1957.

——. *Soubor díla F. X. Šaldy*. Vol. 21. *Kritické projevy—12, 1922–1924*. Prague: Československý spisovatel, 1959.

Škvorecký, Josef. *All the Bright Young Men and Women: A Personal History of the Czechoslovak Cinema*. Trans. Michael Schonberg. Toronto: Peter Martin, 1971.

——. "Bohemia of the Soul." *Daedalus*, Vol. 119, No. 1, 1990.

——. *Talkin' Moscow Blues*. Toronto: Lester and Orpen Denys, 1988.

Štyrský, Jindřich. *Texty*. Prague: Argo, 2007.

Sutnar, Ladislav. *Visual Design in Action*. Ed. Reto Caduff and Steven Heller. Zurich: Lars Müller Publishers, 2015 (facsimile reprint).

Sutnar, Ladislav, and Knud Löndberg Holm. *Designing Information*. New York: Whitney Publications, 1947.

Teige, Karel. *The Minimum Dwelling*. Trans. Eric Dluhosch. Cambridge, MA: MIT Press, 2002.

——. *Modern Architecture in Czechoslovakia and Other Writings*. Trans. Irena Žantovská Murray and David Britt. Los Angeles: Getty Research Institute, 2000.

——. "Mundaneum." *Oppositions*, No. 4, October 1974.

——. *Osvobozovaní života a poezie: studie ze 40. let. Výbor z díla*. Vol. 3. Ed. Jiří Brabec, Vratislav Effenberger, Květoslav Chvatík, and Roberta Kalivoda. Prague: Aurora, 1994.

——. *Svĕt stavby a básnĕ: studie z 20. let. Výbor z díla*. Vol. 1. Prague: Československý spisovatel, 1966.

——. *Zápasy o smysl moderní tvorby: studie z 30. let. Výbor z díla*. Vol. 2. Prague: Československý spisovatel, 1969.

7. Autobiographical Literature

A. Letters and Diaries

Boudník, Vladimír. *Vladimír Boudník a přátelé*. Vol. 2. *Dopisy Hanese Reegena Vladimíru Boudníkovi a Reegenova literární pozůstalost*. Ed. Jan Placák. Prague: Ztichlá klika, 2014.

Coward, Noël. *The Letters of Noël Coward*. London: Knopf, 2007.

Fučík, Julius. *Reportáž psaná na oprátce*. Prague: Torst, 1995.

Ginsberg, Allen. *Iron Curtain Journals January–May 1965*. Ed. Michael Schumacher. Minneapolis: University of Minnesota Press, 2018.

Havel, Václav. *Dopisy Olze*. Brno: Atlantis, 1990.

Jesenská, Milena. *De Prague à Ravensbrück: Lettres de Milena Jesenská 1938–1944*. Ed. Hélène Belletto Sussel and Alena Wagnerová. Villeneuve d'Ascq, France: Presses Universitaires de Septentrion, 2016.

Jirousová, Juliana, and Ivan Martin Jirous. *Ahoj milý miláčku: vzájemná korespondence z let 1977–1989*. Prague: Torst, 2015.

Joyce, James. *Selected Letters of James Joyce*. Ed. Richard Ellman. London: Faber and Faber, 1992.

Juráček, Pavel. *Deník III. 1959–1974*. Prague: Torst, 2018.

Kafka, Franz. *The Diaries of Franz Kafka 1910–23*. Ed. Max Brod. Trans. Martin Greenberg and Hannah Arendt. London: Penguin, 1964.

——. *Dopisy rodičům z let 1922–24*. Ed. Josef Čermák and Martin Svatoš. Prague: Odeon, 1990.

——. *Letter to the Father*. Bilingual ed. Trans. Ernst Kaiser and Eithne Wilkins. New York: Schocken, 2015.

——. *Letters to Felice*. Trans. James Stern and Elisabeth Duckworth. New York: Schocken, 1973.

——. *Letters to Friends, Family, and Editors*. Trans. Richard Winston and Clara Winston. New York: Schocken, 1977.

——. *Letters to Milena*. Trans. Philip Boehm. New York: Schocken, 1990.

——. *Letters to Ottla and the Family*. Ed. N. N. Glaser. Trans. Richard Winston and Clara Winston. New York: Schocken, 1982.

Nezval, Vítězslav. *Korespondence Vítězslava Nezvala: depeše z konce tisíciletí*. Prague: Československý spisovatel, 1981.

Salivarová-Škvorecká, Zdena, ed. *Osočení—Dopisy lidí ze seznamu*. Toronto: Sixty-Eight Publishers, 1993.

Serge, Victor. *Notebooks 1936–1947*. Trans. Mitchell Abidor and Richard Greeman. New York: New York Review Books, 2019.

Škvorecký, Josef. Letter to Louis Armand, 12 September 2010. *Vlak*, No. 4, 2012.

Vaculík, Ludvík. *A Czech Dreambook*. Trans. Gerald Turner. Prague: Karolinum, 2019.

Werich, Jan. *Listování: úryvky z korespondence a článků*. Prague: Brána, 2003.

Zábrana, Jan. *Celý život: Výbor z deníků 1948–1984*. Prague: Torst, 2001.

B. Interviews

Bytová revolta: Jak ženy dělaly disent. Ed. Marcela Linková and Naďa Straková. Prague: Academia, 2018.

Čapek, Karel. *Hovory s T. G. Masarykem*. *Spisy*. Vol. 20. Prague: Československý spisovatel, 1990.

Čáslavská, Věra. "Legendární gymnastka Věra Čáslavská: Můj meč hlavy nestínal." Interview by Martin Hašek. iSport.cz, 4 November 2011.

Čermák, Josef. "Just Wild about Franz Kafka." Interview by Avi Kempinski. *Washington Post*, 4 October 1992.

Clementisová, Lída. "Ženy s podobným osudem: seriál rozhovorů studenta s vdovami po popravených v procesu z roku 1952. 2. Hovoří Lída Clementisová." Interview by Jan Kavan and Alexandr Kramer. *Student*, Vol. 4, No. 13, 27 March 1968.

Forman, Miloš. *The Miloš Forman Stories*. Ed. Antonín J. Liehm. New York: Routledge, 2016.

Ginsberg, Allen. "The King of May: A Conversation between Allen Ginsberg and Andrew Lass, March 23, 1986." *Massachusetts Review*, Vol. 39, No. 2, 1998.

Goldstücker, Eduard. "Interview with Professor Eduard Goldstücker." National Security Archives, CNN broadcasts, Episode 6, *Reds*, 1 November 1998.

——. "Interview with Professor Eduard Goldstücker." National Security Archives, CNN broadcasts, Episode 14, *Red Spring (The Sixties)*, 17 January 1999.

Gott, Karel. "Gott poprvé otevřeně o svých chybách: Anticharta? Mistrně mě zmanipulovali!" Interview by Luboš Procházka. Blesk.cz, 13 October 2018.

——. "Karel Gott exkluzivně o svém spise: Já s StB netančil." Interview by Eliška Bártová. Aktuálně.cz, 29 July 2009.

Grygar, Mojmír. "Rozhovor s literárním teoretikem a historikem Mojmírem Grygarem." *Česká literatura*, Vol. 61, No. 3, 2013.

Hoffmeister, Adolf. *Piš jak slyšíš, kniha interviewů*. Prague: Družstevní práce, 1931.

Hrabal, Bohumil. *Pirouettes on a Postage Stamp: An Interview-Novel with Questions Asked and Answers Recorded by László Szigeti*. Trans. David Short. Prague: Karolinum, 2008.

Illichmann, Carmen T. "Lidice: Remembering the Women and Children." *UW-L Journal of Undergraduate Research*, No. 8, 2005.

Jireš, Jaromil. "Jaromil Jires: 'S'il faut être malheureux, autant l'être dans son pays.'" Interview by Michèle Levieux, *L'Humanité*, 21 August 1999.

Joyce, James. "The Game of Evenings" (interviews by Adolf Hoffmeister with James Joyce in *Rozpravy Aventina*). Trans. Michelle Woods. *Granta*, Vol. 89, April 2005.

Koudelka, Josef. "Invasion 68: Prague Photographs by Josef Koudelka." Interview by Melissa Harris. *Aperture*, Issue 192, Fall 2008.

Kubišová, Marta. "S Kubišovou o Gottovi: Umělce, kteří pracovali za totality, jsem spíš litovala." Interview with Jiří Kubík. Seznamzpravy.cz, 11 October 2019.

——. "Tí, čo boli pri revolúcii, sa na nej stále vezú." Interview by Miroslav Brada. *Britské listy*, 18 August 2003.

Liehm, Antonin. *Trois générations. Entretiens sur le phénomène culturel tchécoslovaque*. Paris: Gallimard, 1970.

Margolius Kovály, Heda. "Other Europe: Jacques Rupnik Interview with Heda Margolius-Kovály, New York, January 10, 1988." At https://www.youtube.com/watch?v=Chq939cXAfU.

——. "Ženy s podobným osudem . . . 1. Vypráví Heda Kovályová-Margoliová." Interview by Jan Kavan and Alexandr Kramer. *Student*, Vol. 4, No. 12, 20 March 1968.

Margolius Kovály, Heda, and Helena Třeštíková. *Hitler, Stalin and I: An Oral History*. Trans. Ivan Margolius. Los Angeles: DoppelHouse Press, 2018.

Menzel, Jiří. "Irony Man." Interview by Steve Rose. *Guardian*, 9 May 2008.

Moravková, Květoslava. "Kdo, když ne my, kdy, když ne teď!" Interview by Pavel Kovář. iForum, 4 November 2009.

Němcová, Dana. "Sedminásobná matka Dana Němcová neúnavně bojovala proti bezpráví režimu." Interview by Markéta Reszczyńská. *Pražský deník*, 27 April 2019.

Němec, Jan. "Everything You Always Wanted to Know about My Heart . . . An Interview with Film Director Jan Němec." Interview by Ivana Košuličová. *Central Europe Review*, Vol. 3, No. 17, 14 May 2001.

Passer, Ivan. "Eclairage intime de Ivan Passer." Interview by Olivier Père. Arte.tv, 2 November 2016.

——. "In-person: Q&A with Director Ivan Passer." Billy Wilder Theater, 14 September 2018, at https://www.cinema.ucla.edu.

Radok, Alfréd. "Alfred Radok." Interview by Antonin J. Liehm. *International Journal of Politics*, Vol. 3, No. 1/2, 1973.

Reinerová, Lenka. "'Here's Looking at You Kid . . .': A Czech Girl in Wartime Casablanca." Interview by David Vaughan. Radio Prague, 21 April 2005.

——. "Lenka Reinerová—Moje století." Interview by Jiří Hrabě. *Vital*, 15 June 2008.

——. "Lenka Reinerova—A Writer Who Keeps the Rich Tradition of Prague German Literature Alive." Interview by David Vaughan. Radio Prague, 22 August 2004.

——. "Lenka Reinerová: Život je nepochopitelný, někdy prapodivný." Interview by Irena Jirků. *Sanquis*, No. 46, 2006.

Scorsese, Martin. "Martin Scorsese on Hereditary, Hugo Haas, and Joanna Hogg." Interview by Kent Jones, 1 October 2019, New York 57th Film Festival. Uploaded on YouTube by Lincoln Center.

Škvorecký, Josef. "Josef Skvorecky: The Art of Fiction No. 112." Interview by John A. Glusman. *Paris Review*, No. 112, Winter 1989.

Šlingová, Marian. "Hovoří Marian Vilbrová-Slingová, doplňuje Jan Šling." Interview by Jan Kavan and Alexandr Kramer. *Student*, Vol. 4, No. 15, 10 April 1968.

Staněk, Tomáš. "Nechat mluvit fakta." Interview by Petr Blažek and Pavel Zeman. *Paměť a dějiny*, No. 2, 2013.

Suchý, Jiří. "Místo emigrace zvolil v roce 1968 návrat do vlasti. 'Nikdy jsem nelitoval,' říká Jiří Suchý." Interview by Jan Herget. Český rozhlas, 8 August 2018.

Vachtová, Ludmila. "Každý máme svoje lobby." Interview by Terezie Pokorná and Viktor Karlík. *Revolver Revue*, No. 43, 2000.

C. Autobiographies, Memoirs, and Reminiscences

Bondy, Egon. *Prvních deset let*. Prague: Maťa, 2002.

Brod, Max. *Život plný bojů*. Prague: Nakladatelství Franze Kafky, 1994.

Čapková, Jarmila. *Vzpomínky*. Prague: Torst, 1998.

Černá, Jana [aka Jana Krejcarová]. *Adresát Milena Jesenská*, Prague: Concordia, 1991.

——. *Kafka's Milena*. Trans. A. G. Brain. Evanston, IL: Northwestern University Press, 1993.

Černý, David, et al. *David Černý*. Prague: Meetfactory, 2017.

Černý, Václav. *Paměti III, 1945–1972*. Brno: Atlantis, 1992.

Demetz, Peter. *Prague in Danger*. New York: Farrar, Straus and Giroux, 2008.

Diviš, Alén. "Vzpomínky na pařížské vězení Santé." *Revolver Revue*, No. 17, August 1991.

Drtina, Prokop. *Československo můj osud*. Vol. 2, Bk. 1. Prague: Melantrich, 1992.

Fodorová, Anna. *Lenka*. Prague: Labyrint, 2020.

——. "Mourning by Proxy: Notes on a Conference, Empty Graves and Silence." *Psychodynamic Practice*, Vol. 11, No. 3, 2005.

Forman, Miloš, and Jan Novák. *Turnaround: A Memoir*. London: Faber and Faber, 1994.

Fry, Varian. *Surrender on Demand*. New York: Random House, 1945.

Fučíková, Gusta. *Život s Juliem Fučíkem*. Prague: Svoboda, 1971.

Goldstücker, Eduard. *Vzpomínky 1913–1945*. Prague: G plus G, 2003.

Hoffmeister, Adolf. *Čas se nevrací!* Prague: Československý spisovatel, 1965.

——. *Hors d'oeuvres: feuilletony, karikatury, epigramy*. Prague: Aventinum, 1927.

——. *Kalendář*. Prague: Aventinum, 1930.

——. *Podoby. Výbor z díla*. Vol. 3. Prague: Československý spisovatel, 1961.

——. *Unwilling Tourist*. Trans. Don Perris. London: John Lane the Bodley Head, 1942.

——. *Vězení*. Prague: Československý spisovatel, 1969.

Honzík, Karel. *Ze života avantgardy*. Prague: Československý spisovatel, 1963.

Hrabal, Bohumil. *Gaps: A Novel*. Trans. Tony Liman. Evanston, IL: Northwestern University Press, 2011.

——. *In-house Weddings*. Trans. Tony Liman. Evanston, IL: Northwestern University Press, 2007.

——. *Svatby v domě*. Toronto: Sixty-Eight Publishers, 1987.

——. *The Tender Barbarian: Pedagogic Texts*. Trans. Jed Slast. Prague: Twisted Spoon Press, 2020.

——. *Total Fears: Letters to Dubenka*. Trans. James Naughton. Prague: Twisted Spoon Press, 1998.

——. *Vita Nuova: A Novel*. Trans. Tony Liman. Evanston, IL: Northwestern University Press, 2010.

Janouch, Gustav. *Conversations with Kafka: Notes and Reminiscences*. 2nd rev. and enl. ed. Trans. Goronwy Rhys. New York: New Directions, 1971.

Kaplický, Jan. *Album*. Prague: Labyrint, 2010.

Klíma, Ivan. *My Crazy Century*. Trans. Craig Cravens. New York: Grove Press, 2013.

Koestler, Arthur. *The Invisible Writing: An Autobiography*. Boston: Beacon Press, 1954.

Kohout, Pavel. *Kde je zakopán pes*. Brno: Atlantis, 2000.

——. *Z deníku kontrarevolucionáře aneb Životy od tanku k tanku*. Prague: Mladá fronta, 1997.

Krull, Germaine, and Jacques Rémy. *Un voyage: Marseille–Rio 1941*. Paris: Stock, 2019.

Lévi-Strauss, Claude. *Tristes Tropiques*. Trans. John Russell. New York: Atheneum, 1964.

Löbl, Evžen. *Sentenced and Tried*. London: Elek, 1969.

London, Artur. *Doznání: v soukolí pražského procesu*. Prague: Československý spisovatel, 1990.

——. *On Trial—L'Aveau*. London: Macdonald, 1970.

Mareš, Michal. *Ze vzpomínek anarchisty, reportéra a válečného zločince*. Prague: Prostor, 1999.

Margolius, Ivan. *Reflections of Prague: Journeys through the Twentieth Century*. Chichester, UK: Wiley, 2006.

Margolius Kovály, Heda. *Under a Cruel Star: A Life in Prague 1941–1968*. London: Granta, 2012.

Miller, Arthur. "The Chelsea Affect." *Granta*, 28 June 2002.

Mlynář, Zdeněk. *Night Frost in Prague: The End of Humane Socialism*. Trans. Paul Wilson. London: Hurst, 1980.

Mucha, Jiří. *Au seuil de la nuit*. Trans. Françoise Tabery and Karel Tabery. La Tour d'Aigues: Éditions de l'aube, 1991.

——. *Living and Partly Living*. Trans. Ewald Osers. London: Hogarth, 1967.

Nakashima, George. *The Soul of a Tree: A Woodworker's Reflections*. New York: Kodansha, 2011.

Neveux, Georges. "La Voleuse de Londres." Program notes, Théâtre du Gymnase, Paris, 1960.

Nezval, Vítězslav. *Pražský chodec*. Prague: Borový, 1938.

——. *Z mého života*. Prague: Československý spisovatel, 1961.

Raymond, Antonín. *An Autobiography*. Rutland, VT: Charles E. Tuttle, 1973.

——. *Antonín Raymond v Japonsku 1948–1976: vzpomínky přátel*. Ed. Helena Čapková and Kóiči Kitazawa. Prague: Aula, 2019.

Reinerová, Lenka. *Bez adresy: neskutečně skutečné přiběhy*. Prague: Městká knihovna, 2019.

——. *Čekárny mého života*. Prague: Labyrint, 2007.

——. *Hranice uzavřeny*. Prague: Mladá fronta, 1956.

——. *Kavárna nad Prahou*. Prague: Labyrint, 2001.

——. *Všechny barvy slunce a noci*. Prague: Městská knihovna, 2019.

Rubin, Susan Goldman, with Ela Weissberger. *The Cat with the Yellow Star: Coming of Age in Terezin*. New York: Holiday House, 2006.

Scheinpflugová, Olga. *Byla jsem na světě*. Prague: Mladá fronta, 1988.

Seifert, Jaroslav. *Všecky krásy světa*. Prague: Československý spisovatel, 1992.

Škvorecký, Josef, and Zdena Salivarová. *Samožerbuch: Autofestšrift*. Prague: Panorama, 1991.

Slánská, Josefa. *Report on My Husband*. New York: Atheneum, 1969.

Šlingová, Marian. *Truth Will Prevail*. London: Merlin, 1968.

Štorch-Marien, Otakar. *Sladko je žít*. Prague: Aventinum, 1992.

Svěrák, Zdeněk a kolegové. *Půlstoletí s Cimrmanem: Legendární divadlo z odvrácené strany*. Prague: Paseka, 2016.

Vondráčková, Jaroslava. *Kolem Mileny Jesenské*. Prague: Torst, 1991.

8. Poems, Plays, Novels, and Other Literary Works

Apollinaire, Guillaume. *The Wandering Jew and Other Stories*. Trans. Rémy Inglis Hall. London: Rupert Hart-Davis, 1967.

Art from the Ashes. Ed. Lawrence L. Langer. New York: Oxford University Press, 1995.

Bezruč, Petr. *Slezské písně*. Prague: Orbis, 1950.

Biebl, Konstantin. *Bez obav: básně z let 1940–1950*. Prague: Československý spisovatel, 1951.

——. *S lodí, jež dováží čaj a kávu*. In *Cesta na Jávu*. Prague: Labyrint, 2001.

Binet, Laurent. *HHhH*. Trans. Sam Taylor. New York: Farrar, Straus and Giroux, 2013.

Bondy, Egon. *Básnické spisy I 1947–1963*. Ed. Martin Machovec. Prague: Argo, 2014.

——. *Básnické spisy II 1962–1975*. Ed. Martin Machovec. Prague: Argo, 2015.

——. *Básnické spisy III 1976–1994*. Ed. Martin Machovec. Prague: Argo, 2016.

Breton, André. *Anthology of Black Humor*. Trans. Mark Polizzotti. San Francisco: City Lights, 1997.

——. *Arcane 17*. Paris: Biro, 2008 (facsimile reprint).

——. *Martinique: Snake Charmer*. Trans. David W. Seaman. Austin: University of Texas Press, 2008.

——. *Nadja*. Trans. Richard Howard. New York: Grove Press, 1960.

Čapek, Josef. *Oheň a touha: Básně z koncentračního tábora*. Prague: Odeon, 1980

Čapek, Karel. *Francouzská poesie*. Spisy. Vol. 24. Prague: Český spisovatel, 1993.

——. *Letters from England*. Trans. Geoffrey Newsome. London: Continuum, 2004.

Carroll, Lewis. *Alice's Adventures in Wonderland*. New York: Appleton, 1866.

Desnos, Robert. "Le pensionnat de Humming-Bird Garden." Excerpt from *La liberté ou l'amour*, at freaklit.blogspot.com.

Eliot, T. S. *Collected Poems 1909–1962*. London: Faber and Faber, 1974.

Epstein, Jennifer Cody. *The Gods of Heavenly Punishment*. New York: Norton, 2014.

Fischl, Viktor. *The Dead Village*. Trans. Laurie Lee. London: Young Czechoslovakia, 1943.

Halas, František. *Mladé ženy Staré ženy*. Prague: Nibiru, 2002.

——. *Naše paní Božena Němcová*. Prague: Městská knihovna, 2000 (e-book).

Hašek, Jaroslav. *The Good Soldier Švejk*. Trans. Cecil Parrott. London: Penguin, 1974.

Havel, Václav. *The Garden Party and Other Plays*. Various translators. New York: Grove, 1993.

——. *Largo Desolato*. Trans. Tom Stoppard. London: Faber and Faber, 1987.

Hemingway, Ernest. *For Whom the Bell Tolls*. New York: Charles Scribner's Sons, 1940.

Hoffmeister, Adolf. *Poprava—Pissoir*. Prague: Dilia, 1991.

Hořejší, Jindřich. *Den a noc*. Prague: Janská, 1931.

——. *Hudba na náměstí*. Prague: CIN, 1921.

——. *Korálový náhrdelník*. Prague: SNKLU, 1961.

——. *Překlady*. Prague: SNKLU, 1965.

Hostovský, Egon. *The Hideout*. Trans. Fern Long. London: Pushkin Press, 2017.

Hrabal, Bohumil. *Closely Watched Trains*. Trans. Edith Pargeter. Evanston, IL: Northwestern University Press, 1990.

——. *Dancing Lessons for the Advanced in Age*. Trans. Michael Henry Heim. New York: Harcourt Brace, 1995.

——. *I Served the King of England*. Trans. Paul Wilson. London: Picador, 1990.

——. *Inzerát na dům, ve kterém už nechci bydlet*. Prague: Mladá fronta, 1965.

——. *Morytáty a legendy*. Prague: Mladá fronta, 2000.

——. *Mr Kafka and Other Tales from the Time of the Cult*. New York: New Directions Books, 2015.

——. *Murder Ballads and Other Legends*. Trans. Timothy West. Bloomington, IN: Three String Books, 2018.

——. *Too Loud a Solitude*. Trans. Michael Henry Heim. New York: Harcourt Brace Jovanovich, 1976.

Jirásek, Alois. *Legends of Old Bohemia*. Trans. Edith Pargeter. London: Hamlyn, 1963.

Jirous, Ivan Martin. *My Itinerary Has Been Monotonous for Quite a While*. Trans. Marek Tomin. London and Prague: Divus, 2017.

Joyce, James. "Anna Livie Plurabelle." Trans. Samuel Beckett et al. *Nouvelle Revue Française*, No. 36, 1 May 1931.

——. "Continuation of a Work in Progress." *transition*, No. 8, November 1927.

——. *Finnegans Wake*. London: Faber and Faber, 1975.

——. *Ulysses*. Paris: Shakespeare, 1922. New York: Dover Books, 2010 (facsimile reprint).

Kafka, Franz. *The Castle*. Trans. Mark Harman. London: Penguin, 1998.

——. *Dearest Father: Stories and Other Writings*. Trans. Ernest Kaiser and Eithne Wilkins. New York: Schocken, 1954.

——. *Selected Short Stories of Franz Kafka*. Trans. Willa Muir and Edwin Muir. New York: Modern Library, 1993.

——. *The Trial*. Trans. Breon Mitchell. New York: Schocken, 2012.

Konrád, Karel. *Robinsonáda: Zabili všechny mládence na rozkaz krále Heroda*. Prague: Hyperion, 1926.

Kozik, Francis [František Kožík]. *The Great Debureau*. Trans. Dora Round. New York: Farrar and Rinehart, 1940.

Kožík, František. *Největší z Pierotů*. 2 vols. Prague: Evropský literární klub, 1939.

Krejcarová, Jana. *Clarissa a jiné texty*. Prague: Concordia, 1990.

Kundera, Milan. *The Book of Laughter and Forgetting*. Trans. Michael Henry Heim. London: Penguin, 1986.

——. *The Book of Laughter and Forgetting*. Trans. Aaron Asher. New York: HarperCollins, 1996.

——. *The Joke*. Trans. David Hamblyn and Oliver Stallybrass. London: Macdonald, 1967.

——. *The Joke*. Trans. Aaron Asher. New York: HarperCollins, 1993.

——. *Life Is Elsewhere*. Trans. Peter Kussi. London: Penguin, 1986.

——. *Life Is Elsewhere*. Trans. Aaron Asher. New York: HarperCollins, 2000.

——. *Poslední máj*, 2nd rev. ed. Prague: Československý spisovatel, 1961.

——. *The Unbearable Lightness of Being*. Trans. Michael Henry Heim. New York: HarperCollins, 1991.

Leppin, Paul. *Others' Paradise: Tales of Old Prague*. Trans. Stephanie Howard and Amy R. Nestor. Prague: Twisted Spoon Press, 2016.

——. *Severin's Journey into the Dark: A Prague Ghost Story*. Trans. Kevin Blahut. Prague: Twisted Spoon Press, 2012.

Lustig, Arnošt. *Dita Saxova*. Trans. Jeanne Němcová. Evanston, IL: Northwestern University Press, 1993.

Mácha, Karel Hynek. *May*. Trans. Marcela Sulak. Prague: Twisted Spoon Press, 2005.

Mareš, Michal. *Andělíčkářka—The Angel-Maker: A Czech-English Parallel-Text Concise Novel*. Trans. David Short. London: Jantar Press, 2011.

Margolius Kovály, Heda. *Innocence; or, Murder on Steep Street*. Trans. Alex Zucker. New York: Soho Press, 2015.

Meyrink, Gustav. *The Golem*. Trans. E. F. Bleiler. New York: Dover, 1976.

Němcová, Božena. *The Grandmother*. Trans. Frances Gregor. Prague: Vitalis, 2006.

Neruda, Jan. *Prague Tales*. Trans. Michael Henry Heim. London: Chatto and Windus, 1993.

Nezval, Vítězslav. *Abeceda*. Prague: Torst, 1993 (facsimile reprint of 1926 Otto ed.).

——. *Alphabet*. Trans. Jindřich Toman and Matthew S. Witkovsky. Ann Arbor: Michigan Slavic Publications, 2001.

——. *Prague with Fingers of Rain*. Trans. Ewald Osers. Tarset: Bloodaxe Books, 2009.

——. *Praha s prsty deště*. Prague: Borový, 1936.

Nezval, Vítězslav, and Jindřich Štyrský. *Edition 69*. Trans. Jed Slast. Prague: Twisted Spoon Press, 2004. (Contains translations of Nezval's *Sexuální nocturno* and Štyrský's *Emilie přichází ke mně ve snu*, as well as Bohuslav Brouk's afterword.)

Rimbaud, Arthur. *Rimbaud: Complete Works, Selected Letters*. Ed. and trans. Wallace Fowlie. Chicago: University of Chicago Press, 1966.

Rothwell, Nicolas. *Belomor*. Melbourne: Text Publishing, 2013.

Salač, Alois Ludvík. *Slezské jařmo*. Plzeň: Česká ročenka, 1925.

Sebald, W. G. *Austerlitz*. New York: Knopf, 2001.

Seifert, Jaroslav. *Dílo Jaroslava Seiferta*. Vol. 1. Prague: Akropolis, 2001.

——. *The Early Poetry of Jaroslav Seifert*. Ed. and trans. Dana Loewy. Evanston, IL: Northwestern University Press, 1997.

——. *The Selected Poetry of Jaroslav Seifert*. Ed. and trans. Ewald Osers. New York: Collier, 1986.

——. *Vějíř Boženy Němcové*. Prague: Orbis, 1940.

Shelley, Mary. *Frankenstein: Or, the Modern Prometheus*. London: Penguin, 2004.

Škvorecký, Josef. *The Cowards*. Trans. Jeanne Nemcova. London: Gollancz, 1970.

——. *Two Murders in My Double Life*. New York: Farrar, Straus, Giroux, 2001.

Slouka, Mark. "The Little Museum of Memory." *Granta*, Vol. 96, 27 December 2006.

Štyrský, Jindřich. *Dreamverse*. Trans. Jed Slast. Prague: Twisted Spoon Press, 2018.

——. *Emilie přichází ke mně ve snu*. Prague: Torst, 2001 (facsimile reprint).

Tomin, Zdena. *The Coast of Bohemia: A Winter's Tale*. London: Hutchinson, 1987.

Toyen. *Specters of the Desert*. Trans. Stephen Schwartz. Chicago: Black Swan Press, 1974.

Triolet, Elsa. *Le monument*. Paris: Gallimard, 1957.

Weil, Jiří. *Life with a Star*. Trans. Rita Klimova and Roslyn Schloss. Evanston, IL: Northwestern University Press, 1998.

——. *Mendelssohn Is on the Roof*. Trans. Marie Winn. Evanston, IL: Northwestern University Press, 1998.

——. *Žalozpěv za 77,297 obětí*. Prague: Československý spisovatel, 1958.

Weislitzová, Věra. *Dcera Olgy a Lea/The Daughter of Olga and Leo*. Prague: Unitisk, 1994.

Wolker, Jiří. *Host do domu*. Prague: Městká knihovna, 2011.

Woolf, Virginia. *A Room of One's Own*. London: Penguin, 2014.

9. Graphic Albums, Photo Books, and the Like

Aleš, Mikoláš. *Špalíček národních písní a říkadel*. Prague: Orbis, 1950.

Heisler, Jindřich. *Aniž by nastal viditelný pohyb*. Ed. Věra Linhartová. Toronto: Sixty-Eight Publishers, 1977.

Kaplický, Jan. *Jan Kaplický Drawings*. Comp. and ed. Ivan Margolius. London: Circa, 2015.

Kolář, Jiří. *Kafkova Praha/Kafkas Prag/Prague de Kafka 1977–1978*. Prague: Alea, 1994.

——. *Týdeník 1968/Newsreel 1968*. Prague: Torst, 1993.

Koudelka, Josef. *Invasion 68: Prague*. New York: Aperture, 2008.

——. *Prague, 1968: Photographies de Josef Koudelka*. Paris: Centre National de la Photographie, 1990.

Krull, Germaine. *Métal*. Paris: Calavas, 1928. Reprint, Cologne: Ann and Jürgen Wilde, 2003.

Lukas, Jan. *Pražský deník 1938–1965*. Prague: Torst, 1995.

Plicka, Karel, and František Volf. *Český rok v pohádkách, písních, hrách a tancích, říkadlech a hádankách*. Illustrated by Karel Svolinský. 4 vols. Prague: Mladá fronta, 2010–2011.

Urbanová, Alexandra, and Zdeněk Tmej. *Abeceda duševního prázdna*. Prague: Zádruha, 1946.

10. Films

Amadeus (Miloš Forman, 1984).

Anna proletářka (Anna the proletarian; Karel Steklý, 1953).

Bílá nemoc (*The White Disease*, or *Skeleton on Horseback*; Hugo Haas, 1937).

The Cabinet of Dr. Caligari (Robert Wiene, 1920).

Casablanca (Michael Curtiz, 1942).

Černý Petr (*Black Peter*; Miloš Forman, 1964).

Daleká cesta (*Distant Journey*; Alfréd Radok, 1949).

Démanty noci (*Diamonds of the Night*; Jan Němec, 1964).

Erotikon (Gustav Machatý, 1929).

Extase (*Ecstasy*; Gustav Machatý, 1932).

The Girl on the Bridge (Hugo Haas, 1951).

La Grande Illusion (*The Grand Illusion*; Jean Renoir, 1937).

Hair (Miloš Forman, 1979).

Hangmen Also Die (Fritz Lang, 1943).

Hoří, má panenko (*The Firemen's Ball*; Miloš Forman, 1967).

if. . . . (Lindsay Anderson, 1968).

Intimní osvětlení (*Intimate Lighting*; Ivan Passer, 1965).

Jan Cimbura (František Čáp, 1941).

Johanes Doktor Faust (Emil Radok, 1958).

Jud Süß (*Jew Süss*; Veit Harlan, 1940).

Kdyby tisíc klarinetů (If a thousand clarinets; Ján Roháč and Vladimír Svitáček, 1965).

Když struny lkají (When the strings moan; Fridrich Fehér, 1930).

Konkurs (*Audition*; Miloš Forman, 1963).

Lásky jedné plavovlásky (*Loves of a Blonde*; Miloš Forman, 1965).

Lidice: A Light across the Sea (Dan Stubbs, 2013).

Metropolis (Fritz Lang, 1926).

Metropolis (Rintaro, 2002).

Na pomoc generální prokuratuře (To help the general procurator; Vlastimil Vávra, 1969).

Na sluneční straně (On the sunny side; Vladislav Vančura, 1933).

Niemandsland (*No Man's Land*; Victor Trivas, 1931).

Night of the Quarter Moon (Hugo Haas, 1959).

O slavnosti a hostech (*A Report on the Party and the Guests*; Jan Němec, 1966).

Obchod na korze (*The Shop on Main Street*; Ján Kadár and Elmar Klos, 1965).

Obsluhoval jsem anglického krále (*I Served the King of England*; Jiří Menzel, 2006).

Olympia (Leni Riefenstahl, 1938).

One Flew over the Cuckoo's Nest (Miloš Forman, 1975).

One Girl's Confession (Hugo Haas, 1953).

Oratorium pro Prahu (*Oratorio for Prague*; Jan Němec, 1968).

Ostře sledované vlaky (*Closely Watched Trains*; Jiří Menzel, 1966).

Otvírání studánek (Opening of the wells; Alfréd Radok, 1960).

Perák a SS (*The Chimney Sweep*; Jiří Trnka, 1946).

Perličky na dně (*Pearls of the Deep*; Věra Chytilová, Jaromil Jireš, Jiří Menzel, Jan Němec, Evald Schorm, 1966).

Pickup (Hugo Haas, 1951).

Pražské jaro (Prague Spring; Alfréd Radok, 1958).

Případ pro začínajícího kata (*The Case for a Rookie Hangman*; Pavel Juráček, 1969).

Pudr a Benzin (*Powder and Petrol*; Jindřich Honzl, 1932).

Rudá záře nad Kladnem (Red blaze over Kladno; Vladimír Vlček, 1955).

Sedmikrásky (*Daisies*; Věra Chytilová, 1966).

The Silent Village (Humphrey Jennings, 1943).

Skřivánci na niti (*Larks on a String*; Jiří Menzel, 1969).

Strange Fascination (Hugo Haas, 1952).

Taking Off (Miloš Forman, 1971).

Theresienstadt: Ein Dokumentarfilm aus dem jüdischen Siedlungsgebiet (Terezín: a documentary film from the Jewish settlement area, 1944).

Tiefland (*Lowlands*; Leni Riefenstahl, 1954).

Toyen (Jan Němec, 2005).

Triumf des Willens (*Triumph of the Will*; Leni Riefenstahl, 1935).

Valerie a týden divů (*Valerie and Her Week of Wonders*; Jaromil Jireš, 1970).

Věra Lukášová (Božena Benešová, 1938).

Věra 68 (Olga Sommerová, 2012).

Žert (*The Joke*; Jaromil Jireš, 1968).

Zítra se bude tančit všude (Tomorrow there will be dancing everywhere; Vladimír Vlček, 1952).

11. Exhibition Catalogs

The Art of the Avant-garde in Czechoslovakia 1918–1938. Ed. Jaroslav Anděl. Valencia: IVAM Centre Julio Gonzalez, 1993.

Bruselský sen: československá účast na světové výstavě EXPO 58 v Bruselu a životní styl 1. poloviny 60. let. Ed. Marie Bergmanová. Prague: Arbor Vitae, 2008.

Celostátní výstava archivních dokumentů: od hrdinné minulosti k vítězství socialismu. Zdeněk Nejedlý. Prague: Ministerstvo vnitra, 1958.

Černá slunce: Odvrácená strana modernity. Lenka Bydžovská, Vojtěch Lahoda, and Karel Srp. Prague: Arbor Vitae, 2012.

České imaginativní umění. František Šmejkal. Prague: Galerie Rudolfinum, 1996.

Československý socialistický realismus, 1948–1958. Tereza Petišková. Prague: Gallery, 2002.

Český a slovenský exil 20. století. Vol. 1. Ed. Jan Kratochvíl. Brno: Meadow Art, 2002.

Český informel (Průkopníci abstrakce z let 1957–1964). Ed. Mahulena Nešlehová. Prague: Galerie hlavního města Prahy, 1991.

Civilisovaná žena: Jak se má kultivovaná žena oblékati/Zivilisierte Frau: Wie sich eine kultivierte Frau ankleiden soll. Ed. Božena Horneková, Jan Vaněk, and Zdeněk Rossmann. Brno: J. Vaněk, 1929.

Crafting a Modern World: The Architecture and Design of Antonín and Noémi Raymond. Ed. Kurt G. F. Helfrich and William Whitaker. New York: Princeton Architectural Press, 2006.

Cyklus výstav Sbírky moderního malířství, tiskové zpravodajství, 1984–1989. Sixteen exhibitions curated by Jiří Kotalík. Cylostyled press releases in archive of National Gallery, Prague.

Deset let Československé lidově demokratické republiky ve výtvarném umění 1945–1955. Prague: Ministerstvo kultury, 1955.

The Dreaming Rebel: Toyen 1902–1980. Ed. Anna Pravdová, Annie Le Brun, and Annabelle Görgen-Lammers. Prague: Národní galerie, 2021.

Expo 58: Between Utopia and Reality. Ed. Gonzague Pluvinage. Brussels: Lannoo Uitgeverij, 2008.

Eyewitness: Hungarian Photography in the Twentieth Century. Péter Baki, Colin Ford, and George Szirtes. London: Royal Academy of Arts, 2011.

The Family of Man. Edward Steichen. New York: Museum of Modern Art, 1983.

50 let československého malířství 1918–1968. Jiří Kotalík. Prague: Národní galerie, 1969.

For New Brno: The Architecture of Brno 1919–1939. Zdeněk Kudělka and Jindřich Chatrný. 2 vols. Brno: Muzeum města Brna, 2000.

"Garakutashu—A Network for Modern Craft and Design." Exhibition brochure, Institute for Art Anthropology, Tamu Art University, Japan, 2021.

George Grosz: Berlin–New York. Ralph Jentsch. Milan: Skira, 2008.

Jindřich Heisler: Surrealism under Pressure 1938–1953. Jindřich Toman and Matthew S. Witkovsky. Chicago: Art Institute of Chicago, 2012.

Adolf Hoffmeister (1902–1973). Ed. Karel Srp. Prague: Gallery, 2004.

Adolf Hoffmeister: Ilustrace. Prague: Galerie Československého spisovatele, 1958.

Hoffmeisterova ironická kronika doby. František Šmejkal. Litoměřice: Severočeská galerie výtvarného umění/Památník Terezín, 2016.

Hořká léta 1939–47/The Bitter Years 1939–47. Vladimír Birgus. Opava: Slezská univerzita, 1995.

Jaro 62: výstava tvůrčí skupiny Mánes, hostí a bloku tvůrčích skupin. Prague: Mánes, 1962.

K výtvarné problematice třicátých let. Prague: Národní galerie, 1964.

Jan Kaplický—Vlastní cestou/His Own Way. Deyan Sudjic. Prague: DOX Centre for Contemporary Art, 2010.

Jiří Kolář Úšklebek století/Grimace of the Century. Marie Klimešová and Milena Kalinovská. Prague: Národní galerie, 2018.

Konec avantgardy? Od mnichovské dohody ke komunistickému převratu. Ed. Hana Rousová. Prague: Arbor Vitae, 2011.

Koudelka: Návraty. Ed. Josef Koudelka and Irena Šorfová. Prague: UMPRUM/Kant, 2018.

Jaromír Krejcar 1895–1949. Ed. Rostislav Švácha. Prague: Galerie Jaroslava Fragnera, 1995.

Jiří Kroha v proměnách umění 20. století (1893–1974), Architekt · Malíř · Designér · Teoretik. Ed. Marcela Macharáčková and Jindřich Chatrný. Brno: Muzeum města Brna, 2007.

Germaine Krull. Michel Frizot. Paris: Hazan/Jeu de Paume, 2015.

Josef Lada. Tereza Petišková. Prague: Obecní dům, 2008.

Laterna Magika: Nouvelles technologies dans l'art tchéque du XXe siècle/New Technologies in Czech Art of the 20th Century. Ed. Marion Diez. Prague: Kant, 2002.

Kamil Lhoták, sic itur ad astra: Obrazy, básně, přátelé/Paintings, Poems, Friends. Anna Fulíková and Nina Machková. Prague: Retro Gallery, 2015.

Mikuláš Medek. Ed. Antonín Hartmann. Prague: Gema Art, 2002.

Mikuláš Medek: Nahý v trní/Naked in the Thorns. Lenka Bydžovská, Karel Srp, and Michal Novotný. Prague: Národní galerie, 2020.

Emila Medková. Lenka Bydžovská and Karel Srp. Prague: Kant, 2001.

Mezinárodní surrealismus. Ed. Jiří Kotalík. Prague: Topičův salon, 1947.

Moc obrazů, obrazy moci/Power of Images, Images of Power. Tomáš Bojar, Jan Třeštík, and Jakub Zelníček. Prague: Galerie U Křižovníků, 2005.

Moderní české malířstvi II: léta dvacátá. Miroslav Lamač and Jiří Padrta. Brno: Dům uměni města Brna, 1958.

"Museum of Modern Art Opens Exhibition of War Caricatures by Czechoslovakian Artists." MoMA press release, 5 May 1943.

Národ svým výtvarným umělcům. Ed. František Kovárna. Prague: Kulturní rada, 1940.

New Formations: Czech Avant-Garde Art and Modern Glass from the Roy and Mary Cullen Collection. Karel Srp and Lenka Bydžovská, with Alison de Lima Greene and Jan Mergl. Houston: Museum of Fine Arts, 2011.

Ohniska znovuzrození: České umění 1956–1963. Ed. Marie Judlová. Prague: Galerie hlavního města Prahy, 1994.

Osada Baba: Plány a modely/Baba Housing Estate: Plans and Models. Tomáš Šenberger, Vladimír Šlapeta, and Petr Urlich. Prague: Czech Technical University, 2000.

Other Air: The Group of Czech-Slovak Surrealists 1990–2011. Ed. Bruno Solarik and František Dryje. Prague: Analogon, 2012.

The Precious Legacy: Judaic Treasures from the Czechoslovak State Collections. Ed. David Altshuler. New York: Summit Books, 1983.

Antonín Raymond 7x. Ed. Dan Merta and Klára Pučerová. Prague: Galerie Jaroslava Fragnera, 2015.

Roky ve dnech: české umění 1945–1957. Marie Klimešová. Prague: Arbor Vitae, 2010.

Seznam děl Jubilejní výstavy Mikoláše Alše. 2 vols. Prague: SVU Myslbek, 1932–1933.

Skupina 42. Eva Petrová et al. Prague: Akropolis/Galerie hlavního města Prahy, 1998.

Skupina Ra. František Šmejkal et al. Prague: Galerie hlavního města Prahy, 1988.

Jindřich Štyrský. Lenka Bydžovská and Karel Srp. Prague: Argo/Galerie hlavního města Prahy, 2007.

Štyrský, Toyen, Heisler. Ed. Jana Cleverie. Paris: Centre Georges Pompidou, 1982.

Ladislav Sutnar: Americké Venuše (U.S. Venus). Ed. Iva Knobloch. Prague: Arbor Vitae, 2011.

Ladislav Sutnar—Praha—New York—Design in Action. Ed. Iva Janáková. Prague: Argo, 2003.

Jan Švankmajer: Dimensions of Dialogue/Between Film and Fine Art. Ed. František Dryje and Bertrand Schmitt. Prague: Arbor Vitae, 2012.

Karel Svolinský 1896–1986. Ed. Roman Musil and Eduard Burget. Olomouc: Nadace Karla Švolinského a Vlasty Kubátové, 2001.

Symboly obludnosti. Stanislav Dvorský, Vratislav Effenberger, and Petr Král. Prague: Galerie D, 1966. Facsimile reproduction in Marie Langerová et al., *Symboly obludností: mýty, jazyk a tabu české postavantgardy 40.–60. let.* Prague: Malvern, 2009.

Karel Teige: Architettura, Poesia: Praga 1900–1951. Ed. Manuela Castagnara Codeluppi. Milan: Elekta, 1996.

Karel Teige, Surrealistické koláže 1935–1951. Rumjana Dačeva, Vojtěch Lahoda, Karel Srp. Prague: Středoevropská galerie, 1994.

V okovech smíchu: Karikatura a české umění 1900–1950. Ed. Ondřej Chrobák and Tomáš Winter. Prague: Gallery, 2006.

Věci umění, věci doby: Skupina 42. Marie Klimešová. Prague: Arbor Vitae, 2011.

Výstava díla Mikoláše Alše 1852–1952. František Nečásek et al. Prague: Orbis, 1952.

Výstava Národ svým výtvarným umělcům. Miloslav Hýsek et al. Prague: Kulturní rada ústředí pro kulturní a školskou práci Národního souručenství, 1939.

Výstava Poesie 1932. Prague: SVU Mánes, 1932.

The World of Tomorrow: Exploring the 1939–40 World's Fair Collection. New York Public Library online exhibition.

Zakladatelé moderního českého umění. Miroslav Lamač, Jiří Padrta, and Jan Tomeš. Brno: Dům uměni města Brna, 1957.

František Zelenka: plakáty, architektura, divadlo. Ed. Josef Kroutvor. Prague: Uměleckoprůmyslové museum, 1991.

12. Dictionaries, Encyclopedias, Chronologies, Directories, Guidebooks, and Other Reference Works

Amtliches Verzeichnis der Straßen, Plätze und Freiungen der Hauptstadt Prag—Úřední seznam ulic, náměstí a sadů hlavního města Prahy. Prague: Deutsche Druckerie, 1940.

Česká divadelní encyklopedie. Prague: Divadelní ústav, n.d. (encyklopedie.idu.cz).

Československo 1966–1971. Přehled událostí: Chronologie. K. Urianek and M. Michálková. Prague: Komise vlády ČSSR pro analýzu událostí 1967–1970, 1991.

Český hudební slovník osob a institucí. Ed. Petr Macek. Brno: Ústav hudební vědy Filosofická fakulta Masarykova univerzita, n.d. (ceskyhudebnislovnik.cz).

Dějiny české literatury 1945–1989. Vol. 2. *1948–1958.* Pavel Janoušek et al. Prague: Academia, 2007.

Dějiny Československa v datech. Miroslav Buchvaldek et al. Prague: Svoboda, 1968.

Dějiny Prahy v datech. Zdeněk Míka et al. Prague: Mladá fronta, 1999.

Encyclopedia of America's Response to the Holocaust. David S. Wyman Institute for Holocaust Studies (enc.wymaninstitute.org).

Encyclopedia of Jewish Women. Jewish Women's Archive (jwa.org).

Holocaust Encyclopedia. US Holocaust Memorial Museum (encyclopedia.ushmm.org).

The International Encyclopedia of Surrealism. Ed. Michael Richardson. 3 vols. London: Bloomsbury, 2019.

Internet Encyclopedia of Philosophy. (iep.utm.edu).

Internetová encyklopedie dějin Brna (encyklopedie.brna.cz).

Kalendárium roku 1968. At totalita.cz.

Kalendárium roku 1969. At totalita.cz.

Kalendárium roku 1970. At totalita.cz.

Kdo byl kdo v našich dějinách v 20. století. Vol. 2. Milan Churaň. Prague: Libri, 1998.

Knihy za ohradou: Česká literatura v exilových nakladatelstvích. Ed. Jan Čulík. Prague: Trizonia, 1991.

Lexikon českého filmu: 2000 filmů 1930–1996. Václav Březina. Prague: Cinema, 1996.

Malá československá encyklopedie. Ed. Bohumil Kvasil et al. Prague: Academia, 1986.

Naučný slovník aktualit. Ed. Zdeněk Tobolka. Prague: L. Mazáč, 1939.

Nová encyklopedie českého výtvarného umění. Ed. Anděla Horová. 2 vols. Prague: Academia, 1995.

Ottův slovník naučný. 28 vols. Prague: Jan Otto, 1888–1909.

Praha avantgardní: literární průvodce metropolí v letech 1918–1938. Kateřina Piorecká and Karel Piorecký. Prague: Academia, 2015.

Praha moderní IV: velký průvodce po architektuře 1950–2000. Zdeněk Lukeš and Petr Kratochvíl. Prague: Paseka, 2015.

Pražské sochy a pomníky. Milan Krejčí. Prague: Galerie hlavního města Prahy, 1979.

Pražský uličník: Encyklopedie názvů pražských veřejných prostranství. Marek Lašťovka et al. 2 vols. Prague: Libri, 1997–1998.

Přehled obcí a částí v ČSR, jejichž názvy zanikly, byly změněny. . . . Prague: Ústřední správa spojů, 1964.

Příručka pro sběratele československých poštovních známek a celin. Alois Dušek et al. Prague: Nakladatelství dopravy a spojů, 1988.

Procházka akční Prahou: akce performance happeningy 1949–1989. Pavlína Morganová. Prague: Akademie výtvarných umění, 2014.

Průvodce protektorátní Prahou. Místa—události—lidé. Ed. Jiří Padevět. Prague: Academia/ Archiv hlavního města Prahy, 2013.

Prvních 100 dnů Charty 77: Průvodce historickými událostmi. Petr Blažek and Radek Schovánek. Prague: Academia, 2018.

Slovník české literatury po roce 1945. Ed. Michal Přibáň. Prague: Ústav pro českou literaturu AV ČR, n.d. (slovnikceskeliteratury.cz).

Slovník zakázaných autorů 1948–1980. Jiří Brabec et al. Prague: Státní pedagogické nakladatelství, 1991.

Wikipedia. English, French, and Czech versions (which differ).

Women in World History: A Biographical Encyclopedia. Ed. Anne Commire. 16 vols. Wakeford, CT: Yorkin, 1999 (encyclopedia.com).

YIVO Encyclopedia of Jews in Eastern Europe (yivoencyclopedia.org).

Židovská Praha: glosy k dějinám a kultuře. Průvodce památkami. Ctibor Rybár. Prague: Akropolis, 1991.

13. Secondary Literature: Monographs, Theses, and Articles

Aberth, Susan L. *Leonora Carrington: Surrealism, Alchemy and Art.* Burlington, VT: Lund Humphries, 2004.

Adler, H. G. *Theresienstadt 1941–1945: The Face of a Coerced Community.* Trans. Belinda Cooper. Cambridge: Cambridge University Press, 2017.

Adorno, Theodor W. *Prisms.* Trans. Samuel Weber and Shierry Weber. London: Spearman, 1967.

Agnew, Hugh. *The Czechs and the Lands of the Bohemian Crown.* Stanford, CA: Hoover Institution Press, 2004.

Alan, Josef, ed. *Alternativní kultura: příběh české společnosti 1945–1989.* Prague: Lidové noviny, 2001.

Applebaum, Anne. *Gulag: A History.* London: Penguin, 2003.

Arendt, Hannah. *Eichmann in Jerusalem: A Report on the Banality of Evil.* New York: Viking Press, 1964.

———. *Essays in Understanding 1930–1954.* Trans. Jerome Kohn. New York: Harcourt Brace, 1994.

———. *The Origins of Totalitarianism.* Boston: Mariner Books, 2001.

Armand, Louis, ed. *Abolishing Prague: Essays and Interpretations.* Prague: Literaria Pragensia, 2014.

Aubert, Nathalie. "'Cobra after Cobra' and the Alba Congress." *Third Text,* Vol. 20, No. 2, 2006.

Augustin, L. H. *Kamil Lhoták.* Prague: Academia, 2000.

Baer, Josette. *"Spirits That I've Cited . . . ?" Vladimír Clementis (1902–1952): The Political Biography of a Czechoslovak Communist.* New York: Columbia University Press, 2017.

Balint, Benjamin. *Kafka's Last Trial: The Case of a Literary Legacy.* New York: Norton, 2018.

Barron, Stephanie, ed. *"Degenerate Art": The Fate of the Avant-garde in Nazi Germany.* Los Angeles: Los Angeles County Museum of Art, 1991.

Barthes, Roland. *Camera Lucida: Reflections on Photography.* Trans. Richard Howard. New York: Hill and Wang, 2000.

——. *Mythologies*. Trans. Annette Lavers. New York: Farrar, Straus and Giroux, 1991.

Bataille, Georges. *The Absence of Myth: Writings on Surrealism*. Ed. and trans. Michael Richardson. London: Verso, 2006.

Batuman, Elif. "Kafka's Last Trial." *New York Times Magazine*, 22 September 2010.

Bauman, Zygmunt. *Modernity and the Holocaust*. Ithaca, NY: Cornell University Press, 2002.

Beck, Evelyn Torton. *Kafka and the Yiddish Theater: Its Impact on His Work*. Madison: University of Wisconsin Press, 1971.

Beckerman, Michael. "The Dark Blue Exile of Jaroslav Ježek." *Music and Politics*, Vol. 2, No. 2, Summer 2008.

——. "How Desperate He Must Feel Sitting There Helplessly: Jews, Gypsies, Czechs . . . and the Chinese . . . from Zápisník to Terezín and Beyond." *Musicologica Brunensia*, Vol. 55, No. 2, 2019.

Bělina, Pavel. *Dějiny zemí koruny české*. Vol. 2. Prague: Paseka, 1992.

Benjamin, Walter. *The Arcades Project*. Trans. Howard Eiland and Kevin McLaughlin. Cambridge, MA: Harvard University Press, 1999.

Binarová, Alena. "Svaz výtvarných umělců v českých zemích v letech 1956–1972: oficiální výtvarná tvorba v proměnách komunistického režimu." Disertační práce, Univerzita Palackého v Olomouci, Filozofická fakulta, 2016.

Birgus, Vladimír, and Jan Mlčoch. *Czech Photography of the Twentieth Century*. Prague: Kant, 2010.

Blažek, Petr. "The Deportation of the King of May: Allen Ginsberg and the State Security." *Behind the Iron Curtain*, No. 2, 2012.

——. "Majáles 1956: Pražská studentská slavnost ve fotografích Antonína Rozsypala." *Paměť a dějiny*, No. 1, 2016.

Bolton, Jonathan. "The Shaman, the Greengrocer, and 'Living in Truth.'" *East European Politics, Societies and Cultures*, Vol. 32, No. 2, 2018.

——. *Worlds of Dissent: Charter 77, the Plastic People of the Universe, and Czech Culture under Communism*. Cambridge, MA: Harvard University Press, 2012.

Borl, Petr. "Chrámy vědění osiřely: Intervenční úsilí představitelů protektorátní správy o zmírnění následků německé akce vůči českému vysokému školství na podzim roku 1939." Diplomová práce, Univerzita Karlova v Praze, 2014.

Bren, Paulina. *The Greengrocer and His TV: The Culture of Communism after the 1968 Prague Spring*. Ithaca, NY: Cornell University Press, 2011.

Brod, Toman, Miroslav Kárný, and Margita Kárná, eds. *Terezínský rodinný tábor v Osvětimi-Birkenau*. Prague: Melantrich, 1994.

Bryant, Chad. "Either German or Czech: Fixing Nationality in Bohemia and Moravia, 1939–1946." *Slavic Review*, Vol. 61, No. 4, 2002.

——. *Prague in Black: Nazi Rule and Czech Nationalism*. Cambridge, MA: Harvard University Press, 2009.

——. *The Thick Line at 1945: Czech and German Histories of the Nazi War Occupation and the Postwar Expulsion/Transfer*. Washington, DC: National Council for Eurasian and East European Research, 2006.

Buben, Václav, ed. *Šest let okupace Prahy*. Prague: Orbis, 1946.

Buber-Neumann, Margarete. *Milena: The Tragic Story of Kafka's Great Love*. Trans. Ralph Manheim. New York: Arcade, 2014.

——. *Mistress to Kafka: The Life and Death of Milena*. London: Secker and Warburg, 1966.

Burian, Jarka M. *Leading Creators of Twentieth-Century Czech Theatre*. London: Routledge, 2013.

Bydžovská, Lenka, and Karel Srp. *Knihy s Toyen*. Prague: Akropolis, 2003.

Čapková, Helena. *Bedřich Feuerstein: cesta do nejvýtvarnější země světa*. Prague: Kant, 2014.

——. "'Believe in Socialism . . .': Architect Bedřich Feuerstein and His Perspective on Modern Japan and Architecture." *Review of Japanese Culture and Society*, Vol. 28, 2016.

——. "Transnational Correspondence: Tsuchiura Kameki, Tsuchiura Nobuko and Bedřich Feuerstein." *Design History* Vol. 8, 2010.

Castro, Colette de. "The Destruction of Bliss: Gustav Machatý's *Erotikon* (1929) and *Ecstasy* (*Ekstase*, 1933)." *East European Film Bulletin*, Vol. 78, October 2017.

Čermák, Josef. *Franz Kafka: Fables et Mystifications*. Trans. Hélène Belletto-Sussel, Paris: Presses Universitaires de Septentrion, 2010.

——. *Franz Kafka: Výmysly a mystifikace*. Prague: Gutenberg, 2005.

Césaire, Aimé. *Discourse on Colonialism*. Trans. Joan Pinkham. New York: Monthly Review Press, 2001.

Cinger, František. *Šťastné blues aneb z deníku Jaroslava Ježka*. Prague: BVD, 2006.

Clybor, Shawn. "Laughter and Hatred Are Neighbors: Adolf Hoffmeister and E. F. Burian in Stalinist Czechoslovakia, 1948–1956." *East European Politics and Societies*, Vol. 26, No. 3, 2012.

Cohen, Gary B. *The Politics of Ethnic Survival: Germans in Prague 1861–1914*. Princeton, NJ: Princeton University Press, 1981.

——. *The Politics of Ethnic Survival: Germans in Prague, 1861–1914*. 2nd ed. West Lafayette, IN: Purdue University Press, 2006.

Combe, Sonia, ed. *Archives et histoire dans les sociétés postcommunistes*. Paris: La Découverte, 2009.

Couffer, Jack. *Bat Bomb: World War II's Other Secret Weapon*. Austin: University of Texas Press, 1992.

Crowley, David. "Humanity Rearranged: The Polish and Czechoslovak Pavilions at Expo 58." *West 86th: A Journal of Decorative Arts, Design History, and Material Culture*, Vol. 19, No. 1, 2012.

Cuhra, Jaroslav. *Trestní represe odpůrců režimu v letech 1969–1972*. Prague: Ústav pro soudobé dějiny AV ČR, 1997.

Čuňas, František Stárek, and Martin Valenta. *Podzemní symfonie Plastic People*. Prague: Argo, 2018.

Dagan, Avigdor, ed. *The Jews of Czechoslovakia*. Vol. 3. Philadelphia: Jewish Publication Society of America, 1984.

Dluhosch, Eric, and Rostislav Švácha, eds. *Karel Teige 1900–1951: L'Enfant Terrible of the Czech Modernist Avant-garde*. Cambridge, MA: MIT Press, 1999.

Doležal, Jiří. *Česká kultura za Protektorátu: školství, písemnictví, kinematografie*. Prague: Národní filmový archiv, 1996.

Douglas, R. M. *Orderly and Humane: The Expulsion of the Germans after the Second World War*. New Haven, CT: Yale University Press, 2012.

Draskoczy, Julie. "The 'Put' of Perekovka': Transforming Lives at Stalin's White Sea–Baltic Canal." *Russian Review*, Vol. 71, No. 1, January 2012.

Drubek, Natascha. "Sich (k)einen Namen machen: Die židovská jména der Honza K." *Slovo a smysl*, Vol. 14, No. 28, 2017.

Duchacek, Ivo. "The February Coup in Czechoslovakia." *World Politics*, Vol. 2, No. 4, 1950.

Dufek, Antonín. *Vilém Reichmann*. Prague: Foto Mida, 1994.

Dvořáčková, Magdaléna. "Pavel Juráček v kontextu šedesátých let." Diplomová práce, Univerzita Karlova v Praze, Fakulta Humanitních Studií, 2017.

Eisner, Pavel. *Kafka and Prague*. Trans. Lowry Nelson and René Wellek. New York: Arts, 1950.

Emanuel, Muriel, and Vera Gissing. *Nicholas Winton and the Rescued Generation*. London and Portland, OR: Vallentine Mitchell, 2003.

Engle, Karen, and Yoke-Sum Wong, eds. *Feelings of Structure: Explorations in Affect*. Montreal: McGill-Queen's University Press, 2018.

Epstein-Mervis, Marni. "Le Corbusier's Forgotten Design: SoCal's Iconic Butterfly Roof." *Curbed Los Angeles*, 24 December 2014.

Evanson, Robert K. "Political Repression in Czechoslovakia, 1948–1984." *Canadian Slavonic Papers*, Vol. 28, No. 1, 1986.

Fanon, Frantz. *The Wretched of the Earth*. Trans. Constance Farringdon. New York: Grove Weidenfeld, 1963.

Fárová, Anna. *Josef Sudek*. Prague: Torst, 1995.

Fárová, Anna, et al. *Josef Koudelka*. Prague: Torst, 2002.

Fijalkowski, Krzysztof, Michael Richardson, and Ian Walker. *Surrealism and Photography in Czechoslovakia*. London: Ashgate, 2016.

Fotiade, Ramona, ed. *Andre Breton: The Power of Language*. Exeter, UK: Elm Bank, 2000.

Frankl, Michal, and Jindřich Toman, eds. *Jan Neruda a Židé: texty a kontexty*. Prague: Akropolis, 2012.

Fraser, James, ed. *The Malik-Verlag: 1916–1947*. New York: Goethe House, 1984.

Freud, Sigmund. "The Uncanny" (1919), trans. Alix Strachey. In *The Standard Edition of the Complete Psychological Works of Sigmund Freud*. Vol. 17 (1917–1919). *An Infantile Neurosis and Other Works*. Ed. James Strachey. London: Hogarth Press, 1955.

Frommer, Benjamin. *National Cleansing: Retribution against Nazi Collaborators in Postwar Czechoslovakia*. Cambridge: Cambridge University Press, 2004.

Fukuyama, Francis. "The End of History." *National Interest*, Summer 1989.

Gallo, Rubén. "Who Killed Leon Trotsky?" *Princeton University Library Chronicle*, Vol. 75, No. 1, Autumn 2013.

Gard, D., I. Main, M. Oliver, and J. Wood, eds. *Inquiries into Past and Present*. Vol. 17. Vienna: IWM Junior Visiting Fellows' Conferences, 2005.

Gates, Eugene, and Karla Hartl. "Vítězslava Kaprálová: A Remarkable Voice in 20th-Century Czech Music." *Tempo*, New Series, No. 213, 2000.

Gdula, Sara. "The New Hope Experiment: An Investigation and Conservation Plan for the Antonín and Noémi Raymond Farm." Master's thesis, University of Pennsylvania, 2018.

Gerwarth, Richard. *Hitler's Hangman: The Life of Heydrich*. New Haven, CT: Yale University Press, 2012.

Giddens, Anthony. *Conversations with Anthony Giddens: Making Sense of Modernity*. Stanford, CA: Stanford University Press, 1998.

Gilbert, Sandra M., and Susan Gubar. *The Madwoman in the Attic: The Woman Writer and the Nineteenth-Century Literary Imagination*. New Haven, CT: Yale University Press, 2020.

Giustino, Cathleen M. "Industrial Design and the Czechoslovak Pavilion at Expo '58: Artistic Autonomy, Party Control and Cold War Common Ground." *Journal of Contemporary History*, Vol. 47, No. 1, 2012.

Glassheim, Eagle. "National Mythologies and Ethnic Cleansing: The Expulsion of Czechoslovak Germans in 1945." *Central European History*, Vol. 33, No. 4, 2000.

Gloaguen, Yola. "Antonín Raymond, an Architectural Journey from Bohemia to Japan in the Early 20th Century." *Friends of Czech Heritage Newsletter*, No. 16, Winter 2016–2017.

——. "Towards a Definition of Antonín Raymond's 'Architectural Identity': A Study Based on the Architect's Way of Thinking and Way of Design." PhD diss., Kyoto University, 2008.

Golan, Galia. *The Czechoslovak Reform Movement: Communism in Crisis 1962–1968*. Cambridge: Cambridge University Press, 1971.

Gordin, Michael P. *Einstein in Bohemia*. Princeton, NJ: Princeton University Press, 2020.

Greenberg, Clement. *The Collected Essays and Criticism*. Vol. 1. *Perceptions and Judgments 1939–1944*. Ed. John O'Brian. Chicago: Chicago University Press, 1988.

Grimberg, Salomon. "Jacqueline Lamba: From Darkness, with Light." *Woman's Art Journal*, Vol. 22, No. 1, 2001.

Gruša, Jiří. *Franz Kafka of Prague*. Trans. Eric Mosbacher. New York: Schocken, 1983.

Gupta, Pankaj Vir, and Christine Mueller. *Golconde: The Introduction of Modernism in India*. AIA Report on University Research. Austin: University of Texas, 2005.

Guzik, Herbert, ed. *Bydlet spolu. Kolektivní domy v českých zemích a Evropě ve 20. století*. Prague: Arbor Vitae, 2017.

Hájková, Anna. *The Last Ghetto: An Everyday History of Theresienstadt*. New York: Oxford University Press, 2021.

——. "The Woman behind the Kindertransport." *History Today*, Vol. 68, No. 12, December 2018.

Hájková, Anna, and Martin Šmok. "Dějiny zapomínají na hrdinky: Nová iniciativa připomíná Marii Schmolkovou, ženu, která zachránila tisíce lidí před holokaustem." a2larm.cz, 13 November 2017.

Halamová, Veronika. *Political Processes in Czechoslovakia 1949–1953: An Instrument of Legitimation of the Communist Regime*. Lublin: El-Press, 2014.

Hannah-Jones, Nikole, Caitlin Roper, Ilena Silverman, and Jake Silverstein, eds. *The 1619 Project: A New Origin Story*. New York: One World, 2021.

Harmetz, Aljean. *Round Up the Usual Suspects. The Making of Casablanca: Bogart, Bergman, and World War II*. New York: Hyperion, 1992.

Hartl, Karla, and Erik Entwistle, eds. *The Kaprálová Companion*. Lanham, MD: Lexington Books, 2011.

Hawes, James. *Excavating Kafka*. London: Quercus, 2008.

Heiting, Manfred. *Czech and Slovak Photo Publications 1918–1989*. Göttingen: Steidl, 2018.

Hochschild, Adam. *King Leopold's Ghost: A Story of Greed, Terror, and Heroism in Colonial Africa*. 2nd ed. Boston: Mariner Books, 2020.

Hockaday, Mary. *Kafka, Love and Courage: The Life of Milena Jesenská*. Woodstock, NY: Overlook, 1997.

Holzknecht, Václav. *Jaroslav Ježek a Osvobozené divadlo*. Prague: SNKLHU, 1957.

Hopkins, David, ed. *A Companion to Dada and Surrealism*. New York: Wiley, 2016.

Hrabová, Martina. "Between Ideal and Ideology: The Parallel Worlds of František Sammer." *Umění/Art*, Vol. 64, No. 2, 2016.

Huebner, Karla. *Magnetic Woman: Toyen and the Surrealist Erotic*. Pittsburgh, PA: Pittsburgh University Press, 2021.

Ichitani, Tomoko. "'Town of Evening Calm, Country of Cherry Blossoms': The Renarrativation of Hiroshima Memories." *Journal of Narrative Theory*, Vol. 40, No. 3, 2010.

Inaga, Shigemi, ed. *A Pirate's View of World History: A Reversed Perception of the Order of Things from a Global Perspective*. Kyoto: International Research Center for Japanese Studies, 2016.

Jangfeldt, Bengt. "Roman Jakobson in Sweden 1940–41." *Cahiers de l'ILSL*, No. 9, 1997.

Jankovič, Milan. "Nad Vančurovými *Obrazy z dějin národa českého* (Podíl rytmičnosti na utváření smyslu)." *Česká literatura*, Vol. 48, No. 4, 2000.

Jasch, Hans-Christian, and Christoph Kreutzmülle, eds. *The Participants: The Men of the Wannsee Conference*. New York: Berghahn Books, 2017.

Jirásková, Marie. *Stručná zpráva o trojí volbě: Milena Jesenská, Joachim von Zedtwitz a Jaroslav Nachtmann v roce 1939 a v čase následujícím*. Prague: Nakladatelství Franze Kafky, 1996.

Judlová, Marie, ed. *Česká kultura na přelomu 50. a 60. let*. Prague: Galerie hlavního města Prahy, 1988.

Kamen, Jiří. *Češi patří k Vídni, aneb třicet dva výprav do Vídně v českých stopách*. Prague: Mladá fronta, 2019.

Kaplan, Karel. *Československo v letech 1945–1948*. Prague: Státní pedagogické nakladatelství, 1991.

——. *Report on the Murder of the General Secretary*. London: I. B. Tauris, 1990.

——. *"Všechno jste prohráli!" (Co prozrazují archivy o IV. sjezdu Svazu československých spisovatelů 1967)*. Prague: Ivo Železný, 1997.

Karas, Joža. *Music in Terezín 1941–1945*. Hillsdale, NY: Pendragon Press, 1990.

Karasik, Mikhail. *The Soviet Photobook 1920–1941*. Ed. Manfred Heiting. Trans. Paul Williams. Göttingen: Steidl, 2015.

Karelová, Magdalena. *Tajemná místa komunismu*. Prague: Albatros, 2018.

Kárný, Miroslav, et al. *Terezínská pamětní kniha: židovské oběti nacistických deportací z Cech a Moravy 1941–1945*. Prague: Melantrich, 1995.

Kieval, Hillel J. *The Making of Czech Jewry: National Conflict and Jewish Society in Bohemia 1870–1918*. New York: Oxford University Press, 1988.

Kind-Kovács, Friederike, and Jessie Labov, eds. *From Samizdat to Tamizdat: Transnational Media during and after Socialism*. New York: Berghahn, 2013.

Kleinová, Nikola. "Emigrace z komunistického Československa a Češi v Dánsku." Diplomová práce, Universita Karlova v Praze, Fakulta Humanitních Studií, 2013.

Klíma, Ivan. "Fictions and Histories." University of California–Berkeley Occasional Papers, 1998.

Klimov, Oleg. "'I Wanted to Be the Devil Myself': The Forgotten History of How a Soviet Photographer Glorified the Gulag's White Sea Canal." *Meduza*, 4 August 2015.

Klímová, Nikola, ed. *SNKLHU Odeon 1953–1995: České knižní obálky v edičních řadách*. Prague: UMPRUM, 2016.

Klingan, Katrin, ed. *A Utopia of Modernity: Zlín*. Blumenthal: Jovis, 2010.

Knapík, Jiří. *Únor a kultura: Sovětizace české kultury 1948–1950*. Prague: Libri, 2004.

Knobloch, Iva, and Radim Vondráček, eds. *Design v českých zemích 1900–2000: instituce moderního designu*. Prague: Academia/UMPRUM, 2016.

Kopáč, Radim, and Josef Schwarz. *Nevěstince a nevěstky: obrázky z erotického života Pražanů.* Prague: Paseka, 2013.

Kouřil, Vladimír. *Jazzová sekce v čase a nečase 1971–1987.* Prague: Torst, 1999.

Kovaříková, Olga. "Cenzura a její vliv na divadelní život v Protektorátu Čechy a Morava." Disertační práce, Pedagogická fakulta, Univerzita Karlova v Praze, 2013.

Kremličková, Ladislava, ed. *Jan Masaryk (úvahy o jeho smrti).* Prague: Úřad dokumentace a vyšetřování zločinů komunismu, 2005.

Kriseová, Eda. *Vaclav Havel: Životopis.* Brno: Atlantis, 1991.

Kruger, Nicolai. "A Modern Marriage: Kameki and Nobuko Tsuchiura at Tatemono-en." *Artscape Japan/Focus,* 2 April 2014.

Kučera, Henry. "Roman Jakobson." *Language,* Vol. 59, No. 4, 1983.

Kundra, Ondřej. *Vendulka: Flight to Freedom.* Trans. Gerald Turner. Prague: Karolinum, 2021.

Kural, Václav. *Místo společenství—konflikt! Češi a Němci ve velkoněmecké říši a cesta k odsunu (1938–1945).* Prague: Karolinum, 1997.

Kusin, Vladimir V. *From Dubček to Charter 77: A Study of "Normalization" in Czechoslovakia, 1968–1978.* Edinburgh: Q Press, 1978.

Lahoda, Vojtěch. *Emil Filla.* Prague: Academia, 2007.

Lamač, Miroslav. *Osma a Skupina výtvarných umělců 1907–1917.* Prague: Odeon, 1988.

——. *Výtvarné dílo Adolfa Hoffmeistera.* Prague: Nakladatelství československých výtvarných umělců, 1966.

Laurence, Charles. *The Social Agent: A True Intrigue of Sex, Lies, and Heartbreak behind the Iron Curtain.* London: Ivan R. Dee, 2010.

Lazo, Pablo. "Dislocating Modernity: Two Projects by Hannes Meyer in Mexico." *AA Files,* No. 47, Summer 2002.

Leclerc, Hélène. "L'exil mexicain de Lenka Reinerová." *Études Germaniques,* Vol. 63, No. 4, 2008.

Leidenberger, Georg. "'Alles z'Unterobsi': Hannes Meyer and German Communist Exiles in Mexico." Submitted for publication. Available at academia.edu.

Lindqvist, Sven. *"Exterminate All the Brutes."* Trans. Joan Tate. New York: New Press, 2007.

Loeffler, Jane C. *The Architecture of Diplomacy: Building America's Embassies.* Princeton, NJ: Princeton Architectural Press, 1998.

Louis, W. Roger, ed. *History of Oxford University Press.* Vol. 3. *1896 to 1970.* Oxford: Oxford University Press, 2014.

Lyotard, Jean-François. *The Postmodern Condition: A Report on Knowledge.* Trans. Geoff Bennington and Brian Massumi. Manchester, UK: Manchester University Press, 1994.

Macadam, Heather Dune. *999: The Extraordinary Young Women of the First Official Jewish Transport to Auschwitz.* New York: Citadel Press, 2019.

Machovec, Martin. *Writing Underground: Reflections on Samizdat Literature in Totalitarian Czechoslovakia.* Prague: Karolinum Press, 2019.

——. "Židovská jména rediviva: Významný objev pro dějiny samizdatu." *A2 Sociální divadlo,* Nos. 51–52, 2007.

Macura, Vladimír. *The Mystifications of a Nation: The "Potato Bug" and Other Essays on Czech Culture.* Trans. Hana Píchová and Craig Cravens. Madison: University of Wisconsin Press, 2010.

Maisel, David. "Proving Ground." Story Institute, n.d.

Manaugh, Geoff, William L. Fox, and Tyler Green. *David Maisel: Proving Ground*. Göttingen: Steidl, 2019.

Margolius, Ivan. *Architects + Engineers = Structures*. Chichester, UK: Wiley-Academy, 2002.

Marková-Kotyková, Marta. *Mýtus Milena*. Prague: Primus, 1993.

Marx, Karl. "Theses on Feuerbach." In Karl Marx and Friedrich Engels, *Collected Works*, Vol. 5. London: Lawrence and Wishart, 1976.

Matthews, John P. C. "Majales: The Abortive Student Revolt in Czechoslovakia in 1956." Working Paper No. 24. Washington, DC: Woodrow Wilson International Center for Scholars, 1999.

McDermott, Kevin, and Matthew Stibbe, eds. *De-Stalinising Eastern Europe: The Rehabilitation of Stalin's Victims after 1953*. Basingstoke, UK: Palgrave Macmillan, 2015.

McLeod, Mike. "The Life, Legacy and Furniture of George Nakashima and a Conversation with Mira Nakashima." *Southeastern Antiquing and Collecting Magazine*, August 2015.

Merhaut, Vladislav. *Grafik Vladimír Boudník*. Prague: Torst, 2009.

Michaels, Jennifer E. "Migrations and Diasporas. German Writers in Mexican Exile. Egon Erwin Kisch's and Anna Seghers' Promotion of Cross-Cultural Understanding." *Studia Theodisca*, Vol. 19, 2012.

Michalová, Rea. *Karel Teige: Captain of the Avant-garde*. Prague: Torst, 2018.

Micka, Alois. "Umění mezi sjezdy." Disertační práce, Univerzita Karlova v Praze, Filozofická fakulta, Ústav pro dějiny umění, 2019.

Mikeš, Jiří. "Svaz českých výtvarných umělců v době normalizace." Magisterská diplomová práce, Masarykova univerzita, Brno Filozofická fakulta, 2013.

Militzová, Anna. *Ani víru ani ctnosti člověk nepotřebuje ke své spáse. Příběh Jany Černé*. Olomouc: Burian a Tichák, 2015.

Mladičová, Iva. "Jan Kotík 1916–2002—monografie." Disertační práce, Univerzita Karlova v Praze, Ústav pro dějiny umění, 2012.

Molella, Arthur P., and Scott Gabriel Knowles, eds. *World's Fairs in the Cold War: Science, Technology, and the Culture of Progress*. Pittsburgh, PA: University of Pittsburgh Press, 2019.

Montserrat, María, Farías Barba, Marco Santiago Mondragón, and Viridiana Zavala Rivera. "Lena Bergner: From the Bauhaus to Mexico." *Bauhaus Imaginista Journal*, Issue 2, 2019.

Moucha, Josef. *Jan Lukas*. Prague: Torst, 2003.

Naimark, Norman M. *Fires of Hatred: Ethnic Cleansing in Twentieth-Century Europe*. Cambridge, MA: Harvard University Press, 1992.

Nakashima, Mira. *Nature, Form and Spirit: The Life and Legacy of George Nakashima*. New York: Abrams, 2003.

Nejdlová, Romana. *Amšel (syn Herrmanna Kafky)*. Prague: Galén, 2013.

Nejedlý, Jan, and Jakub Šofar. *Po práci legraci: lexicon lidové tvořivosti z dob socialismu*. Prague: Albatross, 2016.

Nekula, Marek. *Franz Kafka and His Prague Contexts*. Prague: Karolinum, 2015.

Nohlen, Dieter, and Philip Stöver. *Elections in Europe: A Data Handbook*. Baden-Baden: Nomos, 2010.

Northey, Anthony. *Kafka's Relatives: Their Lives and His Writing*. New Haven, CT: Yale University Press, 1991.

Novokmet, Filip. "The Long-Run Evolution of Inequality in the Czech Lands, 1898–2015." WID. world Working Paper Series No. 2018/06, 2018.

O'Grady, Gerald, ed. *The Banned and the Beautiful: A Survey of Czech Filmmaking 1963–1990*. New York: Public Theatre, 1990.

O'Neill, Patrick. *Trilingual Joyce: The Anna Livia Variations*. Toronto: University of Toronto Press, 2018.

Opelík, Jiří. "Fučík jako kritický vykladač Haškova Švejka." *Česká literatura*, Vol. 2, No. 4, 1954.

Orwell, George. "Notes on Nationalism." *Polemic*, October 1945.

Oshima, Ken Tadashi. *International Architecture in Interwar Japan: Constructing Kokusai Kenchiku*. Seattle: University of Washington Press, 2009.

Overy, R. J. *War and Economy in the Third Reich*. Oxford: Oxford University Press, 1994.

Owen, Jonathan L. *Avant-garde to New Wave: Czechoslovak Cinema, Surrealism and the Sixties*. London: Berghan Books, 2011.

Palmier, Jean-Michel. *Weimar in Exile: The Antifascist Emigration in Europe and America*. Trans. David Fernbach. New York: Verso, 2006.

Parr, Martin, and Gerry Badger. *The Photobook: A History*. Vol. 1. New York: Phaidon, 2004.

Pasák, Tomáš. *17. listopad 1939 a Univerzita Karlova*. Prague: Karolinum, 1997.

Pažout, Jaroslav. "'Chceme světlo! Chceme studovat!' Demonstrace studentů z vysokoškolských kolejí v Praze na Strahově 31. října 1967." *Paměť a dějiny*, No. 1, 2008.

Pearce, Celia, Laura Hollengreen, Rebecca Rouse, and Bobby Schweizer, eds. *Meet Me at the Fair: A World's Fair Reader*. Pittsburgh, PA: ETC Press, 2014.

Pfaff, Ivan. *Česká levice proti Moskvě 1936–1938*. Prague: Naše vojsko, 1993.

Píchová, Hana. *The Case of the Missing Statue: A Historical and Literary Study of the Stalin Monument in Prague*. Prague: Arbor Vitae, 2014.

Pilař, Martin. *Underground, aneb Kapitoly o českém literárním undergroundu*. 2nd ed. Brno: Host, 2002.

Plung, Dylan J. "The Japanese Village at Dugway Proving Ground: An Unexamined Context to the Firebombing of Japan." *Asia-Pacific Journal*, Vol. 16, Issue 8, No. 3, 15 April 2018.

Polizzotti, Mark. *Revolution of the Mind: The Life of André Breton*. New York: Da Capo, 1997.

Pravdová, Anna. *Zastihla je noc: čeští výtvarní umělci ve Francii 1938–1945*. Prague: Národní galerie/Opus, 2009.

Prikryl, Jana. "The Kundera Conundrum: Kundera, *Respekt* and Contempt." *Nation*, 20 May 2009.

Primus, Zdenek. *Umění je abstrakce: česká vizuální kultura 60. let*. Prague: Kant, 2003.

Procházková, Barbora. "Když se řekne kafkárna." *Naše řeč*, Vol. 92, No. 4, 2009.

Ptáčková, Věra. *Česká scénografie XX. století*. Prague: Odeon, 1982.

Pynsent, Robert. "Conclusory Essay: Activists, Jews, the Little Czech Man, and Germans." *Central Europe*, Vol. 5, No. 2, 2007.

Pytlík, Radko. *Pražské kuriosity*. Žďár nad Sázavou: Impresso Plus, 1993.

Rokoský, Jaroslav. "Amnestie 1960." *Paměť a dějiny*, No. 1, 2011.

Rothkirchen, Livia, Eva Schmidt Hartmann, Avigdor Dagan, and Milena Janišová. *Osud Židů v Protektorátu 1939–1945*. Prague: Trizonia, 1991.

Sánchez, Héctor Antonio. "Un aire más puro: itinerario de Benjamin Péret." *Casa del Tiempo*, Vol. 2, Series 5, April 2015.

Sawin, Martica. *Surrealism in Exile and the Beginning of the New York School*. Cambridge, MA: MIT Press, 1997.

Sayer, Derek. *The Coasts of Bohemia: A Czech History*. Princeton, NJ: Princeton University Press, 1998.

——. *Making Trouble: Surrealism and the Human Sciences*. Chicago: Prickly Paradigm Press, 2017.

——. "Prague at the End of History (The Prague Address)." *New Perspectives*, Vol. 27, No. 2, 2019, pp. 149–60.

——. *Prague, Capital of the Twentieth Century: A Surrealist History*. Princeton, NJ: Princeton University Press, 2013.

——. *Prague, Crossroads of Europe*. London: Reaktion Books, 2018.

——. "A Quintessential Czechness." *Common Knowledge*, Vol. 7, No. 2, 1998.

Schonberg, Michal. *Osvobozené*. Prague: Odeon, 1992.

Secrest, Meryle. *Frank Lloyd Wright: A Biography*. Chicago: Chicago University Press, 1998.

Šedivý, Jiří. "The Pull-out of Soviet Troops from Czechoslovakia." *Perspectives*, No. 2, 1993–1994.

Sedláková, Radomíra. *Jak fénix: minulost a přítomnost Veletržního paláce v Praze*. Prague: Národní galerie, 1995.

——. *Sorela: česká architektura padesátých let*. Prague: Národní galerie, 1994.

Ševeček, Ondřej, and Martin Jemelka, eds. *Company Towns of the Baťa Concern: History—Cases—Architecture*. Stuttgart: Franz Steiner Verlag, 2013.

Sheller, Mimi, and John Urry. "The New Mobilities Paradigm." *Environment and Planning A*, Vol. 38, 2006.

Sichel, Kim. *Germaine Krull: Photographer of Modernity*. Cambridge, MA: MIT Press, 1999.

Šíp, Ladislav. *Česká opera a její tvůrci*. Prague: Supraphon, 1983.

Siry, Joseph M. "The Architecture of Earthquake Resistance: Julius Kahn's Truscon Company and Frank Lloyd Wright's Imperial Hotel." *Journal of the Society of Architectural Historians*, Vol. 67, No. 1, 2008.

Skilling, H. Gordon. "The Break-up of the Czechoslovak Coalition, 1947–8." *Canadian Journal of Economics and Political Science*, Vol. 26, No. 3, 1960.

——. "Gottwald and the Bolshevization of the Communist Party of Czechoslovakia (1929–1939)." *Slavic Review*, Vol. 20, No. 4, 1961.

Skřivánková, Lucie, Rostislav Švácha, Martina Koukalová, and Eva Novotná, eds. *Paneláci: Historie sídlišť v českých zemích 1945–1989*. Prague: Uměleckoprůmyslové muzeum, 2017.

Skřivánková, Lucie, Rostislav Švácha, and Irena Lehkoživová, eds. *The Paneláks: Twenty-Five Housing Estates in the Czech Republic*. Prague: Museum of Decorative Arts, 2017.

Šmídtová, Martina. "Pražské jaro 1968 v kulturních časopisech: Literární listy & Listy, Host do domu, Index." Diplomová práce, Masarykova univerzita, Brno, 2007.

Snyder, Timothy. *Bloodlands: Europe between Hitler and Stalin*. New York: Basic Books, 2012.

Sontag, Susan. *Essays of the 1960s and 70s*. Ed. David Lieff. New York: Library of America, 2013.

——. *On Photography*. New York: Picador, 1977.

Soukup, Jiří. "České podoby Franze Kafky před druhou světovou válkou." Disertační práce, Filosofická fakulta, Univerzity Karlova v Praze, 2017.

Spáčilová, Martina. "Zmizelé knihy: Původní české beletristické knihy, které byly na přelomu šedesátých a sedmdesátých let dvacátého století cenzurou z ideologických důvodů 'zastaveny' v různých fázích výroby či distribuce." Diplomová práce, Univerzita Karlova v Praze, Filozofická fakulta, 2014.

Srba, Bořivoj. "K historii fašistické perzekuce českého divadla v letech 1939–1945." *Otázky divadla a filmu*, No. 1, 1969.

Stach, Reiner. *Is That Kafka? 99 Finds*. Trans. Kurt Beals. New York: New Directions, 2016.

———. *Kafka: The Decisive Years*. Trans. Shelley Frisch. Princeton, NJ: Princeton University Press, 2013.

———. *Kafka: The Early Years*. Trans. Shelley Frisch. Princeton, NJ: Princeton University Press, 2017.

———. *Kafka: The Years of Insight*. Trans. Shelley Frisch. Princeton, NJ: Princeton University Press, 2013.

Staněk, Tomáš. *Odsun Němců z Československa 1945–1947*. Prague: Academia, 1991.

———. *Perzekuce 1945: Perzekuce tzv. státně nespolehlivého obyvatelstva v českých zemích (mimo tábor a věznice) v květnu-srpnu 1945*. Prague: ISE, 1996.

———. *Poválečné 'excesy' v českých zemích v roce 1945 a jejich vyšetřování*. Prague: Ústav pro soudobé dějiny, 2005.

———. *Tábory v českých zemích 1945–1948*. Opava: Tilia, 1996.

Staněk, Tomáš, and Adrian von Arburg. "Organizované divoké odsuny? Úloha ústředních státních orgánů při provádění 'evakuace' německého obyvatelstva (květen až září 1945)." *Soudobé dějiny*, Vol. 12, Nos. 3–4, 2005; Vol. 13, Nos. 1–2, 2006; Vol. 13, Nos. 3–4, 2006.

Stehlíková, Eva. "The Laterna Magika of Josef Svoboda and Alfréd Radok." *Theatralia*, Vol. 14, No. 1, 2011.

Suk, Jiří. *Politika jako absurdní drama: Václav Havel v letech 1975–1989*. Prague: Paseka, 2013.

Suk, Marek. "'Jsem člověk, který se těžko podvoluje': Proces s Jiřím Kolářem v roce 1953." *Česká literatura*, Vol. 61, No. 4, 2013.

Suppan, Arnold. "Austrians, Czechs, and Sudeten Germans as a Community of Conflict in the Twentieth Century." Working Paper 06-1. Center for Austrian Studies, University of Minnesota, October 2006.

Švácha, Rostislav, and Marie Platovská. *Dějiny českého výtvarného umění [V] 1939–1958*. Prague: Academia, 2005.

Švehla, Marek. *Magor a jeho doba: Život Ivana M. Jirouse*. Prague: Torst, 2017.

Svobodová, Markéta. *Bauhaus a Československo 1919–1938/The Bauhaus and Czechoslovakia 1919–1938: Students/Concepts/Contacts*. Prague: Kant, 2016.

Szczygiel, Mariusz. *Gottland: Mostly True Stories from Half of Czechoslovakia*. Trans. Antonia Lloyd-Jones. Brooklyn, NY: Melville House, 2014.

Taussig, Michael. *Walter Benjamin's Grave*. Chicago: University of Chicago Press, 2006.

Taylor, A. J. P. *Politicians, Socialism, and Historians*. London: Hamish Hamilton, 1980.

Teichova, Alice. *The Czechoslovak Economy 1918–1980*. London: Routledge, 1988.

Templ, Stephan. *Baba: Die Werkbundsiedlung Prag/The Werkbund Housing Estate Prague*. Basel: Birkhäuser, 1999.

Teughels, Nelleke, and Peter Scholliers, eds. *A Taste of Progress: Food at International and World Exhibitions in the Nineteenth and Twentieth Centuries*. London: Routledge, 2016.

Toman, Jindřich. *Foto/montáž tiskem/Photo/montage in Print*. Prague: Kant, 2009.

———. *The Magic of a Common Language: Jakobson, Mathesius, Trubetzkoy and the Prague Linguistic Circle*. Cambridge, MA: MIT Press, 1995.

——. "The Woman Is Hollow: Toyen's Melancholy In-Sights." *Umění*, Vol. 66, No. 4, 2018.

Tomek, Prokop, and Ivo Pejčoch. *Okupace 1968 a její oběti*. Prague: Vojenský historický ústav, 2017.

Trojanová, Magdaléna. "Časopis 'El Checoslovaco en México' v letech 1942–1945." Disertační práce, Univerzita Karlova v Praze, 2011.

Tuckerová, Veronika. "Reading Kafka in Prague: The Reception of Franz Kafka between the East and the West during the Cold War." PhD diss., Columbia University, 2012.

Tučková, Kateřina. "Skupina RADAR." Diplomová práce, Univerzita Karlova v Praze, Filozofická fakulta, Ústav pro dějiny umění, 2014.

Tvrdíková, Michaela. "Proměny československé emigrace v letech 1948–1989." Diplomová práce, Masarykova Univerzita v Brně, Filozofická fakulta, 2007.

Urban, Jiří. "Několik vět: Posledních pět měsíců komunistické diktatury petiční optikou." *Paměť a dějiny*, No. 1, 2010.

Vajskebr, Jan, and Radka Šustrová. "Německá bezpečnostní opatření v Protektorátu Čechy a Morava na začátku války." *Paměť a dějiny*, No. 3, 2009.

Veverková, Irena. "Mladá léta světově známého architekta Antonína Raymonda." *Slanský obzor: Ročenka Musejního spolku v Slaném*, No. 6, 1999.

Výsledky voleb do Poslanecké sněmovny 1920–2006. Prague: Český statistický úřad, 2008.

Wagnerová, Alena. *La famille Kafka de Prague*. Paris: Bernard Grasset, 1997.

——. *Milena Jesenská*. Prague: Prostor, 1994.

Wawrzycka, Jolanta, and Erika Mihálycsa, eds. *Retranslating Joyce for the 21st Century*. Leiden: Brill Rodopi, 2020.

Weber, Max. *From Max Weber*. Ed. Hans Gerth and C. Wright Mills. London: Routledge, 1970.

Weidenhofferová, Iva, ed. *Konfliktní společenství, katastrofa, uvolnění: Náčrt výkladu německočeských dějin od 19. století*. Prague: Ústav mezinárodních vztahů, 1996.

Wittgenstein, Ludwig. *Tractatus Logico-Philosophicus*. Trans. C. K. Ogden. London: Kegan Paul, Trench, Trubner, 1922.

Wright, F. L. *Drawings and Plans of Frank Lloyd Wright: The Early Period (1893–1909)*. New York: Dover Books, 1984.

Wyman, David S., ed. *The World Reacts to the Holocaust*. Baltimore: Johns Hopkins University Press, 1996.

Zantovsky, Michael. *Havel: A Life*. New York: Grove Press, 2014.

Zarecor, Kimberly Elman. *Manufacturing a Socialist Modernity: Housing in Czechoslovakia, 1945–60*. Pittsburgh, PA: University of Pittsburgh Press, 2011.

Zimmermann, Volker. *Sudetští Němci v nacistickém státě 1938–1945: Politika a nálady obyvatel říšské župy sudetské*. Prague: Prostor, 2001.

INDEX

Page numbers in *italics* refer to illustrations.

A NOTE ON THE TYPE

This book has been composed in Arno, an Old-style serif typeface in the classic Venetian tradition, designed by Robert Slimbach at Adobe.